Encyclopedia of

SOCIAL
MOVEMENT
MEDIA

Editorial Board

Encyclopedia of

SOCIAL MOVEMENT MEDIA

John D. H. Downing

EDITOR

Southern Illinois University Carbondale

Los Angeles | London | New Delhi
Singapore | Washington DC

For information:

SAGE Publications, Inc.
2455 Teller Road
Thousand Oaks, California 91320
E-mail: order@sagepub.com

SAGE Publications Ltd.
1 Oliver's Yard
55 City Road
London, EC1Y 1SP
United Kingdom

SAGE Publications India Pvt. Ltd.
B 1/I 1 Mohan Cooperative Industrial Area
Mathura Road, New Delhi 110 044
India

SAGE Publications Asia-Pacific Pte. Ltd.
33 Pekin Street #02-01
Far East Square
Singapore 048763

Printed in Mexico

Library of Congress Cataloging-in-Publication Data

Encyclopedia of social movement media / edited by John D. H. Downing.
        p. cm.
Summary: Includes more than 250 essays on the varied experiences of social movement media throughout the world in the 20th and 21st centuries.
Includes bibliographical references and index.
ISBN 978-0-7619-2688-7 (cloth)

    1. Alternative mass media—History—20th century—Encyclopedias. 2. Alternative mass media—History—21st century—Encyclopedias. 3. Mass media—Social aspects—History—20th century—Encyclopedias. 4. Mass media—Social aspects—History—21st century—Encyclopedias. 5. Mass media—Political aspects—History—20th century—Encyclopedias. 6. Mass media—Political aspects—History—21st century—Encyclopedias. 7. Social movements—History—20th century—Encyclopedias. 8. Social movements—History—21st century—Encyclopedias. I. Downing, John (John Derek Hall)

P96.A44.E53 2011
302.2303—dc22 2010024806

This book is printed on acid-free paper.

11 12 13 14 10 9 8 7 6 5 4 3 2

Publisher:	Rolf A. Janke
Assistant to the Publisher:	Michele Thompson
Reference Systems Manager:	Leticia M. Gutierrez
Reference Systems Coordinator:	Laura Notton
Production Editor:	Jane Haenel
Copy Editors:	Colleen Brennan, Sheree Van Vreede
Typesetter:	C&M Digitals (P) Ltd.
Proofreaders:	Annie Lubinsky, Sandy Zilka
Indexer:	Julie Grayson
Cover Designer:	Gail Buschman

Contents

List of Entries

Reader's Guide

The Reader's Guide is provided to assist readers in locating articles on related topics. It classifies articles into the following topical categories: Cinema, Television, and Video; Concept and Topic Overviews; Cultural Contestations; Feminist Media; Gay and Lesbian Media; Human Rights Media; Independence Movement Media; Indigenous Peoples' Media; Information Policy Activism; Internet; Labor Media; News; Performance Art Media; Popular Song; Press; Radio; Social Movement Media. Entries are also listed according to the region of the world they address: Africa; Australia and Aotearoa/New Zealand; East Asia; Europe; Latin America; Middle East; South Asia; South East Asia; Transnational; and the United States, Canada, and the Caribbean.

Cinema, Television, and Video

Activist Cinema in the 1970s (France)
Appalshop (United States)
Beheading Videos (Iraq/Transnational)
Berber Video-Films (Morocco)
Black Exploitation Cinema
    (United States)
Challenge for Change Film
    Movement (Canada)
Cine Insurgente/Rebel Cinema
    (Argentina)
COR-TV, 2006, Oaxaca (México)
Deep Dish TV (United States)
DIVA TV and ACT UP (United States)
Documentary Film for Social
    Change (India)
Kayapó Video (Brasil)
Media Education Foundation
    (United States)
Medvedkine Groups and Workers' Cinema
    (France)
Paper Tiger Television (United States)
Political Critique in Nollywood
    Video-Films (Nigeria)
Public Access
Sixth Generation Cinema (China)
Third Cinema
Video SEWA (India)

Concept and Topic Overviews

Alternative Media
Alternative Media at Political Summits
Alternative Media Global Project
Alternative Media: Policy Issues
Anarchist Media
Citizen Journalism
Citizens' Media
Community Media and the Third Sector
Creative Commons
Culture Jamming
Environmentalist Movement Media
Feminist Media: An Overview
Grassroots Tech Activists and Media Policy
Human Rights Media
Indigenous Peoples' Media
Installation Art Media
Leninist Underground Media Model
Media Infrastructure Policy and Media Activism
Mobile Communication and Social Movements
New Media and Activism
Participatory Media
Performance Art and Social Movement Media:
    Augusto Boal
Public Access
Third Cinema
Youth Media
Youth-Generated Media

Internet Social Movement Media (Hong Kong)
Mobile Communication and Social Movements
New Media and Activism
Online Diaspora (Zambia)
Online Nationalism (China)
Radical Software (United States)
Social Movement Media in 2009 Crisis (Iran)

Labor Media

Ankara Trash-Sorters' Media (Turkey)
Industrial Workers of the World Media
   (United States)
Labor Media (United States)
Migrant Workers' Television (Korea)
Sex Workers' Blogs
Social Democratic Media to 1914 (Germany)
Undocumented Workers' Internet Use (France)
Workers' Film and Photo League (United States)

News

Al-Jazeera as Global Alternative News Source
   (Qatar/Transnational)
Alternative Information Center (Israel and
   Palestine)
ANCLA Clandestine News Agency (Argentina)
Barricada TV (Argentina)
BİA Independent Communication Network
   (Turkey)
Citizen Journalism
Democracy Now! and Pacifica Radio (United
   States)
National Alternative Media Network (Argentina)
Non-Aligned News Agencies Pool
OhmyNews (Korea)
Third World Network (Malaysia)

Performance Art Media

Boxer Rebellion Theater (China)
El Teatro Campesino
Indian People's Theatre Association
Madang Street Theater (Korea)
Performance Art and Social Movement Media:
   Augusto Boal
Sarabhai Family and the Darpana Academy
   (India)
Social Movement and Modern Dance (Bengal)
Street Theater (Canada)
Street Theater (India)

Popular Song

Dischord Records (United States)
La Nova Cançó Protest Song
   (Països Catalans)
Lookout! Records (United States)
Music and Dissent (Ghana and Nigeria)
Music and Social Protest (Malawi)
Political Song (Liberia and Sierra Leone)
Political Song (Northern Ireland)
Popular Music and Political Expression
   (Côte d'Ivoire)
Popular Music and Protest (Ethiopia)
Protest Music (Haïti)
Reggae and Resistance (Jamaica)
Rembetiko Songs (Greece)

Press

Alternative Comics (United States)
Alternative Local Press
   (United Kingdom)
Anarchist and Libertarian Media, 1945–2010
   (Federa; Germany)
Anarchist and Libertarian Press, 1945–1990
   (Eastern Germany)
Anti-Anticommunist Media Under McCarthyism
   (United States)
Ballyhoo Magazine (United States)
Belle de Jour Blog (United Kingdom)
Black Press (United States)
Dangwai Magazines (Taiwan)
Fantagraphics Books (United States)
Le Monde diplomatique
   (France/Transnational)
Leeds Other Paper/Northern Star (United
   Kingdom)
Leveller Magazine (United Kingdom)
Love and Rockets Comic Books (United States)
Mother Earth (United States)
RAW Magazine (United States)
Southern Patriot, The, 1942–1973 (United
   States)
Spare Rib Magazine (United Kingdom)
$pread Magazine (United States)
Stay Free! Magazine (United States)
Tehelka Magazine (India)
Wartime Underground Resistance Press,
   1941–1944 (Greece)
Whole Earth Catalog (United States)
Zines

About the Editor

John D. H. Downing was born in England in 1940 and lived there, aside from 2 years as a child in India, until 1980. During that period, he received an undergraduate theology degree at Oxford and graduate sociology degrees at the London School of Economics. During this time, he spent some very formative years in Shepherds Bush, then a high immigration area, and in Stepney during the concluding decades of London's dockland, as well as with a waning Jewish community and a rising Bangladeshi community. His PhD research was on the representations of labor conflict and of people of color in major British news media.

Downing worked in the sociology program at what is now Greenwich University from 1968 to 1980, heading the program from 1972 to 1980. After a year as an exchange professor in the Sociology Department at the University of Massachusetts, Amherst, he was appointed to the Communications Department at Hunter College, City University of New York, in 1981 and worked there until 1990, serving as department chair from 1981 to 1987. In 1990 he was appointed to the Radio-Television-Film Department at the University of Texas, Austin, as John T. Jones Jr. Centennial Professor and worked there until 2003, serving as department chair from 1990 to 1998. In January 2004 he was appointed founding director of the Global Media Research Center in the College of Mass Communication and Media Arts, Southern Illinois University, from which he retired in 2010, though taking up temporary appointments through 2011 at the American University of Paris, Aarhus University, Denmark, and the universities of Helsinki and Tampere, Finland.

His publications focus mostly on social movement media; ethnicity, racism, and media; Soviet Bloc media in the final decades of the Soviet Union; and political cinemas of the global South. His books include *The Media Machine* (1980); *Radical Media* (first edition 1984); *Film and Politics in the Third World* (1987); *Questioning the Media* (coedited with Annabelle Sreberny and Ali Mohammadi, 1990, revised edition 1995); *Internationalizing Media Theory: Reflections Upon Media in Russia, Poland and Hungary* (1996); a substantially revised and expanded version of *Radical Media* (2001); *Sage Handbook of Media Studies* (editor-in-chief, with Denis Mc-Quail, Philip Schlesinger, and Ellen Wartella, 2004); *Representing "Race"* (with Charles Husband, 2005); and *Alternative Media and the Politics of Resistance* (coedited with Mojca Pajnik, 2008). He also served as area editor for international communication in the International Communication Association's 12-volume *International Encyclopedia of Communication* (2008), edited by Wolfgang Donsbach. He is a member of the executive editorial committee of *Global Media and Communication* and will serve as elected editor of *Communication, Culture & Critique* from 2011 to 2013.

Downing was an elected member of the International Council of the International Association for Media and Communication Research from 1996 to 2008, and in 2008 he was elected to a 4-year term as one of two vice presidents of the association. With Clemencia Rodríguez, he cofounded the OURMedia/NUESTROSMedios network in 2001.

Contributors

Wale Adebanwi
University of California, Davis

Stephan Adolphs
University of Lucerne

Angela J. Aguayo
Southern Illinois University

Sevda Alankuş
*Faculty of Communication,
Izmir University of
Economics, Turkey*

Stuart Allan
Bournemouth University

Heather Anderson
*Queensland University of
Technology*

Fabiana Arencibia
*National Alternative Media
Network, Buenos Aires*

Chris Atton
Edinburgh Napier University

Stephen Baker
University of Ulster

Mustafa Berkay Aydın
*Middle East Technical
University, Turkey*

Indrani Bhattacharya
*American Institute of Indian
Studies*

Mario Antonius Birowo
Atma Jaya Yogyakarta University

Lucas Bolo
Barricada TV, Buenos Aires

Lisa Brooten
Southern Illinois University

Karl Brown
Southwestern University

Brigitta Busch
University of Vienna

Mavic Cabrera-Balleza
*Global Network of Women
Peacebuilders*

Çağdaş Ceyhan
Anadolu University

Sandra Gayle Carter
Independent Scholar

Nicolás Castelli
Barricada TV, Buenos Aires

Antoni Castells i Talens
Universidad Veracruzana

Young-Gil Chae
*Hankuk University of Foreign
Study, Seoul*

Sunitha Chitrapu
*Sophia Polytechnic,
Mumbai*

Nishaant Choksi
University of Michigan

Killian B. Clarke
New York University

Troy B. Cooper
University of Illinois

Matthew Crain
University of Illinois

Andrea Cuyo
Barricada TV, Buenos Aires

Daniel Darland
University of Texas, Austin

Bidhan Chandra Dash
Jamia Millia Islamia, Delhi

Heather Davis
Concordia University

Rosemary Day
*Mary Immaculate College,
University of Limerick*

Benjamin De Cleen
*Free University of Brussels
(VUB)*

Jeroen de Kloet
University of Amsterdam

Kevin DeLuca
University of Utah

John D. H. Downing
*Southern Illinois University
Carbondale*

Jesse Drew
*University of California,
Davis*

Bernd Drücke
*Graswurzelrevolution
Redaktion, Münster*

Zoë Druick
Simon Fraser University

Hopeton S. Dunn
*The University of the West
Indies*

Mattias Ekman
Stockholm University

Benjamin Ferron
*Center for Research on Political
Action in Europe, Université
de Rennes II*

Susan Forde
Griffith University

Catherine A. Fosl
University of Louisville

Michael Francis
Athabasca University, Canada

Linda K. Fuller
Worcester State College

Tom Gardner
Westfield State College

Cherian George
Wee Kim Wee School of Communication & Information, Nanyang Technological University, Singapore

Anjali Gera Roy
Indian Institute of Technology, Kharagpur

Tim Gopsill
National Union of Journalists, United Kingdom

Fabien Granjon
Laboratoire de Sociologie et d'Économie Orange Labs, France

Andrée Grau
Roehampton University

Alfonso Gumucio Dagron
Independent Scholar

Jessica Gustafsson
Stockholm University

Gabriele Hadl
Kwansei Gakuin University

Marion Hamm
University of Lucerne

Tony Harcup
University of Sheffield

Adrienne Claire Harmon
University of Texas at Austin

Nicolas Harvey
Institut d'études politiques, Université de Rennes II

Ricky Hill
University of Texas at Austin

Arne Hintz
McGill University

Zheng-rong Hu
Chinese University of Communication, Beijing

Wayne A. Hunt
Mount Allison University, Canada

Rob Hurle
Australian National University

Ip Iam-chong
Hong Kong In-media

Adel Iskandar
Georgetown University

Lukas S. Ispandriarno
University of Atma Jaya, Yogyakarta

Kimio Ito
Kyoto University

Anuja Jain
New York University

Sheena Johnson-Brown
The University of the West Indies

Alex Juhasz
Pitzer College

Mustafa Dawoud Kabha
Open University of Israel

M. Susana Kaiser
University of San Francisco

Sophia Kaitatzi-Whitlock
Aristotle University of Thessaloniki

Sarah Kanouse
University of Iowa

Tilottama Karlekar
New York University

Joe F. Khalil
Northwestern University in Qatar

Lena Khor
University of Texas at Austin

Dorothy Kidd
University of San Francisco

M. J. Kim
MediACT, Seoul

Maria Komninos
National and Kapodistrian University of Athens

Fernando Krichmar
Cine Insurgente, Buenos Aires

Cicilia M. Krohling Peruzzo
Universidade Metodista, São Paulo

Novotny Lawrence
Southern Illinois University Carbondale

Alice Y. L. Lee
Hong Kong Baptist University

Chin-Chuan Lee
City University of Hong Kong

Becky Lentz
McGill University

Carla Leshne
Independent Media Producer, San Francisco

Dennis Ka-kuen Leung
Newcastle University

Anne Lewis
University of Texas at Austin

Elizabeth Lhost
University of Wisconsin, Madison

Ji-dong Li
Chinese University of Communication, Beijing

Yehiel Limor
Tel-Aviv University

Sarah Lubjuhn
Institute of Communication Studies, University of Duisberg-Essen

Linda Lumsden
University of Arizona

John Chipembere Lwanda
Dudu Nsomba Publications

Miranda Ma Lai Yee
*School of Journalism and
    Communication, Chinese
    University of Hong Kong*

María Fernanda Madriz
*Universidad Central de
    Venezuela*

Claudia Magallanes-Blanco
*Universidad Iberoamericana
    Puebla*

Kanchan K. Malik
University of Hyderabad

Oliver Marchart
Lucerne University

Daniel Marcus
Goucher College

Gabriela Martínez
University of Oregon

Patricia Ann Mazepa
York University

Greg McLaughlin
University of Ulster, Coleraine

Michael Meadows
Griffith University

Andrea Medrado
University of Westminster

Mike Melanson
University of Texas at Austin

Stefania Milan
European University Institute

Pradeep N' Weerasinghe
University of Colombo

Assem Nasr
University of Texas at Austin

Heinz Nigg
University of Berne

Afsheen Nomai
University of Texas at Austin

Gisela Notz
*Friedrich-Ebert-Stiftung
    to 2007, Independent
    Author*

Andrew Ó Baoill
Cazenovia College

Ebenezer Obadare
University of Kansas

Alan O'Connor
Trent University

Joseph Oduro-Frimpong
*Southern Illinois University
    Carbondale*

Ariel Ogando
*Wayruro Comunicación
    Popular, Jujuy, Argentina*

Eun-ha Oh
*Southern Illinois University
    Carbondale*

Angela Faye Oon
*Institute of Southeast Asian
    Studies, Singapore*

Andy Opel
Florida State University

Kristin Skare Orgeret
Oslo University College

Camilla Orjuela
*University of Gothenburg,
    Sweden*

Cinzia Padovani
*Southern Illinois University
    Carbondale*

Eugenia María Pagano
Barricada TV, Buenos Aires

Radhika Parameswaran
Indiana University

Vinod Pavarala
University of Hyderabad

Geraldene Peters
*Auckland University of
    Technology*

Petra Pfisterer
University of Vienna

Angela Phillips
*Goldsmiths College, London
    University*

Mojca Planšak
*Centre for Media and
    Communication Studies,
    Central European University*

Judith Purkarthofer
University of Vienna

Prarthana Purkayastha
*De Montfort University, United
    Kingdom*

Jack Linchuan Qiu
*Chinese University of Hong
    Kong*

Courtney C. Radsch
Independent Journalist

Maryam Razavy
University of Alberta

Jane Regan
Independent Scholar

Ellie Rennie
*Swinburne University of
    Technology*

Roopika Risam
Emory University

Clemencia Rodríguez
University of Oklahoma

Bill Rolston
New University of Ulster

Corey Ross
University of Birmingham

Lorna Frances Roth
Concordia University, Canada

Curtis Roush
University of Texas at Austin

Kristen Rudisill
Bowling Green State University

Juan Francisco Salazar
University of Western Sydney

Avi Santo
Old Dominion University

Anne Schumann
School of Oriental and African Studies

Mehdi Semati
Northern Illinois University

Lobna Abd Elmageed Shokry
Egyptian Radio

Jake Simmons
Eastern New Mexico University

Arvind Singhal
University of Texas, El Paso

Ubonrat Siriyuvasak
Chulalongkorn University

David Skinner
York University

Sylvanus Nicholas Spencer
University of Sierra Leone

Debra Spitulnik
Emory University

Annabelle Sreberny
School of Oriental and African Studies, University of London

Rudolf Stöber
Otto-Friedrich-Universität, Bamberg

George Stoney
New York University

Heidi Swank
University of Nevada, Las Vegas

Tai Yu-hui
Southern Illinois University Carbondale

Tedjabayu
Action Network News Agency

Ximena Tordini
Radio La Tribu, Buenos Aires

Celia Tsui Yuen Sze
School of Journalism and Communication, Chinese University of Hong Kong

Vassilis Vamvakas
National and Kapodistrian University of Athens

Ineke van Kessel
African Studies Centre

Jacqueline Vickery
University of Texas

Natalia Vinelli
Barricada TV, Buenos Aires

Patrick S. Washburn
Ohio University

John Whalen-Bridge
National University of Singapore

Karin Gwinn Wilkins
University of Texas at Austin

Wendy Willems
University of the Witwatersrand

Bill Yousman
University of Massachusetts, Amherst

Margaret Zanger
University of Arizona

Ying Zhu
City University of New York at Staten Island

Introduction

You are looking at the very tip of the top of a gigantic iceberg. Indeed, you have the absolute right, if you are a social movement media activist, researcher, or historian and have examined the list of entries, to complain that this particular media project, that particular media project, or even a fleet of media projects seem to be off this encyclopedia's radar.

This editor regretfully agrees. Social movement media represent a dizzying variety of formats and experiences, far greater than mainstream commercial, public, or state media. A single-volume encyclopedia can deal with only a tiny sample. The guiding principles in selection have been to ensure as far as possible that experiences from the global South are given voice; that women are properly represented among the contributors (approximately half); that the wide spectrum of communication formats is included, from graffiti to the Internet; that further reading is provided where relevant in languages other than English; and that some examples are provided of repressive social movement media, not exclusively progressive ones.

The many different terms used to denote such media effectively testify to their huge variety: alternative media, citizens' media, community media, counterinformation media, grassroots media, independent media, nano-media, participatory media, social movement media, and underground media. This is quite apart from subcategories, each with its own cornucopia of descriptors, such as environmentalist media, feminist media, Indigenous media, minority-ethnic media, radical media, rhizomatic media, tactical media, and youth media.

So, think of this encyclopedia as a first edition, a downpayment on a second, much more extensive project hopefully using web and Internet resources even more systematically than in this first edition to provide or link to original texts and to both visual and aural materials. As shown by the list of book-length studies—English-language ones only—that follows this Introduction, research in this field has been thriving over the past decade. This volume deploys an anthropological and social movement perspective on media rather than a technologically based one. Murals, graffiti, popular song, and dance rub shoulders here with video and cinema. Low-power community radio and hi-tech digital networks are in the same dance.

Social movement researchers, however, are likely to complain that the term "social movement" is used in the encyclopedia title without being theorized systematically in the volume, not to mention other nomenclature such as "community" and "network." I have also perhaps cavalierly taken it for granted that social movements can range from the very local to the transnational. This is all true and is the case for two reasons. First, I and others have addressed these definitions and issues elsewhere (readers are encouraged to track down those discussions), thus I resisted simply rehearsing them here (e.g., Atton, 2003; Downing, 2008; Guedes Bailey, Cammaerts & Carpentier, 2008; Juris, 2008; Pajnic & Downing, 2008; Rennie, 2006; Rodríguez, 2001). Second, and probably more important, social movement research, although voluminous at this point in time, has largely been disfigured to date by (a) its virtually obsessive concentration on social movements in the global North (the "New Social Movements" research literature is a perfect case in point) and (b) its splendidly self-confident neglect of communication and media as integral dimensions of social movements. Both these limitations represent conceptual myopia of a high order. I will leave it to those who specialize in social movement research to reflect on how the sociology of knowledge might assist in explaining this myopia's genesis.

Furthermore, although the Nazis, the Rwandan *génocidaires*, the "beheading" videos made by murderous fanatics, and some other examples of venomous movements do find their way into these pages, much less examination of media of extreme right movements occurs in this volume than there might be. They unquestionably demand thorough analysis. The other issue of importance that this volume does not address is the "how-to" of making, distributing, and upgrading social movement media. Kate Coyer, Tony Dowmunt, and Alan Fountain's *The Alternative Media Handbook* (2007) is a model in this regard.

All these issues matter greatly. The dominant forces pushing our planet down at the beginning of this century are antidemocratic and antisocial. Climate change, ocean disintegration, lethal poverty, war—all of which shatters women's and children's lives, in particular—confront us with extreme urgency. A great variety of constructive projects and social movements, small and large, are active spaces of hope. But there is far more agreement and discussion of what should *not* happen and *why* current economic and political structures must be reshaped than actually *how* to reshape them.

For this purpose, the flourishing of social movement media is crucial because they are pivotal vehicles within which global civil society can collectively chew on solutions, float and discard them, track their trajectories, and evaluate them, from the most local and immediate to the international and long term. *If* defiance to the existing order is to be effectively mobilized and *if* other "worlds" are to become realistically possible, then reflecting critically on the experience and potential of these protean media is nothing less than crucial.

Acknowledgments

I owe a great deal to the work of others in focusing my attention on the multifarious forms of media communication over the years—first and foremost, to the many migrant workers I knew in London from the Caribbean, Ireland, south Asia, and west Africa and to the workers in London dockland, whose maltreatment by mainstream media some 40-plus years ago pushed me to explore how other forms of media worked, did not work, and might work better. Second, I owe much to certain research forerunners. I have in mind Celia Hollis, whose 1970 book *The Pauper Press* focused on the early 19th-century "unstamped" unofficial press of Britain's Chartist movement; Hans Magnus Enzensberger, whose 1970 essay "Baukasten zu einer Theorie der Medien" (Constituents of a Theory of Media) pinpointed the liberatory potential of the then new media technologies; and Armand Mattelart, whose pioneering study of Chilean media during the 1970–1973 Popular Unity period came into my hands in spring 1975. His analysis of emergent workers' media in the industrial belts of Santiago and of what he described as Chilean commercial media's Leninist mass agitation against the socialist movement made a huge imprint on my thinking. In 1983 Siegelaub and Mattelart's second volume of their *Communication and Class Struggle* provided uniquely important histories, experiences, and concepts of liberatory media. Though this project is more libertarian and movement oriented, that volume's international and historical scope was in some degree a template for this encyclopedia. Last, I thank the tremendous movement media activists and researchers who have contributed since 2001 to the OURMedia/NUESTROSMedios network.

I owe a great personal debt to certain individuals who were especially helpful in putting together this compendium. Professor Laura Stein at the University of Texas, Austin, assembled the great majority of the U.S. entries, some 20% of the total number. For assistance with varying regions of our planet, I am absolutely indebted to Joe F. Khalil for the Arab region, to Tai Yu-hui for Chinese-speaking Asia, and to Rajamit Kumar for south Asia, all doctoral communication students at Southern Illinois University Carbondale. Regarding sub-Saharan Africa and for general assistance my thanks go to Joseph Oduro-Frimpong, doctoral anthropology student at Southern Illinois University Carbondale, and for German-speaking Europe I thank Professor Werner Maier (Zürich University).

At various points along the way I continued to depend on the ready assistance of (alphabetically by last name) Chris Atton (Edinburgh Napier University), Lisa Brooten (Southern Illinois University Carbondale), Alfonso Gumucio Dagron, Gabi Hadl (Kwansei Gakuin University), Susana Kaiser (University of San Francisco), Shuchi Kothari (University of Auckland), Mojca Pajnik (Peace Institute, Ljubljana), Clemencia Rodríguez (University of Oklahoma), Annabelle Sreberny (School of Oriental and African Studies, London), and Nabeel Zuberi (University of Auckland).

The consistent backing provided to the Global Media Research Center by Deans Manjunath Pendakur, Gary Kolb, and Deborah Tudor, of Southern Illinois University Carbondale's College of Mass Communication and Media Arts, has been crucial in enabling me to address this encyclopedia project. Laura Germann, my assistant at the Center since its foundation, has proved herself a sterling model of perceptive and pleasant efficiency. It has been marvelous to be able to rely utterly on her expertise and readiness to help. The original idea for this unprecedented project came from Margaret Seawell, then acquisitions editor at SAGE. Since then, it has been nursed along by others at SAGE, notably Laura Notton and Sara Tauber, to whose professionalism, patience, persistence, and unfailing pleasantness this project owes a great deal. Special thanks also to my developmental editor at SAGE, Diana Axelsen, as well as to the editorial production team of Jane Haenel, Colleen Brennan, and Sheree Van Vreede.

To Ash Corea, whose warmth, love, inspiration, wit, critique, patience, support, and sparkling cuisine have made my life delectable and this mammoth project feasible, my thanks are beyond all measure.

John D. H. Downing
Global Media Research Center
Southern Illinois University Carbondale

Further Readings

Atton, C. (2001). *Alternative media*. London: Sage.

Atton, C. (2003). Reshaping social movement media for a new millennium. *Social Movement Studies, 2*(1), 3–13.

Atton, C. (2005). *An alternative internet*. Edinburgh, UK: Edinburgh University Press.

Atton, C., & Hamilton, J. F. (2008). *Alternative journalism*. Thousand Oaks, CA: Sage.

Carpentier, N., & Scifo, S. (Eds.). (2010). Community media—the long march. *Telematics and Informatics, 27*(2) [special issue].

Coyer, K., Dowmunt, T., & Fountain, A. (Eds.). (2007). *The alternative media handbook*. London: Routledge.

Downing, J. (1984). *Radical media: The political experience of alternative communication*. Boston: South End Press.

Downing, J. (2001). *Radical media: Rebellious communication and social movements* (Rev. ed.). Thousand Oaks, CA: Sage.

Downing, J. (2003). Audiences and readers of alternative media: The absent lure of the virtually unknown. *Media, Culture & Society, 25*, 625–645.

Downing, J. (2008). Social movement theories and alternative media: An evaluation and critique. *Communication, Culture & Critique, 1*(1), 40–50.

Enzensberger, H. M. (1970). Baukasten zu einer theorie der medien [Constituents of a theory of the media]. *Kursbuch 20*, 159–186/*New Left Review, 64*, 13–36.

Frey, L. R., & Carragee, K. M. (Eds.). (2007). *Communication activism* (2 vols.). Cresskill, NJ: Hampton Press.

Guedes Bailey, O., Cammaerts, B., & Carpentier, N. (2008). *Understanding alternative media*. Maidenhead, UK: Open University Press.

Gumucio Dagron, A. (2001). *Making waves [Ondes de choc/Haciendo olas]*. New York: Rockefeller Foundation.

Hadl, G. (Ed.). (2009). Convergences: International civil society media and policy. *International Journal of Media and Cultural Politics, 5*, 1–2 [special double issue].

Hollis, P. (1970). *The Pauper Press: A study in working-class radicalism of the 1830s*. Oxford, UK: Oxford University Press.

Howley, K. (Ed.). (2009). *Understanding community media*. Thousand Oaks, CA: Sage.

Juris, J. S. (2008). *Networking futures: The movements against corporate globalization*. Durham, NC: Duke University Press.

Mattelart, A. (1974). *Mass medias, ideologies et mouvement revolutionnaire, Chili 1970–73*. Paris: Éditions Anthropos.

Pajnic, M., & Downing, J. (Eds.). (2008). *Alternative media and the politics of resistance: Perspectives and challenges*. Ljubljana, Slovenia: Peace Institute.

Rennie, E. (2006). *Community media: A global introduction*. Lanham, MD: Rowman & Littlefield.

Rodríguez, C. (2001). *Fissures in the mediascape*. Cresskill, NJ: Hampton Press.

Rodríguez, C., Kidd, D., & Stein, L. (Eds.). (2008). *Making our media: Global initiatives toward a democratic public sphere* (2 vols.). Cresskill, NJ: Hampton Press.

Servaes, J., & Scifo, S. (Eds.). (2010). Community media–the long march. *Telematics and Informatics, 27*(2) [special issue].

Siegelaub, S., & Mattelart, A. (Eds.). (1983). *Communication and class struggle: Vol. 2. Liberation, socialism*. New York: International General.

Sreberny-Mohammadi, A., & Mohammadi, A. (1994). *Small media, big revolution: Communication, culture and the Iranian Revolution*. Minneapolis: University of Minnesota Press.

ABORIGINAL MEDIA (CANADA)

See First Peoples' Media (Canada)

ACTIVIST CINEMA IN THE 1970S (FRANCE)

Beginning in the late 1960s, French activist cinema became its most lively and inventive. The advent of portable media—Super-8 cameras, video recorders, editing benches—permitted easier learning of film techniques, and activist collectives multiplied. Argentinean documentary-makers Fernando Solanas and Octavio Getino, French documentarian Chris Marker, France's Medvedkine cinema collective, and French director Louis Malle were some of the leading influences of the period. However, the advent of the established Left parties to parliamentary and presidential power in 1981 saw the decline of this wave.

Background

France's first politically committed films began to be made during the 1936–1937 left-leaning Popular Front government. The Ciné-Liberté (Cinema-Freedom) group produced *La rue sans nom* (Street Without a Name), directed by Pierre Chenal, and *La vie est à nous* (Life Is Ours), by Jean Renoir. Numerous propaganda films concerning demonstrations, strikes, and campaigns were made by the

CGT (a leading Communist union), the Communist Party, or the Socialist Party Union (the SFIO). The SFIO and the Ciné-Liberté group produced a number of documentary films, often very short and harnessing major figures in French cinema, which portrayed cheerful crowds, spirited political speeches, or the solidarity of strikers.

Renoir's *La vie est à nous*, with Jean-Paul Le Chanois and Paul Vaillant-Couturier, produced by the Communist Party, was a prototype of activist cinema, bringing together industry professionals and major political organizations, and making its point with song and heartfelt testimonies. It was banned right up to 1969, but its inspirational influence surpassed its distribution. At the time, it was illegally screened for free in urban neighborhoods that requested it in and out of Paris, circulating with six 35mm copies and two cars mounted to project the 16mm version.

Enter Portable Film and Video

Some of the key collectives in the period beginning in 1968 were Unicité (Oneness), which made *The CGT* in May–June 1968; Les Films du Grain de Sable (Grain of Sand Films), which made *Alertez les bébés* (Warn the Kids); Ciné-Lutte (Cinema-Struggle), which made *Chaud, chaud, chaud* (Hot, Hot, Hot); Medvedkine, which made *Classe de lutte* (Class in Struggle, a twist on *lutte de classe*, meaning class struggle); Arc, which made *Brigadier Mikono*; Slon (acronym for Launch Service for New Works), which made *Nouvelle société* (New Society); Iskra, which made *Image, son, kinéscope*

(Image, Sound, Kinescope); Cinéma Rouge (Red Cinema), which made *Le charme discret de la démocratie bourgeoise* (The Discreet Charm of Bourgeois Democracy); and Ligne Rouge (Red Line), which made *Oser lutter, oser vaincre* (Dare to Fight, Dare to Win). Layerle lists more than 100 collectives and nearly 700 completed films.

Argentinean filmmakers Solanas and Getino, already mentioned, were pivotal influences not only through their uncompromising documentary *La Hora de los hornos* (Hour of the Furnaces) but also via their lengthy manifesto *Hacía un tercer cine* (Toward a Third Cinema), which called for a liberatory cinema practice, sharply distinct from both Hollywood and art film. Chris Marker came out with two notable films in 1967, *À bientôt, j'espère* (Soon, I Hope), on a notable strike and factory occupation in Besançon, and *Loin du Viêtnam* (Far From Vietnam).

The 1968 May–June events opened up a sharp divide between New Wave cinema's focus on marginal, deviant, and upper-middle-class characters, and activist cinema's emphasis on factory workers,' white collar workers,' and farmers' class struggles against capital. Louis Malle's 1972 film *Human, trop humain* (Human, All Too Human) was shot in the Rennes Citroën factory. Other films focused on new social actors, such as immigrants, prostitutes, gays, women, and new critical issues, such as antipsychiatry, ecology, the disabled, regional cultures, third world issues, and antimilitarism. Examples included *Les prostituées de Lyon parlent* (Lyon Prostitutes Speak), *Coup pour coup* (Blow for Blow), *Travailleurs immigrés* (Immigrant Workers), *Avoir vingt ans dans les Aurès* (Twenty years old in Aurès [a Berber mountain region in Algeria]), *Malville, état de siège* (Martial Law in Malville).

Fargier calls this the "wheelbarrow-video" era, when activists took tapes to meeting rooms, cafés, apartments, schools, churches, cinemas, along with tape recorders, monitors, and amplifiers. Enthusiasm for autonomous workers' struggles, independent of union hierarchies or leftist parties' control, mirrored the activists' desire for independence in cinema and audiovisual media production. There was a romantic notion of the collective I, "we film-makers and workers, joined at the hip." But there was equally a vigorous and widespread spirit of mutual assistance in getting these films made.

Several prominent concerns emerged in the development of this activist cinema. One issue involved the professionalization of the filmmakers and the participation of the social actors filmed.

Issues of Professionalism and Participation

There were emblematic arguments regarding the first of these concerning Marker's *À bientôt, j'espère* about the Besançon factory, to which the Medvedkine collective opposed its *Classe de lutte*. In the workers' discussion at the factory following the screening of Marker's film, one worker announced he thought that if Marker really wanted to express the workers' feelings and needs, he had shown himself clueless, and that he had simply exploited the workers in the name of an anticapitalist struggle. Another called Marker a romantic. To be accused of exploiting strikers cut deep.

The Medvedkine group made itself the voice for rupturing the division of labor in film production, proposing that in the last analysis the standard manner of producing these images reproduced the expert–lay domination that needed to be fought against. Similarly the Vidéo-Out collective handed over some of its footage to the workers after their protracted strike at the Lip factory to use as they saw fit, while making their own documentary with the remainder, directed by Marker (*Puisqu'on vous dit que c'est possible* [Because We're Telling You It Can Be Done], 1968). Marin Karmitz worked out the script of *Coup pour coup* in advance with the women textile factory workers.

"Talking heads" predominated in these films in the name of giving voice and agency to the excluded. Those filmed would watch the rushes, and if they disapproved, it was back to the drawing board. In other cases, the screening would be halted to allow for discussion. The ultimate step was to hand over the video camera—though 35mm cameras did not lend themselves to this—to those to be filmed. Indeed, authorless films began to appear. The onslaught of professional expertise was thoroughgoing, though it did not pass without critique. Critics argued that making a film was more than just gathering up images: It required intensive reflection, practice, scripting, and labor.

Toward a Revolutionary Film Aesthetic

A further concern was to seek to draw activist cinema closer to experimental cinema—what one critic, Claude Beylie, called the "Red" avant-garde closer to the "White" avant-garde. But this trend remained largely at a speculative level, with no real impact upon actual productions or even partial reorientations of productions emanating from one side in this debate by adopting an element from the other side. Some feature films, such as *L'an 01* (Year One), directed by Gébé (Georges Blondeaux) and Jacques Doillon, became more tied to current events, but without unseating the hegemony of the witness film or the documentary, which were considered supremely effective in stripping social realities bare.

On the activist side, the tendency was more to reconstruct than document a social movement, using nonprofessional actors, to open up the spectator's mind. This was much in the tradition of Sergei Eisenstein and Russian avant-gardists, but found itself less strongly represented in France than in Britain (e.g., Humphrey Jennings, Peter Watkins, Ken Loach), despite Renoir and the October group, some of Jean-Luc Godard's films, and more recently films by Jean-Louis Comolli and Ginette Lavigne.

French Cinema Since 1981

As noted, the 1981 presidential and parliamentary election brought the Socialist Party and its allies to official power, and many collectives disbanded. Some, such as Iskra, remain active (as of 2009). Some spaces emerged inside the cultural industries, enabling films to be made, such as *Femmes de Fleury* (Fleury Women), a 1992 documentary directed by Jean-Michel Carré about the women's prison at Fleury-Mérogis, Europe's largest such prison, which pulled in over 10 million viewers. Small repertory movie theaters continued to screen films that were, if not activist, then at least politically committed. In the period 1995–1997, the working class experienced a kind of social realist "comeback" in at least half a dozen films that made a mark, although it must be underscored that France's labor militancy of 1995—which included blocking trains from leaving the station and closing down shipyards—seemed to have impacted film scripts for a while. And the Cinémathèque Française, France's metropolitan cathedral of cinema, organized a series of retrospectives of 1970s film collectives' work.

Fabien Granjon
(translated by John D. H. Downing)

See also Documentary Film for Social Change (India); Labor Media (United States); May 1968 Poetry and Graffiti (France/Transnational); Medvedkine Groups and Workers' Cinema (France); November–December 1995 Social Movement Media (France); Paper Tiger Television (United States)

Further Readings

Carré, J.-M. (2004). Les films du Grain de Sable. Entretien avec Jean-Michel Carré [Grain of Sand films: Interview with Jean-Michel Carré]. *CinémAction, 110,* 125–130.

Fargier, J.-P. (2004). L'action cathodique [Cathodic action]. *CinémAction, 110,* 99–103.

Gauthier, G. (2004). Le cinéma et le Front Populaire [Cinema and the Popular Front]. *CinémAction, 110,* 21–26.

Gauthier, G. (2004). Cinéma, vidéo, militantisme et participation [Cinema, video, activism and participation]. *CinémAction, 110,* 59–65.

Hennebelle, G. (2004). Si ce n'est plus l'heure des brasiers, c'est peut-être celle de la reprise [If it isn't the hour of the furnaces any more, then perhaps it's time for a revival]. *CinémAction, 110,* 15–18.

Layerle, S. (2004). 700 films de 1967 à 1981 [Filmography: 700 films from 1967 to 1981]. *CinémAction, 110,* 251–323.

Martineau, M. (2004). Cinéma militant: le retour! [Activist cinema: The return!]. *CinémAction, 110,* 11–14.

Memmi, D. (2004). L'introuvable «peuple» dans le cinéma français [The undiscoverable "people" in French cinema]. *CinémAction, 110,* 46–51.

Roth, L. (2004). L'expérience de Ciné-Citoyen. Entretien avec Laurent Roth [The Ciné-Citoyen experience: Interview with Laurent Roth]. *CinémAction, 110,* 33–37.

ADBUSTERS MEDIA FOUNDATION (CANADA)

The Adbusters Media Foundation (AMF) is a Vancouver-based activist organization with a number of progressive social, economic, and media-related agendas. The AMF, primarily through its bimonthly magazine *Adbusters,* is critical of the advertising industry, accusing it of promoting myriad social, environmental, and health problems that, it argues, are exacerbated through rampant consumerism. The AMF promotes a lifestyle critical of, and counter to, the consumerist frenzy. According to AMF's self-description, "We want to change the way information flows, the way corporations wield power and the way meaning is produced in society" (www.adbusters.org).

The AMF advocates for a number of economic and cultural issues. Media Carta is the AMF's own brand of advocating for media democracy. True Cost Economics argues for a new measure for economic progress. First Things First is a program targeting graphic designers and is aimed at promoting change from within the power structures where they work. Buy Nothing Day, an event held every year the day after Thanksgiving, urges people to reconsider and "downshift" their consumer lifestyle. Mental Detox Week (originally called TV Turnoff Week), encourages people to spend the time they would normally watch television, or engage any type of electronic media, with other activity. The AMF hopes that participation in Buy Nothing Day and Mental Detox Week can lead to larger transformations in people's lives.

Adbusters and the AMF have been closely aligned with the practice of culture jamming, especially in promoting and distributing subvertising texts within the pages of the magazine. The connection between culture jamming, *Adbusters,* and the AMF has been further solidified by cofounder Kale Lasn, who took to referring to the work he and his organization are doing as culture jamming. His 1999 book *Culture Jamming* outlines the tactics he argues will lead to a cultural revolution, with the AMF at the helm. By the late 2000s, AMF oversaw the publication of *Adbusters* with a global circulation of 120,000.

The prominence of subvertising within the pages of *Adbusters* helped to build the magazine's reputation among progressive cultural activists. With the increasing cooptation of subvertising tactics by mainstream advertisers, however, the AMF, with Lasn's leadership, created the Blackspot "anticorporation," a company which markets an ethically produced, Converse All-Star style sneaker called the Blackspot. According to late 2000s advertisements for Blackspot in *Adbusters* magazine, the brand aimed to expand into the music and restaurant businesses in order to promote local consumer cultures.

Afsheen Nomai

See also *Ballyhoo* Magazine (United States); Barbie Liberation Organization (United States); Church of Life After Shopping (United States); Culture Jamming; Environmental Movement Media; Media Education Foundation (United States)

Further Readings

Adbusters Media Foundation: www.adbusters.org
Binay, A. (2005). *Investigating the anti-consumerism movement in North America: The case of* Adbusters. Unpublished doctoral dissertation, University of Texas, Austin.
Harold, C. (2007). *Our Space: Resisting the corporate control of culture.* Minneapolis: University of Minnesota Press.
Lasn, K. (1999). *Culture jam: How to reverse America's suicidal consumer binge.* New York: Quill.
Nomai, A. J. (2008). *Culture jamming: Ideological struggle and the possibilities for social change.* Unpublished doctoral dissertation, University of Texas, Austin.
Rumbo, J. D. (2002). Consumer resistance in a world of advertising clutter: The case of *Adbusters. Psychology & Marketing, 19*(2), 127–148.

ADIVASI MOVEMENT MEDIA (INDIA)

India has about 84 million people considered under the constitutional term *scheduled tribe,* about 8% of the general population. Many of these scheduled tribe groups prefer the political term *adivasi,* or "original inhabitant." The largest concentration of *adivasis* lie in India's far northeast, followed by the "central tribal belt" in the hilly, forested areas stretching from Gujarat to West Bengal. Most adivasis survive on subsistence-level agriculture or migrant labor.

Adivasis have a long history of social struggle, and their media production is almost as old. The

British documented numerous large-scale rebellions such as the 1855 Santal tribe Hul (liberation movement) and the 1895 Birsa movement, each of which mobilized hundreds of thousands, under adivasi leadership, against British and upper-caste exploitation. Other large-scale rebellions also took place. Although print was not widespread then, adivasi authors as early as 1894 began publishing tracts in adivasi languages to unify their communities along political and cultural lines.

Contemporary Adivasi Movement Media

One particularly influential movement has been the *Jharkhand* movement, the oldest autonomy movement in postindependence India. The struggle for Jharkhand, a tribal majority state carved out from Bihar, West Bengal, Orissa, and Madhya Pradesh, began in 1938 with the formation of the Adivasi Mahasabha (the Great Council of the Adivasis). In the late 1980s the movement merged with left parties such as the Communist Party of India (Marxist-Leninist), which attempted to cast the Jharkhand movement as much more than an adivasi struggle but a struggle for all oppressed people, including *Dalits* (the proper term for so-called untouchable castes). In November 2000, a truncated Jharkhand state was carved out solely from Bihar, to the dismay of many activists.

The Jharkhand movement inspired many media. In the 1970s and 1980s, left activists working in Jharkhand began to express a Jharkhandi culture among its various social sectors, including adivasis and Dalits. Activists such as Ramanika Gupta began a media foundation that brought together adivasi and Dalit intellectuals from Jharkhand and elsewhere. Her long-running magazine *Yudhrat Aam Admi* (The Common Man's War Chariot) maintains the spirit of the Jharkhand movement, translating the writings of adivasi authors, poets, and commentators into Hindi.

The movement had a huge impact on the burgeoning adivasi language media as well. Many Santali magazines in the greater Jharkhand area (including West Bengal and Orissa), such as *Nawa Ipil* (New Star), have special issues on the Santal Hul. The imagery in these media is not just commemorative. Through recalling the Hul in magazines, plays, poetry, and feature films, Santals also reiterate their ongoing desire for tribal autonomy.

Recent movements such as the Narmada Bachao Andolan (Save Narmada Movement), started in 1989 against building a huge dam on Gujarat's River Narmada, have also produced a variety of adivasi media. Because most of those affected were adivasi groups, the movement inspired a number of protest songs and protest literature in local adivasi languages. These songs were recorded and circulated by the movement in collections such as *Amu Adivasi* (We, Adivasis): *Tribal Songs From the Narmada Valley Struggle*. These collections featured older *adivasi* struggle songs as well, illustrating how the movement attempts to integrate past protest with contemporary agendas.

Finally, adivasi media have often been deployed to link cultural expression and economic development. The Gujarat-based Bhasha (Language) Center has combined health care, education, microcredit, and other programs with the production of adivasi-language magazines. The magazine *Dhol* (The Drum) allows adivasis to write in their own languages but also circulates information on development projects. Bhasha also publishes *Bol* (Speech), a magazine specifically targeting adivasi children in Gujarat. Unlike mainstream magazines, it features adivasi artists, popular regional adivasi stories, and adivasi history. Bhasha also intends to start an adivasi-only radio station in the area to promote oral education. Bhasha insists economic uplift of Adivasis requires cultural empowerment.

Although only a few examples of adivasi media are noted here, from diverse institutional settings and regional contexts, they illustrate a common thread. Social movements often formulate their claims around universal goals, but for Adivasis they also involve cultural assertion. Their media allow Adivasis to participate in national and international democratic struggles for rights and recognition, while also furthering their unique cultural contributions.

Nishaant Choksi

See also Dalit Movement Media (India); First Peoples' Media (Canada); Indigenous Media (Australia); Indigenous Media in Latin America; Indigenous Peoples' Media; Māori Media and Social Movements (Aotearoa/New Zealand); Moon River Movement Media (Thailand); Zapatista Media (México)

Further Readings

Baviskar, A. (1995). *In the belly of the river: Tribal conflicts over development in the Narmada Valley.* New Delhi, India: Oxford University Press.

Bhasha Research and Publication Center: http://www.bhasharesearch.org.in/Site.html#id=Home

Devy, G. N. (2006). *A nomad called thief.* Hyderabad, India: Orient Longman.

Gupta, R. (Ed.). (2008). *Adivasi sahitya yatra* [The literary journey of the Adivasis]. New Delhi, India: Radhakrishna Publications.

Hembrom, P. (2007). *Shaontal shahityer itihash* [The history of Santali literature]. Kolkata, India: Nirmal Publications.

Munda, R. D., & Mullick, S. B. (Eds.). (2003). *The Jharkhand movement: Indigenous people's struggle for self autonomy in India.* Copenhagen, Denmark: International Workgroup for Indigenous Affairs.

Murmu, N. C., & Hansdah, R. C. (n.d.). *A portal for Santals books & magazines.* http://wesanthals.tripod.com/id39.html

Singh, K. S. (Ed.). (1983). *Tribal movements in India.* New Delhi, India: Manohar Publications.

ADVOCATE, THE (UNITED STATES)

The Advocate is the longest running and most widely distributed gay and lesbian publication in the United States. The monthly magazine's devotion from a queer perspective to news, travel, art, and general cultural interests affords it wide readership not just in North America but also throughout the world. Since its inception, it has been a major source of information for the gay and lesbian community and the most widely cited source of major national publications seeking "gay perspectives."

Born of a newsletter created by PRIDE (Personal Rights in Defense and Education), a Los Angeles group founded in the late 1960s to combat police harassment, *The Los Angeles Advocate,* as it was originally known, was 12 pages long and had an initial print run of 500. Its three main founders were Dick Michaels, Bill Rand, and artist Sam Winston. The trio came together to purchase the publication rights in 1968, prior to PRIDE's dissolution, and by March 1970, *The Los Angeles Advocate* had a run of over 5,000. It was at first sold in gay-friendly establishments for 25 cents to cover the cost of printing. Later that spring, *Los Angeles* was dropped from the title, with the hopes of *The Advocate* gaining a broader readership. By 1974, it was printing 40,000 copies of each issue.

The circulation increase caught the attention of entrepreneur David B. Goodstein, who purchased *The Advocate* in 1975. He made it a biweekly for the next decade, also shifting from a heavily political magazine to a more commercial, glossy publication. Many gay activists resented Goodstein's purchase because of the magazine's somewhat militant roots. *The Advocate*'s lack of acknowledgment and lack of coverage of the 1980s AIDS crisis drew heavy criticism from many within the gay community. Goodstein eventually moved the editorial offices from Los Angeles to San Mateo, near San Francisco, until 1984, when the decision was made to return to Los Angeles.

Between 1990 and 1992, national advertising revenue nearly doubled. In 1992, Sam Watters took over the publication and made it an all-glossy magazine. The magazine's sexually explicit "pink pages" were spun off into a separate periodical. Whereas advertising revenue continued to steadily increase with the magazine's sleek new look, reader response was somewhat varied. Many argued that the removal of sexual ads and erotic fiction caused a "mainstreaming" effect, whereas others were pleased to have a more "wholesome" magazine that spoke to their community.

In November 2005, *The Advocate*'s publisher, Liberation Publications, Inc., was acquired by San Francisco–based PlanetOut Inc., merging the two largest gay-oriented media firms in the United States. In 2008, *The Advocate* was sold by PlanetOut Inc. to Regent Media, owners of LGBTQ cable network here! and *Out* magazine.

Ricky Hill

See also Alternative Media; DIVA TV and ACT UP (United States); Gay Press (Canada, United Kingdom, United States); *Gay USA;* Stonewall Incident (United States)

Further Readings

Iconic American LGBT publication *The Advocate* sold by PlanetOut. (2008, August 26). *PinkNews.* http://www.pinknews.co.uk/2008/08/26/iconic-american-lgbt-publication-the-advocate-sold-by-planetout

Selvin, M. (2005, November 10). Gay media firms to combine. *Los Angeles Times.* http://articles.latimes .com/2005/nov/10/business/fi-planetout10

Streitmatter, R. (1995). *Unspeakable: The rise of the gay and lesbian press in America.* Boston: Faber & Faber.

Thompson, M. (Ed.). (1994). *Long road to freedom: The advocate history of the gay and lesbian movement.* New York: St. Martin's Press.

AIDS

See HIV/AIDS Media (India)

AL-JAZEERA AS GLOBAL ALTERNATIVE NEWS SOURCE (QATAR/TRANSNATIONAL)

Al-Jazeera began as the first 24-hour all-news satellite station in the Arabic language in 1996. Fourteen years later, al-Jazeera is one of the most popular and recognizable global media brands with 10 satellite channels, including sports, documentary, children's, and live parliamentary channels. An initiative of the Emir of Qatar, al-Jazeera incubated a cadre of professional journalists who moved from a defunct BBC Arabic television station that had collapsed as a result of editorial differences with the Saudi funders.

With a startup fund of $140 million, the Doha-based station seemed like a toddler compared to the Arab broadcasting behemoths in Egypt, Saudi Arabia, and Lebanon. However, in a pan-Arab context, with its once-novel focus on political opposition and social taboos, al-Jazeera quickly developed its distinct style. At its inception, unrivalled were its relatively freewheeling approach, its on-the-ground reporting of conflict, and its ability to cover many stories from disparate regions.

Al-Jazeera's ability to do this was also dependent on overcoming access limitations, especially given that some Arab countries banned satellite dishes. Yet by the late 1990s, satellite access had increased exponentially throughout the region, and the technology became pervasive, from rural enclaves to urban communities, from the elite intelligentsia to impoverished refugees. Restrictions became dead letter laws and al-Jazeera's coverage became available to audiences throughout the Arab world and Arabic-speaking communities globally.

From the outset, the station was perceived as an alternative, especially of its critical treatment of Arab regimes (with the exception of its home state Qatar) and its attention to opposition groups and movements. The station also pioneered talk shows, which tackled taboos ranging from the role of women in Islamic societies and sexuality, to interviewing Israeli officials and political dissidents. In a region where most news content was produced by government networks overseen by Ministries of Information, al-Jazeera seemed anomalous given its relative contrast to Qatar's own state television. Even before the arrival of al-Jazeera, Arab publics had held an increasingly cynical and distrustful view of their political and economic establishments. In contrast, the network's approach to news coverage, along with its pan-Arab staff, helped established its image as a genuinely credible regional news broadcaster.

Underscoring its image of courage were a 2001 U.S. missile attack on the al-Jazeera office in Kabul and a 2003 shelling of the Baghdad office, which killed one of its lead reporters, Tariq Ayoub. The publication of a classified memo of an April 14, 2004, conversation between U.S. President George W. Bush and British premier Tony Blair further reinforced the image, where the bombing of al-Jazeera's Doha headquarters was purportedly discussed. A media firestorm followed this incident, and thousands of websites and blogs posted a banner declaring they would publish the "al-Jazeera memo" if it were to be declassified.

Globally Controversial

Although a relative newcomer, al-Jazeera rapidly generated much debate and considerable media research. From glorification to vilification, the station has been described as "radical" and "extremist" by its detractors and as a much-needed alternative by its admirers. Governments around the world have expressed their reservations, including famously from a former U.S. secretary of state calling on the Qatari Emir to muzzle the station during the early days of the 2003 war on Iraq. Regardless of leaning, most commentators acknowledged that al-Jazeera constituted a phenomenon among Arab broadcasters, some arguing it had effectively transformed regional journalism.

Al-Jazeera became particularly known for its unfettered, and sometimes exclusive, access to key news events, including the early days of the U.S.-led wars in Afghanistan and Iraq, as well as for airing numerous videos from al-Qaeda leaders Osama bin Laden and Ayman al-Zawahiri. The station also garnered global attention for its coverage of the 2006 Israel–Lebanon war. More recently, it was the only global network on the ground in Gaza during the Israeli military attack in December 2008–January 2009. During these periods the station solidified its reputation as a go-to source of alternative news for Western news organizations.

Over the years, al-Jazeera has been accused of inciting activism against Arab regimes, violence against U.S. interests, and hatred of Israel. Many believe it is energizing a new pan-Arab sentiment, whereas others believe its antagonistic tone divides Arabs by playing off state nationalisms against each other. Although it has provided a platform for the broadcast of "radical voices," al-Jazeera does not appear to align itself directly with any social movement and instead argues that coverage of polarizing groups is a journalistic imperative.

In recent years, the network has dedicated considerable coverage to political and militia groups, such as Lebanon's Hezbollah and Palestine's Hamas. Nation-states that define these organizations solely as terrorist entities, primarily the United States, Israel, Canada, and the Netherlands, have vigorously objected to al-Jazeera's coverage. Network officials responded that both organizations are very newsworthy, given that sympathetic interest in the Palestinian situation has always been high throughout the region's audiences.

The same critique has been directed at al-Jazeera for its attention to al-Qaeda, and for giving airtime to Israeli officials, a move that challenges other regional broadcasters' boycott of Israeli spokespeople. Although the station has been called "Osama bin Laden's mouthpiece" by U.S. administration officials, it insists it has never adopted al-Qaeda's or any other social movement's ideology. There are no signs of al-Jazeera identifying with any specific organizations in the Arab world, beyond a general sympathy with the underdog.

Al-Jazeera "English"

In 2007, al-Jazeera launched an English-language satellite network. The startup expenditures were around $1 billion, the costliest single media startup in history, and included four broadcasting centers in Doha, Kuala Lumpur, London, and Washington, D.C., as well as one of the most extensive networks of bureaus and reporters in the world, 21 as of 2010. Al-Jazeera English attempts to present news from a novel perspective, choosing to rely on reporters from the nation or region ("native correspondents") and focusing on regions with disproportionately low coverage in the Western networks (e.g., South America, sub-Saharan Africa, South and Southeast Asia, and the Middle East). This has led some to describe al-Jazeera English as the first major transnational network from the global South, with others calling it the voice of an "empire striking back."

However, although the network appeared to have made strides in its first three years, its exact popularity remains unclear. To date, al-Jazeera English had only been able to enter the U.S. TV market via satellite network LinkTV (reaching up to a quarter of households) and two small cable providers in Toledo (Ohio), Burlington (Vermont), and most recently Washington, D.C. Burlington became the site of a high-profile town hall debate following the network's removal due to viewer complaints that it was anti-American. Subsequently, two town hall meetings were held and a majority voted to reinstate the network, citing that it offered a unique alternative to American programming. This was considered a major victory for the network's U.S. profile and for other global news providers trying to break into the U.S. market.

The characterization of al-Jazeera as an alternative medium is hotly contested. The station appears to be an amalgam of both alternative and mainstream. Those arguing it is mainstream note it is built on the corporate sponsor model and utilizes typical U.S. industry-standard marketing, advertising, and public relations instruments. Al-Jazeera's staff are professionals with years of experience. The network also clearly demarcates occupational boundaries that privilege specialization and vocational training. In fact, al-Jazeera is now home to a training facility for journalists and media personnel. Despite falling short on advertising revenues, its budget remains colossal, dwarfing even the most heftily funded Western networks.

However, there is still a considerable evidence in support of the opinion that al-Jazeera is alternative. What it lacks in organizational alterity, it compensates for in content. Several features of its coverage stand out: (a) its open forum for dissent of all stripes, particularly on the uninterrupted and volatile talk shows, unparalleled among the Arab region's state broadcasters; (b) its war reporting, including its emphasis on humanitarian consequences; and (c) its emphasis on native journalism by assigning reporters to report on their locales.

Although al-Jazeera English reaches some 150 million households worldwide, at this time, it remains early to judge the station's success and effectiveness. Nevertheless, the network has become a major social force within global media reform circles, with some of its supporters describing it as the voice of the "postcolony." Its provision of an ongoing combative forum for counter-narratives from the global South is seen as a significant challenge to Western media hegemony.

Adel Iskandar

See also Alternative Information Center (Israel and Palestine); Arab Bloggers as Citizen Journalists (Transnational); Beheading Videos (Iraq/Transnational); Citizens' Media; Peace Media (Colombia); Small Media Against Big Oil (Nigeria); Third World Network (Malaysia)

Further Readings

Downing, J. D. H. (2001). *Radical media: Rebellious communication and social movements*. Thousand Oaks, CA: Sage.

el-Nawawy, M., & Iskandar, A. (2002). The Minotaur of "contextual objectivity": War coverage and the pursuit of accuracy with appeal. *Transnational Broadcasting Studies Journal*. Retrieved on July 22, 2003, from http://www.tbsjournal.com/Archives/Fall02/Iskandar.html

el-Nawawy, M., & Iskandar, A. (2003). *Al-Jazeera: The story of the network that is rattling governments and redefining modern journalism*. Boulder, CO: Westview Press.

Iskandar, A. (2005, Fall). Is al-Jazeera alternative? Mainstreaming alterity and assimilating discourses of dissent. *Transnational Broadcasting Studies, 15*.

Lynch, M. (2006). *Voices of the new Arab public: Iraq, al-Jazeera and Middle East politics today*. New York: Columbia University Press.

Zayani, M. (2005). *The al-Jazeera phenomenon: Critical perspectives on new Arab media*. Boulder, CO: Paradigm.

ALLIANCE FOR COMMUNITY MEDIA (UNITED STATES)

The Alliance for Community Media (ACM) is a nonprofit, member-driven organization of community groups and individuals dedicated to serving the interest of PEG (public, educational and government) cable TV access organizations and community media centers across the United States. Founded in 1976, it represents more than 3,000 such organizations and millions of people who utilize PEG channels to engage with their communities.

Their ranks include multidenominational religious institutions, public school systems, local government agencies and officials, the National Association for the Advancement of Colored People (NAACP), and even NASA, the U.S. space agency. The ACM works with and on behalf of these organizations to ensure that PEG communication is not hindered by legislative or regulatory action, often filing lawsuits on behalf of access networks.

The ACM organizes under the belief that access to communication tools is a right, is the responsibility of the government to provide to its citizens, and should not be a party-political partisan issue. In 2008, the ACM proposed a national policy of "community reinvestment," which would allow PEG access groups more funding, spectrum, and bandwidth use for public interest purposes. This proposal was based on the following four points:

1. Federal protection of the right of the local community to decide the best way to utilize PEG access property

2. A dedication of at least 10% of public airwaves and PEG channel capacity for free speech, diverse viewpoints, local programming, community education, and news

3. The mandate of 5% of gross revenues from service providers, infrastructure creators, and spectrum license holders to support PEG equipment, facilities, training, and services

4. Guaranteed universal PEG access to any individual who requests it

The ACM remains one of the oldest organizations dedicated to preserving public sector cable television. It is their consistent willingness to fight for a democratic media system that has protected cable access stations from corporate and government threats to their continued existence.

Ricky Hill

See also Alternative Media: Policy Issues; Community Media and the Third Sector; Community Radio and Podcasting (United States); Media Activists and Communication Policy Processes; Media Infrastructure Policy and Media Activism; Media Justice Movement (United States); Public Access

Further Readings

Alliance for Community Media: http://www.alliancecm .org

ALTERNATIVE COMICS (UNITED STATES)

Comics have appeared in mainstream newspapers for centuries, but since the 1960s, small press and self-published comics have arisen in the United States to challenge prevailing notions of style, form, and content, ranging from the extremely lowbrow and obscene, to highly intellectual. Sometimes referred to as comix, they represent a diffuse movement of artists, publishing houses, and fan communities that work against the mainstream diet of superhero stories and gag strips. As of the late 2000s, technological advances in printing and computer-aided composition, as well as the Internet's development as a distribution and marketing platform, have led to a significant presence of comics as an intelligent, communicative, and diverse artistic medium.

Underground Comix

Produced on a small scale and with limited resources, the early underground comics were almost always produced by a single person, serving as artist, writer, inker, and the rest. Limited in length, they usually ran fewer than 10,000 copies. They were typified by a low-tech aesthetic, much in the same vein as punk zines. Harvey Kurtzman introduced the idea of comics as an underground movement in *Mad* magazine in 1954, and the movement was significantly tied to 1960s U.S. counterculture.

These comics primarily relied on head shops and the postal service for distribution, though some appeared in underground publications like the *Berkeley Barb* and *East Village Other*. They were produced independently of the large publishing houses, such as DC Comics and Marvel, and were not bound by the Comics Code Authority, the industry's self-regulatory body, leaving them free to tackle taboo subjects, reveling in depictions of sexuality, violence, and drugs.

Important artists of the underground period, lasting until the mid-1970s, included Robert Crumb, Bill Griffith, and Art Spiegelman, whose work appeared in publications like *Zap Comix*, *Armadillo Comix*, *Doctor Wirtham's Comix & Stories*, and *Bijou Funnies*. The underground comics vilified many aspects of mainstream U.S. life—the government, religion, general uptightness—often directly parodying mainstream characters and artists in the process. Unlike mainstream comics' fairly staid and recognizable style, the artists ranged from the seemingly amateurish to the highly polished.

Postunderground

With the collapse of the counterculture and economic stagnation in the mid-1970s, the underground comics saw decline. As a result, a new movement of comic creators arose that utilized more mainstream production models and distribution channels to foster alternatives to the mainstream. From its founding in 1976, publisher Fantagraphics Books became the home of several new talents, such as Daniel Clowes, Chris Ware, and the Hernández brothers, Gilbert and Jaime. Spiegelman started *RAW* magazine, with his wife Françoise Mouly, as a publishing venue for alternative comics in 1980, and it lasted until 1991. Robert Crumb founded *Weirdo* magazine, which ran until 1993 and espoused a more low-art outsider aesthetic than *RAW*. With the growth of comics-specific retailers in the mainstream comics boom of the 1980s, alternative comics found themselves with new outlets for sales alongside their more popular counterparts. As of the late 2000s, many mainstream bookstores also carried alternative comics from publishers like Fantagraphics, Drawn and Quarterly, Top Shelf, and Oni Press.

Some alternative works have achieved significant mainstream exposure and success. Spiegelman's *Maus*, about his father's experiences in the Holocaust, received a Pulitzer Prize in 1992. Clowes's *Ghost World* and *Art School Confidential*, as well as Harvey Pekar's *American Splendor* and Marjane Satrapi's *Persepolis*, have been adapted into major motion pictures. Alternative publications carry politically and culturally subversive comic strips such as *This Modern World, Red Meat*, and *Dykes to Watch Out For*. Alternative book-length comics such as *Blankets, Jimmy Corrigan*, and *Maus* are increasingly available in libraries and taught in high school and college as literary texts.

With the growing popularity of alternative comics and a general decline in censorship in the United States, mainstream publishers adopted some of the experimental features of the alternatives, introducing more stylized works with adult-oriented content. In 1986, DC Comics published Frank Miller's *Batman: The Dark Knight Returns*, which featured a dystopian ultraviolent future Batman, and *Watchmen*, a critical and violent deconstruction of superhero depictions and narratives. Both turned a critical eye on the mainstream comics universe, co-opting the alternative's outsider stance, but their publication by mainstream comics publishers, as well as financial and critical success, made them decidedly mainstream.

Webcomics

Since the advent of the Internet, comics creators have been able to return in many ways to the early ethos of the do-it-yourself underground comics due to the ease of distribution and the ability to foster a close relationship with readers. So-called webcomics allow individual artists to self-publish without the barrier of printing or editorial oversight. Like the link between underground comics and the 1960s drug culture, the webcomics in part correspond with a cyber-subculture of the digitally literate. As a result, many webcomics focus on aspects of geek culture, such as video games, hacking, and the Internet.

The Internet's fluidity allowed the creators to explore the medium outside of page size and layout limitations, employing Scott McCloud's notion of the "infinite canvas." The quality was prone to the same problems as any type of self-publishing, but the experience could be empowering for the creators regardless of talent. Few webcomics were self-supporting, though some artists were able to survive through the sale of books and merchandise like shirts and posters, and many solicited donations from fans to stay afloat. In addition, alternative comics-specific events like the Small Press Expo and the Alternative Press Expo gave the artists an outlet for collaboration, sales, and valuable contact with fans. Prominent webcomics included James Kochalka's *American Elf*, Chris Onstad's *Achewood*, Dorothy Gambrell's *Cat and Girl*, Ryan North's *Dinosaur Comics*, Nicholas Gurewitch's *The Perry Bible Fellowship*, and *Penny Arcade* by Jerry Holkins and Mike Krahulik.

Daniel Darland

See also *Ballyhoo* Magazine (United States); Fantagraphics Books (United States); *Love and Rockets* Comic Books (United States); Political Cartooning 1870s–Present (India); *RAW* Magazine (United States); Zines

Further Readings

Brunetti, I. (Ed.). (2006). *An anthology of graphic fiction, cartoons, and true stories*. New Haven, CT: Yale University Press.

Brunetti, I. (Ed.). (2008). *An anthology of graphic fiction, cartoons, and true stories* (Vol. 2). New Haven, CT: Yale University Press.

Estren, M. J. (1974). *A history of underground comics*. San Francisco: Straight Arrow Books.

Fenty, S., Houp, T., & Taylor, L. N. (2004). Webcomics: The influence and continuation of the comix revolution. *ImageTexT, 1*(2). http://www.english.ufl.edu/imagetext

Rosenkranz, P. (2002). *Rebel visions: The underground comix revolution, 1963–1975*. Seattle, WA: Fantagraphics Books.

Sabin, R. (1996). *Comics, comix & graphic novels: A history of comic art*. London: Phaidon Press.

Sanders, C. R. (1975). Icons of the alternate culture. *Journal of Popular Culture, 8*(4), 836–852.

ALTERNATIVE INFORMATION CENTER (ISRAEL AND PALESTINE)

The Alternative Information Center (AIC) is a joint Palestinian–Israeli nongovernmental organization (NGO), founded in 1984, and active as of the late 2000s. Its website mission statement says it "engages in dissemination of information, political advocacy, grassroots activism and critical analysis of the Palestinian and Israeli societies as well as the Palestinian-Israeli conflict" (http://www.alternativenews.org/index.php?option=com_content&view=section&id=6&Itemid=595).

According to Michel Warschawski, one of its cofounders—a well-known figure in the Israeli anticolonialist movement—the AIC is alternative in two senses. First, it publishes dissenting perspectives and critical information on issues not covered by the mainstream media in Israel and Palestine. For instance, *News From Within*, launched in 1985, publishes many articles on Palestinian political prisoners, torture in Israeli prisons, the Palestinian civil resistance, including the women's movement, the condition of the Jews who migrated to Israel from Arab nations, the Israeli peace movement, and the expansion of settlements in the Occupied Territories. Palestinians and Israelis can be informed as to the internal evolution of their respective societies.

The AIC is also alternative in the sense that it aims at constituting a common political space and partnership for Israeli and Palestinian activists. This partnership is not mere cooperation but a political commitment to reinforce the Palestinian national movement and the Israeli organizations in their concrete opposition to the occupation. This dimension is evident in the numerous connections established between the AIC and left-wing movements in Israel, the Occupied Territories, and internationally—especially the global social justice movement.

Political Trajectory

The AIC's internal organization significantly changed over its first twenty years in step with the evolution of the Israeli–Palestinian conflict. It had been born in the aftermath of Israel's 1982 occupation of southern Lebanon, located in a two-room apartment in Jerusalem, without funds or hierarchical decision making.

Its members—journalists, activists, lawyers, or teachers—began publishing reports, studies, and newspapers. They multiplied contacts with the national and international press. In 1985, the AIC was involved in the negotiations among the Israeli government, the organization Ahmad Jibril, and the Red Cross, for a detainee exchange. This involved 1,115 Palestinian detainees exchanged for six Nahal soldiers, captives since the Lebanon invasion. (*Nahal* is a special Israeli army unit, awarded the Israeli government's top honor in 1984, the Israel Prize.) Two of these soldiers, now veterans, began working in the AIC: Ali Jeda and Ata el-Qeimari.

As of the late 1980s, however, the center experienced government repression. In late 1986, Ali Jeda was arrested in Jerusalem's Old City while collecting information for an article on an attack against Arab residents in the Muslim Quarter. Then in early 1987 the government temporarily closed the AIC and arrested Warschawski. The AIC was accused of connections with an "illegal organization," the Popular Front for the Liberation of Palestine. Warschawski was released in late 1990, after remission of a third of his 8-month sentence.

Overall, during the Palestinian uprising, between 1987 and 1991 (the First Intifada), the AIC reached a peak of activity, playing the role of mediator and advisor between the Palestinian resistance and the Israeli anti-Occupation movement, but also working with international journalists and diplomats.

After the Oslo Agreements (1993–1995), the AIC became a more professional organization. It had 9 employees in 1993 and 17 by 1997. At the same time, the number of volunteers decreased, from 15 in 1994 to 7 in 1997. The AIC benefited from growing donations coming from European and U.S. governments or foundations. Its opposition to the Oslo peace process substantially reduced its international revenue, but the total budget still grew. The AIC became more and more a "classical" NGO.

In 1994, a second office was opened in Beit Sahour (West Bank). New publications were launched, such as *The Other Front*, in 1992, dedicated to reporting Israeli society developments for the Palestinian public; *April 17*, on Palestinian political prisoners, in 1993; *Rou'ya Ukrha* (Another Vision), a magazine in Arabic; and *Mitsad Shen* (The Other Front), a magazine in Hebrew.

In January 1999, however, three leading AIC activists, Elias Jeraysi (editor of *Rou'ya Ukhra*), Inbal Perlson (editor of *Mitsad Sheni*), and Yohanan Lorwin (editor of *News From Within*), were killed in a flash flood. This tragic event ushered in an internal crisis, due to tensions between NGO priorities and a desire to restore a more politicized approach. In August 2000, the AIC began operating from one office in Bethlehem. The staff was reduced to 7, with increased reliance on volunteers. The Second Intifada began in September, and Israel's total closure of the West Bank forced reopening an office in downtown Jerusalem in November.

The AIC established close relationships with the global social justice movement in the 2000s, especially following the 2001 visit of the French farmer trade unionist José Bové to the Occupied Territories. Connie Hackbarth became the new AIC director through 2006. Repression against the Palestinians reached AIC staff member Ahmad Abu Hannya, placed for 6 months in administrative detention without charge by the Israeli Army in 2005.

In early 2007, a new directorship team was elected. Sergio Yahni became program director, Connie Hackbarth executive director, and Nassar Ibrahim political director.

As of the late 2000s, the AIC produced four main print publications: *Rou'ya Ukhra, News From Within, Mitsad Sheni,* and *The Economy of the Occupation*. It had a website in four languages; published books, reports, and booklets; made documentaries; organized alternative tours in the Occupied Territories and conferences; and was involved in many grassroots projects with the Palestinian civil resistance and Israel's anti-Occupation movement.

Benjamin Ferron

See also Arab Bloggers as Citizen Journalists (Transnational); BİA Independent Communication Network (Turkey); Palestinian Interwar Press; Pirate Radio (Israel); Pirate Radio (Lebanon); Zionist Movement Media Pre-1948

Further Readings

Alternative Information Center: http://www.alternativenews .org

Avran, I. (2001). *Israël-Palestine: les inventeurs de paix* [Israel-Palestine: Inventors of peace]. Paris: Éditions de l'Atelier/Éditions Ouvrières.

Warschawski, M. (2002). *Sur la frontière* [On the border]. Paris: Pluriel, Hachette Littérature, Stock.

Warschawski, M. (2006). *The Alternative Information Center: 20 years of joint struggle.* Jerusalem: Alternative Information Center, Latin Patriarchate Press.

ALTERNATIVE LOCAL PRESS (UNITED KINGDOM)

From the 1970s to the 1990s, alternative local newspapers sprang up in towns and cities across Britain, challenging mainstream media's social, political, and journalistic conservatism. This press was diverse, reflecting local conditions and different priorities. Most titles were short-lived but some lasted for 1 or even 2 decades; some were created by disgruntled journalists, but most were the product of people with no training in journalism. Most were monthly, some less frequent, and a few weekly; all relied on unpaid labor, but several also had some low-paid staff. Few survived past the mid-1990s.

They emerged in the context of a number of anticolonial wars and widespread student protests and industrial conflict in Europe. Britain was experiencing the beginnings of the breakdown of the post-1945 economic and political "consensus." There was an upsurge in the confidence and activities of social movements, including feminism, gay liberation, antiracism, antifascism, antinuclear, and antiapartheid, alongside a growth in self-organization within working-class communities as tenants groups, claimants unions, and housing action groups were formed.

There already existed a so-called underground or counterculture press, such as *Oz*, and some young radicals were becoming familiar with U.S. examples, such as the *Village Voice*. All this coincided with the arrival of relatively cheap and easy offset litho printing, heralding a new do-it-yourself publishing culture.

These papers, as they emerged, drew from and reported on the community politics and social movements that had emerged in the wake of 1968. Some of the best-known titles, indicating their geographical spread, included *Aberdeen People's Press, Alarm* (Swansea), *Brighton Voice, Bristol Voice, Cardiff People's Press, Durham Street Press, Exeter Flying Post, Glasgow News, Hackney People's Press, Islington Gutter Press, Leeds Other Paper, Liverpool Free Press, Manchester Free Press,* the *Post* (Hull), *Rochdale Alternative Press,* and *Sheffield Free Press*.

Sales ranged from a few hundred to several thousand. The majority were run by informal collectives or workers cooperatives. They reported "from below" the views and actions of people in a range of local struggles, living on low-income housing estates, community groups, rank and file union activists, unemployed workers, and activists within the women's and gay movements and Black communities. Typically, they acted as a watchdog on the local establishment and the forces of law and order and provided a notice-board to publicize a vast range of alternative and noncommercial events, services, and networks. Many provided free listings or accepted paid advertising from community or political events, local co-ops, and benefit gigs, and their pages could be locations of lively debate. Such papers served and helped constitute what might be referred to as the "alternative public sphere."

However, they were not homogenous. Some, including *Liverpool Free Press* and *Manchester Free Press,* were set up by journalists employed by their local commercial newspaper who felt the need for an alternative outlet on the side. Most, however, were produced by people with no formal journalistic training, who taught themselves while on the job. This emergent press was informed by a libertarian socialist ethos, and those involved were interested not only in producing alternative content but also in developing alternative or "prefigurative" ways of working together. Typically, such publications had relatively open structures, with readers being invited to join in and become producers. With open editorial policies and a shifting population of contributors, an alternative paper such as *Leeds Other Paper*—one of the longest lasting—might change its style and priorities several times within a short space of time.

Many such newspapers would gather for occasional national conferences, and those who met in Leeds in 1984 agreed on the following statement, which is worth quoting in its entirety because it gives the flavor of the times:

> An unambiguous definition of an "alternative newspaper" is impossible, but there seem to be features common to all of them. They are: local; anti-racist; anti-sexist; politically on the left; overtly, rather than covertly, political; not produced for profit; editorially free of the influence of advertisers; run on broadly collective principles. The content and format of individual publications is often determined by their perception of their role as persuasive or informative, by their aims and distribution, and the political allegiance of their contributors. (Harcup, 1994, p. 14)

The precise emphasis of a paper depends on the geographical location and political arena in which it is produced. Whereas some papers, generally in Conservative-controlled areas, can count upon the wide support of the left, others in traditional Labour areas are not guaranteed such support. Thus, their role as critics of the local state will differ. A Labour establishment can be as hostile as a Tory one to the independent critical voice of the alternative newspaper.

Papers in Labour-controlled areas have a contradictory role in that they often want to criticize from the Left, do not want to be identified directly with the Labour Party, but at the same time are loath to provide the Right with ammunition.

Most alternative newspapers are small, their existence precarious. With one or two notable exceptions, their circulations are in the hundreds rather than the thousands. But this tells us nothing about their influence or their value. As virtually all mass media are in the political center or on the right, the voice of the local alternative newspaper is an important counterweight. Small need not mean insignificant.

Many of these papers would swap story ideas and information via a duplicated newssheet distributed by People's News Service, a not terribly successful attempt at providing an alternative to Associated Press and Reuters.

Most, if not all, of the papers depended on free labor, although some managed to pay a limited amount in wages, scraped together from sales, advertising income, and extra money earned from printing or typesetting for groups within the alternative sphere. However, supplies of income and labor became less plentiful as the political and economic climate grew harsher under 18 years of Conservative governments (1979–1997). By the late 1980s and early 1990s, many of the social, political, and cultural networks that had fed into and been reflected by the alternative local press had been damaged if not destroyed. Many who had set up such papers were either exhausted or had moved on, while the generation known as "Thatcher's children" (after Margaret Thatcher, Conservative prime minister, 1979–1990) seemed to have less energy for such projects.

Short-lived though they were, the alternative local papers that emerged in the United Kingdom from the 1970s challenged the hegemony of the local establishment and mainstream media by demonstrating that there was more than one way of viewing the world and—not least—that nonprofessionals could become journalists and create their own media.

Tony Harcup

See also *Dangwai* Magazines (Taiwan); *Leeds Other Paper/Northern Star* (United Kingdom); *Leveller* Magazine (United Kingdom); *Spare Rib* Magazine (United Kingdom)

Further Readings

Atton, C., & Hamilton, J. (2008). *Alternative journalism.* London: Sage.

Aubrey, C., Landry, C., & Morley, D. (1980). *Here is the other news.* London: Minority Press Group.

Bone, I. (2006). *Bash the rich: True-life confessions of an anarchist in the UK.* Bath, UK: Tangent.

Dickinson, R. (1997). *Imprinting the sticks: The alternative press beyond London.* Aldershot, UK: Arena.

Fountain, N. (1988). *Underground: The London alternative press.* London: Routledge.

Harcup, T. (1994). A Northern Star: Leeds Other Paper *and the alternative press 1974–1994.* London: Campaign for Press and Broadcasting Freedom.

Harcup, T. (2003). The unspoken—said: The journalism of alternative media. *Journalism, 4*(3), 356–376.

Harcup, T. (2005). "I'm doing this to change the world": Journalism in alternative and mainstream media. *Journalism Studies, 6*(3), 361–374.

Harcup, T. (2006). The alternative local press. In B. Franklin (Ed.), *Local journalism and local media* (pp. 129–139). London: Routledge.

Royal Commission on the Press. (1977). *Periodicals and the alternative press.* London: HMSO.

Whitaker, B. (1981). *News Ltd: Why you can't read all about it.* London: Minority Press Group.

ALTERNATIVE MEDIA

Alternative media are produced outside mainstream media institutions and networks. They can include the media of protest groups, dissidents, fringe political organizations, even fans and hobbyists. They tend to be produced by amateurs who typically have little or no training or professional qualifications. They write and report from their position as citizens, as members of communities, as activists, or as fans. Alternative media also seek to redress what their producers consider an imbalance of media power in mainstream media, which results in the marginalization (at worst, the demonization) of certain social and cultural groups and movements. As well as being homes for radical content, alternative media projects also tend to be organized in nonmainstream ways, often nonhierarchically or collectively, and very often on a noncommercial basis. In these ways they hope to be independent of the market and open to change.

This entry examines the ways in which alternative media—and, in particular, the term *alternative*—have been defined, explores ways in which such media represent a challenge to media power, and discusses a typology of alternative media. The field theory of Pierre Bourdieu is drawn upon to consider the relationship between alternative and mainstream media production, and subsequently the particular ideology and practices of alternative journalism.

The definition of alternative media as presented here is not limited to political and "resistance" media. It is equally applicable to artistic and literary media (video, music, mail art, creative writing), as well as to forms such as zines and electronic communication. Not only social relations in general but also dominant practices of media production—text, visual forms, even distribution processes—may be transformed, and notions such as professionalism, competence, and expertise can be reassessed.

Defining Alternative Media

The apparent looseness in defining terms in this field has led some critics to argue that there can be no meaningful definition of the term *alternative media*. Whereas *radical* encourages a definition that is primarily concerned with (often revolutionary) social change, *alternative* offers a much looser purchase. Custom and practice within alternative media appear to have settled on *alternative* as the preferred term. Its strength is that it can encompass far more than *radical*, or terms such as *social change publishing*; it can also include alternative lifestyle magazines, an extremely diverse range of fanzine and zine publishing, and the small presses of poetry and fiction publishers.

Furthermore, definitions have historical and cultural contingencies. *Alternative* in West Coast countercultural terms invokes alternative therapies and New Age thinking. *Radical* for some can be as much to do with avant-garde artistic activity as with politics. For zine writers, neither term might be preferable: The even looser *DIY publishing* might replace both. John Downing talks of radical media, an alternative public realm, alternative media, and radical alternative media, but he also refers to counterinformation and popular oppositional culture. His discussion of Oskar Negt and Alexander Kluge's work raises Antonio Gramsci's notion of counterhegemony that, Downing implies, is also a driving force behind the contemporary media he is examining.

The entire range of alternative media might be considered as representing challenges to hegemony, whether on an explicitly political platform, or employing the kinds of indirect challenges through experimentation and transformation of existing roles, routines, emblems, and signs that

Dick Hebdige locates at the heart of counterhegemonic subcultural style. Karol Jakubowicz finds a wider meaning in *alternative*: not simply sects or narrow special interests but a wide-ranging and influential sphere that may include all manner of reformist groups and institutions.

From a sociological point of view, there is a discrepancy between what alternative signifies and what oppositional, counterinformation, and counterhegemony signify. Cultural historian and analyst Raymond Williams distinguished between alternative and oppositional practices. Alternative culture, such as a minority back-to-nature cult, would be for him a very different matter to oppositional culture—for instance, the global ecology movement. Williams hoped that the culture of the new social movements, although being termed an alternative culture, would ideally become an oppositional culture. Certainly the 1977 Royal Commission on the Press judged that the British alternative press of that period expressed attitudes hostile to widely held beliefs.

Alternative media thus becomes both a comparative term and a broader term. Within it may be placed not only the media of politics and empowerment but also the media of popular culture and the everyday. Alternative media may be home to explorations of individual enthusiasm and subcultural identity just as much as they may be homes to radical visions of society and the polity. Rather than relying on the mass media to set the boundaries of political involvement, citizens use their own, self-managed media to become politically involved on their own terms. To become an active participant in the process of media production is a political education in itself. Amateur media practices are always embedded in everyday life practices; they are therefore already located in broader political, economic, social, and cultural contexts. For these reasons, many prefer the terms *alternative media* and *alternative journalism* to describe these practices.

Alternative Media as Challenges to Media Power

Media researchers Nick Couldry and James Curran have argued that the term *alternative media* indicates that indirectly or directly, media power is at stake. This perspective is able to accommodate a range of theories that have been put forward to make sense of alternative media production. These include Downing's theory of radical media, Clemencia Rodríguez's citizens media, and Bob Hackett and William Carroll's notion of democratic media activism, all of which share a common assumption that alternative media are primarily concerned with radical politics and social empowerment, with what political scientist Pippa Norris has called "critical citizens." Couldry and Curran consequently find broader aims in alternative media, aims that may or may not be politically radical or socially empowering.

Couldry has argued that challenges to media power do not necessarily always take place within conventional practices of media production. His studies of protests in England show how they denaturalized mainstream journalism practices that normally are taken for granted (such as what counts as newsworthy, how stories are framed, and how people in those stories are represented). In Gramscian terms, they are hegemonic practices that appear natural; it seems that there is no other way of doing journalism.

Amateur media producers play an important role here. They show that it is possible to reimagine media production and that there are other ways of practicing it beyond its dominant forms. This develops Bourdieu's position, that symbolic power is the power to construct reality. Participatory, amateur media production challenges the mainstream media monopoly on producing symbolic forms. Through more inclusive and democratic forms of media production, alternative media producers are able to rebalance the power of the media, however modestly.

A Typology of Alternative Media

Media researchers Olga Guedes Bailey, Bart Cammaerts, and Nico Carpentier argue that alternative media may serve specific communities by representing them in ways that challenge their image in the local commercial press and that there are media that provide more autonomous and oppositional alternatives, whether in their organization, the forms of representation they use in their journalism, or their methods of distribution. For Bailey, Cammaerts, and Carpentier, these first two types are centered on media production.

The third and fourth types are centered not so much on media but on society: Both use media production to try to effect social and political change. The third type, civil society media, operates with more or less fixed objectives. The fourth type is rhizomatic media (a metaphor of the horizontal underground runner plant taken from Gilles Deleuze and Félix Guattari) that tend to be interconnected, often on a global scale; the network is key to these media, where organization is fluid and often transient. Rhizomatic media are able to mutate as social or political conditions change. To theorize alternative media we need to take account of all four types, to examine how they work with or against each other in different political, social, cultural and geographical contexts. In other words, these four approaches are not exclusive: Community media may be rhizomatic; autonomous media may have a civil society function. Theorized in this way, the practices of alternative media highlight challenges to dominant media practices with respect to structure (the market and the state), agency (participation, the network), and the ideology of journalistic practices (representation).

Therefore, to consider alternative media is to recognize the ongoing interrelation between dominant, professionalized media practices and marginal, amateur practices. The struggle between them is for media power. The emphasis on alternative media as oppositional projects, however, has until recently tended to obscure the relationship between the amateur and the professional. This relationship is particularly relevant when we consider alternative media as forms of journalism, an area of research that has only recently been developed. Alternative media offer opportunities for participating in the world that go far beyond the narrow conceptions of citizens as passive consumers and marginal players in politics and culture. They offer the means to a properly active citizenship. For all the diversity of approaches, there is general agreement among scholars that *citizenship* in some sense is at stake.

Alternative Media and Field Theory

The field theory of Bourdieu offers a fruitful approach to developing a sociology of alternative media. Bourdieu provides a method of understanding culture in society that neither mystifies the creative process nor reduces it to social and economic context. Instead, he provides a framework upon which may be built a complex understanding of cultural production in social life, one that takes into account structural determinants such as economics and politics (power), interactions between individuals and institutions, and the development of taste, social and cultural value, and esteem. He also focuses on interactions, borrowings, and struggles between agents across related fields or subfields (e.g., across mainstream and alternative journalism), as well as within a single field or subfield. Field theory offers more precise terms than *alternative* and *mainstream*.

Rodney Benson, a sympathetic critic of Bourdieu, argues that three expressions of economic capital in journalism are circulation, advertising income, and audience ratings. By distinction, cultural capital lies in journalism that is respected more for its professionalism, its erudition, and its originality. If we understand alternative media in these terms, their general disinterest in economic capital and general lack of mass-popular success or recognition suggest they are in the subfield of small-scale (restricted) production, whereas mainstream journalism is located in the subfield of large-scale (mass) production. Bourdieu's terms (*small-scale* and *large-scale*) have an analytical precision that the terms *alternative* and *mainstream* lack.

It is also important to consider alternative media not only as occupying the subfield of small-scale production but also as able to occupy intermediate positions at the juncture of the two subfields of journalism, or between an activist (or other) field and the journalistic field. Intermediate positions are implied but not discussed by Bourdieu. The low levels of both cultural and economic capital Bourdieu assigns to nonprofessionals might explain the failure of amateur and activist media producers to make any significant impact on large-scale journalistic production. Yet cultural capital might well be achieved at the juncture of the fields of journalism and activism in ways that he does not specify.

Alternative Journalism

In the context of alternative journalism, examples of these activities at the boundaries include the professionalization and normalization of blogs in large-scale journalism and, though perhaps less obviously, the fanzine-like production taking place on large-scale, international social networking sites such as MySpace. Popular music researcher Gestur Gudmundsson and his colleagues' assessment of professional rock journalism as "semi-autonomous" seems to recognize both its intermediate, liminal nature and its movement into large-scale production from its roots in the amateur, underground press and fanzines, accruing cultural capital as it moves. *Liminal,* from the Latin word for "threshold," suggests more than intermediate, rather a moment or a space of opportunity and change.

Alternative news values are bound up not just in terms of what is considered as news but also in approaches to news gathering, who writes such news and how it is presented. These values present a direct challenge to the objectivity ethos that dominates professionalized journalism. This challenge has both a normative and an epistemological aspect. Professionalized journalism is based on the empiricist assumption that there exist facts in the world and that it is possible to identify these facts accurately and without bias. The normative ideal of alternative journalism argues the opposite: that reporting is always bound up with values (personal, professional, institutional) and that it is therefore never possible to separate facts from values. Thus, different forms of knowledge may be produced, which present multiple versions of reality from those of the mass media.

A study by Tony Harcup of alternative and mainstream reporting in northern England found alternative press reporters favored the views and comments of bystanders, quoting street eyewitnesses and conversations overheard in courtrooms rather than official spokespeople. Mark Deuze and Christina Dimoudi studied online journalists in the Netherlands and found similar community impulses at work. They hold out the hope that the Internet will facilitate the development of closer dialogue between journalists and their audiences, resulting in sourcing and agenda setting driven by a range of more heterogeneous interests than in mainstream journalism.

Ideology and Practice in Alternative Journalism

If it is possible to speak of a single ideology of alternative journalism, it lies in the belief that journalism should facilitate, not restrict, the circulation of information and views to enable citizens to make their own assessments. Therefore, a key aim of alternative journalism is to democratize journalism and encourage consumers of news to become creators of news. Many alternative journalists consequently treat nonofficial sources as primary definers in their stories (examples include factory or shop workers, minor government officials, pensioners, working mothers, the unemployed, the homeless, even schoolchildren), actively seeking out "ordinary" people as expert sources in their own lives and experiences.

Media researcher Harcup (1994) calls this kind of alternative journalism "the parish magazines of the dispossessed" (p. 3) and identifies the local alternative press that flourished in 1970s Britain as an exemplary form. These papers were interested in reports that directly affected the lives of working people in their communities. These reports could be significant to the local community, often bypassing the event-driven routines of mainstream news practices.

Alternative journalism will tend, through its very practices, to reassess notions of truth, reality, objectivity, expertise, authority, and credibility. We need to consider alternative journalism practices as socially and culturally situated work, as well as processes of political empowerment. The field theory of Bourdieu offers a sophisticated and nuanced methodology for exploring alternative journalism in relation to professionalized ideologies and practices, as well as to the activism that is so often its wellspring.

Alternative media are characterized by their potential for participation. Rather than media production being the province of elite, centralized organizations and institutions, alternative media offer the possibilities for individuals and groups to create their own media from the periphery. To think about alternative media in this way is to consider it as far more than mere cultural aberration or marginal practice.

Chris Atton

See also Alternative Comics (United States); Alternative Media Center (United States); AlterNet (United States); Citizen Journalism; Citizens' Media; Community Media and the Third Sector; Installation Art Media;

Performance Art and Social Movement Media: Augusto Boal; Zines

Further Readings

Atton, C. (2002). *Alternative media.* London: Sage.
Atton, C., & Hamilton, J. F. (2008). *Alternative journalism.* London: Sage.
Bailey, O. G., Cammaerts, B., & Carpentier, N. (2008). *Understanding alternative media.* Maidenhead, UK: Open University Press.
Benson, R. (2006). News media as a "journalistic field": What Bourdieu adds to new institutionalism, and vice versa. *Political Communication, 23,* 187–202.
Bourdieu, P. (1996). *The rules of art: Genesis and structure of the literary field.* Cambridge, UK: Polity Press.
Couldry, N., & Curran, J. (2003). The paradox of media power. In N. Couldry & J. Curran (Eds.), *Contesting media power: Alternative media in a networked world* (pp. 3–15). Lanham, MD: Rowman & Littlefield.
Deuze, M., & Dimoudi, C. (2002). Online journalists in the Netherlands: Towards a profile of a new profession. *Journalism: Theory, Practice and Criticism, 3*(1), 85–100.
Downing, J. D. H. (with Villarreal Ford, T., Gil, G., & Stein, L.). (2001). *Radical media: Rebellious communication and social movements.* Thousand Oaks, CA: Sage.
Gudmundsson, G., Lindberg, U., Michelsen, M., & Weisethaunet H. (2002). Brit crit: Turning points in British rock criticism, 1960–1990. In S. Jones (Ed.), *Pop music and the press* (pp. 41–64). Philadelphia: Temple University Press.
Hackett, R. A., & Carroll, W. K. (2006). *Remaking media: The struggle to democratize public communication.* New York: Routledge.
Harcup, T. (1994). *A Northern Star: Leeds Other Paper and the alternative press 1974–1994.* London: Campaign for Press and Broadcasting Freedom.
Hebdige, D. (1979). *Subculture: The meaning of style.* London: Methuen.
Negt, O., & Kluge, A. (1983). The proletarian public sphere. In A. Mattelart & S. Siegelaub (Eds.), *Communication and class struggle: Vol. 2. Liberation, socialism* (pp. 92–94). New York: International General. (Original work published 1972)
Rodríguez, C. (2000). *Fissures in the mediascape: An international study of citizens' media.* Cresskill, NJ: Hampton Press.
Royal Commission on the Press. (1977). *Periodicals and the alternative press.* London: HMSO.

Williams, R. (1983). *Towards 2000*. London: Chatto & Windus.

ALTERNATIVE MEDIA (MALAYSIA)

Malaysia provides a case study of media under a soft authoritarian electoral system, where citizens lack the civil and political rights guaranteed in liberal democracies but are relatively free of the brutal repression faced under totalitarian states that deny even the right to vote. Malaysia's media activists are able to operate openly, but they need artful methods—and, sometimes, foreign support—to survive harassment and obstruction. Malaysia also offers striking examples of aggressive, counterhegemonic use of the Internet. Government permits are required for operating print media and broadcasting but not websites. The Internet has therefore become a haven for alternative and social movement media. The government has found it difficult to tame dissent in cyberspace.

The country achieved independence from British colonial rule in 1957. Since then, the same alliance of parties has won every general election. Politics is structured along ethnic lines. The ruling alliance, Barisan Nasional (BN), is led by the United Malay National Organization (UMNO) representing the Malays, who, with other Indigenous groups, made up more than 60% of the country's 25 million people in 2009. Traditionally, UMNO's main BN partners have represented the Chinese and Indian communities (over 20% and 7% of the population, respectively).

BN hegemony has been built on multiracial inclusivity and economic development, both fraught with contradictions, requiring BN dominance to be underwritten by frequent recourse to coercion. For this, the state possesses several instruments, notably the Internal Security Act, which permits arbitrary arrest without warrant and detention without trial. State control has limited severely the mass media's ability to offer news and opinion from diverse and critical perspectives. The national broadcaster Radio Television Malaysia and the Bernama news agency are both owned by the government.

Newspapers are commercially run, as are several television and radio stations, but all require annual permits dispensed at the discretion of government ministers. Most are owned directly or indirectly by the ruling parties, whereas others have owners who are close to the establishment. Licensing laws and other powers over the media have been used to silence the press or replace its management at critical junctures.

Contestation Through Media

Alternative media are not new. In the early 20th century, many Malay and Muslim progress associations emerged, including literary societies that spawned Malay journals. Journalists, poets, essayists, and other writers were important in radicalizing the Malay majority and developing the anticolonial movement. This radical media tradition was swept aside after independence. Especially during the lengthy premiership of Mahathir Mohamad (1981–2003), the BN regime attempted to construct an image of Malaysia as a harmonious society in which discordant voices were neither welcomed nor needed.

Nevertheless, Malaysia has witnessed major waves of protest, each associated with lively alternative media. In 1998, during the Asian financial crisis, Mahathir sacked his restless deputy Anwar Ibrahim, who proceeded to lead a Reformasi movement demanding political reform. In 2007, frustration with BN corruption and ineptitude led to more protests, notably the Bersih (Clean) rally for free and fair elections. The Anwar-led opposition alliance was able to take advantage of the antigovernment mood.

Thus, in the March 2008 elections, the opposition won a historic 5 out of 13 states. Also, for the first time in almost 30 years, the opposition denied BN a two-thirds majority in the federal parliament, ending its power to rewrite the Constitution at will. By 2009, Malaysians were contemplating a major reshaping of the social and political structure, facilitated in part by a complex web of movements and their media. The forces shaping these changes continue to be analyzed. What is clear, however, is that Malaysia is culturally diverse and economically divided, with marginalized groups that would, if they could, use media to define, express, and empower themselves.

One set of antagonisms relates to Malaysia's race-based politics. The most salient tension is between the numerically superior Malays and the economically wealthier Chinese. Such competition, however, is mostly contained within the dominant structure and modes of political participation: The mainstream Malay-language and Chinese-language press reflect the interests of their respective communities. It is instead intra-Malay competition that threatens to undercut UMNO's base and destabilize the regime. Because Malaysia's majority group identifies itself as simultaneously Malay and Muslim, UMNO's main challenge has come from the opposition Islamic party, Parti Islam SeMalaysia (PAS). PAS has published its own newspaper, *Harakah* (Movement), since 1987.

Harakah is perhaps the most powerful of Malaysia's alternative media. The tabloid sells enough copies not only to sustain a full-time editorial team but also to contribute to the party coffers. It used to be published twice a week, but when the Reformasi tide lifted its circulation to more than 300,000 in 1999, the government used its licensing powers to cut *Harakah*'s frequency down to twice monthly. PAS responded by pouring more resources into its new daily Internet edition. *Harakah Daily* (www.harakahdaily.net) became the most sophisticated and content-rich partisan website, and the first to include video.

PAS has had a tenuous relationship with secular opposition parties. Their alliance was formalized under the Pakatan Rakyat (Peoples Alliance), led by Anwar Ibrahim. In the 2008 elections, it apparently succeeded in challenging BN's race-based politics. The PAS rejection of the Malay party's (UMNO's) racial politics enabled it to appeal to many non-Muslim Chinese and Indians. At the same time, Pakatan's secular, multiracial elements, such as the Democratic Action Party (DAP), were able to attract Malays who had come to see UMNO as a corrupt machine for enriching a narrow Malay elite. DAP has a monthly newspaper, *Rocket*, published in English, Chinese, and Malay.

A second ongoing conflict is between the illiberal forces that dominate Malaysian politics and the country's prodemocracy movement. The latter comprises a loose network of opposition parties, nongovernmental organizations (NGOs), and individuals. The NGO *Aliran* (Movement), founded in 1977, publishes a mainly English-language monthly magazine, *Aliran Monthly*, and

a website (www.aliran.com). *Aliran* is based in Penang, the northern island state with a strong tradition of liberal politics and civil society activism.

The country's consumer movement also originated in Penang: The Consumers Association of Penang, which publishes the magazine *Utusan Konsumer* (Consumer Courier), was established in 1970 and campaigns for consumer rights and social justice. *Suaram* (Malaysian Public's Voice) was launched in 1989 in the capital, Kuala Lumpur, and has since emerged as the country's most vigorous human rights NGO. It has a website (www.suaram.net) and e-newsletter *Hak* (Rights), and also publishes an annual Malaysia Human Rights Report.

The most prominent progressive website is *Malaysiakini* (www.malaysiakini.com), a news site founded by two former mainstream newspaper journalists. It received funding from the Bangkok-based Southeast Asian Press Alliance and the Open Society's Media Development Loan Fund. Struggling at first to attract revenue from either advertising or subscriptions, it managed to establish a firmer footing by 2008, when Malaysians' hunger for independent news and analysis remained unmet.

Malaysiakini's independent ownership and freedom from licensing more than compensated for its meager resources and fewer than 15 journalists. *Malaysiakini* was frequently a faster and more credible source of political news than mainstream outlets. In 2008, it claimed more than 1.6 million unique visitors per month, carrying content in English, Malay, Chinese, and Tamil.

Aside from the broad-based alternative media, there are also various single-issue groups. In 2007, members of Malaysia's marginalized ethnic Indian community agitated vociferously for fair treatment under the banner of the Hindu Rights Action Force (Hindraf), using multiple websites to further their cause.

Costs of the country's rapid economic development are highlighted by various NGO media. These include the nature conservation group Wild Asia (www.wildasia.net) and the Center for Orang Asli Concerns (www.coac.org.my), which works with tribal communities. Women's groups, such as the Women's Aid Organisation (www.wao.org.my) and Sisters in Islam (www.sistersinislam.org.my), use the Internet in their advocacy and educational campaigns. Third World Network, which publishes the monthly magazine *Third World Resurgence* and fortnightly newsletter *Third World Economics,* is a Penang-based nonprofit focusing on development and North–South issues.

The Internet Opportunity

Although the Internet did not introduce alternative media to Malaysia, it certainly intensified and diversified media contestations. The government opened up public access to the Internet in the mid-1990s and rolled out an aggressive plan to attract foreign direct investment into information technology. So consumed was it by its "Multimedia Super Corridor" vision that the government guaranteed "no censorship of the Internet" under its 1997 Multimedia Bill of Guarantees. Although it never rejected the use of postpublication punishments, its assurance that it would not attempt to license or block Internet content offered an unprecedented opportunity for alternative communication.

Established organizations such as PAS and *Aliran* developed elaborate online media. Stand-alone websites included *Malaysian Insider* (www.themalaysianinsider.com), the Malay-language *Agenda Daily* (www.agendadaily.com), the Chinese-language *Merdeka* (Independence) *Review* (www.merdekareview.com), and *The Nut Graph* (www.thenutgraph.com).

Individual activists used the Internet to rise to prominence as citizen journalists and political commentators. Jeff Ooi's *Screenshots* blog (www.jeffooi.com) helped to amplify the impact of demonstrations organized by Suaram and other groups. Raja Petra Kamarudin, a key chronicler of the Reformasi protests in 1998, became a thorn in the side of the Abdullah Badawi government that succeeded Mahathir. His *Malaysia Today* site (www.malaysia-today.net) persistently alleged that Najib Razak (deputy prime minister, later prime minister) was linked to the murder of a Mongolian model.

The Internet provided public sphere access but no immunity from repression. Its patience stretched to breaking point by Raja Petra's sustained attacks, the government detained him and shut down his website, ending the government's no-censorship guarantee. The national English-language daily, *New Straits Times,* served a defamation suit on Ooi and another prominent blogger. Such reactions, however, only succeeded in spreading their fame. Ooi, in particular, was able to ride his online popularity into electoral politics, joining the DAP and successfully contesting a parliamentary seat in 2008.

In 2000, Malaysia had just 17 Internet users and 9 personal computers per 100 inhabitants, but the Internet's reach was not as limited as the figures suggest. The Internet was invariably embedded within traditional media as well as faxes and texting. Photocopies and word of mouth helped extend Internet messages into rural Malaysia. Today the typical Malaysian media activist or public intellectual straddles multiple media. A notable example is Amir Muhammad, a filmmaker, blogger, book publisher, and newspaper columnist.

Solidarities and Tensions

Attempts to organize alternative media to lobby for greater freedom of expression have been spearheaded by ad hoc initiatives as well as more established bodies such as *Aliran* and the Centre for Independent Journalism. Although many NGOs are small and personality driven, they are capable of impressive collective action. The Reformasi and Bersih campaigns saw dozens of groups coalesce, using the Internet and mobile phones to coordinate their actions and mobilize the public.

At the same time, the alternative media landscape is crisscrossed by practical (in particular, linguistic) and ideological divides. The deepest of these pertains to the position of Islam in politics and public life. PAS and *Harakah* officially support the extension of Islamic law into more areas of Malaysian life. Its statements regularly put it at odds with the media of other opposition parties and secular progressive NGOs, especially women's groups.

Another significant though less contentious distinction hinges on connections to political parties. At one end of the spectrum lie partisan media, including the many anonymously written tracts that purvey malicious rumors in the run up to elections. At the other end, partly in reaction to what they see as the amorality of electoral battles, lie independent media such as *Malaysiakini,* as well as civil society media. These are not averse to criticizing the opposition either.

Complicating the picture further is the lack of any consistent relationship with the regime. Its overall stability belies a fractured and competitive structure, providing media insurgents with elite allies of varying permanence. For example, agencies promoting investment in multimedia have helped discourage Internet censorship. The government's Human Rights Commission (SUHAKAM) has contributed to educating the administration about international norms of freedom of expression.

Prominent politicians' changing loyalties have also affected the contours of alternative media. Anwar Ibrahim's campaign against his erstwhile colleagues was the single biggest catalyst for alternative media in the country's history. A decade on, the political establishment had fully woken up to the potential of alternative media as tools in intra-elite competition. Thus, in 2007, Mahathir Mohamed, who had condemned *Malaysiakini* while he was in office, gave it a lengthy interview when the mainstream press would not give him a platform to attack his successor, Abdullah Badawi. Mahathir also launched his own blog, http://chedet.co.cc/chedetblog. In 2009, when Najib Razak took over the premiership, Mahathir rejoined UMNO and pledged his support for the new government, apparently ending his brief sojourn in alternative media. Around the same time, a celebrated citizen journalist and founder of a national alliance of bloggers returned to mainstream journalism to become editor of a national newspaper. Malaysia's brand of personality politics, with its fluid alliances and animosities, can thus add an unpredictable dimension to alternative media.

Cherian George

See also Independent Media (Burma/Myanmar); Social Movement Media, 1980s–2000s (Japan); Social Movement Media in 1987 Clashes (Korea); *Suara Independen* (Indonesia); Third World Network (Malaysia)

Further Readings

George, C. (2006). *Contentious journalism and the Internet: Toward democratic discourse in Malaysia and Singapore*. Seattle: University of Washington Press.

Hilley, J. (2001). *Malaysia: Mahathirism, hegemony and the new opposition*. New York: Zed Books.

Loh, F. K.-W., & Khoo, B. T. (2002). *Democracy in Malaysia: Discourses and practices*. Richmond, UK: Curzon.

Nain, Z. (2002). The media and Malaysia's *Reformasi* movement. In R. H.-K. Heng (Ed.), *Media fortunes, changing times: ASEAN states in transition* (pp. 119–138). Singapore: Institute of Southeast Asian Studies.

Ooi, K. B., Saravanamuttu, J., & Lee, H. G. (2008). *March 8: Eclipsing May 13*. Singapore: Institute of Southeast Asian Studies.

SUHAKAM. (2003). *A case for media freedom: Report of SUHAKAM's Workshop on Freedom of the Media*. Kuala Lumpur: Suruhanjaya Hak Asasi Manusia Malaysia.

Weiss, M. L. (2006). *Protest and possibilities: Civil society and coalitions for political change in Malaysia*. Stanford, CA: Stanford University Press.

Weiss, M. L., & Hassan, S. (Eds.). (2003). *Social movements in Malaysia: From moral communities to NGOs*. New York: RoutledgeCurzon.

ALTERNATIVE MEDIA AT POLITICAL SUMMITS

Whenever powerful political leaders gathered in the late 1990s and over the following decade, they were beset by demonstrators and alternative summits, and lobbied by nongovernmental organizations (NGOs). Alternative media were always there, reporting, providing infrastructure, and organizing themselves as alternative media movements.

In the early 1980s, protest movements emerged in the global South against neoliberal policies that removed already skimpy social support structures. Spreading north, what came to be called the altermondialization, global justice, or, more controversially, antiglobalization movement organized around U.N. summits, meetings of multilateral organizations (e.g., International Monetary Fund, World Bank, World Trade Organization), economic elite groups such as the Group of Eight (G8), and free trade negotiators.

By the early 2000s, the "movement of movements" had its own international summits in the form of the World Social Forum and regional social forums. Engaging in summits, many movement organizations generated their own media, newsletters, mailing lists, and video projects. In addition, they were supported by existing alternative media and their international networks, such as the Association Mondiale des Radiodiffuseurs Communautaires (AMARC; World Association of Community Radio Broadcasters), the Association for Progressive Communications (APC), and video activists from the network Videazimut.

Lastly, summit convergences often sparked new networks and media projects. A prominent example of the latter was the Independent Media Center (IMC, Indymedia) network. Mainstream media typically represented summits from the "inside" perspective of powerful governments and, if they reported on protests, positioned the camera with the riot police. In contrast, the first IMC at the "Battle of Seattle" (World Trade Organization protests in 1999) brought journalistic perspectives from inside the crowd to a wide audience through its website.

Alternative media also supported social movement organizing at summits, disseminating information on developments inside the venue, logistics during mobilizations, and background information on the issues. Through participatory and dialogic features, they provided forums for discussing strategies and deepened analyses of movement concerns. For example, how would the Rio Earth Summit have turned out if members of APC had not set up mailing lists, online fora, and websites for NGOs, helping them to coordinate with each other and influence governments?

More recently, media activists have set up so-called tactical media labs alongside summits to share technology know-how. Such infrastructure support has become a standard service that alternative media provide. This not only shapes the outcome of summit mobilizations but also allows NGOs and activists to go home with new skills and infrastructure.

As alternative media people traveled to summits to cover and support social movements, they began to see themselves as a social movement in its own right. AMARC and a few other alternative media organizations, including those of Indigenous media, have long lobbied governments and multilateral institutions for better conditions for alternative media, such as legalization (or at least de-criminalization) of community radio, and for better funding. However,

these actions tended to be isolated by traditional divisions of media technologies used (radio, Internet, video, etc.) and the interests of membership-based organizing. During the World Summit on the Information Society (WSIS, 2003–2005), media activists and researchers from a range of backgrounds worked together, trying to formulate a common agenda and to influence governmental and civil society discourse inside the summit. They also worked with oppositional movements outside.

Alternative media thus became part of the "movement of movements," integral to the success of the other movements. However, other movements did not always recognize this. In the Civil Society section of WSIS and even at the World Social Forum, media activists had to fight hard to get their issues on the agenda.

Moreover, research suggests that alternative media are not immune to existing imbalances of power (based on class, ethnicity, geography, gender, political orientation) and that their efforts to increase people's access to information technologies may conflict with environmentalist goals.

Gabriele Hadl

See also Alternative Media in the World Social Forum; Alternative Media: Policy Issues; Grassroots Tech Activists and Media Policy; Media Activists and Communication Policy Processes; Media Infrastructure Policy and Media Activism

Further Readings

Hadl, G., & Hintz, A. (2009). Framing our media for transnational policy: The world summit on the information society and beyond. In D. Kidd, L. Stein, & C. Rodríguez (Eds.), *Making our media* (pp. 103–121). Cresskill, NJ: Hampton Press.

Hintz, A., & Milan, S. (2007). Towards a new vision for communication governance? Civil Society Media at the World Social Forum and the World Summit on the Information Society. *Communication for Development and Social Change, 1*(1), 13–32.

Kidd, D. (2002, July 20). *Which would you rather? Seattle or Porto Alegre?* Paper presented at OURMedia II conference, Barcelona, Spain. Retrieved May 2, 2010, from http://mediaresearchhub.ssrc.org/which-would-you-rather-seattle-or-porto-alegre/resource_view

ALTERNATIVE MEDIA CENTER (UNITED STATES)

Red Burns and George C. Stoney, both faculty members at New York University's Tisch School of the Arts, created the Alternative Media Center (AMC) in 1970. Stoney had just spent 2 years as executive producer of the Challenge for Change Program (CFC) at the National Film Board of Canada. Burns, also with earlier National Film Board connections, had spent the 1960s as a commercial media executive.

The idea was to reproduce in the United States a nurturing ground for the conceptions and designs fostering community media that had been the CFC objective. An important CFC component was developing the use of the newly available VHS as a device for "democratizing the media." Simultaneously, CFC staff carried out experiments on the use of cable TV channels that both the Canadian and the U.S. government eventually allocated for public access. A Markle Foundation grant to pursue the development of "community cable" soon focused the AMC's activity.

Immediately, the AMC set up a community video center on campus where nonstudent community members could find video training. In the next few months, the AMC set up five systems across the country in locations where Burns persuaded cable companies to provide space, access to cable time, and eventually a partial salary for the AMC-trained coordinators. The AMC went on to develop manuals and to produce sample programs to serve as models for many other community media efforts simultaneously springing up.

In its second year, AMC advertised an internship program offered to nonstudents who could show they had both production skills and understood the "philosophy of open community media for social purposes." Interns also had to persuade their local cable operator to guarantee four things: (1) unrestricted use of a channel, (2) equipment for cablecasting (usually ¾″ in video) in addition to the ½″ rigs the AMC provided, (3) space for training, and (4) half the salary for the coordinator selected by AMC (the other half to come from the Markle grant). In the next 2 years, 24 interns were producing work that was cablecast locally and "bicycled" to other systems, thus becoming influential in spreading the concept soon labeled "public access cable TV."

Frequent visits to the interns by AMC staff and twice-yearly gatherings in New York helped clarify the objectives of what was by then a "movement." At the university, these were codified in a course called Cable and Community. A newsletter helped answer inquiries from across the country and, eventually, across the world, as the use of consumer-grade video equipment became generally available.

While Stoney took a sabbatical to make a long-planned documentary, Burns conducted experiments in the use of electronic media for social purposes. In Reading, Pennsylvania, she and her staff developed an interactive television network for seniors. From 1979 to 1982, they developed and operated a telecom system for the developmentally disabled in Vermont. During this time, they developed the first teletext project using PBS stations' vertical blanking interval, a forerunner of interactive text and graphics.

When the Markle Foundation grant was not renewed, the AMC ended the internship program. However, most interns continued their work, often assisted by organizations like community colleges. Missing the gatherings that had once brought them together at AMC, they founded the Alliance for Community Media, the national body that today links the hundreds of public access centers around the United States and many abroad.

George Stoney

See also Alliance for Community Media (United States); Alternative Media Heritage in Latin America; Community Broadcasting (Canada); Community Radio and Podcasting (United States); Cultural Front (Canada); Public Access

Further Readings

Boyle, D. (1997). *Subject to change: Guerrilla television revisited*. New York: Oxford University Press.

Engelman, R. (1990). The origins of public access cable television, 1966–72. *Journalism Monographs, 123*.

Fuller, L. K. (1994). *Community television in the United States: A sourcebook on public, educational, and governmental access*. Westport, CT: Greenwood Press.

Stein, L. (2001). Access television and grassroots political communication in the United States. In

J. D. H. Downing (with G. Gil, T. Villarreal Ford, & L. Stein), *Radical media: Rebellious communication and social movements* (pp. 299–324). Thousand Oaks, CA: Sage.

ALTERNATIVE MEDIA GLOBAL PROJECT

The Alternative Media Global Project (AMGP) is a collaborative and multilingual website that is devoted to recording research on alternative media throughout the world. Structured around a specialized bibliography, an interactive world map, a long-term chronology, and an online yearbook, the AMGP seeks to centralize the many resources available on alternative media and to make them available to the community of researchers, activists, and actors who work on, with, or for them. The site is built on a Wiki platform. This enables users who access it to contribute or modify content. The Wiki system maximizes customized applications, plus technical and geographical accessibility. As its base, the AMGP uses *Dokuwiki,* an open source program.

The AMGP was launched in 2007 as an initiative of Benjamin Ferron, R. E. Davis, and Clemencia Rodríguez. It became a working group of the OURMedia network. As of 2010, this not-for-profit counted on a network of 60 correspondents, some of them working collectively, out of the 30 countries involved in the project in Africa, the Americas, Europe, Oceania, the Arab World, and Asia. English is the main language of the site, with translations in French, Spanish, and Portuguese.

Project Components

The project includes a section on research, a developing bibliography, a mapping project, a chronology, a yearbook, a blog, and a glossary. These different sections are linked to each other and many external Web resources.

The research section, first, addresses how to define, study, and theorize alternative media. So, should the meaning of *media* be reduced to newspapers, cinema, and broadcasting, or should it include graffiti, posters, flyers, music, dance, theater, documentaries, audiotapes, photos, and blogs? Why are there so many terms for out-of-the-mainstream media: alternative, radical, citizens', community, participatory, free, autonomous, underground, independent, clandestine, pirate, ethnic, dissident, marginal, parallel? Can they be defined only by their opposition to mainstream media? If not, can one term reflect their extreme diversity of form and content? Does their study require specific methodologies or theories? How can other media or social movement research be useful to understand them? Which possibilities and obstacles exist to developing international comparison of alternative media networks and histories?

Second, the multientry bibliography lists research publications, materials produced by community media producers themselves, and articles from mainstream media on alternative media worldwide. Alternative media studies come from several disciplines (information-communication, sociology, history, political science, anthropology). The AMPG hopes to promote cross-disciplinary dialogue. It also aims to facilitate research in specific geographical zones, international comparisons on alternative media networks, and to archive the historical memory of these media. Around 500 references had been classified by 2009 by media technology, country, and theme (e.g., alternative media and anarchism, alternative media in conflict situations).

Third is an interactive world map of hundreds of community radios, independent newspapers, free TVs, alternative video projects, and radical websites. Just 6 months after its creation, this "amazing map," according to the alternative blog *Waves of Change,* had been visited more than 10,000 times. It pinpoints geographically 600 media projects in almost every country in the world.

Each is described, its conditions of birth and development, the difficulties or repression it has faced, its networks of production and distribution, its equipment, coordinators, internal organization, financing, publications, formats, institutional partners, website, address, contacts, logo, and its relationships with other alternative media. This inventory was made possible by a network of correspondents, working with Google Maps. Each correspondent can add important information about his or her geographical area. Internet research and field investigations facilitate gathering and recording relevant information.

Fourth is the chronology from 1700 to the present. In close interaction with the world map, it presents a unique historical overview, from the first revolutionary publications of the 18th century in Europe to the Intercontinental Network of Alternative Communication launched by the Zapatista movement at the end of the 1990s. Conceived as a very simple and interactive source of information, by 2009 it included data on the history of the anarchist, communist, and radical press in Europe and the United States in the 19th century, the birth of the community and Indigenous radio movements in Australia, Africa, and Latin America since the 1950s, the struggles for a New World Information and Communication Order in the late 1970s and early 1980s, the main steps in the emergence of an alternative Internet in the 1990s, and many well-known and little-known aspects of the global history of alternative communication.

Last, the yearbook provides data on alternative media activists and commentators. It also plans to develop a database on alternative media researchers, journalists, activists, and artists, to help researchers study alternative media producers and facilitate connections among practitioners. The blog offers updates about alternative media issues throughout the world (new legislation, conferences, festivals, projects, new books or articles, cases of repression, and announcements). The glossary aims to define the concepts and expressions used to describe alternative media.

Simple, open, and collectively run, the AMGP seeks to serve varied interests: to be an integrative tool for research; to foster contact among activists, communities, and researchers; to make information available on alternative media projects and lessons to be drawn from their experiences; and to promote democratic and critical debate on these subjects.

Benjamin Ferron

See also Alternative Media; Anarchist Media; Citizens' Media; Environmental Movement Media; Feminist Media: An Overview; Human Rights Media; Installation Art Media; Performance Art and Social Movement Media: Augusto Boal

Further Readings

Alternative Media Global Project: http://www.ourmedia network.org/wiki

ALTERNATIVE MEDIA HERITAGE IN LATIN AMERICA

This entry pinpoints the Latin American subcontinent's particular road in developing analyses of alternative media and counterinformation, and briefly maps its landmarks, in order to guide future travelers and help develop a definition of these media as integral parts of the social transformation process.

Definitions and Their Problems

The ambiguities implicit in terms such as *alternative* and *counterinformation* are scarcely novel. The proliferation of terms such as *participatory communication,* *"popular" communication, activist media, emancipatory media, self-managed media, community media, alternative media,* and *citizens' media* highlight different aspects of a (partial) notion of alternative and is, in some measure, influenced by theoretical and conceptual movements in the social sciences from the 1960s to the present.

The problem is that the conceptual indeterminacy from which these terms suffer is usually tedious for those who enjoy poking around among the debates and tensions common in this field of forces. Quite often it operates as a kind of box of odds and ends to shove anything into it that does not fit inside dominant communication or journalism patterns. This ends up putting dissimilar and even contradictory experiences in the same bag, from those in "Third Sector" journalism to the press of social movements and people's political organizations, passing by Latin American revolutionary groups' radio stations—for example, El Salvador's Farabundo Martí National Liberation Front in the 1980s—along the way. This vague label is shared or contested by a neighborhood community newspaper, an experimental art video, and a political intervention video, and by low-power commercial TV stations and community television.

The heart of the matter is that while it is really important to escape from tidy notions that skate over the multiple contexts in which alternative communication can develop—these contexts are fundamental in analyzing what is *alternative*—it is also counterproductive and politically disastrous to stretch the term, which becomes de-politicized through its abuse. This can be seen in how the disruptive content of many such media experiences gets eliminated to suit the dictates of global aid programs, shifting them away from any radical transformational impulse. The background to alternative needs to be restored from a viewpoint that defines it as more than simply "different" and does not divorce it from the politics of social transformation.

The Latin American Background

In Latin America, the experiences of grassroots communication that formed the basis of analysis and practice concerning alternative communication and counter-information refer to a practical and perceptual mold that deeply marks much current social movement media practice in the region. The precedents can be traced back to the end of the 18th century, if we take into account the understanding of the press as a weapon of combat linked to emancipation from Spain, and the place of military information. Thus, the seditious satirical posters that accompanied the first revolts against Spanish rule were media as an expression of resistance and of a project for a new society.

More recently, beginning in the mid-20th century, media began to appear that are usually thought of as founding alternative media history. These are the beginning phase of Radio Sutatenza in Colombia, and the first radio training schools run by the Catholic Church (then its educational and community stations); the Bolivian miners' stations as a form of self-representation by the miners' unions; and Cuba's Radio Rebelde (Rebel Radio) as a media and propaganda space for the 26th July Movement, led by Fidel Castro. Notwithstanding the differences between these examples, this reading of alternative media as a consciousness-raising exercise predominated through the 1960s. This was so whether in education (for literacy, evangelization, health, or liberation) or ideological critique—political interventions, counter-information, de-alienation, or attacks on cultural imperialism.

Refocusing "Alternative" in Relation to Social Movements

This reading of alternative communication does not, however, sideline community participation and social activism as central elements in what is alternative. It permits us to focus on defining alternative in such a way that the dependence of a given media project on a major transformational movement is perceived as the decisive issue. This does not require an organic relationship to it, as with a political party press, but broadly includes that connection along with other communication projects that share a common vision and a general strategy.

Moreover, it must be underscored that alternative objectives in Latin America had a dual birth: the church and the unions. In the former case, certainly not all these activities were part of Liberation Theology (assuming that to mean a transformational project), and it is equally plain that the church had a basic mission: to enlighten and evangelize. This too meant understanding media in terms of extra-communicational goals.

A mass of experiences can be drawn upon as tradition in a number of current attempts to resist neoliberalism. For example, the Latin American Newsreel in Cuba's Film Institute (ICAIC), directed by Santiago Álvarez; Prensa Latina (Latin Press) news agency in the Cuban Revolution's first years; the work of Cine Liberación (Liberation Cinema) and Cine de la Base (Grassroots Cinema), in Argentina; the industrial zone newspapers in Santiago, Chile, during Salvador Allende's government, 1970–1973; Brazil's labor union press and Christian base communities; the Salvadoran guerrilla radio stations; the Nicaraguan political press and transformational theater in the 1980s.

What all these have in common is that they are political and communication endeavors, some linked to more extensive social transformation projects, others directly part of them, which gave them meaning and direction. How else could be interpreted the Agencia de Noticias Clandestina (Clandestine News Agency), set in motion by the Montonero activist and writer Rodolfo Walsh, who was imprisoned and disappeared during the 1976–1982 military dictatorship? (The *Montoneros* were leftist activists within Argentina's complex and long-running Peronist movement.) The agency, an organizational necessity at a time of extreme repression in the whole Southern Cone, could not set up large-scale participatory decision making. An assembly to debate on steps to be taken would have been a very easy target. Nonetheless, who could doubt the agency's alternative status?

Researcher Margarita Graziano commented on this in 1980, writing that alternative has as much to do with power relations as communication, and the transmission of signs and imposition of codes that those relations allow to be expressed. This seems fundamental, if we seek to problematize the relation between communication and politics, or between communication and the construction of people's power. The essence of alternative is based on the articulation of two dimensions, one communicative and the other political, related in turn to the historical and social context within which media practice is inserted. Armand Mattelart and Jean-Marie Piemme proposed something similar, namely to understand the alternative in relation to the production of new social relations.

From an academic point of view, this perspective is generally dismissed as anachronistic, though this renders the social sciences in Rodríguez Esperón's view into a conceptual assembly line where some terms get junked and others mesh perfectly with the sign of the times. In effect, the alternative as a research topic was progressively abandoned in Latin America, following an important body of work produced toward the mid-1980s but thereafter confined to a few locales. Yet, at the turn of the millennium, the political context and the organizational needs of people's struggles were once more rather cautiously reinstating the topic on the debate agenda.

Recent Developments

The current Latin American conjuncture clearly shows the harmful role played by newspaper firms (as interested parties) in destabilization or open coups against the processes of change at work in some nations. Examples include the 2002 Venezuela coup and the Bolivian crisis beginning in 2006 in which the government and the people had to confront secessionists in the wealthy Media Luna half of the country. In this context, it is impossible to wait to carefully frame the necessary responses.

In any case, interpretations of the alternative do not escape the influence of the conceptual shifts in the social sciences, including communication. The larger or smaller interest in this topic rather obviously followed the paradigm change evident since the 1980s and has intensified since then. Interest was declining from the second half of that decade

to the point of practically disappearing in the 1990s, so that the high point in debate occurred in the late 1970s and early 1980s, when there was an attempt to articulate macro and micro dimensions of communication following the failure of national communication policy making.

In Argentina and in general in Latin America, in harmony with the transition to democracy, the critique of political vanguards, and the crisis of omnibus political strategies, the postdictatorship reading of the alternative bore the mark of social movement theory, Michel Foucault's notion of distributed power, and a reemphasis on its cultural over its political dimension. Schematically speaking, the shift from the 1960s and 1970s to the 1980s brought back the idea of community, which was seen as a tangible space (close at hand, small scale) for intervening in the alternative.

Within this framework, daily life seemed a place where hegemony was reproduced but also resisted. A huge shift took place from a paradigm focused on domination to one (coded as democratic) focused on hegemony, which influenced the approximations and practices of alternative communication. In this manner, women, ecologists, Aboriginal rights activists, and, above all, young people reclaimed their means of expression, organized not from a macro vision but from each group's specific status. The phenomenon of FM radio stations set up in Argentina after the last dictatorship, although enormously varied, can be seen from this perspective: radio as expressing a plurality of voices, a safe space for reflection and a place for community participation.

This tendency to focus attention on cultural matters deepened in the 1990s and, far from renewing perspectives anchored in the alternative as tools of a social transformation process, reading the macro from the micro and vice versa, ended by forsaking the centrality of key issues such as social class and inequality. Those concepts, implying class combat, were replaced by the notion of cultural difference, resulting in a perspective in which alternative communication, as Carlos Mangone put it, was more communication than alternative. In this transition, the notion of alternative, which had earlier been thrashed out, took on a new sense. As Rafael Roncagliolo put it at the 1992 AMARC conference in México, the vocation of alternative is not marginality but alteration, change, and transformation of power relations in the cultural domain.

The issue of what is alternative goes beyond the simple practice of communication, inasmuch as this practice is not estranged from societal dynamics and their conflicts. It is not enough to proclaim critical intentions for social transformation if these intentions are not accompanied by a practice that sets out to change reality. As Rodolfo Walsh insisted, it is a question of using language like an object, wielding it like a hammer: Everything that is written needs to be submerged in the new process and needs to serve it, contribute to its forward march—once more, journalism was the appropriate weapon.

Natalia Vinelli

See also Alternative Media; Citizens' Media; Medvedkine Groups and Workers' Cinema (France); Naxalite Movement Media (India); Social Movement Media, 1960s–1980s (Chile); Social Movement Media, 2001–2002 (Argentina); Social Movement Media, Anti-Apartheid (South Africa); Third Cinema; Zapatista Media (México)

Further Readings

Fuentes Navarro, R. (1992). Imperialismo cultural y comunicación alternativa [Cultural imperialism and alternative communication]. In *Un campo cargado de futuro*. Guadalajara, México: ITESO/Maestría en Comunicación. ccdoc.iteso.mx/cat.aspx?cmn= download&ID=945&N=1

Graziano, M. (1980). Para una definición alternativa de la comunicación [Toward an alternative definition of communication]. *Revista ININCO, 1*.

Link, D. (Ed.). (1996). *Rodolfo Walsh: Ese hombre y otros papeles personales* [Rodolfo Walsh: That man and other personal papers]. Barcelona, Spain: Editorial Seix Barral.

López Vigil, J. I. (1997, Autumn). Las radios de nuevo tipo: la estética sin la ética no sirve para nada, entrevista de Ernesto Lamas [Radios of a new type: Aesthetics without ethics is useless, interview with Ernesto Lamas]. *Causas y Azares, 5*, 77–89.

Mangone C. (2005). Qué hay de nuevo viejo, alternatividad y clases sociales [What's new and old, alternativity and social classes]. *Cuadernos Críticos de Comunicación y Cultura, 1*.

Mattelart, A., & Piemme, J.-M. (1981). *La televisión alternativa* [Alternative television]. Barcelona, Spain: Anagrama.

Rodríguez Esperón, C., & Vinelli, N. (2004, September 23–25). *Comunicación alternativa, contrainformación y transformación social* [Alternative communication, counterinformation and social transformation]. Ponencia presentada en la Facultad de Ciencias Sociales, Universidad de Buenos Aires, Argentina.

Roncagliolo, R. (1992, August). Exposición inaugural, 5to. Congreso de la Asociación Mundial de Radios Comunitarias, México [Inaugural exhibition, 5th Congress of the World Association of Community Radio, México].

Simpson Grinberg, M. (1986). Trends in alternative communication research in Latin America. In E. McAnany & R. Atwood (Eds.), *Communication and Latin American society* (pp. 165–189). Madison: University of Wisconsin Press.

Simpson Grinberg, M. (1989). Comunicación alternativa: tendencias de la investigación en América Latina [Alternative communication: Research trends in Latin America]. In M. Simpson Grinberg (Ed.), *Comunicación alternativa y cambio social* [Alternative communication and social change]. México: Premiá. (Original work published 1986)

Vinelli, N. (2007). *ANCLA: Una experiencia de comunicación clandestina orientada por Rodolfo Walsh* [ANCLA: An experience of clandestine communication directed by Rodolfo Walsh]. Caracas, Venezuela: Fundación Editorial El Perro y la Rana. (Original work published 2000)

ALTERNATIVE MEDIA IN THE WORLD SOCIAL FORUM

Alternative media issues have played an increasingly important role within the World Social Forum (WSF), founded in 2001 to oppose the annual procapitalist World Economic Forum in Switzerland (WEF). WSF sought to enable social movements, networks, nongovernmental organizations (NGOs), and other civil society organizations to debate strategies for sustainable development, the environment, democracy, and human rights. Its founders insisted the forum should be held in the global South at the same time as the WEF. The event grew massively, from 10,000 participants in 2001 to more than 130,000 in 2009. It has met in Brazil a number of times, but also in India and Kenya.

The WSF's Communicative Character

The WSF is without doubt a highly communicative event, not only in its intermovement and interactivist dialogues but also in terms of defining communication strategies for the issues, organizations, and struggles involved. The number of seminars and activities concerning alternative media have increased since the 2001 WSF, and as of 2009, alternative media and communication constituted the counterhegemonic section of the WSF program. What follows is a brief survey of developments in this sphere up to the 2009 WSF in Belém, Brazil.

The alternative media context in the WSF process is a tension within the WSF, which can be defined as a movement with specific goals, or as an open space where everyone can participate and hierarchical order is absent. The WSF's Charter of Principles states that the WSF's main goal is to provide a global arena where as many individuals, organizations, and movements as possible can participate in order to discuss and learn from each other's experiences. No final documents or declarations should be the result of the forum, as that would go against the principles and the nature of the forum. However, there have been several attempts to constitute it as a singular, yet diversified, global movement that can communicate as such, and operate as a social and political actor.

Older Alternative Media Organizations

One of the most energetic actors within the WSF process is the global South news agency Inter Press Service (IPS). IPS started in 1964 as a journalists' cooperative as part of the third world anti-imperialist movement, to give a "voice to the voiceless." As of 2009, it published the WSF newspaper *TerraViva,* which covers not only the WSF but also other activities related to the global justice movement. IPS is also responsible for different media campaigns emerging out of the WSF process. Many of its contributors also participate in different social movement media productions.

AMARC (Association Mondiale des Radiodiffuseurs Communautaires; World Association of Community Radio Broadcasters) originated in the 1960s and is one of the oldest networks of community-based media. In the WEF, AMARC organizes discussions and workshops concerning alternative, local, and small media production and facilitates a connection between social movements and alternative media.

Alternative Media Networks

Indymedia or the Independent Media Center (IMC) is probably the best-known alternative media network participating in the WSF process. The initial IMC was developed during the buildup to the 1999 anti–World Trade Organization protests in Seattle. It is an activist-run network, free from NGO or funding or corporate involvements, the absolute opposite of corporate media. By 2009, the IMC network was most active in North America and Europe but was represented worldwide. In the global South, the IMC to late 2008 was particularly strong in Argentina and Brazil. In many parts of the global South, however, absence of easy Internet access greatly lessened Indymedia's potential. One of the most important roles of the IMC within the WSF was to facilitate a link between alternative and mainstream media.

Other important networks participating in the WSF included the Agencia Latinoamericana de Información (ALAI). ALAI is a web-based network of social movements striving to democratize communication at the grassroots level. ALAI produced both a printed and online publication called *América Latina en Movimiento,* addressing issues of social movement activity, organization, and media, and published books on similar issues. Active too in the WSF was the Paulo Freire–inspired radio network Asociación Latinoamericana de Educación Radiofónica (ALER). Both ALAI and ALER have played an important role in strengthening major social movements such as Brazil's rural landless workers' organization Movimento dos Trabalhadores Rurais Sem Terra (MST) and La Vía Campesina (The International Peasant's Voice).

MST has deployed various forms of alternative media in order to mobilize, organize, and strengthen Brazil's landless workers. Through radio broadcasts such as *Vozes da Terra* (Voices From the Land), the monthly newspaper *Sem Terra* (Landless), the weekly newspaper and web source *Brasil de Fato* (Brazil Today, closely connected to the MST and Via Campesina), and still other publications, the MST contributes to a lively and progressive public sphere. Using the Internet to circulate information about marches, campaigns, and collective action has proved valuable. In 2003, MST activists entered the WSF computer labs and replaced Microsoft operating systems with Linux. MST has also built a nationwide communication infrastructure deploying free software (Free/Libre Open Source Software), and thereby dislodging dependency on corporate products.

WSF Alternative Media Initiatives

An example of the WSF functioning to enable action proposals is the space provided to the Campaign for Communication Rights in the Information Society (CRIS). The CRIS campaign challenged the privatization and commodification of information and communication. Within the WSF process, the CRIS campaign assembled various communication initiatives of the global justice movement in preparation for the UN World Summits on the Information Society (2003, 2005). CRIS also provided a platform for social movements dealing with issues connected to information technology and communication. CRIS organized the more institutional, reform-focused communication activists.

Communication rights were a central topic during the CRIS seminars at WSF 2005 and 2007, where CRIS organized meetings to gather concrete proposals. Among the issues addressed was the struggle to define communication rights as fundamental to democracy. Consequently, information, communication, and knowledge needed to be recognized as public goods and services, not as mere commodities, and should therefore remain outside free trade agreements.

Another project connected to the WSF was Media Watch Global (MWG), a media-monitoring project launched at the 2002 WSF by the IPS and *Le Monde diplomatique*. MWG's objective is "to promote the right of citizens around the world to be properly informed," as stated by the then director of *Le Monde diplomatique*, Ignacio Ramonet (2003, p. 1). As of 2008, MWG had at least 10 chapters in Europe, Africa, Latin America, and Asia. Its operation is based on volunteer groups observing media content, producing evidence of biased coverage, and writing letters to editors. MWG covers three fields of mass communication—news, mass culture, and advertising—and produces media critiques focused on the connection between content and corporate structures. It also works within the more liberal media ethics tradition.

An important step toward sharing information, distributing articles, photos, radio, and television was reflected in the web-based initiative of The International Ciranda of Shared Communication (Ciranda). Ciranda—named after a Brazilian community dance—was initiated at the first WSF as a platform for both alternative and mainstream journalists to share their material. Ciranda deploys copyleft principles (a form of licensing that allows distributing and reproduction of the original work) and publishes material relevant to the WSF process. Hundreds of journalists and media producers from all over the world participated in Ciranda, making it one of the most extensive sources of media coverage of the WSF.

Media Challenges in the WSF Process

There have been several WSF-related media and communication initiatives. In 2005, a pre-forum, solely devoted to alternative media and communication, was organized before the WSF, called Information and Communication World Forum (ICWF). It focused on the impact of neo-liberal policies in the information sphere, media reform and information pluralism policies, and alternative media.

Within the WSF, alternative media and communication tend to intertwine and overlap with the work and activities in social movements and other organizations participating. With increased Internet use and the revitalization of older alternative media, alternative media can potentially constitute a counterhegemonic formation within the current global order.

However, the level of activities related to media and communication depended very much on sociogeographical context. The Nairobi 2007 WSF saw a decline, with only 70 workshops, panels, and other meetings on media and communication, less than 5% of the total forum activities. One reason was the impact of immediately pressing African struggles around HIV/AIDS, the privatization of water and other natural resources, imperialist aggression, war, and raw materials looting. Nevertheless, one of the important insights of the earlier WSFs was the necessary integration of media and communication with other social and political activities, an insight that seemed largely overlooked during the 2007 meeting. The impact of alternative media and communication is intertwined with its connection to social movements and progressive grassroots organizations. Media activism is both dependent on, and reinforces, the strength and organizational capability of social movements.

Mattias Ekman

See also Alternative Media at Political Summits; Alternative Media: Policy Issues; Copyleft; Grassroots Tech Activists and Media Policy; Human Rights Media; Indymedia (The Independent Media Center); Participatory Media

Further Readings

Bailey, O. G., Cammaerts, B., & Carpenter, N. (2008). *Understanding alternative media.* Maidenhead, UK: Open University Press.

Bond P. (2007). Linking below, across and against—World Social Forum weaknesses, global governance gaps and the global justice movement's strategic dilemmas. *Development Dialogue, 49,* 81–95.

Ciranda: www.ciranda.net

Costanza-Chock, S. (2006). The globalization of resistance to capitalist communication. In G. Murdock & J. Wasko (Eds.), *Media in the age of marketization* (pp. 221–249). Cresskill, NJ: Hampton Press.

Inter Press Service: http://www.ips.org

León, I., & Burch, S. (2009). The World Social Forum: Current challenges and future perspectives. In J. Sen & P. Waterman (Eds.), *World Social Forum challenging empires* (pp. 292–304). Montréal, QC: Black Rose Books.

Media Watch Global: http://www.mwglobal.org

Patomäki, H., & Teivainen, T. (2004). The World Social Forum—An open space or a movement of movements? *Theory, Culture & Society, 21*(6), 145–154.

Ramonet, I. (2003, October). Le cinquième pouvoir [The fifth power]. *Le Monde diplomatique,* p. 1.

Sampedro, V. (2005). The alternative moment and its media strategies. In F. Polet (Ed.), *Globalizing resistance* (pp. 243–257). London: Pluto Press.

Sen J., & Kumar, M. (with Bond, P., & Waterman, P.). (Eds.). (2007). *A political programme for the World Social Forum? Democracy, substance and debate in the Bamako appeal and the global justice movements: A reader.* New Delhi, India: CACIM & Durban, South Africa: CCS.

Smith, P., & Smyth, E. (2008, March 26–29). *Open spaces, open sources: The World Social Forum and international communication rights in a digital world.* Paper presented at the annual meeting of the International Studies Association, San Francisco, CA.

Teivainen, T. (2007). The political and its absence in the World Social Forum. *Development Dialogue, 49,* 69–79.

Whitaker Ferreira, F. (2006). *Towards a new politics—what future for the World Social Forum?* Delhi, India: Vasudhaiva Kutumbakam.

ALTERNATIVE MEDIA: POLICY ISSUES

Alternative media often emerge under politically adverse conditions such as censorship or oppression, and arise and fade with social movements. However, some want to serve their constituencies long term and make an impact on the overall mediascape. To do this, they need reasonable "framing conditions": policies that at least allow them to exist, better yet support them. Often combined forces from the state and corporate sectors make and administer policies framing them. This entry discusses overall legal and regulatory issues, community radio, copyright and intellectual property, access to distribution, and some broad strategies to respond to problems.

Legislation, Regulation, and Policy

Government policies on free speech, education, and cultural participation are crucial. Direct censorship, together with laws on defamation, libel, *lèse-majesté,* obscenity, indecency, business secrets, copyrights, government secrets, cybersecurity, terrorism, and shield laws for politicians, may all be used to hamper or completely shut down alternative media. Governmental funding and licensing policies are also used to exercise control.

On the other hand, alternative media are also affected by progressive terrorism legislation, regulation relating to online anonymity, and governmental policies relating to Indigenous peoples;

immigration; religion; disabilities; women; sexual minorities; gay, lesbian, bisexual, transgender (GLBT) people; environmental issues; labor issues; or local and national education and development. Where such policies foster access to affordable technologies and telecommunications infrastructures, as well as to technical and critical media skills, they tend to offer opportunities for alternative media making. Also, as a rule of thumb, the better the overall health of the media system (including journalism ethics, cultural diversity, public service regulation, and measures against ownership concentration), the easier it is for alternative media to frame their issues, involve more people long term, and create alternative and counter-publics that can affect social and political changes.

Community Radio

Community radio stations have fought to be decriminalized and for access to public funding ever since the commercial and public enclosures of the airwaves in the early 20th century. Many countries still prosecute nonlicensed broadcasters, while offering no legal way to establish a noncommercial or nongovernmental station. Others, like Japan, now allow noncommercial broadcasters to apply for licenses but have no dedicated policy for them, forcing them to compete with commercial broadcasters for licenses, audiences, and funding. In countries that actively aim to foster community and Indigenous radio, such as Australia, South Africa, and many others, these media can reach large audiences and involve great numbers of people in media making. Yet the devil is in the details: License categories, limits on commercial time, whether there is public funding and how it is administered, who sits on the board of regulatory agencies, how channels are allocated, and how unlicensed stations are treated are hotly contested even in supportive environments.

More radical projects often prefer a hands-off policy: little regulation (even if it means no support) and more toleration. Countries where broadcast laws are rarely enforced, such as Israel, may have a thriving "pirate" sector, including a broad array of political, religious, and quasi-commercial stations.

Some conditions framing alternative media are regulated by multiple actors, from local to global. For example, media education policies may be handled by different ministries and agencies, the police, local governments, school districts, non-governmental organizations (NGOs), media corporations, professional training institutions, or even the computer industry. Policies on development media may come from intergovernmental organizations like UNESCO or the United Nation's Food and Agriculture Organization, local or national governments, or NGOs.

Copyright and Related Rights and Intellectual Property

Many alternative media-makers want to copy, sample, satirize, or simply use for noncommercial purposes materials from popular culture, TV, and mainstream news. Whether they can do this legally or at least with impunity depends on the extent of copyright protection; whether there are exceptions for education, criticism, and reporting (in the United States, "fair use"); enforcement practices; and the availability of works in the public domain or free for noncommercial use.

However, most countries are obliged to comply with binational free trade agreements, the policies of the World Trade Organization and the World Intellectual Property Organization, which tend to favor media industry over cultural and public service values. Nationally, permission to legally use a copyrighted work is often delegated to industry bodies such as the American Society of Composers, Authors and Publishers, whose policies are typically not geared toward noncommercial users.

While commercial media thus carefully guard their own creations, they frequently co-opt and plagiarize styles, slogans, images, and genres developed by alternative media (including the term *alternative*). Many "new" commercial media genres, from call-in shows and reality TV to video-sharing sites, social network sites, "citizens' journalism," and blogging are essentially declawed versions of original alternative media practices (CNN's "i-report" even plagiarized Indymedia's logo). To protect their work against commercial exploitation, while still having it circulate widely through copying, translating, and recycling, some alternative media-makers use Creative Commons licenses. Others attack the system of intellectual property rights by flouting it, refusing to use it, or even trying to disrupt it.

Privacy rights such as anonymous publishing and protection against surveillance are also a big issue for alternative Internet users. Again, these rights are in the hands of multiple actors: The law may stipulate limits and requirements, but commercial entities such as Internet service providers may track users and share information with commercial data miners, law enforcement agencies, and military or political groups.

Distribution

In most countries, important layers of the audiovisual distribution system (e.g., satellite channels, local cable distribution) are business controlled. Alternative media organizations using primarily print and video/DVD, as well as Internet distribution and digital radio, also often find themselves shut out by industry actors. Distribution of DVDs, CDs, and print media to bookstores and newsstands may be controlled by a few companies, who overcharge or wholly refuse to handle noncommercial titles. News portals may lead readers to stories provided by the same few news agencies. In countries without must-carry provisions, terrestrial digital broadcasting infrastructure providers (like cable and satellite providers) can refuse access to noncommercial media-makers. Search engines for mobile phones may be designed to search only commercial databases. In addition, business corporations and their industry associations also often lobby the government against alternative media interests and use alternative media's economic weaknesses to undermine their organizations.

Strategies for Media Activists

Civil society actors naturally play a big role for alternative media. The overall health of civic engagement and social movements is a big factor in their success, as is the degree to which social movement organizations, individual activists, and formal civil society (NGOs, labor unions, etc.) consider alternative media as part of their strategies. For example, many feminist media have symbiotic relationships with social movement organizations. Korean labor unions from the late 1990s to the mid-2000s boosted their own social influence by funding alternative media and supporting their lobbying efforts. Unfortunately, many

social movements still need to make media issues their "second priority." Private philanthropy and foundation policies also influence alternative media by supporting certain types of organizations, and research on them, at the expense of others. Individual academics and educational institutions can work with them through internship systems, events, and collaborative research projects.

The best strategy for alternative media to improve their framing conditions is to network and lobby. Two prominent examples of international umbrella organizations that lobby for alternative media are the World Association of Community Radio Broadcasters and the Association for Progressive Communications, the latter of which supports nonprofit online service providers. However, there are currently no such organizations for other media technologies. The OURMedia/NUESTROSMedios Network fulfills networking functions and helps promote the cause of alternative media in academia, and to foundations, but does not lobby governmental or commercial actors.

The issues facing alternative media are highly diverse, depend on local context and the technologies used, and are overall hard to tackle, making it difficult to build campaigns around more than one issue at the time. Movements with meta-agendas like "communication rights" or "media democracy" are an attempt to address this.

Gabriele Hadl

See also Alternative Media at Political Summits; Alternative Media in the World Social Forum; Copyleft; Creative Commons; Media Activists and Communication Policy Processes; Media Infrastructure Policy and Media Activism

Further Readings

Buckley, S., Duer, K., Mendel, T., & Ó Siochrú, S. (with Price, M., & Raboy, M.). (2008). *Broadcasting, voice, and accountability: A public interest approach to policy, law, and regulation.* Washington, DC: World Bank Group.

Hackett, R., & Carroll, W. (2006). *Remaking media: The struggle to democratize public communication.* Routledge: New York.

Hadl, G. (Ed.). (2009). Convergences: Civil society media and policies [Special issue]. *International Journal of Media and Cultural Politics, 5*(1).

AlterNet (United States)

AlterNet is a progressive online alternative news source that not only serves as a source of original content but also aggregates other alternative media online. It is a creation of the nonprofit Independent Media Institute (IMI), originally founded in 1983 as the nonprofit group Institute for Alternative Journalism (IAJ). It promotes and strengthens the independent press in an increasingly concentrated media landscape. AlterNet plays an important role in the editorial planning of many alternative papers.

As of 2010, Don Hazen was executive editor of the IMI and executive editor of AlterNet. Hazen was the former publisher of *Mother Jones* magazine, another U.S. independent nonprofit publication. The staff largely consists of professional journalists and others with direct experience with the topics about which they write. Whereas earlier incarnations of AlterNet encouraged user-created content, independently produced blogs, other media outlets, and staff writers now generate the site's featured content. Users are encouraged to engage in discussion in the comments section that follows each article. The site has over 30,000 registered users.

The AlterNet of the late 2000s served primarily as a news source and aggregator and less as a newswire, collecting stories from other popular alternative locations such as *The Huffington Post, Democracy Now!* and *The Nation,* while concurrently including stories featured on such mainstream news sources as CNN and *The Washington Post.* AlterNet had 12 areas of special coverage, each with an editor and a weekly newsletter. These were Rights & Liberties, Corporate Accountability & Workplace, Democracy & Elections, Environment, Media Culture, Reproductive Justice & Gender, Health & Wellness, War on Iraq, Water, Immigration, Drug Reporter, and Sex & Relationships.

Thus, AlterNet brings to the forefront topics often reduced to subplots in mainstream media. Mainstream news often breaks down into local news, politics, sports, world news, and business, before moving onto living, arts, and other sections. AlterNet evolved its distinctive direction over time: The very first website listed six subsections, with more traditional categories such as Arts & Entertainment and Books & Authors.

AlterNet acted as an important center for online alternative media, providing a one-stop location for a variety of content from a variety of sources. The latest figures showed that the website received 3 million visitors monthly with over 7.5 million page views. According to the site, many readers came from Google, Digg, and Reddit.

Mike Melanson

See also Indymedia (The Independent Media Center); *OhmyNews* (Korea); Online Nationalism (China)

Further Readings

AlterNet: http://www.alternet.org/about/index.html and http://web.archive.org/web/19980210172648/www .alternet.org/aboutalter.html

Anarchist and Libertarian Media, 1945–2010 (Federal Germany)

Right after the end of World War II, the few anarchists who had survived war and fascism started to reorganize the anarchist movement, which had been shattered during the Nazi dictatorship. On May 20, 1945, German anarchism once again raised its journalistic voice, with the journal *Mahnruf* (Warning Cry), published by Otto Reimers in Hamburg.

In 1947, the journal *Befreiung* (Liberation) was published for the first time in Mühlheim. This newspaper went through several editorial changes and inconsistencies in its content. During its final years in Cologne until its closedown in 1978, it linked old and young anarchists and represented anarcho-syndicalist positions. It had a national circulation of 1,500 copies.

Many early postwar anarchist journals were produced on a duplicator. Not so *Die Freie Gesellschaft* (The Free Society), published by the Föderation Freiheitlicher Sozialisten (Federation of Free Socialists). This "monthly journal for social criticism and free socialism" (subtitle) saw 43 issues between 1949 and 1953.

Anarchism's Renaissance and New Libertarian Media

Neoanarchism was mainly influenced by 1960s anticolonialist liberation struggles. The majority of the antiauthoritarian and Außerparlamentarischen Opposition (APO; Extra-Parliamentary Opposition) movement tried to challenge the U.S.–Vietnam War, which was supported by the authorities of the German Federal Republic and the mass media. The APO also opposed the emergency laws of the "grand coalition," consisting of the Social Democratic Party of Germany and the conservative parties (Christian Democratic Union/Christian Social Union) and Germany's mediascape, dominated by the Springer media conglomerate. They contested Germany's "sclerotic institutions" and their representatives, old-fashioned ideas about morality, and the indifference and complacency of society at large.

In June 1967, after the student Benno Ohnesorg was shot dead by a police officer during a Berlin demonstration against the visit of the Iranian despot Shah Reza Pahlavi, many activists within the Sozialistischer Deutscher Studentenbund (Socialist German Student Union) became increasingly radical. Only a year later, anarchist literature gained currency on a hitherto unimaginable scale. At first, classical anarchist writings were published as pirate editions; later on they were produced in high print runs by big publishing houses. Anarchism saw a renaissance. The new anarchist movement consisted mainly of students, pupils, and apprentices. There was no continuity with the old, working-class anarchists, who looked very skeptically at the younger ones from middle-class families.

Anarchism researcher Rolf Raasch has argued that there were theoretical divisions between the younger and the older generations. The students initially were committed to a critical version of Marxism. Their attempt at mediation between Marxism and Anarchism, cheerfully unconcerned with past grievances, was inevitably repugnant to seasoned anarchists, who had deeply internalized the historical clashes between both movements—not least because some of them had personally experienced Marxist socialism as practiced in the German Democratic Republic.

From February 1968 onward, the neoanarchist movement sharply increased its presence. Neoanarchist, undogmatic, and antiauthoritarian magazines were launched in 1968, particularly in West Berlin. They were models for many subsequent "underground papers." Their scene jargon and their layout, inspired by Dadaism, differed clearly from the magazines of the old anarchists with their tidy composition and simple layout.

Linkeck

Linkeck (Left Corner), which called itself "the first anti-authoritarian paper," was the organ of a Berlin anarchist commune by the same name, founded in 1967. It was published nine times from May 1968 and had a circulation of about 8,000. It became known nationwide because Germany's biggest yellow press daily, *Bild,* ran editorials against the "left terrorist paper." Four *Linkeck* editors were charged with "libel" and "distributing obscene writings." The commune broke up in 1969, due to overwork, legal problems, and internal conflicts. Its paper ceased to be published. The anarchist publishing house Karin Kramer Verlag in Berlin, which still exists, emerged from *Linkeck* in 1970.

agit 883

With a similar layout, *agit 883* was published every 10 to 14 days, beginning in February 1968. It achieved a circulation of up to 7,000. It was a left-wing information bulletin from Berlin, served as a "leaflet for agitation and social practice" (its subtitle) and dealt with current events.

On April 11, 1968, a man "incited" by the politics of *Bild* tried to assassinate student activist Rudi Dutschke. As a reaction, crowds of protesters spontaneously blocked buildings of the Springer media conglomerate to prevent deliveries from its premises (including *Bild*). This conflict went down in history as Osterkrawalle (the Easter riots).

Soon afterward, "urban guerrilla units" emerged. Discussions about the activities of these armed groups were intense in many far left and anarchist papers. In May 1970, the first public statement from the Red Army Faction (*Rote Armee Fraktion,* RAF) was published in *agit 883* under the headline "Building the Red Army Faction." At that time, *agit 883* was a largely uncensored discussion organ of militant left-wing groups with a focus on anarchist and Marxist theories. They rejected the avant-garde claim and the authoritarian dogmatism of those they saw as Leninists with guns (*agit 883* about RAF). They agreed, however, with the internationalist principles of RAF and its perception of the strategic use of violence as an essential weapon against the state and U.S. imperialism.

The *agit 883* editorial collective was frequently raided, the paper often confiscated or banned. After 88 issues and a number of conflicts among the editorial staff, *agit 883* closed down in February 1972. The collective had already split up in 1971 over evaluating RAF.

FIZZ

Former *agit 883* editors left the collective, and in 1971 in Berlin, they formed the militant underground paper *FIZZ*. It declared its solidarity with RAF in contrast to *agit 883*, which appeared simultaneously. *FIZZ* appeared for 1 year. Nine of its ten editions were confiscated and banned. *FIZZ*'s successors were *Berliner Anzünder* (Berlin Incendiary, 1972), *Hundert Blumen* (Hundred Flowers, 1972–1975) and *Bambule* (German prison slang for "shindig," 1972–1974).

MAD

In September 1971, the Föderation Neue Linke (FNL; New Left Federation) published the first edition of *MAD* with "Materials, Analyses, Documents" as its subtitle. When the FNL, which understood itself as a "federation of autonomous, local anarchist and grass-roots groups," dissolved, *MAD* was published as an "anarchist magazine" (subtitle). It published anarchist calls for action and Situationist texts and articles about strategies of industrial struggle. Looking back, one of its editors commented on how important it was felt at that time to show that poetry and revolution belonged together and to include Dadaism and surrealism into the origins of the new anarchism.

After the U.S. "satirical magazine" *MAD* took legal action against the anarchist project having the same name, it was discontinued in 1973, after magazine issue number 4/5 had been published. After that, the anarchist *MAD* was published under the name *Revolte*, until issue number 6/1973 with the subtitle "anarchist journal, formerly *MAD*—anarchist magazine." From 1977 until 1982, *Revolte* was published by Hanna Mittelstädt

and Lutz Schulenburg of the publishing house Verlag Edition Nautilus. From 1981 onward, they published *Die Aktion* as a "journal for politics, literature and art."

Graswurzelrevolution (Grassroots Revolution)

In the summer of 1972, the pilot issue of the *Graswurzelrevolution* (GWR) came out. The editorial collective was inspired in concept and orientation by *Anarchisme et Nonviolence* (Paris), which was published between 1965 and 1974 in the French-speaking regions of Europe as a nonviolent and anarchist paper; by *Peace News,* published in London since 1936; and by *Direkte Aktion—Zeitung für Gewaltfreiheit und Anarchismus* (Direct Action—Newspaper for Nonviolence and Anarchism), which was published in Hannover in 1965–1966. The GWR editorial group was oriented toward movements in other countries, for example, Britain and the United States. Gandhi's methods had undergone further development in the fight against the nuclear bomb and for civil rights, and the "grassroots movement" had taken a new shape.

From its beginning, GWR tried to widen and develop the theory and practice of nonviolent revolution. Besides critique of existing conditions, the GWR tried and continues to try to organize at least the seeds of a just and livable future society. It is the newspaper's declared aim to point out the connection between nonviolence and libertarian socialism, to contribute to the pacifist movement becoming libertarian socialist and the left-wing socialist movement becoming nonviolent in their forms of struggle.

Since issue 52 in 1981, the periodical has been published monthly with a July–August break. Before that, it was published every 2 to 3 months. Since 1989, it has had an eight-page supplement of "libertarian book pages" every October. It has been published by different editors in Augsburg (1972–1973), Berlin (1974–1976), Göttingen (1976–1978), Hamburg (1978–1988), Heidelberg (1988–1992), Wustrow (1992–1995), Oldenburg (1995–1999), and Münster (since 1999). The different editorial collectives each determined their own style. 2009 was GWR's 38th year of publication, circulating between 3,500 and 5,000 copies.

It is the longest-lived anarchist newspaper in the German-speaking area and a leading outlet for grassroots activists.

A special antimilitarist edition of GWR about the war in Afghanistan in 2003 had a circulation of 55,000. The nonviolent-anarchist youth paper *Utopia*, a bimonthly since 2007, is a supplement to GWR. It has a much wider distribution than GWR and in March 2009 it rose from 18,000 to 25,000.

direkte aktion

In November 1977 the first issue of the anarcho-syndicalist paper *direkte aktion* appeared in Hamburg. Initially it was supposed to serve as a regional voice of antiauthoritarian people who were organized in local groups of the Initiative-Freie Arbeiter Union in northern Germany and who had just started.

The editors followed the tradition of the anarcho-syndicalist Freie Arbeiter Union Deutschlands (FAUD; Free Workers Union of Germany), which was smashed by the Nazis. The FAUD had at times 150,000 members and was the most influential anarchist organization in Germany. Its main publication was *Der Syndikalist*, and in 1920 its weekly circulation amounted to 120,000 copies.

The formation of *direkte aktion* is to be seen as an attempt to get a new start for anarcho-syndicalism in Germany. Inspired by the reactivation of the Spanish Confederación Nacional del Trabajo, people from several cities came together to build a new anarcho-syndicalist organization at the beginning of 1977, the Freie ArbeiterInnen Union (FAU; Free Workers Union [*Innen* is capitalized to pinpoint women's activism rather than incorporating it under the masculine *Arbeiter*]). It started with the experience of many people in their work situation and with the politics of the DGB (Federation of German Trade Unions) and its member unions, who were "stifling initiatives from the grassroots."

They argued that the reformist unions were organized undemocratically; they would hold their members dependent on the leadership, and this would mean to keep the capitalist economy in existence. Many people had tried to reform the apparatus from below, but all had failed, were shunted aside, or expelled, or had become part of the union bureaucracy. Another reason to form an anarcho-syndicalist union was the disorganization, isolation, and lack of new perspectives in small groups and individuals among the libertarian-socialist people. They argued that anarcho-syndicalism presented important opportunities for organizing political action on a libertarian basis, to deal with the problem of political isolation, and to create networks and forums for joint discussion.

From July 1978 onward, *direkte aktion* has been published as a joint paper of anarcho-syndicalist initiatives from all over Germany. It continues to be produced bimonthly by changing editorial groups in different cities and has a nationwide circulation of 2,000.

The Anarchist Press in Federal Germany Today

Between 1986 and 1995, at least 310 different libertarian and autonomous periodicals were started but ceased publication to a great extent. Today anarchists start much less anarchist print media mainly because many anarchists are active on the Internet. Ever since 2006, for example, supporters of the Projektwerkstatt Göttingen have published *Fragend Voran* (Questioning Forward), which appears irregularly. Anarchists in Berlin produce *Abolishing the Borders From Below*, which is mainly a voice of anarchist groups in eastern Europe. In Leipzig, the regional anarchist paper *Feierabend* (Quitting Time at Work) is published approximately biweekly with a circulation of 600. The individualist-anarchist *espero* appeared irregularly with a circulation of about 500 since 1994. *Contraste*, published in Heidelberg, is a monthly on workers' self-management. It has a strong anarchist tendency and a circulation of 2,000. In Magdeburg, *Grüne Blatt* (Green Leaf) has an ecological orientation and a circulation of 800. The quarterly *DIE AKTION* (The Action) is a sophisticated intellectual journal about libertarian theory.

Bernd Drücke

See also Anarchist and Libertarian Press, 1945–1990 (Eastern Germany); Anarchist Media; Culture Jamming; EuroMayDay; Free Radio Movement (Italy); Industrial Workers of the World Media (United States); Indymedia (The Independent Media Center)

Further Readings

Drücke, B. (1998). *Zwischen Schreibtisch und Straßenschlacht? Anarchismus und libertäre Presse in Ost- und Westdeutschland* [Between writing desk and street battle? Anarchism and the libertarian press in East and West Germany]. Ulm, Germany: Verlag Klemm & Oelschläger.

Drücke, B. (Ed.). (2006). *ja! Anarchismus. Gelebte Utopie im 21. Jahrhundert* [yes! Anarchism: Lived utopia in the 21st century]. Berlin, Germany: Karin Kramer Verlag.

Jenrich, H. (1988). *Anarchistische Presse in Deutschland 1945–1985* [Anarchist press in Germany 1945–1985]. Grafenau, Germany: Trotzdemverlag.

ANARCHIST AND LIBERTARIAN PRESS, 1945–1990 (EASTERN GERMANY)

After World War I, the anarchist movement in Germany had, for some time, boasted more than 150,000 active members. After World War II, the few anarchists who had survived 12 years of Nazi dictatorship tried to reorganize the movement. In Eastern Germany, in spite of extremely serious obstacles, the movement survived underground in minimal versions but came to play a pivotal role in the latter years of the Soviet system, in significant measure because of some printing concessions reluctantly conceded to the Protestant Church.

Anarchists had a hard time asserting their anti-authoritarian and anti-Stalinist positions, especially in the Soviet Occupation Zone (SBZ, 1945–1949). The SBZ ruling powers and, later on, the Communist German Democratic Republic (GDR) were hostile toward libertarian socialists. Following Lenin, they defined anarchism as a petty-bourgeois, pseudo-revolutionary political and ideological current, objectively functioning to divide the anti-imperialist movement and strengthen monopoly capitalism.

Because paper was scarce postwar and the Soviet Military Administration was repressive, libertarian socialists in the SBZ were able to circulate only a small number of leaflets and circulars. Some activists, like Willi Jelinek, an agitator from Zwickau who tried to organize a libertarian-socialist network in the SBZ as early as 1945, were arrested.

The GDR statist Marxists continued quite successfully suppressing anarchist, or libertarian-socialist, tendencies. In journalism, anarchist groups had hardly any perceptible influence up to the mid-1980s. However, there had been illegal leaflets even in the 1950s and 1960s. Traces of East German subculture did exist—especially in niches created by the well-educated. The Extra-Parliamentary Opposition movement, which came into being in the Federal Republic of Germany in the mid-1960s, and the neoanarchist groups following in its wake, also contributed to the GDR opposition movement.

From the 1970s, GDR oppositionists largely advocated socialism. However, as Wolfgang Rüddenklau, editor of the *Umweltblätter* (Environment Pages) magazine, used to put it, the socialism they wanted was real, democratic, based on workers' councils, or anarchist—quite opposed to the ruling regime. The more explicitly anarchist, being but a small part of a poorly structured opposition, were virtually forced to act in a conspiratorial fashion.

In the GDR's "real socialism," the media published only official opinions and reports approved by the authorities. There was hardly any legal access to other sources of information. There were photocopiers in office and company buildings, but they were under strict surveillance, and their use was limited to an elite group loyal to the party.

The late 1970s brought changes in the media that were inspired by the ideas of grassroots democracy and anarchism. Erich Honecker, the long-time GDR leader, was facing a growing crisis in economic and social policy. To ease tension, in 1978 he entered into negotiations with Albrecht Schönherr, the bishop of the East Berlin Protestant churches. As a result, he granted the church a printing permit for internal information leaflets, announcements, and the like.

In the following years, this printing permit became a loophole heavily used by opposition groups. In the early 1980s, a serious civil rights movement grew up under the auspices of the Protestant Church, completely independent from the ruling Communist Party. Part of this movement became increasingly radical and outspoken about their anarchist positions. In 1982, for example, a politically active group was founded in Dresden's church organizations. It became known throughout the GDR by the name of Anarchistischer Arbeitskreis Wolfspelz (AAW; The "Wolf's Clothing" Anarchist Working Group). With the quiet help of a printer at the newspaper *Sächsische Zeitung,* they managed to circulate leaflets—some of them numbering more than 20,000 copies—and to call people to action.

Other anarchists typed, stenciled, and circulated texts by Mikhail Bakunin, Emma Goldman, Peter Kropotkin, and other anarchist classics. However, due to the poor copying techniques available, many of the texts were nearly illegible.

The first libertarian-socialist, underground periodicals in the GDR appeared in1986. Like almost all the opposition's publications, they were printed and distributed under the relative protection of the Protestant Church.

Kopfsprung (Header [a soccer move], 1987–1991) was the name of an overtly anarchist underground magazine. It dated back to the GDR Protestant Church Congress in 1986 where a group called *Kirche von Unten* (Church From Below, KVU) formed "in opposition to the existing church bureaucracy." This rather atheistic group did not see themselves as a Christian base community acting against highly privileged church dignitaries or as a religious reform group. Instead, they were mainly anarchists and punks acting against the existing system. Over time, rather than remaining a mere "anti" movement, KVU grew up to be a group with positions of its own.

The movement later split into several groups focusing on a variety of topics. In 1986, KVU issued at least three issues of *mOAning-STAR,* a hectographed periodical promoting libertarian-socialist views. The first issue of *Kopfsprung,* edited by an anonymous group, appeared in East Berlin in spring 1987, without stating either date or place of its publication. The next issues were stenciled and duplicated. The typewritten, single-column political texts were embedded in a sparse layout but enlivened by handmade drawings and lyrics.

In 1986, the liberal-left Initiative Frieden und Menschenrechte (Peace and Human Rights Initiative) in East Berlin launched the uncensored *Grenzfall* (Marginal Case), which became widely distributed throughout the GDR. Unlike the *Umweltblätter,* the editors of *Grenzfall* did not consider their project anarchist.

The goals pursued by anarchist groups such as KVU, AAW, and Umwelt-Bibliothek Ostberlin (East Berlin Environment Library) were different. They believed that, by expanding on the freedoms to be gained after a reform of the GDR or by undermining the state structure, they would be able to start the process they wanted—the process of growing a "new society from below."

Umweltblätter/telegraph

In the fall of 1986, *Umweltblätter,* subtitled "Informational Bulletin of the Peace and Environment Circle," appeared in East Berlin, initially published by the Umwelt-Bibliothek, an anarchist group founded that year under the Zion Parish Church's "umbrella." *Umweltblätter,* like most, was stenciled and duplicated in A4 format, with the heading "Internal church information only." Due to the poor print and layout quality, the single-column texts were often difficult to read.

Nevertheless, the small libertarian-socialist movement used *Umweltblätter* as their organ. They tried to "convey an unobtrusively anarchist attitude," as their editor Wolfgang Rüddenklau put it. They primarily published articles dealing with suppressed information on everyday life in the GDR. In winter 1986–1987, *Umweltblätter* disclosed the fact that the upper limits of smog concentration had been exceeded ninefold in Berlin. The GDR authorities were not happy to read this and were not happy about the fact that the periodical was developing into a GDR-wide discussion forum used by a variety of independent environmentalist, peace, and civil and human rights groups. Indeed, the magazine, passed from reader to reader, created a counter-public sphere, in spite of its relatively low nominal circulation of 600 copies.

In November 1987, the controversies between the GDR authorities and opposition groups reached a new pitch. The night of November 24, the secret police—known as the *Stasi* (abbreviation for State Security)—for the first time searched the Protestant Church's premises. Five people were arrested. The raid was aimed at *Umweltblätter,* of which 12 issues had been published by that time, and *Grenzfall.* About 20 Stasi and the state prosecutor's officials confiscated copying machines, manuscripts, and books published in the West.

This prompted public protest and vigils throughout the GDR. Dissidents who had been shunted off to West Germany in earlier years provided a regular flow of information about these events, obtaining international media coverage. In the end all those arrested were released and the charges dropped. *Umweltblätter* continued publishing.

In 1994, Rüddenklau would observe that the Zion Parish Church affair was the beginning of the end of the GDR. From then on, domestic crises repeatedly showed that the regime could no longer rely on the terror that had kept people in fear and secured the GDR's existence. Understanding that the emperor had no clothes, people took to the streets in growing numbers until, in late 1989, the regime broke down.

The successful ending of the Zion affair gave an enormous boost to the opposition's publications. Although the Stasi was successful in stopping *Grenzfall* with the help of repeated technical sabotage carried out by an "unofficial collaborator," *Umweltblätter* simply took over *Grenzfall's* role as a GDR-wide opposition periodical. Correspondents from numerous towns and villages in the GDR forwarded news, comments, analyses, and general descriptions of the situation to East Berlin and had them published in *Umweltblätter*.

In early October 1989, things started happening very fast. The *Umweltblätter* editorial group decided to keep pace by issuing 7- to 10-page newsletters every few days, "as needed." On October 9, when the crisis reached its first crunch point, the magazine appeared under the title *telegraph* for the first time. (This title continues to the present day for a now irregularly appearing publication.)

Troops had been massed against the Leipzig Monday Rally. Armored scout cars and other army vehicles were patrolling the inner city of Leipzig. Rüddenklau recalled in 1994 that printing the first 4,000 copies of the first issue on rickety duplicating machines was a laborious task. These copies sold out to the demonstrators at the East Berlin Gethsemane Church in a matter of 20 minutes. Another print run of 2,000 copies followed while the next issue was being prepared.

From now on, *telegraph* continued at intervals of 7 to 10 days. The editors did their own investigations, and their work was based on anti-Stalinist as well as anticapitalist views. This was how they critically accompanied the transition from one system to another. There were numerous articles on how to come to terms with the past, on the Stasi, and on the partially anarchist opposition movement.

Conclusion

In 1989, the small oppositional scene grew into a mass movement. Hundreds of thousands demonstrated against the powerholders in East Berlin under the slogan, "We are the people!" On November 8, the Politburo resigned and instantly reassembled under the leadership of Egon Krenz.

After the Berlin Wall was opened the next day, GDR libertarian-socialist groups began procuring paper and printing facilities outside church facilities. Contacts with groups and printing collectives in the West intensified. Whereas communists and anti-imperialists rejected the anarchist movement in the GDR as being "anticommunist," many anarchists in the East and the West rejoiced at the fall of the Wall and the "incipient decline of state capitalism."

Anarchism in the GDR contributed more to the fall of communism than is generally known today.

Bernd Drücke

See also Anarchist and Libertarian Media, 1945–2010 (Federal Germany); Anarchist Media; Citizens' Media; EuroMayDay; Free Radio Movement (Italy); Indymedia (The Independent Media Center); Prague Spring Media; Revolutionary Media 1956 (Hungary); *Samizdat* Underground Media (Soviet Bloc)

Further Readings

Drücke, B. (1998). *Zwischen Schreibtisch und Straßenschlacht? Anarchismus und libertäre Presse in Ost- und Westdeutschland* [Between writing desk and street battle? Anarchism and the libertarian press in East and West Germany]. Ulm, Germany: Verlag Klemm & Oelschläger.

Drücke, B. (Ed.). (2006). *ja! Anarchismus. Gelebte Utopie im 21. Jahrhundert* [yes! Anarchism: Lived utopia in the 21st century]. Berlin, Germany: Karin Kramer Verlag.

Rüddenklau, W. (1992). *Störenfried* [Mischief maker]. Berlin, Germany: Verlag BasisDruck.

ANARCHIST MEDIA

Anarchism may be argued to offer a paradigm of radical publishing—not in its popular equation with chaos, but as an approach based on voluntary cooperation. Individual freedom, unfettered by commercial or governmental interference; enterprises run on collective lines; diversity of opinion: These are all anarchist ideals. Anarchism challenges authority, questions its legitimacy, and helps people take control of their own lives and consequently of the societies in which they live. Insofar as it challenges authority, anarchism is against the state and for direct, fully participative democracy. For many alternative publishers, these goals can be realized by writing and publishing.

Anarchist and libertarian media advocates argue that their media (like all radical media) should demonstrate their arguments by practicing "prefigurative politics," the attempt to practice socialist principles in the present, not merely to imagine them for the future. Anarchist media should enable a broad range of political and social possibilities to be proposed and discussed.

The history of anarchist media can be viewed from three major perspectives. The first, primarily historical, views anarchist media as mouthpieces of anarchist organizations, publications to present and develop anarchist theory and practice, the products of political groupings that are more or less closed, intellectually based and elitist.

The second, the principal focus here, addresses more recent developments in anarchism, where media lean more toward collective and nonhierarchical models. Problems and tensions in contemporary anarchist media are as evident currently as historically, as will be noted. This perspective may also include media modeled on anarchist principles (whether they explicitly espouse and promote anarchism or not), that are employed to further the aims of collectively organized protest groups, known in the 1990s as the "New Protest." Internet use is very significant in these recent developments.

A third and final perspective touched upon in conclusion views anarchism through the lens of the personal, where anarchist media become experiments in playful symbolic action.

The Historical Perspective: Organization and Ideology

It is tempting to locate the fountainhead of anarchist media in the 1936–1939 Spanish civil war. This period of the 20th century saw what remains as the sole contribution of anarchist thought to the political affairs of a nation, one with international repercussions. The anarchists of the Confederación Nacional del Trabajo (CNT; National Confederation of Labor) had as their mouthpiece the newspaper *Solidaridad Obrera* (Workers Solidarity). Founded in 1907, the paper endured regular suppression by the Spanish government, but during the war became the largest circulation newspaper (220,000 copies). Dictator Francisco Franco banned it, but it appeared clandestinely, returning to regular weekly publication in 1976 following his death and the CNT's legalization. It was still publishing as of this writing, distributed free in paper and online.

However, the roots of anarchist media lie much further back. Josiah Warren's *The Peaceful Revolutionist,* a four-page weekly first published in 1833, is regarded as the first anarchist periodical in the United States. Anarchism historian John Quail describes Benjamin Tucker's paper *Liberty* (founded in 1881) as the first systematic propaganda defining itself as anarchist that had any effect within the socialist movement. It was *Liberty* that in part prompted the editors of the British anarchist fortnightly *Freedom* to begin publishing in 1886, now one of the longest-running anarchist periodicals in the world. Both *Freedom* and its precursor, the *Anarchist* (which predated *Freedom* by 1 year), offer historians of radical media an important perspective on early anarchist media, a perspective very different from late 20th-century anarchist publishing.

The *Anarchist*'s intellectual base was strong. Writer George Bernard Shaw was one of its contributors, as was Russian anarchist philosopher Peter Kropotkin. Kropotkin was also a significant contributor to *Freedom. Freedom* was established as the organ of the London-based Freedom Group.

Its membership was limited and closed; there was no attempt to build a popular movement. Instead, the paper used the prestige of Kropotkin to distribute the paper through more established groups such as the Socialist League. Despite this elitism, its editors saw their paper as the nucleus for the organization of other autonomous groups. All its contributions were published anonymously, including Kropotkin's. Although this is not the case today (*Freedom* still comes out fortnightly), the tradition of anonymous authorship continues throughout radical media (and predates anarchist media): whether to avoid prosecution or—as is common in contemporary radical media—to implicitly challenge notions of individual authorship and intellectual property rights.

The organization of *Freedom* can be seen as a precursor of what well-known anarchist writer Murray Bookchin has called "affinity groups," where the organization of media takes place on an "anti-mass" level and privileges local groups (affinity groups), connected informally through international networks of solidarity and resource sharing. That said, many anarchist media projects have operated in ways that appear exclusive and elitist. This has nonetheless spurred diverse anarchist media in terms of ideology, organizational methods, and numbers of publications.

Contemporary Anarchism and the "New Protest"

The number of anarchist media projects increased significantly in the last quarter of the 20th century. In the United Kingdom, according to the 1996 edition of the *Anarchist Year Book,* over 20 newspapers and journals were being published, by more than a dozen explicitly anarchist publishers. The numbers would be much higher if titles that employ anarchist organizational methods, but were not explicitly anarchist, were included.

France has long enjoyed many anarchist publications. At the turn of the last century (1880–1914), there were 400 explicitly anarchist press titles. In the period 1968–1983, there were 730. Estimates for the 10 years following are as high as 1,000. These included long-standing titles such as the Fédération Anarchiste's *Le Monde libertaire* (Libertarian World), the French CNT's *Le Combat syndicaliste* (Union Combat, founded in 1946),

and the Organisation Communiste Libertaire's *Courant alternative* (Alternative Perspective), as well as anarcho-punk fanzines like *On A Faim!* (We're Hungry!) and *Soleil Noir* (Black Sun). Current print-runs range from 15,000 for organizational organs such as *Le Monde libertaire* to as little as 300 for regional and urban titles like *Soleil Noir.*

The reasons for this upsurge of publications lie primarily in the development of grassroots political activism in the 1960s outside the established political parties. Methods of organizing media production were further enhanced during the 1970s by what has come to be known as the DIY (do-it-yourself) culture of political organization that developed from the 1970s punk movement. DIY culture emphasizes small-scale, antiparty, and antihierarchical methods of activism that rely less on early 20th-century ideologies of anarchism and more on independently antielitist perspectives. These media also developed out of the so-called New Protest of the 1990s.

The term *New Protest* encompasses a plethora of diverse groups and movements that espoused nonparliamentary direct action tactics. These sprang up, coalesced, or split as choice or necessity dictated. Most had no formal memberships, such as Earth First! or came together temporarily for specific actions, such as the Earth Liberation Front and the radical cyclists' campaign Critical Mass. Others led shadowy existences in an attempt to evade police surveillance, such as the militant animal rights group, The Justice Department. Most had no leaders and no hierarchy. These protests cannot be considered as entirely new but rather as the latest in the line of thriving cultures of resistance using direct action.

Where, arguably, they were new was in the nexus of alliances that came together—animal rights, environmentalism, anticapitalist critiques, squatters' rights, rave culture—and in the highly visible networks of communication and action they developed. Self-organization and DIY politics as channels of resistance were enhanced by a refusal to grant primacy to any particular site or mode of struggle. The global network of Independent Media Centers that make up Indymedia offers a striking example of such anarchy in action, without requiring the network explicitly to proclaim anarchist aims.

Problems and Tensions in Anarchist Media

The anarchist aims of independence, freedom, and collective organization have had their cost. As early as the turn of the 20th century, provincial anarchist papers had challenged *Freedom*'s attempt to function as a national U.K. center for anarchism. Their failure has been attributed to the philosophy of pinprick attacks and piecemeal defense, which John Quail has claimed moved them away from the collaboration with socialist groups normal in early anarchist agitation.

Freedom to publish has its critics in the anarchist movement. In 1990 the Centre International de Recherches sur l'Anarchisme (CIRA) at Lausanne had received, in a few months, 40 anarchist periodicals in English. Rather than see this as a success, the CIRA called instead for consolidation, for putting the money and effort involved in producing 40 journals into an international anarchist weekly. This may be viewed as a plea for the most effective use of people and resources in endeavors always dependent on voluntary labor and limited funds. Pooling scarce resources would not only improve research and news gathering, it would also give a higher profile to a single anarchist journal and its promotion of anarchism to the public. This is unlikely to happen—the fierce independence within anarchist media is too strong for that. Networking and cooperation may be common among participants, but relinquishing one's own titles is not a popular option.

The independence of individual anarchist media projects can just as easily lead to their media being an ideological battleground where competing perspectives on anarchism are played out, not always to the benefit of the promotion of anarchist praxis. This struggle not only leads to ideological division between publications (e.g., between the classical anarchism of *Freedom* and the violent direct action promoted by a paper such as *Class War*), but also has been played out within publications.

The history of *Fifth Estate* provides a striking example. *Fifth Estate* was founded in the United States in 1965, though it did not promote itself as explicitly anarchist until 1975. In the 1990s, it adopted a militant, antitechnology ideology that drew significantly on the primitivist anarchist theory of John Zerzan. Later it distanced itself from anarchism as an ideology, preferring to consider itself as anticapitalist.

The British *Green Anarchist* (founded in 1984) latterly also embraced a primitivist stance that supported violent direct action. Its history is remarkable for the range of organizational approaches it has adopted, usually as a result of internal struggles for editorial control. It began as the work of three people and was run more or less hierarchically. An attempt to bring more people into the editorial process led to more collective decision making but also led to the acrimonious departure of one of its founders. A further shift in organization facilitated the paper's move to a highly fluid collective, where jobs and responsibilities were subject to change and its editing was decentralized to autonomous groups across the country.

Despite the problems that arise when anarchist principles are put into practice, decentralization and autonomy—as syndicalism—have historically played an important part in anarchist practice. During its heyday in the late 19th and early 20th centuries in the United States, the Industrial Workers of the World carried forward the premises of anarchism and syndicalism—and their fluidity and mobility—in a number of ways. It helped to pioneer a flexible, de-territorialized resistance to capitalism that was much less about local industrial confrontations and much more about a variable, general community of labor affinity at specific sites, to be determined by choice and conditions. By being de-institutionalized, tactics and specific actions spread person-to-person through word of mouth, becoming much less the official stance of a union or party and much more a fluid social movement—and thus much more difficult for supervisors, managers, and the state to detect, control, and punish. Its newspaper, *The Industrial Worker,* is still published online.

Where anarchism is a tiny splinter activity, we find fewer titles but often longevity. *Brand* has been published continuously in Sweden since 1898; *Umanità Nova* has been published by the Italian Anarchist Federation since 1920; the Federación Libertaria Argentina has been publishing its journals since 1935; Venezuela's *El Libertario* has been published since 1995. Anarchism in Japan goes back to the early 20th century. The Black Battlefront Company began in 1971 to publish facsimile editions of key journals of Japanese anarchist groups. In 1993, only one journal had national reach and longevity: *Jiyu Ishi,* the journal of the Japanese

Anarchist Federation, which is very much in the style of early 20th century anarchist publishing, aimed at a closed group with few concessions to a wider audience in either style or content.

In the United States and United Kingdom, there have been publications written by and for minority-language groups. For example, anarchist media in Yiddish included *Freie Arbeiter Stimme* (Free Workers Voice, United States, 1890–1977), *Arbeiter Fraynd* (Workers Friend, United Kingdom, 1898–1914), and *Germinal* (United Kingdom, 1900–1908). *Cronaca Sovversiva* (Subversive News, United States, 1903–1918) was aimed at working-class Italian immigrants. Exiled Russian anarchists founded *Delo Truda* (Labour Issues) in 1925 from Paris (later Chicago), which survived a merger to continue publication until 1950.

Anarchist Media and the Internet

Anarchist principles are most vividly practiced by contemporary libertarian media projects on the Internet. The application of anarchist principles to Internet-based practices of political organization and media production by networks such as Indymedia has been termed *cyberanarchism.* By this is meant the establishment of "confederal" structures of community and communication, free from the external coercion of the state and commercial providers of Internet access, and the limits of computer ownership and literacy. This utopian view of technology, however, takes little account of the power asymmetries within the network (North/South, reformist/radical) and its chronic domination by men of European descent. A highly dystopian view appeared in a 1995 editorial in *Fifth Estate,* where the online paper argued that the Internet was the final frontier for advanced capitalism's drive to mechanize everyday life, thereby downgrading the value of direct experience and community life.

Nevertheless, many anarchist publications seized on the Internet as a way of building communities and of establishing global networks of autonomous anarchist projects. Some anarchist groups and commentators saw in the structure and openness of the Internet the prefiguring of an anarchist society. Anarchist publications were among the first alternative print media to move to the Internet. Anarchist use of the Internet can be traced back as

far as 1988 with the establishment of the Anarchy List, yet this did not touch the long-established anarchist media until much later. As late as 2002, *Freedom*'s presence on the Internet was sparse. *Freedom* was not alone in this: *Black Flag,* established as the newsletter of the Anarchist Black Cross in the United Kingdom, was also restricted by the resources it could put into electronic publication, preferring to maintain its quarterly, later biannual, magazine as its primary medium.

The American journal *Practical Anarchy Online* was the first anarchist periodical to become available solely in electronic format in 1992. U.S. journal *Wind Chill Factor* declared in 1993 that the cost of printing 5,000+ copies per month was prohibitive. It decided to publish quarterly in print, and to issue electronic "info-bulletins" in between. The problem of low print runs is very real for anarchist publishers and hinders any widespread dissemination of their titles. Estimates of readership in the United Kingdom were 12,000 for *Class War,* 500 to 1,000 for *Direct Action* and for *Freedom,* and 2,000 for *Green Anarchist.* One would expect the actual copies printed to be at least half of these figures.

Publishing on the Internet requires that only a single "copy" of any document exist to provide mass circulation. This not only dispenses with the notion of circulating copies, it also blurs the distinction between publishing and distribution. Although the Internet does away with the capital requirement for print runs, it nevertheless requires capital and time to enable the origination of documents in machine-readable format. Such a requirement is hardly trivial. Where publishers receive no income from their work, these resources must come from personal funds or be offset by the use of equipment intended for other purposes, such as scanners and computers used in the course of other (paid) employment.

Early uses of the Internet by anarchist groups were more or less fragmented ventures into small-scale electronic media production. These experienced only small increases in the circulation and reach compared to their print precursors and were hard to sustain. By contrast, the development of the McSpotlight website in 1996 demonstrated a more successful strategy based on international networking, a broadening of the protest agenda and the participation of numerous local groups.

McSpotlight was set up to raise awareness of what became the longest trial in English legal history, when the fast-food company McDonald's took members of the anarchist group London Greenpeace to court for publishing and distributing a leaflet allegedly containing defamatory statements about McDonald's, claiming that the company was responsible for the destruction of rainforests to provide land for beef cattle, infringing workers' rights, cruelty to animals, and promoting unhealthy eating. The site provided a nonhierarchical center for a range of diffuse and only informally connected groups and individuals—Bookchin's affinity groups in action. As the site grew to involve more groups, opportunities arose to expand the interests of the site to cover not only the "McLibel" trial but also the practices of multinational corporations in all countries and their links with governments and supra-governmental bodies.

A site that functioned more conventionally as a library and an archive was the anarchist Spunk Press (subsequently known as Spunk Library), which stored many anarchist journals and acted as a distributor for numerous anarchist news services. Established in 1992 in Holland, but with an international editorial group, its aim was to act as an independent publisher of works converted to, or produced in, electronic format and to spread them as far as possible on the Internet, free of charge. Spunk Library's catalog contained essays, speeches, and lectures from prominent anarchists, both historical (Bakunin and Goldman) and contemporary (Bookchin and Chomsky).

What was striking in the case of Spunk Library was the extent to which a given technology could be fully integrated into anarchist praxis. Whereas many paper-based archives of anarchist media and literature operated from private houses, conducting most of their business by mail, with low use and extremely low public profiles (such as the Anarchist Archives Project in the United States and the Kate Sharpley Library in the United Kingdom), Spunk Library Press has considerable visibility and accessibility (www.spunk.org).

A further opportunity for anarchist media to practice prefigurative politics on the Internet is through radical approaches to intellectual property rights. The anticopyright and copyleft movements have their roots in anarchism. Proudhon's

well-known axiom "property is theft" prompted Bookchin to argue for the concept of "usufruct" as a replacement for property rights. Whereas the notion of property rights implies the permanent ownership of resources, usufruct is temporary, based on current needs within a communal framework. What has been termed *electronic non-propertarianism* is an especially powerful concept for web-based media, where usufruct has emerged as a norm for distribution and sharing of media resources: This too is anarchism in action.

Anarchist Media as Play

We have seen the influence of DIY culture on the recent history of anarchist media. The 1980s and 1990s saw a further development of this influence. This time, though, there was an emphasis on printed zines and pamphlets by individual authors (often anonymous or pseudonymous). These occasional and one-off publications used anarchism as the basis for critiques of contemporary society and employed irony, humor, and satire to argue for social change. They tended to use techniques familiar from the Situationist literature of the 1960s, critiquing commodity culture through cartoons and self-consciously overblown rhetoric. The antiauthoritarian philosophy of anarchism was melded with a fascination with the contingent and the playful to produce texts from fictitious groups such as the Fare Dodgers' Liberation Front (*Artful Dodger*), the Institute of Social Disengineering (*Another Year of the Same Old Shit*), and the Society for Cutting Up Men (Valerie Solanas's *SCUM Manifesto*).

Publications like these were not interested in using media in the long-standing tradition of establishing anarchism as a serious alternative to dominant currents of political thought; nor did they seek to promote and establish communication within the more recent activism of autonomous and collective protest groups. Instead, as suggested in the names of publishers such as Play Time For Ever Press, these were the media of a symbolic protest that disrupted and subverted everyday life and challenged taken-for-granted issues. Less than a movement, even less a coherent ideology, such texts nevertheless have a place in the history of anarchist media for providing an enduring "subversive current" that challenges the dominant media as well as anarchist media themselves.

Chris Atton

See also Alternative Media; Citizens' Media; Community Radio Movement (India); Indymedia (The Independent Media Center); Indymedia: East Asia; Youth Media; Zines

Further Readings

Atton, C. (1996). Anarchy on the Internet: Obstacles and opportunities for alternative electronic publishing. *Anarchist Studies, 4*(2), 115–132.

Atton, C. (1999). Green anarchist: A case study in radical media. *Anarchist Studies, 7*(1), 25–49.

Berry, D. (1993). The Anarchist press in France today. *Anarchist Studies, 1*(1), 39–45.

Bookchin, M. (1986). A note on affinity groups. In M. Bookchin, *Post-scarcity anarchism* (2nd ed., pp. 243–244). Montréal, QC: Black Rose Books.

Chan, A. (1995). Anarchists, violence and social change: Perspectives from today's grassroots. *Anarchist Studies, 3*(1), 45–68.

Clement, E., & Oppenheim, C. (2002). Anarchism, alternative publishers and copyright. *Anarchist Studies, 10*(1), 41–69.

Downing, J. D. H. (with Villarreal Ford, T., Gil, G., & Stein, L.). (2001). *Radical media: Rebellious communication and social movement.* Thousand Oaks, CA: Sage.

Epstein, B. (1991). *Political protest and cultural revolution: Nonviolent direct action in the 1970s and 1980s.* Berkeley: University of California Press.

Freedom Press. (1990). Discussion notes on communicating. *The Raven, 3*(4), 377–383.

Kriha, T. F. J. (1994). *Cyberanarchism.* http://www .spunk.org/library/copyrite/comms/sp000877.txt

McKay, G. (1996). *Senseless acts of beauty: Cultures of resistance since the sixties.* London: Verso.

McKay, G. (Ed.). (1998). *DiY culture: Party and protest in nineties Britain.* London: Verso.

Pickard, V. W. (2006). United yet autonomous: Indymedia and the struggle to sustain a radical democratic network. *Media, Culture & Society, 28*(3), 315–336.

Quail, J. (1978). *The slow burning fuse: The lost history of the British anarchists.* London: Paladin.

Ritter, A. (1980). *Anarchism: A theoretical analysis.* Cambridge, UK: Cambridge University Press.

Salerno, S. (1989). *Red November, black November: Culture and community in the industrial workers of the world.* Albany: State University of New York Press.

Spunk Library Manifesto: www.spunk.org

ANCLA CLANDESTINE NEWS AGENCY (ARGENTINA)

A writer, journalist, and revolutionary militant who disappeared during the last military dictatorship in Argentina, Rodolfo Walsh joined the Montoneros revolutionary organization in 1973, where he fulfilled tasks in the Military Secretariat Department of Information and Intelligence, not in the press area. Nevertheless, when the coup took place in 1976, because of the new political situation that was unfolding in the country, he undertook projects that involved both journalism and counterintelligence. These included organizing the Clandestine News Agency (ANCLA).

Walsh had been thinking for some time, as he used to put it, of using language as an object, to wield it as a hammer. His participation in the Cuban news agency Prensa Latina, the Argentine weekly magazine *Semanario CGT*, and the *Noticias* newspaper had allowed him to see the practical possibilities of the press as a means of organization and combat.

In late 1975, when a military coup was only a question of time, Walsh and other comrades began to evaluate the possibility of setting up an emergency plan to obstruct the initial deployment of the new military assault. The proposal had taken into account the tremendous information blockade that would ensue. But the coup accelerated the situation. The level of repression and the consecutive losses forced adaptation, the new phase that was unfolding.

It was in those first harsh days of Argentina's bloodiest dictatorship when the old idea of a clandestine press decisively took shape. In a meeting with a group of four friends with whom he shared responsibility, Walsh finalized the details of what was to be the Clandestine News Agency. Once it was operating he dedicated himself to counterintelligence, and ANCLA came under Lila ("Lidia") Pastoriza's direction.

Basically, the agency came to represent the necessity for media not only efficient in circulating information but, above all, effective as a political instrument. ANCLA had to be a clandestine information forum and also focus an important part of its efforts to acting within the heart of the power structure. In other words, it had to operate as a communication institution but be equally committed to direct action, taking an active part in the resistance struggle against the regime.

Its attack mode of operation was not only because of the oppressive situation but also because of its role as a counterintelligence tool: All military and political activities had to aim to accelerate the contradictions within the groups in power until their unity broke down. That is why ANCLA acted with apparent autonomy from other organizations. Its political practice was founded on a triple objective: to favor popular participation in the communication process, to function as a source of counter-information, and to operate as an instrument of psychological action against the military–economic power bloc.

That is to say, ANCLA had a definite perspective but did not claim to be any particular political group's organ; nor did it focus only on the success of a specific operation. That task belonged to the *Evita Montonera* and the *Montonero* magazines, which were responsible for propagandizing the Montoneros' political line. ANCLA functioned, as Lenin would have put it, as the only ongoing operation capable of drawing up a balance sheet of the full spectrum of political challenges under way at the time. But ANCLA gave battle in the symbolic realm instead.

From June 1976, news reports began to arrive by mail to national newspaper offices, to foreign press correspondents, clergy, the army, and the economic power groups. Concealed under its vague identity, the agency exposed all the information that in those years was systematically denied to Argentineans: the divisions among the military junta, the objectives of the looming economic restructuring plan, the expressions of popular resistance, and the tremendous human rights violations.

ANCLA combined exhaustive analysis of the official press, intercepts from the military's communication network, informants' reports, information received through the Montoneros'

networks, and contributions from neighbors, workers, and students who overcame their fears to bring information to the agency. This made of ANCLA a space where, paraphrasing Walsh, language was used like an object, like a rifle, like a hammer.

Natalia Vinelli (translated by Guillermo Azzi)

See also Alternative Media Heritage in Latin America; Citizens' Media; Miners' Radio Stations (Bolivia); Social Movement Media, 1960s–1980s (Chile); Zapatista Media (México)

Further Readings

Vinelli, N. (2002). *ANCLA: una experiencia de comunicación clandestina orientada por Rodolfo Walsh* [ANCLA: An experience of focused underground communication by Rodolfo Walsh]. Buenos Aires, Argentina: Editorial La Rosa Blindada. http://www.scribd.com/doc/8529148/Natalia-Vinelli-ANCLA-Una-experiencia-de-comunicacion-clandestina-orientada-por-Walsh

ANGRY BUDDHIST MONK PHENOMENON (SOUTHEAST ASIA)

What has been called "angry monk syndrome," a phenomenon in which protesting Buddhist monks from Southeast Asia became a staple of Western media representation, can be usefully related to *Engaged Buddhism*, a term used to describe the participation of Buddhist activists in political struggles. Engaged Buddhists believe that the purpose of dharma is not only to heal the individual but also to contribute to social healing, and so they participate in efforts to raise awareness about political and social problems, including economic and political injustices. If, as many Engaged Buddhists believe, there is no dualistic separation between individual consciousness and social life, then individual transformation and social transformation are interrelated. This entry describes the role of Engaged Buddhism as a foundation of the protests known as "angry monk syndrome" and examines the relationship of such protests to the expression of anger and social protest.

Engaged Buddhism

Angry monk syndrome and *Engaged Buddhism* are not synonymous terms. A review of the latter term illuminates the controversial aspects of the former. The term *Engaged Buddhism* was first popularized by Thich Nhat Hanh, a Vietnamese Zen Buddhist monk and spiritual leader, in his book *Vietnam: Lotus in a Sea of Fire* during the period of the Vietnam War (1959–1975). He used it to describe the interpretation of Buddhism as a path of mindful social action, and he reconfigured the idea of "enlightenment" in ways that were clearly social and even political. His interpretation can partly be understood as a modernist attempt to reverse the image of Buddhism's historical "quietism" and passiveness toward public life.

Thich Nhat Hanh has been a theorist-practitioner of Engaged Buddhism since the early 1960s, a period in which the (anticolonial, pro-Communist) North fought against the (democratic, U.S.-supported) South. Engaged Buddhism usually combines political action with contemplative detachment; Thich Nhat Hanh attempted to avoid partisan attachment to a side and so refused to align himself with either the North or the South, instead actively promoting peace and encouraging people to oppose the war. In 1965, he wrote a letter to Martin Luther King Jr. and met with him in 1966, urging him to publicly denounce the Vietnam War. This led, in 1967, to King's famous speech at the Riverside Church in New York City, his first speech which publicly questioned the U.S. involvement in Vietnam.

Political analysis is often confined to the effects of the most powerful interest groups; Engaged Buddhism, however, is invariably a "weapon of the weak." The Vietnamese monks of this period had some moral authority rather than military force; instead, they utilized what can be called "theatrical activism," meaning forms of public performance designed to generate desirable dramatic effects. One of the most iconic images of the 20th century was that of Thich Quang Duc, the Vietnamese monk in Saigon who set himself on fire on June 11, 1963, in protest of the persecution of Buddhists by the South Vietnamese authorities. His intention for this act of martyrdom was to create a powerful image to draw attention from the Western press. Afterward, Malcolm Browne's Pulitzer Prize–winning photograph received wide international attention, and U.S. President John F. Kennedy is said to have recoiled in horror when he saw it (Brown, 1993, p. 12).

Insofar as it brought world attention to injustice, Quang Duc's death led to an outcome desired by activist monks such as Thich Nhat Hanh. Given the nonviolent methods of Engaged Buddhism and the Buddhist precept about avoiding killing, it was very likely an unintended consequence that, within 5 months, the U.S. government approved a coup against South Vietnam's dictatorial Prime Minister Ngo Dinh Diem, resulting in his assassination.

Engaged Buddhism is controversial among some Buddhists precisely because overt engagement with political processes frequently results, intentionally or unintentionally, in partisan attachment and even violence. Encoded within the iconic image of the utterly serene monk on fire is the rationale for such risky engagement with violent social phenomena: The monk does not hide from the pain of *samsara*, but, calmly sitting in the midst of fire as he was, Thich Quang Duc demonstrated to the world that it is possible to be present within a violent situation without mentally or spiritually succumbing to it. The photograph of the burning man reveals no trace of anger or blame.

"Angry Monk Syndrome"

The phenomenon of "angry monk syndrome" can be considered a subset of those activities referred to as "Engaged Buddhism," but the protests of 2007–2008 have been iconically represented by images of angry rather than serene monks. This "syndrome" made almost daily appearances in international newspapers in the months leading up to the Beijing Olympics. During the same period, monks protesting in Myanmar and, to a lesser degree, in places like Korea were a near-constant topic of media fascination. Angry monks who have protested have been a recurrent historical reality during the past 5 centuries, arising whenever Buddhism has been directly affected by colonial domination, but "angry monk syndrome"—involving not only the historical occurrences but also the repetition and reification of mainstream media—forms a distinct pattern.

In 2007–2008, the syndrome was associated most with Myanmar and Tibet. Whether the monks protested in Myanmar (or Burma), Korea, Nepal, India, or China (or Tibet), the conflicts were fueled by anticolonial resentment and geopolitical maneuvering. Typically, contestants in a soft-power struggle vie for sympathetic understanding from international witnesses in order to improve conditions internally, at the national level. When monks in Tibet react angrily to Chinese government repression, Western media, in part serving their own corporate interests by tapping into fears of a rising China, replay the events endlessly, which then stimulates the monks' will to express anger publicly. If resultant international pressure on China causes a reduction in repression, the protests succeed. Angry monk syndrome, however, does not depend on internal success or failure; Western witnesses can continue to construct themselves as moral agents whether or not the act of witness improves material conditions for Tibetans.

Engaged Buddhism and the Expression of Anger

Political activity typically involves fierce passions leading, in worst cases, to violence. The discourse of Engaged Buddhism explicitly warns practitioners to beware of such unintended consequences, as the emergence of violence undermines both spiritual practice and the development of peaceful social relations. Tibetans rioting in Lhasa in March 2008 may have killed as many as 18 Han Chinese migrants (or colonists). Reports vary and are hard to document because of the lack of a free press in China, but the People's Liberation Army may have shot and killed at least 1,000 protesters. In an act that recalls the archetypal expression of modern monastic political protest, one Tibetan monk, attempting to emulate Thich Quang Duc, set himself on fire in protest.

Engaged Buddhism consistently opposes the promotion of anger, whereas the monks protesting in 2007–2008 expressed anger in the manner typical of non-Buddhist protest marchers. The actors (e.g., the monks) and the script (meaning the verbal expressions of anger) appear to contradict one another. The dynamic tension that gives this syndrome its attention-grabbing drama stems from the belief, in part an Orientalist construction and in part a standard doctrine within Buddhism, that

Buddhist monks are never supposed to indulge in anger. Because Buddhist monks signify the human capacity for self-pacification, this breach constitutes a dramatic symbol of anger.

It is precisely because Buddhist monks are typically understood to have renounced voluntary anger that they have accrued an impressive degree of moral authority, a conditioning factor that gives their anger more international credibility. This is well understood by the monastics themselves, and they have used these displays of "anger" to their political advantage; the term *angry monk syndrome* was picked up by major news outfits around the world, including the *New York Times*, the *International Herald Tribune,* and *Asia Times.*

The rhetorical battle between Tibetan Buddhist monks and the People's Republic of China is a symbolic one. The Tibetans know that it is not a sufficient strategy to attain Tibetan independence or even autonomy, and yet armed insurrection is not a viable option for Tibetans in exile or Tibetans within the borders of contemporary China. The *symbolic* battle, however small a part it can play toward a satisfactory outcome, has certainly helped the Tibetan government-in-exile accrue status with governments around the world, much to the consternation of the People's Republic of China.

It is obviously against Tibetan long-term interests to accede to "powerlessness," but it can be a wise short-term strategy to perform honorable powerlessness in ways that develop their chances of self-determination, hoping to shape perception in ways that will be as consequential as possible. The monks know that a sympathetic viewer will blame not the monks but rather the oppressing state. Buddhist monks will not lose credibility so long as they continue to be perceived as harmless. The necessary condition for media valorization could be called "honorable powerlessness."

The Dalai Lama (the ecclesiastical and temporal leader of Tibet) has become a powerful living symbol of the cultural and religious repression of Tibet by China. He understands his imagistic appeal on the world stage, and he uses his celebrity to perform Buddhist narratives to a world often unfamiliar with them. He alludes to Tibetan history and culture in order to develop support for displaced Tibetans and the Tibetan government-in-exile, and to publicize human rights abuses within

Chinese-occupied Tibet in ways consonant with the principles of Engaged Buddhism.

In the past couple of decades, Engaged Buddhism has grown in popularity in the West. Organizations such as the Buddhist Peace Fellowship and International Network of Engaged Buddhists bring together laypeople, activists, thinkers, and community leaders to engage in activities that have a tangible impact on the world around them, based on Buddhist teachings—exactly what Thich Nhat Hanh meant by following the path of mindful social action.

John Whalen-Bridge and Angela Faye Oon

See also Eland Ceremony, Abatwa People's (Southern Africa); Free Tibet Movement's Publicity; Human Rights Media; Independence Movement Media (Vietnam); Independent Media (Burma/Myanmar); Installation Art Media

Further Readings

Aitken, R. (1996). *Original dwelling place: Zen Buddhist essays*. Washington, DC: Counterpoint Press.

Brown, M. (1993). *Muddy boots and red socks: A reporter's life*. New York: Random House.

Jordt, I. (2008). Turning over the bowl in Burma. *Religion in the News, 10*(3). Retrieved March 17, 2009, from http://www.trincoll.edu/depts/csrpl/RINVol10No3/turning%20over%20the%20bowl.htm

King, S. B. (2005). *Being benevolence: The social ethics of engaged Buddhism*. Honolulu: University of Hawai'i Press.

Monk immolates self in Tibet's Ngaba region: Report. (2009, February 27). Retrieved March 17, 2009, from http://www.phayul.com/news/article.aspx?id=23948

Nhat Hanh, Thich. (1987). *Being peace*. Berkeley, CA: Parallax Press.

Sivaraksa, S. (2005). *Conflict, culture, change: Engaged Buddhism in a globalizing world*. Boston: Wisdom Publications.

ANKARA TRASH-SORTERS' MEDIA (TURKEY)

At the very beginning of the 1990s, increasing clashes in Turkey's Southeast caused considerable migration to large, more affluent cities such as Ankara, Istanbul, Izmir, Adana, and Mersin. The refugees nonetheless met inadequate socioeconomic conditions. Neoliberal policies transformed these people into the urban poor, living on the periphery of big cities and struggling to survive.

The refugees could find only irregular and precarious jobs in the informal sector, such as collecting solid waste. They collected cans, paper, and plastic from garbage dumps for commercial recycling. Youthful migrants were generally the ones involved. At midnight, they tried to find any waste that was easy to collect, carry, and get paid for.

Because they could not legally collect waste, they were defined as lawbreakers; in reality, they transformed the cities' solid waste into a sustainable economy. Aiming to change their image and to call attention to their tough living conditions, as well as to struggle against poverty and police harassment, they formed their own Ankara Recycling Association (KATIK).

Their first initiative was organized in 2003. Twenty trash-sorters showed up at May Day demonstrations with their poster "Don't throw capitalism into the trashcan of history, it's not worth a cent!" To start with they used the initials "AKI" (Waste Paper Workers) to name their organization, and later, in 2005, switched to "Ankara Recycling Association." They were determined to build up the political strength of Ankara's trash-sorters, to work to get them recognized, to improve their working and living conditions. The members were composed not only of trash-sorters but also academics, socialist university students, and trade unionists. The association's principles were solidarity, democracy, volunteerism, equality, transparency, social responsibility, and the public interest.

The Newspaper and the Website

They also began publishing a newspaper, *KATIK*, which supported the trash-sorters' struggles, and then created a website. They tried to highlight urban poverty and people's harsh living conditions by arranging street performances and taking part in demonstrations. The trash-sorters left no stone unturned in their struggle against Ankara Municipality's decision to transfer the waste collection business to professional licensed agencies. The sorters put huge efforts into creating a counter public sphere within the middle class.

It was the municipality's 2007 announcement of its proposed policy that triggered publishing a newspaper. The first issue of *KATIK* was published in February that year. Although KATIK was planned as a monthly, it could not be published as planned due to financial and organizational problems. The seventh issue, the last one, was published in March 2009. They took their first slogan as their masthead: "Don't throw capitalism into the trashcan of history, it's not worth a cent!"

KATIK declared in their first issue that they wanted guaranteed work conditions and to be registered as a group possessing an organizational structure and with health insurance. Mehmet Ali Mendilcioğlu was *KATIK*'s founder and himself a trash-sorter. As he observed, they had no media experience, but they *did* have something to say.

After the fourth issue, *KATIK* volunteers created their own website. The designers were not sorters but university students coming from middle-class socialist families. Their primary aim was to draw attention to the sorters' hard working conditions.

The sorters partly financed *KATIK* from their own irregular income. Their second source was from nongovernmental organizations (NGOs) such as the Union of Turkish Engineers and Architects. They had their own distribution network. KATIK volunteers circulated the newspaper to NGOs, unions, democratic mass organizations, and even to other major cities where trash-sorters live, such as Eskişehir, Adana, and İzmir. Mendilcioğlu confirmed that the newspaper was sold mostly in Ankara, but rarely at newsstands. The price was only 1 Turkish lira (0.4 Euro).

The pictures used were supplied by the Ankara Photography Artists Association. The content was composed of essays, poems, articles on issues with the city government, interviews with NGO directors, and trash-sorters' stories.

KATIK's most important role was giving the trash-sorters the chance to define their own lives in their own words, forming a counter public sphere against the dominant one. The other most important effect of the association and its newspaper was to display how a common counter public sphere could be established among the urban poor and the politically concerned middle class through community media. When community media can make this interrelation, it can create a counter

public sphere far beyond expectations. This was the crucial success of *KATIK* newspaper.

KATIK Life Stories and Poems

Ercan, a trash-sorter, writing in *Katık 3*:

Our city, our universe, the heaven of cheap work-power. We, millions of unemployed are handcuffed, waiting to die in agony for selling our work-power, every minute of the day. Roaming around dumpsters with the hope and eagerness that the job will be better one day. Collecting waste from morning till night, pushing iron carts. We are waiting for the refuse of the rich, in their neighborhoods, in front of their hot spots; hungry or not, cold or hot.

So, There Is Such a Job?

Hamit, a trash-sorter, writing in *Katık 2*:

From time to time people were coming from Ankara to my relatives. When I asked them their jobs, they told me that they were collecting cardboard. I came to Ankara without learning the situation completely . . . It was unbelievably cold. I had come from Cukurova. I was not considering anything but earning money. Cold was nothing for me. On my first day I was restless. I was so keen for someone to get out with me and learn the business. Strange thing, we went eating at uncle's. We ate. I told my nephew we should go out together. My aunt-in-law said "You can't do it. Try another job." I said "Why? Everybody does it. I can too." She said "No, they are used to it." I said "Aunt, I need the job. I left my kids and came here. I have to earn money. I'm determined. I *will* work." My nephew and I hit the streets with just one cart. I found myself in this business. Yes, what we do is trash, but only trash. We began earning from trash.

My Only Witness: Stars and Waste

Anonymous poet, writing in *Katık 4*:

Everybody hides a hope inside
Within the deepest place of the heart
Everyone has a ache in their heart
How many spirits are there in the world?

Lost their tomorrows in the dark
Wrecked hopes, stolen youth
Not one happy day?

Mustafa Berkay Aydın and Çağdaş Ceyhan

See also Alternative Media; Anarchist Media; BİA Independent Communication Network (Turkey); Labor Media (United States); Radio Lorraine Coeur d'Acier (France); Social Movement Media, 2001–2002 (Argentina); Vernacular Poetry and Audiotapes in the Arab World

Further Readings

Acar, H., & Baykara, Y. (2008). *Başkentin Karıncaları* [Ants of the capital city]. Ankara, Turkey: Seçkin Yayınevi.

AFSAD [Ankara Photographers Association]: http://www.afsad.org.tr

Ankara Geri Kazanim Derneği [Ankara Waste Pickers Association]: http://www.angekader.blogspot.com

Atık kâğıt işçileri hasretini kâğıda döktü: Katık [Trash-sorters dumped their longings onto paper: Katık]. (2007, January 12). http://www.ufukcizgisi.net

Atık-kağıttan-dertlerin gazetesi [The newspaper made by sorrows of waste paper]. (2008 June 28). http://www.gundelik.net

Katık: http://www.katikdergi.org

ANTI-ANTICOMMUNIST MEDIA UNDER MCCARTHYISM (UNITED STATES)

Senator Joseph McCarthy's name is permanently associated with the years 1950 through 1954, during which he fanatically denounced Communist subversion, claiming numerous Communist agents were in high places, and with his congressional and news media cohorts spread what has been called "The Great Fear" across the United States. Journalists, broadcasters, filmmakers, educators, civil rights activists, and labor unionists were forced under oath to betray their friends or former friends or to protect themselves and avoid this by invoking the Fifth Amendment—only to have McCarthy publicly smear them as "Fifth Amendment Communists." Many lost their jobs and careers, some were forced to emigrate to seek work, and some were jailed.

Albeit under surveillance by the Federal Bureau of Investigation (FBI), the press of the dogmatic sectarian Left continued, but as usual they were not in the business of providing a forum for opposing views. Political space for independent critical media voices on the Left shrank to almost vanishing point. Very few publications found a voice in it, including the long-running *The Nation* weekly and *The Progressive* monthly on the liberal left, and the weekly *National Guardian, Monthly Review,* and *I. F. Stone's Weekly* that nonparty Marxists—anti-anticommunists—started in 1948, 1949, and 1953, respectively. *The National Guardian* continued until it was taken over by a Maoist group in 1967, and *I. F. Stone's Weekly* continued to 1971. *Monthly Review* celebrated its 60th anniversary in 2009.

At this distance, the nonparty Marxist trio may be hard for some to evaluate easily. Why would their contribution matter then or now?

Then, they were consistent voices in support of labor rights, women's rights, and African Americans' civil rights, in a period when the first matter and the third were defined as Communist issues and, therefore, their advocates probably subversives, traitors, and dangerous people. This was also when women's issues were typically "settled" with male laughter. They also supported independent "third way" positions, such as then-Yugoslavia's Marshal Tito's 1948 declaration of neutrality between Moscow and the West, for which he was excoriated and militarily threatened by the Stalin regime and regarded with extreme suspicion by McCarthy and his allies.

At a time when the nuclear arms race was stepping up, these publications were voices for peace and reason, even though disarmament talk was regarded, at best, as playing into Moscow's hands and therefore dangerous. They opposed the extension of the devastating war in Korea, where U.S. bombing had flattened every city and town in the North to the point there was nothing left to bomb. I. F. Stone published a book-length analysis of the war, painstakingly culled from dissonant reports in the British, French, and U.S. mainstream press, which had no less than 30 publishers reject it before finally Monthly Review Press took it on.

This was at a point when one issue of *Monthly Review* had every single contributor anonymous.

It was when FBI agents would warn news vendors not to sell *The National Guardian* in their kiosks and stores and would visit mail subscribers far away from New York City to pressure them into canceling their subscriptions. It was when the presses had to be meticulously checked before printing the paper because solid objects from time to time mysteriously appeared inside them.

People like James Aronson and Cedric Belfrage of *The National Guardian*, and I. F. Stone, were largely treated as pariahs. The reason Stone began his weekly newsletter was because no one would hire him, despite—and because of—his exceptional record as an investigative journalist. He was a forerunner of today's bloggers, fiercely independent in his view but possessed of incisive writing skills few can or could emulate.

In terms of present-day relevance, keeping those political spaces open has been a significant contribution. As political space opened up in the early 1960s, as the civil rights movement got fully into its stride, and as protests against the Vietnam War increased in volume, it was not uncommon to see *The National Guardian* being carried by demonstrators. *Monthly Review*, a forum for multiple sources of Marxist analysis, demonstrates that when not used as a secular religion, those insights continue to have crucial intellectual traction and political input.

Furthermore, what is termed *McCarthyism* should probably be titled *Hooverism,* after J. Edgar Hoover, who was special assistant for antiradical action in the newly formed FBI in 1917, played a major part in the post–World War I Red Scare and Palmer Raids, and rose to be FBI director until his 1972 death. His legacy endures, healthy as ever, in the national security state. The public's struggle continues too.

John D. H. Downing

See also Black Press (United States); Labor Media (United States); Media Justice Movement (United States); *Mother Earth* (United States); Paper Tiger Television (United States); *Southern Patriot, The, 1942–1973* (United States); Workers Film and Photo League (United States)

Further Readings

Belfrage, C., & Aronson, J. (1978). *Something to guard: The stormy life of* The National Guardian, *1948–1967.* New York: Columbia University Press.

Cottrell, R. C. (1992). *Izzy: A biography of I. F. Stone.* New Brunswick, NJ: Rutgers University Press.

Guttenplan, D. D. (2009). *American radical: The life and times of I. F. Stone.* New York: Farrar, Straus & Giroux.

I. F. Stone: www.ifstone.org

ANTICOLONIAL PRESS (BRITISH COLONIAL AFRICA)

Colonialism in Africa was founded equally on physical violence and on the construction of ideological consent among the African peoples. Nonetheless, certain newspapers were among the most critical agencies in deconstructing the colonial order's discourses. The anticolonial press—with varying levels of strength, breadth, and depth—contested both the discursive hegemony of the imperial powers and their colonial presence. In the absence of democratic representation, the self-advertised mission of the anticolonial press, as the *Lagos Weekly Record* put it in 1919, was to be "the guardian of the rights and liberties of the people as well as the interpreter of their ideals and aspirations."

The anticolonial press was part of the strategic alliance formed by social forces in the colony as they built a rudimentary social movement. The fact this press predated the formal imposition of colonialism in some territories meant it was able to tap into the ties, loyalties, and preferences of existing associational life. This was critical to its survival, as it faced charges of seditious libel, harassment, proscriptions, detentions, and imprisonment.

Most leading journalists were also politicians or activists. Indeed, the Indigenous press largely developed as a platform for the expression of dissent by the colonized. Nnamdi Azikiwe, Nigeria's first president, who had also been one of the most famous anticolonial newspaper publishers and journalists in British West Africa, stated that "the pioneers of the Nigerian press had held their own in establishing a virile press at a time when in a colonial territory, freedom of expression was not respected as a right, but as a privilege" (Azikiwe, 1964).

Given the strategic nature of information sharing and publicity in the struggle against colonialism, the anticolonial movement was driven to search for a space of public representation. The radicalization of the emergent elite and the educated class, fostered by the anticolonial press, helped to shape public opinion, both in the colony and among students and migrant workers in the metropole. The press attracted, even recruited, teeming supporters to the cause of political freedom. And as an anonymous writer put it in 1946, Africa's low literacy level made the reading public far more susceptible to the suggestion of the printed word.

Key Examples

New Era, a weekly newspaper founded in 1855, became the rallying point for anticolonial forces in Sierra Leone. So did the vigorously critical *Western Echo,* founded in 1885 in Gold Coast (now Ghana). The *Lagos Observer,* founded in 1882, proceeded to attack judges on the colonial bench as "amateur lawyers . . . steeped in the most bitter Negro hatred" (May 18, 1882). In 1919, the *Lagos Weekly Record* described the colonial government of Nigeria as an "inglorious administration which constitutes not only a standing disgrace to the cherished traditions of British colonial policy in West Africa but also a positive libel upon the accepted principles of British culture."

In 1902, the *Lagos Standard* (April 30, 1902) articulated the role of the colonial press in these terms:

> Without universal suffrage, without representation of any kind, without a municipality or other agency, by which it may be said that the people have any voice or hand in the government, the press is the only means, feeble and ineffective as it often is, still it is the only means there is of restraining or checking abuses.

Following World War II, against the backdrop of the global anticolonialist wave and specific local grievances against colonial rule, this press became fully radicalized. It was saturated with unequivocal demands for political independence. As the Lagos *Daily Service* argued in 1952, "many Africans yearn for the day when they will be free." In Uganda and Kenya, several newspapers, including vernacular-language newspapers, were established, many of which the colonial government accused of publishing "seditious propaganda."

However, given the press's prestige in this era, the colonized public's admiration for those who published against the colonial order, and the financial success of such papers, anticolonial journalists in Africa were further encouraged to savage the colonists' pretension to a right to rule.

In its discourse of political freedom, the anticolonial press was generally "a militant press: bellicose in temperament, belligerent in posturing and adversarial in language and perception" (Malaolu, 2004, p. 5). It encouraged, popularized, and articulated the social, economic, and political grievances of the colonized peoples. However, the anticolonial newspapers' agendas diverged. While some concentrated on a national front to end colonialism, others focused on intracolonial (i.e., interethnic or interregional) competition for power.

There is no doubt that the newspaper press was central to the struggle for independence in much of Africa. Indeed, the fact that prominent elements in the nationalist movements were also almost always leading journalists meant that the press was doubly critical to the struggle, not only as an important platform for independence campaigns but also as an institutional shelter for anticolonial campaigners and activists.

Wale Adebanwi

See also Boxer Rebellion Theater (China); Independence Movement Media (India); Independence Movement Media (Vietnam); New Culture and May 4th Movements Media (China); Social Movement Media, Anti-Apartheid (South Africa)

Further Readings

Agbaje, A. (1992). *The Nigerian press hegemony and the social construction of legitimacy, 1960–1993.* Lewiston, NY: Edwin Mellen Press.

Anonymous. (1946). An experiment in colonial journalism. *African Affairs, 45,* 80–87.

Azikiwe, N. (1964, May 31). *Pioneer heroes of the Nigerian press.* Lecture delivered at the Jackson College of Journalism, University of Nigeria, Nsukka.

Coker, I. H. E. (1971). *Landmarks of the Nigerian press.* Lagos, Nigeria: Nigerian National Press.

Gadsden, F. (1980). The African press in Kenya 1945–1952. *Journal of African History, 21,* 515–535.

Golding, P., & Elliott, P. (1979). *Making the news.* London: Longman.

Malaolu, O. (2004). *The effects of militant press on Nigeria's democratic evolution.* Unpublished master's thesis, Department of Mass Communications, University of South Florida.

Omu, F. I. A. (1978). *Press and politics in Nigeria, 1880–1937.* London: Longman.

ANTI-FASCIST MEDIA, 1922–1945 (ITALY)

The anti-Fascist movement in Italy included socialists, communists, liberals, Catholics, union members, factory workers, students' and women's organizations, anarchists, and intellectuals. Despite ideological divisions, they were able to form a unified front to fight Fascism and establish a new, democratic country.

Any resistance against Mussolini's power was anti-Fascist: from organizing strikes in the factories of the industrial North, to producing, distributing, or reading subversive publications, to operating or listening to illegal radio stations. In fact, the production of anti-Fascist media, especially during the years of the *Resistenza* (the partisans' armed struggle against Fascism and the Nazi occupation of Italy, March 1943–April 1945), was one of the most prolific in Europe.

Some of the publications were a single page, some came out only once, some were produced by little print-shops, and a few were organs of illegal political parties and anti-Fascist groups in exile. All played a crucial part in Italy's liberation. Their main functions were to organize subversive activities, relay foreign news (e.g., the Spanish civil war, the partisans' anti-Fascist struggle in neighboring Yugoslavia, the Italian Army's war defeats), distribute reports from foreign radio stations, and discuss Fascism's political significance and how to defeat it. In the process, they laid out most of the issues that would dominate Italian politics for decades to come.

Leading Up to the Dictatorship

By the time Benito Mussolini was appointed prime minister in October 1922, a strong journalistic tradition of attacking the government was already in place, dating back to Italy's mid-1800s

Risorgimento movement for the country's unification. In the 1890s, such publications included the magazine *Critica Sociale* (Social Critique, 1891), *Lotta di Classe Giornale dei Lavoratori Italiani* (The Italian Workers' Class Struggle Newspaper, 1892), and the Socialist party newspaper *L'Avanti!* (Forwards! 1896).

In 1918, the revolutionary paper *Il Soviet* began; one year later, three founding members of the Communist Party, Antonio Gramsci, Palmiro Togliatti, and Angelo Tasca, founded *Ordine Nuovo* (New Order), a weekly review of socialist ideas. Journalists were heavily intimidated during Mussolini's first years in power, but antigovernment dailies continued to be published. The Catholic daily *Il Popolo* (The People), organ of the left of center People's Party, began in 1923. In 1924, Gramsci founded *L'Unità* (Unity), the Communist Party's chief organ, which was still in operation in the early 2000s.

The 1920s

When Mussolini was made prime minister, the 1848 press law still provided basic freedoms but had a clause allowing for punishments to "regulate any abuses" of freedom. The Fascist leader seized on this clause, as any antigovernment publication could be defined as an abuse of press freedom.

Paradoxically, the events surrounding the national elections of 1924, and the government crisis that followed, enabled Mussolini to further tighten control of the press and of anti-Fascist activities. After the elections, a Socialist deputy, Giacomo Matteotti, declared in a famous speech to the Chamber of Deputies that many voters had been unable to express their preferences because of widespread Fascist militia intimidation. In the same speech, Matteotti denounced that during the election, campaign publication of pamphlets and opposition newspapers had been blocked, his party's fliers had been seized, and printing plants smashed or forbidden to print anti-Fascist material. This was Matteotti's last speech to the Chamber of Deputies. In retaliation, he was kidnapped and stabbed to death by Mussolini's militia.

After the murder, opposition to *il duce* (the leader Mussolini's preferred title) grew. The so-called Aventine secession, a nonviolent protest against the government organized by a group of deputies who refused to participate in parliamentary activities, threatened a crisis. Even mainstream newspapers denounced Matteotti's assassination and accused Mussolini's Blackshirt militia. It was then in January 1925 that Mussolini defied his opponents and officially proclaimed the beginning of the dictatorship. *Il duce* made explicit reference to the press accusations, which he defined as a "filthy and wretched campaign that dishonored (us) for . . . months" (http://www.storiaxxisecolo .it/fascismo/fascismo10g.htm).

Between 1925 and 1926, new legislation (the so-called Special Legislative Provisions for the Defense of the State, or *leggi eccezionali* [exceptional laws]), outlawed freedom of association, political parties, and freedom of the press. The Italian National Fascist Party was made the only legal party. The infamous secret police was established. The managing editors of all non-Fascist or anti-Fascist newspapers had to be instantly dismissed and a special tribunal was instituted to try political crimes.

In 1927, the Fascist Union of Journalists was founded; in 1928, a national List of Italian Journalists was set up. Anti-Fascist activities continued, although the terror spread by the secret police contributed to a growing sense of defeat and demoralized, for at least a few years, the anti-Fascist resistance.

L'Unità and Other Publications

After a few smaller publications of the Communist Party of Italy (PCd'I) had been shut down, Gramsci and other party leaders decided to establish a new paper to promote the discussion of insightful, critical analysis of fascism, with the purpose of fostering unity between workers and farmers. Gramsci wanted the newspaper, whose title was *L'Unità,* to avoid mentioning the Communist Party, in the hope of evading its banning. Indeed, when it first came out, the paper was discreet. Its first issue subhead in February 1924 was simply "Workers' and Farmers' Daily."

But Matteotti's murder and the ensuing crisis made it untenable for *L'Unità* to avoid a clearer stance and, on August 12, 1924, its subhead changed to "The Organ of the Communist Party." The paper drew on many underground collaborators, including peasants, students, and women, as well as leading anti-Fascist intellectuals for reporting and political analysis.

From summer 1926, Fascist repression against the paper intensified. After Mussolini's attempted assassination in October, Blackshirts vandalized *L'Unità*'s newsroom in Bologna, and the government outlawed it. Thanks to a team of reporters led by Camilla Ravera, Alfonso Leonetti, and Felice Platone, *L'Unità* continued underground publication as a four-page biweekly, often published on rice paper. The first such issue appeared in Milan on January 1, 1927, and on January 10 in Turin. Young Communists organized printing and distribution. During the first years of the regime, prison sentences for reading or distributing the paper went from 3 to 5 years. *L'Unità* remained one of the most important and diffused underground paper during the *Resistenza*. On June 6, 1944, in Rome, official publication of the paper was restored.

Non Mollare! (Hang In There!), whose first issue came out in January 1925, was another important publication and the first anti-Fascist underground newspaper printed in Italy. Written by members of the circle Italia Libera (Free Italy), based in Florence, it set out to disobey the Fascist government's bans and to encourage rebellion against every aspect of the Fascist system. In October 1925, the paper was shut down, and many of those involved fled the country. Those who remained were arrested some years later.

The newspaper *Giustizia e Libertà* (Justice and Freedom) and the magazine *Quaderni di Giustizia e Libertà* (Justice and Freedom Notebooks) were both published in Paris by the anti-Fascist revolutionary movement Giustizia e Libertà (a group close to the Italia Libera circle of Florence). The Justice and Freedom movement, comprising mostly exiled intellectuals, was inspired by liberal ideals, opposed equally to Fascism, Marxist socialism, and the Catholic Church. The main objective of its publications was to propose pragmatic ways to apply the principles of anti-Fascism.

The 1930s

The first half of the 1930s were difficult years for the anti-Fascist movement and its media. Repression grew even more intense as the regime secured a ever firmer grip over press and radio. Mussolini demanded that all newspapers' publishers and their owners (not just their editors) be on board with the dictatorship, in preparation for his Africa campaign (1935–1936).

But the Ethiopian war (1935–1936) and the Spanish civil war (1936–1939) strengthened the commitment of anti-Fascist forces in Italy, as abroad. The struggle against the dictatorship took on fresh international significance. An estimated 3,000 Italians, including members of Giustizia e Libertà and of the PCd'I, fought on the side of the Spanish republicans against Franco's military. During those years, the foundations of the *Resistenza* were established. The experience those fighters gained during Spain's civil war proved very important in organizing against the regime at home. Information diffused by illegal radio stations, in Italy and abroad, about the Spanish struggle for freedom galvanized Italian anti-Fascist forces. By the late 1930s, new clandestine publications were being circulated.

La Resistenza

Historians debate exactly when the Resistenza began, but the week-long strike in March 1943 at the Turin's Fiat factories significantly demonstrated Mussolini's decreasing legitimacy. Hundreds of underground manifestos were distributed in Turin and Milan to provide information about the workers' conditions and to explain the strike. Clandestine publications played a fundamental role in allowing the workers' voice to challenge the regime.

As the Italian Army continued to suffer defeat after defeat, people were growing tired of listening to the censored information coming from official broadcasts. The desire to access other sources was strong, even among the politically inactive. Although it was illegal, many began to listen to Radio London and Radio Moscow. Meanwhile, events were moving fast, and on July 25, 1943, Mussolini was arrested after receiving a no-confidence vote from the Grand Council of Fascism. Immediately, anti-Fascist activists in exile started to come back to reorganize.

In 1942, members of Giustizia e Libertà had formed the Action Party, which, after the Nazi invasion of Italy in September 1943, took a leading role in the organization of partisan brigades and the Comitati di Liberazione Nazionale (the National Liberation Committees), together with other parties and movements, including the PCd'I (which became, in 1943, the Italian Communist Party, or PCI). *Italia Libera* was the Action Party's main publication, and *L'Unità* continued to be the Communist Party's underground paper.

Clandestine radio stations also played a crucial role. One of them was Radio Cora, established in January 1944 in Florence and operated by the Action Party. The station allowed exchange of crucial information between the Allies and the Partisans. In June 1944, the Nazis raided Radio Cora and kidnapped its leaders, most of whom were tortured and killed.

The punishments were extreme for those caught gathering information; producing, distributing, or simply possessing anti-Fascist material; or participating in the operation of illegal radio stations. According to the level of responsibility, they could be jailed, given solitary confinement, tortured, summarily executed, or sent to concentration camps in Italy or Germany. Nonetheless, the number of anti-Fascist media grew exponentially between 1943 and the end of the war.

Among their thousands, there were national newspapers; organs of various parties, like *L'Unità* and *Italia Libera;* as well as smaller publications for students, workers, women, and professional organizations. Small presses, but also large, well-established ones, were used to print subversive material. When possible, presses outside the main cities were preferred. Distribution was carried out through a well-organized network of runners (*staffette*). The success of the anti-Fascist struggle in producing and distributing its media was based on a well-disciplined network and on an absolute solidarity among its members.

On April 25, 1945, Italy's liberation was proclaimed, and many clandestine publications came back into the open. The anti-Fascist media of the previous 2 decades had been the life blood of a movement of political regeneration, which continued to influence the new democracy and the establishment of the new, anti-Fascist republic.

Cinzia Padovani

See also Independent Media (Burma/Myanmar); Revolutionary Media, 1956 (Hungary); Social Movement Media, 1920s–1970s (Japan); *Suara*

Independen (Indonesia); Wartime Underground Resistance Press, 1941–1944 (Greece)

Further Readings

Castronovo, V. (1995). *La stampa italiana dall'unità al fascismo* [The Italian press from unification to fascism]. Bari, Italy: Laterza.

Legnani, M. (1980). La stampa antifascista [The antifascist press]. In V. Castronovo & N. Tranfaglia (Eds.), *Storia della stampa italiana, IV. La stampa italiana nell'età fascista 1926–1943* [History of the Italian press, IV. The Italian press during the fascist era 1926–1943] (pp. 261–365). Bari, Italy: Laterza.

Murialdi, P. (1998). *La stampa italiana dalla Liberazione alla crisi di fine secolo* [The Italian press from Liberation to the end-century crisis]. Bari, Italy: Laterza.

Padovani, C. (2005). *A fatal attraction: Public television and politics in Italy.* Lanham, MD: Rowman & Littlefield.

Pugliese, S. G. (2004). *Fascism, anti-fascism, and the resistance in Italy: 1919 to the present.* Lanham, MD: Rowman & Littlefield.

Richeri, G. (1980). Italian broadcasting and fascism 1924–1937. *Media, Culture & Society, 2*(1), 49–56.

Rosengarten, F. (1968). *The Italian anti-Fascist press 1919–1945.* Cleveland, OH: Press of Case Western Reserve University.

APPALSHOP (UNITED STATES)

Appalshop is a nonprofit media, arts, and education center based in Whitesburg, Kentucky, with a theater division office in Norton, Virginia.

The Appalachian Community Film Workshop began in October 1969 as an Office of Economic Opportunity (OEO) project during the Johnson administration's War on Poverty to train Appalachian youth in film and television technology. The expectation was that the recruits would use their new skills to find employment outside Appalachia. Instead, as they made documentary films about local culture, the issues of youth, and social justice, the trainees dedicated themselves to their home community. With the end of OEO funding in 1974, they formed a nonprofit with the name Appalshop, Inc., to continue making films. These unsentimental films remain of interest as authentic expressions of community seen from the inside.

Appalshop expanded during the 1970s to include Roadside Theater, June Appal Recordings, educational materials, and even publishing. Later, Appalshop added WMMT community radio (1985), the Appalachian Media Institute for youth leadership development (1988), the Seedtime on the Cumberland Festival (1987), and other cultural and educational projects. Recent years have brought the Appalshop archive, an international exchange, and the Thousand Kites project, which addresses issues concerning prisons.

This has enabled the creation of a large body of work, in a wide range of media, which documents the life, celebrates the culture, and voices the concerns of people living in Appalachia and elsewhere in rural America. Through its various divisions, Appalshop presents stories that commercial news and cultural industries do not tell. These stories challenge the "hillbilly" stereotype, support grassroots efforts to achieve justice and equality, and celebrate cultural diversity as a positive social value.

The underlying philosophy is that rural and Appalachian people, along with underserved communities worldwide, must tell their own stories and solve their own problems. In Appalshop, documentary films, coal miners, fast-food workers, prisoners, truck drivers, community activists, high school students, teachers, musicians, and artists speak for a better way of life for their families, their communities, and their country. Appalshop amplifies these voices through a variety of public presentations and educational projects, including film, video, radio, Internet media, music, theater, and community and international exchanges. *Vérité* footage of labor strikes, community protests, work, community life, and performance material has created a remarkable archival record of the region.

Appalshop's location in the central Appalachian coalfields, its 40-year history, and its scope make it unique among American cultural institutions. The National Endowment for the Humanities has recognized Appalshop as one of the nation's most important community-based humanities centers. Jane Alexander, former chairperson of the National Endowment for the Arts, described Appalshop as "the jewel in the NEA's crown." "Appalshop's work has been a cultural beacon, for the people of the Appalachian region, for independent filmmakers, for media arts leaders, and also for people who, like me, celebrate and study the role of independent media in a democratic society," stated writer and cultural activist Pat Aufderheide, director of the Center for Social Media at American University (personal communication, February 27, 2010). Nationally recognized films produced by Appalshop include *The Buffalo Creek Flood* (the National Film Registry); *Stranger With a Camera; Fast Food Women; Morristown, Strangers and Kin;* and *On Our Own Land.*

Anne Lewis

See also Activist Cinema in the 1970s (France); Alternative Media Center (United States); Community Broadcasting (Canada); Community Media and the Third Sector; Documentary Film for Social Change (India); Media Justice Movement (United States); Medvedkine Groups and Workers' Cinema (France)

Further Readings

Appalshop: http://appalshop.org

ARAB BLOGGERS AS CITIZEN JOURNALISTS (TRANSNATIONAL)

Throughout the Arab world, citizen journalists have emerged as the vanguard of new social movements dedicated to promoting human rights and democratic values. After briefly surveying blogging and the expanding connectivity in the Arab region, and citing some instances from Bahrain, Lebanon, and Saudi Arabia, this entry focuses on citizen journalists in Egypt, especially the younger generation.

Citizen journalist-bloggers have been using self-publishing tools to create transnational and subnational activist networks to draw attention to the plight of citizens still waiting for democratic access to public sphere participation. Egypt, Saudi Arabia, Tunisia, and Syria were among the world's top 13 "enemies of the Internet" identified by Reporters Without Borders as "black holes" of press freedom since 2005.

Arab blogs emerged in 2003 in Iraq, but it was not until 2005 that they became central to social movements. Although bloggers emerged as key leaders in social movements throughout the Arab world, Egypt was the country where bloggers most successfully made demands on the government and campaigned for social justice, across ideological divides. Throughout the region, activists deployed the same mechanisms and processes to make claims by blogging, tweeting, Flickring, and Facebooking, to further their calls for social justice.

The blogosphere is a diverse array of personal diaries, journalistic accounts, rants and raves, and opinions, but some blogs focus particularly on politics, society, and news, and seek to report, document, and challenge both institutional media and governments. Blogging is the epitome of citizen journalism. Every blogger can become a citizen journalist with a few keystrokes. Most of the leaders in the Arab region's movements were bloggers who routinely practiced citizen journalism. Like their professional counterparts, such bloggers employed many journalistic principles—credibility, accuracy, witness, investigation, reporting, timeliness—and used similar mechanisms to establish authority, such as eyewitness accounts, sourcing, quotes, images, video, and reputation.

Bloggers differ from their professional counterparts in that they are unabashedly subjective, disavowing objectivity. Citizen journalists are not subject to the same editorial filters or commercial dynamics as professional journalists because they are essentially volunteers. As one blogger put it, "Blogs did for personal publishing what the press did for print publishing—it allowed non tech savvy people to publish" (personal communication).

Blogs can be more dialogical than traditional media because of the comments functions, trackback, and social bookmarking tools. Trackback tools allow users to comment on the original post with a link to their weblog, and social bookmarking tools allow users to share and repost links they like.

The Myth of Low Connectivity in the Arab Region

From 2007, the use of mobile phones enabled unedited, free, instantaneous reporting, challenging the state's ability to control the information environment and pushing mainstream journalists to compete. Easy online publishing tools and the subsequent development of Arabic script and platforms, coupled with increasing levels of connectivity, opened up new possibilities. Low connectivity levels, especially in the poorer Arab states outside the Gulf, are often overstated. As Deborah Wheeler has shown, most global measurement techniques do not account for the high concentration of Internet cafés or shared (often illegal) connections, and therefore skew the picture of Internet usage in this part of the world.

Thus, as blogging gained popularity and Internet connectivity reached a critical mass among the elite and youth, it became a potent part of the "repertoires of contention" of social movements in the Arab world in 2005. (This expression addresses the crucial role of culture and history in shaping activism, focusing on influences from previous experience, exposure to accounts of other social movements, and borrowing.)

The structural conditions were not only technological. Opposition to the U.S.-led war in Iraq and the U.S. government's ongoing emphasis on "democracy promotion" in the Middle East created political opportunities for bloggers, not least in regimes backed by the United States, to invoke their rights to freedom of expression.

In Bahrain in 2005, bloggers led the "Free Ali" campaign, part of Bahrain's broader human rights movement. Ali Abdulemam was a computer engineer and Islamic activist, blogging since 2002, who responded to an apparent liberal shift in Bahrain's policies, used his real name in his blog, and was thrown in jail.

Lebanese bloggers helped create the so-called 2005 Cedar Revolution that forced Syrian troops to withdraw from Lebanon after the assassination of former Prime Minister Rafik Hariri. In 2006, these citizen journalists were at the forefront of the alternative information movement during the Israeli invasion of Lebanon.

Saudi Arabian bloggers launched a campaign in 2007 to free imprisoned blogger Fouad al-Farhan, known as the godfather of Saudi bloggers, and created a blogger's union to support freedom of expression. He, too, had begun to use his own name and was explicitly hostile to terrorism. He was released in 2008.

Egypt as the Motor of Change

It was Egyptian citizen journalist activists who created the template, provided the inspiration, and sometimes even trained activists in other Arabic-speaking countries. A new political movement known as *Kefaya* (Enough) emerged in 2004 among activists and youth just as blogging was starting to gain popularity. *Kefaya*'s manifesto called for civil disobedience and sought to break taboos and establish a right to demonstrate and speak frankly about the country. Over the next 2 years, the movement inspired people to demand change by taking to the streets and speaking out; among them were many of Egypt's early blogger-activists. They used their blogs to publicize, organize, and report on activism, and took advantage of the interest of Western journalists to develop their networks. Having a blog became essential to staying up to date and *being* an activist.

Citizen journalists were crucial to *Kefaya*'s early success. They were not part of the political establishment and thus represented a challenge to the status quo. They multiplied the movement's influence and visibility because mainstream media labeled many of their activities *Kefaya*. And they helped frame and explain Egyptian politics to Western journalists and analysts.

During a 2005 demonstration against a proposed constitutional referendum and in support of judicial independence, women were sexually assaulted by state security forces and hired thugs. The mainstream press remained silent, and bloggers were the only ones to cover the alarming incidents, posting video, images, and eye-witness accounts. After 3 days of silence, Egypt's mainstream media finally began to cover the incidents.

The assaults garnered media coverage by the local and international press, as did the arrests of several bloggers. Suddenly a new category emerged—bloggers. The U.S. media picked up on the story and recognized "blogger" as an organizational identity. International human rights organizations equated them with an existing identity category that could be invoked and politicized—citizen journalists.

Egyptian and other Arab bloggers became beneficiaries of the advocacy granted professional journalists by the Committee to Protect Journalists, Amnesty International, Human Rights Watch, and Reporters Without Borders. These nongovernmental organizations reported on blogger issues, published press releases, advocated for their freedom and protection, pressured governments on their behalf, and offered them the resources of their transnational activist networks. Western mainstream journalists also helped certify particular bloggers as citizen journalists, elevating them to the status of journalist and thus invoking the associated professional rights. This certification by Western authorities definitely helped.

Similar citizen journalism addressed Egyptian police brutality against Sudanese refugees, unannounced bulldozer evictions in Kafr el-Elw village and other locations, and arrests of several prominent bloggers. Bloggers were at the forefront of the movement against violence against women, pioneering coverage of sexual aggression against women and leading campaigns like *Kulna Laila* (We Are All Laila), where 200 women blogged in a single day to protest daily sexual harassment and to create solidarity among women bloggers.

In 2006, Egypt's most famous citizen journalist, Wael Abbas, posted a video of police brutality, garnering a Knight International Journalism award (along with a Burmese blogger), while helping to solidify the movement against torture. Videos of police violence came out of the woodwork as Egyptians sent him videos shot on their mobile phones; people were inspired to publicize and protest torture by posting such documentation on blogs, Flickr, and YouTube. In Egypt, Saudi Arabia, Tunisia, and a host of other Arab countries where bloggers were arrested for writing and organizing, bloggers posted antitorture banners to support a virtual movement against torture, transcending political divisions.

Children of imprisoned Muslim Brotherhood members in Egypt created the *Ensaa* (Forget) news blog to get out information on their fathers' cases. *Ensaa* became a primary information source to media barred from covering the military tribunal. They simultaneously coordinated opposition to military tribunals.

The 2008 "Facebook Strike"

Citizen journalists were overwhelmingly concerned with social justice, and many covered the 2008 strikes, culminating in the April 6 "Facebook strike," involving tens of thousands mobilizing and communicating via Facebook. This had initially been planned in solidarity with striking workers in the city of Mahalla and in light of worsening economic conditions for the population at large. By this time, various groups of citizen journalists had created well-organized networks of correspondents who deployed throughout Cairo and Mahalla and reported back to other bloggers, including several of the more high-profile bloggers who decided to stay off the streets to avoid being arrested. They, in turn, posted the reports and pictures, sent out tweets and ensured live, up-to-the-minute coverage.

Days after the April 6 "Facebook strike," an American graduate student arrested (along with his translator) for photographing demonstrations sent the message "arrested" from his mobile to Twitter, which passed it along to his 48 followers, including several bloggers who in turn sent tweets to their followers, including journalists working for most of the major Western media organizations.

Similarly, when Gaza activist Philip Rizk was arrested in 2009, people in his Facebook and Twitter networks sent out messages about his arrest. Within hours, several major media outlets were reporting on it, though most remained silent on the other Gaza activists arrested in separate incidents on the same day. In each case, supporters contacted their respective universities, embassies, media outlets, and human rights organizations.

The previously mentioned examples demonstrate how and why citizen journalism has become such a powerful process in the repertoire of Arab social movements. First is the multiplier effect, in which an account by one citizen journalist is reposted many times as other activists linked to or reposted original reports on their blogs and Facebook pages, which were sent out in tweets and translated into other languages. Second is the importance of certification by Egyptian and Western authorities, and third, citizen journalist bloggers' position as "switches" connecting various activist, journalist, and personal networks within their countries and in the West.

Bloggers developed into a social movement via relational and nonrelational connections, as young Arabs who did not know each other formed information and activist networks online, and many bloggers sought to take virtual relationships into the real world, by holding *iftars* (the evening meal that breaks the daylong fast during Ramadan), organizing conferences, and meeting up at demonstrations. The young woman who started the Torture in Egypt blog sought out a few of the more famous bloggers to help her improve her blog and reach more people. Conferences about human rights and blogging in Lebanon, Egypt, and Jordan drew the most famous citizen journalists in the region and helped them create networks with bloggers, seasoned human rights activists, and journalists.

Bloggers successfully created collective action frames that resonated with Egyptians, especially youth. The process of creating such frames began at the emotional level as bloggers were moved by stories of torture, wrongful imprisonment, and sexual harassment and inspired by *Kefaya*'s slogan "enough" and calls for change. These emotions influenced them to frame events as part of a larger antitorture campaign and quest for social justice. These citizen journalists then wrote about them on their blogs or uploaded videos. The individual stories became a part of a larger narrative frame deployed by bloggers themselves, and by second-level brokers such as the journalists and human rights organizations that redeployed and legitimated those frames.

Courtney C. Radsch

See also Beheading Videos (Iraq/Transnational); BIA Independent Communication Network (Turkey); Bloggers Under Occupation, 2003– (Iraq); Citizen Journalism; Citizens' Media; Human Rights Media; Independent Media (Burma/Myanmar); Kefaya Movement Media (Egypt); *OhmyNews* (Korea); Social Movement Media in 2009 Crisis (Iran); Women Bloggers (Egypt); Youth Media

Further Readings

Al-Anani, K. (2008). Brotherhood bloggers: A new generation voices dissent. *Arab Insight, 1*(3), 29–38.

Arab Bloggers Union: http://arabictadwin.maktoobblog .com

Faris, D. (2008, Fall). Revolutions without revolutionaries? Network theory, Facebook, and the Egyptian blogosphere. *Arab Media & Society, 6*. http://www.arabmediasociety.com/?article=694

Hakem, M., Hamada, A. A. A., & Eid, G. (2007). *Electronic media and human rights.* Cairo, Egypt: Arabic Network for Human Rights Information.

Haugbolle, S. (2007). From A-list to Webtifada: Developments in the Lebanese blogosphere 2005–2006. *Arab Media & Society, 1.* http://www .arabmediasociety.com/?article=40

Lynch, M. (2007). Blogging the new Arab public. *Arab Media & Society, 1.* http://www.arabmediasociety .com/?article=10

Radsch, C. C. (2008). Core to commonplace: The evolution of Egypt's blogosphere. *Arab Media & Society, 6.* http://www.arabmediasociety.com/ ?article=692

Wheeler, D. L. (2006). *The Internet in the Middle East: Global expectations and local imaginations in Kuwait.* Albany: State University of New York Press.

AUDIOCASSETTES AND POLITICAL CRITIQUE (KENYA)

Audiocassettes of political opposition speeches, former political leaders, and subversive songs have figured prominently in Kenyan opposition politics since 1990. The audiocassette technology enables popular and oppositional usage because it is small, easy to transport and even conceal, relatively inexpensive to reproduce, and cheap to play. In addition, it is oral, thus allowing accessibility to both literate and nonliterate users. This contrasts with the Internet, which requires both print and computer literacy and a fairly high income or a professional job with computer access. Although audiocassettes are a modern communication technology, their functions and even contents are not necessarily new. Songs, praise poems, and other spoken genres expressing political critique in African cultures date back to colonial and precolonial times.

From independence in 1963 through 1982, Kenya was effectively a single-party state, and from 1982 to 1991 a single-party system was constitutional. In the early 1990s, there was widespread agitation for political reform, including critiques of sitting president Daniel arap Moi's (1978–2002) ethnic favoritism toward his native Kalenjin people, to the exclusion of other major groups such as the Kikuyu and Luo.

Numerous protest songs were recorded on audiocassettes and widely circulated during this period. Responding to their incendiary contents, the Kenyan government banned their sale, but their reproduction and distribution continued at multiple levels, including street vendors, music stores, bars, and private homes. Over the 1990s, these songs amplified widely debated issues throughout Kenya and helped focus demands for government change.

Passengers in urban minibuses (*matatus*), the primary mode of public transportation in urban Kenya, became captive audiences for these cassettes, as *matatu* drivers played their commentaries on social and political injustices. Topics included violent evictions in a poor Nairobi neighborhood, the jailing of a former cabinet minister who had lobbied for constitutional changes to create a multiparty state, and the mysterious murder of the foreign affairs minister, who was of the Luo ethnic group and known for his critiques of government corruption.

Many songs on the oppositional cassettes were in the Kikuyu language, and this played into the intensifying ethnic dimension of the multiparty movement. After President Moi banned all informal street vending and the playing of music in *matatus,* people found ways to dodge state scrutiny. For example, some van drivers silenced the music at stops, but played it at high volume once they started driving.

Pressure for reform was pervasive and the Kenyan constitution was amended in 1991 to allow for a multiparty system. Moi won reelection in democratic, multiparty elections in 1992 and 1997. During the subsequent election in 2002, Moi was constitutionally barred from running, and his chosen successor Mwai Kibaki was elected.

Although audiocassettes helped to nurture a prodemocracy political culture in Kenya that is still thriving today, since about 2003 they have been almost completely replaced by CDs and DVDs. Locally produced political music and political comedy are flourishing, as a result of the ease with which CDs and DVDs can be produced and copied and the overall increase in open expression of political dissent more generally. During the 2007–2008 clashes following the disputed presidential election, other media such as text messaging and FM radio hate speech played a large role in political mobilization.

Debra Spitulnik

See also Music and Dissent (Ghana and Nigeria); Music and Social Protest (Malawi); Political Song (Liberia and Sierra Leone); Political Song (Northern Ireland); Popular Music and Political Expression (Côte d'Ivoire); Popular Music and Protest (Ethiopia)

Further Readings

Haugerud, A. (1995). *The culture of politics in modern Kenya.* Cambridge, UK: Cambridge University Press.

Sabar-Friedman, G. (1995). "Politics" and "power" in the Kenyan public discourse and recent events: The Church of the Province of Kenya (CPK). *Canadian Journal of African Studies, 29*(3), 429–453.

B

BALLYHOO MAGAZINE (UNITED STATES)

Ballyhoo magazine debuted in 1931, amid the devastating throes of the Great Depression and the steady rise of modern advertising. Edited by Norman Anthony, former editor of humor magazines *Judge* and *Life,* and published by Dell, *Ballyhoo* flourished despite the economic woes of the nation. *Ballyhoo's* initial run spanned 1931–1939, with attempts to revive the magazine in the late 1940s and 1950s. Within 6 months of its creation, at its peak, nearly 2 million copies had been sold.

Ballyhoo became such a success that companies began to approach the magazine for advertising opportunities. Some were even willing to pay to have their advertisements mocked in the magazine. Beech-Nut Products is said to have been the first paid advertiser to appear in *Ballyhoo* ("Hooey," 1931). The back cover of the February 1932 issue contained a Beech-Nut ad. Thus, while its critiques of advertising, consumerism, and political affairs continued unabated, it also was business savvy.

Ballyhoo's humor took several common forms, including one-frame comics and fictional stories. Like other risqué humor magazines of the period, *Ballyhoo* employed racy cartoons of curvaceous women in various stages of undress.

Perhaps the most prominent form of *Ballyhoo's* humor lay in its advertising parodies. As noted by *Time* magazine, *Ballyhoo* "based its appeal chiefly upon the business of making fun of the advertising business, but knew and pursued the sale of scatology" ("Dirt," 1931). Indeed, the first page of the first issue of the magazine depicts an advertisement for "Old Cold Cigarettes," an obvious parody of the *Old Gold* brand of cigarettes, which promises "NO TOBACCO TO TAINT THE BREATH . . . OR SCRATCH THE THROAT." In this and various other advertisement burlesques, *Ballyhoo* called attention to advertisers' fantastic and often false claims.

Ballyhoo also often ridiculed the policies and politicians of the 1930s, and particularly the policy and political architects of Prohibition. In one spoof, President Hoover was caricatured in a Hoover vacuum advertisement. He was depicted holding a vacuum cleaner and sucking the cash out of people's pockets: "The HOOVER is guaranteed to clean everything and everybody but the bootleggers" (Anthony, 1932, p. 1). Other common targets of *Ballyhoo's* parody were pushy salesmen and enemy political leaders. For instance, Hitler was continually parodied in the pages. *Ballyhoo* uniquely balanced comedy and critique.

Ballyhoo was an anomaly. Whereas other publications and businesses shut down due to economic turmoil, *Ballyhoo* found success. Capitalizing on apprehension over the rise of advertising, the magazine struck a chord with the population. As the publication progressed, and as the world prepared to go to war, *Ballyhoo* became more political. Despite its short life, *Ballyhoo* made a big impact. It was an early critique of American consumerism, and particularly critical of advertising.

Troy B. Cooper

See also Alternative Comics (United States); Barbie Liberation Organization (United States); Culture Jamming; Political Cartooning 1870s–Present (India); Yes Men, The (United States)

Further Readings

Anthony, N. (Ed.). (1932, May). *Ballyhoo*, 2(4).

Dirt. (1931, December 28). *Time*. Retrieved December 9, 2008, from http://www.time.com/time/magazine/article/0,9171,753235,00.html

Hooey. (1931, December 14). *Time*. Retrieved December 9, 2008, from http://www.time.com/time/magazine/article/0,9171,930061,00.html

McFadden, M. (2003). "WARNING—Do not risk federal arrest by looking glum!" *Ballyhoo* magazine and the cultural politics of 1930s humor. *Journal of American Culture*, 26(1), 124–133.

BARBIE LIBERATION ORGANIZATION (UNITED STATES)

In late 1993, the Barbie Liberation Organization (BLO) switched the voice boxes between 300 speaking G.I. Joe dolls and "Teen Talk" Barbie dolls. The dolls were first purchased from stores and then, after the switch was made, returned to store shelves throughout the country in time for Christmas shopping. Barbie, with her exaggerated blondeness, hourglass figure, blue eyes, and scripted voice, was an iconic expression of White male heterosexism. G.I. Joe was the even more long-standing reverse image, of White masculinism.

When consumers unwittingly purchased these products, the boxes containing the dolls also contained a pamphlet with information on the action and the phone numbers of local news media, which they were encouraged to contact. Instructions on how to switch voice boxes in the dolls were also made available by the group. The Oppenheim Toy Portfolio, an organization dedicated to reviewing the safety of children's toys, dubbed the spoof a "terrorist act against children."

The activist collective RTMark claimed to have funded the BLO action with money donated from a veterans' group. But the connection between RTMark and the BLO's 1993 Barbie action was a little less transparent than that. After having formed RTMark, founder (and "yes man") Andy Bichlbaum contacted BLO member (and "yes man") Mike Bonanno to ask if he remembers the activist collective "sponsoring" the action. Bonanno helpfully "recalled" that RTMark had donated $10,000 to the cause; hence, the activity of the BLO is now often considered to be one of RTMark's earliest sponsored actions.

In 1994, the BLO's stunt was referenced in a fifth season episode of the TV animated comedy show *The Simpsons*, titled "Lisa vs. Malibu Stacy" (episode 1F12). After Lisa becomes horrified hearing her new talking Malibu Stacy doll say things like "Don't ask me, I'm just a girl," she complains to some friends at school. One girl mentions there is something wrong with her doll, too, and when she pulls the string, her doll says, "My Spidey sense is tingling. Anybody call for a web-slinger?" (the dialogue refers to the *Spiderman* series).

In 1996, the BLO created a short film about the action called *Operation NewSpeak*. Presented in the manner of a newscast, the video features clips from news coverage of the 1993 action and guests who talk about what the BLO did and how they did it.

Afsheen Nomai

See also Adbusters Media Foundation (Canada); Church of Life After Shopping (United States); Culture Jamming; DIVA TV and ACT UP (United States); Fantagraphics Books (United States); Yes Men, The (United States)

Further Readings

The Barbie Liberation Organization. (2000). *RTMark*. Retrieved December 10, 2008, from www.rtmark.com/blo.html

Bichlbaum, A., Bonanno, M., & Spunkmeyer, B. (2004). *The Yes Men: The true story of the end of the World Trade Organization*. New York: Disinformation Company.

Firestone, D. (1993, December 31). While Barbie talks tough, G.I. Joe goes shopping. *New York Times*. http://www.nytimes.com/1993/12/31/us/while-barbie-talks-tough-g-i-joe-goes-shopping.html?pagewanted=1

RTMark: http://www.rtmark.com

BARRICADA TV (ARGENTINA)

In early 2008, the cultural commission of an Argentinean organization of employed and unemployed workers decided to set up a video workshop in conjunction with Cine Insurgente (Rebel Cinema). The objective was to explore and build a political and communication instrument to serve as a vehicle for collective discussions and political concerns and simultaneously operate as a stage for some new social relations.

The commission drew on the perspectives of a leading Argentinean media activist, Raymundo Gleyzer, who argued in 1970 that cinema is a counterinformation weapon, not a military type of weapon, an information tool for the grassroots, and that this was its added value at that period in the class struggle. Decades later, many activist video and film groups in Argentina are reviving his tradition to bring their struggles, projects, and ways of seeing the world to the screen. Precisely because they consider that building people's power also means building a new revolutionary mentality, Barricada TV's People's News added another "trench" in this "war of position"—in Antonio Gramsci's sense of those terms.

Builders of an audiovisual space of this kind needed to be alert to Gleyzer's warning against reproducing the harmful ways of thought that, even in the name of a collective project, led individuals to emphasize the uniqueness of their contributions to the task. He would say that media activists needed to learn from how a factory worker, bound to the production process for 8 hours a day on a specific task (say, attaching doors in a car factory), is fully aware he is working with a group without whom he cannot finish the product, cannot complete the car. He knows what group labor is, what teamwork is, and he lives it every day. He has developed the sense of working collectively, of joining together with a group to make a specific product.

Thus, holding fast to these insights, and having to build its own agenda from issues emerging from political struggles, Barricada undertook the task of collective training in video skills. In a period of mainstream television dominance and free-market dogma, Barricada TV set out to narrate the world within the news format, but with the collective aim of building a people's news service that could serve as a foundation for the long-held project to set up an alternative TV channel.

Within this setting, after many debates and discussions, including initial camera forays, the notion began to emerge of Barricada TV as a politically active audiovisual group, adopting the format of a people's news bulletin, constructed according to their priorities and challenging dominant media frames. In this fashion, the Barricada collective was embodying the interventions that emerged during the 1990s resistance against neoliberalism in other settings and that, above all, were based in the 2001 rebellion, which, as for many people, combusted in the streets and laid the foundations of the collective's present practice.

In this sense, the Barricada TV collective do not consider themselves artists or to have a primarily aesthetic purpose (though they do not dismiss experimentation), but above all as political and social activists who decide to make videos as a tool to enable people to organize. Thus, Barricada TV is not simply a group of people who dedicate themselves to filming various conflicts and grassroots experiences. First and foremost they are an action group that tries to transform the reality they live.

In this sense too, Barricada TV considers that counterinformation cannot be separated from political intervention in a particular conjuncture. It is from that point that Barricada seeks to help build a counterhegemonic discourse, to strip away mainstream media disinformation, to mobilize, debate, conceptualize, and question their own mode of operation, and basically to acquire fresh comrades for the struggle. The work does not stop with the last edit, but rather in the effective circulation of their video materials and in the public's encounter with them. This is their goal.

Examples of the work of Barricada TV include the various reports on the protests against the 2009 Gaza massacre or the situation of political prisoners in Argentina, made possible by the confidence the collective had established that enabled one of their leaders to be interviewed secretly. Likewise, Barricada TV took part in organizing resistance against the threat of dispossession of the IMPA steelworks, the first of the factories taken back by factory workers. In this instance, the collective's role was to make a video about preparing the factory's defense, though it was edited for tactical reasons: Barricada TV was operating from the same factory with whose workers the collective had an ongoing relation. Central to the Barricada collective's goal is that "telling the story from below" means developing an action agenda based on their political definitions and agreements with sister organizations at the grass roots.

Lucas Bolo, Nicolás Castelli, Andrea Cuyo, Eugenia María Pagano, and Natalia Vinelli

See also Al-Jazeera as Global Alternative News Source (Qatar/Transnational); Deep Dish TV (United States); Industrial Workers of the World Media (United States); Internet Social Movement Media (Hong Kong); Labor Media (United States); Medvedkine Groups and Workers' Cinema (France); Migrant Workers' Television (Korea); Paper Tiger Television (United States); Radio La Tribu (Argentina)

Further Readings

Barricada TV: www.barricadatv.blogspot.com

BEHEADING VIDEOS (IRAQ/ TRANSNATIONAL)

In the 2000s, the production and circulation of videos produced by kidnappers became a common feature of certain news media and dedicated websites. They ranged from a person reading a list of demands to more complex edited sequences, even featuring the decapitation of the kidnapped person. These so-called beheading videos have raised questions about their religious justification, mainstream media's role in their distribution, their psychological significance, and other issues. Less commented upon though no less significant is their use as communication tools by various extremist organizations addressing both their communities and their enemies. To get a better sense of the significance of these videos as alternative media, this entry examines their historical background, production, and circulation.

History of Beheading

Beheading is a social, religious, or judicial sentence carried out in public. Until the early 20th century,

all ancient civilizations (Muslims and non-Muslims alike) practiced it, using swords or axes against condemned criminals. Perhaps the most famous beheadings took place in France during the Reign of Terror (1793–1794) using the specially designed guillotine. In the Arab world, beheading as capital punishment is practiced by close U.S. allies such as Saudi Arabia. In addition, groups affiliated with certain extremist interpretations of Islam have been practicing beheading since the 1980s. Their executions became increasingly visible through the distribution of beheading videos post-9/11.

Public fascination with filmed beheadings is not recent. In 1939, the secret filming of Eugene Weidmann's beheading prompted a decision to cease public beheading in France—and the film is accessible today on Google video. In 1980, an ATV-WGBH documentary, *Death of a Princess*, reenacted the execution of a Saudi princess and her lover. The broadcast of this documentary led to strained relations between Saudi Arabia and the United Kingdom and United States.

In the Arab world, beheading videos also have roots in hostage videos, particularly those associated with Lebanon's hostage crises. Between 1982 and 1992, members of the Iranian-backed Lebanese radical group Hezbollah are believed responsible for the kidnapping of 96 people, mostly Western. The hostages would often appear in videos either reading or listening to a statement prepared by the kidnappers. Although 10 hostages were killed or died in captivity, the kidnappers rarely released videos of their killing. One exception is worth noting. In 1988, U.S. Colonel William Higgins was kidnapped in southern Lebanon while serving with the United Nations. A year and half later, a video circulated on television worldwide featured Higgins beaten up and hanging from a rope.

From the Philippines to Chechnya, beheading videos have been associated with extremist Sunni Islam. In the aftermath of 9/11, beheading videos emerged in association with al-Qaeda, first in Afghanistan and later in Iraq. Since 2004, the kidnapping of foreigners in Iraq has been associated with demands for ransom (usually for non-Americans) or the delivery of messages through beheading videos (Americans). The latter peaked in 2004—starting with the beheading video of Nicholas Berg, whose body was found 2 days before the video emerged on the blogosphere—and subsided after 2006. (Far more Iraqis, including journalists and union activists, were kidnapped and often murdered, though their plight is not in focus here.)

Features of the Beheading Videos

To better understand these videos, the following is a brief description of features common to the Iraq-based beheading videos. The video opens with a graphic caption in Arabic, identifying the organization responsible for the beheading. A fixed camera shot features one or more masked militants standing against a wall covered with banners or flags, usually identifying the group. Unlike the kidnappers, the hostage is sitting or kneeling with face uncovered. One of the militants would read a prepared statement including Islamic references in the form of Qur'anic verses and political assertions, followed by a list of demands. At that point, the video is usually edited to feature the beheading sequence: Using a knife or a sword, a militant slits the neck of the hostage amid cries of *Allahu Akbar* (God is great). The video then moves into a sequence that resembles a music video: Fast cuts of militants mutilating the body, against certain *Anasheed* (religious militant songs) or Qur'anic recitation.

Not only do beheading videos attempt to turn murders into public executions, but they also constitute a significant while repellent instance of alternative media. Given their circulation via mainstream media coverage and the Internet, they reveal a complex array of interpretations, editorial decisions, and audiences. While they provide an Islamic veneer—infidels are beheaded (Christians, Jews, Shi'a, and atheists)—these videos stirred different responses around the world, including condemnation from radical groups like Hamas and Hezbollah. A similar view is shared by Saudi official clerics who believe that such acts, let alone their videotaping, are un-Islamic, unsanctioned, and unjustified.

Beheading videos were circulated on mainstream media, particularly Arab news channels, and on the web. In most cases, screen captures were also featured on the front page of the world press. Similar to the Osama bin Laden audiotapes, which were promoted as news scoops, viewers of Qatar-based news channel al-Jazeera were treated to significant segments of the beheading videos.

In contrast, the Saudi-owned al-Arabiya channel would feature fewer segments of the videos and accompany them with highly critical condemnation. In comparison, Western channels such as the BBC and CNN carefully edited the sequences in accordance with specific editorial and regulatory standards. However, most videos were first seen on the Internet as militant groups promoted and circulated the beheading videos, which were accompanied by written statements. Although first available on radical websites, these beheading videos were also featured on blogs, gore fan sites, and news sites.

These videos operated in tandem with press releases, telephone calls to press agencies, and threat statements. In using shocking visuals, extremists deployed a scare tactic, with their stories saturating the news cycle. Their use aimed to consolidate their power base among their communities and to sway international public opinion. Some have argued that the Iraqi videos were particularly designed to scare off the civilian contractors that the occupation forces deployed in large numbers in order to avoid a military draft.

Joe F. Khalil

See also Al-Jazeera as Global Alternative News Source (Qatar/Transnational); Alternative Media; Extreme Right and Anti–Extreme Right Media (Vlaanderen/ Flanders); Radio Mille Collines and *Kangura* Magazine (Rwanda)

Further Readings

Crew, B. (2003). *The beheading and other stories: The shocking investigation into the barbarism of modern-day Saudi Arabia.* London: Metro.

Furnish, T. (2005, Spring). Beheading in the name of Islam. *Middle East Quarterly, 12*(2), 51–57.

Janes, R. (2005). *Losing our heads: Beheadings in literature and culture.* New York: New York University Press.

Kimmage, D., & Ridolfo, K. (2007). *Iraqi insurgent media: The war of images and ideas: How Sunni insurgents in Iraq and their supporters worldwide are using the media* (RFE/RL special report). Washington, DC: Radio Free Europe/Radio Liberty.

BELLE DE JOUR BLOG (UNITED KINGDOM)

One of the best-known and oft-cited call girl blogs is the blogger-hosted *Belle de Jour,* started in October 2003 and updated on a weekly (and often daily) basis ever since. The blog chronicles the life of the anonymous author, focusing on her working life as well as personal relationships and dating. The blog's title comes from Joseph Keppel's 1928 novel of the same name, which later inspired the 1967 film directed by Luis Buñuel and starring Catherine Deneuve.

In their second annual blog awards, *The Guardian* (London) named *Belle de Jour* the "Best Written Blog" of 2003. One of the judges, Bruce Sterling, remarked that

> an archly transgressive, anonymous hooker is definitely manipulating the blog medium, word by word, sentence by sentence, far more effectively than any of her competitors. It's not merely the titillating striptease aspects that are working for her, but her willingness to use this new form of vanity publishing to throw open a great big global window on activities previously considered unmentionable . . . . She is in a league by herself as a blogger. (Cited in Waldman, 2003, para. 10)

The quality of her writing paired with the intriguing topic of sex work has allowed this blogger to write several autobiographical books under the pseudonym Belle de Jour: *Intimate Adventures of a London Call Girl* (UK), *Further Adventures of a London Call Girl, Diary of an Unlikely Call Girl* (United States), and *Playing the Game.* She also had a regular column in Britain's *Sunday Telegraph* in 2005 and 2006. In September 2007, British television channel ITV2 aired a television spinoff loosely based on *Belle de Jour*'s blogging persona, called *Secret Diary of a Call Girl.* As of 2008, the show was in its second season. In 2008, the U.S. cable network Showtime began airing the series.

The journey from underground blog to mainstream adaptations begs the question of how "alternative" a media format *Belle de Jour* still is. The author has switched sex work for writing (online and offline) and lives off her book earnings. However, she still uses her blog as a space to discuss sex work and provides readers with an uncensored self-representation of a sex worker. Her blog provides links to other blogs intimately related with the sex industry, and she explicitly encourages her readers to visit them; her site functions as a resource to navigate the sex industry blogosphere.

Finally, because of mainstream attention, *Belle de Jour* has been the subject of many reviews, criticism, and interviews (never face-to-face). The *Belle de Jour* blogger uses her blog to critique, comment upon, and deconstruct journalistic reviews, often telling the "behind-the-scenes" truth about interviews and publishing items that did not make it into the original article.

Thus, although the blog's content and context have shifted into a more mainstream sphere, it remains an uncensored and self-distributed source that serves a different purpose than her books or television series (loosely based on the blog). It provides insight into, and commentary on, the sex industry not readily available in mainstream media outlets and facilitates the creation of online sex worker communities and networks.

After keeping her identity a secret for 6 years, Belle de Jour identified herself to *Sunday Times* columnist (and one of her fiercest critics) India Knight on November 15, 2009. Belle's real identity is Brooke Magnanti, a 34-year-old research scientist at Bristol University. While working on her PhD in forensic pathology at Sheffield University, Magnanti ran out of money and spent 14 months as a call girl for a London escort service. Already an experienced scientific blogger, she decided to start writing anonymously about her experiences.

Jacqueline Vickery

See also Alternative Media; Gay Press (Canada, United Kingdom, United States); Sex Workers' Blogs; *$pread Magazine* (United States)

Further Readings

Belle de Jour: http://belledejour-uk.blogspot.com

Walman, S. (2003, December 18). British blog awards 2003: The best of British blogging. *The Guardian.* http://www.guardian.co.uk/technology/2003/dec/18/weblogs11

BERBER VIDEO-FILMS (MOROCCO)

The overarching term *Berber* references Indigenous inhabitants from Morocco to Egypt. *Amazigh* (plural *Imazighen*) also refers to the collectivity of subgroups throughout North Africa, and the collective variety of dialects is Tamazight. Berbers claim a heritage predating the Arab Islamic conquest of North Africa (604–709). In Morocco, three main subgroups are identified by region: northern Riffians speak the dialect Tarifit; central Amazigh speak Tamazight; and southern Chelha speak Tachelhit. Given their widespread geographic and historical presence, activists contest their sociopolitical marginalization. This entry focuses on the production of Berber videos in Morocco, which fill a void created not by neglect, but by repression of cultural identity.

Across North Africa, including Morocco, prior to the 1990s there were no nationally circulating film or television productions depicting Berber culture or utilizing Berber language except for musical productions and folklore. The Moroccan government had repressed most signs of Berber cultural specificity during the 1970s and 1980s by arresting activists, raiding cultural centers, and forbidding the production of culture in Berber language, aside from folklore.

Since the early 1990s, Morocco's gradual reforms have included a lifting of this repression. As a result, Berbers have engaged in the production of their own media in order to maintain a cultural and ethnic specificity in the face of media that only represent others (primarily the state and the Arab ethnic majority). In addition to traditional folklore, local video productions are used to preserve Indigenous and thereby a multivocal national heritage.

Berbers, particularly in the South, the Chelha, have actively produced video features with activists seeking to reify Berber cultural specificity, or video makers moving from music videos to feature productions. Similarly, many of the famous Berber singers have become the actors and actresses of the video-film era. Since the mid-1990s, there have been more than 10 companies (mainly Chelha) developing their own feature films in video format, utilizing Berber language (primarily Tachelhit), locations, actors, and stories.

While a number of video-films were set within Berber urban communities, the majority were filmed in countryside locations, mixing professionals with amateurs, and mostly telling stories concerning Berber life or mythologies. Modern era drama and humor are the dominant genres, though several historical fictions have been produced. In many ways, Berber video producers challenge Morocco's national media and cinematic constructs. Their video-films function diversely as entertainment, but also as political statements of Berber cultural specificity and a testament to Moroccan cultural and ethnic heterogeneity.

Since the 1990s, Moroccan Berber video-films have been privately produced in greater numbers than state-funded movies. At least 75 video-films have been produced, with a number of sequels in the works. These videos have been sold throughout Morocco and also in Europe to accommodate the large number of migrant Berber speakers.

Until *Tilila* (2006), directed by Mohamed Mernich, the state's cinema institution funds, which support feature filmmaking in Morocco, had never funded Berber films. Fewer productions have occurred in Tamazight or Tarifit languages, though this will change with the legalization of the Berber cultural movement and various mechanisms of state funding opening up since 2005 to allow Berber language productions.

Sandra Gayle Carter

See also Adivasi Movement Media (India); First Peoples' Media (Canada); Indigenous Media (Burma/Myanmar); Indigenous Media in Latin America; Indigenous Peoples' Media

Further Readings

Carter, S. G. (2009). *What Moroccan cinema? A historical and critical study, 1956–2006.* Lanham, MD: Lexington Books.

BHANGRA, RESISTANCE, AND RITUALS (SOUTH ASIA/ TRANSNATIONAL)

At the end of the 20th century, the reinvention of *Bhangra*, a Panjabi harvest dance, as an ethnocultural signifier of South Asian identity for young British Asians offers an illuminating instance of the co-option of dance in the cultural politics of identity. The genealogy of Bhangra provides the historical context for the intersection of Sikh nationalism with regional chauvinism in shaping the identity politics of postindependence India.

Its reinvention in the mid-1980s by second-generation British Asian youth recalls earlier moments in its history when it was incorporated in the construction of a regional Panjabi identity after the partition of 1947. This took place through collaboration between the old aristocratic and new institutional elites, who—with the complicity of hereditary performers—linked a marginalized dance genre to postindependence Panjabi identity.

In its appropriation in diasporic identity production as "our roots," Bhangra's constructed character is invariably subordinated to a desire for authentic origins. Even so, its hybridization with Black and White popular musical styles makes it a contested site for the debates on purity and hybridity, as the valorization of hybridity in postmodernist and postcolonialist analysis is complemented by the cult of authenticity.

South Asian Dance History: Control and Resistance

The history of dance in South Asia overlaps not only with systems of control through which bodies are produced, regulated, and disciplined but also with resistance to ruling ideologies and power structures, religious or secular. This is manifested in the simultaneous production and disruption through the body of dance of caste, gender, religious, and regional hierarchies, whether in precolonial, colonial, or postcolonial formations.

Although professional dancing was traditionally stigmatized because of its attachment to outcaste performing communities of *doms* or *bhands*, or women dedicated to singing and dancing such as *devadasis, maharis, kanjaris,* and *tawaifs,* contradictorily the reproduction of dance as an alternative route to godhood in the *bhakti* and *sufi* movements elevated dance to a divine art form. The genealogies of Indian classical dances in bhakti and sufi movements invest them with the transgressive force of their reformist drive, their destabilization of religious, caste, linguistic, and gender hierarchies.

Devadasi belonged to a hereditary caste of woman temple dancers; *mahari* were professional singers and dancers dedicated to Lord Jagannath; *tawaifs,* courtesans patronized by Muslim nobles, contributed to music, dance, theater, and the Urdu literary tradition; *kanjari* is now a derogatory Punjabi term for a dancing girl but mutates a Farsi word for "dipped in gold and fully blossomed."

In anticolonialist movements in South Asia, the production of national identity through the "cultural"—music, dance, painting, literature—similarly made cultural practices a fragmented and contentious site. The hegemonic reconstruction of *kathak* and *bharatnatyam* as dominant symbols of Hindu culture in the Indian nationalist movements of 1920–1940 exhibited two major facets. One was their disengagement from their mixed legacies and traditional social groups; the other, their articulation to new ideologies that assimilated them into an urban, educated class with invented spiritual genealogies.

Transnational Musical Cultures and Bhangra

When British media and academia examined Bhangra's resistivity in South Asian identity narratives, situating it in Britain's cultural politics of Blackness, they heavily stressed its engagement with the country's White racism and exclusionary narratives. But Bhangra's resistance appears to be directed at both dominant White racist and nondominant South Asian discourse through the intersection of race with generation, gender, caste, and sexuality. By calling attention to how this process redefined the "spiritual" Asian—constructed by classical dance and musical genres—as "Kool," this "re-mastered" Bhangra interrogated the way that during the period of cultural nationalism certain musical and dance genres had been enthroned as classical in the production of Indian national culture, as well as how the persistent hierarchization of classical and folk dance had been neatly concealed in a rhetoric of "interdependence."

Through the global visibility that Panjabi harvest dance received through its reinvention in South Asian youth subcultures in Britain, it produced a South Asian space in the British nation to which South Asian identities might be articulated but also contested the notion in India of a monolithic national culture that marginalized regional ones. Moreover, while giving South Asian youth their voice in the diaspora, Bhangra also became instrumental in mobilizing a transnational separatist narrative of Sikhism and the 1980s Khalistan independence movement.

The transnational provenance of these developments is underlined by the fact that the mid-1980s Bhangra revival in Britain intersected with a Bhangra revival in India. Whereas British media paid much attention to afternoon raves and "day jams" at which South Asian youth danced the Bhangra, subverting their parents' condemnation of partying, yet dancing outside the dominant White space from which they were excluded, the Bhangra revolution in India went almost unnoticed. A South Asian youth subculture, converging on Panjabi dance and in the making since the 1980s, transmuted into a global youth culture by the end of the 1990s.

Thus, over the past 2 decades, a transnational Bhangra culture industry, its sites of production and consumption distributed across the globe, has come to challenge the hegemonic hold of Hindi film music on the subcontinent and to cross over into British popular culture. Bhangra's global visibility has produced a transnational Panjabi subculture in which ethnolinguistic signifiers are displayed with visible pride and rustic performers are consecrated as symbols of regional identity. In capitulating to global taste preferences, the Hindi film industry has been compelled to naturalize Panjabi folk dance as Bollywood dance and song, thereby transforming it into national popular music.

As South Asian youth ride through the streets of metropolitan cities playing the Bhangra full blast on their car stereos or dance the Bhangra in clubs from New York to New Delhi to resist the hegemonizing thrust of globalization through their local cultural production, the relationship between resistance and rituals is driven home loud and clear.

Whereas folk dance in India has traditionally served as a counterhegemonic discourse, Bhangra's crossover into national and global popular culture has reconfigured the local and the global while destabilizing generational, class, caste, gender, linguistic, and religious hierarchies. Several resistance movements have converged in Panjabi dance as it gets simultaneously appropriated in the production of a transnational multiple discourse of *panjabiat* (Panjabi-dom), South Asian diasporic identities, and global youth identities. Bhangra's role in the production of new ethnicities underlines the symbolic signification of cultural practices in national and global politics.

Anjali Gera Roy

See also Dance as Social Activism (South Asia); Installation Art Media; Khalistan Movement Media (India/Transnational); Performance Art and Social Movement Media: Augusto Boal; Social Movement and Modern Dance (Bengal)

Further Readings

Banerji, S. (1988). *Ghazals* to *Bhangra* in Great Britain. *Popular Music, 7*(2), 207–214.

Baumann, G. (1990). The re-invention of *Bhrangra*: Social change and aesthetic shifts in a Panjabi music in Britain. *World of Music, 32*(2), 81–98.

Hall, S. (1996). New ethnicities. In D. Morley & K.-S. Chan (Eds.), *Stuart Hall: Critical dialogues in cultural studies* (pp. 441–449). London: Routledge.

Sharma, S., Hutnyk, J., & Sharma, A. (Eds.). (1996). *Dis-orienting rhythms: The politics of the new Asian dance music.* London: Zed Books.

Zuberi, N. (2001). *Sounds English: Transnational popular music.* Chicago: University of Illinois Press.

BİA INDEPENDENT COMMUNICATION NETWORK (TURKEY)

Initiated in 1997 by three nongovernmental organizations—Interpress Service Communication Foundation, the Union of Chambers of Turkish Engineers and Architects, and the Turkish Physicians Association—alongside a group of local media professionals and media academics, Bağımsız İletişim Ağı (BİA; the Independent Communication Network) was launched in January 2001 with an EU grant.

At its founding conference in İzmir, BİA adopted as its major aim to create an outlet for "politically and ethically responsible journalism" and to empower the local media as the "voice of the voiceless" in a country where community and/or ethnic, cultural minority, noncommercial electronic media are restricted by law.

Today, with its news website BİAnet.org, BİA has become a major source for alternatively framed and alternatively focused news, as well as pooling the news dispatched by 130 affiliated local newspapers and radio stations in the initial years when local media were not yet using the Internet as a platform. In this first stage (2000–2003), it also provided basic vocational training for local media journalists, produced radio programs for the program pool, and gave legal counsel and support to journalists and local media owners across the country whose rights to free expression and access to information were seriously restricted.

In its second phase (2003–2006), the project, now known as BİA 2, grew to operate as a "Network for Monitoring and Covering Media Freedom and Independent Journalism." Specifically this meant to cover and promote the implementation of human rights reforms in Turkey, to monitor violations of human rights and their coverage by the mainstream media, and to enhance journalistic and professional ethics from a human rights reporting approach, with particular focus on women's and children's rights.

In this second stage, BİA became a unique location not only for reporting and monitoring human rights violations but also for reporting on human, women's, and children's rights. Assuming that conventional news reporting typically neglects women's and children's rights because of its routine priorities, BİA developed the concept and practice of "human/women's/children's rights–focused reporting." This refers not only to following up rights violations and reframing the news in its entirety from women's and children's rights perspectives but also to redefining conventional news reporting practices.

BİA devoted two subsites to women's and children's issues and produced radio programs named *The Women's Window, Children's Radio,* and *You're Right, You Have Rights.* The program CDs were routinely distributed to 77 radio stations via the BİAnet network and were also published on the website in MP3 format.

During this second phase, BİA 2 took its basic vocational training to a further level, and local media journalists were given human/women's/children's rights news reporting workshops. Since the beginning of the project, BİA training sessions have reached nearly 1,300 local media workers in 62 different localities across the country and BİA has published 15 books of serious quality on basic journalism and human rights reporting. The books are distributed free of charge to journalists from local and mainstream media and to media education programs and related circles.

In November 2006, BİA hosted an Istanbul International Independent Media Forum to create a platform for independent media activists, academics, communication researchers, students, and local journalists from the country and overseas. The conference slogan was "Another Communication Is Possible," and its proceedings are available on the BİA site.

In its third phase beginning in 2007, BİAnet was guided by the same slogan and continued to be an alternative and independent news site with its distinctive women- and children-focused news. Aiming to promote human rights–based news reporting in the mainstream media, BİA training now includes college communication graduates. In its fourth phase, BİA aims to extend its journalistic scope to include the "differently abled," with a particular focus on handicapped women's issues.

BİA is nonhierarchically structured and has an advisory board comprising representatives of local media; prominent human, women's, and children's rights activists; academics; and journalists. Besides two project coordinators, it has an editorial desk with five editors, one reporter, one webmaster, and several freelancers. The editors' responsibilities are regularly rotated. Freelancers and interns from other parts of the country and outside Turkey frequently join the team for shorter periods, alongside academics, human rights activists, journalists, writers, and photographers who voluntarily contribute to BİAnet.

On air since 2000 via the Internet, BİAnet continues to be a unique example of independent media in Turkey, with its alternative news focus in both English and Turkish, quarterly media monitoring reports, ongoing training programs, open access book publications, local media news pool, and legal advising on media issues.

Sevda Alankuş

See also Alternative Media; Ankara Trash-Sorters' Media (Turkey); Citizen Journalism; Citizens' Media; Human Rights Media; Media Education Foundation (United States); Media Justice Movement (United States); *OhmyNews* (Korea)

Further Readings

Independent Media Network: http://www.BIAnet.org
Istanbul International Independent Media Forum: http://BIAnet.org/kitap/76/another-communication-is-possible

BLACK ATLANTIC LIBERATION MEDIA (TRANSNATIONAL)

The emergence of anticolonialist sentiments in Africa, the Caribbean, and the rest of the Americas self-evidently went back to the origins of the slave trade, but the origins of counterhegemonic *strategic* thinking—as distinct from tactical survival thinking—came later. Initially face-to-face sharing of news, then autobiographical accounts by freed former mariner slaves, then a growing body of publications were crucial steps in the long anti-slavery and anticolonial struggle. News of Haïti's successful insurrection traveled from port to port and then gradually inland in the early 1800s via Black sailors, which prompted a basic vision of a different world order. Beginning in the latter 19th century, with Caribbean and U.S. activists such as Martin Delany, Edward Blyden, and Alexander Crummell, a stronger and stronger lettered and transatlantic activism developed, seeking to generate various strategies of liberation from White control.

But it was perhaps particularly World War I's interimperialist carnage and the experiences of African, Caribbean, and African American troops in and directly after that war that operated as a furnace, raising the overall temperature of revolt among people of African descent in and out of the continent itself. Ireland's 1916 anticolonial revolt and partial independence some years later were also very encouraging.

Thus, the first Pan-African Congress, with attendance from the Caribbean, England, and the United States, met in Paris in 1919 to petition the Versailles conference world leaders for African self-government. It was followed by further conferences in 1921, 1923, and 1927 in various cities, including London, Paris, and New York. The immediate impact on colonialism was effectively nil, but knowledge that these assemblies were taking place gave wider inspiration, and some significant individuals became part of an ongoing network of exchange and vision. At its height in 1920–1921, Jamaican Marcus Garvey's Back to Africa movement (the United Negro Improvement Association), though ultimately foundering, also had outposts in a large number of countries.

Newspapers began to emerge, often circulated internationally, as with the news about Haïti, by Black sailors. *The Negro World,* Garvey's own creation, founded in 1918, traveled widely. French and British colonial authorities banned it, though the future first president of independent Nigeria vividly recalled reading a copy as a young man.

One of the ongoing features of this movement, however, was continuing friction between those who wanted it to be part of the world communist movement and those deeply suspicious (like Garvey) of Moscow's motives and principles. Apart from *The Negro World,* it was normally the procommunist publications that were banned—but they were also often the most truculently anticolonialist and antiracist, though arguing that ultimately class, not "race," was foundational.

A leading example of the procommunist newspapers was *The Negro Worker,* also published as *L'Ouvrier Nègre,* which began publication in 1928. Another was *Le Cri des Nègres* (Black Call), which began in 1931. However, the Paris-based newspaper *Les Continents* (The Continents), beginning in 1924, simultaneously attacked French and British colonial rule in Africa but endorsed France's republican ideal and public attitudes in France. *La Dépêche Africaine* (The African Dispatch), beginning in 1928, run by "French" Caribbean activists, critiqued colonialism but sought expanded rights to French citizenship. *La Race Nègre* (The Negro Race), started in 1927 and continuing on to the mid-1930s, took a more truculently anti-imperialist position. It also was wracked at times by disputes between its communist and noncommunist activists.

These and other newspapers often had a short life span and appeared irregularly, but in the Internet and instant e-mail era, it is easy to be blind to the precious impact then of newspapers providing news of anticolonial movements and holding out hope. Claude McKay's 1929 novel *Banjo* gives a vivid impression of life in the port area of Marseille at that time, including the exciting moments when a new copy of one or other of these papers would arrive, in the hands of a Black sailor whose ship had just docked. And of how one copy would circulate.

Another remarkable tri-continental communication network was the *Négritude* (approximately, Black Consciousness) literary movement, beginning in Paris among African and Caribbean students in the late 1920s. Sénégal's future president Léopold Senghor and Martinique's extraordinary political poet Aimé Césaire were among the leaders of this movement. A movement publication, *Revue du Monde Noir* (Black World Review), though only appearing in 1931–1932, served as a major forum. It opened its columns to colonial paternalist viewpoints but also to African American writer Langston Hughes, Haïtian activist Léo Sajous, and exposés of the notorious Scottsboro Boys case in the United States.

This network accidentally resurfaced in Martinique, then Cuba and Haïti, then New York, when leftist surrealist writers André Breton and Cuban Wifredo Lam were interned in Martinique by France's Vichy collaborationist regime. There they had intense contact with Césaire and his wife Suzanne, described by those who knew her as the "soul" of the *Tropiques* surrealist and anticolonialist movement. It was only then that Lam turned his talents to painting, with profound African and Afro-Cuban themes, for which he is best known today.

Césaire had published his long poem of African cultural self-assertion *Cahier d'un Retour au Pays Natal* (Notes From a Return to My Native Land) in 1939. This served as inspiration for African anticolonialists for decades thereafter, including his fellow *martiniquais* Frantz Fanon, whose own books *Black Skin, White Masks* and *Wretched of the Earth* would in turn inspire masses of anticolonial and antiracist activists. It was the fifth Pan-African Congress in Manchester, United Kingdom, in 1945 that really launched the successful postwar African anticolonial movement.

John D. H. Downing

See also Anticolonial Press (British Colonial Africa); Mawonaj (Haïti); Reggae and Resistance (Jamaica); Social Movement Media, 1915–1970 (Haïti); Social Movement Media, Anti-Apartheid (South Africa); Weimar Republic Dissident Cultures (Germany)

Further Readings

Bolster, W. J. (1997). *Black jacks: African American seamen in the age of sail.* Cambridge, MA: Harvard University Press.

Derrick, J. (2008). *Africa's "agitators": Militant anticolonialism in Africa and the West, 1918–1939.* London: Hurst.

McKay, C. (2008). *Banjo.* London: Serpent's Tail. (Original work published 1929)

Palcy, E. (Director). (1994). *Aimé Césaire: Une voix pour l'histoire* [Aimé Césaire: A voice for history; Documentary film, 3 parts]. France: Cinémathèque Afrique.

BLACK EXPLOITATION CINEMA (UNITED STATES)

Between 1970 and 1975, the Black exploitation (*blaxploitation*) movement functioned as a significant alternative to Hollywood's historic misrepresentation of Blacks. The movement emerged through three main social, political, and economic factors: the civil rights movement, the historic misrepresentation of Blacks in motion pictures, and Hollywood's financial problems.

While Dr. Martin Luther King Jr. and swarms of Blacks and liberal Whites protested America's racial discrimination in the streets during the 1960s, performers like Sidney Poitier and Jim Brown fought the battle for equality on the silver screen, challenging the stereotypical roles—the loyal Tom, buffoonish coon, tragic mulatto, over-bearing mammy, and savage buck—that the majority of African American performers had been relegated to playing. Their efforts, combined with Hollywood's financial crisis, led to the emergence of blaxploitation cinema.

Cotton Comes to Harlem

Blaxploitation cinema can be defined as films made by both Black and White filmmakers alike, in the attempt to capitalize on the African American film audience. The first one was *Cotton Comes to Harlem* (1970), directed by Ossie Davis and released by United Artists. *Harlem* chronicles police detectives Coffin Ed Johnson (Raymond St. Jacques) and Grave Digger Jones's (Godfrey Cambridge) efforts to find $87,000 stolen from the Harlem community during a Back to Africa rally.

The film presented a fresh perspective of Black inner city life, cutting against Hollywood's caricatures while establishing the major conventions of the blaxploitation movement: a Black hero or heroine, a predominantly Black urban setting, Black supporting characters, a strong display of Black sexuality, a contemporary rhythm and blues soundtrack, and plot themes that addressed the Black experience in contemporary American society.

Harlem was extremely successful at the box office, accumulating over $8 million in its theatrical run. According to United Artists, an estimated 70% of the gross came from Black audiences. Thus, *Harlem* established Black filmgoers as a viable demographic, launching the blaxploitation movement.

Sweet Sweetback's Baadasssss Song

Although *Harlem* was the first, Melvin Van Peebles's *Sweet Sweetback's Baadasssss Song*, released 9 months later, is often cited as the pioneering blaxploitation movie. This is largely due to the controversy that surrounded *Song* after its release. Written, directed, produced, scored, and starred in by Van Peebles, *Song* opens with a title card that reads, "This film is dedicated to all the Brothers and Sisters who have had enough of the Man."

The film tells the story of Sweetback, a brothel performer, who agrees to pose as a suspect for two White police officers who need to demonstrate to their boss that they are making progress on a case. The police officers answer a call on the way to the station; they arrest a young Black militant whom they handcuff to Sweetback. On the way to police headquarters, the officers take a detour to an oil field where they plan on beating the militant before arriving at their destination. They uncuff him and proceed to abuse him as Sweetback watches.

Refusing to stand by and allow this injustice to continue, Sweetback intervenes, killing the officers. He then goes on the run, using his sexual prowess and Black community assistance to evade the massive police hunt. At the film's end, Sweetback escapes to México and a title card appears onscreen instructing audiences "Look out! Cause a bad-ass nigger is coming back to pay some dues!"

Song's mixture of sexual content and graphic violence created a great deal of controversy, resulting in mixed critical reception from both Black and White scholars and critics. Lerone Bennett Jr.'s *Ebony* magazine article "The Emancipation Orgasm" attacked the film:

> It is disturbing to note Mr. Van Peebles' reliance upon the emancipation orgasm. . . . It is mischievous and reactionary for anyone to suggest to black people in 1971 that they are going to be able to sc**w their way across the Red Sea. (Bennett, 1971, p. 118)

Howard University instructor Don L. Lee described the picture as a moneymaking fantasy that put the "filth" of Van Peebles's "distorted" view of the African American community up on the screen. If Sweetback is coming back to collect some dues, Lee asked, "From whom? The police, the brothers who didn't help him, the most visible elements of our suppression? . . . What about an organized nation that controls the world and ain't worried about no long-lost nigger coming back to collect anything?" (Lee, 1971, p. 48).

In contrast, Huey P. Newton, Black Panther Party minister of defense, commended Van Peebles's depiction. Black critic Sam Washington of the *Chicago Sun Times* also supported *Sweetback*, asserting,

> *Song* is a grotesque, violent, and beautifully honest film that takes no crap from whitey and his over civilized hang-ups while it deals with some

specifics about the black experience. . . . For the first time in cinematic history in America, a movie speaks out of an undeniable black consciousness. (Quoted in Bennett, 1971, p. 112)

Despite the attacks, the film performed extremely well at the box office. Made on a budget of $500,000, the film grossed $10,000,000 by the end of its theatrical release, further demonstrating the power of the Black movie audience.

The Proliferation and the Demise of Blaxploitation Films

Studio executives took notice of *Harlem* and *Song*'s box office success and quickly began producing blaxploitation films across varying genres in an attempt to garner similar financial gains. An influx of films ensued from MGM, Warner Bros., and AIP, featuring performers such as Richard Roundtree, Pam Grier, William Marshall, Tamara Dobson, and Ron O'Neal as strong Black heroes and heroines. The titles included canon blaxploitation films such as *Shaft* (1971), *Superfly* (1972), *Cleopatra Jones* (1973), and *Foxy Brown* (1974), in addition to more obscure pictures like *Blacula* (1972), *Sweet Jesus Preacher Man* (1973), *Mean Mother* (1974), *Black Lolita* (1975), and countless others. A large majority of the films performed well at the box office, helping to reverse a decline in ticket sales that had plagued theaters in the late 1960s.

Although a number of blaxploitation movies were successful, many plots relied heavily upon sexual content and graphic violence. Thus, even at the height of their popularity, blaxploitation films were extremely controversial. Concerned about the impact that the films were having on the Black community, the National Association for the Advancement of Colored People, the Southern Christian Leadership Conference, and the Congress of Racial Equality formed the Coalition Against Blaxploitation (CAB), which consistently criticized Hollywood for depicting distortions of Black life style.

While these groups fought against blaxploitation films, prominent Black figures, such as Gordon Parks Sr. and professional football player turned actor Jim Brown, defended them. Parks noted, "The so-called black intellectuals' outcry

against black films has been blown far out of proportion. It is curious that some black people, egged on by some whites, will use such destructive measures against black endeavors" (quoted in "Black Movie Boom—Good or Bad?"). Brown contended,

The so-called "black" film has made some important contributions not only to black people but to the film industry as a whole. It has allowed black directors, black producers, black technicians, black writers, and black actors to participate on a higher level than ever before. (Quoted in "Black Movie Boom—Good or Bad?")

The controversy, combined with the emergence of the blockbuster, led to the eventual demise of the films. By the end of 1973, surveys revealed that as much as 35% of the audience for the mega-hits *The Godfather* and *The Exorcist* was Black. Hollywood reasoned that the production of crossover films appealing to both White and Black audiences could potentially double box-office revenues. The ensuing years, with *Jaws, Star Wars,* and *Saturday Night Fever* solidified the blockbuster marketing practice.

Although studios ceased producing blaxploitation films, they hold a significant place in motion picture history. Between 1970 and 1975, hundreds of blaxploitation films were produced, presenting an alternative to the stereotyped representations of Black life that had historically plagued Black performers. The films presented strong Black heroes and heroines, predominantly Black urban locales, and funky musical soundtracks by popular artists such as Earth, Wind & Fire, James Brown, Isaac Hayes, Curtis Mayfield, and Marvin Gaye. Thirty years later, films such as *Jackie Brown, Shaft, Kill Bill vol. 1, Baadasssss, Four Brothers,* and *Grindhouse* continued to pay homage to blaxploitation cinema, while relying upon its most prevalent themes in creating new features.

Novotny Lawrence

See also Activist Cinema in the 1970s (France); Black Press (United States); Challenge for Change Film Movement (Canada); Documentary Film for Social Change (India); Medvedkine Groups and Workers' Cinema (France); Sixth Generation Cinema (China); Workers' Film and Photo League (United States)

Further Readings

Bennett, L., Jr. (1971, September). The emancipation orgasm: Sweetback in Wonderland. *Ebony, 26,* 106–118.

Black movie boom—Good or bad? (1972, December 15). *New York Times,* p. 3.19.

Bogle, T. (2003). *Toms, coons, mammies, mulattos, and bucks: An interpretive history of Blacks in American films* (4th ed.). New York: Continuum.

Dunne, S. (2008). *"Baad bitches" and sassy supermammas: Black power action films.* Champaign: University of Illinois Press.

Guerrero, E. (1993). *Framing Blackness: The African American image in film.* Philadelphia: Temple University Press.

Lawrence, N. (2007). *Blaxploitation films of the 1970s: Blackness and genre.* New York: Routledge.

Lee, D. L. (1971, September). The bittersweet of Sweetback/Or, shake yo money maker. *Black World, 21*(1), 43–48.

Martinez, G., Martinez, D., & Chavez, A. (1998). *What it is . . . what it was: The Black film explosion of the '70s in words and pictures.* New York: Hyperion.

Sims, Y. D. (2006). *Women of blaxploitation: How the Black action film heroine changed American popular culture.* Jefferson, NC: McFarland Press.

BLACK PRESS (UNITED STATES)

Black newspapers have existed in the United States since 1827, reaching the height of their power and influence from 1910 to 1950 when they played a major role in setting the stage for the civil rights movement. Then, they began a rapid decline in circulation and never again were the force they once were. Meanwhile, coinciding with the decline, Black magazines quickly rose to become the dominant Black print media.

Early Development

On March 16, 1827, *Freedom's Journal* in New York City became the country's first Black newspaper. Published weekly by a group of free Blacks who wanted to combat local anti-Black sentiments, the first issue informed readers, "We wish to plead our own cause. Too long have others spoken for us" (http://www.wisconsinhistory.org/

libraryarchives/aanp/freedom). The newspaper lasted only slightly more than 2½ years before closing for lack of money. By the end of the Civil War in 1865, there were about 40 Black newspapers in six states and one territory, slightly more than half published in New York State. Burdened by low circulations, little advertising, and shaky funding, along with a high illiteracy rate among potential Black subscribers, it was not surprising that the longest one lasted merely 12 years and the shortest only 2 months.

Among the early publishers, Frederick Douglass stood out. A runaway slave who became an outspoken abolitionist, he started the *North Star* in 1847 in Rochester, New York, and 4 years later merged it with another paper to become *Frederick Douglass' Paper,* which lasted until 1860. The papers' strong and well-written attacks on slavery and other Black injustices attracted national attention and numerous White readers, including reportedly U.S. presidents.

From 1866 to 1905, the number of Black newspapers increased dramatically to more than 1,200. The largest paper, the *New York Freeman,* had a weekly circulation of 5,000, though papers continued to appear and disappear quickly, some within months, mainly because they had little advertising and had to depend on sales. However, as the country's Black literacy rose—from only 5% in 1865 to 55.5% in 1900—the papers became increasingly indispensable to Blacks because they were essentially the only place where they could get news about themselves.

White-owned newspapers virtually refused to write about Blacks unless they were involved in criminal activities or lynched by White mobs, mostly in the South. Incensed by the lynchings and forced to leave Memphis when Whites destroyed her paper and its press in 1892 because of her uncompromising editorials, Ida B. Wells launched a famous antilynching campaign in the Black *New York Age* that lasted until she died in 1931.

Robert Abbott and the Chicago *Defender*

In 1905, Robert Abbott started a fourth Black newspaper in Chicago, the *Defender,* because, according to a friend, he wanted "to express his views on the race question." In 5 years, he had about 10,000 in circulation. Always looking for a way to sell more papers, he made a decision that permanently changed the Black press. His newspaper became sensationalistic as it featured injustices against Blacks, sometimes with large front-page headlines in red, thus appealing to the masses rather than being directed primarily at Blacks with education and money. Within 10 years, his circulation grew to around 200,000, making the *Defender* the largest Black newspaper up to that time, and other Black papers quickly followed his lead.

Abbott primarily boosted his circulation by encouraging southern Blacks to move north. The migration had been going on since the 1870s, but it escalated in the 1910s when 500,000 Blacks relocated, more to Chicago than any other city. The *Defender* played a major role by publishing railroad schedules, letters from Blacks contrasting Chicago life very favorably with life in the South, and outspoken criticism of southern leaders. One column in 1916 (October 7) labeled them "looters, grafters, lazy sinecurists, general 'no-accounts,' persecutors, KILLERS OF NEGRO MEN, seducers, RAVISHERS OF NEGRO WOMEN."

As the migration increased during the decade, southerners became alarmed and angry at how many Blacks were leaving, which hurt the southern economy, and some towns passed laws forbidding the sale of Black newspapers in the city limits. Abbott countered by going to the men who worked as Black sleeping car porters on the railroads, and they threw out bundles of the *Defender* at pre-arranged places as the trains rolled through the southern countryside, rather than stocking the newspapers at the train depots. Thus, the South was unable to stop the *Defender* as well as other Black northern papers from circulating.

World War I and World War II

When the United States entered World War I, the government immediately investigated the Black press heavily under the new Espionage and Sedition Acts, which outlawed anything that might damage the war effort. One outspoken Black socialist magazine, *The Messenger,* lost its second-class mailing permit, which made it unprofitable to mail, and the editor of the Black *San Antonio Inquirer* was sent to a military prison for 2 years for running a letter that criticized the army. The government claimed the letter was "an unlawful attempt to cause insubordination, disloyalty, mutiny, and refusal of duty in the military forces" (Washburn, 1986, p. 20).

In the 2 years following the war, the Red Scare period, the Black press continued to complain about injustices. The Justice Department, pushing for the first peacetime sedition act since 1798–1801, sent Congress reports of what it considered to be dangerous material in Black publications. A congressional bill was drawn up but eventually tabled after heavy public criticism.

Between the world wars, the *Pittsburgh Courier* surpassed the *Chicago Defender* as the largest and most influential Black newspaper, with 190,000 circulation weekly and 14 national editions. By 1940, there were 210 Black papers with a combined circulation of 1.276 million, and studies noted that they had become more powerful than Black ministers because so many people read them each week as they were passed from person to person. Their circulation would grow to 1.808 million by the end of the war with the *Courier* becoming the largest Black paper in U.S. history with a circulation of 350,000.

During World War II, the *Courier* quickly started the famous Double V campaign. This pushed for victory over totalitarian forces overseas, a second victory over forces in the United States that were denying Blacks their rights, and a third in the U.S. South where terror was being sown through lynchings.

As this was going on, *Defender* publisher John Sengstacke met in June 1942 with Attorney General Francis Biddle, concerned that the papers' complaints about injustices were hurting Black morale. He threatened the papers with an Espionage Act indictment but promised to hold off if the papers did not step up their criticism of the federal government any further. However, he said that he hoped they would become more supportive of the war effort, and they did.

Then, in February 1944, two notable events took place for the Black press. The Negro Newspaper Publishers Association became the first group of American Blacks to meet with a U.S. president (Franklin D. Roosevelt), and Harry S. McAlpin of the Black *Atlanta Daily World* became the first Black White House correspondent. Also significant was a massive amount of advertising in the Black papers for the first time from White-owned companies, responding to Congress offering tax breaks to firms if they reinvested profits during the war in new ways.

From Newspapers to Magazines

In 1950, the Black newspapers' circulation and influence began declining precipitously. The White-owned press had begun hiring the best young Black college graduates, paying them more and giving them more readers than the Black papers could offer. As time went on, the White press particularly needed these reporters because they could more easily cover riots in Black areas. The White press also began doing a better job of covering Blacks beyond sports, entertainment, and crime. Thus, for the first time, Blacks found reasons to read White newspapers, making Black papers less necessary.

At the same time, a new breed of Black magazines became quickly successful. Leading the way was John H. Johnson, who started a picture magazine for Blacks, *Ebony*, in 1945. In 1955, it had a circulation of 506,000 and had climbed to 6 million by 1980. He attributed his success to reporting seriously about Blacks rather than using sensational articles and cheesecake photographs of women. Although the success of the magazines continued, the Black newspapers never recovered from their loss of influence.

Patrick S. Washburn

See also Anticolonial Press (British Colonial Africa); Black Exploitation Cinema (United States); Social Movement Media, Anti-Apartheid (South Africa); *Southern Patriot, The,* 1942–1973 (United States)

Further Readings

Buni, A. (1974). *Robert L. Vann of the* Pittsburgh Courier: *Politics and Black journalism.* Pittsburgh, PA: University of Pittsburgh Press.

Ottley, R. (1955). *The lonely warrior: The life and times of Robert S. Abbott.* Chicago: Henry Regnery.

Pride, A. S., & Wilson, C. C., II. (1997). *A history of the Black press.* Washington, DC: Howard University Press.

Washburn, P. S. (1986). *A question of sedition: The federal government's investigation of the Black press during World War II.* New York: Oxford University Press.

Washburn, P. S. (2006). *The African American newspaper: Voice of freedom.* Evanston, IL: Northwestern University Press.

Wolseley, R. E. (1971). *The Black press, U.S.A.: A detailed and understanding report on what the Black press is and how it came to be.* Ames: Iowa State University Press.

Bloggers Under Occupation 2003– (Iraq)

When the Iraq War began in 2003, the United States wanted to avoid mistakes associated with its war in Vietnam when media images eventually helped to turn public opinion against the war. To avoid this scenario, reporters were "embedded" with the U.S. military. The result was predictable: A number of sanitized photos and homogenized press reports appeared.

Equally predictable, there was an enormous demand for accounts that gave an authentic, on-the-ground report of events as they affected the lives of actual people. Quirky, edgy, and gritty, new media sources such as blogs and other forms of mobile technology, such as pictures taken from cell phones, gained an audience. These visual images and these reports had a freshness and immediacy with which standard-issue news reports could not compete.

Some occupation force soldiers started their own blogs, called *milblogs,* focusing on their experiences of the war. A pioneering effort in milblogging came from Colby Buzzell. Buzzell described the sense of numbness and boredom that came from the moral, spiritual, and physical carnage around him. It was a constellation of milblogs, intermilitary e-mail rings, and mobile phones that brought the torture images from Abu Ghraib prison into general circulation. They became an iconic statement about what was wrong with the projection of American force around the world. However, allowing soldiers to act as citizen journalists, reporting on incidents from their own point of view, was highly unsettling for the military top brass, and the practice was banned.

Ongoing, however, were blogs by Iraqis documenting their personal experiences with the war.

One, Salam Pax (a pseudonym that is a combination of the Arabic and Latin words for peace), was the first to gain a widespread following in this regard. He wrote about prewar conditions under the Saddam Hussein regime and then the daily experience of the occupation. His blog was interrupted for a while by telecommunications breakdowns, but he continued his diary on paper until service was restored and he could telecommunicate it.

Numerous others came after him. The best known of the Iraqi women bloggers went by the name of Riverbend. In her blog, Riverbend described what it was like to come from a mixed Sunni and Shi'a background. Her self-styled "girl blog" graphically chronicled what it was like to sit with her brother, "E," atop their roof, watching Baghdad burning and learning to identify various types of automatic weaponry from the sound of their volleys. Her blog was turned into two books and formed the basis of an award-winning play.

The very success of user-generated content posed a strategic problem for the occupation force. Iraqi insurgents also used information technology for their own strategic recruitment and operational purposes.

Wayne A. Hunt

See also Arab Bloggers as Citizen Journalists (Transnational); Beheading Videos (Iraq); Citizen Journalism; Citizens' Media; New Media and Alternative Cultural Sphere (Iran); Women Bloggers (Egypt); Youth Media

Further Readings

Al-Roomi, S. (2007). Women, blogs and power in Kuwait. In P. Seib (Ed.), *New media and the new Middle East* (pp. 139–156). New York: Palgrave Macmillan.

Hunt, W. (2008, Winter). Baghdad burning: The blogosphere literature and the art of war. *Arab Media and Society, 4*. Retrieved February 4, 2009, from http://www.arabmediasociety.com/?article=584

Riverbend. (2005). *Baghdad burning: Girl blog from Iraq.* New York: Feminist Press.

Riverbend. (2006). *Baghdad Burning: More Girl Blog From Iraq.* New York: Feminist Press.

Salam Pax. (2003). *Salam Pax: The Baghdad blog.* London, UK: Guardian Books.

BOXER REBELLION THEATER (CHINA)

The Boxer Rebellion was an anti-imperialist and anti-Christian movement in China's northern provinces in the period 1899–1901. Mainly from the lower social classes, the Boxer groups rose up against the Western powers' invasions that had begun with Britain's Opium War (1839–1842). Feeling was greatly intensified by the Sino-Japanese war (1894–1895), in which large areas of the country were devastated and the northeastern parts occupied, resulting in serious economic disruption and poor harvests.

A striking characteristic of the rebellion was the rebels' superstitious belief that they could fight and survive against Western weaponry. This belief was closely connected to the social influence of Chinese theater practice and ritualistic martial arts. The movement was called *Yihe tuan* (Society of Righteous and Harmonious Fists, known as "Boxers" in English). Hundreds of thousands of poorly organized Boxers believed that bullets could not hurt their bodies because of the martial arts they practiced and the supernatural powers they possessed. Many thought they would be able to burn down the foreign powers' Christian mission compounds with a fan or a breath.

The entire Boxer Rebellion movement was played out on a huge social stage, and the Boxers assumed for themselves the traditional roles in the play, performing according to the scripts of traditional dramas deeply rooted in rural Chinese society for thousands of years. The traditional theater made the imagined story real; the Boxer Rebellion transformed the performance into reality.

Traveling shows performed by theater groups for their deity held special meanings for rural communities. They were often the only public events in the isolated feudal settlements, and they attracted everyone in the neighborhood. Dramatic performances provided a social space for Boxer groups to gather. For example, the Boxer group Big Sword Association attacked a church after a dramatic performance in 1895, and the next year it held a 4-day-long drama performance that attracted more than 100,000 people.

Boxers assumed roles according to the drama. Male Boxers belonging to the Righteous Harmony

Society Movement played the parts of male heroes, and female Boxers belonging to the Red Lanterns played the heroines. The Red Lanterns were mainly girls aged 12 to 18. They wore red dresses, and each carried a fan, a lantern, and a basket. They also practiced ritual exercises to induce their gods to possess them, and they performed as heroines in dramas such as *Fan Lihua*. They believed that they could stop a bullet with a fan, and the bullet would drop into their basket. Through these performances, ordinary farmers were influenced to become Boxers, who could themselves become heroes and heroines, able to fight against Western invaders and even become the new rulers of China, just as in the script of the play.

Boxer groups maintained their viability by combining performance and reality. They fought like warriors in the play and even made new plays based on their wars. For example, after a battle against 200 converted Chinese Christians, the Big Sword Association performed a play based on this battle and named it *Battle in Lu Weibo*. The collective practice of the martial arts attracted more and more poor farmers, the possession of goddess-like characteristics created collective cohesion, and spirit rapping enhanced their psychic resistance, thereby enabling the Boxer Rebellion to spread like wildfire without fear of Western weapons.

Although the movement was crushed by an eight-power colonialist alliance, the tottering Chinese empire collapsed just 10 years later and was replaced by the new republic, led by nationalist leader Sun Yat-sen.

Tai Yu-hui

See also Anticolonial Press (British Colonial Africa); Black Atlantic Liberation Media (Transnational); Independence Movement Media (India); Independence Movement Media (Vietnam); Performance Art and Social Movement Media: Augusto Boal; Social Movement Media, Anti-Apartheid (South Africa)

Further Readings

Zhou, N. (2003) *Imagination and power: Theatre ideology research* [in Chinese]. Xiamen, China: Xiamen Press.

Center for Digital Storytelling (United States)

Many consider the nonprofit Center for Digital Storytelling to have led the way in developing digital storytelling. Inspired by community arts activism, the center trains people of all ages and backgrounds to create stories using digital media. From 1994 through 2008, the Center for Digital Storytelling trained more than 10,000 people.

In the early 1990s, a group of media artists met in the San Francisco Bay Area to explore how to use new digital media to tell stories. These discussions led to the establishment of the Center for Digital Storytelling. The founders believed that hearing the stories of others would enrich everyone's life. The center also provides an outlet for alternative voices by assisting those usually without voice or without know-how to effectively tell their story. The center challenges the elitist notion that only professional artists can create a meaningful story.

The center offers a variety of educational workshops and programs. The teaching has been well crafted and tested to help effectively teach a wide variety of people. People may take the workshop without prior digital skills. The center has a fund to assist those who cannot afford the workshop. As part of the reflective experience of digital storytelling, students are asked to reflect on how their lives have changed after making their digital story.

Personal narratives are key. The center encourages people to construct emotionally direct and thoughtful narratives and to find pictures, artwork, and music to help illustrate them. With the teachers' help, students edit 3- to 5-minute stories using the personal narrative and materials collected. The subject might be a specific political or social issue. Stories include transgender identity, life in the United States, foster care, and communities in South Africa.

By training educators, the center helped digital storytelling to spread. The center provided workshops for K–12 teachers and offered a graduate course through the University of Colorado, Denver, on digital storytelling. In addition, the center developed an intensive training program for digital storytelling facilitators, covering guiding principles, technical training, and curriculum issues. The center also produced a workbook and textbook about the process.

In 1994, the staff journeyed to Bristol, England, for their first international workshop. As of 2008, the center had assisted people in 26 nations on 6 continents to develop digital storytelling projects.

The center's website hosts digital stories for people to watch. The stories are divided into the six categories: Community, Education, Family, Health, Identity, and Place. Furthermore, numerous published articles written by the center are available on the site, which serves as an important information resource.

Adrienne Claire Harmon

See also Alternative Media; Appalshop (United States); *Belle de Jour* Blog (United Kingdom); Citizens' Media; Women Bloggers (Egypt); Women's Radio (Austria)

Further Readings

Center for Digital Storytelling: http://www.storycenter.org

CHALLENGE FOR CHANGE FILM MOVEMENT (CANADA)

The Challenge for Change program at the National Film Board of Canada (NFB), along with its French-language counterpart Société nouvelle (New Society), endures as one of the institution's most notable undertakings. The program was established in 1967, Canada's centennial year, and between 1967 and 1980, 145 films and videos were produced, the majority between 1967 and 1975.

Created as part of Canada's War on Poverty (1965) and meant to publicize the nationalization of social assistance, pensions, and socialized medical care, the program was planned to enable citizen engagement with policymakers through a mediated public sphere. For some analysts, this meant that the program perpetuated the long-standing Canadian tradition of "technological nationalism," attempting to find technological solutions for democratic deficiencies in state-initiated media publics. However, the particular configuration of participatory democracy and technology in this program also characterized the public's mood in the late 1960s and early 1970s, when traditional party politicians seemed out of touch and Canadian philosopher Marshall McLuhan's ideas about mediated environments had taken on popular resonance.

In part, the program was a technological response by establishment English Canada to anxieties produced by Québec nationalism and civil rights activism in the United States. The program was intended to make films and videos within "at-risk" communities where interventionist policy could help corral social change in consensual directions. Impoverished inner-city and rural communities with divisive issues around housing or resettlement were seen as good test cases.

The NFB, a progressive but by no means radical institution founded in 1939, enlisted activists and filmmakers to make the films. Each proposal was vetted by a government committee, and not all were given the green light. For instance, a proposed film on militant trade unions in Québec was quashed. In the 1970s, films about organized labor in a postindustrializing economy and about women's issues came to dominate the program.

Filmmakers and activists associated with the program envisioned a more radical kind of community media than was foreseen by the government policy. Whereas the government vision was of a closed circuit dialogue loop between decision makers and their constituents in a time of economic restructuring, community activists envisioned the formation of widespread, grassroots publics. One was top-down, the other bottom-up. These divergent approaches to social inequality were maintained in uneasy balance.

After a controversial pilot film titled *The Things I Cannot Change* (1967), well-respected U.S. activist and documentary filmmaker George Stoney was brought in as the program's executive producer during what would prove to be its most productive period (1968–1970). (Stoney eventually left to take a job at New York University, where he cofounded the Alternative Media Center.)

From the outset, different sorts of films with different intentions were produced: general information films about social inequality, many of which were broadcast on CBC TV; primers on social activism for use in classrooms and by activist groups (some featuring U.S. community organizer Saul Alinsky); and a series made in Newfoundland outport communities in which film was utilized to convey opinions to people in neighboring communities and to government policymakers. This approach became known as the "Fogo process," perhaps Challenge for Change's most famous legacy.

The celebrated 23 short Fogo Island films are examples of applying film to local decision making. Between 1955 and 1975, 28,000 people in newly annexed Newfoundland province were relocated from outport communities to towns, and people with fishing skills became test cases for retraining schemes. Many of the unemployed collected government assistance, and the Newfoundland government turned to the federal government for help. As Newfoundlanders' welfare was taken over by the newly centralized welfare state, the fate of these citizens became an important barometer of the new federal system. Film titles such as *A Memo*

From Fogo (1972) and *The Specialists at Memorial [University] Discuss the Fogo Films* (1969) give the bureaucratic communication flavor that was one aspect of the program.

Twenty hours of footage shot over 5 weeks were edited down to 5 hours of shorts that could be compiled into variable programs. Many, such as *Dan Roberts on Fishing* (1967), consisted of one person giving his or her views. Colin Low, the series director, called this "vertical" editing, arguing that it was an important way to keep the filmmaker's influence to a minimum. Some have argued that this emphasis on interview subjects also helped forge the "talking heads" convention in social issue documentaries.

But the "process" films were just one aspect of Challenge for Change. Many others were short explorations of the plight of the poor and disenfranchised in more typical documentary form, blending observation and explanation. They were filmed in communities across Canada and tended to emphasize the specificity of the issues in each locale. Because the NFB was located in Montréal, then Canada's largest city, many of the films were made there. *VTR St-Jacques* (1969) is one example. Directed by American expatriate Bonnie Sherr Klein, the film also perhaps best encapsulates the movement within the program toward participatory video. The film documents the emergence of a "citizens committee" in a poor inner-city neighborhood and shows how the use of video cameras and local screenings can enliven direct democracy.

In conjunction with alternative production and distribution centers starting up at the end of the 1960s and early 1970s in cities across Canada, such as Video In (Vancouver) and Vidéographe (Montréal), the program's objectives linked naturally with the political projects of grassroots community broadcasting. Thus, Challenge for Change became a flashpoint for many people involved with community broadcast activism. Many films were made in conjunction with First Nations communities, and between 1972 and 1974 a number were made about women's issues. The establishment of Studio D, the women's studio, in 1975 represented a redirection of much of the energy of Challenge for Change, with many filmmakers associated with the earlier program moving to the newer one.

The Legacy of the Program

The program's legacy is complex. For many, it represented all that is progressive about Canadian public media, a position perhaps unwittingly bolstered by the vocal disapproval of the program by the NFB's famous founding commissioner, John Grierson. However, in recent years, a reassessment of the program has been under way. Perhaps the program defies simple summary as it was composed of such a diverse array of participants. As media historian Ralph Engelman succinctly put it, "Incompatible agendas—liberal, McLuhanesque, and leftist—coexisted uneasily" (1996, p. 234) in the program. Films made under the rubric of the Challenge for Change/Société nouvelle are vivid and exciting evocations of the shifts going on in the late 1960s and through the decade of the 1970s toward nonparty democratic activity and of new visions of mediated publics in Canada and elsewhere.

Zoë Druick

See also Alternative Media Center (United States); Community Broadcasting (Canada); Community Broadcasting Audiences (Australia); Community Media and the Third Sector; Deep Dish TV (United States); First Peoples' Media (Canada); Paper Tiger Television (United States)

Further Readings

Baker, M., Waugh, T., & E. Winton, E. (Eds.). (2010). *Challenge for Change/Société nouvelle: The collection.* Montréal, QC: McGill-Queen's University Press.

Charland, M. (1986). Technological nationalism. *Canadian Journal of Political and Social Theory,* 10(1–2), 196–220.

Engelman, R. (1996). *Public radio and television in America: A political history.* Thousand Oaks, CA: Sage.

Marchessault, J. (1995). Reflections on the dispossessed: Video and the "Challenge for Change" experiment. *Screen, 36*(2), 131–146.

National Film Board of Canada, Challenge for Change/ Nouvelle société film series: http://www3.nfb.ca/collection/films/resultat.php?ids=171718&nom=Challenge+for+Change%2FSoci%E9t%E9+nouvelle&type=liste-serie

Stoney, G. C. (1971/1972). The mirror machine. *Sight and Sound, 41*(1), 9–11.

CHANNEL FOUR TV AND UNDERGROUND RADIO (TAIWAN)

Taiwanese history has demonstrated that without continuous confrontation of the authoritarian regime by social movements and their media, the transformation from authoritarian regime to representative democracy would not have happened. Vibrant social movements over the 1970s forced the Kuomintang (KMT) government—finally in 1987, after 38 years—to lift martial law. The ban on newspapers was lifted in 1988. However, the KMT regime still tried to control electronic media and faced constant challenges from illegal cable television and underground radio, especially during the early 1990s, when both had close opposition party connections.

Television in Taiwan was tightly controlled by the KMT, and three terrestrial stations called the "old three TV stations" were owned by the government, the KMT, and the military. Thus, illegal cable television commonly became known as Channel Four to differentiate it from the existing stations.

Channel Four was very popular because of its variety of choices as compared to the old three TV stations. It ran pirated movie tapes from rental stores, satellite television spillover programming from Hong Kong and Japan, local restaurant shows, and even pornography, at affordable prices. By 1985, 1.2 million people in Taiwan (including 40% of Taipei residents) had watched Channel Four, but initially the KMT regime did not perceive these urban, low-cost illegal operators as a challenge.

However, the establishment of an opposition political party, the Democratic Progressive Party (DPP), in 1986 and the 1987 abolition of martial law thrust the KMT into fierce electoral contests—but still they refused to open up electronic media. To compete with the KMT, DPP politicians became involved in Channel Four and underground radio in order to promote their politicians and for election propaganda. In 1990, the first so-called democratic TV station was established in Taipei county, and it began broadcasting videos of DPP politicians, protests around Taiwan, and election campaigns. This opened up the first political channel.

At its peak, there were as many as 60 democratic TV stations. Before cable television was legalized in 1993, there were already more than 600 illegal cable operators, some of whom had been in operation for more than 15 years, on an island with a population of just 24 million people. According to a 1994 Taiwan Provincial Government survey, the number of system operators and subscribers increased from 125 systems and 800,000 subscribers in 1989 to 625 systems and 2 million subscribers in 1993.

Channel Four was legalized because of internal pressure from cable operators and support from its DPP alliance. Another factor was increased U.S. pressure for greater copyright control of pirated U.S. movies screened on Channel Four. To gain legal status, more than 200 cable operators formed the Cable Television Association in the early 1990s, and in September 1990, 21 Channel Four operators, with DPP support, set up the National Democratic Cable Television Association. In response to the call for legalization, the legislature passed the Cable Television Law in July 1993.

The development of underground radio was similar to the development of Channel Four. In 1949, there were 33 radio stations in Taiwan, mainly controlled by KMT, the government, and the military. In 1959, the KMT had prohibited new radio station applications. But then, to have affordable media to deliver his message, the famous storyteller Wu Le Tian launched Taiwan's first underground radio, Voice of Democracy, in 1991, and the DPP general secretary launched Voice of People in 1992, to prepare for parliamentary elections in 1992 and the Taipei mayoral election in 1994. By the end of 1994, nearly half (24) of the radio stations in Taipei were underground and belonged to members of the opposition political party.

In contrast to other media, underground radio built its own close connection with the popular classes, such as taxi drivers, vendors, farmers, and residents in southern Taiwan, who historically lacked economic, political, and cultural resources. Underground radio hosts encouraged audience participation by using call-in programs to strengthen this imagined community's unity and challenged authority by publicizing officials' phone numbers on the air. Using its fast, powerful, and even forceful mobilization ability made underground radio into "guerrilla media," a major player in the mass movement, able at times to paralyze public transportation.

Channel Four and underground radio challenged authoritarian control over media and ushered representative democracy and party politics into Taiwan. However, they were strongly influenced by partisan politics and became an election tool rather than an alternative media advocate for social justice and broader social reform for people's rights. After legalization, cable television became commercialized and controlled by a few conglomerates.

In 2009, the National Communication Commission announced the issue of the 11th series of radio licenses since 1993, legalizing in all 105 underground stations (180 stations were already legal). However, the problem was not legalization but competition, which led to a combination of commercialization with demagogic broadcasting, which, during elections, has been termed *airwaves terrorism*. The next stage to revive the social movement media spirit would be to disconnect it from partisan politics and build social movements based on real needs and interests.

Tai Yu-hui

See also *Dangwai* Magazines (Taiwan); Internet Social Movement Media (Hong Kong); MediACT (Korea); Social Movement Media in 1987 Clashes (Korea)

Further Readings

Chung, J. E. (2008, May 22). *Political economy of media reform in Taiwan and South Korea in the 1990s: With a focus on the development of cable television.* Paper presented at the annual meeting of the International Communication Association, Montréal, Québec.

Feng, J. (1995). *Taiwan guangbo ziben yundong de zhengzhi jingji* [The political economy of the broadcast capital movement]. Taipei, Taiwan: Tangshan.

Lee, C. C. (2003, May 27). *Liberalization without full democracy: Guerrilla media and political movements in Taiwan.* Paper presented at the annual meeting of the International Communication Association, San Diego, CA.

Chipko Environmental Movement Media (India)

The Chipko (hugging) environmental conservation movement came to public attention in 1973 when a group of women in Mandal village, located in the mountainous Himalayan State of Uttarkhand, "hugged" trees in order to prevent them from being felled. In the next several years, more than a dozen confrontations between women and lumberjacks occurred in Uttarkhand—all nonviolent and effective, enshrining forever the term *tree hugger* in conservation parlance.

In 1974, an especially notable confrontation occurred in Reni Village in Uttarkhand, where a women's group, led by Mrs. Gaura Devi, blocked an army of lumberjacks, singing: "This forest is our mother's home; we will protect it with all our might." They admonished the lumberjacks:

If the forest is cut, the soil will be washed away. Landslides and soil erosion will bring floods, which will destroy our fields and homes, our water sources will dry up, and all the other benefits we get from the forest will be finished. (Nagar, 2006, p. 306)

Stories and photographs of women's bodies in Mandal and Reni villages, interposed between the trees and the gleaming axes of timber cutters, spurred word-of-mouth buzz in neighboring communities and made interesting news copy for local, national, and global media. The notion of "Cut me down before you cut down a tree," generated a lot of media coverage, bringing with it a new humanized morality to abstract environmental concerns.

Two local activists—Chandi Prasad Bhatt, a Marxist, and Sundar Lal Bahuguna, a Gandhian—led the Chipko movement, albeit somewhat independently. They both exuded characteristics that fueled the spread of Chipko, bringing it to national and international awareness. Bhatt and Bahuguna were charismatic and credible, and they spoke forcefully in both Hindi and the local Garhwali dialect. Well networked with journalists, they both wielded a prolific pen, writing with ease in both

Hindi and English and thus mobilizing their rural and urban elite constituencies.

In Uttarkhand, the communication media underlying the Chipko movement was remarkably small-scale and low-tech, emphasizing local knowledge, local resources, local leadership, local language, and locally relevant methods of communication. Poets and singers were frontline motivators, writing verse and songs for public performance to inspire grassroots participation. Ghanshyam Sailani emerged as Chipko poet laureate, penning verses such as the following:

Let us protect and plant the trees
Go awaken the villages
And drive away the axemen.

When Uttarkhand women heard that the lumberjacks were on their way, they would sing such songs and walk toward the forest. The chorus would get louder and strident when the timbercutters arrived. The women would hold hands and form a circle around the tree, hugging it as a group. The lumberjacks were rendered powerless, even with their axes and saws.

The Chipko movement gathered rapid momentum as it rode the wave of spirituality. *Bhagwad kathas* (large prayer meetings) were routinely organized in forest areas, emphasizing that God resides in every living being, including in trees. To protect the trees was a sacred act, blending environmental science with deeply ingrained spirituality.

Chipko's appeal was uniquely wide-ranging. Thus, the movement was co-opted, shaped, and popularized by groups as diverse as local and global journalists, grassroots activists, environmentalists, Gandhians, spiritual leaders, politicians, social change practitioners, and feminists. The feminist movement popularized Chipko, pointing out that poor rural women walk long distances to collect fuel and fodder and thus are the frontline victims of forest destruction. Gandhians accentuated the Chipko movement through symbolic protests such as prayers, fasting, and *padayatras* (ritual marches). Further, Chipko became synonymous with the growth of ecology-conscious journalism in India and around the world.

The media that the Chipko movement generated went beyond just saving trees but, rather, was imbued with the belief that the forest belonged to the people, and only they could ensure its wise use. And, as the movement spread, and generated more media, it humanized environmental concerns for local, national, and global audiences.

In India, the headlines generated by Chipko put the notion of saving forests squarely on the political and public agenda of the country. In the early 1980s, India's prime minister, Indira Gandhi, ordered a 15-year ban on cutting trees 1,000 meters above sea level in the Himalayan forests (she believed that Chipko represented India's "moral conscience"). In subsequent time, this decree was extended to the tree-covered forests of India's Western Ghat and the Vidhya mountain ranges.

Arvind Singhal and Sarah Lubjuhn

See also Community Radio Movement (India); Environmental Movement Media; First Peoples' Media (Canada); Indigenous Media (Australia); Indigenous Media in Latin America; Indigenous Peoples' Media

Further Readings

Bhatt, C. P. (1992). The Chipko Andolan. Forest conservation based on people's power. *Environment and Urbanization, 2*(1), 7–16.

Guha, R. (1989). *The unquiet woods. Ecological change and peasant resistance in the Himalayas.* New Delhi, India: Oxford University Press.

Nagar, D. (2006). *Environmental psychology.* New Delhi, India: Concept Publishing.

Routledge, P. (1993). *Terrains of resistance: Nonviolent social movements and contestation of place in India.* Westport, CT: Praeger.

Shah, H. (2008). Communication and marginal sites: The Chipko movement and the dominant paradigm of development communication. *Asian Journal of Communication, 18*(1), 32–46.

Shepherd, M. (1982). Chipko. North India's tree huggers. In S. S. Kunwar (Ed.), *Hugging the Himalayas. The Chipko experience* (pp. 102–128). Gopeshwar, Uttar Pradesh, India: Dasholi Gram Swarajya Mandal.

CHRISTIAN RADIO (UNITED STATES)

Christian radio in the United States emerged from a desire to broadcast a Christian message;

however, the specifics of what is considered a Christian message vary from program to program. Christian music, educational programs, and talk radio constitute the majority of Christian radio programming. As of 2008, there were 1,600 Christian broadcasting organizations in the United States. Among U.S. radio audiences, 5.5% listen to Christian radio.

One difficulty in studying Christian radio is that there are more than 38,000 Christian denominations. Catholic, fundamentalist, Pentecostal, and mainline Protestant groups maintain differing views regarding what makes a person a Christian, and the various groups often differ politically.

A useful framework for understanding Christian radio is to look at Robert White's (1994) classification of Christian broadcasting models as (a) part of the public sphere, (b) popular among revivalist evangelical movements, (c) answering to institutionalized churches, and (d) as active alternative voices for social change.

Though it is seemingly contradictory for "Christian" to be considered "alternative," because generically Christians are the largest religious group in the United States, the demographic considers itself underrepresented in mainstream media. Mainstream radio plays songs with references to sex, alcohol, and drug use and gang-banging. Thus, some Christian radio focuses on being an alternative to mainstream radio and entertainment.

Christian radio began early in the United States. In 1921, Pittsburgh's Calvary Episcopal Church Sunday service became the first religious radio broadcast in the United States. Yet only 7 years later, Christian radio had to fight for the ability to broadcast. The 1927 Federal Radio Act gave the Federal Radio Commission (FRC) power to assign radio frequencies and hours of operation. The FRC declared that religious broadcasting was propaganda and set obstacles to Christian broadcasting, decreeing that no new licenses would be issued to religious groups. Existing religious groups with licenses were reassigned to weaker channels. Such policies helped foster the sense that Christian radio was separate from mainstream media.

In the 1930s, Christian radio began to purchase airtime from commercial stations, though some stations restricted this, spurring Christian broadcasters to see themselves as alternative to mainstream media. Most Christian shows during this period relied on listener donations, and some very successfully. At first barely able to buy air time, by 1948 *The Lutheran Hour* aired on 684 stations, a third of all stations then in the United States, and received over 30,000 listeners' letters a week.

Politically Conservative Responses

One particular response to these difficulties is National Religious Broadcasters (NRB). The NRB considers one of its main purposes to represent Christian broadcasters and advocate their right to communicate a Christian message. NRB claims to support "the" evangelical worldview and supports making abortion illegal. The NRB also supports teachings disputing evolution, even though the Catholic Church and other Protestant denominations publicly subscribe to it. The association has over 1,400 member organizations but still only speaks for some Protestants. Not all fundamentalists espouse rightist political positions.

Nonetheless, because the NRB represents multiple denominations, it created a seven-point statement to define *Christian*. The NRB created a code of ethics for Christian broadcasters regarding fund-raising and business management, and provided educational programs for broadcasters, covering topics such as Internet radio broadcasting, social networking sites, fund-raising, branding, marketing, governmental policy, media relations, and production skills.

Fundamentalist programming dominates Christian radio today. However, other Christian groups broadcast too. *Day 1,* representing six mainline Protestant denominations, began in 1945. *Day 1* programming contains teachings on reconciliation, women's spirituality, and environmental concerns. *American Catholic Radio,* a weekly program, contains segments on the Saint of the Day and the Catholic catechism. These radio shows are increasingly using the Internet and podcasts to reach their audiences.

Some fundamentalist radio talk shows have received professional acclaim. *Focus on the Family* with Dr. James Dobson from the Christian Right was inducted into the Radio Hall of Fame in 2008. The show, broadcast daily since 1980, is known for its highly conservative teachings on relationships, family, struggles in daily life, and opposition to homosexual marriage. The show is broadcast in

155 nations to more than 220 million listeners. Due to the show's antihomosexuality stance, gay rights activists petitioned to keep *Focus on the Family* out of the Radio Hall of Fame.

The Christian Coalition, a political advocacy group, encourages its members to write Congress and save talk radio. The group claims talk radio is where many conservatives go to avoid mainstream media liberal bias and find out what liberals are really up to. Additionally, in 2008 the Christian Coalition mobilized 3 million letters and postcards to protest a potential FCC ban on issuing more licenses to Christian radio stations and limiting paid airtime. Fundamentalist talk radio often addresses abortion, stem cell research, euthanasia, and gay marriage, then encourages listeners to contact their political representatives to pressure them for a conservative vote. Operation Rescue, an antiabortion group that routinely barricaded abortion clinics and endorsed the murder of some doctors who conducted abortions, used Christian talk radio to gain activists.

Christian music has become commercially successful, and U.S. corporations recognize it as a growth market. It includes such genres as Gospel, Christian rap, Christian metal, Christian punk, Contemporary Christian, and worship music. The Grammy Awards have a separate category for Christian and Gospel music. Viacom and Time Warner promote popular Christian music labels. In 1984, Christian music annual sales were $85 million, and by 2004 topped $720 million. In 2006, 64% of Christian albums were sold in mainstream retail outlets like Wal-Mart and Target.

The commercial success of the Christian music industry, as well as the rise in sales of Christian books, video games, and DVDs, has also supported Christian radio, although as of the late 2000s, many such stations were commercially funded. Their commercials usually conformed to the station's codes, which would reject commercials contrary to their beliefs, such as a strip club ad. Some stations and shows are listener-supported. Because many U.S. churches are non-profit organizations, supporters can also fund Christian radio through tax-deductible donations.

Adrienne Claire Harmon

See also Alternative Media; Beheading Videos (Iraq/Transnational); Extreme Right and Anti–Extremist Right Media (Vlaanderen/Flanders); Online Nationalism (China); Paramilitary Media (Northern Ireland); Tamil Nationalist Media (Sri Lanka/Transnational); White Supremacist Tattoos (United States)

Further Readings

Emmanuel, D. (1999). *Challenges of Christian communication and broadcasting.* London: Macmillan.

Hogan, T. J. (2002). *Redeeming the dial: Radio, religion and pop culture in America.* Chapel Hill: University of North Carolina Press.

Schultz, Q. J. (2003). *Christianity and the mass media in America.* East Lansing: Michigan State University Press.

Ward, M. (1994). *Air of salvation: The story of Christian broadcasting.* Grand Rapids, MI: Baker Books.

White, R. (1994). Models of religious broadcasting. *Media Development, 16*(3), 3–7.

CHURCH OF LIFE AFTER SHOPPING (UNITED STATES)

The Church of Life After Shopping is a New York–based troupe of activists who preach the "gospel of stop shopping" in various locations, including street corners, stores, and churches. The basic action involves Church of Life After Shopping founder, Reverend Billy (aka Bill Talen) preaching while the Stop Shopping Gospel Choir provides accompaniment. Each of these performances resembles a religious revival at a Pentecostal church, as Reverend Billy enthusiastically proselytizes against the evils of rampant consumerism, his hand outstretched to the heavens, while his choir loudly retorts with "Amen" and "Hallelujah" and breaks out in song.

The church advocates tempering the predominant consumerist lifestyle and, instead, building local economies that emphasize neighborhoods and community. Church members attack the corporatization of culture and consider shopping malls and big box stores as inimical to rewarding ways of living. A familiar chant at the church's events includes the word *pushback*, a term intended to encourage consumers to resist corporate developments in their communities.

In 1996, performance artist Bill Talen created the Reverend Billy character when he moved to New York and began to spend time preaching against consumerism on the streets around Times Square. It was there that he famously entered and wandered through the Times Square Disney store, holding an oversized Mickey Mouse doll and calling it the anti-Christ while encouraging shoppers to resist the urge to buy. Reverend Billy's prominence grew from there, and as his activity gained admirers and followers, so too did the church grow.

While Disney stores remained a popular place for the church to congregate, and for Reverend Billy to preach, the group expanded to include other chains, most notably Starbucks. The church entering and preaching within Starbucks in New York became so common that the corporate office issued a memo to stores with one section titled "What should I do if Reverend Billy is in my store?" advising employees how to handle the preacher and the media, should they show up.

By the late 2000s, the Church of Life After Shopping consisted of Reverend Billy, a choir of 35, and a band of 7, with a director of operations (Savitiri D) and choir director (James Solomon Benn). The church has a stage show, a television program (*The Last Televangelist*, broadcast by Deep Dish TV), a film and companion book (both titled *What Would Jesus Buy?*), and a music CD and has been written about in news and features around the world. The church's website lists 23 affiliated groups the church supports and promotes.

Even though the church's title and main focus are consumerism, it is actively involved in campaigns to preserve local spaces from corporate takeover. In 2000, the Church of Life After Shopping was also actively involved in a campaign to save a Greenwich Village house where Edgar Allan Poe once lived. In the mid-2000s, the church combined with a number of preservation and historical societies to oppose a redistricting of Coney Island that these critics feared would lead to destruction of the heart of the historical amusement district.

Afsheen Nomai

See also Adbusters Media Foundation (Canada); Culture Jamming; Environmental Movement Media; Installation Art Media; Performance Art and Social Movement Media: Augusto Boal; Street Theater (India); Yes Men, The (United States)

Further Readings

Church of Life After Shopping: http://www.revbilly.com

Talen, B. (2003). *What should I do if Reverend Billy is in my store?* New York: New Press.

Talen, W. (2007). *What would Jesus buy? Fabulous prayers in the face of the shopocalypse.* Jackson, TN: PublicAffairs.

VanAlkemade, R. (Director). (2007). *What would Jesus buy?* [DVD]. United States: Warrior Poets Releasing LLC. (Distributed by Arts Alliance America, New York)

CINE INSURGENTE/REBEL CINEMA (ARGENTINA)

The Grupo de Cine Insurgente (GCI; Rebel Cinema Collective) was founded under that name in 1997 in Buenos Aires, though some of its members had worked previously on other documentary projects, such as *L'Hachumyajay* (1996), which, in the Wichi language, means "Our Way of Doing Things." This was filmed in Salta Province in Argentina's far northwest, bordering both Bolivia and Paraguay, and home to a number of aboriginal communities. It documented the provincial government's criminal policies toward these communities, giving their members voice to describe their experiences. In one town with an aboriginal majority, the community made the local TV station screen the documentary no less than six times, newly empowered by seeing their issues discussed for the very first time on television.

One of the lessons to be learned from the collective's history is the importance of its extremely close relation to different social movements, demonstrated especially by the locations and situations in which Cine Insurgente screened its works.

GCI's first major project as such was *Devil, Family and Property* (1999), the title a play on "Tradition, Family and Property" (slogan of Argentina's fascist groups). It set out to address a legend in Argentina's northwest in which supposedly the big sugar barons had a pact with a demon, known as *El Familiar,* to whom the barons would feed a number of workers during the harvest season, never to be seen again, in return for prosperity in their business dealings. The filmmakers' vision was that this legend in reality echoed the vicious repression of the 1976–1982 military dictators, in which perhaps 30,000 people were disappeared. In making L'Hachumyajay, they had also heard many stories from village chiefs of the emptying out of their villages in earlier decades as their young people streamed into the sugar mills down in the plain.

The first screening of Devil, Family and Property was as a benefit event for the organizers of a major march in Buenos Aires to commemorate the summary 1976 arrest of some 400 people at a demonstration in downtown Buenos Aires—of whom 33 were never seen again. After the screening, 40 video-copies of the film were sold and thereafter passed from hand to hand. For the second screening in a cinema, the collective put up stickers more than 20 separate times and distributed thousands of fliers, especially at train stations serving large numbers of commuting workers. Serious about engaging the public and not treating it in the typical "audience" mode, the collective organized a roundtable discussion of the film in the cinema and distributed a short questionnaire to those present. They also coordinated publicity with the grassroots station Radio Colectivo de la Tribu (The Tribe).

After running 5 weeks in the cinema, the documentary was then screened at more than 200 exhibitions and sold over 1,000 videotapes, and had more than 100 exhibition screenings outside Argentina. Not least, following the initial screening, the group H.I.J.O.S. (Children of the Disappeared, from the 1976–1982 military dictatorship) proposed an escrache (demonstration) against the owner of the Ledesma company, whose trucks, back in 1976, had transported the police to arrest the 400 demonstrators of whom 33 never returned. She had a mansion in the town of Ledesma but also served as president of the Friends of the Fine Arts Museum in Buenos Aires. So escraches were organized simultaneously in both locations.

In the tumultuous days of December 2001, when masses of Argentineans poured out into the streets to demand the resignation of their government, following the huge financial crisis that had long been building but finally gripped the country by the throat in that month, GCI was extremely active. Early in the month they organized a weeklong screening of cine piquetero (picketer cinema), featuring the shorts and documentaries made by a cluster of militant film groups (such as Worker's Eye, The Fourth Patio,

Grupo Alavío, Counterimage, May First Group). Piqueteros was a term that sprang into widespread use in Argentina at this time to denote the most daring and determined of the street activists.

As the situation exploded on December 19–20, Cine Insurgente, along with other groups, was video recording the street clashes, organizing more than 300 street film projection events, and distributing hundreds of videos. They organized, along with Worker's Eye and Counterimage, an assembly under the slogan "You saw it, you lived it: Don't let them tell you about it!" This was a moment in which documentarians, journalists, artists, photographers, and activists shared daily the most intense discussions and reflections concerning the origins of the crisis, the nature of Argentina's political class, and its dependence upon Wall Street and Washington, D.C.

Since that time, GCI has been involved in a series of further documentaries. These included Por Los Cinco! (For the Five, 2003), concerning five Cubans given double life sentences in the United States for trying to trace the connections of expatriate Cuban terrorist groups allowed to operate freely in Miami. Another was Asamblea: Ocupar es Resistir (Assembly: Occupation Is Resistance, 2004), filmed inside a bank building occupied in summer 2002 by the neighborhood people's assembly. Yet another was Yaepota Ñande Igüiü—Queremos nuestra tierra (We Want Our Land, 2006), detailing the struggles of an Indigenous Guaraní community to recover the ancestral land from which they had been dispossessed in 1996 by the transnational Seaboard Corporation.

In addition, GCI organized tours of its work in Latin America and Europe. It also organized a series of 10 training workshops in video production and editing in fall 2009.

Fernando Krichmar
(translated by John D. H. Downing)

Note: Originally published in El Grupo de Cine Insurgente. In N. Vinelli & C. Rodríguez Esperón (Eds.), Contrainformación: Medios alternativos para la acción política [Counter-information: Alternative media for political action] (pp. 185–199). Buenos Aires, Argentina: Ediciones Continente, 2004.

See also Activist Cinema in the 1970s (France); Documentary Film for Social Change (India); Medvedkine Groups and Workers' Cinema (France);

Radio La Tribu (Argentina); Social Movement Media, 2001–2002 (Argentina); Third Cinema; Wayruro People's Communication (Argentina)

Further Readings

Cinepiquetero/Grupo de Cine Insurgente (2004). *Vos lo viviste: compilado de video informes 2002–03* [You lived it, friend: Compiled video reports 2002–03]. cinepiquetero@datafull.com

Grupo de Cine Insurgente (Producer & Director). (2002). *Las madres en la rebelión popular del 19 y 20 de diciembre 2001* [The mothers (of the Plaza de Mayo) in the people's rebellion of December 19–20, 2001; Documentary VHS]. cineinsurgente@hotmail.com

Grupo de Cine Insurgente (Producer), & Krichmar, F. (Director). (1999). *Diablo, familia y propiedad* [Devil, family and property; Documentary DVD]. cineinsurgente@hotmail.com

Krichmar, F. (2004). El Grupo de Cine Insurgente. In N. Vinelli & C. Rodríguez Esperón (Eds.), *Contrainformación: Medios alternativos para la acción política* [Counterinformation: Alternative media for political action] (pp. 185–199). Buenos Aires, Argentina: Ediciones Continente.

Citizen Journalism

The phrase "citizen journalism" entered the journalistic lexicon in the immediate aftermath of the South Asian tsunami of December 2004. The remarkable range of first-person accounts, camcorder video footage, mobile and digital camera snapshots generated by ordinary citizens on the scene (often people on vacation)—many posted through blogs and personal webpages—was widely heralded for making a unique contribution to mainstream journalism's coverage. One newspaper headline after the next declared citizen journalism to be yet another startling upheaval, if not outright revolution, being ushered in by Internet technology. News organizations, it was readily conceded, were in the awkward position of being dependent on this "amateur" material in order to tell the story of what was transpiring on the ground.

Despite its ambiguities, the term *citizen journalism* appeared to capture something of the countervailing ethos of the ordinary person's capacity to bear witness. In the years since the South Asian tsunami, the term has secured its place in journalism's vocabulary, more often than not associated with a particular crisis event. It is described variously as "grassroots journalism," "open source journalism," "participatory journalism," "hyperlocal journalism," "distributed journalism," or "networked journalism" (as well as "user-generated content"), but there is little doubt that it is profoundly recasting crisis reporting's priorities and protocols.

In tracing its emergent ecology, it is important to recognize the ways in which its diverse modes of reportorial form, practice, and epistemology—typically defined too narrowly around technological "revolutions"—have been crafted through the needs of crisis reporting. In the months following the tsunami, two such crises appeared to consolidate its imperatives, pretty well dispensing with claims that it was a passing "fad" or "gimmick." The London bombings of July 2005, like Hurricane Katrina's devastation that August, necessarily figure in any assessment of how citizen journalism has rewritten certain long-standing reportorial principles.

Particularly vexing for any journalist during a crisis is the difficulty of securing access to the scene. In London, tight security barred entry to Underground (subway) stations, which meant that the aftermath of the explosions was beyond reach and out of sight. On the other side of the emergency services' cordons, however, were ordinary Londoners, some with cell phone cameras. These tiny lenses captured the scene underground, with many of the images conveying what some aptly described as an eerie, even claustrophobic quality.

Video clips taken were judged all the more compelling because they were dim, grainy, and shaky, and—even more important—because they were documenting an angle on an event as it was actually happening. The pictures captured the horror of being trapped underground. Many of these photographs, some breathtaking in their poignancy, were viewed thousands of times within hours of their posting on sites such as Flickr.com or Moblog.co.uk.

It was precisely this quality that journalists and editors were looking for when quickly sifting through the vast array of images e-mailed to them. The director of BBC News recorded that within minutes of the first blast, they had received images from the public, 50 within an hour. The London

Evening Standard production editor Richard Oliver opined that news organizations were bound to tap into this resource more and more in future.

The next month, as Hurricane Katrina caused severe destruction along the U.S. Gulf Coast, citizen journalism was once again at the fore. Voices from within major organizations were quick to concede that it was augmenting their news coverage in important ways. CNN.com's supervising producer observed that Katrina had been the highest profile story in which news sites were able to fill in the gaps when government wasn't able to provide information and where people were unable to communicate with each other.

The AOL News editor in chief forecast that the interactive nature of the online news experience meant it could offer "real-time dialogue" between users joining in to shape the news. In his view, the significance of participatory journalism, in which everyday people are able to take charge of their stories, had taken overly long to be properly acknowledged. Michael Tippett, founder of NowPublic. com, concurred. In underscoring the extent to which journalism is being effectively democratized, he contended that perceptions of the journalist as an impersonal, detached observer were being swept away. He endorsed the power of emotional depth and firsthand experience, rather than the formulaic, distancing approach of conventional journalism.

In the years since Hurricane Katrina, there has been no shortage of crisis events that have similarly figured in appraisals of the changing nature of the relationship between "professional" journalism and its "amateur" alternatives. Examples include citizen reporting of the Buncefield oil depot explosion in the United Kingdom, the Mumbai train bombings, the protesting monks of Myanmar/ Burma, Saddam Hussein's execution, the Virginia Tech University shootings, and the Wenchuan earthquake. During the November 2008 Mumbai hostage crisis, there was much press comment on how citizen journalists used Twitter feeds to relay vital insights. Time and again, Twitter was singled out for praise as the best source for real-time citizen news. Still, if Twitter deserved praise as a useful means to gather eyewitness accounts during a crisis, doubts remained about its status as a trustworthy news source in its own right.

It is readily apparent that what counts as journalism in the "network society" is in a state of flux. Familiar reportorial principles in mainstream news are being recast by competing imperatives of technological convergence and by those of divergence being played out by "the people formerly known as the audience," to use blogger Jay Rosen's apt turn of phrase. It follows that these changing dynamics will necessarily entail thinking anew about the social responsibilities of the citizen as journalist while, at the same time, reconsidering those of the journalist as citizen.

Stuart Allan

See also Arab Bloggers as Citizen Journalists (Transnational); Citizens' Media; December 2008 Revolt Media (Greece); Human Rights Media; Indymedia (The Independent Media Center); Indymedia: East Asia; *OhmyNews* (Korea); Social Movement Media in 2009 Crisis (Iran); Women Bloggers (Egypt)

Further Readings

Allan, S., & Thorsen, E. (Eds.). (2009). *Citizen journalism: Global perspectives.* New York: Peter Lang.

Gillmor, D. (2004). *We the media: Grassroots journalism by the people, for the people.* Sebastopol, CA: O'Reilly.

Lasica, J. D. (2005, September 7). Citizens media gets richer. *Online Journalism Review.*

CITIZENS' MEDIA

As an academic term, *citizens' media* belongs to a large family of concepts that include community media, alternative media, autonomous media, participatory media, and radical media. Benjamin Ferron lists the following terms that are associated with citizens' media: *alternative, radical, citizens', marginal, participatory, counter-information, parallel, community, underground, popular, libres, dissident, resistant, pirate, clandestine, autonomous, young,* and micro-médias.

In 2001, Clemencia Rodríguez coined the term *citizens' media* in her book *Fissures in the Mediascape,* which emerged at the crossroads between Latin American communication and culture scholarship of the 1980s and 1990s and the proposal for a global New World Information and Communication Order (NWICO).

During the 1980s, Latin American communication and culture scholars proposed alternative theoretical frameworks to understand cultural, communication, and media processes. Antonio Pasquali in Venezuela, Paulo Freire in Brasil, Rosa María Alfaro in Perú, Armand Mattelart in Chile, Luis Ramiro Beltrán in Bolivia, Marita Mata and Eliseo Verón in Argentina, Néstor García Canclini in México, Mario Kaplún in Uruguay, and Jesús Martín Barbero in Colombia proposed a series of pioneer conceptual frameworks that allowed Latin America to conceptualize communication and culture in its own terms and questioned theories imported from the global North. Also, Latin American communication and culture scholarship broke off from the "ivory tower" of academia, proposing instead a genre of scholarship deeply engaged with the Indigenous, labor, student, women's, and youth social movements that stirred political mobilizations and profound social, economic, and cultural transformations in the region from the 1970s onward.

During the late 1970s, representatives from third world countries had exposed a scenario of global communication inequities at UNESCO and the United Nations. They protested a situation in which the flow of information and communication from first world countries into third world countries was many times stronger than the reverse, and in which the communication infrastructure in the latter nations was sharply inferior. UNESCO commissioned the 1980 MacBride Report on this situation, which was translated into many languages and widely distributed and debated across the world. It demonstrated that most global media traffic was controlled by a few transnational communication corporations in the United States, Western Europe, and Japan. The MacBride Report also showed that global-South-to-global-South communication was then practically nonexistent.

Solutions proposed by those striving for more democratic communication practices included changing national communication policies, increasing South-to-South communication and information initiatives (such as press agencies), and a code of ethics for the mass media. However, when Rodríguez published *Fissures in the Mediascape* 20 years later, she noted that NWICO had never gotten off the ground. In part, this was because of corporate hostility channeled through the U.S. and British governments, which actually withdrew from UNESCO for 2 decades to punish its initiative, but most particularly because of the need to rethink the democratization of media from a grassroots perspective, closer to people and third world communities than to press agencies, large-scale media, and national information policies.

This new perspective visualized social movements and grassroots organizations and their alternative media as the new key players in the processes of democratization of communication. The hope was now for these newly politicized social subjects (social movements, grassroots organizations, *grupos populares*) to establish their own small-scale media outlets and to spin their own communication and information networks, bypassing the global communication giants. Apart from providing their audiences with alternative information, these new media—labeled alternative media—were expected to divert from the top-down vertical mode of communication. Whereas the big media function on the basis of a hierarchy between media producers and media audiences, where the latter have no voice and are restricted to a passive role of receiving media messages, alternative media were thought of as the panacea of horizontal communication, whereby senders and receivers share equal access to communicative power.

Reconceptualizing the Issues

Rodríguez set herself the challenge to find a theoretical grammar appropriate to the then current terms of the debate. She argued that a relocation of the debate on democratization of communication should go beyond a mere reaccommodation of the same old concepts to a local scale. The new direction for a debate on the democratization of communication should imply finding a new conceptual framework that can capture how democratic communication happens within alternative media. Theorizing the democratization of communication had remained trapped within a vision of politics and democracy rooted in "grand narratives of emancipation" and essentialist concepts of power, citizenship, and political action.

Drawing from Belgian feminist and political scientist Chantal Mouffe's theories of radical democracy and citizenship, Rodríguez proposed *citizens' media* as a term better able to capture processes of social change and democratization facilitated by alternative or community media. This defines media on the basis of their potential to trigger processes of social change. Conversely, *community media* defines media based on who the producers are (i.e., community organizations, grassroots collectives) or the type of broadcasting license granted by the state (i.e., community broadcasting license). *Alternative media* defines media by what they are not (i.e., alternative to the mainstream media, alternative to vertical communication), instead of defining their specifics. Rodríguez also argued that alternative media implies a reactive relationship with dominant media and a corresponding acceptance of a lesser status. Coining *citizens' media*, Rodríguez strove to redirect analysis away from the comparison with mass, commercial media, to focus instead on the cultural and social processes triggered when local communities appropriate information and communication technologies.

Mouffe had broken away from theories that define citizenship as a status granted by the state, and proposed a move to reclaim the term *citizen.* She proposed that a citizen should be defined by daily political action and engagement and argued for citizenship as a form of identification, a type of political identity: something to be constructed, not empirically given. Citizens have to enact their citizenship on a day-to-day basis, through their participation in everyday political practices, as localized subjects whose daily lives are traversed by a series of social and cultural interactions. These are framed by family interactions and relationships with neighbors, friends, colleagues, and peers. Each individual gains access to power—symbolic power, psychological power, material power, and political power—precisely from these interactions. According to Mouffe, when individuals and collectives use their power to redirect and shape their communities, these actions should be theorized as the building blocks of democratic life.

Adopting Mouffe's definition of citizenship, Rodríguez coined the term *citizens' media* to refer to alternative, community, or radical media that facilitate, trigger, and maintain processes of citizenship building, in Mouffe's sense of the term. Rodríguez's citizens' media are those media that promote symbolic processes that allow people to name the world and speak the world in their own

terms. Here, Rodríguez connects Mouffe's notions of radical democracy, citizenship, and political action with Jesús Martín Barbero's theories of identity, language, and political power. According to Martín Barbero, the power of communities to name the world in their own terms is directly linked with their power to enact political actions. In Spanish, Martín Barbero plays with a linguistic pun between the terms *contar* (to narrate) and *contar* (to have a strong presence, to count) and explains that only those who can *contar* (narrate) will *contar*; only those with the ability to narrate their own identities and to name the world in their own terms will have a strong presence as political subjects.

Drawing on Martín Barbero's emphasis on identity and narrative, Rodríguez articulated the significance of information and communication technologies (ICTs). As technologies that allow people to meddle with the symbolic, media and new ICTs are located in a privileged historical position to facilitate communities' appropriation of their own languages to name the world in their own terms, narrate their identities, and express their own visions for a future. Rodríguez's theory of citizens' media also drew from new social movement theories that understand power and resistance as tightly linked with issues of recognition of identity, voice, agency, and narration, as key elements of political representation. According to these approaches, the power of the subaltern to resist is not limited to alignments behind predesigned political agendas. Instead, the power of the subaltern is predicated on the collective ability to articulate a vision of the future expressed via a voice strong enough to become part of the public sphere and to gain political power. In other words, new social movements (e.g., feminism, environmentalism) are understood as collective identities with strong presence in the public sphere, who can clearly articulate notions of self and proposals to build community.

Thus, according to Rodríguez, citizens' media are those media that facilitate the transformation of individuals and communities into Mouffe's notion of citizens and Martín Barbero's powerful subjectivities with a voice. Citizens' media are communication spaces where men, women, and children learn to manipulate their own languages, codes, signs, and symbols, gaining power to name the world in their own terms. Citizens' media trigger processes that allow individuals and communities to recodify their contexts and selves. These processes ultimately give citizens the opportunity to restructure their identities into empowered subjectivities strongly connected to local cultures and driven by well-defined utopias. Citizens' media are the media citizens use to activate communication processes that shape their local communities.

Rodríguez's term *citizens' media* emerged from the need to overcome oppositional frameworks and binary categories traditionally used to analyze alternative media. Whereas *alternative media* defines community media by what they are not— not commercial, not professional, not institutionalized—*citizens' media* defines them by what they spark: processes of change triggered among media participants. Researcher Jo Tacchi and her colleagues have shown how transformative processes activated by citizens' media spill over in concentric circles, beyond the small circles of media producers, to touch the lives of producers' neighbors, extended families, friends, coworkers, and ultimately their audiences.

Furthermore, the term *citizens' media* breaks away from a binary and essentializing definition of power, whereby the mediascape is inhabited by the powerful (mainstream media) and the powerless (alternative media). Instead of limiting the potential of alternative media to their ability to resist large media conglomerates, *citizens' media* accounts for the processes of empowerment, conscientization, and fragmentation of power that result when men, women, and children gain access to and reclaim their own media.

Case Studies of Citizens' Media

Based on qualitative methodologies that range from ethnography to in-depth interviews, oral history, memory workshops, and life stories, Rodríguez carried out case studies of local radio correspondents in Nicaragua, local television in Cataluña, participatory video in Colombia, Spanish-language radio among Latina/o communities in the United States, community radio in Chile, and citizens' media in regions of armed conflict in Colombia.

In her more recent work, Rodríguez has used *citizens' media* as a qualifier instead of a category

that defines the legal status of the medium. In this sense, a medium can have a community broadcasting license and still not qualify as a citizens' medium. A medium with a community broadcasting license will qualify as a citizens' medium only as long as it triggers processes by which local producers recodify their own identities and reformulate their own visions for their communities' futures.

Drawing from Rodríguez's work, communication and media scholars use the term *citizens' media* to refer to electronic media (i.e., radio, television, video) and information and communication technologies (Internet, text messaging, cellular telephony) controlled and used by citizens and collectives to meet their own information and communication needs and strengthen their agency as political subjects. Michael Meadows used the term in his studies of Indigenous and community media in Australia. Usha Sundar Harris adopted the term as the main theoretical framework in her visual ethnography of processes of empowerment among women in Fiji. Heather Anderson used citizens' media to explore prisoners' radio in Australia and Canada. Antoni Castells i Talens theorized Indigenous radio stations in México as citizens' media. According to Castells i Talens, although Indigenous radio is sponsored and controlled by the Mexican state, Mexican Indigenous communities use these communication spaces to strengthen their own processes of self-empowerment.

Media anthropologist Juan Francisco Salazar has used the term *citizens' media* in his work about Indigenous media in general and Mapuche media in particular, to articulate notions of Indigenous citizenship that problematize the equivalence between citizenship and nation. The Chilean constitution only recognizes the existence of ethnic groups within a unitary national state. Several Mapuche communities in Chile appropriate media as a way to perform their ethnic citizenship within a state that recognizes their existence as aboriginal people but fails to recognize any form of Indigenous citizenship or nationality. The concept of ethnic citizenship has been formulated by Mexican anthropologist Guillermo de la Peña, who has revisited Renato Rosaldo's notion of cultural citizenship in his analysis of cultural assimilation in the United States. Hence, the notion of ethnic citizenship is used here to refer to the processes of political and social participation where Indigenous people are able to partake in the public sphere not only as Chilean, Bolivian, or Mexican citizens, but also as Mapuche, Aymara, or Zapotecas.

Based on an ethnography of Bush Radio, a community radio station in Cape Town, South Africa, media scholar Tanja Bosch develops Rodríguez's concept of citizens' media by theorizing community media in light of Deleuze and Guattari's theory of the rhizome. According to Bosch, like the rhizome, community radio cuts across borders and builds linkages. Bush Radio is clearly rhizomatic in terms of Deleuze and Guattari's principles of connection and heterogeneity, multiplicity, and signifying rupture. She argues that Bush Radio is not so much an organization as a rhizomatic organism, held together by a complex set of interlinked networks of relationships and interactions, with the concept of community pulsating as its central life force.

Ongoing Issues

More recently, the term *citizens' media* has been perceived as problematic. Although as defined by Rodríguez, the term is far from state-based understandings of citizenship, the term cannot escape its connotation of inclusion and exclusion based on the legal status of the citizen's rights, a status systematically denied to millions because of their nationality, labor certification, health-care access status, or sexual orientation. As media justice researcher Pradip Thomas has argued, citizenship entitlements as defined by liberal democratic theory—as a birthright and not in Rodríguez's definition as everyday political action—cannot be easily discarded because in their implementation lies security for millions in the global South.

Clemencia Rodríguez

See also Alternative Media; Anarchist Media; Citizen Journalism; Citizens' Media; Feminist Media: An Overview; Indigenous Peoples' Media; Mobile Communication and Social Movements; Participatory Media; Youth Media

Further Readings

Alfaro Moreno, R. M. (2004). Culturas populares y comunicación participativa: en la ruta de las redefiniciones [Popular cultures and participatory communication: On the path of redefinitions]. *Comunicación, 126,* 13–19.

Atton, C. (2002). *Alternative media.* London: Sage.

Bosch, T. E. (2009). Theorizing citizens' media: A rhizomatic approach. In C. Rodríguez, D. Kidd, & L. Stein (Eds.), *Making our media: Global initiatives toward a democratic public sphere: Vol. 1. Creating new communication spaces.* Cresskill, NJ: Hampton Press.

Castells i Talens, A. (2009). When our media belong to the state: Policy and negotiations in indigenous-language radio in Mexico. In C. Rodríguez, D. Kidd, & L. Stein (Eds.), *Making our media: Global initiatives toward a democratic public sphere: Vol. 1. Creating new communication spaces.* Cresskill, NJ: Hampton Press.

Downing, J. D. H. (with Villareal Ford, T., Gil, G., & Stein, L.). (2001). *Radical media: Rebellious communication and social movements.* London: Sage.

Gumucio Dagron, A. (2001). *Making waves: Participatory communication for social change.* New York: Rockefeller Foundation.

Hamelink, C. (1997). MacBride with hindsight. In P. Golding & P. Harris (Eds.), *Beyond cultural imperialism. Globalization, communication and the new international order* (pp. 69–93). Thousand Oaks, CA: Sage.

MacBride Commission. (2003). *Many voices, one world: Towards a new, more just, and more efficient world information and communication order.* Lanham, MD: Rowman & Littlefield.

Martín Barbero, J. (2002). Identities: Traditions and new communities. *Media, Culture & Society, 24*(5), 621–641.

Mattelart, A. (1974). *La comunicación masiva en el proceso de liberación* [Mass communication in the process of liberation]. Buenos Aires, Argentina: Siglo XXI.

McClure, K. (1992). On the subject of rights: Pluralism, plurality and political identity. In C. Mouffe (Ed.), *Dimensions of radical democracy: Pluralism, citizenship, community* (pp. 108–125). London: Verso.

Meadows, M., Forde, S., Ewart, J., & Foxwell, K. (2009). Making spaces: Independent media and the formation of the democratic public sphere in Australia. In C. Rodríguez, D. Kidd, & L. Stein (Eds.), *Making our media: Global initiatives toward a democratic public sphere: Vol. 1. Creating new communication spaces.* Cresskill, NJ: Hampton Press.

Mouffe, C. (Ed.). (1992). *Dimensions of radical democracy: Pluralism, citizenship, community.* London: Verso.

Roach, C. (1990). The movement for a new world information and communication order: A second wave? *Media, Culture & Society* 12(3), 283–307.

Rodríguez, C. (2001). *Fissures in the mediascape: An international study of citizens' media.* Cresskill, NJ: Hampton Press.

Rodríguez, C. (2003). The bishop and his star: Citizens' communication in southern Chile. In N. Couldry & J. Curran (Eds.), *Contesting media power: Alternative media in a networked world* (pp. 177–194). Lanham, MD: Rowman & Littlefield.

Rodríguez, C. (in press). *Disrupting violence. Citizens' media and armed conflict in Colombia.* Minneapolis: Minnesota University Press.

Rodríguez, C., & Murphy, P. (1997). The study of communication and culture in Latin America: From laggards and the oppressed to resistance and hybrid cultures. *Journal of International Communication,* 4(2), 24–45.

Salazar, J. F. (2009). Making culture visible: The mediated construction of a Mapuche nation in Chile. In C. Rodríguez, D. Kidd, & L. Stein (Eds.), *Making our media: Global initiatives toward a democratic public sphere: Vol. 1. Creating new communication spaces.* Cresskill, NJ: Hampton Press.

Thomas, P. (2007). The right to information movement and community radio in India. Observations on the theory and practice of participatory communication. *Communication for Development and Social Change,* 1(1), 33–47.

COMMUNIST MOVEMENT MEDIA, 1950s–1960s (HONG KONG)

The People's Republic of China (PRC) was founded in 1949, a turning point in the cold war. With Hong Kong under British rule, the Chinese communist government was eager to promote communism and get a political foothold in the colony. The promotion of communist ideology in the 1950s transformed into collective anticolonialist actions in the 1960s. Violent rioting broke out in 1967 and lasted 8 months. The pro-China leftist press played an important role in the communist movement throughout the 2 decades. The leftist film studios gave a helping hand too. Both were very visible in the 1967 disturbances.

Left-Wing Films

In the late 1940s, given China's unstable political situation, a number of filmmakers left for Hong Kong. Three left-wing film companies were established in Hong Kong in the late 1940s and early 1950s, namely, the Great Wall Movie Enterprises Ltd., Feng Huang Film Company, and Sun Luen Film Company. During those turbulent times, for a number of filmmakers and actors, leftist beliefs represented hope for the future of China. Initially, the companies' left-wing sponsorship was not apparent. But Feng Huang became a cooperative and received Chinese government support. Around the mid-1950s, the Chinese Communist Party started sending people to Great Wall as well.

In the 1950s, these studios' movies reflected postwar society and communist ideals. Some commented satirically on the hypocrisy of capitalist society (e.g., *Awful Truth,* 1950) and issued veiled pleas to return to the homeland (e.g., *Dividing Wall,* 1952), while others called insistently for the masses to be educated (e.g., *Parents' Love,* 1953). The colonial government was sensitive to left-wing influence, and in 1952, it deported 10 left-wing filmmakers.

The News Media and Leftist Activism

As for the news media, after 1949 Hong Kong became a major site of the struggle for power between the Chinese Communist Party (CCP) and the Kuomintang (KMT, the pro-Western Nationalist Party). Whereas the KMT treated Hong Kong as a bridgehead to counterattack the mainland, the CCP saw Hong Kong as a location to unite overseas Chinese and promote communism. Hong Kong newspapers were divided into leftist, centrist, and rightist factions. Press–party parallelism dominated the media.

In the 1950s, the leftist news media started a movement against U.S. imperialism as part of the cold war. In Hong Kong they opposed both U.S. influence and British rule. In addition, they trumpeted mainland developments and launched political attacks on Taiwan's government. The communist movement in the 1950s and early 1960s did not cause much trouble in the colony until 1967, when the long rioting seriously challenged the colonial government's authority.

The rioting ran from early May to late December. Social order was critically upset. In addition to nonviolent demonstrations and protests, rioters flung stones, set off bombs, committed arson, and physically confronted the antiriot police force. A strike at artificial-flower firms triggered the rioting, turning a labor dispute into large-scale demonstrations against colonial rule. Some analysts have attributed its causes to various earlier labor disputes and agitation by radical leftists inspired by the Cultural Revolution. In fact, no consensus has been reached on the real causes, and it was most likely a mixture of local grievances and the influence of the Cultural Revolution.

The Hong Kong leftists were well-organized and powerful. They had considerable human and capital resources and were supported by the Macau and mainland communists. Most importantly, they had their newspapers to help spread their propaganda.

After the outbreak of rioting, newspapers in Hong Kong were divided into two camps and constituted a media battlefield. Whereas leftist newspapers promoted the rioting, the centrist and rightist press sought to explain the situation, ease public anxiety, maintain social cohesion, and help the government keep order. The former called an end to British rule, but the latter supported the colonial government in order to preserve the status quo.

Communist press theory advocates that during a political struggle, the idea of revolution versus counterrevolution should be spread through the media to fight the enemies at the ideological level. By the mid-1960s, there were 48 newspapers in Hong Kong, 8 of which belonged to the communist camp. Particularly *Ta Kung Pao* and *Wen Wei Po* were guided by communist press theory and mobilized people to participate in the rioting. The newspapers performed the functions of propaganda, education, organization, and mass mobilization.

To foster collective action, the first step the leftist newspapers took was to politicize the events. Thus, *Ta Kung Pao* alleged the rioting was caused by a planned intervention by the Hong Kong government in a labor dispute. It explained that this "savage act" represented British racial oppression of the Chinese. Their second step was to win over the general public in order to build a united front. Through editorials, news reports, and letters from readers, the leftist newspapers supported the formation of the Hong Kong and Kowloon Committee for Anti–Hong Kong British Persecution Struggle and tried to educate their readers that rioting was a patriotic anti-British action. They called upon all Chinese to stand up and join the movement against oppression and to overthrow the British colonial government.

During the prolonged disturbances, their criticisms of the government were highly provocative. Three leftist newspapers were charged with violating local press law and were suspended.

Meanwhile, some filmmakers were also passionately engaged in the movement. Famous movie stars such as Shek Hwei and Fu Che, husband and wife, were outstanding examples, aggressively involved in anti-British political activism. They worked for the left-wing studios. Fu Che was a member of the Hong Kong and Kowloon Committee for Anti–Hong Kong British Persecution Struggle. They were arrested in July 1967 and jailed for over a year.

During the rioting, leftist newspapers were successful at spreading revolutionary messages across the territory. However, the communist press theory they adopted rejected fair and accurate reporting and led to low news credibility. Moreover, the Hong Kong public opted for stability and supported the colonial government in cracking down on the violent rioting in which 51 people were killed. The application of communist press theory did not eventually help the leftists to achieve their political goal.

Impacts of the Movement

Although the movement was defeated, the 1967 rioting fundamentally changed the colonial government's philosophy. A new policy direction was to establish district offices and organize a series of youth activities. The colonial government shifted from only co-opting social elites to actively seeking public support. The Government Information Services and other liaison channels were set up to facilitate communication between the public and the government.

As for the left-wing studios, they continued to operate. Famous actor and director Bao Fong admitted that even after the rioting, he made some films that were very "leftist," such as *The Battle of Sha Chia Bund* (1968) and *Collegiate* (1970). However, the Cultural Revolution exacted great damage on Hong Kong left-wing cinema, and the three studios were never able to reclaim the glories of the 1950s and 1960s.

Alice Y. L. Lee

See also Activist Cinema in the 1970s (France); Documentary Film for Social Change (India); Internet Social Movement Media (Hong Kong); Leninist Underground Media Model; Revolutionary Media, 1956 (Hungary)

Further Readings

Cooper, J. (1970). *Colony in conflict: The Hong Kong disturbances May 1967–January 1968*. Hong Kong: Swindon.

HKU (University of Hong Kong) Student Union. (1978). *Information brochure on Hong Kong Week Exhibition* [in Chinese]. Hong Kong: Author.

Hong Kong Government. (1967). *Hong Kong: Report for the year*. Hong Kong: Government Press.

Lee, A. Y. L. (1999). The role of newspapers in the 1967 riot: A case study on the partisanship of the Hong Kong press. In C. Y. K. So & J. M. Chan (Eds.), *Press and politics in Hong Kong: Case studies from 1967 to 1997* (pp. 33–65). Hong Kong: Chinese University of Hong Kong, Hong Kong Institute of Asia-Pacific Studies.

Sinn, E. (Ed.). (2004, June). *E-Journal on Hong Kong Cultural and Social Studies, 3*. http://www.hku.hk/hkcsp/ccex/ehkcss01

Wong, A. L. (2001). Preface. In J. Au-Yang (Ed.), *An age of idealism: Great Wall & Feng Huang days* (pp. xvi–xxvi). Hong Kong: Hong Kong Film Archive.

Wong, C. (2004). The 1967 leftist riot and regime legitimacy in Hong Kong. *E-Journal on Hong Kong Cultural and Social Studies, 3*. http://www.hku.hk/hkcsp/ccex/ehkcss01/frame.htm?mid=0&smid=1&ssmid=3

COMMUNITY BROADCASTING (CANADA)

Canada is sometimes seen as one of community broadcasting's birthplaces but, particularly in English-speaking Canada, it has not been well supported by government and has often been hampered by a lack of funding and access to other resources.

The Canadian Radio-Television and Telecommunications Commission (CRTC) is charged with regulating all elements of broadcasting in Canada, including community television and radio. The 1991 Broadcasting Act defines broadcasting as a "public service essential to the maintenance and enhancement of national identity and cultural sovereignty" and includes public, private, and community broadcasters as essential parts of the system.

Community Television

Community television in Canada grew out of the National Film Board's Challenge for Change program. Born out of the 1960s social movements, Challenge for Change provided an example of how people might use video to strengthen their communities and inspired people across North America to get involved in video production.

Responding to people who wanted to take up video for community development, the CRTC encouraged cable companies to provide a community channel where these productions might be produced and aired. In 1975, the CRTC made the provision of a community channel—complete with a small studio and equipment—a license condition for most cable operators. However, as an early study by Goldberg showed, the cable licensee and its employees gradually extended their control over programming decisions, productions, and equipment use, and away from the community. The ownership structure tended to block community access and to mainstream both programs and users. This got worse in 1997 when the CRTC ruled cable companies no longer had to fund a community channel.

Recognizing that ongoing concentration of corporate media ownership had resulted in "reduced representation of local voices," the CRTC announced a new community media policy in 2002, designed to increase public involvement and reinvigorate the community channel. Community channels run by large cable operators now had to devote 30% of the schedule to access programming, and several kinds of community television license were created. New licensees include independent program producers who, with varying levels of cable company support, create programs carried on a company channel and community broadcast organizations that are independent from cable companies, other than a requirement that they be carried on the local cable service. These latter organizations sometimes have their own over-the-air signal and may be carried on program distributors other than cable.

However, for the most part, control over community television generally remained with large cable companies. These companies had to contribute over C$100 million annually to the community channel. But there was no oversight as to how these funds were spent, and numerous complaints arose that companies had cut back community programming and created program formats mimicking those of commercial broadcasters. New distribution technologies also presented challenges to community television as satellite broadcasters were not required to carry a community channel.

In 2007, there were 101 English-language community channels and 11 community program services. But while cable companies appeared to be trying to turn community television to a more conventional commercial format, activist and more traditional formats persisted.

For instance, Fearless TV (FTV) is an independent community program producer, founded in 2007 and operating in the downtown east side of Vancouver—one of the country's poorest neighborhoods. FTV is a "cluster" of about 30 volunteers associated with the Downtown East Side Community Arts network and includes artists, residents, journalists, and community activists. Using the local cable licensee's equipment, the group produced about 25 hours of programming over the first 15 months of its operation. Programs generally focus on four core issues: local arts, housing, poverty, and homelessness. They specifically strive to enhance community action, build social networks, help negotiate collective values in the neighborhood, and foster civic participation.

First established in 1994, Telile Community Television is an independent station on Isle Madame, a small island off the southeast coast of Cape Breton Island in Nova Scotia. In the wake of the local fishery's closure, the station was created to strengthen "the island's consciousness of itself as a community; and to disseminate the information which the island's people would need in the process of renewal" (Telile, n.d., para. 2). Initially, programs were just on cable, but the station also launched an over-the-air signal in 2002. Financed largely through a weekly bingo program and local advertising, Telile has three employees. Programming includes local news, council meetings, and community events. Speaking of Telile's role in the community, founding chair Silver Donald Cameron noted,

> You can't participate if you don't know what's going on. . . . You can't have real community, and you can't have real democracy, if you don't have communications. Telile's role is to make sure that people here do know what's going on, and do know how they can participate. That's what Telile is all about. (Telile, n.d., para. 7)

St. Andrews Community Television in St. Andrews, New Brunswick, offers a similar but perhaps less activist approach to community building. First carried on cable in 1993, the station also began broadcasting in 2006 on UHF. The station is financed through bingo, advertising, memberships, and local fund-raising initiatives. It is run by volunteers and produces 14 hours per week of programming that includes a wide range of community news, variety programming, town meetings, and special events.

In an effort to help develop and organize around the interests of community television organizations, the Canadian Association of Campus and Community Television User Groups and Stations was founded in 2007. Perhaps the best hope for community television is the development of nonprofit community-based television associations, coupled with reliable sources of income and guaranteed access to the basic program packages offered by all television distributors.

Community Radio

Community radio has long roots in towns and universities across the country. As politics heated up in the late 1960s and 1970s, radio became a way of organizing and movement building, and stations with a more radical edge began to appear, particularly at the local level. Today, the CRTC recognizes that community radio should be participatory and respond to its communities' concerns. The commission defines a

> community radio station [as a station owned] and controlled by a not-for-profit organization, the structure of which provides for membership, management and programming primarily by members of the community at large, [of which the programming] should reflect the diversity of the market that the station is licensed to serve. (CRTC, 2000, n.p.)

There are several types of community radio station licenses: Types A and B, community campus, and instructional. A and B licenses are issued to nonprofit groups in the community at large. Type A licenses are issued where there are no essentially commercial stations operating in the same language other than those of the Canadian Broadcasting Corporation. Type B licenses are issued where there are commercial stations. Stations on campuses are divided into "community campus" and "instructional" stations. Community campus stations are responsible to the larger community within which the educational institution is based. Instructional stations primarily train professional broadcasters. In December 2007, there were 9 English-language Type A stations, 26 Type B stations, 34 community-campus stations, and a further 9 English-language community stations under development.

Because of the larger role it has played in French/English politics, in general, French-language community radio—particularly in Québec—is better organized and financed than in the rest of the country.

Although sometimes carrying cooperatively produced news and current affairs programs—or even syndicated programming such as *Democracy Now!*—programming is generally developed locally and licensees are expected to inform the public of opportunities for participation and training. Stations generally have three or four part-time paid employees and are programmed by volunteers. Off-campus stations raise funds through a variety of means, including membership fees, fundraising drives, and advertising. Regulations generally impose stronger limits on advertising by community stations than commercial stations, particularly in urban centers.

Because they are largely run by volunteers, these stations are heavily integrated into the communities they serve. Founded in 1975, Radio Centre-Ville (CINQ FM) delivers programming in seven languages to the neighborhood of Quartier Saint-Louis in downtown Montréal. The station is mandated to "give priority access to local residents and groups, particularly those neglected by other media" (www.radiocentreville.com) and serves up a wide range of talk and musical programming designed to engage listeners in local issues and events. It is supported by more than 350 volunteers and serves more than 40 different communities, focusing largely on low-income immigrant groups.

Also founded in the early 1970s, Vancouver's CFRO (Co-op Radio) is similar in focus but tends to be a bit more radical in practice. As the station's mandate states, its

> first priority is to provide a media outlet for the economically, socially or politically disadvantaged. We provide news and perspectives that are not otherwise accessible—information that is not covered by the conventional media or perspectives that challenge mainstream media coverage.

Located in the heart of Vancouver's downtown east side, CFRO is collectively managed by four part-time staff. Most major decisions are made by committee, and 400 volunteers are involved in programming, which includes alternative arts, public affairs, music, and non-English fare. Co-op radio is directly plugged into progressive social movements, and many of the volunteers are organizers.

In the absence of commercial stations in their communities, more rural stations like CHMM in Mackenzie—a town of about 5,000 in the interior of British Columbia—take a more centrist approach in their efforts to build community. Operated by a local not-for-profit radio society, this station acts as a clearinghouse for a wide range of community information, including advertising.

Like their community station cousins, campus stations carry a range of programming, and their political affiliations vary. Policies for them were first promulgated in 1975 and the "community-based campus" designation began in 2000. The boards of directors must include student representatives, volunteers, and community members at large. Regulations steer these stations away from licensed commercial formats.

In terms of income, advertising at these stations is limited to a maximum of 4 minutes in any 1 hour, but they generally also receive a small levy from student tuition. Over the past decade, both station programming and the tuition levy have been the subject of heated political struggles between conservative and progressive student organizations on a number of campuses.

A number of both types of community station are members of the National Campus and Community Radio Association/Association nationale des radios étudiantes et communautaires (NCRA/ANREC). Founded in 1981, the NCRA represents 53 stations across the country. Their Statement of Principles states

that mainstream media fails to recognize or in many instances reinforces social and economic inequities that oppress women and minority groups of our society [and commits members to] providing alternative radio to an audience that is recognized as being diverse in ethnicity, culture, gender, sexual orientation, age, and physical and mental ability.

NCRA representatives regularly appear at CRTC hearings and meet with government and related industry groups on issues such as licensing, regulatory fairness, and copyright. The NCRA houses a program exchange, organizes an annual Homelessness Marathon among member stations, and is developing a weekly news program to share among its members. The organization also hosts a well-attended annual conference with sessions on fund-raising, programming, working with the CRTC, and professional development.

In early 2008, the CRTC announced the creation of the Community Radio Fund of Canada (CRFC). Seeded by a C$1.4 million commitment over 7 years by Astral media, the fund was negotiated through the CRTC as part of a community benefits package that accompanied Astral's purchase of a string of corporate radio stations. It is hoped that further funds will be contributed by the federal government and other sources. The fund will help support stations across the country finance local news and public affairs programming, community access, emerging local artists, volunteer support, and new media technologies.

Although community and campus radio in Canada reaches and represents communities and interests that are marginal for corporate media, the sector also faces serious challenges. To a large part, community radio exists as a patchwork on the margins of a heavily entrenched corporate media system. Many stations have precarious finances and operate under 50 watts. In the face of increasing competition for radio spectrum, they are at risk from much more powerful commercial stations. Moreover, as the broadcast standard switched from analog to digital technology, community stations had no budgets to prepare for the move.

With the economics of corporate media now threatening the disappearance of local programming, community media offer a way to remake the system to be more responsive to, and reflective of, the Canadian public. Whether or not policymakers in Canada will seize this opportunity remains to be seen.

David Skinner

See also Alternative Media Center (United States); Challenge for Change Film Movement (Canada); Community Broadcasting Audiences (Australia); Community Media (Venezuela); Community Media and the Third Sector; Community Radio (Haïti); Community Radio Movement (India); First Peoples' Media (Canada); Street Theater (Canada)

Further Readings

Canadian Radio-Television and Telecommunications Commission (CRTC). (2000, January 28). *Community radio policy* (Public notice CRTC 2000–13). http://www.crtc.gc.ca/eng/archive/2000/PB2000-13.HTM

Canadian Radio-Television and Telecommunications Commission (CRTC). (2002, October 10). *Policy framework for community-based media* (Public notice CRTC 2002–61). http://www.crtc.gc.ca/eng/archive/2002/pb2002-61.htm

Canadian Radio-Television and Telecommunications Commission (CRTC). (2008). *Communications monitoring report, 2008.* http://www.crtc.gc.ca/eng/publications/reports/policymonitoring/2008/cmr2008.htm

DTES Community Arts Network: http://dtescan.wordpress.com

Goldberg, K. (1990). *The barefoot channel: Community television as a tool for social change.* Vancouver, BC: New Star Books.

Lithgow, M. (in press). The (almost) invisible giant: Transformations of practice, policy and cultural citizenships within Canada's community television sector. In P. Mazepa, K. Kozolenko, & D. Skinner (Eds.), *Alternative media in Canada*. Vancouver, BC: UBC Press.

Telile. (n.d.). *History*. http://www.telile.tv/history.htm

COMMUNITY BROADCASTING AUDIENCES (AUSTRALIA)

The Australian community broadcasting sector is one of the oldest in the world, legally enshrined since the early 1970s under the Broadcasting Services Act of 1992. The sector's structure and operations are particularly interesting to community broadcasting movements elsewhere in the early days of officially establishing their own sectors. With almost 450 licensed broadcasters for around 20 million citizens, community broadcasting has grown exponentially since the early 1980s, more than threefold since 1991–1992. Successive Australian governments have rapidly granted licenses, and community groups have seized the opportunity.

The Australian community media sector, with both radio and television stations, is incredibly diverse. Community radio stations broadcast in more than 100 different languages, and 79 community television licenses service regional and remote Indigenous communities (many in the outback and some on remote islands). There are programs for visually impaired listeners (Radio for the Print Handicapped), religious listeners, youth, and marginalized political groups. Six generalist television stations service major cities. In around 40 Australian communities, community radio is the only broadcast service.

This entry summarizes a nationwide study of *why* people choose to use community media rather than other media forms and seeks to define the cultural and social role that community media play in society.

Australia's Broadcasting Sectors

The three tiers of Australian broadcasting consist of the commercial sector; the "public" government-funded Australian Broadcasting Corporation (ABC), and the Special Broadcasting Services (SBS) for multicultural communities; and the community sector. Although community media are considered the third tier, they have the most radio licenses. The commercial radio sector boasts 254, the community sector 450. In terms of audiences and funding, however, the community sector is certainly smaller than either of the others.

Importantly, though, community broadcasting's audience numbers are strong. Recent research indicates about 27% of Australians tune in to a community radio station at least once a week, and 57% at least once a month. This compares with about 64% in an average week who listen to commercial radio and 45% to the public broadcasters. But financially, the comparison reveals a stark contrast: The commercial radio sector annual turnover in the late 2000s was around A\$945 million; the combined ABC and SBS budget just over A\$1 billion, whereas the community radio sector operated with just under A\$51 million.

Despite this disparity in resources, community radio produces more local content, plays more Australian music, and supports a greater diversity of Australian cultures than its commercial counterparts. Additionally, ordinary community members are far more engaged with community media outlets than with either local commercial or public broadcasters, evidenced by the levels of volunteers present in the sector. In 2002, there were over 20,000 regular volunteers for the community radio sector alone, contributing more than \$145 million in unpaid work to the Australian economy each year. Additionally, community media volunteers appeared particularly dedicated, working at least 2½ times longer than volunteers in the general community.

To fulfill their licensing conditions, the community broadcasting sector operators must be not-for-profit; they must represent the community they have been licensed to represent; and significantly, they must encourage their communities to participate in station operations and program content. By advocating the participation of citizens in local broadcasting and thus supporting the community by broadcasting issues and ideas of immediate relevance to their everyday existence, community broadcasting has established itself as a real and relevant alternative to other radio services in many Australian cities and towns.

Australian Community Broadcasting Audiences

Our study of these audiences was informed by 48 audience focus groups around Australia: 25 for general audiences, 10 specifically for minority–ethnic language groups, 8 for Indigenous audiences, and 5 for community television audiences. We also conducted qualitative interviews with community groups who *access* community broadcasting, to determine the "community value" of each station, that is, the level of involvement and interaction between the media outlet and its community. In addition, more than 80 one-on-one interviews were conducted with Indigenous broadcasting audience members in remote regions and similar interviews with program presenters, station coordinators, and various ethnic group representatives.

In all, the fieldwork was gathered over 3 years and provides the first comprehensive view of community broadcasting audiences in Australia. Coupled with the quantitative data gathered by independent research group McNair Ingenuity, this qualitative audience study informs the sector at large, but also policymakers and researchers, about the nature of community media audiences and their primary reasons for listening or viewing.

The project's key findings indicate that the hugely diverse audiences accessed community media for four overarching reasons: (1) they wanted to access local news and information not provided by commercial and/or public broadcasts; (2) they wanted to hear diverse and specialist music formats; (3) community media outlets provided an important "community connection" they could not find anywhere else; and (4) the programming was socially and culturally diverse.

Audiences were quite explicit about the *nature* of what they liked. For example, many found community broadcasters to be accessible and approachable because they sounded "just like us"—like ordinary nonprofessionals. Indigenous audiences loved to hear their own voices on radio and felt Indigenous radio helped to maintain social networks and break down stereotypes about their communities. Minority-ethnic audiences particularly felt community broadcasting was essential in maintaining their cultures and languages and in providing local news and gossip absent from mainstream media. But whereas different audience sectors liked their various outlets for slightly different reasons, they were all united in identifying the key issues noted earlier.

Empowerment is a comprehensive term for most, if not all of the sector's operations, functions, and services. Community media do not empower everyone—some station processes observed during the 1999–2002 and 2003–2007 projects excluded individuals who did not fit the station's overall values and purpose. However, on a continuum of *potential* to empower, community media fare much better than other media. Rather than being subjected to the financial pressures that limit the broadcast options of commercial media, community media outlets in most democracies are free to disseminate the ideas, beliefs, and practices—in other words, the cultures—of a multitude of communities defined by interest, locality, or both. Community media, albeit not without their faults, empower everyday people with media access, the most powerful means for communicating culture.

Audiences additionally felt community media quite simply gave them a sense of being part of the community. At 3RRR, one of Australia's largest and oldest radio stations, located in Melbourne, an audience member summed up the feelings of many, noting the tendency of new technologies like the Internet to contribute to isolation:

> It [3RRR] is something that actually brings the community together, whereas a lot of the stuff in the world today seems to be isolating us. You know, you can get all the information you need, sitting at home in front of your computer. . . . Whereas, this is something that actually gives you a reason to get out and into your community, and a community that is open and accepting of you. (3RRR audience focus group, Melbourne, 2005)

Another participant at the 2FBi focus group, a youth-oriented radio station in Sydney, made a similar observation:

> The sort of product of today's society is that disassociation from your environment and you know, you're another number and you might be on a bit of a treadmill at work. You know what I mean, it's just some sort of meaning to your life as

well. Not that you don't have any elsewhere but you know, I hope you do. Yeah, just being a part of something bigger that's meaningful to you. (2FBi audience focus group, Melbourne, 2005)

Community radio stations were referred to as "social glue" in one community (Tumut, regional New South Wales in eastern Australia), because they broadcast discussions and events of interest and also inform audiences about events and activities taking place in the local area. In Byron Bay, a popular beachside tourist town about 6 hours north of Sydney, an audience member said:

I'd say "community glue." . . . It glues the community together in so many ways, and allows that opportunity to hear in-depth discussion about what matters to the community. The presenters get on air, and then there's a follow-up, so for me it's that nourishing community feeling and sense of understanding about what's going on in the community. (Bay FM audience focus group, Byron Bay, 2005)

A listener from Artsound, a specialist jazz and diverse music station in Canberra, the federal capital, reiterated:

Commercial radio makes me despair for this country and I find it quite depressing. And so listening to Artsound FM reminds me that not everybody belongs to commercial radio land and there is community out there. And in that sense, it's given me a sense of connectiveness and it also reminds me that it's necessary to keep striving for that—that it's not a natural or a given and that's one reason why I will support community radio because it's an alternative to the mass. (Artsound FM audience focus group, Canberra, 2005)

This study of community broadcasting audiences in Australia suggests community broadcasting—in all its diversity—is providing much-needed content that commercial and public broadcasters do not provide. Through its programming and its use of "average" voices on radio and on television, it encourages audience members to access the station and take part in the station's community network, because it suggests a nonprofessional environment

that puts audiences at ease. Importantly, community media are providing local news and information that the commercial broadcasters—which increasingly belong to larger global corporations—are no longer willing to provide.

Susan Forde

Note: The author wishes to acknowledge the contribution of colleagues Associate Professor Michael Meadows, Dr. Kerrie Foxwell, and Dr. Jacqui Ewart to the project upon which this paper is based.

See also Citizens' Media; Community Media (Venezuela); Community Media and the Third Sector; Community Radio (Haïti); Community Radio (Ireland); Community Radio in Pau da Lima (Brasil); Community Radio Movement (India); Free Radio (Austria)

Further Readings

Australian Communications and Media Authority. (2006). *Communications report 2005–06.* Melbourne, Australia: Author. Retrieved December 2, 2007, from http://www.acma.gov.au/CommsReport

CBOnline. (2006). *Community Broadcasting Database: Survey of the radio sector 2003–04 financial year* [Full report]. Sydney: Community Broadcasting Association of Australia.

CBOnline. (2007, December). *Community Broadcasting Database: Survey of the community radio sector, 2005–06 financial period* [Public release report]. http://www.cbonline.org.au/index.cfm?pageId =37,0,1,0

Downing, J. D. H. (2003). Audiences and readers of alternative media: The absent lure of the virtually unknown. *Media, Culture & Society, 25*(5), 625–645.

Forde, S., Meadows, M., & Foxwell, K. (2002). *Culture, commitment, community: The Australian community radio sector.* Brisbane, Australia: Griffith University. http://www.cbonline.org.au/index.cfm?pageId= 14,40,3,835

McNair Ingenuity Research. (2008, July 28). *Community Radio National Listener Survey* [Summary report of findings]. http://www.cbonline.org.au/media/McNair Listners2008/FullNationalListenerSurvey2008.pdf

Meadows, M., Forde, S., Ewart, J., & Foxwell, K. (2007, March). *Community media matters: An audience study of the Australian community broadcasting sector.* Brisbane, Australia: Griffith University. http:// www.cbonline.org.au/media/Griffith_Audience_ Research/reports/CommunityMediaMatters_final.pdf

COMMUNITY MEDIA (VENEZUELA)

As with everything else in Venezuela since President Hugo Chávez came to power in February 1999, public opinion concerning community media is divided between its supporters and opponents. For some, these media articulate the new organizational forms the so-called Bolivarian revolution has put in place to transfer power and voice to historically excluded sectors of the nation. For others, they articulate an authoritarianism that is seeking to colonize the public sphere, to silence democratic dissent, to capture the media system and gear it to indoctrination in support of the president's socialist project.

To understand how Venezuelans have reached this point, some history is needed to provide a context for the complex situation that has allowed the exponential growth of Venezuelan community media, along with the conflictual relationship they maintain with President Chávez's government.

The Context

Venezuelans do not know whether to laugh or cry at the oil wealth that has blessed and cursed them with equal abandon. One Venezuelan minister called hydrocarbons "the Devil's excrement," given the way they contaminate the air, the rivers, governmental ethics, and national morale. No one can reflect on Venezuela, including its community media, without thinking about the challenge black gold incarnates for those nations that enjoy its abundance.

Other nations have repeatedly interfered in the country's internal affairs, all the while that local elites have prospered through their political, economic, and cultural commitments to outside interests. Oil revenues in Venezuela financed inequality, bringing to birth a structure of socioeconomic privilege that guaranteed power to certain complicit and lazy elites in the face of the poverty that the majority of the 28 million people in today's Venezuela have suffered for decades. Up to 1999, oil revenues financed the apparent golden rule of social inequality: 20% of Venezuelans consumed 80% of the wealth, while the other 80% survived on the remaining 20%.

This same logic governed the development of Venezuela's media system. Up to the end of the 20th century, the state owned a television channel and a radio station with two channels (classical and light). This allowed the private commercial sector prime place, given the oligopolistic concentration of ownership in the hands of a few local companies, dependent in their turn on the U.S. consortia that dominate Latin America's technology, news, images, TV series, films, and advertising.

Thirty years of bad governments led this model rentier democracy to crisis in 1989, when the announcement of International Monetary Fund "structural adjustment" policies sparked 3 days of rioting and looting, stamped out by repression on a scale unprecedented in Venezuela's history. In 1992, Chávez, then a lieutenant colonel, led an attempted coup, and when Caracas stayed in the oligarchy's hands, Chávez was allowed to broadcast very briefly to urge his supporters elsewhere to surrender. Those 56 seconds, and his statement that they had only failed "for now" but that "new opportunities will arise again," became mythical and turned him into a new leader of people's illusions.

Thus, in December 1998, opposed by a single candidate representing the traditional elites, Chávez was elected president by the progressive middle class, leftist groups, and the majority of popular voters. He faced almost complete opposition from mainstream media, both then and since then.

Grassroots Media up to April 2002

When Chávez took power early in 1999, only two small community TV stations, TV Boconó and TV Rubio, had been able to obtain licenses, along with some church radio stations and TV operations geared to religious instruction and adult education. There were also a handful of illegal radio stations, such as Radio Catia Libre (Radio Free Catia—a Caracas neighborhood), which broadcast from a moving vehicle to avoid detection.

These grassroots activists pre-1999 broadly included three groups: those with no relation to the organizations that supported Chávez, before or after his ascent; those that were in sympathy with the Bolivarian movement and joined in its activities, but without organic links with the president's mobilization base; and those committed to organic links with both legal and clandestine organizations that contributed to his rise to power. This variety was valuable for the grassroots media movement, guaranteeing it a certain degree of organizational and ideological independence in the face of the new government's national project.

The Librecomunicación (Freecommunication) collective, for instance, was crucial in exerting pressure on the National Assembly to approve the new Telecommunications Law of 2000. The original draft did not really envisage permitting community licenses, and it was thanks to the mobilization of groups such as Onda Libre (Free Airwave), Librecomunicación, and the Committee for Public Service Broadcasting (Comité por una Radio-televisión de Servicio Público), that the act ultimately included various clauses (the 2nd, 12th, and 203rd) that guaranteed community usage, organized via broadcasting nonprofits. That summer, 60 nonprofits applied to the National Telecommunications Commission (CONATEL) for licenses.

The April 2002 Coup and After

During the 24 hours the coup lasted, the would-be president canceled all laws passed since Chávez's election, dissolved the National Assembly, and dismissed all mayors and state governors. Mainstream media kept silent about street and neighborhood protests demanding the president's return. Grassroots media, however, conducted an effective counterinformational campaign. Moreover, members of Caracas community stations such as Catia Libre and Radio Perola (Radio Saucepan) got the public TV channel (Venezolana de Televisión), which had been closed by force the day before the coup, back on the air.

Once Chávez was restored to power, many grassroots groups that previously had simply sympathized with the Bolivarian project began to bind themselves organically to it in their attitudes, their editorial lines, and their street actions. Likewise, the state adopted an aggressive communication policy that transformed it into what has been termed the "Communicator State." From then on, the radio and TV stations that some called "community," others "alternative," and still others "government," multiplied exponentially.

From 1936 through 1999, there had just been one local radio station and two local TV stations,

all other grassroots license applications having been denied. Between January 2002 and November 2008, 266 community broadcasters were registered, 38 of them TV stations. Another 600 licenses were being considered, and a further 1,300 projects were resisting having their status legalized. Nationally, 2,136 broadcasters were transmitting.

Whereas up to 1999 no communication legislation had stipulated community broadcasting rights, since then the 1999 Bolivarian Constitution, the 2000 Telecommunications Act, and the 2002 Public Service Open Community Regulation for Sound Broadcasting and Television jointly did so.

The majority of these new stations, along with print and digital media, which also increased exponentially, belonged to one of three national associations. La Red Venezolana de Medios Comunitarios (ReVeMec; the Venezuelan Community Media Network) had the most independence over time, though they supported the majority of government policies. El Movimiento de Medios Alternativos y Comunitarios (MoMaC; the Alternative and Community Media Movement) was openly committed to the Bolivarian revolution, as per its founding manifesto. La Asociación Nacional de Medios Comunitarios, Libres, y Alternativos (ANMCLA; the National Association of Community, Free and Alternative Media) was sympathetic to Chávez but, given ANMCLA's frequent confrontations, especially with CONATEL, not to his government bureaucracy.

There were also 16 regional networks, such as Cardumen al Viento (Shoal in the Wind) in Nueva Esparta state, Red Café (Café Network) in Táchira state, and REIRME (MAKEMELAUGH) in Mérida state, along with some local associations that housed radio stations, newspapers, and webpages.

Thus, community media were literally everywhere in the country, including various Indigenous radio and TV stations transmitting in their languages or bilingually.

A qualitatively important dimension was media–community interaction. Although not identical everywhere in scale and significance, most of the broadcasting nonprofits maintained active and organic links with their communities and, for the most part, provided program space for community reports on local issues. The strongest exemplars, such as Radio Perola, Radio Negro Primero

(First Black Radio), and Catia Libre in the capital, participated in and promoted street activities, literacy programs, arts and sporting gatherings, along with radio and TV programs entirely produced by children.

Finally, many stations developed groups of community producers as part of licensing conditions. These stations had to provide training workshops for their neighborhoods because of the requirement that 70% of programming had to be locally created.

Disquieting Trends

Along with these gains, other trends emerged that were not just discouraging, but disquieting and even regressive. First, sectarianism was evident in some independent broadcast news operations, denying access to opponents of Chávez's national project. In interviews with community media producers and spokespeople, they frequently would insist—candidly or fanatically—that every opinion was always welcome except for unhealthy criticism of the Bolivarian process or speech hostile to Commander Chávez.

A second worrying aspect was the low technical training of many independent and community producers, mostly because of inexperience in using the language of broadcasting. This led to programming on a poor creative level, both formally and aesthetically. For this reason, programming did not usually get beyond half the 70% required to be made by community and independent producers, so many stations filled the required transmission period with preprogrammed music, turning themselves not into "rock stations with ads," as used to be said of commercial stations, but into "rock stations with politics."

These features were disquieting, but other features of grassroots media behavior and transmissions have to be considered unacceptable. For a start, journalists, radio station operators, and TV operations that were hostile to Chávez's national project were physically attacked by activists. The most indicative case was perhaps the Alexis Vives Collective from the January 23 Precinct, which repeatedly harassed, spray painted, and assaulted the headquarters of the opposition channel Globovisión. Radio Arsenal, from the same precinct, openly supported these activities.

Next must be mentioned the pressure placed on CONATEL by grassroots media collectives to withdraw, refuse to renew, and not permit licenses for the few local broadcast operations that did not support the government.

Third was the growing dependence of these media on direct subsidies, equipment, premises, and advertising supplied by the state. In reality, these radio and TV stations had practically no self-financing strategies to ensure their sustainability over time. Most of them survived on the support provided by the numerous official policies designed to coalesce—or absorb—the grassroots media movements.

On this front, the state developed the following initiatives, among many others:

1. A plan for equipment and antenna supply

2. A plan for constructing and remodeling premises and studios

3. A plan to finance cell phones, with a preferential rate for community reporters

4. A plan to train radio, TV, and newspaper personnel, and webpage designers

5. A plan to develop locally generated technologies and equipment recycling

In the final analysis, the growing interconnection between these media and the Chávez administration turned out to be unacceptable. Some examples follow.

The People's Power Minister of Communication and Information transmitted from the premises of one of these local media, networked via public and community media, a monthly hour-long program titled *Communication in Revolution*. As of 2009, nine such programs were broadcast from Caracas and from Vargas, Bolívar, Miranda, Carabobo, and Zulia states.

The same ministry's webpage, along with the webpages of the National Assembly, the President's Office, Venezuela National Radio, Venezolana de Televisión, and the government online portal, among others, carried direct or indirect links to the various webpages of the community media. In their turn, many pages belonging to these grassroots broadcasters had direct or indirect links to various public bodies of the aforementioned agencies—some, moreover, to the Partido Socialista Unido de Venezuela (PSUV; Unified Socialist Party), of which Chávez was also president.

Participation by this party's activists was frequent on the management boards of various broadcasting nonprofits, despite dual membership being explicitly forbidden by the 2002 regulation.

There was a gap and often a split between a given grassroots media operation's editorial line and the religious, cultural, and political characteristics of its community. The key examples were in those precincts where local and regional opposition candidates had regularly won elections but where, nonetheless, licensed stations supported Chávez's national project and maintained an openly and aggressively confrontational editorial posture toward all other political forces. This caused irritation and a very frosty attitude toward the stations within communities that should see them as theirs.

The outward symbols that premises and activists of the community stations displayed marked them as *chavismo* supporters (shirts, flags, posters of Chávez and PSUV leaders). Right away this visual demarcation would frighten off any non-*chavista* citizen who might be interested in doing radio or TV in the precinct.

Conclusions

In 50 years, local communication movements from Venezuela's grassroots never enjoyed so much activism, so much power, and so much social muscle as they did in the 2000s. At the same time, never before were they so threatened with being disempowered, absorbed, and nullified by the power structure's regressive operations. Never before were they so close to being reduced to the pathetic role of being repeater stations, ventriloquists for the most dogmatic and militaristic and least progressive sector of President Chávez's national project. Still worse, they had never previously been so close to slipping into being ensnared and effectively vanishing, subverted—despite their enormous resources and potential—by the dead weight pulling down the wings of the so-called beautiful revolution.

Although undoubtedly these media represented a new broadcasting circuit in Venezuela, their independence and the elimination of state tutelage would be essential if they were to merit description as community, alternative or free. There is no point waiting day by day for this to happen, or expecting "neutrality" in such a conflictive context. But it is possible to desire and demand independence of judgment and measured passion, and it is vital to soften and break down the polarization destroying Venezuela.

María Fernanda Madriz
(translated by John D. H. Downing)

See also Community Radio (Ireland); Community Radio in Pau da Lima (Brasil); Community Radio Movement (India); Miners' Radio Stations (Bolivia); Peace Media (Colombia); Radio La Tribu (Argentina); Women's Radio (Austria)

Further Readings

Aporrea.org, Section of Media, Alternative, Community and Free Communication: http://www.aporrea.org/medios

Ciudadanía Activa (Active Citizenship): http://www.ciudadaniaactiva.org

López Vigil, J. I. (2008). *Ciudadana radio* [Citizen radio]. Caracas, Venezuela: Ministerio de Comunicación e Información.

Madriz, M. F. (in press). A day of programming on three community radio stations in Caracas. *Anuario ININCO*.

Pasquali, A. (2007). La libertad de expresión bajo el régimen chavista: mayo de 2007 [Freedom of expression under the Chávez regime: May 2007]. *Signo y Pensamiento* [Bogotá], *50*, 264–275.

Venezuelan Ministry of Communication and Information, General Direction of Alternative and Community Media: http://www.minci.gob.ve/medios_comunitarios/41

COMMUNITY MEDIA AND THE THIRD SECTOR

Across every region of the globe, the early days of community broadcasting were full of protest, rebellion, and technical wizardry: mobile broadcasters operating illegally from the back of vans (United States), students barricading themselves in radio studios to avoid closure (Australia), video activists inserting their own productions into cable programming (Italy), and singing the news on air when it was against the King's command to announce it (Nepal). In some countries, community broadcasting has resulted in more sinister outcomes: military attacks, loss of life, and imprisonment (Bolivia and Thailand, for example).

The history of community media contains such extreme episodes because of its challenge to the dominant paradigm of broadcasting control. This entry examines what it means to construct a separate mediasphere for community use. The campaign for community media has been a battle for resources and legislative provision for nonprofit, accessible media outlets, designed to serve those who are not otherwise represented in the media. The "Third Sector" of media requires laws and organizational structures significantly different from those of commercial and public service broadcasting.

Of course, there is much more to community media than the policy limitations imposed upon them. Starting from the policy perspective, however, two broad themes are uncovered: First, it can help us to understand how community media fit within broader structures of the media and society. Second, digital media are radically altering the playing field in terms of community media's core principles: access and participation. The guidelines that determine what, until recently, has been thought of as "community media" arose in the second half of the 20th century when the broadcast media reigned. As the Internet becomes the dominant communicative platform, it is worth revisiting that history in order to determine whether community media is still a relevant concept.

The Beginnings of Community Media

The dominant policy model of community media emerged in the 1960s when countries such as Canada, Australia, and the United States began making provision for community use of the radio spectrum and cable television. The model was refined and promoted through international forums, such as UNESCO's New World Information and Communication Order debates and AMARC (the World Association of Community Radio Broadcasters), as well as at the national policy level. The key elements of community media policy were nonprofit associations, owned and operated by the community they were intended to serve, and designed to provide access, training, and the means to participate in media production.

In reality, community media often relied on government support by way of regulation, resources, or both, and some market interactions for sustainability. However, the motivations for community media were separate from the nation-building aspirations of public service media and were more likely to be local in orientation. Furthermore, even with some form of advertising, money making was not their sole concern. Community media began from cultural or political agendas, along with technical curiosity and an aspiration to be part of the media. Amateurism and volunteerism were common factors of community media endeavors.

Community Media and Community

Without a shared understanding of what community media means, community media activists may find themselves quickly outdated. Does community media mean all amateur media production? What is their relationship to social networking media? Such questions are important because they cause us to consider what belongs in the public domain and what is produced through commercial enterprise. At the policy level, the answers may have implications for resourcing for, and institutional limits upon, community media.

Community media can be difficult to define because the term *community* is so amorphous and diverse. Communities emerge on the basis of hobbies, religion, ethnicity, politics, fandom, sports, sexuality, age, and many other factors. Some endure while others are fleeting. The term *community sector* can refer to clubs, informal networks, and allegiances. Large organizations within the charity sector are also termed *community organizations* when they are run as nonprofit associations. Therefore, the word *community* spans loose networks, affiliations, and highly structured institutions. Community media organizations generally sit somewhere in the middle.

If we break down the concept of community even further, we are essentially talking about *social connectedness*—the way in which we, as individuals, are embedded within our local, cultural, and national context. We do not live in isolation but interact, learn, and survive through other people. Communitarian theory is thus a correction to Western individualist notions of society and human nature, rooted in the Enlightenment era's idea of individual freedom and the free market as the conditions under which society can best function.

Communitarianism does not reject these principles, but adds another layer. Communitarian theorists argue that specific laws and allowances need to be made to accommodate and support community associations, minority groups, and those in need. Community media fit within this framework as a mediasphere deliberately created for community purposes.

The arguments for or against community media rest on one central issue: whether natural affiliations and groups should be regulated, protected, or encouraged. Those that argue in favor of community media believe that without specific structures to support the media of ordinary citizens (as opposed to professional media), many voices will go unheard. On the other side of the debate, some doubt that community media will ever be more than a few ardent media enthusiasts pursuing their own interests, and that commercial and public service media do a better job at representing the world.

Can we ensure that institutional arrangements for community media provide equitable access to all community groups? Do some groups require greater resources and encouragement to participate? Does the licensing process crystallize communities that would otherwise have evolved? Will the social benefit be tangible? For community media organizations, the practical complexity of community arises every day in the way that volunteers are managed, how programming policies get made, and how issues and stories are reported.

To add to the complexity, the social role of community media changes according to the way organizations are structured. In Ireland in the 2000s, community radio was considered an important means for addressing the country's sharply new experience of multiculturalism. Community radio, in this instance, was a policy partly designed to address an area that the market and government could not adequately, or easily, serve. Thus, although community media were governed by the community, they were nonetheless also endorsed, resourced, and protected through law to achieve social outcomes the state considered important to the nation overall.

The operationalization of community may then be a governmental technique to achieve certain ends. Communities exist independently, yet the state can create institutional and legal frameworks to enable community knowledge and networks to accomplish social outcomes. As Nikolas Rose argues, the third space, or community sector, can become the target for the exercise of political power, while remaining outside of politics and even acting as a counterweight to it.

Community Media in the Broadcast Era

In most democracies, the newspaper industry has largely acted independently of regulation. Broadcasting, however, was managed by government agencies and legislation. In cable, community television operators have had to negotiate with commercial infrastructure owners, who were in turn answerable to regulators. As Thomas Streeter points out, broadcasting and cable were essentially an administrative space, where the government granted access. Thus, community media have positioned themselves as an attempt to take back a portion of the airwaves—seeing spectrum as a shared resource owned by the people to be held in the public trust.

The reasons for licensing community media have varied. In Europe, community broadcasting challenged public service broadcasters' dominance. It formed part of broadcasting's decentralization, which at that time contested dominant notions of the public interest. In some cases, such as the U.K. community television pilots, community media were supported by the commercial sector as a means to demonstrate their community service— sourly framed in some quarters as an alliance between mercenaries and missionaries. This encouraged suspicion of community media, which was also thought to be too amateur, thereby lowering broadcasting standards. Public service media traditionally existed to discipline tastes and create an informed citizenry. In contrast, community broadcasting was seen as displaying low quality and generating questionable benefits.

In the United States, the main challenge to community media has come from the commercial sphere. Thousands of micro-radio (local, low power) broadcasters emerged in the 1990s, all operating illegally. After considerable lobbying, Congress okayed low power community licenses in 2000. This was incredibly important, but these stations are small and get bumped (pushed out) if a major broadcaster successfully claims they interfere with that broadcaster's signal.

Access television in the United States, otherwise known as PEG (public, educational, and government channels), also faced significant threats stemming from commercial television expansion. From the late 1970s, municipal authorities negotiated access channels and funding with cable companies during the franchise agreement process. With the advent of digital broadband, telecommunication companies (in particular AT&T) began providing video-on-demand services via cable. The legislation that paved the way for video-on-demand undermined municipal power over franchise agreements and led to a significant decline in access funding.

In Australia, where community broadcasting had strong legislative endorsement and provision, the principal threat has come from digital broadcasting. Australia's first community radio stations began appearing in the 1960s. In 1992, the government created a specific community broadcasting license, enshrining community broadcasting in legislation as the third tier of broadcasting (previously, stations operated under experimental and educational licenses). More than 400 community radio stations and a handful of community television stations emerged as a result. When digital television and radio transmission were introduced (2001 and 2009, respectively), the community sector found itself marginalized, with most new channels handed over to incumbent commercial and public service broadcasters or set aside for spectrum auctions.

All in all, community media did not have an easy run during the broadcast era and its status was marginal at best. Critics argued community media would never be able to compete with the professional media for audiences, that they are aesthetically inferior or a waste of resources, including spectrum. And that's just in Western democracies. Where community media emerged outside of this context, they have had even tougher issues to contend with.

Democracy and Development

The rapid growth of communications technology has had a contradictory influence on community media in the global South as well as in newly democratized states. On the one hand, digital information and communication technologies have assisted burgeoning civil society networks, which are in turn making strong demands for access to media platforms, including television and radio. However, in some parts of the globe, the rush by governments to reform communications policy has been haphazard and exclusionary.

Community media have emerged as a strong force in Asia. Historically state-run media have typically served undemocratic governments or military regimes in many parts of the region. Moreover, commercial media outlets do not necessarily produce the level of information and debate needed in liberal democracies. Community media are largely a response, often motivated by activist causes. However, coming late to community media has meant that campaigners, groups, and policymakers have been able to learn from the experience of other countries. India developed its policy for community media in late 2006, allowing communities to own and manage FM radio stations. Previously, communities and nongovernmental organizations (NGOs) had been forced to buy airtime from government stations.

One of the most valuable models of community television is South Korea's RTV, established in 2002. South Korea is a global North nation that had been subject to despotic rulers and political upheaval up until the late 1980s. South Korean community media developed with a strong commitment to minority representation and democratic values. RTV is a cable and satellite provided channel, run via a nonprofit organization, dedicated to openness, independence, and fairness. Openness refers to the access policy, whereby members of the general public can submit programs for screening, free of charge. Independence describes the programming and operations of the station.

Fairness, however, is what distinguishes RTV from many other community television channels. To achieve this, RTV established two committees to oversee program planning, selection, and grants. These committees are intentionally separate from station management and give priority to under-privileged and minority groups as well as to issues neglected by mainstream media. By providing funding, training, and free equipment loans to programmers, RTV nurtures small production groups based around social justice issues. Regular programs included migrant and Korean workers' news, disabled rights, and media education. In 2007, RTV had a budget of 3.17 billion won (US$3.4 million at the time), including 1.5 billion won (US$1.6 million) in grants from the government's Broadcasting Promotion Fund. Approximately 800 million won (US$800,000) went directly to programmers.

In 2008, RTV experienced a dramatic change of fortune when the government withdrew its financial support. Why was RTV's government-derived budget terminated? South Korea had elected a new president, Lee Myang-bak, in 2007. The former Hyundai Corporation chief executive officer began pursuing aggressively free-market policies. A publicly supported, community-run television channel did not fit this agenda.

In the global South more widely, community media projects are often funded through donor agencies to build democratic media or to provide health, education, and peace information and to promote participation and community ownership. Since the 1990s, NGOs began to direct their funding toward projects that are run by local people with respect for cultural difference and language maintenance. Donor agencies and NGOs thus began implementing community media on a participatory media model.

Community media can be an important factor in creating social change, particularly in places where the media are tightly controlled. Outcomes, however, are not always clear-cut. First, there is the issue of sustainability. What happens when project money runs out? In the global North, community media often depend on volunteers. Relying on an unpaid work ethic can be a problem where adequate labor conditions and basic survival needs are not being met. The idea that civil society can exist in any context needs questioning.

The other issue facing development-centered community media is how outcomes are measured. Grant-based funding systems, backed by donor agencies, expect measurability and major social outcomes. Yet community media

projects may never be able to solve issues that stem from deep-seated poverty, conflict, and political disenfranchisement. Community media projects are often judged upon criteria that they will never be able to meet. Has a community media project failed if tangible socioeconomic outcomes are not achieved? Are there other, less immediately visible outcomes, such as long-term skills or personal empowerment, which are also important? When we attempt to define communities as knowable and measurable entities, we are missing the point. The strength of community media lies in their unpredictable nature, diverse strategies, and surprising results.

Transitions and Complexity in Community Media

Gaining access to the tightly controlled space of broadcasting has been such a difficult endeavor that, for a long time, advocacy arguments dominated descriptions and theoretical assumptions. The overarching discourse surrounding community media was that they could counteract mainstream media biases and democratize the airwaves. Although there is some truth in that, we also need to acknowledge the more mundane, sometimes conservative, qualities community media bring into the media environment.

When access is implemented through communications policies, a range of voices, opinions, and ideas will become part of the mediasphere. Not all will be progressive, or compelling. The reality is that community media involve ordinary folk producing all kinds of content, some of which may be narrow in focus, prejudiced, unskilled, or uninformed. Furthermore, we know that community media is democratic in that it promotes free speech, but often its outcomes are small-scale and transient.

For many people, participation in community media is a matter of self-expression, creativity, and experimentation, rather than engagement with a media political practice. Rather than viewing community media as a singular, cohesive project, community media theorists are now acknowledging them as a complex, transient terrain. Community media practice is a cultural strategy that occurs on multiple fronts rather than as a united movement.

New Media

The rules are now changing as digital platforms become more dominant. The Internet fulfilled early community media activists' vision: If technology could be made accessible and affordable, then people would participate on a massive scale. Yet if access and participation have been achieved via the Internet, do governments need to continue setting aside resources for community media use? The question, although rarely spoken, is surely on the minds of those who govern broadcast spectrum.

Not so long ago, community media were the most obvious means for nonprofessionals to participate in media production. Now, anyone can easily create, distribute, or contribute to informational and creative works. In direct contrast to the traditional media, these sites and activities are not always easily identifiable as community, commercial, or public service media. We are witnessing a convergence not just across platforms but across the three traditional media sectors.

However, essential differences remain. Community media outlets are focused on social needs, training, not-for-profit business models, open technologies, and community governance. Furthermore, the Internet is not free from government or corporate control. Nation-states restrict access through filters, laws, and surveillance. Corporations can control access via infrastructure ownership, proprietary measures, and search engines. In contrast, online community media groups are often dedicated to open source technologies and philosophies. This keeps information and technological innovations in the public domain.

Community media are therefore important in terms of information rights. Retaining community media (as a media objective and as a sector) will provide spaces where we can participate in the media without having to worry about commercial use of private data, and where technologies are open and collaborative rather than proprietary and closed. At the content level, this may also entail trustworthy, independent, and diverse viewpoints.

Although in theory anyone can participate in media production and distribution via the Internet, deeper media engagement requires skills and an understanding of the limits and responsibilities of communication. Community media organizations provide training and media experience, a kind of media workplace where ideas and skills are shared.

Community media outlets thereby act as intermediaries between the amateur and the professional, allowing people to participate in sophisticated production, yet with a high degree of self-direction. Participating also means getting access to an established audience. The responsibility that comes with that can bring real competencies and ethical standards.

Conclusion

Community media have rarely been a central concern in broadcasting policy. What they represented in the broadcast era, however, was a significant challenge to the various ways the airwaves were used and managed. They defied the assumption that top-down public institutions should decide what the public should be watching and listening to. And they sought to hold commercial media to account by questioning corporate control of information and the fact that nation-states sanctioned that power. Most importantly, community media brought a range of new voices into the mediascape and helped pave the way for a new media paradigm where diversity and participation are celebrated.

By looking at the debates and theories that surround the governance of community generally, we can see that the struggles over community media in the broadcast era are inseparable from important questions of democracy and individual liberty. From a policy perspective, the status of community media is essentially a matter of how we manage, assist, endorse, or deny the natural zone of social connectedness.

In the digital era, making a case for community media requires new thinking. Communities and individuals can now be seen and heard without having to overcome substantial regulatory barriers. Therefore, describing community media according to access and participation no longer adequately distinguishes community media from other media. But we do need to consider what structures are required to ensure that social benefits flow from media participation. Our descriptions of community media need to refocus attention away from access and participation and toward information rights and digital literacy.

Information rights, then, mean more than net neutrality and anticensorship. For community media, they mean open source technologies, privacy in terms of data use, and dedication to editorial openness. In terms of digital literacy, we need to expand our definitions beyond basic training and use toward an understanding of how producers engage with audiences and the creation of new content forms through experimentation and collaboration.

For communications theory, this means looking at users and audiences, not just production. Where community media researchers have mostly focused on participation and individual or community empowerment via self-expression, it is important to consider the way in which different kinds of media are received in the digital environment. That means reexamining why people listen to, read, or watch community media. The answer will help to define the role of community media into the digital age.

Community media can play an important role in assisting us to navigate the new media environment, make ethical choices about what kind of media we participate in, and enable us to participate at all levels: technical, production, and organizational decision making. Widespread participation in the media via digital technologies doesn't necessary mean that the role of community media is over. In fact, from this perspective, it has barely begun.

Ellie Rennie

See also Alternative Media; Citizens' Media; Community Radio (Ireland); Community Radio Movement (India); Copyleft; Creative Commons; Grassroots Tech Activists and Media Policy; Media Infrastructure Policy and Media Activism; Migrant Workers' Television (Korea); Participatory Media; *Radical Software* (United States)

Further Readings

Escobar, A. (1995). *Encountering development: The making and unmaking of the third world.* Princeton, NJ: Princeton University Press.
Jacka, L. (2003). "Democracy as defeat": The impotence of arguments for public service broadcasting. *Television and New Media, 4*(2), 177–191.
Lewis, P. M. (1978). *Community television and cable in Britain.* London: British Film Institute.
Rennie, E. (2006). *Community media: A global introduction.* Lanham, MD: Rowman & Littlefield.
Rodríguez, C. (2001). *Fissures in the mediascape.* Cresskill, NJ: Hampton Press.
Rose, N. (1999). *Powers of freedom: Reframing political thought.* Cambridge, UK: Cambridge University Press.
Streeter, T. (1996). *Selling the air: A critique of the policy of commercial broadcasting in the United States.* Chicago: University of Chicago Press.
Walzer, M. (1995). The communitarian critique of liberalism. In A. Etzioni (Ed.), *New communitarian thinking* (pp. 53–70). Charlottesville: University Press of Virginia.
Wilkins, K. G. (Ed.). (2000). *Redeveloping communications for social change.* Lanham, MD: Rowman & Littlefield.
Young, I. M. (1990). The ideal of community and the politics of difference. In L. J. Nicholson (Ed.), *Feminism/postmodernism* (pp. 300–323). New York: Routledge.

COMMUNITY RADIO (HAÏTI)

Haïti's 1991–1994 military regime ended after 3 years of steady resistance inside the country, coupled with predemocracy mobilization in North America and Europe. President Jean-Bertrand Aristide made an agreement with the Clinton administration that allowed him to return to power, but only in exchange for making drastic neoliberal economic reforms. A muted and compromised Aristide came back to the National Palace accompanied by some 20,000 Marines, the second of Haïti's U.S. military occupations.

The conditions initially mattered little to most people. The brutally repressive police and army were gone; the muzzle was off again. A second explosion of political communication appeared to be in the making. But a combination of factors—some of them peculiar to Haïti, others common in the global South—meant a much less encouraging scenario was in play. Haïti's community radio experience provides important lessons.

Community Radio or People's Radio?

All over the country, but especially in the capital, grassroots groups and the nonprofits that supported them immediately got back to holding press conferences and seminars to air complaints, issue manifestos, call for strikes, or form new political parties. *Libète* (published in Kreyòl, or Haïtian Creole) and other newspapers were once again on street corners. Dozens of new commercial radio and television stations sprang up, and shuttered ones reopened, partly because new communications technologies made low power equipment more affordable.

The real communication revolution was in community radio. Taking Latin American *radios populares* (people's radio stations) as their models, youth groups, farmers' organizations, nongovernmental organizations (NGOs), and unions set up stations in many small towns and villages. Between 1995 and 2000, more than 30 community and people's radio stations launched. (In Haïti, organizations claimed their stations were *radyo popilè* or "people's radios," rather than "community radios," if they considered themselves part of a political and/or social movement struggle.)

Many of the more radical stations had names like Farmer's Voice Radio, People's Liberation Radio, Rebel, People's Voice Radio, Wozo, and Tènite stations (*wozo* is a bamboo plant that, even in violent storms, "bends but does not break" according to the Haïtian proverb; *tènite* is a grass that withstands brutal sun and heat). The founders said their stations would be part of a struggle for "total, complete change," for "another kind of society," for "justice."

But most were not strictly homegrown. Foreign and local NGOs and UNESCO, excited about taking part in the reconstruction of Haïti's democracy, rushed into the country with huge funds for equipment and training. They hired trainers, organized seminars, and even helped create programming. In some cases, the NGOs went so far as to go into the field and handpick which towns would receive the stations, setting up the "grassroots" organizations themselves.

A study by Regan—assisted by the Haïtian NGO Sosyete Animasyon Kominikasyon Sosyal (Society for Social Communication), one of the two NGOs that did most of the training—showed that overwhelmingly, the new stations did not deliver on their promises of resistance and rebellion. Although grassroots groups' drive to set up the radios was certainly real, many, if not most, lacked the organizational, ideological, and perhaps even the political capacity to do so. In an atmosphere where unconscious paternalism often overpowered

the avowed belief in empowerment, the challenges were even greater. Local and foreign NGOs either failed to grasp the conditions for such stations' success or, anxious to get on the air, decided to overlook them in the rush.

Radio Enriquillo's Father Rouquoy was one of the champions of the movement. He acknowledged the stations were set up hastily, with more concern for equipment than organization, as the Regan study cites him as saying,

> I remember that there was a big discussion in Washington and some said, "But they won't be able to manage them! It will be disorganized!" But I said, "That's not what's important now. It's important for everyone in Haïti, all the community organizations, to get a little radio station. Let's organize that, and afterwards we'll see how we can organize them, how we can coordinate them."

Most of the groups were collections of like-minded young activists, usually dominated by one or several men, without a broad base or mechanisms through which community members could participate. Top-down leadership marginalized participation within the groups also, and as the decade wore on, most of the once-flourishing popular and social movement organizations had dwindled to small handfuls of members. Some scholars have argued that in fact, many of these organizations had lost their vision as early as 1990, back when Aristide—an icon of Haïti's post-Duvalier social and political movements—morphed from priest to presidential candidate. Many had felt they must choose between supporting his candidacy or continuing their more radical struggles for land reform and social and economic justice, and they usually chose the former.

Additional Obstacles to People's Radio

In addition, repression prior to and during the 1991–1994 military regime had eliminated or scared away many of the grassroots organization leaders and members who had steered clear of electoral politics. Repression continued—albeit at a much lower level—after Aristide's return. Several of the new community or people's radio stations, specifically those critical of the government, were threatened or attacked by local police or local elected officials from Aristide's Lavalas party. Following the coup, the Lavalas and other smaller parties recruited heavily among grassroots organizations. Station activists became operatives, government employees, and even candidates for political office.

Finally, the economic factor cannot be overlooked. The poorest country in the hemisphere, Haïti's economic and social indicators declined steadily throughout the 1990s. Unemployment was at least 60% during the late 1990s and, according to the World Bank, two thirds of Haïti's rural residents lived below the absolute poverty line. Economic pressure on station volunteers on the one hand, and the seductive power of foreign money on the other, impacted even the most idealistic grassroots organizers.

The NGOs' decision to rush in with equipment and funding also dealt a brutal blow to the stations' local credibility. For decades dependent on both foreign assistance and remittances, Haïti is afflicted with what many call a "culture of dependency." The foreign funding increased this mentality among the stations' backers on the one hand, and on the other, convinced community members that they did not need to contribute money for basic running costs.

The lack of financial commitment from the stations' communities can also be explained by the fact that most of the stations did not encourage or empower local residents. Although people were clearly proud of having "their own" radio station, it was seen more as telephone than radio, because participation was limited to the delivery of messages—about a cockfight, a funeral, or a stolen goat—not for public debate.

Creative Associates International

By 2004, 7 of the 30 stations born between 1994 and 2000 were off the air. Most of the rest were run as private stations by a small group of people (mostly men), contracted with Creative Associates International (CAI), which calls itself an NGO. In reality, CAI is a U.S. government–funded institution with close State Department ties, which has won hundreds of millions to carry out "democracy enhancement" projects around the world: supporting the Nicaraguan contras in the 1980s, rewriting

school textbooks for Iraq in the 2000s. Haïti's community radio movement offered a direct line to Haïti's rural masses.

CAI quickly got most of Haïti's fledgling stations on board. In exchange for a CAI contract, they got more powerful audio equipment and generators and could send dozens of volunteers to free CAI seminars. In turn, they were required to play a 12-part educational radio play and to open up their management to all community members, even those whose public record was hostile to democracy. Stations were required to adhere to "balance and neutrality" (which in a polarized and unequal situation begs the critical question of balance between what, and neutrality toward what).

By the time the project ended in 2005, CAI had spent over $600,000 on equipment, had signed up 40 stations, had increased the coverage of CAI-affiliated stations to 80% of Haïtian territory, had trained 122 radio professionals, and had hosted two national conferences.

A few of the community and people's stations resisted CAI's clarion call. Not surprisingly, these were the few stations embedded in the community and backed by a still-existing organization. Most notable was Radio Voice of the Peasant (RVP), founded by Mouvman Peyizan Papay (MMP; Papaye Peasant Movement). Of the nearly 30 stations Regan's study surveyed, RVP was the most participatory, encouraging community members to become "reporters" and relying on its neighbors for donations of cash or, in many cases, produce, which RVP could sell to buy gasoline for the generator.

The morphing of the other stations—from political and social movement–oriented to merely local radio stations—came as no surprise, as the democratic movement was also at perhaps its lowest point in 20 years. As the Regan study reports, one radio station member said, "The popular struggle has been broken" and noted its consequences for radios, which were supposed to represent the demands of the masses. "We were supposed to accompany the movement, but if the movement is dead, what is our role?" Thus, as Haïti's more radical social movement organizations weakened and even disappeared, so too did the "people's" or "grassroots" aspects of the new radio stations.

Jane Regan

See also Community Broadcasting (Canada); Community Media and the Third Sector; Community Radio (Sri Lanka); Community Radio in Pau da Lima (Brasil); Community Radio Movement (India); Community Radio Stations (Brasil); Miners' Radio Stations (Bolivia); Radio La Tribu (Argentina); Social Movement Media, 1991–2010 (Haïti)

Further Readings

Creative Associates International, Inc. (2006). *Media Assistance and Civic Education Program (RAMAK) final report.* http://pdf.usaid.gov/pdf_docs/PDACH582.pdf

Jean, J.-C., & Maesschalck, M. (1999). *Transition politique en Haïti—radiographie du pouvoir Lavalas* [Political transition in Haïti—X-ray of the Lavalas power structure]. Paris: L'Harmattan.

Regan, J. (2008). Baboukèt la tonbe!—The muzzle has fallen! *Media Development, 2,* 12–17.

René, J. A. (2003). *La séduction populiste: essai sur la crise systémique haïtienne et le phénomène Aristide, 1986–1991* [The populist seduction: Essay on Haïti's systemic crisis and the Aristide phenomenon]. Port-au-Prince: Bibliothèque nationale d'Haïti.

COMMUNITY RADIO (IRELAND)

As of 2009, there were 21 licensed community radio stations in Ireland. This may seem small, but Ireland has just over 4 million people. The experience these stations have to share with community media activists internationally is valuable as they have developed a philosophy of community radio forged from collective reflection on their experience. This philosophy is encapsulated in a definition of community radio employed by the regulatory authority but developed by the community stations themselves. Sharing a vision and a set of core aims, these 21 stations, in a wealthy and developed nation, work primarily with the marginalized population and usually in a community development manner. The regulatory authority has an open, friendly relationship with the stations they license, a partnership devoted to community building and to empowering individuals through their participation in broadcasting.

There are two types of Irish community stations currently licensed. These are defined in terms of geographic communities and communities of interest. Sixteen serve geographic communities. They range from the 10,000 people scattered over a rugged terrain of 300 square miles, including two off-shore islands, served by Connemara Community Radio, to one quarter of Dublin's population, nearly 250,000 people, served by NEAR FM. Communities of interest licenses have been granted to students in three major cities (Cork, Galway, and Limerick), named respectively Cork Campus Radio, FLIRT FM, and Wired FM; to a Christian faith community in Cork; and to the scattered community of Irish speakers living in greater Dublin.

History and Aims

The 1988 Broadcasting Act broke the 62-year legal monopoly of the public service broadcaster, RTÉ, and allowed for the licensing of independent, commercial, and community radio. A regulatory authority, that underwent several name changes—from Independent Radio and Television Commission (IRTC), to Broadcasting Commission of Ireland (BCI), to Broadcasting Authority of Ireland (BAI)—was established to license and monitor the sector. Licensed commercial, local, and national radio stations began broadcasting in 1989, but community groups had to wait longer.

In 1993, two community stations, both in Dublin, were granted licenses as a result of successful political lobbying. The demand continued for other community stations to be licensed. The regulatory authority decided to establish an 18-month pilot project to examine the viability of community stations before issuing long-term licenses. Invitations to participate were advertised in the press in 1994, and in 1995, 11 community stations began broadcasting.

One of the key achievements arising out of this pilot project, apart from the survival of nine of these stations 4 years later, was the development of a definition of *community radio*. This definition declares that any group seeking a community radio license must be representative of their community in ownership, management, and programming and must operate on a not-for-profit basis. The station must be open to participation at the levels of membership, management, operation, and programming, and it must be able to define the community it serves.

This definition enables stations with diverse perspectives, coming from very different types of communities, to work together as a sector and as a movement. It facilitates the licensing and support of community radio stations in a clear and transparent manner. It prevents other groups from laying claim to community credentials and licenses when, perhaps, they are solely music oriented and profit driven.

Another significant outcome of the pilot project was the establishment of the Community Radio Forum of Ireland, now called Craol, the Irish word for "to broadcast." All licensed community stations on air are members of this network, and community groups aspiring to broadcast are welcomed and supported in making their applications. Craol's work is assisted by the regulatory authority through easy access to its officers, advice on scheduling and the care of volunteers, and through a number of funding schemes for development, evaluation, and training.

The network initially had one paid executive, supported by a volunteer committee elected by stations and organized as a cooperative. This appointment and the website together greatly facilitated communication among community radio activists. Craol organized many training events throughout the year in diverse locations and for specific needs. Its single biggest event is a national training festival or Féile. Hosted by a different station each year, Féile invites up to 150 participants for a weekend of training, learning, and networking. Stations choose different participants to go each year so that learning is maximized and shared on return with others.

Ownership and Management

Community radio in Ireland is changing extremely fast, and the following account describes developments up to early 2010. Each of these licensed stations was owned by the community it had been licensed to serve. Sometimes this was in partnership with an existing community development body. This was the case with Radio Pobal Inis Eoghan (ICR) in County Donegal in the north of the country and Radio Corca Baiscinn (RCB) in County Clare on the western seaboard.

More stations were owned by cooperative societies (co-ops) that anyone in the target community could join for a nominal fee. Shares were unlimited in number but did not pay dividends. Shares were used to fund-raise and to sharpen awareness of collective ownership. They formed a minimal part of the station budget. Each person or organization had only one vote, regardless of the number of shares purchased. Examples of this type of station included NEAR FM and Dublin South FM, both in the capital city.

Some community stations opted to form limited companies, but here too, nondividend shares were offered to all members of the community at a nominal price. Campus community radio stations were owned by the students in partnership with their institution or their student union or both.

No matter which model, each of Ireland's community stations had a board of management, democratically elected, to develop long-term policy and run the station. These boards had to comprise community members and, in every case, the majority of board members were volunteers. A gender balance had to be ensured. This was a licensing requirement, but in almost all cases it was reflected in practice.

In most stations, a paid manager, assisted by a subcommittee or executive of volunteers nominated by this board, managed the station day to day. Irish community radio stations collectively devised a circular-flow model of continuously linking management to community listeners that now forms part of BCI community radio policy. (The term *circular flow* is derived from economics, where it denotes the flow of goods between producers and households.)

Finance

Almost every Irish community radio station depended on other paid staff to assist the manager. How these were funded often proved problematic. They varied considerably over time as Ireland moved from widespread unemployment, through the boom of the Celtic Tiger phase, and back into recession. Stations varied in their reliance on government-funded back-to-work and disability employment schemes and on positions provided through grant-aided projects.

It is a basic tenet of the community radio movement and a contractual condition for Irish community radio stations to be funded from a variety of sources. Advertising was allowed, capped by the regulator at 50% of all income, but this percentage had not been reached by any Irish community station as of 2009. This was partly because commercial advertisers did not show interest and also because activists were keen to maintain their editorial independence.

The greatest single sources of funding for Irish community radio stations were grants from government departments, nongovernmental organizations, and the European Union. Stations rarely managed to secure funding to make programs. Instead, they depended on funding for training or for interventions with marginalized or disadvantaged sectors. Examples included adult literacy work by Community Radio Castlebar, a training project by West Dublin Access Radio with reformed drug addicts, a production course with young people with disabilities in Wired FM, and a multitude of projects involving the participation of new immigrants and disaffected youth in nearly every station in the country.

Other sources of income included local sponsorship, fund-raising in the community, off-air commercial activity such as studio rental, equipment training, and membership shares. As of 2009, no funding agency recognized the important contribution of these stations to developing their communities. This meant that the costs had to be met from elsewhere. However, stations survived, carefully choosing the projects for which they applied for funding to match their aims and ethos.

The regulatory authority supplied significant funding, but it could not be spent on operating expenses. A number of specific schemes assisted stations in developing key areas, such as the Féile, discussed earlier, the Community Radio Support Scheme (CRSS), and the Sound and Vision Scheme.

The CRSS funded evaluations, both internal and external, to enable the station to assess its performance—for example, its relationship with its community or its long-term planning. Sound and Vision was paid for from the television license fee. It funded new programs on Irish culture, heritage and experience, adult literacy, and the Irish language. Launched in 2005, it brought significant funding, and therefore security, to community stations, enabling them to focus on program making. It undoubtedly improved the quality of programming, funding documentary, drama, and experimental sound projects, and in the process developing the expertise of community stations.

Programming and Target Groups

The voices heard on air are probably the most obvious signifiers of public participation in any community station. Through its programs and the voices, a community may first assess the station's relevance. This means that talk programming predominates on most. Although all stations play music and many programs are music oriented, the priority for stations is speech-based, issue-driven programming across a range of genres. The magazine format predominated.

Community volunteers made up the majority of the presenters and producers, as a matter of policy. An average of 80 people participated on a weekly basis in each station.

Community of interest licenses established stations for specific groups within the wider community. However, all geographically based stations also targeted segments of their community in order to support and empower those excluded from or ignored by mainstream media and society. These included women in the home, the elderly, disaffected youth, new immigrants, and the disabled.

By working with other agencies who care for those on the margins of society, Irish stations formed part of the efforts to build a more inclusive and democratic society. They sought to foster long-term relationships with disengaged and disempowered individuals and groups.

Sometimes a station would provide on-air training leading to programs that got broadcast, and that might be the extent of the intervention. More frequently, they put together training programs in the areas of personal development, communication and broadcasting skills, and community activism. The aim of Irish community radio stations was to enable different sectors of the community to interact with each other through the station and to cooperate in the community building project for all.

Rosemary Day

See also Community Broadcasting (Canada); Community Media (Venezuela); Community Media and the Third Sector; Community Radio in Pau de Lima (Brasil); Community Radio Movement (India); Free Radio (Austria); Peace Media (Colombia); Women's Radio (Austria)

Further Readings

Broadcasting Commission of Ireland. (2001). *Community radio policy document*. Dublin: Broadcasting Authority of Ireland. http://www.bai.ie

Craol: http:www.craol.ie

Day, R. (Ed.). (2007). *Bicycle highway: Celebrating community radio in Ireland*. Dublin, Ireland: Liffey Press.

Day, R. (2008). *Community radio in Ireland: Participation and multi-flows of communication*. Cresskill, NJ: Hampton Press.

Oireachtas na hEireann, Broadcasting Bill 2008, Section 64: http://www.oireachtas.ie/documents/bills28/bills/2008/2908/b2908s.pdf

COMMUNITY RADIO (SRI LANKA)

Sri Lanka was the first South Asian country to do community broadcasting, starting with Mahaweli community radio (MCR) in 1981. Under the Mahaweli Project (1978–1987), 1 million displaced and landless people were resettled in mainly agricultural zones. MCR's aim was to use radio to motivate them to take an active part in this project. Thus, communication for development was the core of community radio. UNESCO offered consultancy assistance to MCR, and the Danish International Development Agency gave it funds.

MCR's first stage was under the Sri Lanka Broadcasting Corporation (SLBC). After a few years' experimental programs, MCR established small community radio stations focusing on particular sectors of the Mahaweli Project, Giradurukotte (1985), Mahailluppalama (1987), and Kothmale (1989).

The latest initiative, however, Uva Community Radio, began in 2003 outside the Mahaweli Project under a pilot United Nations Development Programme (UNDP) project titled Area-Based Growth with Equity Programme (ABGEP). They are contrasted in the following section.

Pioneer MCR Experiences

MCR program production primarily seeks solutions to development issues in settlers' daily lives, as identified by the community. The MCR acts as a bridge between the community and the authorities, its programs produced by a community-based team rather an individual. The production process would commence with a short visit by a producer to a village, meeting the villagers in public places, on farms, and even on the road, and having a discussion with them. The discussion would proceed at a relaxed pace to encourage settlers to speak freely and fully about their problems.

During this visit, villagers' communication needs and development issues would be identified, and a date and place to produce radio programs set. On the due date, the MCR production team would move into the village with mobile equipment. They would camp out there for 4 days, mixing freely with villagers, speaking the local dialect, and trying to live as typical villagers. The purpose was to enable the villagers to be the focal point in the production process.

The villagers would gather at a common place in the evening to plan and produce programs. Under the guidance of MCR producers, the program would be planned through discussing major local problems and suggesting varied solutions. The community decided on the program title, format, and content, and participated in speaking in the program. Recording or live broadcasting was done the same or the following day. If recorded, at end of the recording it was played back to the villagers to get their comments and approval to broadcast it. As a result of this process, the villagers were empowered as broadcasters, their voice heard within the public sphere.

MCR program formats were identified by the community, who would frequently use folk media formats to present their own problems and alternatives through radio. The folk media are multiple, flexible, and alternative. Folk media artists could always be found among the villagers. David's research suggests that integrating folk media with community radio provides a powerful tool for social control as well as a means of solving community problems. The MCR experience shows this method of community participation is highly valued among community members.

Democratic Community Participatory Radio: Uva Community Radio

Uva Community Radio (UCR) was also set up under SLBC auspices, with funding from UNDP and Uva Provincial Council, and UNESCO support. UCR's aim was to encourage community participation in planning, implementing, and evaluating ABGEP projects. Accordingly, UCR pioneers conceived of the station as programmed, managed, and owned by the community.

The next task was to identify a suitable mechanism to mobilize the community from the UCR's 1.8 million people constituency, spread over a vast area. The first challenge was how to reach this target audience. For this purpose, a group of 40 multiethnic volunteers were selected as communicators. First, they were given training in theoretical and practical aspects of community mobilizing, community broadcasting, and social marketing. Second, they were given the responsibility to mobilize the community in their own neighborhoods.

The first community meeting they organized was held at a small village school. Almost a hundred people attended this meeting, representing different community groups in the area. First, the community members divided into small groups. Afterward, they were asked to list the radio programs they listened to and their reasons for listening to them. They were also asked to identify participatory opportunities in, and weaknesses of, these programs. They tagged programs they would like to broadcast if a radio station were established in their area. Finally, they were allowed to present their fact list in front of the whole community.

These discussions focused on people's media needs and the need for a community radio station. By the end of the meeting, community participants concluded that the government and the business class owned the mainstream media but that none of them would fulfill the community's needs or allow community voices to be heard. This naturally led to explanation of the proposed community radio station. The community members decided to meet again to discuss their role in it.

A few weeks later, around 150 participants gathered again. This time they agreed to form a community organization for the new radio station, run by a core group. The criteria for selecting this group were suggested by the radio pioneers and agreed on by the community members.

Those chosen were neither political activists nor officeholders in a volunteer organization. They represented various professions and were of both genders. This organization was named the Knowledge Society. By following this model, by 2003 about 178 Knowledge Societies were established in Uva Province by UCR communicators. In each Knowledge Society, a volunteer group was also established. The same training given the communicators was given to these volunteer groups. Accordingly, 4,500 volunteers were trained. The task of producing programs for the proposed community radio was assigned to volunteers.

After the Knowledge Societies had been established, two district conferences were held with participation by core groups of the Knowledge Societies. The first took place in the Badulla district and about 1,000 representatives participated, with 450 attending the second conference, held in Monaragala district. Widely discussed in the conferences were modes of community members' involvement in the proposed radio programs, along with their management structure and ownership. Finally, district and provincial Knowledge Society Federations were established.

The next step was to form a legal management structure to ensure that communities would maintain ownership of the UCR. A group of provincial officials, SLBC officers, provincial council members and representatives of Knowledge Societies participated in a workshop to this end. Participants agreed that a majority of places on the UCR management board should be given to Knowledge Society representatives, with the rest to be appointed by Uva Provincial Council. The chairperson and the station manager should be selected by a majority of board members.

Political Thickets

Meanwhile, the next issue emerged. The UPC began work on erecting the UCR station and finding its staffing. Under the 13th Amendment of Sri

Lanka's constitution, central government power was devolved to provincial councils. Thus, an Uva Provincial Act was drafted to establish a community radio station. The provincial governor also represents the central government in the provincial council, but when he submitted the bill to the central government's solicitor general, he was informed the 13th Amendment would not permit the provincial council to do this.

UPC civil servants then decided to present the bill as a white paper to the provincial council and so make a legal framework to establish the station. However, the provincial councilors delayed approving the white paper. Meanwhile, there was a national election. The ruling People's Alliance was defeated, and the United National Party came into power. Even though provincial power remained with the People's Alliance, Sri Lanka's political culture would not countenance setting up a provincial station without central government approval. And under the Broadcasting Act, the minister alone is empowered to issue broadcast licenses. So far Sri Lanka's governments had issued radio licenses only to business families, and no policy or legal framework existed to establish community radio stations.

Cutting Through the Dilemma

Meanwhile, the construction of the community radio station building had been completed. The community had mobilized to participate in owning and managing the station. In addition, the station equipment, ordered through ABGEP, had arrived in Sri Lanka. The law required a license for the station and its frequency, as well as for Customs to release it. The process of establishing UCR came to a crucial point.

The only alternative was to discuss the issue with SLBC and ask for the equipment's release under a SLBC license. As a result, a Memorandum of Understanding was signed by the SLBC and UPC, which gave the ownership and the management of UCR to the SLBC and UPC. The crucial component of UCR, the community, was left out.

UCR went on the air in March 2003. Though the community lost direct participation in owning and managing it, they still had the opportunity to participate in its programs. In the memorandum signed between SLBC and UPC, both agreed to

implement the program guidelines already prepared by the community. Accordingly, the community could utilize the 30 minutes of air time allocated by the UCR for each Knowledge Society to achieve their unmet daily needs. The Knowledge Societies were able to produce and broadcast their programs without any undue influence and restrictions. They created an environment in which the community could contribute actively to development and democracy. Uva Province was empowered as a result.

Discovering Similarities and Differences

There are significant differences between MCR and UCR. MCR is owned and run by the government. In contrast, UCR had achieved editorial independence in its attempt to become owned and run by the community. Some media and development practitioners have identified UCR as the most independent and influential community radio in Sri Lanka to date.

A further key difference is that MCR attempted to use the radio to facilitate individual farmers' empowerment. By contrast, UCR prepared the necessary community mobilization for group empowerment via a structure of collective ownership, management, and programming. UCR also tried to build an independent democratic movement in the province. The UCR case reveals that citizens can contribute to democracy and the development process when they are made the real owners of community radios. But in spite of their differences, both UCR and MCR face similar challenges, such as marginalization, the lack of legal framework, and the lack of funds.

Pradeep N' Weerasinghe

See also Community Radio in Pau da Lima (Brasil); Community Radio Movement (India); Indigenous Radio Stations (México); Miners' Radio Stations (Bolivia); Participatory Media; Peace Media (Colombia)

Further Readings

Area-Based Growth with Equity Programme (ABGEP) (Project SRL/971101). (2000). Colombo, Sri Lanka: UNDP. http://erc.undp.org/evaluationadmin/downloaddocument.html?docid=433

Arnaldo, C. A. (2000). *Assessment of technical proposals to establish Uva Community Radio* (Project SRL/97/101). Kuala Lumpur, Sri Lanka: UNESCO.

Center for Policy Alternatives and International Media Support. (2005). *Study of media in Sri Lanka*. Colombo, Sri Lanka: Author.

David, M. J. R. (1986). *An evaluative study on the impact of a settlement-based Community Radio*. Colombo, Sri Lanka: SLBC.

Jayaratne, T., Pinto-Jayawardena, K., Guneratne, J. A., & Silva, S. (2007). Legal challenges and practical constraints: A comprehensive study of "community radio" in Sri Lanka. *Law & Society Trust, 18*, 1–62.

Jayaweera, W., & Jayarathna, T. (Eds.). (2003). *In search of solutions: The UCR's values and standards*. Colombo, Sri Lanka: UPC & SLBC.

Karunanayake, N. (1986). The Mahaweli Community Radio in Sri Lanka: A promising experiment. *Media Asia, 13*(4), 209–214.

Librero, F. (2004). *Community broadcasting: Concept and practice in the Philippines*. Singapore: Eastern Universities Press.

Selvakumaran, N., & Edirisinha, R. (1998). *Mass media laws and regulations in Sri Lanka*. Singapore: AMIC.

UNESCO. (1983). *Mahaweli Community Radio: Project findings and recommendations* (Serial no. FMR/COM/DCS/83/218 [FIT]). Paris: UNESCO. http://unesdoc.unesco.org/images/0005/000559/055973eo.pdf

Valbuena, V. T. (1988). *Mahaweli Community Radio Project: An evaluation*. Singapore: AMIC.

COMMUNITY RADIO AND NATURAL DISASTERS (INDONESIA)

Indonesia's location on the Pacific Ring of Fire, sandwiched between three continent plates in a tropical region, creates the potential for earthquakes, eruptions, tsunamis, floods, landslides, and droughts. In disasters, information is crucial. In many cases in Indonesia, community radio's role is clear in its responses to the challenges faced by those coping with disaster.

Mass media under Suharto, concentrated in big cities and dominated by the state and major firms, had failed to serve many localities. In the post-Suharto period, media democratization campaigns began in the legislature. During the Megawati administration (2001–2003), under civil society

pressure, Broadcasting Law 32/2002 was enacted, which, for the first time in Indonesian history, legally acknowledged the existence of community broadcasting. Previously, community radio was illegal and operated clandestinely.

Additionally, the regional autonomy movement post-Suharto, where villages became a focus for the democratic movement, contributed to the establishment of community radio. Activists used community radio to empower villagers, to foster a strong civil society to counteract the power of local government and enable participation in the development process. At of 2009, thousands of community stations had been set up. (The total would only be known once the registration process had been completed.)

Community Radio and Civic Action in Natural Disaster Management

The post-tsunami experience in Aceh in 2004 illustrated the vital role of community radio in the affected areas. Aceh, the westernmost Indonesian province, was worst affected. Along hundreds of kilometers of coastline in this province, 180,000 people were killed and houses and buildings flattened, leaving more than 500,000 homeless.

The 2004 tsunami also killed many journalists, destroyed media infrastructures and telephones, and washed away parts of roads. Several days afterward, Aceh still had zero media communication. Half of the 30 radio stations were damaged, including Radio Republik Indonesia (RRI), the state-owned radio. RRI lost all 26 staffers. The tsunami isolated already devastated areas because of communication infrastructure damage. The Acehnese had no means to communicate with one another and with people in other regions. As a consequence, the first news about this disaster was reported at 8:30 a.m., hours after the tsunami, by Detik.com, an online Jakarta website. Television broadcasters had problems reaching the region and, as a result, could only report the event by noon.

Radio was the only viable communication medium. Thanks to their social network, several community radio volunteers from other regions in Indonesia worked on community radio projects to help the Acehnese establish community radio. The post-tsunami projects in Aceh provided a first experience for the volunteers in handling disaster response.

Community radio in Aceh began by helping people in the emergency. More recently, it developed as a tool for recovery and reconstruction. Community radio covered local issues and content in order to heal the public's trauma, as well as to entertain and educate community members in the recovery and reconstruction phases.

A good example was the use of *nazam* (traditional Aceh poems), often aired on a number of stations. These poems consisted of religious messages, aimed at helping survivors recover from their grief. *Nazam* were also used to express people's feelings, for example, their hope for a peaceful situation in Aceh. Samudera FM, a community radio operated by refugees from the tsunami-affected areas in North Aceh, broadcast religious programs to heal the trauma of Acehnese who had been affected by conflict and the tsunami. Community members came to the studio voluntarily to entertain each other in order to try to recover from their grief.

Another community station, SeHa FM Community Radio—SeHa abbreviates *seunang hatee* (happy feeling)—was managed by young refugee camp dwellers and aired field reports on the situations, problems, and opinions of survivors living there. Suara Meulaboh community radio conducted vox populi interviews with local inhabitants. Samudera FM community radio reported and discussed the conditions and problems faced by people living in camps and barracks. This helped build close relations between the community and their radio because it helped them voice their aspirations. Community radio also functioned as entertainment media by airing song requests. In this way, they helped heal their community and their own selves.

Community Radio in West Sumatra: Spontaneous Action

Based on experiences of natural disasters in other regions in Indonesia, community radio volunteers were better prepared to respond to the emergency caused by a 5.8 earthquake in West Sumatra on March 6, 2007. The earthquake killed 66, injured hundreds, destroyed about 10,000 homes and buildings, and displaced more than 6,500 people.

Although there had been no emergency-response training, community radio volunteers in West Sumatra had learned that knowledge was crucial during the emergency-response period. Two hours after the earthquake, communication infrastructures were collapsing. The only information came from RRI. Because RRI was located in Padang, the provincial capital, most of the information was dominated by Padang's crisis. As a result, there was a lack of information for victims and medical teams in remote areas.

The earthquake disrupted wide areas, most of them rural, cutting off roads and isolating some areas. The condition of victims worsened, as most affected areas were in mountainous regions not easily reached by land transportation. Some areas, due to topography, could not be covered by radio from Padang or other cities. Those areas were known as blank-spot areas. As a result, inhabitants were isolated from aid distribution. They urgently needed a form of communication to describe their plight.

Community radio volunteers in West Sumatra realized radio could help the victims. They decided to go to these areas to establish emergency radio. Four community radio stations in Solok (Radila FM Community Radio and Semarak Community Radio) and Padang Pariaman (Suandri FM Community Radio and Bahana FM Community Radio) operated as emergency stations immediately after the earthquake.

Community radio allowed local people and government and aid agencies to be informed of the situation and to coordinate help and distribution logistics. Community radio volunteers collected data about the need for milk, bandages, mineral water, baby food, instant noodles, and tents. Then they broadcast these needs widely to connect supply and demand.

Soon after the earthquake, rumors began to circulate about an impending tsunami and another earthquake. To reduce their impact, community radio informed survivors of the real situation from the Indonesian Meteorological and Geophysical Agency and provided timely information about aftershocks.

In Paninggahan, West Sumatra, a local inhabitant said that community radio had helped calm people after the earthquake because it gave clear information about the situation. In this village, community radio also helped victims to release their stress. Locals joined in the radio programs to entertain each other. They sent greetings to their friends and families by radio, which covered areas surrounding Singkarak Lake. They could update people on their situation and encourage each other to recover from their grief and the destruction.

To support their activities, the Community Radio Network of West Sumatra applied two strategies. First, they dropped volunteers in the affected areas to set up emergency radio. Because their station budgets had no available funds, volunteers had to use their own money. They came from various community stations surrounding the affected areas. They alternated in working for 3 to 4 days at a time.

Second, they used their networks to obtain support from people outside the disaster locations. They got support from the Community Radio Network of Indonesia, the Combine Resource Institution, and the Indonesian Press and Broadcasting Society. The capacity to work together played an important role in community action, as communities drew upon their own resources to solve problems.

Emergency community radio played its role only for a limited time during the emergency-response period, about 3 months after the disaster. After that, the emergency community radio officially ceased operation. Recently, however, community radio was revived by locals to broadcast other programs.

Mario Antonius Birowo

See also Community Media (Venezuela); Community Radio (Sri Lanka); Community Radio in Pau da Lima (Brasil); Community Radio Movement (India); Participatory Media; Peace Media (Colombia)

Further Readings

Afrizal, R. B., & Prakoso, I. (2009). *Berbagi kisah dari seantero negeri upaya-upaya penanggulangan bencana oleh radio komunitas* [Stories of community radio in disaster management]. In A. Nasir, E. Wijoyono, & A. Tanesia (Eds.), *Mengudara Menjawab Tantangan* [On air to answer challenges] (pp. 19–47). Yogyakarta, Indonesia: Combine Resource Institution.

Birowo, M. A. (2006). *Community radio movement in Indonesia: A case study of Jaringan Radio Komunitas Yogyakarta (Yogyakarta Community Radio Networks)*. Retrieved January 12, 2007, from http://mediaasiaconference.humanities.curtin.edu.au/pdf/Mario%20Antonius%20Birowo.pdf

Haryanto, I., & Ramdojo, J. J. (2009). *Dinamika Radio Komunitas* [The dynamic of community radio]. Jakarta, Indonesia: LSPP.

Internews. (2007). *Internews assesses media needs after West Sumatra earthquake, 21 March* [Press release]. http://www.internews.org/prs/2007/20070321_indo.shtm

Sen, K., & Hill, D. T. (2000). *Media, culture and politics in Indonesia*. Melbourne, Australia: Oxford University Press.

COMMUNITY RADIO AND PODCASTING (UNITED STATES)

Podcasting is a term for a collection of tools and techniques that facilitate the publishing of audio files online. In simple terms, every time podcast publishers make an audio file available on the Internet, they also update a special kind of text file, called an RSS file, to note the existence of the audio file and its location. Listeners can choose to "subscribe" to a podcast using specialized client-end software. That software periodically checks for updates to the RSS files of the podcasts to which the listener has subscribed and, when it notes an update, can download the relevant audio file without further intervention by the listener. Many content management systems, in particular those designed for weblog production, include this podcast publishing function, as do sites such as YouTube. At the client end, there are a variety of applications that facilitate podcast subscription and downloading.

Podcasting differs from webcasting in that the content produced is portable and available on demand. Clients can transfer downloaded files to other devices and listen when and where they choose. In addition, through the choices available regarding which feeds to subscribe to, or which files to play or skip, listeners have highly granular control over their audio diet akin to control over individual music tracks, rather unlike broadcast radio.

Economics

The economics of podcasting differ from that of radio, community radio in particular. One of radio's distinctive features is its cost model. Although the capital costs can be significant, the operating costs can be quite low, and there is no additional cost for each extra listener. Newspapers have an additional cost for each extra copy printed, and this can limit readership size. With radio, the transmitter's power acts to limit the listening area, but within that area, the station is available to all who chose to tune in. Podcasting costs, in contrast, are heavily unit-based, as podcasting relies on transmission through the Internet, and thus bandwidth costs increase as audiences grow.

Community radio in the United States depends heavily on a repeated "pledge drive" funding model. Internet distribution has posed challenges for that model. First, Internet users are heavily acclimated to content being largely free at the point of use. Second, community stations frequently base their call for funds on providing content not otherwise available within their area. However, particularly with syndicated content, this is often no longer so, as audience members can access programming directly through producer websites, or through webstreams and/or podcasts provided by other affiliate stations.

Access

Community radio has provided a means for individuals to pool resources and thereby generate services that would not be possible for a single individual. Community stations also serve as an overarching brand that can be promoted more readily to audiences than a scatter of program brands. For many producers, those advantages are likely to continue in the digital era.

However, the combination of digital editing tools and podcasting has lowered the entry barriers for those seeking to create audio content independently. In addition, the subscription dimension of podcasts facilitates the development of niche audiences. The barriers that remain are, however, significant. Planning and production of audio content, particularly on an ongoing basis, can require a significant time commitment. Thus, those who have previously been unable to engage in media production due to work and family commitments may continue to be excluded, though the wide availability of digital editing tools means that it is now easier for production to be done from home or in other nontraditional settings.

Localism

It may be incorrect to describe localism as a defining characteristic of the community radio sector—many stations feature syndicated content, or programming that is not explicitly focused on local concerns—but community stations do most often have a commitment to serve a local community. Internet distribution raises questions as to how far this local focus is solely a product of signal strength and how the relationship between place and content will develop in the future.

The availability online of content once only available from local community stations poses particular questions, both practical and esoteric. These stations always used to tout their provision of this content to solicit listener donations, or to draw in audiences, but now such arguments have lost some traction. Stations that have drawn together multiple social movements, rationing airtime among varied interests, must now deal with potential listeners who have access to far more content in any particular area of interest than can be provided on air—and with producers who can reach dispersed audiences without necessarily needing a host radio station.

How does distribution of station content through the Internet fit with, or affect implementation of, a local community commitment? On the plus side, Internet transmission gets to areas the signal does not currently reach, and to members without radios (or who prefer to use the Internet). It makes content available on demand, or that does not fit within the broadcast schedule. On the negative side, however, this can disenfranchise those community members without ready Internet access.

Some community stations primarily serve communities of interest, such as fans of a certain form of music or the LGBTQ (lesbian, gay, bisexual, transgender, queer) community. In such cases, podcasting and Internet distribution provide exciting opportunities, yet there are certain network realities that suggest that only a limited number of outlets focused on a particular audience are likely to thrive online. For stations adopting Internet distribution, the various spaces available to producers and schedulers demand scheduling that recognizes their varied audiences. These spaces may share a common brand or identity, but each will be suited to the display of a different set of content. Whereas early experiments generally duplicated over-the-air content on the Internet, more ambitious and varied uses of the multiple spaces now available will emerge.

Regulation and Policy

The limited availability of broadcast spectrum, as well as the perceived need to police its orderly allocation, has long been used to justify licensing regimes that control who can gain access to the airwaves. With few exceptions, governments limit who can take to the airwaves and frequently subject broadcasting to greater restrictions on content than other media (e.g., acceptable language or balance in political coverage). Such restrictions are often not applied to content distributed online.

Radio stations that adopt online distribution find, however, that they are bound by additional copyright restrictions and other Internet-specific regulatory concerns. Whereas U.S. radio stations are exempt from paying music royalties to the holders of performance rights, Internet-based transmissions require them. Internet transmission also requires payments to holders of songwriter copyrights, on top of any broadcast use payments.

Beyond costs, copyright law may prevent certain types of use that would be permissible in broadcasting. Again using U.S. copyright law as an example, there are limitations in the number of tracks from any individual artist or album that an Internet radio producer may include in any single period. Programming focused exclusively on the work of a single artist would only be permissible in a broadcast.

U.S. law, drafted before podcasting, also provides that on-demand transmissions (which contain licensed music content) cannot be less than 5 hours in length, with material not being available for more than 2 weeks. This constrains how stations can make content available online, with some stations adopting the creative solution of stitching together multiple editions of 3-hour shows in order to create a single 6-hour piece.

The differing regulatory structures can provide arbitrage opportunities, in which the distribution platform can be chosen based on the nature of the content available and the regulations applying to each platform. This in turn facilitates content creation that otherwise might fall foul of national regulations and which would, in consequence, not have reached production even 10 years ago. Producers and management are finding themselves involved in a new set of policy debates, distinct from those traditionally of interest to radio stations, such as network neutrality and intellectual property.

Andrew Ó Baoill

See also Community Broadcasting (Canada); Community Broadcasting Audiences (Australia); Community Media and the Third Sector; Community Radio (Haïti); Community Radio (Ireland); Low-Power FM Radio (United States); Prometheus Radio Project (United States)

Further Readings

Cecil, M. K. (2007). *Pathways to community: An ethnographic study of podcasting implementation in a community radio station.* Paper presented at the International Communication Association, San Francisco, CA. http://www.allacademic.com/meta/p171145_index.html

Lewis, P. M. (2002). Radio theory and community radio. In N. W. Jankowski & O. Prehn (Eds.), *Community radio in the information age* (pp. 47–61). Cresskill, NJ: Hampton Press.

Neumark, N. (2006). Different spaces, different times: Exploring possibilities for cross-platform "radio." *Convergence: The International Journal of Research Into New Media Technologies, 12,* 213–224.

COMMUNITY RADIO IN PAU DA LIMA (BRASIL)

The view of Pau da Lima seen from the top of the hills is astonishing. Crammed together and built on top of each other, thousands of houses help create a brick-colored mosaic. At first sight, Pau da Lima is just another *favela* (slum) in Salvador da Bahia, Brasil (sometimes simply called Bahia). Nevertheless, a closer look reveals a nuanced environment. In 2007, Salvador's population was over 2.8 million. Pau da Lima, approximately 200,000 people, is one of its 18 boroughs and a heterogeneous and multifaceted community.

This diversity is also reflected in the different forms of media found in the neighborhood. As of the late 2000s, there were local newspapers, one "lamp post" radio, and four unlicensed FM radio stations. This entry discusses two of them in detail: the lamp post radio station and one of the FM stations.

Radio Pop Som

Radio Pop Som (Pop Sound) was founded in 1998 by Elson Simão Rocha, a resident for over 25 years. This station's programs have been aired through loudspeakers, connected by wire to a central station, and placed on lamp posts on the streets, thus the expression "lamp post radio." As of 2009, there were 22 loudspeakers in busy places, such as bus stops, grocery stores, and churches. Elson wanted to avoid a rather bureaucratic and time-consuming federal licensing process for an FM station. For the lamp post station, he only needed a city hall authorization, cheaper and easier.

The station employed three residents and was on air Monday through Friday from 9 a.m. to noon and 3 to 6 p.m., and Saturdays from 9 a.m. to noon. The programming added to Pau da Lima's loud sonic environment by competing with other speakers placed on car roofs and on the backs of bicycles, which were constantly in motion advertising local events and shop offers. The station played eclectic music genres, such as country music (música popular brasileira) and dance music. The disc jockey (DJ) played different styles according to the "moods of the day" and, in his words, "contributed to creating a soundtrack for the streets" (personal communication).

Radio Pop Som also had connections with the city's public health department and with a well-established public health research institute, linked to the Federal Ministry of Health. As the institution had been conducting research on infectious diseases in Pau da Lima for over 10 years, members of their field research team often met with the station's staff in order to suggest health campaigns. Hence, the station aired public health messages such as tips on how to prevent the proliferation of the dengue fever mosquito.

The station was funded by selling advertising to local shop owners. This price was R$50 (approximately US$30), almost 300 times cheaper than a mainstream FM station. This guaranteed the sustainability of the station but did not allow for significant profits. Hence, contrary to the notion of community media as not-for-profit in nature, the station was commercial. Interestingly, listeners perceived this as crucial for the local economy, which had a vibrant marketplace residents were quite proud of. Local shop owners appreciated the affordable advertising, which helped keep them competitive.

Star FM

Community radio was legalized in Brasil in 1998. However, this did not help foster a more democratic media environment. The law said stations could typically only broadcast within a 1-kilometer radius. The license process could take a long time, be extremely complicated, and often unfair. Many applications were simply filed or forgotten, unless the applicant had a political connection. These stations could be subject to severe repression by the federal police, resulting in transmitters being confiscated or even the arrest of station staff. The Pau da Lima FM stations reflected these constraints, and as of 2009, all were unlicensed. (Their names and the names of their staff have been changed.)

Star FM was founded in 2001 by Eduardo Andrade, an engineering student and resident. Six other community members worked as presenters. Star FM aired daily, 6 a.m. to 11 p.m. The programming consisted of various national and foreign music genres, ranging from gospel to pagode (a subgenre of samba) to mainstream U.S. pop. Each DJ had a good degree of autonomy and played songs according to their tastes and to listeners' requests, which might have contributed to the station's eclectic format. The programming also included bulletins about community events, current affairs, and health tips. Besides phoning in, listeners could participate in the station's programming by calling the presenters on their mobile phones or talking to them face-to-face.

However, what distinguished Star FM from the other stations was its close relationship with some of Pau da Lima's social movements, such as the Grupo Resistência Comunitária (Community Resistance Group). These members were young residents who met regularly to discuss issues such as racism, religious intolerance, and social inequality. Working together with the group, the station aired a weekly reggae program called *Star Reggae*. During it, presenters would explain reggae's origins and draw out the cultural similarities between Jamaica and Brasil, especially their African roots.

In a city known as the African capital of Brasil, where people of African descent make up more than 80% of the population, Star Reggae attracted a loyal audience, not only in Pau da Lima but also in neighboring districts. In addition to fostering a sense of self-esteem in the community, this program also questioned Brasil's "myth of racial democracy," the claim that its racial relations are remarkably peaceful and that discrimination is only class based.

Challenges

The Pau da Lima stations had limited participation as only a relatively small number of community members were directly involved in actually *making* programs. Both of these stations had abandoned training schemes, because of the lack of staff with available free time to run them and the lack of money to pay the trainees.

The community radio legislation was unhelpful, and stations were often confronted with business, religious, and political interests. Local politicians often helped stations get licenses in exchange for campaigning for them on the radio. At the same time, many stations sold program slots to the thriving evangelical churches. This was also the case in Pau da Lima. At the time of research, Star FM had three daily slots dedicated to evangelical programs.

Yet stations such as Radio Pop Som and Star FM represented bottom-up projects, carried out by Pau da Lima residents who cared about the community rather than by development groups, which often had prepackaged ideas about community radio. Moreover, both these radio initiatives played

important roles in Pau da Lima's everyday life. Blasting from the loudspeakers, Radio Pop Som helped keep the local economy healthy and fit well with the sonic rhythms of the streets. Connecting Salvador with Kingston, Star FM's reggae program helped disturb the oppressive silence of racism.

Andrea Medrado

See also Citizens' Media; Community Media and the Third Sector; Community Radio (Haïti); Community Radio (Ireland); Community Radio Movement (India); Indigenous Radio Stations (México); Low-Power FM Radio (United States); Reggae and Resistance (Jamaica); Women's Radio (Austria)

Further Readings

de Lima, V. A., & Lopes, C. A. (2007). *Coronelismo eletrônico de novo tipo (1999–2004): as autorizações de emissoras como moeda de barganha política* [A new form of electronic authoritarianism: Broadcast licenses as currency for political bargain-making]. Observatório da Imprensa & Instituto para o Desenvolvimento do Jornalismo. http://www .observatoriodaimprensa.com.br/download/ Coronelismo_eletronico_de_novo_tipo.pdf

Jankowski, N., & Prehn, O. (Eds.). (2002). *Community media in the information age: Perspectives and prospects*. Cresskill, NJ: Hampton Press.

Reis, R. (2006). Media and religion in Brazil: The rise of TV Record and UCKG and their attempts at globalization. *Brazilian Journalism Research, 2*(2), 167–182.

Silveira, P. F. (2001). *Rádios comunitárias* [Community radio stations]. Belo Horizonte, Brasil: Del Rey.

COMMUNITY RADIO MOVEMENT (INDIA)

Bertolt Brecht lamented in the late 1920s that radio had been reduced to only an "acoustical department store." He pleaded for turning radio into "something really democratic" by making it a medium of two-way communication, enabling true participation by citizens in public affairs. In many ways, the history of the struggle for community radio in India, which culminated in November 2006 in a new Indian government policy permitting community radio, has been an effort to realize his plea to use radio to build a robust civil society.

The fight to free the radio spectrum has been a key element in contesting the global march of capitalist media industries and the unidirectional flow of information and communication from the northern metropolitan countries to the rest of the world. This movement is also concerned with providing a means of expression to a wide spectrum of social actors who have been socially, culturally, geographically, economically, and politically excluded from power.

A historic judgment delivered by the Supreme Court of India in 1995 ruled that "airwaves constitute public property and must be utilized for advancing public good" *(Union of India v. Cricket Association of Bengal,* 1995). Following this judgment, community radio campaigners struggled through most of a decade to create not-for-profit radio stations, owned and run by local people, typically in rural areas.

Earlier Initiatives

Using radio for development was a cornerstone of official policy, yet no attempt to solicit even public feedback was made until 1956, when an experiment was conducted with United Nations Educational, Scientific and Cultural Organization (UNESCO) assistance in 150 villages in Maharashtra State. Based on a Canadian model, it was designed to establish two-way communication between village audiences and radio producers. By the mid-1960s, little more was heard of this development communication experiment. All-India Radio remained centralized and lacking in editorial independence. AIR has a network of local radio stations, but they have not proven locally relevant as they are not community-run.

In the 1970s, an experimental FM station was set up in Tamil Nadu State. The project successfully elicited listener participation and could have been a workable model—but not if staffed by AIR professionals with no local connection or commitment.

Radio shifted to a highly commercialized model in 1999. In 2005, Phase II of the FM policy made access much simpler for private firms, with 330 frequencies in 90 cities up for bidding. Radio entertainment in India witnessed a revival of sorts.

However, no one seemed to have an ear for the rural voices that were seeking a "radio of our own," despite their periodic acknowledgment in a series of government committee reports proposing a comprehensive national media policy. In 2003, these long-standing demands yielded only a "campus" avatar of community radio, permitting "well-established" educational institutions to set up FM stations on their premises. It was mere tokenism to claim that urban campus radio would provide space for the marginalized, rural, or poor populace to disseminate their own messages, and to challenge the mainstream understanding of social issues. The government long resisted demands for opening up this sector, claiming that secessionists or subversive elements would misuse the medium.

The Long Campaign for Community Radio Licensing

In 1996, the Bangalore-based communication campaign group VOICES convened a gathering of radio broadcasters, policy planners, media professionals, and not-for-profit associations to study how community radio could be relevant to India, and to deliberate on appropriate policies. A declaration was signed calling for the establishment of community broadcasting. A suggestion was put forward that AIR's local stations should allocate regular airtime for community broadcasting. Requests were also made for licenses for nongovernmental organizations (NGOs) and other nonprofit groups to run community stations. Subsequently, UNESCO made available a portable "briefcase radio station" kit to VOICES to do experimental broadcasts for hands-on learning in preparation for setting up an independently run community station.

A UNESCO-sponsored workshop in 2000 in Hyderabad issued the "Pastapur Initiative" on community radio that urged the government to take to its logical conclusion the intent to free broadcasting from state monopoly, by making media space available also to communities. This landmark document urged the government to create a three-tier structure of broadcasting in India.

The spirited campaigning and innumerable representations by organizations, academics, and individuals led the Ministry of Information and Broadcasting (MIB) to organize a workshop in

May 2004 in New Delhi, supported by UNDP (United Nations Development Programme) and UNESCO, to design an enabling framework for community radio. The workshop brought together a large number of community radio enthusiasts, academics, NGOs, and policymakers, who worked out a set of recommendations that would allow community groups to run their own stations. When the Telecom Regulatory Authority of India issued a consultation paper later that year, they arrived at largely the same formulations.

In July 2004, MIB prepared a draft policy based on the May consultations. Subsequently, community radio groups in India launched an online petition, urging the inclusion of communities' rights within the policy and an end to discrimination against rural and poor communities. In October 2005, the draft policy was referred to a group of ministers, who took about a year to give approval, after deliberating upon several contentious issues such as advertising, news and information, license fee, and spectrum availability. These intense advocacy efforts and passionate debates about community radio broadcasting for the social sector finally culminated in November 2006 with an inclusive community radio policy approved by the Cabinet.

The new policy permitted NGOs and community-based groups with a record of development work to set up community radio stations (CRSs). Each CRS had to have an ownership and management structure reflective of the community. At least 50% of content had to be generated with local participation, and the programs had to be in the local language and dialect(s). Restricted advertising was permitted for up to 5 minutes per hour. The license was issued for 5 years and was nontransferable.

The license holder is required to adhere to the provisions of the AIR program and advertising code. This governs norms such as good taste, decency, and respect for religions, communities, and friendly countries. The policy did not permit any CRS to broadcast news and current affairs programs or politically partisan material.

The application procedure for other than government-recognized educational institutions was not simple and required clearances from several ministries. For this reason, more than 2 years after the policy's announcement, only 3 of the 48 functioning CRSs in India are owned by development organizations. All others are campus stations.

Civil Society Initiatives in Rural India

Even as the government was dithering over this legislation, a few community-based organizations had initiated radio projects in rural India. Some made use of available spaces within the state sector of broadcasting whereas others, fearing co-optation and appropriation, steadfastly resisted the offer to use state radio. In the absence of a license, they continued to creatively engage in narrowcasting, that is, playing back programs on a tape recorder or reaching people through cable television.

In 1998 the Deccan Development Society, an NGO working with poor, rural, Dalit women in Zaheerabad in Andhra Pradesh State, set up a station with UNESCO assistance. Programs produced by members of the community were narrowcast through tape recorders in the village *sangams* (autonomous women's groups). This CRS—Sangham Radio—finally went on the air in 2008 as India's first rural community radio after securing a license under the new policy.

In 2001, VOICES/MYRADA started an audio production center, Namma Dhwani (Our Voice), in Budikote village in Karnataka State and cablecast via TV programs made by rural men and women trained in radio production basics. This project was due to be officially licensed by 2010.

The Kutch Mahila Vikas Sangathan (KMVS), an NGO working with rural women in Kutch area villages in Gujarat State, offered a different model. KMVS built on its long development work and, by purchasing a commercial slot, started airing a 30-minute sponsored Kutchi language program on AIR's Radio Bhuj in 1999. They then acquired the AIR slot for two subsequent series and called themselves Ujjas (Light) Radio. Owing to the vast geographical area in which KMVS functions, different blocks or communities applied for separate licenses to operate their own CRSs. These stations planned to seek capacity-building from Ujjas.

Chala Ho Gaon Mein (Come, Let's Go to the Village) was a community radio program supported by the National Foundation for India and produced by community representatives of Alternative for India Development, a grassroots-level NGO in Jharkhand. From August 2001, the program was broadcast from Daltongunj, a backward region in the Palamau district of the state, by using the AIR slot of the local station on terms similar to that of KMVS in Bhuj. The organization acquired its license and was set to launch its CRS.

Other initiatives that merit mention here are the Heval Vaani (Voice From the Heval Valley) and Mandakini ki Awaaz (Voice of the River Mandakini), set up in Uttarakhand State by a media and development NGO, IdeoSync. Also, Bundelkhand Radio, of Development Alternatives, started airing programs as a second rural station in 2008.

A New Beginning

The setting up of CRSs in India may be looked upon as an ongoing struggle for reclaiming the radio commons. The creation of an autonomous community radio sector would go a long way to foster a counter public sphere in which dissonant experiences and knowledge of the marginalized can be freely articulated, exchanged, debated, and developed. Several NGOs and media activist groups, which had campaigned and networked for nearly a decade to set up local radio for development, came together in 2007 to form the Community Radio Forum (CRF). CRF promotes setting up community stations and lobbies for policy changes to strengthen the progressive aspects of community radio policy and to further simplify and democratize licensing procedures.

Vinod Pavarala and Kanchan K. Malik

See also Chipko Environmental Movement Media (India); Community Radio (Sri Lanka); Community Radio in Pau da Lima (Brasil); Indigenous Radio Stations (México); Miners' Radio Stations (Bolivia); Peace Media (Colombia); Radio La Tribu (Argentina)

Further Readings

Pavarala, V., & Malik, K. K. (2007). *Other voices: The struggle for community radio in India*. New Delhi, India: Sage.

COMMUNITY RADIO STATIONS (BRASIL)

Brasil's community radio stations have their own special features, achievements—and a record of civil disobedience. They are public, with no money-making goals, and historically created and run, in most cases, collectively. They perform an important role in the process of informing and mobilizing around issues that concern the lives of impoverished and marginalized social sectors.

Their activities began after more than 2 decades of the military dictatorship imposed on the country beginning in 1964 in the context of social movement activism, of community associations, and of progressive sectors of Christian churches, which were seeking to find solutions to major social problems and mobilizing in struggles to reestablish democracy.

Their programming is alert to the public interest, is responsive to organized groups from subordinate classes and/or their localities, or contributes to their social development. Among other items, they broadcast cultural materials created from among the same groups their programs aim to serve. They function as informal "schools" for media practice. They struggle to acquire the right of freedom of expression by operating and the empowering technologies that help to make it feasible.

Brasil has four contrasting models: community licensed stations, unlicensed free stations (or free community stations), loudspeaker stations, and Internet community stations.

The licensed stations transmit on low power FM, are managed by local community organizations, and are meant to reach small urban and rural areas. They are governed by Law 9.612 (1998) and regulated by Decree 2.615 (1998), which permits them to function solely in the name of community associations or nongovernmental organizations. The same law requires a minimum of five local legally registered nonprofits to form a single association with the objective of running the frequency. The Federal Ministry of Communications authorizes community stations.

Free stations operate the same way, but without a license. Conservative writers call them "pirate" or "clandestine" stations, but the stations reject both terms, since they have no financial goals and publicize their locations and frequencies. It should be emphasized that Brasil's FM community stations came into being without legal protection in the 1970s and 1980s (the law is dated 1998). Hundreds of thousands continue in this mode. While illegal under the law, they are socially valid by reason of the emancipatory work they develop.

Loudspeaker stations are also known as radio mailboxes or radio trumpets. They are small grass-roots sound systems that transmit their messages through loudspeakers or sound amplifiers. They are fixed to public lamp posts or other tall objects and on church towers. There is evidence of these dating back to the 1950s, but they blossomed in the 1980s. They are a particular type of "station" connected to social movements and community associations, such as churches (especially Catholic churches), and are used at times by media activists on behalf of citizens and communities for information, mobilization, and education, to challenge the blockages placed on legal use of the spectrum.

In other words, with no possibility of sharing the FM or AM spectrum, and at various moments in Brasil's political history when violent repression was launched against anyone daring to offend against the broadcasting laws, alternative communication channels were created, community radio being one. Its first emergence was as "people's radio" or "community radio" via loudspeakers, preceded by megaphones and then FM community radio on a specific frequency, and then by community FM proper, as specified in the 1998 law. Recently it has adopted Internet and web radio.

The recourse to loudspeakers was a way of escaping punishment under the telecommunications law, as community groups needed no authorization or special concession to operate loudspeakers. Activists affectionately call them "people's radio," meaning they are the only form of radio the public has real access to and can operate according to its own standards. In Brasil, a country of contrasts, this radio mode continues to fulfill an informative and educational role relevant to many regions. Many neighborhoods have no local or community station, and the commercial stations' programming comes from major cities, whose issues and topics often have a tenuous relationship to these localities.

Internet community stations (webcasters/Internet-only) are typically run by groups or communities with similar interests or experiences in common, based on language, ethnicity, or gender relations. Their operation tends to be less collective than that of community stations with a local base.

Although the community radio law and subsequent decrees envisage civil society, not-for-profit, and community action uses, a perhaps even larger number of stations operating under it are commercially motivated, linked to local political elites, or connected to religious groups (and used for evangelization, publicity, or even proselytizing, but without involvement in community affairs). This situation provokes controversies and misunderstandings in the community radio sector. For example, the commercially based stations run defamatory campaigns against the genuine community stations, accusing them across the board of being pirate or clandestine, which damages their real social contribution.

Faced with a choice, the commercial stations usually opt for the golden calf. The state radio stations often function as propaganda organs for the political party in office, canvassing for votes or calming their critics. The genuine community stations try to ensure effective channels for participation, not just at the microphone, but in producing and distributing programs and in other station activities, such as evaluation and program planning.

Legal Aspects

The 1998 law imposed a number of difficulties on community radio. One of its restrictions set the same community frequency for the entirety of Brasil. Yet in the vast city of São Paulo, this frequency was inaccessible for about a decade because of the zone's topography. Channel 198 was set for the city and 35 districts of Greater São Paulo at 87.4 FM, a very unfavorable point on the dial.

The city's first permission for a functioning community frequency was not until August 2007, located experimentally on another specific channel (199/87.7) and in the first instance assigned to São Paulo's Rádio Heliópolis. The transmitter was restricted to less than 25 watts, over a 1-kilometer radius and with a 30-meter aerial by law. Commercials were banned, and no public funds were made available to guarantee the station's continuance. Furthermore, only territorially based communities were recognized as having the right to use the channel. This excluded migrant workers from the rest of Latin America, Indigenous peoples, women's movements, and other potential users.

These obstacles were ones that the community radio movement was trying to overcome—through individual activists; through its national body, the Associação Brasileira de Radiodifusão Comunitária (Brazilian Community Radio Association) or ABRAÇO ("hug"); through similar organizations in the states and other forces struggling for democracy. A number of legislative proposals were put forward and study commissions formed, but after more than 10 years no substantial advance had been made, because the major commercial media defeated any attempt to democratize communication in the country. The federal government and congressional majorities were on their side. Moreover, a number of senators, deputies, and city councilors owned stations themselves.

The National Communications Agency (ANATEL) and federal policy close hundreds of community stations each year for unlicensed transmission. The policy is aggressively enforced and based solely upon complaints registered by ANATEL. Despite this, many stations reopen, others change addresses to make ANATEL's financial oversight harder or go to court to demand the right to operate a radio station. An index of the frequency of the latter is that in recent years a single sympathetic judge, now retired, acceded to around 100 temporary injunctions and permits favorable to community stations.

A rebellious mentality has been a feature of community stations in Brasil from the very beginning. Starting up as free community stations before the 1998 law was in place, there were estimated to be around 20,000 such stations by the end of the 1990s. Despite ANATEL's harassment, shutdowns, trials, and spontaneous closures, in the first decade of the 21st century, ABRAÇO still reckoned there were about 15,000 stations, around one quarter licensed.

Many disregarded the 1-kilometer and no-advertising rules. The Ministry of Communication's authorization process was painfully slow (some cases had been waiting 3, 5, or even 10 years) and nontransparent in defining what constituted a genuinely representative community association. A number rebelled by breaking the ANATEL seal on their doors and returning to remove the radio equipment. Others got temporary restraining orders on ANATEL decisions. Still others obtained new equipment through local community support.

At a time when civil society has been organizing innumerable collective projects to improve people's living conditions, there is a pressing need to use radio to create a communication channel to inform, mobilize, and discuss issues of local public concern in terms set by the community itself. Community bodies know that a station under their control can contribute to informal education and expand the ways citizens exercise their rights and duties. These cover freedom of expression, equal opportunity for political participation, enjoyment of one's cultural heritage, the right to communicate, and even every citizen's right to be informed and have access to the means of communication.

When the state refuses these rights, civil society manages to advance them by exerting them in practice, going ahead and broadcasting anyway. Those who pursue the matter through the courts invoke the Brazilian Constitution and the American Human Rights Convention (the San José Pact), which guarantee Brazilian citizens the right to full freedom of expression through whatever means.

As Paulo Silveira argues, when the government exceeds its constitutional rights (e.g., through unjust laws) or, through political insensitivity, spurns and neglects the public's reasonable concerns, then either the public accepts its dominion and becomes inactive and dependent on government favors, or it rebels in order to exercise its citizenship, beginning with civil disobedience and culminating in civil revolution. Civil disobedience, Silveira proposes, is salutary in a certain respect because it helps the government to redirect its mistaken path and also brings society back from its inertia.

This form of disobedience in Brasil only inconveniences the government, ANATEL, or commercial media owners, who in general operate in a much more aggressive fashion through their business associations. Local publics do not distinguish between licensed and unlicensed stations, or they do not care about the distinction. Sometimes they assemble at their station sites to resist the ANATEL "visitations" that always have the police present.

Cicilia M. Krohling Peruzzo
(translated by John D. H. Downing)

See also Community Media and the Third Sector; Community Radio (Ireland); Community Radio in Pau da Lima (Brasil); Community Radio Movement (India); Free Radio (Austria); Indigenous Radio Stations (México)

Further Readings

Bahia, L. M. (2008). *Rádios comunitárias: mobilização social e cidadania na reconfiguração da esfera pública* [Community radio stations: Social mobilization and citizenship in the reconfiguration of the public sphere]. Belo Horizonte, Brasil: Autêntica.

Kuhn, F. (2005). *O rádio entre o local e o global: fluxo, contrafluxo e identidade cultural na internet* [Radio between from local to global: Flow, contraflow, and cultural identity on the Internet]. São Bernardo do Campo, Brasil: UMESP.

Machado, A., Magri, C., & Masagão, M. (1986). *Rádios livres: a reforma agrária no ar* [Free radio: Agrarian reform on the air]. São Paulo, Brasil: Brasiliense.

Peruzzo, C. M. K. (2004). *Comunicação nos movimentos populares: a participação na construção da cidadania* [Communication in people's movements: Participation in the construction of citizenship] (3rd ed.). Petrópolis, Brasil: Vozes.

Peruzzo, C. M. K. (2006). Rádio comunitária na Internet: empoderamento social das tecnologias. [Community radio on the Internet: Social empowerment technologies]. *Revista Famecos 30,* 115–125. http://www.revistas.univerciencia.org/index.php/famecos/article/view/497

Silveira, P. F. (2001). *Rádios comunitárias* [Community radio stations]. Belo Horizonte, Brasil: Del Rey.

COPYLEFT

The concept of a "copyleft" was first introduced in the 1970s and is a form of copyright, a licensing of intellectual property, which sets out the terms of that property's use and distribution. Unlike copyright, which reserves all rights for the producer(s) of a piece of work, copyleft reserves some or no rights for the work's creator(s). Copyleft puts the work into the public realm, where, depending on the degree of freedom in the particular license used, the work can be changed, reproduced, used, or distributed. As opposed to the familiar copyright symbol ©, copyleft is signified by a backward "c" inside a circle (which, with splendid irony, is unavailable in standard

Unicode). Although the official General Public License is offered only in English, there are 18 unofficial translations of the license, from Spanish to Farsi, with several more under way. Creative Commons, the nonprofit corporation that works to spread copyleft licensing, notes 52 countries that have adopted Creative Commons license legislation and 8 other countries with legislation pending.

Copyleft is often thought of in terms of software, though it can also apply to music, art, writing, and other forms of information. One of the first examples of copyleft in the software world was with Tiny BASIC, a simplified version of the BASIC programming language developed in 1975. In the credits for the software was a copyleft symbol with the phrase "ALL WRONGS RESERVED."

The GNU General Public License (GPL), written by Richard Stallman in 1989, is a commonly used implementation of copyleft in the modern software world. Copyleft's strongest implications may indeed lie in the realm of software, as it allows for collaboration that would otherwise be impossible under copyrighted software. Some primary examples of software that have flourished under the GNU GPL are the many forms of Linux now freely available, the popular web browser Firefox, and the open-source alternative to Microsoft Office, Open Office. By putting these programs under a copyleft agreement, their users are able to not only modify and improve the software but also create free alternatives to what may otherwise be expensive programs.

A guarantee that a subsequent work derived from copylefted information will remain free under the same terms is key to a strong copyleft agreement. This is to ensure that the information will never be taken and copyrighted for exclusive use, negating the original intentions. Copyleft agreements can come in varying degrees, depending on the terms of the agreement. Whereas the GNU GPL generally applies to software, another license, the GNU Free Documentation License, was written by the Free Software Foundation to copyleft accompanying manuals and documentation.

Creative Commons is a similar form of rights preservation to copyleft. The Creative Commons website describes the license as in between full copyright, wherein all rights are reserved, and the public domain, wherein no rights are reserved. Creative Commons works to create a license that protects a work's author from being exploited while trying to contribute to community and cooperative efforts. Licenses are available online.

Mike Melanson

See also Alternative Media: Policy Issues; Creative Commons; Grassroots Tech Activists and Media Policy; Media Infrastructure Policy and Media Activism; Media Justice Movement (United States); *Radical Software* (United States)

Further Readings

Creative Commons: http://creativecommons.org
Free Software Foundation: http://www.fsf.org/licensing/licenses
GNU Public License: http://www.gnu.org/copyleft/copyleft.html
Jones, S. (Ed.). (2003). *Encyclopedia of new media: An essential reference to communication and technology.* Thousand Oaks, CA: Sage.

COR TV, 2006, Oaxaca (México)

On August 1, 2006, thousands of women took over the installations of the Corporación Oaxaqueña de Radio y Televisión (COR TV) in the city of Oaxaca. They held control for 21 days, transforming the programming, and serving as a voice for their social movement and for marginal sectors struggling against the state's neoliberal government. This unprecedented event shook the nation and undoubtedly changed the ways in which many viewed media. It set a precedent of what women can do when faced with a fundamental need to communicate to defend their and their people's needs.

COR TV's Background, the Teachers' Strike, and the APPO

COR TV is a public broadcasting corporation, operating radios 680 AM and 96.9 FM, and Oaxaca TV, a broadcast television station known as Channel 9. The goals for these public channels are to produce and disseminate programs promoting the state's development and supporting local cultures. Its slogan, "The radio and television of the Oaxacan people," announces that these public media belong to and serve the people. There is also a general consensus that over time many of COR TV's public service objectives have been undermined to serve state government interests.

COR TV's directors were always from the same political party as the state governor, mostly from the Partido Revolucionario Institucional (PRI; Institutional Revolutionary Party). Other members of its administration, too, were mostly aligned with the elected governor. The profound significance of these alliances became clearer during the dramatic events throughout 2006. It was then that many members of the public, along with unions and various civil society organizations, formed a coalition from which the social movement Asamblea Popular de los Pueblos de Oaxaca (APPO; Popular Assembly of the Peoples of Oaxaca) emerged.

APPO's formation was triggered by police repression against striking teachers. In May 2006, thousands of teachers went on strike asking for better salaries, better school conditions, and provisions of breakfast and books for poor students. Governor Ulises Ruíz Ortíz, elected in 2004 on a platform of promising to not allow marches, blockades, or encampments, rejected most of their demands.

By the end of May, the teachers had set up plastic tents, occupying the main *zócalo* (town square) and surrounding streets in downtown Oaxaca. Although not everybody supported this, sentiment soon turned against Ruíz Ortíz. At dawn on June 14, the governor sent about 1,500 riot police to the *zócalo* to take the sleeping teachers by surprise, which created an unexpected but widespread backlash against him. Brutal police behavior in evicting the teachers sparked tremendous solidarity with them.

University students and citizens went to the streets, confronting the police and demanding the governor's resignation. This turned into a day-long battle between the police and teachers, along with their citizen supporters. Whereas the police were heavily armed, teachers and citizens defended themselves with stones and sticks. Hundreds, including police officers, were badly injured and hospitalized. To make things worse, COR TV, and corporate media like Televisa and TV Azteca, justified the police violence.

From that moment on, the demand for the governor's resignation united people from different levels of Oaxacan society. A few days later at a large public forum, the movement formally adopted the title Asamblea Popular de los Pueblos de Oaxaca (APPO). The APPO was unusual in not having a leader; rather, it was a grassroots social movement with a representative council.

APPO's council would constantly consult the people through public forums on every new action, whether marches, blockades, barricades, or negotiations with the government. Besides trying to force the governor's resignation, APPO sought to create a permanent space where all citizens could exercise their constitutional rights and engage in transforming their society. Major discussions revolved around the need to attain self-governance, disposing of the repressive government as well as the neoliberal policies that had hit middle and lower classes hard.

COR TV and other mainstream media were meanwhile framing the APPO as a corrosive and destabilizing force.

COR TV's Takeover

Women were an important factor in this social movement because a great majority of teachers are women. However, women were not at center stage until the unprecedented takeover of COR TV on August 1, 2006.

As the struggle continued through June and July, the toll grew of political prisoners, badly injured, and corpses. The women called for a march that emulated women's marches in Argentina and Chile, which had experienced devastating dirty wars in the 1970s. The march, set for August 1, would be named *la marcha de las cacerolas,* or the Saucepans March (a familiar form of demonstration in some Latin American countries). Thousands of women walked to the zócalo, banging pots and calling for the governor's resignation. Once in the zócalo, the women spontaneously decided to go over to the station to request some airtime to express their views and concerns. Approximately 200 women walked in to speak

with the general director while a thousand or more waited outside.

Although the general director rejected their petition, the takeover that followed was peaceful. The women used the legal argument that the people have the right to revoke the public airwaves entrusted to the state if the state does not serve the interests of the people. They felt that this public media organization was privileging the views of the governor and those in power. Using COR TV's slogan, "The radio and television of the people of Oaxaca," they argued that they, the people of Oaxaca, were now in charge of their radio and television stations.

The general director turned over the building to them, probably because she and other employees felt intimidated by the thousands of women outside the building. This was a unique moment in this social movement and in the history of civil society's demands for rights over spectrum allocation and use of public airwaves. This action challenged both mainstream media as an institution, and the state as rightful possessor of the airwaves.

The women successfully aired their first radio and television broadcasts that very afternoon. A few employees who were APPO sympathizers aided them along with a few communication students from the local university who were called in to help. Over the next several days, employees were not allowed to remain, and university communication students and media aficionados provided all the technical support. With COR TV under their control, women came to center stage, energizing the population to stand firm and forcing the national media to pay closer attention to the conflict in Oaxaca.

Radio Cacerola and Channel 9

The women renamed the stations. The radio station became Radio Cacerola in honor of the August 1 march. The television station was still known as Channel 9, but adopted the slogan, "All power to the people." A group of APPO women and men volunteered to take charge of programming. Some had media experience, others not. The programs were primarily focused on content rather than format. This became one of the most interesting experiments in media democracy. The way in which the movement made use of the public airwaves served to mobilize thousands across the state. Listeners and viewers seized the opportunity to unite their voices with this emerging social movement.

The women's control over COR TV helped the movement gain momentum and created a central space from which to articulate the movement's purpose day by day, consolidating social and political cohesion. This demonstrated the power of the people over the state, and the actual physical structures of the stations, including the transmission towers, became symbolically reconquered spaces.

One of the most important strategies was to allow people in the state of Oaxaca to access microphones and cameras. They spoke about the long-standing needs and experiences of their communities as well as the current situation. Radio shows operated as an open forum to which people could call in, raising questions about the movement, the governor, democracy, and other pressing issues. For the most part, people called to affirm the movement and denounce social injustice, although there were also those calling to disagree. There was an open debate over the airwaves as never before.

The Programming

Those in charge of programming encountered the familiar challenge: filling airtime. This was a major issue, particularly for the television station. The radio had a more steady flow of programming throughout the day, beginning early in the morning and ending at around 11 p.m. Programs varied from news to music to public forums to gender issues. The television station operated on and off, sometimes from 1 p.m. to 9 p.m., and other times only throughout the afternoon.

As certain radio programs became a staple, some tensions and contradictions at the core of the movement began to surface. The lack of editorial control and programming direction made the radio a site that, for better or worse, different political tendencies could use to debate and disagree. In some instances, this seemed very democratic, but in others, it revealed internal fissures composed of dozens of radical left organizations, a more moderate left, and those in the center who had begun to support the APPO's call for social reform and more transparent governance.

Although such tensions and contradictions were not as evident in the television broadcasts, lack of content began to reduce its use for information or entertainment. For the most part, television programming showed old documentaries about Cuba, Nicaragua, and other countries that underwent major uprisings. There was a constant replaying of videos about the dawn eviction from the zócalo, produced by a local video collective Mal de Ojo (Evil Eye) and by citizens who had run into the streets with their consumer cameras. Other documentaries featured the work of Canal 6 de Julio, an independent video organization that covers issues not touched by corporate or state-run media.

Sometimes they would produce live roundtables discussing women's health issues, problems facing Indigenous communities, and other social problems across the state. The approach of many of these live programs was radically different to what audiences were used to getting on Channel 9, and many liked these programs.

However, some people within and outside the movement began questioning the tone of some programs because they did not want the movement to appear as a promoter for radical left ideologies, including armed struggle. Many did not want to see the public airwaves become a mouthpiece for those who still believed in authoritarian revolutionary models. The urgency of keeping up the fight against the governor while providing space for different voices and identities did not allow going into depth in the programming or resolving tensions in the broadcasts. Nevertheless, people still made use of Channel 9 and Radio Cacerola.

Finally, on August 22, 21 days after the women's bold and assertive act, the government sent a group of paramilitaries to cut the transmission signal of both radio and television, suddenly leaving the movement without a voice and a center. The women who were at the forefront of the radio and television operations promptly called for action and organized the takeover of 12 private radio stations in town. They had become aware of the significant power of media and were not willing to relinquish this newfound power to control mainstream media. They held control of those 12 stations for a few days until the stations' managers entered into an agreement with APPO guaranteeing the stations' return in exchange for more balanced coverage of the situation.

Gabriela Martínez

See also Community Radio in Pau da Lima (Brasil); Feminist Media: An Overview; Free Radio Movement (Italy); Indigenous Radio Stations (México); Peace Media (Colombia); Radio La Tribu (Argentina); Radio Lorraine Coeur d'Acier (France); Zapatista Media (México)

Further Readings

Congreso de Estado Libre y Soberano de Oaxaca. (1993). *Decreto ley 159.* http://www.congresooaxaca.gob.mx/lx/info/legislacion/111.pdf

Davis, N. (2007). *The people decide: Oaxaca's popular assembly.* Natick, MA: Narco News Books.

Esteva, G. (2007). The Asamblea Popular de los Pueblos de Oaxaca: A chronicle of radical democracy. *Latin American Perspectives, 34,* 129–144. Retrieved March 2, 2008, from http://lap.sagepub.com/cgi/content/abstract/34/1/129

López, C. B. (2007). *Oaxaca: Insula de Rezagos: Crítica a sus gobiernos de razón y de costumbre* [Oaxaca: Island of Backwardness: Critique of the "usos y costumbres" of its governments]. Oaxaca, México: Editorial Siembra.

Martínez, G. (2008). *Civil disobedience and community media at the birth of a social movement.* Paper presented at the International Association for Media and Communication Research conference, Stockholm, Sweden.

Osorno, D. E. (2007). *Oaxaca: La primera insurección del siglo XXI* [Oaxaca: The first insurrection of the 21st century]. México: Grijalbo.

Stephens, L. (2006, September 12). Women play key role in Oaxaca struggle. *North American Congress on Latin America (NACLA).* Retrieved March 2, 2008, from http://nacla.org/node/1408

Creative Commons

Creative Commons is a nonprofit organization founded in 2001 to promote an expansion of copyright law to allow greater access, use, and repurposing of creative works. Free culture advocate Lawrence Lessig is among the organization's founders. Since 2005, the organization has expanded to scientific works with its project Science Commons. The group offers licenses that can be applied by copyright owners to their work to allow or prohibit certain uses. Originally focused on U.S. copyright law, the group has expanded its licenses to be compatible with copyright laws in more than 50 countries.

As opposed to blanket retention of rights by intellectual property holders, the licenses allow some rights to be granted to the public. The organization draws on an idea of a "public commons" of creative content that allows the public to interact with creative works with a greater degree of freedom than increasingly restrictive copyright laws allow, believing that more sharing leads to a more robust society. Somewhere between the "all rights reserved" of copyright, and the public domain, with "no rights reserved," Creative Commons argues for "some rights reserved" by the copyright holders, with the rest given over to the public.

Creative Commons draws inspiration from the GNU General Public License, which allows software writers to release their proprietary code for others to use, modify, and redistribute without restrictions. The Creative Commons licenses expand this open source ethos to all creative works.

The organization offers six licenses for use, depending on the copyright holders' preferences. All licenses require attribution when using the work but do not limit users' ability to copy and distribute it. Copyright holders can choose to prohibit commercial use of the work and stipulate that the work not be modified or truncated in any way. Licenses can also request the users "share alike," or make any modified versions of the work available for further modification under a compatible and similar licensing scheme. A creative work can be released under a basic "Attribution" license, with no restrictions on use beyond a credit to the creator. At the same time, a work can be licensed under the most restrictive license "Attribution Noncommercial No Derivative Works," which prohibits commercial use of the work and any modification or truncating.

Creative Commons licensing is facilitated primarily by the Internet and is particularly well suited to digital content, though it can be applied to any creative work. Photograph-sharing website

Flickr.com allows its users to apply Creative Commons licensing to their pictures through built-in mechanisms. The Creative Commons site offers code that web authors can include in their sites—often using the phrase "some rights reserved"—to denote licensing schemes and to link back to the Creative Commons sites so potential users can get more information. As a result of the technical nature of applying the licenses, their effective use is most common in global North countries and relies on the existence of a cultural dialogue about intellectual property.

Daniel Darland

See also Alternative Media: Policy Issues; Copyleft; Media Infrastructure Policy and Media Activism; *Radical Software* (United States)

Further Readings

Boyle, J. (2008). *The public domain: Enclosing the commons of the mind.* New Haven, CT: Yale University Press. http://www.law.duke.edu/boylesite
Creative Commons: http://creativecommons.org/about
Lessig, L. (2003). The Creative Commons. *Florida Law Review, 55*(3), 763–777. http://homepages.law.asu.edu/~dkarjala/OpposingCopyrightExtension/commentary/LessigCreativeCommonsFlaLRev2003.htm

CULTURAL FRONT (CANADA)

The tone and style of alternative media during the interwar period in Canada are indicated by a 1930 cover of *The Militant Youth,* a Ukrainian-Canadian journal written by and for children. It featured a screaming boy with a noose around his neck: "Lynched Negro Worker" "Stop Lynching!" Such an explicit graphic is an early example of "agit-prop"—media combining agitation and propaganda—expressing outrage as an emphatic call to action. Its opposition to social injustices and inequalities across national and social borders signaled the convergence of several battles in an emerging Cultural Front.

The metaphor of "the Cultural Front" draws attention to how movements and media develop, intersect, and network through what Michael Denning distinguishes as the "politics of allegiance" and the "politics of form." The former describes how a number of different organizations and groups come together in a network with a common purpose. The politics of form encompasses the cultural producers, their modes and means of communication, and the venues necessary for production and exhibition.

Origins of the "Popular Front"

In 1930s Canada, these networks forged a social movement initially characterized as the "popular front." Historically, the term identifies a formal coalition among a range of socialist and communist political parties which formed Popular Front governments in Spain and France in 1936. Facilitating a popular front was also a specific strategy of the Communist International at the time, which sought alignment among progressive political parties and activist groups in many countries with a view to avoid war but defeat fascism.

Such alignments were exemplified in Canada in the formation of umbrella organizations such as the Canadian League Against War and Fascism (1934), bringing together various groups by drawing attention to the intersection between civil rights, political economy, communication, and culture. Such groups included communist, socialist, and labor political parties, labor unions and unorganized workers, associated women's groups (including the Women's International League for Peace and Freedom), and radical religious groups such as the Fellowship for Christian Social Order.

The Canadian League Against War and Fascism was complemented by a push for a "united front" of youth organizations, bringing together labor, pacifist, political, and religious organizations in youth congresses. This resulted in a Bill of Rights of Canadian Youth (1936), which implored the federal government to guarantee a holistic set of rights connecting economic security, ethical and creative labor, and culture, health, and education, as inseparable and interdependent.

Although the politics of allegiance was volatile because of conflicts over rival goals and methods, the energy and mobilization of the Cultural Front grew from the politics of form. This meant cultural action from below, both opposed and alternative to the dominant structuring of culture in sports, drama, and education. It equally meant expanding communication through producing a whole range of alternative media.

The Cultural Front in Sport

An amalgamation of local sports clubs into the Workers' Sport Association of Canada, for example, opposed the commodification of sports, with the associated construction of large premises for paying spectators, and media and corporate promotional budgets (exemplified by Canada's National Hockey League). It distanced itself from the individualism, nationalism, patriotism, and militarism imposed on most amateur sport organizations and aimed to facilitate public alternatives that did not discriminate by age, gender, or social class.

Sport was seen as a social activity for physical and spiritual development, which needed to be accessible in terms of time available to participate in free or public facilities. It was also political, involving agitating for such access and unrestricted participation. Its publications included a regular magazine, pamphlets, and promotion and support of the Worker's Olympics (held every 4 years from 1921 to 1937). Whereas the International Olympic Committee's Olympic Games were based on national identification, individual performance, and restricted competition, the Worker's Olympics stressed international solidarity and had no limits on either participation or performance.

The Cultural Front in Drama

Articulating the Cultural Front in drama meant reclaiming creative performance as inclusive, opposed to the exclusive and structured practice of professional theater. A number of mobile and fixed stage drama groups developed into the Progressive Arts Club, later establishing a Theatre of Action. Small but active mobile troupes performed in the streets, public parks, and community halls and traveled to parades, demonstrations, and strikes, producing agit-prop in dramatic form for large rallies such as those of the Canadian League Against War and Fascism.

They were complemented by the numerous drama circles, musicians, choirs, and other creative groups that were housed in community halls, or immigrant "labor temples," in towns and cities across Canada. Community, independent ownership of these halls was crucial in securing a public space for the creative politics of the Cultural Front. They included libraries, printing presses, reading rooms, and classrooms, for developing civic knowledge and communication skills.

The Cultural Front in Adult Learning and Education

The Cultural Front included alternative developments in adult learning. The Workers' Educational Association (WEA) challenged the state education system, which directed workers to "vocational" schools, and equally challenged universities' restricted public access, segregated disciplines, and curriculum based on positivism, "scientific management," and corporate requirements. The WEA worked to contribute to the development of critical thinking in its "education for citizenship" and to democratize adult education through courses combining political economy with civics, drama, public speaking, and journalism.

Its regular publications—written by students and teachers—combined education with activism focused on labor and social legislation, such that by 1935, it established two research institutes to advance participation in government policy making. The WEA was an innovator in the use of radio to facilitate adult long-distance education and, supported by its own production facilities and film library, use of film, photo slides, and radio to provide classes and promote discussion groups.

The WEA teachers and writers were part of a new radical literary movement of the Cultural Front, intent on combining creative writing skills with progressive activism. A literary style called *reportage* emerged in Canada in a variety of genres, including poetry, novels, and literary journals. It drew attention to social realism (starvation, violence, the exploitation and oppression of the working class) and socialist realism (advocating the elimination or alleviation of oppression). Cultural Front writers sought to demonstrate that rebellion and revolution were not foreign to Canada or communistic, but an integral part of its history. Although these publications were small and relatively short-lived, owing to the Depression and the ideological limits of Canadian commercial publishers, the writers had better access in this alternative press.

Cultural Front Media

There was by then a common Cultural Front view that independent control over production, distribution, and exhibition of communication was essential. Ranging from mimeographed bulletins to a daily newspaper, the alternative press of the Cultural Front included the immigrant press; the many union publications; the socialist and communist party newspapers; "radical" religious and pacifist publications; and thousands of pamphlets addressing unemployment, hunger, war, and fascism. The labor temples were essential printing facilities, and where financially possible, formal publishing houses such as the Finnish Publishing Co. Ltd., the (Ukrainian) Worker-Farmer Publishing Association, and the union-supported Mutual Press Ltd. were established to produce the wide range of publications. Most of the labor press was situated in Winnipeg, which was, up until the late 1930s, *the* center of labor publication in North America.

Frequency and reach of the Front's immigrant-language press depended on the group's size, as well as its organization and finances. Although its overall content was similar to the nationalist, religious, and commercial immigrant press, it differentiated itself by its focus on social class and the international exploitation of labor. The titles included the words *workers, working people,* or *labor,* later changed to *people's* to reflect the shift to a popular or united front. These papers were predominantly communist leaning, but included a range of political expressions including Trotskyist, socialist, and social-democratic positions. Less dogmatic papers preferred to emphasize *independence, truth,* or *freedom* in addition to working class or labor unity. Press editors were almost always male, yet there were dedicated women's and youth publications, such as the communist-leaning *The Militant Youth,* and these publications were expressions of women's and youth activism.

The immigrant labor press was complemented by a political party press, which included the Communist Party of Canada (CPC) and the press of the fledging democratic-socialist party, the Co-operative Commonwealth Federation (CCF). Encouraging the development of an activist press was also, from 1933, the goal of the Associated Labor Press, which was intent on becoming a critical news bureau and distribution agency. Although the Depression caused many commercial newspapers to close, the CPC published a daily newspaper beginning in 1936. Political differences evident in the immigrant labor press were also expressed in polemics between the CPC and the CCF, as each sought to discredit the other. The organized labor press did little to encourage movement unity. Written primarily by union leaders, it focused on interunion rivalry and reified prevailing divisions in labor's ranks (radical vs. corporatist, national vs. international, skilled vs. nonskilled) and reinforced divisions of gender, race, and ethnicity.

As the threat of fascism and another war loomed large, Cultural Front media included flyers, pamphlets, posters, almanacs, calendars, and books advertised in the newspapers, distributed in the street, and posted in labor temples, union halls, and on street corners. Pamphlets were usually on a specific topic, such as capitalism, imperialism, war, and fascism, and included republications and explanations of government proceedings, international socialism, and activist methods. Photographs, cartoons, sheet music, and radical lyrics were also distributed in alternative bookstores and through the immigrant and party press.

Art displays and poster exhibitions on socialism were part of the youth congresses, and like the poets and writers who wrote in the alternative press, individual artists adopted socialist realism in their work. Radical religious and pacifist publications critiqued capitalism and engaged in polemics, distributed by a small number of "peace libraries," on the relationship of socialism, religion, and pacifism.

The combination of unemployment, hunger, and the Depression, together with the rise of fascism and the enlistment of Canadian volunteers in the Spanish Civil War, made for potent inspiration as Canadian activists searched for ways of articulating them through media and culture. These forms were inevitably limited in comparison to commercial, conservative religious, and government media that consistently sought to discredit or destroy challenges to the dominant power hierarchy.

Less limited by media ownership and control were the many marches, parades, and rallies in streets, parks, and on government grounds. It was there that participants confirmed the movements' existence and made the Cultural Front most visible, and it was there where governments used violence and restrictive laws to contain the movement.

On each site of the Cultural Front, a central challenge was to keep politics and culture together despite the drive to structure them into separate regimes of sport, education, theater, and literature, distinct and politically separate from labor. Indeed, this was not a so-called old social movement solely concerned with labor and limited to political and economic concerns, but one that emphasized the connections between labor, politics, communication, and culture as manifest in capitalism, imperialism, fascism, and war. It is through identifying both the politics of affiliation and the politics of form that we see the battles of the Cultural Front still endure.

Patricia Ann Mazepa

See also Challenge for Change Film Movement (Canada); Citizens' Media; Community Broadcasting (Canada); Indian People's Theatre Association; Labor Media (United States); Street Theater (Canada); Workers' Film and Photo League (United States)

Further Readings

Berger, T. R. (1982) *Fragile freedoms, human rights and dissent in Canada.* Toronto, ON: Clarke, Irwin.

Bray, B. (1990). *Against all odds: The Progressive Arts Club's production of* Waiting for Lefty. *Journal of Canadian Studies, 25*(3), 489–504.

Denning, M. (1996). *The Cultural Front: The laboring of American culture in the twentieth century.* London: Verso.

Doyle, J. (2002). *Progressive heritage: The evolution of a politically radical literary tradition in Canada.* Waterloo, ON: Wilfred Laurier Press.

Kidd, B. (1996). *The struggle for Canadian sport.* Toronto, ON: University of Toronto Press.

Patrias, C. (1994). *Patriots and proletarians: Politicizing Hungarian immigrants in interwar Canada.* Montréal, QC: McGill-Queen's University Press.

Radforth, I., & Sangster, J. (1981, Autumn/Spring). A link between labour and learning: The Workers' Educational Association in Ontario, 1917–1951. *Labour, Le Travail, 8/9,* 41–78.

Socknat, T. P. (1987). *Witness against war: Pacifism in Canada, 1900–1945.* Toronto, ON: University of Toronto Press.

CULTURE JAMMING

Culture jamming appropriates a dominant cultural form and then alters it in a way that becomes a comment on the form itself, often with a critical edge. The goal is to disrupt the easy flow of cultural communication taking place through corporate texts and products and to expose underlying processes or assumptions that are commonly taken at face value. It is a tactic used by activists associated with a wide variety of social movements, including the anticonsumerism and antiglobalization movements. Its success is ultimately tied to viewers' ability to see through the façade of similarity to the criticism embedded in the "jam."

Culture jamming has been associated with the Dada, surrealist, and Situationist movements. For many of the artists and activists who worked within those milieus, everyday objects became the means through which they expressed critiques of contemporary society and culture. The term *culture jamming* is credited to collage band Negativland, who, in their release *Jam Con '84,* likened culture jamming to the practice of jamming broadcasting. They argue that cultural communication can be jammed in much the same way, because the jammer interferes with cultural communication in an attempt to inscribe it with alternative meaning that is critical of the original.

The analogy is not exact, given that broadcasts are jammed to block their message entirely, but in doing this, culture jammers work with the same iconography and aesthetics as their targets, within the same cultural, and sometimes geographical, spaces. However, the texts which these activist artists massage to reinscribe with critical content tend, at least at a rapid glance, to resemble what they critique. What results is a nuanced form of critique where the jammer's reworking of the original may be entirely missed.

A wide variety of cultural objects serve as the targets of culture jamming activity; advertisements, pop cultural icons and products (such as logos, dolls, and compact discs), and websites serve as a few examples. Perhaps the most commonly cited and experienced culture jamming form is the *subvertisement.* An original advertisement is the starting point for this activity, of which the content is then subtly, or not so subtly, altered while staying true to the original's aesthetic features. Subvertising is done on small and large scales, with magazine, television, and billboard advertising serving as catalysts. Subvertisements are used to critique anything from the specific product to advertising practices and consumer culture in general.

Culture jamming can be expanded to apply to cultural processes and behaviors. In the activity of media hoaxing, for example, culture jammers lead journalists to believe they are presenting an honest story when, in fact, the story is completely made up. Prominent media hoaxer Joey Skaggs uses this tactic to point out the flaws in journalistic practices. The Yes Men's numerous pranks posing as World Trade Organization officials at trade conferences around the world serve as an example of culture jamming that attempts to disrupt common perceptions of globalization by upsetting expectations of the organization's behavior and policy.

It is through the upsetting of common expectations that culture jamming is expected to have most of its critical power. Ideally, at the moment a viewer realizes that what he or she is experiencing is not an original, a critical reassessment of the cultural norms associated with that form should follow. In this way, culture jamming challenges people to think critically about the ideologies that sustain a host of social, cultural, and economic practices. It is used by activists associated with any number of social movements. And its creative nature means that any specific tactics enacted are limited only by the practitioners' imagination.

The main criticisms of culture jamming are tied to the tactic's mode of address. Some argue that the predominantly rhetorical nature of culture jamming's critique of structures of inequality leaves them firmly intact. For example, much of the culture jamming activity of the anticonsumerist organization Adbusters Media Foundation has been critiqued as merely a comment on consumerism, rather than affecting the material conditions that give rise to any social and cultural problems stemming from consumerism.

Another criticism centers on the texts and notes the cultural level at which criticism is offered. Not only can cultural critique cloaked in the language and aesthetics of the target be easily missed, but it is also ripe for appropriation from above. In this case, culture jammers must rely heavily on the viewers' cultural capital, that they can spot the jam, flesh out the critique being offered, and then be motivated to act.

Many critics, however, miscalculate the potential for change when culture jamming is used by activists. For example, rather than conceiving culture jamming as a force that should immediately change the material relations of society, the activity can serve an educational and inspirational role. Educationally, it can help to illuminate social and cultural problems people may not have thought of before, encouraging them to change their behavior or even join a wider activist movement. This is culture jamming's consciousness-raising potential. Moreover, culture jamming can be a powerful way of organizing and maintaining a community of activists around common ideals and goals. This can be extremely important to a social movement's longevity and strength.

Afsheen Nomai

See also Adbusters Media Foundation (Canada); Barbie Liberation Organization (United States); Installation Art Media; Performance Art and Social Movement Media: Augusto Boal; Yes Men, The (United States)

Further Readings

Carducci, V. (2006). Culture jamming: A sociological perspective. *Journal of Consumer Culture, 6*(1), 116–138.

Dery, M. (1993). *Culture jamming: Hacking, slashing and sniping in the empire of signs.* Westfield, NJ: Open Media.

Haiven, M. (2001). Privatized resistance: *Adbusters* and the culture of neoliberalism. *Review of Education/ Pedagogy and Cultural Studies, 29,* 82–110.

Harold, C. (2007). *Our space: Resisting the corporate control of culture.* Minneapolis: University of Minnesota Press.

Heath, J., & Potter, A. (2005). *The rebel sell: Why the culture can't be jammed.* Toronto, ON: Harper Perennial.

Klein, N. (2000). *No logo.* New York: Picador.

Lasn, K. (1999). *Culture jam: How to reverse America's suicidal consumer binge.* New York: Eagle Brook.

Negativland. (1985). Crosley Bendix reviews JamArt and cultural jamming. On *Jam Con '84* [CD]. El Cerrito, CA: Seeland.

Nomai, A. J. (2008). *Culture jamming: Ideological struggle and the possibilities for social change.* Unpublished doctoral dissertation, University of Texas, Austin.

DALIT MOVEMENT MEDIA (INDIA)

In India, the movement of "untouchables" against the caste system is generally known as the Dalit movement. The word means "crushed" or "broken to pieces" in the Marathi language. The movement has long used popular cultural forms effectively to fight caste oppression.

Emergence of the Dalit Movement

Historically, the relationship between the Dalits and popular cultural form emerged mainly as a result of two factors: (1) the "cultural labor" imposed on the Dalits within the hierarchy of caste occupations, and (2) the fact they were required to work with animals' skins, which the upper castes found sacrilegious to touch, to make musical instruments. Thus, there existed many forms of music, dance, and theater chiefly designed for the upper castes' entertainment but played and performed by the Dalits. Many of these cultural forms persisted as oral traditions, as the caste system denied the Dalits access to literacy.

The emergence of a concerted movement against caste oppression in the 19th century reinvented these popular cultural forms as movement media, as sites of resistance and contestation. Two such popular forms are noteworthy: *powada* (a praise song exclusively performed by lower caste males in Maharashtra State) and *tamasha* (a popular form of folk theater).

Conventionally, the lower castes used to compose powadas in praise of the dominant ruling castes. It is in this art form the Dalit movement found a militant cultural expression. For example, one well-known powada presents King Shivaji—a popular icon in Maharashtra and India at large for his brave feats in the 1600s against the Mughal emperors—as the leader of the lower castes and attributes his achievements to the strengths and skills of his lower caste armies rather than his court.

Cultural hegemony has enabled a degree of consent among Dalits to the exploitative caste practices. Jotirao Phule and Bhimrao Ambedkar, pivotal late 19th- and early 20th-century Dalit leaders respectively, identified education as the most important means for reconstructing consciousness to liberate the Dalits from this "mental slavery." During those centuries, even though print media became powerful within the Dalit movement, the majority of the lower caste masses were illiterate. Consequently, the Dalit movement invented a new genre of tamasha—the *jalsa*—as a form of movement media to communicate with the masses.

The content was sharply altered: instead of religion, reform and revolt. A typical tamasha begins with a *gan* (devotional offering to the God), but in the jalsa, with a *gavlan* (a comic act by an "effeminate" male performer), followed by the performance of *lavani* (a spiritual and erotic ballad performed by lower caste women). The key element of the new jalsas was the *vag* (extempore satirical performance), which often praised modern science and education, ideas of rights and equality, and was built around mockery of the oppressive brahminical religious practices. One of Phule's famous compositions, titled "The World Leans," critiqued the rich men who bid for the sexual services of the tamasha dancers.

In *Ambedkari Jalsa*, the plots and themes were organized around Ambedkar's principles of equality, fraternity and liberty. Instead of the conventional respectful *Johar Maibap!* greeting to a landlord, the plot would begin with the slogan *Jai Bhim!* in praise of Bhimrao Ambedkar (and also a traditional friendly greeting among Indian Buddhists). However, jalsas highlighted their difference from the tamashas by omitting the erotic lavanis, which most social reform movements considered vulgar—but thereby excluded women performers. The Dalit movement in rural India during Ambedkar's leadership also used the *kalapathak* tradition, a folk musical theater that involves a director/lyricist and in which actors are also the chorus and write their own roles.

Dalit Literature

Immediately after Ambedkar's death in 1956, a young generation of urban educated Dalits, pouring out of the educational institutions established by him, initiated the Dalit Panthers and Dalit literature movement in the Maharashtra region. Both movements were inspired by his struggle against caste oppression. These movements gave new meaning to the word *Dalit*, which became a symbol of change and revolution. Writing to critique the persistence of caste-based social order in postindependence democratic India became a way for the Dalits to express their anger and frustration. The Dalit literature movement was designed to develop a counterhegemonic ideology against the logic of the caste system.

The movement's first imperative was to overcome the hegemonic grip of Hindu culture. A significant proportion of Dalit literature, therefore, was devoted to scathing denunciation of Hinduism. The language used was often deliberately provocative, blasphemous, and even obscene, designed to scandalize dominant caste values. Dialect and colloquialisms were deployed to demonstrate freedom from caste-Hindu culture. The following extract of a poem is a classic example: *O Parameshwar* [God] / *You are* / *Like an aged husband* / *An object*

of fun, who is / *The lord of his wife* / *Only in name . . .*

However, the Dalit literature movement also reflected a process of social change and stratification. Within it may be discerned a middle class and institutionally established group, who write about the Dalit masses. Emerging perhaps in opposition is a younger, more radical organized group, more oriented toward political activism. Existing alongside these two is an older, less-educated group of folk-poets, who represent continuity with the jalsa tradition and whose work is more easily accessible to the Dalit masses. The agenda and purpose of Dalit literature is different for each group.

Dalit Rangabhoomi (Theater)

The persistence of the traditional caste order in independent India emerged as a central theme in Dalit literature, but it remained confined to the educated urban intelligentsia. However, close on its heels emerged Dalit theater, which attempted to put into practice the agenda and ideology of the Dalit literature movement. The Abhinav Kala Niketan (Home of the Acting Arts), established in the 1970s, used street theater to spread a new Dalit awareness. Through their street plays, they presented a slice of the Dalits' everyday lives.

The plays were based on actual or plausible incidents related to the lives of the Dalits. The objective was to make them as real as possible, transcending the difference between art and life, or actors and audiences. The scripts were not fixed, and oftentimes the themes were suggested by the audience surrounding the pressing problems of that particular locality. Many of the plays depicted a new resolve on the part of Dalits to struggle for their rights. Some of the plays were like soap operas; each year, as new atrocities came to light, they got woven into the play.

One particularly striking treatment of the Dalit condition in independent India was in the "free play" titled *Day of Death or Day of Liberation*. The action was staged as a trial and debated whether freedom exists in India. The parties at stake were named as caste, capitalism, and dictatorship on the one hand, and minorities, untouchables, and slaves on the other. There were two other characters, named "freedom" and "citizen." Soon it appears that the judge sides with the former group, and toward the end "freedom" is carried away to be cremated.

In the context of increasing exclusion of Dalit artists from mainstream theater, the Dalit Ramgabhoomi Sanstha (Dalit Theater Organization) emerged in 1979 and put together a play depicting the emergence of Dalit consciousness. The play *Kalokhachya Garbahat* (In the Womb of Darkness) chronicled the Dalit movement and narrated the dismal story of the cruelty, brutality, and prejudices of Dalit life. The ending of the play is its most significant part, as in it, the main character took up a scythe and killed a Patil (a dominant caste in Western India). In his final address the narrator, who played a role akin to a Greek chorus, held society responsible for putting the scythe in the hands of the Dalit. The play depicted the dangerous consequences of the Dalit masses' continuing oppression and warned that the point of no return was rapidly approaching.

Theater has become a very appropriate media format for contemporary Dalit mobilization. There are currently more than 40 theater groups existing in different parts of the country. Many write their own plays; a few adapt plays from U.S. Black theater. For example, the Delhi-based Ahwan Theatre has two plays, titled *Devadasi* (Servant of God) and the translation of Langston Hughes's *Mulatto*. Some try to revive the old tradition of popular cultural forms. The theater has also supported a Dalit puppeteer group from Rajasthan State.

Bidhan Chandra Dash

See also *Adivasi* Movement Media (India); Dance as Social Activism (South Asia); Indian People's Theatre Association; Naxalite Movement Media (India); Social Movement Media, Anti-Apartheid (South Africa); Street Theater (India)

Further Readings

Dangle, A. (1994). *Poisoned bread: Translations from modern Marathi Dalit literature.* Mumbai, India: Orient Longman.

Gokhale, J. (1993). *From concession to confrontation: The politics of an Indian untouchable community.* Mumbai, India: Popular Prakashan.

Guru, G. (2004). *Dalit cultural movement and dialectics of Dalit politics in Maharashtra* (2nd ed.). Mumbai, India: Vikash Adhyayan Kendra.

Joshi, B. R. (Ed.). (1986). *Untouchable! Voices of the Dalit liberation movement.* London: Zed Books.

Limbale, S. (2004). *Towards an aesthetic of Dalit literature: History, controversies and considerations.* New Delhi, India: Orient Longman.

O'Halon, R. (2002). *Caste conflict and ideology: Mahatma Jotirao Phile and low caste protest in nineteenth-century western India.* London: Cambridge University Press.

Rege, S. (2002, March). Conceptualising popular culture: *Lavani* and *powada* in Maharashtra. *Economic and Political Weekly, 37*(11), 16–22.

Zelliot, E. (2001). *From untouchable to Dalit: Essays on the Ambedkar movement* (3rd ed.). New Delhi, India: Monohar.

DANCE AS SOCIAL ACTIVISM (SOUTH ASIA)

Dance is not the most obvious medium for dealing with political issues. It cannot easily contextualize, argue, or analyze. Yet as anthropologist Felicia Hughes-Freeland (2008) proposes: "Dance is more than it appears: it is a site of latent resistance and concealment, and a source of tactics which works against other institutional locations" (p. 28). One could argue that this is because intrinsically dance is always constructed around tensions and conflicts within the body.

South Asian choreographers use their artistic practice as political activism, creating powerful works that encourage people's awareness and understanding of different contemporary issues, such as gender discrimination, dowry deaths, homosexuality, AIDS, world debt, domestic violence, or ecological issues. It would be unusual for people to have their first encounter with such subject matter through dance; most probably go to the theater already half aware and convinced about the political issues raised. Nevertheless, the very experience of the live engagement with the artists strengthens and sharpens people's awareness, often giving them a longer lasting impression than, for example, reading a newspaper article on the same topic. Artists are therefore often directly political and engage in conflict awareness, if not necessarily resolutions, through their dance practice, the narrative content of their works, and the kinds of movement vocabulary they use.

This entry focuses on choreographers and dancers in South Asia who dance, despite the danger this puts them under, in countries where such practices are actively discouraged. It presents some examples of historical attitudes toward dance in Malaysia and Pakistan and also discusses dancers and choreographers who have chosen to create overtly political works.

The Act of Dancing as Activism

Dancing itself can be a political act when regimes consider such bodily practices as inappropriate. In such instances, dancers may often not describe their practice as "dance." Rather they will deploy another label, such as "exercise," to remove the stigma attached to dance. For example, Malaysian dance scholar Mohd Anis Md Nor has described how while working in the 1980s for an American doctorate, he hesitated to give prominence to 1930s studies by Jeanne Cuisinier, as they described practices of dance by traditional Malay healers, practitioners, and patrons of magic. He was concerned that the ultraconservative Muslim regime in Kelantam might respond to his research by entirely stamping out traditional Malay dances.

Similarly, Maneesha Tikekar has discussed how Pakistan largely has a culture hostile to the performing arts, with objections to dance as well as drama. Before Partition in 1947, Lahore had been a center for the arts, including dance, but after Partition, anything smacking of Indian culture had to be rooted out, beginning with music and dance. This did not mean, however, that dance disappeared entirely. Following the 1957 invitation of the prime minister of then both West and East Pakistan, a Bengali, Huseyn Shaheed Suhrawardy, to set up a dance academy, the dancers Jayakar and Neelima Ghanshyam moved from Kolkata to Karachi. Moreover in the 1970s, Prime Minister Zulfikar Ali Bhutto founded the Pakistan National Council for the Arts, the National Institute of Folk Heritage, the National Dance Academy, and the National Film Corporation. After his 1979 execution, however, his successor General Muhammad Zia-ul-Haq imposed martial law and instituted an "Islamization" program.

By the 1980s, strong restrictions had been put on artists, especially dancers. The renowned *kathak* practitioner, Naheed Siddiqui, for example, moved

to England. Similarly, the Ghanshyams were hounded out of the country in 1983. Vigilantes began attacking their house, which doubled as their dance institute, smashing windows and spray-painting graffiti on the gate threatening "Islamic punishment" to anyone found singing and dancing there.

Despite facing tremendous difficulties, Sheema Kirmani, a leading dancer and vocal campaigner in Pakistan, cofounded Tehrik-e-Neswan (Women's Movement) in Karachi in 1981, a company specializing in plays about women. She has commented on how hard it was to recruit women because their male relatives were prone to consider the stage dishonorable. Dancers trained by the Ghanshyams continue to dance and teach students from liberal families, but this takes place mainly in private residences. When it performed at Karachi University for International Women's Day in 1983, the company received threats, and the moment a man and a woman would come on stage together, shooting would start. Yet, when asked about the stigma attached to dance, Kirmani insists it is only the agenda of a small minority. She points out how she danced in front of 10,000 people at the Karachi World Social Forum in 2006 and in front of thousands at a conference in 2007.

Choreographies as Political Messages

A number of choreographers create works about political and social issues they hold dear as a way of engaging themselves and their practices in the world. British Asian choreographer Darshan Singh Bhuller, for example, argues that making dances is his way of "facing up to horror and evil." The Belgian Moroccan choreographer Sidi Larbi Cherkaoui says he sees everything he does as communication, and whether it is dancing or giving an interview, it is, in his view, political.

Many South Asian choreographers have similar approaches. Working with dance genres often directly linked to texts and where the separation between drama, dance, and mime does not exist to the same extent as in the West, South Asian choreographers can often be much more explicit than their Western counterparts in expressing specific messages, political or otherwise. Gujarati dancer and choreographer Mallika Sarabhai, for example, argues that it makes more sense for her to express in dance the horrors of caste violence than to perform classical Hindu myths of *bhakti* and the love for Shiva. She labels herself a dancer-activist. Similarly, the journalist and writer Asif Farrukhi described Kirmani's work as celebrating and exploring personal and social issues, and Kirmani herself sees her artistic and activist identity merging in her fight for social equality, peace, and justice.

Younger generations of South Asian choreographers and dancers continue to engage with the world in this way. The Bengali Prarthana Purkayastha, for example, working within the contemporary Navanritya (New Dance) genre, creates choreographic work with a social conscience. In 2004, she choreographed *From Hecabe*—the legendary Trojan queen who saw her children massacred—as her artistic response to the horror of the Beslan school massacre in Russia, in which Chechen terrorists took more than 1,000 people hostage, mainly children, and which ended in a massacre when Russian commandos retook the school. In 2007, she choreographed *The Wife's Letter,* a solo performance based on "Streer Patra" (1914), a controversial short story written by Nobel laureate poet Rabindranath Tagore, where a 28-year-old Bengali woman, Mrinal, tells her husband she is leaving, because she rejects the unjust traditions that put her at his family's mercy, and will take no more of his insensitivity.

Conclusion

If, as mentioned earlier, dance is not as effective as drama in communicating political messages, it may be useful to reflect as to why artists should chose to work in this way and why audiences enjoy their performances. Dance is a practice that focuses on embodiment, and it can be seen as a somewhat privileged medium for dealing with communication that deals with this panhuman experience. Indeed, Judith Mackrell, dance critic for the London newspaper *The Guardian,* has argued that dance not only expresses raw feelings but may be more powerful and subtle than text when it comes to capturing the visceral dynamics of emotion, the sensual texture of experience.

The late ethnomusicologist John Blacking argued that the arts had the potential to be powerful because they provide a way of discovering something about oneself and especially about the world of feelings. They are effective, he claimed, because the roots of our humanity are to be found not in ratiocination, but in the quality and intensity of feelings, as expressed primarily in nonverbal communication and ritual.

A great deal of time, energy, and resources are devoted in dance to the construction of extraordinary bodies with capabilities unavailable to most people. It is through these bodies that the stories, ideas, and aesthetic ideals proposed by different performance genres are transmitted in memorable ways to their audiences. Social dance can also be part of a subterranean symbolic politics of resistance, although to examine such a double meaning embedded in the dance is beyond the scope of this entry.

Andrée Grau

See also Bhangra, Resistance, and Rituals (India/Transnational); Indian People's Theatre Association; Installation Art Media; Performance Art and Social Movement Media: Augusto Boal; Sarabhai Family and the Darpana Academy (India); Social Movement and Modern Dance (Bengal); Street Theater (India)

Further Readings

Claus, P. J., Diamond, S., & Mills, M. A. (Eds.). (2003). *South Asian folklore: An encyclopedia: Afghanistan, Bangladesh, India, Nepal, Pakistan, Sri Lanka.* New York: Taylor & Francis.

Farrukhi, A. (Interviewer). (n.d.). Sheema Kirmani. *Mag4you.* Retrieved March 26, 2009, from www.mag4you.com/spotlight/Sheema+Kirmani/9382.htm

Hughes-Freeland, F. (2008). *Embodied communities: Dance traditions and change in Java.* Oxford, UK: Berghahn Books.

Mackrell, J. (2003, February 12). Dance away the heartache. *The Guardian.* http://www.guardian.co.uk/stage/2003/feb/12/dance.familyandrelationships

Mackrell, J. (2004, June 5). The power to provoke. *The Guardian.* http://www.guardian.co.uk/stage/2004/jun/05/dance.music

Malik, I. H. (2006). *Culture and customs of Pakistan.* Westport, CT: Greenwood Press.

Pak Tea House: http://pakteahouse.wordpress.com

Sarwar, B. (2008, June 30). Struggling to dance. *Pak Tea House.* http://pakteahouse.wordpress.com/2008/06/30/struggling-to-dance

Scott, J. C. (1992). *Domination and the arts of resistance: Hidden transcripts.* New Haven, CT: Yale University Press.

Tikekar, M. (2004). *Across the Wagah: An Indian's sojourn in Pakistan.* New Delhi, India: Promilla/ Bibliophile South Asia.

Van Erven, E. (1992). *The playful revolution: Theatre and liberation in Asia.* Bloomington: Indiana University Press.

DANGWAI MAGAZINES (TAIWAN)

The term *dangwai* means "outside the party" and denotes the crop of illegal media that emerged in Taiwan to challenge the harsh one-party rule imposed in the late 1940s. After his defeat by the Communists, Chiang Kai-shek took his quasi-Leninist Nationalist regime (Kuomintang, or KMT) and fled to Taiwan in 1949. He declared martial law and suspended constitutional rights, in the name of anticommunism. Freezing press licenses effectively put the party-state and Chiang's mainland loyalists in control of the media (owning half of the 31 papers, a majority of radio stations, and all three television stations). However, the regime did not ban small media (political magazines and, later, crude cable service). Dissenters turned to resource-poor, low-cost, small-scale, and technologically crude channels of communication. Run by a small group of political activists rather than professional journalists, these "guerrilla media" rose from the margin to wage "hit and run" battles with state censors and the mainstream media. They attacked the authoritarian party-state, challenging its patron–client system, its rigid control, and its hegemonic myths and fake consensus. More important, they became integrated into political movements as powerful organizational and ideological instruments.

In the 1950s, the liberal *Free China Monthly* advocated that Taiwan implement democracy to fight against the Communists, only to anger the authorities. A liberal alliance of intellectuals and politicians was crushed when they tried to launch an opposition party. *Internal colonialism*—elite minority rule of mainland Chinese over the majority of local Taiwanese—defined Taiwan's identity politics along ethnic lines from the beginning.

Taiwan Political Review and Democratic Change

After a 15-year interlude, emerging local politicians regrouped and in 1976 published the *Taiwan Political Review.* This magazine was presented explicitly as a political project to mobilize grassroots support rather than as an intellectual assertion by the 1950s liberal elites. It challenged the KMT's legitimacy claims—especially the "one China" myth that bolstered the mainlanders' power privileges—but was closed down after only five issues.

While monopolizing central power, the KMT incorporated local elites and allowed local elections to boost its legitimacy. In 1977, opposition candidates for the first time captured important seats and won 30% of the popular vote in local elections. They were emboldened to form a loosely organized *Dangwai* (Outside the Party) body, a name adopted to avoid being banned as an unauthorized political party but also to signal distance from the KMT regime.

In the late 1970s, the title of *Free China* was changed to *Formosa,* and the magazine became the focus of Dangwai's organizational and media efforts. The title change suggested that anti-KMT and domestic power redistribution took precedence as the movement's primary themes against the larger background of anticommunism. *Formosa* energized movement leaders, and legislators were elected to coordinate political rallies via the magazine's 21 offices throughout Taiwan. When the United States recognized the People's Republic of China in 1979, the KMT arrested almost all Dangwai leaders at a protest rally. This watershed event garnered international attention and brought censure from the U.S. government. The authorities killed *Formosa* magazine, but public sympathy sent more of the victims' spouses and defense lawyers into office in subsequent elections. Dangwai magazines sprouted like grass. They raised public consciousness and legitimized counterideologies. They raised funds and coordinated political activities, while cementing an in-group identity within the movement. They formed a united front, forcing the regime and pro-KMT media to answer inconvenient questions. Press freedom was hard fought, with appeal to such empowering Western ideologies as "the public's right to know" and "checks and balances."

By the late 1970s, two privately owned newspaper groups had replaced state press organs as the center of editorial gravity. The *United Daily News* sided with the KMT's conservative wing, and the *China Times* endorsed its liberal wing. They were generally unsympathetic to the Dangwai's "unruly" practical politics and yet found themselves constantly disparaged by Dangwai publications for their timidity and hypocrisy. Given its audience reach and certified status, however, the mainstream press was crucial in promoting the abstract concepts of democracy, press freedom, and the rule of law. Moreover, its reporters were found to have contributed to understaffed Dangwai magazines—under pseudonyms—the bulk of trenchant Dangwai critiques of KMT misbehavior.

The1980s: Fragmentation, Success, and Disappearance

In the 1980s, ideological rifts and competition grew more intense among Dangwai camps. Each faction ran several organs, sniping at each other while attacking the KMT as the common enemy. The censors hardened their repression by imprisoning more Dangwai publishers, acting on tips to impound their publications at the printers. This round of repression turned out to be its last surge before democratic change set in. State repressive power suddenly lost its magic, for Dangwai figures regarded going to jail as a badge of honor.

At this time the Dangwai magazines grew adept at playing "hide and seek" games with the censors. They deliberately wrote something to provoke the censors and, hence, public curiosity. Unfortunately, they were mired in rough competition for a niche in the saturated market, and the manufacture of sensational and even unethical exposés, inside stories, and gossip led to their gradual decline in credibility. After martial law was lifted, Dangwai magazines faded from the landscape of a more liberal media order.

Chin-Chuan Lee

See also Channel Four TV and Underground Radio (Taiwan); Communist Movement Media, 1950s–1960s (Hong Kong); Social Movement Media in 1987 Clashes (Korea); *Suara Independen* (Indonesia)

Further Readings

Lee, C.-C. (1993) Sparking a fire: The press and the ferment of democratic change in Taiwan. *Journalism Monographs, 138*, 1–39.

Lee, C.-C. (2000). State, capital, and media: The case of Taiwan. In J. Curran & M.-J. Park (Eds.), *De-westernizing media studies* (pp. 124–138). London: Routledge.

Lee, C.-C. (2001). Rethinking political economy: Implications for media and democracy in Greater China. *Javnost—The Public, 8*(4), 81–102.

Lee, C.-C. (2004). *Beyond Western hegemony: Media and Chinese modernity*. Hong Kong: Oxford University Press.

DECEMBER 2008 REVOLT MEDIA (GREECE)

The protests that started in Greece on December 6, 2008, after the police killing of 15-year-old Alexis Grigoropoulos, lasted for more than 2 weeks. Whereas the political parties and the media system stood unable to cope with the cruel incident and the young people's rage, the new media as well as face-to-face communication were the basic vehicles to organize the longest and most violent nationwide riots in Greece since the Metapolitefsi (the period after the military junta fell in 1974, and democracy was restored).

School and university students, leftists, and anarchists were the protagonists of a youth revolt coordinated by texting, e-mails, special groups and personal messages on Facebook, journalistic blogs, and the Athens Independent Media Center (IMC). Significantly, this mobilization was achieved completely outside the mainstream parties and the media system, both of which were taken by surprise, especially in the early days. The streets of the capital and other big towns were taken over by students, while occupations and demonstrations broke out all over the country. The crucial moments—daily marches to police stations, parliament, and ministries; sit-ins; invasions of broadcast stations and theaters; the raising of a banner on the Acropolis; and the burning of the Christmas tree in Athens' central square, right by the parliament building—were first announced and systematically covered by new media.

During the December days, all the new media—both the more prestigious ones, such as blogs and forums, and the more popular ones, such as social networks and sites—brought together and directed the flow of information in a "struggle for interpretation." The mainstream media system and especially commercial TV, incapable of understanding or controlling the flow of events, were reduced to following and reporting, for the most part, information originating via the Internet.

This, then, was the first time since the advent of commercial television in Greece in the 1980s, that television could not set the agenda, with the result that most channels, particularly the private ones, expressed strong support for the young rebels, positing an artificial distinction between them and the *koukouloforoi* (the hooded ones, so-called because of their ski masks, gas masks, and *keffiyes*), who, according to other sources, played a decisive role in the mobilizations.

Prior Media Activism

The deregulation of broadcasting and the entry of private capital into the media industries in the late 1980s ended the political parties' hegemony over the press. However, despite the optimism of deregulation's early days, the new hegemony of publishers/entrepreneurs did not strengthen the public sphere, but rather replaced it with an extremely commercialized public space. As a result, the younger generation, as well as university-educated audience members, felt alienated. Consequently they were attracted by the new modes of interactive communication and the new virtual communities, which provided both a needed and an attractive alternative to the monolithic power of mainstream media.

One of many responses was the Athens Independent Media Centre, created in 2001. This quickly attracted much attention and appeal, though it was clearly linked to, and disseminated the (often violent) agenda of, anarchist groups, on the rise since the late 1980s. Today, athens.indymedia.org is the 99th most popular worldwide site in Greece (according to Alexa web information database) and the second most popular link among Greek blogs (according to blogs.sync.gr). It produced independent social issue information devoid of commercial objectives, which even people not identifying with anarchism perceived as a source of free, interactive, and on-the-spot communication. This was due to the up-to-the-minute news it offered, with text, photographs, streaming audio, video, and hyperlinks to alternative information sources.

Another response worth noting was the rapid expansion of the Greek blogosphere beginning in 2005. This expansion is also contributing to the formation of a novel oppositional public sphere. Most blogs were being written by younger journalists who experimented with new forms of journalism unfettered by media industry restrictions. These blogs adopted a satirical, humorous style, often systematically exposing political scandals.

The escalating impact of these blogs pushed certain journalists, such as the well-known political reporter Stelios Koulouglou (www.tvxs.gr), or the scandalmonger Makis Triantafylopoulos (www.zougla.gr) to start blogs of their own. In addition to journalists, veteran politicians, and opinion leaders, there were radical political activists, ecologists, and young people of the "700 Euro generation" (so called because of their low salaries or the unemployment they face despite their qualifications). Extreme nationalists also joined in.

The most famous bloggers displayed strong political and topical concerns, even when they cultivated idiosyncratic perspectives (e.g., pitsirikos .blogspot.com). In the 2007 elections, 29 of the 50 most popular blogs did political journalism, and 16 were critical of the two major parties, the conservatives (New Democracy) and the socialists (PASOK). Some of these blogs (e.g., anadasosi .blogspot.com) orchestrated a silent, environmental demonstration of thousands of people in black in the center of Athens to protest the devastating fires all over Greece in summer 2007.

Some of the Internet's new facets, such as Indymedia (the Independent Media Center), blogs, webcams, social network sites, forums, and chat rooms, with their great appeal to younger generations, have contributed to the emergence of a new oppositional public sphere. Thus, Internet use in Greece should not be seen simply as the expression of a new sociability or access to infotainment, but rather as a manifestation of discontent against the traditional media and of circumscribing them.

Three Political Dimensions of Internet Use

The fresh dimensions the December 2008 revolt created and highlighted, especially concerning new media, were as follows.

First was rebellious young people's spontaneous creation of new sites, blogs, and radio stations (e.g., katalipsiasoee.blogspot.com, katalipsipoly-texneiou.blogspot.com, syntonistikogrigoropoulos .blogspot.com, eleftherosgalaxias.blogspot.com, katalipsisxolistheatrou.blogspot.com). Pupils, students, and all kinds of activists, who participated in the occupation of schools, universities, and public buildings, regarded the Internet, and particularly its audiovisual applications, as ideal for spreading their messages and publicizing their actions and viewpoints without being filtered through traditional media.

New sites, run by young people who were members of the Far Left parties, and sites that reproduced the Indymedia style, set out to communicate slogans, announce protests, orchestrate occupations, and organize cultural events and discussions. At the same time, the most influential blogs with a journalistic and even a sensationalist profile instantly reproduced and disseminated this information (e.g., prezatv.blogspot.com, troktiko.blogspot.com, press-gr.blogspot.com, kourdistoportocali.blog spot.com).

Second was the impressive transformation of social network sites into fora of political opinion and activism. Facebook became a prominent tool of protests by dozens of determined groups expressing their sorrow for Grigoropoulos's killing, with thousands of members participating with comments and coverage about the events. (One such group, ALEXANDROS GRIGOROPOULOS (R.I.P.), had 136,000 members.)

The extraordinary radicalization of Facebook was manifested the first days of the riots, when a plethora of new groups were formed (only one had over 13,000 members) to express solidarity with the burning of the Christmas tree, which became a locus of symbolic resistance until the New Year. Artists' groups and anarchists kept on destroying the celebratory image of the tree by decorating it with garbage and rotten meat.

Third, the Internet combined with the streets of Athens and other big towns to become conjoined spaces, where an unprecedented mixture of violent, imaginative, and emotive events, happenings, and demonstrations took place. The mistrust of police authorities and the defiance of their violence were common themes expressed in both three-dimensional and cyberspace. Facebook fans, the followers of Indymedia, and the "new journalism" of bloggers interacted and converged in an unprecedented way, creating momentum throughout the December revolt.

This insurgency was fueled by the anger and disillusionment of many groups, youths, pupils, students, and anarchists, most of whom belonged to middle-class families but who felt the globalized economy has relegated them to a precarious, indeed extremely unsafe, future (the 700 Euro Generation). Their experience resembled that of the migrant workers and the unemployed, who also joined the protests.

In the revolt, the young people—who had grown up in the economic prosperity of the post-dictatorship period and were part of the consumer society—used new media and traditional forms of contestation massively to reject all established institutions. This explains why these "children of the revolution" were greeted with either hope or fear all over the world.

Maria Komninos and Vassilis Vamvakas

See also Anarchist Media; Citizen Journalism; Indymedia (The Independent Media Center); Indymedia and Gender; Indymedia: East Asia; Political Graffiti (Greece); Social Movement Media in 2009 Crisis (Iran); Youth Protest Media (Switzerland)

Further Readings

Douzinas, C. (2009, January 9). What we can learn from the Greek riots. *The Guardian* (UK). Retrieved April 16, 2010, from http://www.guardian.co.uk/commentisfree/2009/jan/09/greece-riots

Komninos, M. (2001). *From the forum to the spectacle: The transformation of the public sphere in Greece, 1950–2000* [in Greek]. Athens, Greece: Papazissis.

Panayiotopoulos, P. (2009). Suffering and revolt of the "included." Some keys to understand the revolt of December 2008. *European Forum for Urban Safety.* Retrieved April 16, 2010, from http://www.fesu.org/index.php?id=30102&L=0

Vernardakis, C. (2008). Blogs in Greece of 2008. Political culture and the new public sphere. *Monthly Review,*

47. Retrieved April 16, 2010, from http://www
.monthlyreview.gr/antilogos/greek/periodiko/arxeio/
article_fullstory_html?obj_path=docrep/docs/arthra/
MR47_erevna_FS/gr/html/index

Vulliamy, E., & Smith, H. (2009, February 22). Children
of the revolution. *The Observer* (UK). Retrieved
April 16, 2010, from http://www.guardian.co.uk/
world/2009/feb/22/civil-unrest-athens/print

Deep Dish TV (United States)

Deep Dish TV is the first public-access television series to be distributed nationally by satellite in the United States. Since 1986, Deep Dish has organized documentary series featuring the work of hundreds of alternative media producers investigating national and international issues from progressive perspectives. It demonstrated the viability of using satellite transmission for low-budget productions, providing programming to hundreds of individual access channels.

Beginnings

Deep Dish was started by DeeDee Halleck and Paper Tiger Television, a video collective that since 1981 has been producing a series on media, culture, and politics for Manhattan public access TV. Their goal is to provide viewers nationally a chance to see video work by producers from around the United States and the world. Public access had grown in the United States on a city-by-city basis, and videomakers producing within the access system had few possibilities to show their work more widely. Producers had sometimes sent tapes to a station, asking staff to forward them to other access facilities after use, a cumbersome process known as "bicycling." With the spread of satellite cablecasting in the 1980s, the opportunity arose to create an informal network of access stations to receive simultaneous transmissions.

Paper Tiger TV issued a call to access and independent producers to submit short works on high-profile issues of the mid-1980s—homelessness, the collapse of family farms, and U.S. government interventions in Central America, among others—and compiled the pieces into a 10-hour series dubbed Deep Dish Television. The collective rented time on a commercial satellite and made the programming available free of charge to access centers, educational channels, and home dish owners. Paper Tiger members coordinated publicity efforts and compiled a database of access stations interested in the programming, for future distribution campaigns. The series provided enhanced visibility to many producers, displayed the achievements of the access community, expanded the availability of programming for access stations, and countered mainstream media reportage on a range of controversial issues.

For its second season in 1988, Paper Tiger decentralized editorial control to access producers from around the country, and Deep Dish TV established its own central staff in New York City to fund-raise, publicize the series, and handle distribution. The second series once more collected small pieces and excerpts from larger works into hour-long shows, organized by theme, such as AIDS and labor rights, or by originating community, such as work by youth, senior citizens, and Latina/o producers. Deep Dish also began distributing single-work, long-form productions to augment its compilations.

In 1990, faced with the drive toward war in the Persian Gulf and the accompanying mainstream news jingoism, Deep Dish distributed the *Gulf Crisis TV Project (GCTV)*. The four-part series was distributed to access and public television stations and enjoyed significant international exhibition as well, including on Britain's Channel 4. *GCTV* showed the possibilities for timely responses by independent producers to pressing issues of the day, combining camcorders, satellite distribution, and a publicity and distribution infrastructure to reach audiences in numbers and locations previously out of reach for low-budget, alternative productions.

Later Productions

Subsequent Deep Dish seasons have included *Sick and Tired of Being Sick and Tired* (on health care, 1994), *Shocking and Awful* (the second war against Iraq, 2005), and *Waves of Change* (grassroots media from around the world, 2008). Deep Dish produced the first season of the television edition of the radio news program *Democracy Now!* with Amy Goodman, and in 1999 collaborated with alternative producers to create *Showdown in*

Seattle, a series of nightly reports on the protests against the World Trade Organization talks in Seattle. *Showdown in Seattle,* shown on access channels and the satellite network Deep Dish TV through Free Speech TV, achieved new heights of viewership for alternative media reportage. This effort to immediately counter mainstream coverage through video and the Internet spawned the Independent Media Center movement.

Deep Dish series continue to play on access channels, on the Dish Network via Free Speech TV, and on DirecTV via Link TV. Older Deep Dish programs can be accessed through archive. com, seen on the Deep Dish channel on YouTube, and ordered from www.deepdishtv.org.

Daniel Marcus

See also Alliance for Community Media (United States); Alternative Media Center (United States); Barricada TV (Argentina); Documentary Film for Social Change (India); *Gay USA;* Paper Tiger Television (United States); WITNESS Video (United States); Workers' Film and Photo League (United States)

Further Readings

Halleck, D. (2002). *Hand-held visions: The uses of community media.* New York: Fordham University Press.

Stein, L. (2001). Access television and grassroots political communication in the United States. In J. D. H. Downing (Ed.), *Radical media: Rebellious communication and social movements* (pp. 299–324). Thousand Oaks, CA: Sage.

DEMOCRACY NOW! AND PACIFICA RADIO (UNITED STATES)

By the beginning of 2010, the alternative daily news program *Democracy Now!* hosted by Amy Goodman and Juan González, was available on more than 800 radio and television stations across the United States, including college stations, the Pacifica network, and PBS stations, as well as being podcast and available through BitTorrent. It was carried on both cable and satellite (via Dish Network on both Link TV and Free Speech TV).

Democracy Now! began in 1996 on the almost venerable Pacifica Radio Network—in social movement media terms—which started with one station (KPFA, Berkeley) in 1949 and expanded over time to stations in Los Angeles, New York City, Houston, and Washington, D.C. The program was initiated at the New York City station, WBAI. During a protracted internal confrontation at KPFA between Pacifica's board of directors and the staff in 2000–2001, the program moved to Downtown Community Television, a long-term alternative video documentary project in Manhattan.

In 2001, *Democracy Now!* added television. It receives no financial support from any government or corporate source, or from the Corporation for Public Broadcasting, though it has received relatively small amounts from some foundations.

The program repeatedly addresses and keeps alive issues that mainstream news media are prone to cloud over or avoid altogether, whether in U.S. domestic or foreign policies. Topics covered by the program include media policy reform, health care policy reform, capital punishment, global economic depression, planetary ecology, the wars in Iraq and Afghanistan, and events in Pakistan. Certain distinguished artists and thinkers have been profiled, such as Native American singer Buffy Sainte-Marie and jailed African American journalist and writer Mumia Abu-Jamal.

Frequent guests on the program include linguist and political activist Noam Chomsky, anti-Zionist activist Norman Finkelstein, African American commentator Michael Eric Dyson, British Middle East correspondent Robert Fisk, African American actor and activist Danny Glover, long-term environmental campaigner Ralph Nader, leading Indian peace activist Arundhati Roy, and investigative journalist Greg Palast. Notable international interviewees include former U.S. president Jimmy Carter, Bolivian president Evo Morales and Venezuelan president Hugo Chávez, and Jean-Bertrand Aristide, U.S.-ousted former Haitian president.

Amy Goodman is a long-term campaigning investigative journalist and was WBAI news director for 10 years before cofounding *Democracy Now!* She was well known for her exposés of U.S.-sanctioned Indonesian army violence against Timor-Leste's independence movement and of the Chevron Oil Corporation's collusion with Nigeria's military in crushing protests in a heavily polluted oil area.

Juan González is former president of the National Congress for Puerto Rican Rights and of the National Association of Hispanic Journalists. He received widespread commendation for his 2002 book *Fallout*, which exposed government cover-ups regarding health hazards at the 9/11 massacre site.

As of early 2010, *Democracy Now!* is the only nationwide alternative broadcast news source. Other news sources such as the online *Huffington Post*, the *Nation* weekly, and *Z Magazine* contribute to allowing people in the United States information and perspectives typically denied them or just dismissively noted by mainstream news media. But the ongoing daily commitment of *Democracy Now!* to using all electronic channels to open the public's eyes is an unparalleled contribution toward a genuinely democratic information society.

Goodman has traveled throughout the United States and beyond, promoting the program and speaking on the political practices of mainstream news media. She is no stranger to the dangers of direct conflict, as when she and other *Democracy Now!* activists were arrested for filming a police crackdown on protestors against the Republican Party's presidential nomination convention in 2008. Even this flouting of law by law enforcement, however, paled by comparison with her and her colleague's near murder at the hands of the Indonesian military in Timor-Leste.

The speaking style on the news program, however dramatic or painful the topics, is businesslike and leaves the subject matter to speak for itself. The website archives every single show, going back to 2001.

John D. H. Downing

See also Anti-Anticommunist Media Under McCarthyism (United States); Deep Dish TV (United States); Human Rights Media; Labor Media (United States); Low-Power FM Radio (United States); Media Justice Movement (United States); Paper Tiger Television (United States)

Further Readings

Democracy Now! http://www.democracynow.org

Downing, J. D. H. (2001). *Radical Media: Rebellious communication and social movements* (Chap. 21). Thousand Oaks, CA: Sage.

Land, J. (1999). *Active radio: Pacifica's brash experiment.* Minneapolis: University of Minnesota Press.

Stern, M. J. (2005). The battle for Pacifica. *Journal of Popular Culture, 38*(6), 1069–1087.

DISCHORD RECORDS (UNITED STATES)

Dischord Records is an independent record label that releases punk and experimental records from exclusively Washington, D.C.–based artists. Founded in 1980, the label was set up by Jeff Nelson and Ian MacKaye as a do-it-yourself project to release records from their own bands, as well as those of their friends. Dischord went on to release over 150 records from early D.C. punk acts like Fugazi, Shudder to Think, and Nation of Ulysses to more contemporary experimental groups like Faraquet, Medications, Black Eyes, and Q and Not U. The label's success and wide popularity has done nothing to dull its definitively DIY (do-it-yourself) ethics, radical politics, and strict independence.

From its inception, the label has been rooted in punk ideals and subversive political aspirations. According to Charles Fairchild, these punk ideals assert that pop music can draw upon its populist roots to work both to confront and negate mainstream society. By producing and distributing music entirely outside of elite control and corporate practices, subversive art can be created and disseminated without the threat of immediate compromises or marginalization by market forces. For the D.C. punk scene, the Dischord record label serves to release the art of its community, outside of the control of the corporate music industry and against the industry's typically exploitative artist relations.

To accomplish artistic self-determination and economic independence, the label's organizational form has maintained an informal structure, as well as cooperative relationships with its artists. Dischord does not place bands under contract and forgoes any ownership of the recording, allowing bands to maintain complete rights to their work. Signed bands also retain full creative license. Song content, packaging, liner notes, and other artistic and design elements are the undisputed territory of the artist.

Dischord also operates more equitably with its associated artists. Bypassing the major labels' heavily litigated deals and exploitative practices, Dischord splits all profits from record sales equally between the band and the label. Dischord also handles distribution scrupulously. Records are sold primarily through direct sales to independent record stores, as well as mail order. For higher volume and international distribution, Dischord works with Southern Records, an independently owned distribution company founded in 1974 that has worked with the Dischord label since the 1981 international release of the first Minor Threat record. Dischord completely bypasses large chain retailers and distribution corporations.

As a small-scale operation geared to redress some of the worst music industry tendencies, Dischord functions as a radical media outlet, insofar as it acts in opposition to the dominant paradigm and maintains a typically underground profile. Unfettered by the logics of industry capital, Dischord Records is still releasing records after operating independently for over 25 years, according to their own strict counterhegemonic and procommunity ethics.

Curtis Roush

See also Copyleft; Creative Commons; Lookout! Records (United States); Political Song (Liberia and Sierra Leone); Popular Music and Protest (Ethiopia)

Further Readings

Fairchild, C. (1995). "Alternative music" and the politics of cultural autonomy: The case of Fugazi and the D.C. scene. *Popular Music and Society, 19*(1), 17–35.

Goshert, J. C. (2000). "Punk" after the Pistols: American music, economics, and politics in the 1980s and 1990s. *Popular Music & Society, 24*(1), 85–107.

O'Connor, A. (2008). *Punk record labels and the struggle for autonomy: The emergence of DIY.* Lanham, MD: Lexington Books.

Thompson, S. (2004). *Punk productions: Unfinished business.* Albany: SUNY Press.

DIVA TV AND ACT UP (UNITED STATES)

DIVA TV (Damned Interfering Video Activist Television), founded in 1989 during the height of the U.S. AIDS activist movement, is a video-documenting affinity group of ACT UP (the AIDS Coalition to Unleash Power). ACT UP is a diverse, nonpartisan group of individuals united in anger and committed to direct action to end the AIDS crisis. Its website proclaims, "We advise and inform. We demonstrate. WE ARE NOT SILENT."

Founding members of DIVA TV include Bob Beck, Gregg Bordowitz, Jean Carlomusto, Rob Kurilla, Ray Navarro, Costa Pappas, George Plagianos, Catherine Saalfield, and Ellen Spiro. The extensive media produced by DIVA TV in its several manifestations (over 700 camera hours) documented ACT UP and community responses to AIDS. According to Saalfield, DIVA TV was "organized to be there, document, provide protection and counter-surveillance, and participate. . . . [It] targets ACT UP members as its primary audience and makes videos by, about, and, most importantly, *for the movement*" (cited in Juhasz, 1997, p. 37).

ACT UP was founded in 1987 in New York City and is often acknowledged for reenergizing civil disobedience tactics in the United States. Video has always played a central role in the AIDS activist movement. AIDS video activists used newly available camcorders to form a local response to AIDS, to rebut or revise mainstream media representations of AIDS, and to form community around a new identity, PWA (Person With AIDS, as opposed to AIDS "victim"), forced into existence by the fact of AIDS.

In her *Camcorderists Manifesto*, Ellen Spiro, another DIVA TV founder, insists that

> camcorder footage contributes to a broader analysis of an event by offering an alternative to broadcast media's centrist view. It has the power to add a dimension to the chorus of voices heard, providing a platform for seasoned activists and concerned community members, rather than the same old authoritative experts giving their same old scripted raps. (Cited in "Media Praxis," 2008)

DIVA TV understands, critiques, and celebrates the central role of media in determining the meanings, policies, and histories of AIDS. In its first year, the group produced three tapes documenting AIDS activism. *Target City Hall* chronicled ACT UP's March 28, 1989, demonstration against New

York City Mayor Ed Koch's administration for its refusal to respond adequately to the AIDS crisis. *Pride* covered the 20th anniversary of the city's gay and lesbian pride movement. *Like A Prayer* consisted of five 7-minute perspectives on the ACT UP/WHAM (Women's Health Action Mobilization) demonstration "Stop the Church" at St. Patrick's Cathedral on December 10, 1989, to protest Cardinal John O'Connor's responsibility for neglecting the crisis. About this work, Saalfield explains, "Here protest is the process, communication is our form of resistance, and everyone has a say" (quoted in Juhasz, 1997, p. 37).

Like many activist collectives that hold themselves to radical and communal standards, by 1990 this initial configuration of DIVA TV had folded. "DIVA TV has long been more of a state of mind than a collective," it stated on its 2008 website. It was revived in 1990 by new ACT UP member James Wentzy, who committed his energies to producing AIDS Community Television (ACT), a half-hour public access show devoted to programming for greater advocacy, coalition building, and greater public awareness of AIDS activism. From January 1, 1993, until 1994, Wentzy produced more than 150 half-hour programs, airing many times monthly in New York. Many of the shows were also aired by ACT UP affiliates across the country. From 1994 to 1996, he produced more than 40 programs called *ACT UP Live*, a live call-in weekly public access television series sponsored by ACT UP/New York.

Like the first DIVA TV collective, Wentzy produced video that covered the AIDS crisis as AIDS activists see it, including *The Ashes Action* (1992) and *Holding Steady Without Screaming* (1995): "What is unique about what I'm doing is twofold: it's the only weekly series in the world devoted to covering AIDS activism, and it's political. All activists see the crisis as a *political* problem" (quoted in Juhasz, 1995, p. 71). Since 1996, Wentzy has continued to document ACT UP demonstrations, political funerals, and public lectures under the DIVA TV moniker, and in 2003 he produced *Fight Back, Fight AIDS: 15 Years of ACT UP*. The work of DIVA TV is archived in the AIDS Activist Video Collection (1993–2000) at the New York Public Library.

Alex Juhasz

See also Advocate, The (United States); Anarchist Media; Deep Dish TV (United States); Gay Press (Canada, United Kingdom, United States); *Gay USA*; Human Rights Media; Stonewall Incident (United States); WITNESS Video (United States)

Further Readings

Juhasz, A. (1995). *AIDS TV: Identity, community and alternative media*. Durham, NC: Duke University Press.

Juhasz, A. (1995). So many alternatives: The alternative AIDS video movement (Pt. 2). *Cineaste*, 21(1–2), 37–39.

Media praxis. (2008, December 18). In *Encyclopedia of activist media*. http://aljean.wordpress.com/2008/12/18/encyclopedia-of-activist-media

Saalfield, C. (1993). On the make: Activist video collectives. In M. Gever, J. Greyson, & P. Parmar (Eds.), *Queer looks* (pp. 21–37). New York: Routledge.

Spiro, E. (1991, May). What to wear on your video activist outing (because the whole world is watching): A camcordist's manifesto. *The Independent*, 14(4), 22.

DOCUMENTARY FILM FOR SOCIAL CHANGE (INDIA)

In the latter half of the 20th century, independent documentary films became an important medium for political expression in India. Despite attempts at government censorship, such films remain an important source of political critique, and alternative circulation networks are being developed. This entry reviews the emergence of the independent political documentary beginning in the 1970s and examines the impact of alternative films especially after the Vikalp Film Festival held in Mumbai in February 2004.

Independent Political Documentary in the 1970s and 1980s

By the early 1970s, the optimism of the early years after India's independence gave way to growing anger and disillusionment. Wars, famines, and spiraling inflation contributed to a simmering discontent that Prime Minister Indira Gandhi attempted to quell in 1975 by imposing a national emergency. The brutal repression of civil liberties during the emergency catalyzed the political documentary movement. A wave of documentaries throughout the 1970s critiqued and revealed the oppression of those years. These included Gautam Ghose's *Hungry Autumn* (1974), Utpalendu Chakrabarty's *We Want Freedom* (1977), and Tapan Bose and Suhasini Mulay's *An Indian Story* (1981).

The most influential documentary filmmaker to emerge at this time was Anand Patwardhan. His *Waves of Revolution* (1974) documented the non-violent revolutionary movement in Bihar State led by JP Narain just before the emergency. *Prisoners of Conscience* (1978) focused on the condition of political prisoners during the emergency. These were "guerrilla" films in the truest sense: made on limited budgets and borrowed equipment, and circulated only in underground screenings.

Patwardhan continued to make his distinctive documentaries through the 1980s and 1990s. Films such as *Bombay Our City* (1985), *In the Name of God* (1992), and *Father, Son, and Holy War* (1995) reflected his enduring concerns with social injustice, especially with the growing political force of rightist Hindu nationalism. Most of his films faced state censorship, and he spent much of his time engaged in legal battles, most recently for *War and Peace* (2002) on the India–Pakistan nuclear arms race.

Patwardhan's work inspired a new generation of political filmmakers in the 1980s as the growth of television and video contributed to a boom in documentary film production. Many were women, mobilized by the growing women's movement of the time. Prominent were Reena Mohan, Deepa Dhanraj, Manjira Datta, Nilita Vachani, and the women of the Media Storm Collective. Women's issues, and the rise of Hindu nationalism as a political force, became the prime focus of political documentary. For the most part, these films were issue-based, made in the collective voice. Individual experiments with aesthetics and form were considered antithetical to political documentary.

Experimentation, Censorship, and the Vikalp Movement

In the 1990s, satellite television and the influx of transnational brands and images dramatically transformed India's media landscape, presenting challenges as well as opportunities for political documentary filmmakers. Transnational networks and digital technology made filmmaking more accessible to many. But the social and political context in which these changes happened raised new concerns. Many documentary filmmakers grew evermore concerned by growing inequalities and the divisive force of religious nationalism. They particularly focused on stories that were glossed over in mainstream media.

At the same time, the voice of the political documentary seemed jaded, ineffective, and overly didactic to many filmmakers in this changed context. Amar Kanwar's *A Season Outside* (1998) broke new ground in its use of an intensely personal, poetic voiceover, a challenge to "activist" documentaries that relied on direct interviews as a means of conveying truth. Kanwar continued to experiment with the form and aesthetics of the political in films such as *A Night of Prophecy* (2002) and, most recently, *The Lightning Testimonies* (2007). Filmmakers such as Madhusree Dutta, Paromita Vohra, Rahul Roy, and Saba Dewan, to name just a few, did likewise.

Though they had different approaches to form, a concern with social and economic injustices in an age of globalization united them. And eventually, the large-scale pogrom against Muslims in Gujarat State in 2002 galvanized them. Several documentary films emerged from the Gujarat carnage, the best known of which was Rakesh Sharma's *Final Solution* (2004). *Final Solution* was censored in India despite winning awards at international festivals.

In 2004, the government-sponsored Mumbai International Film Festival rejected *Final Solution*, along with several other political documentaries. In response, documentary filmmakers organized a parallel film festival that showcased the censored films. *Vikalp,* or "alternative," as the festival was called, received a great deal of public attention, and gave political documentary films an unprecedented degree of visibility.

In many ways, Vikalp was the beginning of a movement. Though the Vikalp festival was not replicated on the same scale, Vikalp coalesced as a network of political documentary filmmakers, committed to building alternative circulation networks and creating a parallel space for films as political critique. With the growth of an alternative network of festivals in the later 2000s, political documentary emerged as an increasingly vibrant form of critical political practice.

Tilottama Karlekar

See also Media Against Communalism (India); Sarabhai Family and the Darpana Academy (India); Social Movement Media in the Emergency (India); *Tehelka* Magazine (India); Women's Movement Media (India)

Further Readings

Dutta, M. (2002). *Making of the nation and language of documentary films in India.* Retrieved May 2, 2010, from http://www.madhusreedutta.com/images/article_4_Cinema_India.doc

Films for Freedom: http://www.freedomfilmsindia.org

Garga, B. D. (2007). *From Raj to Swaraj: The non-fiction film in India.* New Delhi, India: Penguin.

Patwardhan, A. (n.d.). [The films of Anand Patwardhan]. Retrieved March 26, 2009, from http://www.Patwardhan.com

E

EL TEATRO CAMPESINO

A notable U.S. example of radical street theater has been El Teatro Campesino (the Farmworkers' Theater). It became known through the later success of one of its key members, Luís Valdez, and his brother Daniel, whose *Zoot Suit* became a popular Broadway musical and a 1981 movie, but the theater group's beginnings were anchored in the labor struggles of Chicana/o and migrant Mexican farmworkers on huge California plantations in the 1950s and 1960s. By the late 1960s, some 100 such street theater groups were in operation, but El Teatro Campesino was the spark.

The California labor struggles from 1965 onward were often led by the UFW (the United Farm Workers of America), the unofficial union founded in 1962 by César Chávez, Helen Chávez, and Dolores Huerta. Official unions often sided with the big farmers in disputing the UFW's right to negotiate wages and conditions. Part II of documentary maker Hector Galán's PBS series *Chicano!* graphically recounts this story. Earlier centuries of struggle by poor farmers, *peones*, slaves, and seasonal day-laborers were another more diffuse but powerful source, whether in México or within the southwestern United States.

Popular oral traditions of commentary, protest, and ridicule based on these grievances fed into the productions of El Teatro Campesino. So did a well-established popular Mexican theatrical form, the traveling *carpa* (tent) performance, whose performance space was, literally, a collapsible tent, taken from site to site on a truck or even a mule cart. It had brightly painted backdrops, often a single naked electric lightbulb, and plain benches for the audience, and it offered live music, dance, and a series of comic sketches (*actos*) with both earthy and fantastic subjects.

As with African American dance in the era of slavery, the performers' use of their bodies as a communication instrument was especially important, sometimes almost more important than the words themselves. As Broyles-González (1994) explains, "Understanding a performance . . . entailed an apprehension of tone, of silences, of body movement, of images, of sounds in all their variety. . . . The performance aesthetic capitalized on mime" (p. 18).

Language was another crucial feature of the performances. Spanish and English intermingled in the deft deployment of both that is sometimes referred to as "Spanglish," but also *calós* (local mixed dialects from different Chicana/o neighborhoods) functioned as yet a third language. This blend made performances hard to understand for second-language Spanish speakers, but tremendously rich and rooted for the actual audiences.

Both in *carpa* theater and El Teatro productions, the script was an approximate guide, discussed in common beforehand, but performances were intensely interactive: As Broyles-González (1994) notes, "Improvisation [depended] most notably on . . . audience response and participation. . . . Essential to this process [was] each individual's split-second timing and capacity to think on [his or her] feet" (p. 17). A key character in *carpa* was the underdog, *el pelado/la pelada*: irreverent, ribald, irrepressible, at one and the same time truculent and scared, winner and loser, scruffily dressed, a trickster figure combined with man/woman of the people. Humor, often farcical, was a key component.

Commentators have often suggested the influence of Brecht and other radical theater exponents on El Teatro Campesino, and certainly the San Francisco Mime Troupe had been a formative influence on Luís Valdez. The iconic Mexican comedian Cantínflas (Fortino Mario Alfonso Moreno Reyes, 1911–1993), a Chaplinesque figure, was also a source of inspiration.

Broyles-González insists, however, without discounting such influences, on the very strong Indigenous roots of the company. Its members drew in considerable detail upon Mayan and Aztec religious cultures in developing a theater philosophy anchored in a philosophy of existence. Rejecting the segregation between performance and personal life frequent in mainstream theater culture, or between social justice activism and religion, they sought to develop a single interpretive basis both for their performance training and for their vision of El Teatro Campesino's contribution to Chicana/o communities' struggles. Accounts of El Teatro's work often stress their support of the UFW, or their lead in the revival of Chicana/o awareness in literature, history, the arts, and politics, but omit their endeavor to revalorize the core Indigenous component of *Mexicanidad*.

In 1967, the Teatro Campesino moved to Del Rey, California, to start El Centro Campesino Cultural. Classes sprang up in English, Spanish, history, drama, puppet-making, music, and political activism. A major 1968 production was *La Conquista de México* (The Conquest of México). This emphasized two themes: the way disunity among different Indigenous peoples opened the way to Spanish victory in México and Perú, and the parallels with gringo domination of Chicanas/os. In 1969, as their reputation grew, they began to perform in Los Angeles and as far away as a cultural festival in France. In 1970, they created a five-scene *acto*, *Vietnam Campesino*, focused on the disproportionate number of Chicano soldiers dying in the Vietnam War.

For some critics, the shift to national and even international performances more and more risked withering the project's roots in everyday labor and community struggles. For others, such as Luís Valdez, it was a vital step toward the mainstreaming of Chicana/o culture, which he considered all-important for the future position of Chicanas/os and Latinas/os in the United States. For some, telling the story of El Teatro Campesino has focused far too much on the particular contribution of Valdez, to the detriment of the large and crucial contributions of the project's cultural workers, not least its women activists.

Thus, the Teatro Campesino intriguingly illustrates the frequent importance for radical media of engaging with local popular cultural traditions, including theatrical traditions. It shows how important spontaneity is in radical theater and how all these elements interlocked in this instance with political support for the labor movement.

John D. H. Downing

See also Boxer Rebellion Theater (China); Cultural Front (Canada); Indian People's Theatre Association; Madang Street Theater (Korea); Performance Art and Social Movement Media: Augusto Boal; Street Theater (Canada); Street Theater (India)

Further Readings

Broyles-González, Y. (1994). *El Teatro Campesino: Theater in the Chicano movement*. Austin: University of Texas Press.
Galán, H. (Producer). (1996). *Chicano! History of the Mexican-American civil rights movement* [TV documentary series, 4 episodes]. United States: National Latino Communications Center, Galán Productions, and KCET Los Angeles.
Huerta, J. S. (1977). Chicano agit-prop: The early *Actos* of El Teatro Campesino. *Latin American Theater Review, 10*(2), 45–58.

ELAND CEREMONY, ABATWA PEOPLE'S (SOUTHERN AFRICA)

The word *Abatwa* is a Zulu word for "Bushman" or San. The San are considered the aboriginal population of southern Africa and comprise numerous communities totaling about 110,000. The history of the Abatwa, as of other hunter–gatherer peoples, is one of exploitation and abuse, but it is also a history of creativity and survival. The Eland Ceremony is a combination of performance art and installation art media.

In the Drakensberg Mountains of KwaZulu-Natal, South Africa, there are Zulu speakers who have begun reasserting an aboriginal or San identity and use the term *Abatwa* as an ethnonym. These people live in an area of southern Africa where there are no recognized extant communities of San descent.

The area contains thousands of rock art images left behind by the San peoples long assumed to be extinct or assimilated into the dominant African communities. The Abatwa began asserting their presence around 1999 to no or very limited avail, but there are now more than 1,500 individuals recognized, and many more are expected to come forward.

The Eland Ceremony

In 2003, the Abatwa created a ritual to celebrate their San ancestry and to make a public statement of their San ethnicity. Previously, they had had limited success in being fully recognized as San descendants. Largely through the work of Frans Prins, they obtained some legitimacy in academic circles. By drawing on this academic legitimacy, they were able to leverage access to the rock art site and to garner some interest from the media and local politicians.

The ceremony was linked to the designation of the Drakensberg as a World Heritage Site and the opening of a rock art tourism venture. The ceremony involved the sacrifice of an eland as well as prayers at the rock art site in the Kamberg Nature Reserve. The eland was the main figure painted in the rock art and for the San is a spiritual animal. The most important rituals were kept secret and private among the Abatwa but were followed by a public feast for the entire community. Although the ceremony failed to become an annual affair, it successfully reasserted their presence in the area, with consequences for rock art conservation and for their organizing of a community.

This community has very limited means and very limited access to media, let alone the ability to create media. Their first media foray was to feature their culture and history as a major part of the documentary film shown to visitors at the Kamberg Nature Reserve. Their community leader then became a vocal member of the Kamberg Rock Art Trust, which involves state heritage organizations, museums, and tourism boards. They have been able to assert their cultural identity and so to change how tourism is practiced in the reserve.

Ritual Pollution

The Abatwa treat the rock art sites as sacred. They wish for people to view them but are deeply concerned about their physical and spiritual preservation. Visitors to the rock art site at Game Pass Shelter, one of the main tourist sites, now engage with Indigenous knowledge and practice. Tourists must ritually cleanse themselves by rubbing themselves with specific grasses; this ritual acknowledges the Abatwa and adds to the tourism experience.

So the challenge remains for the Abatwa to continue pressing for their identity rights and access to their heritage as they simultaneously champion rock art conservation.

Michael Francis

See also Adivasi Movement Media (India); First Peoples' Media (Canada); Indigenous Media (Australia); Indigenous Peoples' Media; Installation Art Media; Māori Media and Social Movements (Aotearoa/New Zealand); Performance Art and Social Movement Media: Augusto Boal

Further Readings

Francis, M. (2009). Contested histories: A critique of rock art in the Drakensberg Mountains. *Visual Anthropology, 22*(4), 327–343.

Francis, M. (2010). The crossing: The invention of tradition among San descendents of the Drakensberg, KwaZulu-Natal, South Africa. *African Identities, 8*(1), 79–105.

Prins, F. (2009). Secret San of the Drakensberg and their rock art legacy. *Critical Arts, 23*(2), 190–208.

South African San Institute. (2002, December). *Annual report.* Kimberley, Northern Cape Province, South Africa: Author.

ENVIRONMENTAL MOVEMENT MEDIA

A paradox lies at the heart of the environmental movement. Often characterized as comprising tree huggers, Luddites, and New Age hippies, the environmental movement is and always has been the highest of high-tech social movements with respect to media technology. The form and substance of the environmental movement's messages have been inextricably linked to and born of the new media of the moment. The paradox is that the environmental movement emerges as a reaction to the excesses of industrialism, while simultaneously depending on the technological products of industrialism.

Taking media seriously suggests a complementary history of environmental activism that can account for its impressive global force. While the environmental movement has clearly been inspired by solitary curmudgeons scribbling in the wilderness (such as Henry David Thoreau and Edward Abbey), people around the world have been moved by image-based media campaigns to save their places and their world. This entry charts the impact of high-tech media in enabling people to see the planet anew and motivating them to act on their new visions.

Origin Stories and Landscape Photography

The origin myth of environmentalism usually posits Henry David Thoreau or John Muir as the fount of eco-wisdom that challenged industrialism and inspired the environmental movement. There is no need to downplay Thoreau or Muir. Still, it is worth noting that such tales imagine Thoreau as the lone heroic individual at Walden Pond or Muir as the irrepressible explorer of the High Sierras, while little noting that their efforts relied on the medium of writing and the technologies of the printing press and a distribution system for books and magazines. In addition, Muir was both subsidized by, and an ally of, Southern Pacific Railroad.

More significantly, such origin myths overshadow a parallel tale of the role of new media technologies in the founding and propagation of environmentalism. Long before *Walden* became an American classic and Muir set foot in Yosemite,

the new medium of photography conspired with industry to play a pivotal role in preserving Yosemite Valley as the world's first wilderness park.

Yosemite Valley

The fundamental role of landscape photography in the creation of Yosemite as the world's first wilderness area created "for the benefit of the people, for their resort and recreation, to hold them inalienable for all time" (Yosemite Grant, 1864) points to the crucial role of images in environmental politics and confirms that such image politics did not start with the advent of television. Survey photographer and Yosemite's first major documentarian Carlton Watkins embodied the multiple discourses of his time—romantic and artistic, to be sure, but also commercial, industrial, and technological. This is reflected in the breadth of his subjects, from the wilderness landscapes of Yosemite to the industrial mining at Mariposa. Watkins established dual legacies as both founder of landscape photography and chronicler of industrial progress, celebrator of sublime nature and creator of the technological sublime.

Watkins's early photos of Yosemite highlight, more than anything else, the sublime. Watkins's photography transforms the spectacular sublime into the domestic spectacle, the private possession of tourists, East Coast urban dwellers, and armchair adventurers. Yosemite is captured. It is at the mercy of the viewers. Viewers can contemplate the image at their leisure, put it away, return to it later, compare it to other collected images, and, indeed, own it, so that sublime nature is now commodified nature, a private possession, nature as cultural capital. The sublime is further domesticated within the photographs themselves as Watkins often created a safe space for the spectator—the beautiful place—from which to view the sublime spectacle. This dynamic, at work in many of the photographs, is particularly evident in the photograph "Yosemite Falls."

In "Yosemite Falls," the beautiful literally frames the sublime. An idyllic meadow occupies over a third of the photograph. In the immediate foreground is a flat space ringed by flowering plants, grasses, and four trees, resembling a picnic site. The trees occupy entirely the left and right sides of the frame, creating a frame within the frame. Within this treed frame, positioned in the upper center of the photograph, is the spectacular sight of Yosemite Falls cascading down the cliffs of the canyon. The cascading plume rives the canyon walls and links to the washed-out sky.

The twice-enframed sublime is domesticated and commodified, a view for the taking, the common currency of the tourist trade. In the union of the sublime and beautiful is born the tourist gaze. The beautiful foreground gives the tourist a pleasing place from which to view the spectacular spectacle of the sublime. Positioned in the meadow, viewers experience the scene at ground level. From the picnic site, viewers gaze across a wide expanse of meadow to the cliffs and Yosemite Falls. Apprehending the scene from this plane envelops viewers within a garden rather than positioning them at the actual edge of a precipice. Watkins anticipates and constructs a sublime experience in which comfort displaces risk as the spectator replaces the participant. The distanced position of the spectator obviates the emotional experience of the sublime. In a sense, Watkins's images blaze a trail for the tourist at the expense of the adventurer and hollow out the sublime, leaving only spectacle.

Although interested in art and profit, not nature, Watkins's photos played a role in the birth of environmentalism. The initial proposal to preserve Yosemite Valley originated, notably, with industry—the tourist industry. Israel Ward Raymond, the California agent of the Central American Steamship Transit Company, forwarded a draft of a preservation bill and Watkins's 1861 photographs of Yosemite to California Senator John Conness, who introduced the bill to Congress in March 1864. The legislation passed, and President Abraham Lincoln signed it into law on June 30, 1864, thereby deeding Yosemite Valley and Mariposa Big Tree Grove to the State of California. The legislative protection of this national "natural" landscape placed preservation policy as the cornerstone of American environmental politics.

Watkins imaged a Yosemite devoid of human markings, a pristine wilderness where one could glimpse the sublime face of God. In picturing a nature apart from culture, Watkins was obeying the dictates of the nature/culture dichotomy central to Western civilization, wherein "Nature"—ontologically divided from culture—serves as a

source of resources, artistic inspiration, spiritual awe, emotional succor, and Otherness. The creation of Yosemite as the world's first wilderness area reveals the foundational role of images created by the new medium of the camera and promulgated by the new tourist industries, especially railroads. Yosemite became a template for preservation politics, with images deployed as a key rhetorical strategy. The camera makes manifest a certain vision of nature and makes "real" pristine wilderness.

It must be stressed that the camera creates pristine wilderness untouched by humans. Already by the time of Watkins's 1860s trips to Yosemite, there were hotels, stores, farms, and logging mills in the valley. The Ahwahneechee had lived in Yosemite Valley for centuries and had created the beautiful vistas by annually burning the brush on the valley floor. In creating his wilderness photos, Watkins chose not to photograph people and their artifacts. In addition, he would sometimes manipulate the landscape, clearing brush and trees in his way. Finally, the technological requirement of extended exposure times in early photography made capturing action impossible and people difficult. The camera, not God, created sublime, Edenic wilderness.

Yellowstone

The process of saving Yellowstone in 1871–1872 was remarkably similar to that of Yosemite. Ever since 1808 when John Colter of the Lewis and Clark expedition provided the first descriptions by a white person of Yellowstone's geysers and bubbling hot springs, Yellowstone had been known as "Colter's Hell." Yellowstone's reputation as "hell on earth," "the place where hell bubbles up," is evident in many place-names in the region—Devil's Glen, Devil's Slide, Devil's Hoof, Hell Roaring River, Fire Hole Prairie. By 1870, financier Jay Cooke of Northern Pacific Railroad realized that his railroad's right-of-way to the Pacific passed by Yellowstone, a potential site to attract travelers. In the first U.S. Geological Survey to Yellowstone in 1871, the survey's leader, Ferdinand Hayden, was mindful of the effects of Watkins's esteemed photos of Yosemite and arranged to have the photographer William Henry Jackson along. Cooke, also cognizant of the power of images, arranged to have the painter Thomas Moran accompany Hayden's survey.

Hayden included a preservation recommendation in his official report. Crucial to these efforts were the photographs by Jackson and the illustrations and watercolors by Moran. Hayden distributed Jackson's photos and 400 copies of Langford's *Scribner's* article with Moran's illustrations, along with Moran's watercolors. Jackson and Moran's art served to verify the fantastical accounts of Yellowstone. Jackson's photographs served a reality-certifying function while Moran's watercolors confirmed the otherworldly coloring of the region. Together, they documented Yellowstone as a sublime place.

Moran's paintings intensified the sense of a sublime Yosemite. Moran's watercolors supplemented Jackson's photographs, filling in the otherworldly hues of the alien landscape (and explaining the moniker *Yellowstone*). In a word, the watercolors are fantastical. Yellowstone's astonishing colors are richly displayed in Moran's "The Castle Geyser, Upper Geyser Basin." The watercolor largely approximates Jackson's Castle Geyser photo perspective, but a few steps to the right so that the hot spring pool occupies the left foreground and the Castle Geyser is in the right center. Six minuscule figures in front of the geyser attest to scale.

The colors, of course, are strikingly different. Castle Geyser gleams an unearthly white. The crater pool, named Circe's Boudoir, is stunning shades of blue, lighter on the edge to dark in the center like a clear sky just after the sun has set. Beautiful blue rivulets leak from the pool. Three months after the Yellowstone Park Act was introduced, President Ulysses S. Grant signed it into law on March 1, 1872. Their art helped to transform the image of Yellowstone from Colter's Hell to America's Wonderland. Northern Pacific Railroad helped continue this iconic transformation in the coming decades through the proliferation of these images in pamphlets and guidebooks. Indeed, Northern Pacific Railroad's corporate logo became "Yellowstone Park Line."

Ansel Adams Imaging the American Wilderness

Watkins, Jackson, and Moran haphazardly blazed a trail that others followed, most notably landscape photographer and political activist Ansel Adams.

Since its founding in 1890, the Sierra Club had been interested in preserving Kings Canyon, California. Sensing an opportunity in the 1930s with the Roosevelt administration, the Sierra Club decided to send Ansel Adams with his portfolio of Kings Canyon photographs to Washington, D.C., to lobby Congress. Adams combined his photos into a book, *Sierra Nevada: The John Muir Trail*. When published in 1938, he sent a copy to Secretary of Interior Harold Ickes. Ickes took the book to the White House and showed it to the President Franklin D. Roosevelt, who was so impressed Ickes gave him the book. With the president's support, in 1940 Congress passed a bill establishing a 454,600-acre Kings Canyon National Park. National Park Service director Arno B. Cammerer wrote to Adams in 1940: "A silent but most effective voice in the campaign was your own book *Sierra Nevada: The John Muir Trail*. As long as that book is in existence, it will go on justifying the park" (quoted in Turnage, 1980, para. 27).

Adams's lobbying effort and his book *Sierra Nevada: The John Muir Trail* merit attention both as art and environmental advocacy. Both the Sierra Club and Adams were conscious of imitating the earlier successful efforts to use Watkins's photographs of Yosemite Valley and Jackson's photographs of Yellowstone to preserve those places. Adams's efforts on behalf of Kings Canyon, however, represent the first time that the roles of artist, environmental advocate, and lobbyist were consolidated in one person. This tripartite persona is one that Adams would don the rest of his life.

This Is the American Earth (1960) is perhaps Adams's greatest success in this regard. A collaboration with the writer Nancy Newhall and Sierra Club Director David Brower, it was designed both as art and to galvanize support for the Wilderness Act. Immediately upon publication, Brower sent a copy of the book and a letter seeking support for the Wilderness Act to all the members of the U.S. Congress. These lobbying efforts helped pass the Wilderness Act of 1964:

A wilderness in contrast with those areas where man and his works dominate the landscape, is hereby recognized as an area where the earth and its community of life are untrammeled by man, where man himself is a visitor who does not remain.

Even an artist as exacting as Adams was very aware of his work as rhetoric and the need for environmental activism to exploit new media, as he made clear in a 1961 letter to Newhall:

It was seriously important to see the *American Earth* book on TV. Not only was it a new "transcription" of the concept, but it seemed to have its own and different aesthetic. I had the feeling that the screen was showing what the people who read the book really see; that is, what the average spectator (to whom the book is addressed) really sees. We often lose out in that we, as "experts," look upon things such as photographs with highly trained eyes and minds. . . . But it is to the spectator that the image is really addressed, and our problem is to discover what *he* sees in our images. . . . I believe we should do a lot of serious thinking about this medium, and work towards better esthetic and mechanical controls. The scope and size of the audience for even the little educational photography films is frightening. (Adams, 1988, p. 268)

The success of *This Is the American Earth* enabled Brower to fund a series of Sierra Club coffee table books combining sublime landscape photography with text, often exalted quotes from the likes of Thoreau ("In wildness is the preservation of the world") and Muir ("the range of light").

When the U.S. government decided it would be a good idea to build two dams in the Grand Canyon, Brower launched an image campaign anchored by the book *Time and the River Flowing: Grand Canyon* (1964) and full-page ads in *The New York Times*, *The Washington Post*, and other major newspapers. In *Time and the River Flowing*, the Sierra Club deployed photographs, a product of modern industrial culture now being used to preserve wilderness from that very same culture, to convey a compelling vision of sublime wilderness. Photos depicting grand vistas, canyon walls, waterfalls, and endless innovations in natural architecture dominate the book. There are also images of people at play in the Grand Canyon and images of the damages of dams, suggesting nature as a source of sustenance for humans and the need for humans to be careful.

In its construction of nature as sublime and as sustenance, the book and advertising campaign were an appeal to an elite, urban class versed in the cultural meanings of the sublime and appreciative of wilderness as an aesthetic and recreational resource. The Sierra Club's imagistic appeal was a resounding success and the U.S. government abandoned the dam plans.

Silent Spring: Giving Voice to Nature

A classic Adams photo, "Moonrise, Hernandez, New Mexico, 1941," provides a bizarre footnote to another watershed environmental event in the 1960s—the publication of Rachel Carson's *Silent Spring*. Carson's book gave birth to a new branch of environmental activism. In focusing on the pesticide pollution of the planet, Carson contested the post–World War II arrogance of the chemical industries that "man" could control nature. Americans were so oblivious to the dangers of pesticides that one can watch film clips of children at the time chasing the DDT (dichlorodiphenyltrichloroethane) fog truck down the street as if it were selling ice cream, their forms disappearing into the DDT fog. In place of the domination of nature, Carson argued for the interrelatedness of humans with all things in nature and emphasized an ethic of the balance of nature.

From this perspective, the pollution of nature inevitably entails the pollution of people. *Silent Spring,* then, set the stage for a humanist environmentalism, the environmental justice movement, wherein caring for the environment shifted from sublime wilderness to people and the places they inhabit. *Silent Spring* also inspired President John F. Kennedy to direct the President's Science Advisory Committee to examine pesticide issues. Their report would vindicate Carson's work.

Although in the old medium of print, *Silent Spring* was a media event. First serialized in the *New Yorker* and then a best-selling book, *Silent Spring* spurred activism, policy changes, and new laws, but it also fomented an intense antienvironmental backlash in print and on television. In a sense, *Silent Spring* inspired the creation of the antienvironmental movement and "greenwashing" (companies' practice of falsely advertising their products and policies as environmentally friendly). As the public relations agent for the Chemical Manufacturers Association, E. Bruce Harrison orchestrated the industry assault on Carson and

Silent Spring. After smearing Carson, Harrison would go on to found the first antienvironmental public relations agency and invent the practice of greenwashing.

As part of the campaign to demonize Carson as a hysterical woman, the chemical industry distributed pamphlets extolling the virtues of poisons and stoking the fear of insects. One such scare pamphlet, "Once upon a springtime," trumpets pesticides as the cure for the dangers of the Black Death, malaria, the yellow plague, typhus, famine, flies, and *digitaria sanguinalis* (crabgrass) phobia (which apparently afflicted suburban housewives). Among images of housewives, plague victims, fruits, vegetables, rodents, flies, locusts, and farms, Adams's "Moonrise, Hernandez, New Mexico, 1941" was reappropriated to provide the anchoring centerfold image for the pamphlet.

The ability of industry to appropriate environmental causes and images through public relations, greenwashing, and raw political power left Carson with a mixed legacy. Carson changed the world's public perspective, children no longer chased DDT fog trucks, and DDT was banned in the United States in 1972. Yet, DDT is still exported to other countries, and the world is annually doused with billions of pounds of untested poisons that decimate wildlife and cause an array of human health problems.

Whole Earth in Space

The apotheosis of camera activism occurred during the *Apollo* space missions and was as accidental as its beginnings with Watkins. It was midmorning on Christmas Eve, 1968, when the *Apollo 8* crew, Frank Borman, James Lovell Jr., and William Anders, emerged from the dark side of the moon and were struck by the earth rising over the moon. Reflecting the National Aeronautics and Space Administration's (NASA's) technical mind-set, Anders's photograph is historically recorded as Photograph #AS8-14-2383 but is popularly known as "Earthrise." Although "Earthrise" was not a scheduled photographic target, it became one of the most widely circulated images of the 20th century, along with another NASA photograph, #AS17-148-22727 or "Whole Earth," taken on December 7, 1972, aboard *Apollo 17.*

Utilizing unprecedented vantage points, these images provided a worldview that shattered conventional notions of the earth and suggested a holistic, ecological vision. In seeing an isolated, fragile earth, people saw a planet needing protection. As astronaut Anders remarked,

The Earth looked so tiny in the heavens that there were times during the Apollo 8 mission when I had trouble finding it. I think that all of us subconsciously think that the earth is flat or at least almost infinite. Let me assure you that rather than a massive giant, it should be thought of as the fragile Christmas-tree ball we should handle with care. (Quoted in Cosgrove, 1994, p. 284)

These images of the earth are not the earth. Yet, as is the magic of photographs, they became the earth. They are not the earth in at least two respects: (1) They are flat, two-dimensional photographs, and (2) they violate our ideas and experiences of the earth. So, "Earthrise" and "Whole Earth" are photographs. So, AS8-14-2383 and AS17-148-22727 are earths devoid of dimension, of weight, of depth, of smell, of sound, of movement, of history, of context. They give us the earth as radical illusion. This radical illusion interrupts, shatters, silences our ideas of the earth, our visions, and our dreams.

In these images, we see that the earth is not what we thought. It is utterly other—the earth as inhuman. It is a world we do not know, a world we have not seen before. It is the earth from an inhuman perspective. All human markings are gone. No buildings. No roads. No human activity. An earth devoid of human politics and cartography and morality. No nations. No names. No lines of latitude and longitude. But it is not a natural world, either. There are no trees, rivers, animals, mountains, or lakes. Finally, it is not a Western world from a Western orientation—the North on top of the South and dominating. These images are the earth askew, singular, insoluble, unintelligible, and enigmatic. Yet it is also an earth alone in a sea of endless blackness, a fragile globe. "Whole Earth" and "Earthrise" transformed the way people see the world, inspiring Earth Day and becoming the iconic banner for numerous environmental activities.

The Public Screen and Image Events

On June 27, 1975, 50 miles off the coast of California, six Greenpeace activists in three inflatable rubber Zodiacs and armed with one film camera confronted the Soviet whaler *Vlastny* (Imperious). One Zodiac managed to position itself between the whaler and a whale, putting their bodies on the line on behalf of the whale. The Soviets fired anyway, narrowly missing the activists and killing the whale. Though the Greenpeacers lost the whale, they won the media war. The confrontation was captured on film and became the image event seen on televisions around the world. As then Greenpeace activist Robert Hunter (1979) noted, "With the single act of filming ourselves in front of the harpoon, we had entered the mass consciousness of modern America" (p. 231). The next year the Soviets gave up the whaling hunt; a decade later, commercial whaling was banned internationally; and Greenpeace became the largest environmental organization in the world.

With this action, Greenpeace introduced direct action image events into the repertoire of environmental activism. Instead of sublime landscape photographs designed to inspire letter writing and lobbying, videotaped image events capture people intervening on behalf of nature. This move from scene to action is facilitated by advances in video camera technology and marks an epistemic break in ways of knowing the world. The cascade of new media technologies favors the propagation of image events and the decline of speeches and more traditional forms of media activism. Television, video cameras, cable, videocassettes, DVDs, computers, the Internet, cell phones, and YouTube in a cacophonous concert transform the mediascape from the deliberation of the public sphere to the direct action and image events of the public screen.

The concept of the public screen recognizes that most public discourse today takes place via "screens"—televisual, computer, and cell phone. The starting premise, then, is that television and the Internet in concert have fundamentally transformed the media matrix that constitutes our social milieu, producing new forms of social organization and new modes of perception. The public screen is a constant current of images and words, a ceaseless circulation abetted by the technologies of new media.

Whereas the public sphere, in privileging rational argument, assumed a mode of perception characterized by concentration, attention, and focus, the public screen promotes a mode of perception that can be characterized best as "distraction." The public screen conceptualizes distraction not as a lack of attention but as a necessary form of perception when immersed in the technologically induced torrent of images and information that constitute public discourse in the 20th and 21st centuries. The public screen favors images over words, emotions over rationality, speed over reflection, distraction over deliberation, slogans over arguments, the glance over the gaze, appearance over truth, the present over the past.

Speaking for the Trees

EarthFirst! is one of the many groups that have adopted and adapted Greenpeace's deployment of image events on the public screen. They have pioneered multiple tactics to attract attention in this age of distraction, including tree-sitting as a way of saving ancient forests. In December 1997, Julia "Butterfly" Hill, an ex-waitress and car accident victim, climbed Luna, a 1,000-year-old redwood and potential victim of a chainsaw massacre. So began the longest tree-sit in U.S. environmental protest history.

Butterfly lived in the tree for over 2 years. During that time, she overcame El Niño winds and rains; harassment by Maxxam (the company that "owned" the tree and hoped to turn it into cash via the medium of picnic tables and hot tubs), which included fly-bys by helicopter and an attempt to starve her out through a security guard blockade; the atrophying of her legs, and the general travails of living on an 8 × 6 platform 180 feet up a tree. During her time in the tree, Butterfly managed to become the public face of Earth First! and to successfully articulate the inextricable link of wilderness and social issues. She managed to do this through the siting of her protest, her bodily presence in the tree, and her rhetoric.

The particular tree-sit that Hill joined had started in October 1997 and was significant for its location. It was not in pristine wilderness but on a hillside above the town of Stafford, California. The Earth First!ers chose this location after a mudslide caused by clear-cutting destroyed seven homes in Stafford. Significantly, Stafford is a lumber town. Belying the stereotype, then, this Earth First! tree-sit linked wilderness and social concerns.

Butterfly's use of her body and the redwood Luna suggests her awareness of the image landscape she was operating in. A former model, Butterfly realized that a pretty face and a striking image are irresistible to the media. In her self-presentation on her website, two types of images predominate. First, there are close-ups of Butterfly, barefoot and hugging Luna, her traditionally pretty white face framed by her windswept long, black hair. It is a face that is both pleasing and comforting, a cliché of small-town America. Second, there are long-range shots that give more of a sense of the grandeur of Luna. Among the most spectacular are those of Butterfly standing on the very pinnacle of the ancient redwood, hundreds of feet in the air, arms outstretched toward the sky, hair flowing in the wind, tenuously tethered to the tree by her feet. In thus deploying her body, Butterfly turned her protest into an image event worthy of the public screen.

The longer Butterfly dwelled in Luna, the more of an international image event she became. Though neither well-educated nor a veteran environmentalist, Butterfly proved to be a savvy student of media politics and a remarkably disciplined rhetorician. A steady pilgrimage of print and television journalists traveled to Luna, many ascending the tree, to interview Butterfly. In addition, Butterfly's solar-powered technology was her umbilical cord to the media worlds of radio and the Internet. In TV and radio interviews and on her website, Butterfly deftly wove together wilderness issues, human concerns, and a critique of corporate practices, while placing wilderness as the ground for environmental and social concerns. In the end, Maxxam capitulated, agreeing to preserve Luna and a buffer zone.

The environmental activist tactic of staging image events went global in two ways. First, groups like Greenpeace exported their tactics internationally, and local groups around the world adopted such tactics as tree-sits, road blockades, and chain-ins for mass media broadcast. Second, media effectively amplified Greenpeace and their image events into worldwide household images, so that via media an event that happened in one place happened as an image event in every place. For example, Ailun Yang, Greenpeace China's campaign manager for climate and energy, remembers Greenpeace image events from her childhood in a relatively cloistered China:

> People know Greenpeace quite well because in the 80s and 90s CCTV showed a lot of whaling images. . . . In those days, it meant to show how miserable people in capitalist countries are and the need for those heroes on the boats chasing the bad guys. (Yang, personal communication, March 2008)

Embracing the paradox of tree huggers armed with high-tech media, the environmental movement's immersion in new media continues apace. The examples are legion. Al Gore's PowerPoint show and movie *An Inconvenient Truth* transformed him into the global warming guru, Oscar winner, and Nobel Peace Prize Laureate while making climate change an accepted reality. PETA (People for the Ethical Treatment of Animals) has used miniaturized camcorder technology to clandestinely videotape and expose the myriad forms of animal cruelty undergirding industrial civilization. And, of course, major environmental groups have elaborate websites, Facebook and MySpace pages, Second Life presences, and YouTube clips. Saving the world always has been and remains a social movement dependent on the tools of media.

Kevin DeLuca

See also Alternative Media; Chipko Environmental Movement Media (India); Citizens' Media; Eland Ceremony, Abatwa People's (Southern Africa); Human Rights Media; Indigenous Peoples' Media; Installation Art Media; Moon River Movement Media (Thailand); Performance Art and Social Movement Media: Augusto Boal

Further Readings

Abram, D. (1997). *The spell of the sensuous*. New York: Vintage Books.

Adams, A. (1988). *Ansel Adams: Letters and images 1916–1984* (M. S. Alinder & A. G. Stillman, Eds.). Boston: Little, Brown.

Angus, I. (2000). *Primal scenes of communication: Communication, consumerism, and social movements.* Albany: State University of New York Press.

Cosgrove, D. (1994). Contested global visions: *One-World, Whole-Earth,* and the Apollo space photographs. *Annals of the Association of American Geographers, 84*(2), 270–294.

Cox, J. R. (2006). *Environmental communication and the public sphere.* Thousand Oaks, CA: Sage.

Dale, S. (1996). *McLuhan's children: The Greenpeace message and the media.* Toronto, ON: Between the Lines.

DeLuca, K. M. (1999). *Image politics: The new rhetoric of environmental activism.* Mahwah, NJ: Erlbaum.

Harold, C. (2009). *OurSpace: Resisting the corporate control of culture.* Minneapolis: University of Minnesota Press.

Hunter, R. (1979). *Warriors of the rainbow: A chronicle of the Greenpeace movement.* New York: Holt, Rinehart & Winston.

Turnage, R. (1980). *Ansel Adams: The role of the artist in the environmental movement.* http://www.anseladams.com/content/ansel_info/conservation.html

EuroMayDay

EuroMayDay is a Europe-based transnational movement network that emerged from the global movement against neoliberal globalization. It aims to put the issue of increasing precarity of living and working conditions on the political agenda. In mobilizing against neoliberal welfare and labor reforms, it seeks to bring together a wide range of activists from the overlapping fields of art, media, culture, and politics as well as migrants and precariously employed service industry workers.

The term *precarity* refers to the rapidly growing scenario of flexible exploitation (low and insecure pay, intermittent income, variable working hours, and shifting workplaces), and everyday insecurity (high risk of marginalization because of low wages, welfare cuts, and high cost of living). Rather than demanding a return to stable working conditions and fixed job-identities, the movement developed wider claims extending to "social rights," such as access to transport, housing, information, culture, education, and, most importantly, a basic income to replace vanishing social security entitlements.

The EuroMayDay Parades

The movement is most visible in the annual EuroMayDay parades of "the precarious." These processions are timed to coincide with the International Day of Workers Struggles, May 1. At the same time, they sharply differ from traditional trade union marches, not only in their demands but also in their extensive use of radical media. In their endeavor to produce "new political subjectivities," EuroMayDay activists draw on popular culture to create imageries of precarity. For instance, they "subvertize" mass-cultural formats like comics, psycho-tests and games, or *détourn* (hijack) rituals taken from the popular traditions.

The first MayDay parade was organized in 2001 in Milan by activists and subvertizers from the group ChainWorkers, together with the militant trade union CUB (Confederazione Unitaria di Base), and supported by Milanese and Roman *centri sociali* (squatted culture centers) in order to give visibility to temporary workers, part-timers, freelancers, and other service laborers. In 2004, the MayDay parade was held simultaneously in Milan and Barcelona—and in cyberspace, where 17,000 carefully designed avatars marched in a net-parade through a digital urban landscape. Media and other activist collectives embedded in their respective local political scenes succeeded in devising a transnationally resonant event.

In October the same year at *Beyond ESF*, an autonomous event coinciding with the European Social Forum in London, activist groups concerned with labor, migration, and urban issues formed, in conjunction with several media collectives, the transnational EuroMayDay Network. In the so-called Middlesex Declaration (2004), they declared their intention to launch a "structured network of labor radicalism and media activism" and

> to hold a common EuroMayDay . . . on May 1st in all of Europe's major cities, calling for angry temps, disgruntled part-timers, frustrated unemployed, raging immigrants and labor activists to mobilize against precarity and inequality, in order to reclaim flexibility from managers and executives: we demand flexicurity against flexploitation. (para. 3)

By 2009, EuroMayDay parades had taken place in 15 countries and 41 European cities, including Barcelona, Berlin, Copenhagen, Hamburg, Helsinki, Liège, Maribor, Naples, Paris, Seville-Málaga, and Vienna. The protest format of MayDay parades was also adopted by precarious workers in Japan. The number of participants ranged from less than 100 (Hanau, Germany, 2008) to more than 100,000 (Milan, Italy, 2005). The shared web-portal Euromayday.org provided links to dedicated local EuroMayDay websites. In 2008, a web-feed was established to include multilingual content from these local websites.

More important for the movement, however, was the innovative employment of media *at* the parades.

Media at the EuroMayDay Parades

It was not by coincidence that EuroMayDay activities focused on innovative media uses. Many Milan-based initiators of the EuroMayDay parades worked in the "creative" industries and were familiar with "the persuasive power of pop culture and advertising" (Chainworkers, archived website 1999–2002, http://www.ecn.org/chainworkers/chainw/who.htm). Activists and theorists associated with the movement used a post-*operaist* analysis to explain the importance of mediation. (*Operaismo*, from the Italian word for "worker," has been an enduring current in Italian leftist politics, foregrounding workers' agency in bringing about socioeconomic change.) They assumed that in post-Fordist societies, besides labor and welfare changes, life itself was turned into a means of production. Skills like abstract thinking, language, imagination, emotions, and aesthetic tastes became part of the production process. In turn, economic production increasingly moved into the spheres of communication, knowledge, information, emotion, and desire.

For this type of labor, post-operaist theorists coined the term *immaterial labor*. Although most prevalent in the "creative" industries, they regard it as central to contemporary economic processes. If the production of imageries, concepts, symbols, relationships, and emotions is at the economy's core, media production can be seen as an important starting point for social movement activity rather than merely an auxiliary tool for counterinformation.

At MayDay parades, this orientation resulted in a flood of imageries, slogans, and concepts relating to the struggles of what was called "precariat" (with reference to the Fordist "proletariat") printed on posters, cards, T-shirts, and stickers; translated into songs transmitted from sound systems; performed at the parades; and web-disseminated as digital film, photo, graphics, and sound. Intended to proliferate and to be contagious, this imagery first spread on alternative media like Indymedia or the magazine *greenpepper*. It also reached mass media, commercial social network platforms like Facebook, and advertising campaigns. Overall, the MayDay parades aim at the production of new political subjectivities through direct action, theoretical production, linguistic innovation, and the creation of new scenarios for the imagination.

Imageries of Precarity: San Precario and Superheroes

A powerful example of the "imageries of precarity" is the figure of San Precario, patron saint of precarious workers, equipped with his own prayer, colorful iconography, hagiography, and rituals. With his appearances in the context of EuroMayDay, this invented saint made visible issues arising from the increasing casualization of the workforce. Small prayer cards with the image of the saint and a reworked version of the Lord's Prayer were distributed. Drawing off the Catholic tradition of carrying a saint's statue in processions in urban spaces, activists performed prayer-chanting processions and sermons relating to precarity in unlikely locations like supermarkets and other chain stores. Among the miracles performed by San Precario were sudden price reductions. Disseminated in print and digital formats, the concept of San Precario traveled across Europe. It was reenacted in multiple localities, mainly in Catholic areas and often in the guise of the female saint Santa Precaria.

A second example is the concept of precarious superheroes or *imbattibili*, which envisaged the practices needed to survive in precarity as superhero powers. Starting in Milan and picked up in several other cities, mainly in Italy, Germany, and Spain, these *détourned* comic figures came to embody the multifaceted condition of precarity. Over a couple of years, whole series of superheroes appeared: uploaded on EuroMayDay websites; mediated in the format of collection cards, leaflets, and stickers during EuroMayDay parades; and embodied by dressed-up activists. At the 2007 G8 (Group of Eight) Heiligendamm protest, a block of activists in superhero costumes carrying speech bubbles with their demands pointed to the issue of precarity. In some cases, the superhero figure was used in direct actions. A report on Indymedia describes how in Hamburg in 2006, just before the annual EuroMayDay parade, some activists dressed as superheroes entered a delicatessen supermarket and helped themselves to a trolley-load of delicatessen, which they distributed to precarious workers. The police tried to catch them with several police cars and a helicopter, but to no avail. This intervention became the talk of the town and also circulated in the international mass media.

"Social Media"

The EuroMayDay movement of the precarious aimed at building a trans-European public space from below. In this process, activists used a wide range of digital and traditional alternative media in performative rather than representative ways. This concept is described by the Italian initiators of the EuroMayDay parades as "social media": media that allow face-to-face interactions among precarious workers, political activists, and protesters. This type of mediation process tries to develop a collective identity in which different features of precarious workers' daily lives come together and, as a result, are able to spread struggles against precarity.

Oliver Marchart, Marion Hamm,
and Stephan Adolphs

See also Adbusters Media Foundation (Canada); Alternative Comics (United States); Culture Jamming; Fantagraphics Books (United States); *Love and Rockets* Comic Books (United States); Performance Art and Social Movement Media: Augusto Boal; *Stay Free!* Magazine (United States); Yes Men, The (United States); Zines

Further Readings

Hamm, M., & Adolphs, S. (2009). Performative repräsentationen prekärer arbeit: Mediatisierte bilderproduktion in der EuroMayDay-Bewegung [Performative representations of precarious labor: Mediated image-production in the EuroMayDay movement]. In G. Herlyn, J. Müske, K. Schönberger, & O. Sutter (Eds.), *Arbeit und nicht-arbeit: Entgrenzungen und begrenzungen von lebensbereichen und praxen* [Work and nonwork: Limitations and delimitations of life areas and practices] (pp. 315–340). München, Germany: Mering.

Marchart, O., Adolphs, S., & Hamm, M. (2007). Taktik und taktung. Eine diskursanalyse politischer online-proteste [Tactics and timing. A discourse analysis of online political protests]. In M. Ries, H. Fraueneder, & K. Mairitsch (Eds.), *dating.21. Liebesorganisation und verabredungskulturen* [dating.21. The organization of love and the culture of appointments] (pp. 207–224). Wien, Austria: Transcript.

Marrazzi, C. (2008). *Capital and language: From the new economy to the war economy.* Cambridge, MA: MIT Press/Semiotext(e).

Mattoni, A. (2006). Multiple mediation processes in contemporary social movements: Six years of EuroMayDay parade in Italy. Paper presented at the Conférence Identifier, s'identifier—Faire avec, faire contre, Université de Lausanne, Switzerland. Retrieved February 26, 2009, from http://www.unil.ch/webdav/site/iepi/users/cplatel/public/atelier_3/Mattoni.pdf

Mattoni, A. (2008). ICTs in national and transnational mobilizations. *tripleC: Open Access Journal for a Global Sustainable Information Society, 6*(2), 105–124.

Middlesex Declaration of Europe's Precariat. (2004). Retrieved June 2, 2010, from http://www.euromayday.org/2005/middle.php

Raunig, G. (2004, June). La inseguridad vencerá: Anti-precariousness activism and MayDay parades. *Transversal, 7.* Retrieved February 24, 2009, from http://eipcp.net/transversal/0704/raunig/en

Tarì, M., & Vanni, I. (2005). On the life and deeds of San Precario, Patron Saint of precarious workers and lives. *Fibreculture, 5.* Retrieved February 24, 2009, from http://journal.fibreculture.org/issue5/vanni_tari.html

Vanni, I. (2007). How to do things with words and imageries: *Gli Imbattibili.* In M. Stocchetti & J. Sumalia-Sappanen (Eds.), *Images and communities: The visual construction of the social* (pp. 147–170). Helsinki, Finland: University of Helsinki Press.

Virno, P. (2004). *A grammar of the multitude: For an analysis of contemporary forms of life.* Cambridge, MA: MIT Press/Semiotext(e).

EXTREME RIGHT AND ANTI–EXTREME RIGHT MEDIA (VLAANDEREN/FLANDERS)

This entry reviews extreme right and anti–extreme right media in Vlaanderen, the Dutch-speaking northern region of Belgium. Because the success of the Flemish Vlaams Belang (VB; Flemish Interest) far exceeds that of the extreme right in the French-speaking South, and because the French-speaking and Dutch-speaking public spheres are quite separate, this entry is limited to Vlaanderen.

Both sides complain about the mainstream media. Put simply: For the VB, the mainstream media are left wing, "politically correct," and controlled by the political establishment. From the anti–extreme right's perspective, the media treat the VB too much like a conventional right-wing party. Both camps develop strategies to get mainstream media access and have links to more alternative media but also communicate through their own media and public events.

The VB and the Extreme Right in Vlaanderen

The Vlaams Belang was formerly the Vlaams Blok (Flemish Bloc), which was founded in 1978 as the result of a split within the Flemish nationalist Volksunie (People's Union) over Belgium's official language policy, a trigger for continuing strife for many decades now.

The VB's electoral success remained rather limited until the local elections of 1988 when it gained a significant number of city council seats, especially in Antwerp and surrounding cities. It is often said that this was due to the party's heightened attention to "the immigrant problem." The national elections of 1991 marked the definitive breakthrough, with the VB gaining more than 10% of Flemish votes. The VB continued to grow over the next decade, receiving up to almost 25% of votes in the 2004 Flemish elections.

A few months before those elections, the VB was legally found guilty of racism. The court ruled that in its propaganda, the party "clearly and repeatedly promoted discrimination against foreigners." The VB renamed itself Vlaams Belang, but both party leaders and critics stressed that the new party consisted of the same people, with no substantial change in agenda. After 2004, however, the VB's growth halted or at least slowed. But it remained a very important political player in Flemish and Belgian politics.

Extreme Right Media

The VB has the biggest media budget of all the Flemish political parties. It produces its own media and also spends on mainstream media publicity (though several papers refuse to publish its propaganda), on billboards, and elsewhere. The VB, far more than other parties, spreads the word year-round in Vlaanderen and Brussels and does not limit its propaganda to election seasons.

Both its central office and local sections publish several free member and nonsubscriber magazines with wide distribution. The party has a very active website that includes press releases, comments on current events, columns by the party president, videos of VB actions, cartoons, and more. The VB also hosts the website criminaliteit.org (crime.org), where it posts news items about crime, advice on how to prevent it, and "wanted" and "missing" person messages. Website visitors can post their crime stories, published as "men's and women's street testimonials."

The VB's in-house publisher Egmont publishes VB party members' books and other publications on Flemish history and politics. VB programs produced by the Nationalist Broadcasting Foundation were broadcast on the public broadcaster VRT until 2001, when VRT put an end to "third-party programs" that assigned airtime to Flemish political parties. In 2005, the party started its own radio station (VB6015) with a weekly 2-hour show broadcast on digital short wave, which could be downloaded on MP3. But legal problems soon blocked VB6015, because Flemish media law states broadcasters must be independent from political parties.

For many years, the VB's main slogan was "Our Own People First." This slogan was and still is chanted by its followers at party gatherings. The VB uses simple and often harsh imagery to convey its message. Viciously anti-immigrant images—the kind that informed the court's decision in the racism trial—were the boxing glove (with the slogan "In Self Defense"), and the broom ("Big Clean-Up").

In 2005 Antwerp VB parliamentary representative Philip Dewinter caused some surprise by using a heart as a symbol in his "A Heart for Antwerp" campaign. Dewinter, who had always been both a hardliner and very popular, attempted in this way to appeal to an even broader public. Other recurring images were a young Flemish family—husband, wife, and two children (white)—looking forward to the future, and the lion, the symbol of Vlaanderen (the Flemish flag depicts a lion, and the Flemish "national" anthem is called "The Flemish Lion").

The VB is the only extreme-right political party in Flanders, but numerous organizations are close to it, including the Nationalist Student Union, the activist group Voorpost (Outpost), and the think tank Verbond van Nederlandse Werkgemeenschappen Were Di (Union of Dutch Working Societies—Defend Yourself). They provided the VB with an ideological rationale and spread this ideology by organizing debates, meetings, and publications such as Voorpost's *Revolte* and Were Di's *Dietsland-Europa* (Dietsland literally means Dutchland and refers to the goal to unite all the territories of the ethnically Dutch). They also organize demonstrations against multicultural policies and in favor of Flemish secession.

Furthermore, the extreme right is active in conventional media, for example, through VB sympathizers' letters to the editors and newspapers' website forums. Also, both VB parliamentary representatives and other extreme-right activists used blogs and video sites such as YouTube to spread their message.

A special role is played by *'t Pallieterke* (the name refers to the 1916 book *Pallieter* by Flemish nationalist Felix Timmermans), a conservative Flemish nationalist newsweekly. *'t Pallieterke* is independent of the VB and sometimes critical of the party, but considered close to it. Some of the often satirical contributions in *'t Pallieterke* are written by VB members under an alias.

The most important Flemish nationalist public event is the Yser pilgrimage. For years, the extreme right attempted to shift rightward this annual commemoration of Flemish soldiers killed in World War I. After years of struggle over this symbol among different nationalist factions, the extreme right decided to organize its own annual event, the Yserwake (Yser Funeral Wake). Another event with high symbolic value, where nationalist politicians from different parties are present, is the Flemish National Song Fest, where singing of traditional Flemish songs is combined with speeches demanding Flemish secession.

Anti–Extreme Right Movement Media

The huge indignation and protest that followed the VB's 1991 electoral success represented the real breakthrough of the anti–extreme right movement. Anti-VB resistance focused mainly on the VB's immigration policy. Resistance against the VB was and is thus mainly antiracist, but this can be seen as the pivotal issue in a broader progressive struggle. The anti-VB movement was most active from 1991 to 1994 but continued its fight and managed to get broad popular support on a number of occasions.

There were also a number of state-subsidized institutions that attacked discrimination and racism. The Centre for Equal Opportunities and the Struggle against Racism (CGKR) played a crucial role in the battle against the VB—and was strongly opposed by the VB. But the focus here is on anti–extreme right media. The anti-VB movement was more loosely—and often quite spontaneously—organized than the extreme right party and its associated organizations. Its financial resources were also far less than the VB's. These are two of the reasons why anti–extreme right media were less structured and continuous. Nevertheless, communication played a crucial role for the anti–extreme right movement.

One of the main strategies followed by the anti–extreme right movement was to show "the real face" of the VB, a strategy summarized by journalist Hugo Gijsels's 1994 book *Open Your Eyes Before the Vlaams Blok Closes Them*. The underlying assumption was that if people knew what the VB really stood for, they would not vote for it. This led many organizations and individuals to try to inform (and warn) the public. Investigative journalists published books about the VB, and antiracist organizations published brochures for the general public and teaching material for schools.

Additionally, blogs from organizations such as Blokbuster (linked to the Left Socialist Party, a movement for a genuine socialism) and the Anti-Fascist Front (verzet.org [resistance.org]) contributed to this unmasking project. On channels such as YouTube there are many critical documentary videos and reportages about the VB. In 2005 several individuals and organizations combined to start Blokwatch, a website dedicated to informing the public about the VB.

However, in 2007, the website volunteers decided the VB was no longer an acute danger to democracy, and stopped updating the website. The site is still online and includes information on VB ideology and parliamentary representatives, on groups with VB connections, and on research and journalistic coverage on the Flemish extreme right. Blokwatch also published a daily review of press coverage of the extreme right and cartoons satirizing the VB. It also distributed anti-VB stickers and posters, posted an online petition calling for the cutting of the state funding of the VB, and published the book *What You Need to Know About the Vlaams Belang*.

By explaining the VB's racist project, and showing its links with the Flemish extreme right organizations mentioned earlier and with the international extreme right movement, antiracists tried to show the VB was a racist party. Slogans such as *Nie Wieder Fascismus* (Fascism Never Again) and images of VB representatives with Hitler moustaches, raised right arms, or Nazi military helmets served the same purpose, not least in Belgium, with its history of being a major theater in both world wars.

After the VB's 1991 election success, progressive forces felt the need to show that there were large groups against the extreme right. The most important player in this popular mobilization was called Hand in Hand. The main communication strategy of this network of civil society organizations, including the peace movement and labor unions—who played different roles in the battle against the extreme right—was to express broad popular protest through mass demonstrations (in 1992, 1994, 1998, and 2002).

Through mobilizing large numbers of people, Hand in Hand aimed to show that the VB was not the voice of the "silent majority." By promoting rather general aims of tolerance and democracy, Hand in Hand managed to create a broad alliance and mobilize tens of thousands of people. Hand in

Hand's most famous campaign image illustrates its broad post-1991 pro-multiculturalism message: a dark-skinned boy and a white-skinned boy, arms wrapped around each other, each with a black eye. Hand in Hand used a variety of media outlets and called on media personalities to raise awareness and mobilize broadly. Financial support from civil society organizations was important here.

Another reaction to 1991's election disaster was Objectief 479.917. Objectief 479.917 succeeded in collecting more than 479,917 signatures—the number of extreme right votes in the 1991 elections—against the extreme right to show the numerical strength of the anti–extreme right. It also organized demonstrations.

In 2006, Hand in Hand was one of the organizations behind the Street Without Hate campaign. After a young man's racist shooting of a little girl and her Malinese nanny, more than 100,000 posters were distributed in Antwerp. A national initiative followed later. By hanging the posters on their windows, people showed their disapproval of racism and violence. Similar, but more explicitly focused on the elections, was the Red Triangle against the extreme right: A person wearing the red triangle pin showed that he or she would not vote for the extreme right and supported a multicultural and progressive society.

The most recent large-scale mobilization for tolerance and against the extreme right was the 2006 "0110" concert "for tolerance, against racism, extremism, and gratuitous violence." Held one week before the local elections of October 8, 2006, these four city concerts with big-name performances from every musical style attracted about 100,000 people. Performances by popular Flemish artists were considered especially important because they showed that not only "alternative" or "elitist" artists were against the extreme right and challenged the VB's pretense to speak for "the ordinary people."

The concert "0110" wanted to be more than rockers doing their left-wing thing. To make this clear, artists and their management organized the concerts completely independent of political parties, but also of the (progressive) civil society actors traditionally part of the antiracist struggle. For some artists—including organizer Tom Barman of Antwerp rock band dEUS—the concerts were explicitly against the extreme right, for others less so. Some other artists—such as Helmut Lotti—refused to call their participation a political statement against the extreme right and preferred the broad "tolerance" label.

The antiracist movement also tried to formulate solutions for and strategies against the extreme right's success. Charta '91, for example, was a reaction of intellectuals against the VB after the 1991 elections. It played an important part in political debate in the years following but is not active today. Charta '91 was a think tank that analyzed the reasons for the extreme right's growth and developed strategies for a progressive counterforce. It produced texts and organized debates. It came up with the idea of a *cordon sanitaire* (literally: quarantine line, for the containment of viruses) to contain the VB by not entering into coalitions with it, which was signed by all the other Flemish parties. In the years following, the VB attacked the *cordon* and many politicians and commentators questioned this containment strategy. The anti-VB movement counterattacked, continuously warning against the danger of the VB through op-ed pieces and in other ways.

More radical and often radical left organizations such as Blokbuster and the Active Left Students also organized counterdemonstrations against VB and other extreme right organizations' meetings and demonstrations. Access to university campuses was an important symbolic dimension, and they both attempted to prevent VB representatives from participating in debates at universities and protested against Nationalist Student Union events. These confrontations sometimes led to violent clashes.

A Continuous Struggle

The VB reacted in a number of ways. Frequently, anti–extreme right groups got portrayed as extreme leftists, implying the VB represented the majority, and its opponents a radical minority. When the anti-VB message was one of tolerance and democracy, the VB argued these were vague terms with no meaning and an attempt to mislead people into opposing the VB. The VB tried to reduce a generic statement against the extreme right to a partisan strategy against the major opposition party, the VB. And the VB steadfastly rejected the accusations of racism that were the core of the anti–extreme right message, as an unscrupulous way to de-legitimate reasonable Flemish nationalist opposition.

At times, the VB mocked and parodied antiracist campaigns. Hand in Hand, for example, was countered with a poster depicting a departing airplane and the slogan "Hand in Hand Back to Their Own Country." Although much antiracist communication was either serious or almost naïve (the Hand in Hand poster), mockery and parody are also part of the antiracist communication toolbox. The entire Blokwatch website, for example, was at one point an exact copy of the VB website's structure and look. Also, on blokwatch.be, Dewinter's "A Heart for Flanders" became "Hard for Flanders."

The effectiveness of antiracist initiatives in Belgium is hard to evaluate. The *cordon sanitaire* has proven efficient in keeping the VB from governing. And the anti-VB movement has proven successful in showing public disapproval of the extreme right, in moments when the extreme right danger was most acute—around elections or as a reaction against extreme right violence. But the movement did not succeed in stopping the VB from becoming one of the biggest extreme right parties in Europe.

Benjamin De Cleen

See also Christian Radio (United States); Media Against Communalism (India); Radio Mille Collines and *Kangura* Magazine (Rwanda); *Southern Patriot, The, 1942–1973* (United States); Tamil Nationalist Media (Sri Lanka/Transnational); White Supremacist Tattoos (United States)

Further Readings

De Witte, H. (Ed.). (1997). *Bestrijding van rascisme en rechts-extremisme. Wetenschappelijke bijdragen aan het maatschappelijk debat* [Fighting racism and right wing extremism. Academic contributions to the societal debate]. Leuven, Belgium: Acco.

Detant, A. (2005). The politics of anti-racism in Belgium: A qualitative analysis of the discourse of the anti-racist movement Hand in Hand in the 1990s. *Ethnicities, 5*(2), 183–215.

Van Aelst, P. (2000). De anti-racistische protestgolf in België [The antiracist protest gap in Belgium]. In T. Sunier (Ed.), *Emancipatie en subcultuur: sociale bewegingen in België en Nederland* [Emancipation and subculture: Social movements in Belgium and the Netherlands] (pp. 98–119). Amsterdam: Instituut voor Publiek en Politiek.

FANTAGRAPHICS BOOKS (UNITED STATES)

Located in Maple Leaf, Washington State, Fantagraphics Books is a publishing house specializing in alternative comic books, graphic novels, magazines, and adult comics. Founded in 1976, the company has persisted in publishing works that push the boundaries of aesthetics and storytelling in comic form, pushing for comics' acceptance as a legitimate art form by focusing on book-length works. Founder Gary Groth wanted comics in the mainstream, using mass marketing techniques instead of relying on niche outlets. Fantagraphics has energetically tried to overcome negative perceptions of comics and enable artists to find audiences.

Fantagraphics emerged when the U.S. underground comics movement of the 1960s and 1970s matured. Those were largely self-published by a single artist and distributed through loose networks of specialty stores and underground publications. Fantagraphics, and some other peers, emerged as that movement declined and its artists gained more mainstream acceptance and, most importantly, mainstream shelf space. As of the late 2000s, books published by Fantagraphics could be found at most mainstream book retailers in the United States. The company opened its own bookstore in Seattle in 2006.

Initially only publishing the comics news and criticism magazine *The Comics Journal*, by the 1980s the company had expanded to publish works

that mainstream publishing houses like Marvel Comics and DC Comics—who published primarily fantasy and superhero comics—were avoiding. In addition to new works, Fantagraphics publishes retrospectives and anthologies of work by underground and mainstream artists of the past.

Important publications include *Love and Rockets* by Gilbert and Jaime Hernandez, as well as works by Chris Ware, Robert Crumb, and Daniel Clowes. Anthologies like *Mome, Blab*, and *Blood Orange* allow newer artists to find larger audiences. Topics are as varied as the company's mission of publishing fiercely original work would suggest, while also pushing aesthetic boundaries. Works have dealt with ethnic and cultural identity, sexuality, and social alienation, ranging in tone from satire, to action, to black comedy, to crude humor. The works have garnered critical acclaim from both comic and mainstream critics.

Fantagraphics' success has only been moderate as a business, though the acquisition of Charles Schulz's wildly popular comic strip *Peanuts* in 2004—a project slated to end in 2016—has lent it some economic stability. Despite several financial struggles, Fantagraphics has found ways to continue fulfilling its stated mission of supporting artists by providing them an avenue for publication, while also cultivating a strong fan base from which to draw support.

Daniel Darland

See also Alternative Comics (United States); Alternative Media; *Love and Rockets* Comic Books (United States); *RAW* Magazine (United States); Zines

Further Readings

Bennett, P. (1998, August). Trading on comics: The business of selling comics and graphic novels to the trade. *Publisher's Weekly*, pp. 32–40.

Matos, M. (2004, September 15). Saved by the beagle. *Seattle Weekly*. http://www.seattleweekly.com/2004-09-15/arts/saved-by-the-beagle

FEMINIST MEDIA, 1960–1990 (GERMANY)

Within the social and feminist movements of the 21st century, the opportunities opened up by the Internet and other electronic communication media may lead to a dismissal of feminist newspapers and magazines as nothing of consequence. But they had a remarkable, if checkered, history, and the issues they opened up are a long way from being settled.

History

In Germany, feminist publications existed long before the 1960s, beginning with the newspapers—repeatedly banned—of the 19th- century suffrage and the social-democratic feminist movements. Saxony's press law prohibited women from editing their own papers. It stated: "The editorial responsibility of a newspaper can only be taken on and continued by men" (Peters, 1995, p. 122).

Frauen-Zeitung (Women's Newspaper) was the first in 1848 in Cologne, but it was closed after the third issue. Likewise, Leipzig's *Frauen-Zeitung*, started in 1849, was banned in 1852 due to its "dangerous influence" on women. A little longer was granted to others, such as *Neue Bahnen* (New Paths), started in 1866; *Die Frau*, published from 1863 to 1916; and *Centralblatt des Bundes Deutscher Frauenvereine* (Central Paper of the Federation of German Women's Associations), founded in 1899.

The first proletarian women's newspaper, *Die Staatsbürgerin* (The Citizeness), published in 1884, was banned 6 months later due to its "incitement to class hatred." *Die Arbeiterin* (The Working Woman) ran from 1890 to 1891. The most important organ of the proletarian women's movement was *Die Gleichheit* (Equality). After 1933, all of these newspapers disappeared.

The Newspapers of the New Women's Movements

The new women's movements of the 1960s and 1970s had their own newspapers and magazines. Few exist today. They constituted unique forms of public media in that they were movement organs, often locally. Some were also national. Examples include *Schwarze Botin* (Black Woman Messenger), anarchist-oriented (1976–1986); *Frauen gemeinsam sind stark* (Women together are strong), which alternated publication in different cities; *Frauen und Film* (Women and film); and lastly *Courage*, whose pilot appeared in 1976, and *Emma*, 4 months later.

After the new women's movement had passed its formation phase, the 1970s saw the beginning of feminist counterculture projects. From 1978, the magazine *beiträge zur feministischen theorie und praxis* (contributions to feminist theory and practice) enriched the plethora of feminist print media. *Wir Frauen* (We Women), evolving from a circular of the Demokratische Fraueninitiative (Women's Democratic Initiative), became a magazine in 1982. It became very professional over the years, a model of maintaining a critical perspective. Its political articles, attacking exploitation, wars, racism, sexism, the wasting of ecological resources, neoliberal globalization, and many other topics, still make excellent reading. The magazine's website, www.wirfrauen.de, contains a detailed overview of many other feminist newspapers and magazines.

Two major journals were published too. *Feministische Studien—Zeitschrift für interdisziplinäre Frauen- und Geschlechterforschung* (Feminist Studies—Journal for Interdisciplinary Women's and Gender Research) first appeared in 1982 and continues to be published biannually. The radical feminist and lesbian magazine *Ihrsinn* ran from 1989 to 2004 (*Ihrsinn* is a pun—*Irrsinn* means "insanity," while *Ihrsinn* would translate as "her intelligence.")

The Newspaper *Courage*

Courage was founded as a self-managed project inside the new feminist movements. The idea for the autonomous, leftist-feminist newspaper *Courage* stemmed from a small circle of Berlin women actively involved in the autonomous feminist movement who knew each other from the Women's Center in the Kreuzberg neighborhood. They brought various concerns to 48 Bleibtreustrasse (*Courage*'s office) but were unanimous in believing "we need a newspaper that supports women taking over political responsibility and encourages them to demand privileges and power." They wrote this on a green flyer, now yellowed with time.

Their target audience was rebellious women who questioned society's foundation on the oppression of women and other "minorities" and who wanted to launch perspectives for change. There were to be numerous articles about the history of women, the job market, continuing education, psychology, sexuality, medicine, women's movements, the church, justice, and culture. Women of all ages and professions were targeted, even those not actively involved in the women's movement.

Mother Courage, the camp cook of Brecht's *Mother Courage and Her Children,* was on the flyer. Soon, somebody made the suggestion to choose the Grimmelshausen version of the wandering Courage as symbol of the pugnacious, self-directed woman:

> Zest and esprit mark her life's battle. Her curiosity is infinite and keeps her alive. Her outlook makes trifles important, makes minor matters essential. She defends her liberty with all means. Courage—the self-directed woman—is not a starry-eyed idealist but neither is she satisfied with the status quo. She lives and thinks in alternative ways. This is what *Courage* stands for. No more and no less. (Duden, 1976, p. 1)

The women disregarded the warning voices of friends, parents, and others who tried to get them to see that this project would need money. They sent out invitations anyway to a women's festival in Berlin. It was a wild success. Women came in droves. The first printing bill could be paid from the entrance fees and pilot issue sales (5,000).

When rumors arose that Alice Schwarzer, soon afterward to be owner-editor of *Emma* (Germany's long-running women's magazine), was also planning to launch a newspaper, *Courage* offered to cooperate. However, the women were relieved to be rejected. They hurried, and the first issue appeared in September 1976. *Emma* appeared in print 4 months later.

The *Courage* women had empowered themselves and defined their program themselves. Work started at 10 a.m. They had little practical prior knowledge and even less money, but they were full of idealism, self-assurance, and fervor. The founding mothers invented new working structures and experimented with many other projects. All tasks had to be done by everyone and be equally valued. There was to be no hierarchy (this soon had to be modified). They established the departments, the paper's sections, and its priorities.

It was both a painstaking and a passionate time. *Courage* informed relentlessly about events, debunked myths, denounced grievances, and tackled previous taboos, and rapidly became famous. The *Courage* women's maxim was that *Courage* was a kind of regulatory force that channeled chaotic opinions and theories. By the end of the 1970s, the newspaper was selling over 70,000 copies. Very few editors had prior journalistic training. For an entire year, they worked as volunteers; however, after the initial 2 years, the women were able to live well off their uniform wage.

In the beginning, *Courage* could only be obtained via Berlin's magazine distributors and at Berlin news vending kiosks, but soon it became well known beyond the city. It went from 5,000 (pilot) to 20,000 (third issue). In February 1977, 2 weeks after *Emma* appeared (circulation: 20,000), *Courage*'s circulation reached 35,000. Sales climbed to 70,000 in the late 1970s. However, this breathtaking success could not be maintained. (*Emma,* according to inside sources, had managed, by 2010, to reach over 100,000.)

With *Emma*'s appearance, bitter controversies broke out among the women's movements. Over and over, Schwarzer's autarchy was critiqued. *Emma,* right from the beginning, had business model structures that the women's movement frowned upon. *Emma*'s content evolved around the dispute between different interpretations of feminism, especially heated regarding a military draft for women. Schwarzer advocated equality of women in all areas, whereas the *Courage* collective rejected military service in general. *Courage* was now under fire from the male press and *Emma.*

These conflicts found their way into the collective. For 2½ months, *Courage* went from monthly to weekly—and then suddenly was gone. The once so-euphoric members of the collective had fallen out. In 1984, *Courage* had to declare bankruptcy. The women's movement has missed an important outlet ever since.

beiträge zur feministischen theorie und praxis

In a quest for greater theoretical clarity, the nationwide Verein sozialwissenschaftlicher Forschung und Praxis für Frauen (Association of Social Science Research and Practice for Women) was founded in 1978. In that year, the association edited the first issue of *beiträge zur feministischen theorie und praxis* (contributions to feminist theory and praxis), which called itself the "oldest and biggest magazine of the autonomous women's movement." It especially set out to offer a discussion forum for theoretical arguments over feminist political practice, as evinced within the numerous projects that had sprung from women's movements.

The magazine's 69 colorful issues contained a broad spectrum of national and international feminist insights and discussions. The first issues were published by Verlag Frauenoffensive (The Woman's Offensive Press). In 1983, a small editorial group developed a new concept for the journal and independently produced three issues annually. The first issue of this second phase was titled "Against Which War—for Which Peace?"

Over the years, this magazine produced material still used today in many ways by women's movements, in political education, by women's representatives, in the context of unions, churches, universities. The magazine *beiträge zur feministischen theorie und praxis* not only discussed recent topics but also initiated debates, became an important medium for cross-linking women's projects, and developed into a political theoretical discussion forum of the autonomous women's movement. In the magazine, only women had a voice.

Major congresses, conferences, public events, and lectures resulted from the initiatives of *beiträge*—for example, congresses on "The Future of Women's Work," "Women Against Gene and Reproductive Technologies," "Women Against Racism." On the occasion of the "Women's Strike Day" on March 8, 1994, *beiträge* took over one of the two nationwide coordinating centers.

The magazine *beiträge* was often caught between two stools: For women academics, the magazine was too political; for activists, it was too aloof and theoretical. After multiple disputes (not only among the staff but also within the women's movements) about the so-called White middle-class feminism that excluded migrant women, Afro-German women, and Jewish women, the magazine identified itself as antiracist and felt connected to Black feminism.

Regrettably, the magazine's activities became less and less visible as time passed. On March 7, 2008, one day before International Women's Day and 30 years after its first issue, *beiträge* closed. "Just as the women's movement lost its force, with the emergence of gender studies *beiträge* gradually lost its discussion base," wrote the progressive Berlin daily *Tageszeitung* in its editorial of February 22, 2008. Circulation had decreased from 3,000 copies per issue a decade before to 600. Furthermore, it had become increasingly difficult for the volunteer editorial team to recruit volunteer authors. From the original 1983 collective, only one woman remained.

One cofounder told *Tageszeitung*, "Each branch of gender studies now has its own journal." She did not expect any editorial progeny: "Young women are blind to structural discrimination." She conceded that the *beiträge* project had reached its natural term: "The second women's movement is over. The third has to be led by other women. And they will most certainly find other forms for it" (all quotations from *Tageszeitung* editorial, February 22, 2008). But its demise left another gap in the sparse feminist print media scene.

The Loss of a Secure Place

In both projects, feminist utopias of self-managed cooperation were put to the test. The editorial offices were places full of life and fantasy where new ideas germinated. The women themselves often queried the necessity of "women's nooks." It is a paradox of feminist politics that exclusion is needed to overcome women's exclusion. The whole purpose of the collective was to self-run the organization's aims, content, and format. In both projects, all decisions were made collectively. Each rejection and each acceptance of an article was discussed in the group.

Of course, there were informal hierarchies and different responsibilities within the autonomous groups and projects. These differences often led to destructive and paralyzing conflicts in which some proved more assertive than others. The idea of the autonomous project as a nonhierarchical space, virtually in an extraterritorial relationship vis-à-vis patriarchy, proved extremely problematic in the medium term. In the end, the collective's members had to discover that they could not avoid competition and the profit motive.

The examples of *Courage* and *beiträge* are quite dismaying, for they demonstrate how impotent feminist structures seem to be when dealing with conflicts. *Courage* failed, among other reasons, because of this incapacity. *beiträge* also experienced staff attrition. For a long time, it survived only because a few members invested some funds in the project—in addition to volunteering their work. Because all were "volunteers," they earned their living through outside jobs. This created different conditions, but probably not less conflict potential, than conventional work.

The hope that women, just because of their womanhood, would be less elitist and less competition-oriented than men was prone to disappointment. High-minded political insistence on equality and the abolition of the division of labor was abandoned. Already in 1998 *beiträge* noted, "In this project it is no longer possible to share complete knowledge and complete experience" (Erhardt, 1998, p. 7).

However, at the beginning of the 21st century, the issues the new women's movement raised have in no way been settled. Those aims must not be given up, even if they cannot be realized under current conditions and in the face of powerful opponents, such as the internationally organized pro-life advocates (anti-abortion activists). To address them, more methods and media are needed to cross-link feminists with each other.

Gisela Notz (translated by Christina Voss)

See also Feminist Media: An Overview; Indymedia and Gender; Sarabhai Family and the Darpana Academy

(India); Women Bloggers (Egypt); Women's Movement Media (India); Women's Radio (Austria)

Further Readings

Duden, B. (1976). In eigener sache. *Courage, 1.*

Erhardt, H. U. (1998). Die ersten zwanzig jahre. Beiträge zur feministischen theorie und praxis [The first 20 years: Essays on feminist theory and praxis]. *Metis: Zeitschrift für Historische Frauenforschung und feministische Praxis, 13.*

Hüttner, B. (2006). *Verzeichnis der AlternativMedien 2006/2007* [Alternative media register 2006/2007]. Neu-Ulm, Germany: AG SPAK Bücher.

Notz, G. (2006). *Warum flog die Tomate: Die autonomen Frauenbewegungen der Siebzigerjahre* [Why the tomato flew: The autonomous women's movements of the seventies]. Neu-Ulm, Germany: AG SPAK Bücher.

Notz, G. (2007). *Als die Frauenbewegung noch Courage hatte* [When the women's movement still had courage]. Bonn, Germany: Friedrich-Ebert-Stiftung.

Peters, L. O. (1995). *Ihr literarisches und publizistisches werk.* In J. Ludwig & R. Jorek (Eds.), *Auftrag der Louise Otto Peters Gesellschaft.* Leipzig, Germany: Leipziger Universitäts-Verlag.

Plogstedt, S. (2006). *Frauenbetriebe: Vom Kollektiv zur Einzelunternehmerin* [Women's projects: From collective to individual entrepreneur]. Königsstein, Germany: Ulrike Helmer Verlag.

Susemichel, L., Rudigier, S., & Horak, G. (Eds.). (2008). *Feministische Medien: Öffentlichkeiten jenseits des Malestream* [Feminist media: Public spheres beyond the malestream]. Königsein, Germany: Ulrike Helmer Verlag.

FEMINIST MEDIA: AN OVERVIEW

If women's roles as decision makers are invisible in information and communication structures, tools, and processes, including the media, women will never be a part of actual social, economic, and political decision-making processes. If women do not take part in all areas and all levels of decision making, their rights will never be protected and there will never be gender equality and gender justice.

This is the general reality in terms of where women are located within the media and in the larger society, as reflected in media's portrayal of women's images. This entry first reviews the scale of the problem women face and then examines women's activism in digital media, community media, and alternative media projects, and in exerting pressure on communication policymakers.

Underrepresentation of Women and Minorities

Fewer women than men have access to the media, and fewer people from minority groups have access. If a woman is from a minority group, she has fewer opportunities to be in the media. And less still if she is a lesbian, is a person of color, or represents a minority religion. Access, in this regard, refers to both visibility of women in the media and the space available to them to use or work within media organizations.

The findings from the Global Media Monitoring Project (GMMP), coordinated by the World Association for Christian Communication, illustrated this. In 1995, 17% of news subjects were women, and 83% were men. In 2000, when the project was carried out again, women were found to be just 18% and men 82%. In 2005, the third time that the GMMP was conducted, there were 21% women and 79% men—still four men for every woman who appeared in the news.

A similar trend was evident in South Africa over the same period. Only 17% of news sources were female; less than 10% of the sources for politics, economics, and sports stories were women. Only 8% of politician sources were women even though 18% of the members of parliament in the region are women. Media statistics in the United States are in line. A report by Media Matters for 2005 and 2006 stated that men outnumbered women by 4 to 1 as guests on Sunday morning talk television shows.

A second Media Matters report revealed the continuing lack of women and minorities in U.S. prime-time cable news. Women were less than 50% of the guests on a single one of the three cable networks, and on some they comprised as little as 18%. Women in Congress received fewer total newspaper articles; fewer mentions in front-page, national, foreign, metro, business, and sports articles; fewer issue-based articles; and fewer mentions and quotes in newspaper articles than their male

counterparts. Northwestern University's Media Management Center 2006 report revealed that women were only 29% of top managers in newspaper companies.

Furthermore, among the few women who climbed the media ladder, many did not represent women's interests. They saw themselves as one of the boys and did not challenge the patriarchal and hierarchical structures and profit-oriented agendas of corporate media.

Stereotyping Gender

Men are portrayed in news and entertainment media as aggressive, independent, and in charge. The same media depict men in traditional, stereotypical ways, such as macho men who degrade and victimize women. Although some nontraditional portrayals and coverage occasionally surface, many researchers have found that women are generally portrayed as young and fair, slim and beautiful, and preoccupied with men and children. In the news media, once again in relation to sourcing, men are more likely to be quoted on stories about politics, business, religion, science, defense, and security issues. Women, on the other hand, are more likely to be quoted in coverage of issues such as health, home, food, fashion, travel, and education.

Media stereotypes have led to many real-life problems, one of which is the distortion of women's self-image. Women are made to believe that there is always something wrong with their looks. In Asia, Africa, and Latin America, media continuously convey the message that in order to be beautiful and attractive to the opposite sex, one should have a fair complexion. To be dark is not acceptable. This message is used to aggressively promote skin-whitening products. On the other hand, in North America and Europe, light-skinned women are pressured to get a tan because it looks healthy and is fashionable.

Normalizing Inequality, Discrimination, and Violence Against Women

Media stereotypes of gender reinforce traditional relationships between women and men, sending the message that such relationships are normal and therefore should not be challenged. Much research suggests that there is a correlation between exposure to sexually explicit and sexually violent material and increased negative attitudes toward women. Such negative attitudes often lead to violence against women where the common interpretation is that the female victim (survivor) is responsible or partially responsible for what happened to her.

Women victims (survivors) of violence are often interrogated in the news media and their characters and physical attributes subjected to scrutiny. One journalist in the Philippines reported in a celebrated rape-murder case that the victim was wearing "micro-shorts" when the incident happened.

Because most media—especially government and corporate media—do not allow people to speak for themselves in their own authentic voices, there are inaccuracies, distortions, and misrepresentations of reality, often with negative consequences for social justice.

Although some may argue that the issues discussed so far only apply to government and corporate media (often referred to as mainstream media), the following discussion of women's engagement in digital media and community media reviews their current situation and opportunities in this newer arena.

Digital Media

The upsurge of new information and communication technologies (ICTs), particularly the Internet, has in many ways dismantled the barriers for women's entry into the media. The new ICTs have allowed more women to produce and distribute media materials that accurately and adequately articulate their issues, concerns, and aspirations. They have also enhanced the reach of older communication media such as print, radio, and television.

However, although the new ICTs offer a broad range of opportunities, their development has also increased the divide between those who have access to such technologies and those who don't. Moreover, there is a widening gender divide within the digital divide. Across the world, women are confronted with economic, social, cultural, and political barriers that limit or prevent them from accessing the new ICTs. In many developing countries, subscription to the Internet costs more than the average worker's monthly income. Women not only earn less than men, but they also have fewer opportunities to be trained in using digital technologies.

Gender statistics on Internet usage are scant and uneven. There are different levels of disparity between global North and South nations. But studies by Women in Global Science and Technology (WIGSAT) and by the UNDP have demonstrated that there is a long way still to go to achieve parity. Furthermore, the sale of video games such RapeLay (a video game that simulates sexual assaults on women) and widespread use of the Internet for sex trafficking are indications that new problems emerge along with new developments.

Community Media

The community-based ownership and nonprofit orientation of community media present more opportunities for women's access to the media. Because these media place less emphasis on formal education, youth, and physical appearance, more women are able to access this type of media. Issues such as reproductive health, abortion rights, and women's political participation often find space in community media when they are deemed too sensitive, too political, or are dismissed as women's issues by government and corporate media.

Community media take various forms, such as community newspapers, community wall news (*peryodikit* in some parts of the Philippines, from the Spanish *periódico* and the Tagalog *dikit* "post"), community bulletin boards, community TV, and community radio. In some places, there are community telecenters that combine Internet café, telephone calling station, and community radio.

Community radio serves both as a campaign and as an organizing instrument, as in the case of the Radio Suara Perempuan (Women's Voice Radio) in Pariaman, West Sumatra. Radio Suara Perempuan was initiated by Nurhayati Kahar, founder of the Institution for Victims of Violent Acts to Women and Children. Kahar and her group use community radio to raise awareness of violence against women and children and generate support for their campaign to eliminate it. From what was initially a taboo subject, more and more women in local communities in Pariaman are now coming out to give their views on the issue.

In Jordan, Amman Net community radio covers women's issues more broadly than the other stations and dedicated airtime for women's groups to discuss their activities during a 16-day campaign against gender violence, when no other stations would. In Mozambique, women community radio broadcasters formed the Network of Women in Community Radios in 2003 to "encourage activities seeking to ensure that women enjoy the same rights, duties and opportunities as men."

In Fiji, femLINKpacific uses community radio to hold the government accountable to its commitment under UN Security Council Resolution 1325 on Women, Peace and Security. femLINKpacific produces radio programs that highlight women's role in peace building and conflict resolution in the Pacific context.

People's participation in governance is greatly influenced by how the media report and interpret political events and issues, and how media influence the political process and shape public opinion. In an environment where people have access to and control of the media, as illustrated by the examples of community radio productions cited, people's capacity to contribute to and influence policy and decision making is enhanced.

Community radio has a number of attributes that make it an effective tool in promoting women's participation in decision-making processes and governance structures. It is not beholden to corporate and government interests, which allows it to speak to issues independently. It uses local language, which makes the information and the discussions on issues accessible to local communities. It transcends literacy barriers, which allows and encourages a great number of women to use it as their primary source of information and channel of communication.

However, even in the community media sector, there are issues of women's underrepresentation and negative and stereotypical portrayal. For example, a 2006 study conducted by Isis International and AMARC Women's International Network–Asia-Pacific showed that 45% of community radio staff and volunteers in the Asia Pacific region are women, but only 28% of them are in leadership positions. However, because of its community-based and people-controlled nature, these issues are confronted to a much lesser degree. Given this reality, community radio remains an effective tool in promoting people's ownership of and participation in development processes that ultimately will guarantee accountability, transparency, effectiveness, efficiency, and responsiveness—all essential elements of good governance.

Challenges for Feminist Media Activists

The women's movement challenged the media from within and without, and continues to do so. Women have protested the negative, stereotypical, and distorted images of women and men in the media. They have also fought against discrimination against women within media organizations.

One of the biggest problems feminist media practitioners confront is being categorized as "advocacy" journalists, their viewpoints dismissed as biased and glibly labeled propaganda. Because of this, the blogs and articles they produce are not picked by the mainstream. Because of the "advocacy journalism" label, feminist perspectives in mainstream media will likely be found only in op-ed pages until audiences, writers, publishers, broadcasters, editors, and producers all come to terms with the fact that the traditional ideal of objectivity in the media does not exist.

What's the point of aspiring to be in the mainstream when you want to be alternative?—one might ask. But feminist media practitioners want to challenge the mainstream by influencing its culture and practices from within. A key part of this entails educating their colleagues to write news and produce media materials from a gender lens. A second priority is that feminist media practitioners want to reach the widest audience possible. The third, which builds on the first two, is to discontinue the "ghettoization" of feminist perspectives, the stereotyping and isolation of views that challenge patriarchy.

In development and social movement circles, where one might think feminist media would be better appreciated and feminist media practitioners' issues would resonate, the struggle is also uphill. Feminist media projects have great difficulty in getting funded. They are not a priority for the international donor community for several reasons. One is that women's media projects—communication projects in general—are often regarded simply as information-sharing initiatives. Women's media and communication projects are not seen as integral to the development process, let alone as development projects themselves.

Another reason why fewer funds are allocated to such projects is the belief that women's and gender issues are already mainstreamed. In the 1990s, following the adoption of the Nairobi Forward Looking Strategies and the Beijing Platform for Action, women's media projects flourished. Even major companies like the Australian Broadcasting Corporation produced very progressive, women-focused programs such as *Women Out Loud*. But in the 2000s, the assumption is widespread that women and women's issues are mainstreamed everywhere, including in the media—in actuality leaving women nowhere.

Women's Responses

Feminist media practitioners are claiming their spaces in the media, and they are doing this globally and from all fronts. They established their own media organizations to produce and distribute media materials; these organizations include Africa Woman and Child Feature Service, Feminist International Radio Endeavor (Costa Rica), fem-LINKpacific (Fiji), and Women's International News Gathering Service (WINGS; Canada). They train the media how to be more gender-sensitive (Isis International, Manila). They monitor the media and educate audience members to analyze the media (Southern Africa Media and Gender Institute/Women's Media Watch, South Africa).

These feminist advocates also create venues for dialogues and partnerships between grassroots women's organizations and the media (International Women's Tribune Centre). They train women in the news media to provide them with the skills they need to succeed in their career and become leaders in newsrooms (International Women's Media Foundation). They have also used the law to challenge the exclusion of women from decision-making positions within media structures, and oppose blatant sexism in the media.

At the policy level, women have lobbied governments, the United Nations, and regulatory agencies to develop and implement policies that they hoped would transform women's roles in media institutions and media's portrayal of women. One such policy is the Beijing Platform for Action (BPFA), the most comprehensive agenda for women's

empowerment to date, adopted by 189 governments at the Fourth World Conference on Women in Beijing in 1995. The BPFA cites women and media as one of the critical areas of concern and it has two strategic objectives:

1. Increase the participation and access of women to expression and decision-making in and through the media and new technologies of communication.

2. Promote a balanced and nonstereotyped portrayal of women in the media.

Since the women's movement took up the issue of women and media 40 years ago, inroads have definitely been made in terms of women's media representation and visibility. However, the problems are complex and deeply rooted, and there are no easy solutions. Women need to always be vigilant and aware that much more work needs to be done. This is especially so as new developments take place.

It is also important to view the issue of women and media intersectionally, taking into account the perspective of the global South. The issue of gender is inextricably linked to other factors of domination and subordination, such as race, caste, class, ethnicity, religion, and sexual orientation. It is also linked to the multiple global crises—the financial, food, and environmental crises. As such, it is an integral component of anticorporate globalization movements and other social movements.

In addition, challenging stereotypical and negative portrayals of women and men can be seen as imperative in terms of journalistic ethics. When half of the population is not equally visible, when diverse women's images are not adequately and accurately portrayed, there is a violation of basic journalistic standards.

Women need to be in the newsroom, in the boardroom, and at the government and intergovernmental policy levels. Women's equal access to the media and their decision-making structures affect the media's portrayal of women. Diverse and positive images in the media will help women see what they can be to their fullest potential. The reflection of such images will help normalize a world in which women and men, young and the old, minority and majority govern together, exchanging ideas and solutions, creating a world that is better for everyone.

Mavic Cabrera-Balleza

See also Alternative Media; Citizens' Media; Feminist Media, 1960–1990 (Germany); Feminist Movement Media (United States); Participatory Media; Sex Workers' Blogs; Women Bloggers (Egypt); Women's Movement Media (India); Women's Radio (Austria)

Further Readings

Cabrera-Balleza, M. (2005). Developing and evolving a feminist agenda in the information society. In A. Ambrosi, V. Peugeot, & D. Pimienta (Eds.), *Word matters: Multicultural perspectives on information societies* (pp. 214, 230–233). Montréal, QC: C&F Éditions.

Cabrera-Balleza, M. (2008). Community radio as an instrument in promoting women's participation in governance. In M. Solervicens (Ed.), *Women's empowerment and good governance through community radio: Best experiences for an action research process* (pp. 16–17). Montréal, QC: AMARC.

Gallagher, M. (2005). *Who makes the news? Executive summary.* Retrieved June 2, 2010, from http://www.whomakesthenews.org/reports/2005-global-report.html

Gurumurthy, A., Parminder, P. J., Mundkur, A., & Mridula, S. (Eds.). (2006). *Gender in the information society: Emerging issues.* New York: UNDP-APDIP/Elsevier.

Huyer, S. (2004). *Gender, ICT and the information society: A global view.* [PowerPoint presentation]. Brighton, Ontario, Canada: Women in Global Science and Technology (WIGSAT). http://archive.wigsat.org/huyerAITEC.ppt

Internet Demographics for USA. (2008). Retrieved May 6, 2009, from http://techcrunchies.com/internet-demographics-for-usa

Northwestern University Media Management Center. (2006). *Women in media 2006: Finding the leader in you.* Retrieved May 6, 2009, from http://www.mediamanagementcenter.org/research/wim2006.pdf

Schwartz, A. (2004). *A look at the origins and significance of the Southern African Gender and Media Awards summit.* Retrieved April 20, 2009, from http://www.awid.org/eng/Issues-and-Analysis/Library/Why-should-we-be-watching-gender-and-media-activism-in-Southern-Africa

Spears, G., & Seydegart, K. (2000). Global media monitoring project. World Association for Christian Communication. Retrieved April 20, 2009, from http://www.whomakesthenews.org/reports/global-media-monitoring-project-2000.html

Tanesia, A. (2008). Women as producers of information in Indonesia. In V. Solervicens (Ed.), *Women's empowerment and good governance through community radio: Best experiences for an action research process* (pp. 74–75). Montréal, QC: AMARC.

World Bank. (n.d.). *Engendering ICT toolkit: Indicators for monitoring gender and ICT.* Retrieved May 6, 2009, from http://web.worldbank.org/WBSITE/EXTERNAL/TOPICS/EXTGENDER/EXTICTTOOLKIT/0,,contentMDK:20272986~menuPK:562601~pagePK:64168445~piPK:64168309~theSitePK:542820,00.html

FEMINIST MOVEMENT MEDIA (UNITED STATES)

The second wave of the American women's movement was an outgrowth of progressive organizing of the 1960s, including the civil rights, youth, and antiwar movements. Betty Friedan's *The Feminine Mystique* (1963), and other protofeminist texts (like those of women avant-garde filmmakers, including Maya Deren, Shirley Clarke, and Carolee Schneemann, all working in the 1950s and early 1960s), set the stage for this movement by beginning to articulate women's discontent, "a problem without a name."

Then, women who were radicalized and given a set of critical vocabularies through the 1960s protest movements began to add their critique of gender to shared movement concerns about personal freedom, social justice, and structures of domination. Women spoke out about sexism within these radical communities, as well as how issues like discriminatory work practices, female sexuality and health, day care, education, abortion, and lesbianism were left largely unaddressed by these movements. However, the feminist movement adamantly shared with the New Left a critique of the politically conservative role of the mainstream media and a commitment to the progressive possibilities within what B. Ruby Rich would call "cine-feminism."

In the 1960s and 1970s, feminists organized around several media concerns, including women's lack of employment within the industry, sexist and stereotypical depictions of women found within dominant media, the creation of a distinctly feminist media education and institutions, and the invention of new languages for avant-garde feminist media-making and criticism.

Differences within feminism often led to debate among the creators of these various projects (particularly between "activist" media-makers and "academic" theorists), fueling several streams of movement media with often contradictory aims. The mid-1980s brought a backlash against feminism (part of a general quieting of the U.S. Left). This coexisted in perhaps contradictory ways with "postfeminism" claims—some thought feminism's gains large enough to assert sexism had been vanquished—and in this climate, the feminist media movement slowed.

Discrete feminist practices, on the other hand, continued unabated and in ever greater numbers, due in large part to the ideas, images, and institutions created during the movement's heyday. Although most feminist media institutions closed along with most countercultural organizations due to de-funding, feminists visibly continued to contribute to dominant media, to teaching, to writing, and to media activism. Feminists professionalized, inhabiting positions of cultural power, just as they have dispersed, bringing their multiple interpretations of gender inequality to other, ongoing movements. Meanwhile, global feminist media movements have taken on an urgency of their own, learning from, challenging, and adapting the concerns and practices of this highly productive, earlier U.S. tradition.

Professional Media Employment

Feminists were quick to understand that controlling images was central to shaping ideology. They also understood that women were almost entirely unrepresented in the media professions, within both mainstream and alternative domains. The early golden days of Hollywood had seen only four women directors: Ida Lupino, Lois Weber, Alice Guy-Blaché, and Dorothy Arzner. The alternative media were no better. Very few women directed films or were trained in media production. Until 1980, women directed less than 1% of all studio films.

Thus, demands for women's inclusion across the media workforce were some of the first demands the movement made. Activism in this vein occurs to this day because women's representation in this field remains far lower than in other professions. The national organization Women in Film, founded in 1973, continues to support women's networking and career growth in chapters across the United States. In 2007, less than 7% of working directors were women, according to Martha Lauzen, a scholar who tracks the industry through an annual study titled *The Celluloid Ceiling*. It took until 2010 for the first woman—Kathryn Bigelow, for *The Hurt Locker*—to win top director awards from either the Academy of Motion Picture Arts and Sciences or the Directors Guild of America in the United States.

Images of Women

In the early 1970s, several highly influential books introduced the histories and analyses of women's representation to feminist politics. Kate Millett's *Sexual Politics* (1970), Marjorie Rosen's *Popcorn Venus: Women, Movies, and the American Dream* (1973), and Molly Haskell's *From Reverence to Rape: The Treatment of Women in Movies* (1974) all looked at the stereotypical sexist depictions of women created by a male-dominated industry. Using sociological and historical approaches, these books catalogued common and recurring patriarchal movie roles for women, which represented them with maximum sexuality and limited agency. In Hollywood, women were inevitably seen as sexual objects, suffering mothers, man-hating spider-women, or dependent girls. They were fated to inhabit stories organized around either their successful romance and marriage or their punishment for crimes (of hypersexuality or other forms of transgression).

Feminists demanded more complex (or positive) images of women. Some feminists demanded more positive images of women, others more balanced and complex images. All wanted a cinema that would expand to include women's concerns and a female point of view. Moreover, feminists of color, lesbians, and others marginalized within mainstream feminism, began to enumerate their particular stereotyping (or absences) within this more global analysis, also demanding self-representation and greater visibility.

Feminist Institution-Building

As was true for the U.S. counterculture more generally, feminists understood that beyond critiquing the workings of dominant, patriarchal institutions, the movement needed to form parallel institutions that would enable women's media-making with feminist principles. With a large social presence in the 1960s and 1970s, a smaller number holding out through the de-funded Reaganite 1980s, and a few victors continuing into the present, feminists founded a vast array of media institutions for exhibition and conversation, archives, artist collectives, media centers, festivals, conferences, journals, production education, distribution, and funding.

For example, 1971 saw the First International Festival of Women's Film and the First Annual Women's Video Festival, both in New York. More than 100 films from the United States, Canada, and Europe were screened. In the next few years, as many as 50 more such festivals took place in the United States alone. Feminist film festivals, conferences, and seminars began to flourish internationally as well, including a celebrated if controversial set of feminist screenings at the Edinburgh Film Festival in 1972. Feminist production and distribution collectives also flourished. During the feminist media movement's heyday, women could make, fund, watch, talk about, write about, and distribute films within a lively interactive network of feminist institutions.

As of 2010, however, there were only about five women's film festivals held annually in the United States, with about the same number internationally. Feminist distribution companies, journals, and funding sources have similarly declined in number, as feminist aims have lost funding, have become incorporated into the larger goals of progressive media organizations, or have been institutionalized in academia.

Feminist Film and Video

Empowered by the women's movement and the feminist institutions mentioned earlier, women started at that time making their own films and videos to self-represent female experience and feminist demands. Expanding upon then-contemporary theories of consciousness-raising, film proved an ideal vehicle for the representation of women's voices, which were bent upon expressing their shared experiences and interpretations of patriarchy through a public discourse that could motivate further analysis and change.

Inspired by the feminist credo "The personal is the political," a significant majority of feminist media focused on biographical or autobiographical images of women, with feminist historical or political concerns arising out of this self-exploration. Making use of newly available handheld consumer technology, in particular video (which was cheaper to purchase, easier to use, and initially not dominated by men), many women were able to bypass sexist media education and professionalism altogether, while a small but growing number of women also began to make their work inside Hollywood.

Furthermore, women began attending, and then teaching within, film and art schools. Beyond increasing the number of educated women practitioners, these feminist teachers were changing media education by serving as role models as well as by establishing feminist methods for approaching technology and production. In great and continuing numbers, women began producing an eclectic array of media dealing with feminist issues as diverse as women's sexuality, employment, mothering, abortion, history, labor, and debates within feminism over racism and homophobia within the movement. A guiding feminist vision was often also found within media connected to other political movements, such as civil rights, queer politics, antiglobalization, antiwar, and environmental activist media.

Feminist Film Theory

As the feminist film movement expanded the places and processes by which women encountered film, women scholars were radically rethinking media studies' relation to film texts. Feminists strove to position, within the heart of film scholarship (where it has stayed to this day), their radical analyses concerning the ways that classical cinema is organized around the production of patriarchal definitions of women.

Much of this work was initially inspired by Claire Johnston's essay "Women's Cinema as

Counter Cinema" (1973) and Laura Mulvey's essay "Visual Pleasure and Narrative Cinema" (1975), both of which relied upon feminist interpretations of contemporary critical theory emerging from psychoanalysis, structuralism, Marxism, and semiotics. Moving past the earliest studies, which had focused on images or roles of women, foundational feminist film theory set out to understand the patriarchal structures undergirding dominant systems of representation, relying in particular upon psychoanalytic concepts of the "male gaze" and identification and Marxist-inflected semiotic discussions of ideology.

Staunchly antirealist, and quickly anti-essentialist, these film scholars did not support the kind of political and personal feminist cinema described earlier—rooted in self-discovery, self-knowledge, self-representation—for in the critical theory they were investigating, the self was in crisis. They argued that realist representation could enable neither ideological nor formal analysis, nor could it break from the structural limitations of cinematic institutions where pleasures in looking were rooted in patriarchal systems of desire, knowledge production, and identity formation.

Feminist film scholarship looked at form, or signifying systems, inspiring a critical look at classic cinema and a celebratory analysis of avant-garde, experimental film. A feminist countercinema developed, in close conversation with this more academic tradition. Feminist countercinema attempted to radically reconfigure traditional practices of looking by developing alternative forms and experimental techniques to create a viewer self-aware of the patriarchal structures of cinematic spectatorship and storytelling.

Since the 1990s, feminist media scholarship has grown beyond and challenged the narrow if seminal concerns of this early tradition, in directions as diverse and dispersed as is feminism itself. Contemporary feminist media scholarship adds theoretical considerations of difference (including race, nation, and sexuality) to rethink spectatorship, textuality, and authorship. It engages with televisual and digital production where feminists play a larger role in the construction and viewing of images. It researches women's multiple roles in the history of cinema and focuses upon international and transnational feminist media, as well as the diverse practices of American feminists.

In this way, although feminist movement media may be a thing of the past, feminist practices continue to radicalize media, in relation to gender and its associated issues, and contribute to political explorations of the themes, forms, institutional practices, and analyses of global media.

Alex Juhasz

See also Barbie Liberation Organization (United States); Feminist Media, 1960–1990 (Germany); Feminist Media: An Overview; Women's Movement Media (India); Women's Radio (Austria)

Further Readings

Foster, G. A. (1995). *Women film directors: An international bio-critical directory*. Westport, CT: Greenwood Press.

Juhasz, A. (2001). *Women of vision: Histories in feminist media*. Minneapolis: University of Minnesota Press.

Kuhn, A., & Radstone, S. (1990). *The women's companion to international film*. London: Virago Press.

Rich, B. R. (1998). *Chick flicks: Theories and memories of the feminist film movement*. Durham, NC: Duke University Press.

Rosenberg, J. (1983). *Women's reflections: The feminist film movement*. Ann Arbor, MI: UMI Research Press.

FIRST PEOPLES' MEDIA (CANADA)

Canadian Indigenous media evolved with a distinct relationship to social movements and activism. From the time of their conception in the 1960s and 1970s, First Peoples' media, policies promoting cultural and communication rights, and participatory community development were yoked together. This established a crucial connection between communications and politics in First Nations' self-assertion. In order to gain territorial, political, and economic power through negotiating constitutional treaties with the federal, provincial, and territorial governments, Indigenous leaders recognized early on how powerful the tools of communications would be in furthering their interests. Consequently, many became engaged in politics soon after having held positions of responsibility in media. This entry describes the evolution of First Peoples' media, its programming, and its impact throughout Canada.

Indirectly influenced by the grounded documentary film approach of John Grierson, first National Film Board (NFB) commissioner in the 1940s and 1950s, the success and showcasing of two NFB film production workshops on Baffin Island in the early 1970s triggered the self-organization of many media projects for First Peoples. Simultaneously, Telesat's Anik Satellite became operational in 1973, offering live television from southern Canada and improved telecommunication services to those living in northern and remote regions.

Anik A, the NFB experience, and an experimental Anik-B intercommunity video/audio project *Inukshuk* (1978–1981) soon demonstrated to Canadian funding agencies that accessible communications infrastructures to link isolated communities would make good economic, cultural, and political sense. Ordinary citizens could appropriate the satellite's technical potential to communicate their own (inter)cultural, sociopolitical, and economic development goals within and beyond their own territories. Their publicly mediated voices could contribute to their constituency groups' politicization. The politics of communications and the communication of politics were seen to be integrally tied together in the development of First Peoples' media.

Northern media activists proceeded through several stages. After the Inukshuk project's positive evaluation in 1981, 13 regional Native Communications Societies (NCSs) emerged, all acknowledged in 1983 in a Northern Broadcasting policy framework. The policy's implementation vehicle—Northern Native Broadcast Access Program—provided financial support for the weekly production of 20 hours of radio and 5 of television in northern Indigenous languages.

After this, NCS leaders banded together to demand consistent funding and distribution capacity under their own control. Several of them applied for and received licenses from the Canadian Radio-Television Telecommunications Commission (CRTC; Canada's regulatory agency) to become network broadcasters. From 1983 to 1986, federally funded programming from the NCSs was intraregional, with minor exceptions of occasional "outside" contract work.

In the late 1980s, Northern Native Broadcasting, Yukon, took the bold initiative to move beyond the cultural, territorial, and political borderlines to negotiate a contract for a half-hour program *Nedaa* (Your Eye on the Yukon) on public broadcasting's Newsworld service. This had the long-range consequence of opening small spaces for Aboriginal broadcasting within mainstream Canadian media and of stimulating debate over how to build cross-cultural alignments for political, social, and cultural activist purposes.

Funding Northern Canada broadcasting was not a problem by the end of the 1980s; the challenge was exhibition. A major federal lobbying strategy was undertaken, and Television Northern Canada (TVNC) was established as a pan-Northern distribution service in 1991, the year in which communications access rights for Aboriginal peoples were enshrined in Canada's Broadcasting Act. TVNC became the vehicle through which First Peoples would publicly represent their Northern perspectives.

Not surprisingly, exposure to each other's NCSs programming stimulated public dissatisfaction with its territorial limitations. First Peoples wanted multidirectional communication flows and the integration into their broadcasts of feature films and independent producers' work from other parts of Canada.

By 1997, TVNC's pan-Northern successes convinced its board and staff to pursue the establishment of a nationwide network. Though controversial, due to cable companies' opposition to carrying it as a mandatory national channel, the CRTC approved TVNC's application on February 22, 1999, and granted Aboriginal Peoples Television Network (APTN) carriage on basic cable and satellite services throughout Canada, with a small monthly subscription fee in the South. APTN has operated since September 1, 1999, and was also a crucial information support for the creation of Nunavut, Canada's first Inuit-governed territory in that year. On September 1, 2005, its license was renewed for another 7 years.

Impact of First Peoples' Media

First Peoples' media content consists of a range of programming topics and genres: information programming, fictional and historical drama, Indigenous sports (lacrosse), comedy, cooking shows, variety shows, news and current affairs, quiz and talk shows, and children's programs, among many others, each of which has a consistent inflection toward Aboriginal viewpoints. It serves several purposes, as Ginsberg and Roth (2002) have pointed out, including

> documenting traditional activities with elders; creating works to teach young people literacy in their own languages; engaging with dominant circuits of mass media and political struggles through mainstream as well as alternative arenas; communicating among dispersed kin and communities on a range of issues; using video as legal documents in negotiations with states; presenting videos on state television to assert their presence televisually within national imaginaries; or creating award-winning feature films. (p. 130)

Beyond the broadcasting sectors (community, regional, and national), multiple websites and feature films, such as those produced by Isuma Igloolik Productions (*Atanarjuat: The Fast Runner, The Journals of Knud Rasmussen*), form a burgeoning independent production and distribution sector. The narration of Indigenous stories and the retelling of their histories for circulation beyond the local has become an important force in claims for land and cultural rights, and for developing alliances with other communities and states. Recently, Isuma TV launched a web-based, open-access Aboriginal film exhibition site, which provides an excellent complement to existing First Peoples' media in Canada and elsewhere.

The cultural persistence evident in First Peoples' multiple media platforms has the potential to disturb the encompassing but narrow aesthetic of Canada's commercial media. In becoming national media citizens in control of their own information services and public intellectual perspectives, First Peoples activists have used media to mediate sociopolitical relationships and coalitions and to interrupt the Canadian assimilationist project to absorb minority cultures into the Anglo-French ascendancy.

In the televisual joining together of Canada's regions, First Peoples have taken charge of new media venues and are using them in ways consistent with their own priorities, cultural orientations, and pedagogical strategies. As a growing social movement, they have tackled technological and administrative challenges at many levels and have pushed for and gained new mediating structures. Northern and Aboriginal media policies, innovative practices, technological infrastructures, funding programs, a burgeoning feature film industry, a dedicated broadcasting channel, and an international public all represent new resources in Canada. First Peoples' versions of Canada's history, their knowledge, and their cultural practices are now the preferred content of their own media undertakings. These coexist and collaborate with those owned and operated by other Canadians; North, Central, and South Americans; and members of the international community.

Lorna Frances Roth

See also Adivasi Movement Media (India); Eland Ceremony, Abatwa People's (Southern Africa); Indigenous Media (Australia); Indigenous Media (Burma/Myanmar); Indigenous Peoples' Media; Indigenous Radio Stations (México); Māori Media and Social Movements (Aotearoa/New Zealand)

Further Readings

Aboriginal Peoples Television Network: http://www.aptn.ca
Ginsburg, F., & Roth, L. (2002). First Peoples television. In T. Miller (Ed.), *Television studies* (pp. 130–131). London: British Film Institute Publishing.
Isuma TV: http://www.Isuma.tv
Roth, L. (2005). *Something new in the air: The story of First Peoples television broadcasting in Canada.* Montréal, QC: McGill-Queens University Press.

FREE RADIO (AUSTRIA)

Austrian free radio is a recent example of community media in central Europe and is, despite its relative youth, rather varied in terms of content and organizational structure. Its German title is *Freies Radio* or *Lokalradio* (free or local radio). These terms refer to independence and freedom of expression as well as to its local orientation. Free radio stations are not targeted to a specific community but provide a platform for diverse marginalized voices and opinions in a particular locality. The Austrian free radio scene is part of a more variegated social movement media scene that also consists of print and Internet media as well as Vienna's community TV station. (All data in this entry refer to findings of Purkarthofer, Pfisterer, and Busch's 2008 study *Ten Years of Free Radio in Austria*; see Further Readings.)

Overcoming the Monopoly in Austria

Austria's struggle for free radio frequencies started in the late 1970s and 1980s throughout the country and was intensified by different pirate radio actions. From the beginning, the political and social dimensions of these efforts were very important. In spring 1989, the European Federation of Free Radios organized a public broadcast in Vienna on media pluralism, which ended with the transmitter being confiscated. Several pirate radio initiatives founded a Pressure Group Freies Radio in 1991 and worked actively to end the broadcasting monopoly in most of Austria's federal states.

In 1989, the Radio AGORA association applied to the authorities for a local license to open a multilingual and noncommercial radio station. When it was rejected, they filed a grievance with the European Court for Human Rights. Their core argument was based on the restricted access of the Slovene-speaking minority to multilingual audiovisual media in the region, which was discriminatory and violated its media pluralism rights. The Court took up the grievance together with a grievance by Austrian commercial broadcasters, and in 1993 the Austrian national broadcasting monopoly was abolished. AGORA's argument was cited in the Court's ruling, which states that private broadcasting monopolies should be checked and that the rights and needs of specific groups of listeners and viewers should be catered for in the interests of media pluralism.

This ruling, by explicitly strengthening minority rights, went beyond earlier decisions ending national monopolies in several other European states. In 1993, the government decided on the Regionalradiogesetz (Regional Radio Act), which became the basis for the first licenses distributed in early 1995. However, except for one license in Salzburg and a second in Vienna for noncommercial radio stations, only economically powerful regional print media were given the available licenses. The rejected applicants, among them the noncommercial free radio stations, filed a grievance with the Constitutional Court, which subsequently cancelled the previously assigned licenses. After an amendment to the Regional Radio Act, in which the newly founded Association of Austrian Free Radios (VFRÖ) played a major role, a larger number of frequencies were announced (8 on the regional level and 40 on the local), and in subsequent years they increased in number again slightly.

The Austrian Community Radio Landscape

Austria has a threefold broadcast system: a strong nationwide public service, with 3 nationwide and 9 regional 24-hour radio stations; a number of commercial stations with regional licenses; and 13 free radio stations. The mandate for nationwide broadcasting gives the public broadcaster Österrischer Rundfunk (ORF; Austrian Broadcasting) priority for strong frequencies, whereas noncommercial and commercial stations only get weaker, local ones. The mountains in large parts of the country require several transmitters even for a relatively small area, a difficult and costly challenge. But even in cities, the assigned frequencies and the transmitters in place do not cover every location in their areas.

By the end of 2008, 15 out of 16 VFRÖ stations were broadcasting via ground signal (13 full licenses) or the Internet. Some began as pirate projects in the 1970s, but the most recent had started only in autumn 2008. Austria's Free Radios Charter, which includes ethical and organizational principles, dates from 1995 and continues in force in a slightly altered version for all VFRÖ members.

Staff numbers ranged from 2 activists in one case to more than 500 volunteers at Vienna's Radio ORANGE. Most volunteers produced regular radio shows, with a smaller number working in administration (projects, programming, special events, and committees).

With the stations' background in pirate radio and a variety of leftist political and social movements, organizational and participation issues have always figured in the stations' everyday work. Many tried diverse models of direct democracy and formed constitutions giving volunteers and staff the right to vote and to develop the organizational structure. Whereas in the beginning the legal struggle for licenses was the focus, the first years of broadcasting brought the challenge of organizing a regular day-to-day service to maintain the programming and the volunteers' commitment.

From its beginnings, an outstanding feature of Austrian free radio was its self-definition as noncommercial. Advertising is rejected to support independence in reporting. Funds are drawn instead from public funding, cultural events announcements, sponsorship of particular shows, and mutual public relations and outreach work among noncommercial projects. Thus, there are no commercial breaks. Paid cultural announcements have their own format and program slot, sponsorship is announced at the beginning and end of a show, and reciprocal support work is done via reporting on other projects, or in flyers and the monthly program bulletin. However, recent debates have focused on the need for affordable advertising for local ethnic businesses and cultural events. Music shows especially can promote local concerts and festivals, and staff from nonprofit organizations frequently host shows as part of their outreach activities.

Diversity of Opinion, Pluralism

Airtime is mainly allocated by indices of social and media marginalization. Whereas at the start the paramount aim was simply to fill the 24 hours, as time went by new shows were more and more carefully selected. To achieve internal pluralism, free radio stations tried to involve as many different people as possible and to let them speak from their own standpoint. This strategy also led to new and experimental radio formats, which might be at odds with radio's genres and conventions but may also challenge audiences' listening habits.

Broadcasts in free radio stations often show close links to local social or cultural initiatives. Over their first decade, some have been very successful in positioning themselves as an important niche-medium for social, political, and cultural affairs.

Free radio turned out to be a place where it was possible to speak about experiences that need a safe environment under the speakers' control, because radio guarantees both publicity and anonymity. This especially benefits topics like HIV/ AIDS, sexual abuse, or violence, as well as people who feel their place in society is precarious or unstable. Sensational, audience-grabbing handling of personal stories is avoided and thus radio becomes a channel for a respectful way of talking about trauma, taboos, and social problems.

Free radio was also a major platform for broadcasts in migrants' and minority languages. The public broadcasting service was continually refusing or cutting down air time for languages other than German, thus failing its mission. In contrast, free radio stations allow for linguistic diversity and a variety of opinions in their programs, so that people's individuality is taken into account and their reduction to ethnic categories is more likely to be overcome. In this way, free radio stations have been actively working on leaving behind essentialist views of identity and the former notion of ethnic "colorfulness."

Empowerment and Media Education

Free radio stations also define themselves as learning and teaching environments, so the large number of volunteer producers is central to their mission. The stations became important in media training, and many who begin their career in the free stations went on to work in other media or in public relations. Besides acquiring journalistic and technical skills, volunteers described a boost in self-confidence as a benefit brought about by their new activity. Certain qualifications can be transferred directly to other areas, and radio work develops networks and teamwork, as well as social skills through cooperative activity.

Participants are prompted to reflect upon journalistic practice, such as editing or interviewing; they learn how to communicate issues to different audiences; and they start to question communicative and journalistic routines. Volunteers can draw on the accumulated knowledge of an experienced organization.

Places of Negotiation and Social Involvement

It is an essential merit of free radio to make social diversity heard. More than any other media institution, it is committed to marginalized communities and viewpoints and manages to get many of them on the air. Free radio uses this access to the public to improve social life according to community perspectives, and show a keen willingness to support environmental protection, health care issues, education, human rights, and sociopolitical counterinformation.

In programs as well as in the stations themselves, there is space for encounters that foster interaction with other people and their opinions. For the negotiation of conflicts, it is essential for all parties to know where they stand and to be able to represent themselves. Over time, radio work empowers participants to better know their own positions and experience what others think and why. This empowerment touches also a wider circle of people occasionally involved in a show who are committed to active listenership and social action. Yet linguistic, financial, educational, physical, and technical barriers remain, and stable funding needs to be found for current measures to involve disadvantaged persons over the long term.

Regional Relevance and Translocal Networks

An outstanding strength of the free stations is their simultaneous local relevance and translocal interconnectedness. Cultural locations, musical groups, and social initiatives especially profit from a station's ties to its locality. For institutions and nongovernmental organizations, the stations are not only a way to inform the public but also a focal point where interests meet and ideas emerge. In addition, free radio stations also arrange translocal networks and seize various opportunities in order to link up different local audiences: Cross-border collaborations in neighboring regions brought forth creative multilingual formats as well as collaboration on the basis of common languages. Free radio offers interesting and sustainable job opportunities.

The value of a translocal perspective consists in maintaining connectedness to the local and yet breaking its narrowness. Issues and areas previously regarded as marginal move to the center and can be considered from a new perspective.

Conclusion

The Austrian free radio experience has been fairly successful, and there is potential for further expansion of more diverse programming and structural diversity.

After 10 years of intensive organization and development, two major obstacles persist: signal quality and inadequate funding. Existing funding does not cover every station's basic costs, and the situation varies from province to province. Stable funding in particular is essential to make better use of the stations' potential to contribute to social cohesion and pluralism.

In comparison to its neighboring countries, Austria's free radio is deeply rooted in a social movement scene and politically active. This clear difference from mainstream media is a challenge for the audience and their listening routines. But it needs to be seen as an important alternative to mainstream journalistic practices, whether through multilingual broadcasting, addressing taboos openly, or actively dismantling broadcasting barriers. Free radio stations reflect more than other media the linguistic diversity of Austrian society and have been implementing accessibility for people who, for various reasons, are denied a public voice. The innovative formats and aspects of free radio journalism regularly win official awards. Important changes in a media system often start from its margins and can advance from there to the mainstream.

Judith Purkarthofer, Petra Pfisterer,
and Brigitta Busch

See also Community Broadcasting Audiences (Australia); Community Media and the Third Sector; Community Radio (Ireland); Community Radio Movement (India); Free Radio Movement (Italy); Free Radio Movement, 1974–1981 (France); Low-Power FM Radio (United States); Prometheus Radio Project (United States); Women's Radio (Austria)

Further Readings

AMARC. (2007). *Community radio social impact assessment.* AMARC Global Evaluation. http://www.amarc.org/documents/books/AMARC_Evaluation_book_June-10_2007.pdf

Bonfadelli, H. (2008). *Migration, medien und integration. Forschungsbericht zuhanden des BAKOM* [Migration, media and integration. Research report for BAKOM]. Zürich, Switzerland: Universität Zürich, Institut für Publizistikwissenschaft und Medienforschung.

Busch, B. (2004). *Sprachen im disput. Medien und öffentlichkeit in multilingualen gesellschaften* [Languages in dispute: Media and the public sphere in multilingual societies]. Klagenfurt, Austria: Celovec.

Busch, B. (2006). Changing media spaces: The transformative power of heteroglossic practices. In C. Mar-Molinero & P. Stevenson (Eds.), *Language ideologies, policies and practices: Language and the future of Europe* (pp. 206–219). New York: Palgrave Macmillan.

Day, R. (2008). *Community radio in Ireland: Participation and multi-flows of communication.* Cresskill, NJ: Hampton Press.

Knoche, M. (2003). Freie radios—frei von staat, markt und kapital(ismus)? Zur widersprüchlichkeit alternativer medien und ökonomie [Free radio stations—Free from the state, market and capital(ism)? On the contradictoriness of alternative media and economy]. *Medienjournal: Zeitschrift für Kommunikationskultur, 4,* 4–19.

Knoche, M., Grisold, A., Hirner, W., Lauggas, M., & Wagner, U. (2001). *Endbericht zum forschungsprojekt entstehung und entwicklung freier nichtkommerzieller radios in Österreich* [Final research report on the origin and development of free noncommercial radio stations in Austria]. Salzburg, Austria: Auftraggeber BM für Verkehr, Innovation und Technologie.

Lewis, P. (2008). *Promoting social cohesion: The role of community media.* Report prepared for the Council of Europe's Group of Specialists on Media Diversity. Strasbourg, France: Council of Europe. http://www.coe.int/t/dghl/standardsetting/media/Doc/H-Inf(2008)013_en.pdf

Peissl, H., & Tremetzberger, O. (2008). Community medien in Europa [Community media in Europe]. *RTR: Nichtkommerzieller Rundfunk in Österreich und Europa, 3,* 115–258. http://www.rtr.at/de/komp/SchriftenreiheNr32008

Purkarthofer, J., Pfisterer P., & Busch, B. (2008). 10 jahre freies radio in Österreich. Offener zugang, meinungsvielfalt und soziale kohäsion–eine explorative studie [Ten years of free radio in Austria: Open access, opinion diversity and social cohesion—an exploratory study]. *RTR: Nichtkommerzieller Rundfunk in Österreich und Europa, 3,* 11–113. http://www.rtr.at/de/komp/SchriftenreiheNr32008

Verband Freier Radios Österreich. (2006). *Charta der freien radios Österreichs* [Austria's Free Radios Charter]. http://www.freie-radios.at/article.php?ordner_id=27&id=54

Free Radio Movement (Italy)

In a climate of intense cultural, social, and political change, when even the public broadcaster, Radiotelevisione Italiana (RAI), was breaking away from the decades-long control of the Christian Democratic Party, the free radio, or *Libertà d'antenna* (Antenna Freedom) movement in Italy was the expression of the desire for more freedom of communication coming from expanding sectors of civil society. The free radio movement had deep roots in the country's history of rebellious, antigovernment, and antiestablishment communication: from partisan radio stations during the antifascist resistance period, to pirate stations, to local and community radio. The radio movement, which began in the early 1970s, soon included a multitude of illegal stations that mushroomed across the peninsula, from north to south, in the main cities as well as in provincial towns. It is difficult to gauge how many stations there were, as most of them had a very short life, ranging from a few days to a few months. Some, however, broadcast for a few years, while others became viable operations and were still on the air in the late 2000s.

The Legislative Context

Early attempts to jam official radio frequencies and use radio for subversive politics date back to 1970 with Radio Gap, broadcasting in the northeastern town of Trento on the frequency assigned to the news bulletin of RAI's first channel. Together with Radio Sicilia Libera (Radio Free Sicily), those first pirate radio stations demonstrated an early interest in radio's potential.

State broadcasting monopoly, first established in 1952, was placed under review by the Constitutional Court in 1974. Two years later, its decree ended that monopoly over local broadcasting. Unfortunately, legislation regulating the private broadcasting sector only passed in 1990, leaving the sector prey for entrepreneurs and commercial interests. Indeed, by the early 1980s, the season of the "hundred flowers" (as the growth of independent radio and TV stations was called) had drawn to an end, with the consolidation of the commercial TV sector in magnate Silvio Berlusconi's hands. Many radio stations found themselves competing for advertising and soon organized into national networks. This contrasted with the initial local flavor and noncommercial nature of many stations.

Radio for Democratic Communication

Most of the politically oriented stations that proliferated in the mid-1970s were run by the Far Left, the New Left, Communists, Socialists, labor unions, rightist Catholic associations such as Comunione e liberazione (Communion and Liberation), as well as by the neofascist Movimento Sociale Italiano, which was closely connected to Radio University. Among the stations motivated by progressive political aspirations were Radio Popolare, Radio Alice, and Radio Cora.

Radio Popolare (People's Radio) was founded in 1976 in Milan by a small group of people wanting to escape narrowly defined political affiliations and create a forum for everyone on the Left to communicate with each other. Radio Popolare distinguished itself for its imaginative use of programming, which included not only political news but also satire, music, and live studio performances. It was based on a form of diffused ownership, where listeners could purchase shares of the cooperative, so as to have a more tangible stake in the station. In 1992, it became part of the Radio Popolare network. Some critics contend that Radio Popolare became less politically engaged as time passed; it was still in operation in the late 2000s.

Another rebel radio station of the mid-1970s—for style, language, and use of technology—was Radio Alice, founded in Bologna in 1976 by an outgrowth of the A/traverso (A/aslant) collective. Its creators were hackers, pirates of technology and language, true innovators of the counterculture scene of the 1977 movement.

For its active reporting role and—as conservative media and the police often contended—for its support of the urban guerrilla activities and riots in Bologna in March 1977, Radio Alice was shut down on several occasions and frequently raided by the police. Radio Alice was a powerful source of information because it broadcast events almost as they were unfolding in the streets, so that anyone listening to the radio could join the demonstrations. Its innovative use of the medium included pranks such as on-air trick phone calls to well-known politicians and counterfeit news, a practice known as Dadaist politics, later imitated by various satirical publications in Italy. By the time it was definitively shut down later in 1977, Radio

Alice had become a legend in the youth movement: Experimental and imaginative, it was the epitome of what a free, really free radio, should sound like.

Another subversive station was Controradio. Founded in Florence in 1975 by an activist cooperative close to the Autonomia Operaia (Workers Autonomy) movement, Controradio represented another very important platform for the youth movement of 1977. Soon, the station distinguished itself for its pioneer role as a forum for experimental punk music, the first radio to do so in Italy. By the 1980s, it had become the station of the avant-garde pop music scene in Florence. It was still in operation in the late 2000s.

A New Language

In part, the free radio movement, which inspired similar movements in France, Japan, and elsewhere, was born out of the desire to find new modes of expression, to escape the narrowly defined terrains of political organization and language, and to develop a lateral communication outside mainstream channels. The language of speakers on these stations, for example, was stylistically very different from RAI broadcasts. Theirs was a more immediate, everyday idiom, intended to provide a closer connection between the station and its community of listeners.

A fundamental feature of some of the most progressive radio stations of those years was that they did not impose programs on their audiences. Quite the contrary, every form of communication, be it a phone-in show or a music show, was part of a project to make radio a vehicle for voices coming from outside. Radio was, indeed, supposed to be the voice of the people. Radio Popolare and Radio Alice, for instance, were the first stations to experiment with what was defined as "phone-in political action," when callers reported on the air what was happening with the students' demonstrations. Contributions from informal correspondents, who would call in from telephone booths, did not just inform the audience about what was happening, they also proposed which actions needed to be taken. Radio programs became such an important form of active political intervention that the Communist Party city officials then running

Bologna's city government and the *carabinieri* (the military police) deemed Radio Alice an "intolerable threat" and joined forces to close it down.

Commercial and Political Interests

Although the stations, inspired by a commitment to promote more democratic forms of communication, were a crucial part of the free radio movement, it would be a mistake to identify the movement only with those stations. Commercial interests and the need to find new advertising opportunities also played a crucial role in lobbying for the development of free (i.e., commercial) radio and TV stations.

Furthermore, institutional political parties, some losing influence over Italy's political and cultural life, saw in the establishment of independent broadcasting potential new venues to reach voters and influence public opinion. While financial and industrial groups were lobbying in the name of "antenna freedom," exponents from both the centrist Socialist Party and the Catholic Church were also unofficially encouraging the birth of independent radio and TV stations.

Local Broadcasting

The ubiquitous growth of independent radio stations was in line with broader requests from civil society for stronger regional and local institutions, including the decentralization of broadcasting. Indeed, although in 1975 a new, regional TV channel (RAI3) had been established, Rome was still playing a central role, leaving only a limited part of TV production to Milan, Turin, and Naples, and radio production to Florence.

Independent radio stations also offered an opportunity for local businesses to advertise their products and the opportunity for many young people living in the outlying neighborhoods and provincial towns to share information about what was happening in their communities. The local character of radio stations was often a source of pride: In opposition to the Roman accent of the majority of the announcers on RAI radio channels, local broadcasters would insist on speaking their local dialects, a key everyday issue in Italian life.

Conclusion

Although independent radio stations born out of a desire to provide progressive and more democratic forms of communication were not the only ones promoting the Antenna Freedom movement, they distinguished themselves for their use of innovative languages, the introduction of experimental technologies, the creation of new genres, and the popular music they shared with their publics. Some of those stations were so controversial that, as in the case of Radio Alice, they attracted the curiosity even of those who had different political positions.

Criticism of the Antenna Freedom movement came from a variety of political fronts and intellectuals, including those on the institutional left. They lamented that, in the absence of broadcasting regulation, those who advocated for freedom of antenna contributed to the sector's commercialization by paving the way for private capital to play an increasingly active role in the ownership and control of broadcasting in Italy. For instance, during those years, *L'Unità*, the Communist Party daily, categorically refused to use the expression "free radio," preferring "private radio."

However, the experience of the free radio stations cannot be reduced to the history of what later became the large commercial networks. Indeed, the "really free" among those stations—an integral part of the youth movement of the late 1970s—were a living disproof of the thesis that the media are always manipulated by the power structure and that they unavoidably encourage social homogeneity. Although the majority of those rebel stations had a short life, they remain a source of inspiration for the possibilities of the medium and for the different, radical forms of democracy and active political participation that they supported.

Cinzia Padovani

See also Citizens' Media; Community Radio (Ireland); Community Radio Movement (India); Free Radio (Austria); Free Radio Movement, 1974–1981 (France); Women's Radio (Austria)

Further Readings

Berardi F., & Guarnieri, E. (Eds.). (2002). *Alice è il diavolo: Storia di una radio sovversiva* [Alice is the devil: History of a subversive radio]. Milan, Italy: Shake Edizioni Underground.

Dark, S. (2009). *Libere! L'epopea delle radio italiane degli anni '70* [Free! The epic of Italian radio in the '70s]. Viterbo, Italy: Stampa Alternativa.

Downing, J. D. H. (2001). *Radical media: Rebellious communication and social movements.* Thousand Oaks, CA: Sage.

Eco, U. (1994). Independent radio in Italy. In R. Lumley (Ed.), *Apocalypse postponed* (pp. 167–176). Bloomington: Indiana University Press.

Finardi, E. (1976). *La radio* [Video]. Retrieved April 21, 2009, from http://technorati.com/videos/youtube. com%2Fwatch%3Fv%3Di40xTbLu6RM

Kogawa, T. (1993). Free radio in Japan: The mini FM boom. In N. Strauss (Ed.), *Radiotext(e): A special issue of Semiotext(e)* (pp. 90–96). New York: Autonomedia.

Lewis, P. (1984). Community radio: The Montreal conference and after. *Media, Culture & Society, 6,* 137–150.

Moliterno, G. (2000). *Encyclopedia of contemporary Italian culture.* New York: Routledge.

Ortoleva, P. (2006). Introduzione [Introduction]. In P. Ortoleva, G. Cordoni, & N. Verna (Eds.), *Radio FM 1976–2006: Trent'anni di libertà d'antenna* [FM radio 1976–2006: Thirty years of antenna freedom] (pp. 19–23). Bologna, Italy: Edizioni Minerva.

Padovani, C., & Calabrese, A. (1996). Berlusconi, RAI, and the modernization of Italian feudalism. *Javnost/ The Public, 3*(2), 109–120.

Stivale, C. (1985). *Pragmatic/machinic: Discussion with Félix Guattari.* Retrieved March 23, 2009, from http:// webpages.ursinus.edu/rrichter/stivale.html

FREE RADIO MOVEMENT, 1974–1981 (FRANCE)

The use of radio in political upsurges began in earnest in 1917 when the cruiser *Aurora*'s transmitter broadcast to Petrograd that the Bolshevik revolution had taken place. Since then, a decisive dimension of radio has been the innovations, especially in semiconductors, that have shrunk the transmission and reception apparatus and made audiovisual communication in general, radio in particular, more and more accessible. In the 1970s, a variety of radio initiatives sprang into life that were associated with specific political struggles,

whether revolutions, social critiques, or national liberation movements, and often at the local level. Brazil, for example, would see hundreds of pirate radios and even some TV operations supporting agrarian reform.

In France, up to the Socialist Party's 1981 electoral victory, conflict over the airwaves took the form of challenging the state's broadcasting monopoly and its striking remoteness from people's actual lives. The free radio movement was designed to provide alternative sources, to reveal the realities of the ordinary public's oppression and alienation, and to combat the apathy and inertia perceived as the effect of mainstream media. The harsh critiques of official media that surfaced during the 1968 May-June events in some sense gave birth to this movement, peopled—as one radio collective put it in 1978—by those who lived in the real world, who worked, struggled, and dreamed but who were systematically evacuated from the airwaves.

In 1974, two students, Antoine Lefébure and Jean-Luc Couron, launched the journal *Interférences* to develop a thorough critique of official media and to encourage experiments in alternative media. Radio's affordability and technical simplicity made it, in their view, an ideal entry point eventually to create multimedia and audio centers that they termed *Réseaux Populaires de Communication* (People's Communication Networks).

Lefébure put this into practice in the same year by starting Radio Active, which was loosely connected to the antinuclear movement. This sparked some other mostly brief radio experiments, but without significant consequence. Only when, in 1977, ecologist Brice Lalonde scored a surprise victory in municipal elections was there an initiative to begin a network of "green radio stations." One such station was Radio Verte (Green Radio) in Paris. Although not very effective as a station, Radio Verte got huge coverage; this resulted in free radio becoming defined as "a public problem."

Radio Verte Fessenheim

France's first major free radio station was Radio Verte Fessenheim (RVF), which began in 1976–1977 to challenge the Alsace media's silence about local opposition to a nuclear power station being constructed in the town of Fessenheim. The station had a network of transmitters across the borders of three countries: in Alsace (France), in the German canton of Bade, and in northern Switzerland, a zone locally called Dreyeckland (Three-Corner Land). This triple location enabled the station to service the antinuclear movement across a substantial territory, to dodge police raids, and to escape broadcast jamming. Often its initial function was to mobilize—for example, to summon people to assemble where the police were about to disperse demonstrators occupying the construction site.

RVF was based on a participatory model, opening up the airwaves to those struggling to defend their jobs or their environment. Forty or so activists kept the station operational clandestinely, while a legally constituted group (Friends of Dreyeckland) was the station's official face. Many decisions about coverage were made on the spot at the grass roots. Technical skills were taught, including interview formats.

RVF's founders then started a second free station, La Voix des Travailleurs Immigrés (Immigrant Workers' Voice), and similarly opened up training to these workers, many from Morocco. The purpose was to ensure their voice was heard in community affairs and to create a means of communication from the public, organized by the public.

Other stations sprang up, inspired both by RVF and by the experiments in free radio then burgeoning in Italy, especially the mythic Radio Alice in Bologna. Radio 44 started in Nantes, Radio Libre Populaire (Free People's Radio) in Saint-Nazaire, Radio Beau Délire (Beautiful Delirium Radio) in Villeneuve-d'Ascq, Radio Campus and Radio Libre 59 in Lille, Radio Abbesses Écho (Radio Echo Abbesses) in Montmartre, Radio 93 in Villetaneuse, Radio Larzac/Barbe Rouge (Red Beard) in Toulouse, Radio Pomarèdes in Béziers, to mention only some. Radio Fil Bleu (Radio Blue Thread) in Montpellier was prominent, though conservative in politics and very commercially driven. Many others faced jamming, arrests, and equipment confiscation, especially of transmitters.

Two free radio federations emerged: the Association pour la Libération des Ondes (Airwaves Liberation Association) and the Coordination des Radios Libres (Free Radio Stations Joint Committee). The former was started by some very prominent intellectuals (including Gilles Deleuze, Michel Foucault, Félix Guattari, Serge July). The latter emerged out of the epic Larzac confrontation between the army, which wanted to build a base there, and local farmers, led to some extent by José Bové, the environmental activist.

1978: The Movement Grows

The movement somehow grew in tandem with its repression. Beginning in 1978, jamming intensified, trials multiplied as a result of cases brought to court by the state monopoly broadcaster, and a new law (the Lecat law) provided for a month in jail and a fine up to 100,000 francs for breaking it. Charges, fines, and confiscations steadily grew in number. Some stations went off the air (e.g., Radio Oya, Radio Mirabelle, Radio Trottoir, Radio Joufflu).

Yet some stations managed to resist the onslaught, and other new stations came into being, especially in the Paris outskirts and out in the provinces. There was also a new development: stations that were definitely illegal, but which enjoyed support from town councils, unions, and political parties (especially the Socialist Party). They did not always conform to free radio practices, but news media and the public linked them together. These institutionally backed stations gave the free radio movement its second wind and a (somewhat unreal) image of dynamism. The political system was unsure how to handle this type of support, became embarrassed, and in the absence of any real strategy, elected to respond piecemeal.

Leftist town councils then started to launch projects, which sometimes never gelled. The political parties attempted to run short-run experiments, but it was the social struggle stations that mostly discussed them. Characteristically the party stations did not explicitly challenge the principle of the state's broadcasting monopoly. The Communist Party and the Communist trade union Confédération Générale du Travail (CGT) only attacked the state's abuse of monopoly power and so refused to ally themselves with the movement. They had no long-term goal and were only interested in responding to particular moments of crisis while they lasted.

SOS Emploi (SOS Job), launched by the local Socialist Party trade union Confédération Française Démocratique du Travail (CFDT) in 1978, and Lorraine Cœur d'Acier (Heart of Steel, Lorraine) started by the CGT in 1979, were both geared to the steelworkers' struggles at that time in the town of Longwy and reflected those short-term mobilization goals. There were some 40 other CGT stations from 1979 to 1981, set up to supply information about labor struggles typically absent from mainstream media. Some of these institutionally backed stations, like Lorraine Cœur d'Acier or Radio Riposte (a Socialist Party station), given the harsh repression they underwent, gave the movement fresh visibility.

Two Opposite Directions

Far from being homogeneous, and despite the efforts of the CGT, the CFDT, and other union initiatives, the free radio movement was divided into opposing positions, sometimes fiercely contesting each other. There were the apolitical and would-be professional, business, and long-term projects, happy to take advertising. And there were the "movement stations," geared to activist mobilization, uninterested in profits and happy with low-tech.

Yet even within their ranks, there were those (e.g., the CGT stations) who wanted to generate effective counterinformation to challenge mainstream news sources but had no problem with traditional information formats. Others were closer to autonomist politics and a "perspectivist" position, concerned with developing more multivoiced and engaging radio formats, thwarting the typical arrogation of the right to speak by representatives, journalists, or experts (e.g., Radio Dédalus, Radio Rocket). One collective in 1978 insisted that the public did not need another information business, even on the left, to reluctantly, kindly, or generously apportion times to speak, but needed, rather, an open space where ordinary people's practices and everyday experiences were expressed in their own languages.

The really effective clampdown on free radio stations followed the Socialist Party candidate's electoral triumph in 1981. Private noncommercial stations were authorized in November that year with temporary and revocable contracts. Meanwhile, even though court cases against free radio activists came to a halt, jamming continued, transmitter size was limited, and equipment continued to be confiscated from stations that did not satisfy the eligibility requirements and that were then excluded from the FM band. In 1982 the state's monopoly was wound up, but advertising was provisionally banned.

Some stations seized the chance to become more professional and commercial. In 1984 advertising was permitted, in 1986 radio networks were authorized, and 620 stations proceeded, for the most part, to go commercial. Verte Fessenheim, Lorraine Cœur d'Acier, and Radio Libre Paris (Free Paris Radio) were, by then, distant echoes.

Fabien Granjon
(translated by John D. H. Downing)

See also Free Radio Movement (Italy); Miners' Radio Stations (Bolivia); Radio La Tribu (Argentina); Radio Lorraine Coeur d'Acier (France); Radio Student and Radio Mars (Slovenia); Women's Radio (Austria)

Further Readings

Bénetière, J., & Soncin, J. (1989). *Au cœur des radios libres* [At the heart of the free radio stations]. Paris: L'Harmattan.

Cardon, D., & Granjon, F. (2005). Médias alternatifs et médiactivistes [Alternative media and media activists]. In É. Agrikoliansky, O. Fillieule, & N. Mayer (Eds.), *L'altermondialisme en France: La longue histoire d'une nouvelle cause* [Global justice movement in France: The long history of a new cause] (pp. 175–198). Paris: Flammarion.

Charrasse, D. (1981). *Lorraine Cœur d'Acier* [Lorraine Heart of Steel]. Paris: Maspéro.

Cheval, J.-J. (1997). *Les radios en France: Histoire, état, enjeux* [French radio stations: History, condition, issues]. Rennes, France: Apogée.

Collectif Radio Libre Populaire. (1978). *Les radios libres* [The free radio stations]. Paris: Maspéro.

Collin, C. (1982). *Ondes de choc: De l'usage de la radio en temps de lutte* [Shock waves: Radio usage in times of struggle]. Paris: L'Harmattan.

Lefebvre, T. (2008). *La bataille des radios libres, 1977–1981* [The free radio stations battle, 1977–1981]. Paris: INA/Nouveau Monde Éditions.

Lesueur, D. (2002). *Pirates des ondes* [Pirates of the airwaves]. Paris: L'Harmattan.

Peyrault, Y. (1991). *Radio libertaire: La voix sans maître* [Libertarian radio: The voice with no master]. Paris: Éditions du Monde Libertaire.

FREE TIBET MOVEMENT'S PUBLICITY

The movement for a significantly autonomous or fully independent Tibet is now decades old, and supporters have sought numerous avenues to publicize their cause globally. The government of the People's Republic of China (PRC) argues that Tibet has always been a part of China and that the first map showing it as separate was a British colonial map of India some 200 years back designed to further Britain's imperial sway. Many Tibetans and their worldwide supporters point to the highly distinctive character of Tibetan language, culture, and history, and to the PRC government's repression of open debate and demonstrations on the subject within Tibet and indeed within China at large.

In 1959, the Dalai Lama and many of his government ministers escaped into India. Prime Minister Nehru granted him and his entourage asylum in the remote mountain settlement of Dharamsala, close to Tibet's border. The then 24-year-old Dalai Lama's flight garnered much attention in Western media, which referred to him as the "God-King."

Soon after his escape, the Dalai Lama established a government-in-exile in Dharamsala. He proceeded to contact world leaders and international news media about the occupation of his country by the People's Republic of China (PRC). The isolationist policies previously pursued, however, left the Dalai Lama and his ministers ill-positioned to negotiate modern diplomacy.

In the 1960s, political and media attention focused away from the Tibetan refugees for several reasons. When the Cultural Revolution began in the middle of the decade, Tibet's borders with Nepal and India were closed, and people and information coming out of Tibet significantly decreased. Simultaneously the cold war escalated, the Vietnam War expanded significantly, the civil rights and other U.S. social movements burgeoned, student movements exploded worldwide, and the news media had a full agenda.

In the early 1970s, President Nixon's 1972 visit with Mao Zedong and the subsequent Western move to a "one China" policy positioned the West less favorably to assist the Dalai Lama. Yet with no widespread support for the Free Tibet movement, there was little that the Tibetan refugees and their advocates could accomplish. Dharamsala's remoteness did not help.

Only in 1987, when pro-independence demonstrations erupted in Lhasa and stone-throwing demonstrators were met with semiautomatic gunfire, killing many, was there a shift. International media, mainly due to the presence of many foreign journalists in Lhasa at the time, covered the confrontation extensively. The PRC's violent response shocked and unified exiled Tibetans, their Western supporters, and many passive sympathizers. Soon afterward, a large number of organizations emerged working for Tibetan independence, or autonomy within the PRC. Among these were the Free Tibet Campaign (1987 founding), the International Campaign for Tibet (1988), and Students for a Free Tibet (1994).

More visible to the larger public, though, were the many celebrities (e.g., Richard Gere, Harrison Ford, Goldie Hawn, Julia Roberts, Sting, Björk, REM, and Adam Yauch) and movies (e.g., *Seven Years in Tibet, Kundun*) contributing to the movement for Tibet. Richard Gere was arguably the most vocal celebrity. In 1993, after making a speech during the Oscar ceremonies against Chinese policies in Tibet, Gere was banned as a presenter by the Academy of Motion Picture Arts and Sciences. He also established the highly visible Gere Foundation, which provides grants for organizations working to preserve Tibet's culture.

The Beastie Boys' Adam Yauch also significantly contributed. He organized the first Tibetan Freedom Concert in San Francisco in 1996, an annual event that continued through 2001, drawing large crowds and generating substantial publicity. These concerts brought the Tibetan freedom movement to the greater public, increasing both awareness and activism.

Since the early 1990s, the Tibetan government-in-exile has also been tapping into the media to promote autonomy for Tibet. Its first such use of the media occurred in 1993 at the UN World Conference on Human Rights in Vienna. The Tibetan delegation was able to attract significant media attention to a decision to ban the Dalai Lama from speaking at a nongovernmental organization (NGO) conference held in parallel with the UN conference. Tibetans in Vienna generated online dispatches and faxes internationally to supporters, NGOs, governments, and the press. The resulting public pressure precipitated a reversal of the ban, allowing the Dalai Lama to give his speech.

Groups of Tibetan young people in exile have long advocated for their independence or autonomy. One particularly vocal group, the Tibetan Youth Congress (TYC), was formed in 1970 and has consistently challenged what it views as the government-in-exile's slow progress in regaining the homeland. Their efforts have focused on demonstrations, boycotts, and hunger strikes. In 1998 in New Delhi, at the end of one such hunger strike that lasted more than 40 days, a Tibetan set himself on fire as Indian police were dispersing the crowd. Pictures of this Tibetan man engulfed in flames saturated the media, as did discussions of Tibet and its occupation. Whereas self-immolation is extremely rare within the Free Tibet movement, hunger strikes, protests, and marches occur regularly in Dharamsala, where not only the exile government but also more than 7,000 Tibetan refugees reside.

Not all Tibetan refugees, though, participate in these efforts to free Tibet. Tibetans who have newly arrived in the refugee communities from Tibet as well as the elderly, who are more likely to remember and have lived in Tibet as a child, are best represented at such events. According to one Tibetan youth born in exile, young people like him are more likely to participate in such events during their college years, leaving these activities behind as they move into adulthood.

The 2008 riots in Lhasa brought only a slight shift in these demographics. The writer of this entry spent 10 weeks in Dharamsala in summer 2008, and observed and participated in several weekly marches. The elderly and those newly arrived from Tibet were decidedly in the majority. Similarly, a protest march organized by the TYC from Dharamsala to the Tibetan border, which enjoyed significant media attention, was made up of many older Tibetans, those newly arrived, and a slightly larger number of youth born in exile.

The Free Tibet movement in all its incarnations brought the Tibetan cause to the world through its use of and presence in the media. A brief survey of articles in *The New York Times* from 1959 to 2009 highlights the impact this movement has had on garnering media coverage. After a spike soon after the Dalai Lama's 1959 flight, media attention dipped significantly. It began a slower but notable upward trend in the 1980s, especially in the years that followed the 1987 Lhasa confrontation and then again following the 2008 Lhasa riots. Where this trend would move was increasingly uncertain. The Dalai Lama's health problems emphasized that the well-known visage of the "God-King," who was 75 in 2010, would not be the face of the Free Tibet movement for too much longer.

Heidi Swank

See also Angry Buddhist Monk Phenomenon (Southeast Asia); Human Rights Media; Independent Media (Burma/Myanmar); Online Nationalism (China); Performance Art and Social Movement Media: Augusto Boal

Further Readings

McLagan, M. (1996). Computing for Tibet: Virtual politics in the post–cold war era. In G. E. Marcus (Ed.), *Connected: Engagements with the media* (pp. 159–194). Chicago: University of Chicago Press.

Powers, J. (2000). The Free Tibet movement: A selective narrative. In C. S. Queen (Ed.), *Engaged Buddhism in the West* (pp. 218–246). Boston: Wisdom Publications.

G

GAY PRESS (CANADA, UNITED KINGDOM, UNITED STATES)

A history of the gay press is also the story of a social movement to fight discrimination and change public opinion. The most complete list of lesbian and gay periodicals contains more than 7,200 titles published worldwide from the 1890s to the 2000s. This includes small-circulation magazines of the 1950s and local newsletters about AIDS treatments in the 1980s. The main emphasis in this entry is on the press that emerged in the 1970s with the modern gay movement.

However, mention should be made of the first magazine to be openly sold for homosexuals in the United States. *ONE* magazine (1953–1969) won an important Supreme Court case in 1958, *One, Inc. v. Olesen*, in which the Court ruled that the distribution of the magazine through the mail did not violate obscenity laws. This judgment led indirectly in 1967 to the founding of *The Advocate*, which started as a countercultural paper and campaigned against police harassment in Los Angeles.

The period after the Stonewall Rebellion of June 1969 in New York City saw the emergence of a radical gay liberation movement and a militant press with titles such as *Gay Flames*, *Gay Sunshine*, and *Come Out!* This militancy of the early 1970s was not shared by *The Advocate*, which increasingly became a commercial lifestyle magazine, though it soon dominated the field of gay journalism in the United States. The *New York Native* (1980–1997) played a vital role in covering the AIDS crisis in the early 1980s, but later its coverage became erratic.

The relation between the activist social movement and the gay press can be best observed by looking at other important but less commercial papers. These included *Gay Community News* in Boston, *The Body Politic* in Toronto, and *Gay News* in London. These were closely identified with a radical political and cultural movement in the 1970s. They were not simply magazines but were often centers for organizing campaigns and political protests. Their listings of community organizations and events connected readers with a social movement.

The intellectual and social ambience of papers like *The Body Politic* and *Gay Community News* was lively. There were intense internal debates about gay businesses exploiting the movement, about the meaning of gay rights, about conservative and antipornography feminists who were accused of homophobia, and, in the 1980s, about issues of race and diversity within the gay social scene.

Sophisticated activists doubted the value of simply including homosexuality in human rights legislation. As well as dealing with everyday issues such as workplace discrimination and child custody for gay parents, they wanted to broadly challenge relations of gender and social class. It was realized that not all readers shared this political radicalism. "Gay rights" was therefore a slogan that could unite a broad-based movement. Buying a gay newspaper was at times an act of courage, and before the era of computer dating, the classified ads for those seeking sexual partners were often the most popular part of the paper.

News magazines such as *The Body Politic* (1971–1987) did more than simply report the news; they were political actors. Those involved had sometimes been active in radical politics and turned to the gay movement in part because of homophobia on the left. They brought with them an analysis of social class and the state, and practical experience in political organizing.

The Body Politic was twice prosecuted by the state for obscenity and had to defend itself in drawn-out and expensive legal battles. At the same time, the Toronto police responded to gay men's increased visibility in the late 1970s and early 1980s by making mass arrests at gay bathhouses. *The Body Politic* fought back, organizing several large demonstrations in Toronto. At the same time, it produced a monthly magazine of Canadian and international news, features, and reviews, which sold about 10,000 copies. This was accomplished with a mostly volunteer collective and a small paid staff.

Gay Community News (GCN; 1973–1992) was published in Boston, a national center of lesbian and gay activism. A photo of the collective in 1983 shows an equal number of men and women, whereas *The Body Politic* was dominated by gay men. GCN was a weekly newspaper with a circulation of about 5,000 copies and, like *The Body Politic,* had constant financial problems. Major advertisers were scared of supporting the radical gay press.

GCN was also a hub of lively social and intellectual life. In her memoir of the paper, Amy Hoffman says that for her it was "the center of the universe." In 1982, the offices of the paper were destroyed by fire set by an arsonist, but the paper recovered and continued for another decade. Hoffman suggests that as the mainstream press gradually began to cover gay issues in the 1980s, there was less need for a gay weekly newspaper.

Gay News (1972–1983) grew out of community meetings in the winter of 1971 and 1972, at the height of the militant gay movement in England. Its first editor, Denis Lemon, was not interested in a collectively run paper and soon took personal ownership and control. The fortnightly paper published news, features, and book reviews, and eventually had a circulation of about 18,000.

Although there were some volunteers, it was mostly put out by an underpaid staff of some 20 people crammed into a small house. The staff were union members, perhaps typical for England but unheard of in North America. There were the usual differences in perspective between gay men and lesbians at the newspaper, including, in this case, a tendency for women to expect a more collectively owned and managed paper. Some of the *Gay News* staff were involved as individuals in political activism, including the Campaign for Homosexual Equality. Denis Lemon became well known in 1977 because of a private prosecution brought against *Gay News* by conservative morals activist Mary Whitehouse. *Gay News* was thought by many people to be a nonprofit community organization, but it was sold by Lemon to its marketing manager in February 1982. The undercapitalized company was soon in a financial crisis that led to the collapse of the paper a year later.

These papers articulated gay activism and radical publishing, but it was never easy. There were always tensions and differences between lesbians and gay men. There were debates over content, sometimes simplified as being over material oriented to the commercial gay scene versus more political or intellectual perspectives. The reality was a readership with very different levels of education and cultural capital.

All three papers were deeply affected by the AIDS crisis in the 1980s, but this is not the only reason for their demise or transformation. There were unresolved issues of the meaning and goals of the gay movement. The tension between being a social movement and a publisher was often expressed in struggles between the model of a volunteer-run collective versus a regular business. Neoliberal attacks on workers' rights and social welfare through the 1980s made it more difficult for people to participate as volunteers or low-paid staff. Businesses catering to the gay scene brought much-needed advertising income but also pressures to tone down political activism.

In many respects, the radical gay movement of the 1970s failed or was defeated in its fundamental goals of transforming gender relations and society. It did, however, have substantial long-term effects on everyday life. It is now sometimes possible for gays and lesbians to walk down the street holding hands.

Alan O'Connor

See also *Advocate, The* (United States); DIVA TV and ACT UP (United States); *Gay USA*; *$pread* Magazine (United States); Stonewall Incident (United States); Women's Radio (Austria)

Further Readings

Hanscombe, G. E., & Lumsden, A. (1983). *Title fight: The battle for* Gay News. London: Brilliance Books.
Hoffman, A. (2007). *An army of ex-lovers: My life at the* Gay Community News. Amherst: University of Massachusetts Press.
Johnson, P. A., & Keith, M. C. (2001). *Queer airwaves: The story of gay and lesbian broadcasting.* New York: M. E. Sharpe.
Miller, A. V. (2000). *Our own voices: A directory of lesbian and gay periodicals, 1890s–2000s.* Canadian Gay and Lesbian Archives: http://www.clga.ca
One, Inc. v. Olesen, 355 U.S. 371 (1958).
Streitmatter, R. (1995). *Unspeakable: The rise of the gay and lesbian press in America.* Boston: Faber & Faber.

GAY USA

Gay USA is a weekly, hour-long TV news program hosted by journalist-activists Andy Humm and Ann Northrop, and produced by Bill Bahlman. The show, on the air since 1985, focuses on current political and social issues affecting LGBTQ (lesbian, gay, bisexual, transgendered, queer) communities locally, nationally, and internationally. It also includes interviews, human-interest stories, and entertainment features. *Gay USA* is aired on Manhattan Neighborhood Network cable access in New York City, nationally on the Dish Network channel Free Speech TV, and is available worldwide in the form of downloadable podcasts from the website.

Gay USA was preceded by *Pride and Progress,* another show hosted by Andy Humm. It was part of Gay Cable Network's (GCN's) original programming lineup and is best known for award-winning

coverage, focused on LGBTQ issues, of the Democratic and Republican National Conventions. GCN is credited with being the first television network to cover stories related to the HIV/AIDS epidemic.

Andy Humm has been a gay activist since 1974 and also served as spokesperson for New York City's Coalition for Lesbian and Gay Rights. He has been with *Gay USA* since its inception and was one of a handful of reporters covering the 1980s AIDS crisis. He has extensive experience as a print journalist. He has interviewed prominent individuals such as Bill Clinton, Jesse Jackson, and Gloria Steinem and has appeared as a guest on *CBS Evening News* and the *Charlie Rose* TV interview show.

Ann Northrop has produced news for *CBS Morning News* and ABC's *Good Morning America.* Her passion for activism led her to join ACT UP (AIDS Coalition to Unleash Power) in New York City in the late 1980s, and she was arrested many times for civil disobedience. As well as hosting *Gay USA,* Northrop also regularly anchors the news slot of the satellite TV show *Dyke TV.*

Producer Bill Bahlman has an extensive activist and journalist background. He served as the Gay Activists' Alliance Executive Committee chair and helped found ACT UP. He was also anchor and news director for the cable show *Out* in the 1980s and 1990s, a worthy competitor to *Gay USA.*

Gay USA is one of the longest running and most consistent voices within LGBTQ media. Its commitment to consistently cover queer news stories from a noncorporate perspective, as well as to challenge definitions of queer news, is a much-needed service to the communities it represents.

Ricky Hill

See also *Advocate, The* (United States); Diva TV and ACT UP (United States); Gay Press (Canada, United Kingdom, United States); *$pread* Magazine (United States); Stonewall Incident (United States); Women's Radio (Austria)

Further Readings

Johnson, P. A., & Keith, M. C. (2001). *Queer airwaves: The story of gay and lesbian broadcasting.* New York: M. E. Sharpe.

GRANDMOTHERS OF THE PLAZA DE MAYO (ARGENTINA)

Abuelas de Plaza de Mayo (The Grandmothers of the Plaza de Mayo) is an organization created in 1977 by women looking for their disappeared grandchildren, either toddlers kidnapped with their parents or babies born in captivity. During Argentina's last dictatorship (1976–1983), pregnant political prisoners were kept alive until the moment of giving birth. Their babies were then seized as spoils of war and appropriated by families of the military or their civilian accomplices (the Grandmothers use the term *appropriation* to differentiate the practice from adoption). The mothers were then killed. An estimated 500 children suffered this fate.

For more than 30 years, finding these children has been the focus of the unyielding activism of the Grandmothers. This search consists in investigations—literally detective work—and the development of media strategies and campaigns. The seized babies have grown up (they were in their 30s in 2009); hence, the Grandmothers concentrate their efforts on reaching young people and promoting the notion that if they were born during the dictatorship and have doubts about their identity, they should contact the Grandmothers. This is the first step of the investigation leading to DNA testing and confirmation of identity. At the beginning of 2009, 97 appropriated grandchildren had recuperated their identities.

Identity is at the core of the Grandmothers' activism and the focus of their media messages. The goal is to create awareness in society that there are still 400 young people whose biological families are looking for them. The carriers of these messages range from books to theater performances, including television programs and activities centered on sports and music. In this search for identity, there is the double task of reaching the public with appealing messages and educating the public about state terrorism. Posters, printed ads, radio spots, and television commercials promote these campaigns by reproducing the message "If you doubt your identity." The Grandmothers have several publications, including their monthly bulletin, available in hard copy and online, and various

books with a thorough compilation of data and images documenting the organization's history and its achievements.

"For Identity" projects are crucial components of the Grandmothers' search. The pioneer venture was *Teatro × la Identidad* (Theater for Identity—in Spanish, the multiplication sign × is expressed as *por*, "for"; its use replaces the word *por*). This annual cycle of free performances launched in 2000 is a collaboration of the Grandmothers, playwrights, actors, and directors. Most of the plays address the appropriation of babies, issues of identity, and everyone's right to know who they are. There are usually brief presentations by Grandmothers and actors who link the play to the campaign for identity. Other events have included *Deporte × la Identidad* (Sports for Identity)—sport competitions—and *Rock × la Identidad* (Rock for Identity)—concerts by popular musicians. Under the banner "Art and Culture for Identity," and to place this matter in spheres related to the arts, the Grandmothers have joined photographers, filmmakers, choreographers, and musicians to organize tango, dance, film, and photography contests. These projects broaden the spaces for discussion of the Grandmothers' struggle, particularly among the younger generations. For the Grandmothers, all their media efforts are aimed at recuperating grandchildren so their campaigns entertain to promote investigations and add allies to their cause.

The most atypical, certainly alternative, project with a human rights message was *Moda × la identidad*. Designer Teo Gincoff based his 2007 fashion line on identity in honor of the Grandmothers for being the maximum referent of the right to identity. Milo Lockett's artwork with Grandmothers' themes decorated the T-shirts. Inspired by the images of Grandmothers marching in the rain, Gincoff designed raincoats with a 1970s style. He produced orange garments because it is the color of the Grandmothers' media brochures. His collection had clothes in dark colors to symbolize the years of terror and long collars partially covering the face and hiding the identity of the wearer. For his lines' presentation, Gincoff invited as model an actress who played the daughter of a *desaparecido* in a successful television serial. If we add the presence of several Grandmothers and supporters at the event, and the fact that 100 of the T-shirts were given away to the public, we conclude that the designer managed to perform an act of memory in the often frivolous sphere of the fashion world. The broadcast of the fashion show for over 3 months by a TV fashion channel meant another opportunity to broaden the promotion of the Grandmothers' human rights message.

The latest project was *Televisión × la Identidad* (Television for Identity), a cycle of three programs honoring the Grandmothers' 30th anniversary, broadcast in October 2007 by Telefé, a major television network. It presented the organization's work through fictional representations of real cases of recuperated grandchildren. The cycle was a success and showed the potential of commercial television as a vehicle for transmitting memories of state terrorism. It generated good ratings, won several awards, including the 2008 Emmy International for best television miniseries, and prompted an increase in calls to the offices of the Grandmothers by young people thinking that they might be children of *desaparecidos*. One month after its broadcast, the network and the newspaper *Página 12* joined forces for the massive distribution of a DVD of the programs and donated the proceeds to the Grandmothers. Thus, *Televisión × la Identidad* kept reaching large audiences after its broadcast.

The Grandmothers have received one of the buildings at the ESMA compound (a former torture center in Buenos Aires) and will operate the Casa de la Identidad there. The creativity that the organization has shown over the years suggests that this project will set new parameters in the search for identity. This center will probably incorporate all of the Grandmothers' media projects—music, sports, television, film, fashion, dance, theater. Judging by what they have done so far, it seems that the Grandmothers are not shy of exploring new venues to get their message across. The fact that they have recuperated almost 20% of the appropriated children suggests that their strategies work.

M. Susana Kaiser

See also H.I.J.O.S. and *Escraches* (Argentina); Human Rights Media; Mothers of the Plaza de Mayo

Further Readings

Abuelas de Plaza de Mayo: http://abuelas.org.ar
Arditti, R. (1999). *Searching for life*. Berkeley: University of California Press.

Interviews by Author

Estela de Carlotto, President of Abuelas de Plaza de Mayo, July 9, 2008.
Milo Lockett, July 1, 2008.
Rosa T. de Roisinblit, Vice President of Abuelas de Plaza de Mayo, October 31, 2007.
Teo Gincoff, July 5, 2008.

GRASSROOTS TECH ACTIVISTS AND MEDIA POLICY

The term *grassroots tech groups* (also called *radical tech groups*) refers to groups voluntarily providing alternative communication infrastructure to civil society activists and citizens and operating with collective organizing principles. They aim at counteracting commercial as well as state pressures on information content, media access, and media users' privacy. Grassroots tech groups usually offer website hosting, e-mail and mailing list services, chats, and other tools such as anonymous remailers and instant messaging; they also provide platforms to self-produce information. They enable movements for political change to get direct and participatory access to the web and media.

Based on an experimental do-it-yourself ethos, some were pioneers of Internet development in the early 1990s, and many have since then contributed to web innovations. Examples include the Spanish SinDominio (NoDomination), the Italian Autistici/Inventati, the German Nadir, the British Plentyfact, the North American riseup.net, and the open-publishing platforms of the Indymedia network.

A typical radical tech collective would consist of half a dozen volunteer activists often, but not necessarily, based in the same town. Some have weekly meetings for strategic discussions and decisions, some even operate a computer lab or an Internet café, but most communication takes place online. Daily tasks include managing webservers and listservs, and larger projects may include developing software tools, such as content management systems or encryption programs, which other civil society activists can use.

They become more visible when they step out of cyberspace. Radical tech groups have established media centers at major protest events such as those against G8 and G20. Indymedia UK, for example, have set up tents with computer equipment in the middle of actions and action camps to allow activists to write and upload reports directly from the street. The group Nadir once transformed a countryside barn in a remote north German village into a high-tech media hub that enabled thousands of environmental activists to send their reports on a protest against nuclear waste shipments to a global audience. The New York–based group May First/People's Link ran the communication infrastructure of the Social Forum of the Americas.

Characteristics and Rationale

The common characteristics and rationale of grassroots tech groups include the following:

1. *Autonomy:* self-run alternative communication infrastructures, entirely distinct from the commercial and state realm.

2. *Emancipation:* free from dominant providers of information and communication channels and their overarching business and government control.

3. *Direct action:* initiating an alternative production mode.

4. *Collectivism:* horizontal consensus building and a rejection of formal leadership and representation, with voluntary contribution of knowledge, skills, time, and financial support.

5. *Service provision and "meta-activism":* while being an intrinsic part of other movements (e.g., environmentalism, antiracism, antifascism), they provide communication services for the latter and raise awareness on privacy and knowledge issues.

Grassroots tech groups are an integral part of "radical," "alternative," or "civil society" media. They adhere to their main characteristics, such as grassroots ownership and control, nonprofit social objectives, and democratic and participatory

structures, and most either provide alternative content or assist others in doing so. Nevertheless, they have been largely off the research map and even farther from policy support. While policymakers, as with the 2008 European Parliament report on Third Sector media, have begun to get behind community media, grassroots tech groups have rarely enjoyed positive recognition.

Thus, although recent forms of multi-stakeholder network governance have allowed nongovernmental actors to participate in policy making, and although fora such as the World Summit on the Information Society (WSIS) and the Internet Governance Forum (IGF) have opened the door for many civil society groups, only well-resourced organizations have been able to respond. Many who are building an information society in their everyday practices—such as grassroots tech groups, free software developers, or creators of community wireless networks—have been unable or unwilling to attend such fora. This robbed WSIS and similar gatherings of significant participation from grassroots information and communication technology activists.

Policy Inclusion Obstacles

Interviews with some of their members referenced in the 2009 study by Hintz and Milan illuminate the attitudes of these grassroots tech groups toward such arenas for policy debate and decisions and identify their priorities. Whereas many civil society groups have tried to render policy processes more inclusive, grassroots tech groups hold back. They regard civil society inclusion in large policy debates, such as UN summits and multi-stakeholder fora, as "decorative"—a "puppet theatre" whose main purpose is to "legitimize the decisions taken by corporations, governments, lobbies." (*Note:* All quotations in this entry are from interviews conducted in 2008 by Hintz and Milan, who published their findings in 2009.)

Instead, they primarily or even exclusively create actual communications infrastructure. As one group member said,

I don't think we need to focus on "asking" or "having a voice." I think we have "to do," "keep doing" and keep building working structures and alternatives that are diametrically opposed to the ways capitalism forces us to function in our everyday lives. Our job, as activists, is to create self-managed infrastructures that work regardless of "their" regulations, laws or any other form of governance.

Their response to policy challenges is to develop technical bypasses and, if necessary, technological self-defense. As tech activists are volunteers, their scarce time and energy play a further role: "If I have to choose between debating issues of governance, or setting up a Public Access Point at the No Border Camp, I'm afraid I'll choose the second."

This approach is rooted in a cultural and political framework that includes anarchist thought, do-it-yourself culture, and cyber-libertarianism, and it overlaps with the values of early Internet pioneers, who advocated minimal state regulation and maximum freedom for technical experts and civil society actors to develop infrastructures according to public needs.

Grassroots tech groups are deeply affected by policy development and enforcement, but they view these largely as threats, not opportunities. They observe how state and business activity can lead to enclosure of previously free spaces of communication. State repression is identified as the primary threat, despite the Internet's supposedly global and borderless nature.

Grassroots media projects have been facing surveillance and harassment in many countries, including Western democracies, due to their support for dissident social movements. Some have had their equipment confiscated and apartments raided by police, activists have been arrested, some even targeted via antiterrorism laws. Increasing state surveillance—for example, through new legislation on data retention—provides further challenges, according to the Hintz and Milan (2009) study, as it "forces us to disclose information about our users to the government." The expansion of intellectual property regulation, too, has challenged the groups' objective of enhancing free knowledge exchange.

Business players, too, have interfered with grassroots tech groups' operations, partially in a technical sense (e.g., domain name filters provided by telecommunication companies), partially through legal means. Several groups have faced libel cases and have not had the resources to properly defend themselves even though they were in compliance with the law. Overall, the major source of threats is seen coming from those who dominate transnational policy processes in general—governments and large businesses.

Policy Priorities

Grassroots tech groups prefer to limit regulatory action to enhancing freedom of information and user/citizen civil rights. Core demands are for open technical standards and network neutrality; the right to anonymity, privacy, and freedom of expression; and the free flow of knowledge and information. Antimonopoly regulation and privacy protection are seen as crucial to prevent excessive interventions by powerful private and state actors. In particular, state interference in communication infrastructures needs to be curbed by limiting surveillance practices and ensuring citizens' rights, including the right to political dissent.

This policy catalogue has been developed and confirmed at media activist meetings, such as the alternative series of events WSIS?WeSeize! which took place parallel to the first WSIS summit in Geneva in 2003. WSIS?WeSeize! promoted the development of autonomous and civil society media infrastructures, highlighted openness to counter state- and business-led privatization and control policies, criticized state censorship and surveillance as well as the privatization of ideas through intellectual property law, and discussed the exploitation of intellectual and informationalized labor.

Grassroots techs are, however, highly skeptical of whether government- and business-led transnational policy dialogue can achieve progress in these fields. As one said in the Hintz and Milan (2009) interviews, "I am not convinced at all that any major institution or international body would try to regulate, or create policy, in a way that it would not favour states and corporations." Furthermore, they doubt that state officials in international policy processes have the necessary knowledge to regulate complicated technical issues. Another interviewee complained, "Stakeholders who have decision-making powers demonstrate their utter ignorance of the systems that they are supposed to govern."

Rather they prefer to establish policy dialogue between "democratically chosen groups of technical experts that operate in a very open and transparent way." They strongly advocate self-regulation by the information providers and, where possible, the end-users, grounded in "non-binding standards that gain popularity based on their quality, usefulness and ease of use/implementation."

Multi-Stakeholderism Revisited

If this type of policy process is to be legitimate, a broad range of actors have to be included within policy agendas and fundamental barriers to global governance arenas must be lowered. Channels should exist through which grassroots tech groups can have their objectives represented. However, as this brief overview suggests, the most straightforward recipes for inclusion—such as providing financial assistance—may not be sufficient. Grassroots tech groups' strong priority for setting up practical alternatives to mainstream content, infrastructure and organizational models, coupled with their deep skepticism towards current policy processes, and their core values of autonomy, diversity, and rejection of centralist decision making, make even "inclusive" policy arenas unattractive for them. A forum such as WSIS or IGF would thus need to respond to transform itself more fundamentally.

Grassroots tech groups are only one example of how a growing number of social movements, civil society groups, and citizen initiatives are structured in ways incompatible with current institutional processes. As collective enterprises, they regard consensus decision making and consultation of all members as foundational, and they therefore reject political representation. Assigning decision-making power to a single representative in a policy forum conflicts with their principles of equality and horizontality.

Grassroots tech groups thus point to an evolving disintegration of traditional forms of formal organization. This affects (a) organized civil society, with the nongovernmental organization format increasingly giving way to looser forms of network cooperation, and (b) international (interstate) policy making. Developing a response may require new democratic but nonrepresentational models of decision making, with a stronger focus on concepts such as "organized networks" and

"constituencies." This would involve a radical decentralization of global governance and a bottom-up approach to policy making, which would place those directly affected by policy measures at the center of governance efforts.

Conclusion

Grassroots tech groups play an often neglected but crucial role in social movement media, primarily as providers of alternative information and communication infrastructure. They offer a distinct policy agenda that centers on privacy, information rights, openness, and self-regulation. Developing alternative infrastructure and technological "bypasses" around laws and regulations is valued more than participating in policy dialogue with governments and the private sector. They are "beyond-ers," largely operating beyond policy processes, neither insiders, who pursue active engagement in institutional processes, nor even outsiders, who adopt confrontational forms of protest at established policy fora.

Their political agenda enriches the debate, but it also leaves some question marks. Their strong focus on self-regulation resonates with both cyber-libertarian myths and the policy preferences of the private sector, while lacking concern with structural factors that interfere with free self-regulation, such as North–South imbalances.

Grassroots tech groups provide us with a view on the deficiencies of current multi-stakeholder global governance. If transnational policy making is to be democratic, participatory, and thus legitimate, it should involve the concerns of all key actors. However, an inclusive process still led by the "old" powers of the governmental and intergovernmental realm or the "new" powers of the business realm will remain unacceptable to many. Rather, they point to the need to create new governance mechanisms that reflect the aspirations, skills, roles, and organizational structures of all actors who make a relevant contribution.

Arne Hintz and Stefania Milan

See also Alternative Media: Policy Issues; Anarchist Media; Copyleft; Environmental Movement Media; Human Rights Media; Indymedia (The Independent Media Center); Media Activists and Communication

Policy Processes; Media Infrastructure Policy and Media Activism; *Radical Software* (United States)

Further Readings

Bennett, L. (2003). New media power: The Internet and global activism. In N. Couldry & J. Curran (Eds.), *Contesting media power* (pp. 17–38). Lanham, MD: Rowman & Littlefield.

de Jong, W., Shaw, M., & Stammers, N. (2005). *Global activism, global media.* London: Pluto Press.

European Parliament. (2008). *Report on Community Media in Europe,* 2008/2011(INI), approved September 25, 2008. http://www.europarl.europa.eu/oeil/FindByProcnum.do?lang=en&procnum=INI/2008/2011

Hintz, A. (2009). *Civil society media and global governance: Intervening into the World Summit on the Information Society.* Münster, Germany: Lit.

Hintz, A., & Milan, S. (2009). At the margins of Internet governance: Grassroots tech groups and communication policy. *International Journal of Media and Culture Policy, 5*(1), 23–38.

Lovink, G., & Rossiter, N. (2005). Dawn of the organised networks. *Fibreculture Journal, 5.* Retrieved April 30, 2008, from http://journal.fibreculture.org/issue5/lovink_rossiter.html

H.I.J.O.S. AND *ESCRACHES* (ARGENTINA)

H.I.J.O.S. is an organization of daughters and sons of *desaparecidos* (disappeared people), political activists, and people forced into exile during the last Argentine dictatorship (1976–1983). The acronym stands for *Hijos por la Identidad y la Justicia contra el Olvido y el Silencio* (Daughters and Sons for Identity and Justice Against Forgetting and Silence). The group was created in 1995 and soon achieved local notoriety for the specific characteristics of its activism, in particular for its *escraches*.

Escraches are a new form of public protest. The word *escrachar* is an Argentine slang term meaning "to uncover." For H.I.J.O.S., *escrachar* is "to reveal, to make public the face of a person that wants to go unnoticed." Escraches are campaigns of public condemnation through demonstrations that are well covered by the media and aim to expose the identities of the dictatorship's hundreds of torturers and assassins who benefit from impunity laws.

In mobilizing public support, H.I.J.O.S. relies on announcements placed in newspapers and flyers. Marchers invade the neighborhoods where torturers live and walk the streets carrying banners and chanting slogans such as *Alerta, Alerta, Alerta los vecinos, que al lado de su casa está viviendo un asesino* (Alert! Alert! Alert all neighbors, there's a murderer living next door to you!), or *Como a los nazis les va a pasar, a donde vayan los iremos a buscar* (It'll happen to you, just like the Nazis— wherever you go, we'll go after you).

They inform the community about the atrocities committed by the former torturers and hand out fact sheets about the person targeted, including photo, name, address, activities during the dictatorship, human rights abuses in which he is implicated, and current job. The demonstration ends in front of the torturer's home with a brief "ceremony"—a few speeches, street theater performances, and music. Marchers then "mark" the torturer's home by spraying slogans on sidewalks and walls. Red paint symbolizing blood is usually splattered on building walls.

H.I.J.O.S.'s escraches were developed within a political and cultural environment of legalized impunity that succeeded the dictatorship for 2 decades, a process that could be described as the "normalization" of living with major human rights abusers. This meant accepting that *represores* (the generic term for torturers and murderers) had the right not to be behind bars. In 1998, when escraches reached their peak, hundreds of criminals benefiting from amnesties were free to wander in public places, were television talk show guests, had become "democratic" politicians, and were even defined as kindly parents of children they had kidnapped, after having tortured and/or disappeared the children's real parents. A few such faces and names were well known, but hundreds of represores went unknown to the majority of the population.

In aiming for public exposure and humiliation, the escraches' goal was to curtail the access to societal spaces that represores had gained, to tear off the protective shield of anonymity. Lacking judicial power, H.I.J.O.S. wanted to ensure the neighbors knew their faces and their crimes. Escraches, thus, contested denial and ignorance by making people realize that those responsible for massive atrocities might be their kindly neighbor or the father of their daughter's best friend. The strategy played a key role in challenging impunity and political amnesia. The symbolically powerful tactics of bringing back the past into the contemporary public sphere compels society to face its failure to administer justice and to define its position toward past human rights violations and campaigns for accountability.

Impunity laws were nullified in 2005, but many represores still are unknown. H.I.J.O.S. has continued with its escraches, targeting not only represores but also their accomplices. Because the dictatorship also introduced the neoliberal policies implemented throughout the 1990s, H.I.J.O.S. organized escraches connecting past political repression and present economic distress. They labeled as *genocidas económicos* (economic genocidal agents) those who implemented policies that resulted in hunger, unemployment, wealth concentration, auctioning of state enterprises, and destruction of the domestic market. Escraches have been launched against head offices of top figures from the financial establishment, many of them beneficiaries of the dictatorship's economic policies.

H.I.J.O.S. has also made a point of uncovering members of those sectors that condoned, collaborated, and benefited from the repression. There was an escrache at the National Museum of Fine Arts targeting a board member whose family, members of the country's ruling oligarchy, owned a major plantation, where during a 1976 "blackout," dozens of workers were kidnapped and many remain disappeared. Other escraches have targeted bishops, recalling the church hierarchy's complicity with the repression.

H.I.J.O.S. developed follow-up memory activities, so the momentum gained with the escrache did not fizzle out. One tactic was the "mobile escrache," in which activists revisited the residences of several represores. Demonstrators went around on bikes, in cars, or in chartered buses, and stopped briefly at different houses over a 2- to 3-hour span. Another activity was to return to the neighborhood in the days following an escrache. In

a public space, H.I.J.O.S. showed photos taken during the escrache, broadcast from the site, and organized screenings and performances. The escrache thus became ongoing with active community participation.

There were also international escraches organized by H.I.J.O.S. outside Argentina (many members grew up in exile). One escrache targeted an infamous torturer residing in México who was eventually extradited. H.I.J.O.S. Roma organized an escrache denouncing the meeting of an Argentine minister with Italy's premier Berlusconi as a "mafiosi" encounter.

H.I.J.O.S. should be credited with limiting the represores' social and spatial freedom. Escraches trap torturers and assassins by building metaphorical jails, so that represores recognized by a particular community are, in the hopes of the H.I.J.O.S., isolated within that environment. Escraches also show that in these times of "cyber encounters," it is still effective to take to the streets.

M. Susana Kaiser

See also Anti-Fascist Media, 1922–1945 (Italy); Grandmothers of the Plaza de Mayo (Argentina); Human Rights Media; Mothers of the Plaza de Mayo (Argentina); Social Movement Media, 1991–2010 (Haïti)

Further Readings

H.I.J.O.S.: www.hijos-capital.org.ar

Kaiser, M. S. (2002). *Escraches:* Demonstrations, communication and political memory in post dictatorial Argentina. *Media, Culture and Society, 24*(4), 499–516.

Kaiser, M. S. (2008). The struggle for urban territories: Human rights activists in Buenos Aires. In C. Irazábal (Ed.), *Ordinary places/extraordinary events: Citizenship, democracy, and urban space in Latin America* (pp. 170–197). New York: Routledge.

HIV/AIDS Media (India)

The world is now decades into the HIV/AIDS crisis and there is no vaccine in sight. One of the epidemic's hot spots is South Asia, with India alone harboring almost 5 million HIV-positive cases. In a general climate of doom and gloom, India has also taken some notable strides in strategically and innovatively communicating HIV/AIDS messages through mediated interventions.

The Red Ribbon Express

On World AIDS Day 2007, the Red Ribbon Express, a special train, was flagged off from New Delhi's Safdarjang Railway Station by Mrs. Sonia Gandhi, president of the ruling Congress Party. The train's mandate included halting at 180 stations and reaching more than 50,000 villages in India with critical information on HIV prevention. During each station stop, six performing teams, each with ten artists, disembarked from the train on a fleet of bicycles to visit dozens of villages. They used folk media and street theater to spread messages about stopping HIV infection and fighting AIDS stigma and discrimination. Another group of young campaigners traveling by buses covered an even larger area than the cyclist performers. Many of these on-the-ground events were covered by local, regional, and national media.

Further, the Red Ribbon Express was a traveling education and exhibition vehicle, equipped with interactive touch screens. It had an auditorium to host sessions for *anganwadi* (child care center) workers, self-help groups, and young people's and women's nongovernmental organizations. A separate coach provided six cabins for one-on-one counseling, testing, and medical services. Considered groundbreaking, the Red Ribbon Express was hailed as one of the largest mass mobilization efforts on HIV/AIDS undertaken anywhere in the world.

Media Efforts

Between 2001 and 2007, a unique partnership between the BBC World Service Trust, the Government of India's National AIDS Control Organization, and Doordarshan (the country's public broadcaster) led to the broadcast of an award-winning detective television series, *Jasoos Vijay* (Detective Vijay). This reached more than 70 million people with engaging messages about HIV prevention and reducing AIDS-related stigma and prejudice.

Early in the series, for example, Detective Vijay is commissioned by an urban family to check out the background of a young rural woman whom they wish their son to marry. When Vijay arrives in her village, he discovers the young woman is missing and her family is trying to cover up her disappearance. When her body is found in the village well, Vijay investigates how she died. Through a maze of intrigue and suspense, Vijay discovers that the young woman was a childhood friend of a village outcast, who was ostracized by the community because he was HIV-positive. She was killed because of her association with an HIV-positive person.

Through 153 episodes of *Jasoos Vijay,* viewers were treated to multiple cliffhangers and multiple denouements. Various theory-based strategies were employed to enhance the engaging narrative: the use of a celebrity epilogue-giver; the posing of multiple dilemmas (such as "How did she die"?) to stimulate audience reflection and elaboration; an emphasis on mystery to build suspense and audience involvement; and the raising of key social dilemmas surrounding HIV/AIDS, designed to deconstruct prevailing social values, beliefs, and norms about HIV/AIDS.

Jasoos Vijay was part of a larger mass media campaign in India to encourage open and informed discussion of HIV and AIDS in India. Other campaign elements included more than 2,500 promotional TV advertisements, billboard hoardings, celebrity endorsements, and a novel youth reality television show, *Haath Se Haath Milaa* (Hand in Hand Together). Set aboard two buses (one for boys, one for girls), the youth contestants journeyed through five targeted low HIV-prevalence Indian states—Rajasthan, Haryana, Delhi, Uttar Pradesh, and Uttaranchal. The buses, equipped with bunk beds, cooking facilities, television cameras, and a presenter, visited cities, villages, university campuses, ancient forts, and temples, constituting the youth journey of a lifetime.

During the journey, contestants competed to resolve challenges: They may be challenged to buy a condom in a pharmacy in full view of others, or be asked to role-play in a game where they are challenged to creatively decline the advances of the opposite sex. In so doing, the participants and the audience members learn skills to live life to the fullest, to protect themselves from HIV/AIDS, and to have more compassion for those living with AIDS.

Both *Jasoos Vijay* and *Haath Se Haath Milaa* represent creative examples of how popular mediated entertainment formats can be suitably adapted for health education. Both programs were rigorously evaluated and yielded significant desirable changes among viewers in knowledge, attitudes, and practices related to HIV prevention, reducing AIDS-related stigma, and the like.

The mass-mediated campaigns surrounding the Red Ribbon Express and the *Jasoos Vijay* television program hold important lessons for media scholars and practitioners about creatively breaking the silence on AIDS and spurring ground-based, community-centered action.

Arvind Singhal

See also Community Radio Movement (India); DIVA TV and ACT UP (United States); Participatory Media; Sex Workers' Blogs

Further Readings

Beger, G. (2007, December 6). *"Red Ribbon Express" rides the rails to raise youth AIDS awareness in India.* http://www.unicef.org/infobycountry/india_42022.html

Jasoos Vijay campaign: http://www.bbc.co.uk/world service/trust/whatwedo/where/asia/india/2008/03/080229_india_hiv_project_jasoos.shtml

Singhal, A., & Rogers, E. M. (2003). *Combating AIDS: Communication strategies in action.* Thousand Oaks, CA: Sage.

Singhal, A., & Rogers, E. M. (2004). The status of entertainment-education worldwide. In A. Singhal, M. J. Cody, E. M. Rogers, & M. Sabido (Eds.), *Entertainment-education and social change: History, research, and practice* (pp. 3–20). New York: Routledge.

Singhal, A., & Vasanti, P. N. (2005). The role of popular narratives in stimulating the public discourse on HIV and AIDS: Bollywood's answer to Hollywood's *Philadelphia. South Asian Popular Culture, 38*(1), 3–14.

HONG KONG IN-MEDIA

Hong Kong In-Media is an advocacy group for independent media closely associated with the social movements in Hong Kong, Mainland China, and other Asian regions. It originated during the 2003 mass rally against Article 23, which strengthened the Hong Kong government's powers to restrain freedom of speech and association. Most of the founding members were activists, progressive academics, and journalists engaged in social movements and publishing independent magazines during the 1990s. They saw the 2003 confrontation as a turning point in Hong Kong's recent democratic struggles. They decided to set up various alternative media platforms in response to shrinking autonomy and freedom in mainstream corporate media and to the thriving political voices on the Internet.

Hong Kong In-Media's first project was to set up inmediahk.net, a local portal website in Chinese, which sought to facilitate public engagement in citizen journalism. It learned from the experience of the Independent Media Centers, Korea's *OhmyNews'* idea of "citizen reporters" and other innovative independent media practices elsewhere in Asia.

The structure of inmediahk.net is formally non-hierarchical in terms of authority, though it maintains an editorial team for daily management. The website users can contribute and publish their stories, commentaries, and videos instantly without editors' approval. Its citizen journalists and media activists are involved in a wide range of local and international issues. They extensively covered the 2005 anti–World Trade Organization (WTO) protest and presented a more complete picture of the anti-WTO organizations than most mainstream media.

They were also first to stir up the "citizen journalism" controversy and its challenge to professional journalism in Hong Kong. In response, some journalists in Hong Kong also criticized Hong Kong In-Media for doing politically biased reports. In recent years, the citizen journalists have actively engaged in the local historical conservation movement, the campaign against censorship, and community movements. Inmediahk.net has already become one of the most popular alternative media, particularly in Hong Kong's social and cultural movement issues.

Inspired by global experience in the anti-WTO protests, Hong Kong In-Media additionally developed interlocals.net, a cross-border network for media activists and citizen media organizations from different regions to exchange news and information. In early 2009, it published *Info-Rhizome: Report on Independent Media in the Chinese-Speaking World,* which covered the recent development of independent media in Hong Kong, Mainland China, Malaysia, and Taiwan.

This book was a project intended regularly to update new developments in independent media in these four regions and further extend to other Asian regions in the future. It aimed at setting up an agenda for collaborative research and activism. It has already built a network of independent media workers and researchers in those four Chinese-speaking communities.

Although the initial funds partially came from European foundations, it is largely funded by individual supporters who give small-amount donations (around HK$100) monthly. While many Hong Kong NGOs are funded by government and overseas foundations, Hong Kong In-Media manages to keep a high proportion of individual donations. It sees strong and active civil society as the primary support for independent media over the long term. It attempts to develop a model for small nongovernmental organizations and independent media in Hong Kong and other Chinese communities.

Ip Iam-chong

See also Alternative Media (Malaysia); Communist Movement Media, 1950s–1960s (Hong Kong); Indymedia (The Independent Media Center); Indymedia: East Asia; Internet Social Movement Media (Hong Kong); *OhmyNews* (Korea)

Further Readings

Ip, I., & Lam, O. (Eds.). (2009). *Info-Rhizome: Report on independent media in the Chinese-speaking world.* Hong Kong: Hong Kong In-Media. http://interlocals .net/?q=node/314

HUMAN RIGHTS MEDIA

The media are central to issues related to human rights. Everything related to the monitoring, protection, promotion, and enforcing of human rights depends on communication. This entry describes the efforts of organizations, institutions, and individuals in lobbying and organizing for the recognition and enforcement of human rights through the use of a great variety of media.

In Buenos Aires, a group of women wearing white scarves, mothers of people who disappeared during the last dictatorship, perform their weekly march demanding truth and justice. In London, during G20 protests, a witness documents the police clubbing a demonstrator who died moments later; almost immediately these images are up on an interactive website for the world to see and demand accountability. On International Women's Day in Tehran, a young man with a scarf on his head is wearing a T-shirt with the inscription "Death to Patriarchy." In California, a comic-strip style booklet on sexual harassment is distributed among day laborers, most of them immigrant women. In the United States, on the television show *Freedom Files,* a woman explains her opposition to the death penalty and why she lobbied against the execution of her daughter's murderer.

Human rights activists in practice have demanded and exercised the right to communicate, even without any official acknowledgment of the endorsement of this right in UN documents and often risking their lives in extremely dangerous situations. They have been, and are, pioneers in developing human rights media and in highlighting the centrality of the right to communicate. Article 19 of the 1948 Universal Declaration of Human Rights (UDHR) ensures the right of every individual to "freedom of opinion and expression," which includes the freedom to "seek, receive and impart information and ideas through any media and regardless of frontiers." The People's Communication Charter, an unofficial initiative, outlines specifics of several communication rights and is an important reference for those working to ensure those rights.

This entry first discusses the concept of human rights and its definition in various international legal documents. It then describes the two central goals of human rights media—documentation and intervention—and examines their producers and their audiences, as well as the formats in which they appear. Lastly, it presents a series of examples that convey the variety of human rights media in different global contexts and political environments, and fulfilling diverse goals. It concludes with a look at the impact of human rights media and how it can be assessed.

Human Rights and Violations Defined

Contemporary human rights violations include but are not limited to political repression, torture, death penalty, gender violence, genocide, abuse, and discrimination based on race, gender, religion, and class. Particularly vulnerable groups include children, women, religious and ethnic minorities, refugees, homosexuals, and HIV-positive people. Examples in the 21st century include abuses linked to immigration, human trafficking, lack of environmental protection, use of children as soldiers, land rights, economic exploitation, privatization of resources such as water, slave labor, and child prostitution.

International legal instruments define most human rights abuses that we face, as do institutions such as UN human rights bodies. But monitoring bodies often lack enforcement power. This is why human rights media have become tools to promote compliance with national and international law.

Two major documents complement the UDHR and categorize rights in five main areas. The International Covenant on Civil and Political Rights, also known as first-generation rights, specifies rights to freedom from state interference in civic and personal life. The International Covenant on Economic, Social and Cultural Rights, known as second-generation rights, specify where states must intervene and provide for their citizens. Third-generation rights, or solidarity rights, include the right to peace, development, and a healthy environment. In addition, there are several conventions such as the Convention on the Elimination of All Forms of Discrimination Against Women, the Genocide Convention, the Convention of the Rights of the Child, the Convention on the Elimination of All Forms of Racial Discrimination, and the Convention on the Protection of the Rights of All Migrant Workers and Their Families.

There are debates about how these Western-shaped rights apply globally—how far they privilege individual rights over the collective ones that are essential to Indigenous communities. Discrepancies also focus on priorities for the global North and global South, as some countries favor certain rights over others—for example, civil over economic rights. Worldwide, however, activists concur human rights are indivisible. For we cannot talk of respect for human rights if people can vote but cannot afford health care, or if they have access to free education but are banned from voicing their political opinions.

Abusers are first and foremost governments, and within governments, abuses may stem from individuals, organizations, institutions, or a corrupt legal system. But corporations, including those that benefit from repressive and dishonest governments, are major violators of human rights. Some are guilty of poisoning food supplies, disregarding workers' safety, or benefiting from sex tourism. Thus, while there is much to ask from governments, there is also need to denounce complicities and demand corporate responsibility.

Human Rights Media: Documentation and Intervention

The objectives of human rights media center on the activities of documentation and intervention. The goals of documentation can be summarized as follows:

1. To expose, monitor, and denounce human rights violations

2. To identify the perpetrators, including governments, corporations, structures, institutions, and individuals

3. To identify potential solutions

4. To offer an alternative human rights framing of issues

5. To document successes in stopping abuses

6. To establish records of past violations

Through advocacy and outreach, intervention seeks to achieve the following goals:

1. To broaden the sphere for the discussion of human rights

2. To alert mainstream media so issues become routinely and prominently covered

3. To educate at all levels

4. To gain new supporters for the cause

5. To propose and generate actions to monitor and stop the abuses

6. To use testimonies and memories about past human rights violations to search for truth and justice, and to foster reconciliation processes

Human Rights Media: Producers and Their Publics

Producers of human rights media include activists, human rights groups and organizations, and official institutions. Historically, the media have been tools to disseminate human rights information. Access to and use of the media are central for human rights work.

Individuals may act on their own but be part of a larger movement. This is common where civil and political rights are abused, such as when someone in a dictatorship risks scribbling graffiti denouncing a crime or calling for resistance or action on any public surface (e.g., messages on walls, in public restrooms, or prison cells).

However, human rights organizations are the main producers of human rights media and cannot function without media. From the moment that a small group of individuals decides to join forces to address human rights abuses up to the point where they become a formal organization, they must develop media strategies both for building their group and for communicating their concerns and demands to society. The larger international nongovernmental organizations (NGOs) are Amnesty International and Human Rights Watch, which are joined by an array of local, regional, and international organizations and community groups.

Institutions funded by federal and local governments also produce and distribute human rights media. This may lead, at worst, to the co-optation of issues and their manipulation to serve the political goals of governments, but we still need to identify aspects of their media campaigns that may parallel activist concerns. Examples include the national broadcasts of the government-organized Truth and Reconciliation Commission hearings in South Africa, which, for over a year, investigated severe human rights violations during the previous apartheid era (1948–1994).

Selecting the spheres and spaces to circulate and distribute Human Rights media to reach the public requires a careful identification of audiences. Are they local, national, or international? Are producers targeting society at large or governments, corporations, organizations, institutions, specific individuals, opinion leaders, and celebrities who can amplify the message and influence or modify policy?

Activists may shoot footage and then edit and frame their images for specific audiences and different purposes, producing one video for legal evidence and another to strengthen international solidarity networks. In many cases, it is about reaching anybody that may reproduce the message, as was the case when activists filled Chinese corporations' fax machines during the 1989 Tiananmen Square events with solidarity messages, letting China's public know that the world was watching.

In their quest to reach audiences, human rights media formats must attract attention and compete with multiple stimuli. Often, entertaining the audience is a way of engaging it and has a potentially greater impact in generating responses and actions. This is the case with human rights music concerts as a medium to connect with younger generations.

Human Rights Media Formats

Human rights media cover a broad spectrum, including publications, demonstrations, radio, street theater, songs, videos, hunger strikes, and T-shirts. Activists worldwide have historically appropriated then-new technologies for their campaigns: transistor radios during the Algerian liberation struggle (1956–1962), audiocassettes in Iran during the 1978–1979 revolution that ousted the royal regime (the Shah), text messaging in the Philippines in 2001 to bring down the government. Cell phones, in particular, are turning into key tools for the monitoring and promotion of human rights, as are new portable computers and digital cameras. The Internet has become essential for organizing and action. Having a website is a requisite to operate with efficacy, as it allows for community building, the sharing of information, and the posting of calls for action. This is especially relevant for transnational activism, making rapid global connection increasingly possible.

The access to high-tech formats does not imply the replacement of low-tech ones. Radio coexists with text messaging, uploading videos from a cell phone, printed zines, and street theater. People may sign petitions online but also attend protests announced via texting. A video of the police beating demonstrators is uploaded from a phone to a website at the same time that a flyer calling for action is downloaded to be printed and given away in a busy intersection. A video downloaded from a website to a DVD allows screenings at locations without Internet access and can be brought to other audiences if uploaded into a mobile phone. Moreover, access to cyberspace is increasingly available due to wireless technology, and those who do not own equipment can rent time at machines located in cyber coffee shops or kiosks.

Human Rights Media: Case Studies

This selection of case studies is intended is to show their variety and creativity, to highlight initiatives that are central for global human rights activism and focus on some recent trends. Some major formats such as radio and print publications are not addressed here.

Demonstrations and Marches

This low-tech format is characterized by the physical presence of activists in highly visible locations. Many of these events incorporate performance, street theater, and music. Others are silent marches, sit-ins, vigils, or hunger strikes. Taking to the streets and occupying public spaces is one essential way to transmit the messages.

Vigils by groups protesting the death penalty are customary at the doors of U.S. prisons on execution days. There are vigils and silent marches when the community comes together to denounce police brutality in places as far apart as New York and Buenos Aires. When these take place at night, often illuminated by candlelight, there can be almost a mystical feeling. Boycotts and pickets also take place, such as those demanding workers' economic rights—for example, the Justice for Janitors' pickets in the United States in the late 1990s that led to the negotiation of better wages and basic benefits. In 2005, farmworkers' highway protests, supported by consumer boycotts, prompted the

U.S. fast-food chain Taco Bell to pay a surcharge on produce to increase the workers' pay. Around the world, sit-ins and protests demand peace at the gates of military bases or denounce sweatshops at corporate headquarters.

Hunger strikes have been used to demand respect for human rights and get media attention. People have fasted, often until their death, for many reasons: Palestinian prisoners protesting conditions in Israeli jails; Indigenous groups in México City's huge central square denouncing conquest and genocide during the quincentennial of the "discovery" of the Americas; information policy activists in Tunisia opposing the 2005 World Summit on the Information Society held there, despite Tunisia's human rights violations; Jennifer Harbury at the doors of the White House demanding accountability for the death by torture of her husband, a Guatemalan guerrilla leader, and denouncing the decades-long genocide of Mayan citizens in that country.

Performances

The examples here belong to what may be a "border fringe" between demonstrations and theater performances. They often take place in public spaces but incorporate performative elements. Some of these theater projects, however, use traditional indoor spaces but may at times venture into the streets. Most of these performances are inspired by activist theater, closely linked to Latin American grassroots movements during the 1970s.

Relevant examples include *El Teatro Jornalero* in San Francisco, California, a company of Latin American immigrant workers, many of them day laborers. Their performances often adapt traditional plays to illustrate their plights and the discrimination they suffer, but plays have also taken place at the Mexican border to denounce the harassment and killing of immigrants.

For over 3 decades, Yuyachkani, a Peruvian theater collective, has been producing theater committed to documenting and exposing abuses. Among their most powerful performances were those during the public hearings of the Peruvian Truth Commission in 2001–2002. Actors used the streets as their stage to denounce the crimes that the commission was investigating. In some instances, victims approached the actors to confide their ordeals, as they found it easier to talk to them than to the prosecutors. The performance broadened the sphere for the discussion of human rights crimes and turned the streets into annexes of the buildings where the official commission operated.

Thousands of activists gather every year at the gates of the School of the Americas in Fort Benning, Georgia (United States). They demand the closing of an institution that trains Latin American military officers, many of them major human rights abusers. Speeches, music, and performances denounce violations across the globe. In 2004, demonstrators chanted *Presente!* as each name was read aloud of individuals slaughtered by the institution's graduates, each name celebrated by thousands of raised hands, waving crosses, flags, or fists. The strip leading to the military base became a stage to perform a massive act of memory. There were also demands for issues ranging from the death penalty to torture in Guantánamo and Abu Ghraib; activists lay on the floor simulating mutilated corpses and washing American flags soiled with blood.

Artworks

Art is a category with many subdivisions. There are paintings, sculptures, photography, graffiti, monuments, and memorials, all of which have examples of human rights communications. The locations for exhibiting these works are museums, galleries, parks, or the streets. Photography was a pioneer technology used to document human rights violations. Sebastião Salgado's photos of famine in Sudan and landless families in Brazil made it to the front page. In many places, walls are the "popular newspapers" for people without access to other media.

Monuments and memorials play roles in processes of remembering past abuses. In Buenos Aires, the monument to the victims of state terrorism is engraved with names of the disappeared. People look for those they knew and stand silently in contemplation. Comparable dialogues occur at Horst Hoheisel's countermonument in the former Nazi concentration camp at Buchenwald. A stainless steel plate placed on the ground, constantly heated to body temperature of 98.6 degrees Fahrenheit (37 °C), represents the absence of those who died there by bringing back their humanity through their body heat. This interaction with death happens each time that a visitor touches the monument and feels the warmth.

There are also "mobile" memorials, collectively made, which keep changing depending on what is added and where they are exhibited. Examples include the AIDS Memorial quilt, which toured a series of U.S. cities, with every patch commemorating a victim of the epidemic; and the Clothesline Project, decorated T-shirts hanging from a clothesline expressing the emotions of women affected by violence.

Popular Music

Examples include the Holocaust commemorations by Israeli musicians and the Argentine counterculture groups that managed to turn hip-hop into a cry against torture and disappearance. In locations as diverse as the Philippines, the United States, Latin America, and South Africa, lyrics that protest, denounce, demand social change, write memories, celebrate, and call for action are expressed in genres that include salsa, rap, rock, folk, reggae, and punk and address issues such as domestic violence, apartheid, agrarian reform, women's oppression, and racial profiling. Concerts help to broaden the spheres for discussion of abuses and to develop solidarity networks; they are political spaces where ideologies and meanings are articulated and debated. By attending concerts, singing, and dancing to the beat of these songs, people participate in the distribution and promotion of human rights messages.

Amnesty International was the pioneer in using music for its campaigns. Its 1988 *Human Rights Now!* tour, featuring concerts in different parts of the world, commemorated the 40th anniversary of the UDHR with participation of musicians such as Peter Gabriel, Bruce Springsteen, and Tracy Chapman. This tour inspired other tours, concerts, and CDs promoting awareness and benefiting other human rights causes, such as poverty in Africa or AIDS.

For the 60th anniversary of the UDHR in 2008, Link TV produced the music video *The Price of Silence*, available for download on iTunes, and with proceeds benefiting Amnesty International. In it, some of the world's top musicians perform songs addressing the Darfur conflict, domestic female abuse in India, war, violence and corruption in Colombia, and poverty in Uruguay.

Film

Filmmakers have a long tradition of engaging with human rights issues. Political repression, torture, genocide, or the violence and devastation caused by corporate greed have been portrayed in both narrative and documentary films. Documentaries address many human rights abuses. For example, *Total Denial* (2006) exposes the violations of the Burmese people's rights, including displacement, forced labor, torture, and killings, by the military junta during the building of a gas pipeline by an international corporation. *The Greatest Silence* (2007) portrays the massive rapes and mutilation of women in Congo.

Human rights–themed films win prestigious awards. *Taxi to the Dark Side* (2007), exposing torture in Abu Ghraib and Afghanistan, received the 2008 Oscar for best documentary. That same year, Amnesty International gave an award to *Sleep Dealer* (2008), an allegory of globalization through the science-fiction portrayal of immigration, outsourcing, Tijuana's *maquilas,* and corporations' pillage of natural resources.

Human Rights film festivals are mushrooming worldwide. By showing thought-provoking films, festivals offer spaces to discuss issues, connect with activists, and promote actions to stop the abuses. The annual Human Rights Watch International Film Festival complements theater screenings with a traveling festival that institutions and schools can rent. In 2008, linked to the Nobel Peace Prize ceremony in Oslo, Norway held its first Human Rights Human Wrongs film festival. There are also the 3 Continents festival in South Africa; the annual international Human Rights Film Festival in Buenos Aires; the Human Rights Arts & Film Festival in Melbourne, Australia; Basic Trust, a 2002 festival co-organized by the Tel Aviv Cinémathèque and Al Quds University in Palestine, with screenings in both Tel Aviv and Ramallah, focusing on the use of film in peace-building processes.

In addition to their theater releases, screenings at educational and cultural institutions, DVD sales and rentals, and online streaming all multiply the audiences exposed to these messages. Indeed, it is hard to assess the reach and impact of a human rights film considering only its box office performance.

Television

Making it to prime-time television with a human rights message is the goal of many activists. Entertainment education projects have used soap operas for social change in campaigns ranging from reproductive rights in India to literacy in Latin America. In South Africa, *Soul City* portrayed stories about AIDS, sexual abuse, and violence against women. In Argentina, *Television for Identity* was a tool in the campaign to find the children stolen from their executed parents by the 1976–1983 military dictatorship.

The *Freedom Files* television series was created by the American Civil Liberties Union in 2005 and broadcast by PBS and cable channels. Its episodes have addressed several issues, affecting mostly U.S. citizens: the curtailment of constitutional rights in the name of national security, the Patriot Act's restrictions of freedoms, surveillance through wiretapping of phone calls and monitoring of e-mails, the government's use of torture and rendition programs, gay and lesbian rights, the juvenile criminal justice system, racial profiling, immigrant rights, and the death penalty.

Human rights broadcasts now often direct audiences to their websites, which contain teaching guidelines for educators and community organizations, calls for action, further information about the issues discussed in the episodes, and online discussions.

Locally Generated Multimedia Projects

In some cases, the community participates in the production of videos. Organizations integrate these videos in interactive websites that allow uploading and downloading of materials, a combination of high and low-tech media, and online activities with public events. The following international, regional, and local projects illustrate how documentation is complemented by advocacy and intervention.

Just Vision documents grassroots peace building by Palestinian and Israeli civilians. They produce documentaries and maintain a website about joint efforts to end the bloodshed and resolve the conflict. They have managed to bring nonviolent peace-building efforts to page one, prompting coverage in major media outlets such as *The Wall Street Journal* and al-Jazeera. By widely screening some of their documentaries, they have spread their message to audiences worldwide, including to opinion leaders and decision makers.

Border Stories is a web-based documentary showcasing films from both sides of the U.S.–México border, putting a face to countless stories of people living in that region dividing the developed and underdeveloped worlds. This mosaic of films portrays the challenges they face, how their rights to live in freedom and working for a just salary are affected, the rationale of American anti-immigrant vigilante groups, and reflections by those attempting to cross into the United States.

Guerrilla Griots' Human Rights Media Arts Center, a project from Ithaca, New York, is a collective of mostly young people of color. Their activism focuses on issues affecting marginalized communities, including immigrants, such as environmental policies, the justice system, and prisons. They challenge mainstream media stereotypes by making their own media (e.g., music videos), but they also work on renewable energy projects. They reach out to the community by hosting public educational events.

Most of the documents and videos posted on these websites rely on the stories of people whose rights have been violated or who are challenging structures that curtail the full exercise of their rights. Storytelling is central, and there is an increasing role of oral history in human rights media projects. This is particularly relevant in the aftermath of mass political violence. While official truth commissions create a space to talk about the past and secure media coverage, other initiatives by NGOs fulfill the role of what Louis Bickford calls "unofficial truth projects" and also have great impact on the victims recounting their ordeals and those who listen to them. Examples include projects in Cambodia and the former Yugoslavia that produce videos based on the material gathered through oral histories. Thus, we can consider the projects discussed earlier as examples of unofficial truth projects.

Video Games and Other Tools

Video games have a growing niche focusing on social change and human rights education. Playing requires responses. Interactivity allows exploring different perspectives to assess conditions and propose solutions. The relevance of empathy in games has the potential for their use in human rights work. Players of all ages can entertain themselves while they learn about global conflicts, poverty, or the environment.

Examples include *PeaceMaker,* where players can bring peace to the Middle East and win the Nobel Prize or worsen the region's situation. *Darfur Is Dying* explores the genocide taking place and explores initiatives to stop the crisis. *ICED–I Can End Deportation* allows the player to take the role of an illegal immigrant and experience the effects of unfair immigration laws. *The Redistricting Game* teaches about the U.S. political redistricting process, the abuses that undermine the system, and proposals to improve it. *Perspectives on the U.S. Criminal Justice System* presents different stories about the same case illustrating how one person's incarceration affects families and communities.

New technologies allow for innovative virtual reality installations set in the Second Life site, as with these collaborations between Peggy Weil and Nonny de la Peña: *Walljumpers* is about jumping over the world's border fences and illustrates the futility of human contention by separations such as the Berlin wall and the fences dividing México and the United States and Israel and Palestine. *Gone Gitmo* is a virtual Guantánamo prison; users can experience being detained, hooded, transported, dressed with the orange jumpsuit, and locked inside a cage for an indefinite period.

Tools and Resources for Activists

Amnesty International and Human Rights Watch are key resources for activists and policymakers. Their websites give information about the state of human rights worldwide, conflicts by region, situations demanding urgent responses, advocacy opportunities, educational kits, and success stories from courageous activists. Hundreds of organizations follow comparable patterns. For example, the Business & Human Rights Resource Centre focuses on corporations as abusers and also potential enforcers of human rights. Their website features news and reports about corporations' records on human rights and their impact worldwide.

To provide techniques to document and monitor abuses, design databases, and systematize documentation centers is the mission of HURIDOCS (Human Rights International Documentation Systems), a global network of organizations that include intergovernmental organizations, human rights institutes, NGOs, and networks. Activities focus on helping organizations acquire the knowledge and the skills for efficient use of communication technologies. The Human Rights Connection, a network of New York organizations that includes the Center for the Study of Human Rights at Columbia University, promotes global activism and human rights education. The network provides practical advice on how to use technology, work with the news media, develop studies, plan advocacy campaigns, raise funds, and manage the challenges and dangers of working in human rights.

Assessing the Impact of Human Rights Media

"Internal" effects impact the individuals producing human rights media, generating cohesion, unity, and contributing to the creation of a movement, which are essential first steps for the development of strategies to reach the larger community. "External" effects relate to the achievement of the goals outlined within the functions of documentation and intervention and range from informing to modifying policy. These may be the slow and gradual building of a movement, the broadening of the public sphere where issues are discussed, and the increase in lobbying efforts to enforce laws protecting rights.

Evaluating the impact of human rights media, however, is not an easy task, and it varies depending on the situation and the context. How people learn about human rights issues and act upon this knowledge is a complex process. Moreover, the impacts of human rights media are usually the outcome of a combination of factors, in which these media interact with educational campaigns and legal battles, as is the case with the transmission of memories of human rights abuses in Argentina. As the following examples suggest,

however, somebody listened, understood, and took action, and this resulted in verifiable improvements of human rights conditions.

A journalistic project investigating forced labor by a Nike contractor in Malaysia was broadcast in Australia in 2008. The report about slavery and the violations of the rights to just employment shamed Nike and helped to liberate 7,700 workers enduring those conditions. In 2007, an Internews investigative report exposed a web of human trafficking in West Africa that was sending children to Europe for prostitution. The report, which included photos and videos, was used to prosecute traffickers, including Ghanaian immigration officials, and for a sting operation that rescued 17 girls.

In the former Yugoslavia, the Videoletters project became a tool for pacification and reconciliation in a region devastated by violent ethnic wars. Members of factions that fought against each other recorded videos explaining their actions and reasons for them and sent them to former neighbors and friends who turned into enemies during the war. Recipients answered in video format, starting a conversation about the past, present, and future. By showing the videos on public television in the region, the project contributed to broadening the sphere for dialogue between former enemies.

WITNESS lists triumphs in several of their projects. In the Democratic Republic of Congo, the screening of incriminatory videos about child soldiers to officials of the International Criminal Court led to arrests for alleged war crimes. In Senegal, a video exposed the devastating effects of land mines. In response, the government pledged record funding for women land mine victims, including for prostheses free of charge. In the United States, a video exposed widespread abuses in California's juvenile prison system. Days after its screening at the Capitol, the Senate introduced legislation to fix problems denounced in it.

M. Susana Kaiser

See also Citizens' Media; Grandmothers of the Plaza de Mayo (Argentina); Independent Media (Burma/Myanmar); Indigenous Peoples' Media; Installation Art Media; Mothers of the Plaza de Mayo (Argentina);

Peace Media (Colombia); Performance Art and Social Movement Media: Augusto Boal; Social Movement Media, 1960s–1980s (Chile); Women's Movement Media (India)

Further Readings

Amnesty International: http://www.amnesty.org

Bickford, L. (2007). Unofficial truth projects. *Human Rights Quarterly, 29*(4), 94–1035.

Border Stories: www.borderstories.org

Business & Human Rights Resource Centre: http://www.business-humanrights.org

El Teatro Jornalero: http://www.cornerstonetheater.org/content/index.php?Itemid=111&id=203&option=com_content&task=view

Games for Change: http://www.gamesforchange.org

Gone Gitmo: http://gonegitmo.blogspot.com

Greenwald, R., & Perez, R. R. (Producers). *The freedom files* [Television series]. New York: American Civil Liberties Union. http://www.aclu.tv

Gregory, S. (2006). Transnational storytelling: Human rights, WITNESS, and video advocacy. *American Anthropologist, 108*(1), 195–204.

Guerrilla Griots: http://www.guerrilla-griots.org

Human Rights Connection: http://www.humanrightsconnection.org

Human Rights International Documentation Systems (HURIDOCS): http://www.huridocs.org

Human Rights Watch: http://www.hrw.org

Internews Every Human Has Rights Media Awards: http://media-awards.everyhumanhasrights.org

Just Vision: http://www.justvision.org

Kaiser, M. S. (2005). *Postmemories of terror: A new generation copes with the legacy of the "dirty war."* New York: Palgrave Macmillan.

Link TV. (2008). *The price of silence.* Available at http://www.linktv.org/humanrights

The Redistricting Game: http://www.redistrictinggame.com

Rubio Zapata, M. (2008). *El cuerpo ausente (performance política)* [The absent body (political performance)]. Lima, Perú: Didi de Arteta S.A.

360 degrees: Perspectives on the U.S. Criminal Justice System: 360degrees.org

Videoletters Project: http://www.videoletters.net

Walljumpers: http://walljumpersproject.blogspot.com

Weissman, R. (2005). Victories! Justice! The people's triumphs over corporate power. *Multinational Monitor, 26*(7/8), 35–47.

WITNESS: http://witness.org

INDEPENDENCE MOVEMENT MEDIA (INDIA)

Resistance against the British began long before the 20th century, when the British East India Company expanded its powers in eastern India, particularly in what are now known as West Bengal State and Bangladesh. This entry describes the role of independence movement media dating from the mid-19th century and continuing until Indian independence in 1947. The influence of media from this time in Indian history can still be seen today in street theater.

Evolution of the Independence Movement

One of the earliest events of the Indian independence movement was the 1857 revolt by *sepoys* (Indian soldiers) in the East India Company's army. Variously known as the Sepoy Mutiny, the Rebellion of 1857, or India's First War of Independence, the 1857 revolt threatened the East India Company's power in today's Delhi, Bihar, Uttar Pradesh, and Madhya Pradesh. The British government dissolved the company and took direct control.

Leading figures of the rebellion, including the *Rani* (Queen) of Jhansi and Mangal Pandey, became folk heroes represented in images and performances that were part of successive waves of the independence movement. Independence agitation grew more insistent from then onward into the 20th century, from the 1885 founding of the Indian National Congress (INC), to Mahatma Gandhi's return to India in 1915, to the 1920–1922 Noncooperation and 1942–1044 Quit India movements. In 1947 Britain withdrew, but not without having very hastily partitioned the subcontinent into the nations of India and Pakistan, instigating the largest short-term migration in history to that date, with 15 million refugees.

Initially not invested in eliminating British rule in India, the INC split in 1907 and became the main organizing body of the independence movement. Socially conscious religious groups such as the Arya Samaj and Brahmo Samaj also became involved in the independence movement, focusing on social reforms that created national pride among the masses. With the 1905 British partition of Bengal, the Bengali public—angry at British divide-and-rule tactics and failure to consult the people—engaged in widespread boycotts, with INC support. Common INC posters depicted India as an elderly man contemplating three paths: civil disobedience, violence, and collusion with the British.

The Vernacular Press and "Vande Mataram"

Vernacular newspapers such as the *Amrita Bazaar Patrika* and the *Bengalee* made important contributions to India's burgeoning nationalist sentiment, and by the early 20th century, there were more than 500 vernacular newspapers. A few were run by British people sympathetic to the nationalist cause, though most were run by Hindu entrepreneurs. Vernacular presses were unrestrained in their critique of British rule and the lack of representation of Indians within government.

The colonial government had strengthened its hold over vernacular presses in 1878 with the Vernacular Press Act, an act known to Indians as the "Gagging Act," suppressing nationalist writings within vernacular-language (but not English-language) newspapers. Due to significant censorship programs in the wake of this act, the well-known Bengali paper *Amrita Bazaar Patrika* (Amrita Bazaar Newspaper) became an English-language paper to circumvent censorship. But vernacular presses only grew more resilient in the 20th century. Even at times when the nationalist movement was waning or being repressed by colonial rule, the vernacular press served as critics of government, as educators, and as promoters of nationalism.

The song "Vande Mataram" (I Bow to Thee, Mother) became a rallying cry during the independence movement, particularly among the masses after Bengal's partition. Leaders within the independence movement, including India's Nobel Prize–winning poet Rabindranath Tagore, sang the song publicly in support of independence. One of India's earliest filmmakers, Hiralal Sen, featured "Vande Mataram" prominently in his documentary on antipartition demonstrations in Calcutta in 1905, one of the first political films in India. Additionally, Indian freedom fighter Lala Lajput Rai created a newspaper called *Vande Mataram,* a venue for nationalist engagement, in Lahore.

The Noncooperation Movement's Symbols

In 1915, Gandhi returned to India from South Africa, having waged campaigns of nonviolent resistance to colonial repression within the Indian community there. Working with urban and rural poor, Gandhi organized the masses against discrimination and extortionate taxation. The Indian independence movement grew more fervent with the Rowland Act, designed to contain sedition and prohibit public gatherings, and the 1919 Jallianwallah Bagh massacre in Amritsar, when on the Sikh New Year's Day, British General Dyer instructed troops to shoot without warning into an unarmed crowd of demonstrators.

As a result, the Noncooperation movement became the first nationwide nonviolent people's movement, spearheaded by Gandhi and the INC. In 1921, Gandhi became INC head, with a platform for eradicating poverty, ending untouchability,

seeking women's rights, and achieving Indian independence. As the Noncooperation movement continued, Indians withdrew their children from British schools, boycotted English goods, and shut down factories. Posters reading "Buy Swadeshi" (self-sufficiency), advocating purchasing of Indian-made goods, appeared in cities, advertising Indian-owned companies with slogans such as "India's Pride, Nation's Wealth." Other posters, sponsored by the INC, depicted Gandhi sitting in a tree alongside Indians engaged in noncooperation, while a soldier attempted to bring them down.

In the 1920s, Gandhi began urging Indians to wear homespun cloth called *khadi,* handmade cloth of cotton, silk, or wool made on a *charkha,* or spinning wheel. Gandhi advocated this versatile fabric for all seasons as a mode of rural self-reliance. Consequently, khadi became an important symbol for the Swadeshi movement, representing economic self-sufficiency and independence. Khadi was worn by Indians, including Gandhi himself, and angry masses burned or symbolically destroyed foreign textiles. In 1946, Margaret Bourke-White captured her iconic photograph of Gandhi with his charkha. Before allowing Bourke-White to take his photo, Gandhi made her learn to use the spinning wheel, which she did. Today, official rules stipulate that the flag of India may only be made out of khadi.

Also known as the Salt *Satyagraha* (truth and love force), the Salt March began on March 12, 1930, as a protest against the British salt tax. In one of his earliest organized nonviolent protests, Mahatma Gandhi led a march from his *ashram* (religious residence) outside Ahmedabad, Gujarat State, to the coastal village of Dandi to make salt from seawater, circumventing British taxation laws. On April 6, Gandhi broke the salt laws and millions followed suit. With his followers, Gandhi planned to take over the Dharasana Salt Works, but he was arrested on May 5, 1930. With nearly 100,000 people jailed because of the salt campaign, which sparked mass civil disobedience, the Salt Satyagraha remains one of the most memorable campaigns of the Indian independence movement, garnering the attention of the global media. British policies stayed in place for a time. But the Salt Satyagraha informed the British that their ability to retain their colonial holdings depended on Indian acquiescence, clearly ebbing fast.

In the 1920s and 1930s, political theater became an important trend in the independence movement. Plays such as Kallakuri Narayana Rao's *Padmavyuham* (Army Configuration of the Lotus, 1919) and Damaraju Pundarikakshudu's *Gandhiji Vijayam* (Victory of Gandhi, 1921) used historical and mythological frameworks as allegories for contemporary conditions under British domination. Playwrights were influenced by, and they participated in, the expanding anticolonial movement, and performances of such plays played no small role in creating and mobilizing national identity toward independence.

The Quit India Movement

The Bharat Chhodo Andolan (Quit India) movement began in 1942 as result of INC demands for immediate British withdrawal. In July, the INC demanded independence, threatening mass civil disobedience if their demands were not met. In August, the All India Congress Committee passed the Quit India Resolution, and Gandhi advised nonviolent resistance to the British. The message found expression in multiple media. Political graffiti with slogans, propaganda, and even caricatures of Gandhi driving the British out of India began appearing in New Delhi, Calcutta, and elsewhere. Progressive vernacular literature emerged as well, particularly in novels in the Marathi and Kannada languages by Nagnath S. Inamdar and Basavaraj Kattimani, and in S. Sitarama Sastri's poetry.

Plays during the Quit India movement explicitly focused on political liberation. These include Jasti Venkata Narasayya's *Congress Vijayam* (1946) and Pattigodupu Raghava Raju's *Delhi Kota* (From Delhi to Kota, 1946). The Praja Natya Mandali (People's Theatre Movement) provided a forum for revolutionary drama. Sunkara Satyanarayana and V. Bhaskara Rao's plays, produced by the Praja Natya Mandali, used folk forms such as storytelling and dance to communicate political messages. Audiences, however, found these performances too propagandistic.

Multiple issues relating to Indian independence found their voices in the work of the Indian People's Theatre Association (IPTA). From the violence of World War II, to famine and starvation in Bengal, to British repression of the Quit India movement, IPTA's goal was to use theater and other traditional performance-based art forms to fight British imperialism and the Axis powers, while enlightening middle-class and working-class consciousness. IPTA plays used stark realism, often in the social realist tradition, portraying the masses' plight. IPTA sponsored plays and street theater all over India in regional vernacular languages, aiming to broadly reach audiences.

IPTA's most influential performance, however, was the 1944 play *Navanna* (New Harvest). This four-act play told the story of luckless Bengali peasants during the 1943 Bengal famine. Deeply committed to bridging divides between culture and politics, IPTA became an influential part of the Indian Left, while remaining a deeply respected cultural movement. Although the original core group disbanded in 1947, IPTA's legacy remains alive in politically active street theater groups still working in India today.

Roopika Risam

See also Adivasi Movement Media (India); Anticolonial Press (British Colonial Africa); Boxer Rebellion Theater (China); Indian People's Theatre Association; New Culture and May 4th Movements Media (China); Political Cartooning, 1870s–Present (India); Street Theater (India)

Further Readings

Chandavarkar, R. (1998). *Imperial power and popular politics.* Cambridge, UK: Cambridge University Press.
Menon, V. P. (1997). *Transfer of power in India.* Hyderabad, India: Orient Longman.
Purohit, V. (1988). *Arts of transitional India, 20th century.* Mumbai, India: Popular Prakashan.
Trivedi, L. (2007). *Clothing Gandhi's nation.* Bloomington: Indiana University Press.
Vilanilam, J. (2005). *Mass communication in India: A sociological perspective.* New Delhi, India: Sage.
von Tunzelmann, A. (2007). *Indian summer: The secret history of the end of an empire.* New York: Henry Holt.

INDEPENDENCE MOVEMENT MEDIA (VIETNAM)

Vietnamese history is replete with attempts by outsiders to invade the country, inevitably followed by Vietnamese reaction, both violent and subtle, to oust them. For thousands of years the Chinese have been repelled, though they have sometimes occupied the country for extended periods. The 18th century brought Europeans to the area. French national prestige, coupled with the need for cheap natural resources, demanded colonies to compete with the British Empire and led to the French colonization of Vietnam, Laos, and Cambodia—rationalized as a "civilizing" mission for these ancient cultures.

In 1802, French adventurers helped Nguyễn Phúc Ánh establish the Nguyễn dynasty, installing him as Emperor Gia Long. The southern part of Vietnam was colonized by 1867. After military defeats, a one-sided treaty in 1883 set up a "protectorate" over the central and northern parts. The royal court ruled these two sections on behalf of the French.

The colonial authorities were constantly troubled by rebellion. Much early opposition was led by Confucian scholars, who circulated written material among students and acquaintances, often condemning the royal court for selling out to the French. Phan Bội Châu was probably one of the most famous of these scholars, moving to Japan and later to China, setting up schools for Vietnamese youth to learn politics and the arts of insurrection. His writings and those of his compatriot, Phan Chu Trinh, deeply impressed young activist Nguyễn Ái Quốc, later to be known as Hồ Chí Minh.

Poetry and Anticolonial Resistance

The French colonial government pressed heavily upon the Vietnamese population, setting up monopolies on alcohol, salt, and opium and placing taxes on almost everything. An anonymous poem circulating in 1905–1906 recounts:

All the varieties of taxes,
They increase them endlessly
The land tax is hardly paid
When the tax on buffaloes and cows is due,
Tax on dogs; tax on pigs
Tax on matches; tax on alcohol; tax on ferries;
tax on cars
Tax on markets; tax on tea; tax on tobacco
. . . .
We want to scream to tear off the sky
We want to draw out our swords.

In the early days of the resistance to colonialism, poetry was a popular way to share despair and grievances and to build political opposition.

Vietnamese poetry is often expressed in a unique form, known as the *lục-bát* (six-eight) form, in which lines of six and eight syllables alternate in a complex rhyming scheme that is easily memorized to be sung and recited; this form of poetry was popular in the villages. *Ca dao* poems can be proverbs and sayings, love poetry, or political weapons.

By the 1930s, the scholars' protests were widely seen as ineffective, and, at the same time, modern political parties were developing—usually cruelly repressed by the colonists. Hồ Chí Minh formed the Vietnamese Communist Party in Hong Kong in 1930 by drawing together disparate elements within Vietnam and activists operating in southern China. The party was not very effective inside Vietnam until after Hồ Chí Minh had returned to northern Vietnam in 1941. At that time, he formed the Việt Minh, an alliance of independence-minded groups dominated by the Communist Party.

The Communist Press: Beginnings

About 90% of the Vietnamese population lived in rural areas, and one of Hồ Chí Minh's first concerns was to engage these mainly illiterate people. He began by publishing a small newspaper *Việt Nam Độc Lập* (Independent Vietnam!) in 1941 and wrote the first issues on stencils and printed them using a flat rock and a roller in a river bed, in the mountainous province of Cao Bằng. The newspaper was not free, but it spoke of ordinary people's concerns. It carried international news too, which, in pre-broadcast times, was almost unprecedented. In Vietnam, newspapers were only available to the wealthy in the big cities, but here was a newspaper specifically for poor rural people. It carried hope for a Vietnam independent of any colonial oppressor. Each issue carried a little section called the "Culture Garden" with some poetry, sometimes with a political message, sometimes just for pleasure. New issues of *Việt Nam Độc Lập* were produced about every 2 weeks, and copies were carried around the country by Việt Minh cadres, who either read them aloud or chose a villager who could read to do so.

In 1942, Hồ Chí Minh also wrote and published *Lịch sử Nước Ta* (A History of Our Country), which was a brief account of Vietnam's history starting from the origin legends, which date back to around 2000 BCE. His list of dates accurately predicted Vietnam's independence 3 years later. The booklet, like *Việt Nam Độc Lập*, was handwritten and produced using the kind of tools available to the intended audience. *Lịch sử Nước Ta* is written entirely in verse, using the *lục-bát* form. The Việt Minh also mounted a mobilization and awareness campaign during World War II, one of the highlights of which was a large anti-illiteracy campaign targeting the village folk of Vietnam. There were night classes for the farmers, and people of all ages were involved, often the young ones teaching their elders how to read and write the new script. Many older people would know only a few rudimentary Chinese characters, whereas the youngsters had learned the quasi-Latin *quốc ngữ* script used today.

Media were central to the effort to oust the French. The very first Việt Minh armed unit, organized by General Võ Nguyên Giáp in 1944, was named the Vietnam Propaganda Liberation Force. It would later become the formidable army that defeated the French in 1954. Việt Minh media were so successful that in mid-August 1945 a more-or-less peaceful revolution occurred throughout Vietnam, followed by Hồ Chí Minh's Declaration of Independence on September 2 and the formation of a popular front government.

Postwar Independence Media

By 1947, the Việt Minh had built up a great deal of credibility where it mattered—among the 90% of rural Vietnamese. The Việt Minh ran a successful propaganda campaign in the rural areas in order to mobilize the farmers to help the war effort against the French. The media took the form of posters, songs, performances, leaflets, and personal interaction between cadres and villagers. The posters were produced in the simple manner pioneered by Hồ Chí Minh, but with more use of color if materials were available. They used devices that had great appeal to the rural population—poetry in the *ca dao* form, girl–boy dialogues, and pictures along traditional village lines. Many posters referenced unique aspects of Vietnam's minority cultures.

Pamphlets and posters warned villagers how to avoid becoming bombing targets, how to reconstruct bombed villages, and how to avoid malaria. People were told about holding markets and schools early in the day or late at night, to avoid the daylight hours, and to be careful where they put their washing to dry so as not to make targets for the bombers. They were encouraged to sew for the soldiers, to transport rice to the front, and to encourage, hide, and support the guerrillas. Always the French *colons* were defined as the enemy, not all French as such.

The Việt Minh government remained intact, albeit pursued by the French, providing services in those areas under its control—some areas were controlled by the French by day and the Vietnamese by night. Schools were set up, along with information and cultural services and construction advice services.

The success of these activities in mobilizing the population became evident in the historic 1954 Điện Biên Phủ battle. The French Expeditionary Force built an "impregnable" stronghold near the main road to Laos, in the mountains, but they had not foreseen the dedication and determination of the Vietnamese people. Hundreds of thousands (some say millions) of people worked to lug huge artillery pieces up through difficult mountain passes and to position them, unknown to the French defenders, above the fortifications. The French camp fell on May 7, 1954, and Hanoi was liberated on October 10.

Blocking the ideals of Hồ Chí Minh and other nationalist Vietnamese leaders, a temporary division of Vietnam into two parts was forced upon them by the cold war. In the southern part of the country, the United States encouraged the regime to ignore the elections promised for 1956; thus, conditions were in place for what is now known in the West as the "Vietnam War" (within Vietnam as the "American War"). This time the enemy was the authoritarian regime in Saigon and the invading Americans.

Characteristics of Việt Minh Media

The Việt Minh media demonstrated effective communication principles. First, they were based on verifiable truth. The French colonists were, indeed, cruel and exploitative. This was a fact obvious to those in the rural areas, as can be seen by the poetry and folk sayings that have been collected from that time.

Second, the media were expertly targeted. Most used materials that villagers themselves could use; indeed, much was produced in the villages. The contents told stories of village life, of community planning, of village leaders, of the farmers and their interests, of men and women who cared for each other. Folk tales were adapted to carry the message so that, for example, one could see Mr. Toad teaching in the literacy campaign, or carpenters competing with each other to build school desks. Third, the media carried simple messages about action that could be taken by ordinary people. There were clothes to sew for the soldiers, food to be carried to the front, guerrillas to be fed and hidden, and village defenses to be built up. Some of the contents urged young men and women to join the Liberation Army, and many of the songs showed a yearning for the end to fighting and a hope for national reunification.

Rob Hurle

See also Anticolonial Press (British Colonial Africa); Communist Movement Media, 1950s–1960s (Hong Kong); Independence Movement Media (India); Indian People's Theatre Association; Palestinian Interwar Press; Vernacular Poetry Audiotapes in the Arab World

Further Readings

Chapuis, O. (2000). *The last emperors of Vietnam: From Tu Duc to Bao Dai*. Westport, CT: Greenwood Press.

Fall, B. B. (1967). *Hell in a very small place: The siege of Dien Bien Phu*. Philadelphia: Lippincott.

Hồ Chí Minh. (2001). *Lịch sử Nước Ta*. Hanoi, Vietnam: NXB Chính Trị Quốc Gia for Bảo Tàng Tân Trào—ATK. (Original work published 1942)

Lockhart, G. (1989). *Nation in arms: The origins of the People's Army of Vietnam*. Sydney, Australia: Asian Studies Association of Australia in association with Allen & Unwin.

Marr, D. G. (1981). *Vietnamese tradition on trial, 1920–1945*. Berkeley: University of California Press.

Marr, D. G. (1995). *Vietnam 1945: The quest for power*. Berkeley: University of California Press.

McFarland, B. (1993). *The end of the Vietnamese monarchy*. New Haven, CT: Council on Southeast Asia Studies, Yale Center for International and Area Studies.

Nguyễn Đạo Toàn, Lê Hữu Cảnh & Nguyễn Công Quang (Compilers). (2006). *60 Năm Tranh Cổ Động Việt Nam 1945–2005*. Hà Nội: Bộ Văn Hóa—Thông Tin, Cục Văn Hóa—Thông Tin.

Nguyễn Khắc Viện. (2007). *Vietnam: A long history* (7th ed.). Hà Nội: NXB Thế Giới. (Original work published 1987)

Phạm Mai Hùng (Head Compiler). (2000). *Báo Việt Nam Độc Lập (1941–1945)*. Hanoi, Vietnam: NXB Lao Động for Bảo Tàng Cách Mạng Việt Nam. (Originally published as newspaper series)

Prados, J. (2007). Assessing Dien Bien Phu. In M. A. Lawrence & F. Logevall (Eds.), *The first Vietnam War: Colonial conflict and cold war crisis* (pp. 215–239). Cambridge, MA: Harvard University Press.

Triều Văn Hiển, Trần Hải Nhị, Lê Thị Thúy Hoàn, & Ngô Thị Ba (Compilers). (2007). *9 Năm Kháng Chiến Qua Tranh Tuyên Truyền Cổ Động* [9 years of resistance war through propaganda paintings and posters] (Lê Thị Thúy Hoàn, Trans.). Hà Nội: SAVINA for Bảo Tàng Cách Mạng Việt Nam.

Truong Buu Lam. (1967). *Patterns of Vietnamese response to foreign intervention: 1858–1900*. New Haven, CT: Yale University Southeast Asian Studies.

Truong Buu Lam. (2000). *Colonialism experienced: Vietnamese writings on colonialism, 1900–1931*. Ann Arbor: University of Michigan Press.

INDEPENDENT MEDIA (BURMA/MYANMAR)

Burma's border-based media have a long history, including clandestine radio stations such as the ethnic Karen-controlled Radio Kawthoolei, named after the Karen homeland, which began broadcasting in 1949 and continued intermittently during the 1970s and 1980s. Journals and information sheets of various kinds in a range of languages have long been published in the border areas, which are also home to reporters and stringers who travel into and out of Burma reporting for the international broadcasting networks.

Burmese exile media range from the stable and continuous to more ephemeral forms of media such as stickers, posters, and leaflets produced outside and then smuggled into Burma and slapped on walls, posts, fences, and even military vehicles.

In the first decade of the 21st century, most Burmese exile media had an online presence and were moving toward multimedia production. But

Burmese Internet use began much earlier and in the mid-1990s was often lauded in international news reports as a harbinger of a new international cyberactivism.

Burma's Official and Exile Mediascape

Media are highly censored in Burma, which was renamed Myanmar in 1989 by the country's military dictatorship in a top-down move denounced as illegitimate by the country's democratic opposition movement. All broadcasting and daily newspapers are controlled by the State Peace and Development Council. There is a private sector of weeklies and monthlies that grew significantly during the late 1990s and early 2000s, but these publications must be cleared by the censorship board, the Press Scrutiny and Registration Division.

The Burmese are able to receive otherwise inaccessible information through international broadcasters such as the BBC, Voice of America, Radio Free Asia, and radio and television from the Oslo-based Democratic Voice of Burma (DVB). In the early 2000s, the al-Jazeera International English edition also became popular with those who could afford satellite dishes. Less than 1% of the total population has access to the Internet, and those who do take risks if they use it to access political information.

There is virtually no space for independent Burmese journalism. Even the types of critical commentary found in traditional Burmese entertainment are strictly curtailed, and there is no government tolerance for media devoted to social change. Independent media are only able to develop and grow outside of the country.

A critical year for Burma and its media was 1988, when dissidents fled to the country's border areas after the military regime reacted to massive street demonstrations by killing thousands. These areas between authoritarian Burma and the relatively freer communications environments in Thailand, China, Bangladesh, and India became home to a variety of new Burmese media in exile. These media have varied goals and target audiences but a common purpose in working for political change in Burma and an end to militarization and violence.

Burmese print media produced in exile generally fall into two broad categories. The first is composed of a few well-funded, widely read, and increasingly professional exile media that are "unmarked" in terms of ethnic identification, including *The Irrawaddy* and Mizzima News Agency (in English and Burmese) and *New Era Journal* (in Burmese). These media cover the activities of a wide variety of groups in Burmese society and address important issues in international news, especially issues relevant to Burma. Beginning in the mid-1990s, there also emerged a number of media identified with the country's ethnic minority groups, produced primarily although not exclusively from locations along the border. Several such media have become significant voices, putting the ethnic nationalities "on the map" for outsiders interested in the situation in Burma and for the other groups in the democratic opposition.

The Internet and Burma's "Spiders"

The BurmaNet listserv, founded in 1993, quickly became the primary source of daily information for most Burma watchers. The impact of the Internet and BurmaNet took the Burmese regime by surprise, and it soon recognized that effective control of communication required new strategies. Despite protests from some listserv subscribers, in 1994 BurmaNet's editors decided to allow military representatives to post messages to the listserv and to include excerpts of these messages in BurmaNet news summaries in the interests of free speech and full debate. BurmaNet arguably became the most significant forum for discussion between the regime and the opposition.

Reaching a peak in the mid-1990s was the high-profile Internet campaign spearheaded by the Free Burma Coalition, an umbrella organization coordinating international groups. At its height, it claimed member groups in more than 100 universities and high schools in the United States and other countries and that it was the largest cyber-campaign devoted to human rights in a single country. Activists often began their online postings with "Dear fellow spiders," in reference to the campaign's motto, "When spiders unite they can tie down a lion."

This Internet and use of information and communications technology enabled more complex flows of information between those inside and outside Burma. Information obtained by exile media and then posted to BurmaNet would get picked by the wire services and other news agencies, including international Burmese-language broadcasters, who then broadcast much of the information back into Burma. The DVB in Oslo would have had difficulty surviving without the Internet, which was both a source of information and a tool enabling field reporters to send reports as e-mail attachments rather than having fax or dictate them over the phone. Even those without Internet access are affected by the increased number of sources it makes available to traditional media.

Editorial Independence: A Debate

Many of the Burmese exile media were initially established as propaganda arms of opposition political groups, and since 1988, the staff of these media have debated the degree to which they should become independent. While many assert their independence, others argue Burmese media must promote unity and motivate people to work for democracy. The move to demand independence may have, at least initially, stemmed as much from funding agencies as from a genuine desire for freedom from political power-holders. A great deal of self-censorship still occurs within the exile media with regard to opposition political groups.

Nevertheless, Burmese journalists in exile have become increasingly insistent about using their press freedoms to promote media independence, despite challenges from opposition political groups. They have come to contest the view that press freedoms can be granted and argue that they must be continuously fought for and protected.

The transformation of the DVB since 1988 is indicative of changes in other exile media during this period. The DVB was established in 1992 as the official voice of the opposition leadership in exile, the National Coalition Government of the Union of Burma (NCGUB). From the start, there was contention among political leaders regarding control of the station, its budget, and programming.

After heated debate, the DVB staff was promised independence in its operations as long as it continued to open each broadcast with the statement, "This is the Democratic Voice of Burma of the National Coalition Government of the Union of Burma." The staff acknowledges the early unwritten policy never to criticize the opposition organizations. They saw DVB's role as informing people inside Burma about the human rights violations perpetrated by the regime, about international support for change in Burma, and about the opposition organizations' activities.

In those early days, many staffers were themselves politically affiliated, which made critical reporting on the opposition problematic. If they wrote about abuses within a rival organization, a process of accusations and counteraccusations would follow. They saw their job as working to reduce friction and forge consensus and believed that, under the circumstances, freedom of speech and total independence were inappropriate.

These attitudes changed gradually through training in journalism and ethics and ongoing discussions. The station dropped its opening NCGUB reference in 2002, and in 2008 the staff marked DVB's 15th anniversary by officially declaring the station's independence from the NCGUB. Despite the heated debate this provoked, the staff remained adamant that their biggest contribution toward democracy in Burma was to develop their skills as independent journalists beholden to no political groups. Like many other exile media groups, the DVB staff came to see the source of their legitimacy as the credibility gained from independent reporting, including critiquing opposition groups and their leaders when they deem it necessary.

The Saffron Revolution and Cyclone Nargis

The role of Burma's exile media in reporting on the tumultuous events of the 2007 Saffron Revolution and the 2008 devastation brought on by Cyclone Nargis had a paradoxically beneficial impact on the media's development. It improved their networks inside Burma and increased their profile and legitimacy among international media.

The 2007 uprising was sparked by skyrocketing fuel prices brought on by unannounced cuts in government fuel subsidies. By late September, tens of thousands of monks, nuns, and ordinary civilians took to the streets to call for dialogue between the military and the opposition National League for Democracy (NLD), and for the release of political prisoners, including Nobel Peace Prize Laureate and NLD leader Aung San Suu Kyi. International news reports dubbed the protests the "Saffron Revolution," referring to the saffron-colored robes associated with Buddhist monks, who took the lead in the demonstrations.

After a few days, the regime cracked down, and at least 80 people remained unaccounted for, with hundreds wounded and thousands arrested. In the wake of the protests, the government instituted martial law, banned foreign journalists from entering the country, and instituted a blackout on all news related to the protests. But unlike in 1988, when few journalists were able to document the protests and the military's violent reaction, this time courageous Burmese citizen reporters and bloggers made use of their cell phones, digital cameras, and Internet access to upload images of the protests and of soldiers beating monks and civilians. Bloggers provided regular updates that were then taken up by international and Burmese exile media and circulated worldwide.

The regime began targeting those on the streets with cameras. A disturbing cell phone video of the shooting death of Japanese photojournalist Kenji Nagai circulated widely in international news. At least 15 Burmese journalists were arrested on suspicion of sending images and information to foreign news agencies, as were artists, intellectuals, comedians, and singers accused of supporting the protestors.

At first, the regime did not realize the key role of the Internet in getting information out of the country so quickly, but once they understood, they cut off mobile phone services and blocked all Internet access for 2 weeks, after which censorship was tightened. The crackdown continued for months as the regime continued to arrest activists. In one high-profile case, computer expert and blogger Nay Phone Latt was arrested in January 2008 and sentenced to 20 years in prison.

In May 2008, tropical Cyclone Nargis hit Burma; it was the deadliest natural disaster in the country's recorded history. Heavy winds ripped off roofs, downed trees and power lines, and collapsed buildings, and huge waves swept away entire villages in the Irrawaddy Delta region. The official death toll was grossly underestimated as the regime tried to reduce the disaster's political impact by keeping foreign reporters and aid workers from reporting on the full extent of the damage. Aid workers critiqued the regime's secrecy, obsession with security, and restrictions that led to

delays in relief efforts and many more deaths than might have otherwise occurred.

For several weeks, foreign journalists and aid workers waited in vain in Thailand for visas after the regime had refused them entry. Nevertheless, reports emerged from inside Burma of authorities confiscating aid, arresting aid workers for refusing to hand over the aid, or demanding that aid recipients provide physical labor in return. Reports also accused the regime of forcing survivors out of emergency camps and back to their destroyed villages. Estimates were that as many as 130,000 may have been killed and 2 to 3 million left homeless.

Burma's exile media, as they already had networks established inside the country, were crucial in getting information out during both these tragedies. Their audiences skyrocketed. Editors of the more established media outlets—such as Aung Zaw of *The Irrawaddy,* Soe Myint of Mizzima News Agency, and Aye Chan Naing of the DVB—took on a new role as analysts for international news outlets.

The urgency of these events also resulted in increases in funding for some of these media. After the Saffron Revolution, the Mizzima News Agency was able to hire 10 new staff members and open a bigger office in Thailand. In the aftermath of Cyclone Nargis, Mizzima also opened a temporary Bangkok office to cover the work of aid agencies based there. These varied media were also able to strengthen their operations inside Burma, hiring new stringers and further developing the network of journalists inside and outside Burma that constitutes the foundation for the free media of Burma's future.

Lisa Brooten

See also Angry Buddhist Monk Phenomenon (Southeast Asia); Free Tibet Movement's Publicity; Independence Movement Media (Vietnam); Indigenous Media (Burma/Myanmar); Media Activism in the Kwangju Uprising (Korea); Social Movement Media, 1960s–1980s (Chile); Social Movement Media in 1987 Clashes (Korea)

Further Readings

Amnesty International. (2008, January 25). *Myanmar: Arrests increasing four months on.* http://www.amnesty.org/en/for-media/press-releases/myanmar-arrests-increasing-four-months-20080125

Aung Zaw. (2008). The cyber dissident. *The Irrawaddy, 16*(3), 24–26, 28–29.

Brooten, L. (2003). *Global communications, local conceptions: Human rights and the politics of communication among the Burmese opposition-in-exile.* Unpublished doctoral dissertation, Ohio University, Athens.

Danitz, T., & Strobel, W. P. (1999). *Networking dissent: Cyber-activists use the Internet to promote democracy in Burma.* Washington, DC: U.S. Institute for Peace.

Reporters Without Borders. (2008). *Burma—Annual report 2008.* http://www.rsf.org/article.php3?id_article=25624

Smith, M. (1999). *Burma: Insurgency and the politics of ethnicity* (2nd ed.). London: Zed Books.

Yeni. (2008). Burma: The censored land. *The Irrawaddy, 16*(3), 20–23.

Indian People's Theatre Association

As the cultural wing of the Communist Party of India, the Indian People's Theatre Association (IPTA), founded in 1943, had two main aims. One was to energize traditional rural and folk art forms; the second was, through them, to mirror contemporary social realities, promote the awareness of human rights, and spread national consciousness and patriotic fervor.

The founding of IPTA in 1943 was one of the attempts made by the Communist Party of India to fight for democracy by uniting the fragmented left-wing groups across India through an organized nationwide cultural movement. The need for such an organized cultural mass movement became extremely clear from severe social turbulences such as the Bengal famine (1942–1946). Owing to an intense scarcity of food in the rural areas of Bengal (because of the British colonial government's large-scale export of food grains to feed British troops in Europe and the Pacific theater), millions of farmers and laborers in rural Bengal died of starvation. The famine also brought many thousands of hungry folk from rural areas to big cities such as Calcutta. In October 1943 alone, 3,363 corpses had to be disposed of in Calcutta.

Such widespread devastation and man-made calamity shocked and enraged intellectuals and artists within and beyond Bengal. The rage and the protest against the colonial authorities began to be enacted through theater, music, poetry, and dance. Social and political agitation adopted cultural forms of expression.

IPTA's Work

The IPTA in Bengal, along with the Friends of Soviet Union and the Anti-Fascist Writers and Artists Association, began to operate in earnest from 46 Dharmatala Street in Calcutta. Its work reflected the domestic conflict between South Asian nationalism and British imperialism, but also the Soviet Union's mortal struggle against Nazi fascism. IPTA's agenda was achieved through a departure from the elitist model of performance that ruled conventional theaters in Bengal at the time. IPTA delved instead into Indigenous folk models of theater, music, and dance for inspiration and expression.

IPTA's constitution, adopted at the All India IPTA Conference held in Bombay in September 1943, explained its objectives as including the development of theater, music, dancing, and other fine arts and literature in India, "as an authentic expression of the social realities of our epoch and the inspirer of our people's efforts for the achievement of peace, democracy, and cultural progress." It also set itself educational objectives via schools, lectures, libraries, and exhibitions, and a publishing program for general education and artistic training.

The IPTA set up "squads" in eight Indian states—Bengal, Bihar, the United Provinces, Maharashtra, Gujarat, Andhra Pradesh, Kerala, and Karnataka—and at the national level an All-India Committee and eight state-level Provincial Committees. IPTA's key players were not only urban educated intellectuals but also folk artists and farmers. With its caption *People's Theatre Stars the People,* it roped in performers and artists from villages and, in its cultural programs, consistently featured folk songs and dances that engaged with contemporary sociopolitical themes from different states.

The IPTA Bengal Squad's active participants collaboratively created some startling productions in the 1940s. A major milestone in the history of Bengali theater was reached through the staging of playwright Bijon Bhattacharya's *Nabanna* in October 1944. Set against the background of the Bengal famine, the play had as its protagonist the character of Pradhan Samaddar, a farmer, and followed the turbulent events that he and his family faced during the food crisis. The first staging of *Nabanna* resulted in a run of 35 performances at theaters and public gatherings in Bengal, often to audiences of several thousands.

Also in 1944, *Bhookha Hai Bengal* (Hungry Bengal), produced by IPTA-Bombay and choreographed by Shanti Bardhan, was performed across numerous towns and cities in Gujarat and Maharashtra. It is said that during one of its performances in Bombay, attended by film industry stalwarts, the leading actor-director Prithviraj Kapoor was so moved that he got up on stage, announced "I must do something for hungry Bengal" and with his cap in hand, begged for donations from the audience. He and his colleagues raised 20,000 rupees for famine victims in Bengal (approximately 250 British pounds or 370 U.S. dollars, a considerable sum in 1940s India).

Bhookha Hai Bengal became a milestone in Indian modern dance presentation, making a substantial impact on the consciousness of a pre-Independence India that was grappling with severe social problems. Other IPTA dance productions by Bardhan, such as *Spirit of India* (1945) and *India Immortal* (1946), as well as plays performed across several Indian states, confirmed IPTA's reputation as one of India's most vociferous cultural projects, with a strong commitment to contemporary social issues.

Prarthana Purkayastha

See also Dance as Social Activism (South Asia); Performance Art and Social Movement Media: Augusto Boal; Sarabhai Family and the Darpana Academy (India); Social Movement and Modern Dance (Bengal); Street Theater (India)

Further Readings

Bardhan, G. (Ed.). (1992). *Rhythm incarnate: Tribute to Shanti Bardhan*. New Delhi, India: Abhinav Publications.
Bharucha, R. (1983). *Rehearsals of revolution: The political theatre of Bengal*. Honolulu: University of Hawai'i Press.
Bhatia, N. (2004). *Acts of authority, acts of resistance: Theatre and politics in colonial and postcolonial India*. Ann Arbor: University of Michigan Press.
Chatterjee, M. (2004). *Theatre beyond the threshold: Colonialism, nationalism and the Bengali stage 1905–1947*. New Delhi, India: Indialog Publications.

INDIGENOUS MEDIA (AUSTRALIA)

Australia's 517,200 Aboriginal and Torres Strait Islander people make up 2.5% of the population. Key social indicators reveal their conditions remain well below the non-Indigenous population. They have won access to their own forms of media only following persistent campaigns and applying technological creativity and ingenuity.

The Indigenous Press

The first identified publication produced by an Aboriginal organization was the *Aboriginal* or *Flinders Island Chronicle*, published in 1836. More than 100 years later, the first known Torres Strait Islander publication was a typewritten newspaper published in 1938. Few details exist of others until the 1950s, although many small, community-based newsletters had "spread the word." Some used local Aboriginal languages and became a resource for the language renaissance that emerged from the Homelands and Outstation movement in the Northern Territory and North Queensland in the late 1970s. Aboriginal land council newsletters increased dramatically during the land rights protests of the late 1960s and 1970s and have remained an important source of news on these issues. Also in the 1970s and 1980s Aboriginal responses to racist media representations took the form of demands for some control over their representation.

The perceived threat to languages and cultures in remote Indigenous communities from satellite television set the publishing wheels in motion again in the 1980s with a wide array of newsletters and magazines emerging from communities and government departments. The Northern Land Council in Darwin began publishing the monthly newspaper, *Land Rights News*, in 1976 as a roneoed newsletter, and this remains the longest-running

Indigenous newspaper in Australia. Throughout the 1980s, *Black Nation*, edited by Ross Watson, raised Aboriginal community concerns surrounding Australia's 1988 Bicentenary and Expo in Brisbane. Watson went on to become the first station manager of Murri Radio 4AAA in Brisbane in 1993—the first state capital city Indigenous community station.

The 1990s saw a resurgence in Aboriginal newspapers led by the successful Lismore-based monthly, the *Koori Mail*. Another regular publication was *Land Rights Queensland*, published by the Foundation for Aboriginal and Islander Research Action (FAIRA) Corporation from 1994 until 2001. The *National Indigenous Times* was launched in 2002 and arguably remains the most critical of the three current Indigenous-focused newspapers published regularly. A lack of access to culturally relevant media training has meant that there are few Indigenous people working in the Indigenous print media industry either as journalists or in sales and marketing. It is not unusual, therefore, to find non-Indigenous Australians occupying key roles in these papers.

The Rise of Broadcasting

It was not until the late 1970s that Indigenous broadcasters began to gain access to the airwaves, largely through the emerging community radio sector (then called public radio). The first Aboriginal radio program went to air on 5UV in Adelaide in 1972. By the early 1980s, Indigenous broadcasters were involved in community radio stations in the Northern Territory, Queensland, and New South Wales. During this period, Indigenous broadcasters also began broadcasting weekly on the Australian Broadcasting Corporation's (ABC) regional services and through the Special Broadcasting Service (SBS).

More than 100 licensed Remote Indigenous Broadcasting Services (RIBS)—small radio and television stations—serve their audiences in remote parts of Australia with a further 25 radio stations in regional and urban areas. Each represents a local Indigenous media association and many broadcast in local languages. Most of the small, remote stations are engaged in re-transmitting available satellite programming, with a handful having access to sufficient resources to enable local

production. The Central Australian Aboriginal Media Association (CAAMA) was one of the earliest of these and has been an important role model. In 1985, CAAMA became the first Aboriginal community station in Australia. Since then, it expanded to become a major production house for Indigenous audio and video. Several other regional Indigenous media groups have also become major production hubs.

The ABC established working relationships with regional and remote Indigenous media associations throughout the 1980s, leading to several applying for their own community radio licenses. The ABC employs Indigenous broadcasters to produce two national Indigenous radio programs— *Awaye!* (a word from the Central Australian Arrernte language which means "Listen!" or "Listen up!") and *Speaking Out*—and a television program, *Message Stick*.

Policy Polemics

The federal government decision to adopt satellite broadcasting for remote and regional Australia in the 1980s raised the ire of Indigenous people. There was little negotiation with remote communities where English was the second, third, or fourth language. The federal government held a series of regional inquiries, setting up four Remote Commercial Television Services (RCTS), with minor concessions to produce culturally-relevant programming. The successful licensee for the Central Zone RCTS was a consortium of Aboriginal organizations known as Imparja (an Arrernte word which means "footprints") Television. It began broadcasting from Alice Springs in Central Australia in 1988.

The opposition to satellite television from remote communities triggered two key investigations into Aboriginal media uses—Eric Willmot's *Out of the Silent Land* and Eric Michaels' *The Aboriginal Invention of Television*. Michaels based himself in the remote community of Yuendumu, 300 kilometers from Alice Springs, and worked with the Warlpiri to set up a pirate television station, showing that Indigenous people could produce (or "invent") their own kind of television. A similar venture was underway at the same time with Anangu-Pitjantjatjara-Yankunytjatjara peoples in Pukutja (Ernabella), about 800 kilometers south. During the 1980s, each community amassed around 1000 hours of locally produced videotapes of social and cultural activities, most of which were re-broadcast to their local audiences.

These "pirate" television activities influenced the federal government to introduce the Broadcasting for Remote Aboriginal Communities Scheme (BRACS), designed to give communities some control over incoming satellite television signals—in theory, at least. Around 80 targeted remote communities were given a package of equipment allowing them to switch off undesirable programs and to "broadcast" their own. However, there was no money for training or maintenance, and BRACS units quickly fell into a state of disrepair in most communities.

The scheme, while good in theory, was mismanaged from the start, with some suggesting it was set up to fail. It remains in a modified form today but the vast majority of communities with a BRACS unit now use it simply to watch mainstream television—precisely what it was set up to avoid. By the early 1990s, a study revealed that just 20 of the 250 Indigenous languages spoken in Australia at the time of the British invasion were being actively transmitted to and used by children.

The Indigenous media sector in Australia developed in a virtual policy vacuum. One underlying problem was Indigenous media's ongoing heavy dependence on government funds. The first national review of the Indigenous media sector in 1998, *Digital Dreaming*, made 131 recommendations, including the establishment of a dedicated Indigenous broadcasting program production fund. Two years later, the Australian Government's Productivity Commission publicly acknowledged for the first time that Indigenous media were fulfilling a dual role—providing a primary level of service for communities and acting as a cultural bridge between Indigenous and non-Indigenous people.

In 1991, the community at Yuendumu, along with three other communities in the Tanami Desert, experimented with compressed videoconferencing and satellite technologies creating the Tanami Network. Later expanded into the Outback Digital Network, it was used to mediate a wide range of social and cultural activity, including successfully reuniting prisoners in Alice Springs prison with their families many hundreds of kilometers away. The cumbersome and high-maintenance videoconference units have given way to desktop

technologies but at its peak, the network linked around 60 remote Indigenous communities across Australia.

In more recent times, the convergence of broadcasting, computing, and telephony has meant Indigenous communities have had to become familiar with digital technologies, which they have used enthusiastically and creatively to enable communication largely still based on traditional frameworks. Interestingly, some of the "old" technologies like high frequency radio have been enlisted again because they are cheap, trouble-free, and enable communication over vast distances. In the Anangu-Pitjantjatjara-Yankunytjatjara Lands in Central Australia, it is common for such old and new technologies to be melded to meet the needs of local communities.

The Sector Today

Three national Indigenous newspapers target diverse audiences across the country and there is a growing Indigenous online presence, but community radio and television remain the major communications media for Aboriginal and Torres Strait Islander people. In addition, there are two Indigenous commercial stations—radio 6LN in Carnarvon in Western Australia—and Imparja Television, based in Alice Springs. Two Indigenous organizations in Western Australia operate semi-commercial broadcasting licenses—Goolarri Television, owned by the Broome Aboriginal Media Association and Ngarda TV, run by the Juluwarlu Aboriginal Corporation in Roebourne.

There are two Indigenous community radio networks—the National Indigenous Radio Service (NIRS) and the National Indigenous News Service (NINS). A regular Indigenous Community Television service (ICTV) started in 2001 broadcasting on a shoestring budget around 20 hours a day of locally produced television, using a spare Imparja Television channel. It included contributions from the Remote Indigenous Broadcasting Services (RIBS) PY Media, Warlpiri Media, Pilbara and Kimberley Aboriginal Media (PAKAM), Ngaanyatjarra Media, Top End Aboriginal Bush Broadcasters' Association (TEABBA), and other local producers.

Following a 2005 federal policy decision, in July 2007 the National Indigenous Television service (NITV) controversially supplanted ICTV by taking over the only available community television channel in remote and regional Australia. In 2010, the majority of Australian audiences could access NITV only through pay TV or a free-to-air community channel in regional and remote areas. NITV was supported by an A$48 million federal government initiative, but over 4 years. This amount paled when compared with the most recent *annual* revenue for the Aboriginal Peoples Television Network in Canada (C$36 million) and Māori Television in New Zealand (NZ$34 million). The significance of Aboriginal and Torres Strait Islander languages and cultures are ignored in Australia's Broadcasting Services Act—another key departure from similar legislation in Canada and New Zealand.

Community Uses of Indigenous Media

The first comprehensive audience study of the Indigenous broadcasting sector, completed in 2007, confirmed that where local radio and video production were being undertaken regularly, these media represented an essential service for Indigenous communities. Indigenous audiences across Australia confirmed that their local media play a critical role in maintaining social networks. They saw their media playing an important educational role as well as representing a primary source of news and information, apart from word of mouth.

It may be that the Indigenous media sector is the most effective in fostering reconciliation between Indigenous and non-Indigenous Australia by promoting cross-cultural dialogue. Most Australians are unaware of the burgeoning Indigenous music industry, and it is Indigenous radio, in particular, that has given voice to countless musicians. Indigenous media in Australia continue to represent critical cultural resources for Aboriginal and Torres Strait Islander peoples.

Michael Meadows

See also Adivasi Movement Media (India); Eland Ceremony, Abatwa People's (Southern Africa); First Peoples' Media (Canada); Indigenous Media (Burma/Myanmar); Indigenous Media in Latin America; Indigenous Peoples' Media; Indigenous Radio Stations (México); Māori Media and Social Movements (Aotearoa/New Zealand)

Further Readings

Ginsburg, F. (1991). Indigenous media: Faustian contract or global village? *Cultural Anthropology, 6*(1), 92–112.

Langton, M. (1993). *"Well, I heard it on the radio and I saw it on the television": An essay for the Australian Film Commission on the politics and aesthetics of filmmaking by and about Aboriginal people and things.* Sydney, Australia: Australian Film Commission.

Langton, M., & Kirkpatrick, B. (1979). A listing of Aboriginal publications. *Aboriginal History, 3*(2), 120–127.

Meadows, M., Forde, S. Ewart, J., & Foxwell, K. (2007). *Community media matters: An audience study of the Australian community broadcasting sector.* Brisbane, Australia: Griffith University. Retrieved October 10, 2008, from http://www.cbfonline.org.au

Meadows, M., & Molnar, H. (2002). Bridging the gaps: Towards a history of Indigenous media in Australia. *Media History, 8*(1), 9–20.

Michaels, E. (1986). *The Aboriginal invention of television: Central Australia 1982–1985.* Canberra, Australia: Australian Institute of Aboriginal Studies.

Molnar, H., & Meadows, M. (2001). *Songlines to satellites: Indigenous communication in Australia, the South Pacific and Canada.* Leichhardt, Australia: Pluto Press.

Rose, M, (Ed.). (1996). *For the record: 160 years of Aboriginal print journalism.* St. Leonards, Australia: Allen & Unwin.

INDIGENOUS MEDIA (BURMA/MYANMAR)

Indigenous media are increasingly important in the multiethnic opposition to the brutal military dictatorship in Burma (renamed Myanmar by the regime in 1989). These media reflect the need of Burma's ethnic minority groups to protect themselves against the regime's assimilationist and genocidal policies, but also to avoid being overlooked by dissidents from the ethnic Burman majority.

Although Burmese Indigenous media have existed in various forms for decades, they began to flourish in the mid-1990s, produced primarily, although not exclusively, from locations along

Burma's borders. Several of these media have become significant voices, putting the Burma's Indigenous groups "on the map." They also complicate notions of "Indigenous media" by incorporating information from a variety of non-Indigenous sources, and by actively cooperating with nongovernmental organizations (NGOs) and others outside their communities.

Indigenous Groups, Violence, and the Burmese Democracy Movement

More than 100 different languages and dialects have been identified in Burma, though reliable comprehensive data do not exist. The 1974 constitution recognized seven ethnic states—Chin, Kachin, Karen, Kayah (Karenni), Mon, Rakhine (Arakan), and Shan. There are other large minority groups in the country as well, including the Lahu, Naga, Pa-O, and Wa, and Burma is also home to populations of Chinese, Tamils, Bengalis, and others of South Asian origin. Estimates, albeit contentious, suggest that ethnic majority Burmans comprise approximately 69% of the population.

When the British colonized Burma, they divided it into Ministerial Burma in the central regions and the Frontier Areas, in which Indigenous peoples remained semiautonomous. The British used Indigenous minority soldiers to police the Burman majority who were agitating for independence, which sharpened tensions after Burma's 1948 independence. In 1962, a coup brought the military to power under the leadership of General Ne Win, who led the country into isolation while the military waged war against the country's ethnic minority populations.

After decades of mismanagement led the United Nations to accord Burma Least Developed Country (LDC) status in 1987, massive student-led street demonstrations broke out in 1988. Even conservative estimates claim the regime slaughtered thousands in response. Many students and other dissident leaders fled to the country's border areas, where they met the Indigenous peoples, who had long been struggling against the military regime. Initial mistrust, caused by decades of regime propaganda that had stereotyped the ethnic minorities as ruthless and disloyal, eventually gave way to cooperation built upon the recognition of a similar goal: an end to military rule. This led to the birth

of Burma's contemporary multiethnic democracy movement.

However, the Indigenous groups realized that despite their common enemy, their interests also differed. The Burman groups, struggling primarily for democracy, were not especially concerned with the non-Burmans' desire to protect their right to self-determination. Some Burmans even perceived this agenda as a distraction from pressing issues of political change.

It is not surprising, then, that a key motivating factor in the development of Indigenous media was to provide Indigenous peoples with a means to express themselves freely regarding concerns they faced as minority groups. For some, it provided an opportunity for their people to break the cycle of fear that prevented them from speaking openly.

That fear was all too real. In 2008, Human Rights Watch noted the Burmese military's ongoing attacks against civilians in ethnic conflict areas, forced labor, sexual violence against women and girls, extrajudicial killings, torture and beatings, and confiscation of land and property. More than 40,000 civilians were displaced that year by counterinsurgency and security operations, adding to an estimated 450,000 or more internally displaced people in eastern Burma. The Burmese army and paramilitaries used land mines extensively, including near civilian settlements and food production sites.

Self-Determination and Other Goals of Indigenous Media

In the years since 1988, both the Burman dissidents and the Indigenous groups have established new media in exile, operating outside the constraints of the strict censorship inside Burma. But the Burman dissidents had an advantage. Unlike the discourse of self-determination used by Indigenous groups, the Burmans' discourse of democracy and human rights fit comfortably with Western foreign policy concerns. As a result, most Indigenous media in the 1990s and 2000s in the border areas or in exile were founded several years later than the ethnically "unmarked" and better funded exile media founded by those who fled Burma after the 1988 uprising.

Nevertheless, Indigenous media developed significantly since then, honing their skills and establishing websites. These have made their news reports more accessible to other Burmese independent media and to international audiences. They have worked to educate outsiders about the impact of foreign investment, such as the likely effect on local communities of the project by the Unocal and Total corporations to pipe Burmese natural gas to Thailand.

By providing a forum for discussion of issues affecting their groups, the Indigenous media perform what Viswanath and Arora call the "cultural transmission" function, helping revive or reinforce ethnic identity and pass it to the next generation. As only religious groups are allowed to teach non-Burmese languages in Sunday school or in the monasteries, many groups producing ethnic media strive to preserve literacy in their national languages for cultural survival. Saw Thaw Thi, an editor of the Karen journal *Kway K'Lu* (named for a traditional horn used to communicate between villages), explained to this writer that they publish the journal in order to raise the level of Karen literature and culture in Karen society.

Karen literature used to be taught in Karen schools but, because of restrictions on ethnic language teaching, is now prohibited. *Kway K'Lu* provides a place for its development, through articles on traditional cultural practices, the retelling of old stories, and the creation of new ones. Cartoons are another way *Kway K'Lu* transmits traditional values. According to Saw Thaw Thi, many older Karen are alarmed that the standards of Karen literature have been declining, and that many of the Karen young people do not seem to appreciate their culture. Like other Indigenous media, *Kway K'Lu* tries to address these concerns.

Indigenous media also educate their publics about international political events and their relevance to Burma, and sustain their audiences' motivation to improve their own situation and oppose the regime. Some of these media have been reformatted to fit in a back pocket or have modeled their covers to look like legal Burmese publications so they are more easily smuggled inside Burma. Indigenous media involve their communities in the production process to varying degrees, and they encourage feedback.

From Human Rights to Human Interest

In the aftermath of the 1988 uprising, funding for human rights abuse documentation and for the promotion of Burmese independent media led to opportunities for Burman and Indigenous groups for training in Western-style journalism, new office space, and access to new information and communication technologies. However, training sessions for Indigenous groups in exile initially focused on documenting human rights abuses rather than journalism, as this documentation could be useful for lobbying international organizations and for posting on the many websites devoted to human rights violations in Burma.

Many Indigenous media developed out of these efforts. They outlined the Universal Declaration of Human Rights and discussed the rights of women, children, ethnic minorities, and Indigenous peoples. They also taught their audiences about democracy and how it functions in other countries, and about patterns of genocide or ethnic cleansing not only in Burma but elsewhere in the world as well.

By the early 2000s, however, stimulated by training and pressure from funding agencies, many Indigenous media organizations began to expand their focus. Journalism training encouraged them to think about their long-term viability and to work to gain larger audiences by developing more diverse and creative content. Many felt that relentlessly recording the regime's abuses had come to be merely demoralizing for audiences. Although important for advocacy campaigns targeting the international community, that unitary focus also reinforced images of Indigenous peoples as simply victims.

Nevertheless, while Indigenous media have made great strides, they still lag behind the more developed, ethnically "unmarked" Burmese independent media in terms of skills, funding, and overall recognition. An important effort to address these concerns has been the development of the Burma News International network, consisting largely of ethnic minority media groups.

Burma News International

Burma News International (BNI) was formed in 2003 to promote Burma-related news in South Asia and Southeast Asia and to open up discussion among media groups and help support their development, especially those with a focus on Burma's

Indigenous communities. BNI's mission includes creating knowledge and understanding about the different ethnic nationalities and regions of Burma. BNI began with four founding members and has grown to include ten, eight representing ethnic minorities: Kaladan Press (Rohingya), Khonumthung News Group (Chin), Narinjara News (Arakan), Kachin News Group, Independent Mon News Agency (IMNA), Kao Wao News Group (Mon), Kantarawaddy Times (Karenni), and Shan Herald Agency for News. The two ethnically "unmarked" members are Mizzima News and Network Media Group. BNI functions by appointing a member journalist as duty editor, who is responsible for checking stories posted by member organizations, writing editorials, and overseeing the weekly news package, all distributed through the BNI website.

BNI has played a key role in helping Indigenous media groups obtain funding and training opportunities and in raising their profile through the network website. BNI members are committed to assisting its least developed members. Each group has reported benefiting from membership and acknowledges that perhaps the most exciting aspect of the network is its unparalleled potential as a collective. Working together, these groups offer the most comprehensive media coverage of the country, given their unparalleled reach into the rural areas to bring to light stories other media are unable to provide.

The best example is the first collective project undertaken by BNI. This was a nationwide survey conducted in 13 of the country's 14 administrative subdivisions, including in ethnic minority areas not normally researched. The survey assessed public attitudes toward the national referendum on the military-backed constitution scheduled for May 10, 2008. The survey was reportedly the most comprehensive and statistically representative poll of eligible voters ever, consisting of questionnaires and face-to-face interviews with more than 2,000 Burmese voters, including farmers, traders, day workers, students, and housewives. The results showed a low level of awareness regarding the details of the constitution and widespread resistance to the coercive nature of both the constitution drafting process and the referendum procedure.

On May 2, Cyclone Nargis slammed into Burma. This was the largest natural disaster in Burma's recorded history, yet despite the devastation, the military regime pushed on with the referendum, postponing it only in the hardest hit areas of the country. As widely expected, the military regime announced that more than 92% of voters had approved the constitution. Unfortunately, the devastation of Cyclone Nargis overshadowed the importance of BNI's pioneering collective research effort. Nevertheless, the survey demonstrated the network's potential to poll the opinions of Indigenous peoples in hard-to-reach areas of this troubled country, where people quietly struggle and succeed daily in surviving the direst conditions with creativity and dignity.

Lisa Brooten

See also *Adivasi* Movement Media (India); First Peoples' Media (Canada); Independent Media (Burma/Myanmar); Indigenous Media (Australia); Indigenous Media in Latin America; Māori Media and Social Movements (Aotearoa/New Zealand); Zapatista Media (México)

Further Readings

Brooten, L. (2008). "Media as our mirror": Indigenous media in Burma (Myanmar). In P. Wilson & M. Stewart (Eds.), *Global Indigenous media: Cultures, practices and politics* (pp. 111–127). Raleigh, NC: Duke University Press.

Burma News International: http://www.bnionline.net

Human Rights Watch. (2008). *Burma: Events of 2008.* http://www.hrw.org/en/node/79297

Smith, M. (1999). *Burma: Insurgency and the politics of ethnicity* (2nd ed.). London: Zed Books.

Steinberg, D. I. (2001). *Burma: The state of Myanmar.* Washington, DC: Georgetown University Press.

Viswanath, K., & Arora, P. (2000). Ethnic media in the United States: An essay on their role in integration, assimilation and social control. *Mass Communication and Society, 3*(1), 39–56.

INDIGENOUS MEDIA IN LATIN AMERICA

Among the most impressive and radical transformations in Latin America since the 1990s is the emergence of new Indigenous movements. As of

2010, the Indigenous population was 50 million, constituted by more than 400 culturally diverse nations, groups, or tribes, inhabiting the big metropolises as well as some of the most varied, remote, and rich ecosystems. Many are farmers, and several groups live in ways they have done for centuries. Many others are urban professionals, global citizens, and international experts in different fields of knowledge. Together they have generated a great variety of media projects over recent decades, projects which, like such Indigenous movements elsewhere, have done much to reassert Indigenous rights and maintain Indigenous cultures as living expressions of distinctive values.

The Resurgence of Indigenous Self-Assertion

Until recently, research on cultural pluralism had pictured Latin America as an exception, where Indigenous and ethnic groups did not mobilize politically; where ethnic diversity did not give way to sustained ethnic violence; where states did not explicitly target ethnic groups and pass minority-ethnic legislation. However, the resurgence of Indigenous social movements in Latin America post-1992 has proved the contrary.

These movements are diverse, yet they all indicate a resurgence of a latent ethnic consciousness. Most of the 18th century saw notable Indigenous people's rebellions and resistance movements, such as the uprisings of 1780 in Perú led by Túpac Amaru II, and 1781 in Bolivia under the lead of Túpac Katari. In the early 19th century, and during the 1910–1920 Mexican Revolution and the 1952 Bolivian Revolution, Indigenous organizations played a crucial role in independence struggles across the continent. Still, until the early 1990s, the historical silencing and immobilization of Indigenous resistance movements is perhaps a core feature of Latin America, with a legacy of dictatorships and, more recently, neoliberal policies serving to compound the issue.

Indigenous social movements began resurging strongly in Latin America after the "commemoration" of the 5th century of European "discovery" of the Americas in 1992 and the Zapatista uprising in Chiapas, México, in 1994. Paradoxically, the immense media coverage of the Zapatista struggle concealed other similar cultural and ethnic mobilizations surfacing in other countries. Their vigor in Ecuador, Bolivia, Guatemala, and México, challenging and sometimes directly impacting national politics, powerfully illustrated Indigenous peoples' self-reassertion into the Latin American states' mental maps. México, Perú, Guatemala, Colombia, Venezuela, Bolivia, and Ecuador have formally acknowledged the multicultural base of their societies. In Guatemala, Ecuador, and Bolivia—and, more recently, Colombia—these mobilizations clearly showed the eruption of Indigenous discourses, which challenged centuries of imposed silence and racist denial.

The Indigenous demands are complex because they demand a revision of the very idea of a nation-state, of development, and of multiculturalism. In some countries, for example, the demands are as simple as seeking the state's legal recognition of Indigenous peoples as nations (*pueblos*) and not just ethnic minorities (Costa Rica, Chile); in other cases there have been fully fleshed demands for autonomy and self-determination (México, Ecuador, Bolivia, and, later on, Chile). In Ecuador, strong Indigenous organization has been critical in deposing two presidents. In 2005, Bolivia elected Evo Morales, its first Indigenous head of state.

Indigenous organizations have targeted their demands to more political participation and the rethinking of the whole democratic apparatus of the countries, demanding pluricultural states. This is also the case in Perú, Bolivia, Colombia, and México, where the national constitutions have been amended to confirm the pluricultural foundation of these nations. Most Indigenous demands also address the access to, and control of, natural resources (Nicaragua, Panamá, Perú, Brasil), with the right to be consulted and to veto multinational corporations operating in protected areas. This includes protection from bio-piracy and collective rights to land and territory. Other complex demands deal with the right to intercultural bilingual education (Chile, Perú, Paraguay, Guatemala) and intercultural health policies (Perú, Panamá), while others also deal with specific Indigenous women's rights (Guatemala), Indigenous territories (Brasil), collective intellectual property rights, and the right to independent access to and ownership of media outlets.

Indigenous Media Projects

Despite the renewed visibility of Indigenous affairs in transnational politics, mainstream national media in Latin America, both public and commercial, do not offer spaces for participation for and by Indigenous peoples, or even basic mechanisms for intercultural communication between Indigenous and non-Indigenous societies. The highly concentrated commercial media in Latin America impede the open communication environment needed to enable civil society, especially Indigenous groups, to participate in the political deliberations that affect them. Indigenous issues continue to be stereotyped as folkloric or criminalized as civil disobedience that allegedly endangers the internal security of the rather still unstable Latin American democracies.

With commercial and public national media failing to open up spaces for Indigenous participation, Indigenous peoples have created their own networks, including radio, video, and online media, and have actively appropriated media narratives and technologies as practices of self-representation and self-determination in an active process of making and representing culture from their own perspective. An Indigenous video movement has emerged strongly since the 1990s, particularly in México, Bolivia, Brasil, and Ecuador, and to a lesser extent in Guatemala, Colombia, Perú, Chile, Venezuela, and Argentina, which exists in parallel and in relation to the many mechanisms by which Indigenous nations have been engaging directly in global policy and governance processes since the 1980s. In creating, imagining, and reinventing traditional social relationships through the moving image, Indigenous organizations have found new forms of cultural resistance and revitalization. At the heart of the emerging Indigenous video movement, we see a process grounded in the local struggles for political self-determination, cultural and linguistic autonomy, and legal recognition, with potentially transnational and pan-American implications.

Indigenous media now occupy a significant place not only within local cultures and communities but also in national and global media discourses, policies, industries, and funding structures. Many scholars situate this in relation to broader cultural activism, arguing that media of "minoritized people" may be understood as counterhegemonic cultural production in response to dominant mass media forms.

Indigenous media are at once a form of political activism, an emerging genre, and a practice of intercultural dialogue. Indigenous media has also become an independent field of cultural production by and for Indigenous peoples, situated at the crossroads of contemporary politics of cultural identity and representation. As such, they challenge the modern binary logic of self/other, and the politics of representation of cultural purities, between the so-called traditional and modern.

At the 2003 World Summit on the Information Society in Geneva, for instance, the Indigenous organizations present quickly and clearly critiqued the main documents that came out of the summit. They pointed out that they failed to include the fundamental proposals made during the preparatory meetings, especially regarding the urgency of developing autonomous Indigenous communication platforms. Like other organizations present at the summit, Indigenous groups also emphatically criticized the technocratic and deterministic view assumed in the Plan of Action, where the engine of social change seemed to have been defined as digital information and communications technology access, rather than more basic human rights and freedoms.

In the larger picture, Indigenous video calls for the decolonization of media practice, typically influenced by the dominant industry's filmmaking and videomaking conventions or by non-Indigenous producers, funding agencies, and NGOs. Indigenous organizations and individuals have been creating distinctive media projects, structures, and networks that demonstrate how effective coordinated local mobilization and transnational networking might be in allowing Indigenous peoples to challenge the "indigenist" rhetoric of development, modernization, and citizenship officially perpetuated all across Latin America.

Indigenous video production in Latin America is positioning itself as a field of cultural production separate from national cinema, popular and community video, and tactical media practices. It inhabits its own representational space and is starting to create parallel circuits of production, dissemination, and reception of cultural materials, which, for some, indicates the end of the hegemony of the literate and the beginning of decolonizing the intellect. In many ways, the appropriation of video has functioned as a sort of "reverse conquest," where Indigenous organizations and community media producers have been slowly conquering back their rights to self-representation.

The Coordinadora Latinoamericana de Cine y Comunicación de los Pueblos Indígenas (CLACPI; Latin American Council of Indigenous Film and Communication) is an organization created in 1985, which now serves as a network of Indigenous media organizations and as a biannual film and video festival. It has been critical in creating a discursive space for Indigenous media in Latin America, generating along the way new spaces of participation within national media discourses (production, circulation, and reception). From 1996 onward, it has been a network primarily run by Indigenous communicators, and since 2008, it has been directed by Jeannette Paillan, a prominent Mapuche media-maker from Chile.

The CLACPI festivals constitute a fluid Indigenous mediascape for a growing Indigenous imagined community. In Bolivia, for example, a national plan for Indigenous communication has been developed by several Indigenous and non-Indigenous civil society organizations since 1996, with funding from European development agencies. It has remained completely independent from national government and is managed principally by Indigenous organizations such as Coordinadora Audiovisual Indígena Originaria de Bolivia (CAIB; Bolivian Indigenous Media Organization). The proposed new Bolivian policy framework for autonomous Indigenous communication is a broad-based vision that contrasts notably with other realities in Latin America. In several countries, there has been concerted civic action to reform the media, but very few cases among these have incorporated Indigenous perspectives or the need to integrate the "Indigenous question" into national media policy reform.

Mapuche Media in Chile

Evolving Mapuche communication practices in the past couple of decades have roots in historical contradictions but have been prompted by the re-democratization that followed military rule in 1990. They also coincide with what has been described as a new pan-American movement of Indigenous reemergence in Latin America. Mapuche media are firmly established in local social solidarities and have had a remarkable impact on local communities. Today they also play an important part in challenging both national and state policy and law as well as corporate commercial media discourses and practices. They are an important element of new civil society media formations and, more importantly, Mapuche media practices open up new discursive avenues from which to challenge corporations' and the state's ever-increasing shrinkage of spaces for meaningful debate.

Given how Chilean media have historically included and excluded groups of citizens, the new public social space formed by Mapuche video activists and online networks is increasingly becoming a small-scale counter public sphere in John Downey and Natalie Fenton's terms. Mapuche communities, particularly urban ones, are at the center of a particular historical moment during which central government ideals of nation building confront them. Media makers are an integral part of this moment, with a responsibility to help articulate reinvigorated Mapuche social formations at the public, national level.

Alternative media have become a major zone for several Mapuche professionals. A new mediated Mapuche imaginary constructed from within was evident in videos such as Jeannette Paillan's *Wallmapu* (the name of the Mapuche nation/territory, the size of Portugal). The same is true of the newspaper *Azkintuwe* (The Lookout), which provides alternative and citizen journalism by and for Mapuche audiences in both Chile and Argentina. Both draw attention to the ways in which Mapuche cultural resistance and desire for a better society are projected through communication technologies. Paillan's documentary is the first audiovisual countertelling of official histories of contact and colonization of the Mapuche, made by a Mapuche filmmaker, in which a different ideological construct of the Wallmapu (past and present) is presented. In similar form, *Azkintuwe* grew out of a counterinformation collective called Lientur. It became an indispensable alternative voice in the formation of alternative and counterpublics, emphasizing Mapuche culture and progressive politics; it is also becoming a news agency reporting from the field and an online news service.

More importantly, the appropriation of technologies of imagination and information is a self-conscious political process. Paillan has insisted she makes films to try to help alter, not just describe, Mapuche realities and that she would be delighted to make fewer films were Mapuche realities to change. But perhaps the most important impact of an emergent Indigenous public opinion is that the peoples, historically defined by their conquerors' discourses, are now developing the means to create their own self-definition.

This new Indigenous activist imaginary expressed through communications media provides political resources and values—not only through internal mobilization and solidarity but also via transnational communication and cross-cultural communication. The Mapuche diaspora around the world was quite significant, due to the particular situation of several hundred Mapuche individuals—including political activists, farmers, and professionals—whom the dictatorship exiled in the 1970s. The development of a Mapuche "activist imaginary" through Internet use has become, in the words of Faye Ginsburg, a renewed "resource of hope," raising fresh issues about citizenship and the formation of the public sphere inside conventional thinking on polity and civil society.

For Mapuche activists, media-makers, political leaders, and intellectuals, video and the Internet have started to be conceived as active instruments of intervention in Chilean national politics. An intricate network of websites has made possible the circulation of images not available anywhere else—the circulation of informed ideas, debates, and public opinion. Perhaps the main feature of this transformation is the reconceptualization of Wallmapu, a complex concept that embraces the notion of nation (*pueblo*) in terms of not only cultural identity but also, in certain cases, the demand for political and territorial autonomy.

In Chile, these demands arise primarily from Mapuche intellectuals based in big urban center like Temuco, Concepción, and Santiago, or activist organizations in rural areas like Lumaco, Arauco, and Malleco. In any case, they formulate a specific political framework for understanding the current situation of Indigenous radio, the emergence of Indigenous video and the Internet, as well as a wider revitalization of Indigenous cultural politics in general, characterized by a wave of Mapuche poetry, video art, music, and traditional arts and crafts.

Juan Francisco Salazar

See also COR TV, 2006, Oaxaca (México); First Peoples' Media (Canada); Indigenous Media (Australia); Indigenous Media (Burma/Myanmar); Indigenous Radio Stations (México); Māori Media and Social Movements (Aetearoa/New Zealand); Zapatista Media (México)

Further Readings

Coordinadora Latinoamericana de Cine y Comunicación de los Pueblos Indígenas (CLACPI; Latin American Council of Indigenous Film and Communication): http://www.clacpi.org

Ginsburg, F. (2000). Resources of hope. In C. Smith & G. K. Ward (Eds.), *Indigenous cultures in an interconnected world* (pp. 27–47). Sydney, Australia: Allen & Unwin.

Native Networks/Redes Indigenas: http://www.nativenetworks.si.edu

Paillan, J. (Writer/Director). (2002). *Wallmapu* [Documentary film; in Spanish & Mapudungun]. Santiago, Chile: Lulul-Mawidha.

Salazar, J. F., & Cordova, A. (2008). Imperfect media: The poetics of Indigenous video in Latin America. In M. Stewart & P. Wilson (Eds.), *Global Indigenous media: Cultures, poetics, and politics* (pp. 39–57). Durham, NC: Duke University Press.

INDIGENOUS PEOPLES' MEDIA

Indigenous media are made by and for Indigenous peoples eager to take control over media representations of their lives and communities. They are usually closely associated with movements for Indigenous rights, such as struggles over land, control of natural resources and intellectual property, cultural survival and autonomy, and political and economic justice. Indigenous media have often emerged to counteract common images of Indigenous peoples, either as timeless, unchanging, and backward or as criminal and suspect.

Many Indigenous media-makers are engaged in the creation of what Faye Ginsburg calls "screen memories," attempting to recover collective histories erased in the dominant culture's narratives and in danger of disappearing forever. Whereas print media are perhaps the easiest to set up, radio remains the most accessible and affordable for most Indigenous groups, although television and films are also vibrant and growing sectors for Indigenous production. Productions range from small-scale community projects to major international undertakings, such as feature films. Although most Indigenous media are produced by and for Indigenous communities, many also target non-Indigenous audiences, appearing at film festivals, human rights forums, UN proceedings, and other international venues.

Indigenous media have often been at the forefront of political struggles, such as with conflicts between Indigenous and commercial fisheries in Alaska and the struggle to pass the Alaska Native Claims Settlement Act, an achievement met in 1971. Perhaps the best known of these struggles is the effective use of media by the Zapatista movement in Chiapas, México, but there are many such struggles. Many Indigenous media-makers are activists in their communities, using media to strengthen their activist work. Others are (or were) also professional mainstream journalists.

Working definitions of *Indigenous peoples* usually denote peoples who inhabited an area prior to colonization, invasion, or settlement by outsiders; who consider themselves culturally distinct; who have their own political, economic, social, and cultural structures; who are only partly integrated into the dominant nation-state; who are usually discriminated against or disadvantaged; and who desire to affirm their identity and self-determination.

There is no universally acknowledged definition, and *indigeneity* is increasingly difficult to define, especially given recent changes in transport, migration, and global media. Increasing commodification of indigeneity in the global marketplace muddies the picture further, especially as the dominant society determines the commodity value of "tribal authenticity." Jeff Himpele argues that indigeneity is a collection of conscious discourses and strategies embedded in a global environment of non-Indigenous activists, human rights discourses, nongovernmental organizations (NGOs), and other organizations.

Indigeneity, from this viewpoint, constitutes a cultural performance, closely linked to struggles

for self-determination. Indigenous media are platforms for this performance and for struggles for equitable treatment. (Indigenous media are at times referred to as ethnic or ethnic minority media, although not all ethnic groups are minorities, and not all ethnic minority media can be considered Indigenous.)

National and Transnational Policies Regarding Indigenous Peoples

Indigenous media cannot be separated from the larger geopolitical environments in which they exist. States deal differently with Indigenous peoples within (and often straddling) their borders. Some protect Indigenous peoples through legislation and in other ways. Some establish Indigenous media to promote development or to preempt Indigenous peoples from developing independent media. Some still employ the assimilationist or even genocidal policies historically targeted at Indigenous peoples.

States also respond variously to calls for Indigenous communication rights. Canada and Australia have worked to serve remote communities with a variety of media projects, services, and experiments, in contrast to Russian and U.S. neglect. In some countries, public service media air Indigenous programming. In a few cases, Indigenous groups operate commercial media. In the early 1980s, for example, the Australian Broadcasting Corporation established working relationships with regional Indigenous media associations, and the corporation's Indigenous Broadcasting Unit has continued that work.

The transnational Indigenous rights movement grew in strength during the last 3 decades of the 20th century, working to include Indigenous rights in international law and in the practices of international and transnational organizations and networks. The World Council of Indigenous Peoples (1975–1996) was the first global effort by Indigenous peoples to protect their rights throughout the world. It was one of the first NGOs to be granted consultative status at the UN Economic and Social Council.

Other organizations working to support Indigenous peoples' rights include the nonprofit organization Cultural Survival, which has supported local Mayan broadcasting stations and

Guatemala's Indigenous Radio Network. The International Labour Organization's Article 169 on Indigenous and Tribal Peoples is a strong international mechanism for the protection of Indigenous rights. Its basic principles emphasize nondiscrimination, protections for the specificity of Indigenous cultures, and expectations that Indigenous peoples be consulted and be able to set their own priorities in projects that will affect them.

Indigenous groups have also strengthened their transnational networks by participating in major international conferences, such as the 1992 UN Conference on Environment and Development (the "Earth Summit"), the 1995 World Conference on Women, the 1996 Social Summit, and the 2001 World Conference against Racism. Indigenous organizations were also represented at the UN-sponsored World Summit on the Information Society in 2003 and 2005, where they were quick to point out the lack of attention to proposals regarding the need to develop autonomous and Indigenous communication platforms.

The United Nations has also been an important venue for work on issues facing Indigenous peoples. In 1982, the UN Economic and Social Council established the Working Group on Indigenous Populations (WGIP) within what is now the Sub-Commission on the Promotion and Protection of Human Rights. The WGIP began in 1985 to draft *The Declaration on the Rights of Indigenous Peoples,* finally adopted by the UN General Assembly in 2007. This declaration is the most comprehensive statement of Indigenous peoples' rights to date, and its emphasis on collective rights is previously unmatched in international human rights law.

UNESCO also works to strengthen Indigenous media through training programs, funding for media development, and the development of online resources for journalists and media practitioners. The United Nations declared 1993 as the International Year for the World's Indigenous Peoples, and in 1994, the General Assembly launched the International Decade of the World's Indigenous Peoples (1995–2004). This resulted in the establishment in 2000 of the UN Permanent Forum on Indigenous Issues to coordinate matters relating to Indigenous peoples. In light of the need for continuing attention to the world's Indigenous peoples, a second Decade of the World's Indigenous Peoples began in 2005.

Transnational networking by Indigenous peoples has broadened efforts at self-determination by creating both local and international coalition politics. The resulting movement has successfully promoted globalization from below by those peoples whose cultures are most affected by global corporate interests. As a result, Indigenous peoples in several parts of the world have experienced a cultural revival, in which Indigenous media have played a key role.

Concurrently, transnational Indigenous media networks have grown, challenging state borders and the state-controlled communications that often aid in the oppression of Indigenous peoples. The World Association of Community Radio Broadcasters supports community broadcasting worldwide, including Indigenous broadcasters. In 2008, after years of international networking, the first meeting was held of the World Indigenous Television Broadcasters Network, with attendees from Australia, Canada, Fiji, Ireland, Norway, Scotland, South Africa, Taiwan, and Wales.

The first International Film and Video Festival of Indigenous Peoples, held in México in 1985, was the result of a collaborative effort of Indigenous media organizations throughout the hemisphere, organized by the Latin American Council of Indigenous Peoples' Film and Communication. Since then, Indigenous film festivals have blossomed around the world, and Indigenous films have made inroads at more mainstream film festivals as well.

Historical Development of Indigenous Media

These media developed unevenly, depending in the 20th century on state policies regarding broadcasting's role within nation building. The very earliest were print media, such as the first Aboriginal publication in Australia in 1836, the *Flinders Island Chronicle,* and the *adivasi* tracts of the late 19th century in India. Broadcasting came later, such as Alaska's first Indigenous broadcasts in the 1930s and Burma's clandestine Karen ethnic minority radio, beginning in 1949.

The 1970s were a pivotal decade, as Indigenous broadcasters had begun to gain real access to the Australian and Canadian airwaves by then. Indigenous community radio has since remained the fastest-growing sector of Australia's broadcasting environment. In 1988, the world's first Aboriginal-owned commercial television station began broadcasting in Australia. In Canada in 1982, the Inuit Broadcasting Corporation was founded, the first Native-language television network in North America. The first broadcast outlet run by and for Black South Africans was formed in 1992. And in 1999, the world's first national broadcast network run and produced by Indigenous peoples, the Aboriginal People's Television Network, was established in Canada.

The development of Indigenous media was often motivated by specific events or concerns, such as protests over land rights in Australia in the late 1960s and 1970s. A wave of Indigenous media production in the 1980s and 1990s resulted from concerns about racist mainstream media representations and the perceived threat to Indigenous languages and cultures from the introduction of satellite television. Aboriginal linguist Eve Fesl described satellite TV as a "cultural nerve gas," and the former president of the Inuit Broadcasting Corporation, Rosemarie Kuptana (1982), was widely quoted describing mainstream television's impact on the Native people of northern Canada as similar to a neutron bomb "that destroys the soul of a people but leaves the shell of a people walking around" (para. 22).

Indigenous media projects have also been sites for activism on the part of some anthropologists. *Through Navajo Eyes* (1972), where researchers gave cameras to seven adult Navajos to learn about how they perceive the world, was seminal. The Navajo Film Project played an important role in the shift to Indigenous self-representation and, along with other Indigenous media projects, benefited from anthropology's 1960s intellectual crisis, in which the power relationship between those filming and those filmed was vigorously critiqued. This crisis roughly coincided with opportunities for previously marginalized groups to begin representing themselves through new media technologies. A strong body of ethnographic research on Indigenous media began in the late 1980s, yet only as the 21st century began did other disciplines begin to fall in step. Toward the end of the 20th century, scholars in fields as diverse as media studies, literature, linguistics, education, and political science began to recognize the growing importance of Indigenous media.

The Internet has also played a key role in more recent Indigenous media development, program distribution, and networking, creating a transnational solidarity that has helped to contest the power relation between national minorities and majorities. This has resulted in an explosion of recent Indigenous news programming, film, music, and other media, clearly linked with the international movements of Indigenous peoples, which Valerie Alia calls the "New Media Nation." This "nation" is transnational, although individual members may be subject to state regulations and control.

Funding of Indigenous media is often problematic. Most are nonprofit, with informal organizational structures. While some may run advertisements, others operate with the support of foundation grants, government subsidies, or local bodies such as community centers or churches. The more established Indigenous media projects also sustain themselves through video sales and university lectures, such as the Chiapas Media Project/Promedios, a binational NGO that provides equipment and training to Indigenous communities in Chiapas and Guerrero states, México. In some cases, Indigenous media-makers have moved into the mainstream commercial or public media with their own productions.

Indigenous media practitioners have at times also had to face negative attitudes toward their work from local people in their own communities. It can be difficult to understand the value of locally produced media as contrasted with collectively constructing a house or harvesting a crop.

Common Goals of Indigenous Media

Survival

In the most extreme cases, these media provide a platform for Indigenous groups whose very existence remains threatened by assimilation or state-sponsored violence. In Burma, for example, Indigenous media produced in the country's rebel-held border areas report on the multiple forms of human rights violations perpetrated by the country's military dictatorship against Indigenous groups. This can of course be dangerous, and Indigenous media are themselves often targets of state-sponsored violence. In Burma, those caught with Indigenous media products are subject to arrest or worse. In Guatemala, the Public Ministry conducts periodic raids on Indigenous Mayan radio stations, all of which remain unlicensed and therefore vulnerable. In Colombia, Indigenous media practitioners have often been assassinated, disappeared, or forced into exile for their efforts to bring state-sponsored violence to light.

Culture and Identity

A central goal of many Indigenous media is to keep alive traditions and traditional values and pass them on to the next generation by showcasing Indigenous practices and knowledge and the wisdom of a community's elders. The maintenance of Indigenous languages is also a key component to the growth of Indigenous media, through peoples' desires to communicate in their local languages and to allow the languages to evolve and remain alive for their young people. Some of these media may also unintentionally encourage assimilation into the mainstream. Stephen Riggins suggests that all such media play a "dual role" with a balance of "assimilationist-pluralist functions" that varies over time.

Some Indigenous media seek to break away from dominant frameworks of media production, so as to develop Indigenous frameworks that respect local community values and processes. These media are often run by volunteers or minimally paid part-time staff. They often rely on consensual decision making and media production, or other forms of participatory communication that involve the community. In addition, Indigenous media provide a means through which Indigenous groups can set their own news agenda, focusing on the stories they consider most important.

Self-Determination

Although media have often been complicit in the processes of colonialism and assimilation, they also offer options for Indigenous reworking of histories, cultures, and identities through what Ginsburg has called a "rhetoric of self-determination." Media have played an important role, for example, in the shaping of an Inuit identity and nationalism in Canada; in connecting Inuit across geographical, linguistic, and cultural divides; and ultimately providing an important rationale for their land claims settlement. Such efforts can threaten not only the

interests of a society's dominant group(s), but even the agendas of democratic activists, who may argue that Indigenous struggles for autonomy undermine the collective strength of multiethnic alliances working to push for social change.

Education

Many Indigenous media work to educate their people about the relevance of national and international politics to their specific situation, adapting national or international news to reflect the local literacy level and cultural terms of reference. Indigenous media also inform their audiences about their rights under international law, about the role of international organizations, and about concepts such as genocide, ethnic cleansing, and democracy. These media often try to challenge the patterns of oppression that lock local communities into a narrow understanding of their plight as a result of their own failure, emphasizing instead the structural forces beyond their immediate control and the similar situations facing other Indigenous peoples.

Call to Action

Many Indigenous media work to develop their audiences' motivation to struggle in whatever ways they can, while resisting dependence on outside help. Indigenous media-makers in Oaxaca, for example, expressed concern that their community did not have enough *conciencia de lucha* (the experience and determination in standing up for themselves) to fight for their rights. Other Indigenous media call on their audiences, both local and global, to struggle for justice on a global scale.

Perhaps the best known of such media work is the campaign by the Zapatistas, especially their use of cell phones and the Internet, to oppose regional, neoliberal free trade agreements such as NAFTA and CAFTA. The Chiapas Media Project/Promedios and the Mexican film *Moojk/Maize*, two examples among many, present critiques of consumerism and neoliberalism that urge audiences to join Indigenous peoples in their struggles for global justice.

Questioning Indigenous Media

Indigenous media have been important expressions of Indigenous identities and self-determination, yet questions have been raised over their authenticity, especially those in which Indigenous peoples collaborate with outsiders from dominant groups. Such critiques are answered by charges that they establish a dangerous essentialism, ignoring the hybrid cultural formations inevitable in a globally interconnected world, and are ethnocentric, demanding an "authenticity" in Indigenous media not required of other media.

Ginsburg argues that it is important to ask questions about the actual authorship of media productions, but outsiders working with Indigenous producers are often careful to emphasize reciprocity and exchange so that they speak with, rather than for, the people with whom they work. Some have become long-term residents of Indigenous communities. For other scholars, authenticity is found only in hybrid media. These debates have increasingly made clear that media representations are subjective interpretations of a situation based on the producers' particular location within levels of power relations.

One significant issue facing Indigenous media producers is how to deal with the political consequences of simplistic images of Indigenous peoples, such as the romantic primitivist emphasis on exoticism, universality, agelessness, and nostalgia. Harald Prins has called the dilemma this raises the "primitivist double-bind," in which primitivism simultaneously reduces Indigenous peoples to the "noble savage" stereotype, yet provides them with a model of self-representation that they can (and do) exploit for their own political purposes. This is a form of "strategic essentialism," where a group takes on but also exploits the essentializing category.

Himpele has distinguished between the enactment of *indigeneity* by Indigenous peoples for self-representation and self-determination, and *indigenism,* the romanticization of Indigenous rituals, music, dress, and divine entities by non-Indigenous or even urbanized Indigenous people. Such indigenism stems from nostalgia for the depoliticized, romantic, and unchanging past represented through mainstream media images.

Such indigenist rhetoric is also employed by states in the name of development, modernization, and citizenship. In Bolivia, Indigenous media-makers have recognized the power of romanticized indigenist images and, in a process of "indigenized indigenism," often incorporate such images to seek control over common media representations.

Case Study: Isuma Productions and *Atanarjuat*

The work of Igloolik Isuma Productions (IIP), the Arctic's first independent Inuit production company, created in 1991, demonstrates the complexities facing Indigenous producers wishing to engage with international audiences. IIP created the first feature written, produced, and acted by the Inuit, *Atanarjuat, The Fast Runner* (2001), arguably a watershed in the history of North American popular cinema.

The film draws from a 2000-year-old Inuit oral legend warning against the effects of jealousy and selfishness on communal life. *Atanarjuat* is part of a growing body of work by Inuit media-makers that, since the 1970s, has self-consciously engaged in the interrelated projects of political activism (especially campaigns for sovereignty), nation building, and a reconceptualization of cultural identities in response to dramatic social changes.

Atanarjuat gained much attention at international film festivals, remaining in the top 60 North American Films for 23 consecutive weeks and generating US$3.7 million. Screened at the National Gallery of Canada, the Museum of Modern Art in New York, the American Film Institute, the Museé d'Art Moderne in Paris, and the Museum of Northern Peoples in Hokkaido, it enjoyed success in Europe and elsewhere, winning several prestigious awards, including the Cannes Film Festival *Caméra d'Or,* the coveted prize for first directors. This film established Indigenous filmmaking as part of the national cinema of Canada. In addition, IIP has been successful in generating film jobs and training through *Atanarjuat* and its productions since then. Echoing Inuit traditions, IIP also uses consensual decision making in its productions.

Nonetheless, the film's funding and distribution problems spotlighted the difficulties facing Indigenous media-makers. They began filming with a modest C$200,000 from 17 sources and then applied to Telefilm Canada (TC), the government's main funding source for independent filmmakers, for the remaining C$2 million needed. *Atanarjuat*'s producers did not apply for TC's Aboriginal Production Fund, capped at C$200,000. But TC officials underestimated the film's importance, failed to place the proposal in the broader competition, and informed the producers that "Aboriginal funds" had already been allocated, thus confining Aboriginal producers to underresourced "media reservations" as Ginsburg put it. Only after protests were the filmmakers granted additional money. After the film's debut, IIP sued their international sales agent for depriving them of revenue. These difficulties demonstrate the need to rethink the problematic nature of many arts policies and the categories they construct, and to strategize to protect Indigenous media-makers from exploitation.

However, Avi Santo argues that IIP's global marketing and distribution strategies placed unexpected limitations on their local cultural and economic goals. To gain non-Indigenous international recognition, *Atanarjuat*'s producers had to transform complex cultural practices to conform to stereotypical assumptions about Aboriginal "authenticity." This example of the "primitivist double-bind" demonstrates how the global market constrained the production process yet, simultaneously, sustained local media production and helped legitimate Indigenous identities transnationally. Although the crossover nature of *Atanarjuat* worried some, Lucas Bessire argued it revealed "the co-constructed nature of imagery" and Aboriginals' struggle to recast alienating categories as part of their quest for independence and dignity.

Lisa Brooten

See also Adivasi Movement Media (India); Berber Video-Films (Morocco); COR TV, 2006, Oaxaca (México); First Peoples' Media (Canada); Human Rights Media; Indigenous Media (Australia); Indigenous Media (Burma/Myanmar); Indigenous Media in Latin America; Indigenous Radio Stations (México); Māori Media and Social Movements (Aetearoa/New Zealand); Peace Media (Colombia); Zapatista Media (México)

Further Readings

Alia, V. (2009). Outlaws and citizens: Indigenous people and the "New Media Nation." *International Journal of Media and Cultural Politics, 5*(1–2), 39–54.

Bessire, L. (2003). Talking back to primitivism: Divided audiences, collective desires. *American Anthropologist, 105*(4), 832–838.

Ginsburg, F. (2002). Screen memories: Resignifying the traditional in Indigenous media. In F. Ginsburg,

L. Abu-Lughod, & B. Larkin (Eds.), *Media worlds: Anthropology on new terrain* (pp. 39–57). Berkeley: University of California Press.

Ginsburg, F. (2003). *Atanarjuat* off-screen: From "media reservations" to the world stage. *American Anthropologist, 105*(4), 827–831.

Himpele, J. (2008). *Circuits of culture: Media, politics, and Indigenous identity in the Andes.* Minneapolis: University of Minnesota Press.

Huhndorf, S. (2003). *Atanarjuat, the Fast Runner*: Culture, history, and politics in Inuit media. *American Anthropologist, 105*(4), 822–826.

Kuptana, R. (1982). *Inuit Broadcasting Corporation presentation to the CRTC on cable tiering and universal pay TV.* Retrieved June 2, 2010, from http://www.inuitbroadcasting.ca/Resources/neutron_e.htm

Molnar, H., & Meadows, M. (2001). *Songlines to satellites: Indigenous communication in Australia, the South Pacific and Canada.* Leichhardt, Australia: Pluto Press.

Pack, S. (2000). Indigenous media then and now: Situating the Navajo Film Project. *Quarterly Review of Film and Video, 17*(3), 273–286.

Prins, H. (1997). The paradox of primitivism: Native rights and the problem of imagery in Native survival. *Visual Anthropology, 9*(3–4), 243–266.

Roth, L. (2005). *Something new in the air: The story of First Peoples television broadcasting in Canada.* Montréal, ON: McGill-Queens University Press.

Salazar, J. F. (2009). Indigenous video and policy contexts in Latin America. *International Journal of Media and Cultural Politics, 5*(1–2), 125–130.

Santo, A. (2008). Act locally, sell globally: Inuit media and the global cultural economy. *Continuum: Journal of Media & Cultural Studies, 22*(3), 327–340.

Wilson, P., & Stewart, M. (Eds.). (2008). *Global Indigenous media: Cultures, poetics, and politics.* Durham, NC: Duke University Press.

INDIGENOUS RADIO STATIONS (MÉXICO)

Indigenous radio stations in México have proved to be contested territory. México hosts the largest Indigenous population in Latin America. Close to 11 million people do not have Spanish as their native language, share little—culturally, economically, and socially—with other Mexicans, and for almost 5 centuries have been persecuted and marginalized. In the 19th and 20th centuries, official history books glorified their archaeological past and their fierce resistance to 16th-century Spanish conquerors, but simultaneously the close to 60 Indigenous peoples constituted a nuisance to the Mexican state's modernization project.

From the state's perspective, Indigenous peoples had to undergo *castellanización* (Castilianization— i.e., they had to abandon their languages and adopt Spanish). Since the 1960s, to achieve *castellanización,* the federal government had tried to create radio stations in remote Indigenous regions. In the late 1970s and early 1980s, this project became a contradictory reality: The stations were to teach Spanish and modernize Indigenous peoples, but also to fight poverty, encourage grassroots participation, promote Indigenous traditions, and, paradoxically, defend Indigenous cultures.

However, the mostly Indigenous staff concentrated on the latter goals, and *castellanización* soon disappeared from everyday practices and explicit station objectives. The stations soon became multipurpose: The state used them to increase its presence in Indigenous areas, but Indigenous audiences and radio workers seized the airwaves with different agendas that sometimes coexisted, but often clashed, with official goals. Even though these stations belonged to the government, and sometimes acted accordingly, their programming and daily operations also constituted an example of the public appropriating media.

The Negotiation of Rule

México constitutes an unusual case in the history of alternative communication and grassroots organizations. Throughout most of the 20th century, an authoritarian party managed to control the three branches of government and the media, and attempted to co-opt social movements too. The hegemonic hand of the one-party system, led by the Partido Revolucionario Institucional (PRI; Institutional Revolutionary Party), was everywhere, in unions, farmers' organizations, and Indigenous movements.

Occasionally, the state relied on the use of force to repress dissident movements. In the late 1950s, for instance, the police jailed thousands of railroad unionists who had challenged the official union. Ten years later, in 1968, a student rally in

Tlatelolco was crushed in a massacre that left several hundred demonstrators dead. Meanwhile, the mainstream media reported a kinder, happier, pro-PRI reality. Broadcasting in México was almost exclusively private but not independent. On one occasion, Emilio Azcárraga, then owner of the TV monopoly Televisa and one of the wealthiest businessmen in México, defined himself as a "PRI soldier." The press, also private, was controlled through bribery, direct censorship, and state control over newsprint supply.

In spite of all this, however, a more complex reality hid beneath daily Mexican society. Everyday life showed that power and rule were not always in the hands of the state, the government, or the PRI. Rather, governance was attained through a complex negotiation. Thus, when the state created Indigenous-language radio stations, what was meant as a preemptive strike against independent Indigenous community media became a space of resistance, a school for social and media activists, and a role model for future, alternative media.

Indigenist Radio

In 1948, the Mexican government created its own branch of Indigenous affairs, the Instituto Nacional Indigenista (INI; National Indigenist Institute), an organization that was replaced in 2003 by the Comisión Nacional para el Desarrollo de los Pueblos Indígenas (National Commission for the Development of Indigenous Peoples). It was the INI that had installed the first Indigenous-language radio station in Guerrero State in 1979. During the following 2 decades, the government created 24 more such stations and organized them as a network.

One was shut down in 1990 in the southern state of Tabasco. Four others broadcast in low-power FM from children's orphanages in the Maya area of Yucatán. The remaining 20 programmed music and shows about agriculture, health, human rights, news, Indigenous culture, and other social interest topics. The stations received no advertising funds, and donations were, in general, difficult to accept because of tight regulatory policies. The stations' total dependence on state funds lost them a great degree of autonomy but also protected them from the intervention of local non-Indigenous commercial and political interests.

Because the initiative came from the INI and not from a grassroots, Indigenous movement, the stations call themselves "indigenist" rather than "Indigenous," a distinction that has been welcomed by academics and Indigenous activists alike. However, over the years, these radio stations have developed a participatory approach to communication. The birth of the stations was based on the use of media for development and social change, with explicit references to Paulo Freire and Emile McAnany. Their explicit objectives included opening the medium to Indigenous participation, so as to forge grassroots media. The Mexican case is unique in that a "bottom-up" model of communication was applied to the Indigenous population from "the top," and in that the process of state formation turned indigenist media into spaces for negotiating governance.

Most indigenist radios developed in a relatively calm environment for the first decade, but 1994 marked a turning point. On January 1, 1994, a guerrilla group occupied several towns in the southern state of Chiapas and declared war on the Mexican government. In a matter of days, the Ejército Zapatista de Liberación Nacional (EZLN; Zapatista Army of National Liberation) managed to present itself as a grassroots movement that fought for Indigenous rights. A clever communication strategy and a charismatic leader quickly gave the EZLN a significant number of supporters both in México and abroad, especially among social movements and intellectuals.

The rebels included indigenist media in their agenda from the early days of the uprising. Exactly 2 months after its first public appearance, the EZLN presented a list of demands to the government. The 10th demand read:

> The guarantee of the Indigenous peoples' right to truthful information at the local, regional, state, national, and international levels with an Indigenous radio station that is independent of the government, managed by Indigenous people and operated by Indigenous people.

Since then, the apparent top-down/bottom-up contradiction of state-promoted grassroots media was sharpened by the tension, political and armed, between the government and the EZLN. Indigenist radio stations were caught in the crossfire. The EZLN accused them of serving as counterrevolutionary tools, but the state mistrusted the closeness of the stations' staff and programming to Indigenous communities and to some EZLN ideals.

Radio Stations as Spaces of Negotiation

The actors involved in the negotiation and the role they play vary from station to station. They can include the station staff, local nongovernmental organizations, Zapatista guerrillas and their supporters, local politicians and landlords, religious organizations, federal employees, religious and community leaders, and audience members.

Several stations begin and end each day by playing the Mexican national anthem in Indigenous languages. The state has used the network for its campaigns. At the beginning of the 1990s, the government introduced a national identity document and organized a nationwide campaign with the slogan, "Come and have your picture taken." These messages were translated into Maya and other languages and were broadcast to ensure that Indigenous peoples would not remain unregistered.

Simultaneously, the state has mistrusted some stations and their potential for subversive ideology. In the early 1980s, a time of particularly intense turmoil in Central America, even some music was perceived as problematic. In some stations, one can still find back covers of vinyl discs with marks next to the songs that could not be broadcast. Chilean singer Violeta Parra's song "Gracias a la vida" ("Thanks to Life"), for instance, has a thick NO written with a black marker.

After the 1994 Zapatista insurrection, control policies became stricter. INI forced some stations to broadcast news only from Notimex—the official news agency—or even required them to fax every story to INI's headquarters. Direct censorship gradually disappeared as the tension diminished, but throughout the first decade of the 21st century, the stations still knew they were under surveillance. It would be unfair, however, to say that the role of federal institutions was exclusively one of control. On numerous occasions, the indigenist institution also sheltered and protected the radio stations from the pressures of local and state politicians and landlords.

Indigenist radio stations also serve the interests of Indigenous actors. At times with the complicity of headquarters, at other times with their tolerance, and at yet others without their knowledge or even against their opposition, radio workers developed mechanisms to adopt, adapt, or resist indigenist policies. Almost all these workers came from Indigenous areas and spoke their languages on the air.

An implicit policy of negotiation circulated among radio workers. As if it were a semi-secret motto, the sentence "everything can be said as long as you know how to say it" circulated for years among radio workers and indigenist officials. This premise allowed for the broadcast of Zapatista communiqués in Chiapas, interviews with opposition-party leaders, or criticism of government policies and state abuse of human rights.

In general, communities appreciate the radio stations. Even the EZLN has shown respect toward their work. During the 1994 uprising, the Zapatistas seized two government-owned stations, one belonging to the state of Chiapas, the other the indigenist station in Las Margaritas. When they abandoned the stations, the guerrillas behaved in opposite ways. Whereas they destroyed equipment, material, and installations in the state government's station, they left the indigenist station intact when they abandoned it.

Another revealing case occurred in 1999 during a consultation the EZLN organized throughout México. Chiapas activists traveled all around the republic to promote participation by the citizenry; according to organizers, they reached 3 million people. On their way through Oaxaca, an indigenist worker who sympathized with their cause transported EZLN delegates in the station's pickup truck with the inscription "Poder Ejecutivo Federal" (Federal Executive Branch) written on the door. That night, the activists even slept in the INI video production center.

Policies and practices are also malleable in actions that are not necessarily linked to freedom of speech, such as flexible and creative budgeting, the weaving of local alliances that make the federal government uncomfortable, or the interpretation of history from Indigenous, unofficial points of view. The space for negotiation is ample, as long as the integrity and authority of the state are not openly questioned.

Antoni Castells i Talens

See also Community Radio Movement (India); COR TV, 2006, Oaxaca (México); Indigenous Media in Latin America; Zapatista Media (México)

Further Readings

Castells i Talens, A. (2004). *The negotiation of indigenist radio policy in Mexico.* Unpublished doctoral dissertation, University of Florida, Gainesville.

Cornejo Portugal, I. (2002). *Apuntes para una historia de la radio indigenista en México* [Notes for a history of indigenist radio in México]. México City, México: Fundación Manuel Buendía.

Ejército Zapatista de Liberación Nacional (EZLN). (1995). *EZLN: Documentos y comunicados* [EZLN: Documents and communiqués]. México City, México: Era.

Frattini, E., & Colías, Y. (1998). *Tiburones de la comunicación* [Communication sharks]. México City, México: Océano.

Joseph, G. M., & Nugent, D. (Eds.). (1994). *Everyday forms of state formation: Revolution and the negotiation of rule in modern Mexico.* Durham, NC: Duke University Press.

Ramos Rodríguez, J. M. (2005). Indigenous radio stations in Mexico: A catalyst for social cohesion and cultural strength. *The Radio Journal, 3*(3), 155–169.

Secretaría de Agricultura y Recursos Hidráulicos— Comisión del Río Balsas. (1977). *Anteproyecto para la instalación de una radio difusora en Tlapa, Gro* [Draft project to install a radio station in Tlapa, Guerrero]. México City: Author.

INDUSTRIAL WORKERS OF THE WORLD MEDIA (UNITED STATES)

The Industrial Workers of the World (IWW) was founded in 1905 and is one of the oldest existing labor unions. The Wobblies, as they are commonly referred to, originally used both song and the independent union papers, *The Industrial Worker* and *Solidarity,* in their attempts to further their cause.

The *Preamble to the IWW Constitution*, printed on the back of every bright red membership card, reads,

> The working class and the employing class have nothing in common. There can be no peace so long as hunger and want are found among millions of the working people and the few, who make up the employing class, have all the good things of life.

The IWW aims to unite workers along class divisions to seek better conditions in the workplace. Members use direct action such as strikes, propaganda, and boycotts in their efforts.

The IWW has also used song in its efforts to spread its message. Two prominent songwriting figures early on were Joe Hill and Ralph Chaplin. Hill wrote parodies of Christian songs, such as *There'll Be Pie in the Sky When You Die (That's a Lie)*, a parody of *In the Sweet By and By*, so that union members could sing their own lyrics alongside Salvation Army bands, in an interesting form of culture jamming. Chaplin penned the lyrics of *Solidarity Forever*, the Wobblies' anthem, as well as editing both *The Industrial Worker* and *Solidarity*.

The Wobblies were well known for their songs, which exemplified their often-combative stance at rallies, strikes, demonstrations, and picket lines. For example, *Solidarity Forever*, written to the tune of *John Brown's Body*, reads in the second stanza:

> *Is there aught we hold in common with the greedy parasite*
> *Who would lash us into serfdom and would crush us with his might?*
> *Is there anything left to us but to organize and fight?*
> *For the Union makes us strong.*

The Wobblies also used print media to spread their message within the broader union movement. *The Industrial Worker*, first printed in 1906, continued publication into the 21st century with 10 issues a year. *The Industrial Worker* attempted not only to reach out to those not part of the organization but also to serve as a lateral form of communication between members and local branches.

Circulation in 2010 was just over 4,000 copies per month.

The other IWW publication, *Solidarity*, merged with *The Industrial Worker* in the 1930s. *The Industrial Worker* is printed by union labor, and the editor is elected by the membership via a rank-and-file vote for a 2-year term. *The Industrial Worker* can be downloaded for free from the IWW's website and can be found in print format at many radical bookstores. It focuses on labor issues and news directly relating to union members. To further facilitate member communication, the IWW website hosts message boards, chat rooms, and member blogs.

In addition to providing labor movement news, *The Industrial Worker* offers a variety of IWW-related clothing, patches, posters, decals, CDs, and books, including *The Big Red Song Book*, the book of Wobbly songs dating back to 1909.

Mike Melanson

See also Alternative Media; Citizens' Media; Labor Media (United States); Workers' Film and Photo League (United States)

Further Readings

Industrial Workers of the World: http://www.iww.org
Industrial Workers of the World. (n.d.). *General campaigns, projects and publications of the IWW*. http://www.iww.org/en/projects
Industrial Workers of the World. (n.d.). *IWW documents: Culture, history, and library*. http://www.iww.org/en/culture

INDYMEDIA (THE INDEPENDENT MEDIA CENTER)

The Independent Media Center (IMC) was born in Seattle, Washington, in late 1999, during mass demonstrations against the neoliberal mandates of the World Trade Organization (WTO). A loose coalition of media activists, social movement organizers, and open-source computer designers, realizing that the mainstream media would not adequately represent the demonstrators' varied perspectives on global social justice, opened a downtown storefront dubbed the Independent Media Center. One hundred fifty volunteers reported on the week of teach-ins, street protests, and cultural activities, for a variety of old and new media. These included a daily newspaper, a low-power FM radio station, the national Pacifica Radio network, and a documentary video project.

In addition, a team of computer designers set up a powerful new website, indymedia.org, with an open source design, and "open publishing" capacities, which provided a 24/7 forum for anyone with Internet access to upload text, audio, photographs, or video content to or from anywhere in the world. The IMC outperformed the mainstream media, providing reports for alternative and commercial media across the planet. Most notably, the website received a million and a half hits from all over the world.

The Seattle IMC rejected the commercial media international news model, in which a corps of professional journalists, relying on a small number of powerful government and corporate sources, package information for global audiences through the branded channels of a handful of transnational media corporations. They also turned down the approach of the international nongovernmental organizations (INGOs), whose professional spokespeople mostly stick to the narrow talking points of reform they think acceptable to the mainstream press and policymakers.

Instead, the IMC critiqued both models and set about to assemble a corps of volunteers who would combine accurate reporting with perspectives infused by their commitment to social and economic justice. They also opened up their site to the interactive participation of people underrepresented in corporate and public service models of media production and content.

This practical demonstration of a collaborative way of making media, and of harnessing the global capacity of the Internet to produce and circulate multimedia information, resonated with activists in the emerging global justice movement. The IMC quickly became their platform of choice. The numbers of Indymedia centers grew during the ensuing wave of international protests against the WTO and its parallel organizations, such as the International Monetary Fund, the World Bank, the Free Trade of the Americas, and the G8/G20. By 2004, the global Indymedia network included 150 autonomously operated local centers, complemented by transnational technical support and special media production teams, and a shared technical infrastructure, in more than 50 countries.

The IMC was the first global site to adopt easy-to-use interactive web features, which later became an accepted part of the web 2.0 menu. However, equally important was the network's "DNA" of participatory democracy which informed every activity, from the consensus-based forms of decision making of each media production team and autonomous site, to the open publishing, archiving, and collaborative software. As the network grew, teams developed new ways to promote local and transnational cooperation, from easier language translation functions, to more participatory forms of discussion, production, and editing.

The technical crew espoused the collaborative problem-solving ethos of the Free and Open Source Software (FLOSS) movement and built the site with free software and open source code. The resulting decentralized network structure spurred the IMC's rapid growth as centers everywhere could quickly share the resources. Many centers shared servers, operating code, systems of content management, and the basic webpage logo and layout. After signing onto a common agreement with the network, each center was encouraged to manage itself, making central overhead costs minimal. However, most participants were deeply critical of funding models based on government, foundation, or INGO support, and no consensus was ever achieved as to how to sustain such a complex transnational operation; almost all of the sites relied on volunteer labor and donations.

When the intense initial wave of protests waned in 2001, the global IMC shifted to providing news reports from a wide diversity of social justice movements. These varied from worldwide protests against the war in Iraq, to regional, national, and local campaigns for political, social, economic, and environmental justice.

Several solidarity teams set up in centers of global conflict, such as Palestine and Iraq, or Africa and Latin America, where there were fewer digital technology resources. Intraregional projects enabled collaboration across arbitrary national borders originally established by the colonial powers. For example, Indymedia Estrecho linked collectives from Spain, the Canary Islands, and

Morocco, while the Oceania hub aggregated features from across Southeast Asia and the Pacific region.

The Global and the Local

Many IMC sites also began to experiment with different ways of utilizing media. In Urbana-Champaign, Illinois, for example, the IMC created a multimedia center in a former post office, started a free monthly paper funded by local labor groups, and helped organize a new community radio station.

In many countries of the global South, which had very few Internet hookups or even phones, IMC activists worked with the existing circuits of social movement communications. In México's Chiapas State, the birthplace of the Zapatista movement, whose approach to radical grassroots democracy had inspired many "IMCistas," the IMC team provided extensive training for local organizations in using audiotapes and radio. In Brazil, they also began primarily off-line, using existing community radio and video networks, video screenings in poor neighborhoods or public places, or printed news-sheets, distributed in schools, workplaces, and neighborhoods.

In Ecuador, the IMC organized three independent film festivals of social documentaries from Latin America. In Argentina, the IMC teams facilitated the video documentation of groups of unemployed workers, youth, neighborhood activists, and the Mapuche, an aboriginal people.

The astonishing pace of development was not without growing pains. Like many of its radical media precursors, the IMC Network had to deal with constant problems of sustainability, uneven and unequal distribution of financial, technical, and social resources among people around the globe, difficulties in overcoming long-standing social power differences among volunteers, and attacks from hostile governments and individuals. In addition to these problems, they faced the difficulties inherent in sustaining a more democratic communications model in an increasingly enclosed corporate media environment.

IMCs were consistently raided by national and international security agencies, for example, in Canada, Italy, Spain, the United Kingdom, and the United States. Several sites, especially the global Israel and Palestine IMCs, were systematically attacked. For example, in 2002, in advance of the meetings of the European Union in Barcelona, the Spanish police announced they were tracking the IMC and other alternative information networks. In October 2004, just before a European Social Forum meeting on Communication Rights, the U.S. Federal Bureau of Investigation seized the hard drives of servers in the United States and United Kingdom, which linked 20 IMC sites, claiming they were elements in an "international terrorism investigation." After an international solidarity campaign, the servers were returned, and the IMC discovered that the Italian and Swiss governments had prompted the actions.

IMC's openness also made it vulnerable. For example, the innovative text messaging and Internet reports during the New York protests against the Republican National Convention in 2004 provided both demonstrators and police with up-to-the-minute reports.

Free Expression, Censorship, and Archiving

Partly in response, many local centers and the network as a whole began to practice more content selection, editing, and control of spam/flames, although many of the original crews protested this turn toward gatekeeping. By 2004, the global Newswire Working Group routinely cleared duplicate posts and commercial messages and hid hostile posts to encourage wider participation. Several sites, such as IMC Germany, explicitly filtered the newswire for racist, fascist, sexist, and anti-Semitic content, as well as for newness or originality of analysis.

By 2005, the growth of the global network began to slow. Many of the sites imploded, as the end of highly visible international street protests halted recruitment. Local teams were less able to sustain the long hours of unpaid work or to overcome differences of political perspective or social power. In addition, the IMC began to be eclipsed as the platform of protest in many countries. YouTube, Facebook, and similar commercial sites adopted their open publishing features. By 2007, those social justice organizations, with easy access to digital equipment and broadband, were routinely posting their reports to these commercial services. At the same time, a new generation of digitally rich youth no longer turned to the IMC as a media outlet.

However, the IMC continued to provide news, information, and commentary not readily available anywhere else. It was the first-on-the-scene in 2008, as Greek students demonstrated against their right-wing national government, and again, in 2009, during the resistance to the right-wing coup in Honduras. In addition, specialized teams provided more thematic features about social justice campaigns of students, Indigenous people, immigrants, and peace activists, for example. In the face of serious deficits in local and international mainstream news coverage, the IMC's timely multimedia coverage of protests, and links to other informational sites around the world, ensured their relevance.

Dorothy Kidd

See also Alternative Media at Political Summits; Anarchist Media; Indymedia and Gender; Indymedia: East Asia; *Radical Software* (United States)

Further Readings

Brooten, L. (2004). Digital deconstruction: The Independent Media Center as a process of collective critique. In R. Berenger (Ed.), *Global media go to war* (pp. 265–279). Spokane, WA: Marquette Books.

Downing, J. D. H. (2003). The Independent Media Center movement and the anarchist socialist tradition. In N. Couldry & J. Curran (Eds.), *Contesting media power* (pp. 243–257). Lanham, MD: Rowman & Littlefield.

Kidd, D. (2003). Become the media: The global IMC network. In A. Opel & D. Pompper (Eds.), *Representing resistance: Media, civil disobedience, and the global justice movement* (pp. 224–240). Westport, CT: Praeger.

Studies of Indymedia: https://docs.indymedia.org/Global/ImcEssayCollectionSimple

INDYMEDIA AND GENDER

Indymedia philosophy owes much to critiques of hierarchy and power developed by feminist movements. All IMCs in the network are committed to the development of nonhierarchical

and antiauthoritarian relationships, from interpersonal relationships to group dynamics (Principles of Unity No. 6). However, activists have pointed out that in terms of gender, this commitment remains largely unfulfilled.

First, there are sexist and/or heterosexist (homophobic) postings on the newswire. In a well-known example, a male-supremacist group tried to take over the newswire and comment functions of IMC Québec. This is a problem in the design and usage of IMC resources, especially the open publishing function.

Second, there exist sexist and/or gendered patterns within IMC collectives and discussion spaces. Identified issues include absence and invisibility of non–male-gendered people, a division of labor along lines of gender, higher levels of appreciation for traditionally "male"-gendered work ("tech-arrogance," prevalent in the early stages of the network), verbal and physical harassment, silencing, male aggressiveness, an emphasis on dramatic confrontational politics as opposed to "slow burn" issues, and assumptions about behavior based on gender, class, and ethnic and cultural origin.

These issues are not unique to Indymedia but common to most cultures and therefore the social movements situated in them. Media networks like the Association for Progressive Communications and the World Federation of Community Broadcasters (AMARC) have tried to address these problems by developing women-specific initiatives and programs. In the Indymedia network, a system of online discussion lists has allowed activists to raise critiques and develop solutions.

Important English-language discussion groups include the *IMC-Women* listserv, a women-only online community, which galvanized a debate on gender issues throughout the network and affected a change in 2003 in policy admission procedures; the *IMC-ANTIPATRIARCHY* listserv, established in 2002 for people of all genders, and the *IMC-queer* listserv. *IMC-women-tech* supports women working on technological issues in the network. *IMC-women-website* is a project to establish an IMC with a gender focus. For Portuguese speakers, there is also *CMI-mulheres*. Important other resources include the "Leftist Techies" survey conducted by the IMC activist Blue in 2001, and "An open letter to other men in the movement"—a newswire posting discussed and circulated in 2002.

Based on an analysis of English-language gender-related discussions, Brooten and Hadl found that by 2008, IMC activists had begun to develop the following approaches. One was to move beyond notions of victimizers and victimized, by recognizing multiple and shifting subject positions and each individual's degree of complicity in patterns of domination. Another was to acknowledge prevailing hierarchies in the surrounding culture.

Actions undertaken included creating a safe and welcoming environment, if possible by setting up a women's collective; improving meetings by providing attentive and fair facilitation; rethinking the consensus decision-making model to include attention to people and issues unnoticed or absent; and having multiple decision-making models. Longer term actions included rethinking the value certain kinds of work are assigned according to the gender traditionally associated with them, and moving away from the currently dominant "openness" and "anticensorship" philosophy to a "communication commons" model.

Brooten and Hadl concluded that because introspection, self-reflection, and critical discussion were an integral part of Indymedia culture, the system of interlocking online and off-line discussion spaces should allow for expanding this introspection throughout the international network.

Gabriele Hadl

See also Feminist Media: An Overview; Feminist Movement Media (United States); Indymedia (The Independent Media Center); Indymedia: East Asia; Women Bloggers (Egypt); Women's Radio (Austria)

Further Readings

Brooten, L., & Hadl, G. (2009). Gender and hierarchy: A case study of the Independent Media Center network. In D. Kidd, L. Stein, & C. Rodríguez (Eds.), *Making our media* (Vol. 1). Cresskill, NJ: Hampton Press.

INDYMEDIA: EAST ASIA

The Indymedia movement became very active in East Asia from 2002 to 2005. Of the many groups that formed, however, some never made it beyond the planning stages (e.g., in Hong Kong, Korea, and Thailand), and others (e.g., IMC Taiwan and IMC Burma) succeeded at setting up sites and joining the international network of IMCs, but were active only for a short period. In many cases, local initiatives fulfilled similar functions, and thus local activists felt no particular need for an IMC.

For example, in the late 1990s, Korean activists had pioneered open publishing software prior to Indymedia's formation, and there were already a large number of social movement–oriented online services, such as Jinbonet. People interested in setting up a multilingual IMC Korea (especially organizing around migrant issues) lacked resources and support from the local media activist community. In Hong Kong, knowledge about the Indymedia network was limited, but local activists started a similar project, INmediaHK. IMC Taiwan (twIMC), at its peak in 2003–2004, offered an interesting mix of news in Chinese about local movements and activist news in English from abroad, but activists soon became more involved in a blogging project, Twblog.net, now discontinued, which they felt more closely corresponded to their needs.

However, many of these projects lacked Indymedia's horizontal organizing, commitment to open source software, and/or international network. To address the last issue, Korean social movement sites often add English-language features during key phases in movement activity. INmediaHK works closely with interlocals.net, a regional content exchange project.

As of 2009, there were three active IMCs in the region. IMC Jakarta joined in 2004. It had a very active newswire and editorial page, with most content in Bahasa Indonesia, the country's official language written in Roman script. IMC Manila was the survivor of a series of splits and fallouts, involving IMC Philippines, IMC Quezon City, and several projects that tried to be independent alternatives to IMC-affiliated sites. Most content is currently in English (the language of education in the Philippines), and the editorial collective seemed to be a small anarchist group.

IMCjp (Japan) was the only IMC that published in Asian script and was an early example of a multilingual IMC, bridging Japanese and English social movement news. Set up by a loose association of activists to cover the 2002 antiwar demonstrations, it was long relatively unknown in the Japanese activist community. It finally gained some recognition for G8 protest reporting and collaborating with the Japanese G8medianetwork in 2008.

Challenges faced by IMCs in Asia include language barriers within local collectives (e.g., IMCjp members include Japanese-only and English-only speakers) and Anglo-centrism within the Indymedia network. The latter has manifested itself technologically in software hard to adapt to Asian scripts (IMC Burma lost momentum before successfully addressing this issue on their site), including the global IMC mailing list server, and organizationally by a process for joining the network that requires a high level of English skill. A frustrated Taiwanese activist wryly signed his postings to the New-IMC list (which is responsible for accreditation), "Don't hate the English, be English," a take-off on the Indymedia slogan "Don't hate the media, be the media."

Another issue in some places (e.g., Korea) was "IMColonialism." English-speaking activists from the global network often offered help with setting up local IMCs but sometimes went too far in taking the initiative without understanding local conditions. East Asian IMC activists tried to connect regionally, for example, through Asia-Pacific meetings, the IMC-Oceania project, and personal contacts.

Gabriele Hadl

See also Alternative Media; Alternative Media (Malaysia); Anarchist Media; Indymedia (The Independent Media Center); Indymedia and Gender; Internet Social Movement Media (Hong Kong)

Further Readings

Downing, J. D. H. (2003). The IMC movement beyond "the West." In A. Opel & D. Pompper (Eds.), *Representing resistance: Media, civil disobedience, and the global justice movement* (pp. 241–258). Westport, CT: Praeger.

Hadl, G., & Huang, S. (2007). IMC Taiwan (2003–5): Archeology and memory. *Interlocals.* http://interlocals .net/?q=node/144

INSTALLATION ART MEDIA

Installation art describes artworks that the audience physically enters or that take into account the physical and conceptual relationships among objects, the space in which they are arranged, and the body of the viewer. This admittedly broad definition suggests the sheer diversity of artworks grouped under this category. Installations may employ ordinary or "found" objects; industrially fabricated materials; traditional visual art forms; organic material such as soil, blood, or food; screen-based media like film or video; the performing arts; lighting and sound design; and even scent. They may be full of sensory stimuli or visually restrained, even nearly invisible. Installations may transform a gallery's white cube into a seemingly autonomous world or employ the social, physical, and historic characteristics of the place where they are produced, as site-specific artworks do. Some installations may invite extended, individual contemplation, whereas others spur the audience to group action.

Thus, it is impossible to speak in broad strokes about installation art. The term itself was not even settled until the late 1980s, when major museums began to commission artists to produce original works, often with very high production costs, for their galleries. Today, installation art often calls to mind large-scale, museum-based, and highly capitalized projects that require small armies of technical advisers, production assistants, and professional fabricators. However, installation art has a much longer history, beginning with some of the politicized cultural movements of the early 20th century, continuing through the unmarketable, ephemeral "environments" of experimental artists of the 1950s and 1960s, and coming into its own in the 1970s and 1980s alongside artistic engagement in feminist, gay rights, and antiwar movements.

While canonical art histories tend to downplay the ways that some installation art has furthered political goals, tensions between art's symbolic and sensory roles and the more goal-directed needs of social movements have often complicated attempts for artists to work within groups dedicated to achieving political change. Particularly in the

Euro-American tradition, which has traditionally prized artwork for its alleged universalism and transcendence of time, place, and politics, artists are often ambivalent about "instrumentalizing" their work in pursuit of specific social aims. Some of the most successful examples of art installations in social movements have involved the politics of representation: Marginalized groups have often successfully used art in general, and installation art in particular, to demand cultural and political visibility on their own terms. Finally, the existence of a distinct genre known as "installation art" may be coming to a close, as artists today are increasingly employing varied strategies in their work, of which recognizable art objects and art experiences are only a small part.

A Prehistory of Installation Art

Although the term *installation art* did not even exist 50 years ago, art historians have traced it to early 20th-century European avant-gardes. The term *avant-garde* originally meant a small, highly skilled group of soldiers who would explore the terrain ahead of a larger army. In a cultural sense, avant-garde refers to people and artworks that are challenging, innovative, or ahead of their time. Traditionally the avant-garde existed in conflict with established social norms and dominant aesthetics. Although some were committed to "art for art's sake," other avant-gardes extended their critiques to more political issues. The tension between the purely aesthetic and more politicized approaches to art continues.

The Dada movement, which arose in Europe in reaction to World War I's colossal industrialized slaughter, is one avant-garde associated with the prehistory of installation art. Dada artists attacked the basic philosophies of the warring European empires, rejecting their official values of beauty, art, and rationalism for their inability to direct away from war. Radical experiments in music, poetry, and theater were performed at the Cabaret Voltaire, which opened in 1916 in Zurich, Switzerland, a neutral country. These performances often mined the detritus of an emerging consumer culture, obscured the boundaries between audience and performer, and engaged all the spectators'

senses—all of which would prove highly influential in installation art. Other Dada groups were active in Europe and the United States and developed techniques that would revolutionize graphic design, literature, dance, and music.

However, the movement is better characterized as cultural rather than political. Although political issues were fiercely debated in the pages of various Dada publications, relatively few artists outside of the Berlin group became directly involved with antiwar organizing. Dada's most savage critiques were often leveled at the art world itself. In 1917, Marcel Duchamp famously entered a urinal (which he purchased at a hardware store and signed with a pseudonym) into a New York art exhibition that had claimed it would exhibit all entries. Whether offended by the symbolism or unwilling to accept an industrial object as art, the artists running the exhibition chose to hide *Fountain*, as it was satirically titled. Duchamp had exposed the exclusivity and conservatism of even the self-described avant-garde.

After the Dada movement disintegrated in the early 1920s, a former member of Berlin Dada, Kurt Schwitters, began what some art historians consider the first installation. Between 1923 and 1937, when he fled the Nazis, Schwitters slowly transformed several rooms of his home in Hannover, Germany, into a total sculptural environment he called the *Merzbau*. Using largely low-cost materials such as newspaper, cloth, wire, dead flowers, and glue, Schwitters obsessively constructed and re-constructed a highly personal artwork resembling at times a cave or cathedral and featuring intimate grottoes and shrines. Although a very private viewing experience that did not address the world beyond the studio, *Merzbau* contrasted with the European system of valuing artworks that was based on craft mastery, expensive materials, and, above all, the ability for collectors to buy and sell art objects. It would inspire later artists who became discouraged with art's role as a capitalist commodity.

Some artists associated with Dada, especially from the Paris group, went on to work as Surrealists in the 1920s and 1930s. Surrealism also viewed Enlightenment rationalism as a root of violence and oppression, but the Surrealists more often used traditional art media, such as painting; acknowledged a relationship to art history; and created work that was often beautiful. Surrealists were fascinated with the power of the unconscious mind and the theories of Sigmund Freud. Several Surrealist manifestos explicitly linked the liberation of the imagination with political revolution, and many Surrealists were actively involved in communist, leftist, and anticolonial political movements. The Surrealists were aware of the tensions between their political sympathies and the prestigious art venues for their work. They began exhibiting artwork in ways that they hoped would liberate the imagination and at the same time disrupt market-oriented art spectatorship and collection. In 1938, the International Surrealist Exhibition in Paris brought together more than 300 individual works in a specially designed environment now widely seen as a precursor to later installation art. Paintings and sculptures were hung tightly together on walls, doors, and pedestals while found objects were strewn around the gallery. In one corner, Salvador Dalí installed a pond, complete with water lilies, moss, and reeds, beside an antique-style bed with rumpled sheets. Like later installation art, the exhibition engaged all the senses; the smell of roasting coffee wafted through the space while recordings of screaming psychiatric patients assaulted spectators' ears. To top it all off, the exhibition opening was held in complete darkness, and visitors were given flashlights to explore the space and view the artwork. The exhibition intentionally overloaded the senses and provoked the subconscious mind to overcome habitual ways of thinking, viewing, and feeling.

Another avant-garde movement, Constructivism, arose in Russia in support of the Bolshevik Revolution's official goals of social and economic equality. Constructivist artists were dedicated to finding a visual and material vocabulary for expressing communist values and producing a revolutionary consciousness. They believed that the bold, unfamiliar language of abstraction and modernism could shock the viewer into seeing the world in a fresh way, and they produced countless propaganda posters and advertisements for new, state-run enterprises. Most often identified as a precursor of installation art is Vladimir Tatlin's proposed *Monument for the Third International*, which would have stood 100 meters higher than

the Eiffel Tower. Fabricated of steel and inspired by what Tatlin described as a "machine aesthetic," the tower would have symbolized the strength of the new Soviet Union's industrial workers, even as it also provided space for the public meetings and screenings that the new citizen needed. The utopian project suggested that space could embody revolutionary values and actually produce new kinds of social relationships for the viewers who entered it—an idea that continues to inspire some installation artists today.

The fate of Constructivism highlights some of the tensions that often have complicated artists' attempts to work with social and political movements. The belief that people need to be "shocked" comes across as more than a little arrogant. Not everyone wanted to be shocked—including many ranking Soviet officials. Constructivism and other avant-garde approaches were often criticized for being too difficult for the common people to understand, too similar to Western "bourgeois" art, and too abstract to succeed as propaganda. Constructivism was eventually banned, along with any other experimental art, when Joseph Stalin declared Socialist Realism the Soviet official artistic style in 1932.

This conflict is often replayed when artists work with campaigns for social and political change, which sometimes want artists to spread their message engagingly and understandably. Politically sympathetic artists, especially those trained in Europe or the United States, are often concerned that nuance and subtlety will be lost in the process. Often, like the Zurich Dadaists, artists are more interested in critiquing the underlying structures of belief that they see as producing the social conditions they abhor than intervening directly to change those conditions. This tension has produced a subtle but important difference between "activist" and "critical" art.

Critique or Activism?

Western aesthetic theory has evaluated artwork on narrow assumptions, usually ignoring the very specific cultural origins of these assumptions. Works of art were to be beautiful, without being merely pretty, and certainly not cute. Good art was autonomous of context, specific knowledge, or any special relationship to the audience. The best art was believed to be transcendent and universal: A masterpiece would be so judged in any time and place. Clearly, artwork produced within a social movement could clash with these assumptions. An artwork addressing injustice may very well not be beautiful. A play written for an activist organization is not autonomous, and a poster addressing a topical or local issue may not aspire to be universal. Although these assumptions have been roundly rejected, most recently by feminism, queer theory, and postcolonial criticism, they remain so deeply rooted that they continue to influence even their critics.

The notion of artistic autonomy has been particularly persistent. Cultural theorist Theodor Adorno provided one of the most influential Marxist defenses of artistic autonomy when he criticized political artists for presenting didactic, propagandistic work that oversimplified political complexity, debased the intelligence of the audience, and opted for a tidy dualism of good and evil. For Adorno, artistic autonomy could be repurposed for liberatory ends, a way to perpetually interrogate society, to ask the questions that unsettled one's own political allies—in other words, an open-ended "criticality" over a topically specific "activism." Adorno argued that formal innovations were important because they unsettled received beliefs.

Meanwhile in the 1950s and 1960s, a group of young, largely male, American artists were rediscovering the work of earlier European avant-gardes and beginning to create expanded sculptural "environments" that blurred the line between viewer and participant. In the late 1950s, Allan Kaprow began to create large, sculptural assemblages composed of paper, found objects, and other low-cost materials. Over time, the assemblages required greater physical engagement by the viewer and are now seen as among the first examples of installation art. In *Penny Arcade* (1957), viewers had to move and peer around strips of cloth hung in front of wall-hung pieces; in *Words* (1962), viewers physically entered a two-room space and were asked to rearrange words painted on cardboard piece hung on the gallery wall.

Around the same time, Kaprow began to produce what he called Happenings, or loosely scripted events in which the audience was asked to perform particular tasks singly or as a group,

thereby obliterating the distinction between performer and audience. Although there was rarely topical political content to the work and the degree of participation remained controlled by the artist, Kaprow sought to physically, intellectually, and emotionally engage the viewer. He implicitly suggested that a participatory art was more populist and democratic than an art object meant to be appreciated from afar, and he traced a connection between his projects of the early 1960s and the counterculture that arose soon afterward. Like Adorno, however, Kaprow preferred art that enacted a political stance through its *form* rather than promoted a political position through its *content*.

For some artists, however, the Vietnam War, anticolonial, and Black Power movements, the New Left, second-wave feminism, and the hippie counterculture were too urgent to be ignored. By 1969—the year after the assassinations of Martin Luther King Jr. and Robert Kennedy and the same year that the Stonewall raid touched off the gay liberation movement—many artists had come to see themselves as a political force. Organizations like the Art Workers' Coalition, the Guerilla Art Action Group, the Black Emergency Cultural Coalition, Angry Arts Against the War in Vietnam, and the Women Artists in Revolution were founded, and members often began their activism by singling out the part of the power structure that most immediately touched artists' lives: major art institutions. Over the next few years, these and other grassroots groups sponsored frequent protests, targeting museums with defense industry ties, exhibitions that excluded women and minorities, and a system of sales that enriched art galleries at the expense of artists. For many of these politicized artists, the only rational decision was to abandon traditional forms like painting and sculpture that could easily be sold to hang in a million-dollar home or become just another part of an investment portfolio.

As an art form that seemed to resist commodification, installation art proliferated alongside other developing forms like performance art, video art, process art, and earth art. New, artist-run galleries, often operated collectively, opened in former industrial lofts, church basements, and temporary storefronts. Installation art seemed to embody precisely the revolution in form that Adorno advocated. Whereas "autonomous" paintings and sculptures existed apart from the viewer as "masterpieces," installation art required a physical encounter between the viewer and the artwork. This dependence of the art on viewer participation was associated with a culture of openness and a politics of radical democracy.

Moreover, by the early 1970s, poststructuralist theory had begun to identify Western culture's enthronement of vision over the other senses with a drive to impose order through differentiation, control, and domination. Installation art's emphasis on multisensory, embodied experience implicitly challenged this. Finally, the immersive quality of installations meant that there was no single "correct" perspective from which they could be viewed; each individual viewer had his or her own unique experience of the work of art. This was in keeping with attacks against the supposed "universality" of Western culture leveled by feminist and anticolonial movements. Installation art seemed an almost intrinsically "critical" form in Adorno's sense.

However, even during the height of the ferment, relatively few artists employed explicitly political themes or content in their work or became politically involved in other ways. Perhaps Adorno may have reinforced many artists' individualistic impulses by giving them a political rationale to make work the art establishment would embrace.

The artists who most fully realized the potential of installation art to work reciprocally with social movements were those for whom the art world was not a safe bastion. Women, gays and lesbians, and people of color faced routine discrimination in the art world in the 1960s, 1970s, and beyond, and the work of these artists demonstrates that political installation art can be *both* formally innovative *and* activist. These artists used installation to liberate their own consciousness from oppression and to articulate an identity in opposition to the stereotyping and discrimination of the dominant culture.

Womanhouse and the Feminist Art Program

Recognizing that female art students were often openly ridiculed and harassed by their male colleagues and professors, the artist Judy Chicago founded the first feminist art programs in the United States, at California State University–Fresno in 1970 and, with Miriam Schapiro, at the

California Institute of the Arts in 1971. Chicago and Schapiro wanted to create a collaborative, mutually nurturing and emotionally responsive environment in keeping with feminist values, in opposition to the highly competitive, individualistic ethos of mainstream art schools. The program used techniques developed by women's "consciousness-raising" groups and encouraged students to explore the political aspects of their personal lives in their artwork.

In 1971–1972, the feminist art class took over an abandoned Los Angeles mansion slated for demolition. Under the direction of Chicago and Schapiro, 21 female students transformed the entire building into a cooperative installation called *Womanhouse.* The installation explored the gendered nature of domestic space, simultaneously challenging patriarchal ideas of "a woman's place," celebrating women's bodily experiences, and proclaiming the creativity of feminine-associated art forms such as embroidery, cooking, lacemaking, and quilting.

In *Nurturant Kitchen,* by Vicki Hodgetts, Susan Frazier, and Robin Weltsch, every surface of the room was painted pink, even the appliances, to symbolize the kitchen as the ultimate feminine space. Plastic fried eggs were fastened to the ceiling and morphed into breasts on the walls to symbolize the dual sexual and caregiving roles assigned to women. As in Kaprow's environments, visitors were invited to interact with the objects: The breasts were soft and spongy to the touch, and the kitchen drawers could be opened to reveal collaged imagery of exotic vacation locales.

Another installation was Faith Wilding's *Womb Room,* a much more minimal environment, which cocooned the visitor in exquisite crochet work and invited contemplation. Judy Chicago's own contribution, *Menstruation Bathroom,* confronted the viewer with a visceral tableau crammed with thousands of feminine hygiene products, many of which appeared to be used. Chicago's bathroom was particularly unsettling to many visitors at the time, and her insistence on locating feminist politics in the bodily experiences of womanhood has been criticized more recently as heavy-handed and dangerously simplistic.

Nevertheless, *Womanhouse* was a powerful example of feminist pedagogy that transformed the lives of many of the female students. The project, visited by nearly 10,000 people and reviewed in *Time* magazine, provided a powerful set of images and stories that reinforced the work of feminist organizers in other sectors.

Chicano Art Movement and the Border Arts Workshop

The Chicano art movement was another artist effort that grew from a broader social and political struggle. The term *Chicano* is used to describe politicized Mexican Americans. It connotes identification with one's Mexican, Spanish, and Indigenous heritage in opposition to accepting the categories of White America (such as Hispanic) or the pressure to assimilate. The movement began in the mid-1960s when activists supporting United Farm Workers' labor struggles began producing graphics. The art movement grew quickly as both vernacular and college-trained artists used visual means to express frustration and rage at a deeply racist society and inspire others to resist.

Like feminist artists, Chicanas/os wanted to celebrate the popular, culturally specific visual expressions that were devalued by mainstream aesthetics. Chicano art embraced so-called low culture—the world of advertising imagery, bright colors, plastic knick-knacks, and "folk" art motifs—and created work that was a celebration of life and a nose-thumbing to middle-class White ideas of taste and decorum. While much of the art took the forms of mural painting, posters, and sculpture, many installations were also created by artists who identified with the Chicana/o art movement, especially Chicana feminists. Artists like Amalia Mesa-Baines were inspired by the tradition of home altar-making that was an important part of Mexican religious expression, often tended by women. In *An Ofrenda for Dolores del Río* (1984), Mesa-Baines placed the 1940s Hollywood film star at the center of an elaborate altar festooned with lace and covered in candles and ritual objects, celebrating her as a bilingual, binational heroine, whose successful career on both sides of the border suggests cultural and personal possibilities beyond assimilation.

The Border Arts Workshop/Taller de Arte Fronterizo (BAW/TAF) was an outgrowth of the Chicana/o art movement founded in San Diego in 1984 by the artist David Avalos and the Centro Cultural de la Raza. The group, which included dozens of collaborators over the years, organized scores of events on the U.S.–México border between 1984 and 2000 to address issues of migration, binational culture, immigrant rights, and the militarization of the border. BAW/TAF sponsored and produced installations, videos, performance art, direct actions, and public dialogue that brought together artists, writers, activists, scholars, and ordinary people from both sides of the border. Their "artwork" was as much organizing experiences and discussions as it was producing objects. The BAW/TAF was less interested in "shocking" the viewer than in using accessible images, forms, and experiences to generate dialogue around pressing social issues.

Artists and the AIDS Crisis

One of the most serious social issues of the 1980s was the AIDS pandemic, yet in the early years of the disease there was next to no public dialogue about it. The disease had claimed 30,000 lives in the United States (and tens of thousands more around the world) by the time then-president Ronald Reagan publicly uttered the word *AIDS* in 1986. In 1987, activists, frustrated with previous efforts to draw attention to and destigmatize the disease, founded the AIDS Coalition to Unleash Power, better known as ACT UP. ACT UP was dedicated to using direct action to end the AIDS crisis.

The New Museum of Contemporary Art invited ACT UP to produce an installation about their work. They created *Let the Record Show* in the museum's storefront window to frame the disease as a political and human rights issue, not a matter of personal failing. They featured an enlarged photograph of Nazi officials at the Nuremberg Trials, with cutouts of U.S. officials placed in the role of defendants. Each figure had a marker at its feet with a quotation reflecting a "do nothing" or "blame the victim" approach to the crisis. An LED display cycled through statistics about the disease. The installation, visible to the public even without entering the museum, was so successful that members of ACT UP created their own group in 1988 and began to produce art about AIDS exclusively. This group, called Gran Fury, primarily produced graphic art and leveraged its good relationships with major art institutions to gain access to public spaces, such as billboards, that they never would have been able to get on their own.

Gran Fury was not the first artistic group to address the AIDS crisis. The collaborative effort known as Group Material, initiated in 1980, became known for their installations and public actions on many topics, including what they saw as the interlocking issues of AIDS, the crisis of affordable housing, and the future of democracy. Group Material's work took the form of visually spare installations that joined together documents, videos, slogans, pictures, art objects, and consumer products that revealed various aspects of the complex issues they addressed. Like the Border Arts Workshop, Group Material transformed curation—the selection of objects and programming of events—into its own form of art. Although their work was much less visceral than Gran Fury's, Group Material believed that the process of sorting through the information they presented and engaging in discussion, even argument, in the events they put on was itself a model of the democratic process that is necessary to address any political and social crisis.

Indigenous Rights

By the 1980s, university-trained American Indian artists were beginning to receive some recognition from art institutions for work that drew on installation, performance, and video art and addressed issues of representation and politics. Native artists like Hachivi Edgar Heap of Birds (Cheyenne/Arapaho) used the opportunity to openly contest how American history has been told and for whom. Heap of Bird's 1990 project *Building Minnesota* consisted of 40 signs commemorating the 40 Dakota warriors executed by Abraham Lincoln in 1862 and 1865 for fighting in the Dakota War. The bilingual signs, in English and Dakota, visually mimicked the look of historical markers and were installed in a historic district of Minneapolis as a reminder of the genocidal price of American "progress."

Other Native artists produced work blurring the boundaries between performance and installation. James Luna (Luiseño) is best known for his *Artifact Piece* (1985–1987), a "living installation" in which he donned a loin cloth and lay in a glass display case in San Diego's Museum of Man. The project addressed the early anthropologists' practice of kidnapping Indigenous people and forcing them to live in displays, but it also questioned how far the museum and its spectators had moved on—especially when legal protection for sacred Native American gravesites was not yet established. Viewers expecting a mannequin were shocked that Luna's figure was alive and quite unsettled when he reversed the power of their gaze by looking back at them. Luna's piece was so influential that it was restaged in 2008 by Erica Lord (Athabaskan/Dena'ina). Her reenactment, which was presented with Luna's cooperation at the National Museum of the American Indian, brought issues of gender to the forefront while focusing attention on whether anthropologists' and museum practices had in fact improved.

The End of Installation Art?

All of these installation artworks underscore the near impossibility of differentiating installation artwork from other forms of artistic expression. Were the BAW/TAF and Group Material curators, organizers, or artists? Were Gran Fury and Heap of Birds' signs graphic design, intervention, or installation? Was *Artifact Piece* an installation or a performance? As installation art has been mainstreamed by museums interested in introducing contemporary art to patrons who want a good show, it has become harder to find someone who self-identifies as an "installation artist." Rather than play taxonomic games, more and more artists are taking a tactical, even pragmatic, approach to their work.

The Argentinean artist group Ala Plástica (Plastic Wing) is exemplary of this approach. From 1991, the artists were active in a small town just south of Buenos Aires. It is one of the most polluted spots in the world. Rather than presenting alarming images to shock a distant audience into action, critiquing the dualistic man versus nature thinking underlying environmental problems, or producing experiences to enable people to think differently about ecology, Ala Plástica worked with their neighbors—fishermen and farmers, scientists and teachers—to create programs that work simultaneously on the level of policy and metaphor. For example *Junco/Emergent Species* (1995) was a project that reinvigorated the ability of a particular reed to purify coastal waters. Following extensive research, the native reed species was replanted, community organizing was undertaken to secure continued local government support, and educational programming was undertaken to renew the local people's connection with the plant, which had been a significant part of Indigenous life for hundreds of years. The installation art portion of the project involved site-specific, ephemeral constructions of reeds on the site, as well as a gallery installation that presented visitors with the many layers and strategies of the project.

However, Ala Plástica believed that all of their work, not merely the portion that can be exhibited, is art. They insisted that art constitutes a distinctive mode of engaging with human and natural realities. Unlike Adorno, they insisted that this change be made manifest in results. Artists like Ala Plástica are taking installation art's promise of democracy, multisensory experience, and attention to multiple perspectives and turning it into a method for aesthetic engagement, with the physical installation only one outcome among many, and possibly not the most important one.

It is premature to declare the "end" of installation art. However, it is likely more and more artists will find ways to reinvent both art and social movements through their work, perhaps finally overcoming the impasses of art and politics that marked the 20th century.

Sarah Kanouse

See also Anarchist Media; Environmental Movement Media; Feminist Media: An Overview; Indigenous Media in Latin America; Performance Art and Social Movement Media: Augusto Boal

Further Readings

Ala Plástica: http://www.alaplastica.org.ar

Ault, J. (Ed.). (2002). *Alternative New York, 1965–1985.* Minneapolis: University of Minnesota Press.

Bishop, C. (2005). *Installation art: A critical history.* New York: Routledge.

Gaspar de Alba, A. (1998). *Chicano art: Inside/outside the master's house.* Austin: University of Texas Press.

Lippard, L. (1984). Intersections. In *Flypunkter/Vanishing point.* Stockholm, Sweden: Moderna Museet.

Reiss, J. H. (1999). *From margin to center: The spaces of installation art.* Cambridge, MA: MIT Press.

Suderburg, E. (Ed.). (2000). *Space, site, intervention: Situating installation art.* Minneapolis: University of Minnesota Press.

INTERNET AND THE FALL OF DICTATORSHIP (INDONESIA)

In the mid-1990s in Indonesia, the political opposition's uses of the Internet even managed to help topple a strongman (General Suharto) who, until his unanticipated resignation in May 1998, had been Asia's longest reigning postwar ruler. He had seized power in 1965 with U.S. support and then engineered a bloodbath of over half a million opponents, real and supposed. His regime was notorious for its corruption, and his army for savage suppression of dissent, especially during its attempt to annex eastern Timor (now the nation of Timor Leste) after Portuguese colonial rule collapsed there in 1974.

In the 1990s, however, Indonesian students, nongovernmental organizations (NGOs), and journalists marked a new era by speeding the regime's downfall. Intense discussions about democracy and human rights were held in cyberspace and then disseminated through photocopying downloaded materials. Many militant actions were also coordinated on the Internet.

As a result, endeavoring to keep a grasp on the Internet became close to an obsession for the regime. Try as it might, the state apparatus seemed unable to predict or contain its rapid growth. The other crucial if paradoxical aspect of the situation was that in Indonesia—even up to 2010—the Internet was still free of censorship, though certainly not of political surveillance. Thus, although activists belonging to the "illegal" faction of the opposition Indonesian Democratic Party (PDI) might be living clandestinely and under assumed names, they were free to convey their propaganda on the web, and even insult the head of the armed forces and the president.

This meant that notwithstanding the draconic Anti-Subversion Law, a small desktop or laptop combined with a telephone connection enabled them to speak their minds without much fear of official retribution. Their words and ideas could travel throughout the country and even beyond its borders. Many came to use a number of simple but powerful encryption tools such as Pretty Good Privacy (PGP), smuggled in from the United States by human rights activists, which shielded Internet users from repression. Further safeguards were available through the anonymity offered by Hotmail, Yahoo, and Iname, among others. In addition, very few security forces or intelligence service staff at that time were Internet-savvy.

Role of the Indonesia Postal Service

The arrival of PC (personal computer) clones and subsequent proliferation of pirated software enabled students and other computer buffs to demonstrate their creativity in both software and hardware. Initially, business applications had predominated. But in 1996, the Indonesia Postal Service agency decided to expand its business by opening Internet service providers (ISPs) in every provincial capital. It is no exaggeration to say that 1996 was the year cyberspace routes opened up for Indonesia.

By 1998, Indonesian subscribers already numbered some 100,000. Many belonged to the professional and managerial class although there were also some members of the small upper class, both business people and bureaucrats. Students and NGOs were among the earliest and most enthusiastic adopters.

An interesting development was the emergence of small commercial Internet sites in big cities, usually cafés or telecenters. In university towns especially, these were cheap and hence extremely popular among students. From these sites, many activists and students were able to receive news about events not fully reported in mainstream media. Because every café also provided a printer for hire, users could obtain hard copies. Photocopied printouts of alternative news were then distributed to the grass roots.

Student Networks and the Apakabar Mailing List

Indonesian students studying abroad had discovered the Internet's many uses earlier than their compatriots at home. Many of these began using it for academic exchange through online conferences they created, as well as through listservs and mailing lists. Student networks soon sprang up, such as IndozNet for those studying in Australia, ISNet for

Muslim students, and ParokiNet for Catholic students. Cyberspace also enabled them to debate topics considered taboo back home, such as the Indonesian government's human rights abuses and repressive policies.

One free mailing list in particular was widely used at that point, namely Apakabar, founded by an expatriate U.S. citizen, John McDougall. In 1984 he had set up a company to sell research findings and quality articles from the Indonesian media. McDougall also disseminated the data he compiled to various newsgroups and Internet conferences. Building upon the rapid take-up of this service, in 1990 he set up Apakabar (which means "How are you?" in Indonesian), which—very importantly—offered anonymity to users.

Apakabar offered views from the radical to the moderate, from prodemocracy activists to intelligence officers masquerading as ordinary citizens. These latter were supposed to counter any negative information about the regime, and they did their job using both polite and crude language. But Apakabar aficionados were almost always able to spot which ones were bogus, and they countered their material so effectively that most agents retired from the fray. Indeed, only a few seemed able to cope with using such a democratic—at times near-anarchic—medium.

The roles of Indonesian NGOs in Internet use were increasingly important. Already in 1990, the Legal Aid Institute (Indonesian acronym LBH) began to post reports on the Internet about the human rights situation in Indonesia on Apakabar. However, only in 1995 when LBH posted an Urgent Action (UA) on Apakabar, was cyberspace finally acknowledged as a key site of contestation between prodemocracy activists and regime supporters.

This UA, consisting of three short sentences, protested the murder, most probably by the armed forces, of Marsinah, a woman labor activist who had been leading a strike in East Java. In less than 6 hours after the UA was posted, the fax machines in the Office of the President, the Ministry of Foreign Affairs, and the Ministry of Defense and Security were jammed with hundreds of protests from around the world. This dramatically transformed Marsinah, a young and unknown village girl from East Java, into a global workers' heroine. It also set off an NGO-instigated online information war against the regime.

Mainstream Media Censorship and the Internet's Spread

The 1994 crackdown on three leading magazines—*Tempo*, *DeTIK*, and *Editor*—generated a further push into Internet use. There were already websites and listservs run by Indonesian journalists and academics, ever more openly challenging the regime's heavy-handed control over mainstream media. Fearing they would be closed down as well, the rest of Indonesia's media had practically surrendered to the authorities. But ex–*Tempo* staffers and management decided to go online and developed *Tempo Interaktif*. This was the first step in professional journalists' use of the Internet as a tool of dissent. Student activists downloaded *Tempo Interaktif* stories, made hard copies, and sold them on campuses and to NGOs.

People thirsty for accurate information about Indonesia began flocking to the web. The emergence of sites such as SiaR, MateBEAN, MeunaSAH, MamberaMO, KDPNet and AJINews, which complemented materials offered by other sites and listservs, fed this demand.

These information developments are widely recognized as having been pivotal in strengthening people's conviction that it was time for the Suharto regime to go. Among the most explosive material, made available only on the Internet, was a list of the staggering assets of the Suharto and Habibie families and their cronies, compiled by George Junus Aditjondro. This was downloaded, photocopied, and circulated while Suharto was still in power. After Suharto's ouster, mainstream media finally began to quote Aditjondro's research, and it subsequently appeared in book form.

The SiarList mailing list featured the *GoRo-GoRo*, a collection of political jokes against Suharto and his supporters. This became immensely popular and was widely disseminated. The jokes were eventually published in book form in a print-run of tens of thousands.

Censorship of mainstream media did not vanish overnight even after the regime had fallen. Consequently, young journalists, frustrated that their reports were cut at key places, posted the full text on the Internet. Some even formed an online discussion group called Kuli Tinta (Ink Slave). The SiarList continues like a news agency, with political and economic news as well as articles on human rights.

Direct Internet access was not the only point of access to these materials. For those without it, child newspaper vendors sold hard copies of downloaded news at low prices. These sold very well, but the children were unwittingly putting themselves at risk. In 1996, the police arrested two university instructors on the charge of possessing paper versions of downloaded Siar news items, and even arrested two children for selling downloaded photocopies.

Efforts to Control and Censor

In Indonesia, claiming the young needed protecting from pornography and guerrilla politics, the Suharto government threatened restrictive actions. Senior military officials also attacked postings for being "divisive," for "inciting," or for "endangering political stability."

Interference in Internet flows was present but not systematic in the period leading up to Suharto's downfall. E-mail sometimes failed to reach its destination or was delayed for several days. E-mail addresses known to be used by dissidents were thought to be subject to censorship attempts by unknown individuals within certain ISPs. In the days leading up to the huge student demonstrations in 1998, ISP access in Jakarta was very difficult. Although it may have been that too many people were trying to use the system simultaneously, many observers believed the ISPs were being compelled to sabotage the system.

A number of conglomerates, such as mining transnational Freeport McMoran, apparently censored postings from certain mailing lists. Every posting from any of these lists would be returned to the provider from which they were sent with the note "User Name Unknown." A number of sensitive postings were also discarded, giving as reason "Address Unknown."

Almost all advocacy NGOs in Indonesia agreed early on that the Internet would not necessarily shield them from official retaliation. Eventually, they concluded that in addition to using commercial ISPs, they also needed e-mail access that did not have any direct link to the Internet. In 1994, this community developed a restricted e-mail system called the NusaNet Consortium. Initially, five cities operated as NusaNet subhosts. NusaNet also played a major role in disseminating alternative news from the Internet to the NGO community. According to its users, the NusaNet e-mail system and the newsgroups within it were fairly secure because they generally used the PGP encryption system.

Infiltration attempts appeared at that time mostly to focus on East Timor/Timor Leste. In February 1997, hackers, apparently from Portugal, infiltrated an Indonesian Ministry of Foreign Affairs website regarded as having disseminated lies about East Timor. The hackers managed to change the webpage, altering "Welcome to the Department of Foreign Affairs, Republic of Indonesia" to "Welcome to the Department of Foreign Affairs, Fascist Republic of Indonesia."

In 1996, Portuguese hackers had also penetrated the Research and Technology Ministry's homepage, which had been producing enthusiastic accounts of the technological progress under then Minister B. J. Habibie. The attack was to mark the fifth anniversary of the Santa Cruz tragedy in which Indonesian soldiers shot dead a still undetermined number of unarmed proindependence Timorese demonstrators. Such hacker attacks were repeated on various official Indonesian government sites, including the armed forces, the police, the Ministry of Defense and Security, and the ruling party Golkar. In retaliation, pro–Indonesian government hackers attacked a Portuguese website known as the "den" of computer activists.

The Internet in Indonesia's Future

Today, the Internet continues to be crucial to Indonesia's future and is still regarded as an alternative channel for views and news that would otherwise remain unheard and unwritten. Although Indonesian authorities control media less than before, reports still go unpublished and vital information does not get out. The Internet has continued as the one venue where people can say the otherwise unsayable and get access to information that mainstream media avoid. Given rocketing print media costs, the Internet may even become the main news platform, in Indonesia as elsewhere.

Tedjabayu

See also Alternative Media (Malaysia); Community Radio and Natural Disasters (Indonesia); Independent Media (Burma/Myanmar); Social Movement Media (Philippines); Social Movement Media, 1980s–2000s

(Japan); Social Movement Media in 1987 Clashes (Korea); *Suara Independen* (Indonesia)

Further Readings

Aditjondro, G. J. (1997, September 3). Suharto and his family: The looting of East Timor. *Green Left Weekly.* http://www.greenleft.org.au/1997/288/16097

Aditjondro, G. J. (1998). *Dari Soeharto ke Habibie, Guru Kencing Berdiri Murid Kencing Berlari: Kedua Puncak Korupsi, Kolusi dan Nepotisme Rezim Orde Baru* [From Suharto to Habibie: Two crests of corruption, collusion and nepotism]. Jakarta, Indonesia: Pijar Indonesia dan Masyarakat Indonesia Untuk Kemanusiaan.

Aditjondro, G. J. (2006). *Korupsi Kepresidenan, Reproduksi Oligarki Berkaki Tiga: Istana, Tangsi dan Partai Pennguasa* [Presidential corruption, a tripod of oligarchic reproduction: The palace, the military, and the ruling political party]. Yogyakarta, Indonesia: LKiS (Institute for Islamic and Social Studies).

Ford, M. T. (2003). *NGO as outside intellectual: A history of non-governmental organizations' role in the Indonesian labour movement.* Unpublished doctoral thesis, University of Wollongong, New South Wales, Australia.

Hill, D. T. (1996). *The press in New Order Indonesia.* Perth: University of Western Australia Press.

Hill, D. T., & Sen, K. (1997, April). Wiring the warung to global gateways: The Internet in Indonesia. *Indonesia Magazine, 63,* 67–89.

Hill, D. T., & Sen, K. (2005). *The Internet in Indonesia's new democracy.* London: Routledge.

Mahdi, W. (1995, April). *The Internet factor in Indonesia: Was that all?* Paper presented at the 54th annual meeting of the Association for Asian Studies.

Steele, J. E. (2005). *Wars within: The story of* Tempo, *an independent magazine in Soeharto's Indonesia.* Jakarta, Indonesia: Equinox Publishing.

INTERNET SOCIAL MOVEMENT MEDIA (HONG KONG)

A few years after Great Britain handed over Hong Kong to China, Hong Kong joined the Internet activism bandwagon. By 2007, household penetration rates of personal computer and Internet service in Hong Kong were 71.7% and 67.1%, among the highest in the world. Over the past few years, Internet social movement media (ISMM) have played a unique role in Hong Kong in scrutinizing the government, and they have become a new mobilizing power, a platform for discussion of current affairs, and a social networking platform among politically active people.

Although the spread of new communication technologies was an essential condition for this development of social movement media, it also had much to do with social and political sea changes. On July 1, 2003, half a million people took to the streets expressing their discontent at Hong Kong's National Security Bill, which they were worried would undermine freedom of expression in Hong Kong (population about 7 million). They also protested against the government's ineffective administration and demanded universal suffrage. It was the biggest political movement since the colonial era, and thus it drew much international attention.

In 2004, several radio talk show hosts resigned, claiming political suppression by the Chinese Central Government and the Hong Kong government, and the public again felt suffocated by another freedom of speech crisis. Because "freedom of speech" is commonly held by Hong Kong people as the core value that defines their local identity with regard to the authoritarianism of Mainland China, they felt it urgent to arrest this seemingly worsening situation.

Triggered by this panic, a number of Internet social movement media emerged, ranging from independent media websites, Internet video, and Internet radio to online discussion forums (see Table 1).

All together they have constituted an energetic force for democratization from below, particularly advocating citizen participation in social affairs. Therefore, *Internet social movement media* in this entry refers to the independently owned and operated noncommercial Internet platforms whose emergence was triggered by the July 1 protest and thereafter became an impetus to further movement growth.

Independent Media Websites

The last wave of independent print media in Hong Kong can be dated to the 1970s and 1980s magazines such as *The 70's Biweekly, War Message, October Commentary,* and *Young Plant,* which were closely tied to the torrent of social movements at that time (union movement, democracy movement, official language movement). Succeeding this tradition in the new information age, Inmediahk (www.Inmediahk.net) is now the most influential independent media website in Hong Kong.

Inmediahk was established in 2004 by a group of renowned public intellectuals, veteran media practitioners, and social activists. Because of its popularity, Inmediahk is well known among young people, but what also makes it so prominent is that its members actively participated and even initiated numerous social movements, such as the anti–World Trade Organization protest in Hong Kong in December 2006 and the Star Ferry Pier preservation movement in 2007. (The pier played a pivotal role in the 1960s anticolonial movement.)

Throughout, Inmediahk took up a dual role as a voice for both reporters and activists, reporting

Table 1   Different Forms of ISMM in Hong Kong

	Internet Column	*Internet Radio*	*Internet Video*	*Discussion Board*
Exemplar	Inmedia HK	People Radio Hong Kong	RebuildHK	E-politics21
Date of founding	October 2004	June 2004	June 2003	June 2003
Background of leading figure(s)	Cultural critics, academics, and veteran media practitioners	Veteran social activists	Professional video producers	A group of young active netizens
Agenda(s)	Universal suffrage, cultural policy	Universal suffrage, minority interests	Universal suffrage	Universal suffrage

what they were doing and what they would do next. In response to criticism that their practices did not abide by objectivity and impartiality, Chu Hoi-Dik, their leading figure, made it clear the organization was independent but not neutral. Whether or not people agreed, it was always the fundamental belief that ISMM should go beyond the confines of mainstream media.

The difference between Inmediahk and its predecessors was not only in its agenda but also in inclusiveness. For Inmediahk, people could post their articles or give feedback on others' work as long as they had registered online. An Inmediahk survey found their readership shared similar political attitudes: prodemocracy, antidiscrimination, and pro–minimum wage. About half of the readers were college-educated. Inmediahk succeeded in constructing an online community, even though it was loosely organized.

Internet Radio

Hong Kong citizens cannot legally set up a non-commercial FM radio station. The ratio of population to radio channel (FM, AM, & shortwave) is over half a million to one, higher than that of Singapore, South Korea, or Taiwan. Three broadcasters own all 13 channels. Yet the radio industry has held firmly to the tradition of speaking for the people, not for the power-holders. As Hong Kong democracy is underdeveloped, radio talk shows have taken up a surrogate democratic function and have acted as a popular chamber, channeling dissident voices and also bolstering their power to challenge the government.

As in many countries, there is a group of activists performing civil disobedience with micro-FM broadcasting in order to expand freedom of speech. But most people want to play it safe, opting for Internet radio. Benefiting from streaming technologies, for example, shoutcast.com, and the easy availability of broadcasting equipment, people can set up their own online radio channels. Examples include Openradio (www.openradiohk.com), People Radio Hong Kong, Myradio (www.myradio.com.hk), and 71 Radio.

Internet radio can enable Hong Kong people to reclaim and enact their right of radio broadcasting, and it also offers a new space with looser regulations and legal measures than traditional radio.

Sensitive political issues (e.g., Falun Gong, or Taiwan independence), social issues (e.g., sex, homosexuality), and subcultures (e.g., *anime*, comics) can be addressed without fear.

Internet Video

Also, with low-price equipment and accessible Internet platforms, independent video producers could quickly respond to current affairs, producing the videos on their own, uploading them to their own websites, and doing e-mail advertising. Rebuildhk (www.rebuildhk.com) was the most successful case. There were local groups ceaselessly producing alternative videos and films for years, for example, Videopower, which uses videotapes or discs to capture the world from firsthand experience. Those videos are mostly documentaries in realist style that tend to reflect the plight of grassroots people, the issues mainstream media would normally ignore. The videos are usually shown in small theaters and community town halls to small audiences. Other independent video groups, for example, Vartivist, also use the Internet as a broadcast platform, but with a small audience. What made Rebuildhk's videos so influential was that their contents resonated with Hong Kong's collective memory.

To arouse public interest, Freeman Lo, the founder of Rebuildhk, chose video clips from mainstream television news, sound bites from politicians, and matched them with oldies music to construct his version of "the Hong Kong story." His most remarkable work was a music video of a 1970s oldie, *Under the Lion Rock*, a classic song embodying the soaring spirit and togetherness of Hong Kong people at that time. Historical clips showing Hong Kong's development (images of skyscrapers, efficient transportation) were edited together with current news clips showing people participating in political activities, to convey a message: We did it before for economic development, we can do it again for our political development, as long as we stand together steadfastly.

This combination of emotional narrative and rhetoric echoed in the hearts of many and thus facilitated the strength of the July 1 protest. Due to its mass appeal, the website had more than 1 million clicks in its first two years, and it even attracted much mainstream media attention to this new phenomenon. Although this kind of remixed video achieved popularity by appropriating mass culture, its dependence on mainstream TV materials also limited its inventiveness and space for oppositional perspectives, because sources available had been preselected by mainstream media. Therefore, its claim to challenge hegemony remains in doubt.

Online Forum

Online forums are the most participatory and interactive form of ISMM. E-politics 21 is an example. Triggered by the July 1 protest, a group of young people launched an antiestablishment and prodemocracy online forum. They circulated information about current affairs and did culture jamming, such as creating and re-creating political jokes, photos, and badges. Some became popular after mainstream media covered them. E-politics 21 also served as the information and discussion center of the three forms of ISMM already mentioned.

Moreover, E-politics 21 also jumped from online to the real world. Not only did it cooperate with Internet radio stations such as PRHK in large-scale projects, such as the "2004 Hong Kong legislature election broadcast initiative," but it also organized its members into a group to join prodemocracy protests. In the protests, they wore their own T-shirts and carried their own banners to declare "netizens want universal suffrage," which showed their strong identities as active Internet users. As with Inmediahk, E-politics 21 succeeded in constructing a political identity among its community of users.

ISMM as People's Channels?

ISMM have several unique characteristics. The first lies in their citizen journalism activity. Departing from elitist professional journalism, Internet media can operate in the "open publishing" mode, encouraging content contribution and interactivity from the public. Moreover, whereas traditional journalism embraces objectivity and impartiality, public journalism emphasizes speaking for the powerless, to enhance equality, justice, and democracy.

Yet like mainstream media, ISMM need editors in charge of layout, editing the articles for length, and compiling articles into a special theme issue; radio program supervisors to oversee station development and be responsible for daily operation; and online forum facilitators to maintain orderly discussion. There is still hierarchy in the ISMM production process, but it is less entrenched than in mainstream media.

Second, to avoid political or commercial interference, ISMM practices the "gift economy" more effectively than their print predecessors. Although most ISMM financial sources come from fundraising at public events and through the leading figures' personal networks, online donations also became significant via PayPal. Not least, the media contents are offered in "open source" mode, free for download, use, transfer, or even re-creation. An economic cycle of "gift" exchanges has thus been formed.

Having analyzed different ISMM, the key question is can they develop as people's channels? The answer is in part yes. The Internet is a mixed blessing for social movement media. On one hand, unlike traditional media, it has enabled a relatively egalitarian and automatic public space. People can stay true to their opinions, without bothering much about subsequent economic and political backlash.

On the other hand, ISMM inevitably exclude the "information have-nots." Internet radio's live audience is no more than a thousand even for the most popular program. ISSM influence cannot be comparable to mainstream media. As a result, ISMM in Hong Kong in 2010 was still "small-circle media," popular mainly among politically interested and active young people.

In the future, if ISMMs concentrate on expanding their impact rather than just focusing on producing media content, the next steps would be to strengthen cooperation among ISMMs, to challenge official media policies, and, most important, to engage in public education about the necessity and urgency of what they are attempting. As social movement media, the most crucial element is still support from those many Hong Kong people who take freedom of speech and expression as a hallmark of their citizenship.

Dennis Ka-kuen Leung, Celia Tsui Yuen Sze,
and Miranda Ma Lai Yee

See also Anarchist Media; Channel Four TV and Underground Radio (Taiwan); Citizen Journalism; Citizens' Media; Copyleft; Creative Commons; Hong Kong In-Media; Indymedia (The Independent Media Center); Indymedia: East Asia; Online Nationalism (China)

Further Readings

Chan, J. M., & So, Y. K. (2001). The surrogate democracy function of the media: Hong Kong citizens' and journalists' evaluations of media performance. In S. K. Lau, M.-K. Lee, P.-S. Wan, & S.-L. Wong (Eds.), *Indicators of social development: Hong Kong 2001* (pp. 249–276). Hong Kong: Hong Kong Institute of Asia-Pacific Studies & Chinese University of Hong Kong.

Gillmor, D. (2004). *We the media: Grassroots journalism by the people, for the people.* Sebastopol, CA: O'Reilly.

Ip, Y. C. (2007). *Small media, big event* [in Chinese]. Hong Kong: Step Forward Multimedia.

So, Y. K., & Lee, Y. L. (2007). The radio phone-in talk show as the people's council in postcolonial Hong Kong. In Y. S. Cheng (Ed.), *The Hong Kong Special Administrative Region in its first decade* (pp. 827–852). Hong Kong: City University of Hong Kong Press.

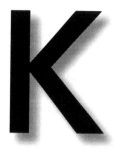

KAYAPÓ VIDEO (BRASIL)

Kayapó video is an important example of how the adoption of new technologies can help Indigenous communities not only to better communicate with other groups, including at the national and international levels, but also to strengthen their identity and culture.

The Kayapó are one of a group of Indigenous Gê-speaking tribes that inhabit the Amazon River Basin of Brasil. Their territory in the State of Pará, made up of tropical rainforest, is mostly contained in six reserves that cover a combined area of some 100,000 square kilometers, which is approximately the size of Portugal. As of 1993, roughly 14 Kayapó villages were left, with a total population of approximately 5,000. The name Kayapó means "resembling apes"; it was not picked by the tribe itself but given to them by the neighboring Indian tribes.

In 1985, photographer Monica Frota and two anthropologists started the Indigenous video initiative *Mekaron Opoi D'joi* (he who creates images) in the language spoken by the Kayapó tribes in Brasil. Once the Kayapó had the video cameras in their own hands, they used them for the preservation of the cultural memory of the community, recording their rituals.

They soon switched to exchange political speeches and to document their protests against the Brasilian state. The political dimension of the project was a logical development; the Kayapó showed a high level of understanding of how media interacted with public opinion. Their image of high-tech Indians quickly gained the front pages of important journals, including a cover of *Time* magazine, when they denounced the construction of a hydroelectric dam in Altamira that would flood their land. They successfully sought political and financial support from non-Indigenous public opinion, nongovernmental organizations, and governments, both in Brasil and abroad, to compel the Brasilian state to recognize legally their territory and their rights to control its resources.

One important source of support was the increasingly positive evaluation of non-Western cultures, which is associated with anthropology and multicultural movements. Another source of support was the growing movement in defense of human rights. Most important of all was environmentalism, according to Terence Turner, the U.S. anthropologist who supported the Kayapó video initiative. Turner said that from the moment they acquired video cameras of their own, the Kayapó made a point of making video records of their major political confrontations with the national society.

Instead of just being subjects of documentary films, the Kayapó quickly understood the advantages of video technology as a communication tool for transforming their social and political reality. Thus, the appropriation of video tools by the Kayapó strengthens the notion that people can master their own history, as long as they can master their own representation in the media. Video has been perceived as a key way for economically deprived communities to gain some measure of democratic control over information and communication sources currently controlled by either the state or multinational corporations.

Alfonso Gumucio Dagron

See also Eland Ceremony, Abatwa People's (Southern Africa); Indigenous Media (Australia); Indigenous Media (Burma/Myanmar); Indigenous Media in Latin America; Indigenous Radio Stations (México)

Further Readings

Turner, T. (1992). Defiant images: The Kayapó appropriation of video. *Anthropology Today, 8*(6), 5–16.

KEFAYA MOVEMENT MEDIA (EGYPT)

On December 12, 2004, the first demonstration directly attacking the regime of Egyptian President Hosni Mubarak was organized by the fledgling social movement Kefaya (Enough). It was the first of a series of protests that the movement staged against Mubarak and his National Democratic Party (NDP) over the course of the next 10 months. *Kefaya* means "enough" in Egyptian colloquial Arabic and became the de facto name for the movement formally called the Egyptian Movement for Change. It was also a simple and powerful rallying cry that was widely employed in the movement's media tactics. Formed in August 2004 as a social movement coalition, Kefaya united activists with all manner of political and ideological backgrounds—Nasserites, socialists, liberals, and Islamists—under the common goal of opposing the continued oppressive control of Egypt's political climate by the Mubarak regime and the NDP.

Among Kefaya's most clearly stated demands were (a) the end of Mubarak's rule, (b) the distribution of decision-making powers beyond the presidency, and (c) preventing the president's son, Gamal, from succeeding his father as president. These goals were largely shaped by three events in 2005: (1) a May referendum to approve a constitutional amendment permitting direct multiparty

presidential elections, (2) the presidential elections in September, and (3) the October and November parliamentary elections. Throughout this period, the Kefaya movement maintained a consistent presence in the streets of Cairo, organizing regular protests, clashing with law enforcement officials, and attracting a significant amount of both domestic and foreign attention.

Initially the movement's media tactics were conventional. Leaders were wary of confrontational tactics and used relatively cautious techniques that avoided chanting and shouting. They stood shoulder to shoulder in silent defiance of the security forces and the regime, with the slogan Kefaya emblazoned across yellow stickers that were stuck onto their chests and mouths. On one occasion, they organized a candlelight vigil that was similarly devoid of chanting or shouting.

But as its protests continued, Kefaya adopted several catchy slogans that embodied its pointed message of opposition to Hosni Mubarak and his regime: *La li' Tamdid! La li' Tawrith!* (No to Succession! No to Inheritance!); *Yasqut, Yasqut, Hosni Mubarak!* (Down, down with Hosni Mubarak!); and *Kefaya Mubarak! Kefaya Hizb al Watani! Kefaya al Qami'a* (Enough of Mubarak! Enough of the NDP! Enough of Oppression!). It also spread its message through newspaper advertisements, text messages, online chat rooms, and a movement website. These mediums were used not only for disseminating the movement's call for reform but also for publicizing the date, time, and location of their protests.

As Kefaya gained momentum, several different submovements began to form, oriented around various middle-class professions—Lawyers for Change, Professors for Change, Engineers for Change, Doctors for Change, and Journalists for Change. Among the most active of these spin-off movements was the one formed by the movement's student and youth members: Youth for Change. Because so many of Kefaya's participants were students and young adults, this submovement quickly grew in number and by mid-2005 had taken on an identity somewhat of its own. It began to coordinate its own protests and held separate meetings. It was also the source of some of the most creative innovations with regard to media.

Youth for Change quickly tired of Kefaya's emphasis on more conventional forms of protest.

They started to experiment with music and with the idea of "protest theater," which they used to spread the word of Kefaya's activities and to alert nonactivists to the regime's many injustices. They developed a protest technique called the "flash protest," in which a group of 20 to 30 activists would pop up in a square in Cairo and protest for 15 minutes, while handing out flyers to citizens who expressed interest. Then, before the security forces could arrive, the protesters would melt away into the streets and alleyways and then reconvene in another square.

They also developed variations on the Kefaya banner. Although posters and banners were common at all the protests, they began to publish the Kefaya slogan on other materials. Sometimes these would be small bits of yellow paper that they would toss like confetti into the streets. At one point, they even placed the slogan on hundreds of yellow balloons, which they then released into the sky at one of the protests.

The movement's media tactics therefore started conventionally and later became more innovative as young people took a more active role in planning and coordinating protests.

Killian B. Clarke

See also Arab Bloggers as Citizen Journalists (Transnational); Street Theater (Canada); Street Theater (India); Vernacular Poetry Audiotapes in the Arab World; Women Bloggers (Egypt); Youth-Generated Media

Further Readings

Shahin, E. E.-D. (2005). Egypt's moment of reform. In M. Emerson (Ed.), *Democratisation in the European neighborhood*. Brussels, Belgium: Centre for European Policy Studies.

KHALISTAN MOVEMENT MEDIA (INDIA/TRANSNATIONAL)

Khalistan (land of the *khalsa,* or pure) is the name of a proposed independent Sikh nation within contemporary India. Although the Khalistani movement is rooted historically in the vision of Guru Gobind Singh, the 10th and final Sikh leader in the 1600s, in the 18th-century establishment of a Sikh capital in Mukhlispur, and in the early 19th-century kingdom of Maharaja Ranjit Singh, the contemporary Khalistan movement was born in the 1970s. From the 1980s, it became a global network, using media, and especially the Internet, to sustain and develop its growth.

India's politics played a vital role in its creation. Among the issues for many Sikhs were governance rights in Punjab State, the decentralization of resources and power, clashes resulting from the "Green revolution" in agriculture, and overall the perceived discrimination against Sikhs by India's government.

Jarnail Singh Bhindranwale (1947–1984), a charismatic Sikh preacher, played an important role during this time of political unrest. He strongly opposed worldly vices and called for a return to the pure roots of Sikhism. Despite his controversial status (some Sikhs considered him a liberator, others an extremist), Bhindranwale became an important figure in the Sikhs' struggles.

His movement quickly gained grassroots support and escalated into an intensive armed campaign. But in 1984, the Indian government, in an attempt to eliminate Bhindranwale (who together with his followers had taken up refuge in Amritsar's Golden Temple, the holiest Sikh shrine), stormed the site in Operation Blue Star. The attack resulted in the death of hundreds (including Bhindranwale himself) and in the Temple's desecration. Two of Prime Minister Indira Gandhi's Sikh bodyguards subsequently assassinated her, and this killing helped catalyze the murderous riots in which some 10,000 individuals perished in Punjab State alone.

Political, economic, and religious turbulence in Punjab State during this period renewed the call for an independent Sikh homeland, and the Khalistani movement, at its peak, seized the imaginations of many Sikhs both at home and abroad. Khalistan as an ideology remains a viable aspiration among some segments of the Sikh population.

Global Khalistan Movement Media

The Sikh diaspora (roughly one million live outside of India, with large pockets in Canada, the

United States, and Britain) has played a particularly important role in the engineering of the Khalistani movement. Outside Punjab State, groups have been able to raise enormous funds toward the cause and to lobby various government bodies, the United Nations, and Amnesty International. In 1993, Khalistan was admitted as a member of UNPO, the Unrepresented Nations and Peoples Organization. Most importantly, however, these diaspora Khalistani movements have been successful in conveying their missions using various forms of media communication relating issues unfolding in Punjab State to Sikhs around the world. These movements link members of the Sikh community with one another and allow them to expound their ideology globally.

One of the earliest proponents of the Khalistan movement, and leader of the British arm of the Khalistan Council, Dr. Jagjit Singh Chauhan (1929–2007), often relied on international media to bring attention to the Khalistan cause. Notably, in 1971, he published a full-page advertisement in the *New York Times* denouncing the oppression of Sikhs in India and proclaiming an Independent Sikh state. Having amassed a great deal of support from Sikhs worldwide, Chauhan eventually declared himself president of the Republic of Khalistan and issued Khalistan passports, postage stamps, and currency.

International groups and proponents of the Khalistan movement such as the Khalistan Council, the Babbar Khalsa, the International Sikh Youth Federation, Sikh Lionz, the World Sikh Organization, and the Council of Khalistan also rely heavily on written and electronic media in relaying their platforms to Sikhs around the world. E-mails, newsgroups, and mailing lists remain important means of communication among these groups and Sikhs around the world.

Over the years, these and other groups also have depended extensively on the Internet in advancing their cause. Websites such as www .khalistan.com, www.khalistan-affairs.org, www .khalistan.net, and www.sikhlionz.com are crucial for the dissemination of news, campaign information, press releases, and articles related to Khalistan, as well as for providing links to other sources of related interest.

The Internet also has become a particularly important forum for the promulgation of video, audio, and pictorial materials intended to raise awareness to the alleged atrocities committed against Sikhs in India. For example, Khalistanis often use sites such as YouTube to post videos showing the desecration of the Golden Temple following Operation Blue Star as well as the slaughter and torture of innocent Sikhs. Also made readily available are archived speeches by Bhindranwale that Khalistanis often employ to inspire individuals toward the separatist cause.

Perhaps the most influential form of media associated with the global Khalistan movement, however, has been the use of images of martyrs, or what Mahmood refers to as "massacre art." Pictures of tortured and mutilated Sikh corpses have been crucial in providing a disturbing perspective on the Khalistan cause. Often referred to as martyrs or *shahid*s for their heroic deaths, these pictures circulate in books, magazines, websites, and in most pro-Khalistani *gurdwaras* (Sikh places of worship).

These often highly graphic depictions play a central role in not only equating the struggle of the martyr with struggles faced by some of the early Sikh gurus (thereby linking the present with the past) but also in alerting people toward what many Khalistanis consider the tumultuous relationship between Sikh subjects and the Indian State. These graphic images, together with descriptions of oppression and abuse, are remarkably abundant on Khalistani websites.

In addition to depictions of tortured bodies, most Khalistani movements also portray Bhindranwale as the martyr par excellence. Often in Sikh parades and more pro-Khalistani *gurdwaras*, Khalistanis publicly display his pictures together with banners that declare *Khalistan Zindabad* (Long live Khalistan), *Bhindranwale Zindabad* (Long live Bhindranwale), "We love Khalistan," "Sikh homeland Khalistan," and "Khalistan is the only solution."

The popularity of online Khalistani groups also has increased. For instance, they exist on both MySpace and Facebook, where people worldwide can meet as a virtual community and blog, share opinions, sell related merchandise (Khalistan T-shirts and bracelets), and share music, pictures, and stories pertaining to the cause.

Music also has been an important media form in the global Khalistan movement. Compilations such as *Khalsa Revolution* (Vols. 1 and 2) and *Flight to Khalistan* include lyrical pieces describing Sikh struggles and stressing the importance of fighting for independence. Songs have such titles as "Wake-up Call to the Youth" and "Welcome to Khalistan." Often, music is available for purchase and download.

Maryam Razavy

See also *Bhangra*, Resistance, and Rituals (South Asia/Transnational); *La Nova Cançó* Protest Song (Països Catalans); Naxalite Movement Media (India); Tamil Nationalist Media (Sri Lanka/Transnational)

Further Readings

Axel, B. K. (2001). *The nation's tortured body: Violence, representation and the formation of a Sikh diaspora.* Durham, NC: Duke University Press.

Dhillon, S. (2007). *The Sikh diaspora and the quest for Khalistan: A search for statehood or for self-preservation?* (IPCS Research Papers 12). New Delhi, India: Institute of Peace and Conflict Studies.

Mahmood, C. K. (1997). *Fighting for faith and nation: Dialogues with Sikh militants.* Philadelphia: University of Pennsylvania Press.

Razavy, M. (2006). Sikh militant movements in Canada. *Terrorism and Political Violence, 18*(1), 79–93.

Tatla, D. S. (1999). *The Sikh diaspora: The search for statehood.* London: UCL Press.

KURDISH "MOUNTAIN" JOURNALISM

The old Kurdish adage "no friend but the mountains" expresses the ability of the Kurds to survive centuries of enemy onslaughts from the snowy peaks of their rugged homeland and is manifest even in the development of 20th-century journalism in Iraqi Kurdistan. "Mountain journalism was a journalism of resistance to the oppression against us," says renowned poet Sherko Bekas. Iraqi Kurds used media in their opposition to the Ottoman Empire, the British colonial government, the Hashemite monarchy, and successive Arab Ba'ath regimes, all of them more or less intent on assimilating or destroying Kurdish cultural identity and political aspirations.

From tiny villages and mountain hideouts, Iraqi Kurds broadcasted radio programs in Kurdish and Arabic for a largely illiterate population. From hidden rooms or even isolated caves, *Peshmerga* (those who face death) fighters cranked out news bulletins, magazines, and scores of books on crude presses for clandestine distribution. Circulation was small, as possession was likely to result in arrest at least, death at worst.

"Mountain" journalism or "mountain" media designates clandestine publishing in general, but more specifically, it refers to an intense period of media production that began in 1975 with the "new revolution" against the Iraqi central government. The term was coined by Kurdish political leaders to distinguish their media from the propaganda the Ba'athist government was cranking out during the same period. Aside from news bulletins, between 1984 and 1988, Iraqi Kurds produced more than 80 books in the mountains, including the *Peshmerga Handbook* and volumes of resistance poetry.

It reached its zenith from 1984 to 1988, when it was stopped short by the *Anfal* genocide campaign. The *Anfal* was a systematic series of military campaigns led by Ali Hassan al-Majid (the notorious "Chemical Ali") to destroy the mountain-based Kurdish rebellion. Nearly 200,000 Kurds were killed in scorched earth operations that destroyed more than 1,200 villages and included dozens of documented chemical attacks. The rebellion was destroyed, as was mountain journalism.

Iraqi Kurdish journalists generally describe mountain journalism as an effort to (a) reveal the Iraqi government's crimes against the people, (b) raise political and social awareness, (c) mobilize the public to stand up to the government, and (d) convey the positions of the various political parties. The Patriotic Union of Kurdistan, the Kurdistan Democratic Party, and the Kurdistan Communist Party were the three largest during this time period, all involved in producing clandestine media.

Although Iraqi Kurds now enjoy a good measure of autonomy with a strong regional government, Kurds in Turkey, Iran, and Syria still suffer repression and generally lack the ability to publish or broadcast freely. For them, the spirit of "mountain journalism" continues.

Margaret Zanger

See also Berber Video-Films (Morocco); Free Tibet Movement's Publicity; Independence Movement Media (India); Independence Movement Media (Vietnam); Palestinian Interwar Press; Vernacular Poetry Audiotapes in the Arab World

Further Readings

Alpinar, Z. (2008). Kurdish international broadcasting. In W. Donsbach (Ed.), *The international encyclopedia of communication* (pp. 2624–2626). Malden, MA: Blackwell.

Black, G. (1993). *Genocide in Iraq: The Anfal campaign against the Kurds.* New York: Middle East Watch.

Hassanpour, A. (1996). The creation of Kurdish media culture. In P. Kreyenbroek & C. Allison (Eds.), *Kurdish culture and identity.* London: Zed Books.

McDowall, D. (2004). *A modern history of the Kurds* (3rd ed.). London: I. B. Tauris.

Randal, J. C. (1998). *After such knowledge, what forgiveness? My encounters with Kurdistan.* Boulder, CO: Westview Press.

LA NOVA CANÇÓ PROTEST SONG (PAÏSOS CATALANS)

In the 1960s, Catalan culture experienced an explosion of songwriting and music challenging the Franco dictatorship. In less than a decade, *Nova Cançó* (New Song) became an outlet for dissent, one of the most important mass culture movements in the country, and a keystone for Catalan cultural revivalism.

The Catalan Countries, as the Catalan-speaking territory is generally known, comprise an area of 11 million people, spread throughout Catalonia, Valencia, and the Balearic Islands in the Spanish State, Northern Catalonia in the French State, and the independent state of Andorra. The area has known intensive cultural and political repression for centuries. In the early 1700s, Spanish was imposed, including in schools, and Catalan was persecuted for some 260 years, with brief periods of tolerance.

In response, the defense of language rights has traditionally been an intrinsic part of Catalan struggle for autonomy, especially since the 19th century. Language is the main trait of Catalan national distinctiveness.

The Need for New Songs

After the Spanish Civil War (1936–1939), the Fascist government outlawed Catalan again and suppressed a Catalan autonomous government that had lasted less than a decade. Many cultural expressions were prohibited, including the national flag, the national anthem, and the national dance. The policy of Franco, often described as one of cultural genocide, took the Catalan nation to the verge of extinction.

In the late 1950s, two Catalan intellectuals, Miquel Porter-Moix and Lluís Serrahima, began discussing the effects of the dictatorship on the language. The elite-driven clandestine movements to defend Catalan, they noted, were increasingly separated from the people, who used Catalan only interpersonally, and accepted Spanish as the exclusive language of public life.

Porter-Moix and Serrahima thought that songs would be an effective way to awaken language activism. Every Thursday from 10 p.m. to 2 a.m., they met and composed a song. Soon other intellectuals joined them. Rather than exploiting the rich tradition of Catalan folk songs, they invented a totally new Catalan song movement, appealing to the people (especially young people) inspired by contemporary popular sounds such as the French *chanson*, Negro Spirituals sung in the U.S. Civil Rights Movement, and Italian songs.

Sixteen Judges

As the group of intellectuals interested in forming a song movement grew, so did the need to create songs with higher quality. The intellectuals called themselves *Els setze jutges* (The sixteen judges), inspired by a tongue-twister that Catalans brag is unpronounceable for any non-Native speaker: *setze jutges d'un jutjat mengen fetge d'un penjat,* which would roughly translate as an absurd and rather macabre sentence, "sixteen judges from a court eat a hanged man's liver."

The Sixteen Judges were only three at first—Miquel Porter-Moix, Remei Margarit, and Josep Maria Espinàs—but they intended to recruit other singers until they actually became 16. Using their own vehicles and covering their own expenses, they toured the Països Catalans on weekends, generally with just a guitar. At first, they performed for small audiences during theater intermissions, in the facilities of local organizations, or libraries. Although Catalan was illegal in almost all aspects of cultural life, including print and electronic media, the singers took advantage of a legislative void that did not explicitly forbid singing Catalan. Additionally, the movement was initially discreet. Once the regime realized the political potential of Catalan songwriting, prohibitions of concerts began, but by then the movement had become unstoppable.

The work of the Sixteen Judges soon caught the attention of local committed businessmen, who created Edigsa and Concèntric, two recording labels that produced and distributed their records, and La Cova del Drac, a club where Catalan singers could perform. The Sixteen Judges got to 16 members in 1967. Some, such as Maria del Mar Bonet, Lluís Llach, and Joan Manuel Serrat, became successful professional singers. Others, like Valencian Raimon, were vital contributors to the success of the *Nova Cançó*.

Within a few years, the Sixteen Judges were not only inspiring dozens of young Catalans to compose songs in their language but also attracting other intellectuals, writers, and artists to collaborate with the song movement. Painter Joan Miró, for example, designed the cover of an LP for Raimon and another for Maria del Mar Bonet. Poets wrote lyrics. Churches, local choirs, and rock groups adapted and performed the work of songwriters, and students turned some songs into political anthems at anti-Franco rallies.

Censorship and Resistance

Tied to the success of the movement was an increasing politicization of the lyrics. Catalan identity affirmation and anti-Franco resistance became synonymous for the song movement. Raimon would make audiences sing, if not cry, when he passionately sang *Diguem No* (Let's say No): "We've seen men full of reason / locked up in jail. / No, / I say no / We say no / We do not belong to this world."

As soon as singers became popular, however, bans began. Before every concert, artists had to submit the list of songs to be performed. Censorship worked arbitrarily. Some songs were banned at times and not at others, specific words were forbidden, and sometimes concerts had to be canceled because the authorities prohibited them. Often, the police would surround the facilities of concert halls, and clashes would erupt after, or even during, the show.

To evade censorship, singers played with the meaning of words. The ineptitude of censors helped. For example, officials forbade the title of "Let's say No," which Raimon replaced by *Ahir* (Yesterday). They also banned the words "we've seen men full of reason locked up in jail," which became an equally poignant "we've seen how they hushed many men full of reason."

Singers created and shared with one another words audiences understood right away, but censors missed. *Night, dusk, stake, fear, death, silence, clouds, storm,* and *shadows* were some of the code words for oppression, Franco, and government. *Day, dawn, light, boat, flowers, walk,* and even *little chicken* meant people, hope for liberation, and the Països Catalans. By the time government officials understood a metaphor and banned a song, the audiences had learned it by heart. Authorities would forbid a singer from performing it, but the public would sing it anyway at the end of the concert.

In the case of Lluís Llach, censors went as far as to forbid him to talk during his concerts. After a 1975 concert, Llach was arrested by the police and accused of stirring up the public with the way he looked at them. Several singers received death threats, and in 1971, Llach fled to Paris 2 hours after finding that Franco himself had referred to him as a traitor. In France, Llach kept singing in Catalan with considerable success, and Jean-Paul Sartre even wrote the program for one of his concerts.

After Franco's death in 1975, prohibitions continued for a few years. Although some singers kept performing for still another two or three decades, the *Nova Cançó* faded away in the 1980s. The 1990s witnessed a resurgence of music performed in Catalan, known as *Rock Català*. Dozens of performers who had been children at the end of Franco's regime readopted the idea of using Catalan to sing and contributed to "normalize" its use. Most groups disappeared after a decade, with the notorious exception of *Els Pets*, which began playing in the mid-1980s as a small rock band (agricultural rock, as they called it, to emphasize their rural roots) and in 2007 held the top position with the most sold CD in the Països Catalans for several weeks.

A Third Wave

During the first decade of the 21st century, music in Catalan enjoyed a third comeback, reaching an unprecedented diversity of genres and performers, ranging from reggae and hardcore punk to jazz and avant-garde experimentations, often with the influence of sounds from African and Latin American migration. Some performers, such as Roger Mas, or *Anna Roig i l'ombre de ton chien* (Anna Roig and your dog's shadow) still fit the category of songwriters in the original, *chanson* spirit of *La Nova Cançó* but with a radical reinvention of the genre. Other bands, such as Valencia's *Obrint Pas*, Catalan *Mesclat*, or Majorca's *Oprimits*, continued the tradition of political involvement, composing songs that advocated social justice and Catalan independence. One of the most notorious protest groups during the first decade of the 21st century, Obrint Pas, often sings with an energetic rage:

> I sing to the storms of your world
>   and to the paths that your rudders have
>   followed
> I sing to the borders that can be erased with
>   one's fingers
> I sing to the flags that we burned tonight.

Antoni Castells i Talens

See also Music and Social Protest (Malawi); Popular Music and Political Expression (Côte d'Ivoire); Popular Music and Protest (Ethiopia); *Rembetiko* Songs (Greece)

Further Readings

Fuster, J. (1985). Pròleg [Prologue]. In E. Climent (Ed.), *Lluís Llach: Poemes i cançons* [Lluís Llach: Poems and songs] (9th ed., pp. 9–19). Barcelona, Spain: Tres i quatre.

Hargreaves, J. (2000). *Freedom for Catalonia? Catalan nationalism, Spanish identity and the Barcelona Olympic Games*. Cambridge, MA: Cambridge University Press.

McRoberts, K. (2001). *Catalonia: Nation building without a state*. Don Mills, ON, Canada: Oxford University Press.

Porter-Moix, J. (1987). *Una història de la cançó* [A history of the song]. Barcelona, Spain: Departament de Cultura de la Generalitat de Catalunya.

Servià, J-M. (1982). *Lluís Llach: Un trobador per a un poble* [Lluís Llach: A troubadour for a people]. Barcelona, Spain: Puntual.

Vázquez-Montalbán, M. (1968). *Antología de la "Nova Cançó" catalana* [Anthology of the Catalan "Nova Cançó"]. Barcelona, Spain: Ediciones de Cultura Popular.

LABOR MEDIA (UNITED STATES)

Given that working people make up the majority of the U.S. population, one would expect the voices and perspectives of workers to be well represented in media. In fact, however, labor media are considered a form of alternative, nonmainstream media in the United States. This entry reviews the history of labor media in the United States and then examines their functions today, as voices for both specific unions and broader social movements. It then describes some of the communication strategies currently being used by labor media. The entry concludes with a look at the role U.S. labor media may play in the future.

Historical Development of Labor Media

From the early trade union militancy of the Knights of Labor following the Civil War through the end of the Great Depression and the powerful Congress of Industrial Organizations (CIO) organizing drives of the 1930s, there have been many media outlets with a labor perspective. Newspapers, journals, and newsletters were valuable communication tools in working-class activity during these times. In the early part of the 20th century, there were at least a dozen daily labor papers and hundreds of weekly publications.

One of the largest was the socialist newsweekly *The Appeal to Reason* published in Girard, Kansas.

The *Appeal*, whose circulation ranged from 500,000 to 1,000,000 readers, was affiliated with Eugene Debs, one of the most powerful and popular labor leaders of his time. The Industrial Workers of the World (IWW) published many newspapers to assist in their organizing drives and strike activities. Their publications, such as *The Industrial Worker* and *Solidarity*, were integral to IWW demands for workers' speech rights. The IWW editors were frequently arrested and their papers shut down, only to spring up again with new editors in another locale.

During the 1930s organizing drives, hundreds of labor publications flourished, in large cities and small towns, catering to many different trades and in dozens of different languages. Their titles reflect the wide regional diversity of labor media: the *Seattle Union Record, Butte Daily Bulletin, Oklahoma Daily Leader,* and *New York Call.* The labor press had its own press bureau, Federated Press, modeled after the Associated Press. Federated Press had full-time labor reporters in New York City, Chicago, and Washington, D.C., and stringers in many other states and internationally as well.

Labor's voice was not limited to print, however. Many labor radio programs could be heard on the radio dial, from small, low-power community radio programs to the powerful WCFL of the Chicago Federation of Labor. Labor media on such a mass scale disappeared or were marginalized substantially in the 1950s, as a result of a combination of McCarthy-style repression, a growing consumerist culture, and organized labor leadership's "great compromise" that relegated unions' role to service and contract enforcement and away from active political participation. Even with the demise of labor's independent media voice, labor issues were still represented in mainstream media, as almost every major paper in the United States still had a labor writer focused on union issues. By the 1980s, although mainstream newspapers had business sections devoted to business viewpoints, there were no labor writers left at any major U.S. media outlet.

Labor Media Today

Since their decline, labor media have been primarily relegated to the specific newspapers and journals of each respective union or to social movements agitating for labor militancy or union reform. Labor union media are not geared toward a national, general audience but toward specific union memberships, their retirees, and external allies.

This is not say that content is only narrowly relevant. Many publications do have broad appeal, offering analysis on everything from the economy, environmentalism, and foreign policy to sports, recipes, and crossword puzzles. Labor union activists firmly believe that all working people are each other's natural allies, and thus, labor media actively address the concerns of all workers, organized or not.

The circulation of many union publications often surpasses that of large urban newspapers. *AFSCME Works*, for example, with a circulation of 1.7 million, is delivered to more people than the *New York Times*. The National Education Association's *NEA Today* has a circulation of 2.7 million, higher than any U.S. newspaper. *Solidarity*, the journal of the United Auto Workers, reaches more than one million people, as do the *Teamster* and several other labor journals.

Labor Media and Broader Social Movements

At times, union publications have taken on wider importance through leading roles in social movements. *El Macriado* (Sassy Brat), the newspaper of the United Farm Workers under César Chávez, could be seen far beyond the fields of California's central valley. The Black Eagle emblem had readers in many urban areas and locations with Spanish-speaking workers.

The United Electrical Workers (UE) newspaper, *UE News*, became more influential during the 1960s, as the UE was one of the first unions to oppose the war against Vietnam. Similarly, the *Dispatcher*, voice of the International Longshore and Warehouse Union (ILWU), covered the anti-apartheid movement in South Africa closely and urged U.S. workers to act against the apartheid regime. The efforts of the ILWU were praised by Nelson Mandela in a speech in Oakland, California, shortly after he was freed from prison.

New Communication Strategies

Unions do not limit themselves to publications, and frequently use other media as well, including radio, theater, posters, buttons, and T-shirts. The United Farm Workers Union benefited tremendously from broadcast media generated by its sister organization, the National Farm Workers Service Center, which owns radio stations in the Central Valley of California, Arizona, and Washington state. Labor cartoonists such as Fred Wright, from the UE, and independent artist Gary Honapacki have developed audiences far beyond their respective unions. Guerrilla theater, marches, demonstrations, sit-ins, picketing, billboarding, parades, and other interventions into public space also serve as part of the arsenal at the disposal of labor.

Actions that thrust workers into the public realm have been very successful at breaking the barrier that often stands between the public and the very real people that mediated text, voice, and image represent. Often such action plays a critical role in making visible a workforce that is seldom considered, as when Justice for Janitors brought thousands of custodial workers into downtown financial centers, or when thousands of strawberry pickers marched through shopping areas to convey their message.

Dissident groups within labor unions have played a substantial role in labor media. The Dodge Revolutionary Union Movement, an African American auto workers' group and forerunner of the League of Revolutionary Black Workers, developed around a newspaper, the *Inner City Voice*. The newspaper gave them a platform to lead a struggle against the entrenched conservative leadership of the United Automobile Workers union and the racist policies of the Detroit automobile industry. Reform movements in the Teamsters Union, the United Mine Workers, and other large unions have all developed a strong media presence in order to organize members to unite against union corruption or sclerotic bureaucracy. *Labor Notes*, an influential labor newsletter based in Michigan, serves as an important clearinghouse for union news and developments in union reform efforts and labor militancy.

Labor groups have been in the forefront of incorporating electronic media into their communications strategies. Public access TV has generated many labor-focused television programs, such as *Labor Beat* in Chicago. The online bulletin board service Labornet, based at the Institute for Global Communications (IGC), began as an early form of social networking among labor activists, years before the World Wide Web became popular. Labor computer networks facilitated information sharing and concerted labor action among workers worldwide.

The growth of community radio and more recently low-power FM radio stations has contributed to a strong group of labor radio programs, such as the Workers Independent News Service, based in Wisconsin. Unions rely to a large degree on the latest media technologies to keep their memberships current, to deliver contract information, to organize new workers, and to agitate for workers' rights. The Labortech conference has served as an important means to share notes and resources for labor activists to use communications technology effectively.

Many labor media activists remain convinced that labor should pool its many resources to create a national and daily source of media content that could bring labor's perspective to the national audience. There have been some national attempts to bring labor media back into the mainstream. One of the more successful was *We Do the Work*, a labor television program syndicated to PBS stations nationwide, that was eventually discontinued for lack of funding. Labor media advocates see a national media strategy as critical to building workers' political power beyond labor contracts and work conditions to address critical national issues like human rights, arts and culture, universal health care, and political change.

Jesse Drew

See also Barricada TV (Argentina); Cultural Front (Canada); Industrial Workers of the World Media (United States); Miners' Radio Stations (Bolivia); Paper Tiger Television (United States); Prometheus Radio Project (United States); Social Movement Media, 1980s–2000s (Japan); Workers' Film and Photo League (United States)

Further Readings

De Caux, L. (1970). *Labor radical: From the Wobblies to the CIO*. Boston: Beacon Press.

Dubofsky, M. (1969). *We shall be all: A history of the IWW*. New York: NY Times Book Company.

Godfried, N. (1997). *WCFL: Chicago's voice of labor, 1926–78*. Urbana: University of Illinois Press.

McChesney, R. W. (1992, August). Labor and the marketplace of ideas: WCFL and the battle for labor radio broadcasting, 1927–1934. *Journalism Monographs, 134,* 1–40.

Milkman. P. (1997). *PM: A new deal in journalism, 1940–1948.* New Brunswick, NJ: Rutgers University Press.

Morais, H. M., & Cahn, W. (1948). *Gene Debs: The story of a fighting American.* New York: International Publishers.

Shore, E. (1988). *Talkin' socialism: J. A. Wayland and the role of the press in American radicalism, 1890–1912.* Lawrence: University of Kansas Press.

Le Monde diplomatique (France/Transnational)

Founded in 1954, *Le Monde diplomatique* (LMD) is a French monthly specializing in international politics. Most articles are written by academics, many of them not French. LMD gives considerable space to regions neglected by the rest of the French press (e.g., sub-Saharan Africa and Latin America). Since the 1970s, the newspaper has had a radical left-wing editorial line and has been involved with some activist movements since the 1990s. LMD's policy is international in its circulation: In 2009, it was routinely translated into 25 languages, and its paper version circulation alone was nearly 2.5 million, plus its important webpage.

Originally, LMD's readers were expected to be diplomats; at that time, French was very important in those circles, and LMD targeted itself to diplomats and their families. LMD was neutral regarding the cold war, and had no editorial column. Most articles were written by *Le Monde*'s foreign correspondents—the national newspaper of record—and by diplomats and politicians who set out their government's official views.

Nevertheless, in 1973, with the arrival of a new editor in chief, Claude Julien, the monthly changed drastically. Julien could be characterized as a Christian socialist; he had also been active in the French Resistance. In the 1950s, he worked for a French newspaper in Morocco but was expelled for criticizing the colonial regime. Afterward, he started to work for *Le Monde*. Conflicting with

the daily's hierarchy, Julien transformed LMD in the early 1970s and brought it closer to the model of a journal of ideas. At this time, LMD took on a radical left-wing editorial line, close to the anticolonial and "Third World-ist" movements.

LMD gradually increased its autonomy from *Le Monde*. Most articles were now written by outside contributors, many from universities or independent journalism. In the 1980s, LMD started to employ permanent journalists as sub-editors to rewrite articles submitted by external contributors. This kept the editorial line cohesive but also made academics' writing accessible.

By the 2000s, there were approximately 10 permanent editorial journalists, each competent in certain fields: certain regions (e.g., United States, Western Europe, sub-Saharan Africa, and Latin-America) and questions (e.g., international law, economics, media, and new technologies). Most did not write more than three articles a year. Their work was to find new outside contributors, to commission articles, to rewrite them, and to defend their fields in editorial meetings. They operated like bureau chiefs.

In the mid-1990s, some LMD journalists decided to leap into activism. They initially created a readers' association, Les Amis du *Monde diplomatique* (Friends of LMD), to raise funds to create an affiliate. LMD had achieved editorial autonomy around 1980 but wanted to enlarge it by diversifying and controlling a part of the stock. Many local *Les Amis* associations sprang up in French cities and some foreign capitals (Montréal, London, Genève, and Brussels). They mainly organized public conferences with journalists and major outside contributors. Through this affiliate both journalists and readers could veto any change in company status and the appointment of a new director.

LMD also helped create certain global social justice associations: ATTAC, Media Watch Global, and the World Social Forums. In all three cases, LMD's editor Ignacio Ramonet wrote an editorial appealing to LMD readers to get involved. The large worldwide circulation of the newspaper helped to mobilize activists, especially "elitist activists" and "leftist intellectuals," LMD's main readership.

However, leaping into activism led to some internal disputes, notably concerning journalistic ethics. Some journalists had had a long communist press career before joining LMD, and had been both fired, and expelled from the Communist party, for being too critical of the USSR and the French Communist Party. They opposed any political interference in editorial policy. This conflict culminated in 2007 with the resignations of an editor in chief and his assistant, protesting against ATTAC and LMD overlap. Journalists who were previously academics were generally more favorable to mixing political activism and journalism.

Today, the newspaper generally has 28 pages and is illustrated by artistic pictures or reproductions. The place of international relations and organizations decreased since the collapse of the Communist regimes. Most articles now cover domestic issues in foreign countries. Since the 1990s, a "balkanization" of the editorial line has become evident, with great autonomy for editorial journalists in their fields. Christian socialism, neo-communism, leftist republicanism, and libertarianism are the four main political families in LMD.

Nicolas Harvey

See also Alternative Media; *Bhangra*, Resistance, and Rituals (South Asia/Transnational); Online Diaspora (Zambia); Online Nationalism (China); Radio Lorraine Coeur d'Acier (France); Tamil Nationalist Media (Sri Lanka/Transnational); WITNESS Video (United States); Zapatista Media (México)

Further Readings

Agrikoliansky, É., Fillieule, O., & Mayer, N. (Eds.). (2005). *L'altermondialisme en France: La longue histoire d'une nouvelle cause* [The global social justice movement in France: The long history of a new cause]. Paris: Flammarion.

Harvey, N. (2007). As tipologias dos pesquisadores engajados: Sobre o engajamento de colaboradores acadêmicos do Le Monde Diplomatique [The typologies of committed researchers: On the commitment of *LMD*'s academic collaborators]. *Revista Comunicação e Espaço Publico, 10*(1–2), 138–149.

Harvey, N. (2009). Internationalisation du Monde diplomatique: Entre *cosmopolitisation* et homogénéisation éditoriale [Internationalization of *LMD*: Between *cosmopolitanization* and editorial harmonization]. *Pôle Sud, 30,* 85–98.

Szczepanski, M. (2006). Le commercial et le militant. Usages croisés du Monde diplomatique [Commercialism and activism. Conflicting applications of *LMD*]. In *Journalisme et dépendances* (pp. 239–272). Paris: L'Harmattan.

LEEDS OTHER PAPER/NORTHERN STAR (UNITED KINGDOM)

Leeds Other Paper was one of the alternative local newspapers created in towns and cities across Britain during the 1970s to challenge the social, political, and journalistic conservatism of most mainstream media. Although many lasted just months or even weeks, *Leeds Other Paper* survived for 20 years (1974–1994). It was notable for its long record of investigative journalism as well as reporting local events from below. The newspaper also operated as a notice board and meeting place for individuals, groups, and movements engaged in a range of social, cultural, and political activities.

Leeds Other Paper, commonly known as *LOP*, published its first issue in January 1974 in the industrial city of Leeds in the north of England. It declared itself to be the "Leeds libertarian socialist newspaper"; the tagline was soon dropped but the ethos remained throughout. The paper was the product of a group of young radicals, mostly anarchist ex-students, who found their views and activities either ignored or trashed in mainstream media; their answer was to become the media.

The tone was set from the first issue:

Leeds Other Paper exists to provide an alternative newspaper in Leeds, i.e. a newspaper not controlled by big business and other vested interests. It is our intention to support all groups active in industry and elsewhere for greater control of their own lives. The production will be intermittent at first—we are not professionals and we are few in number. We hope to grow, however, into a regular newspaper. If you wish to help in any way—articles, contacts, distribution, etc.—your assistance will be greatly appreciated.

The paper established a monthly cycle before increasing to fortnightly in 1976 and weekly in

1980; it remained a weekly until it ceased publication. In 1991, it changed its name to *Northern Star*, partly in homage to a radical Chartist paper launched in the city in 1837, but mainly in an unsuccessful attempt at attracting more readers from beyond Leeds. Sales, mainly through local newsagents and in friendly pubs, were usually around 2,000 copies weekly, occasionally rising to approximately 3,000 or more. Advertising was only from noncommercial sources and alternative projects. The paper's finances were always precarious, often being rescued by readers' donations and special events.

Initially staffed by unemployed workers or in people's spare time, from 1978 *LOP* was run as a formal workers' cooperative with a low-paid staff. But people dropping in off the streets—offering to help do anything, unpaid, from writing articles to collating the printed pages—played a vital role throughout most of the paper's existence. There was no editor, and for most of its existence, *LOP*'s editorial meetings were open to contributors and readers alike, who would discuss everything from the ideological meaning of a story to the correct use of an apostrophe. This democratic and "prefigurative" method of organizing was reflected in the paper's content, which emphasized stories about people struggling, individually and/or collectively, for control over their own lives.

In common with other British alternative local press examples, *LOP*'s news agenda was constructed to counter mainstream journalism shallowness. Whereas "straight" reporters often seemed content merely to get the latest line or angle on a story, *LOP* contributors were encouraged to cover issues in both depth and breadth. A 1980s internal discussion document put it:

> We are committed to doing justice to the subjects we cover. This means well-researched, in-depth articles often and *LOP* stories are longer on average than those in the commercial press. . . . We should be conscious of the need to slow down our readers—to reverse the in-one-ear-out-the-other process—and create lasting impressions.

Sometimes this could result in thousands of predictable words about yet another damp house, accompanied by a gray photograph of a miserable tenant pointing to an indiscernible gray patch in the corner of a gray room. At others it meant worthy but dull pieces about faraway international events, the local connection being that some Leeds group was currently campaigning about it. It could certainly be a grim read. "My mum finds it so depressing she barely looks at it," commented one reader.

But it could produce genuinely uplifting copy about people in struggles, from the collective revolt of low-paid public sector workers in 1978–1979 (the United Kingdom's "winter of discontent") and the national miners' strike against pit closures in 1984–1985, via individual battles against bureaucracy, to the establishment of battered women's refuges—and vivid moments, as when frustrated tenants dumped uncollected rubbish on the desk of the official in charge of Leeds' garbage disposal service.

In addition to reporting such events in glorious detail, *LOP* had a long record of investigative journalism, which included revealing a major local employer's use of carcinogenic chemicals; exposing the government's secret *Protect and Survive* instructions on preparing for nuclear attack; uncovering mortgage lenders who discriminated against low-income inner-city areas; and exposing a shadowy organization called the Economic League, which supplied employers with "do-not-employ!" lists of trade union and political activists. Alongside this radical journalism was a lively "what's on" guide with free listings of campaigns, concerts, cinemas, clinics, claimants' unions, and co-ops.

Although always fiercely independent, often idiosyncratic, and occasionally truculent, *LOP* was part of the left in its broadest sense. When the waves of community, social, and workplace activism eventually ebbed—on which it depended for its subject matter, its readership, and its supply of volunteers—the paper's days were numbered. Dwindling sales, mounting debts, increasing staff turnover, declining contributors, chronic undercapitalization, a zero promotion budget, and burnout of the "1968 generation" that had given birth to it, all took their toll. The final issue was in January 1994.

A former *LOP* member remarked: "It was only a grotty little thing produced on a few sheets of recycled paper that 2,000 people would buy, but that doesn't measure up to the impact it had over the years. It had a profound effect on Leeds in its small way." That *LOP* survived as long as it did was an achievement in itself. The history of alternative media suggests that 20 years is a landmark few projects achieve and that the echoes of such media continue to reverberate long after the physical product stops.

Tony Harcup

See also Alternative Local Press (United Kingdom); Alternative Media; Anarchist Media; Citizens' Media; Community Media and the Third Sector; *Leveller* Magazine (United Kingdom); *Spare Rib* Magazine (United Kingdom)

Further Readings

Harcup, T. (1994). *A Northern Star: Leeds Other Paper and the alternative press 1974–1994*. London and Pontefract, UK: Campaign for Press and Broadcasting Freedom.

Harcup, T. (1998). There is no alternative: The demise of the alternative local newspaper. In B. Franklin & D. Murphy (Eds.), *Making the local news: Local journalism in context* (pp. 105–116). London: Routledge.

Harcup, T. (2003). The unspoken—said: The journalism of alternative media. *Journalism, 4*(3), 356–376.

Harcup, T. (2006). The alternative local press. In B. Franklin (Ed.), *Local journalism and local media* (pp. 129–139). London: Routledge.

Harcup, T. (2009). It wasn't all about Arthur: Alternative media and the miners' strike. In G. Williams (Ed.), *Shafted: The media, the miners' strike and the aftermath* (pp. 61–71). London: Campaign for Press and Broadcasting Freedom.

LENINIST UNDERGROUND MEDIA MODEL

During the 20th century, the Leninist underground model of alternative or radical media had considerable influence across the planet. Its influence was to be observed in three forms: in the organization of underground media, in the publications of Marxist parties of one stripe or another, and in the media of Stalinist regimes. The focus in this entry is principally on the first of these.

The pivotal source of this model was Lenin's famous booklet *What Is to Be Done?* first published in 1902, 3 years before the epochal St. Petersburg insurrection, 15 years before the Bolshevik Revolution. Lenin wrote it against the background of the Tsarist regime's political repression, which banned all political parties seeking to voice working-class challenges; banned all strikes as criminal, even anti-state, activities; and had an extensive secret police presence, a large informer network, and severe punishments for those found producing, distributing, or reading revolutionary publications. (Stalin's regime would far surpass even these achievements.)

The issue, then, that Lenin wanted to solve was how, under these political conditions, to develop a stable organizing center for the revolutionary movement across Russia, Ukraine, and the other component units of the Russian empire—one that would not be perpetually liable to be hauled off to jail or worse, decapitating the movement's leadership. A clandestine political party was one element in his solution, led by full-time organizers to be still more disciplined and efficient on a hierarchical military model than the Tsarist state's apparatus of repression. An all-Russian newspaper strictly controlled by the party was another, which in this case was titled *Iskra* (Spark), Lenin's imagery being one of the newspaper as "an enormous pair of smith's bellows that would fan every spark . . . into a general conflagration."

In Section V of the booklet, Lenin outlined his vision of the revolutionary newspaper as a "collective organizer," issued at least four times a month. He compared Russia's political situation at the time he was writing to having lots of bricks and bricklayers, but no one to provide the line along which to build. Without organized teamwork, the bricks would be laid haphazardly, and the Tsar's police could "shatter the structure as if it were made of sand and not of bricks."

The paper would expose political and economic issues all over Russia as material for talks, readings, and informal discussion and to give the full story on issues only hinted at in the legal press or by embarrassed government admissions. It would help the revolutionary movement overcome its dispersed fragmentation that made each local upsurge easy to contain. It would enable sustained and flexible political activity, in Lenin's argument, both in periods of calm and in sudden unanticipated crises. Its network of underground distributors and readers would constitute the party's active and growing core.

But the party leadership's policies on all significant issues would be absolutely binding as regarded the newspaper's contents, a transmission mechanism. Only on topics not yet defined by party policy would it be an opinion forum.

Not surprisingly, in situations of political repression across the planet this model has proved very attractive, whether under South Africa's apartheid regime (1948–1994), Franco's fascist dictatorship in Spain (1939–1975), the Suharto military regime in Indonesia (1965–1998), Argentina's murderous military junta (1976–1982), and elsewhere.

Ironically, the model also operated—as a result of political conditions, not because of Lenin's influence!—in the top-down organization of Poland's Catholic parishes during the sovietized regime (1945–1989), seeking to avoid secret police surveillance. It also operated in part in the underground *samizdat* publications in the Soviet bloc, which played a role over the long haul in decomposing the system. Tragically, it was redeployed in the USSR after 1917 as the model for the new state's media, and in turn served as a media template for imitator regimes.

John D. H. Downing

See also Communist Movement Media, 1950s–1960s (Hong Kong); *Samizdat* Underground Media (Soviet Bloc); Social Movement Media, 1920s–1970s (Japan); *Suara Independen* (Indonesia)

Further Readings

Lenin, V. I. (1961). What is to be done? Burning questions for our movement. In *Collected works* (Vol. 5, pp. 347–529). Moscow: Foreign Languages Publishing House. (Original work published 1902)

LEVELLER MAGAZINE (UNITED KINGDOM)

The *Leveller* magazine (1975–1985) was essentially a journalistic enterprise. It was firmly rooted in the British left and was involved in all kinds of socialist, feminist, anarchist, and antiracist activity, but its members saw themselves primarily as journalists, even those who were not. Its founders were working journalists—if on the fringes of the profession. Their objective was not to bring about revolution or even social change, although all wanted them and wanted to put their skills at the service of those engaged in such struggles. But they were producing a journalistic product, and they were very proud of it.

One of the most remarkable features of its collective practice was the way that nonjournalists were brought in and encouraged to develop their skills. At any one time, the collective's shifting membership would have a dozen or so people actively engaged, only about half journalists.

It never had an editor. Each issue was produced by two "coordinators," informally elected each time. Generally, one would be a working journalist and one not: There were academics, students, planners, environmentalists, full-time activists, budding politicians, teachers, artists, poets, a couple of accountants, a builder, and an architect. People just turned up, and no one bothered with who they were. There was even a political police (MI5) spy, Tony Jones, a perspiring and pinstriped city gent who came across as a kind of left-wing groupie. Everyone had suspicions, but all were perfectly friendly to him, and when he was exposed in *The Guardian* daily, people felt sorry for him.

It was an extraordinarily successful collective venture. Although there were political rows—with one important one that led to a group splitting away—they never interfered with production. The more dominant journalistic personalities, and there were one or two, were kept firmly in line because they were willing to be. Cooperation was the phenomenon at work, although comradeship is the word that would have been used. It was a combination of the anarchic and the efficient that is rarely achieved. Everyone put the magazine first. There were a few who wanted to demand attention or hijack debate, but they simply failed, gave up, and left.

The *Leveller*—whose name came from an egalitarian 17th-century Civil War group that agitated against Cromwell's republic from the "left"—defined itself as "socialist feminist," a label people were happy with until a grouping within the collective, women and men among them, began to argue for "feminist socialist." Theirs were more postmodern politics, less connected to the class-based politics of the majority.

In hindsight the fact that an intense debate over this ran for months and led to the group breaking away might seem absurd to some, but the debates were of a high standard, delving deeply into the political turmoil of the time, and conducted in a comradely way. The breakaway produced a rival magazine called *Desire*. It was an inspired publication, but no second issue emerged.

Most members were independent leftists, although there were a few Communists and others. Trotskyists did not care for its libertarian attitudes; when the first issue was sent for comment to David Widgery, the finest revolutionary writer of that generation, he posted it back with "HOW PREDICTABLE AND BORING" scrawled over the cover, although like others he remained friendly on a personal level.

Although the *Leveller* was a collective, it came into existence largely because of one man. Dave Clark had the idea, brought a widening group of people together, provided the drive that expanded it from an unknown monthly to a 10,000-selling fortnightly, and kept it going through the rough patches. He was a speedy and dynamic character, a compulsive worker, and a natural entrepreneur. He was much mocked for his autocratic tendencies, and much loved. When Clark left the collective in the early 1980s, he launched an independent weekly newspaper, the *Southwark News*, which is still going 25 years later, although Dave Clark himself died in the late 1990s.

Finances were meager. Nobody ever earned a penny working for the *Leveller*. It was sued for libel over a story on donations to a right-wing employer-financed group of wreckers within the trade union movement—a characteristic *Leveller* investigation. The magazine, which had set itself up as a limited company, did not fight the case; it simply dissolved the company and, with the advice of friendly radical lawyers, set up a new one, *Leveller Magazine* (1979) Ltd.

There was more legal excitement over an Official Secrets case that brought the *Leveller* to national attention. In 1977, it was involved in a campaign against the deportation of two American journalists, Philip Agee and Mark Hosenball.

Agee was a former CIA officer and whistle-blower; Hosenball was an investigative journalist for *Time Out* magazine who had collaborated with Duncan Campbell, a British journalist, on an article exposing the activities of the Government Communications Headquarters (GCHQ), the U.K. government's U.S.-linked electronic spying center.

Through the *Leveller*, Campbell was put in touch with a former signals intelligence officer, John Berry and another *Time Out* reporter, Crispin Aubrey. All three were arrested under the Official Secrets Act. This became the ABC (Aubrey, Berry, Campbell) case. When they appeared in court, the crown called "Colonel B" as a secret witness to testify on the supposed national security damage. *Leveller* journalists and friends at *Peace News* found out his name—Hugh Johnstone—and published it.

The *Leveller*, *Peace News*, and the National Union of Journalists, whose paper *The Journalist* had also published the name, were now prosecuted for contempt of court. This was the Colonel B case. Five founding members of the collective appeared with the others in the High Court. They represented themselves and made stirring political speeches, which did not stop them from being convicted; however, they were given only fines, and even these were dropped on appeal.

The *Leveller* grew out of alternative politics, but it was a phenomenon of the printing revolution then taking place, with electronic typesetting and cheap litho printing—ironically on a Trotskyist newspaper's presses. There was much hype about the ease of producing small magazines, which was never really fulfilled, and the *Leveller* itself—a 32-page A4 magazine with spot color—did not last that long. It began to run out of steam around 1983, moved out of its central London squat to a hippy commune in south London, losing all its seasoned journalists, and folded a year or so later.

From time to time people suggested reviving it, but there was little demand. The *Leveller* was really a product of politics with the then Labour Party in government. When the Conservative government took power in 1979, the imperative for the left was to unite in opposition; the kind of debate exemplified by the *Leveller* became a luxury few wanted to afford.

Tim Gopsill

See also Alternative Local Press (United Kingdom); Alternative Media; Anarchist and Libertarian Media, 1945–2010 (Federal Germany); Anarchist Media; *Leeds Other Paper/Northern Star* (United Kingdom); *Spare Rib* Magazine (United Kingdom)

Lookout! Records (United States)

Lookout! Records is an independent record label that has been specializing in the release of punk and pop-punk records since 1988. Founded by *Maximum Rock and Roll* columnist Lawrence Livermore, the label was moved from Laytonville, California, to its current home in Berkeley, California, in 1990 to serve the burgeoning pop-punk scene, featuring bands such as The Queers, The Riverdales, Screeching Weasel, and Green Day. Tied to the DIY ethics of its local scene, Lookout! Records is known for operating in equal partnership with its artists and supporting community organizations, such as the Gilman Street Project.

Based in part on the independent model exemplified by Dischord Records, Lookout! promotes a collaborative relationship with their signed artists. All profits from released records are split equitably between the label and the artist. Once the label's production investment is recouped, 60% for the subsequent profits go to the band. The label also demands little of its signed artists, leaving creative control over production and touring strategies to the discretion of the bands. In its early days, production and distribution were typically minimal operations—new releases would start off as small runs of approximately 1,000–1,500 copies for a 7" or 12" vinyl record, keeping advertising costs and initial investment low. As the label became more successful, Lookout! partnered with independent distribution companies around the United States to expand national reach—Mordam and Revolver in the Bay Area; Taang!, Dutch East India, and Caroline on the East Coast.

Along with more equitable artist relations, community involvement is a critical element for the DIY punks involved with Lookout! Records. The label works in concert with the Gilman Street Project, a community center and punk venue started in part by the *Maximum Rock and Roll* zine. Organized around anarchist nonprofit principles and managed collectively, the Gilman Street Project serves all ages as a music and performance venue, a meeting place for political groups, and a practice space for local bands. The collective meets twice a month to discuss club policies and bookings—membership into the collective costs only $2. At its inception, the Gilman Street Project served as the only independent Bay Area punk venue, thereby concentrating the enthusiasm and activity of the punk scene around a central community location. Lookout! Records offered opportunities to produce and release records to these incipient local acts and thus provided a crucial role as a media outlet for their surrounding community.

Since the late 1990s, Lookout! has been criticized for compromising many of the punk ethics of their earlier days. Under attack by critics in punk zines and disaffected bands, the label has been accused of reneging agreements with artists and working with larger corporate distributors. Indeed, it dropped their independent distribution deal with Mordam in 2000. New owner Chris Applegren, who bought Lookout! in 1998, has since signed a distribution deal with RED, a Sony-owned company that handles sales and promotions for more than 50 record labels.

Although considered compromised by some, Lookout! Records continues to release records independently and to support its Bay Area community through work with the Gilman Street Project.

Curtis Roush

See also Creative Commons; Dischord Records (United States); Popular Music and Protest (Ethiopia); Protest Music (Haïti); *Rembetiko* Songs (Greece)

Further Readings

Fairchild, C. (1995). Alternative music' and the politics of cultural autonomy: The case of Fugazi and the D.C. scene. *Popular Music and Society, 19*(1), 17–35.

Goshert, J. C. (2000). "Punk" after the Pistols: American music, economics, and politics in the 1980s and 1990s. *Popular Music & Society, 24*(1), 85–107.

O'Connor, A. (2008). *Punk record labels and the struggle for autonomy: The emergence of DIY.* Lanham, MD: Lexington Books.

Thompson, S. (2004). *Punk productions: Unfinished business*. Albany: SUNY Press.

LOVE AND ROCKETS COMIC BOOKS (UNITED STATES)

Love and Rockets is a series of comic book stories by brothers Gilbert and Jaime Hernández, often referred to as Los Bros Hernández. At times a third brother, Mario, has also contributed. The series was published by Fantagraphics Books from 1982 to 1996, and then taken up again in 2000. As of the late 2000s, the series was ongoing. The brothers also published individual works under different titles using characters from the series. The comic features character-driven, soap opera–like stories that center on interactions between Latino and Anglo culture, marrying magical realism, punk aesthetics, and traditional comic book art.

The brothers illustrate and write their comic stories independently, maintain their own distinct groups of characters and storylines within the series, and employ different aesthetics and story-telling styles, while uniting around issues of Chicano life. The series primarily features strong female characters, with narratives focusing on their relationships and changes over time. Early narratives included some science fiction and super-hero elements, but the brothers later shifted to more realistic storytelling. The brothers have also aged their characters during their 20+ years of publication, running counter to more mainstream comic book convention, where characters like Superman, Archie, and Donald Duck are ageless.

Jaime uses a photorealistic style of clean, sharp lines, creating highly contrasting spaces of light and dark. His stories center on four women and their relationships, especially in the Southern California punk scene. Two, Hopey and Maggie, have an off and on relationship with each other, and the narrative is typified by an overall lack of definition, both in their relationship with each other, their sexual identities, and their goals in the face of a complicated landscape of Chicano, Latino, and U.S. cultures and subcultures. In addition, flashbacks, shifting storylines, and changing points of view over time contribute to a fluidity of identity and social position.

Gilbert's work, in the fictional Central American village of Palomar, follows village dynamics and its members with attention to character detail almost like William Faulkner's. Gilbert employs a more surrealistic, fluid, and cartoonish visual style than his brother, which extends to the story-telling as well, with frequent usage of magical realism. Gilbert's main character is the strong-willed and highly sexualized Luba, for a time Palomar's mayor before moving with her family to the United States. Gilbert's stories are not exclusively centered in Palomar, but frequently they center on tension between small-town life and modern culture, as well as between familial and intergenerational relationships in Luba's constantly expanding family.

The series' life span, approaching 30 years at the time of writing, coincided with the expansion of alternative comics from underground to main-stream, facilitated by the emergence of publishers, distribution channels, and retailers devoted to fostering alternative comic books.

Daniel Darland

See also Alternative Comics (United States); Alternative Media; Black Exploitation Cinema (United States); Fantagraphics Books (United States); *RAW* Magazine (United States); Zines

Further Readings

Aldama, F. L. (2006). *Spilling the beans in Chicanolandia: Conversations with writers and artists*. Austin: University of Texas Press.

Constant, P. (2007, April). Punk comix. *The Progressive*.

Hatfield, C. (2005). *Alternative comics: An emerging literature*. Oxford: University Press of Mississippi.

Royal, D. P. (2007). Palomar and beyond: An interview with Gilbert Hernandez. *MELUS*, 32(3), 221–246.

LOW-POWER FM RADIO (UNITED STATES)

The history of low-power FM radio (LPFM) in the United States is intimately tied to enduring debates about the influence of commercial advertising on media content. This entry describes the origins of

LPFM and the evolution of the legal framework that governs it.

Historical Background

In 1948, the Federal Communications Commission (FCC) initiated a "Class D" FM license designed to open up radio broadcasting opportunities to educational institutions. Initially, these stations were limited to 10 watts, broadcasting between 88 and 92 MHz, and had a broadcast radius of 3–5 miles. Class D licenses allowed high schools and universities an affordable means to offer training opportunities to students. Interest in the Class D license was slow to emerge, in part because in 1944, the FM band was assigned a new set of frequencies, making previous FM radios obsolete. Eventually, Class D FM stations were allowed to broadcast up to 100 watts, and as the popularity of FM radio grew, so too did the interest in these educational stations.

Class D stations faced further challenges after the 1967 Public Broadcasting Act and the establishment of the National Public Radio network. This act created new rules for noncommercial stations to be eligible for public funding, making it harder for smaller stations to meet the new standards. In 1978, the FCC began to phase out Class D stations by forcing them to upgrade to more than 100 watts or move to the commercial segment of the spectrum (93–108 MHz). By the early 1980s, almost all the Class D stations had been shut down and low-power FM broadcasting was moved to the margins, where pirates and activists picked up the cause.

On November 27, 1986, Mbanna Kantako, a blind African American living in the John Jay Holmes housing project in Springfield, Illinois, went on the air from his living room with a one-watt transmitter. With this act, Kantako is said to have launched the "micro radio movement." Kantako named his station WTRA after the Tenants Rights Association (TRA) he had helped to organize. Initially broadcasting two nights a week, Kantako eventually expanded his air time and renamed his station, "Black Liberation Radio."

In 1990, a federal court ordered Kantako to shut down his station. With the help of the National Lawyers Guild (NLG) Committee on Democratic Communication, Kantako developed a legal response that defended his First Amendment rights "in the face of the world wide monopolization of communication resources by commercial interests." However, because no commercial broadcaster had brought interference charges against Kantako, his legal arguments were never made before a judge.

United States v. Dunifer

The legal framework developed by the National Lawyers Guild in the Kantako case was applied in the legal decision that set the precedent for the micro radio community, *U.S. v. Dunifer*. Stephen Dunifer began Free Radio Berkeley in 1992 in the San Francisco Bay Area. By 1993, the FCC had ordered him to forfeit his equipment and pay a $20,000 fine for illegal broadcasting. Dunifer responded by filing an administrative appeal. The FCC asked the courts for an emergency injunction to stop his broadcasting, but Judge Claudia Wilken refused the injunction, marking the first time any court had rejected FCC efforts to stop an unlicensed broadcaster from accessing the airwaves.

Among the arguments put forward by Dunifer and the NLG was that the 1934 Communications Act required broadcasters to use the "minimum amount of power necessary to carry out the communication desired." By using available bandwidth and a small transmitter, Dunifer and other activists at the time were demonstrating that low-power FM stations were possible, even in a crowded spectrum market such as the Bay Area of California.

After a series of court cases, Dunifer was enjoined from broadcasting, and in 1998, Judge Wilken wrote "The United States had failed to show a probability of success on the constitutional issues raised by Mr. Dunifer" (*U.S. v. Dunifer*, 1998). This case became the road map for other micro radio activists and helped promote a movement that was putting new stations on the air faster than the FCC could shut them down.

Evolving Technologies and Public Policy

The emergence of the Internet allowed micro radio activists to share technical and legal information, resulting in more than 1,000 illegal stations by the late 1990s. In 1998 alone, the FCC shut down more than 250 illegal LPFM stations. This mobilization of media activism was supported by groups such as the Prometheus Radio Project, which maintained a website that served as a clearinghouse about all things LPFM. In addition, activists used the Micro Radio Network, a listserv that allowed members to debate the merits of various strategies and tactics in their efforts to demonstrate that the frequency spectrum could accommodate the addition of small stations.

This strategy allowed the public to learn the potential of LPFM. These micro-stations also became lightning rods for educating the public about LPFM because every time the FCC shut down a station, local news media covered the story. This provided an opportunity for the activists publicly to debate LPFM, and the FCC's refusal to allow small-scale local radio.

After more than a decade of activism, legal challenges, and thousands of registered public comments, the FCC passed *Report and Order 99-25* in January 2000, establishing the process of licensing LPFM stations. This rule established them as noncommercial, low-power stations, in two classes, 100 watt and 10 watt, with ownership limits of one station per owner. By using the second adjacent channel space as a technical standard for LPFM, the FCC greatly expanded the number of potential stations that could be created by the new law.

The National Association of Broadcasters, joined by National Public Radio, challenged this technical standard, claiming their stations would be subject to interference by the new LPFM stations. This dispute was resolved by Congress, not by the FCC. In the fall of 2000, Congress passed the *Radio Broadcasting Preservation Act* (s. 3020, 2000), curtailing the initial FCC proposal for LPFM licensing. Congress established a more rigorous technical standard of third adjacent spacing that reduced the number of potential LPFM stations from more than 10,000 down to roughly 1,000.

In 2005 and 2007, the FCC amended their rules on LPFM licensing in an attempt to promote the growth of the service. Nevertheless, by early 2009, the FCC had only issued slightly more than 1,300 licenses, with fewer than 900 stations actively on the air. Many LPFM advocates argue that the low number of stations is a result of both the restrictive technical standards, especially in urban areas, combined with the noncommercial designation that means local non-profit stations are forced to compete with their local NPR affiliate for audience contributions.

The story of micro radio in the United States is perceived by many as groundbreaking—where commercial media interests were successfully challenged and where localism and the public interest components of media policy regulation were reinvigorated. Others argue that the limited licensing of LPFM essentially blunted the edge of micro-radio activism, offering a small concession that served to maintain commercial dominance of the radio broadcast spectrum. Micro radio has become a critical story for citizens taking part in national media reform efforts. The legal and tactical lessons learned serve as a case study of citizens working to change media policy and increase local content and viewpoint diversity across the radio dial.

Andy Opel

See also Citizens' Media; Community Broadcasting (Canada); Community Media and the Third Sector; Community Radio (Haïti); Community Radio (Ireland); Community Radio and Podcasting (United States); Community Radio in Pau da Lima (Brasil); Community Radio Movement (India); Free Radio (Austria); Free Radio Movement (Italy); Free Radio Movement, 1974–1981 (France); Miners' Radio Stations (Bolivia); Prometheus Radio Project (United States); Radio La Tribu (Argentina)

Further Readings

Klinenberg, E. (2007). *Fighting for air: The battle to control America's media*. New York: Metropolitan Books.

Opel, A. (2004). *Micro radio and the FCC: Media activism and the struggle over broadcast policy*. Westport, CT: Praeger.

Soley, L. (1999). *Free radio: Electronic civil disobedience*. Boulder, CO: Westview Press.

United States v. Dunifer, 997 F. Supp. 1235 (1998). (N.D. Cal. 1998).

Walker, J. (2001). *Rebels on the air: An alternative history of radio in America*. New York: NYU Press.

Madang Street Theater (Korea)

Madang is a type of participatory political street theater. It was developed in the 1970s and was derived from Korea's traditional but regionally diverse *Tal-chum* (mask dance), in which a group of actor-dancers wear masks defining stock characters (the monk, the grandma, or the nobleman), both speaking their lines and dancing. The themes are often subversive and mostly mock ruling class greed, hypocrisy, and allied vices. Although each play has a basic structure, details vary considerably from one performance to another, as audience participation is important.

As opposed to conventional stage-plays where the audience merely watches, *Madang*, following its roots, does not differentiate audience from players, and the drama is complete only with audience participation. Sharing emotions (mostly sorrow and anger), as well as unifying and enlightening the audience, are all important aspects of *Madang*. Rather than having a seamless sequential flow, *Madang* has several *madangs*, or sequences, which are independent stories on their own and are loosely connected one to another.

The themes often fall into four categories: nationalist, anti-capitalist, environmentalist, and populist. It is not certain exactly when and how *Madang* was first born, but the ferocious capitalist growth in 1970s Korea produced a huge sector of low-wage factory workers and urban poor, along with marginalized farmers. Against them was the new rich class, which exploited workers to the extreme and was supported by the dictatorship, to which this class gave its ready allegiance. Mainstream popular entertainment mostly glossed over these conflicts and hardships, and the mainstream stage was overly elitist, with Western or experimental themes that alienated working-class audiences.

In such an environment, this new type of drama-play emerged, with a rich legacy from the traditional culture. The plays actually talked about working-class people and their issues, cheered them up, and sometimes even advised what to do in tough situations. Audiences were invited to talk freely, speak their hearts, and interact with everyone present. This was the power of *Madang*: It provided education and entertainment at the same time. It is why *Madang* often became a part of or even a prelude to a demonstration. After the play, audiences, instead of going back home, would assemble into a group together and go out to demonstrate.

Eun-ha Oh

See also Anti-Fascist Media, 1922–1945 (Italy); Media Activism in the Kwangju Uprising (Korea); MediACT (Korea); Resistance Through Ridicule (Africa); Street Theater (Canada); Street Theater (India)

Further Readings

Choi, W., Yu, T., & Lee, D. (2003). *Hankook eui Juntong-keuk Kwa Hyundai-keuk* [Korean traditional theater and modern theater]. Seoul, South Korea: Books Hill.

Māori Media and Social Movements (Aotearoa/New Zealand)

Generally speaking, contemporary forms of Māori media in Aotearoa/New Zealand have developed in tandem with Māori social movements for *Tino Rangatiratanga* (Indigenous sovereignty). The concerns of these social movements came to the fore-front in the late 1960s to the early 1980s, a period identified by some as the "Māori Renaissance" because of a noticeable resurgence in articulations of political and cultural identity among Māori in the face of continuing expression of settler colonialism within state and civil society.

With a paucity in early years of other kinds of visual record, much of the energy and history of these social movements were documented by leading photographers, with the most significant work produced by Māori photographer John Miller. Much of his work covered community events and nonviolent protests. However, at the time of the 1981 Springbok Tour protests—comprising a rainbow social movement coalition, but including Māori activists expressing their anger at the racism existing within both Aotearoa and apartheid South Africa—Miller's photographs revealed the lengths the state will go to suppress civil dissent. Miller's images included police in full riot dress armed with clubs and shields beating demonstrators, alongside military barricading of the rugby grounds.

Māori involved with various women's, youth and quasi-socialist political groups contributed to the ferment of the late 1960s and 1970s. Many eventually came together to form *Ngā Tamatoa* (Warrior Youth), which initially drew influence from the Black Power movement of the United States. Although Māori activists worked within *pākehā* (white/European) groups, MOOHR (Māori Organization on Human Rights) and Te Hokioi (a large predator eagle—now extinct) were two Māori-based organizations that seeded the intellectual and activist interventions of Ngā Tamatoa. During the 1970s, the shape of Tamatoa shifted, reflecting the different political emphases of members within the group so that liberal tendencies held sway over radical ones. Common to the different factions was an emphasis on addressing the alienation of tribal groups from their lands and other resources as well as the significance of *Te Reo Māori* (Māori language) for the movement toward Indigenous self-determination.

In 1975, the government set up the Waitangi Tribunal, responding (initially in a limited way) to Māori dissent expressed through direct actions such as lengthy *hīkoi* (long walk/walks) that involved critical mass participation. Key events included the 1975 Māori Land March, whose catchcry "not one more acre of Māori land" encapsulated the ethos of other protests such as the Raglan golf course dispute of 1978 and the 506-day Takaparawha (Bastion Point) occupation. Professor Ranginui Walker has noted the impact of this challenge on New Zealand's myth of racial harmony and how these "occupations and marches were quite spectacular media events, on television and radio, . . . beamed into the sitting rooms of the nation and worse still, into the international arena" (Walker, n.d.). Other less spectacular protest actions also took place such as the Ngatihine forestry block dispute, which mobilized both mainstream press and TV, as well as alternative media forms (university and left-wing newsletters, photography, and video) to keep the issue publicly visible.

Government research in the early 1960s and late 1970s identified a near extinction of the Māori language. Accordingly, much of the effort of Ngā Tamatoa was directed toward setting up language-learning initiatives such as *kōhanga reo* (language nests) and, for the liberal activists, soliciting government support. A legislative high point occurred in 1985 when Māori were successful in having the Waitangi Tribunal recognize the status of Māori language as *taonga* (treasure) and the need for the government to guarantee that status through active measures of support. In 1987, Te Reo Māori was recognized as an official language of Aotearoa/New Zealand through the Māori Language Act.

Although print media forms such as newspapers and magazines were used effectively for Indigenous self-representation (such as the MOOHR and Te Hokoi newsletters), the ability of aural and visual media to conduct voice has been considered by some to fit best with Māori oral tradition and cultural expression. Indigenous representation and self-representation through electronic media have depended on infrastructure and resources, often via government funding or access to media institutions.

At times, this has been a strained relationship. Notably, in 1996, Indigenous filmmaker Barry Barclay camped for 3 days outside the offices of NZ on Air (the Broadcasting Commission) to protest at the absence of public funding for Māori television drama. Barclay's cultural interventions as an activist, filmmaker, and writer ranged from television and film (both grassroots and industry) to policy, culminating in an articulation of spiritual guardianship protocols for Indigenous cultural works expressed through his 2005 book *Mana Tuturu: Māori Treasures and Intellectual Property Rights.*

Because radio is less resource intensive than film or television, stations have exemplified more readily a community media ethos run according to the particular needs of *iwi* (tribes) and *hapū* (subtribes). The first Māori language radio broadcast was in 1936 through the government-regulated ZB networks, which nominally served Māori communities during the next decades. It was not until 1983 that a nongovernmental Māori language radio station *Te Reo o Poneke* (the voice of Poneke [Wellington]) began to broadcast briefly in Wellington, the capital, and became the basis for the establishment of an iwi radio network in 1988. By the late 1980s, two kinds of Māori radio network were in operation—a government-resourced pan-Māori network and a community-based iwi network. After much lobbying, by the early 1990s the government recognized that an iwi-based radio network was the most appropriate way in which to support diversity and began to channel frequency management, funding, and infrastructural resources in that direction.

In 2004, the Māori Television service (MTS) went to air, 11 years after the establishment of *Te Māngai Pāho* (Council for [Māori] Broadcasting), which is the government broadcasting funding agency mandated to support Māori language. This period was difficult, with Māori broadcasting initiatives such as the short-lived pilot channel Aotearoa Television Network (ATN), having to navigate bureaucratic impediments, inadequate funding, limited time frames, and the negative biases of mainstream news organizations.

Although hopes for an alternative, Māori public sphere were realized in part through the advent of MTS, the risk has been real of the diversity of tribal representation becoming homogenized through MTS's replication of mainstream television's production and aesthetic norms. That said, there might be promise in the parallel flows of mainstream television and MTS of some kind of emergent bicultural community.

Currently, however, the alternative Māori public sphere lies in the transformative online initiatives of web networks, such as the progressive *Aotearoa* and *New Zealand Māori Internet Societies,* and the radical *Aotearoa Café* initiated by activists such as Te Rangikaiwhiria Kemara, Teanau Tuiono, and others. The Societies mobilize national and international infrastructural change to enable self-defining presences for Māori on the Internet.

Aotearoa Café was modeled initially on Aotearoa Indymedia. At times a place for radical discussion, the site was temporarily shut down, computers confiscated, and activists arrested for a period after the infamous police raids on the homes and settlements of Tūhoe iwi, where police intimidated individuals and family groups under the aegis of terrorist suppression legislation enacted by the government in the wake of 9/11.

Since the mid-1990s, Internet access has enabled Māori groups to circumvent infrastructural ties with the government, but because less than half the Māori population have "at-home" access, it will be some time before the Internet can offer a democratically accessible alternative. Nonetheless, the coexistence of progressive and radical tendencies within the online alternative Māori public sphere echoes the energies of groups such as Ngā Tamatoa, evoking the sense of history residing in a popular Māori proverb: "The future is our past before us."

Geraldene Peters

See also Adivasi Movement Media (India); Eland Ceremony, Abatwa People's (Southern Africa); First Peoples' Media (Canada); Indigenous Media (Burma/Myanmar); Indigenous Media in Latin America; Indigenous Peoples' Media

Further Readings

Barclay, B. (2005). *Mana Tuturu: Māori treasures and intellectual property rights.* Auckland, New Zealand: Auckland University Press.

Beatson, D. (1996). A genealogy of Māori broadcasting: The development of Māori radio. *Continuum, 10*(1), 72–93.

Harris, A. (2004). *Hīkoi: Forty years of Māori protest*. Wellington, New Zealand: Huia.

Miller, J. (2003). John Miller: Media peace award recipient. *Photoforum, 69*. Retrieved April 16, 2009, from http://www.photoforum-nz.org/index.php?pageID=27

Poata-Smith, E. S. Te Ahu. (2001). *Political economy of Māori protest politics, 1968–1995: A Marxist analysis of the roots of Māori oppression and the politics of Māori resistance*. PhD dissertation, University of Otago, Dunedin, New Zealand.

Smith, J. (2006). Parallel quotidian flows: MTS on Air. *New Zealand Journal of Media Studies, 9*(2), 27–35.

Smith, J., & Abel, S. (2008). Ka whawhai tonu mātou: Indigenous television in Aotearoa/New Zealand. *New Zealand Journal of Media Studies, 11*(1), 1–13.

Stuart, I. (2005). The Māori public sphere. *Pacific Journalism Review, 11*(1), 13–25.

Walker, R. (n.d.). *Historical context of the treaty of Waitangi*. Retrieved April 18, 2009, from http://www.anewnz.org.nz/paper_comments.asp?paperid=69

MAWONAJ (HAÏTI)

The use of allusion and metaphor is typical of the way Haïtians speak and is part of *mawonaj*, which is the Haïtian cultural practice that got its name from the "maroons," the runaway slaves on many Caribbean islands, including Haïti and Jamaica. The term "Maroon" is derived from the Spanish *cimarrón* (runaway slave), and in turn from *simarron*, which is a word for "stray arrow" that Cuba's Taíno people used for their own escapees from Spanish enslavement.

Only about half of Haïti's adults can read and write, usually in Kreyòl (Haïtian Creole), which is the mother tongue of all Haïtians but only was made an official language in 1987. Despite Kreyòl's legal legitimacy and prevalence, most of Haïti's printed words—in books, newspapers, and government documents—are in French, which is spoken by only a tiny elite confined to a few coastal cities. Fully 80% to 90% of the population remains monolingual.

Ironically, the tongue that evolved out of French and some West African languages so the French could command their slaves has also been a revolutionary communication tool. Speaking or writing Kreyòl can be an act of resistance in and of itself. Because speaking French is essential to social promotion, political actors, artists, or journalists who use Kreyòl are doing more than merely communicating with the historically excluded popular masses. They are also resisting the centuries-old status quo.

Haïti's culture of resistance and yearning for freedom is heard over and over at the most popular level of the Kreyòl language in songs, stories, and proverbs. Proverbs are full of critical social commentary via allusions, metaphors, symbols, and coded messages. They show how most of Haïti's people—who, more than two centuries after the slave army wrested freedom from the French masters in a bloody revolution and founded the world's first black republic, remain as impoverished as their forefathers—are well aware of the unfair class and "race" relations in their country.

Some examples are as follows: *pale franse pa lespri* (speaking French doesn't mean you're smart); *Konstitisyon se papye, bayonèt se fè* (the constitution is paper, the bayonet is steel); *bourik travay, chwal galonnen* (the donkey works, the horse gallivants); *bay kou, bliye—pote mak, sonje* (the hitter forgets—the scarred one remembers); *rayi chyen, di dan li blan* (hate the dog, praise its white teeth); and *kreyon pèp la pa genm gonm* (the people's pencil has no eraser). This last proverb originally referred to "God's pencil," but during the 1986–1990 democratic and popular movement, "the people" replaced "God" as the one who remembers injustices.

Not surprisingly, none of these examples explicitly attack the powerful. The stand-in for the military regime is the bayonet, "speaking French" stands in for the bourgeoisie, and animals are often used as proxies for class relations.

Mawonaj is an unspectacular, slow, and patient form of communication activism that seeks out autonomous moments to reflect socially on injustice, privilege, and naked power. Political speeches, proverbs, story tales, graffiti, painted murals, theater, and sometimes even newscasts are full of puns, allusion, and double meanings, especially during periods of political repression.

Jane Regan

See also Parodies of Dominant Discourse (Zambia); Political Jokes (Zimbabwe); Protest Music (Haïti); Resistance Through Ridicule (Africa); Social

Movement Media, 1915–1970 (Haïti); Vernacular Poetry Audiotapes in the Arab World

Further Readings

Averill, G. (1997). *A day for the hunter, a day for the prey—popular music and power in Haiti.* Chicago: University of Chicago Press.

MAY 1968 POETRY AND GRAFFITI (FRANCE/TRANSNATIONAL)

The year 1968 was packed densely, like 1848 and 1989, with tumultuous political confrontations, beginning with the Tet Offensive in Vietnam. As decades lengthened, those were often thought to be progressive, at least in terms of good intentions, although 1968 also saw Soviet tanks crush then Czechoslovakia's attempt to humanize the Soviet system, the assassination of Martin Luther King Jr., the rise of Enoch Powell's racist demagoguery in Britain, the vicious military coup-within-a-coup in Brazil, an anti-Semitic movement in Poland, and the slaughter of many hundreds of protesting México students in México City. Nonetheless, the students' and workers' mass protests in France in May–June 1968, at one point numbering 10 million out on strike, stood out as beacons globally, an international symbol of collective self-assertion and resistance.

Among its most enduring legacies were its words, in poetry and graffiti, which captured the imagination of countless people across the world, especially (although not exclusively) in the then student generation. Among the most famous were "All power to the imagination!" and "We will not be free until the last capitalist is hanged with the guts of the last bureaucrat."

The first was a riff on the famous slogan of the 1905 St. Petersburg uprising, repeated again in the revolutionary months of 1917, "All power to the *soviets!*" (spontaneously formed councils of workers, soldiers, and farmers). Since then, *soviet* had become "Soviet," a byword for organized state repression and asphyxiating officialdom. Switching from "soviet" to "imagination" excoriated the Soviet system in passing but sought to recuperate

the visionary energy that had flamed fiercely in masses of people in the year of its birth.

The second was, wittingly or not, an adaptation of a favorite toast going back at least to the early 1800s in London's working-class bars and dives, proposing that freedom would not be ours until the last exploiter had been hanged. Someone wrote it up in large letters on a pompous mural in the main lecture theater in the Sorbonne University (since then, the Paris university authorities, having had the mural restored, scarcely ever let anyone use the lecture theater or even go inside it).

Other pungent aphorisms included the following:

It is forbidden to forbid. Freedom begins by forbidding one thing: interference with the freedom of others.

The walls have ears. Your ears have walls.

Be salted, not sugared.

Consume more and live less!

Only shitheads ideologize!

Beneath the *pavés* is the beach.

Pavés refers to the cuboid cobblestones common on central Paris streets, which were pried up and used as missiles against riot-police charges. Underneath them, after their use, is a world free for enjoyment.

These and many more sparked similar creativity elsewhere, whether in the much longer running Italian political movement of the 1970s—as in *Noi vogliamo tutto!* (We want the *lot!*)—or in 1968's social movement poetry broadsides in the United States.

John D. H. Downing

See also Activist Cinema in the 1970s (France); Free Radio Movement (Italy); Free Radio Movement, 1974–1981 (France); Political Graffiti (Greece); Vernacular Poetry Audiotapes in the Arab World; Youth Protest Media (Switzerland); Youth-Generated Media

Further Readings

Feenberg, A., & Freedman, J. (2001). *When poetry ruled the streets: The French May events of 1968.* Albany: New York State University Press.

Sullivan, J. D. (1997). *On the walls and in the streets: American poetry broadsides from the 1960s*. Urbana: University of Illinois Press.

Viénet, R. (1992). *Enragés and situationists in the occupation movement, France, May 1968*. London: Autonomedia.

MEDIA ACTIVISM IN THE KWANGJU UPRISING (KOREA)

The Kwangju Uprising (May 18–26, 1980) was a popular explosion in Kwangju City against Korea's long tunnel of military dictatorship since General Park's 1961 coup d'état. Park had framed the Constitution to ensure his lifetime presidency, and just advocating abolishing this clause could result in imprisonment, even death. However, in October 1979 he was assassinated by a close associate. Despite the public's eager anticipation of a democratic regime, 2 months later, a group of military officers—the New Military Group (NMG)—staged another coup d'état, which was led by Major-General Chun.

During the previous months, the labor movement had become more active, especially in the mines. More and more groups, especially students, participated in demonstrations to end martial law and support democracy. The NMG declared martial law and specially prepared troops for suppressing demonstrations. From February 1980, soldiers were confined to their barracks and had intensive training in crushing demonstrations violently. They were drilled to hate the demonstrators and assured they were Communist controlled, in a period when Communists were identified as the most evil of enemies.

The NMG also arrested nationally renowned politician Kim Dae Jung and his associates and mercilessly tortured them, claiming Kim was a spy and subversive supported by Pyongyang. When prodemocracy demonstrations calling for an end to martial law and for Kim's release swept the country and grew in size, the New Military Group decided to strengthen martial law. As of the morning of May 18th, political activity of any sort was totally banned, not least assembling at or organizing demonstrations.

However, the citizens of Kwangju, which is a midsized city in the Southwest and one of Kim's political bases, would not submit to the decree. This led to a direct confrontation between trained military personnel and unarmed civilians. Somewhere between 200 and 2,000 people were killed during a weeklong massacre (the figures vary depending on the source). The military called its planned maneuver Operation Fantastic Holiday.

On the 18th of May at around 10 a.m., hundreds of students assembled and shouted slogans like "End martial law!" Then, the troops were ordered to attack. They took over the city and treated people with extreme cruelty, demonstrators and passers-by alike. Those arrested would be forced to confess they were under Kim's control to support the scenario that Kim was leading a rebellion inspired from Pyongyang. The soldiers had poles with axe heads embedded in them. They arrested people, stripped and bound them, and used long swords to cut off women's breasts. Even young children on their way home were murdered, and pregnant women were stabbed in their stomachs. The violence of the troops was such that even the police would beg the citizens to return home before they were killed. Downtown Kwangju became pure hell.

It later emerged that the troops had been starved for 3 days before they arrived, and that they had been plied with *soju*, a powerful liquor, right before they arrived. Together with their months of drilling and their belief they were confronting Communist enemies, all and any violence was green-lighted, whether people were armed or unarmed.

At first, Kwangju's citizens were simply demonstrating against a second military dictatorship. However, faced with such extreme brutality, they felt the urgent need to arm themselves to survive. In the beginning, they were an unorganized and unarmed mass, but as time went by, they organized what they called the "Citizens' Army," which was headquartered at City Hall. They formed spontaneous organizations and had solid support from the Kwangju public. In the midst of their struggles, alternative media also sprang up.

Social Movement Media

During the uprising, various forms of alternative media were deployed. The city was blocked from the outside world: Phone lines and transportation were cut. There was no way for them to inform the world what was actually going on. Even the food supply was cut off from outside. People had limited resources, but they invented various media out of what little they had. Among them were pamphlets, loudspeakers on trucks, and sounding car horns—and setting fire to established broadcast stations.

One of the most important forms of media were the pamphlets. From May 18 to May 21, three different organizations spontaneously produced their own. One was published by a Junnam University student group and another by Yoon Sang Won and the *Deulbul Yahak* team: *Deulbul* means "wildfire," and *yahak* was a volunteer school for the poorly educated, especially for young factory workers. During the 1970s, the *yahaks* had been a major adult education initiative and grassroots political activity.

The third pamphlet series was published by a cultural activist group, *Kwangdae* (Clown). When they got together to form a single team led by Yoon, their individual pamphlets merged. The joint pamphlet was called *Tu-Sa-Hoe-Po* (Activists' Pamphlets), and it spread news and gave directions to the citizens of Kwangju.

They quickly formed a team to create a production system. They used three primitive duplicating machines and worked all night to produce 5,000–6,000 copies daily. Women hid them under their clothes and carried them downtown to distribute, because their surveillance was less absolute. On May 25th, they moved to a Young Womens' Christian Association (YWCA) building and formed a publicity team. Thanks to the YWCA rotary press, they could now make 40,000 copies daily.

The first issue of *Too Sa Hoe Bo* was out on May 21 and released eight issues until the 25th; then, the title changed to *Min Joo Shi Min Hoe Bo* (Democratic Citizens' Pamphlets), which indicated a shift from activists to something embracing a broader audience. The last issue would have been the tenth, but soldiers swooped down on their office.

In a sense, the Kwangju massacre did not even exist in the public domain. TV only broadcasted the official account, which was that a group manipulated by North Korea had attempted a rebellion. Even that news was brief, and the channel was filled with the usual entertainment programs that had nothing to do with the desperate cries coming from Kwangju. All media were under NMG control and there was hardly any way to communicate among citizens.

In such circumstances, these pamphlets were valuable. They were one of the few media that broadcasted the massacre and also directions for action in response. The pamphlets helped coordinate activities in Kwangju and gave them urgently needed news: where dead bodies were stored in City Hall and at which streets the struggle had been the most severe the previous day. Pamphlets lasted longer and their content was more detailed than placards, posters, and street loudspeakers, and they could reach a wider readership at the city's outer edge.

The citizens of Kwangju also invented their own broadcasting system. As the mainstream media poured out the NMG version, a group of citizens burned down the broadcasting stations. It was an expression of their despair and feeling of betrayal that the ongoing massacre was not to be found in any mainstream media sphere. Instead, they invented a street broadcasting system with trucks equipped with miniature microphones and amplifiers. The speakers were mostly women with firm and expressive voices. Chun Ok Joo and Cha Myumg Sook were among the most famous.

Chun Ok Joo was an active movement participant, whereas Cha Myumg Sook was an ordinary girl doing a tailoring course. On her way home, when she found that her school was closed, she saw a Citizen Army group on the street. She joined the broadcasting team on the spot. They broadcasted from the street for days and nights, leading the demonstrations and encouraging additional participation. Their news gave updates on the struggle. They would ask "Soldiers, don't you have tears and blood?" and invite more citizen engagement: "Our friends and brothers are dying. . . . Let's join together and help them out!" They would ride trucks around the downtown to spread the news and ask for more participation.

However, single individuals also participated spontaneously. They would bring their own megaphones and shout to the crowd. One of the earliest and most famous incidents was late afternoon on the 19th, when a middle-aged woman in front of the train station started to speak through a megaphone. "I am not a communist and just an ordinary woman, but I had to come out because I saw our own children bleeding and dying. Let's be courageous and help them out. Let's all join them and defend ourselves!" This passionate and truthful appeal encouraged citizens, and they turned into thousands, heading toward downtown. As this incident shows, this street broadcasting was powerful in giving direction to and uniting an otherwise dispersed mass.

Train stations, downtown *Keumnamno* (Kwangju's main street), and the City Hall area were among the standard sites the loudspeaker trucks would pass by. There were only a handful of trucks, but the effect was huge. As their influence grew, the troops were ordered to arrest the speakers, but they were unreachable as they were surrounded by hundreds and thousands of demonstrators. On the eve of the last day, the broadcasting went on all night throughout the city, asking for participation in the final combat. They anticipated the impending final battle, so the truck ran through residential streets all night long, asking for more participation and pleading with citizens to join the Citizen's Army at City Hall. "*Kwangju shimin Yeorobun!* (Dear fellow citizens of Kwangju!) Join us in City Hall!" The desperate and vulnerable female voice resonated all night throughout the night. It was an unforgettable night and an unforgettable voice for the citizens of Kwangju.

The people in Kwangju also invented creative ways to amplify their demonstrations. Buses and taxis joined demonstrations and participated by turning on their headlights and sounding their horns. They formed a marching troop with their automobiles and entered the evening square with high beams on, sounding their horns to the rhythm of songs and slogans from the crowd. Demonstrators followed the cars. With 200 taxis and many buses together, they marched to the square. Other cars on the streets also responded spontaneously by flashing their lights and sounding their horns. Even big trucks with heavy machinery joined the march. In the evening, the people carried torches to express and amplify their anger and hope.

Although alternative media in the Kwangju uprising were organized in a spontaneous way out of bare scraps, they also had their roots in the

movement legacy developed in the 1970s. Oppressed by military dictator Park, no public media could advocate people. Instead, people had invented alternative media and thus formed strong movement organizations. *Deulbul Yahak* and the *yahak* movement were noted above, but *Kwangdae* had been a cultural activist group with its roots in that tradition in the 1970s. Cultural movement groups in the 1970s worked hard on alternative means of expressing working-class feelings by new forms of street drama (*Madangkeuk*) and *Noraekeuk*, a sort of musical with social messages. Such experiences and networks were helpful for alternative media during Kwangju uprising. In turn, the Kwangju experience led to subsequent development of alternative media in the 1980s.

Kwangju became the symbol and the spiritual source of contemporary Korean social movements. It stood for the ruthless military dictatorship, for the power of people, and for solidarity (during the week, a lot of ordinary citizens volunteered to help the Citizen's Army with food, water, tissues, and other necessities). During the week's massacre, no looting was ever reported despite the total chaos. The Kwangju experience became the theme of hundreds of movement songs, poems, novels, plays, films, and paintings.

The Kwangju resistance also affected alternative media forms. Car demonstrations became common in the 1980s, and political pamphlets became much more systematic and ongoing. The spirit of solidarity in Kwangju became one of the most precious values for the emerging social movement in Korea. It dictated the style of popular and student entertainment throughout the 1980s.

Eun-ha Oh

See also Anti-Fascist Media, 1922–1945 (Italy); Independence Movement Media (Vietnam); Madang Street Theater (Korea); MediACT (Korea); *Suara Independen* (Indonesia)

Further Readings

Kang, J. (2003). *Hankook Hyundaesa Sancheck* [A walk through the history of modern Korea], vol. 1. Seoul, South Korea: Inmul kwa Sasang.

Shin, G., & Hwang, K. (Eds.). (2003). *Contentious Kwangju: The May 18 uprising in Korea's past and present.* Lanham, MD: Rowman & Littlefield.

Yu, S., & Jung, S. (2003). *Memories of May 1980—A documentary history of the Kwangju uprising in Korea.* Seoul, South Korea: Minjuhwa Undong Kineom Sa-eop-hoe.

MEDIA ACTIVISTS AND COMMUNICATION POLICY PROCESSES

Institutional policy arenas often provide "windows," that is, temporary opportunities for activists to raise their concerns and influence the political environment. The way activists respond to such a window depends on their cultural backgrounds and ideological values, as well as on whether they perceive it as a potential gain or a threat. Media activists have been observed to adopt "insider," "outsider," or "beyond" strategies. "Insiders" interact directly and cooperatively with power holders. "Outsiders" question the legitimacy of power holders and address them through protest and disruptive action. "Beyonders" seek to bypass the whole process and to create "alternatives" to top-down power relations.

Media activists might adopt a mixed repertoire that uses distinct tactics according to the policy window. However, a distinction remains in ideological background and values between those who would act "inside" and those who refuse to do so. Whereas social movements in general often focus predominantly on the distinction—and sometimes connection—between inside and outside activities, media activists are particularly strong in the "beyond" sphere, as the core of media activism is to produce and construct new and alternative communication infrastructure.

Mobilizing "Inside"

The 2005 Council of Europe (CoE) Ministerial Conference on Mass Media Policy in Kiev was one of the first instances when civil society organizations were invited to contribute to a media policy "window." Activists from the umbrella organization Community Media Forum Europe (CMFE) participated in a nongovernmental organization forum, which was attended by more than 50 civil society organizations and was held in parallel to the official summit. Forum participants agreed on amendments and appointed spokespeople for the conference, who advocated freedom of expression and protection of journalists. Their amendments on human rights standards, editorial independence, and transparency were accepted for inclusion in the final conference documents.

Following Kiev, the CMFE became involved in a CoE commission on media pluralism that contributed to drafting policy documents and gained observer status. The group helped to establish the community media sector as a legitimate policy stakeholder and to introduce the issue of "community media" in the policy discourse. The CMFE thereby accepted the rule of the game, thus recognizing institutions as legitimate power holders.

The UN World Summits on the Information Society (WSIS; 2003–2005) provided a similar opportunity to engage in a transnational arena on communication policy. Civil society networks such as the Communication Rights in the Information Society (CRIS) campaign attended WSIS, attracted by the promise to participate "on equal footing" with governments and business actors. CRIS's repertoire was defined and constrained by the UN process, which negotiates among states and produces declarations. Several umbrella organizations that represent grassroots media activists, such as the World Association of Community Broadcaster and the Association for Progressive Communication, equally interpreted WSIS as an opportunity to get involved, get legitimized, and get their issues recognized.

Being inside does not necessarily mean "harmonizing." Activists inside WSIS criticized many of its outcomes and occasionally threatened to replace insider with outsider tactics, or to distribute "subversive" information. However, acting within institutions comes at a price. Being "inside" forces activists to interact under institutions' rules, which might compromise internal democratic processes for the sake of efficient representation. There is a risk of dampening critical perspectives. Media activists, who tend to be loosely organized, face procedural challenges of admission and accreditation, which might prevent their access to policy arenas. As nonprofessionals, they might also lack the financial resources and the policy language expertise for participating effectively.

Mobilizing "Outside"

On October 11, 2008, protests against surveillance measures, such as the collection of telecommunications data, the surveillance of air travelers, and the biometric registration of citizens, took place under the motto "freedom not fear—stop the surveillance mania!" in more than a dozen countries around the globe. Protesters demanded a cutback in state and corporate surveillance, chanting slogans like "we are here and we are loud because they are stealing our data."

In Berlin, 50,000 people took part in the largest protest march against surveillance in Germany's history, which was publicly supported by more than 100 civil liberties groups, professional associations, unions, and political parties. Protests in Rome, London, Madrid, Buenos Aires, and Tokyo included art performances, lectures, surveillance camera mapping, rallies, distributing privacy software, and video projections. Coalitions of media and other civil society activists thus brought the highly technical issues of data protection and privacy to the streets, protesting current initiatives by national governments and the European Union to increase surveillance of citizens' electronic communication and movements.

The "freedom not fear" protests showed how media activists interact with institutions "from the outside." Some chose this tactic because they did not have access to the institution or the policy arena, and others chose it because they rejected the rules of the game and did not accept the institution as legitimate. Still others chose this strategy because they sought to add public pressure to "inside" involvement. "Outsiders" adopted tactics of mass mobilization (campaigns, rallies, demonstrations, and cultural resistance) and disruption (blockades). They addressed policy makers, but they expressed fundamental opposition either to a particular policy or to the policy process as such.

Whereas the global social justice movement has focused on disruption and mass protest, these "outsider" tactics are rarer within media activism. Communication policy processes are generally difficult to frame for mobilization and often are distant from the immediate concerns of a nonexpert public. The international protests against surveillance were an exception, and the particularly successful German campaign was enhanced by the issue's connection to the historical memory of surveillance under the Nazi and Communist regimes. Organizers used viral marketing and pop culture references to market the issue and connect with nonmedia activists. However, events elsewhere remained smaller.

Other examples of these "outsider" interventions include the U.S. Media Reform movement's street protests and campaigns against the Federal Communications Commission's plan to dilute media monopoly rules and European media activists' protests during the Geneva anti-G8 protests in 2003 against the World Intellectual Property Organization's probusiness intellectual property policies. British activists' struggle to legalize community media in the 1980s and 1990s saw collaborations between "insiders" and pirate broadcasters who started a campaign called "Free the Airwaves," but outside the institutional arena.

Mobilizing "Beyond"

In Geneva in mid-December 2003, heads of governments and international institutions discussed the future of the information society at the WSIS summit. Meanwhile, in the city center, media activists created the PolyMediaLab, which was a self-organized space as part of the "WSIS? We Seize!" initiative: four days of workshops and strategic planning to show that "an information society can rise from the grassroots, thanks to free knowledge and technologies which can be infinitely shared." Some hundred radical techies, hackers, and communication experts met to share technical skills, develop independent media, and promote alternative modes of media production. In the large hall there were fancy laptops, recycled desktops, people typing and eating, chatting online and offline, and skill-sharing workshops streamed over the web to participants around the globe.

Thus "WSIS? We Seize!" participants took the opportunity of a UN gathering to meet and discuss their own agenda for the "information society," but presented no demands to the global leaders. Instead they put their ideas directly into practice and created an "information society" from the bottom up. One evening, they screened a satirical movie on intellectual property rights on the white walls of the WIPO building, having invited WSIS participants by generating a mock WSIS official invitation to the event.

"Beyond-ers" typically act independently from institutional processes, as illustrated by one activist's comments recorded in interviews conducted by the writers in 2008:

> I don't think we need to focus on "asking" or "having a voice." I think we have "to do," "keep doing" and keep building working structures and alternatives that are diametrically opposed to the ways capitalism forces us to function in our everyday lives. Our job, as activists, is to create self-managed infrastructures that work regardless of "their" regulation, laws or any other form of governance.

"Regardless of" suggests independence from institutional arenas and rejects the latter's relevance. The "beyond" is an autonomous zone, alternative to hegemonic structures and procedures.

"Beyond" strategies thus focus on pre-figurative action: By creating a different system, at both the "material" and "symbolic" levels, media activists seek to transcend a mainstream system that they consider governed by distorted values and illegitimate actors. "Beyond-ers," like "outsiders," criticize institutional policy processes as undemocratic top-down interventions. Yet they go further. Creating parallel pre-figurative realities, they generate a "new world" and redefine social structures from scratch, engaging in an explosion of power as we know it. As the Indymedia slogan goes: "Don't hate the media, be the media." This approach is linked particularly to anarchist currents in contemporary social movements, and it is at the basis of many social centers but also neighborhood assemblies and other experiences of self-organization.

"Beyond-ers" react when their activities and values are threatened by laws, regulations, forms of control, and police repression. The tactical repertoire that they prefer even in these cases includes control circumvention, creation of technical "bypasses" to evade regulation, and "hacking" of norms and conventions. As one activist put it: "Our main tactic is just avoid all the laws, just sneak a way around it." To do that, they use their technical skills, create encryption, move servers to other countries, and generally develop creative solutions that allow them to be one step ahead of regulatory efforts.

Stefania Milan and Arne Hintz

See also Alternative Media in the World Social Forum; Alternative Media: Policy Issues; Grassroots Tech Activists and Media Policy; Media Infrastructure Policy and Media Activism

Further Readings

Cammaerts, B., & Carpentier, N. (Eds.). (2007). *Reclaiming the media: communication rights and expanding democratic media roles*. Bristol, UK: Intellect.

Day, R. J. F. (2005). *Gramsci is dead. Anarchist currents in the newest social movements*. London: Pluto Press.

Hackett, B., & Carroll, B. (2006). *Remaking the media: The struggle to democratize public communication*. London: Routledge.

Hintz, A. (2009). *Global governance and civil society media*. Münster, Germany: LIT.

Jordan, T. (2002). *Activism! Direct action, hacktivism and the future of society*. London: Reaktion Books.

Kingdon, J. W. (1995). *Agendas, alternatives and public policies*. New York: Longman.

Milan, S. (2009). *Stealing the fire. A study of emancipatory practices in the field of communication*. Unpublished manuscript, European University Institute, San Domenico di Fiesole, Italy.

Mueller, M., Pagé, C., & Kuerbis, B. (2007). Democratizing global communication? Global Civil Society and the campaign for communication rights in the information society. *International Journal of Communication, 1*, 267–296.

MEDIA AGAINST COMMUNALISM (INDIA)

Communalism, the strife between Hindu and Muslim communities, has been a part of the Indian social and political fabric for decades. The term is normal in South Asia to refer to what elsewhere is often called religious sectarianism, although the wellsprings of both typically include powerful economic and political vectors, not simply religious ones.

With the 1992 demolition of Babri Masjid, which was a historical 16th-century mosque claimed by the militant Hindu Right to be the god Ram's birthplace, the subsequent conflagration that consumed Mumbai in 1992–1993, and the Gujarat genocide of 2002, these communal conflicts took on a qualitatively new dimension. Although the state began erasing from its archives any "official" audiovisual record of these atrocities, the mainstream news media coverage of these issues continued to be highly problematic. Thus, cinematic, literary, and Internet critiques of the *Hindutava* movement, which sought to desecularize the Indian state and Hindu-ize Indian national identity, played a seminal role in combating communalism.

Magazines and Cinema

Magazines like *Communalism Combat, Manushi,* and *Tehelka* actively challenged the *Hindutava* project and created a discursive space for engaging in a dialogue and critique of its implication within the civil society. *Communalism Combat* is a monthly magazine published by Sabrang Communications and Publishing Private Ltd. It was first published in August 1993 by its editors Teesta Setalvad and Javed Anand as an act of activist journalism in response to the Babri Masjid demolition and the ensuing Mumbai riots.

Manushi, which derived its name from the Sanskrit word *manush* meaning "human being," was started in 1978. It is published by Manushi Trust as a nonprofit journal. In its editor and founder Madhu Kishwar's own words, the journal

> aims to provide a platform that would provide space both for intellectual quests, investigations and debates as well as activist interventions. One of our consistent endeavors has been to bridge the divide between analysis and activism, rather than pitch them against each other. (Manushi website, accessed May 13, 2010)

Tehelka is a weekly magazine that began in 2000 as a news website and garnered national and international attention through exposés of match fixing in Indian cricket and corruption in Indian defense dealings.

Independent documentary cinema, which narrates the trauma and violence of sectarian assaults and interrogates the social dynamics of power and subversion in civil society, is another powerful site for combating communalism. Documentary representations interrogate the Hindu right's use of audiovisual technologies for political mobilization and indoctrination. Developing spectator citizens, they have a distinctive aesthetic and cinematic sensibility, which is visible in the work of documentary filmmakers like Anand Patwardhan, Rakesh Sharma, and Amar Kanwar.

These documentaries have a complex nexus of production, circulation, exhibition, and consumption within India. There is no state funding and infrastructure, and they are screened on national TV channels. They have long battles with state censorship, and mostly are viewed only at film festivals nationally or internationally, or at screenings by nonprofit organizations, educational institutions, film clubs, and forums.

Working in these material conditions, filmmakers view their art as an intervention. They raise questions about the dangerous *Hindutava* constructions of masculinity within the discourses of "potent Hinduism" and "The Hindu Man," which validate violence in the name of God. They address Muslim citizenship and identity; the persistence and nature of violence, especially against Muslim women and children; the sectarian versus "secular" role of the state and the police; the ghettoization of communities; and the political indifference of the middle classes at large.

Hindi cinema is also an important site that engages with the historical trauma of communalism and interrogates the catastrophic politics of memory continuously mobilized by the militant Hindu right. It has been informed by the work of filmmakers like M. S. Sathyu Govind Nihalani, Saeed Mirza, and Mani Ratnam. Employing melodrama, these representations function as an alternative site of cultural memory and constructions of nationhood. Ira Bhaskar's doctoral dissertation (2005) underlines how this cinema is invested deeply in "visions, desires, the formations of subjectivity and in the notions of community."

Cyberspace

Cyberspace has emerged as an important site to combat communalism. It has not only facilitated a new public arena for independent documentary cinema, but also, through online digital media archives like *Pad.ma,* has provided an engagement with images, intentions, and effects present in video footage; conventional video production, editing, and spectatorship have tended to disfavor these resources. Much of the video footage in this archive addresses communal conflicts and their media representations. The archive's design enables various types of viewing and contextualization, from an overview of themes and timelines to much closer readings of transcribed dialogue and geographical locations. Online blogs like the Social Science Research Council's *The Immanent Frame: Secularism, Religion and the Public Sphere* emerged as powerful sites for scholars to debate the advent of a post-secular age and the resurgence of politicized religion all over the world.

Anuja Jain

See also Documentary Film for Social Change (India); Sarabhai Family and the Darpana Academy (India); *Southern Patriot, The,* 1942–1973 (United States); *Tehelka* Magazine (India); Women's Movement Media (India)

Further Readings

Bhaskar, I. (2005). 'The persistence of memory": Historical trauma and imagining the community in Hindi cinema. PhD dissertation, New York University.

Lal, V. (2005). Travails of the nation: Some notes on Indian documentaries. *Third Text* 19(2), 175–185.

Ludden, D. (2005). *Making India Hindu: Religion, community, and the politics of democracy in India.* Delhi, India: Oxford University Press.

Manushi: http://www.manushi-india.org/ morethanajournal-acause.htm

Needham, A. D., & Rajan, R. S. (2007). *The crisis of secularism in India.* Durham, NC: Duke University Press.

Varadarajan, S. (2002). *Gujarat: The making of a tragedy.* New Delhi, India: Penguin Books.

Waugh, T. (Ed.). (1984). *"Show us life": Towards a history and aesthetics of the committed documentary.* Metuchen, NJ: The Scarecrow Press.

MEDIA EDUCATION FOUNDATION (UNITED STATES)

The Media Education Foundation (MEF) was launched in 1991 by Professor Sut Jhally at the University of Massachusetts, Amherst. His goal was to use video technology to make cutting-edge research on the social impact of mass media accessible to students and the wider public. Jhally, who is a specialist on advertising, recognized that society, particularly its youth, is shaped more and more by a visually mediated culture, awash in commercial and, often, dangerous values. MEF seeks both to use and to subvert commercial media imagery to encourage critical reflection and media literacy.

Jhally's first video started as a classroom experiment. *Dreamworlds: Desire, Sex, and Power in Music Video* critiqued the representation of women in what was then young people's most popular media format, the music video. Jhally had been showing his students examples of music videos while discussing their representations of women. For greater efficiency and impact, Jhally edited together fragments of some 200 clips and replaced much of the music with his critical commentary. That approach worked well with his students, so he decided to share the video with other faculty, sending out a flier advertising its availability.

When MTV threatened a lawsuit over alleged copyright infringement, Jhally prepared to defend his Fair Use right for the purpose of critical commentary. He sent a press release and a copy of MTV's "cease and desist" letter to the major print media, and articles appeared in publications ranging from the *Los Angeles Times* to *Time* magazine. The publicity generated by MTV's attempt to censor Jhally's work through legal intimidation helped generate greater sales of the video. When the University of Massachusetts expressed legal concerns, the proceeds were used to start MEF as a nonprofit organization separate from the university and to produce a second video on cigarette advertising aimed at children called *Pack of Lies.*

From that beginning, MEF has grown to become the nation's leading producer and distributor of educational videos fostering critical thinking about media. Starting in a small office space in Northampton, Massachusetts (where the *Teenage*

Mutant Ninja Turtles creators got their start), executive director Jhally, a very small staff, and a few interns, cobbled together the equipment to produce additional videos on race, gender, advertising, violence, news, and entertainment. MEF began making videos accessible to classrooms across the country, with speakers bell hooks, Noam Chomsky, Michael Eric Dyson, Mary Pipher, Edward Said, George Gerbner, Stuart Hall, Jean Kilbourne, Robert McChesney, Edward Herman, Naomi Klein, Jackson Katz, Henry Giroux, Mark Miller, and others.

In 1995, MEF borrowed money from supporters to print and mail thousands more catalogs and brochures to schools. Doctoral students Nina Huntemann and Matt Soar also developed MEF's first web page, which won a National Communication Association award as the best student-designed website. Teachers around the country found the videos struck a strong chord with their students, many of whom were uneasy with aspects of commercial media culture but lacked the vocabulary to articulate their critical thinking.

Demand for MEF's videos remained strong enough for MEF to add to its productive capacity while beginning to pay back those early loans from supporters. Although MEF received a few small grants in its early years and more significant philanthropic support from donors in the 2000s, it grew largely based on sales. This gave MEF an independence that many nonprofits lack.

In its 10th year, MEF expanded to encompass the offices, studio, and editing suite it now occupies in Northampton's former firehouse. It also grew to a staff of 12 to manage production, marketing, distribution, development, and financial management professionally. MEF was now better positioned to provide critical responses and educational resources to counter commercial media's social impact.

Beginning with Mary Pipher's video *Reviving Ophelia,* MEF reached out to high-school educators in addition to their college audience. Two of their most popular videos, *Killing Us Softly 3: Advertising's Image of Women,* with Jean Kilbourne, and *Tough Guise: Violence, Media, and the Crisis in Masculinity,* with Jackson Katz, have been screened in numerous high schools and colleges across the country. As a result of MEF's efforts, millions of young people now can view and

respond to alternative viewpoints on the media's representations of women and men, and can consider the negative impact of these images on gender relations and the culture at large.

Yet new commercial media technologies and genres present new challenges. For instance, MEF produced the first video of its kind on video games called *Game Over: Gender, Race, and Violence in Video Games,* produced by Nina Huntemann. It provides a critical inside look into the world of video games (where few adults have trodden until recently) that forms the entertainment environment for millions of young people, principally boys, but increasingly girls, sometimes for hours each day. Similarly, Jhally and anti-violence educator Jackson Katz teamed up to produce *Wrestling with Manhood,* a critical examination of professional wrestling and its marketing of violence, bullying, and brutality to young boys.

Although MEF's critique of the commercial media system always addressed power and social justice, they took an explicitly political turn with the release of a series engaging with geopolitical conflicts. *Peace, Propaganda and the Promised Land* focused on Israel and Palestine, comparing British and American media coverage of that conflict. *Hijacking Catastrophe,* which was released just before the 2004 election, is a forceful examination of the neoconservative project in the United States and the manner in which the George W. Bush administration capitalized on the events of 9/11 to push through a preexisting agenda dominate the Middle East.

Hijacking Catastrophe became MEF's most widely distributed film and opened new possibilities for reaching a wider audience. Screened in theaters across the country, it received positive critical attention in publications such as the *New York Times,* the *Washington Post,* and the *New Yorker. War Made Easy,* which featured media critic and journalist Noran Solomon, analyzing war propaganda from Vietnam to Iraq, likewise was met with wide-ranging critical approval as it was shown in theaters nationwide. And *Blood and Oil,* based on Michael Klare's book of the same name, connected U.S. Middle East policy over the decades to corporate and governmental aims to control dwindling petroleum resources.

However, MEF did not neglect its original focus on gender representation and consumer culture, releasing films such as *Consuming Kids* on the commercialization of childhood, *Big Bucks, Big Pharma* on the marketing of prescription drugs, and updating Jhally's original film on popular music and gender images under the title *Dreamworlds 3*.

MEF also became the key educational distributor of films by other critically oriented documentarians, most notably Byron Hurt's acclaimed film on rap music, race, and masculinity, *Hip Hop: Beyond Beats and Rhymes*; this film was screened at the Sundance Film Festival and was broadcasted on PBS. Films such as this, as well as MEF's many other productions, are imbued with the spirit of dissenting alternative media exemplified by the dual meaning of the MEF slogan: *Challenging Media*.

Tom Gardner and Bill Yousman

See also Adbusters Media Foundation (Canada); Alternative Media; Citizens' Media; Documentary Film for Social Change (India); Youth Media

Further Readings

Media Education Foundation: http://www.mediaed.org

MEDIA INFRASTRUCTURE POLICY AND MEDIA ACTIVISM

To many, even media activists, policy making about communication infrastructure resources might seem both bewildering and elusive: bewildering because of its sheer breadth, interrelatedness, and complexity, and elusive because it necessarily requires constant responses to technological innovation and change. Yet, social movement actors who depend increasingly on electronic media for their work should be as concerned about how media systems are governed as they are about producing social movement media.

Many social, economic, political, cultural, and financial activities depend on access to communication infrastructure resources such as the airwaves and cable TV, as well as telephone and computer networks. Social movement media in particular are being empowered by one critically important resource: the Internet. An expanding blogosphere, mobile phones, wikis, and social networking services enabled by Web 2.0 such as MySpace, Twitter, and Facebook combine to increase the reach of social movement media.

Attention should be given not only to the strategic *uses* of these resources as contributions to democratic public spheres but also to the policies that give form *to* these electronic public spaces for speech. These policies, which make it possible to access and use electronic communication resources, are equally important to research and political organizing. Typically these "open spaces" are corporately owned and in principle can be shut down as and when their owners choose.

What broadcasting, telecommunications, and Internet policy share is their connection to the infrastructure necessary to be informed citizens or consumers, and for people to speak and be heard. It is essential to realize the fundamental role that these forms of communication infrastructure continue to play in shaping the possibilities for freedom of expression.

The "Commons" and "Enclosures"

David Bollier's notion of the "commons" helps to consider the importance of communication infrastructure resources to the freedom of expression. Generally speaking, resources are those things to which one turns for help when in desperation, such as a recourse or refuge. For example, managing the public airwaves can be set within a discussion about forests, minerals, lakes, and rivers; government research and development investments; public schools; and various kinds of cultural spaces, both physical and electronic.

Bollier worries that these and many other public resources are being "enclosed" in much the same way that in the mid-1500s through the 1800s, English common land was fenced off and privatized, mostly by the already wealthy. Bollier also warns about the contemporary enclosures of the "information commons." We view evidence of this in the concentration of media property ownership, the privatization of public databases and the public airwaves, centralized programming of previously local radio broadcasting, and escalating control of the flow of public knowledge through aggressive corporate litigation using intellectual property rights law.

Communication infrastructure policies that govern the availability and use of these resources matter to social movement researchers and activists. First, they literally produce, through a political process, the electronic spaces in and through which public debate and deliberation occur. Second, they are also important foci for political contestation about those spaces. This perspective is echoed throughout the Civil Society Declaration to the 2003 World Summit on the Information Society, which argued that universal access must be ensured to people for information essential for human development. Infrastructure and the most appropriate forms of information and communication technologies must, therefore, be accessible for all in their different social contexts, and the social appropriation of these technologies must be enabled.

Defining Infrastructure

The word *infrastructure* carries many meanings. Webster's dictionary proposes the following definition:

An underlying base or foundation especially for an organization or system; and the basic facilities, services, and installations needed for the functioning of a community or society, such as transportation and communications systems, water and power lines, and public institutions, including schools, post offices, and prisons.

Susan Star and Karen Ruhleder expand this to include several additional features that emerge when talking about information infrastructures:

1. They are rooted within other technological and social structures.

2. They invisibly sustain other tasks.

3. Infrastructures have "reach"—they often expand beyond a single location, event, or point in time.

4. They are often taken for granted by those who use them but seem somewhat foreign to those who do not.

5. They often both shape and reflect the values, customs, and practices of those who build and maintain them.

6. They often connect fairly seamlessly to other infrastructures because they share design standards and conventions but inherit whatever limitations or benefits are inherent in the base on which they might be installed. (Star and Ruhleder give the example of fiber-optic networks installed alongside railroads.)

7. Finally, infrastructures often only become noticeable when they break, as when a server goes down or when a power failure occurs.

Hence, we can think of infrastructure in a multitude of ways, for example, as physical, social, or even symbolic. Increasingly pervasive and ubiquitous communication infrastructure resources present attributes of all of these.

In the field of communication, physical infrastructures include telephone networks and cell towers, broadcasting and cable television systems, satellite networks, and the interconnected servers, computers, and software that make up the largest network of networks: the Internet. Three types of regulation often govern how available, affordable, and useable is this ensemble of infrastructure resources. Generally speaking, *broadcasting policy* allocates licenses for use of the radio-frequency spectrum resource (i.e., the airwaves). *Telecommunications policy* determines aspects of telephone systems and, by extension, the computer networks that depend on them. *Internet policy* is an emerging area of policy that has to do with governing Internet-related resources such as the domain name system (.com/.org/.edu/.net and country abbreviations such as us/mx/ca/fr/de/ru/cn/in).

Telecommunications resources are often considered unique among other forms of infrastructure. Robert Horwitz notes that telecommunications is a peculiar infrastructure because it is central to the circulation of ideas and information. The regulation of telecommunications is more complicated and interesting than that of transportation precisely because it bears so directly on democracy.

Similarly, Oscar Gandy discusses telecommunications infrastructure not as a physical thing, but as something that acts as a medium for the exchange of ideas, information, and knowledge among people and their associated networks, institutions, and cultures. He suggests a broadened definition of infrastructure (of which telecommunications is only one part) that includes three domains: technical, economic, and cultural. The technical domain includes for him not only hardware and software but also the technical knowledge and values that engineers and developers embed into the design and engineering process. To Gandy, economic and cultural infrastructure also includes the structures and workings of institutions that make up markets, in addition to the values that determine how people acquire and use resources in the marketplace.

Part of this *social* infrastructure vitally includes legislative, judicial, and regulatory bodies. Their infrastructure operations undergird or subvert freedom of expression, which is defined as follows in Article 19 of the Universal Declaration of Human Rights:

> Everyone has the right to freedom of opinion and expression; this right includes freedom to hold opinions without interference and to seek, receive and impart information and ideas through any media and regardless of frontiers.

What is important here is the fact that freedom of expression is connected not only to issues of content but also "through any media" to all the *means* of expression, including the communication infrastructure.

It follows that communication infrastructure policy making, especially Internet policy, focuses primarily on information *distribution* issues. These, however, are often decided on by elite specialists through many corporate, legislative, judicial, lobbying, and regulatory processes. Expert decision making concerns such things as who gets licenses to use the radio-frequency spectrum, where cable television companies can dig and install their cable lines, how telephone companies should charge for their services, which telephone traffic they can and cannot interfere with, whether Internet service providers should or should not be regulated as intermediaries between telephone networks and consumers, whether companies that provide telecommunications services can give the government the names of its customers in the interest of national security, and how technologies that support networks are designed.

On the international level, these legal issues multiply, as Drake and Jorgensen rightly note: telecommunications and media regulation, digital convergence, radio frequency spectrum management, technical standardization, Internet governance, trade in networked goods and services, competition policy, intellectual property, privacy and consumer protection, freedom of speech and censorship, network security and cybercrime, cultural and linguistic integrity, development of the global digital divide, e-commerce, e-government, e-education, and e-everything. As they emphasize, these interdependent issues overlap to form "the elements of a single overarching policy space": It is impossible to address security effectively without considering privacy, intellectual property without considering freedom of speech, trade without considering consumer protection, and so on across the board. Media activism cannot operate autonomously in a bubble, shielded from these interrelated processes.

Indeed because of the Internet's importance as a "critical infrastructure" for commerce, health care, education, and government, issues of national security often enter in. In the aftermath of the terrorist attacks on New York City in 2001, the U.S. Congress passed the U.S. Patriot Act, which affected citizens' privacy rights in several troubling ways. In the name of national security, some telecommunications companies gave customer account records to the government to assist in wiretapping and other government surveillance activities. Along with others working to protect privacy rights, the Citizens Lab and the OpenNet Initiative at the University of Toronto have documented myriad privacy and surveillance problems around the world as cybersecurity issues have become a more prominent aspect of communication infrastructure governance and policy.

Finally, communication infrastructure can also be thought about in a *figurative* sense. It is the symbolic "speaking space" to which French social analyst Michel de Certeau referred in a statement that telecommunications practices have reorganized the speaking space—a space that has been represented alternately as virtual and nonmaterial, as an electronic public sphere and as "cyber space" with no clear location or territorial boundaries.

Conclusion

Communication infrastructure policy can enable, protect, or restrict political and cultural expression as a result of decision making that determines the availability, affordability, accessibility, and use of electronic media resources such as networked computers and the Internet, mobile phones, and television and radio. The policy issues in this field concern both the production of content (broadly conceived to include news and information, entertainment, or even personal information and communication) and its distribution, exhibition, or exchange using a variety of interdependent electronic media resources. Some of these resources are regulated, but many are not. Media activists' opportunities might be enhanced, stifled, or shut down, depending on policies in force. They urgently need to be conversant with the issues if they want social movement media to thrive.

Becky Lentz

See also Alternative Media at Political Summits; Alternative Media in the World Social Forum; Alternative Media: Policy Issues; Grassroots Tech Activists and Media Policy; Media Activists and Communication Policy Processes

Further Readings

Benkler, Y. (2000). From consumers to users: Shifting the deeper structures of regulation towards sustainable commons and user access. *52 Fed. Comm. L.J. 561.*

Bollier, D. (2003). *Silent theft: The private plunder of our common wealth.* New York: Routledge.

Braman, S. (2004). Where has media policy gone? Defining the field in the twenty-first century. *Communication Law and Policy, 9*(2), 153–182.

De Certeau, M. (1998). *The practice of everyday life. Volume 2: Living and cooking.* Minneapolis: University of Minnesota Press.

Drake, W., & Jørgenson, R. F. (2006). Introduction. In R. F. Jørgenson (Ed.), *Human rights in the global information society: Information revolution and global politics* (pp. 1–19). Cambridge, MA: MIT Press.

Gandy, O. (1992). Infrastructure: A chaotic disturbance in the policy discourse. In National Information Network (Ed.), *A national information network: Changing our lives in the 21st century* (pp. ix–xxxiv). Nashville, TN: Institute of Information Studies.

Goldsmith, J., & Wu, T. (2006). *Who controls the Internet? Illusions of a borderless world.* New York: Oxford University Press.

Lessig, L. (2006). *Code: And other laws of cyberspace, version 2.0.* New York: Basic Books.

May, C. (2002). *The information society: A skeptical view.* Cambridge, UK: Polity Press.

McChesney, R. W., Newman, R., & Scott, B. (Eds.). (2005). *The future of media: Resistance and reform in the 21st century.* New York: Seven Stories Press.

Mueller, M. (2004). *Ruling the root: Internet governance and the taming of cyberspace.* Cambridge, MA: MIT Press.

Star, S. L., & Ruhleder, K. (1996). Steps toward an ecology of infrastructure: Design and access for large information spaces. *Information Systems Research, 7*(1), 113–114.

Webster, F. (2006). *Theories of the information society* (3rd ed.). New York: Routledge.

Working Group on Internet Governance. (2005). Retrieved May 13, 2010, from http://www.wgig.org/docs/WGIGREPORT.pdf

Zittrain, J. (2008). *The future of the Internet—and how to stop it.* New Haven, CT: Yale University Press.

MEDIA JUSTICE MOVEMENT (UNITED STATES)

The media justice movement (MJM) is a grassroots network composed of disenfranchised communities united by a broader vision of media's roles in achieving social justice than commonly found in the U.S. media reform (MR) movement. The MR movement leadership's primary goals are, depending on the issue, to bring about or to block national policy changes in the communication sphere. The goals of the MJM do not reject that stance but go further to define the issues below as equally pivotal.

MJM demands more diverse media representations, positive communication rights, good training programs in communication technology uses, media education to enable more effective community-level public relations, and a more accessible and sustainable information infrastructure to serve the entire public. All these goals are recognized as necessarily embedded within the various movements pushing for social justice on a whole variety of fronts. The communication dimensions, while separable analytically, are judged inseparable in reality.

MJM's immediate antecedent is the environmental justice movement, which has challenged mainstream understandings of the environment and environmentalism since the 1980s. The environmental justice movement has examined the unequally heavy burden that a harmful environment places on poor and minority communities, has called for the inclusion of all people affected by environmental problems in related decision-making processes, and has formulated a vision of a healthy and sustainable environment.

As with the environmental justice movement, the MJM links media reform to social justice and civil rights issues, explores the disproportionate effects of an undemocratic media system and cultural environment on minority communities, and asks for the democratic inclusion of these communities in media and cultural policy and practice.

Media justice is a term discussed first at a Highlander Research and Education Center gathering in New Market, Tennessee, in 2002. The conversation occurred among a small number of grassroots organizations recognizing the need to find links to, and maintain the connections between, issues of public policy and media advocacy as they relate to long-term goals of social justice, economic justice, and effective organizing across marginalized communities. The broad idea of media justice soon became an organizing catalyst for many regional grassroots activist groups whose missions include various forms of activism and justice.

These groups shared similar ideas, values, actions, and strategies for change and began to coordinate under the banner *Media Action Grassroots Network* (MAG-NET). MAG-NET represents the first creation of a national coalition within the United States of media justice groups, with member organizations located in Oakland, Albuquerque, Seattle, New York, Philadelphia, San Antonio, and rural Kentucky.

MAG-NET operates under a 10-point platform released at the 2007 U.S. Social Justice Forum in Atlanta, Georgia, which highlighted the main tenets of the unified media justice movement. These were Representative and Accountable Content; True Universal Media Access: Full, Fast, and Free for All; Public Airwaves—Public Ownership; Community-Centered Media Policy; Corporate Media Accountability and Just Enforcement of

Media Rules; Redefine and Redistribute First Amendment Rights; Cultural Sovereignty and Self-Determination; Full and Fair Digital Inclusion; Another Media is Possible—If We Fund It; and Full and Fair Representation in the Movement for Media Reform.

Through these tenets, media justice organizers hoped to create a distinct space within, but separate from, the more mainstream MR movement. This "space" they viewed as necessary to center an analysis of power on race, class, and gender. MJM was a unique arena for oppressed communities to strategize and work toward an inclusive and empowering mediascape as a core dimensions of a more just and democratic society.

Ricky Hill

See also Alliance for Community Media (United States); Copyleft; Creative Commons; Environmental Movement Media; Grassroots Tech Activists and Media Policy; Low-Power FM Radio (United States); Media Education Foundation (United States); Media Infrastructure Policy and Media Activism; *Radical Software* (United States)

Further Readings

Center for Media Justice: http://centerformediajustice.org

Cox, R. (2006). *Environmental communication and the public sphere.* Thousand Oaks, CA: Sage.

Funding Exchange Media Justice Fund. (2009). *A field report: Media justice through the eyes of local organizers.* http://www.fex.org/assets/418_hjmjflocalorganizers2.pdf

Media Action Grassroots Network: http://www.mediagrassroots.org

Reclaim the Media: http://www.reclaimthemedia.org/media_justice

MediACT (Korea)

MediACT's motto is "Act through media, a new window to the world." It is a public local media access center located in Seoul, South Korea. It was started in 2002 to support alternative and participatory media activities, including (a) independent film making, (b) the establishment of public access structures in tandem with media policy development, and (c) activation of systematic media education and its continuation as a lifelong process.

MediACT emerged as a public institution whose facilities are funded by the Korean Film Council, which is an organization the central government funds to promote Korean cinema within the country and overseas, and an independent activist organization managed by the Association of Korean Independent Film & Video. MediACT provides an infrastructure for media activism. Its strategy focuses on the potential to create a new public media sector based on both shifting media access possibilities and the ongoing political democratization in South Korea.

MediACT is located within a history of Korean movements for media democracy that emerged in the late 1980s in efforts to overcome censorship and the broadcasting monopoly. Some of those movements have included activists involved in alternative film and video, a citizens' media monitoring movement, and a trade union movement inside the media. A first phase for public access was made possible through these struggles.

After the 1996 abolition of censorship and the passing of the 2000 Broadcasting Act, a second phase of public access support emerged. This legislation included the requirement that the Korean Broadcasting System broadcast viewer-produced programs, that cable and satellite operators do the same via a regional or a public access channel, and that public funds should support these productions.

As a result, the fight to extend the terrain of public media began to be shaped by several issues. Securing funding and integrating public access more broadly into public media policy was a major one. But others included contending with a rise in corporate media power, engaging with the introduction of new information and communication technologies and broadband technologies, and countering neoliberal policies and their attendant social crises and attacks on basic human rights. This platform took concrete shape through the establishment of local media access centers, the introduction of media education in and out of schools, lobbying for detailed public access policies, and training and organizing local media activists in a national network.

In short, within less than two decades of struggle, South Korea's media landscape became distinguished by real public access to terrestrial, cable, and satellite channels; funding for media education; a vibrant network of access centers; and growing Internet activism, including both Internet uses for social change and Internet democracy advocacy.

MediACT is located in the hub of Seoul downtown and within its 600-m² space houses an auditorium, an audio recording room, seminar rooms, and a wide array of low- and high-end multimedia production and post-production facilities. The basic concept includes a notion of universal service to the public, including undocumented migrant workers, and selective services targeting minoritized groups, communities, or constituencies working for social change. As of 2009, 15 full-time staff were working vigorously to make these projects possible with broad participation from other activists and citizens.

The outcomes of MediACT programs are extensive and noteworthy. MediACT has been a long-standing advocate of local media access centers and has actively empowered thousands of local media activists, independent filmmakers, and various networks of people to build these in almost all regions of South Korea and across different groups. MediACT played an especially critical role in the second phase of struggle for public access by launching the National Media Activist Network, which includes more than 100 civil society organizations and local media activists.

Through media education outreach and consultation, MediACT has catalyzed ongoing dialogue and change among migrant workers; people with disabilities; the elderly; women; teachers; children; gay, lesbian, bisexual, and transgender communities; soldiers; and people in regions outside of Seoul.

With regard to resources for media practice, MediACT has played an important role in developing various media education curricula, media activism strategies, and strategic frameworks. The focus has been to do whatever might be needed to overcome traditional barriers to democracy. One is the habit of dividing movements according to perceptions of their different communication technology uses. Another is the frequent disconnect between the mainstream media reform movement and the community media movement. MediACT has launched a broad coalition to sustain and extend the public media, Media Action, as well as to articulate a civil society position and strategy on Internet Protocol television, the content rating systems, media convergence laws, and intellectual property matters

MediACT has produced the *World Through Media*, a broadcast media education program shown on national public access satellite cable channel RTV, which broadcasts debates on media education and introduces the public to various communication rights issues. Since 2003, MediACT also publishes *ACT!* an online monthly journal that covers various subjects including the historical and current structures of national and transnational media movements, and *off-ACT*, an offline journal.

MediACT has been active in the field of international exchange, introducing experiences and case studies inside and outside of South Korea and providing internship programs and trainings for foreigners on topics that have included public interest media, the struggle against privatization of public communications resources under neoliberal "free trade" policies, media convergence, culture and film policy, media access center construction, and media curriculum development.

Developing media curriculum was critical to the launching of MediR, a local media access center in Tokyo. MediACT representatives have also been active in other translocalized networks including Videazimut, the Campaign for Rights in the Information Society, and the OURMedia/ NUESTROSMedios Network. They have provided training for people interested in building an inter-Asia media activist network and have participated in supranational policy settings as representatives of civil society, including the 2003 UN World Summit on the Information Society in Geneva. Solidarity activities have included sponsoring and supporting the Human Rights Film Festival, the Labor Film Festival, the Migrant Workers Film Festival, the Seoul Independent Documentary Film & Video Festival, and Indieforum screenings.

As of 2010, MediACT's profile had emphasized collective attempts to clarify the multiple registers of public access and to strengthen sites for democracy and self-expression. Fresh challenges included further developing a "publicly funded alternative media" sector, new "public audio visual media culture policies," and a bill of electronic communication rights.

Given the instability imposed by the realities of securing government and public financial resources, sustaining its unique model of center activity is also an ongoing challenge. When asked about its future prospects, MediACT staff contend that its aim is to avoid getting trapped into fund-raising for MediACT, because no organization is forever and because one organization's success can never bring about social change to the extent needed. Although some might see MediACT as core of a network of more than 20 local media access centers, it had in fact tried to decentralize the movement and to explore new models of sustainable social movements, and was moving into a third phase of media movement struggle.

M. J. Kim

See also Copyleft; Creative Commons; Deep Dish TV (United States); Media Education Foundation (United States); Media Justice Movement (United States); Migrant Workers' Television (Korea); Paper Tiger Television (United States); *Radical Software* (United States)

Further Readings

Gumucio Dagron, A. (2001). Labor news production. In A. Gumucio Dagron (Ed.), *Making waves: Stories of participatory communication for social change*. New York: Rockefeller Foundation.

Hackett, R., & Zhao, Y. (2005). The campaign to democratize communication. In R. Hackett & Y. Zhao (Eds.), *Democratizing global media: One world, many struggles* (pp. 289–312). Lanham, MD: Rowman & Littlefield.

Jo, D.-W. (2004, June). *Re-considering active audiences: South Korean experiences in strengthening "media democracy."* Paper presented at Asia Pacific Forum on Active Audiences, Ritsumeikan University, Kyoto, Japan.

Jo, D.-W. (2005). *Social media-communication system and communication rights movement.* Paper presented at Theoretical Seminar on Mediactivism, Seoul, South Korea.

Kidd, D., Rodríguez, C., & Stein, L. (Eds.). (2009). *Making our media: Global initiatives toward a democratic public sphere* (2 vols.). Cresskill, NJ: Hampton Press.

Kim, M. (2003). *Framing the communication rights: Korean context—brief primer.* Paper presented at the Preparatory Meeting for the World Forum on Communication Rights, Geneva, Switzerland.

Kim, M. (2007). *Expanding public media space and media activism in Korea, Reclaim the Media online.* http://www.reclaimthemedia.org/communications_rights/expanding_public_media_space_and_media_act

MediACT. (2004). *Debating the strategy for media activism: Renewal of agenda + regeneration of internationalism.* Seoul, South Korea: MediACT.

Ó Siochrú, S. (2005). Finding a frame: Towards a transnational advocacy campaign to democratize communication. In R. Hackett & Y. Zhao (Eds.), *Democratizing global media: One world, many struggles* (pp. 289–312). Lanham, MD: Rowman & Littlefield.

OURmedia/NUESTROSmedios. (2006). *About us.* http://www.ourmedianet.org/general/about_us.html

MEDVEDKINE GROUPS AND WORKERS' CINEMA (FRANCE)

The Medvedkine film collectives of the 1960s and 1970s borrowed their name from Aleksandr Medvedkin, a Soviet filmmaker (d. 1989) known as the inventor of "locomotive cinema." This was a 1930s project in which the crew traveled around the USSR filming workers and farmers at their jobs, edited the rushes rapidly, and screened the finished product on the spot to those they had filmed. The choice of name, therefore, fit the 7 years' worth of worker-made films produced at Besançon and Sochaux, which are two mid-sized, heavily industrialized towns at that time.

Besançon

The film that launched the Medvedkine Groups was the 1967 Chris Marker film *À bientôt, j'espère* (Soon, I hope), which had been made at the request of striking workers in a Besançon textile factory and by members of that neighborhood's cultural center (Centre Culturel Populaire de Palentes-les-Orchamps, CCPPO). The strike, and then occupation, had been called to protest management's decision to fire some workers and reduce bonus levels.

The documentary showed the uncertain and poverty-stricken life the workers led, as well as its impact on people's friendships, their families, and their emotional and cultural lives—which underscored that money alone would not compensate for these deprivations. The film aimed to allow workers to speak eloquently about their situation, and also to serve as a stimulus to the workers' own reflection on the importance of class conflict, their possible tactics (especially factory occupation), and specific aspects of domination such as women's labor.

When screened to the Besançon workers, the film was not well received. They complained that neither the harsh factory-floor discipline nor women's labor, nor the solutions the workers themselves had come up with, had been touched on. They roundly declared Marker clueless. On the contrary, instead of snuffing out this embryonic collaboration, the stormy encounter set in motion a close collaboration in making films that put testimony to working conditions at the center, including their impact on the rest of the workers' lives. Marker himself commented without bitterness that although he and his crew had been well meaning, they were outsiders, and a workers' liberation cinema simply had to be their own work once they had the equipment in their hands. Then, they themselves would proceed to show what a strike is like, as well as real factory conditions.

The consequence was a program of critical co-development between trained filmmakers and worker filmmaker apprentices. From this productive dialogue between the producers of mass consumer commodities and cultural goods producers came the Medvedkine Groups' first real film in 1968, titled *Classe de lutte* (Fighting class). Made by the workers with the help of Marker's crew—all of 45 names were credited as directors—the film set out to demand the workers' right to have cultural respect, to have a voice, and to handle their own media representation. One woman worker, who was just a worker's wife in *À bientôt, j'espère*, became the principal character. The audience could witness her double struggle against management and the strike organizer. Central to the film were several themes, such as the processes of coming to political awareness, getting rid of certain prejudices, activism, solidarity, daily life, and women's situations or the hankering for culture; all of these were defined collectively. It was not an outside import, but an activist tool for information and self-expression. It won the World Federation of Trade Unions prize in 1969.

From 1967 to 1974, 15 films were made by a handful of workers in Besançon's Rhodiaceta and Peugeot factories, with film stock, laboratory processing, and audio enhancement as needed from Marker and the *Slon* film collective. The CCPPO housed the footage and an editing table. Most films were banned in France but traveled widely abroad. The Besançon Medvedkine Group made *Rhodia 4X8* (1969); *Lettre à mon ami Pol Cèbe* (Letter to my friend Pol Cèbe [a CCPPO activist deeply involved in the film projects]), 1971; *Le traineau-échelle* (The sledge-ladder), 1971; and a 1969–1970 trilogy on factory conditions titled *Nouvelle Société* (New Society) in mocking allusion to the announcement by France's then prime minister of a "New Society" national program that he guaranteed would benefit all.

The trilogy was made up of short segments, each one closing with a freeze frame of workers (many of them migrants) and of a young girl with their gaze fixed past the camera on something presumably important. In fact, that image had been shot in May 1968 at the conclusion of a speech by a striking Peugeot worker, who urged construction workers to strike in solidarity with the automobile workers. It was borrowed from a 1970 documentary made by the Sochaux Medvedkine Group.

Sochaux

Through the CCPPO, some workers at the Peugeot factory in Sochaux became interested in developing a cultural activism alongside standard union activism. Some conventionally minded union and leftist party officials tried to discourage this as a diversion from the "real struggle," but the appeal of independent activism proved greater. Their vision resulted in *Sochaux, 11 Juin 1968*, which is an iconic example of a cinema committed to denouncing a brutal state that, in league with management, organized vicious repression of workers' struggles.

June 11 marked the auto workers' 22nd day out on strike, at the close of France's May–June social unrest. The riot police attacked not only the strikers but also those seeking to return to work, resulting in two dead and 150 injured, with several people requiring amputations. Images of the clash were shot by a taxi driver using a Super-8 the workers had lent him. Bumped up to 16 mm and edited by Marker, they were then screened around the country in a 20-minute film, in conjunction with testimonies from workers present at the confrontation. The film used a crop of cinema techniques: plot-sequence, use of stills, Super-8 color images, black and white subtitles, testimonies in close-up, fades to black, silence, and multiple voices, from management-speak to wall-slogans, to factual information from a former worker who said simply to the camera, "There's 18,000 Peugeot workers who do that every day. 18,000 . . . 18,000."

Later came *Trois quarts de la vie* (Three quarters of a lifetime), 1971; *Weekend à Sochaux*, 1972; and *Avec le sang des autres* (With other people's blood), 1975. These worker films focused on the degrading effect of capitalist labor on daily life—how it bruises bodies and alienates minds. Their makers saw them as acts of resistance blending cold analyses with good humor, theater, games, fiction, debates, and distancing tactics.

Avec le sang des autres was the last one, but it was not strictly a Medvedkine style of film. Its professionally trained director Bruno Muel acknowledged as much when he paid tribute to the workers with whom he had discussed it at length during its making, but it was not their film in the full sense. Nonetheless, it valuably documented life on the assembly line. Thirty-five years later, when it was reissued in DVD format, Muel insisted that other Medvedkine groups would pop up one day or another, under other forms and other names, in other conditions, and probably, he forecasted, with even more anger and, he hoped, as much joy.

Fabien Granjon
(translated by John D. H. Downing)

See also Activist Cinema in the 1970s (France); Anarchist Media; Cine Insurgente/Rebel Cinema (Argentina); Documentary Film for Social Change (India); Labor Media (United States); May 1968 Poetry and Graffiti (France/Transnational); Third Cinema

Further Readings

Anonymous. (2002). *Groupe Medvedkine, le cinéma autrement* [Medvedkine Group, a different cinema]. *L'Image, le Monde*, #3. Paris, France.

Foltz, C. (2001). *L'expérience des groupes Medvedkine (Slon 1967–1974): Histoire d'une aventure cinématographique révolutionnaire* [*The experience of the Medvedkine Groups (Slon 1967–1974): Story of a revolutionary film-making adventure*. Mém. de maîtrise en études cinématographiques [MA thesis in Cinema Studies], Université Paris 1 Panthéon-Sorbonne, Centre Pierre Mendes, France.

Gauthier, G. (2004). De *Slon* à *Iskra* [From *Slon* to *Iskra*]. *CinémAction*, 110, 119–124.

Iskra Collective. (2006). *Les groupes Medvedkine* [Motion picture]. Paris: Éditions Montparnasse/Iskra. DVD + text.

MIGRANT WORKERS' TELEVISION (KOREA)

Migrant Workers Television (MWTV) was established in December 2004 to try to secure human rights for migrant workers in Korea. It evolved from the Migrant Social Movements of the early 1990s. As of 2009, other Korean media projects dedicated to migrant workers' rights in Korea included Salad TV, Osan Migrant Worker Radio (OMWR), Sungseo Community FM (SCFM), and Migrant Network TV (MNTV). However, MWTV is unique in that it was the first and only independent channel established and managed mainly by migrant workers themselves. OMWR and MNTV are affiliated with progressive Korean Churches, SCFM is affiliated with a labor union, and Salad TV is managed by Korean activists.

MWTV's manifesto to "represent the voices of migrant workers in Korea" signals the project's determination to realize the self-reliant collective power of migrant workers in Korea. Unlike other organizations, the migrant workers assume central roles in managing the institution. To understand MWTV's central concerns and roles requires understanding the historical development of migrant social movements in Korea.

Migrant Social Movements and MWTV

Historically, Korea's development has been shaped mainly by struggles between different political and economic groups within a relatively homogeneous national culture. However, with neoliberal globalization, low-paid foreign workers have increased in number rapidly since the late 1980s. Mostly originating from economically less developed Asian countries (China, Vietnam, Philippines, Thailand, Indonesia, Mongolia, Sri Lanka, Uzbekistan, Pakistan, Bangladesh, Nepal, and Burma), labor migration has accelerated the ethnic diversification of the Korean working class. The government projects the number will reach a million in 2010.

However, it is clear that neither government bureaucracies nor private industries were prepared to provide adequate conditions for the migrant workers. Until 2003 when Korea government changed its mandate on the migrant workers from a guest worker program to an Employment Permit System (EPS), the migrant workers were not considered as "laborers" but as "trainees," which means that they were systematically excluded from any labor protection.

Thus, it was not rare in the workplace for migrant workers to suffer severely from exploitation, racist abuse, industrial accidents, sexual abuse, illegal layoffs, and so forth. Being "illegal," they are constantly threatened by tough government crackdowns and forced deportations. Some even die while trying to escape immigration raids. Thus, it might not have been truly accidental when nine undocumented workers detained in Yosoo immigration detention center in 2007 were not rescued from an accidental fire in the building. "The Modern Slave," which is a metaphorical description of the migrant workers, denotes their harsh and unjust living and working conditions.

The Foreign Workers Employment Bill to initiate the EPS in 2003 was a small but essential measure to remedy the serious rights violations for migrant workers. The bill's adoption is a significant victory achieved by almost a decade of struggle. The so-called migrant social movements (MSMs) are organized and mobilized by the diverse ideological, national, and ethnic communities to achieve basic rights for the foreign migrant workers. Since the initial protests in 1993 motivated by the tragic suicide of a Chinese migrant worker, MSMs have challenged and sometimes changed the laws and policies afflicting migrant workers in Korea. Moreover, the movement also has challenged Korean civil society to create new forms of collective action with the increasing engagement of migrant communities in the movement.

It is in this historical conjuncture that MWTV emerged out of the changing social-cultural relations in Korea. It was established in the 2004 aftermath of the demonstration at the Myoundong Sanctuary in Seoul, which ran from November 2003 to November 2004 and was organized to demand legal status for migrant workers and measures to protect labor.

The participants were constituted of various migrant communities, Korean radical labor movement groups, unions, media activists, and human rights advocates. Throughout the sit-in, migrant workers strengthened their communities, generated a network of activist groups, increased their knowledge about the structural problems in Korea, and discussed possible alternatives. It was clear that the movement enables the migrant workers to develop the capacity and consciousness capable of organizing collective actions for social changes.

The creation of MWTV was also first discussed by migrant workers and Korean activists in the movement. They had observed how their demands and realities were easily altered or silenced by the dominant mass media. It was urgent to have their own information media to share information and perspectives to change their working and living conditions in Korea. Using the networks, resources, and knowledge acquired through movement participation, MWTV members successfully launched the first program in April 2005 over the satellite and cable network of RTV (Channel 531), which is the citizens' access channel in Korea.

MWTV Programs

MWTV is organized to expand its agency as both migrant community media and social movement media. As of 2009, it broadcasted two regular programs, the *Multilingual Migrant Worker News* and the discussion talk show *The World of Migrant Workers*. The choice of the particular program formats is the conscious decision to meet the urgent needs of migrant workers to access information and participate in public discussions on the various issues about migrant communities, along with social, political, and economic problems both domestic and international.

Whereas the media messages tended to focus on demanding that the government stop immigration raids, adopt a labor permit system, legalize undocumented workers, and legalize a migrant workers trade union, issues such as the democratization movements of Burma and Nepal, oppositional movements against the Korea–U.S. Free Trade Agreement, and the Iraq war were also given priority. The different levels of media messages—migrant, domestic, and international—signify the multilayered issues and objectives of the migrant social movements that possess the potential to develop into transnational movements for international political, economic, and social justices.

However, MWTV can also be conceived as a movement organizer, as it often provides programs, producers, and production skills for organizing public demonstrations and migrant community events. They also try to educate migrant communities to organize networks of immigrant media producers.

The MWTV activists often call themselves "cultural producers." They envision MWTV as an effective and necessary project to transform the discriminatory and exploitative culture of Korea. The annual Migrant Workers Film Festival and media workshops of MWTV are also organized to enrich the ways of mobilizing the migrant workers and to provide opportunities for the migrant communities to express and reflect on their problems and concerns in relation to life in Korea.

Young-Gil Chae

See also Black Exploitation Cinema (United States); Industrial Workers of the World Media (United States); Labor Media (United States); MediACT (Korea); *OhmyNews* (Korea); Undocumented Workers' Internet Use (France)

Further Readings

Chae, Y.-G. (2008). *Immigrant media and communication processes for social change in Korea: A case study of Migrant Workers Television.* PhD dissertation, University of Texas at Austin.

Lim, T. C. (2003). Racing from the bottom in South Korea? The nexus between civil society and transnational migrants. *Asian Survey, 43*(3), 423–442.

Migrant Workers Television: http://www.mwtv.kr

Miners' Radio Stations (Bolivia)

Historically, Bolivian miners' community radio stations are the most powerful paradigm of participation and ownership of community media. This entry explains the role of these stations and describes their impact and current status.

There are six fundamental reasons for the significance of the miners' radio stations. The first is their early date. There is no evidence on the exact date of the initial broadcast, but the first station started in the period 1947–1948. It is true that Radio Sutatenza, Colombia, which was created by a Catholic priest, was in operation in 1947. However, this was a station "for" the community, managed by Father Salcedo, and it only lasted as a local station for about a year. The miners' stations were controlled from the start by the miners themselves. They were politically advanced at the time and were fully aware of the potential of developing their own media. Radio *La Voz del Minero* (The Miner's Voice), the first one, set the principles for all the rest.

The second is longevity. The miners' stations lasted more than 50 years and several are still in operation, although perhaps with lesser importance now that mining is no longer Bolivia's main revenue source, and many state mines have closed since the early 1990s. Few community media experiences worldwide can show a half-century history in their development without fundamentally altering their principles and ownership over the years. Among those that have lasted longest is *Radio Nacional de Huanuni*. Many stations were attacked and destroyed during military coups, and their archives and equipment were stolen, but they were put back in operation as soon as space for democratic activity reopened.

The third is ownership. How many community media projects can claim that they are owned completely by their constituency? Furthermore, ownership at miners' radio stations has not been an issue of who owned the equipment or frequency, but particularly the *agency* (or capability, as Amartya Sen would define it) that acquired ownership of the communication process itself. This experience helps to understand the distinction emblematically between "access" and "participation"; the first is a generous opportunity given to people to grab the microphones for a while, and the second means active involvement in decision making related to all aspects of the communication process.

The fourth distinction is scope and number. Contrary to examples of single rural or urban community radio in the world—which can be interesting and deserve all the case studies they have generated—the miners' stations constituted from their inception an extensive phenomenon with a growing number of stations in various mining communities, reaching 26 during the early 1960s.

The fifth distinction is social and political impact. Often, we value a community media project because of its relevance to a small population; but in the case of the miners' stations, besides their commitment to the miners and their families, they had also important influence over the surrounding rural areas, where Quechua or Aymara peasants live, through their ongoing socially oriented programming. Furthermore, during political crisis, as during the July 1980 military coup when the military had shut down all commercial stations in the urban areas, stations would link up and air the only national source of information.

The sixth distinction is sustainability. Whereas many stations have started with support from international or local nongovernmental organizations, religious organizations, universities, multilateral or bilateral cooperation agencies, and even governments, Bolivian miners' stations were created, one by one, by their own organizations and sustained by the workers by a 1-day salary from each worker. Yet, this financial self-support—although unique if compared with other community media experiences worldwide—is not the most important factor. Social sustainability, which is the key to long-term sustainability, allowed miners' radio stations to enjoy continuous and permanent support from their constituency, including during extreme political crises (military coups), when men, women, and children would build a human circle around the stations to protect them.

To say the least, miners' radio stations opened the path to the community media movement in Latin America, to the point that today there are approximately 10,000 licensed community radio stations in the region, with Perú, Bolivia, Brazil, and Ecuador accounting for about one half of the total in operation. Many more are not yet licensed.

The variety of community stations is enormous and includes mainly thousands of rural stations for Indigenous and farmer communities; many of them are so isolated that "their" station is the only contact with the rest of the country and the rest of the world.

This growth has been possible despite harsh persecution not only from governments but also from mainly unsympathetic private media owners who feel their monopoly over commercial media is threatened by the explosion of locally based media outlets. In Guatemala, the association of private media owners constantly attacks what they label as "pirate" stations, including many that have been created and are managed by small Mayan communities, in agreement with the 1996 Peace Accords that clearly establish the right to communication of the Mayan population—the overwhelming majority. In the name of the "freedom of information" of private media owners, the small Mayan stations are often shut down by the police, who act against them more forcefully than against the drug-trafficking mafia.

An important pending issue in the communication rights agenda is the enactment of appropriate legislation that recognizes, protects, and promotes community media in the region. The absence of clear policies and legislation opened the door for abuses and censorship in countries like Guatemala, Argentina, or México. However, there is also legislation designed to limit and control the spread of community media, such as currently in Chile or Brazil, where small stations have been restricted to minimal transmitter power.

On the bright side, countries such as Perú, Ecuador, or Bolivia generally promote and protect community media, and Uruguay—followed by Argentina in October 2009—was the first to pass legislation to reserve at least one third of the spectrum to community media, including the upcoming digital frequencies.

Alfonso Gumucio Dagron

See also Citizens' Media; Community Radio (Ireland); Community Radio (Sri Lanka); Community Radio in Pau da Lima (Brasil); Community Radio Movement (India); Indigenous Radio Stations (México); Low-Power FM Radio (United States); Radio Andaquí and the Belén Media School (Colombia); Radio La Tribu (Argentina)

Further Readings

Gumucio Dagron, A. (2001). *Making waves: Participatory communication for social change.* New York: The Rockefeller Foundation.

Gumucio Dagron, A., & Cajías, L. (Eds.). (1989). *Las radios mineras de Bolivia.* La Paz, Bolivia: CIMCA-UNESCO.

Herrera-Miller, K. (2006). *¿Del Grito Pionero . . . al Silencio? Las radios sindicales mineras en la Bolivia de hoy.* La Paz, Bolivia: Fundación Friedrich Ebert (FES).

Huesca, R. (1995). A procedural view of participatory communication: Lessons from Bolivian tin miners' radio. *Media, Culture & Society, 17,* 101–119.

O'Connor, A. (Ed.). (2004). *Community radio in Bolivia: The miners' radio stations.* Lewiston, ME: The Edwin Mellen Press.

Mobile Communication and Social Movements

A notable development in contemporary social movements is the usage of mobile communication devices, which not only facilitate grassroots mobilization and coordination but also, arguably, transform the social movements themselves. This development has resulted from the unprecedented diffusion of portable technologies such as the Palm Pilot, global positioning system, and especially the mobile phone. According to the International Telecommunications Union, by the end of 2007 for the first time in history, there was more than one telephone for every two human beings in the world, which would be impossible without the phenomenal spread of mobile phones, especially among young and low-income people.

Mobile communication has brought to social movements more than just more technological devices. Rather, it reflects the global shift toward more flexible forms of informational politics, especially what Manuel Castells has termed "mass self-communication" or the new spaces for public sphere activity outside inherited political and media institutions. This entry briefly reviews the notion of "swarming," which encompasses interactions between texting and mainstream media coverage of social movements, some immediate pluses and minuses of these developments, and some potential trends.

"Swarming" Tactics and Mobile Phones

The first widely publicized incident of mobile phones being used in social movements was in 1999 when anti–World Trade Organization (WTO) demonstrators found innovative use of their Nextel walkie talkies during the so-called "Battle of Seattle." Because of newly available connectivity, activist groups could coordinate collective action and carry out systematic tactics of "swarming" (i.e., the congregation of a large number of protestors to block parts of the ministerial meeting physically), and then rapid dispersion before the arrival of extra police. By this time, the demonstrators would be congregating at another location, following the military strategy of dynamic, non-linear warfare.

This was not an entirely new mode of protest, but mobile media allowed activists to carry out their "swarming" campaigns much faster and more simply, and at a larger scale. The effect of such "flash mobilization" was so impressive that Howard Rheingold argued it was a harbinger for "smart mobs," where total strangers could form instant solidarity to struggle for a collective goal.

Adding mobility and perpetual contact to the phone leads to a quantum leap for the old device to serve as the basis for new modes of socio-political mobilization, for the emergence of what Manuel Castells views as "instant communities of practice" that turn a proposal for action into a communication generating multiple responses supporting the action.

This is at the core of the concept "mobile civil society," which was proposed by Castells and others who argue that mobile phone usage in social movements can lead to a new form of civil society. It enables independent communication from individual to individual and group to group; it is collectively intensive but with strongly personal dimensions. This bypasses mainstream media and enables an alternative public space.

The "Battle of Seattle" remains a prototype for demonstrators to protest the injustice of economic globalization at WTO and G8 meetings, from Montréal in 2000 to Geneva in 2001, from Cancún in 2003 to Hong Kong in 2005. Whereas mobile devices now are routine in activism, the shock effect has seemingly declined because the security forces have kept pace. At the 2004 Republican National Convention in New York, for example, police were reported to have infiltrated text-message networks of anti-Bush protesters. Meanwhile, the number of participating activist groups and individuals increased to the point that more "central management" was required through such organizational platforms as TxtMob and Rockus. This altered the decentralized and spontaneous person-to-person pattern and was also more prone to be blacked out by the phone company, either intentionally or unintentionally.

Texting, Mainstream Media Coverage, and Mobilizing

Over the years, two additional types of mobile civil society action have emerged. One is the usage of texting to mobilize a protest, followed by the use of mass media and/or the Internet to sustain public attention and produce actual consequences. The best example is perhaps the 2001 People Power II movement in Manila, when mobile-equipped demonstrators took to the streets during the impeachment trial against then-president Estrada.

Whereas texting mobilized activists (known as Generation Txt) to congregate at the historical site of People Power I in 1986 that overthrew dictator Marcos, the rest of the demonstration was organized more or less conventionally, receiving constant TV coverage and increasing support from the Catholic hierarchy and the military. Although People Power II has been remembered as one of the earliest cases of "smart mobs," it in fact did not involve much "swarming" because the events all took place in one fixed site of historical significance with little mobility by protesters.

A more recent protest was the 2007 anti-PX environmental movement in Xiamen, Fujian Province, China. PX stands for Paraxylene, a toxic chemical product. With investment from Taiwan, a 300-acre, $1.4 billion plant producing PX was being constructed, but text messages started to circulate about its environmental hazards. The text messages led to street demonstrations as well as a deluge of newspaper articles, TV reports, and weblog discussions. These conversations generated broader support from across the country as well as from higher-level authorities. As a result, the project was halted, making it China's first successful cell phone–based civil society mobilization, although their role was only in its first phase.

Use of Mobile Communication in Elections

The next important mobile civil society form of action is during election seasons, which unlike the foregoing are entirely predictable. However, Barack Obama's "Txt HOPE" campaign was part of normal procedures. This role for mobiles is, therefore, not to subvert but to mobilize voters who are willing to "vote for change" in an election. One of the earliest cases was the 2002 South Korean presidential election, when Roh Moo-Hyun became the unexpected winner thanks to mobile-equipped *Nosamos* (meaning "people who love Roh Moo-Hyun," Roh being pronounced "Noh" in Korean).

Another case was the 2004 parliamentary election in Spain shortly after the Madrid bombing, when the ruling party was voted out because of a fast texting campaign discrediting the ruling party as liars for conveniently blaming Basque rather than Islamist terrorists. "Swarming" played no role because rallies were banned on Election Day, and activists only needed to get reluctant voters to cast their ballots. Subversion was not at issue because the goal was to use the system to elect more progressive politicians or political parties.

Thus, this is indeed a global phenomenon with incidents of mobile-facilitated movements happening across the planet. There is no linear relation between mobile phone ownership, which is closely correlated with income level, and the level of mobile civil society activity. The Philippines had rather low mobile phone penetration at the time of People Power II, but its mobile civil society movement happened much earlier and with much greater effect than in countries such as Japan, Sweden, or even the United States. Technology's role is therefore secondary to the dynamics and needs of civil society.

Pluses and Minuses of Mobile Phone Uses in Political Challenges

On the one hand, mobile communication messages convey more trust and credibility, especially at times of emergency when the general public believes that an imminent threat is about to impact their lives directly. There has first to be a perceived danger, after which mobiles can be effective catalysts in the mobilization and coordination process because the citizens can now be reached "anytime, anywhere."

On the other hand, mobile phones are relatively limited in their capacity to foster democratic deliberation. As Vincente Rafael argues in his analysis of People Power II, the text messages enable technical connections on a large scale, but do not enhance the quality of their messages' content and thus do not by themselves dislodge enduring systems of power. Rafael and Raul Pertierra both point out that Estrada was the only Philippine president who won by an undisputed landslide, and yet was overthrown by the upper-class mobile-equipped Generation Txt, despite his popularity among poor Filipinos who could not afford mobile phones. Indeed, digital exclusion is not solved so easily among the world's most disadvantaged groups.

Even if everyone texts, the mobile phone is still inadequate for sustained democratic discussion. Anti-corporate globalization activists still need face-to-face meetings, although they can use their mobiles to coordinate subsequent street actions. During the Obama presidential campaign and the anti-PX protest, there was a mixture of mobile communication with traditional mass media and Internet (especially weblog) communication, because the latter provide more room for sustained public exchange.

Future Potential

However, it is also the case that once made part of this cluster of media, mobile phones can also help foster a long-term "community of practice," beyond "flash mobs." This was shown by the growth of the *Nosamos* into a sustainable political force, with its own democratic mechanisms and its increasing independence from the formal political parties in South Korea, even from Roh Moo-Hyun and his cabinet.

These ongoing trends show that the relation between mobile technology and social movements has become increasingly similar to traditional politics. Successful social movements are necessarily based on existing political struggles, and they are shaped, constrained, and contested in the political contexts of the specific civil societies with their own legacies. Thus, this new departure is also about expanding existing tendencies within activist groups and sociopolitical structures, but along a more evolutionary than revolutionary path.

Finally, it is important to note that mobile-facilitated social movements also face increasing control by the authorities. As mentioned, the U.S. security agencies had infiltrated text messaging networks of anti-Bush protesters in New York in 2004. Similar instances have been reported elsewhere in Europe and Asia, whereas powerful SMS filtering and censorship systems have been developed and commercialized in China. During protests in Nepal in 2005, King Gyanandra shut down the national mobile phone network to prevent communication among activists.

In other instances, governments and state-owned mobile networks have engaged in "proactive" messaging (propaganda through SMS spamming) to promote the establishment's agenda, as shown by Berlusconi's mobile message campaign in 2004. Despite all these efforts to squelch mobile-facilitated activism and give it a top-down spin, we have observed incessant grassroots social movements against mainstream politics in Europe and America, and a new wave of mobile civil society incidents in China and Nepal. Perhaps these control efforts might be viewed as nonetheless contributing to the overall maturing of mobile civil society as a new instrument for grassroots social movement organization over the long run.

Jack Linchuan Qiu

See also Alternative Media; AlterNet (United States); December 2008 Revolt Media (Greece); Grassroots Tech Activists and Media Policy; Media Infrastructure Policy and Media Activism

Further Readings

Castells, M. (2007). Communication, power and counter-power in the networked society. *International Journal of Communication, 1,* 238–266.
Castells, M., Fernández-Ardevol, M., Qiu, J.-L., & Sey, A. (2006). *Mobile communication and society.* Cambridge, MA: MIT Press.
Cody, E. (2007, June 28). Text messages giving voice to Chinese. *Washington Post,* p. A1.
Harfoush, R. (2009). *Yes we did: An inside look at how social media built the Obama brand.* Berkeley, CA: New Riders.
Juris, J. S. (2008). *Networking futures: The movements against corporate globalization.* Durham, NC: Duke University Press.
Katz, J., & Aakhus, M. (Eds.). (2002). *Perpetual contact: Mobile communication, private talk, public performance.* Cambridge, UK: Cambridge University Press.
Pertierra, R. (2006). *Transforming technologies; altered selves: Mobile phone and Internet use in the Philippines.* Manila, Philippines: De La Salle University Press.
Qiu, J. L. (2008). Mobile civil society in Asia: A comparative study of People Power II and the Nosamo Movement. *Javnost–The Public, 15,* 5–24.
Rafael, V. (2003). The cell phone and the crowd: Messianic politics in the contemporary Philippines. *Public Culture, 15*(3), 399–425.

MOON RIVER MOVEMENT MEDIA (THAILAND)

Dam construction has been a key controversy between the people and the state throughout Thailand's intensive socioeconomic modernization (1960s–1990s). Although water control is vital for fishing and agriculture, the state exercised its power to alter water usage regardless of local needs. Most dams were for hydroelectric power, although the Electricity Generation Authority of Thailand (EGAT) often claimed their objectives were multipurpose. Emerging in the 1990s, the Moon River Movement became the key driving force to protest against EGAT's Pak Moon Dam project. The movement initiated many unprecedented and courageous public communication actions to struggle for their community rights and found its real strength in alternative media. It was led by Wanida Tantiwitayapitak, who died in 2007 at age 52.

In the early 1980s, the government proposed to build the dam in the Northeastern province of Ubonrachathani. The dam would produce 136 megawatts for the lower Northeastern region. Villagers from five districts (Kongjiem, Pibunmangsaharn, Taansum, Warinchamrab, and Muang) began to network against the project. Despite their continuous protests, the National Peacekeeping Council, which staged a military coup in February 1991, started the construction by deepening the riverbed with heavy explosives. The river Moon is known for its rich variety of fish and its key role as breeding ground for fish and other species from the Mekong and Moon rivers, because of its rock formations. The dam would prevent this crucial annual breeding from taking place and would destroy the lives of more than 4,000 families who depended entirely on fishing for their livelihood.

Protest Strategies During Construction

The Moon River Movement's initial 1990 objective was to stop this EGAT project. Nevertheless, their petitions went unheeded. Peaceful protest at the site turned violent after EGAT rejected their demand for 3 years' compensation and 15 *rai* (0.6 ha/1.5 acres) of land per family. In 1993, the first confrontation between villagers opposing the dam and those supporting it resulted in 31 casualties. This conflict caught local media attention but little national coverage.

Subsequently, EGAT agreed to the movement's five-point demand: clear indication of flood water levels, financial compensation for lost homes and land, new land for villagers with lost homes, research on the dam's fishery impact, and compensation for any public health hazard. Yet when the dam was completed in 1994, EGAT refused to pay compensation. Only after 5 months of vigorous demonstrations did EGAT finally pay the 3-year compensation (35,000 *baht* a year) for the loss of fishing livelihood.

But the protest did not end here. The movement found the dam had seriously damaged the river. Its abundance was lost along with their fishing. They had to rethink their strategy to restore the habitat and their livelihood. This was in 1995, precisely when the Assembly of the Poor was organized.

The Assembly of the Poor was a social movement made up of 125 networks concerning 205 cases on land use, agriculture, fishing, dams, public health care, housing, and large state development projects. The Assembly of the Poor had approximately 180,000 members. In 1997, the Assembly of the Poor organized a 99-day protest in front of Government House to press their demands. They gained huge TV and press publicity. With a great deal of public pressure, the government of Prime Minister Chavalit Yongjaiyudth (New Aspiration Party) resolved the villagers should receive 15 *rai* of land or 500,000 *baht* per family for the loss of their livelihood.

In 1998, the Democrat government reneged. It was the turning point for the Moon River Movement. To demand financial compensation was viewed as a thing of the past. The movement demanded a radical change, to encompass the rehabilitation of the river and its environs in hope of a brighter future for their fishing livelihood. Villagers began to build a temporary village next to the dam and campaigned for public support. They requested EGAT to open the floodgates so the fish could swim upriver and breed in their natural habitat. With this major shift, the movement had to come up with new communication strategies to build public support.

The Movement's Multipronged Media Strategies

During their struggles, both the Assembly of the Poor and the Moon River Movement learned they could not rely on mainstream media to publicize their case or cover their position on local power and democratic participation. They concluded they would attempt to struggle for some space within mainstream media but must become self-reliant by informing their own networks as much as the public and their opponents. Prasitiporn Kanonsri, who was an information and media specialist for the Assembly of the Poor, stated bitterly that "since complaints and petitions did not bring any positive result from the authorities, the best solution is to communicate directly with society."

In 1999, the Moon River Movement set up three major strategies—cultural communication, alternative media, and an information center—to shore up the movement's identity and achieve the ultimate goal of reclaiming their fishing livelihood.

The first step was the creation of a new village called *Mae Moon Man Yuen* (Moon River Forever) located next to the dam. This was the base to demonstrate the local villagers' right to self-governance. The organizing principles were equality, participation, and transparency in an ideal democratic community. This was contrary to the state's and EGAT's secretive operation on the Pak Moon dam project, which excluded local participation and the right to make decisions regarding their livelihood.

In its discursive struggle against the state, the movement organized regular cultural activities to build up their own confidence and communicate with the local and national public. They campaigned with a long *Thamma Yatra* (Nature March) alongside the Moon River to inform local communities and to rally their support.

Local histories and rituals were used to reaffirm their Northeastern cultural and ethnic identity. There was a Baaisri ceremony by the movement's elders to welcome academics, students, and non-governmental organization (NGO) activists who visited *Mae Moon Man Yuen*. There were prayers and rituals for the river's longevity. Exorcism rituals such as burning salt and pepper were used against the evil forces destroying the Moon River.

Popular music and dance were used for both reflection and entertainment. *Mohlam* (Northeastern singing), with the bamboo pipe as its key musical instrument, was recorded in an album called *The Cry of Mae Moon*. The songs narrated the movement's struggle. Some lyrics told the stories of people in similar harsh plights. The songs begged the government to sympathize with the poor and those affected by large development projects. It was sung in the Northeastern language and Central Thai to communicate with both local listeners as well as the general public.

Alternative media or small media were viewed as an effective means of independent communication. Villagers learned to produce banners, flags, bulletin boards, pamphlets, newsletters, and public statements for seminars, conferences, and public hearings. Children and adults worked side by side with students and volunteer groups to produce campaign messages. Some appeared in the video documentary *When the Fisherman Rebelled,* and in the research report "Mae Moon: The Return of the Fisherman." These alternative media also merged movement campaign materials with local resources that generated interesting hybrid forms of communication. Bamboo utensils were made for sale, such as fans, *kratibs* (sticky-rice containers), hats, and equipment such as fishing nets. Producing these brought back a lost awareness among the young generation of the close relationship between nature and people's livelihood on the river.

The third major strategy was the information center. The movement set up its information center to communicate with the public and to ward off any distortion by EGAT and the mainstream media. Systematic news evaluation and records of events provided the movement with accurate and up-to-date analysis of the situation. They also worked with Friends of the People (FOP), the secretariat, and information center of the Assembly of the Poor. In this way, the movement could produce its own news agenda. The information center and FOP used the Internet to send out regular statements and news updates with photos to local and international networks, as well as the mainstream media. The NGO's portal (http://www.thaingo.org) was an important communication space, as it could bypass mainstream media.

Notwithstanding these initiatives, the movement still had to work with the mainstream media. There was no escape, because national newspapers, television, and radio reached the national audience easily on a daily basis. Although the movement's public communication methods were similar to a public relations organization, they had to work doubly hard to convince mainstream media that their agenda was newsworthy. The movement included elders, organizers, academics, and civil society activists, who volunteered to supervise the media campaign and in the process became key information sources. The social standing of a large number of these sources made their interviews highly credible. They also organized press conferences, seminars, and public discussions. Combining these kinds of public communication was far more effective than merely giving interviews.

Apart from media outreach, the Moon River Movement devised many political and tactical moves to build public consensus around the issue. The civil disobedience actions took place during the Democrat government (1998–2001), when their demands were stalled or turned down. In 2000, the movement confronted EGAT and peacefully took over the dam. The government reluctantly set up an ad hoc committee to follow up on the resolution to open all the dam floodgates for 4 months.

After 2 months, the movement came to protest in front of the Government House to press their case. Totally disregarded by the government, the movement decided to use disruptive measures. Approximately 200 villagers broke into the Government House compound after the evening Buddhist Lent ceremony. Young and old, women and children were beaten and imprisoned. But, because of intensive media and public pressure at home and abroad, the government hastily released the protesters and agreed to look into the matter again.

The movement pressed further by staging a 3-day hunger strike. It gained public sympathy and the government complied with the movement for an open hearing at Thammasat University in Bangkok. The Minister for Public Energy was held accountable while villagers appealed convincingly to thousands in the auditorium. The event was broadcasted live on Channel 11 to the whole nation.

In 2001, the new government, led by the Thai Rak Thai party, agreed to open all the floodgates of Pak Moon dam for 4 months to rehabilitate the river. EGAT, however, refused to comply with the order. It took the prime minister to visit the dam and order EGAT to open all eight gates. The habitat was restored and the river was teeming with fish after the gates were open. By the end of 2001, the government renewed the agreement with the movement that the gates should remain open another 12 months and research should be carried out on the dam's full environmental impact.

However, the tide turned again in 2002. EGAT lobbied the government to revert to the initial agreement. The floodgates were to open for 4 months during the breeding season and closed for 8 months to store water for electricity generation and agriculture. Although research by a Ubonrachathani University team showed that the opening of the floodgates would not destabilize the level of electricity generation, the government supported EGAT.

The movement, therefore, made a radical demand that the gates should be open for 5 years based on the university's research finding. The government reluctantly organized a meeting at Government House to negotiate with 30 movement representatives. It was the first of its kind. The meeting was chaired by the prime minister, with villagers, academics, and ministers sitting side by side. With live television broadcasted on Channel 11, representatives of the movement were given equal opportunity to state their case. No clear agreement was reached from the negotiating table. The prime minister then went to the dam and asked the National Statistical Office to carry out a public opinion survey regarding the opening of the gates. The survey showed that most people wanted them closed for 8 months. In 2003, the cabinet resolved that each year the gates were to open for 4 months and closed for 8 months.

Although the Moon River Movement's hope to rehabilitate the river completely failed to materialize, it was partially successful in reclaiming the river and their livelihood. Media and creative public communication strategies played a central role in forming the much-needed public consensus. They could pressure the government and EGAT, and not least the mainstream media, to focus on the problem. With broad and strong networking, the villagers took political action as citizens to demand their community rights. In this process, they opened up new media spaces and set unprecedented models of public communication, such as open negotiations and public hearings within Thailand's highly limited and controlled public sphere.

Ubonrat Siriyuvasak

See also Alternative Media; Chipko Environmental Movement Media (India); Community Radio and Natural Disasters (Indonesia); Environmental Movement Media; *Whole Earth Catalog* (United States)

Further Readings

Chalermsripinyorat, R. (2002). *Politics of representation: Assembly of the poor and the usage of media in the making of a social movement in Thailand.* MA thesis, Southeast Asian Studies Program, Graduate School, National University of Singapore.
Kunnawat, P. (2002). *The Pak Moon Dam opposition group and the process of public communication.* MA thesis, Faculty of Communication Arts, Chulalongkorn University, Bangkok, Thailand.
Pintobtang, P. (1998). *Politics on the street: 99-day protest of the Assembly of the Poor and the history of demonstrations in Thai society.* Bangkok, Thailand: Research and Textbook Center, Krerk University.

MOTHER EARTH (UNITED STATES)

Emma Goldman's anarchist magazine *Mother Earth* was one of the most influential radical periodicals during its run from 1906 through 1917, when the federal government banned it and imprisoned and deported its antiwar publisher.

The text-heavy monthly espoused anarchist values of individual freedom and offered provocative critiques of the emerging corporate state. Russian immigrant and factory worker Goldman (1869–1940) gained notoriety in 1893 when she helped Alexander Berkman prepare to kill steel mogul Henry Clay Frick in response to his company's Homestead lockout violence. She never was indicted, although Berkman served 14 years. Goldman was jailed for 10 months in 1893–1894 for inciting to riot. A charismatic public speaker, Goldman introduced American-born audiences to European radical traditions and European immigrants to American political ideals, both on the podium and in *Mother Earth*. After friends financed the magazine's launch in New York in March 1906, publisher Goldman frequently invoked in its pages the individualist philosophy of American icons such as Thomas Jefferson, Ralph Waldo Emerson, and Henry Thoreau.

Goldman appointed Berkman editor after his release in 1908. She spent much time on the road lecturing for radical causes and raising funds to support the magazine. Its contents reflected the anarchist reverence for nature and pastoral life and its repugnance at capitalism and government. Essays disparaged organized religion and marriage as infringements on freedom. It campaigned for aid for striking workers in Lawrence, Massachusetts, and elsewhere. Goldman and others reviewed books and theater, translated works by Fyodor Dostoevsky and Leo Tolstoi, and occasionally they published poetry, fiction, or plays. Contributors included Margaret Anderson, Louise Bryant, Voltairine de Cleyre, John Coryell, Floyd Dell, Mabel Dodge, and Ben Hecht. Noted illustrators Robert Minor and Man Ray created some of its covers. Despite its somberness, its rich mix of radical thought extended the magazine's influence beyond its estimated circulation of 5,000 copies.

Mother Earth's celebration of sexuality influenced the free-love attitudes of Greenwich Village radical intellectuals, especially the independent "New Women" who admired Goldman. One of *Mother Earth*'s biggest contributions was its fight for birth control. Its first brush with the law occurred when anti-obscenity crusader Anthony Comstock held up mail delivery of the January 1910 issue, which contained a Goldman article exploring the economic roots of prostitution. *Mother Earth* also supported Margaret Sanger's birth control battles. In April 1916, after Goldman was convicted and jailed for lecturing on birth control in New York, *Mother Earth* issued a special in-depth birth control number on the issue.

Its focus switched in 1917, however, when Goldman opposed American entry into World War I. Federal agents raided *Mother Earth* in June 1917 and arrested Goldman and Berkman, who was then editing his own anarchist journal, *The Blast*, upstairs from the *Mother Earth* office. Convicted under the Espionage Act, they were sentenced to 2 years in prison and $10,000 fines. Colleagues struggled to publish *Mother Earth* through August 1917, its final issue. In October, a *Mother Earth Bulletin* surfaced, but it was suppressed that December. On December 21, 1919, in the midst of the postwar Palmer Raids on leftist activists, Goldman was deported to Russia on a technicality concerning her citizenship status.

Linda Lumsden

See also Alternative Media; Anarchist Media; Citizens' Media; Environmental Movement Media; Feminist Media: An Overview; Labor Media (United States); Prisoners' Radio

Further Readings

Goldman, E. (1910). *Mother Earth, 5*. Available online in GoogleBooks.

MOTHERS OF THE PLAZA DE MAYO (ARGENTINA)

Every Thursday since 1977 at 3:30 p.m. in the Plaza de Mayo of Buenos Aires, a group of women wearing white scarves holds a silent march circling the central monument of the square. They are the *Asociación Madres de Plaza de Mayo* or Mothers of the Plaza de Mayo, mothers of the *desaparecidos* (disappeared people). The march is a ritual of both resistance and commemoration performed at a highly symbolic location, and it is one of the most intriguing memorializations of the Argentine dictatorship (1976–1983), in which an estimated

30,000 people disappeared. For half an hour, the cry against repression and the quest for justice are embodied in a public demonstration that activates society's collective memory.

The Mothers' Communication Strategies

From the start, the Mothers created a style aimed at galvanizing a paralyzed society. Theirs was an assertive conquering and remapping of urban territories through marches and performances. In choosing a site for their struggle, the Mothers took over the square facing the Congress building, a location that goes back to the colonial days when the *Plaza Mayor* was the town's heart. Plaza de Mayo is a landmark of Argentina's political life. By placing their resistance to repression in this site of memory, the Mothers marked the space with an alternative historical meaning. At the peak of the terror, their marches in this "liberated" zone became a constant reminder of the repression. Indeed, the Plaza is the Mothers' indisputable territory. As supporters chant, "*La plaza es de las madres y no de los cobardes*" (the plaza belongs to the mothers and not to the cowards).

There are parallels between the Mothers' style and popular theater performances. The Mothers staged demonstrations at literally any location where they could be witnessed. Just as street theater combines script with improvisation, the Mothers responded creatively to external circumstances. If authorities asked one Mother for her identification, then all the Mothers would hand in theirs; if one Mother was arrested, then dozens of Mothers would declare themselves jailed.

The Mothers managed to convey the presence of the *desaparecidos* in the streets through compelling visual images. For the first presidential elections after the dictatorship (1983), large posters, each with a life-size silhouette symbolizing a *desaparecido* with her/his name and date of disappearance, were posted on walls throughout Buenos Aires. Thousands of silhouettes became witnesses to and participants in the electoral process. While people went out to vote, the *desaparecidos* had also taken to the streets.

The Mothers were extremely creative in using graffiti to mark public territories and to press their agenda into official celebrations. On occasions, they painted gigantic white scarves, the symbol of their struggle, on street surfaces where military parades took place. Because they "decorated" the street at the last minute, the authorities had no time to erase it, resulting in images of troops marching over asphalt with painted accusations against them.

Beyond their strong street presence, the Mothers have an impressive record as media producers, to include radio programs, a website, a publishing house, and weekly and monthly publications. These are complemented by the educational activities at their university and the events (exhibits and concerts) at their cultural centre *Nuestros Hijos* (Our Children), located in one of the buildings that housed the ESMA (Navy Mechanics School), which is a former torture center. Thus, their campaigns cover many fronts. They founded their university but zealously guard their "liberated territory" and keep on marching every Thursday.

Implications

The Mothers' activism began during a reign of terror that had stamped out most public resistance. When the Mothers first got together, their purpose was to inform society that their children were disappearing. The task was to find ways to communicate their grievance in a way that would move people to action. They needed to counter the official silence; reach the Church, politicians, unions, foreign governments, and organizations; and build support networks. By taking the issue of disappearances to the public sphere, they were the main visible resistance to the repression.

Since their irruption into the public sphere in the midst of the repression in 1977, the Mothers redefined what "public" means, which is at the core of human rights struggles in the country. By turning motherhood into a public activity, they crucially reset the boundaries of politics and political spaces. By conquering and remapping territories, both physical and metaphorical, they shaped the style and scope of human rights activism.

The Mothers also set new parameters in their use of communications as a key tool for their struggle. For three decades, their campaigns evinced consistency between their political position and their messages, their ability to operate with limited resources—their capacity to turn anything into a medium—and their use of symbols and symbolic spaces. They exhibited amazing creativity in content and format, resulting in a style aimed at shocking and being heard. Their strategies presented a new aesthetic practice of alternative and radical communications, resulting from their new way of doing politics.

Post-Dictatorship

After 1983, the Mothers' communication actions centered on placing human rights on the politicians' agenda and demanding actions from the new government. The democratization process had a promising beginning: a truth commission, and trials of the military junta. However, it was soon followed by a process of legalizing impunity, only overturned by the nullification of impunity laws in 2005. The Mothers continued to be memory-activists of recent history through demands for justice and punishment for the culprits, challenging the responses of post-dictatorship governments, and vindicating their disappeared children's political commitments via projects inspired by their ideals (e.g., building houses in shantytowns).

The Mothers' messages have undeniably influenced policy and action, lodging human rights issues in Argentina's public sphere and on the political agenda. Their communication practices definitely established guidelines for the Argentine human rights movement.

M. Susana Kaiser

See also Grandmothers of the Plaza de Mayo (Argentina); H.I.J.O.S. and *Escraches* (Argentina); Human Rights Media

Further Readings

Kaiser, M. S. (1993). *The "madwomen": Memory Mothers of the Plaza de Mayo.* MA thesis, Department of Communications, Hunter College of the City University of New York.

Kaiser, M. S. (2008). The struggle for urban territories: Human rights activists in Buenos Aires. In C. Irazábal (Ed.), *Ordinary places/extraordinary events: Citizenship, democracy, and urban space in Latin America* (pp. 170–197). New York: Routledge.

MURALS (NORTHERN IRELAND)

Political murals played a significant role in the bitter conflict, which erupted again from 1969 onward between nationalists and loyalists and between locals and the British armed forces in Northern Ireland. However, Northern Ireland boasts a continuous mural painting tradition older than that in México.

The first mural was painted in Belfast in 1908 and depicted King William III on his white horse at the Battle of the Boyne. The Dutch Prince William challenged his father-in-law King James II for the English throne and was successful after several decisive battles in Ireland, including that at the Boyne in 1690. James was a Catholic and William a Protestant, so his victory entrenched the Protestant domination of land, wealth, politics, and culture in Ireland.

With the formation of the Northern Ireland state in the early 1920s, the image of William came to stand for Protestant solidarity. Protestants of all classes and backgrounds came together on July 12, the anniversary of the Battle of the Boyne, to celebrate what they shared in common: their religion and their commitment to the United Kingdom of Britain and Northern Ireland. Given his iconic status as the representative of this ethnic identity, William was the dominant figure in unionist murals over the next six decades. Although not initiated directly by the one-party unionist state in Northern Ireland, the painting of murals became in effect a civic duty—as did the huge marches on July 12th, and the annual erecting of arches, flying of bunting, and painting of curbstones in British national colors.

Nationalists in Northern Ireland, corralled into a partitioned state against their will, were excluded from such celebrations. But more fundamentally, the sectarian nature of the state ensured that they did not have the same access to cultural expression that unionists had. Their culture went on in church halls, sports grounds, and private places out of sight of unionist sensitivities. They could not have easily painted political murals even if they had wanted to.

That changed in 1981. The escalation of violent political conflict over the previous decade led to high rates of imprisonment of political activists.

Initially, they had special recognition as political prisoners; in particular, they did not have to wear a prison uniform. The removal of that status in 1976 triggered a prolonged period of resistance, which culminated in 10 republican prisoners starving themselves to death. In support of their demands, nationalists and republicans marched, demonstrated, and for the first time, began to paint murals.

The first republican murals focused on the hunger strikers and their demands, as well as on the armed struggle of the groups from which they had emerged, the Irish Republican Army (IRA) and the Irish National Liberation Army. Thus, throughout the 1980s, depictions of armed and masked activists were not uncommon. But republicans had a wider range of themes on which to draw, including Irish history and mythology. Key events in Irish history—such as the famine of the mid-19th century or the Easter Rising in Dublin in 1916—were represented, as was the mythical Irish warrior Cuchulainn, who took on the might of an invading army single-handedly. There were frequently murals on contemporary themes as well, whether current political struggles, election murals, or the condemnation of state repression, such as the use of rubber and plastic bullets that killed 14 people, 9 of them children. Finally, from the start, republicans also painted murals on international themes; identifying as they did with the struggles of people elsewhere against imperialism, colonialism, and state repression, they drew parallels with South Africa, Palestine, and Cuba.

During the 1970s and 1980s, unionist mural painting went through two major transformations. The first was the virtual disappearance of depictions of King William. Unionism had begun to splinter under the combined pressure of the Civil Rights campaign, the IRA onslaught, and the intervention of British politicians, administrators, and generals in the internal affairs of the Northern Ireland state. There was much less of a sense of unity and solidarity and, therefore, less need for a symbol depicting those things. Instead, unionists tended for a while to paint inanimate objects—flags, the British crown, an open Bible, and so on.

The second, and more radical, transformation occurred in 1986. The governments in London and Dublin signed an agreement that for the first time gave Dublin some official say in the affairs of the north; unionists were galvanized into action. In the midst of the mass protests, murals in unionist areas became militaristic suddenly and dramatically. For the next decade and a half, whichever loyalist paramilitary group was in charge in an area—whether the larger Ulster Defense Association or the smaller Ulster Volunteer Force—determined what was painted in the area. Each group painted self-promotional representations of their activists, masked, armed, and ready for war. What was once a unionist mural painting tradition—representing the common denominator of identity—became a singularly loyalist phenomenon. As republicans painted on a wide range of themes, loyalists painted endless variations of masked men with guns. One rare exception was the minority of murals that referred to events around the time of World War I. Unionists had organized against the possibility of the British government conceding Home Rule for Ireland, to the point of forming an illegal army, the UVF, in 1912. With the outbreak of war, the UVF joined the British army and became the 36th Ulster Division. At the Battle of the Somme in France in July 1916, this Division was decimated, with more than 5,000 killed, injured, or lost in the first two days of battle. Murals depicting the UVF organizing against Home Rule or the silhouetted soldiers of the 36th Ulster Division were to be found in areas supporting the contemporary UVF.

In August 1994, after secret talks with the British government, the IRA declared a cease-fire, to be followed 6 weeks later by the loyalist groups. In addition, in 1998, the Belfast—or Good Friday—Agreement opened the way to the eventual devolution of government in Northern Ireland under an administration where power was shared between nationalists and unionists. Against the expectations of many, former antagonists in the Democratic Unionist Party led by firebrand preacher Rev. Ian Paisley and Sinn Féin, who was linked to the IRA, worked together.

Republican and loyalist muralists contributed to and responded to these developments in different ways. Initially, republicans painted their demands on the walls—such as the release of political prisoners, the repatriation of British troops, and the disbandment of the local police force. Republican murals were supportive of the Good Friday Agreement, while at the same time demanding that the promises of that Agreement—for example, the right of nationalists to live "free from sectarian harassment"—be realized. A clear decision was made to remove some of the previous iconography of war; thus, there were few murals after 1998 that displayed IRA members with masks and guns. The only murals with guns were now confined to memorials to dead comrades, and if there were depictions of IRA members, they were portraits of actual people devoid of masks.

Removing this one theme from their repertoire did not curtail the activities of republican muralists who continued to have a wide range of other themes on which to paint. Irish history and mythology continued to be a rich vein to mine, as did the continuing resonance of struggles elsewhere. Thus, in recent years, murals have been painted on the plight of the people in Gaza, the hunger strike of Turkish political prisoners, and the Basque struggle for autonomy. Heroes of international struggles have also been painted, such as Che Guevara, Malcolm X, Martin Luther King, Rosa Parks, and Frederick Douglass.

Loyalist muralists have had a more difficult task for two reasons. First, large sections of the loyalist paramilitary groups were at best ambivalent about the peace process. Some loyalists tried to politicize their movement in the same way as republicans had politicized theirs. Others descended into a form of warlordism, with turf wars over control of drugs and weapons. In the feuds that followed, murals often became harbingers of trouble to come as well as victims of that trouble when it arrived. In this atmosphere, there was little pressure from within loyalism to alter their murals. In time, this changed, and coupled with external pressure and the carrot of government funding from a "reimaging" program, most loyalists came to accept the need for alternative iconography. This is where the second difficulty became apparent. Given their overdependence on military iconography, what were loyalists to paint if that option was removed? Unlike republicans, they did not have a wide range of other themes on which to paint. Some answers have involved painting sporting heroes such as soccer legend George Best, or iconic images of the past, such as the Titanic, built in Belfast in 1911. But as of the time this article was written, a core set of themes to declare the identity, aspirations, and future of loyalism eludes its muralists.

Bill Rolston

See also Adbusters Media Foundation (Canada); *Love and Rockets* Comic Books (United States); Political Graffiti (Greece); Political Jokes (Zimbabwe); Resistance Through Ridicule (Africa); Vernacular Poetry Audiotapes in the Arab World

Further Readings

Rolston, B. (2003). *Drawing support 3: Murals and transition in the North of Ireland*. Belfast, Northern Ireland: Beyond the Pale Publications.
Rolston, B. (2009). "The brothers on the walls": International solidarity and Irish political murals. *Journal of Black Studies, 39*(3), 446–470.

MUSIC AND DISSENT (GHANA AND NIGERIA)

Despotic and corrupt regimes in Africa sanction arrest, torture, imprisonment, and extra-judicial killings of their critics. Critiquing authoritarian governments is a hazardous enterprise. There seems little to no avenue for those who seek to expose political abuses and economic mismanagement. Yet in both Ghana and Nigeria, one witnesses "political music critique" in the genres of *Highlife* and *Afrobeat*, respectively. One common element is how artists creatively adapt and fuse diverse African rhythms and lyrics with foreign music elements.

In Ghana's "political" Highlife, sociopolitical critique is constructed through an oblique communication aesthetics. Here, artists use devices such as the sung-tale metaphor, proverbs, allegories, innuendos, and circumlocution to satirize, protest, and comment on sociopolitical issues. Such indirectness allows artists to disclaim political motives effectively within their songs.

This form of music is typical in most of the folktale songs of Nana Kwame Ampadu. His use of the folktale lampoons political anomalies and calls for the reinstatement of ideal political principles. Ampadu's popular folktale song *Ebe Te Yie* (Some are favorably seated), which is situated in an imaginary animal kingdom, highlights social injustice and the stifling of free speech. The imagery, like George Orwell's *Animal Farm,* mirrors undemocratic conditions in Ghana. Ampadu's *Obiara Wo Dee Etumi No* (Every force is subject to a superior power) consists of two tales situated in animal and human realms. The song's moral is not to overestimate one's prowess, as this can lead to humiliation in the face of a greater power. This song was released at a time when a military coup in Ghana toppled a previous military government. Thus, the song acted as a capsule version of contemporary events.

Whereas Ghanaian political Highlife music is meshed in indirection, Nigeria's political Afrobeat is much more overt in its critique. Fela Anikulapo-Kuti, who created this music genre, did not conceal his biting critiques of corrupt and oppressive Nigerian leaders. This confrontational style caused various military and civilian governments to imprison, intimidate, and physically abuse Fela. Some of Fela's songs like *Expensive Shit* draw on his jail experiences to satirize bluntly and lampoon the absurd excesses of the Nigerian police force.

In this song, Fela notes that human beings, and some animals like goats and monkeys, normally are not interested in their own "shit" or in spending time where they defecate. However, Fela reveals that he is aware of some "fools" and "stupid" people who take extreme interest in other people's feces, with the aim of using the feces as evidence to imprison and murder. Fela is referring to his own treatment by the police at one point and makes it clear that the people he is referring to are located at Alagbon—the location of the feared Police Central Intelligence Division. Fela's political critiques also targeted the Nigerian military, which massively disrupted democratic governance in that country. In a scathing indictment of the military in *Zombie,* Fela depicts the Nigerian military as robotic morons lacking common sense and critical thinking.

Africans under dictatorial governments refuse to celebrate victimhood and cower in silence. Although such critiques are not from the people per se, the artist, as a cultural voice of the oppressed, conveys themes symbolically that celebrate the resilience of the deprived and expose the gluttony of the dominant.

Joseph Oduro-Frimpong

See also Music and Social Protest (Malawi); Political Song (Northern Ireland); Popular Music and Political Expression (Côte d'Ivoire); Popular Music and Protest (Ethiopia); Reggae and Resistance (Jamaica)

Further Readings

Nyamnjoh, F. B. (2004). Global and local trends in media ownership and control: Implications for creativity in Africa. In W. Binsbergen & R. van Dijk (Eds.), *Situating globality: African agency in the appropriation of global culture* (pp. 57–89). Leiden, the Netherlands: Brill.
Olaniyan, T. (2004). *Arrest the music! Fela and his rebel art and politics.* Bloomington: Indiana University Press.
Scott, J. C. (1990). *Domination and the arts of resistance: Hidden transcripts.* New Haven, CT: Yale University Press.
Yankah, K. (2000). Nana Ampadu and the sung tale as metaphor for protest. In K. Anyidoho & J. Gibbs (Eds.), *FonTomFrom: Contemporary Ghanaian literature, theatre and film* (pp. 135–154). New York: Rodopi.

MUSIC AND SOCIAL PROTEST (MALAWI)

The main influences that shaped the role of music in social protest in Malawi were colonialism, the two World Wars, poverty, gender inequality, postcolonial dictatorship, disease, and Malawi's oral culture. Given the repressive colonial and postcolonial governance and the controlled electronic and print media, protests about social conditions and poverty could only be subtle and oral. There was also a lack of strong nationalist political leadership between 1915, when John Chilembwe's nationalist uprising was put down, and 1944, when the African National Congress was founded. During this period, protests tended to be diffuse and localized at community or area levels; traditional and popular music were often their vehicle.

Low national literacy rates from the 1890s to the present ensured that orality remained the main mode of communication. But orality, in the form of music, given its universality and ambiguity, gave an equality of protest, however muted, to most

Malawi associations and groups. Music is an integral aspect of daily life in most Malawi cultures.

The Colonial Era

Colonialism, which was formalized when Malawi became a British Protectorate in 1891, marked an end to the slave trade but brought settlers who occupied much of the arable land. This loss of land and independent labor to the settlers, and the resulting estates and the emigration of men to the mines, contributed to rural poverty. Songs composed during this period—many beginning as work songs—referring to *atsamunda* (settlers) were resurrected during the 1949–1961 fight for self-government. The songs protested the harshness of colonial labor practices such as *thangata* (indentured labor) and *machila* (the sedan chair the colonists had Africans carry them in). Several of these songs and laments survive to this day.

During both World Wars, Malawi was a major source for the King's African Rifles. This disproportionate recruitment of Malawians was resented for many reasons: unfair colonial taxes and land policies, the harsh war conditions, the lack of compensation for dead African soldiers, and the poor prospects for those who survived the war. Traditional songs were appropriated as marching songs by African soldiers and used to raise morale, to soften the considerable military discomforts, and to forge their identity as *Nyasa* (lakeland) soldiers, distinct from other African soldiers. Some songs described the tribulations of the "German war" or *nkhondo ya azungu* (the white men's war). Many protest songs from this era made their way into traditional dances and work songs.

After returning from the wars, Indigenous soldiers formed social organizations that mixed Western and traditional elements, *beni*, *malipenga*, and *mganda* being the most famous. *Beni* and *mganda* were not just dances but social movements with, in some cases, political overtones. These syncretic entertainment dances combined elements of Western military culture with local music, instruments, and dance, as well as social male bonding and political protest. The Tonga *mganda* societies, for example, sang *Tingupangana* (We agreed), a reminder to the

colonial power that Malawi was a temporary protectorate to be given back to the natives "once they were educated."

Between the wars, increased migration and soldiers' deaths contributed to rural poverty. This influenced the evolution of some female musical traditions. New dances like *chiwoda* emerged, and new meanings were injected into existing ones like *chimtali*. *Chiwoda* (as in "to order") referred to the "mail ordering" of brides by migrant workers. Their agents often found them the best-looking brides at "sexy" *chiwoda* dances. *Chiwoda* music also had an element of protest at the labor migration system. It also enabled migrants to keep their identity by marrying Malawi women, if only by *chiwoda*. *Chimtali*, popular in Malawi's central region, included lyrics like *Kuntandizi* (To the mines), which bemoaned the cruelties of migrant labor: "What shall I do? I lie awake sleepless," the woman declares in the song.

Christianity promoted using hymns, discouraged "tribal" songs, and attempted to "educate" Malawians into Western music and "choirs." However, the concept of *makwaya* (choral music) was appropriated, indigenized, and used to carry protest. Examples were the nationalist songs *Tiyende pamodzi ndi mtima umodzi* (Let us march together in harmony)—a song with huge emotional pull—and *Chitaganya ndiyo nyumba ya Welensky* (The Federation is Welensky's project), the latter sung to the tune of the hymn *John Brown's Body*. (Federating modern-day Malawi, Zambia, and Zimbabwe was a colonial settler project to hang on to their power and privileges; Welensky was the settlers' leader.)

Tussles between Christianity and colonialism, and traditional cultures were viewed in the resilience of initiation traditions like *jando*, *nyau*, and *chinamwali*. Some songs from these traditions leaked into the public arena and became proud markers of cultures holding on to their own traditions against colonialism and Christianity. Christians were sometimes derided, in song, as *osavinidwa* (the uninitiated).

Post–World War II

Soldiers returned with enhanced social and economic aspirations, strengthening the nationalist cause. Music reflected their frustrations and expectations. Urban, more Western-influenced musical traditions, like *makwaya* (choirs), reflected the aspirations of shanty town and urban African life. *Kuchipatala ndinagonako* (I was once admitted to hospital) by Robert Namangwale noted the dire state of African hospitals. The Paseli Brothers' *Ndifera moyenda* (I will die in my travels) and Wilson Makawa's *Chitukutuku* (The exile) bemoaned the increase of labor migration. By the 1950s, well-articulated issues of class and race, as distinct from colonialism as racial power, were already a significant part of musical discourse as exemplified by Chakwana and Baluti's *Ndidzakwera ndege* (I will travel by plane [first class]) and Ndiche Mwalale's *Musamuone kumanga thayi* (Necktie or no necktie).

The 1949 famine, the weather-related environmental degradation, and subsequent worsening of poverty generated many songs. Many, like *1949 kunali njala* (There was hunger in 1949) and *Napolo* (Flash flood), were recorded or maintained in oral tradition, and are still current.

Apart from the famine, the period 1944–1959 was charged politically, encompassing as it did the expectations of returned soldiers, the increasing political frustrations of educated nationalist Africans, and resistance to the imposition of the Central African Federation. The colonial government's response was repression. Musicians reflected the political protests as in Thailo and Kapiye's *Dziko lino ndi lathu* (This is our land) and Kasiya and Chironga's *ABanda akangana ndiAzungu* (Banda has argued with Europeans).

It could be argued that the emotional impact and release of music allowed the nationalist struggles to be conducted more peacefully. Nationalist songs like *Kamuzu amenya nkhondo ndimau okha* (Dr. Banda fights his battles with words only) emphasized the movement's peaceful nature. In contrast, many nationalist songs reflected an underlying autocracy within the nationalist movement. Dissenters or "traitors" were viciously abused in song.

After "self-government'" began in 1961, African leaders realized that they had to kick-start economic development and initiated a frenzy of self-help projects. They attempted to use music to instill a spirit of self-help in the rural areas. At the same time, songs like *Dziko linapita ndi chuma* (They took our rich land) blamed "colonialists for neglecting Malawi."

Independence and the Banda Years

But this happy phase lasted barely 3 years. In 1964, 2 months after independence, a cabinet crisis split the government, heralding 30 years of dictatorship. The government, exploiting the self-help initiatives and those of the Malawi Women's League, organized all adult women into praise singers for Dr. Banda in the *mbumba* (women folk) movement. Most men, while enjoying the spectacle of dancing women singing well-crafted and drum-accompanied songs, resented the *mbumba* movement. They saw it as a tool to emasculate and silence all Malawi males politically.

Some *mbumba* members, however, had reservations about the one-party system and resented some male party leaders for sexually exploiting young women. A subterranean protest was often detectable within *mbumba* ranks. In 1978, after Albert Muwalo, Banda's ruthless deputy, was hanged for treason, the *mbumba* sang *Chikhala chodziwa, Ngwazi* (Had we known, Leader) implying that President-for-Life Banda had chosen the wrong deputy! Yet Malawi's gendered culture excluded women from urban popular music, depriving them of a public voice. Women's grievances continued to be channeled largely at personal and family levels in *pamtondo* (pounding) songs.

The *beni* and *mganda* traditions, moreover, having been exploited by Banda for their anticolonial sentiments, became suspect after independence because of their military-style organizational structures, political satire, social commentary, and politically ambiguous lyrics. They were viewed as sites of protest against his dictatorship.

From the late 1960s, men, particularly the young, developed a counter voice to *mbumba*. Given their political marginalization, limited education and employment prospects, and poverty, they found a voice through the creation of a jazz band tradition. *Jazz* was a syncretic, syncopated musical form that combined traditional Malawian, other African, and Western pop elements, mostly played on homemade instruments. In the music, they were able to critique the Banda regime in a coded, subtle manner that evaded the censors.

Their live performances, free-form lyrics, and use of metaphors and double-meaning expressions as needed provided a voice for many rural, shanty-town, and urban youths. Songs like *Mitala* (Polygamy) by Mikoko Band critiqued the regime's neglect of rural people. Jazz band culture consti-tuted an alternative social movement to the one-party youth league's hegemony. Many popular and accomplished bands, acoustic and electric, emerged from the jazz band movement.

Urban performers, like Afro-jazz musician Wambali Mkandawire and the big band Malawi Police Orchestra, even while entertaining those in power, also used coded lyrics to criticize autoc-racy. The Malawi Police Orchestra used a popular football song, *Sapota* (Football supporter), to appeal for "freedom to support the football team of your choice," a thinly veiled appeal for multi-party democracy.

Because of the close association between music and drama in Malawi, drama groups also exploited music for protest. Drama often featured rural people in rags to portray poverty, and the politi-cal party "chairman" was often viewed usurping the village chief's powers. Poverty was portrayed subtly in song as urbanites not remitting money home, rather than the government failing to deliver the goods.

From the early 1970s, music was instrumental in challenging the monopoly role of the Malawi Broadcasting Corporation (MBC). The MBC played "safe" music and censored dissenting views. The hunger for music led to bottle stores, bars, and canteens exploiting radio cassettes as alternatives to the MBC. These places became cen-ters where, despite the censorship, a greater range of music could be played (and radio stations heard), breaking the MBC monopoly. They also became centers of increased social interaction and communication, oral and musical, a significant step in a dictatorship.

1994: The Multiparty Scenario

After a multiparty system was instituted finally in 1994, there was initial hesitation as to how the new freedoms could be used and to what level they would be tolerated. Musicians found a voice much faster than journalists did. As corruption acceler-ated, hospitals deteriorated, school standards fell, and prices rose, musicians—some of whom had reappropriated traditional titles like *alangizi* (coun-selors) and *aphungu* (prophets)—articulated these concerns in popular songs performed on modern-ized "traditional" or appropriated Western (e.g., reggae) templates.

Zili kudula (Things are expensive) by The Ravers became the first song banned by the new democratic regime. Musicians tackled subjects ranging from class, politics, famine, freedom, reli-gion, and HIV. In Charles Nsaku's *Ndiphike nyemba* (Let me cook beans), the driver asks his heartless boss for a meal break after working non-stop for 3 days.

The new government's perceived neglect of the HIV/AIDS epidemic spurred musicians (who had lost many colleagues to the disease) to cam-paign for increased HIV treatment resources. The epidemic had brought Christian and donor funding for gospel music, and this facilitated buying computers, making popular music pro-duction much easier. Musicians, both religious and secular, benefited. A much freer range of music resulted.

Despite the funding sources, as a group musi-cians produced generally balanced arguments for more resources, prevention, diagnosis, and better treatment. Their arguments were made with good humor, as in Joe Gwaladi's *Edzi ndi dolo* (AIDS is mighty), which took the medical profession to task for their impotence. Even Malawi gospel, in its "reward in heaven" discourses, seemed, wittingly or unwittingly, to highlight the level of suffering and poverty in Malawi.

Since 1994, both the Bakili Muluzi and Bingu wa Mutharika regimes, like the one-party regime before them, continued rigid control over the MBC. In the context of a weak opposition and limited print media, musicians became a powerful voice protesting the injustices of present-day Malawi, where many still live below the poverty level. In the new century, jazz has married hip-hop, producing a harsher, more strident musical voice easily carried electronically and much harder to censor. Examples of this syncretic music include songs like Lawrence Mbenjere's *Liyanja achuma* (Suits the rich) and Evance Meleka's *Tidzatuluka m'munda* (We shall come out of the fields). Both contain trenchant Marxist critiques of present-day Malawi.

John Chipembere Lwanda

See also La Nova Cançó Protest Song (Països Catalans); Political Song (Northern Ireland); Popular Music and Political Expression (Côte d'Ivoire); Popular Music and Protest (Ethiopia); *Rembetiko* Songs (Greece); Youth Rock Music (China)

Further Readings

Chimombo, S., & Chimombo, M. (1996). *The culture of democracy: language, literature, the arts & politics in Malawi, 1992–94.* Zomba, Malawi: WASI.

Chirambo, R. (2002). Mzimu wa soldier: Contemporary popular music and politics in Malawi. In H. Englund (Ed.), *Democracy of chameleons* (pp. 103–122). Uppsala, Sweden: Nordic Africa Institute.

Chirwa, W. J. (2001). Dancing towards dictatorship: Political songs and popular culture in Malawi. *Nordic Journal of African Studies, 10*(1), 1–27.

Kamlongera, C., Nambote, M., Soko, B., & Timpunza-Mvula, E. (1992). *Kubvina: An introduction to Malawian dance and theatre.* Zomba, Malawi: CSR.

Lwanda, J. (2008). The history of music in Malawi. *Society of Malawi Journal, 61*(1), 26–40.

Lwanda, J. (2008). Poets, culture and orature: A reappraisal of the Malawi political public sphere, 1953–2006. *Journal of Contemporary African Studies, 26*(1), 71–101.

Ranger, T. O. (1975). *Dance and society in eastern Africa 1890–1970.* London: Heinemann.

Rotberg, R. (1966). *The rise of nationalism in central Africa: The making of Malawi and Zambia.* Cambridge, MA: Harvard University Press.

NAIROBI SLUMDWELLERS' MEDIA (KENYA)

More than 60% of Nairobi's population live in informal settlements where access to sanitation and electricity is minimal and poverty and illness are constant threats (African Population and Health Research Center, 2002). Mainstream media do not address such issues. Instead, scandals of corruption and party politics dominate the commercially driven information flow. When mainstream media do cover events in the slums, the information often is related to violence and crime. This has a demoralizing effect on slum-dwellers and increases their alienation.

Since 2006, several small media projects have emerged in the slums designed to counterbalance mainstream media ignorance and to provide the slums with useful news and information. One is Koch FM, which in 2006 started broadcasting in Korogocho, Nairobi's fourth largest slum (approximately 150,000 residents). Apart from Homa Bay Radio, which ran for a couple of years in the 1980s, Kenya had had little community broadcasting, and Koch FM was the first community station in a Kenyan slum. A group of local youngsters from different communities started the station in order to transform Korogocho by addressing poverty, lack of service delivery and governance, sexual abuse, public safety, drug abuse, crime, and unemployment. They identified the crucial need for a communication platform to supply relevant information for people's participation and involvement in solving their problems.

Startup and Growth

With help from some Norwegian friends, a down-loaded manual for building a transmitter, and a disused container to house the studio, the station became a reality. Yet when they started broadcasting, they were unaware it was illegal. The station came to attention when it was featured on Kenyan television news. A visit from the Ministry of Information and Communication followed. The station learned that a license and an assigned frequency were needed.

A 6-month struggle ensued with the CCK (Communications Commission of Kenya), the police, and the Ministry of Information and Communication. They were told several times that the idea of having a station in a slum was ridiculous and would never happen in Kenya. At the end of 2006, though, they finally received a permit and a frequency.

Koch FM's establishment opened up the possibility for other neighborhoods. In 2007, new community stations started in two other Nairobi slums: Pamoja FM in Kibera and Ghetto FM in Majengo. Other community radio stations came to include Kenyatta University radio, Shine FM, and Education Communication Network (ECN), all linked to different educational institutions, and Kapkara FM, Mangelete community radio, and Radio Lake Victoria outside Nairobi.

Contents

Koch FM's slogan is "edutainment." The station entertains the Korogocho residents while educating them on issues of health, environment, advocacy, and human rights, often working closely with other civil society groups. To reach more listeners, they broadcast in Kiswahili, East Africa's lingua franca. Although Kiswahili and English are Kenya's official languages, the country has more than 40 Indigenous languages. Therefore, broadcasting in Kiswahili can also be understood as part of a conscious strategy to create unity among the different ethnic groups, which make up the slum's population.

Discussions are mixed with local music, preferably from the Korogocho community in order to promote local talents. Music, arts, and sports are all important activities for the youth in the slums, because they provide a tool of expression and offer the hope of improving one's future. Koch FM also broadcasts local, national, and international news as long as it is seen to affect the community.

Besides the station's daily operation, Koch FM is involved in community outreach activities to ensure that Korogocho benefits from government programs. For example, it stimulates residents' awareness of the possibility of gaining funding for infrastructure development and economic aid. The station has also introduced community notice boards around Korogocho to inform the residents what is happening in their neighborhood.

Organization

Koch FM is registered as a community-based organization (CBO) and is funded both by Norwegian Church Aid and the Open Society Institute. It has a formal/legal structure consisting of a Chairman, Vice Chairman, Secretary, Treasurer, and an operational structure similar to a commercial radio station with a station manager, a deputy, department managers, and staff. The major difference is that everyone is a volunteer because the funding does not cover staff.

Most people involved are youth in their early 20s who have grown up in the slums and are driven by the vision to transform the slums. By involving themselves in these projects, they help the community but also keep themselves occupied and learn skills and a profession that might give them a paid job in the future.

According to the Economic Commission for Africa (2005), unemployment rates are high among youth in the slums and often go hand in hand with destructive behavior. Getting young people involved in different projects is thus one way to combat a growth in crime. Many projects can almost be described as youth clubs—springboards for motivated individuals to achieve a better life. Unfortunately, the turnover of volunteers is high as the lack of payment eventually forces many to seek paid employment elsewhere. Consequently, reaching the objective of transforming the slums is not an easy task because of these projects' lack of sustainability.

Legal and Financial Conditions and Challenges

Community radio operates under the same laws as other broadcasters because there is no specific community media legislation. However, their 3-year licenses restrict their reach to 2 km. Nor are they allowed commercials. Consequently, community media are entirely dependent on funds from sponsors and private well-wishers. Yet the funds received barely cover running costs. The poor slum infrastructure with frequent power cuts requires petrol generators, which are very expensive to run, thus forcing Koch FM to go off-air frequently. The sustainability of community radio is a difficult problem.

Moreover, the crisis of funding also affects community radio stations on more personal levels. Community and alternative media are often characterized by their flat organizational structure and absence of hierarchies. Even though the people working for community radio are all volunteers, staff are often disappointed with management because of the lack of transparency in the way funds are received and allocated, causing both frustration and distrust. Regardless of whether their suspicions are grounded, this lack of trust is a major predicament because it damages the volunteers' motivation. Working without pay is already a significant challenge for a slumdweller, and without financial support from private funds or a welfare system, it is easy to understand why many feel taken advantage of.

Conclusion

Nairobi is one of the most socioeconomically divided cities in the world, and these media projects are initiatives with great potential. They challenge the negative image of the slums, which dominates mainstream media, arouses public awareness, teaches work skills, and encourages slumdwellers to go on fighting to improve their lives. Furthermore, community radio played a positive and important role during the postelection violence in 2008, by promoting peace and unity rather than ethnic division. Up to the time of writing, the challenges facing community media in Nairobi's slums unfortunately negatively impacted their ability to serve their communities and to fulfill their potential.

Jessica Gustafsson

See also Audiocassettes and Political Critique (Kenya); Community Broadcasting (Canada); Community Media and the Third Sector; Community Radio (Haïti); Community Radio Movement (India); Social Movement Media, Anti-Apartheid (South Africa)

Further Readings

Abdi, J., & Deane, J. (2008). *The Kenyan 2007 elections and their aftermath: The role of media and communication* (Policy briefing #1). London: BBC World Service Trust.

APHRC. (2002). *Health and livelihood needs of residents of informal settlements in Nairobi City* (Occasional Study Report 2002). Nairobi, Kenya: African Population and Health Research Centre.

Economic Commission for Africa. (2005). *Meeting the challenges of unemployment and poverty in Africa* (Economic Report on Africa 2005). Addis Ababa, Ethiopia: Author.

Maina, L. W. (2006). *African media development initiatives: Kenya research findings and conclusions.* London: BBC World Service Trust.

Quarmyne, A. (2006). *From Homa Bay to Ada—lessons on community radio, access and participation.* Paper presented at UNESCO World Press Freedom Day Conference on Media, Development and Poverty Eradication, Colombo, May 1–2, 2006.

Wamucii, P. (2007). *Scoring for social change: A study of the Mathare Youth Sports Association in Kenya.* PhD dissertation, Ohio University, Athens.

NATIONAL ALTERNATIVE MEDIA NETWORK (ARGENTINA)

The *Red Nacional de Medios Alternativos* (RNMA) was envisioned in 2004, almost 30 years after the beginning of the 1976–1983 military dictatorship in Argentina, in the southwestern city of Neuquén, where a conference proposed its formation. Its mission, defined at a subsequent 2005 conference of some 150 grassroots media activists in the western city of Mendoza, pivoted in many ways on the atrocities committed by the regime.

The main conference discussion document placed front and center the question of memory: remembering the 30,000 people the regime seized and vanished, and their political visions; the children kidnapped from their parents and brought up under other identities; the state terrorism that was connected to U.S. imperialism; the foreign debt whose repayment was crippling the lives of a majority of Argentineans; and the complicit roles of Argentina's major news media. Indeed, it pinpointed the value of public political amnesia for the smooth functioning of the political class.

An earlier version of the network had taken shape after the tumultuous days of December 2001, in which the sustained and massive protests by Argentines at the ruinous economic collapse brought about by the neoliberal regime's policies saw four presidents come and go within a single month, and the president finally in place repudiate the International Monetary Fund (IMF) national debt. This earlier grouping was the Alternative Media Forum (FODEMA, Foro de Medios Alternativos), whose priority was to enable grassroots media activists to have access to a forum in common in which they could share resources as well as discuss tactics and strategies, without doing so in response to a competitive or sectarian dynamic.

By 2009, RNMA had an active web presence as a news distributor, as an Internet radio channel, and as a web publisher of basic information concerning media technologies. It also organized periodic conferences for media activists, for example, its fifth such gathering in November 2008 in Córdoba.

The news RNMA distributed on its website began in January 2008 and was from a variety of social movement sources. In mid-March 2009, for example, it carried reports on the continuing case of a Neuquén teacher, killed 2 years earlier by a police teargas grenade fired at close quarters; a new radio law proposed by the government to replace the law instituted by the military dictators; an emerging flashpoint around job cuts; rain flooding in an impoverished Buenos Aires neighborhood; a demonstration by 300 homeless families from a single area; and defending the rights of Córdoba's community radio station.

Earlier that year in January and the previous December, it also carried international news about the devastating Israeli military assault on the civilian population of Gaza and provided a series of ten names and numbers of international aid workers, with the languages they spoke, for alternative journalists to contact. Mostly the news was domestic or from neighboring countries, such as Bolivia and Paraguay. News items often carried photos and were posted on average every 1 or 2 days.

The Internet radio station in spring 2009 was running eight programs a week of political news and discussion, mostly at the weekend, and in between programs played folk and popular music with fractal images on the screen.

Fabiana Arencibia
(translated by John D. H. Downing)

Note: Originally published in Foro de Medios Alternativos. Aportes para la construcción de un colectivo de medios alternativos [Contributions to the construction of an alternative media collective]. In N. Vinelli & C. Rodríguez Esperón (Eds.), *Contrainformación: Medios alternativos para la acción política* (pp. 123–133). Buenos Aires, Argentina: Ediciones Continente, 2004.

See also Barricada TV (Argentina); Radio La Tribu (Argentina); Social Movement Media in 1987 Clashes (Korea); Wayruro People's Communication (Argentina)

Further Readings

Foro de Medios Alternativos. (2004). Aportes para la construcción de un colectivo de medios alternativos [Contributions to the construction of an alternative media collective]. In N. Vinelli & C. Rodríguez Esperón (Eds.), *Contrainformación: Medios alternativos para la acción política* [Counter-information: Alternative means of political action] (pp. 123–133). Buenos Aires, Argentina: Ediciones Continente.

RNMA: http://www.rnma.org.ar

NATIONAL SOCIALIST GERMAN WORKERS' PARTY (NAZI PARTY) TO 1933

In both popular memory and mainstream historical narratives, the Nazis often feature as the most renowned propagandists of the 20th century. They not only established a sprawling web of bureaucratic control over the German media, thus ensuring a government-supporting film, radio, and newspaper industry, but also proved remarkably adept at creating genuinely popular cultural fare as well as staging impressive multimedia spectacles designed to bolster the dynamic image of the movement and its charismatic leader, Adolf Hitler. Popular perceptions often differ little from the postwar verdict of the powerful minister Albert Speer, who famously described the Third Reich as

> a dictatorship which made complete use of all technical means in a perfect manner for the domination of its own nation. Through technical devices such as radio and loudspeaker 80 million people were deprived of independent thought. It was thereby possible to subject them to the will of one man. (Huxley, 1958, p. 25)

Although this supposed propagandistic genius is often greatly exaggerated, as a government the Nazis undoubtedly devoted an unusually large amount of time and resources to the media, more than most other governments at the time and far more than any preceding regime in German history.

It is worth noting, however, that before the Nazi party took power in January 1933, its media and propaganda efforts were based on a fundamentally different footing. For reasons of cost and access, the vast bulk of its work prior to 1933 was focused not on the relatively new and glamorous media of film and radio, for which the Nazis are most often remembered, but rather on the press, postering, and assemblies.

Press

From the very beginning of the party's history, the Nazis were keen to expand their journalistic influence. Despite the party's status in the early 1920s as an obscure right-wing movement, founding a national newspaper was deemed a key priority. The *Völkischer Beobachter* (*VB*, Volkish Observer), a preexisting paper in financial difficulties, was purchased for this purpose in 1921 along with the Franz Eher Verlag that published it. Thenceforth the Eher Verlag, as the Nazi publishing house, was chaired by Hitler and directed by Max Amann, a wartime acquaintance of Hitler. At the outset the *VB* was merely a small and marginal newspaper with little reach beyond Munich; in this sense it closely reflected the Nazi party itself. Yet during the course of 1922–1923, in the context of rising international tensions and runaway hyperinflation, its editor Alfred Rosenberg gradually lifted the paper's profile. In early 1923, it increased its publication frequency from twice weekly to daily, and its circulation quickly grew to around 25,000–30,000 copies. However, after the Nazis' unsuccessful putsch attempt in November 1923, the *VB* was banned, only to return in spring 1925 with a mere 5,000 subscribers. It was only at the end of the 1920s that the paper finally regained its 1923 circulation high point.

By this time, however, the *VB* was only one of numerous Nazi party publications. These included not only the weekly magazine *Illustrierter Beobachter* (Illustrated Observer), founded in 1926, but also a sizable Nazi regional press, which by 1930 numbered some 60 publications in all (albeit primarily small weekly papers, many of them short-lived). The parliamentary elections in September 1930 marked the breakthrough for the Nazi press, as for the party itself. Soon afterward the *VB* launched a Berlin edition, and by the middle of 1931, its nominal circulation had swelled to more than 100,000 (circulation figures were not audited in Germany at the time, so they are not wholly reliable). Furthermore, the number of party periodicals nearly doubled during 1931–1932, the most prominent among them the rabidly anti-Semitic *Der Stürmer* (The Stormtrooper), edited by Franconian party leader Julius Streicher, and the tabloid *Der Angriff* (The Attack), edited by the party's propaganda chief and future Propaganda Minister Joseph Goebbels.

Despite this rapid growth, the actual impact of the Nazi press on the party's electoral fortunes seems to have been slight. Circulation figures never remotely kept pace with the party's electoral returns. At the end of 1932, Nazi press circulation is estimated to have been at a maximum of around 750,000, which represented only 5% to 7% of the total circulation in Germany compared with the party's winning one third of the vote. The party press was thus confined largely to the hard-core membership. Nazi periodicals contained relatively little of interest for the general reader and tended to function more as intraparty newsletters for members and activists. Insofar as the press aided the Nazis in electoral terms, the party probably owed more to the papers associated with rival right-wing parties than to its own publications.

Posters, Assemblies

The use of posters, marches, and other means of making a mark on the visual environment were at least as important for the Nazi movement as the press. The innumerable demonstrations and the visual props they used were a central concern from the beginning. They not only gave the rank and file something to do but also were a ritual for marking territory and literally for occupying public space. This was especially the case at election time, as party members marched incessantly and covered every available urban surface with posters in what has been described as a "war of images" with their archrivals, above all, the Communists, whose agitation techniques were remarkably similar. Nazi posters were insurrectionary in tone, heavily dependent on stereotypes, and highly suggestive of movement. Recurring motifs were the muscle-bound proletarian giant or the anonymous fist dealing a smashing blow to podgy capitalists and scheming Marxists. Hyper-masculine forms denoted determination and dynamism, and flowing red flags and banners signaled insurrectionary opposition to the liberal-democratic republican system.

Film, Radio

Compared with the press, postering, and marches, the Nazi movement made little use of film or radio before entering government in 1933. The reasons for this were the twin problems of cost and access. German radio, effectively a federalized state-run monopoly since its inception in 1923, was conceived under the Republic as a strictly nonpartisan medium from which all party-political broadcasts were banned. Access to the microphone was simply beyond the Nazis' reach before 1933. Film, as a private industry, posed no such barriers, although the costs of production nonetheless kept Nazi efforts within very narrow limits. To be sure, the Nazis were very interested in film; Propaganda Chief Goebbels considered it the most powerful medium of all and considered Soviet films as models for Nazi cinematic art. But party finances were meager for filmmaking, and few outside backers were willing to invest in such films given the possibility of police banning them (as happened in Prussia in 1931 to the Nazi film *Kampf um Berlin,* or Fight for Berlin). Even so, the party managed to produce a small handful of films during the 1920s—including documentaries of Hitler's trial in 1924, the party conferences in 1926 and 1929, as well as *Kampf um Berlin* (made in 1929). Yet such efforts were by and large amateurish given the party's lack of cinematic know-how and shortage of funds. Further efforts to organization film production were also hampered by the perennial and endemic in-fighting within the Nazi movement, including the rivalry between Joseph Goebbels, who directed the party's Reich Film Agency, and Gregor Strasser, who ran its Reich Organisational Directorate.

Hence, conventional views about Nazi propaganda wizardry have always been exaggerated, not least because of the exculpatory implication that the German electorate was thereby tricked. The party's utilization of the media prior to entering government was neither as effective nor as important as is often assumed; indeed, its popular message of national rejuvenation and strong leadership needed little selling in depression-era Germany. Yet the necessary corrections to the image of Nazi propaganda genius do not change the fact that they were well ahead of their rivals in their techniques of political communication before 1933.

Corey Ross

See also Anti-Fascist Media, 1922–1945 (Italy); Beheading Videos (Iraq/Transnational); Christian Radio (United States); Extreme Right and Anti–Extreme Right Media (Vlaanderen/Flanders); Radio Mille Collines and *Kangura* Magazine (Rwanda); Wartime Underground Resistance Press, 1941–1944 (Greece); Weimar Republic Dissident Cultures (Germany); White Supremacist Tattoos (United States)

Further Readings

Evans, R. J. (2003). *The coming of the Third Reich.* London: Allen Lane.

Fulda, B. (2009). *Press and politics in the Weimar Republic.* Oxford: Oxford University Press.

German Propaganda Archive: http://www.calvin.edu/academic/cas/gpa/posters1.htm

Hanna-Daoud, T. (1996). *Die NSDAP und der Film bis zur Machtergreifung.* [The NSDAP and film up to the seizure of power]. Cologne, Germany: Böhlau.

Huxley, A. (1958). *Brave new world revisited.* Retrieved May 28, 2010, from http://teacherweb.com/CA/EastlakeHighSchool/MrGillet/BNW_Revisited_1958.pdf

Mühlberger, D. (2004). *Hitler's voice: The Völkischer Beobachter 1920–1933.* Bern, Switzerland: Lang.

Paul, G. (1990). *Aufstand der Bilder. Die NS-Propaganda vor 1933* [Rise of the images: National-Socialist propaganda before 1933]. Bonn, Germany: Dietz.

Schoch, R. (Ed.). (1980). *Politische plakate der Weimarer Republik 1918–1933* [Political posters in the Weimar Republic]. Darmstadt, Germany: Hessisches Landesmuseum.

NAXALITE MOVEMENT MEDIA (INDIA)

The Naxalite movement greatly influenced leftist politics in India, Bangladesh, and Nepal. On May 24, 1967, some farmers of the Naxalbari region (West Bengal State) killed a police officer. The next day, in response, the police shot dead nine women and two children. In the immediately preceding years, a major Communist Party of India split in 1964 had already produced the more radical Communist Party of India (Marxist). The Naxalbari incident sparked ideological debates among Communist tendencies on whether or not to support armed agrarian revolution, which ultimately resulted in a third Indian communist party. In 1968, the Maoist Communist Centre (MCC) emerged, and in 1969, the Communist Party of India (Marxist-Leninist) was also born. Furthermore, in 1977, emerged the CPI (ML) New Democracy. Mainstream media categorized all their adherents as Naxalites. In the 2000s, a major Naxalite resurgence took place, involving groups such as the CPI (Maoist), which itself is partly composed of the MCC.

In Bengal, the Naxalbari wave shook the traditional base of society, politics, and culture. The CPI (ML), however, never promoted its own cultural front or directly controlled the media mentioned below (except party bulletins and slogans). Rather, party workers, supporters, and sympathizers created and nurtured these media forms (songs and literary works) individually or collectively.

Within the long history of the communist movement in India, the Naxalite movement was unique in involving educated, urban, upper-middle-class youths with the working class. Despite being from traditional middle-class families, women took an active part in the movement and fought side by side with their male comrades. A considerable number of women stopped wearing traditional symbols worn by Hindu married women. Caste barriers vanished as party workers tried to abandon all forms of class distinction.

Revolutionary Songs (*Gana Sangeet*) and Slogans

Famous folk artists like Gaddar (Andhra Pradesh) and Phaguram (Madhya Pradesh) began traveling throughout the nation propagating Naxalite ideology through musical performance. Instead of absolute dependence on the gods' will, folk artists sang of the better future they believed their own common people would bring.

The number of songs produced in first 2 years of the Naxalite movement alone exceeds the number produced by the entire cultural movement (*Gana Natya Andolon*) of India's other communist parties. Some songs merely captured the spirit of the movement, whereas others directly discussed party issues like election boycotts, annihilation of class enemies, and freeing political prisoners. These songs were composed throughout the movement's history.

Until the late 1980s, cultural groups like Dishari, Nishantika, Gana Bishan, Ayani Goshthi, and Opera Group operated cultural programs on special occasions such as May Day, Lenin's birthday, and Naxalbari Day. Ajit Pandey, Protul Mukherjee, Dilip Bagchi, and Nitish Ray composed several popular songs. Perhaps for the first time in Indian history, educated middle-class youths composed songs in dialect or tribal languages (e.g., Rajbanshi and Santhali) to communicate the real nature of the struggle.

The Naxalites called for armed revolution and the annihilation of "class enemies." Other Indian communist parties limited their activities to farmers' and workers' rights. The Naxalites, however, directly attacked the democratic system. Former CPI (ML) party activists say that people in certain localities often changed the party slogans to make them more aggressive. Many young people were shot dead by the police or killed by members of rival parties while writing slogans on walls. Slogans like *khatom obhijan cholche, cholbe* (annihilation is going on, it will go on), *nirbachon boycott korun* (boycott election), *chiner chairman amader chairman* (the chairman of China [Mao Zedong] is our chairman), and *parliament shuorer khoar* (parliament is a pigsty) challenged the very basis of Indian parliamentary democracy.

Poetry, Fiction, and Magazines

It was not only a group of enthusiastic young people who were afire with new political ideology and exploded against feudal oppression, armed struggle, government-organized genocides, and torture of political prisoners, while calling openly for "red terror." Established poets like Manish Ghatak and Birendra Chattopadhyay also sympathized with the Naxalite movement's re-evaluation of the sociopolitical system. New, now famous names in poetry (e.g., Indu Saha, Nabarun Bhattacharya, Kamalesh Sen, and Srijan Sen) emerged from the movement.

Between 1967 and 1970, the media focus was primarily rural, on *zaminders* (landowners) and moneylenders, and on the "revisionist" character of the other communist party leaders, who in forming West Bengal's government had abandoned their earlier promises. After 1970, the conflict shifted toward urban areas and the enemy became the police, the CPI (M), and Congress party members. From 1970 to 1971, cities and suburbs witnessed the mass killing of alleged Naxalites.

Much Naxalite literature featured prominent female characters, not only as mothers, sisters, or lovers, but also as communist party workers. Writers like Mahashweta Devi (her *Hazar Churashir Maa* [Mother of Corpse 1084] and *Sarsatiya, Chetti Munda o Tar Teer* [Chetti Munda and His Arrow]) demonstrated that caste struggle and class struggle were identical in village society. Samaresh Basu (*Oder Bolte Dao* [Let Them Speak], *Siddhanta* [Decision], *Gantabyo* [Destination], and *Mahakaler Rather Ghora* [Horses of the Chariot of Time]) viewed the Naxalites as lost, violent youngsters driven by irrational passions, whereas Sunil Gangopadhyay (*Kendobindu* [Central Point] and *Payer Talar Mati* [Soil Under the Feet]) portrayed them more positively.

Theater and Cinema

The movement's immediacy changed conventional theatrical presentation altogether. A physical stage, lights, microphones, and makeup became less important. The first street play supporting this movement was Amal Ray's 1967 *Bharoter Vietnam* (India's Vietnam), which was followed by hundreds of others, mostly by young supporters and active party workers. Famous actor-director Utpal Dutta's *Teer* (Arrow) was the first professionally performed play based on the Naxalbari incident. Manoranjan Biswas, Shukdeb Chattopadhyay, Amal Ray, and others later formed the first Naxalite theater journal, *Natyaprasanga*. Class oppression, genocide, and police torture became common themes. Writers also adopted imagery from international events such as the French revolution and the struggle in Vietnam.

The CPI (M-L) dismissed the use of feature film as a political medium. Only in certain films by socially concerned directors like K. Abbas (*Naxalite*), Satyajit Ray (*Pratidwandi* [The Adversary]), Mrinal Sen (*Calcutta '71, Interview*), Buddhadeb Dasgupta (*Grihajuddha*), and Gautam Ghose (*Hungry Autumn, Kalbela*) do we find glimpses of the uncertainty and unrest of that period. A film on Aluri Sitharam Raju (a South Indian tribal leader) was made in

Andhra Pradesh. The Bollywood movie *Lal Salam* portrayed the leading female character as a Maoist leader.

Press

The magazines *Deshabroti* (Bengali), *Liberation* (English), and *Jana Yuddh* (Hindi, Punjabi) operated under the party's strict supervision. After 1977, some independently published magazines began to voice their support for the Naxalbari movement.

The MCC had started its party organ in 1968, named *Dakshin Desh* (Correct Nation). Other early Naxalite newspapers in 1976 included *Chingari* (Flicker, in Hindi; *Sphulinga* in Bengali) in Bihar state; *Ishtahar* (Manifesto), distributed in both Bihar and West Bengal; and *Red Tidings*, in 1978. All three were published by the Central Organizing Committee of the CPI (ML). A different Naxalite organization, the CPI (ML) New Democracy, operating openly in West Bengal, but underground elsewhere, began *Lal Jhanda* (Red Flag) in 1977.

The most active Naxalite group in the 2000s was the CPI (Maoist), with its own newspaper *People's War*, published since 1984, and translated into all the major languages.

Indrani Bhattacharya

See also Adivasi Movement Media (India); Dalit Movement Media (India); Documentary Film for Social Change (India); Indian People's Theatre Association; Khalistan Movement Media (India/Transnational); Zapatista Media (México)

Further Readings

Bhattacharya, A. (Ed.). (1992). *Naxalbarir probhabe shilpo sahityo chalacchitro* [Art, literature and film under the influence of the Naxalite movement]. Kolkata, India: Naya Istahar.

Dasadhikari, S. (Ed.). (1995). *Ganasangeet sankhya* [Leftist political songs]. Kolkata, India: Jalarka.

Dasadhikari, S. (Ed.). (1996). *Sottorer shohid lekhak shilpi sankhya* [Martyr writers and artists of the 70s]. Kolkata, India: Jalarka.

Ghose, N. (1988). *Naxalbari andolon o Bangla sahityo* [Naxalite movement and Bengali literature]. Kolkata, India: Karuna.

New Culture and May 4th Movements Media (China)

The New Culture Movement began in 1915, and the May 4th Movement in 1919, both with strongly nationalist and anti-imperialist objectives. After the 1911 revolution that abolished the imperial regime in China, the Returning to the Ancients and Respecting Confucius Movement emerged, supported by the new northern warlord government. However, China's defeat by foreign powers promoted the questioning and reappraisal of millennia-old Chinese values and further inflamed nationalist feeling. All this sparked the New Culture Movement, inaugurated by the *New Youth* journal (*Xin Qing Nian*), established in 1915 by Beijing University professor Chen Duxiu. Thus, the movement's center was Beijing University.

The movement had two phases: the initial one (1915–1917) counterposed feudal, especially Confucianist, thought and superstition to democracy and science, and proposed a new naturalistic vernacular writing style (*Bai Hua Wen*), replacing the difficult 2,000-year-old classical style (*Wen Yan Wen*). Chen Duxiu and U.S.-educated scholar Hu Shi were the leaders in this period, along with Lu Xun, Li Dazhao, and others. In the second phase beginning in 1917, the movement became influenced by Marxism and increasingly political, bringing Chinese Communism to birth. Li Dazhao led this phase. It was a movement among intellectuals, nearly all being Beijing University professors.

Then China's diplomatic humiliation by the colonial powers at the Versailles Peace Conference touched off the May Fourth Movement. On May 4, 1919, more than 3,000 students from 13 Beijing colleges or universities gathered together in Tiananmen Square, shouted out slogans, and displayed a placard written in a student's blood (*Give Back Our City of Qingdao*). Then students in other parts of the country responded one after another. The movement attacked the government as weak-kneed, showing intense dissatisfaction and anger at the Allied Powers' betrayal of China and their own government's inability to secure Chinese interests. Student leaders of the movement included Luo Jialun, Fu Sinian, and Duan Xipeng.

Indeed students acted as vanguard in the movement's early phase, and the working class as its main force later. From early June, workers and businessmen in Shanghai also went on strike, and people from 150 other cities in 22 provinces took part in different ways. Under intense public pressure, the government had to release students it had arrested and dismiss the cabinet ministers who had advocated accepting the Versailles decision. When China's representatives in Paris refused to sign the peace treaty later that month, the movement had its first victory. This wing of the New Culture Movement was deeply anti-imperialist and anti-feudal.

The Movements' Media

Magazines, slogans, and language played a very important role in both movements. Intellectuals and students used them to promote their ideas and demands.

The *New Youth* magazine both launched the New Culture Movement and was the core fortress or battlefield of the new culture. More than 300 intellectuals, including those named above, published their essays in this magazine. Chen Duxiu published his famous essay "Advice for Youth" containing the main propositions of New Culture (democracy and science). The magazine had a circulation of more than 1,000 initially, 15,000–16,000 at its peak, and spread nearly all over China.

As the New Culture Movement advanced, Beijing University students (e.g., Fu Sinian, Luo Jialun, and Xu Yanzhi) founded their own reform journal titled *Xinchao* (Renaissance) on January 1, 1919. Although it only published 12 issues, it was so important that it was enthroned as *New Youth's* companion. It took high-school students as its main readers, to "let the high school students survive the poison of feudalism." The first issue printed 13,000, up to 15,000 by the May 4th Movement.

A magazine called *The Pacific Ocean* also promoted the May 4th Movement. This was founded by returned intellectuals in early 1917 in Shanghai who had received education and training abroad (mainly from the United Kingdom). Other magazines that played a role in the movements included *Comments Weekly, The Citizen, New Education, China Youth,* and *Liberation and Reconstruction.*

Slogans were one of the most powerful media in both movements then, and even are so today. The most popular slogan in the New Culture Movement was "Democracy and Science," whereas slogans from the May Fourth Movement included "Struggle for sovereignty externally, get rid of the national traitors at home," "Do away with the 'Twenty-One Demands'" (Japan's 1915 claims on northern China), and "Don't sign the Versailles Treaty." These communicated the soul and aims of the movements around the country.

Vernacular Chinese took the place of Classical Chinese, and new literature and drama sprang forth, such as Hu Shi's *The Greatest Event in Life,* which encouraged free love. A new experimental literature inspired by Western forms also became highly popular, such as Lu Xun's satires and short stories. The most famous was *The Lunatic's Diary,* the first short stories written in vernacular Chinese.

Besides the above, there were many fliers, pamphlets, and a new dress style. Leading pamphlets included *The Communist Manifesto* and *Awareness* and filters like *The Beijing Academic Circles Declaration.* The dress style became a combination of Chinese and Western, with the Chinese tunic suit, the *cheongsam,* and a one-piece dress being the most popular styles.

Many scholars put these movements together and call them the May 4th and New Culture Movements, and they interpret them as the Chinese Renaissance. Actually, both movements had great influence on Chinese history and culture. First, the trends of thinking became more diverse. Second, traditional Chinese culture and Western culture began to collide and influence each other. Third, media assumed a more and more important role in cultural movements and in movements for a new society.

Zheng-rong Hu and Ji-dong Li

See also Boxer Rebellion Theater (China); Independence Movement Media (India); Independence Movement Media (Vietnam); Online Nationalism (China); Social Movement Media, Anti-Apartheid (South Africa)

Further Readings

Li, K., & Li, S. (Eds.). (2004). *The modern history of China.* Beijing, China: China Book Company.

Li, Y. (2004). *The publisher of the New Youth-Su Xinfu.* Chen Duxiu Studies. Retrieved November 25, 2007, from http://www.chenduxiu.net/ReadNews.asp?NewsID=389

Ren, S. (2007). *The details of the May 4th Movement. History teaching* (vol. 11). Retrieved December 25, 2007, http://en.wikipedia.org/wiki/New_Culture_Movement

New Media and Activism

Magazines, newspapers, and books routinely publish essays on how to harness a new media skill set: digital video production, mobile (cell phone) device production, blogging/vlogging, and online social networking. In this evolving mediascape, citizens are no longer passive consumers but agents in creating and distributing their own content. Broadly, this content is often humorous in nature and includes anything from comedy sketches to unintentionally released amateur video clips like *Star Wars Kid* or the *Don't Tase Me Bro* video.

As much as there seems to be a recreational, commercial culture feature of this content, it is also sometimes politically oriented and occasionally agitational. For example, a group of local activists, organizing protestors at the 2008 Republican Convention in Minneapolis, created a humorous video to welcome like-minded citizens to the city and to direct them to an informational website for the massive demonstrations planned. Similarly, numerous environmentalist movements from around the United States record and stream video of local environmental degradation. These video tours ask viewers to bear witness to the consequences of illegal dumping of hazardous waste. How social movements continue to harness these new media practices for social change is worth serious consideration.

Time magazine identified "video snacking" as a central practice of the evolving new media consumption patterns of the 21st century. The article noted, among other things, that consumption of streaming video is growing and frequent during office lunch breaks. Web content providers have long known that usage spikes at midday during the workweek and, as a consequence, create content specifically for that window. These new practices are commercial in orientation, but they are also emerging from the grassroots. Outside of commercial interests and for ends that frequently challenge the assumptions of the mass media establishment, citizens are increasingly engaged in this new form of digital public address.

Often identified as "user-generated content," this new media skill set enables average citizens to circumvent the gatekeeping of commercial media and traditional channels of political discourse with self-produced content, ranging from recorded public speeches to I-Witness Video accounts of political struggle. Despite the tens of millions online watching and reading about these videos, participating in the creation of content, sharing them with others on Twitter and Facebook, and writing about them on blogs, little scholarly attention has been paid to what kind of cultural and political work these new media practices can accomplish.

In their book, *Digital Generations,* David Buckingham and Rebekah Willett suggest there is a growing cadre of citizens who are crossing the line toward more activist forms of participatory media culture. Echoing this sentiment, Martha McCaughey and Michael D. Ayers note in their book *Cyberactivism* that in recent years small and large networks of wired activists have been creating online petitions, developing public awareness websites connected to traditional political organizations, building spoof sites to make political points, and creating platforms to propel real-life protest.

Yet many skeptics identify mass media use with the private sphere and personal life, in no way uniting private people into an active public, and equally see new media practices as discouraging political debate and public organizing, as merely fostering informal sociability with no specific institutional power. Because blogging, Twitter updates, and Facebook associations require little discussion, center on expressiveness, and lack the close weave of institutional affiliation, publics brought together through them are thought less viable as activist movements.

Yet in practice the success of large-scale protest to support immigrant rights in California was largely attributed to organizing on Facebook. Numerous local and international movements use sites such as YouTube to gain publicity for their causes. New sites such as Twitter were instrumental in giving a platform to Greek protest movements in December 2008 and to state-silenced protestors in the streets of Iran after the 2009 presidential election.

Yet the acquisition of political information is morphing. According to interviews and recent surveys, younger citizens tend to be not just consumers of news but conduits as well—sending out e-mailed links and videos to friends and their social networks. And in turn, they rely on friends and online connections for news to come to them. In essence, they are replacing the professional filter of prominent newspapers. As a result, new media modes of expression are increasingly becoming the public commons of the new millennium and a growing site of grassroots political struggle. Two important components of this emerging digital resistance are the use of social networking sites and viral distribution.

Social Networking

The emergence of social networks sites in the last decade has significantly impacted social relations. Through friend lists on MySpace, associations on Facebook, and microblogging on Twitter, social network sites allow people to find, meet, and contact each other more easily.

How people are organized into social networks varies. Facebook and LinkedIn used existing communities such as students and alumni or business connections to create a base layer for activity surrounding their site. However, other sites are directly organized around activism. Change.org enables people to form communities around social issues like global warming and Net Neutrality. These networks connect people to organizations, making overall social networks more useful.

Facebook is by far the most popular social networking site, reporting at least 400 million users worldwide, with more than 200 million users logging on once a day as of 2010. Although there is nothing particularly activist about popular social networks sites such as Facebook and MySpace, social movements have been enthusiastic about adopting this easy and economical tool for organizing, especially for global activism.

Facebook houses thousands of groups organized around social contestation, protest, and political agitation. Facebook groups have popped up protesting everything from text-messaging fees to national protests in opposition to California's

2008 Proposition 8 seeking to bar gay marriage. In 2008, one Facebook lobby opposing the U.S. government's copyright proposals had more than 90,000 members. In Canada, the government of Ontario province responded to a Facebook protest of almost 150,000 users against proposed limits on the number of passengers allowed in cars driven by teens by swiftly dropping the proposal.

This fact has led to some problems with oppressive governments where activism is tightly restricted and Facebook has become the online social and political organizing tool of choice. Bloggers in the United Arab Emirates and Iran sometimes complain that Facebook is being blocked entirely. There are indications that governments implicitly and explicitly interested in suppression of political speech are becoming savvy to these new media trends and are developing strategies to combat them. In April 2007, Facebook removed an Arab gay rights group after the company received complaints from the Egyptian and Saudi governments.

In other instances, citizens with perceived freedom of political speech in countries like the United States, Australian, and Canada also report a steady stream of censorship. Bloggers in the United States have indicated that political discourse is often identified as spam within the networking system and deleted. However, innovation and ingenuity in technology use seem to sidestep many government censorship efforts. The spontaneous actions of citizens to circulate protest images on Facebook and Twitter after the Iranian government censored the international press are good examples of ingenuity in technology use supplanting censorship efforts. As a result of its primarily social function, Facebook can serve as a forum for human rights groups in all countries that would otherwise suppress political speech. One of the ways political speech is finding its way into homes and public spaces is through viral distribution.

Viral Video and Distribution

Viral videos are previously recorded and/or mashed-up media clips that gain widespread popularity through the process of Internet sharing, typically through e-mail or instant messages, blogs, and other media-sharing websites such as YouTube, Facebook, and MySpace.

Viral video sharing is a kind of culture exchange, a digital spontaneous discussion. Videos and other content such as public notes and microblogging in the form of status updates can become viral if they are compelling and resonate with the people who check into them. Within weeks or just hours, a popular video on YouTube can spread internationally through "viral" networks of individual users and community sites sharing the video clips.

Viral content has a relatively short shelf life. Although its texts persist in the online environment for great lengths of time, long enough for there to be viral video classics, for most viral video, there is an almost wildfire-like quality to their circulation, peaking after less than a week and then settling into a steady stream. When most viral content peaks in circulation, blogs and networking sites and even traditional media outlets begin to register and create public discourse about these texts. Viral content exists outside but also ahead of the curve of most commercial media. This is why viral videos are often covered by commercial media months after their initial Internet eruption.

After the contested results of Iran's 2009 presidential election, outraged citizens took to the streets in protest. Although the government immediately closed off all communication and reports of social upheaval, the social networking site Twitter and the distribution of viral video clips on Facebook and YouTube told the story of citizens outraged and taking to the streets, victims of violent state oppression. The only proof of political suppression to the outside world was the numerous video clips recorded on cell phones and circulated in this nontraditional format.

In many instances, viral video functions as a "hyper-visual" discourse. Hyper-visuality is the electronically and culturally connected, nonsequential discourse that branches out and allows multiple choices for readers to explore the potential grounds for political action.

However, there is a convoluted relationship between consumer culture and viral content, potentially dampening the medium's social movement usefulness. There is also a prominent commercial strain present in the circulation of viral content. Viral video as a term is likely derived from a trend known as viral marketing, which is an attempt to address through unconventional means those turned off by traditional advertising.

It is important to study viral communication for its multiplicity. Distinctions between its modes should be based on classifying the reception, circulation, and uptake of these media works online. This focus would expand the potential scope of understanding viral video as a tool of social change and identify media clips that create specific locations around which to anchor public debate, social contestation, and political resistance.

Conclusion

How social movements create change from or with new media practice is a complicated process, involving much more than circulating user-generated content and using mobile devices. Cross-media use and technological innovation have prompted multidirectional media communication, where audiences can consume public discourse and produce it with the help of the Internet. The Internet has become an important companion to media consumption, facilitating the organization of like-minded citizens into activist publics. Use of these new media has forged strategies for communication that reconceptualize political models of social change by overcoming geographical divides through virtual space. However, traditional strategies for political engagement such as protest, petition, and public face-to-face interaction were not routinely abandoned for "new" Internet strategies of agitation. On the contrary, the Internet facilitated citizens organizing for action in the streets. The study of new media practices should be assessed in terms of their rhetorical force and how they function in the broader public culture and in the process of social change.

Angela J. Aguayo

See also Arab Bloggers as Citizen Journalists (Transnational); Bloggers Under Occupation, 2003– (Iraq); December 2008 Revolt Media (Greece); Mobile Communication and Social Movements; New Media and Alternative Cultural Sphere (Iran); Social Movement Media in 2009 Crisis (Iran); Women Bloggers (Egypt)

Further Readings

Atton, C. (2002). News culture and new social movements: Radical journalism and the mainstream media. *Journalism Studies, 3,* 491–505.

Atton, C. (2003). Reshaping social movement media for a new millennium. *Social Movement Studies, 2,* 3–15.

Atton, C. (2004). *An alternative Internet: Radical media, politics and creativity.* Edinburgh, UK: Edinburgh University Press.

Ayers, M. D., & McCaughey, M. (2003). *Cyberactivism: Online activism in theory and practice.* New York: Routledge.

Buckingham, D., & Willett, R. (Eds.). (2006). *Digital generations: Children, young people and new media.* New York: Routledge.

Critical Art Ensemble. (2001). *Digital resistance: Explorations in tactical media.* Brooklyn, NY: Autonomedia.

Dartnell, M. (2006). *Insurgency online: Web activism and global conflict.* Toronto, ON, Canada: University of Toronto Press.

Della Porta, D., & Tarrow, S. (2005). *Transnational protest and global activism: People, passions and power.* Lanham, MD: Rowman & Littlefield.

The Virtual Activist Training Guide: http://www.netaction.org/training

NEW MEDIA AND ALTERNATIVE CULTURAL SPHERE (IRAN)

We are still living with the repercussions of the 1979 Iranian revolution that toppled the Western-backed monarchy of Shah Reza Pahlavi and established an "Islamic" Republic. That revolution was remarkable not only for the geopolitical developments that it ushered in but also for the role of media in energizing the political movement that culminated in the revolution. The sermons and declarations of Ayatollah Khomeini, the revolution's charismatic leader, were disseminated on audiocassettes and flyers via clandestine networks to mobilize the masses to oppose the monarchy. Such media were characterized as "small" because they bypassed the government-controlled "big" media of television, radio, and newspapers.

Khomeini pronounced the guiding principles of the revolution as establishing "Islamic" culture and society, where individuals *willingly* live, follow, and embody Islamic values but as *prescribed* by the Islamic government. Article 2 of the new constitution expresses the Islamic Republic's commitment to "cultural independence"; yet Article 3 calls for media to propagate "moral values" in accordance with the government's definition of Islam.

Such contradictory tendencies characterize the Islamic Republic's cultural scenario. On the one hand, a theocracy constantly reaffirms its commitment to revolutionary establishment of an Islamic culture. On the other, there is a decline in religious practices and a growing secularization of private life, especially in younger generations—but where 70% of the public is under the age of 30. Thus, many Iranians, especially young people, live by their own values, some in clear violation of the government-prescribed vision. The official culture and media have to coexist with unofficial popular culture.

This coexistence is fraught with tension. Rap music, for example, is part of an "underground" culture because the government deems it "un-Islamic." Yet an alternative cultural sphere has been created that arguably engulfs the official public culture. This is the context for considering the significance of alternative media in today's Iran.

Official and Alternative Media

Official media in Iran include the government-owned and -operated IRIB (Islamic Republic of Iran Broadcasting). IRIB is an enormous organization with a wide range of production and distribution. It offers 7 terrestrial television channels and 14 radio networks. Nonterrestrial broadcasting includes external television and radio services, beaming programming in 27 languages.

Domestic broadcasting offers a wide range of popular programs (sports, entertainment, news, and public affairs) and is far from monolithic, although the news reflects official views. The newspaper industry is commercial and dynamic, although constantly under government pressure. Much of the struggle between the pro-government voices and those of reformers is played out publicly when a newspaper is shut down and then reconstituted with another name, with mostly the same staff.

The alternative cultural sphere is constituted by a range of media and cultural practices that might be entirely banal in other contexts. These include satellite television, Internet and blogging, mobile phone technology, and other digital technologies.

Although satellite dishes are illegal, the government does not seriously enforce the law. As a result, many Iranian households receive, for a small one-time fee, more than 40 Persian-language foreign satellite TV channels from outside Iran (including antigovernment ones). They also receive hundreds of foreign-language satellite TV channels offering a wide range of entertainment and news programming (including CNN International, Voice of America, BBC, and the recently launched Persian-language BBC TV).

The Internet has fast become a medium with significant social and political implications. There are currently 700,000 registered weblogs in Iran. Farsi (Persian) was once tied with French as the world's third most common blogging language. It is now in the top 10. Although weblogs have allowed for a wide range of expression unavailable in official media, the Internet's significance lies in its capacity to evade government control. Bloggers can be arrested if they choose to reveal their identities, but for a host of reasons the government cannot shut down the Internet. The production and circulation of rap music as "underground music," for example, would be impossible without the Internet, file sharing, and mobile phones.

Mobile Phones

The mobile phone has provided a cultural space in which alternative discourses, cultural forms, and ultimately social transformation can be possible. Although by 2010 it was estimated that 50% of Iranians would have one, the recent arrival of cheap "pay-as-you-go" phones via Irancell, a privately owned company, has dramatically increased access. The implications are as follows.

First, although politicians have used mobile phones during elections to mobilize supporters, they provide a potentially threatening networking and thus mobilizing capability. Second, they have facilitated discreet relationships, especially among the youth, that are not always welcomed by parents or the government, such as dating and extramarital relationships. Third, they have helped blur the lines between private and public spheres by making private moments available to a wider public. Images and video clips of dancing in private ceremonies and other explicit contents have flooded cell phones via Bluetooth technology.

Fourth, they have provided a platform for protest and for bypassing or challenging the state's hegemonic discourses. As an example, after gasoline rationing was announced—this in a major oil-producing country—the volume of text messages was so great that the authorities temporarily limited access to SMS in some areas. There is a never-ending supply of jokes that diminish the status of the president or tarnish the aura of religious authorities. Video clips of an individual pretending to be an ayatollah while dancing was a popular file for some time. President Ahmedinejad was reportedly angered when he received a joke on his cell phone that said he did not wash himself regularly.

When the government recently celebrated the launch of the first Iranian-made communication satellite, cell phones were flooded with jokes such as follows: When the Iranian satellite reached Venus, it told her to cover her hair because space was now Islamic. Even popular programs on state TV are reinterpreted to challenge the authorities, as when one character's dream was restated as the president's dream, with a corresponding witticism.

In other instances, cell phones provided an alternative discourse altogether. To the government's dismay, many text messages celebrate pre-Islamic forms of Iranian national identity. Many Iranians exchanged messages to observe March 8, International Women's Day, instead of the religiously inspired day designated by the government.

In all these cases, we see a trend. Communication media such as cell phones not only challenge official media discourses, but also they contribute to the gap that separates the official media and culture from the larger popular "underground" culture. We should also note how alternative uses of media technology intensify the process. If audio-cassettes and other "small media" of yesterday facilitated the 1979 revolution, today's new media technologies enable an alternative cultural sphere that forwards the social transformation to a different, and hopefully better, future for Iran.

Mehdi Semati

See also Arab Bloggers as Citizen Journalists (Transnational); December 2008 Revolt Media (Greece); Kefaya Movement Media (Egypt); Mobile Communication and Social Movements; Social Movement Media in 2009 Crisis (Iran); Women Bloggers (Egypt)

Further Readings

Alavi, N. (2005). *We Are Iran: The Persian blogs.* Brooklyn, NY: Soft Skull Press.

Rahimi, B. (2008). The politics of the Internet in Iran. In M. Semati (Ed.), *Media, culture, and society in Iran: Living with globalization and the Islamic state* (pp. 37–56). London: Routledge.

Semati, M. (Ed.). (2008). *Media, culture, and society in Iran: Living with globalization and the Islamic state.* London: Routledge.

Sreberny-Mohammadi, A., & Mohammadi, A. (1994). *Small media, big revolution: Communication, culture, and the Iranian Revolution.* Minneapolis: University of Minnesota Press.

NON-ALIGNED NEWS AGENCIES POOL

The Non-Aligned News Agencies Pool (NANAP) was an international news exchange created in the mid-1970s by a coalition of nations organized under the broader Non-Aligned Movement (NAM). The NAM was a political faction of newly sovereign and developing nations that struggled for self-determination and for economic and cultural justice in the polarized Cold War period. NANAP was created to facilitate the exchange of domestic and international news produced by and for developing nations that sought to challenge the "First World's" global communication dominance. Facing Western hostility toward attempts to reform international communications regimes as well as increasing political instability within the NAM, NANAP faded away in the mid-1990s. In 2005, the NAM News Network, an online version of NANAP, was resuscitated under Bernama, Malaysia's national news agency.

The Non-Aligned Movement and News Dependence

The Cold War dominated international relations post–World War II. Both the United States and the USSR strained to expand their influence across the globe. Scores of new nations came into being based on former colonies. The political project of the Non-Aligned Movement (NAM) was forged from decolonization movements and was formally constituted in the early 1960s. Throughout the 1960s and 1970s, the NAM crafted an anti-imperialist political platform that defined Western economic and cultural domination as mutually reinforcing. In partnership with UNESCO, NAM launched twin campaigns in which peoples of developing nations sought self-determination in a New International Economic Order (NIEO) and in a New World Information and Communication Order (NWICO).

The call for NWICO emerged in part as a response to the global dominance of the Associated Press, United Press International, Reuters, and Agence France-Presse. Despite the fact that NAM countries hastened to establish national and regional news agencies of their own, global news flows remained overwhelmingly controlled by Western firms, whose much longer histories allowed for significant infrastructure and resource advantages. Collectively, those firms largely monopolized international news flows, typically focusing on stories of concern to the West. Framing information for Western audiences within a commodity model of news production, these agencies not only negatively skewed developing world realities, but also they created international news dependency on their product. Absent the resources needed to employ foreign correspondents, domestic news agencies and media outlets in non-aligned nations often had no choice but to rely on them.

The Non-Aligned News Agencies Pool

Through a series of conferences from 1973 to 1976, NAM leaders created NANAP as a practical step toward redressing global news imbalances. In 1975, news agencies in 12 non-aligned countries officially began using the NANAP for multilateral information exchange. Yugoslavia's Tanjug was the first national news agency to coordinate the collection and redistribution of news among non-aligned countries. By 1976, Tanjug reported that NANAP had 40 participating agencies.

Despite this, NANAP's deployment and uptake among non-aligned countries was perpetually uneven. A few well-established contributors produced large percentages of the content distributed. Such disproportion reflected the postcolonial material realities of news media and communications infrastructure and professional development within non-aligned countries. Nevertheless, by 1981, NANAP had 87 participants and was transmitting 40,000 words per day in four languages, although in 1978, the Associated Press was transmitting more than a million words a day in nine languages.

NANAP insisted that its purpose was to complement Western agencies, disseminating news to non-aligned nations about development issues ignored or misrepresented by Western agencies. NANAP was not a supra-national news agency itself but an exchange mechanism among non-aligned countries' news agencies, functioning as an equal partner in all Pool endeavors. NANAP worked via regional redistribution centers to which member agencies sent articles and photographs for retransmission after translation into English, French, Spanish, and Arabic. The Pool relied heavily on teleprinter networks for distribution. It was thus a hub-and-spoke operation, facilitating low-cost, entry-barrier transmission among non-aligned media outlets.

NANAP's Downfall

Despite apparent progress in its formative years, by the mid-1980s, the NANAP had crested. Its downfall occurred in the context of mounting international criticism, harsh developments in Western foreign policy, and broader historical disjunction within NAM as the Cold War came to a close.

Initially NANAP was largely ignored outside of NAM, but as it grew, the Pool began to garner strong opposition from policymakers, media executives, and news professionals within the dominant international information system. The main charges were that the criticized coverage of non-aligned countries by Western agencies simply reported their harsh realities objectively; that calls for NWICO were empty rhetoric put forth by authoritarian regimes to hide their intentions to suppress media freedom; and that all NANAP news stemmed from state-controlled sources and thus lacked credibility. In sum, the core argument against the Pool was that it ultimately worked to restrict the "free flow" of information in the world.

NANAP had also aligned itself with the call for NWICO, which was based on the argument that "free flow" actually amounted to one-way flow, dominated by entrenched forces. The hostility of Western news agencies toward NANAP can be perceived as motivated by a desire to protect their established monopolistic positions.

The late 1970s and early 1980s saw the United States grow increasingly hostile to UNESCO and the NWICO movement and, by extension, to NANAP. The Reagan administration and its allies put immense pressure on UNESCO to reverse its stance on international communications policy. The United States began to tie bilateral relations with individual countries to their UN voting patterns in attempts to strong-arm NAM countries away from group solidarity. Western mainstream media and conservative policy groups launched an all-out assault on the alleged UNESCO support for state-controlled news and restricting press freedoms. The United States and United Kingdom withdrew from UNESCO in 1984 and 1985, slashing the organization's budget and harming its credibility. This effectively pulled the platform out from underneath non-aligned solidarity on issues of communications reform and dissolved a key pivot of the NAM's political strength.

As the USSR disintegrated and the global geopolitical map was dramatically reconfigured, NAM faced political crisis. The founding principle of non-alignment lost its political potency as the United States became the sole superpower. As the NAM sought greater cooperation with the Global North to get integrated into the emerging global economy, priorities shifted away almost entirely from news flows and NANAP.

NAM had never constituted a cohesive political bloc. Within the coalition there were dozens of individual nations, each with various stakeholders. In addition to significant rivalries, cultural differences, and ideological oppositions, no consensus existed on how to define, prioritize, or implement international communications reform. Yugoslavia's collapse in the 1990s greatly undermined NANAP's viability by disempowering Tanjug. Absent Tanjug's contributions and leadership, NANAP grew rapidly weaker. By the mid-1990s, it suffered heavily from poor financing and lack of staffing, and faded into disuse.

In 2005, Malaysia's Prime Minister proposed a NAM News Network (NNN) to modernize the defunct NANAP and carry out a revitalized non-aligned communications agenda. NNN's stated mission was to promote news and information from a developing country perspective and be a working platform for a reinvigorated Non-Aligned Movement. Malaysia offered financial support and the services of Bernama, the Malaysian national news agency, to serve as NNN's coordinating body. Going live in 2006, the NNN website functioned as a central hub to which accredited news organizations from NAM countries could both upload and download their news items and photographs.

Matthew Crain

See also Alternative Media (Malaysia); Alternative Media in the World Social Forum; Alternative Media: Policy Issues; Indymedia (The Independent Media Center); Third World Network (Malaysia)

Further Readings

Boyd-Barrett, O. (1980). *The international news agencies.* London: Constable.

Boyd-Barrett, O., & Thussu, D. K. (1992). *Contra-flow in global news: International and regional news exchange mechanisms.* London: Charlie Libby & Company.

Indian Institute of Mass Communication. (1983). *News agencies pool of non-aligned countries: A perspective.* New Delhi, India: Allied Publishers Private Limited.

Ivacic, P. (1978). Toward a freer and multidimensional flow of information. In P. C. Horton (Ed.), *The Third World and press freedom* (pp. 135–150). New York: Praeger.

NNN: http://www.namnewsnetwork.org

Pinch, E. T. (1978). The flow of news: An assessment of the non-aligned news agencies pool. *Journal of Communication, 28*(4), 163–171.

Prashad, V. (2007). *The darker nations: A people's history of the Third World.* New York: New Press.

Rosenblum, M. (1978). The Western wire services and the Third World. In P. C. Horton (Ed.), *The Third World and press freedom* (pp. 104–126). New York: Praeger.

Tatarian, R. (1978). News flow in the Third World: An overview. In P. C. Horton (Ed.), *The Third World and press freedom* (pp. 1–54). New York: Praeger.

November–December 1995 Social Movement Media (France)

During these months in 1995, strikes and huge demonstrations, especially in provincial French cities, responded to the crisis of representative democracy and a global neoliberalism completely in thrall to the financial markets. Specifically, they constituted a counteroffensive to the government's attempt to discard the pension system. Moreover, students who rejected a proposed disruption of the higher education system, and new collective actors such as unemployed workers, undocumented workers, the homeless, together with the left wing of the traditional union federations (CFDT, FO, CGT), breakaway reform unions, and public service workers, combined to defend their pensions and social security entitlements. Leftists in traditional unions played a crucial role. Social struggles on such a scale had not been seen in France since May–June 1968.

This 1995 mobilization unequivocally opposed the shift to private insurance schemes, to selling off public services, and to the steady downward pressure on wages and household income. In riposte, the demonstrators demanded multiple rights: to education, work, housing, health care, and other services, often beginning with one of these, but always enlarging the terrain toward addressing every dimension of social life. Their explicit rejection of charity as a solution to social ills was an important precursor to France's vigorous *alter-mondialiste* (global justice) movement, which exploded into life a few years later.

With respect to media, this social movement was noteworthy on at least two grounds: in the first place, the coverage dominant media kept in place for the movement, and in the second place, the way associations and unions rapidly adopted the most recent communication tools, leading to new information activism repertoires.

As regards the first, media coverage of the events was symptomatic of the status quo in both French journalism and politics, in response to activist critique of France's social formation. How information is handled is in itself a political issue, especially in terms of whether public support is

forthcoming. The coverage in the dominant press and broadcasting outlets took pains to present the struggle as taking place between people hanging on to their "privileges," which were blocking the "essential reforms" needed to modernize a "frozen France (*une France bloquée*)." Major media instantly greeted the government's plan as a bold attempt to release France from its inertia.

The public did not see things this way, and the movement's birth was in part caused by a chasm between government and people, and equally between the people and the mainstream public sphere, which seemed to be speaking for the governing classes. Those opposed to the government's plan were typically defined as ill-informed and dim, and their organizations as a dangerous mob lost in the shadows of stupidity. Rejection of the government's plan was termed "loony tunes (*coup de lune*)," a "huge collective fever," a "phantasmagoria," a "carnival," a "schizophrenic slide," and "a movement in which reality is often fogged over by fantasies and the irrational," threatening France's prosperity and holding its citizens to ransom.

One striker went on record commenting that the media were caught up in their own reality, never allowing ordinary French people to speak, or only giving the microphone for 30 seconds to someone unused to public speaking. Indeed, as time went by, the movement began to be pulled from the headlines. One *Le Monde* journalist noted how other journalists wishing to report on the strike were looked at askance by their superiors. The evening before, the paper had announced the movement was running out of steam in the provinces. The mediacrats were blowing the whistle on playtime.

For the strikers, their pitiful share of prime time dwindled to almost nothing. From the end of November to mid-December, their voices never went beyond 10% of the pages devoted to the movement, and averaged just more than 5%. When they were referred to, the coverage varied from the picturesque to the anecdotal, individual subjective interviews serving to marginalize the collective issues in the conflict. Yet public opinion polls were pretty routinely supportive of the movement's goals, despite the dislocations caused by strikes.

The existence, however, of a unified front made up of activist networks that were geographically scattered posed a series of questions to the movement's organizers about how to organize collectively, how to finance the mobilization, how to shape it, and how to sustain a multi-polar movement. In response, associations and joint committees, more than unions, early on made decisive use of the Internet.

This facilitated multiple exchanges and the creation of virtual workshops to discuss and prepare mobilizations. It enabled alternative modes of marshalling skills and of developing new activist repertoires (e-mail calls to action, alert networks, virtual sit-ins, online petitions, and mail-bombing). It also permitted new cooperative methods of information production, circulation, and use, along with new arenas of public expression (websites, listservs, fora), all of them forming practical critiques of dominant media.

This phenomenon emerged during the 1995 movement, hardly at all conceptualized at the time, but forming the basis for initial steps toward political activism. For the first time, the Internet became seriously considered as a platform on which to argue for and justify social demands, and to ensure at least some coverage of political actions, in the attempt to expand the potential for public mobilization, and still more important to create public sympathy. Its capacity to circulate information and explanations allowed the struggle to transform people's uneasiness with the way they were forced to live their lives into a sense of injustice and scandal, and to anchor it in terms of basic tenets of fairness.

However, stressing the importance of horizontal networks among movement actors and becoming simultaneously producers and distributors of information were not to be equated to a comprehensive defiance of professional journalists. Although the Internet opened up spaces for public expression freed from established information production and distribution circuits, these were also perceived as potentially attractive to those same journalists. Activists were always aware that the principal forum in which their challenges were covered remained the major media, which needed to be understood as crucial players in any political mobilization. It was vital to try to engage those media, even if not to attract their political sympathy, in order to win public support.

Fabien Granjon
(translated by John D. H. Downing)

See also Labor Media (United States); May 1968 Poetry and Graffiti (France/Transnational); Online Diaspora (Zambia); Undocumented Workers' Internet Use (France); Women Bloggers (Egypt); Zapatista Media (México)

Further Readings

Acrimed (Action-critique-médias). Observatoire des médias: http://www.acrimed.org

Aguiton, C., & Bensaïd, D. (1997). *Le retour de la question sociale: Le renouveau des mouvements sociaux en France* [The return of class issues: The resurgence of social movements in France]. Lausanne, France: Éditions Page deux.

Brandily, M. (2003). *Le Monde* en 1995: Au service du peuple? [*Le Monde* in 1995: At the public's service?]. http://www.acrimed.org/article1107.html

Granjon, F. (2001). *L'Internet militant: Mouvement social et usages des réseaux télématiques* [The activist Internet: Social movement and uses of telematic networks]. Rennes, France: Apogée.

Neveu, E. (1997). *Sociologie des mouvements sociaux.* Paris: La Découverte.

Neveu, E. (Ed.). (1999). Médias, mouvements sociaux, espaces publics [Media, social movements, public spheres]. *Réseaux, 17,* 17–85.

OHMYNEWS (KOREA)

South Korea is frequently described as "the most wired country in the world" and, as such, as one of the world's leading "webocracies." *OhmyNews*, typically described as an "online newspaper," shares features with the Independent Media Centers but has different imperatives. Its aim since its launch in February 2000 has been to call on ordinary people to provide a form of reporting that serves as an alternative to the mainstream, conservative media while striving to ensure that the news site generates a financial profit. "My goal was to say farewell to 20th-century Korean journalism, with the concept that every citizen is a reporter," declared Oh Yeon Ho, the site's founder. "The professional news culture has eroded our journalism," he added, "and I have always wanted to revitalize it. Since I had no money, I decided to use the Internet, which has made this guerrilla strategy possible."

This "guerrilla strategy," as Oh has described it, has proven to be successful, not only in financial—which is unusual for an online news organization—but also in journalistic terms. As of 2010, most stories on the site—some 80%—were written by ordinary citizens (approximately 70,000) keen to try their hand at journalism. The content for the remaining 20% was prepared by 65 staff writers and editors, some of whom covered major stories, while others assumed responsibility for editing and fact-checking the material sent in by "amateurs," such as students, office workers, police officers, and shopkeepers. Oh's view was that reporters are everyone with news stories who share them, not some exotic species.

The site's founding principle—"Every Citizen Is a Reporter"—is that participants e-mail a news or opinion item (or a blend) regarding whatever topic interests them. Overall editorial policy is significantly fashioned by the emphases of the collective response, which means in a practical sense that diverse publics are shaping the news agenda. Citizen reporters are openly encouraged to identify stories neglected by mainstream media. The site's editors sift through approximately 200 items a day on average to rank them for relative newsworthiness before making a judgment about what prominence to assign them.

Priority items go to the top of prominent pages, whereas those of a more specialized interest are relegated to back pages (there are "basic," "bonus," and "special" items). Such decisions determine, in turn, the payment awarded to the citizen reporter. A highly valued item could earn as much as US$20, although a more typical sum would be a small fraction of that amount. Even for *OhmyNews* editors (mostly drawn from the ranks of citizen reporters), the sense of reward is greater than the payments involved. "We are becoming very powerful," Bae Eul-sun, a member of the editorial team, commented. "The pay is lousy, but it is very satisfying to work here because I really feel like I can change the world little by little."

The news site's reputation for investigative reporting was hard-won. Editors interact with citizen reporters on discussion forums, answering questions but also negotiating story ideas, angles, and possible sources. However, statistics gathered by the site indicate that approximately three quarters of citizen reporters were male and that the largest age group was made up of people in their 20s. This pattern has drawn criticism. Other critics have complained that little pretense is made of objectivity; rather, citizen reporters typically make their personal point of view explicit, thereby inviting a more dynamic relationship with the reader than that derived from dispassionate, conventionally professional journalism. Its advocates consider this departure from the bland strictures of impartiality to be a virtue.

In any case, *OhmyNews* did not assume any formal responsibility for the accuracy of content. Reporters posted using their real identities and with an agreed code of ethics (copyright for what they write is shared between them and the site). To date, only a handful of stories have sparked legal repercussions, none of them serious enough to test this policy. The site has also fallen victim to hoaxes and must always guard against public relations or marketing people posing as citizen reporters to try to pass off advertisements for a commercial product or service as news. Oh's policy was to put everything out there and to let people judge the truth for themselves.

Firmly ensconced as a household name in Korea, *OhmyNews* has averaged approximately 2 million page views each day, with major stories sending those figures skyrocketing. It was Oh's ambition to make the site the "epicenter of world opinion," a strategy that simultaneously informed *OhmyNews International*—an English-language site launched in February 2004—aggregating news reports from 6,000 citizens in more than 100 countries. Additional initiatives have included the introduction of "Thumb News" to facilitate visual content sent via cell telephones and the 2007 launch of the *OhmyNews* Journalism School.

Oh insisted that his primary motivation was to see the *OhmyNews* philosophy, namely "citizen participatory journalism," spread around the globe. This simultaneously reflected a political project. "OhmyNews is a kind of public square in which the reform minded generation meet and talk with each other and find confidence," Oh contended.

"The message they find here: we are not alone. We can change this society" (Schroeder, 2004).

Stuart Allan

See also Citizen Journalism; Citizens' Media; Internet Social Movement Media (Hong Kong); MediACT (Korea); Online Nationalism (China)

Further Readings

Allan, S. (2006). *Online news: Journalism and the Internet*. Maidenhead, UK, and New York: Open University Press.

Schroeder, C. M. (2004, January 18). Is this the future of journalism? Newsweek.com. Retrieved May 13, 2010, from http://www.newsweek.com/id/53873

ONLINE DIASPORA (ZAMBIA)

Electronic message systems are important forms of small media in many social movements. In some cases, they use an e-mail messaging system as their core communication system. Initiatives are announced and coordinated, and members are linked to each other.

Sometimes a group messaging system serves a more general communication purpose and only periodically functions for targeted social action. One example includes Zambia_group on Yahoo!Groups, used by Zambian nationals for both political discussions and information exchange. This Yahoo! group has been active since 2002 and was preceded by Zambia-list, which was created in the mid-1990s by two Zambian PhD students at the University of British Columbia using the university listserv system. In 1996, Zambia-list was migrated to a server at Abilene Christian University in Texas and in the late 1990s and early 2000s to a server at the University of Maryland.

Increasingly inexpensive service providers, affordable personal computers, and Internet cafés have enabled a dramatic proliferation of new ways of communicating, forming community, and maintaining diasporic identities. In 1997, at one of its historical peaks, Zambia-list had approximately 250 subscribers and between 40 and 60 daily messages.

In 2009, its successor Zambia_group had 320 members and approximately 30 daily messages.

The majority of regulars are Zambians in North America and the United Kingdom. Others include Zambians in Japan, Belgium, South Africa, Swaziland, and Botswana, as well as Zambians living at home. A vibrant online community of Zambians is fostered by this discussion group, similarly to Eritrean, Nigerian, and other diasporic communities.

Most online discussions are about the Zambian president, political accountability, government policies, the Zambian economy, and Zambian identity. Other postings include humorous material and discussions about world events, soccer, and religion. At several points, the Zambia-list ("Z-list") members banded together to write political protest letters to Zambian and international media outlets.

In 1995, the list was used to create a collective letter to decry the country's plummeting economy, political corruption, and violent political factionalism. The letter, drafted and revised on Z-list over several weeks, was signed by 40 individuals and was published in Zambia's leading independent newspaper, *The Post*. It called on then Zambian president Frederick Chiluba (1991–2002) to work harder to foster a healthy climate of multiparty democracy and to make a complete shift to a more transparent and accountable government. Chiluba was elected as Zambia's second president in 1991 in the nation's first multiparty elections since 1968.

For 27 years, Zambia had been ruled by its first president, Kenneth Kaunda (1964–1991). For most of that period, Kaunda's party dominated, with other parties being banned. The shift to a multiparty system in 1990 and Chiluba's election in 1991 promised a new era of democracy, but midway into Chiluba's first term, many Zambians worried that the political culture of the single-party state had not been fully eradicated. Although the Z-listers' letter did not have a direct effect, the themes it raised subsequently recurred in *The Post* editorials and other columns. It illustrates how online diasporas can put political pressure on their home governments and potentially play watchdog roles in national politics.

Debra Spitulnik

See also AlterNet (United States); Internet Social Movement Media (Hong Kong); Online Nationalism (China)

Further Readings

Bernal, V. (2006). Diaspora, cyberspace, and political imagination: The Eritrean diaspora online. *Global Networks*, 6(2), 161–179.
Spitulnik, D. (2002). Alternative small media and communicative spaces. In G. Hyden, M. Leslie, & F. F. Ogundimu (Eds.), *Media and democracy in Africa* (pp. 177–205). London: Transaction.

ONLINE NATIONALISM (CHINA)

Nationalism is fundamental to contemporary identity politics and is intensified by globalization. It also constitutes a defining dimension of modern Chinese politics from the 1919 May Fourth movement to the 1949 communist victory to the Chinese government's high-tech strategies. The year 2008 marked when China surpassed the United States for the world's largest population of Internet users. It was also the Beijing Olympics year, a global media spectacle akin to the 1997 Hong Kong handover, which provided ample room for the celebration of Chinese nationalism, inside and outside China—but equally for its contestation by Taiwanese, Tibetan, or Uyghur activists.

The difference between 1997 and 2008 is that a much larger proportion of the content and activities concerning Chinese nationalism have migrated from mass media to the Internet. As a result, the landscape of Chinese online nationalism has become increasingly complicated in ways that reflect crucial trends in the offline world.

The migration was not unique to China. Media roles in nation-building are well documented in the USSR, Germany, and Japan in the first half of the 20th century and post–World War II in newly independent nations such as Malaysia. The Internet's global spread means that national myths can be reproduced, amplified, and, in some cases, reflected on among a larger group of citizens beyond the scope of the political establishment. This is the general trend of "Internet nationalism," or "long-distance nationalism," as Benedict Anderson put it in citing the websites of exiled Argentineans.

The rise of Chinese online nationalism is a specific instance of this general shift. However, given the tight mass media control in China, online nationalism carries special weight. User-generated content in Internet forums has developed closer affinity to grassroots and alternative social movements because of the technical difficulties of censoring decentralized content. Christopher Hughes's seminal hypothesis of 2000 was that online nationalism might represent a rare opportunity for identity politics in China to go beyond the official line of "building socialism with Chinese characteristics" and, in so doing, break the domination of the party-state and official mass media.

The actual development of Chinese online nationalism, however, does not fit so neatly with the original hypothesis. For one thing, Chinese netizens, mostly in mainland China, have to operate within the media and social environment dominated by the traditional stakeholders. Many are members of the elite or the emerging urban middle class who benefit from the existing structure and, therefore, would likely engage in communication that reproduces the official line.

Is then online nationalism a truly progressive force or merely an instrument for conservative identity politics? Answers to this question vary over time and across issues, although the general patterns can be summarized in four basic transformations: (1) the gradual decline of overseas movers and shakers of Chinese online nationalism, and the rise of domestic "angry youth"; (2) increasing state influence over online nationalism discussions and subsequent collective actions; (3) the shift of online nationalism from political to economic realms; and (4) the surge of discursive practice, and simultaneous shrinkage of collective action into haphazard and unconstructive activities (epitomized by the so-called "human flesh search engines").

The Emergence of Domestic "Angry Youth"

Tiananmen Square in 1989 was one of the very first moments when activists deployed Internet and e-mail as powerful tools of struggle. That movement was not purely "nationalist," although nationalism played an essential role in it as in so many other social movements in China today. But most participants of the 1989 Internet- and e-mail–based mobilization process were overseas students studying in U.S. and European universities. Their domination in Internet forums, especially in discussion groups and mailing lists but also on websites and bulletin boards, was a most notable feature of Chinese online nationalism at this early stage.

This was also very visible in the web-based mobilization after Suharto's fall in 1998, when Indonesian mobs were reported to have committed serious crimes against ethnic-Chinese citizens. Much information used for mobilization against the reported atrocities was collected and circulated by overseas Chinese students following the Tiananmen model. Although some crucial information (e.g., photographs) was later proven flawed, the online campaign successfully led to small-scale demonstrations in front of the Indonesian Embassy in Beijing and Indonesian consulates in other cities, as well as in foreign cities with a Chinese student population. This was the first instance of multicity student protests in China and beyond, after the Tiananmen backlash.

The next turning point was the anti–North Atlantic Treaty Organization (NATO) demonstration after the bombing of China's Belgrade embassy in 1999, which produced much larger protests than the 1998 anti-Indonesian demonstrations but crucially saw the birth of *Qiangguoluntan* ("Strong Nation Forum," QGLT), a prominent platform of online nationalism hosted and moderated by *People's Daily Online*, the Communist Party's Internet division.

Until then, most outspoken online nationalism forums had been either outside China, maintained by overseas Chinese students, or in Chinese universities, whose scope of social influence was limited to a few campuses and to a small number of the elite. However, the rise of *Qiangguoluntan* marked a new phase in domestic online mobilization. Overseas students' leadership, with its own grassroots organization and alternative understandings of Chinese nationalism, began to take second place to Mainland dynamics.

This trend continued as online nationalism went through a quantum leap after 1999, not only in absolute numbers but also in terms of its broader impact on society and media, domestic or foreign. The trend was further fueled by a series of events like the 2001 U.S.–China spy-plane standoff, and recurrent issues over Japan's reactionary revision of its history textbooks. In a few years, a whole new generation of "angry youth" (*fenqing*) emerged as a stronghold of online nationalism, moving beyond the stereotype of a young man shouting slogans in Beijing or Shanghai.

Increased State Control of Online Nationalism

The 1999 birth of *Qiangguoluntan* signified a new era of heightened state control, both shaping nationalist discourse in cyberspace from the top down and hegemonically internalized in the minds of the *fenqing*. They can be hypercritical about everything, except nationalism itself, and their vehement attacks on alternative opinion—operating within state-sanctioned parameters—facilitate the attainment of state goals.

Qiangguoluntan's messages are constantly screened by *People's Daily Online*. The forum was originally called the "Anti-NATO Bombing Forum" (*Kangyi beiyue hongzha luntan*) but was later renamed the Strong Nation Forum. Although it has evolved over the years from a purely nationalist to a multi-issue arena, such as leftist discussions, anti-corruption, and other public issues, it remains one of the most representative state-run online nationalism forums. Moreover, *Qiangguoluntan* as a model of 24/7 surveillance and censorship over online discussion forums has been emulated by large commercial portals such as Sina.com, whose well-staffed "customer service" team is dedicated to filtering content that has gone beyond official limits.

Qiangguoluntan is one of the most obvious instances of multifarious state control over online nationalism. So is the closure of forums that used to host alternative nationalistic expressions, for example, bbs.pku.edu.cn and ytht.net. Another important indicator is the relative "silence" of nationalist mobilization for more than 3 years after China's 2001 accession to the World Trade Organization (WTO). Before, there had been at least one or two major online nationalist movements resulting in real-world protests. But during the WTO honeymoon, the Chinese authorities generally succeeded in managing cyberspace identity politics until a new anti-Japanese campaign erupted in 2005. In other words, the party-state was able to enfold Chinese online nationalism within its own agenda, be it under the headings of "peaceful rise," "harmonious society," or "economic globalization."

Events leading up to the 2008 Olympics again showed the hegemonic power of state nationalism in Chinese cyberspace, and its problems. This time, China.com, another website with considerable official backing, acted as a central node of connection among nationalistic *fenqing*. The perceived enemies included old foes like "Chinese traitors" (*hanjian*) inside China, who dared to challenge nationalist myths, as well as new ones like France, which has been seldom previously targeted but singled out this time because of the debacle of the Olympic torch relay in Paris and the support some French politicians gave to the Dalai Lama.

Again, overseas Chinese, especially students, played a prominent role during the global torch relay and in the campaign against foreign media epitomized by anti-CNN.com, a website designed to expose "lies and distortions by the western media" on Tibet. This was for practical reasons because the relay events occurred in foreign cities and average netizens inside China do not have easy access to international sources such as CNN. Most important, unlike in the pre-1999 period, the messages circulated among overseas Chinese, such as "CNN is a liar" and "Protect the torch as it symbolizes China's pride," were no longer alternatives to state nationalism. Even Chinese online nationalism outside China has grown to have more affinity with Beijing's version, following the general trend of increased official control, which is consistent with basic change in the entire society, not just in cyberspace.

A Shift to Economic Issues

In the first 3 years after China entered the WTO, there were undercurrents beneath the surface of simple "silence," despite apparently effective state control. One crucial transformation was the shift of online nationalism from political to economic realms, and from "hard" heroic street protests at critical moments to "soft" Chinese "banal nationalism" circulated in the everyday lives of Chinese netizens.

This banal nationalism is closer to Roland Barthes's idea of the nation as a myth that reproduces dominant ideologies than to the turbulent May Fourth movement's challenge to the political status quo. It is obviously more in sync with the state's emphasis on stability. However, even the flood of economy-oriented banal nationalism cannot guarantee perfect peace in cyberspace or in the streets. Every now and then, advertisements by multinational corporations (e.g., Nike and Citroën) or their products (e.g., Japanese computer games) were singled out for smearing China, Chinese culture, and the Chinese people. Although most of these are relatively low-intensity expressions with little power beyond the online forums, they provide an ongoing training ground for the *fenqing*, whose political libido is there to be activated in response to major events.

The shift to economic issues has led to large-scale consumer nationalism campaigns in recent years, especially the anti-Japanese and the boycott-Carrefour movements in 2005 and 2008, respectively. Some resulted in more violent street protests than others. Although few so far produced long-term effects in foreign countries, most nonetheless cause public relations crises for the multinationals. In this sense, the stress on economic issues added to the tool kit of online nationalism, particularly after China's WTO honeymoon was over. The Chinese state was now troubled by constant trade-related issues. Chinese products, from toothpaste to toys, were increasingly portrayed as "hazardous." These frictions fed into online nationalism.

Discursive Online Nationalism

As noted, the co-evolution of state control and web-based discussion led to the mushrooming of discursive online nationalism, accompanied by a general decline in collective actions. *Fenqing* are a telling indicator. They are angry because they are full of discontent, whose origins may lie in deep-seated problems such as unemployment and official corruption and have nothing to do with the national myth. But their discontent needs an outlet, and online nationalism may be a convenient catharsis in uneventful periods, while they are to be enlisted at dramatic moments.

Another indicator is nationalistic hacking, which was much more prominent before China entered the WTO, when spontaneous collective hacking or website jamming was a common part of online nationalism campaigns. An obvious example was the Sino–U.S. spy-plane incident that produced the so-called "first world hacker war." Although the hacking of foreign websites by Chinese nationals continues, the origins are more often traced to organized activities within China's Internet security/cyberwar apparatus rather than to the spontaneous networking of grassroots nationalists.

Nationalistic *fenqing* are often too cynical for collective action. When they act, it is difficult to have a broad consensus over time because the discursive process contains more catharsis for instant gratification than self-reflective deliberation about collective goals and long-term strategies. This mode of online nationalism development and its problems are most clearly shown by the so-called "human flesh search engines" (*renrou sousuo yinqing*), which hunt down individuals and/or their families perceived as enemies of China and punish them using whatever means.

An example is a pro-Tibet demonstrator who almost grabbed the Olympic torch in Paris. His photo was posted online, and within a few days, he was "hunted down" with his name, home address, and contact information, along with other personal information being exposed in Internet forums. An overseas Chinese student expressed sympathy for pro-Tibet protestors on her campus. She was also "hunted down" as a "traitor," and her parents' home in China was identified by the "human flesh search engine." The next day, a photograph of feces, supposedly delivered to her parents' front door, was posted online. Such is the molecularized "collective action" that represents the worst of Chinese online nationalism, so far away from the original hypothesis that the Internet might give rise to China's civil society with its own healthy sense of national pride.

Jack Linchuan Qiu

See also Alternative Media; Citizens' Media; Free Tibet Movement's Publicity; Internet Social Movement Media (Hong Kong); New Culture and May 4th Movements Media (China); Sixth Generation Cinema (China); Youth Rock Music (China)

Further Readings

Anderson, B. (1983). *Imagined communities: Reflections on the origin and spread of nationalism.* London: Verso.

Barthes, R. (1972). *Mythologies.* New York: Hill and Wang.

Billig, M. (1995). *Banal nationalism.* London: Sage.

Conklin, D. B. (2003). *The Internet, email, and political activism: The case of Tiananmen Square.* Paper presented at the European Consortium for Political Research Workshop #20, Edinburgh, Scotland.

Feigenbaum, E. (2003). *China's techno-warriors: National security and strategic competition from the Nuclear to the Information Age.* Stanford, CA: Stanford University Press.

Hughes, C. (2000). Nationalism in Chinese cyberspace. *Cambridge Review of International Affairs, 13*(2), 195–209.

Hughes, C. (2006). *Chinese nationalism in the Global Era.* London: Routledge.

Hung, C.-F. (2003). Public discourse and "virtual" political participation in the PRC: The impact of the Internet. *Issues & Studies, 39*(4), 1–38.

Li, T. (1990). Computer-mediated communications and the Chinese students in the U.S. *The Information Society, 7,* 125–137.

Smith, C. (2001, May 6–12). The first world hacker war. *New York Times*, p. 2A.

Wang, J. (2005). Consumer nationalism and corporate reputation management in the global era. *Corporate Communication, 10*(3), 223–239.

PALESTINIAN INTERWAR PRESS

During the British Mandate of Palestine (1920–1948), the Palestinian press shaped public opinion. It provided a platform for public discussion of national and extranational issues. Its growth and expanding readership reflected the intensity and importance of newspapers as an alternative medium of expression.

Neutrality and Partisanship

The Palestinian political system during this period was split between two rival camps: the *Majlisiyyun* (parliamentarians) and the *Mu'aridun* (the opposition). Presenting itself as a neutral party, the press served as a third group mitigating internal conflicts and disagreements. However, the two camps enlisted professional journalists in their power struggle. Eventually, newspaper publishers and editors, and even regular journalists, served as members of the various national institutions representing the Palestinians. For example, the Palestinian Executive Committee, which was founded in 1920 and active until 1934, included as members the most senior journalists of the period: 'Issa al-'Issa, 'Izzat Darwaza, 'Issa al-Bandak, and Boulous Shihada.

Despite its "integration" and involvement in internal disagreements, the press was critical of representative political institutions. At times, columnists advocated moves toward a tougher approach to the Mandate authorities, calling for the abandonment of collaboration and embracing more effective and even violent methods. The influence of the press increased with the weakening of the Palestinian Executive Committee, which dissolved after the death of its president, Mousa Kathim al-Husayni, in 1934.

Press Publishers

As a political family, the Husaynis represented a handful of Palestinian families engaged in newspaper publishing. During the Mandate, the Husaynis published several newspapers including *al-Liwa* (The Contingent), *al-Shabab* (youth), *al-Wihda* (Unity), and *al-Wihda al-'Arabiyya* (Arab Unity).

The Husaynis financially supported several journalists and editors, including Emil al-Ghouri. A U.S. graduate, he was instrumental in editing and shaping all the newspapers belonging to the Husayni camp after his return to Palestine in 1935. In addition, the Husaynis employed exiled journalists from neighboring Arab countries. The Palestinian press provided a haven of freedom for journalists such as Muhammad Chirqas, Othman Qasim, and Kamil 'Abbas, and other experienced Arab journalists who relocated to Palestine such as Khayr al-Din al-Zirakli, Sami al-Sarraj, 'Ajaj Nuwayhid, and Muhammad Chirqas.

The Palestinian press benefited from the well-established journalistic practices of Egypt, Syria, Lebanon, and Iraq. Motivated by strong commitment to pan-Arab nationalism, those journalists contributed to the intensification of the pan-Arab orientation in Palestinian press during the latter half of the 1930s.

Contested Issues

The Palestinian press provided a platform for debating contested issues and reflected a microcosm of local and regional politics. One issue was the ideological orientation of the Palestinian National Movement: local Palestinian nationalism (*watani-yya filastiniyya*), the pan-Arab national orientation (*qawmiyya 'arabiyya*), the pan-Islamic orientation (*al-jami'a al-Islamiyya*), or the Eastern League ideal (*al-rabita al-sharqiyya*). Another discussion centered on the relationship between Palestinians and British Mandate, also concerning the Palestinian position regarding the Jewish settlements.

In the 1920s, *Filastin* (Palestine) and *Mir'at al-Sharq* (Mirror of the East) represented local Palestinian nationalism. By the 1930s, Filastin retracted its support of this ideal and joined those stressing the pan-Arab ideal such as *al-Yarmuk*, and in certain instances *al-Karmil*. This tendency intensified with the publication of the newspaper *al-'Arab* (1932) of the al-Istiqlal (Independence) Party and reached its peak with the publication of *al-Difa'* (Defense) in 1934, as well as *al-Kifah* (Struggle) and *al-Liwa* (The Contingent) in 1935. The pan-Islamic current was represented mainly by *al-Sirat al-Mustaqim* (The Straight Path) from 1924 and *al-Jami'a al-Islamiyya* (Islamic Group) from 1932.

Until 1929, most newspapers printed a few hundred copies with the exception of well-established newspapers such as *Filastin* and later *al-Jami'a al-'Arabiyya*, which occasionally reached 3,000 copies. After the Western Wall Uprising of 1929 and the ensuing riots, the demand on newspapers increased as a reflection of the public interest in information and opinion. The large daily newspapers *Filastin* and *al-Difa'* printed an average of 7,000–8,000 copies. Other dailies such as *al-Liwa*, *al-Jami'a al-Islamiyya*, and *al-Sirat al-Mustaqim* typically printed 2,000–4,000 copies, and weeklies such as *al-Karmil* and *al-'Arab* printed 1,500–2,000 copies. During this period, sensational events and points of tension in the Palestinian national struggle increased the number of copies printed by hundreds and even thousands.

The press reached the height of its public influence during the Great Strike (April–October 1936). The demands of the strike were threefold: an end to Jewish immigration, a prohibition of land sales to Jews, and national independence. Although the strike failed to achieve its goals, the Palestinian press was successful in rallying leaders of youth organizations and political parties. The press also encouraged the wider public to pressure the traditional leadership to support the strike. The press and the leaders of the popular committees who joined it might be credited with the achievement of founding the Arab Higher Committee, which was one of the (brief) high points reached by the Palestinian National Movement during the Mandate period.

The relationship between the Press and the traditional leadership was antagonistic. At the center was the debate around the Jewish Settlements and the struggle against the British Mandate. From its inception, the Palestinian press mostly displayed opposition and hostility toward the Zionist enterprise and perceived it as an existential danger to Palestinian Arabs. This position was expressed mainly by objecting to the sale of Arab land to Jews and in promoting a social and economic boycott of Jewish settlement.

To clarify this danger, the Arabic press initiated a huge campaign against Jewish society, describing it as permissive, materialistic, and corrupt. As tensions between the Palestinians and the settlers intensified, the press spoke out against the arming of the Jewish Settlement and in support of organizing, training, and arming Arab youth. The newspapers praised actions of the underground groups in the early 1930s against British and Jewish targets, and even developed legends concerning their leaders.

The British authorities recognized the increasing influence of the press and did everything they could to limit and suppress it through a list of laws and regulations limiting the freedom of the press and of the journalists. During the Great Strike, for example, the authorities not only stopped at suspending the newspapers but also detained and exiled any journalist who expressed support for the strikers or for continuing the strike.

During this period there were approximately 253 journalists, 233 Palestinians, 19 from neighboring Arab countries, and one Muslim from

India. Approximately 187 were Muslims and 65 Christians; 190 journalists belonged to urban families from the three large cities, Jaffa, Jerusalem, and Haifa. Until the early 1930s, journalists from rural settings were a minority but their numbers increased considerably during the Great Strike as they covered the rural resistance groups.

Mustafa Dawoud Kabha

See also Independence Movement Media (India); Independence Movement Media (Vietnam); New Culture and May 4th Movements Media (China); Zionist Movement Media, Pre-1948

Further Readings

Abu Ghazala, A. (1967). *Arab cultural nationalism in Palestine, 1919–1948.* Tripoli, Libya: Institute for Palestine Studies.

Al-Kayyali, A. (1985). *Tarikh Filastin al-Hadith* [The modern history of Palestine]. Beirut, Lebanon: al-'Aqqad.

Ayalon, A. (1995). *The press of the Arab Middle East: A history.* New York: Oxford University Press.

Kabha, M. (2007). *The Palestinian press as shaper of public opinion 1929–1939: Writing up a storm.* London: Vallentine Mitchell.

Khalil, A. (1967). *Al-Sihafa al-'Arabiyya fi Filastin* [The Arabic press in Palestine]. Damascus, Syria.

PAPER TIGER TELEVISION (UNITED STATES)

Paper Tiger Television was founded in 1981 as a volunteer-based video production and distribution collective. The collective has produced hundreds of half-hour programs on media, cultural, and political issues, which have been exhibited regularly on public access channels and in university classrooms, museums, and art spaces. The Paper Tiger series has been one of the foremost examples of the use of public access television to create and distribute guerrilla video and intellectual critique.

The series began when producer and media activist DeeDee Halleck invited communication scholar Herbert Schiller to host a series of shows on the ideology and economics of the *New York Times.* Using Schiller's presentations as a model, Halleck organized a fluid group of videomakers into a collective, and followed with critiques of other major media outlets such as *Time* magazine, CBS *Evening News,* and the *New York Post,* usually presented by a single host from the ranks of academia, media and political activism, or production, from Donna Haraway to Simon Watney to Jill Godmilow.

The analyses were informed heavily by left social theory, political economy, feminism, and multiculturalism, often focusing on the media institution's politics, its links to corporate America through advertising and shared ownership, and its ideological range of representations. The productions were determinedly amateurish and playful, with handwritten graphics, painted backdrops, and camera work showing the production process involved. The aim was to demystify television as a technology and institution, and to inspire viewers to become producers, presaging the 1990s camcorder revolution.

Most episodes were shot live in New York and were originally telecast on a weekly slot on Manhattan public access, the usual opening credit being "It's 8:30. Do you know where your brains are?" With a small paid staff to handle administration and distribution, the collective was mostly operated on a volunteer basis, stressing consensus decision making, shared roles in making shows, and the virtues of collaboration with a range of cultural critics and other media producers.

Throughout the 1980s, the focus of the series expanded to encompass broader media and cultural issues, highlight the achievements of alternative media projects, and address specific political controversies. In 1986, the collective initiated and produced Deep Dish Television, which was the first national series distributed through public access channels, and it helped to develop Deep Dish as an independent, ongoing entity. Collective members in San Francisco and San Diego started producing contributions to the Paper Tiger series, and the group organized retrospectives of its work at the Whitney Museum of American Art in New York (1985) and the Wexner Center for the Arts in Columbus, Ohio (1991), as well as contributing to many other installations and screening series.

In the 1990s, the increased use of camcorders led to more shows constructed in the editing room and the decline of live production. The exploration of political and social issues began to take precedence over critique of media outlets, although the collective remained involved in organizing for media reform and public access systems. Paper Tiger members helped to produce the *Gulf Crisis TV Project* (1990) in response to the first war in the Persian Gulf, which was distributed nationally on public access and public television channels, and internationally on Great Britain's Channel 4 and other systems. Paper Tiger TV producers also helped to organize the alternative media coverage of the World Trade Organization protests in Seattle in 1999, telecast as *Showdown in Seattle* on *Free Speech TV*. The collective also ran production workshops for schools and youth groups.

Paper Tiger continues to create shows with a new generation of producers, who have plans to reintroduce more live shows while negotiating the new media environment of do-it-yourself production that the collective prophesied decades ago.

Daniel Marcus

See also Activist Cinema in the 1970s (France); Alternative Media Center (United States); Barricada TV (Argentina); Deep Dish TV (United States); Medvedkine Groups and Workers' Cinema (France); Workers' Film and Photo League (United States)

Further Readings

Boddy, W. (1990). Alternative television in the United States. *Screen, 31*(1), 91–101.

Halleck, D. (2002). *Hand-held visions: The uses of community media.* New York: Fordham University Press.

Larsen, E. (1995). When the crowd rustles the tiger roars. *Art Journal, 54*(4), 73–76.

Marcus, D. (Ed.). (1991). *Roar! The Paper Tiger Television guide to media activism.* Columbus, OH: Wexner Center for the Arts and Paper Tiger Television.

Paper Tiger Television: http://www.papertiger.org

Stein, L. (2001). Access television and grassroots political communication in the United States. In J. H. Downing, *Radical media: Rebellious communication and social movements* (pp. 299–324). Thousand Oaks, CA: Sage.

PARAMILITARY MEDIA (NORTHERN IRELAND)

Republicans/Nationalists wanted the region unified with the Irish Republic, and Loyalists/Unionists wanted it to remain part of the United Kingdom; both sides had paramilitary bodies. Each camp ran its own news media, which were significantly different in many respects from more mainstream news media. Between both Loyalist and Republican alternative presses on the one hand, and mainstream media on the other hand, there were three key ideological differences. First, alternative publications contextualized events historically. Second, mainstream news concentrated on the individual's role in the political process, whereas the alternative press insisted on the centrality and agency of "the people." Third, mainstream news discourse centered on consensus and the resolution of conflict, whereas the alternative press accentuated dissent and the inevitability of conflict.

The paramilitaries or their political allies printed and distributed irregularly, sometimes illegally, newspapers, news sheets, and pamphlets voicing their views. They revealed a very different picture of the conflict and the peace in Northern Ireland. No respecters of objectivity, they spelled out their message in stark terms and freely gave offense. They also displayed at times a remarkable degree of self-denial and some deeply contradictory thinking about political realities.

Yet, such alternative publications—however offensive or illegal—asked difficult questions about the peace process and its optimistic, liberal orientation, questions absent from official public discourse. Even a summary survey of their responses to key moments in the process gives insight into why sectarianism and armed dissent remained as direct challenges to visions of a new and peaceful Northern Ireland.

Two political events had a significant bearing on attitudes to the Northern Ireland peace process. The first event was local, the 1988 "Good Friday Agreement" that created the architecture of a political settlement and a return to regional government for the first time since 1972. The second event was global, the 9/11 attacks, and the ensuing "war on terror." How did republican and loyalist print media view these events?

The Good Friday Agreement

The Good Friday Agreement was signed on April 10, 1998, to international acclaim. Here, it seemed, was a model of conflict resolution that might be applied in other trouble spots around the world. On a local level, there was a remarkable degree of media consensus in support of the agreement. The three regional daily newspapers—the Nationalist *Irish News* and the Unionist *News Letter* and *Belfast Telegraph* all regarded it as an opportunity for Northern Ireland to break from its violent past. The local broadcast media were less explicit but nonetheless underscored the official preference for a political settlement founded on balanced representation.

With only a few exceptions, the alternative presses of Loyalism and Republicanism expressed fundamental opposition to the agreement and rejected mainstream media accounts as little more than official propaganda. A survey of these publications reveals some interesting contradictions and tensions not so much between as within Loyalists and Republicans.

An Phoblacht/Republican News is a weekly, paid-for newspaper that, throughout the conflict in the North, supported the armed campaign of the Provisional Irish Republican Army (IRA), and subsequently the strategy of Sinn Féin, its political ally, to search for a political rather than military solution. It was no surprise, then, that the paper welcomed the agreement as a "new phase" in the republican struggle. However, other dissident republican publications (e.g., *Saoirse*) rejected it outright as a "con trick," and one that merely "restructured British rule in Ireland" (*Sovereign Nation*).

On the loyalist side, *Combat,* a newspaper supportive of the Ulster Volunteer Force and its political ally, the Progressive Unionist Party, were alone in its explicit support for the agreement that, it claimed, safeguarded Northern Ireland's place within the United Kingdom. This interpretation was selective given that the agreement also guaranteed the option of a united Ireland if the majority of the electorate so wished, a provision that other more extreme publications were quick to highlight.

Leading the Way, a paper supportive of the Loyalist Volunteer Force, which opposed not only the agreement but also the paramilitary cease-fire of the time, warned its readers that they were just "a small step away from a United Ireland." Similarly, *Warrior,* published by the Ulster Defense Association, perceived in the agreement a "comprehensive time-linked programme of Rolling Irish Unification" (Autumn 1998).

The Good Friday Agreement came about amidst local and international factors that helped bring some antagonists around the table and made it difficult for them to back away. The unprecedented cooperation between the British and Irish governments, and the significant sponsorship of the U.S. administration, seemed to fit into the post–Cold War, "New World Order" of political and humanitarian intervention into civil conflicts in the Middle East, Africa, and the Balkans.

However, the 9/11 attacks shifted the global order back to confrontation and conflict. President Bush declared that countries had to decide whether they were with the United States or against it in its pursuit of the terrorists and their international sponsors. Let us discuss how Northern Ireland's paramilitary organizations translated the rhetoric of "war on terror."

September 11 and the "War on Terror"

Loyalists and Republicans viewed September 11, 2001, through the prism of local politics. Sinn Féin was being pressured at the time on the IRA's foot-dragging on turning in its weapons and its alleged links with the Colombian paramilitary group Revolutionary Armed Forces of Colombia (FARC). Throughout the summer of 2001 until September 11, Loyalist groups were getting bad press around the world with news of their sometimes violent picket of a Catholic primary school in North Belfast, where sectarian tensions were escalating despite the peace process. Mindful perhaps of President Bush's tough antiterrorist rhetoric, Loyalists and Republicans seemed suddenly anxious to disclaim the label "terrorism" to describe their actions over the decades of the Northern Ireland conflict.

Loyalist publications broadly welcomed America's determination to tackle terrorism so long as that also included the Irish Republican variety. The *Orange Standard* argued that given republican involvement with FARC, attempts by Sinn Féin to distinguish republican violence from that perpetrated on September 11 was "unlikely to convince any rational person" (October 2001).

The paper also noted America's ambiguous attitude to Irish Republicanism in the past but drew some comfort that the attacks would at last evaporate "lingering sympathy in the free world with terrorists of any kind" (October 2001).

On a similar note, the Scotland-based Loyalist paper *Red Hand* played mischief with America's pledge to exact vengeance on the terrorists and the countries that harbor them. "On the face of it," it remarked, "this does not augur well for Dundalk" (a safe-haven border town in the Republic for the IRA; October 2001). Not even the New York Fire Department (FDNY), who are recognized as the September 11 heroes, escaped Loyalist contempt. *Warrior* reported a street collection by local fire fighters in aid of the FDNY and reminded readers of the New York firefighters' historical sympathies for militant Irish Republicanism. It quoted a Loyalist spokesperson saying, "These people never held any street collections when innocents were massacred by the IRA" (October 2001).

By contrast, Republican responses to September 11, 2001, were more defensive and cautious. *An Phoblacht* condemned the attacks unequivocally, whereas a columnist wrote that those responsible "stepped outside the moral frame for resistance movements" (September 20, 2001). A later edition published Sinn Féin leader Gerry Adams's keynote speech at the annual party conference in which he described terrorism as "ethically indefensible," implying that the IRA was not and never was a terrorist organization. The only critical note in the paper was a warning against indiscriminate and short-sighted U.S. retaliation (October 4, 2001).

The Irish Republican Socialist Party newspaper *The Starry Plough*, however, struck a more strident tone, condemning both U.S. imperialism and the religious fundamentalism that inspired the September 11 attacks. Some Loyalists interpreted its opposition to U.S. foreign policy as evidence of virulent anti-Americanism in Republican thinking. The Ulster Loyalist Information Services Network (ULISNET) compared loyalist solidarity with the U.S. to the "slavish devotion (of republicans) to . . . various Palestinian terrorist organisations and Islamic fundamentalists." Republicans, it asserted, seemed happy to glad-hand corporate America at lucrative fund-raisers, yet still harbor "deep seated hatreds for America and an anti-imperialist analysis of American foreign policy" (October 2001).

Yet, Loyalism also had its anti-imperialist streak. The journal *Ulster Nation* argued that the "tragic events of 11th September 2001 are a direct result of Washington DC's hegemonistic policies . . . an attempt to impose a New World Order." In effect, Washington brought the assault on itself because of its "interventionism and arrogance" (October 2001).

Conclusions

With their instinctive attraction to liberal consensus, both commercial and public service media failed to register in public opinion a deep-seated unease and fear about what the Good Friday Agreement truly represented. This response was demonstrated in successive elections since the agreement was signed in 1998, with political parties once regarded as extreme eclipsing and then displacing the politics of moderate, constitutional Unionism and Nationalism.

By contrast, the alternative press seemed to offer a more accurate reflection of the political tensions and contradictions that perhaps explained the persistent crises that beset the restored regional government until the St. Andrew's Agreement in 2007. They were also much more critical in their analysis of September 11 and the "war on terror" than their mainstream counterparts.

Thus, alternative media sometimes articulate the opinions of diverse constituencies better than mainstream news outlets, which for political and commercial reasons have a vested interest in deferring to power and/or striving for consensus. This fact also underscores their significance as evidence for historians, social scientists, and media scholars.

Greg McLaughlin and Stephen Baker

See also Alternative Media; Murals (Northern Ireland); Peace Media (Colombia); Political Song (Northern Ireland); Tamil Nationalist Media (Sri Lanka/Transnational)

Further Readings

Atton, C. (2001). *Alternative media*. London: Sage.
Baker, S. (2005). The alternative press in Northern Ireland and the political process. *Journalism Studies, 6*(3), 375–386.

Baker, S., & McLaughlin, G. (2010). *The propaganda of peace: The media and conflict transformation in Northern Ireland*. Bristol, UK: Intellect Books.

Downing, J. D. H. (2001). *Radical media: Rebellious communication and social movements*. Thousand Oaks, CA: Sage.

McLaughlin, G., & Baker, S. (2004). The alternative media, the "War on Terror" and Northern Ireland. In R. Ottosen & S. Nohrstedt (Eds.), *U.S. and the others. Global media images on "The War on Terror"* (pp. 191–201). Oslo, Norway: Nordicom.

PARODIES OF DOMINANT DISCOURSE (ZAMBIA)

Parodies of state discourse in Africa are pervasive and are part of dynamic local verbal cultures. They are often related to other local performance modes such as indigenous theater, music, or oratory. As in these latter traditions, word plays, metaphors, altered intonations, and jester-like figures are used to launch both veiled and not so veiled political commentary. Parodic discourse is often central in social movement media such as cartoons, bumper stickers, and protest banners. Parodic discourse also enters into more diffused forms of critique that are not tied to a particular social movement. Parodies of dominant discourse often blur the line between playful humor and political contestation, between entertainment and biting critique.

In Zambia, key terms used by the state and prominent state-related institutions are common targets of parody. During the final years of President Kaunda's (1964–1991) rule, the country's national motto, "One Zambia, One Nation," was parodied in many forms, including: "One Zambia, Two Nations," to stress the extreme divide between the nation's rich and the nation's poor. A new era of economic liberalization and political pluralism ensued in the early 1990s with the election of Zambia's second president Frederick Chiluba (1991–2002). By the late 1990s, Chiluba's party's slogan "The Hour Has Come!" was reworked as "The Hour Is Sour!" to express disillusionment over the failure to deliver on campaign promises.

During this period, the acronym for the World Bank induced Structural Adjustment Program (SAP) was reinterpreted in the local Bemba and Nyanja languages as *Satana Ali Paano* (Satan is here), to highlight what were perceived as the disastrous effects of economic restructuring. Similarly the name of the Zambian government trucks manufactured by the former East German company IFA was interpreted as designating "International Funeral Association" and *imfwa* ("death" in the Bemba language), because the vehicles were involved in so many fatal road accidents.

In early 2001, President Chiluba, who was nearing the end of his second term, supported debate about a constitutional amendment to allow presidents to run for a third term. At the time there was a constitutional restriction on more than two terms. When supporters from Chiluba's rural homeland in the Luapula Province pronounced the English phrase "third term," it sounded more like *sadi temu,* reflecting the lack of "th" and "r" sounds in their native Lunda language. Opponents created a word play on the pronunciation and claimed that a third term for Chiluba would amount to a "sad term." The constitutional amendment initiative failed. Chiluba's chosen successor Levi Mwanawasa (2002–2008) ran instead and was victorious.

Some scholars argue that parodies of state discourse have little real impact on the course of events. Others claim that they are powerful forms of resistance in repressive environments. In either case, they are part of ongoing forms of political commentary at the level of everyday face-to-face communication, and they might be integrated into other forms of small media to amplify their force.

Debra Spitulnik

See also Audiocassettes and Political Critique (Kenya); Political Graffiti (Greece); Political Jokes (Zimbabwe); Political Song (Northern Ireland); Resistance Through Ridicule (Africa); Yes Men, The (United States)

Further Readings

Mbembe, A. (2001). *On the postcolony*. Berkeley: University of California Press.

Spitulnik, D. (2002). Alternative small media and communicative spaces. In G. Hyden, M. Leslie, & F. F. Ogundimu (Eds.), *Media and democracy in Africa* (pp. 177–205). New Brunswick, NJ: Transaction.

PARTICIPATORY MEDIA

The term "participatory media" signifies communication technologies and processes that *embody* ethical approaches to media production and distribution; these approaches are founded on inclusion and promote social justice and humanitarian ideals. Although the production process is central to defining media as participatory, their goals, technologies, organizational processes, and political-economic structures are also involved. Media systems function in similar ways to formal educational institutions, with the potential to instill hegemonic values or to encourage critical thinking. Praxis is a term used to describe the potential for research to inform action through the ability continually to articulate and answer critical questions.

Participatory media privilege an approach to human interaction that enhances the physical, social, political, economic, cultural, and spiritual well-being of all communities. Participatory communication engages in dialogue, leading to thoughtful action to facilitate our achievement of basic needs, as well as political and human rights. The broader political context has potential to facilitate as well as constrain participation. The economic context contributes as well through the allocation of resources to particular programs and institutions designed to foster the public good—or to limit social change, through redirecting resources away from public toward elite agendas. Following a Marxian model, some advocate participatory media to build collective resistance to overcome poverty. Freirean approaches build on this concern with economic deprivation to incorporate attention to issues of respect and dignity, raising political consciousness through dialogic communication.

Interest in participatory media emerges from a variety of approaches and strategies. Development communication approaches, which are often critiqued for promoting one-way government communication flows to citizens without response or dialogue, began in the 1970s to acknowledge at least rhetorically the need for more participatory strategies. Prominent critiques of the classic model also raised concerns about imposing Westernized models that benefited few while most continued to suffer and about focusing on individuals while neglecting structural motivations and constraints.

Thus, there emerged a growing recognition of the value of participatory strategies as more effective and more ethical than other social change strategies. As the term became more popular, however, the meaning of participation became more cloudy, used in a wide variety of ways to address many different agendas.

"Participatory": Its Varied Senses

In some models, the horizontal flows of information within and across communities are valued as the most appropriate way to engage in social change. Advocates stress the diversity of approaches that could be used, arguing against a universal trajectory of political engagement. Some refer to this as a "multiplicity" of participatory strategies. Through an optimistic lens, this model assumes that communities have the power needed to facilitate their own transformation. A more cynical stance, however, would suggest that although this form of participation might be necessary for social change, without adequate resources or strategic advocacy it would not sufficiently enable needed shifts in power relations.

Building on this approach, others value participatory communication for its potential to facilitate dialogue, not merely in sharing information, but in creating a space in which consciousness of oppression can be generated and acted on. This next level of action suggests a different agenda for participatory approaches, moving beyond internal communication toward a more critical stance against agents of oppression. To illustrate, a Friends Service Committee sponsored a Border Committee of Working Women project among workers in the *maquiladora* industries in México to advocate for better working conditions. Within small working groups, women were encouraged to share experiences of discrimination and to rehearse conversations to address supervisors. This framework privileges the potential for advocacy.

Growing interest in participatory media also emerged from those interested in alternative media, community media, and public journalism, as well as those working in social movement organizations. Attention to social movements situates social change within grassroots collective action, not the bureaucratic agendas typically advanced by development institutions. Community and alternative media privilege media production as a critical venue for public engagement. Public journalism shares these ideals, recognizing the importance of serving public interests.

A case in point was the Movement of People's Correspondents in Nicaragua in the 1980s in its initial phase, when villagers and urban workers took up reporting roles to convey a richer picture of national issues than professional journalists usually mustered. From this, we are reminded of the importance of considering the economic structures of media production and distribution, as well as a need for providing public space for perspectives not present in mainstream media industries. Participatory media offer a valuable resource as a public communication domain as well as a potential channel for asserting resistance and mobilizing action.

Given the variety of appropriations of the term "participatory media," diverse approaches to communication are implied. A "transmission" model is adapted to include participatory devices for building more effective communication strategies. A "ritual" model supports participatory media as a means to assert identity and community dialogue. A "critical" approach emphasizes the potential for participatory media to promote active resistance.

These models build on assumptions regarding the direction of information flows. Communication processes considered in participatory media models include attention to bottom-up flows of information, as well as horizontal flows within and across communities. These linear models of communication emphasize the value in providing technical information and support by sharing knowledge and teaching skills.

Dialogic Models

Other frameworks consider the potential for dialogue to mobilize support and communicate to authorities. A dialogic model values media for their potential to inspire individual reflection and collective action. Dialogue might help people with similar concerns build cohesive strategies toward resolving problematic conditions. Through this process, individual experiences can be viewed as a part of broader social problems, moving from episodic anecdotes toward illuminating broader patterns. To illustrate, one person's experience with unemployment or discrimination becomes more resonant as a collective experience when shared with others in similar situations.

At another level, dialogue between public communities and political leaders holds the potential not only to build more respectful policies but also to co-opt legitimate concerns into other political agendas. When direct meetings are not possible within constituencies or across groups, media might be used to approximate dialogue.

Given that dominant media institutions might foster hegemonic control over ideological production in ways that serve the political elite, participatory media serve a competing role in offering alternative perspectives. For example, the consumption highlighted through advertisements and through the status accorded to wealthy characters celebrates capitalism, which implicitly justifies extreme differences in access to material goods. To promote a campaign that people "buy nothing" on a particular day, in opposition to this privileging of consumerism, might require a noncorporate distribution mechanism.

Although some justify the importance of supporting participatory media instrumentally, the ethical foundation of participatory approaches operates as their distinctive feature. The moral justification for participatory communication more broadly finds grounding in the right to communicate, as a critical component of human rights and social justice. As identified by the 1980 MacBride Commission Report *Many Voices One World,* the right to communicate connotes an interest in respecting the dignity and equality of people in diverse environments. The rights to information access and production are included in this broader right to communicate. The principle of equality, which refers to peoples' abilities to participate in decision making as well as their access to resources, is underlined.

One clear division in approaches to participatory communication lies in the attention accorded to process over outcome. A process orientation focuses on causes of oppression, considering long-term strategies, and it follows the participatory model as an ethical end in itself. An outcome orientation, however, engages in participatory practices as an effective tool toward a particular purpose but one typically defined by an organization prior to community consultation.

An example of the latter approach is how some entertainment education projects use "participation" to justify holding focus groups, sounding out members of the public to determine what channels offer the best access and how messages can be sensitive to social and cultural norms. These informants offer their responses to the language used, the subject of information, the sources presented, and the symbols invoked. These campaigns are then typically redesigned, but their goal remains the same.

Organizational Processes

Participatory approaches to media production draw attention to the participants involved as well as to their decision-making processes. First, there is an assumption that members of the community expected to benefit should be constituents of the media production team. The involvement of local participants is believed not only to create more accessible and appropriate content but also to approximate an inclusive process of communication, based on the idea that all communities have a right to communicate, to narrate their own stories, to project their own images, and to engage in collective dialogue. Moreover, the decision-making process should involve a participatory model of power sharing.

Participatory media processes differ in the extent to which decisions are made by members of a community or organization and the extent to which those persons making decisions are connected with the beneficiaries. Community members might participate in decision making through representation on advisory boards, being hired or volunteering to work directly on projects, or being consulted on specific issues. Informants might help determine which problems need to be addressed, how best to implement projects, and how to assess their effectiveness. Each type and focus of participation implies a different level of involvement.

Within this process the question arises, how would outside media professionals contribute to or detract from the participatory process? Although some would advocate their exclusion to strengthen the work of the community team, others would allow outside staff and volunteers to contribute. This latter approach seems more palatable within a participatory model, once a clear decision-making process ensures that the authority to make allocative choices, in terms of budgeting and programming, does not exclusively belong to outsiders.

The specifics of the participatory process can be somewhat complicated, however. Often, the ideal of privileging local insiders is preferred to relying too heavily on "outside experts," who are believed to have insufficient understanding of and sympathy for local concerns and perspectives. Determining who might be inside as opposed to outside becomes challenging, however, when location alone does not deliver cohesiveness automatically. Gender, class, ethnicity, sexuality, and religious affiliation complicate simplistic boundaries privileging insiders.

Another process factor is the mode of decision making. Participatory approaches encourage discussions to be engaged in an inclusive, horizontal manner regarding the allocation of resources as well as program content. Media might promote local managers to encourage public involvement in media production. This involvement might also take place in the form of consultation with the public. A more far-reaching approach to inclusion would advocate self-management, such that public constituents control decisions over policies, finances, and programs. Shared decision making would be valued over hierarchy. This process of decision making involves a dialogic approach to praxis, in which collective consciousness recognizes oppressive conditions, giving rise to thoughtful critiques that guide reasoned strategic action.

Organizational processes include a need for accountability. Research and monitoring offer ways in which media organizations might make their work more transparent and, therefore, accessible to assessment. Participatory research involves a process of improving media production through incorporating assessments of media production, distribution, and reception. This research can take the form of monitoring, which encompasses describing decision-making processes to make them transparent for discussion, or of evaluating, which encompasses assessing the ability of media projects to achieve their goals. Within a participatory model, these approaches to monitoring and evaluating are designed to build on community knowledge as well as directly benefit community conditions.

Participatory action research begins by seeking collective analysis of problems and solutions, and then by exploring the conditions that might help support or constrain the potential of these strategies. The focus of research attention is not only within the community itself but also reaches toward understanding the broader power structures within which communities attempt to achieve their goals. In this latter vein, participatory research might be a praxis of resistance against economic, social, physical, political, and psychological exploitation.

Structural Conditions

Participation cannot realize equitable distribution of political and economic power unless structural resources support it. Funding structures as well as political decision-making structures contribute to these conditions.

Participatory communication relies on a political context in which democratic acts are supported, enabling listening as well as speaking among all people not just government officials, and toward the collective well-being, not just individual benefits. Considerations of power become important within broader contexts as well as in the specific situations of media production. Power over the ability to narrate histories as well as project perspectives might be contingent on access to media technologies, in addition to possessing the needed skills and opportunities.

Broader political structures have the potential to inhibit as well as facilitate participation. Some of the repercussions of the Kheda Communication Project, part of the SITE development program in India, speak to this issue. Project television crews encouraged rural informants to speak on camera of their experiences with exploitation and corruption. As the televised documentation of injustice began to air, laborers felt more confident in airing their grievances, and they initiated a strike to improve their wages. Consequently, these laborers' homes were burned, and the project stopped. Thus, when signaling resistance against those in power, participation can lead to devastating consequences.

Empowerment, like participation, holds a variety of meanings used by diverse groups. At an individual level, empowerment might refer to agency in interpersonal interaction, in resisting dominant ideologies, or in fighting against unjust practices. Empowerment might also signify greater collective agency in community engagement or organizational resources, requiring strategic allocation of financial and political resources.

Funding of media is assumed to affect both the processes as well as content of media production. Concern with funding structures might refer to the agendas of the funders, as well as to dependency on a single donor. Funding might entail private commercial institutions with profit as a central motivating factor, or government institutions, with particular political agendas supporting partisan rather than collective benefits.

The ability of Bolivian miners to sustain local public radio stations addresses these concerns with structural independence. For many years, these radio stations were supported financially and managed by miners' unions in the Bolivian highlands. Control over radio programming and content was facilitated through the economic autonomy generated by relying on volunteer staff and the workers' financial contributions. These stations offered a space for dialogue separate from that of the state, but notwithstanding that level of autonomy, many were intermittently subject to military attacks.

Communication Technologies

Current issues about the technologies best suited to participatory ideals concern their potential for interactivity and appropriateness in given cultural contexts. Historically, advocates of participatory models urged communication practitioners to value "small" over "big" communication technologies. Concretely, this meant supporting community radio stations over television networks. These debates tended to assume that the size of the enterprise, the number of staff and financial resources needed, and the range of reception might correspond better with potential for local control. Another thread within this broader argument is a concern for self-reliant, independent media production.

Appropriateness of particular technologies and formats within particular cultural settings is another dimension. Radio has been perceived as a particularly useful vehicle for participatory communication, in contrast to television, given its relatively lower costs and increased accessibility. Folk media, referring to channels and formats of communication strategies with an historical connection to a cultural community, might also be considered as offering more culturally relevant communication styles to particular groups. For example, some development strategies have used theater, music, and dance as culturally relevant folk media to entertain while educating audiences with a particular message. However, actual audience response is an open question, in that these performances can as easily rely on structured passivity among audiences, as on building in audience participation opportunities.

Interactivity is another central concern in promoting the potential for media to offer participatory and dialogic opportunities. For example, websites can offer a way for political agencies to transmit information about their policies and programs in a hierarchical flow of information just as easily as they might provide a space for feedback. For example, the internet offers a prime opportunity for some to consume male supremacist pornography and to engage in sexual harassment. However, websites organized in a way to allow for feedback allow many women to share information, to mobilize and advance collective actions, and to work against problematic dominant stereotypes.

Similarly, radio programs can transmit information in a linear fashion or offer public debate through call-in programs. Whereas some radio shows broadcast information giving time to government officials, others offer an opportunity for public questions and official response. The People's Parliament radio program in South Africa, for instance, allows people to call in questions and politicians to respond. The exhibition of films and theater performances has the potential to include discussion and debate, promoting these as springboards for more interactive dialogues. Folk media, such as puppet theater and musical events, might also be flexible formats for public participation.

Whether media technologies allow interactivity also depends on which messages are produced and how. If the content of the communicative message, whether channeled through a television program, theater performance, or website, is restricted to the perspective of a dominant organization, then participatory ideals of providing alternative perspectives are lost. For example, a Song and Drama Division financed through India's government might promote a particular vision of modernization just as easily as it might offer a vehicle for expressing concerns about oppressive practices. Television dramas used to educate as well as entertain can promote visions of social mobility that privilege individual acts of consumption and integration into

a market system; conversely, community concerns with political corruption could be leveraged into relevant dramas highlighting the importance of integrity and accountability.

More recently, cell phones and computers have garnered attention for their interactive potential, but historically, radio and video were favored for their participatory potential. Participatory programs have encouraged the use of radio and video, not only for being more affordable and accessible but also for resonating with oral traditions and for not requiring literacy. For example, a project employed in Newfoundland known as the "Fogo" process, using portable video recorders to record local concerns, shared these perspectives across island communities and then protested the destruction of local fishing businesses to government authorities. Other projects have replicated this program, such as the work of the nonprofit group Center for Research and Popular Education in Colombia, supporting local women's video production work.

Given a supportive political climate and economic foundation, media have the potential to leverage participatory processes of decision making. Contingent on how communication technologies are used to create an interactive space, participatory media might offer a valuable resource toward building and sustaining communities.

Karin Gwinn Wilkins

See also Alternative Media; Arab Bloggers as Citizen Journalists (Transnational); Citizen Journalism; Citizens' Media; Community Media and the Third Sector; Feminist Media: An Overview; Kurdish "Mountain" Journalism; Women's Movement Media (India)

Further Readings

Downing, J. D. (2001). *Radical media: Rebellious communication and social movements*. Thousand Oaks, CA: Sage.

Freire, P. (1983). *Pedagogy of the oppressed*. New York: Continuum.

Gumucio Dagrón, A. (2001). *Making waves: Stories of participatory communication for social change*. New York: Rockefeller Foundation.

Hemer, O., & Tufte, T. (Eds.). (2005). *Media & global change: Rethinking communication for development*. Göteberg, Sweden: Nordicom.

Huesca, R. (2002). Participatory approaches to communication and development. In W. B. Gudykunst & B. Mody (Eds.), *Handbook of international and intercultural communication* (pp. 499–518). Thousand Oaks, CA: Sage.

Jacobson, T., & Servaes, J. (Eds.). (1999). *Theoretical approaches to participatory communication.* Cresskill, NJ: Hampton Press.

MacBride, S. (Ed.). (2004). *Many voices, one world: Communication and society. Today and tomorrow.* Lanham, MD: Rowman & Littlefield. (Original work published 1980)

Mody, B. (1991). *Designing messages for development communication: An audience participation-based approach.* New Delhi, India: Sage.

Mody, B. (Ed.). (2003). *International and development communication: A 21st-century perspective.* Thousand Oaks, CA: Sage.

Morris, N. (2003). A comparative analysis of the diffusion and participatory models in development communication. *Communication Theory, 13*(2), 225–248.

Rodríguez, C. (2001). *Fissures in the mediascape: An international study of citizens' media.* Cresskill, NJ: Hampton Press.

Servaes, J. (1999). *Communication for development. One world, multiple cultures.* Cresskill, NJ: Hampton Press.

Trigueiro, O. M. (2008). *Folkcomunicação e Ativismo Midiático.* João Pessoa, Brasil: Editora Universitaria UFPB.

Wallack, L., Dorfman, L., Jernigan, D., & Themba, M. (1993). *Media advocacy and public health: Power for prevention.* Newbury Park, CA: Sage.

Wilkins, K. (Ed.). (2000). *Redeveloping communication for social change: Theory, practice & power.* Boulder, CO: Rowman & Littlefield.

Williamson, H. A. (1991). The Fogo process: Development support communications in Canada and the developing world. In F. Casmir (Ed.), *Communication in development* (pp. 270–287). Norwood, NJ: Ablex.

Peace Media (Colombia)

Various regions of Colombia have suffered for decades from armed violence from paramilitary groups working for major landowners, from narcotics traffickers, and from guerrilla forces. Many communities have been devastated by being caught in the middle. In contexts where armed groups corner unarmed civilian communities, citizens' media are essential in processes of peace-building; citizens' media strengthen democratic institutions, improve governance, increase citizens' participation, decrease corruption, and repair social fabrics torn by war.

The end of the cold war left a geopolitical landscape in which the predominant type of armed conflict happens within national borders. Interstate conflicts have largely been supplanted by conflicts between the state and armed antagonist groups, such as extreme left or right guerrillas, ethnic and/or religious factions, or resource-based mafias (i.e., cocaine, heroin, and diamonds). From 1989 to 2005, 90 intrastate conflicts were recorded, whereas the number of interstate conflicts and wars was only 7. As opposed to traditional interstate wars, generally waged among official armies, intrastate conflicts increasingly target civilians. Current conflicts involve issues of identity (i.e., ethnicity and religion), politics, and resources, and armed violence increasingly impacts civilians' everyday lives, local democratic institutions, and the cultural/social fabric of their communities.

Peace Media Initiatives

The author's research on citizens' media in contexts of armed conflict in Colombia found two different modes in which communities use local radio, television, photography, video, and Internet technologies. In moments of crisis, when local communities are victimized by armed groups, citizens' media help communities find crucial information about food, shelter, medicine, and other logistical support. In crisis situations, these media also serve as impromptu forums where communities can discuss how to respond to the crisis and make collective decisions. However, Colombian citizens' media pioneers insisted in interviews that their long-term peace-building efforts are more important than their response in moments of crisis. This entry explores each of these two modes in which communities use their media to buffer armed conflict.

In moments of crisis, when unarmed civilians are under attack by armed groups, these media play important roles meeting the communities' information and communication needs. The following three examples illustrate this type of use:

In an isolated mountain village high in the Colombian Andes, *Santa Rosa Estéreo*, a small citizen-controlled radio station mobilized an entire community when one of its leaders was kidnapped by a guerrilla organization. In response to a challenge posed by guerrilla commandos, the community radio station organized a caravan of 400 people who piled up in every available bus, truck, or car. After a 10-hour journey through mountain passes and guerrilla-built roads, the caravan reached the guerrilla camp. Men, women, and children set up tents and cooking fires on the central plaza of the guerrilla camp while leaders made their demands known. The civilians would not leave until the hostage had been released. The guerilla commandos were overwhelmed by the presence of so many civilians and decided to free their victim. The triumphant caravan returned to town where the entire village celebrated with a feast, dancing, and music—the sounds of which were all transmitted by the radio station. By disrupting the sense of hopelessness and impotence induced by indiscriminate attacks of armed violence on civilians, the radio station facilitated a series of communication processes that restored feelings of self-reliance and solidarity that ultimately allowed this community to overcome the crisis through collective action.

In December 2001, the town of Belén de los Andaquíes in southern Colombia was attacked by the Revolutionary Armed Forces of Colombia (FARC)—the main guerrilla group operating in the country. Residents were terrified by gunfire, explosives, and the presence of hundreds of armed guerrilla in the small downtown. People hid under their beds, locked their doors, and surrendered to the fear and isolation imposed by war. In the middle of the chaos of combat, *Radio Andaquí*, the local community radio station, opened an alternative communication space. Transmitting traditional Colombian Christmas carols and asking people to turn up the volume in their receivers, the radio station created an alternative to fear and isolation. Soon, dozens of civilians had come out onto the central plaza waving white flags. The Christmas carols, transmitted by the station and amplified by the church's loudspeakers and people's home radios, created a "symbolic shield" that allowed people to overcome the terrifying effects of violence. The radio station was able to generate a sense of togetherness and collective agency in the community, successfully countering the fear and isolation wrought by violence.

In 2000, for several weeks the FARC imposed a regime in which all economic and transportation activities had to stop in the Colombian southern region of Putumayo. In an effort to support their listeners, eight community radio stations linked their broadcastings and made their microphones available to local communities. In situations where people lost contact with loved ones, relatives, friends, and neighbors used the linked broadcastings to send messages from one part of the region to another, informing each other of their whereabouts, and thus reassuring each other. A community radio station called *La Hormiga* (The Ant) facilitated a discussion among schoolteachers as they tried to make decisions on how to continue the school year despite the difficult conditions. *Ocaína Estéreo*, another community radio station, helped the community locate and bring in scarce food and medicines; once the food had reached local stores, the station monitored prices, thus preventing store-owners from taking advantage of the crisis situation by hiking food prices.

Combating the Culture of War

War's impact on civilian communities, though, is not limited to direct attacks. Armed groups recruit the children of these communities and inject massive doses of mistrust, individualism, fear, suspicion, and uncertainty into the people's lives. Armed groups replace the rule of law by the use of force. Local democratic institutions are weakened. Armed groups corrupt, co-opt, or threaten local government officials. Levels of impunity increase, and governance and accountability are replaced by corruption and bribery. Local elections are bought out or boycotted by armed groups. Warring factions impose friend/foe ideologies that diminish citizens' participation in local decision-making processes. Tanks invade public spaces, sand trenches are dug, and armed men patrol parks and plazas, severely restricting freedom, mobility, and people's use of social spaces to create and maintain social bonds. The presence of armed groups erodes traditional bonds of solidarity, togetherness, and trust among civilian communities; armed groups commonly recruit informants and supporters among civilians. Individuals and families learn to mistrust neighbors, friends, and distant relatives, and they descend into severe states of isolation. As isolation and terror mount, feelings of impotence and victimization overcome civilians. Weapons and aggression are normalized. Managing and resolving everyday life conflicts by force and weapons is perceived as normal and effective. Intolerance of difference increases extremist and sectarian ideologies. Armed groups impose militaristic regimes that opt to annihilate anyone with different views, opinions, or beliefs.

Little by little, war erodes the social, democratic, and cultural fabric when civilian communities have to live side by side with armed groups for years. If well designed, citizens' media can help repair the devastation of armed violence in the everyday lives of civilians. First, when in the hands of the people, information and communication technologies (ICTs) can become powerful tools allowing civilian communities to strengthen processes of good governance, transparency, and accountability. A local election overseen by a community radio station, or a public budget scrutinized by civic groups in front of community television cameras, increase the legitimacy of public institutions. These media technologies have the potential to transform private political and institutional processes into public sphere events, thereby solidifying people's trust in democratic institutions and the rule of law.

Three Dimensions of Peace Media Activism

The first dimension concerns these media and the democratic process. The second is their operation as agents in the constructive "stealing away" of young people from a cultural dynamic of normalized violence and militarization. The third is the opportunity they give the adult community to reinterpret their bitter experiences of being caught up in protracted armed conflict, and to reduce their mutual isolation born of terror. For example as regards the democratic process, AREDMAG, a network of 19 municipal community radio stations in the Colombian region of Magdalena Medio,

created and maintains a series of radio broadcasts that strengthen local democratic elections, citizens' participation in local government and collective decision-making processes, and citizens' monitoring of local government officials. *La Trocha Ciudadana* (The Citizens' Path) is a program that explains the government agendas and platforms of each candidate in local elections for municipal mayor and local commissioner. The program insists that voting is an action of great privilege and responsibility, thus encouraging citizens to take their vote seriously and advising against selling one's vote. *Rediciones de Cuentas* (Public Bookkeeping) are live broadcasts in which local mayors explain in public how municipal budgets were spent in the last 6 months. When a mayor is reluctant to hold a public bookkeeping session, community radio stations broadcast daily messages insisting that the community is waiting for it.

There were numerous cases of weekly radio and television programs produced by citizens who take on the role of overseers of local government institutions. *La Cantaleta* (The Tirade), a program led by Doña Marta Calderón in Caquetá; *Chachareano* in Magdalena Medio; and weekly programs in *Custodia Estéreo* in Guainía monitor every corner of their communities, watching for new potholes in the streets, denouncing malfunctioning streetlights, or criticizing mediocre trash collection. Programs such as these strengthen the rule of law and the notion that peaceful coexistence is strongly associated with citizens' participation in decision-making processes, good governance, accountability, and transparency on the part of local governments. It was evident that good communication between governments and the people they govern is the number one condition to peace building. When citizens' media open up to these self-appointed community watchdogs, their monitoring talent becomes an asset for the entire community.

Second, it may be said that Colombian citizens' media "steal" children and youth from war and cultivate ideologies of peaceful coexistence well grounded on local cultures. Most citizens' media initiatives in the author's year-long research heavily involved children and youth. The *Colectivo de Comunicaciones de Montes de María* offer video, television, and radio production training to hundreds of local children and youth; AREDMAG, a community radio network in Magdalena Medio, includes several radio production collectives in local schools as well as weekly radio programs produced by children and youth; similarly, "stealing" children and youth from armed groups and involving them in their own media productions are the main goals of *Radio Andaquí* and the *Escuela Audiovisual Infantil de Belén de los Andaquíes* in Caquetá and also of *Custodia Estéreo*, a school radio station in Inírida, Guainía.

When citizens' media are truly open to participation and profoundly grounded on local knowledge, languages, and aesthetics, they become powerful tools to keep children and youth away from armed groups. Repeatedly, in regions engulfed in armed conflict, children and youth involved in their own media production opt for nonaggressive ways of being and interacting, learn to appreciate difference and to manage conflict in peaceful ways, and greatly improve their academic performance. In general, these children tend to become community leaders, deeply committed to building a peaceful future for their communities, and passionate about the well-being of their local cultures and local environments (children who grow up exploring their communities through the lens of a camera or recording the sounds of their natural environments with a microphone and a recorder tend to fall in love with their local culture and nature). Citizens' media well grounded in local schools or working in strong alliances with local schools are particularly well positioned to reach out to children and youth.

Third, as tools designed precisely to craft symbolic products and processes, ICTs occupy a privileged position in helping communities reconstitute symbolic universes that have been disrupted by violence. In producing their own radio, video, or television programming, civilian communities can begin reconstituting webs of meaning, allowing them to make sense of their experience of armed conflict and war. When communities have access to their own media and can develop their own communication competences as media producers, they can use citizens' media to narrate, interpret, remember, and share the lived experience of violence. Citizens' media facilitate communication processes in which civilians recreate traditional solidarities and form new solidarities, return to public places once abandoned in terror, and organize collective actions. ICTs trigger communal processes that, one step at a time, bring civilians out of the isolation and terror imposed by armed violence and back into the public sphere.

In contexts of war, unarmed civilian communities use communication and media to repair that which armed violence has shattered. People whose lives are woven with violence use these media to resist and overcome the negative impact of war. It is critical to maintain a keen awareness of the centrality of cultural issues in our efforts to understand both armed violence and peace-building initiatives by local communities. We must recognize the ways armed violence impacts the cultural and social fabric of communities, and how civilians use culture, communication, and media to overcome this violence.

Clemencia Rodríguez

See also Citizens' Media; Feminist Media: An Overview; Human Rights Media; Indigenous Peoples' Media; Radio Andaquí and the Belén Media School (Colombia)

Further Readings

Aqrabawe, T. Internews Network—Afghanistan: http://www.internews.org

Center of Innovation for Media, Conflict, and Peacebuilding, U.S. Institute of Peace: http://peacemedia.usip.org

Common Ground Production—Search for Common Ground—global: http://www.sfcg.org/programmes/cgp/programmes_cgp.html

El Gazi, J., & Duplat, T. CaracolaConsultores—Colombia: http://www.caracolaconsultores.com

Rolt, F. Radio for Peace Building—West and Central Africa and Sri Lanka: http:// www.radioforpeace building.co.uk

Siemering, B. Developing Radio Partners—Mongolia, Sierra Leone, Southern Africa: http://www .developingradiopartners.org

PERFORMANCE ART AND SOCIAL MOVEMENT MEDIA: AUGUSTO BOAL

Augusto Boal was a theater practitioner and theorist responsible for developing a system of innovative sociopolitical, interactive, and proactive performance methods designed to empower oppressed groups to both recognize how oppressive power structures function and engage in performances of social resistance. In addition to organizing social action among marginalized groups, Boal's theatrical techniques are used internationally in "educational, communal, and therapeutic contexts" to teach historically privileged and marginalized people about the intricacies of power deployment among dominant ideological systems.

Whereas several social movement theories involve direct political action on behalf of their actors (e.g., dramaturgical analysis), most often carried out in public social spheres, Boal's theatrical *contexts* define the social movement. In other words, Boal's techniques function as a rehearsal process where individuals practice resisting oppressive ideological structures to define their practices of resistance in everyday life. In Boal's terms, performance provides a space where "a catharsis of the revolutionary impetus is produced" and "dramatic action substitutes for real action" (Boal, 1985, p. 155). His work was related closely to fellow Brazilian activist Paulo Freire's vision of educational transformation.

History and Political Climate

Responding to the oppressive politics of a series of military-based Brazilian governments that held power from 1964 through 1985, Boal sought to reinvent the role of the theater in São Paulo, Brazil. In the early 1950s, the dominant local theater scene had been dominated by the esthetics of Teatro Brasileiro de Comédia, which was theater "made by those who have money, to be seen also by those who have it" (Boal, 1985, p. 160). From 1956, *The Arena Theater*, where Boal first experimented with his theatrical techniques aimed at revolutionary change, went through many incarnations and ultimately became a venue for Brazilian playwrights to talk about Brazil to a Brazilian audience. During this time, Arena closed its doors to European playwrights and staged several plays that critiqued the Brazilian government, as well as the right-wing politics of South America at large. Notable performances included Boal's *Revolution in South America* and Roberto Freire's *People Like Us*. These plays, as well as most of the plays Arena

produced, functioned as political resistance in theatrical form.

In 1971, Arena's members were targeted by military dictator General Garrastazu Médici for their blatant refusal to obey recently imposed censorship laws. Boal was arrested, imprisoned, and tortured. The evidence against him was a list of adjectives: subversive, rebellious, and author of antigovernment texts. After a series of letters addressed to the government arrived demanding Boal's release (several internationally), he was exiled and traveled to Buenos Aires. Soon after, Arena shut down. Boal spent the next 5 years in Argentina, where he produced many plays and published what is arguably his most influential text, *Theatre of the Oppressed*.

Theatre of the Oppressed

Unsatisfied with the extent to which he had included his audiences in his productions in his earlier work at Arena, Boal developed a genre of theater that he called Theater of the Oppressed (TO). Boal's theatrical system broke down traditional dramatic structures (e.g., audience and performer, character and actor) in an attempt to demonstrate how oppressed and/or marginalized people could use theater to attack the ruling classes' control. Thus, the "Joker" system was born.

Boal proposed that the Joker system synthesized all the experiments carried out at Arena and coordinated them in a collaborative effort between a facilitator of a theatrical experience, which Boal calls the Joker, and "the people," those who are deeply constrained by the social conditions of their time. He positioned TO as a "weapon to be wielded by the people" and a "rehearsal of revolution."

Philosophical Origins of TO

TO, in its form and function, critiqued traditional dramatic modes borrowed from Aristotelian tragedy. Boal considered Aristotelian theater, and Aristotle's view of poetics in general, "coercive" in that it assumed an apolitical relationship between theater and politics. Aristotle's error, in Boal's view, was his failure to recognize the inherent political choice involved in arguing for a separation between poetics and politics. Boal argues that Aristotelian tragedy relies on, reflects, and ultimately supports the way that power plays itself out within hierarchical social structures.

In place of Aristotle's approach, Boal drew heavily on Brechtian criticisms of theater and fashioned a "theatre made by and for the people." Whereas traditional theater would use a cast of actors to provide an aesthetic that seemingly "reflected" current social systems through a traditional dramatic structure (plot, setting, mood, character, etc.), Boal integrated his audiences into the production.

He used a method called trigger scripting, which facilitates communication between audiences and actors and provides a structural method through which performance scripts are created during the performance itself. In TO, audience members are encouraged to stop the production if they view something problematic emerge, such as a poor representation of a marginalized person, or an insufficient response to an oppressive gesture. Not unlike the conventions of Newspaper Theater, Forum Theater, or Playback Theater, audience members might step into the scene and demonstrate a correct portrayal of, or response to, the given issue within the scene.

Boal insisted the point is to "change the people—'spectators,' passive beings in the theatrical phenomenon, into subjects, into actors, transformers of the dramatic action." This involvement produces what he called the "liberated spectator," a spectator who launches into action. In an interesting shift from how social action is traditionally perceived, Boal argued, "No matter that the action is fictional; what matters is the action!" (Boal, 1985, p. 122).

ALFIN

A well-documented use of TO as an "organizing" force took place in the cities of Lima and Chiclayo, Perú. *Operación Alfabetización Integral* (Operation Total Literacy, ALFIN) was a 1973 campaign launched by Perú's then-revolutionary government. Boal's task was difficult in that he was working with a population with more than 45 different languages. Aside from teaching Spanish, the government was interested in introducing artistic language into the mix so people could use other forms of speaking to express themselves and address their problems. This form of theater, or *simultaneous*

dramaturgy, was used by *The Arsenal* (Boal's term for his performers and the theatrical techniques they employed) as a mechanism that could function as a "sum of all imaginable languages." Boal worked with groups enrolled in ALFIN to demonstrate how theater could be a language through which marginalized people could speak.

He developed a series of techniques designed to empower participants to become agents in their quest for literacy. One method through which this occurred was entitled *Breaking of Oppression.* To clarify the context of this method, Boal uses the term *repression* to refer to a specific action carried out by a body acting on behalf of an oppressive structure on a body that is a victim of that structure. Boal asked the participants to remember a time when they were repressed by a dominant system (e.g., masculinism and capitalism), embodied that repression, and then performed it against their will. The participants were then instructed to stage a scene with other actors that reflected that moment.

After the scene ended, the group members were asked to restage the scene, this time rejecting the repression. A discussion followed the performance, whose function was to devise strategies for combating such repression in everyday life. The goal of *Breaking of Oppression* was to teach participants the relationship between the phenomenon (the scene), in this case the moment where one was repressed—perhaps because of literacy issues—and the legal system, in other words, how hierarchical systems repress the power of marginalized people.

Boal in Europe

After the 1975 death of Argentinean President Juan Perón, the political climate in Argentina became dangerous for Boal because of his teachings of resistance and outspoken critiques of the government. He self-exiled to Lisbon in 1976. After 2 years and a difficult time securing funding from the Ministries of Culture and Education, Boal then took a lecturer position at the Sorbonne.

Feeling a sense of freedom and opportunity in Paris, Boal immediately established The Center for the Theater of the Oppressed (CTO). This allowed him to experiment with the potential of his methods outside their original sociopolitical contexts.

Although still concerned with issues of oppression, Boal's next venture considered how oppression manifests itself psychologically. *The Rainbow of Desire: A Boal Method of Theatre and Therapy* relocated Boal's previous theory from the socio-political to the socioindividual, to the individual-political, and back again. Best understood as a form of new social movement and most likely influenced by his European context, *Rainbow of Desire* addressed oppression in broader and perhaps more responsible terms than Boal's previous work.

In his book by the same name, Boal told a story of how his previous methods had failed to translate to several of his audiences. One story in particular, the story of Virgilio, demonstrates the failure of the mobilization strategies that appeared in Boal's earlier work. Boal's theater often contained a violent message, a violence aimed at subverting oppressive governments. In one production, Boal and his cast sang of "letting the blood spill" to a group of marginalized people. After the show, Virgilio approached Boal and suggested that they do just that, they "let the blood spill." Virgilio asked Boal and his cast to join him in taking arms against the oppressive government and that they do it that day after lunch.

Boal tried to explain to Virgilio that his weapons were merely theater and that he had no intentions of killing anyone, but he was pressed by his audience to act on behalf of his message. Boal told them that he did not actually know how to shoot and that he felt as if his involvement would be little more than a hindrance to them.

Boal recounted that moment to describe a turning point in his practice as well as his recognition of his privileged position as a theater practitioner who spoke of revolution in broad and metaphorical terms. Boal was a White male with a PhD from Columbia University, and his cast of performers at the time, *The Arsenal*, were also white men. After this incident, Boal stepped away from broad definitions of oppression and decided to consider how individual bodies might react to such messages, even when they are presented in theatrical form. Boal never again wrote plays that gave advice.

Boal's work entered into a self-critical stage, where he focused on combating the "cop in the head." Maintaining TO as his theatrical base, his techniques began to focus on combating systems of oppression as they manifest in fear and emptiness from within, through group interactions.

Legislative Theatre

In 1986, when military rule was over, Boal returned to Brazil on a 6-month contract with the government to use TO methods to strengthen public education. In 1989, he established The Center for the Theatre of the Oppressed (CTO) in Rio de Janeiro. However, in 1992, CTO Rio had to disband because of a lack of funding. In a gesture that was supposed to function as a send-off for the organization, Boal ran in the presidential election, using TO methods as campaigning strategies. Initially, Boal felt as if he had no chance of winning, but TO caught the attention of the newspapers and other media because of its imagistic, theatrical form. CTO Rio gained popularity with their methods, which focused on giving audiences a voice through theater in legislative decisions. CTO campaigned throughout Rio de Janeiro with the goal of transforming the public's priorities into law. The campaign was ultimately successful, and Boal was elected as one of six members of a leftist party on Rio's city council from 1992 to 1996.

Boal's status provided a means to fund CTO Rio and allowed Legislative Theatre to move beyond a method of campaigning. *The Arsenal* provided a space for the people of Rio to address their community concerns by workshopping solutions to their problems. Boal believed that a legislature should not make laws for the people, but it should instead be a governing body though which the public makes laws. As of the end of the first decade of the 2000s, CTO Rio was actively practicing the methods aimed at providing a space for the oppressed citizens of Rio de Janeiro to dialogue about their situations in legislative and community arenas. In 2008, he was nominated for a Nobel Peace Prize for his international efforts to fight oppression. He died in May 2009.

Jake Simmons

See also Adbusters Media Foundation (Canada); Chipko Environmental Movement Media (India); Environmental Movement Media; Indian People's Theatre Association (India); Installation Art Media; Madang Street Theater (Korea); Music and Social Protest (Malawi); Social Movement and Modern

Dance (Bengal); Street Theater (Canada); Street Theater (India)

Further Readings

Babbage, F. (2004). *Augusto Boal*. New York: Routledge.

Boal, A. (1985). *Theatre of the Oppressed*. New York. Theatre Communications Group.

Boal, A. (1995). *The rainbow of desire: The Boal method of theatre and therapy*. New York: Routledge.

Boal, A. (1998). *Legislative Theatre: Using performance to make politics*. New York: Routledge.

Boal, A. (2001). *Hamlet and the baker's son: My life in theatre and politics*. New York: Routledge.

Freire, P. (2000). *Pedagogy of the oppressed*. New York: Continuum.

Rodríguez, J., Rich, M., Hastings, R., & Page, J. (2006). Assessing the impact of Augusto Boal's "Proactive Performance:" An embodied approach for cultivating prosocial responses to sexual assault. *Text and Performance Quarterly*, 26(3), 229–252.

PIRATE RADIO (ISRAEL)

From the beginning of the 1980s onward, pirate radio ("pirate" is a term long in use to refer to commercially motivated but unlicensed stations, some of which play a dissident anti-establishment role as well) almost became a national sport in Israel. At least 300 pirate stations began operating in the mid-1990s. This figure was more than 20 times larger than the number of legal radio stations (two national stations and 14 local) broadcasting at that time.

Unlike the United States, where often pirate stations owners could have received licenses but refused to do so in the spirit of the First Amendment, Israel's pirate stations were forced to operate illegally because of numerical limits on stations. Thus, we can consider the illegal, or pirate radio, as an alternative to the mainstream media.

Although several pirate radio stations operated during the 1960s and the early 1970s—all run by amateurs, most of them youngsters—illegal broadcasting as a major phenomenon has its roots in 1973. That year, a famous Israeli bohemian and restaurant owner Abie Nathan bought an old ship and transformed it into a floating broadcasting station named *Kol Hashalom* (The Voice of Peace). Its purpose was to promote peace in the Middle East, and it broadcasted in three languages: English, Hebrew, and Arabic. It imitated 1960s offshore pirate broadcasting in Western Europe.

Although to a great extent Israel adopted the European model of government or state-controlled broadcasting, it was not in a hurry to follow Europe's example of deregulation. In fact, the authorities chose to turn a blind eye to the pirate stations, particularly the veteran *Kol Hashalom*, thus encouraging the establishment of additional stations.

There were two main reasons for this decision, one political and the other social. The silent authorization of *Kol Hashalom*, which was aligned with the political left and began operating under the Labor Party, expressed its dissatisfaction with official radio's failure to fulfill the government's expectations. This was similar to the frustration of many European governments, and some researchers believe deregulation was to punish the national broadcasters that did not serve the authorities as they wished. In Israel, deregulation was not officially instituted until the early 1990s, but *Kol Hashalom*'s continuance can be viewed as effective deregulation, as well as a punishment for the national stations.

The second largest pirate station, *Channel 7*, which was aligned with the political right and the National Religious Party, began to operate in the late 1980s under a right-wing government. This was a replay of the previous situation. The government was not satisfied with national radio, which was perceived as a left-wing mouthpiece. Not only was no action taken against Channel 7, but also it was actually supported. Ministers and Parliament members even gave interviews on the channel's current affairs programs.

For a long time, the authorities also refrained from enforcing the law against the small, local pirate stations that had sprung up all over the country. Speedy and severe measures only were taken against pirate stations when their broadcasts interfered with airport and military base frequencies.

There was also a social aspect to the green light granted the pirates. These stations responded to a broad variety of social and communication needs that had not previously found expression on the national stations. Ethnic minorities, music lovers of various kinds, Orthodox religious circles, and even the gay community set up their own stations that answered their communities' specific needs. The pirates really did create an alternative mediascape. Furthermore, the fact the pirate stations had been left alone for years weakened the pressures on the government to institute deregulation officially and enable the establishment of additional stations.

Additional Factors

Three factors contributed, each in its own way, to the proliferation of the phenomenon, over and above the forces from above and below just noted. One was technological. Broadcasting equipment (all the pirates broadcast on FM) is simple, inexpensive, and accessible. It can be bought "off the shelf" in Europe and smuggled into Israel freely, hidden, for example, in microwave oven boxes. Israeli technicians take advantage of their knowledge to build transmitters to serve the pirate stations.

The second factor was the limited deregulation of radio broadcasts in the early 1990s, when 14 regional radio stations, which were operated by franchise owners, were granted permits. Entrepreneurs quickly set up pirate stations to get broadcasting experience in the hope their proven experience would help them acquire a franchise. These entrepreneurs encouraged others, even if they did not want a legal franchise, to follow suit.

The third factor consisted of the Ministry of Communications, the police, and the courts. Although the ministry attempted to move against pirate radio, on many occasions it received clear signals from the government to refrain from taking action against certain stations. As a result, the ministry did not view the pirate stations as a real problem, except when they interfered with vital frequencies. Thus, personnel and resources were not allocated to fight pirate radio.

The police force did not consider the problem particularly important, mainly because it was busy with other problems such as Palestinian terrorists, car thefts, and other serious crimes. The courts, for their part, were lenient. The maximum penalty was 3 years imprisonment and a fine equivalent to US$750,000. In most cases, they imposed penalties equivalent to a few hundred dollars, and only in 2008 was the first "pirate" sent to jail.

Three Station Types

The three categories are amateur, commercial, and ideological. Stations in the first category are operated mainly by young people. They do not require vast resources, because they all have a stereo and CDs at home. Most broadcast irregularly and infrequently. Their range is limited and their life span usually is short. They only broadcast music, usually according to the owner's or his friends' taste. They have little talk, if any. These stations have no income and are operated as a hobby.

The second type is commercial. All these are local or regional, and most only broadcast music, although in some isolated cases they broadcast talk shows, mainly call-ins from listeners or competitions with prizes. Many specialize in ethnic music, such as Greek, Russian, Iranian, Iraqi, or Yemeni. Their fate depends not only on escaping legal problems, but also primarily on their profitability. Thus, even when some owners were put on trial, they restarted broadcasting shortly afterward, because the low fine was no deterrent.

The third type is ideological. Although some of these sell advertising to enable them to buy long-range transmitters and enhance their programs, their basis is not commercial. The fragile coalition structure, which characterized the Israeli political map over many years, particularly since the 1980s, gave some small political parties, mainly from the religious sector, tremendous power. They took advantage of this to set up pirate stations. Because of their political clout, the authorities usually refrained from taking action against these stations.

Although firmer action, at least compared with the past, was taken in the first decade of the 21st century, it seemed the government did not have the power, and in some cases the will, to close down all pirate stations, and many continued to operate.

Yehiel Limor

See also Alternative Information Center (Israel and Palestine); Alternative Local Press (United Kingdom); Free Radio (Austria); Free Radio Movement (Italy); Free Radio Movement, 1974–1981 (France); Pirate Radio (Lebanon)

Further Readings

Caspi, D., & Limor Y. (1999). *The in/outsiders: The mass media in Israel*. Cresskill, NJ: Hampton Press.

Limor, Y. (1998). *The pirate radio in Israel—a research report* [in Hebrew]. Jerusalem, Israel: The Hebrew University.

Limor, Y., & Naveh, C. (2008). *Pirate radio in Israel* [in Hebrew]. Haifa, Israel: Pardes.

PIRATE RADIO (LEBANON)

Lebanon has always been regarded as a fertile ground for thought and expression despite limits on free speech that the Lebanese people still face. There is a constant struggle between dominant and dissident powers to carve a space for liberty of expression. Pirate radio—locally known as "unofficial" radio—is a key example.

Background

In 1938, Radio Orient, which was run by the French mandate authorities, was the first to start broadcasting. Its goal was to counter Nazi propaganda from Radio Berlin. When French troops withdrew in 1946, the Lebanese government inherited the station, which it renamed Radio Lebanon. It was then the only licensed station. It reflected the ruling elite's views while virtually denying access to any opposing views. News and other programs provided a sanitized version of events, exclusively serving the status quo. This monopoly over the airwaves became the center of controversy in the years to follow.

Soon after World War II, the Arab world witnessed many convulsive changes. The 1948 establishment of the state of Israel, the ensuing displacement of Palestinians, and the rise of nationalist movements fueled by Egyptian leader Gamal Abdul Nasser's ideology were among the key factors that reshaped the region. Arab states used radio to serve their ideologies and agendas, as well as influence neighboring countries.

The Lebanese government, however, avoided involvement in regional tensions. Moreover, it overlooked the surge of arms in Palestinian refugee camps dispersed through urban neighborhoods all over Lebanon and ignored the guerrilla training undertaken by the various political factions. Instead, the government chose to focus on the image of Lebanon as the "Switzerland of the Middle East," catering to tourism and banking industries that made Lebanon the regional business hub. It viewed no need to improve the technical standards of the national radio station.

First Wave of Rebel Radios: 1958

Lebanon became increasingly polarized by the abundance of conflicting ideologies sweeping the region. The Nasserist and other Arab nationalist movements gained support among Palestinians and leftists. In response, Lebanon's Christian communities, which were often economically well placed, felt a grave threat to their livelihoods and political influence. The rifts grew larger and soon took a sectarian form. The volatile situation finally erupted in 1958 as combat broke out between a coalition of leftist pro-Palestinian Muslim parties and the Phalangists, which was a Maronite Christian right-wing party.

Radio Lebanon made many efforts to reestablish national unity and restore calm. But the station remained an exclusive government mouthpiece. The events it reported were tailored to suit the elite's ideology, and it deliberately overlooked facts damaging to the government. Factions opposing the regime could not broadcast their viewpoints. Their only resort was to use alternative measures. Combat on the streets was soon accompanied by a war over the airwaves.

Radio stations sprouted up virtually overnight. *Sawt al-'Uruba* (Voice of Arabism), *Sawt Lubnan* (Voice of Lebanon), and *Sawt al-Muqawamah al-Sha'abiyah* (Voice of the People's Resistance) took to the airwaves, each representing one of the many political camps with a stake in the conflict. The programs produced can be described at best as unprofessional and haphazard. Schedules mostly consisted of news, anthems, and patriotic songs and were created on the spur of the moment, depending on the latest developments. After 9 months of clashes, the government finally regained control. The broadcast mayhem ended, and Radio Lebanon was once again the only radio station broadcasting on Lebanese territory.

The wave of unlicensed stations deepened the political discord significantly. The government realized the immediate need to prevent renegade broadcasts from recurring. In 1959, it increased its station's medium and shortwave capacity to cover all parts of Lebanon. Production standards and program quality improved significantly. However, the agenda remained the same. The public continued to perceive Radio Lebanon as a mouthpiece for the government and the ruling elite.

Civil War: 1975–1990

Control over broadcast media tightened as tension between the major political movements continued to build up. A full-blown civil war started in 1975, polarizing the country even more along sectarian lines. The Phalangists were fervently against the armed Palestinian presence, but a national front representing the diverse Muslim factions (Sunni, Shiite, and Druze) called for the eradication of Israel and its Lebanese sympathizers, the Phalangists.

The official state radio attempted to stay neutral. The programs were sanitized to the extent that a listener could not tell that a war was going on. As a result, people resorted to foreign stations such as the British Broadcasting Corporation and Radio Monte Carlo to learn about the latest developments in their own neighborhoods.

The warring factions needed outlets of their own. The 1958 rebel radios resurfaced within months. Several political movements started radio outlets of their own, although not all lasted. Only parties with a well-funded, well-organized, and professionally run operation continued over the years to follow.

Regardless, unofficial stations increased steadily. Political groups found it easy to launch their broadcasts as a result of the lawlessness. Furthermore, they were enabled by foreign states' investment in the conflict. The civil war physically manifested regional conflicts and the global cold war between the superpowers. Also, the fact that some parties had their own mouthpieces prompted their competitors to start their own.

Voice of Lebanon (VL) and Voice of Arab Lebanon (VAL) stood out in this array. VL, a Phalangist station, was the first to begin broadcasting. At first, it operated from two separate apartments where senior Phalangist officials lived. One location served a news bureau, and the other broadcasted patriotic anthems and plays that often proclaimed a homeland that "will never kneel before any attempts for domination" and frequently glorified Lebanon's Phoenician roots.

Later, as it became enormously popular domestically and abroad, VL moved to Ashrafieh, which is a Christian district of Beirut. Throughout the war, when telephones and other means of communication suffered drastically, the radio provided a huge service by creating a channel of communication for families separated by the war. For example, it created *Reunion With the Beloved*, a program that aired recorded messages from listeners assuring relatives abroad of their safety and well-being. VL reached such a high level of journalism and entertainment that it was often quoted by international news agencies.

VAL, however, was a mouthpiece for the left-wing Independent Nasserist Movement *Murabitun*. VAL was supported covertly by Libya and the USSR. From 1975 to 1982, this station played a key role in rallying support among its Arab nationalist followers. It also catered significantly to the public's needs. During militia street battles, announcers read the names of casualties, emergency clinic reports, and messages from callers regarding the whereabouts of family members. For hours, listeners would tune in to hear messages such as "Salami Abul-Mouna is trapped in his office and assures his family in Verdun that he is safe." In other instances, the station was the only source to notify the fire department or the Red Cross of fires and casualties.

During Israeli air raids or bombing forays against the Phalangists, the station played military and nationalist songs, and sound bites from Nasser's speeches that were interrupted frequently by news flashes on the latest developments. Egyptian anthems reminiscent of Nasser's revolutionary era in the 1950s were not uncommon. During the 1982 Israeli invasion, for example, one song played incessantly, chanting "my homeland, my homeland, my homeland, to you goes my love, my heart, and my soul." As besieged Beirut residents lived through the Israeli blitzes and the ensuing human carnage, they were solaced by songs of freedom, pride, and camaraderie.

Similarly, the other stations were as diverse and colorful as the militias they represented. Across the board, the militias used radio to accuse their rivals of breaking cease-fires, committing atrocities, or running venomous propaganda wars. For instance, when militias in predominantly Muslim West Beirut were busy infighting, their radio mouthpieces would accuse VL of fueling their conflict and distorting the facts to serve its own Phalangist agenda. VL's minute-by-minute reports on the combat among its "traditional foes" gained it credibility with an unlikely audience: a community beyond the trenches.

Curiously, one station was funded directly by a private U.S. organization. The U.S. evangelical George Otis founded the Voice of Hope in an area in south Lebanon controlled by pro-Israeli Southern Lebanon Army militia leader Saad Haddad. Otis created this station reportedly with funds exceeding US$600,000, which were mostly provided by singer/actor Pat Boone. The objective was to inspire people for peace with the "word of God" by presenting pieces from the Scripture and playing wholesome country music. Interspersed with gospel pieces and the "Nashville sound" were speeches by Haddad inciting listeners to action against the Palestinians and their allies.

The flourishing radio set industry enabled a new social phenomenon: a population hooked on transistor radios. People were glued to their sets to hear breaking news on the fighting and cease-fires, as well as on their currency's fluctuating exchange rate against the U.S. dollar. Any missed opportunity to sell and buy currency at one of the exchange shacks found on every street corner meant a significant loss for the many who jumped on the currency dealing wagon. In periods when daily life reached a level of normalcy and in the congested streets of the greater Beirut region, radio stations such as Radio One 105.5 FM provided the latest in Western music. Relying on pirated disks and programming, along with minimal staffing and maintenance expenses, this wide array of radios thrived on substantial advertising revenues.

Postwar

By 1990, when the Taef Accord ended the civil war, approximately 180 unlicensed stations were on the air. With an amended constitution, the government hastily announced intentions to reorganize the radio spectrum and shut down all unlicensed stations. The result was the Law of Audiovisual Media Organization, which purported to regulate the spectrum and grant "responsible freedom of expression" with the purpose of nation building, reconciliation, and postwar development.

However, this limited the number of outlets severely given the law's definitions of "responsible expression." The government established quotas and technical criteria for licensing radio stations. Many stations could not meet these conditions. In addition to the official government station, Radio Lebanon, the stations authorized to broadcast "information" were VL, Voice of the People, Radio Lebanese Liberty, Voice of Tomorrow, and Voice of Light.

Although political parties came to enjoy more representation through their own radio outlets, freedom of expression is far from being achieved. Under the law, only the major political groups can access the airwaves. The Lebanese state might boast of nurturing civil society and democracy, but a large segment of society is still underrepresented. There is multiparty representation over the airwaves, but the political agenda is still set by those in power, while dissident voices remain silenced.

Assem Nasr

See also Al-Jazeera as Global Alternative News Source (Qatar/Transnational); Citizens' Media; Community Radio (Ireland); Pirate Radio (Israel); Radio La Tribu (Argentina)

Further Readings

Boyd, D. A. (1999). *Broadcasting in the Arab world* (3rd ed.). Ames: Iowa State University Press.

Dajani, N. H. (1992). *Disoriented media in a fragmented society: The Lebanese experience.* Beirut, Lebanon: American University of Beirut Press.

El-Khazen, F. (2000). *The breakdown of the state in Lebanon: 1967–1976.* London: I. B. Taurus.

Halwani, M., & Al-Abid, A. (1978). *Al-Anthimah al-Ithaiyah fi al-Duwal al-Arabiyah* [Broadcasting Systems in the Arab States]. Cairo, Egypt: Dar Al-Fikr al-Arabi.

Kraidy, M. M. (1998). Broadcasting regulation and civil society in postwar Lebanon. *Journal of Broadcasting & Electronic Media, 42*(3), 387–400.

Markaz al-I'lam wa al-Tawthiq. (1980). *Itha'at Sawt Lubnan* [Voice of Lebanon Radio]. Beirut, Lebanon: Author.

Nassif, I. (2001). *Al-I'lam fi Lubnan: Dirasah qanuniyah* [Media in Lebanon: A Policy Study]. Beirut, Lebanon: Manshurat al-Jamia al-Lubnaniyah.

POLITICAL CARTOONING, 1870s–PRESENT (INDIA)

From their origins in the comic-satiric journals of Victorian Britain, India's 19th-century vernacular equivalents critiqued the inequities of British rule; the foibles of Westernized elites; the shortcomings of commercial, consumer culture; and the insecurities of squabbling nationalist politicians. Illustrated newspapers, pictorial magazines, and picture books developed as new genres, but the illustrated comic-satiric journal proved particularly fruitful for Indian editors and publishers. It spread to the farthest reaches of the subcontinent, expressing frustrations with British rule and uniting India's disparate populations under the nationalist banner. The images reflected myriad perspectives scattered across India and did so in dozens of Indian languages.

Origins and Production

Political cartoons appeared in some of the first newspapers published in India. The English-owned *Bengal Hurkaru* and the *Indian Gazette* in the 1850s were the first periodicals in India to include political cartoons, but Britain's illustrated comic-satiric periodicals like *Punch* (1841–1992), *Fun* (1861–1901), and the *Pall Mall Gazette* (1865–1921) gave a great boost to this genre. From this inspiration, India's burgeoning printer-publishers became enamored of the comic-satiric form and began to produce their own journals in this vein. The English-owned *Delhi Sketch Book* was the first of its kind to appear in India. This paper lasted for 7 years, until the uprisings of 1857–1858 interrupted its publication. During its lifetime, the comic features of the *Delhi Sketch Book* highlighted the precarious relationship between Britons and natives living in India. These social divides would become a particular point of interest in later illustrated comic-satiric journals from British and Indian perspectives.

Partha Mitter credits a cartoon published in the Bengali newspaper *Amrita Bazar Patrika* (Amrita Bazar Newspaper) in 1872 as the first to appear in an Indian-owned, vernacular-language periodical, but the most memorable cartoons appeared in the journals inspired by *Punch*. Bombay's Anglo-Gujarati

Hindi Punch (1889–1931), which took pride in producing more than a dozen images in its weekly issues, and Lucknow's weekly Urdu-language *Avadh Punch* (1877–1936) were two of the longest-running and most successful illustrated comic-satiric publications in India.

Political and Social Subjects

Despite numerous press control laws, political cartoons published in vernacular papers used new genres of illustrated journalism to voice opposition to many injustices of colonial rule. In the 1870s, cartoons appearing in the *Sulav Samachar* pinpointed collusion between European medical and court personnel and European offenders, allowing Europeans to go scot-free for crimes against poor Indians. Some cartoons foreshadowed the passing of the 1882 Ilbert Bill that was meant to rectify this abuse.

Avadh Punch attacked the notorious colonial Salt Tax by bringing it to life in an exaggerated, caricatured form. *Hindi Punch* attacked the burdens of Britain's tax policies by showing a famished Indian cow carrying the weight of Britain's military on its back. In addition to condemning the injustices of British rule, political cartoons also brought the faces and foibles of British politicians into the homes of Indian readers. Interest in the comic sketches of famous British officials inspired the publication of collections like Harishchandra Tâlcherkar's 1903 volume *Lord Curzon in Indian Caricature.*

Political cartoons in India addressed both British rule and the complexities of Indian society. They caricatured the excessive consumption and inequalities of the Raj and also provided sharp visual reminders of famine's continued presence across India and the ineffectiveness of the colonial government's anti-plague policies. Cartoonists in early 20th-century Bengal loved to lampoon the greedy Brahmin (the priestly class, supposedly immune to fleshly delights), and his voracious appetite for food, wealth, and wine. Gaganendranath Tagore's caricatures portrayed grossly obese Brahmins gorging themselves on carnal luxuries. The artists of *Hindi Punch* expressed similar distaste for the caste system, using a grotesque, large-bellied, bald-pated figure wearing a Brahminical sacred thread to represent "caste." These publications also attacked *sati* (widow burning) and child marriage.

It was, however, in the context of the Indian nationalist movement that the visual vitality of the political cartoon mixed effortlessly with Indian political activities. During its early years, periodicals like *Hindi Punch* followed the meetings and conventions of the Indian National Congress. The paper published dozens of cartoons on the early 20th-century split in the Congress between the so-called moderates and extremists, demonizing one position and exalting the other.

However, it was not until Gandhi rose to the national political stage that political cartoons and pictorial journalism became central to the movement. Then the symbols of Indian nationalism became cornerstones of the political cartoonist's repertoire, and mechanically reproduced images became central to India's political self-perceptions. Gandhi offered cartoonists the spinning wheel, hand-spun cotton *khadi* cloth, the Gandhi cap, and the humbleness of his own body as vibrant political symbols for the future Indian nation. Using these symbols, political cartoonists worked hand in hand with the nationalist leaders' serious engagement with journalism.

Cartoon and Caricature in Post-Independence India

Cartoon and caricature continued to be effective forms of social and political media in post-independence India. Whereas colonial publications caricatured figures like Lord Curzon, post-independence cartoons featured leading Indian politicians, film stars, and other celebrities. Prime Minister Nehru, identified by his Kashmiri cap and long button-down coat, appeared in numerous cartoons. Cartoonists also invoked the figure of Gandhi regularly, even after his death in 1948, as a way to critique contemporary political and social practices. Gandhi's bald head, large ears, wire-rimmed glasses, and *dhoti* (cloth wrap) made him easy to identify.

Other subjects of ridicule included prominent leaders of the Congress Party, India's administrative bureaucracy, and the general inefficiencies of the state. Cartoonists retained much of the traditional dress and attire to identify various religious groups, classes, and occupations. India's prime minister at the time of writing, Manmohan Singh, remained an easily identifiable figure with his light-blue turban and wispy, white beard.

Even in the age of digital media, political cartoonists continued to prey on the shortcomings and bureaucracies that plague contemporary Indian government and the idiosyncrasies and imperfections of India's upper classes. Although the dangers of communal backlash or court fines make some editors wary, many consider the creations of local or nationally syndicated cartoonists a vital part of their paper's content. The black-and-white lithographic prints of the late 19th century gave way to colorful sketches in the 21st century, and the relative anonymity of pre-Independence cartoonists to the notoriety of several important post-independence cartoonists, including Abu Abraham (1924–2002), R. K. Laxman (1924–present), and Mario Miranda (1925–present). Today, the political cartoon remains a powerful tool of political and social critique in India.

Elizabeth Lhost

See also Anticolonial Press (British Colonial Africa); Independence Movement Media (India); Political Graffiti (Greece); Resistance Through Ridicule (Africa); *Tehelka* Magazine (India); Yes Men, The (United States)

Further Readings

Abraham, A. (Ed.). (1987). *The Penguin book of Indian cartoons*. New York: Viking Penguin.

Hasan, M. (2007). *Wit and humour in colonial North India*. New Delhi, India: Niyogi Books.

Mitter, P. (1994). *Art and nationalism in colonial India, 1850–1922: Occidental orientations*. Cambridge, UK: Cambridge University Press.

Pinney, C. (2004). *"Photos of the Gods": The printed image and political struggle in India*. London: Reaktion.

Tarlo, E. (1996). *Clothing matters: Dress and identity in India*. Chicago: University of Chicago Press.

Venkatachalapathy, A. (2006). *In those days there was no coffee: Writings in cultural history*. New Delhi, India: Yoda Press (distributed by Foundation Books, New Delhi).

POLITICAL CRITIQUE IN NOLLYWOOD VIDEO-FILMS (NIGERIA)

Nollywood, the independent Nigerian video film industry, emerged in the late 1980s and early 1990s. The producers, like those in Ghana, began with VHS tape but now use digital equipment. This is partially responsible for the "video boom" in Nigeria. "Nollywood" indexes two things: the prolific number of video-movies released every year and how they have become popular culture products in Nigeria, in the continent at large, and beyond.

However, these videos do not have an overt ideological axe to grind, as is often the case with art cinema from "Francophone African" countries. The video movie producers are interested in capturing the interest of their African audiences, and at least not to risk losing money. Most video-films explore everyday Nigerian issues, including vigilante justice, romance, and not least Pentecostalist Christianity versus witchcraft beliefs and practices. Unlike the "Afrobeat" music of Fela Anikulapo Ransome-Kuti, most seem to avoid explicit political critique, maybe because of the decades of brutal military rule under which the industry emerged.

With the return to democracy in 1999, however, "political" Nollywood videos have emerged. Some carry virtually open critiques, whereas others have indirect and/or symbolic targets. For example, *Grasshopper 1* (Loved Power, 2001) and *Grasshopper 2* (Died in Power, 2001) explicitly deal with the corrupt and nightmarish dictatorial regime of Sani Abacha (1993–1998). Despite the producer's disclaimers that the film is fictitious, the characters use fake names of easily identifiable people (one character is called Professor Nobel, an obvious alias for doughty Nobel literature prize-winner and Human Rights activist Wole Soyinka).

Another instance is *The Last Vote*, which revolves around an honest state governor who refuses to condone the corrupt, unscrupulous practices of those who financed his run for office. This mirrors a long-running political battle in the early

2000s between Enugu state governor Chimaroke Nnamani and Chief Jim Nwobodo, an Igbo political godfather.

Saworide (Brass Bells, 1999) and its sequel *Agogo Eewo* (Taboo Gong/The Sacred Gong, 2002) fall within the symbolic critique category. Here, the actions of a Yoruba traditional king and his subchiefs are used implicitly to critique corruption, usurpation of power, and despotic regimes in 1990s Nigeria. The film uses local proverbs and Yoruba metaphysics to underscore dislike for greed and authoritarianism, and desire for accountability and democracy.

Ekun Oko Oke (The Indomitable Tiger, 2002) is also an allegorical film that details the story of a resolute activist who opposes the actions of an evil ruler. The film *Alaga Kansu* (The Local Council Chairman, 2002) portrays the selfishness and gluttony of local politicians.

All these Nollywood films, just like *Akobi Gomina 1 & 2* (Governor's Heir, 2002), which advocates for more women to participate in public office, convey a call for good governance. Furthermore, they reference undemocratic practices under various military regimes in Nigeria's political history. These issues are either explored through explicit references or allegory.

Thus, Nollywood has a political cinema genre. Such video-movies are not produced in the same quantity as in the witchcraft/occult genre; however, they constitute a visible departure. As the industry continues to mature, as the National Film and Video Censors' Board begins to loosen its hold, and as democratic governance becomes entrenched, we might witness a perceptible increase in "political" Nollywood video-films.

Joseph Oduro-Frimpong

See also Audiocassettes and Political Critique (Kenya); Music and Dissent (Ghana and Nigeria); Parodies of Dominant Discourse (Zambia); Political Jokes (Zimbabwe); Small Media Against Big Oil (Nigeria)

Further Readings

Adeoti, G. (2009). Home video films and the democratic imperative in contemporary Nigeria. *Journal of African Cinema, 1*(1), 35–56.

Adesokan, A. (2009). Practicing "democracy" in Nigerian films. *African Affairs, 108*(433), 559–619.

Haynes, J. (2000). *Nigerian video films.* Athens: Ohio University Press.

Haynes, J. (2006). Political critique in Nigerian video films. *African Affairs, 105*(421), 511–533.

McCall, J. C. (2002). Madness, money, & movies: Watching a Nigerian popular video with the guidance of a native doctor. *Africa Today, 49*(3), 79–94.

POLITICAL GRAFFITI (GREECE)

"The tongue has no bones, but can crush bones." This Greek proverb stresses the power of effective speech and how powerful people fear it (which largely accounts for the lack of civic communication options in Greece even today). People who possess that power have used graffiti to transmit their messages into an otherwise rather inaccessible public domain. Surfaces of walls, on both public and private property, are expropriated for the purpose.

Graffiti developed in Greece over the 20th century mainly as an expressive tool of the radical, downtrodden, and excluded. They responded to social turbulence, foreign occupation, civil war, dictatorship, and struggling peace movements. Graffiti messages have voiced youth unrest and social conflict. They have thrived in politically repressive periods, becoming omnipresent, pointed, even spectacular and impossible to ignore. By the 21st century, they established a stable rapport with the public, articulating concepts or projects normally excluded from mainstream media. They have transcended taboos, publicizing ideas or views otherwise intolerable, suppressed, or approaches pertaining to lateral, imaginative thinking.

During the 20th century, the gradual broadening of literacy in Greece released waves of the urge to articulate wishes, demands, or grievances. Such waves grew remarkably in World War II and also notably in the 1960s, when higher education, previously an upper-class preserve, was opened to young people from all social classes. Campuses became hubs of fresh ideas and radical activism, vividly articulated on university walls. Greece's *University Asylum* law that bans law enforcement officials from setting foot on campuses—at the time of writing a hotly debated issue—has always secured space and protection to "creative dissidents." Similarly, among those driven by poverty from the countryside in the 1960s, tough conditions in the towns fed rising public expressiveness.

These ambitions to address the public turned graffiti into virtually a "local mass medium." This accounts also for official hostility toward graffiti and their creators. The audacity to address illegally all or even "the many" appeared intolerable. Indeed, in Greece, free public communication has been submerged during dictatorial regimes, and successive governments almost hostile to civil society during the paternalistic liberal phases. Despite galloping advances in communications technology, the public at large never had access to sustained community media, whereas mainstream media have been controlled mainly by either corporate or state forces.

Three Phases of Political Graffiti

Phase A occurred between the world wars, particularly during the Metaxas dictatorship from 1936 and up to the end of World War II. As is evident from Theodoros Angelopoulos's films *Days of 1936* (1972) and *The Traveling Players* (1975), graffiti was at that time a key medium for horizontal public communication. They evolved as the prerogative of the then-illegal parties of the Left, particularly the strong Communist Party. Indeed, during Greece's occupation by the Axis powers (1941–1945), graffiti proved vital to organize popular resistance against famine, repression, and forced labor. This resistance even vaulted over the gender gap. In the National Liberation Front youth movement, girls at night painted slogans on walls or made cardboard megaphones to shout defiant messages across city rooftops.

Phase B, the longest phase, included both the first 7 years of military rule (1967–1974) and three successive political scenarios during the 1973–1983 decade. Particularly during the military junta that in 1967 had seized power with U.S. approval, university wall graffiti throbbed with radical "communicative traffic." In spring 1973, the first political scenario began, namely an epic ongoing struggle at Athens Polytechnic (the *Polytechneion*) and student anti-junta riots. The May 1968 revolt in France, as well as other contemporary movements, heartened Greek students in their struggle, and graffiti became an important weapon. These tumults continued through the junta's eventual collapse in July 1974.

The next scenario in phase B encompassed the transitional period 1974–1981, when Greece returned to democratic politics, abolished the monarchy by popular referendum, adopted a new constitution and legalized all political parties, notably the Communist Party. Through such steps, Greece, under the conservative governments of the New Democracy Party, gradually achieved its *Metapolitefsi*, which was the change over from a criminal dictatorship to the rule of law and respect for elementary freedoms.

The third and final scenario of phase B was that of 1981–1983, after the landmark 1981 electoral victory of the Socialist Party *PASOC*, when the country moved toward a relative empowerment of the subordinate classes. Graffiti captured the tensions and flavor of each period and played a part in Greece's gradual transformation. However, the "national" or "public" interest was conceived variously, at this point, by different classes, generations, and citizens of varied educational levels. Wall messages reflected clearly these sophisticated and divergent realities.

In the current *phase C,* graffiti continue to play an alternative communication role. However, contemporary graffiti have become broadly diversified and commercialized. Attempts to "naturalize" and take over graffiti by nonradical forces were evident in the bright colors and nondescript contents, which often occupied public spaces with trendy graphic "noise."

Graffiti Texts

Textual graffiti have represented the largest segment of graffiti and vary widely in expressive forms. Messages comprised anything from summons to protest rallies, to humorous or teasing commentary, or calls for solidarity or thoughtful reflection. The thematic range of graffiti texts is enormous, and the contents full of word play, for this is the terrain of ambiguity, paradox, farce, or subcultural trivia. Puns and innuendos are mixed with interpersonal attacks, whereas repartee is issued with delicate irony, in criticizing locally brewed attitudes. For instance, sarcasm about

sexuality in the wall-command: "Spare your virginity for old age."

Giannis Dimaras's 1981 book title—*Empros ston Etsi poy Charaxe o Tetoios* (Forward to Thingummy, That Was Proclaimed by What's-His-Name)—is a good illustration. This is a much-renowned parody of leftist "leadership" and of a slogan whose original version might have been, for instance, the "Forward on the Path That Was Opened Up by Mao." Although locally embedded, writers are not cut off from their international counterparts. "Happy New Fear!" spotted in Thessaloniki old town, riffs off a contemporary English slogan, revealing international networking across graffiti-writing movements. Similarly, the provocative slogan "The Aegean Belongs to Its Fish" is a sour peremptory dismissal of the seemingly perpetual friction between Greek and Turkish governments in the eastern Mediterranean.

Messages are discursive or provocative, ideological or propagandistic, sometimes urging specific political tactics. Graffiti contents are full of sarcasm, outcry, feelings of disaffection, cynicism, or pained exclamations. Wall writing is unavoidably ephemeral and transient, because of, among other things, the endless battle between night-shift graffiti writers and the daytime white washers of walls. This tense relation entails a communication guerrilla "hit and run" tactic.

Graffiti messages have redeeming effects in times of repression and systematic censorship, and they are experienced as oases of freedom in conditions of political suffocation. The same messages, however, when there is freedom of expression, might be perceived negatively. Graffiti writers then lose the aura of brave heroes of the night. Such shifts suddenly recast wall-writing communities as disconnected ghettos rather than sympathetic activists.

Yet, graffiti contents were always sources of counterinformation or supplementary information, offsetting official propaganda or dominant media bias. Such communicative folklore was not neutral or indifferent, but confrontational. It commanded freedom and grabbed it via the Eleventh Commandment on a wall message: "It is forbidden to forbid." Student graffiti dealt also with democratic self-enlightenment, as in the call "Kill the cop you have inside you!" The endless tug of war of individualists versus collectivists is addressed in another distinguished motif "Apart from imperialism, there is also loneliness." In a narcissistic-existentialist fit, one writer declared: "God is dead, Marx is dead, and I'm not feeling too good myself lately," to which another retorted cynically: "So what?"

The trouble, in Dimaras's view, is that even within "wall-writing" subcultures, people only want to talk, not to listen. And this evidently is a serious matter for political communication. So do graffiti versions of this one-way communication habit risk imploding insurgent movements? Walking through the imaginary "Museum of Greek Graffiti," others respond cynically: "The right to protest has proved the ideal method to control the moves of chess pawns, as planned."

The Political Culture of Struggle and Lament

Poetry has always been significant in Greek culture, so it could hardly be missing from graffiti. Poetic texts or references abound; "Do not neglect to bring water along, our future is anticipated arid" urges Michalis Katsaros (2005). Nicholas Assimos joins in with his melancholy *Cheretismata* (Greetings to Power), uttering his frustration in view of still-born promises of political participation, much-loved verses rendered into memorable songs by Manos Loizos: *Fovame* (I Fear), "I fear all that will be done for me, without me."

Notwithstanding such anxieties, graffiti gave voice to various, mainly Left, youth, or subcultural movements, who took to the walls to force access into the otherwise enclosed public domain. Anarchists were, at the time of writing, by far the most visible among wall writers. Their inputs were broadly recognizable because they carefully forged their distinctive ideology, style, and signature. Dimaras, who charted this phenomenon, often referred to graffiti writers as "bent down." Yet, graffiti signal political struggle and celebrate insubordination. As a 2007 slogan in the center of Athens testified, "We save petrol by burning cars."

A salient graffiti slogan at the time of writing was also title of Georgios Peponis's 2008 book *The Walls Belong to the Masses*. In this perspective, graffiti are common land, not to be monopolized by particular political groups or issues. In effect, however, graffiti project mostly political claims or factional controversies, generational or

subcultural concerns, and occasionally even interpersonal matters.

Sophia Kaitatzi-Whitlock

See also Culture Jamming; December 2008 Revolt Media (Greece); May 1968 Poetry and Graffiti (France/Transnational); *Rembetiko* Songs (Greece); Wartime Underground Resistance Press, 1941–1944 (Greece)

Further Readings

Assimos, N. (ca 1982). *"Greetings to Power," & "I Fear," lyrics made into popular songs* [in Greek]. Athens, Greece.

Dimaras, G. (1981). *Empros ston etsi pou charaxe o tetoios* [Forward to thingumy, that was proclaimed by what's-his-name] [in Greek]. Athens, Greece: Kaktos.

Katsaros, M. (2005). *Kata Saddoukaion* [The Gospel according to the Sadoucheans]. Athens, Greece: Ellinika Grammata. (Original work published 1953)

Mazower, M. (1993). *Inside Hitler's Greece: The experience of occupation 1941–1944*. London: Yale University Press.

Peponis, G. A. (2008). *The walls belong to the masses.* Athens, Greece: Pontiki.

POLITICAL JOKES (ZIMBABWE)

In the early 2000s, the Zimbabwe government increasingly began to restrict the operation of foreign and local privately owned news media. These media often published critical reports on government's role in the growing economic and political crisis and mediated the discontent expressed by emerging civil society organizations and a new opposition party Movement for Democratic Change (MDC), which was established in 1999.

Furthermore, rejecting demands from civil society organizations to liberalize the airwaves, the Zimbabwe African National Union-Patriotic Front (ZANU-PF) government retained a monopoly through the Zimbabwe Broadcasting Corporation (ZBC). Because of the dire economic situation in the 2000s, few Zimbabweans could afford access to alternative news sources such as satellite television, private newspapers, or the Internet. Hence, most became dependent on the ZBC, which mainly represented ZANU-PF views.

In this context, political jokes and rumor emerged as important social movement media, challenging state-controlled media interpretations of the crisis. In the numerous queues for fuel, cooking oil, and sugar, which grew in length over the 2000s, Zimbabweans actively debated the state of the country regardless of their fears of openly discussing it. In "francophone" Africa, these informal media have often been referred to as *radio trottoir* (sidewalk radio).

Jokes were transmitted in queues, public transport, beer halls, and hair salons, and they began to be shared through special joke sections in private newspapers, on cellular telephones, via e-mail newsgroups like ZvaJokes, and websites such as *Nyambo* (joke, in chiShona). Cellular telephones, in particular, were important because these media were relatively accessible to Zimbabweans as compared to satellite television, Internet, and privately owned newspapers. In 2007, 9 out of every 100 Zimbabweans owned a cellular telephone.

Jokes should be understood both as a response to an environment in which public talk and oral culture are common and as a reaction to the strenuous attempt to crush dissent. Because of their particular mode of dissemination, jokes were virtually beyond government control. Jokes responded to government's efforts to promulgate a racialized "party nation" and mocked the declining credibility of the ZBC. The disillusionment with the ZBC is well captured in the following joke, which narrates a visit by a traveling Zimbabwean to an electronics shop in the United Kingdom:

In the United Kingdom last year I was shopping for things to take home to Zimbabwe when I came into this shop selling television sets. The shop attendant was showing me this latest TV that obeys spoken commands. He said "CNN," and we flipped into CNN, then "BBC," and we had it on the screen at once. I asked how much it was and he told me 300 pounds. I was shocked by the price, and I replied, "Nonsense!" but then to my amazement there was Judesi Makwanya on ZBC News Harare.

This joke dismissed ZBC's television content as "nonsense" and counterposed the ZBC to the BBC and CNN. But it reversed the contrast often invoked by the Zimbabwean government, which claimed the ZBC to be patriotic, as opposed to the BBC and CNN, which are defined as foreign governments' tools to promote regime change.

Whereas state-sponsored music jingles and television programs sought to draw Zimbabweans into supporting the ruling party's project of the *Third Chimurenga* (The Third Liberation Struggle), ordinary Zimbabweans balked at being addressed as willing "patriotic" subjects, that is, loyal party supporters. Jokes engaged with the particular style, language, and mode in which ZANU-PF politicians presented themselves on the ZBC, and they commented on the way in which the ZBC gave the government elites free rein.

Popular humor mocked President Robert Mugabe and other regime leaders. After the huge media coverage of Pope John Paul's death in 2005 and of the handshake between Mugabe and Prince Charles at the funeral, the following SMS joke circulated: Dear Lord, you have misunderstood me, I said: "Please take BOB not POPE" (i.e., "Bob" = Robert Mugabe). It also came in response to remarks made by Zimbabwe's Catholic Archbishop, who was a fervent critic of Mugabe and was quoted as having said that all Zimbabweans were praying that the Lord would soon take Mugabe away.

The practice of joking defied government's efforts to monopolize the public sphere. The technologically mediated practice of joking through e-mail and SMS, reverberating in countless retellings on the street and in homes, contributed to the dissemination of alternative imaginaries to those of the state. Hence, jokes and rumors should not strictly be viewed as "countertexts" but as interventions that constituted alternative media in their own right.

However, although rumors and jokes challenged those in power temporarily, the Zimbabwean government introduced a range of measures to gain control over public speech. The 2002 Public Order and Security Act and the 2006 Criminal Law (Codification and Reform) Act imposed severe restrictions on the publication or communication of false statements prejudicial to the state and of undermining the authority of, or insulting, the president. In the wake of the introduction of these new laws, many Zimbabweans were arrested and some charged for uttering statements deemed to insult or undermine the president.

Wendy Willems

See also Barbie Liberation Organization (United States); Parodies of Dominant Discourse (Zambia); Political Graffiti (Greece); Popular Music and Protest (Ethiopia); Resistance Through Ridicule (Africa); Yes Men, The (United States)

Further Readings

Ellis, S. (1989). Tuning in to pavement radio. *African Affairs, 88,* 321–330.

Nyumbo: http://www.nyambo.com

Obadare, E. (2009). The uses of ridicule: Humour, "infrapolitics" and civil society in Nigeria. *African Affairs, 108,* 241–261.

Spitulnik, D. (2002). Alternative small media and communicative spaces. In G. Hyden, M. Leslie, & F. F. Ogundimu (Eds.), *Media and democracy in Africa* (pp. 177–205). Uppsala, Sweden: Nordic Africa Institute.

Willems, W. (2009). *Imagining the power of the media: Global news, nationalism and popular culture in the context of the 'Zimbabwe crisis (2000–2007).* PhD dissertation, University of London.

ZvaJokes: http://groups.yahoo.com/group/ZvaJokes

POLITICAL SONG (LIBERIA AND SIERRA LEONE)

Innocent, who is a popular Sierra Leonean pop musician, said of his work,

> My mission is to sing against the odds in society. If the APC (All Peoples Congress Party) falls short, they will receive a song worse than (the one I last sang against) the SLPP (Sierra Leone Peoples Party). My singing is an ongoing crusade on corruption, bad government and unemployment. I am not just singing for singing sake.

This was indicative of the passion that young people in postwar Sierra Leone and Liberia cultivated for singing as a social movement medium.

However, realizing its huge potential, the political class has sought to channel its energies in their favor by supporting countersongs and offering financial inducement for praise singing. Thus, singing has become a site of struggle between members of the political class and the masses.

Two War-Weary Nations

Sierra Leone and Liberia are two small neighboring countries on the west coast of Africa. They are both richly endowed with natural resources, and their capitals (Freetown and Monrovia, respectively) were founded as sanctuaries for freed slaves returning from the Americas, England, and different parts of west Africa. However, in the early 2000s, both were emerging from bloody and destructive civil wars, characterized by horrific human rights violations.

Prolonged periods of bad governance manifested in (among other things) corruption and intolerance of opposing views contributed significantly to the outbreak of these wars. The one-party government system in both these countries had failed to make them economically viable, in spite of their natural resources.

After the cessation of hostilities, both countries are engaged in postwar governance reform with the help of the international donor community and funding agencies, which have now made democratic good governance a pre-condition for the receipt of aid and loans. Promoting the right to freedom of expression is an important part of this governance reform program.

Young Musicians and Free Expression

Postwar governance reform as of the mid-2000s was gradually producing a public space conducive to free expression. In general, the young people, who for long did not have much say in governance, considered this a welcome opportunity to make known their views and influence political decisions. Although they constituted the bulk of the population and hoped to become future leaders, they also often anticipated a bleak future and expressed disappointment at the attitudes and performance of their current leaders. Their frustration is compounded by growing social problems, which include illiteracy, unemployment, and drug abuse.

The euphoria with which these youths embraced the right to free expression was manifested in, among other things, the singing of songs with political undertones. Through the lyrics of pop songs like "Mr. Government" in Sierra Leone and "Greedy People" in Liberia, young people became vocal not only in denouncing vices like ethnic favoritism, corruption, injustices, and bad governance in general but also in advocating what they considered urgently needed change. This expressive development was a far cry from what obtained in the prewar period.

Although singing had long been an important part of the cultural expressions of the peoples of Sierra Leone and Liberia, such songs, whether traditional or pop, were used rarely to denounce politicians. However, the arrival of Jamaican reggae songs like "Send Another Moses" and "System Dread" in the 1970s helped to encourage the idea that music can be a powerful medium of political protest. Although people, especially youths, identified with some lyrics of these reggae songs and sought to relate them to their own contexts, the political atmosphere existing then did not favor the composition, recording, and distribution of such songs. However, the desperation of urban youths to earn a living in these war-battered economies coupled with the hopeful climate of postwar democratic reform spurred the rise of many young musicians. Some enthusiastically took to U.S. hip hop and rap.

The artists often poured their invectives out on the political elites, but some were open-minded enough to condemn the rest of the public (especially other young people) who through their own laziness, indiscretion, and political passivity allowed themselves to be manipulated into cooperating with treacherous politicians.

The buildup to the 2005 elections in Liberia and the 2007 elections in Sierra Leone showed these songs had more than an entertainment value. New songs were released through which the artists demonstrated a fascinating capacity to mold public opinion and mobilize support. Party-owned and party-aligned radio stations often used them to denounce their rivals and to galvanize support. Political campaign rallies saw jubilant and enthusiastic supporters chanting lines and choruses of these songs, using them to throw accusations at rival camps. At times, this activity resulted in violent clashes, as in the case of the 2007 Independence masquerade in Freetown.

It was "Injectment (Eviction) Notice" and "Landlord," sung by Innocent and Orbah, respectively, which dominated the air waves during the electioneering period in Sierra Leone. The former's song cast aspersions on the government. It considerably undermined its popularity and, through its melodious chorus, repeatedly appealed for its eviction from power. An English translation is: "These people should be evicted. They have to be evicted! Except they are evicted, peace would never reign. Evict them now, evict them now!"

Unlike Innocent, Orbah sang in the government's favor. In fact, his song was a direct response to Innocent's. The lyrics portrayed the government of the day as a landlord who could not be evicted from his land by his tenant. Understandably, this song became popular among members and supporters of the then-ruling SLPP.

The election changed the government. But postelection songs like "We Want Food on the Table" and "The Eye Is Closely Watching" constantly reminded the new administration about its election promises and the need to deliver or be eventually voted out of office like its predecessor. A translation of part of the last-named song says: "It is time to change. . . . The eye is closely watching. It is time to turn over a new page / Not time to damage / But time to manage."

These songs have the advantage of appealing not only to reason but to emotions and sentiments. Because the songs are mostly in the lingua franca (Pidgin), they cater for nationwide audiences, and because copyright laws are often disregarded in these countries, CDs and cassettes are multiplied easily and distributed widely. Lyrics are often printed and peddled without permission from artists.

Music, as an increasingly attractive tool for political expression by young people in these two countries and in Africa generally, has enormous potential to raise political awareness and arouse change. For this to be realized fully, the young musicians should exercise their right to freedom of expression responsibly by recognizing the rights of others and refraining from using lyrics that reasonable members of the public, rather than the government, agree might risk inciting violence. They should also resist the temptation to be seduced financially and manipulated into praise-singing for unscrupulous politicians.

Sylvanus Nicholas Spencer

See also La Nova Cançó Protest Song (Països Catalans); Music and Social Protest (Malawi); Political Song (Northern Ireland); Popular Music and Political Expression (Côte d'Ivoire); Popular Music and Protest

(Ethiopia); *Rembetiko* Songs (Greece); Youth Rock Music (China)

Further Readings

Benga, N. (2005). Meanings and challenges of modern urban music in Senegal. In T. Falola & S. J. Salm (Eds.), *Urbanization and African cultures* (pp. 155–165). Durham, NC: Carolina Academic Press.

Borszik, A.-K. (2007). *Die Interventionsmusik aus Guinea Bissau.* Berlin, Germany: Skyron.

Bright, E. (2004). Africa raps back: Reflections on hip hop from Tanzania and South Africa. In A. Schröder (Ed.), *Crossing borders: Interdisciplinary approaches to Africa. Afrikanische Studien* (Vol. 23, pp. 77–97). Münster, Germany: LIT Verlag.

Collins, J. (1992). *West African pop roots.* Philadelphia, PA: Temple University Press.

POLITICAL SONG (NORTHERN IRELAND)

There is an inseparable interrelationship between Irish history, politics and music. Rebel songs have been both acts of verbal sedition against the British rulers of Ireland and a source of inspiration and mobilization for Irish resistance. Opposition to British rule in the Six Counties of Northern Ireland, especially from 1969 to the 1990s, was heir to this popular political song tradition.

In the mid-19th century, Thomas Davis of the Young Irelanders wrote several stirring ballads that have come down to the present day, such as "A Nation Once Again" and "The West's Asleep." Similarly, a rebellion half a century earlier, that of the United Irishmen, provided many songs that also are still sung, such as "Boolavogue," which is the story of a priest who led the rebels in Wexford. Each successive stirring of Irish militant republicanism produced its songs that quickly went into the canon. The Fenian Brotherhood's anticolonial raids into Canada in the late 19th century produced "Ireland Boys Hurrah!" whereas the Easter Rising in Dublin in 1916 provided the haunting "Foggy Dew" and the War of Independence the plaintive "Kevin Barry," which is about a teenage rebel hanged by the British.

The uneasy political settlement of 1920, which led to the partition of Ireland, continued to stir republicans to resistance. In each decade of the succeeding century, they engaged in military activity both on and off the island of Ireland, and these activities led to new songs. The abortive "border campaign" of 1956–1961 produced the stirring "Sean South, as well as the more thoughtful and indeed self-critical song of Dominic Behan, "The Patriot Game." Both songs are about young men of the Irish Republican Army (IRA) killed in the campaign. The melody of the latter was "borrowed" by Bob Dylan for his "God on Our Side."

The conflict in Northern Ireland between 1969 and the mid-1990s was fertile soil for rebel songs. Whether it was heroic exploits, such as IRA prison breaks (for example, "The Helicopter Song," about the escape of three top IRA men from Mountjoy Prison in Dublin in 1973) or songs praising the Provisional IRA (for example, "My Little Armalite") or condemning British repression (for example, "The Men Behind the Wire," about internment without trial in 1971), there was for some time a virtual republican hit parade in operation, with each most popular song ousted by the song about the next major exploit or atrocity. To bring these songs to live audiences, there was a plethora of groups, such as the Wolfe Tones, Wolfhound, and the Freemen.

The protest by IRA prisoners between 1976 and 1981 in particular launched many classic songs, not least "The H Block Song"—"I'll wear no convict's uniform, nor meekly serve my time / That Britain might make Ireland's fight 800 years of crime." Such songs served not only to mobilize support outside the prisons but also to sustain the prisoners themselves. For example, the writings of Bobby Sands, who was the first prisoner to die on hunger strike in 1981, recount how they had impromptu concerts each evening as they shivered naked except for a blanket in cells where the walls were caked with their own excrement.

Sands also wrote two songs—"I Wish I Was Back Home in Derry" and "McIlhatton"—which were later recorded by Ireland's premier folk singer Christy Moore. Moore was relatively unusual in terms of his sympathetic stance. He wrote and recorded several songs directly referring to events in the north, such as "On the Bridge" (about the strip searching of women republican prisoners), "The

Boy From Tamlaghtduff" (about the second hunger striker to die, Francis Hughes), and "Minds Locked Shut" (about "Bloody Sunday," the British army massacre of 14 civil rights marchers in Derry in 1972). Other folk artists tended either to avoid direct political engagement in their songs or to pen lyrics that condemned violence, such as James Simmons's "Claudy" (about an IRA bomb that killed seven people in the village of that name), Tommy Sands's "There Were Roses" (about sectarian murders), and Paul Brady's evocative and sarcastic "The Island": "And that twisted wreckage down on main street will bring us all together in the end, while we go marching down the road to freedom." Few artists other than Moore were consistent about including state violence in their condemnation.

Distancing oneself from the violence of northern politics was even more de rigeur when it came to pop and rock music. These genres do not easily lend themselves to political commentary. So, arguably the most famous export of the Northern Ireland music scene, Van Morrison, reinvented himself along the way as a Celt but studiously avoided any reference to the conflict in his native Belfast. Those artists who went against the grain tended to address themselves to condemning violence. Whether such songs can be judged as whimsical or banal, the fact is that they did little to inform the public about the complexity of the war in the north of Ireland. Spandau Ballet's "Across the Barricades" in effect places the story of Romeo and Juliet in Belfast, whereas Simple Minds's "Belfast Child" takes the haunting melody of the traditional song "She Moves Through the Fair" as a vehicle for the wish that the Belfast child will sing again. Some artists went further: Paul McCartney urged Britain to "Give Ireland Back to the Irish," whereas fellow Beatle John Lennon tackled the issue of anti-Irish racism in "The Luck of the Irish."

U2 took a different tactic. Fearful that their hit song "Sunday Bloody Sunday" could be read as a rebel song, lead singer Bono took to introducing it with the words, "This is not a rebel song." Perhaps in response, Sinead O'Connor used this disclaimer as the basis of the title of her ironic "This Is a Rebel Song," wherein the relationship between Britain and Ireland is portrayed in the metaphor of a difficult love affair: "How come you've never said you love me / In all the time

you've known me / How come you never say you're sorry / And I do."

In the 1980s, punk musicians tended to be more enthusiastic about tackling the Irish issue, with British groups such as the Au Pairs condemning strip searching of women prisoners ("Torture") or the Pogues' protest at the jailing of the Birmingham Six. Punk bands based in Northern Ireland had a more difficult time and tended either to avoid politics altogether (such as the Undertones) or condemn all violence in pursuit of an "Alternative Ulster" (Stiff Little Fingers). One rap band, New York–based Black 47, was unapologetic in its pro-republican stance in songs such as "Unrepentant Fenian Bastard."

Finally, one could listen to the entire output of rebel song groups, folk artists, and pop and rock entertainers on the Irish conflict and hear little about the unionist or loyalist viewpoint. There were a few exceptions, such as the contribution of the British fascist group Skrewdriver: "Smash the IRA." For the most part, it was left to the loyalists themselves to compose and perform their own odes of self-praise, such as "There'll Always Be an Ulster" and "I Was Born Under a Union Jack" (to the tune of "I Was Born Under a Wandering Star"). These new songs joined several traditional favorites such as "The Sash My Father Wore" and the stirring account of a sectarian attack on Catholics in 1849 ("Dolly's Brae") in the loyalist canon. Although performed to enthusiastic audiences in loyalist drinking clubs, none of these songs ever managed to break through to a more general audience.

For those songs from whichever genre did break through, there was another obstacle of censorship. Under Section 31 of the Broadcasting Act, the Irish government in effect banned the broadcasting of all political songs between 1971 and 1993, which included not only the songs of Christy Moore but also the traditional rebel ballads sung by such world-famous groups as The Clancy Brothers. The Pogues were among those who fell foul of the British broadcasting ban, which existed between 1988 and 1994.

Bill Rolston

See also *La Nova Cançó* Protest Song (Països Catalans);
  Music and Dissent (Ghana and Nigeria); Music and
  Social Protest (Malawi); Political Song (Liberia and
  Sierra Leone); *Rembetiko* Songs (Greece)

Further Readings

McLaughlin, J. (2003). *One green hill: Journeys through Irish songs*. Belfast, Northern Ireland: Beyond the Pale Publication.

Rolston, B. (1999). Music and politics in Ireland: The case of loyalism. In J. P. Harrington & E. J. Mitchell (Eds.), *Politics and performance in contemporary Northern Ireland* (pp. 29–56). Amherst: University of Massachusetts Press.

Rolston, B. (2001). "This is not a rebel song": The Irish conflict and popular music. *Race and Class, 42*(3), 49–67.

POPULAR MUSIC AND POLITICAL EXPRESSION (CÔTE D'IVOIRE)

Zouglou is a popular music style of Côte d'Ivoire identified primarily by its outspoken social commentary and its dance with angular arm movements. It started as a percussive music sung to the accompaniment of a tam-tam (*jembe*), glass bottles, and rattles, but in studio recordings keyboards and synthesizers are essential components. The term *zouglou* emerged between 1990 and 1991 at the student residence at Abidjan University during a turbulent time in the early 1990s when students and professors were at the forefront of a movement demanding political pluralism. Their demands included press freedom and the dismantling of the single party state run by then-president Félix Houphouët-Boigny and the Côte d'Ivoire Democratic Party (*Parti Démocratique de Côte d'Ivoire*, PDCI). They were initially met with repression, but eventually political parties and elections were legalized.

Students used *zouglou* and its dance form to protest against their deteriorating living and working conditions, as the effects of economic crisis became unbearable. This was most clearly reflected in the dance. In the original version, the dancers lifted their arms to the sky to signify an appeal to God to help students in their hardship. Then, the dancers stretched their arms downward, to show they are blocked, because after years of studies, they cannot find work.

This is the symbolism that made *zouglou* the most distinctive and well known of many of musical styles popular in Côte d'Ivoire, including West African reggae, *coupé-decalé,* and hip hop. As urban music, *zouglou* is not associated with any particular region or ethnic group—it is a national music drawing on an eclectic mix of local rhythms and melodies and is internationally recognized as quintessentially Ivorian.

As this new style gained popularity across the country, youth from the ghettoes of Abidjan also took up *zouglou,* and many singers from these quarters used it to express their anguish at an uncertain future and the increasing poverty. As of 2010, *zouglou* groups consist of a lead vocalist and one to three backing singers, predominantly male. Some of today's most famous *zouglou* bands include *Magic System, Yodé & Siro, Espoir 2000,* and *Garagistes. Zouglou* distinguishes itself through its use of *Nouchi,* the French street-slang spoken in Abidjan, and its use of very direct, outspoken texts rather than of subtly coded messages. *Zouglou*'s pervasive use of satirical humor has also won it many listeners and great acclaim.

Thus, *zouglou* in a real sense became street poetry, and its main themes criticized social problems. It also critiques the political elite and thus gained a reputation as socially and political engaged music, even though *zouglou* musicians make it clear that they are not adherents of any party. They do, however, view it as part of their role as musicians to criticize the ruthless behavior of those in power.

Zouglou and Political Unrest

A rapid overview of the political changes in Côte d'Ivoire since 1990 allows a closer understanding of *zouglou*'s significant political messages and enduring role as music of social comment.

In April 1990, Houphouët-Boigny legalized opposition parties and multiparty politics. He won the October 1990 election against established opposition leader Laurent Gbagbo of the Ivorian People's Front (*Front Populaire Ivorien,* FPI). When he died in 1993, Henri Konan Bédié, who was the leader of the National Assembly, took office as prescribed by the constitution Houphouët-Boigny had designed. In protest, Alassane Dramane Ouattara, Bédié's main rival, quit as prime minister. Several PDCI members favoring Ouattara's economic policies broke away to form the

Rassemblement des Républicains (RDR). Bédié viewed this as a grave threat and issued a decree barring Ouattara from running in the 1995 elections, asserting that his nationality was suspect and that he might actually be from Burkina Faso.

Bédié's strategy also revived the concept of *Ivoirité*. This had the negative effect of creating Ivoirians of different degrees, "pure" and "mixed," and questioning the nationality of urban migrants from the north. *Zouglou* artists, such as Yodé & Siro, denounced this political use of *Ivoirité* in their song *Tu sais qui je suis* (You know who I am). As mentioned earlier, *zouglou* represents a pan-Ivorian identity that transcends ethnicity.

As a result of Ouattara's exclusion, the RDR and the FPI boycotted the 1995 elections, which Bédié therefore won. In December 1999, General Robert Guéï overthrew Bédié, stating that he had no presidential ambitions and promised free elections in 2000. At this time, *zouglou*, along with reggae, had become key channels for raising political awareness and mobilization, and both genres were recognized as helping to build up the dissatisfaction that prompted Bédié's overthrow.

Zouglou's contradictory political status, however, became apparent during the country's ensuing political crisis. In the October 2000 election, General Guéï declared himself president. Mass demonstrations ensued, Guéï fled the country, and Gbagbo was declared president. In September 2002, after a failed coup against Gbagbo, the rebels, later known as the New Forces (*Forces Nouvelles*) under the leadership of Guillaume Soro, gained control of the northern half of the country.

To mobilize against the rebellion, Charles Blé Goudé, who is the founder of the Alliance of Young Patriots (*Alliance des Jeunes Patriotes*), used *zouglou*, but thereby was accused of propping up President Gbagbo. Therefore, although *zouglou* presented itself as resistance music against the rebellion, it was dismissed by some as propaganda. Many artists insisted their songs were to uphold the constitutional institutions that were under attack, and that the lyrics' calls for peace and unity were to denounce the war and call for reconciliation.

CD and cassette compilations released in the local market at this time were termed "patriotic albums" and featured many well-known artists. Such albums included *Libérez mon pays* (Free my country), *Prends ma main* (Take my hand), and *David vs. Goliath*. The titles in themselves provide an interesting commentary on local views of the crisis. Despite a general assumption that musicians received money for these patriotic contributions, musicians have maintained that this was not the case. (They did, of course, benefit financially from extensive airplay.)

In March 2007, a new agreement was signed between the president and Soro, under which Soro became prime minister. *Zouglou* artists were still critical of the ruling powers and continue to voice important issues in their songs, such as the unresolved issue of national identity or the 2006 toxic waste scandal. *Zouglou* remained Côte d'Ivoire's number one music, and its singers still attacked political abuses and addressed social issues.

Anne Schumann

See also *La Nova Cançó* Protest Song (Països Catalans); Music and Social Protest (Malawi); Political Song (Liberia and Sierra Leone); Political Song (Northern Ireland); Popular Music and Protest (Ethiopia); *Rembetiko* Songs (Greece); Youth Rock Music (China)

Further Readings

Akindès, S. (2002). Playing it "loud and straight": Reggae, *zouglou*, mapouka and youth insubordination in Côte d'Ivoire. In M. Palmberg & A. Kirkegaard (Eds.), *Playing with identities in contemporary music in Africa*. Uppsala, Sweden: Nordiska Afrikainstitutet.

Blé, R. G. (2006). Zouglou et réalités sociales des jeunes en Côte d'Ivoire [*Zouglou* and young people's social realities in Côte d'Ivoire]. *Africa Development, 31*(1), 168–184.

Fellows, C. (2000). *Ivory Coast: Songs and soldiers*. Retrieved May 31, 2010, from http://www.bbc.co.uk/worldservice/africa/features/rhythms/ivorycoast.shtml

Konaté, Y. (2002). Génération zouglou [*Zouglou* generation]. *Cahiers d'Études Africaines, 42*, 777–796.

Schumann, A. (2009). Popular music and political change in Côte d'Ivoire: The divergent dynamics of *zouglou* and reggae. *Journal of African Media Studies, 1*(1), 117–133.

Solo, S. (2003). Zouglou et nouchi, les deux fleurons pervertis de la culture urbaine [*Zouglou* and nouchi, the two perverted gems of urban culture]. *Africultures, 56*, 121–127.

POPULAR MUSIC AND PROTEST (ETHIOPIA)

Popular music might have a central role to play in societies where the mainstream media do not allow for freedom of expression. The case in point here is Ethiopia, which is a country that, throughout the past decades, has experienced conflicts in which people find themselves caught up with little or no say in their government. In Ethiopia, local popular music has outperformed its imported rivals. Whereas newspapers or talk shows mostly reach the elite, a wide variety of audiences engages with popular culture. Popular music production is best understood as an interactive process in which the musician on one level speaks to "the people" and on another level speaks of and on behalf of them.

Music has always played an important role in Ethiopian culture. It is as important as it is diverse. Music has been part of all significant social movements, from ancient battles, through the periods of Haile Selassie's imperial reign and the military Derg regime, to the contemporary situation. Music is important in religion; traditional Orthodox Church songs are chanted by priests at specific times of day both in the cities and in rural areas, whereas other forms of traditional music are influenced by Muslim traditions.

Cultural isolationism has emerged from Ethiopia's unique history and location. Known as the only African country never colonized, Ethiopia enjoyed a spiritual and political independence for thousands of years, violated only briefly by Mussolini in the 1930s. This historical resistance is also found in Ethiopian popular music. Bob Marley converted Emperor Haile Selassie's historic UN speech for Africa in 1963 as the lyric for "War!" where both freedom and unity for Africa were firmly proclaimed to the world. The fact young people actually prefer listening to music in local languages to English is a unique tendency in the globalized English-speaking world.

Currently, in Ethiopia popular musical expressions are important for discourses of citizenship and belonging. Tewodros Kassahun *aka* Teddy Afro is a good example of how popular music can provide alternative sites of resistance and challenge prevailing political discourse. At the release of his second album *Yasteseryal* (It Heals) right at the

time of the 2005 general elections, Teddy Afro showed an intuitive grasp of projecting the right songs at the right time. He became an important voice in the national exchange of ideas, which articulated many expectations and represented a landmark in terms of voter turnout. The period represented more openness, but it was also characterized by more sensationalism in the media, particularly in the blooming private press.

Against this setting, *Yasteseryal* appeared and summarized the history of the past 50 years of Ethiopia. The lyrics are about love, forgiveness, and unity. They describe an embattled nation in search of new directions and repeatedly stress the need to improve and change the country. The album revealed both a timely strategist who knew his market and the cultural industry's rules, and a national poet. The record sold more than 1 million copies in a few months, and it became the biggest selling Ethiopian music album ever.

After the 2005 general elections, optimistic prospects for more openness expired when a series of serious human rights abuses occurred in their aftermath. Shortly after *Yasteseryal*'s release, the Ethiopian state broadcaster banned many of its songs and videos. No restriction was officially announced, but the songs were nevertheless prohibited from radio and TV. Through interviews with radio disk jockeys (DJs), it emerged that banning was via notices pinned up in the studio prohibiting certain songs. Among those were titles by a whole list of talented artists: In addition to Teddy Afro, these artists included Aster Awoke, Gosaye Tesfaye, Moges Teka, Fikre Addis, Neka Tibebe, Monica Sisay, Ephrem Abebe, Simachew Kasa, Hibist Tiruneh, Kebede James, and Solomon Tekalegn.

Censorship is harder to prove when there is no official documentation; indeed, its existence might be censored efficiently through threats. In interviews with radio DJs, it became clear that self-censorship was widespread, and in numerous subtle ways, DJs were discouraged from playing songs (assumed to be) critical of the government.

How lyrics were judged oppositional is interesting. In the case of *Yasteseryal,* several songs clearly reflected the public's voice challenging the ruling political discourse. To a certain degree, the singing of/listening to a song could be seen as an opportunity to demonstrate one's support for the opposition. Resistance can take many forms, depending on the severity of state oppression.

Although some texts, at least from an outsider's perspective, do not seem radical or politically challenging, the songs apparently hit a national nerve at a decisive moment in Ethiopian history. The symbolic value of the songs was probably as important as a source of popular and political protest as the actual lyrics. In some of the songs, however, as in the title song "Yasteseryal," the public's sense was explicitly voiced that the "new" politicians were similar to their predecessors.

The song begins with a description of the downfall of Emperor Haile Selassie, passing through the Derg's 17-year military rule, with its massacres and expulsions from the country, and ending with the advent of the current rulers. The leaders switched, but vengeful killings and detentions never ceased, and nothing changed in the real battle for the country's poor. In these lyrics, protest is unambiguous.

In Ethiopia, it became clear that banning a song brought attention to the song and gave it more protest credentials. Furthermore, it turned out that small record shops played a vital role in serving as "narrowcasters" and amplifiers for so-called protest music. A typical shop is only a few square meters, built of simple wood and covered from floor to ceiling with copies (legal and illegal) of CDs and DVDs, along with posters of local and international stars. Hence, the tiny record shops not only promote the music they sell by playing it through big loudspeakers but also represent a place where the topics raised by the songs' lyrics can be commented on, further developed, and discussed.

As in most public arenas in Ethiopia, women were in minority here, but several young women nevertheless said that they liked to take part in the discussions unfolding in the record shops and stressed that women singers, for instance Aster Awoke, have been important in giving women more cultural space. The small shops offered an alternative arena of expression and discussion in a situation where official media could scarcely do so.

A major weakness of this alternative public sphere is, of course, that it does not communicate with the state. However, Kimani Gecau has shown how songs with a narrative form might approximate a kind of oral journalism. We might argue that this is the case with these oppositional songs,

where the small record shops provide the communication medium. In a commonsensical manner, the singers mobilize a variety of methods to describe Ethiopian society and communicate its people's histories. Some of the protest texts re-expressed the meanings people made out of their lives, lived out daily within social relations of power and inequality. Thus, in a socially conscious manner, the music can be used as a vehicle for conveying messages and might play a role in contesting and disrupting political authority.

Kristin Skare Orgeret

See also La Nova Cançó Protest Song (Països Catalans); Music and Social Protest (Malawi); Political Song (Liberia and Sierra Leone); Political Song (Northern Ireland); Popular Music and Political Expression (Côte d'Ivoire); *Rembetiko* Songs (Greece); Youth Rock Music (China)

Further Readings

Gecau, K. (1996). *The world has no owner: Everyday resistance in popular songs of Africa*. Retrieved May 31, 2010, from http://www.wacc.org.uk/wacc/publications/media_development/archive/1996_2

Kwaramba, A. D. (1997). *Popular music and society: The language of Chiumurenga music: The case of Thomas Mapfumo in Zimbabwe*. Oslo, Norway: University of Oslo.

Orgeret, K. S. (2008). When will the daybreak come? Popular music and political processes in Ethiopia. *Nordicom Review, 29*(2), 231–244.

Prague Spring Media

This entry touches on the years preceding the 1968 Prague Spring, when Czechs and Slovaks—in their then single nation-state under Soviet domination—saw themselves as taking purely pragmatic steps to redistribute power away from the top, but not to challenge Soviet control. It mainly addresses the events of 1968, up to the Soviet invasion of August 21, and the extraordinary week that followed.

Western commentators saw the Czechs and Slovaks as reinstating parliamentary democracy; some Western leftists subjected them to suspicious scrutiny, in case they really were restoring capitalism, and the Soviet bloc oligarchs regarded them with genuine panic. Reforming Czechs and Slovaks found it incomprehensible and frustrating that their perfectly reasonable discussions should be given such loaded interpretations, particularly when their own consensus was for organizing a self-managed socialist order.

The historical character of Czech culture was a factor here. From the 15th-century revolt of Jan Hus and his followers against established religious and political authority, Bohemia and Moravia had represented an island of commitment to religious tolerance and to some degree even democracy, in a Europe of sectarian strife and absolutist kingdoms. These powerful democratic and pluralistic traditions, although repressed under the Nazis from 1938 to 1945 and under Stalinism from 1948, were very far from dead.

The country's emergence from Stalinism was pioneered in the main by filmmakers, economists, sociologists, writers, and certain magazine journalists. Film, especially animated film, was organized in small workshops, which made them hard to supervise closely, and cartoons can concentrate political critique very effectively. When the economy stagnated, economists' views had to be taken seriously. Sociologists, studying actual life, became willy-nilly spokespeople for everyday experience, as contrasted to government definitions of reality. In particular, the Writers' Union played a significant part. Its publishing house, by a historical quirk was not state owned, and it also administered a Literary Fund which allowed the Writers' Union limited autonomy.

The Writers' Union's first big victory against their sovietized state had been in 1963, to rehabilitate Franz Kafka as an eminent national writer. Given his meticulous dissection of unaccountable state power in *The Trial* and *The Castle,* the vote was politically vital in context.

The two key magazines were the Czech weekly *Literární noviny* (Literary News) and the Slovak weekly *Kultúrny život* (Cultural Life). Magazine writers enjoyed a little more freedom than journalists. Indeed, *Literární noviny* came to be under virtual self-management during 1967, as a result of disputes between the Party and the Writers' Union about who should fill its leading posts. Routinely at that time, up to a third of the material in *Literární*

noviny would be confiscated—an index of its writers' continually bucking against censorship.

Matters came to a head in the fourth Writers' Union Congress of June 1967. Speaker after speaker rose to attack censorship. The powers that be banned *Literární noviny,* threatened to abolish the Writers' Union and seize the Literary Fund, and put a colonel in charge of a new, safe *Literární noviny.* The Slovak Writers' Congress publicly denounced the changeover.

The power structure was terrified that the plague might spread to the daily press. In the period leading up to 1968, journalists began engaging in unprecedented public question-and-answer sessions. They were often a great deal more forthcoming on air or in print.

The *Literární noviny* confrontation was pivotal in the January 1968 Communist Party decision to depose the party leader Antonín Novotný, who was in power since 1953. With his imminent removal, *Literární noviny*'s challenges began to be echoed in major media.

The impact was astonishing. At once, people isolated in the Stalinist social order started to discover their common frustrations and aspirations. There were live TV broadcasts of a several-hour-long youth meeting and of an open discussion meeting in a farm cooperative. In March, 17,000 people met in Prague, with the meeting broadcasted live by radio. It went on for 6 hours and contained many moving pleas for justice for those wrongly imprisoned and executed in the 1940s and 1950s, as well as for a democratized socialism. The group voted overwhelmingly for Novotný's resignation.

Journalists went for the first time behind the scenes at party conferences, and were given immediate reports of debates within the Presidium (Cabinet). Broadcasters asked people live what they thought about the issues of the day. Readers' letters pages had to be expanded. Novotný's own son, who was the director of an educational publishing house, was exposed as having lied about his graduation.

In the *Songs With a Telephone* radio show, leading figures were telephoned on the air and asked questions about public policy, after which listeners were able to respond with critical comment. The defense minister gave a particularly poor TV interview. Soon afterward, he resigned, embarrassed out of office. The trade union newspaper editorialized on how to know when to resign. Some days later, the union federation chief resigned.

Perhaps the tensest radio interviews were with people whom the regime had tortured in the 1940s and 1950s, or with their former prison guards. One TV program actually brought together some of those who had been tortured with their former tormentors. Of all issues, this had been the most absolutely censored, for it laid bare the real character of the post-1948 regime. Justice for those deeply or irrevocably wronged in that period was a major preoccupation of political debate.

People were buying six or seven daily newspapers, and some listened to the radio until 3 a.m. Both radio and TV might be on in the same room, listeners attending to one and the other, depending on what was being said.

Even leading reformers considered the media were out of line. One bluntly asserted that once the journalists had talked themselves out, it would be necessary to clip their wings. Journalists themselves changed rapidly. Some took financial inducements to early retirement. Others became suddenly and unpredictably radicalized. The party newspaper's reactionary editor was simply outvoted at editorial meetings. Most importantly, many media executives stepped down and were not immediately replaced. In their absence, the media really became self-managed.

In several cases. journalists wrote contrary to their editors' instructions, but nothing usually happened because the press was now defined as free. In other cases, they went straight into writing stories about how and why they were being censored. Journalists generally began debunking the political codewords prevalent in the previous official discourse, such as "the readjustment of prices" (price increases), "love of truth" (readiness to denounce one's neighbor), and "love of humanity" (relentless repression of dissent). They widely defined responsible citizenship as developing "critical distrust of the government."

The story of these media in the Soviet occupation's first week is extraordinary. They helped destroy the original plan quickly to form a pro-occupation government and to liquidate reformist leaders.

Post office telecommunications staff actively cooperated with media workers, deploying the radio transmitter network installed against a potential

NATO attack, but now against the Soviet Warsaw Pact forces. Stations broadcast 24 hours a day, giving news, urging people to stay calm, dispelling Soviet claims, announcing the plate numbers of secret police cars, and even giving weather reports to farmers. Transmitters in large enterprises both broadcasted and jammed Soviet broadcasts. There were frequent reassertions of unity between the Czech and Slovak peoples. Programs were also broadcasted in minority languages: Czechoslovakia's quarter of a million Gypsies were addressed in Romany, and other broadcasts were in Polish, Hungarian, Ruthenian, and Russian. After 5 days, there were four different TV channels operating secretly, as against the normal two.

Then, the blanket descended for 21 years, muffling most voices. The Jazz section of the Czech Musicians Union became a significant focus of dissent from 1979 to 1986, even after it was shut down in 1984, and the tiny Charter 77 group also set up an oppositional nucleus, although its members, including Czechoslovakia's first president Václav Havel, were frequently arrested and interned. By the middle of the 1980s, more than 1,000 individuals had signed its call for civic rights, an act of courage given that it usually had consequences.

John D. H. Downing

See also Anarchist and Libertarian Press, 1945–1990 (Eastern Germany); Leninist Underground Media Model; Revolutionary Media, 1956 (Hungary); *Samizdat* Underground Media (Soviet Bloc)

Further Readings

Jezdinsky, K. (1973). Mass media and their impact on Czechoslovak politics in 1968. In V. V. Kusin (Ed.), *The Czechoslovak reform movement 1968*. Santa Barbara, CA: ABC-CLIO.
Skilling, H. G. (1989). *Samizdat and an independent society in Eastern and Central Europe*. Columbus: Ohio State University Press.
Wechsburg, J. (1969). *The voices*. New York: Doubleday.

PRISONERS' RADIO

Defining prisoners' radio is no easy task. Each program has its own unique format and there are minimal, if any, formal networks linking such ventures. Broadly speaking, there are two distinct types of prisoners' radio; those that primarily focus on providing information about prison issues and those that mainly play requests and dedications. This being said, it is quite common for programs to act as a hybrid, incorporating both to varying degrees.

An all-encompassing definition should include at least some of the following: song requests to and from prisoners, their families and friends, often with accompanying personal messages; news stories, interviews, documentaries, and other information that relates to prison and justice issues; and broadcasting from either inside a detention center or working with those directly affected to produce their own content. Prisoners' radio can also involve former prisoners, social justice activists, and/or government representatives as well as radio broadcasters and the occasional prison staff member.

There is, however, a third category, namely a closed-circuit radio station within the institution. In Britain, two national prison radio networks have connected internal stations with formal education and training, and the U.K. Prison Radio Association was recognized for such work with four prestigious radio awards in 2009, against competition that included the BBC.

Internationally, radio that operates for, or by, prisoners and broadcasts to the wider public exists almost exclusively within the community radio context. This is not surprising given the noncommercial nature of prisoners' programming. In addition, the laws governing prisoners' access to the media, and journalists' access to the incarcerated, are complex and daunting, and as a result, there are few examples of government or commercial broadcasters facilitating media for prisoners.

This does not mean to say that prisoners' radio *should* belong exclusively to the domain of community broadcasting, or that mainstream radio stations do not at times produce high-quality programming that deals with prison issues. The community broadcasting sector does, however, focus on community participation and, therefore, seems to be better equipped and perhaps more prepared to address the issues of prisoners directly.

When prisoners can to engage in their own radio production, they can be viewed as participating in a form of meaningful community activity,

which might be beneficial to the prisoners themselves and the wider audience (including family and friends). As such, prisoners' radio has the potential to be citizens' media in action.

On the most basic of levels, program content might be dictated by requests and letters that drive program narratives, either directly or by providing comment and ideas for the presenters' spoken word contributions. At its most interactive, prisoners' radio works directly with prisoners to produce content and (in limited situations) whole broadcasts that can be heard outside of the immediate prison community. Beyond this, there is also the participation of other communities of interest to consider—that of friends and family, activist and support organizations as well as the broadcasters themselves and the wider listening audience.

An alternative criminal justice discourse is promoted through the actual program content, contributing to multiple levels of public sphere activity. Whereas request and letter-based programs cater to a localized (and specialized) audience, information-based shows tend to broadcast to a wider, global community. Prisoners' radio programs act to create counter-publics, because they expose alternative ideas about prison and criminal justice to a wider audience, seeding the wider public sphere. This is important, considering the dearth of information circulating about prison and prisoners' issues in mainstream media.

Prisoners' shows also create enclave publics, where prisoners and their loved ones communicate with one another and discuss issues of importance from the inside out. This is a means of exercising control within an environment that, by its very nature, exists to disempower.

It is important to remember that organizing a prison broadcast does not automatically guarantee that all prisoners will have the confidence, or even the desire, to participate. The access or availability might be present, but there will still be boundaries to participation. These boundaries are created not only by the system itself, through guard strikes or when potential participants are being held in solitary, but through everyday issues such as shyness, which is exacerbated by the unfamiliar, and public, form of expression that defines radio.

Prisoners' radio broadcasting beyond the immediate prison environment has been identified in several countries, most predominantly in Australia,

Canada, Britain, the United States, South Africa, Jamaica, and certain South American countries.

Heather Anderson

See also Alternative Media; Citizens' Media; Community Broadcasting Audiences (Australia); Community Media and the Third Sector; Community Radio (Ireland); Free Radio (Austria)

Further Readings

Beyond the Bars, Australia: http://www.3cr.org.au/ merchandise_beyond_the_bars
Free FM, Jamaica: http://portal.unesco.org/ci/en/ev.php-URL_ID=26640&URL_DO=DO_TOPIC&URL_SECTION=201.html
Jailbreak, Australia: http://www.2ser.com/programs/ shows/jailbreak
Locked In, Australia: http://www.4zzzfm.org.au/ nowplaying/index.cfm?action=dsp_show&showID =12&day=2
Prison Radio, U.S.: http://www.prisonradio.org
Prison Radio Association, UK: http://www .prisonradioassociation.org
The Prison Show, U.S.: http://www.theprisonshow.org
Stark Raven, Canada: http://www.vcn.bc.ca/august10/ organizations/stark_raven.html

PROMETHEUS RADIO PROJECT (UNITED STATES)

Founded in 1998 by a small group of ambitious former micro-radio/low-power radio operators in Philadelphia, the Prometheus Radio Project is part of a larger, national movement working against corporate media consolidation. Prometheus's drive is to create an inclusive and representative media system and to help marginalized communities use legal means to gain access to the airwaves. The Project emphasizes the necessity of a culturally and content diverse media environment as critical to the political and cultural health of the United States. Its work is to foster easily accessible and affordable media outlets, diversity (both demographically and in programming), and the technical knowledge necessary.

This group quickly became leaders within a nationwide movement focusing on the legalization and expansion of low-power FM radio (LPFM) stations. Prometheus held events, which were known as "barn-raisings" after the Amish tradition of a community combining forces to build a vital structure. At its barn raisings, Prometheus would convene with a community to "raise" an LPFM station within the neighborhood. These events brought together many LPFM advocates, activists, lawyers, students, radio engineers, musicians, and all kinds of other people from around the country. All these individuals were committed to building a physical radio studio, raising an antenna, and holding the first on-air broadcast. These activities typically took place over 3 days.

The group also hosted workshops covering various topics, which ranged from basic radio engineering, legal issues, Federal Communications Commission (FCC) regulatory powers, and radio as a tool for social organizing. More than 10 communities had built LPFM radio stations with the organization's assistance at the time of writing. Prometheus Radio Project had also been active outside the United States, helping build stations with local community groups in Guatemala, Nepal, Colombia, Jordan, Kenya, and Tanzania.

Prometheus Radio Project was also instrumental in challenging the FCC on its media ownership regulations. In 2003, the FCC Commissioners made a 3–2 decision to relax ownership regulations governing media outlets and strengthen media concentration. Prometheus soon took the FCC to court. In *Prometheus Radio Project v. the FCC*, broadcast and civic groups such as Media Alliance and the National Council of the Churches of Christ came together with Prometheus in an attempt to bar the FCC from moving forward with its plans.

On September 3, 2003, the Third Circuit Court of Appeals issued a stay, keeping the new lax regulations from being enacted until the lawsuit was complete. In 2004, Prometheus Radio Project won, with the judges ruling 2–1 to require the FCC to cancel its plan. The FCC's concocted index (the so-called "Diversity Index") providing its basic rationale to encourage more concentrated media ownership, was explicitly struck down. The FCC appealed to the U.S. Supreme Court, which declined to hear the case, leaving the appeals court ruling in force.

Ricky Hill

See also Alternative Media; Citizens' Media; Community Media (Venezuela); Community Radio Movement (India); Free Radio (Austria); Low-Power FM Radio (United States); Media Infrastructure Policy and Media Activism; Media Justice Movement (United States); Radio La Tribu (Argentina)

Further Readings

Blofson, K. (Prometheus Radio). (2007). Internet radio interview. http://www.liberadio.com/2007/10/09/interview-with-kate-blofson-prometheus-radio-monday-october-8-2007

Gregor, A. (2003, September 1). What's Spanish for "big media?" *Columbia Journalism Review*. Retrieved May 31, 2010, from http://www.allbusiness.com/buying_exiting_businesses/3483798-1.html

Prometheus Radio Project: http://www.prometheusradio .org

PROTEST MUSIC (HAÏTI)

Verbal communication in Haïti is full of subversive allusion and coded messages—part of a cultural practice referred to as *mawonaj*. Thus, almost anything spoken in Kreyòl—which Haïti's mother tongue but only was made an official language in 1987—can become a tool of resistance and even mobilization. Speaking or "sending" coded criticism through double-entendre-heavy phrases or messages is known as *voye pwen* (sending a point), and for as long as anyone can remember, popular music, including religious songs, have been used to send *pwen* against repressive regimes.

Chan pwen (point songs) are common in *rara* celebrations—boisterous all-night carnivalesque processions organized to honor *Vodou* spirits, usually during Lent. Musicians play drums, differing lengths of bamboo, and sometimes the *lambi* (conch), one of the symbols of the slave revolt movement because its call reportedly mobilized runaway slaves. *Vodou* believers, *rara* participants, and fans who just want to have a good time follow the indications of the *kolonèl* (colonel) and the *majòn jon* (drum major) and dance and sing their way through the streets or down country paths.

During repressive regimes, even though a *rara*'s leader or sponsor or even most fans might not be politically progressive, the mere massing of hundreds and even thousands of Haïti's poor majority in the streets opened up a carnivalesque counter public sphere. And although many *rara* songs and rhythms honor deities, they are also full of obscene language, which can simultaneously be about political resentment as well as sex. Indeed, a *rara* procession's songs can turn from spiritual to sexual to political at a moment's notice, and the particular historical and political context can also give traditional songs new meaning.

For example, the *Vodou* song phrase *Kote moun yo?* (Where are the people?), which was first recorded in the 1950s by a Vodou-Jazz orchestra, became a *chan pwen* during the 1991–1994 coup d'état period. When *rara* processions chanted it through the dark streets in Port-au-Prince, everyone understood it referred to the thousands who had fled the country, or the hundreds of disappeared activists, or maybe even exiled president Jean-Bertrand Aristide.

Commercial bands—especially the *rasin* or "roots music" bands whose musical style combines *rara* music, *Vodou* songs, and rock and roll—also use *pwen* in their albums and in Carnival parades. Recycled traditional *rara* songs create social solidarity and remind the elite of the potential power of the disenfranchised.

In 1990, when a military regime was running the country, Boukman Eksperyans' 1990 Carnival song *Kè m pa sote* (My heart doesn't leap) caused a major political controversy. Like many *rasin* songs, it incorporated a *Vodou* chant—in this case, dedicated to the god of war—and also contained *pwen* references to "assassins," "frauds," "paranoiacs," and "idiots." The regime debated blocking the band from Carnival, but eventually allowed them to join the procession. It was a fatal error. The phrase "My heart doesn't leap" immediately surfaced in most street carnival and *rara* bands and became a defiant proclamation sung and chanted during the protests that brought the regime down only a few months later.

The power of music was to be seen—and heard—again, 2 years later. About 4 months after the 1991 coup, the band RAM added the phrase *Kote moun yo?* to its anti-embargo song *Anbago* (embargo). The Organization of American States had imposed an embargo to try to pressure the junta to step down. When the band asked the carnival crowd to sing along, soldiers cut off the electricity, a tribute to the music's power.

No matter the political context, Carnival is always a time for contestation. Originally 2 days long, the celebrations were extended to 3 days during the first U.S. occupation (1915–1934) as a way of assuaging the population's frustration. The celebrations also include street performers who put on skits ridiculing corrupt judges or the Tonton Macoutes, the regime's notorious enforcers. Some costumes recall past oppressors, like the much-reviled *Chaloska*, a ludicrous character with giant red lips based on the soldier Charles Oscar Étienne who, in 1915, executed more than 160 political prisoners in an attempt to thwart a coup.

During the first Duvalier dictatorship, more radical political organizations and activists attempted to use Haïtian popular culture as a way to reach the masses. In the 1960s, communist students formed groups with names like *Karako Blè* (the blue clothing then worn by farmers), *Lambi* (Conch) and *Vaksin* (a drum), and performed skits and wrote songs in Kreyòl, which had only recently been embraced by Haïti's *indigéniste* intellectuals. When, however, in 1968 two major communist groupings formed PUCH (United Haïtian Communist Party), Duvalier stepped up his campaign against all left organizations, driving most members and sympathizers into exile.

Students and other cultural activists continued organizing in exile, forming the *kilti libète* (freedom culture) movement in New York, Boston, and Montréal. Influenced by the Maoist belief in the revolutionary potential of the peasantry, they embraced *Vodou* more openly. The 1975 album liner notes of *Atis Endepandan* (Independent Artists), which were produced in New York, acknowledged *Vodou* and *rara*, and said they wanted to "popularize the struggles of the masses, to make revolutionary propaganda and political education."

Even though the movement did not survive the 1970s, it did help define the *mizik angaje* (politically committed music) and *chanson patriyotik* (patriotic song) for a generation. The *kilti libète* performers were soon joined outside of Haïti by other artists forced into exile, like troubadour "Manno" Charlemagne, poet Jean-Claude Martineau, and the Frères Parents (The Parent brothers), influenced by liberation theology.

During the second Duvalier dictatorship (1980–1986), exiled singers, playwrights, and poets developed a rich culture of resistance that criticized speaking French instead of Kreyòl, the state, and the bourgeoisie, as well as international organizations and Washington, all of whom, they sang and wrote, stood by as the Haitian people suffered. When the dictatorship ended, many *angaje* artists returned and attacked the greed, violence, and corruption of Duvalier's successors in power. Some entered politics—Charlemagne eventually became mayor of Port-au-Prince, one of the Parent brothers (Clark) became a senator, and his sister Lydie served as mayor of Pétion-ville.

Music and dance are also deployed by enemies of social change. The carnival-style *koudyay*, from *coup de jaille* (spontaneous gush), is a standard tool of all politicians and political parties. Koudyays are orchestrated celebrations where a powerful entity—the government, a local strong man, a politician—supplies music, food, drink, and transportation to a street party or march accompanied by music. People can have some fun, and provide the semblance of popular support. During repressive regimes, like the Duvalier dictatorship, only those in power could sponsor *koudyays*. In a more open situation, *koudyays* could also be used to contest power.

Aristide's last 2 years before his violent ouster saw dueling *koudyays*. As his popular support slipped and before contestation turned violent, his government supplied posters, T-shirts, banners, and trucks blasting music. Demonstrations of his loyal followers would swell with revelers. The opposition did the same thing. Successfully organized *koudyays* can change local and even national politics, because—as they scraped by on less than US$1 daily—most Haitians have few other reasons to celebrate.

Jane Regan

See also Community Radio (Haïti); Mawonaj (Haïti); Music and Social Protest (Malawi); Political Song (Liberia and Sierra Leone); Reggae and Resistance (Jamaica); Social Movement Media, 1971–1990 (Haïti); Social Movement Media, 1991–2010 (Haïti)

Further Readings

Averill, G. (1997). *A day for the hunter, a day for the prey—popular music and power in Haïti*. Chicago: University of Chicago Press.

McAlister, E. (2002). *Rara!—Vodou, power and performance in Haïti and its diaspora*. Berkeley: University of California Press.

PUBLIC ACCESS

Access might refer to cable television programming that is public, educational, and/or governmental (PEG), prepared and delivered by private citizens or nonprofit groups and institutions on a first-come, first-served basis. Or it might refer to ideological, cultural, even physical individual or group involvement in media that could include print, broadcasting, and/or any number of existing or emerging technologies. (Fuller, 2006, p. 20)

Enabling and encouraging citizen involvement in media, public access manifests itself across a range of technologies and treatments, but its core concern is participation in social movements ensuring freedom of speech and personal, aesthetic expression. Informational and/or educational in content, it evolves from grassroots activism by nonprofessional media producers interested in issues that might be personal and/or worthy of public attention.

In its purest form, public access operates nonhierarchically, produced by artistic, advocacy-oriented volunteers. Whereas analogies have been drawn to Gutenberg's invention of the printing press in the 15th century and the innovation of community media in the 20th century relative to citizen access, public access has expanded into examples such blogging, map making, podcasting and iPoding, text messaging by both senders and receivers, web-zining and web-logging, wikiers, digital storytelling, video-blogging, and any number of cyberactive experiments.

We see its application on websites such as MediaChannel.org, the Our Media/Nuestros Medios network, the Independent Media Center ("Indymedia"), and the Alternative Media Global Project, at the World Summit on the Information Society, conferences of the International Association for Media and Communication Research, and any number of alternatives, even guerilla media resources. And so, we have entered the 21st century with entirely new means of communication and activism demanding access for the public.

Historically, it has argued that the inspiration for citizen engagement in pluralism owes a debt to Canadian documentarian Robert Flaherty's 1921 film *Nanook of the North*, and Canada has played a significant role in the development of public access. Although radio has been impacted by principles and practices inherent in its application, the introduction of cable technology in the 1970s in the United States took John Stuart Mill's social libertarian theory, First Amendment guarantees of free speech, and Federal Communication and Supreme Court mandates for localism and viewer rights to new levels for noncommercial television. Operating rules included the following:

1. Access is to be first come, first served, and nondiscriminatory.

2. A prohibition on the presentation of any advertising material designed to promote the sale of commercial products or services (including advertising by or on behalf of candidates for public office).

3. A prohibition on the presentation of any lottery information.

4. A prohibition on presentation of obscene and indecent matter.

5. Permission of public inspection of a complete record of the names and addresses of all persons or groups requesting access time.

Stories abound. Dale City, Virginia, claims operation of the first community-operated closed-circuit television channel in the United States, whereas Grassroots TV of Aspen, Colorado, is said to be the country's first and oldest community cable television station—celebrating its 39th anniversary in 2010. *Alternative Views*, produced in Austin, Texas, since 1978, remains one of the longest running public access television programs in the country, and the investigative, alternative collective Paper Tiger has been airing since 1981. Then, with corporate takeovers by companies such as Comcast, Time Warner, Verizon, AT&T, and others since the 1980s, dedicated supporters of the system cannot help but turn to independent media watchdog organizations and scholars to monitor events. As of today, Rob McCausland of the Alliance for Community Media, a national membership organization representing more than 3,000 PEG access centers, has indicated that local programmers produce some 20,000 hours of new programs per week, serving more than 250,000 organizations annually through the efforts of an estimated 1.2 million volunteers.

Public access, we continually realize, situates itself at the heart of democratic dialogues. Reporting on experiences with a tele-village community project in Grand Forks, North Dakota, Lana Rakow (1999, p. 82) stated,

> We can bring our expertise in the history and theory of communication technologies to the table, along with our access to funding sources through grant writing and our knowledge of research processes. We can generate public discussion of the issues of public access and participation both locally and nationally.

So, public access, as we have long known, still remains a critical component of citizen journalism and peoples' participation.

Linda K. Fuller

See also Alternative Media Center (United States); Deep Dish TV (United States); DIVA TV and ACT UP (United States); Medvedkine Groups and Workers' Cinema (France); Paper Tiger Television (United States); Video SEWA (India); WITNESS Video (United States); Workers' Film and Photo League (United States)

Further Readings

Couldry, N. (2000). *The place of media power: Pilgrims and witnesses of the media age.* London: Routledge.

Dichter, A. (2003). Is this what media democracy looks like? *Media Development, 4,* 15–18.

Downing, J. D. H., with Ford, T. V., Geneve, G., & Stein, L. (2000). *Radical media: Rebellious communication and social movements.* Thousand Oaks, CA: Sage.

Fleming, M. (2003). *The Communication Rights in the Information Society Campaign (CRIS) mobilizes for the World Summit on the Information Society.* Independent study for Clemencia Rodriguez, University of Oklahoma, Norman, OK.

Fuller, L. K. (1994). *Community television in the United States: A sourcebook on public, educational, and governmental access.* Westport, CT: Greenwood.

Fuller, L. K. (2006). *Community media: International perspectives.* New York: Palgrave Macmillan.

Gillespie, G. (1975). *Public access cable television in the United States and Canada.* New York: Praeger.

Gillmor, D. (2006). *We the media: Grassroots journalism by the people, for the people.* Sebastopol, CA: O'Reilly Media.

Gumucio Dagron, A. (2001). *Making waves: Participatory communication for social change.* New York: Rockefeller Foundation.

Huesca, R. (2003). Tracing the history of participatory communication approaches to development. In J. Servaes (Ed.), *Approaches to development* (pp. 1–36). Paris: UNESCO.

Linder, L. R. (1999). *Public access television: America's electronic soapbox.* Westport, CT: Praeger.

Ostertag, B. (2006). *People's movements, people's press: The journalism of social justice movements.* Boston: Beacon Press.

Rakow, L. F. (1999). The public at the table: From public access to public participation. *New Media & Society, 1*(1), 74–82.

Stein, L. (2002). Democratic talk, access television and participatory political communication. In N. Jankowski & O. Prehn (Eds.), *Community media in the information age* (pp. 121–140). Cresskill, NJ: Hampton Press.

Van de Donk, W., Loader, B. D., Nixon, P. G., & Rucht, D. (Eds.). (2004). *Cyberprotest: New media, citizens and social movements.* London: Routledge.

RADICAL SOFTWARE (UNITED STATES)

Radical Software, which was the first magazine devoted to the emerging alternative video subculture in the late 1960s and early 1970s, published 11 issues from 1970 to 1974. It was founded as a project of the Raindance Corporation, an alternative media think-tank started in 1969 by artist and radical media activist Frank Gillette, filmmaker Ira Schneider and *Time* magazine reporter Michael Shamberg. The Raindance Corporation, which was then a collective focused on cybernetics, media, and ecology, produced Michael Shamberg's *Guerrilla Television* (1971) and *Video Art: An Anthology* (1976), which was one of the first compilations on the subject. *Radical Software* was devoted to examining the media power structure and the role of communication and media in society.

The journal often featured computer-generated graphics and comics on topics such as guerrilla television, techno-realism, and Marshall McLuhan. The journal advocated pushing the limits of traditional video to liberate it from corporate control and conventional aesthetics. *Radical Software* served as the voice for an emerging movement influenced by early 1960s rough-cut *cinéma vérité.* The journal also served as a forum for opposing groups and viewpoints within the underground video movement.

The 1968 public introduction of the first portable video camera, the Sony Portapak, which opened up to the public the power of video production, was an epochal event for the editors. They concluded there was a distinct shift in the media power structure, with the conglomerates no longer monopolizing the means of communication.

According to the first editorial page of the first issue of *Radical Software* in 1970, "Power is no longer measured in land, labour or capital, but by access to information and the means to disseminate it" (http://www.radicalsoftware.org/volume1nr1/pdf/VOLUME1NR1_0002.pdf). For the magazine's creators, the freedom of information was a sought-after ideal. Their optimism and assertions were far too sweeping, but the Portapak did give the average citizen power to create video and then disseminate it on public access television.

The magazine itself did not display a typical copyright symbol, but instead a circle with an "x" inside, which was meant to signify their wishes for the information to be copied freely. Although similar to the idea of "copyleft," which uses a backward "c" inside a circle as its symbol, Radical Software's use of their symbol predated copyleft by several years.

The publication fell victim to many of the same pitfalls as other zines. The group did not have a cheap method of distribution; instead, they would drive across country with the first run and often giving out copies for free. As a result, profits were elusive.

Mike Melanson

See also Alliance for Community Media (United States); Alternative Comics (United States); Alternative Media

Center (United States); Copyleft; Deep Dish TV (United States); Paper Tiger Television (United States); Zines

Further Readings

Boyle, D. (1997). *Subject to change: Guerrilla television revisited*. New York: Oxford University Press.

Halleck, D. (2001). *Hand-held visions: The uses of community media*. New York: Fordham University Press.

Radical Software: http://www.radicalsoftware.org

RADIO ANDAQUÍ AND THE BELÉN MEDIA SCHOOL (COLOMBIA)

Radio Andaquí began broadcasting on April 21, 1996, and the Children's Media School was founded in 2005, in Belén de los Andaquíes, in the southern department of Caquetá. Since the mid-1970s, the region has experienced the arrival of coca economies, drug traffickers, and left-wing guerrilla organizations.

Radio Andaquí

In times when armed conflict was dormant, Radio Andaquí developed programs that invited citizens— and especially children and youth—to reappropriate their own visions of themselves and their region. In contrast with most other Colombian community radio stations where the license was granted to a local nonprofit organization, Radio Andaquí's license belonged to the people of Belén.

Radio Andaquí developed a fascinating series of citizens' communication initiatives, such as *La Cantaleta,* a daily program conducted by self-designated municipal ombudswoman Marta Calderón. In her show, Calderón literally yelled at anyone who did not meet their civic responsibilities. These might be the mayor's neglect of street lights and garbage collection, or mule cart owners who did not pick up their animals' droppings, or people not keeping their backyard pigs clean, allowing bad odors to affect everyone.

The *Radio Andaquí* program schedule included programs providing environmental information, shows by and for children, programs about local

farming issues, and discussions of current public issues. Exploring ways to bring "radio technology to wherever people are, not the other way around" (Alirio González, founder of *Radio Andaquí*), this community radio station even developed a "radio-cycle," a mobile radio unit installed on a tandem bicycle.

The Children's Media School

The Children's Media School (*Escuela Audiovisual Infantil de Belén de los Andaquíes*, EAIBA) offered audio and video production education, and Internet access and training for children and youth. EAIBA was founded in 2005 to encourage girls and boys to produce and disseminate multimedia stories, chronicles, features, and news stories about local events, perspectives, problems, and ways of life.

With a population of 12,000, the municipality of Belén de los Andaquíes sits where the Colombian Andes intersect with the Amazonian plateau—a place rich with natural beauty. Since colonial times, extractive economies and consecutive waves of immigrants have permeated local cultures, and the region has become labeled as a "no-man's land." As children and youth immerse themselves in their own symbolic production in the forms of their own radio programming, they explored the nature of the region and its unique history, characters, natural resources, and cultural capital.

In 2007, during the *Children's Media School's* experiment, 13-year-old Maira Juliana Silva produced a reportage about how the arrival of cellular phones impacted her community, and 12-year-old Jordan Alejandro Moreno produced a news report about how the carcass of a poisoned dog caused the death of 13 vultures and numerous fish, with serious consequences for the local environment.

Any boy or girl from the municipality, older than 8, could approach EAIBA with a story she or he wanted to tell. The school offered her/him diverse ways to narrate the story. To develop the narrative, the child worked closely with a tutor, and together they developed a digital soundtrack that—in a second step—would be illustrated with digital photographs edited and animated, using Flash or another animation software. The child produced her/his own images and sounds taking a digital photography camera and a digital mini-disk recorder to the local scenarios of her/his story. The final product was a 2-minute digital visual narrative animated and layered with a sound track, which EAIBA called a "photovideo."

EAIBA's photovideos were premiered at a public street presentation. Each photovideo was projected on a big screen placed out in the street in front of the home of the producer or the protagonist, thus transforming the street into a public sphere where the municipality's inhabitants could see and discuss local issues. Subsequent presentations of the same photovideo are done through the local cable television channel and in local schools' classrooms; finally, each photovideo was uploaded in the school's blog. The children themselves maintained the school blog with comments and entries about their work. The local community radio station broadcasts the times and places of each of these public presentations.

EAIBA articulated its goals as follows:

1. *No camera without a story* (the number one condition to begin the process is for the child to approach the school with a local story s/he wants to tell—the school does not teach anything that the child does not need for the completion of her/his project).

2. *Technologies connect to our locality* (when a child observes his/her context through a digital camera, s/he falls in love with it, leading to taking his/her place in the community and awareness of his/her role in the construction of a collective future).

3. *We narrate what we do and who we are* (so we can discover where we want to go).

4. *We "steal" children from war* (this initiative intends to offer local children and youth an alternative to a life in the ranks of armed groups and/or drug trafficking).

Clemencia Rodríguez

See also Citizens' Media; Youth Media; Youth-Generated Media

Further Readings

Escuela Audiovisual: http://escuelaaudiovisualinfantil
.blogspot.com

Radio La Tribu (Argentina)

Radio La Tribu (The Tribe) was founded originally in June 1989 as an underground station by a group of Communication students. It is located in the center of Buenos Aires. Its activists like to call it the station "without listeners," not because they revel in being irrelevant, but exactly the opposite: Those who tune in are activists, not passive units in commercial broadcast ratings. "Switch off *La Tribu* and make radio yourself!" is its motto.

As of 2009, the station had 35 paid activists, 300 people involved overall, and approximately 55 different programs each week, with a great variety of content. In the morning, programming centered on national and international news with a political and cultural agenda. Music-wise, the focus was on independent music from all over the world, to include poetry and dance interspersed with news of social movement challenges. In the later afternoon and early evening, the station featured independent rock, cultural shows, live studio performances, and interviews. There were reports from factories that had been taken over by their workers, from union activists, from *escraches* (protest actions against the torturers and organizers of the savage 1976–1982 repression in which the military dictatorship took away some 30,000 people and disappeared them forever), and about aboriginal peoples and farming communities.

In the fierce confrontations of December 19–20, 2001, the station set up a network of locally based correspondents so the voices of those demanding the government's resignation could be heard as directly as possible, as well as the voices of those engaged in demonstrations, *escraches*, pickets, and meetings. Thereafter, every 2 weeks, *La Tribu* set about broadcasting the entire day in a particular location outside the studio, including its local hospitals, colleges, cultural centers, and community radio stations throughout Greater Buenos Aires.

La Tribu began as a refuge for a small group involved in communication and leftist political activism. With time, internal debates, and a lot of work, the station began to be built up as a space for meetings, exchange, and production by various groups that brought up initiatives to transform daily life in all spheres: political, cultural, artistic, and environmental. In this fashion, the agenda was expanding and deepening simultaneously.

Opening a cultural space, a bar with artistic activities, also meant an important leap forward in the project's repercussions. Making La Tribu's house a place for alternative groups to meet enriched the radio station's ambit. Another important decision the collective took was to produce a digest of its 20 years' experience in running an alternative media outlet to be shared with other collectives, groups, and social organizations via the Training Center. The decision to dedicate effort and time to constructing networks was another important moment in the project's life. La Tribu also participates actively in the development of community media in conjunction with AMARC, the World Association of Community Broadcasters.

The most recent task undertaken regarded action plans for free cultural exchange. In 2008, the *Fábrica de Fallas* (The Error Factory) festival was organized, representing the first Free Culture and Copyleft festival in Argentina. For 2 days, 400 people took part in informal lectures and discussions that sought to find common ground between the "techies" and the "social activists" and weaving denser networks for political action. The festival also organized a liberated projects fair, with free licenses (books, music, and photographs), a computer to copy free music, and the chance to install free operating systems in people's own computers.

La Tribu's Working Philosophy

With 20 years' experience, the radio collective had wrestled over time with many core issues facing social movement radio. As they wrote in 2004:

> Those media . . . set out in principle to transform dominant reality into open situations. It's likely that if we view each action in itself we see an isolated transgression or a deed without larger consequences. But insofar as spaces where there is resistance, disobedience and the construction of various collectives and organizations form into networks, the chances increase of constructing the society we desire in the here and now.

They continued:

> At any point in time, people have stronger desires than their everyday activities show, and that fact

allows them to alter what they say and do. In a society whose power relations are reproduced in every social setting, daily activities also emerge to let us wield power over our own lives. *La Tribu* operates to escape from the power structure's grammar, to multiply collective, non-capitalist practices, to enlarge the movements' transformative potential. *La Tribu*'s activity is in a communico-cultural space at the cross-roads of the circulation of ideas, of accounts of reality, of what is considered "information," music, art, cultural identities, cultural production, the multiplication of communicative tools. With explicitly "political" practices that go way beyond the notion that an intervention is politically effective only when accompanied by explicitly ideological language. For us political activity doesn't mean diffusing an ideology, but being active in areas where the reproduction or transformation of domination is at issue.

Bringing this down to the dilemmas of everyday practice, *La Tribu* posed some problems as the process by which people get to be "transmitters," the limits of editorial diversity, conflicts between artistic and political objectives, budget issues, developing good programming, tensions between individual and collective work, whether to encourage individual contributors or only members of groups and movements, should members of these latter see themselves primarily as part of *La Tribu* or the organization in which they have been active:

> The process by which someone gets to be a "transmitter." The problem of "What is the limit of editorial pluralism?" The tension between aesthetics and content. Finance. Constructing suitable programming. The relation between individuals and collective work. . . . Do we bring together activists from organizations and social movements, or individuals who belong to neither? Is the correspondent from *La Tribu* in an organization, or the organization's correspondent in *La Tribu*? How to maintain an editorial line that respects diversity of views?

Multiple Activities—and Finance

By 2009, *La Tribu* was active on multiple fronts. It was online as well as over the air, ran a webpage and an active blog, and was podcasting. It had archived a series of programs back to August 2006. It also ran a bookstore, a bar, and a performance space. It published books and CDs and produced video documentaries. It offered technical training courses in all aspects of community radio to children, to teens, to activists in approximately 30 aboriginal community stations in Argentina, and to farmers' stations in a region 1,000 km north of Buenos Aires. On December 31st, the station throws a street party with some 4,000 people dancing in the New Year.

Station finances come from its training programs, the cultural space (events, book and CD sales, and the bar), independent productions, advertising, and parties. There are eight "departments": the radio itself; the training program, the cultural space, business management, projects, institutional communication, technical upkeep, and improvement. Strenuous efforts are made to keep the station management and the station's finances transparent, on the philosophy that a community project can only flourish if its finances are everybody's business. Debates on policy are often long. But the station's working ethos is that to be constantly a work in progress.

Ximena Tordini
(translated by John D. H. Downing)

Note: Originally published in Colectivo de La Tribu. La radio es sus consequencias [The radio station is its consequences]. In N. Vinelli & C. Rodríguez Esperón (Eds.), *Contrainformación: Medios alternativos para la acción política* (pp. 167–177). Buenos Aires, Argentina: Ediciones Continente, 2004.

See also Alternative Media Heritage in Latin America; Free Radio Movement (Italy); Free Radio Movement, 1974–1981 (France); National Alternative Media Network (Argentina); Protest Music (Haïti); Women's Radio (Austria)

Further Readings

Colectivo de La Tribu. (2004). La radio es sus consequencias [The radio station is its consequences]. In N. Vinelli & C. Rodríguez Esperón (Eds.), *Contrainformación: Medios alternativos para la acción política* (pp. 167–177). Buenos Aires, Argentina: Ediciones Continente.
Colectivo de La Tribu. (2005). FM La Tribu, Buenos Aires, Argentina. In A. Geerts, V. van Oeyen, & C. Villamayor (Eds.), *La práctica inspira: La radio populary comunitaria frente al nuevo siglo* (pp. 303–311). Quito, Ecuador: Latinoamericana de Educación Radiofónica.
Free Culture and Copyleft Festival 2008: http://culturalibre.fmlatribu.com/?page_id=9
La Tribu Blog: http://blog.fmlatribu.com
La Tribu Radio Online: http://www.fmlatribu.com

RADIO LORRAINE COEUR D'ACIER (FRANCE)

When the French government announced in December 1978 that the steel industry would be downsized, costing 6,000 jobs especially in Lorraine in eastern France, the public locally in Longwy rapidly took action in the form of general strikes and demonstrations. Unexpectedly, the workers also initiated information media independent of the mainstream.

The first action was a pirate radio sponsored by the Socialist Party trade union (CFDT), *SOS Emploi* (SOS Job). Started the same month, it broadcasted clandestinely for 45 minutes every day. It took its mission as a struggle to open people's eyes, a struggle against fatalism or panic, a struggle to mobilize effectively, to be heard over the din of competing opinions, and fundamentally, to respond to the irrepressible desire to communicate that grew stronger by the day.

The following March, the Communist trade union (CGT) followed suit and launched *Lorraine, Coeur d'Acier* (LCA, Lorraine, Heart of Steel). Originally meant only to run a few days, it ended up broadcasting for 18 months, allowing the Longwy workers to reflect on their situation and make up their minds based on information they generated.

The difference between it and *SOS Emploi* is that whereas *Emploi* defined itself as a free radio at the service of the struggle, LCA from its start was a working-class organ in the struggle. It refused to operate underground and broadcasted several hours a day. At that time, a recent Communist Party congress had publicly defined the party's policy as one with respect for all currents on the left and openness to a variety of opinions. As a result, LCA did not function as a transmission belt for the CGT but as a means to engage with much wider circles of opinion than simply CGT activists. Thus, it was neither a pirate station nor a free station, and it was created to expand the resistance movement—even though the form union mobilization took was partly out of synch with the steelworkers' own struggle.

The CGT hired two journalists, Marcel Trillat and Jacques Dupont, as the station's linchpins who on live broadcasts, rejection of censorship, and a microphone open to everyone. Even though a clear priority was to transmit union organizing information, listeners could phone in at any time and speak live without being filtered. The right of reply was defined as fundamental. The station was set up in Longwy-Haut's town hall, and people could come in and be present as broadcasts were taking place. They could speak, not just be spoken for.

Listeners could intervene in radio discussions by telephone, with the same right to speak as the presenter or the invited guest on the show. There was not a single authoritative voice, but a variety of voices; the listener phoning in had the same right to change the subject or query the way a topic was being handled as the presenter or guest.

Moreover, having the public so deeply involved as presenters, as journalists, as technicians, meant that the station addressed the entire local situation, engaging with culture, education, health care, recreation and other topics, not just the fierce labor struggle. Thus the station greatly expanded the traditional union dimension of the struggle, transcending prior forms of organization located simply in the steelworks.

There was no tightly organized program schedule, but a series of discussion programs were put together as needed. Some of the more long-running programs included *La revue de presse* (Press Review, daily); *Le passé présent* (How We Got Here, long invited interviews); *La parole aux immigrés* (Immigrant Workers Speak); *Les mini-Coeur d'acier* (Mini-Hearts of Steel, children and teens). Also, people put together many occasional programs on various topics, including nuclear power, the local health care system, abortion rights, and freedom in Soviet bloc countries. Some of these stayed in people's active memory for a long time afterward. Cultural programming was conducted with a steady commitment to accessibility and popularization, and to sharing knowledge between workers and intellectuals.

In March 1979, when LCA was set up, the labor struggle was already slowing, and by May it had almost died away. There were practically no broadcasts about the strike, and the station itself almost imperceptibly became the main object of contention. In mid-May, a demonstration protesting the jamming of the station was met with a violent police response.

With the slackening of the steelworkers' strike, the station shifted its broadcasts to local issues: an office workers' strike in a transport firm, support for a local judge under attack from his superiors, and a mobilization around an immigrant workers' hostel. These went far beyond the specifics of union struggles, and the station became more and more independent of the CGT. The CGT responded by pulling its funding and firing without warning the two journalists who had done so much to make the station what it was. It then set up a "new formula" LCA in November, in the neighboring town of Nancy, that operated as a conventional propaganda instrument targeted at Communist Party members. The following January, the police definitively shut down LCA-Nancy.

Fabien Granjon
(translated by John D. H. Downing)

See also COR TV, 2006, Oaxaca (México); Free Radio Movement (Italy); Free Radio Movement, 1974–1981 (France); Labor Media (United States); Small Media Against Big Oil (Nigeria)

Further Readings

Charrasse, D. (1981). *Lorraine cœur d'acier* [Lorraine, heart of steel]. Paris: Maspéro.

Collin, C. (1982). *Ondes de choc: De l'usage de la radio en temps de lutte* [Shock waves: Radio usage in times of struggle]. Paris: L'Harmattan.

Donati, M. (1994). *Cœur d'acier: Souvenirs d'un sidérurgiste de Lorraine* [Heart of Steel: Memoirs of a Lorraine steelworker]. Paris: Payot.

Hayes, I. (2006). Radio Lorraine Cœur d'Acier: Longwy 1979–1980. Ce que le monde ouvrier dit de lui-même [Radio Lorraine Coeur d'Acier, Longwy 1979–1980: What the workers' world says about itself]. In F. Granjon (Ed.), *ContreTemps* (Vol. 18, pp. 76–84). Paris: Textuel.

RADIO MILLE COLLINES AND *KANGURA* MAGAZINE (RWANDA)

Radio Mille Collines (Thousand Hills) and *Kangura* magazine were two of the principal media used in the carefully planned genocidal campaign that took place in Rwanda during April–July 1994, resulting in the slaughter of approximately 800,000 Tutsi and Hutu citizens, predominantly the former, according to Amnesty International's estimates.

The slaughter was devised and led by well-placed individuals of Hutu ethnicity based in the north, who had run Rwanda's politics and economy for the previous two decades. They anticipated correctly an invasion from neighboring Uganda to dislodge them, mostly composed of a sizable Tutsi community that some 30 and 35 years before had fled from violent clashes. The killings were conducted largely by long-unemployed young Hutu villagers organized into a vigilante militia *Interahamwe* (those who fight together). They were coordinated via a national network of village mayors (*bourgmestres*).

Kangura Magazine

Kangura (Wake him up!) was a magazine founded in 1990 published every 2 weeks, 4 years before the genocide, by an extremist group Coalition for the Defense of the Republic. Literacy at that time was low in the countryside, but it was frequently read at public meetings and *Interahamwe* gatherings.

Its language and cartoons were unremittingly violent, explicitly proposing genocide as the solution to Rwanda's economic and political problems. It also diffused fake documents, especially the concocted *Ten Hutu Commandments*, which is similar in intent to the 19th-century's notorious *Protocols of the Elders of Zion* concoction alleging a global Jewish conspiracy to rule the world. The *Commandments* document asserted the Tutsi planned total domination of Rwanda, which only a war to the death could avoid.

Kangura also took pains to present Tutsi women as a major internal menace. It reiterated a myth that they were sexually promiscuous and manipulative, cold-heartedly seducing supposedly open-hearted and naïve Hutu leaders along with United Nations and Belgian soldiers, to protect Tutsi supremacy. Its venom especially spilled over on to prominent Hutu women alleged to be Tutsi friendly, notably Prime Minister Agathe Uwilingiyimana, whom for example *Kangura*'s cartoons repeatedly portrayed naked in sexually compromising poses. She and many other women

were raped and murdered as part of the genocidal campaign. As a result of vicious and effective portrayals in *Kangura* (and a dozen similar publications) portraying Tutsi women as threatening Hutu survival and seducing Hutu husbands, some Hutu women raped other women with sticks.

Radio Mille Collines

Radio Mille Collines (RMC) was founded in August 1993 by the northern Hutu elite. Radio was especially important given rural illiteracy levels. RMC's initial purpose was to counter the invading returnees' army transmitter, which consistently highlighted the government's failures and corruption, and insisted on the national importance of Hutu-Tutsi cooperation. Initially, RMC broadcasted just 3 hours each day over the government station channel, but then in January 1994, RMC installed a powerful new transmitter of its own. Its language initially was attractive to many because of its liveliness in contrast to the government broadcaster.

This liveliness showed itself nonetheless to poisonous effect in the lyrics of a popular singer Simon Bikindi and in the verbal dexterity and "radio voice" of its chief announcer Kantano Habimana. The station endlessly referred to Tutsis as cockroaches, insects, snakes, rats, and infiltrators, alleging they were systematically massacring and raping women, and disemboweling their victims.

When the genocidal massacring began, the station would announce gloatingly that "the work" (of genocide) was proceeding well; Habimana and his colleagues would read the names of leading Tutsis and Hutus who were to be exterminated, as well as locations where *Interahamwe* slaughter activities should be focused. At that point, both RMC and Radio Rwanda, which had been taken over by the *génocidaires*, were almost the only nationwide source of news, especially in the countryside.

John D. H. Downing

See also Anti-Fascist Media, 1922–1945 (Italy); Beheading Videos (Iraq/Transnational); Christian Radio (United States); Extreme Right and Anti–Extreme Right Media (Vlaanderen/Flanders); Media Against Communalism (India)

Further Readings

Chrétien, J.-P., Duparquier, J. F., Kabanda, M., &
Ngarambe, J. (2002). *Rwanda: Les médias du
génocide* (2nd ed.). Paris: Éditions Karthala.

Des Forges, A. (1999). *Leave none to tell the story:
Genocide in Rwanda.* New York: Human Rights
Watch/Fédération Internationale des Ligues des Droits
de l'Homme.

Holmes, G. (2008). The postcolonial politics of
militarizing Rwandan women: An analysis of the
extremist magazine *Kangura* and the gendering of a
genocidal nation-state. *Minerva Journal of Women
and War, 2*(2), 44–63.

Kellow, C. L., & Steeves, H. L. (1998). The role of radio
in the Rwandan genocide. *Journal of Communication,
48*(3), 107–128.

Thompson, A. (Ed.). (2007). *The media and the
Rwandan genocide.* London: Pluto Press.

RADIO STUDENT AND RADIO MARS (SLOVENIA)

Slovenia was the only republic that survived the violent collapse of former Yugoslavia without much bloodshed; it joined the European Union in May 2004, adopted the Euro currency in 2007, and is defined as the region's most successful example of political and economic transition. Within these processes, student movements (Radio Student, Ljubljana) and activism for emancipation from the state (Radio Mars, Maribor) helped to create crucial social changes. However, the true collective value of Slovenia's social movement media was in their exploration of participatory techniques and more democratic forms.

Slovenia had a relatively long tradition of participatory media. Community radio was historically significant in promoting a sense of national belonging in the 1980s. The beginnings of social movement media were in 1969, when Radio Student was established by the University Students Association in the capital, Ljubljana. Radio Mars in Maribor, the second biggest city, was planned as early as 1984 but established in 1990 to broadcast the creative contemporary music absent from the airwaves.

From its inception, Radio Student was one of the few local bastions of independent journalism,

and the only broadcast channel open to cultural "new waves." In the 1970s, it was listened to mostly for its music. It was also the first station in former Yugoslavia to have DJs who presented and reviewed the latest alternative music releases. The explosion of punk rock and independent musical production of the late 1970s coupled with the developing economic and political crisis in Yugoslavia in the early 1980s gradually shifted Radio Student's main focus to social and political issues.

The 1980s marked the establishment of Radio Student's widely respected school of journalism practice, which moved to the forefront the disruption of taboos and limits on freedom of speech, but also journalism's ethical principles. Its reputation in the region around Ljubljana was always high, in part because of its specific style of announcers and technicians who gave a distinctive touch to the programs and to the station's classic and unrivaled radio jingles.

Both Radio Student's and Radio Mars' primary objective was to publicize and investigate frequently ignored student issues, as well as those of marginalized social groups; in so doing, they also educated their listeners. Radio Student always promoted tolerance, respect for differences of opinion, freedom, truth, solidarity, and multiculturalism, but on two levels: educational and practical.

During the civil wars in Croatia and Bosnia from 1991 to 1996, Radio Student obtained first-hand information from its network of correspondents and independent radio stations. It was also the only media source in Slovenia with a regular weekly program in Serbo-Croatian, dealing primarily with the issues of refugees from the war-torn regions and their constant fight for survival.

Obstacles to Further Development

During the 2000s, capitalist interests and, consequently, media policy were two obstacles to participatory media development. As Radio Student and Radio Mars proved, ethnic groups, minorities, and civil society can become active media partners only through participatory media and, thus, really share their activities and daily problems in a wider public sphere. Slovenia's social movement media also ensured the recognition of cultural differences and civil debates that commercial media mostly neglected.

Despite this notable role in the Slovenian and European media landscape, because of the country's nontransparent media policy, the stations cannot develop and prosper as they should and could. The blame also lies with the enormous rise of commercial stations over the 1980s, because 90% of the frequencies, including all the higher range ones, were allocated before 1994, when the first Mass Media Act took effect. Nonetheless, it is clear that Radio Student and Radio Mars are in no way obsolete and will remain on the media landscape for generations to come.

Mojca Planšak

See also Alternative Media; Citizens' Media; Community Media and the Third Sector; Community Radio (Ireland); Community Radio Movement (India); Migrant Workers' Television (Korea); Women's Radio (Austria); Youth Protest Media (Switzerland)

Further Readings

Hamilton, J. (2000). Alternative media: Conceptual difficulties, critical possibilities. *Journal of Communication Inquiry, 24*(4), 357–378.

Hrvatin, S. B., & Lenart, K. J. (2004). *Media ownership and its impact on media independence and pluralism.* Ljubljana, Slovenia: Peace Institute.

Planšak, M. (2009). *Free and community media through the prism of politics.* MA thesis, University of Nova Gorica, Ljubljana, Slovenia.

Radio Mars: http://www.radiomars.si

Radio Student: http://www.radiostudent.si

RAW MAGAZINE (UNITED STATES)

RAW is a comics and art anthology magazine published from 1980 to 1991; it published for 11 issues in two volumes. Founded by Art Spiegelman and Françoise Mouly, the magazine published alternative comics, art, and illustrations primarily from the United States and Europe, as well as Argentina, Japan, and Congo. The magazine's run coincided with a decline in the underground comics movement and the rise of a more mainstream alternative comics market. The magazine took a self-consciously intellectual approach, and Mouly saw it as a way to counter the definition of comics as low-culture products driven by action and humor.

Spiegelman had edited *Arcade: The Comics Revue,* which was similar to *RAW,* with Bill Griffith (creator of *Zippy the Pinhead*) from 1975 to 1976, but its tone and content were much more light-hearted and closer to the underground ethos than *RAW.* Spiegelman had found the *Arcade* experience difficult and was initially skeptical of *RAW*'s chances. Initially funded in part by a street guide to New York City's SoHo district, self-published and self-printed by Mouly, *RAW* financed itself from issue to issue through direct sales.

Mouly and Spiegelman printed fewer than 5,000 copies of the first issue, and many submissions were unpaid from their friends and acquaintances. Eventually, *RAW* worked with publishers Pantheon and Penguin before ceasing publication so Spiegelman and Mouly could pursue other ventures, feeling that increase in publishing outlets for alternative artists meant *RAW* was no longer necessary.

The first volume was in the then-popular large-format of new wave and fashion magazines, but its second volume went to a smaller size. The early, large-format issues were typified by graphical experimentation, do-it-yourself construction—hand-stapling, glued-on pages, and die-cut and torn covers—and often included unusual inserts, such as bubble gum, playable vinyl records, sticker sheets, and stand-alone comic books, all of which had to be stapled or glued in by hand. The second volume issues were less graphical and more narrative. Topics included socially relevant works on the rightist political culture of the Reagan presidency and South Africa's *apartheid* regime, while also challenging decency rules in some explicit imagery and language.

RAW provided a venue for Spiegelman to publish serially his book-length work *Maus* drawn from his father's experiences as a Jew in Poland before and during the Holocaust, as well as Spiegelman's own difficult relationship with his father. *Maus* depicts the people as anthropomorphized animals, with the different ethnic groups each represented by a different species. Most notably, the Jews are depicted as mice, whereas the Nazis are drawn as cats. The work won a Pulitzer Prize Special Award in 1992; it has been used to teach about the Holocaust in classrooms and is the subject of some of the limited scholarship on comics and graphic fiction.

Daniel Darland

See also Alternative Comics (United States); Alternative Media; Fantagraphics Books (United States); *Love and Rockets* Comic Books (United States); Social Movement Media, Anti-Apartheid (South Africa); Zines

Further Readings

Bolhafner, J. S. (1991). Art for art's sake: Spiegelman speaks on *Raw*'s past, present and future. *The Comics Journal, 145,* 96–99.

Chandler, P. (2004). *Raw, boiled and cooked: Comics on the verge.* San Francisco: Last Gasp.

Sabin, R. (1996). *Comics, comix & graphic novels: A history of comic art.* London: Phaidon Press Limited.

Spiegelman, A., & Mouly, F. (1987). *Read yourself raw.* New York: Pantheon Books.

REGGAE AND RESISTANCE (JAMAICA)

Reggae is the heartbeat music of the Jamaican people. This distinctive style, which originated in the 1960s from the harsh urban spaces of Kingston, the capital, can now be heard in varied forms around the world. It has served as a potent medium for Jamaican and other social movements.

Leading up to Jamaica's independence in 1962, there was active experimentation with new popular cultural forms. This music genre emerged mainly from the urban working class and from rural, poor, city migrants. This loose resistance and survival movement brought together all those who felt the full brunt of the declining economic conditions that were the legacy of more than three centuries of British colonial rule.

The classic reggae anthem *Rivers of Babylon* (1972) best symbolizes these struggles and emerging anticolonial worldview. It was adapted from Psalm 137 and remains an enduring medium of lyrical resistance, with a haunting baseline message played on African drums by the celebrated group Count Ossie and the Mystic Revelation of Rastafari.

The anticolonial and religious overtones of the Rastafari reflected in it presaged the combative lyrical content that was to become the social movement's soundtrack throughout Jamaica's early decades of independence.

Jamaican music's journey has four interrelated but distinct forms that dominated specific periods. The first is the pre- and post-independence dance craze called *ska* (circa 1960–1966). The rocksteady era followed (1966–1968), giving way to the more sustained and dominant form of reggae that emerged in about 1969 and has lasted through the current era. Then came dancehall, which started in approximately 1983. Despite overlaps, continuities, and shared meaning, each form conveyed its own mood and message.

Ska and Rocksteady

The ska era, which embodied a lively flailing dance and cheerful lyrics, reflected the optimism of the young generation that grew up with the hope of casting off the colonial yoke and building "the new Jamaica." Although this genre might seem the least overtly political, speaking of neighborly love, unity, and hope for a better life, it also embodied demand for political change and social reform.

This was reflected in such tunes as *Freedom Song* and *Forward March*. Ska featured emerging artists such as Prince Buster, Desmond Dekker, and the celebrated guitarist Ernie Ranglin. It was influenced by U.S. rock as well as folk forms such as the traditional *Mento,* the spirituality of *Revival,* and the *Buru* drumming used by early Rastafarians.

Ska evolved into the more sedate rocksteady, which reflected a country beginning to come to grips with tough social conditions after independence. This dance movement began Jamaican music's shift into soulful social messaging. It was a time of simmering social discontent, official State repression of radical thought, and upper-class abhorrence of the energized Rastafari movement.

Rocksteady songs such as *Cry Tough* were influenced by the growing "rude boy" culture and concerns about the increasing crime rate. "Rude boys" were mostly urban youth, usually unemployed, who adopted tough-guy posturing as a means of survival. However, some songs were ambivalent toward the "rude boy" lifestyle. Songs such as *Rudie Bam Bam* cautioned young men to mend their unruly ways while boosting their potential to challenge an oppressive class system.

From as early as the rocksteady period, there were recordings of rastafarian songs. These expressions were the foundation for the more potent era of globally influential music, expressive dance, and social commentary that today is called reggae.

Rasta and Reggae Music

Bearing the unmistakable lyrical incantations of the Rastafari community that had by now heavily populated Jamaican cultural space and reflecting the baseline of *Buru* and *Nyabingi* drumming, reggae took the nation and later the world by storm. The Rastafari movement took its name from Ethiopia's crown prince Ras Tafari, who was later to be known as Emperor Haile Selassie. Coronated in 1930, he was the longest reigning black king and a descendant of the biblical King Solomon and the Queen of Sheba. His historic 1968 visit to Jamaica greatly intensified Rastafari's prominence.

By the early 1970s, reggae had become a medium of protest and for promoting Rastafari ideology. It spawned countercultural artifacts (flags, drums, headgear, and clothing lines) as well as terms such as *livity* (upright living), *irie* (good, positive vibes), *ital* (unsalted food), and *I and I* (me), among many others.

The reggae message openly resisted the dominant social, political, and religious order, which is represented by the biblical "Babylon." As leading reggae musicians such as Burning Spear, Bob Marley, Rita Marley, and Peter Tosh became adherents of the Rastafari faith, a wide cross-section, including artistes, students, upper- and middle-class youth, and intellectuals also began to defy their parents and authority figures to embrace the movement and the music it promoted.

Reggae music also reflected strongly the wider pan-Africanism and self-reliance advocated by Jamaica's first national hero, Marcus Mosiah Garvey, and his hemispheric black consciousness movement. The Rastafarian successors to Garvey's ideology urged "living clean," peace and love, respect for the African heritage, and repatriation to Africa.

Bob Marley emerged as the main standard bearer of this expanding Rastafari movement. His music and image also became the international face of Jamaican cultural expression all over the world. The highly acclaimed low-budget film *The Harder They Come* (1972), starring reggae artiste Jimmy Cliff, projected this message widely.

Reggae as Palette

As a counterhegemonic social and political force, reggae propagated political resistance, peace, anti-poverty struggles, the fight against police oppression, anticolonialism, black nationalism, antiracism, social injustice, class conflict, sacramental use of marijuana, and the celebration of Rastafari as a religion. Songs spoke about love for humanity and embraced ethnic diversity. The subject of romantic love also influenced the creation of a subgenre known as "lovers' rock."

Against the backdrop of the reggae rhythm, therefore, was painted a wide range of social and political messages, reflecting a growing global movement in opposition to the dominant planetary order. It inspired freedom fighters and oppressed populations in many battle zones, including those of South Africa and Zimbabwe, fighting for liberation against the evils of apartheid and settler rule.

Despite this, Jamaica's radio stations in the 1970s and 1980s still favored rhythm and blues, pop songs, and soul music. Often, reggae was restricted to weekends, late nights, or in daily 2–3 hour off-peak blocks. The mobile sound systems that could play three to four locations were vital in creating demand for reggae on radio. In 1990, the first 24-hour reggae station, IRIE FM, hit the airwaves, skillfully carving out its own niche market. It later grew into the leading radio station by consistently playing Jamaica's music. Many other channels opened up to this popular music form.

Reggae as Political Medium

Reggae and Rastafari also played a role in shaping the political movements of the 1970s and early 1980s, highlighted by the 1972 election of Michael Manley as prime minister. Manley's socialist mandate promised justice and equality to the nation's underclass and stimulated the involvement of many Jamaican musicians.

Manley skillfully manipulated his own political image into the persona of the biblical "Joshua," who led his people into the land of freedom and plenty. During the 1972 election campaign, he was also often seen carrying a carved walking stick, which was dubbed his "rod of correction," a gift from Haile Selassie. This association played into the rising popularity of Rasta and reggae music and galvanized the middle class's younger generation. The musical revolution and the vision of Rastafari were now leading the way for social transformation.

The charismatic political leader commissioned or appropriated several supportive songs from reggae practitioners. "Better Must Come" became a slogan for Manley's party. "Joshua Desire" and "Let the Power Fall on I" were among the reggae compositions that helped to fashion this political movement. Manley won the election by a landslide.

The new opposition leader Edward Seaga also recognized this affinity and drew on his years of experience as music producer to organize musical bandwagons featuring popular singers to accompany his party at rallies. Manley was returned to power in 1976, but by the start of the 1980s, there was widespread disillusionment with his socialist experiment and with the International Monetary Fund's economic policies he was forced to adopt. The heady days of idealism were gone, and the country was in an economic tailspin.

The movement for radical social transformation was derailed by Manley's 1976 State of Emergency, an attempt to stem the election-linked violence sweeping the country. Authorizing security forces to detain anyone who seemed to threaten public safety gave rise to hits such as "Ballistic Affair" and "Sipple Out Deh" (It is slippery/dangerous out there). The same musical movement that had helped Manley into power was now singing a different tune. The opposition had become strident and violence increased all around.

In December 1976, Bob Marley and his manager Don Taylor were shot and wounded at the singer's house. Marley's single "Ambush" reflected his concern that the fight for political power had turned brothers into enemies. Two years later at the "One Love Peace" Concert, Marley used the appeal of reggae in a gesture of unity to have Manley and Seaga join hands during the playing of the hit song "Jammin."

Manley's 1980 defeat election was a turning point in the trek to socialist transformation and in the tone, character, and message of the popular music. The national agenda refocused on market-driven policies in line with "Reaganomics" and "Thatcherism." The government submitted to the IMF's insistent demands for deregulation, removal of food price controls, and other supports. Ordinary Jamaicans managed culturally by turning musically inward and finding other creative expressions.

The Rise of "Dancehall"

Reggae was played initially in inner-city dancehalls, a local music space where political, social, and cultural issues could be aired live through movement, dress, and even lyrical confrontations. The promoters and producers, often the owners of the dancehall sound systems, put on the dances and disseminated the best tunes that emerged. Prominent sound system operators in reggae's early days included Sir Coxsone's Downbeat, Trojan Sound, and King Edwards the Giant. The Big Three also operated their own labels and distribution. Together, they formed the cradle of dancehall.

By the mid-1980s, "toasting," which is the style of talking or chanting over the rhythm that was so widely used earlier in dancehalls, was to become a dominant form. The music operators would introduce new songs, dances, and catch phrases with a variety of vocalizations. This marked the beginning of DJ-ing (disc-jockeying) in Jamaica, with U-Roy recognized as the dancehall recording pioneer. Although some undertones of social resistance remained and some Rastafarian chants could still be heard, dancehall was more about personal gratification and individual self-expression.

In the meantime, conventional reggae music and the reputation of Marley, Jimmy Cliff, Peter Tosh, and other leading reggae performers were growing rapidly outside of the country even as the faster paced dancehall rhythms also grew. Jamaican migrants took both forms across to the United States, Canada, Britain, and elsewhere. Music historians have especially noted DJ Kool Herc, a Jamaican who operated his sound system in New York, as the pioneer whose style of toasting influenced the birth of rap and hip hop.

Dancehall's catchy tunes and faster rhythms mirrored the changes in Jamaican society. Some lyrics sparked controversy, promoting homophobia, whereas others celebrated sound clashes and toasting skills, commented on ghetto violence and domestic poverty, glorified guns and girls, and explored sexual and gender relations explicitly.

Some of dancehall's critics have decried the music, pointing to some of its rawer lyrics featuring violence, drugs, misogyny, and a "get rich quick" mentality that contradicted reggae's values. Supporters have argued that like reggae, dancehall had become the new message, the latest driving force of social resistance for poverty-stricken people. For certain, music once again formed the medium through which the poor and oppressed articulated their counterstrategies for survival within the inner city and under conditions of unremitting economic crises.

Conclusion

The real transformative power of reggae's art form has been its role in articulating the concerns of a succession of social movements over decades. The message in the music persists and has been conveyed in different languages by Jamaican and non-Jamaican reggae and dancehall artists in far-flung venues.

It has, in the process, helped define "Jamaica" as a distinctive global brand. Despite reggae's upward social mobility, the music remains a force for innovation and popular expression, transcending entertainment to serve as a medium for resistance, struggle, and renewal well beyond the shores of Jamaica.

Hopeton S. Dunn and Sheena Johnson-Brown

See also Black Atlantic Liberation Media (Transnational); Community Radio in Pau da Lima (Brasil); Music and Social Protest (Malawi); Political Song (Liberia and Sierra Leone); Popular Music and Protest (Ethiopia); Protest Music (Haïti)

Further Readings

Chevannes, B. (1995). *Rastafari: Roots and ideology.* Kingston, Jamaica: UWI Press.
Cooper, C. (2004). *Soundclash: Jamaican dancehall culture at large.* New York: Macmillan.
Hope, D. (2006). *Inna di dancehall: Popular culture and the politics of identity in Jamaica.* Kingston, Jamaica: University of the West Indies Press.
Katz, D. (2003). *Solid foundation: An oral history of Reggae.* London: Bloomsbury.
Nettleford, R. (1978). *Caribbean cultural identity: The case of Jamaica.* Kingston, Jamaica: Institute of Jamaica.
Potash, C. (1997). *Reggae, Rasta and revolution: Jamaican music from Ska to Dub.* London: Prentice Hall.

REMBETIKO SONGS (GREECE)

From the Homeric poems of the 8th century BC to the present day, politics is immersed in and continually expressed through cultural forms in Greece. In particular, song and politics have been inextricably linked. *Rembetiko* songs (pl. *Rembetika*) are related closely to such music, yet its politics emerges mostly in subtle and indirect ways as it articulates despair, impoverishment, resignation, or even aggressive feelings of denunciation or defiance. The political element often reaches, but only just, to the level of recounting atrocities or collective grievances. *Rembetiko* also celebrated individual freedom at a time when family and clan bonds were still tight and personal relations subject to authoritarian or paternalist stances.

Indeed, the contemporary category *tragoudi* (song) originates directly from the ancient Greek theatrical form of *tragodia* (tragedy), the most brilliant of which dealt with deeply political and moral issues, in classic if not unsurpassable ways. The *Rembetiko tragoudi* is a particular type of urban popular song that was developed as the specific cultural expression of the dominated, impoverished underclass.

It reached its most distinct creative force, indeed its culmination, in lamenting the modern Greek tragedy of expulsion from Turkey in 1919–1922 and the horrors that ensued. The people who expressed themselves with *Rembetiko*, the subculture of *Rembetes* (the word's origin is disputed, but roughly signifies idlers/outsiders/musicians), had political demands yet lacked accepted means to communicate them, either because of being excluded from the mainstream or simply refusing to do so. Following their deepest needs and irrepressible urges, they advanced self-created, exquisite forms of musical expression, on the basis of

Greek popular song, the rhythms of Byzantine music, and cultural loans from other non-Greek traditions.

The urban subculture of *Rembetika* combines also other features such as their internal slang idioms as well as an assorted set of specific dances. For instance, the *zeibekiko*, a solitary, meditative dance in which the dancer improvises her/his moves "personally" along tunes played in 9/8 or 9/16 rhythms, presents a haphazard "poetry in motion," as if issuing gestural statements, now assertive and happy, now melancholy or resigned, expressing grief or frustration, because it was from bitterness that the *Rembetes* drank in bars and danced, trying to forget. During times of tension, crisis, or political rupture, the importance of such inner expressive forms, emanating from the stomach, are paramount for self-defense, curing or at least assuaging deep inner pain and feelings of loss and devastation.

Geopolitical Origins

The origins of *Rembetiko* lie in the outskirts of prosperous Greek cities of the late 19th century, both in Greece proper and in the Ottoman Empire, such as Ermoupolis, Thessalonica, Nafplion, Constantinople, Alexandria, and Smyrna. All the origin cities are ports, which explains the special bond of *Rembetiko* lyrics to the sea. By all accounts, the prosperous Greek city of Smyrna in present-day Turkey was one of the two birth places of *Rembetiko*, the other being Thessalonica.

Smyrna at the turn of the 20th century was also "Islam's City of Tolerance," lying opposite the Greek islands of Chios and of Samos. Ever since Greek independence (1830), this proximity had provided a fine cultural bridge between the West and the Levant. In Smyrna lived also a growing, uncompromising underclass of displaced Greeks, downtrodden bohemians, and plain idlers, who lived on the edge of the law. This diverse underclass had the opportunity to create its own particular expressive works.

Similarly, the osmosis between the ethnically diverse groups and cultures and the constant mingling of dissimilar cultural elements and sources fostered a truly cosmopolitan crucible that gave birth to *Rembetiko*. Outcast locals, refugees, traveling artists, and dilettanti found diversion in *Rembetiko* culture and its intriguing appeal. In this way, these social groups articulated and forged an alternative, secular politics of identity—amid an Islamized society—thereby claiming the right to individuality, cultural taste, and personal choice.

The lyrics suggest that *Rembetes* valued their freedom. Likewise, they celebrated love and indulged in love affairs and in unconventional sex. They also sang of various types of nostalgia and, above all, of their yearning for the seemingly unobtainable value of equality. This is significant precisely because the cosmopolitan Greek city of Smyrna, politically, was under Ottoman rule, and then under the nationalistic Turkish regime of Kemal Atatürk after World War I. *Rembetes* sang, then, of their yearning for emancipation. The subculture thus expressed early on insubordination toward those in power. One type of 19th-century *Rembetiko* were the *manes*, sung in the *Café Aman*, which according to Panagiotis Kounadis describe social injustice, emigration, and workers' grievances. The following *mane* might seem just a love song, but certainly it includes a message about political freedom—in conditions of subordination, ambiguity has always been a tactic of the oppressed:

> *From the sigh that I express tremble and shake the streets entirely*
> *Tremble the Bazaars of Smyrna and the Bridges of Istanbul alike.*

Political Watersheds in the Evolution of *Rembetico*

However, as Greek refugees fled en masse to Athens, Piraeus, and Thessalonica, *Rembetiko* migrated entirely to the western Aegean's shores. *Rembetiko*'s evolution has been divided into three periods, determining *Rembetiko*'s evolution from a fringe subcultural form to an acclaimed expressive culture: the original period up to the 1922 Asia Minor Catastrophe and the Greek-Turkish "population exchange" of 1923; the "classical period" (1922–1940), including the Metaxas dictatorship that began in 1936; and the "working-class period" (1940–1953) of World War II, bringing the Nazi occupation and the civil war that followed.

Apart from the perennial themes of love, death, and life; existential agonies; and betrayal, *Rembetiko* particularly in its post-1922 "Greek phase" continued to praise the values of equality and self-determination, but grew additionally "class conscious."

In addition, the *Rembetiko* way of life helped forge the emancipation of women. Women enjoyed a lot of freedom in *rembetika* dialogues and lyrics. Both women and men wrote lyrics and sang *rembetika,* and both freely frequented their and their tavernas, typically a late-night activity. In that sense, the *rembetisses* were the first Greek feminists, the first to manifest and actually live and painfully carry through their personal emancipation. This aspect projected a divergent model of gender relations from those that prevailed either in the Ottoman-Muslim world or in early 20th-century Greece.

The Collective Grounding of Rembetika

So, the *Rembetes* not only found refuge, diversion, and self-expression through this music, but also forged a radical, alternative lifestyle. Song lyrics, often conceived and written by a group, lamented the evils of class society, being forced to flee for one's life, or the pain of emigration and the loss of parting—yet also about comradeship, group solidarity, and compassion in the face of injustice. In this sense, *Rembetiko* functioned as a source of social cohesion and as survival mechanism for the downtrodden.

Such words or pleas chanted melodically and passionately, always in closed, cramped urban settings, bound people together, even if individual *rembetes* were initially unconnected and scattered. *Rembetika* were, thus, genuine creations of the lowest social classes—outcasts, ex-prisoners, the oppressed, refugees from savage wars, victims of poverty and social injustice, and the misfits under conservative regimes. The sighs that fill *Rembetiko* lyrics come from people whose lives are filled with sorrows and suffering, and people who want to forget their cares for a night at *stekia* (night clubs) in their effort to challenge life's emptiness.

The Outcome of a Cultural Osmosis

Rembetiko's uniquely Greek mingling of diverse musical styles, tunes, rhythms and instruments was likely a result of the Aegean Sea's geopolitical position as a nexus of eastern, western and African currents. *Rembetiko* also had several sub-categories, enabling the creation of sophisticated hybrid forms. However, the osmosis identified in *Rembetiko* culture is part of a long and broader process of cultural osmosis that has characterized Greek culture ever since antiquity.

During the Ottoman period, the *Rembetiko* ethos fostered a quiet, yet defiant mood in such cities as Smyrna and Constantinople. It also encompassed self-indulgent practices pursued in the famous *tekedes,* where customers became immersed in the pleasures of opium and other drugs (legally until 1920), or the *tavernas.* This nonconformist lifestyle indicated a generally insubordinate attitude. But later, when *Rembetiko* left behind subcultural habits such as idleness, Vassilis Tsitsanis, who was one of the most revered *Rembetiko* composers and bards, sang in his piercing and poignant voice: "Don't sit fiddling with your beads; it is work that makes men of us."

Likewise, the *Rembetiko* ethos gradually became class conscious, explicitly political and subversive in a different guise. Significantly, Tsitsanis sang his famous "Hail, Proud and Immortal Working Class," which celebrated the dignity of labor. Indeed, the echo of these verses vibrates in the chest of many Greeks still today. A host of *Rembetika* was collected by Kounadis that belong to the category of working-class songs. The dynamism of the *Rembetiko* ethos, then, is evidenced in the fact that while *Rembetiko* itself underwent a process of social change, core *Rembetiko* elements and attitudes have been adopted broadly in Greece's mainstream culture.

The Feature Film *Rembetiko* (1983)

Director Costas Ferris produced a remarkable recreation of this epoch, which attributes distinctly political claims to *Rembetiko* regarding the international controversies of early 20th-century Greece, notably in relation to Turkey. Significantly, the song *Mana Hellas* (Mother Greece), with lyrics written by the contemporary poet Nikos Gatsos, criticizes the nationalist ideology of "Great Greece" of that time and the disastrous 1919–1922 campaigns against Turkey. Likewise, the film's song *Tis Amynis Ta Paedia* (The Defense boys; i.e., the

Venizelos Party) touches on the tense and prolonged 1920s controversy between the republican forces of the fledgling "democracy" and the authoritarian, foreign-imposed Greek monarchy. So, although *Rembetiko* started out as the song of the insubordinate idlers of Smyrna, by midcentury, *Rembetika* had developed and were adopted by working-class and other radical Greek movements within Greek society.

Precisely, the fear of this power explains why the dictator Ioannis Metaxas prohibited *Rembetika* as soon as he seized power in 1936.

Sophia Kaitatzi-Whitlock

See also *La Nova Cançó* Protest Song (Països Catalans); Music and Social Protest (Malawi); Political Song (Liberia and Sierra Leone); Political Song (Northern Ireland); Popular Music and Political Expression (Côte d'Ivoire); Popular Music and Protest (Ethiopia); Social Movement Media, 1960s–1980s (Chile); Wartime Underground Resistance Press, 1941–1944 (Greece)

Further Readings

Damianakos, S. (2001). *The sociology of the Rembetico* [in Greek]. Athens, Greece: Plethron. (Original work published 1976)

Ferris, C. (Director/Writer), & Leonardou, S. (Writer). (1983). *Rembetiko* [Motion picture]. Greece: Greek Film Center.

Holst-Warhaft, G. (2002). Politics and popular music in modern Greece. *Journal of Political and Military Sociology, 30*(2), 297–323.

Kounadis, P. (2008). *Hail proud and immortal labour* [in Greek]. Athens, Greece: Federation of Trade Unions of Greece.

Milton, G. (2008). *Paradise lost: Smyrna 1922, the destruction of Islam's City of Tolerance*. London: Sceptre/Hodder & Stoughton.

Petropoulos, E. (1996). *Rembetica songs* (8th ed.) [in Greek]. Athens, Greece: Kedros. (Original work published in 1979)

RESISTANCE THROUGH RIDICULE (AFRICA)

T'oro ba ti k'oja ekun, erin la fi n rin (Laughter is the only adequate response to an extremely sorrowful situation) (Yoruba proverb)

Starting in the early 1970s, most African countries have endured a combination of economic crisis and political instability. The postcolonial state has mostly failed to deliver on the extravagant promises made by the emergent political elite in the heady days of anticolonial agitation. Rather than encapsulating the collective will, the postcolonial state has become a standing impediment to the achievement of public good. In most of sub-Saharan Africa today, the state is either in full retreat or has already completely alienated itself from the citizenry at large. And because it remains, by and large, in near-exclusive control of the means of coercion, the state continues to impose its will on society, even as its moral legitimacy continues to erode.

How do ordinary people deal with this kind of situation, particularly the all-pervading uncertainty that is one of its many products? On what kinds of political and cultural resources do they draw in combating the rigors of social life, the depredations of an irresponsible elite, and the overall surrealism of social life? A straightforward answer is that people use different means, which range from forming self-help associations to fomenting rebellion against the state. African political sociology is replete with numerous examples of both. Yet, in their attention to these visible "coping strategies," scholars have tended to neglect other instruments of engagement and/or resistance that, although not as structured, nonetheless retain a degree of potency. One example is humor.

Africans' capacity for jokes can be found in the common observation that, despite harsh material circumstances, Africans still evince a zest for life unmatched even in the so-called industrial democracies where people's living standards seem radically better. A 2003 *New Scientist* survey of more than 65 countries found that Nigerians are the happiest people in the world. Patrick Chabal's book on social life in Africa is titled *Africa, the Politics of Suffering and Smiling*, thus affirming the cultural paradox that on the continent, ridicule continues to crackle in spaces and places where almost everybody agrees there is little or no cause for cheer.

If that is the case, then the critical questions arising are: What purpose do jokes serve for the pulverized African subject? Who are the targets of such humor? How useful or effective is humor in challenging the structures of domination? Or, to paraphrase Cameroonian scholar Achille Mbembe, beyond creating pockets of indiscipline, can humor really make serious inroads into the sovereign power's material base?

In attempting to answer these questions, it must be emphasized that while jokes are the focus here, they are best seen as "irregular" weapons in the arsenal of the weak, not only in Africa, but in most societies throughout human history. The most penetrating accounts of these unconventional resistance tools have been rendered by James Scott, Jeffrey Herbst, and Forrest Colburn, among others.

However, with respect to jokes, there is a major difference in that they are not necessarily the preserve of the subordinated classes. The moral ambiguity of jokes is that they can be and are often used by holders of political and economic power. Thus, although the subaltern might revel in ribaldry, at the same time, members of the ruling elite have been known to amuse themselves by poking fun at those they view (and treat) as "losers" in the social struggle. Essentially, then, humor is a double-edged sword.

Yet, scholars have invariably considered subaltern humor more deserving of interrogation because of its capacity to illuminate power relations in any social formation. Through the jokes people tell about specific social actors, it is possible to gauge where the wind of opposition is blowing, to determine whether or not the society is "open" or "closed," and to view what ideas ordinary people have about their rulers. In this sense, jokes are like a thermometer for measuring the sociopolitical temperature. Thus, Alan Dundes argues that where there is political anxiety, jokes express it; indeed, there is a ratio between political repression and the frequency of jokes.

Because most postcolonial regimes in sub-Saharan Africa have been authoritarian-personalist and because regular avenues for spitting out legitimate grievances are by and large disabled, humor has emerged as an outlet through which ordinary people come to terms with, subvert, deconstruct, get even with, or get out of (momentarily at least), the state and its shambolic practices.

As was discussed previously, for the most part, the targets of ridicule are the state and/or its agents; "powerful" individuals; and bungling government agencies. One example of linguistic sabotage is the description of the famously unreliable national power supply company the National Electric Power Authority (NEPA) as "never expect power always" or "never expect power at all." When NEPA transmuted to NEP Plc (although with no discernible change in its established incapacity to supply power), civic opprobrium was quick: "never expect power, please light your candle." These days, and arguably with one eye on the public's justifiable derision at its service, the official name has been changed to Power Holding Company of Nigeria, which a dubious public has renamed "Power Hoarding Company of Nigeria," or more commonly, "Problem Has Changed Name," a clear reference to the company's continuing failure to provide regular electricity.

On other occasions, however, ordinary people also make fun of themselves, partly in self-criticism, partly as an indictment of the system that subtly incorporates even the unwilling, and at other times as an expression of contempt for fellow subalterns who commit class suicide and make their peace with the powers that be. In these and other instances, jokes encode a sign about the totality of the prevailing situation.

The uses of ridicule are, therefore, apparent: to cause the power structure to recognize its own vulgarity; to (literally and metaphorically) desacralize the public sphere; to articulate discontinuities in the prevailing order; to exercise agency in the context of its denial, therefore attaining a form of political participation amid alienation; and last, to challenge official narratives of meaning and propose subaltern alternatives. It is, perhaps, as a result of these and its other functions that G. A. Fine hypothesizes that humor has the capacity to sustain the morale and cohesion of groups.

One important achievement of humor is that a people muffled by the prevailing order seem automatically to regain their "voice." But then what? Arguably, the most persistent criticism of ridicule as resistance is that it is incapable of inflicting fatal damage on the power structure and causing a fundamental shift in power relations. Achille Mbembe has argued that, like other acts of the dominated, humor or ridicule could ultimately result only in the "mutual zombification" of both the dominant and those whom they apparently dominate.

Although this critique is valid, we should bear in mind that subaltern humor is sometimes its own end. The process of "letting off steam" is deeply symbolic and counterdiscursive, and in the act of calling attention to the grossness of power, the alternative attains a tangible moral victory, even if its political impact cannot be calibrated.

Ebenezer Obadare

See also Barbie Liberation Organization (United States); Citizens' Media; Music and Social Protest (Malawi); Parodies of Dominant Discourse (Zambia); Political Jokes (Zimbabwe); Yes Men, The (United States)

Further Readings

Bond, M. (2003). The pursuit of happiness. *New Scientist, 180,* 40–44.

Chabal, P. (2009). *Africa, the politics of suffering and smiling.* London: Zed Books.

Dundes, A. (1987). *Cracking jokes: Studies of humor cycles and stereotypes.* Berkeley, CA: Ten Speed Press.

Fine, G. A. (1984). Humorous interaction and the social construction of meaning: Making sense in a jocular vein. *Studies in Symbolic Interaction: A Research Journal, 5*(5), 83–101.

Mbembe, A. (1992). The banality of power and the aesthetics of vulgarity in the postcolony. *Public Culture, 4*(2), 1–30.

Mbembe, A., & Roitman, J. (1999). Figures of the subject in times of crisis. In P. Yaeger (Ed.), *The geography of identity* (pp. 153–186). Ann Arbor: University of Michigan Press.

Obadare, E. (2009). The uses of ridicule: Humour, "infrapolitics" and civil society in Nigeria. *African Affairs, 108,* 241–261.

Scott, J. C. (1990). *Domination and the arts of resistance: Hidden transcripts.* New Haven, CT: Yale University Press.

Watts, M. (1992). Languages of everyday practice and resistance: Stockholm at the end of the nineteenth century. In A. Pred & M. J. Watts (Eds.), *Reworking modernity: Capitalisms and symbolic discontent.* New Brunswick, NJ: Rutgers University Press.

REVOLUTIONARY MEDIA, 1956 (HUNGARY)

The Hungarian revolution of 1956 was the largest spontaneous uprising against Communist rule in Eastern Europe until 1989. On October 23, 1956, student demonstrations rapidly snowballed into a revolutionary crowd numbering more than 200,000. The Soviet Army intervened to restore order, but was beaten back by revolutionaries armed with little more than makeshift anti-tank weapons and desperate courage. Imre Nagy (1896–1958), a reform communist, became the leader of the revolution and sought to balance the revolutionaries' demands with the threat of Soviet intervention. His tightrope act was ultimately unsuccessful, and the Red Army crushed the revolution in November. However, the revolution had profound repercussions that lasted for the remainder of the cold war.

Hungary Before 1956

World War II ended for Hungary as it did the other nations of Eastern Europe: in ruins, and either occupied outright by the Red Army or firmly within the Soviet sphere of influence. However, despite the Red Army's occupation of the country and the preference shown the Communist Party in allocating ministerial positions, something like a genuine public sphere persisted throughout this brief (1945–1948) period. Every political party enjoyed the right to mobilize its constituents, publish a party newspaper, and broadcast advertisements on the (state-run) radio. After 1948, however, the communists—led by one of Stalin's most ardent disciples, Mátyás Rákosi (1892–1971)—silenced their opponents one by one, and Stalinization proceeded apace.

Communism in Hungary, as throughout Eastern Europe, was modeled on the Soviet example. Industrialization and collectivization were the priorities, and propaganda and terror were the primary means toward these ends. Small farms were absorbed into collectives, and the resultant surplus population was channeled into industrial production in enormous factories in Budapest, Miskolcs, and elsewhere. The standard of living fell precipitously, and rationing was reintroduced for flour, eggs, meat, lard, and other staples.

Oppression, spearheaded by the State Security Authority (*Államvédelmi Hatóság,* ÁVH), was the order of the day. In the period from 1948 to 1956, the state conducted 1.7 million investigations, and more than 930,000 resulted in convictions. (The population in 1956 was 9.8 million.) Many members of the oppositional intelligentsia and the former bourgeoisie were imprisoned on trumped-up charges, but the general public also faced stringent punishment for the slightest transgressions. For instance, one could be sentenced to 8 years in jail for slaughtering pigs illegally, 5 years for embezzling funds worth under half an unskilled worker's monthly salary, or 2 years simply for making an antiregime remark while standing in a breadline.

This system muted but did not silence oppositional politics. Surveys conducted by Radio Free Europe (RFE), the United States Information Agency, and others reveal a shadow public sphere continuing its conversation *sotto voce* beneath the drone of official discourse. Although the regime prohibited listening to western broadcasts and sought to jam them, these measures seem to have been almost entirely ineffective. Many Magyars recounted listening to RFE, Voice of America, the British Broadcasting Company, and a host of other stations (primarily Paris, Monaco, Luxembourg, and Madrid). These sources provided the information necessary to debunk the regime's propaganda; moreover, the European sources provided a welcome alternative to U.S. propaganda. Although Hungarians could not criticize the regime openly, they did not stop talking politics and they were not entirely cut off from the outside world: The public sphere was not silenced by Stalinist rule, but instead it went underground.

Stalin's death in 1953 ushered in profound changes. In Hungary, Rákosi was replaced by Nagy, a reform communist who embarked on a program of "third-way" or reform socialism: reintroducing some market elements (especially in retail, a perennial problem for centralized economies), increasing consumer goods, and lessening terror substantially. Many prison and work camp inmates were set free, and stories of their innocence—as well as the torture and deprivation to which they were subjected—began to circulate widely. The state-sanctioned literary weekly *Irodalmi Újság* (Literary Gazette) became the major outlet for veiled criticism of Stalinism. It published articles and poems by writers such as István Örkény, László Benjamin, and Sándor Csoóri, who decried the hardships caused by Stalinism even as he confessed his—and by implication, the entire intelligentsia's—culpability for supporting it. *Irodalmi Újság* sold out as soon as it hit the stands, and copies were passed along enthusiastically from reader to reader. However, Nagy's fortunes shifted with the political winds

blowing from the Kremlin, and he was ousted in 1955. Rákosi was reinstated, the ÁVH was unleashed once more, and the minimal improvements vanished swiftly. *Irodalmi Újság* was reined in and Nagy was deposed, but he was not jailed or executed. He became the leader of the swiftly growing group of oppositional intelligentsia.

Thus, as of early 1956, the key elements of the revolutionary ferment were established. Working-class animosity toward the regime, partially appeased by its concessions after 1953, had reescalated. Significant elements of the intelligentsia, quiescent prior to 1953, were now mobilized against the regime. Hungarians of all walks of life had been appalled by revelations of the regime's totalitarian tactics. Nagy became the focal point for this burgeoning rebellious sentiment. Most importantly, the Stalinist system had relaxed its iron control in 1953; this raised the possibility that it could be forced to do so again.

Revolution

In February 1956, Soviet leader Nikita Khrushchev delivered his dramatic midnight speech at the Soviet Twentieth Communist Party Congress, in which he denounced some of his predecessor's horrific policies. News of the "Secret Speech" swiftly leaked out of the Kremlin: It was broadcasted throughout Eastern Europe by RFE and other Western news media and had major repercussions in Poland and Hungary. In Poland, demonstrations in June were bloodily suppressed, but the appointment of the popular Władysław Gomułka averted Soviet intervention successfully. The events in Hungary swiftly took a much more radical turn.

In March 1956, the regime allowed the formation of the Petőfi Circle (named after Hungarian national poet Sándor Petőfi, a major figure in the 1848 revolution against Austrian rule). The circle was originally a discussion group sponsored by the Communist youth organization, but its speakers delivered ever more scathing criticisms of the regime even as its numbers swelled from hundreds to thousands. At one particularly acrimonious June meeting, the famous Marxist philosopher György Lukács was received warmly for his criticism of the "assembly-line" nature of the Communist educational system and the stifling influence of censorship in academia. The Petőfi Circle was shut down later that month after a meeting on the topic of press freedom had drawn more than 7,000 participants.

However, by this time students in Budapest, Szeged, and elsewhere had become accustomed to open critiques of the regime—and discussing them much more freely than before. Popular dissatisfaction grew steadily throughout the summer. On October 6, 1956, the official reinterment of László Rajk (the victim of a 1949 show trial, executed on trumped-up charges but subsequently officially exonerated) drew a crowd of more than 100,000.

On October 22, 1956, students in Budapest announced a demonstration in sympathy with the unruly Poles. Despite a proclamation banning public gatherings, two separate groups of students, one from the Technical University on the Danube's Buda side and the other from the Arts Faculty in Pest, converged on Bem Square in north Buda in the early afternoon of October 23. (Józef Bem was a Polish general who had fought for Hungary in the 1848 Revolution.) Magyars from all walks of life rapidly joined in. By the time the two groups met, they numbered in the tens of thousands; by the time night fell and the revolutionary crowd surged back across Margaret Bridge to Parliament, more than 200,000 individuals participated. At this time the regime reinstated Nagy in an attempt to avert complete chaos. He got off to a bad start by addressing the crowd as "comrades," and according to most accounts, the rest of his speech did not go over well either. Soon thereafter, the Stalin monument was toppled, and fighting broke out at the radio station when the regime refused to broadcast the revolutionaries' demands.

These demands rapidly snowballed beyond what Nagy could grant without inviting Soviet intervention. The Kremlin might have agreed to renegotiate trade agreements and other limited demands. However, the revolutionaries also demanded civil rights, a free press, the right to strike, multiparty elections by secret ballot, the withdrawal of Soviet troops, and other measures that would have toppled communist rule in Hungary and set a dangerous precedent for Communist regimes in neighboring countries.

For the next several days, fighting raged in Budapest and the other cities. Most rebels were working-class men in their 20s. They acquired their weapons from the army and regular police, and they fought the Red Army units and the ÁVH in pitched battles throughout the capital and the other cities of Hungary. In most places, the party-state's authority evaporated almost overnight.

Two striking political developments occurred during these 11 days of freedom. First, the Smallholders' Party and other pre-1948 parties all resumed operations swiftly; their newspapers were up and running by the first week of November. They were joined by a slew of new parties and organizations from all points on the political spectrum, which added to the revolutionary tumult. Second, workers' councils formed throughout Hungary as workers spontaneously organized at the shop-floor level, taking direct control of their factories and sending delegates to present their demands to the broader revolutionary government. These workers' councils can be interpreted as a manifestation of genuine, grassroots, praxis-driven socialism: a phenomenon largely foreign to the supposed "workers' states" of Eastern Europe.

A slew of leaflets, pamphlets, and other revolutionary print media deluged the public as these groups sought to define their stances on the issues of the day; however, radio broadcasts were the most important form of media during the revolution. Although the Nagy-led Budapest revolutionaries controlled Radio Budapest (swiftly renamed Radio Kossuth after Lajos Kossuth, Hungary's other famous 19th-century revolutionary) more radical groups of revolutionaries seized radio stations in Miskolc, Győr, and other major cities. They severely complicated Nagy's attempts to lay down the law from Budapest. Radio Miskolc consistently broadcasted a maximalist line, calling for neutrality and withdrawal from the Warsaw Pact even as Nagy sought to negotiate this delicate point with Khrushchev. Radio Győr was even more radical: As the mouthpiece of the "Trans-Danubian National Council," it announced on October 31, 1956, that it would not recognize Nagy's revolutionary government unless it took a stronger line against the Soviets. Although the resurgent public sphere indeed voiced the opinions of a broad cross-section of Hungarian society, these more radical elements served only to alarm the Soviets and, ultimately, make Nagy's task impossible.

Events on October 30, 1956, seem to have tilted the balance in favor of Soviet intervention. On that day, fighting broke out between ÁVH troops and revolutionaries at Republic Square in Budapest. ÁVH members fired on both the rebels and Red Cross workers attempting to pull wounded fighters out of combat. The ÁVH troops eventually surrendered but were then summarily executed by an enraged mob. At the same time, the Suez Canal crisis came to a head, dominating Western news media as Egypt reasserted control over the canal, against British, French, and Israeli military forces. Khrushchev decided to crush the rebellion.

On November 4, 1956, 16 divisions of Soviet troops invaded Hungary. They were unstoppable. Nagy took refuge in the Yugoslav embassy but was soon seized by the Soviets, who spirited him away to prison in Romania. A total of 2,500 Magyars were killed, and more than 193,000 Magyars (roughly 2% of the entire population) fled the country. Isolated skirmishes continued to occur after the last bastion of the revolution, the working-class district of Csepel Island, was crushed on November 11, 1956.

Resistance continued into December as the Central Workers' Council of Greater Budapest (*Nagybudapesti Központi Munkástanács*, KMT) called a general strike. The leaders of the KMT were arrested on December 9, 1956, but the strike went ahead as planned. Sporadic strike activity continued into January 1957, at which point the death penalty was announced for refusal to return to work or provocation to strike. On July 16, 1958, Nagy and several other leaders of the revolution were tried for their roles in the "counterrevolutionary conspiracy," executed, and buried in unmarked graves.

After 1956

The invasion was condemned by the United Nations and most non-Communist countries. Many Western European Marxists lost their faith in the Soviet system. The Italian Communist Party lost about 10% of its members, and numerous prominent left-leaning French intellectuals—chief among them Albert Camus and Jean-Paul Sartre—spoke out against the invasion as well. The USA also condemned the invasion, but the Eisenhower White House quietly shelved the "rollback" rhetoric that had characterized its pre-1956 foreign policy. During the revolution, Radio Free Europe had broadcasted several incendiary statements as well as rebroadcasts of the regional, more radical radio stations' content; it was blamed by both domestic and foreign critics, as well as by many Hungarian refugees, for inflaming revolutionary passions and even promising American intervention. Although

subsequent research has largely exonerated RFE of these charges, RFE's shoddy performance during the revolution led to its thorough reorganization in the post-1956 era.

In a sense, the Hungarian revolutionaries lost the battle but won the war. János Kádár (1912–1989) led the restoration of communism in Hungary. The initial crackdown was followed by a series of reforms in the 1960s, as elements of the market economy were reintroduced. As a result of these reforms, Hungary became "the happiest barracks in the Soviet camp." The standard of living became higher than anywhere else in Eastern Europe besides the German Democratic Republic, and Magyars enjoyed many freedoms unequalled elsewhere behind the Iron Curtain. Finally, as the communist system collapsed in the 1980s, Nagy made a spectacular "reappearance." He had become a symbol of resistance to communism in the intervening years, and his rehabilitation was one of many demands leveled by Hungarian dissidents. He was finally rehabilitated and his body properly reinterred on the anniversary of his execution in July 1989. The collapse of communism in Eastern Europe occurred a few months later.

Karl Brown

See also Leninist Underground Media Model; Prague Spring Media; *Samizdat* Underground Media (Soviet Bloc)

Further Readings

Békés, C., Byrne, M., & Rainer, J. M. (Eds.). (2002). *The 1956 Hungarian Revolution: A history in documents.* Budapest, Hungary: Central European University Press.

Gati, C. (2006). *Failed illusions: Moscow, Washington, Budapest, and the 1956 Hungarian revolt.* Washington, DC: Woodrow Wilson Center Press.

Izsák, L. (1998). *Rendszerváltástól rendszerváltásig, 1944–1989* [From regime change to regime change]. Budapest, Hungary: Kulturtrade.

Litván, G. (Ed.). (1996). *The Hungarian revolution of 1956: Reform, revolt, and repression, 1953–1963.* London: Longman.

Lomax, B. (1976). *Hungary 1956.* New York: St. Martin's Press.

Valuch, T. (2001). *Magyarország társadalomtörténete a XX. század második felében* [A social history of Hungary in the second half of the 20th century]. Budapest, Hungary: Osirisf.

S

SAMIZDAT UNDERGROUND MEDIA (SOVIET BLOC)

Although many factors came together in the collapse of the former Soviet bloc, *samizdat* media were a formidable element in the brew. The Soviet system was launched originally in the midst of the bloodbath of World War I in the name of peace, bread, and justice, and inspired much 20th-century social justice and media activism. This was because activists around the world were frequently sustained by a myth of astonishing Soviet achievements, genuinely ignorant of or perversely blind to the appalling repression in the revolution's homeland and its colonized nations. Yet it was the very underground *samizdat* media repressed by the Soviet bloc authorities that—for nearly 30 years—helped accelerate the bloc's collapse.

The word *samizdat* means "self-published" in Russian and was coined in opposition to *gosizdat* (state-published), which was stamped on every copy of every newspaper, magazine, and book published in Soviet Russia. Associated terms are *magnitizdat* (unauthorized reel-to-reel audiotape copies) and *tamizdat* (published "over there," i.e., smuggled out, printed in the West, and smuggled back).

The unromantic resonance of "self-published" outside its Soviet bloc context—it sounds like a personal blog at best—is no guide to its political charge in its own setting. This entry focuses on two settings within the Soviet bloc: Russia and Poland.

Russia

After Stalin's death in 1953, the next 11 years saw cautious and contested steps by Khrushchev, his successor up to 1964, to soften the horrifying repression and media blackout of the previous three decades. The best known single sign was the 1962 publication of a short novel in a literary journal *Novy Mir* (New World), which was written by Aleksandr Solzhenitsyn and provided some details of his daily life in Stalin's huge chain of prison camps. This topic was banned completely in Soviet media until then.

However, after Khrushchev was ousted, his successors mounted a major 1965 show trial of two other writers for publishing *tamizdat* work, and he gave them harsh prison sentences. Other writers, who had hoped previously that curbs might continue to soften, took their cue and continued writing—but now underground. There had been small and occasional precedents earlier, but this event marked the start of a movement. The movement accelerated after "Prague Spring" in 1968, when Soviet troops crushed Czechs' and Slovaks' attempt to create open and nonrepressive reforms within the Soviet bloc.

The standard production mode was to use a manual typewriter with up to nine carbon copy sheets interleaved one each between blank pages, making 10 typed sheets in all, the legal maximum. The typing usually stretched to the margins and left no blank space top or bottom to use paper to the maximum. The copies made lower down would, of course, be increasingly blurry. Those who received one of these illicit publications were expected to retype it with at least four copies and distribute them onward, and so on.

Typing paper was not always easily available and not in large quantities. Individuals who bought more than relatively small amounts might be reported for suspicious behavior. The political police (KGB) kept each typewriter's distinctive key impressions on file—some manual machine keys were typically slightly out of alignment—to enable them to check the source of any illicit document they discovered. Later, when photocopiers came into use, access to them was strictly hemmed about by procedures and restrictions. Punishments were severe for being found responsible for any phase in *samizdat* production, circulation, or possession.

Samizdat and *tamizdat* contents were varied. It is possible that most were religious, emanating from banned Christian bodies such as Baptists or Catholics in western Ukraine, sects such as Jehovah's Witnesses, and religious Jewish groups. But they also contained poems, banned novels old and recent, short stories, political essays, the actual history of the Stalin era, plays, memoirs, satires, reports on court and prison issues for detainees, excerpts from official documents (including the barely obtainable Soviet Penal Code, and international human rights legislation), biographies of KGB and prison camp executioners, portions excised from the Soviet published versions of literary works, extreme rightist tracts, and Ukrainian nationalist publications.

The best known publication in the West at the time was the bimonthly *Chronicle of Current Events*, which methodically and nonemotively recorded specifics of arrests and human rights violations. Another important rhizomatic network without echo in official media was an environmentalist movement, with sympathizers at high levels, some of them reactionary nationalists who were horrified by the pillage of the landscape.

Magnitizdat, paradoxically, was both larger in circulation but less frowned on. Reel-to-reel tape recorders became widely available in the 1960s and were used intensively to reproduce and circulate the songs of the so-called "guitar poets," whose lyrics challenged the bounds of Soviet codes more mildly. Three of the most iconic were Vladimir Vysotskii, Aleksandr Galich, and Bulat Okudzhava. Galich's best known (*We're No Worse Than Horace*) ran:

Untruth roams from page to page
Sharing its experience with the next untruth
What's softly sung, booms
What's whispered, thunders
No concert hall. . . . No claque
A Yaooza tape-recorder
And that's it!
That's all we need!

Many of the lyrics, however, were much less directly political or not at all political in tone. Some KGB "intellectuals" were among Vysotskii's earliest admirers—but also modernizers (in Soviet terms).

As audiocassettes became more common, Western rock music began to circulate within the younger generation, in conscious violation of official bans. Often, it was first available to the children of the privileged via their parents who had permission to travel to the West, and then it circulated from there. Again, the lyrics rarely were directly subversive, but the experience of collectively flouting a stupid ban imposed by a stupid and sclerotic older generation in power was enlivening.

By the early 1980s, when not one but three visibly geriatric Soviet leaders died in quick succession (Brezhnev, Andropov, and Chernenko), the stage was set in some respects for rapid change and the energetic 54-year-old Mikhail Gorbachev. The latter soon declared publicly that the unofficial culture of everyday Soviet life, realistic, cynical, impatient for change, fed over decades by these and other "underground" sources, and the official bureaucratic sham culture, represented a form of social schizophrenia intensely damaging to the country's prospects. As controls gradually lessened over the latter 1980s, the underground torrent of dissent became an overt flood with astonishing speed. The USSR—the second superpower—was officially disbanded in 1991. Many factors contributed, but these underground media—over decades—were significant agents.

Poland

Of the many other factors contributing, the vigorous role of Polish dissent and its *samizdat* media were also important. The 1953 workers' revolt in

Eastern Germany and the 1956 Hungarian revolution aside, Poland—with the largest population in East-Central Europe—had been the most energetic opponent of Soviet control and its own sovietized regime. Substantial working-class challenges were mounted in 1956, 1968, 1970, and 1976.

In the later 1970s, opposition began to coalesce in two main quarters: the shipyard and dock workers' communities in the Baltic ports (Sczeczin, Gdynia, Sopot, and Gdańsk); and a group of disparate Warsaw intellectuals around the 1976 *samizdat* newspaper *Robotnik* (The Worker), some leftist, some Catholic, and some humanitarian, who had the courage to list their names on the newspaper. Courage was needed; although the regime stopped short of Stalin's traditional methods, activists were arrested, beaten up, and harassed continually. One woman ran into an attempt to have her small daughter thrown out of preschool. A miner lost his bonuses, was put on the lowest pay scale, had his windows painted over, had cow dung put under his front door, and his wife was told—she had distant relatives in West Germany—that there was no future for her in Poland, and that she should leave for the Federal Republic.

These oppositional forces came together in the illicit union movement known as *Solidarność* (Solidarity). The movement culminated in a long-running strike and occupation of the Gdańsk shipyard in summer 1981. It grew to more than ten million members nationally, and after a tense autumn, it was brought to a halt for many years by the declaration of martial law in December. However, the role of *samizdat* publications was significant both in feeding the growth of collective dissent up to the formation of *Solidarność,* and in beginning rapidly to regroup an oppositional underground public sphere once the immediate shock of martial law had dissipated.

In 1977, several new publications had emerged, such as the *Information Bulletin* (after the paper of the same name from the 1944 Warsaw Uprising), *Głos* (Voice), *Spotkania* (Meetings), *Opinia*, and others. ROPCIO (Movement in Support of Human Rights) was tied closely to the monthly *Opinia*. During 1977–1980, a stream emerged, then a river, and finally an avalanche of underground publications, which represented a wide range of viewpoints on how to deal with the Polish crisis.

Initially reproduced by the classic Soviet *samizdat* method, the technology gradually became more and more sophisticated—and correspondingly subject to stiffer and stiffer fines and sentences if people were caught.

The central node in this publication system, although not its only outlet, was the publishing house NOWA (*Niezależna Oficyna Wydawnicza,* Independent Publishing House). At its peak, NOWA was using no less than five tons of paper a month, and it had printed more than 200 pamphlets, journals, and books: an incredible achievement for a venture defined as illegal by the authorities and repressed whenever the opportunity arose.

People began to display its titles and those of the émigré press openly on their apartment bookshelves. Then, people started to read this material openly on buses and trains and in other public spaces. Finally, it became extremely chic to have read a wide range of underground publications. Several distribution points for this literature came to be well known and intensively patronized.

In addition, there were important symbolic radical communications. There were cartoons of *Solidarność* leader Lech Wałesa that portrayed him as everyman, as trickster, and as antihero, a sharply different message to the grandiose and aggressive depictions of Communist Party leaders in official media. Two iconic messages of defiance were the big wooden cross first set up where the regime had machine gunned the striking Gdańsk workers in 1970, and then the 139-foot steel triple cross erected later in its place.

Even a year after martial law was imposed, the deputy chief of the political police said his squads had seized more than a million leaflets, silenced 11 radio transmitters, found 380 printing shops, and confiscated nearly 500 typewriters. One of the first major messages from these sources after martial law was a detailed set of instructions on how to make your own copy machine.

With Gorbachev's accession to power in Moscow in 1985, it gradually became clear that his base wanted to avoid another Hungary 1956 and another Czechoslovakia 1968. The increasingly assertive Polish opposition began to flex its muscles, and the flood of *samizdat* publications built up again. By now, they were coming to be publicly on sale once a week at Warsaw University and in other places. The regime's collapse came peacefully in 1989, signaling that violence was in abeyance as an option in dealing with not only Polish unrest but also Russian, Ukrainian, and other Soviet bloc unrest.

Conclusions

Important stories must be told about other Bloc countries, not least the Czech Republic, Hungary, and Eastern Germany (the GDR). Together, they are significant testimony to the long-haul power of these miniscule media within the social movements they drank from and nourished. This is also an appropriate moment to acknowledge that a key part of this alternative media story also belongs to the BBC, Deutsche Welle, Voice of America, Radio Liberty, and Radio Free Europe. Their entire history is far too extensive to include here, and also it has its shadow side, but their crucial role—when they were not being jammed—was often to broadcast *samizdat* to a wider public than could possibly have accessed it directly. They were funded and designed to expand the global interests of U.S. and Western corporate power, but only to recognize that dimension of their operation is to be singularly tunnel visioned.

John D. H. Downing

See also Anarchist and Libertarian Press, 1945–1990 (Eastern Germany); Leninist Underground Media Model; Prague Spring Media; Revolutionary Media, 1956 (Hungary)

Further Readings

Blumsztajn, S. (1988). *Une Pologne Hors Censure* [Uncensored Poland]. Paris: Solidarité France-Pologne.

Bushnell, J. (1990). *Moscow graffiti*. Evanston, IL: Northwestern University Press.

Downing, J. D. H. (2001). Samizdat in the former Soviet bloc. In J. D. H. Downing, *Radical media: Rebellious communication and social movements* (pp. 354–387). Thousand Oaks, CA: Sage.

Joo, H.-M. (2004). Voices of freedom: "*Samizdat.*" *Europe-Asia Studies*, 56(4), 571–594.

Komaromi, A. (2004). The material existence of Soviet samizdat. *Slavic Review*, 63(3), 597–618.

Ryback, T. (1989). *Rock around the Bloc*. New York: Oxford University Press.

Saunders, G. (2002). *Samizdat: Voices of the Soviet opposition*. New York: Pathfinder.

Semelin, J. (1997). *La liberté au bout des ondes: Du coup de Prague á la chute du mur de Berlin* [Freedom to the end of the waves: From the Prague coup to the fall of the Berlin wall]. Paris: Belfond.

Smith, G. S. (1984). *Songs to seven strings*. Bloomington: Indiana University Press.

Sarabhai Family and the Darpana Academy (India)

In 1949, the dancer Mrinalini Sarabhai and her husband, the scientist Vikram Sarabhai, set up the Darpana Academy for Performing Arts in Ahmedabad, in Gujarat state, India. By 2009, this institution, which is currently directed by their daughter Mallika, boasted a theater, a conservatoire, a contemporary performance company, and folk dance and drama groups.

Both founders' families were committed financially and personally to the independence movement, and from its inception, Darpana was committed to diversity and social justice. To this day, it employs people of different social, religious, and cultural backgrounds, and it hosts a multiplicity of projects in slums and tribal areas, addressing domestic violence, health, and other concerns alongside projects where the artistic agenda is central but that also tackle social issues. The philosophy of Darpana is that the performing arts can be an effective medium to bring about social change.

Darpana Philosophy and Practice

Mrinalini became a *bharatanatyam* dancer, learning the classical style that was being reconstructed as part of a movement that revalorized the Indian heritage after years of subjugation to the British. While continuing this repertoire, she chose also to develop her art to make people reflect on social injustices current in India. Over the years, she challenged the subordination of women, dowry deaths, deforestation, and pollution. Her daughter Mallika is trained in the classical styles of *bharatanatyam* and *kuchipudi,* and also she creates multimedia performances engaging with social issues. Mallika's son Revanta Sarabhai and his younger sister Anahita Sarabhai, both of whom are *bharatanatyam* dancers, are engaged similarly with the family ethos, making three generations using the arts to forward social justice.

Mallika's artistic production is always political and feminist. Although she wants her works to be judged on artistic merit, as it is through their aesthetic dimension that the message will gain its potency, their advocacy is at their core. For her, art and activism are not separate. After her 1985 success as *Draupadi* in Peter Brook's *The Mahabharata*, she developed more politically and socially focused works. *Shakti—the Power of Women* (1989) addressed the female principle in myth, literature, and history, and in the turbulence and uncertainty of contemporary India, exposing the marginalization of women through the male interpretation of myth and history. Feeling that *Shakti* spoke too little to villagers, Mallika next created *Sita's Daughters* (1990). This piece was developed in discussion with women activists concerning the most pressing problems, which could be explored through performance. The work tackled issues of rape, female feticide, and infanticide, as well as the damaging role models for women offered by the male-dominated readings of mythology.

A major turning point came in 1992 with the traumatic destruction of the Babri Masjid (the Mughal Emperor Babar's mosque) in Ayodhya, when fundamentalist Hindus destroyed the mosque to reclaim the supposed birthplace of Ram, perhaps the most popular of Hindu deities, murdering Muslims in horrific acts of violence. When government ministers celebrated the event, she was deeply shocked. This led her to set up the Center for Nonviolence through the arts under Darpana's auspices and to create *V . . . Is for Violence* (1996), a work that explored violence in everyday life, not just from the victim's perspective but also from that of the perpetrators.

Another key moment came in February–March 2002, with the Godhra massacre and its aftermath, when 58 Hindu pilgrims were burned to death in a train, which ushered in an anti-Muslim pogrom. There had been communal riots in 1969 and 1992–1993, but the state government at the time publicly disapproved and pleaded for harmony. In contrast, in 2002, it encouraged anti-Muslim violence openly. According to Bikhu

Parekh, most Gujarati media were progovernment, provocative, and grossly biased. Mallika decided that her activism could no longer be solely artistic and began a direct battle with the Gujarati state government, which almost obliterated her artistic livelihood.

Hindu Fundamentalism Ascendant

In the last quarter of the 20th century, Hindu fundamentalist parties gained support throughout the country, especially in Gujarat but also nationally in 1998 with the electoral victory of the BJP party. Although Mallika's activism had been confined to her artistic practice, it had largely been tolerated. As the BJP's power increased, however, and its lack of respect for human rights became more apparent, Mallika became more publicly confrontational. Her crusade quickly became paralleled by a state government harassment campaign. Whenever Darpana engaged in building work, for example, government officials questioned its planning permission, health, and safety, or anything else to delay the work. Similarly, Darpana's accounts were regularly scrutinized, in search for the smallest irregularity, but to no avail.

The 2002 Godhra massacre spurred Mallika into action. She published an article in *The Times of India* titled, after Zola in the Dreyfus Affair, *I Accuse.* Personal threats against her started that night. Yet, she continued and filed, with two others, a Public Interest Litigation in the Supreme Court of India against the government of Gujarat for its involvement in the anti-Muslim pogrom. As with other activists for inter-communal harmony, the state government tried to terrorize her into silence, assuming she would withdraw the litigation. Mallika, however, continued both the litigation and her work with Darpana even after she was issued an arrest warrant after a spurious accusation of illegal human trafficking, and she had to go underground. From hiding, she directed *Colours of the Heart* (2003), a collaboration with British Pakistani singer Samia Mallik, and she planned overseas tours, as Darpana needed to earn money to pay its staff, having lost all its sponsorship. Civil liberties group throughout the country and overseas came to her support, yet the saga lasted to December 2004, when the case was dropped. The harassment, however, continued.

Mallika: From Artist to Politician?

Although *Colour of the Heart* continued the trend of women-centered work, Mallika also revisited Gandhian ideals. For example *Unsuni: Unheard Voices* in 2007 examined the marginalized and ignored, the beggars knocking at car windows at traffic lights, and the children running across the street delivering tea. It focused on their resilience in face of adversity. *Unsuni* was performed throughout the country and was linked to discussion groups where spectators were encouraged to create a grassroots movement to change their environment. Working with Revanta and Anahita, it was aimed at young people, encouraging them to look at India's reality, and to critique the West's hypercapitalism and consumerism. She presented these issues in November 2009 in the performance talk she gave at TEDIndia: *Ideas Worth Spreading* in Mysore, which was to be developed in Oxford, United Kingdom, in 2010 at TEDGlobal.

In 2008, she collaborated with her mother on *Khadi Gaatha,* a short performance piece that traced the history of handlooms in India (the *Khadi* movement, used by Gandhi as part of the Quit India movement to remove the British Raj). They used the metaphor of weaving (the warp and the weft) to create links with Hindu mythology and the Vedas. Similarly, *SVA Kranti* (2008), a solo piece, was about women the world over taking up nonviolent struggles to change society.

What the state government's harassment campaign achieved, therefore, was to make the artist activist revisit the Gandhian heritage and rethink her position within India. In 2009, it also helped transform an activist artist into an artist-politician, when Mallika decided to run as an independent for a lower house seat in Ghandinagar, the capital city of Gujarat. Mallika's voice had not been silenced. She came in a respectable third and seemed to want to continue.

Andrée Grau

See also *Bhangra,* Resistance, and Rituals (South Asia/Transnational); Dance as Social Activism (South Asia); Indian People's Theatre Association; Installation Art Media; Performance Art and Social Movement Media: Augusto Boal; Social Movement and Modern Dance (Bengal); Street Theater (India)

Further Readings

Biswas, S. (2009, April 11). *Dancer steps into Indian politics.* BBC News, South Asia. Retrieved May 17, 2009, from http://newsvote.bbc.co.uk/go/pr/fr/-/hi/south_asia/7989395.stm

Chatterjee, A. (2004). In search of a secular in contemporary Indian dance: A continuing journey. *Dance Research Journal, 36*(2), 102–116.

Grau, A. (2007). Political activism and South Asian dance. *South Asia Research, 27*(1), 43–55.

Grau, A. (in press). Dance, militancy and art against violence: The case of Mallika Sarabhai. *Dance Research.*

Joshi, P. K. (Ed.). (1992). *Vikram Sarabhai: The man and his vision.* Ahmadabad, India: Mappin.

Lynton, H. R. (1995). *Born to dance.* London: Sangam Books.

Massey, R. (1991, January). Mallika Sarabhai. *The Dancing Times,* January.

Parekh, B. (2002). Making sense of Gujarat. *India Seminar.* Retrieved March 18, 2004, from http://eledu.net/rrcusrn_data/Making%20sense%20of%20Gujarat.pdf

Sarabhai, M. (1992). My father Vikram. In J. Padmanabh (Ed.), *Vikram Sarabhai: The man and his vision* (pp. 32–37). Ahmadabad, India: Mappin. (Original work published 1984)

Sarabhai M. (2004, March 6) Straight answers: Mallika Sarabhai, danseuse, on International Women's Day. *The Times of India.*

Sarabhai, M. (2009). *Dance to change the world.* TEDIndia. Retrieved November 27, 2009, from http://www.ted.com/talks/mallika_sarabhai.html

Sex Workers' Blogs

Blogs often function as sites of identity negotiation and community building, allowing marginalized groups of people to create safe spaces to speak. Sex workers (particularly escorts, erotic masseuses, and call girls, rather than street walkers, porn stars, or strippers) make their voices heard on the Internet through blogs, and many sex workers find supportive and diversified communities through blogging.

In a Western society that shuns and silences sex workers, their voices and stories often go unheard. Although many documentaries and scholarly articles devote curious and concerned attention to the sex industry, the actual voices of sex workers remain problematically absent. For this reason, there are many contradictory assumptions associated with sex workers—they are alternately imagined as helpless victims, as sex addicts, as desperately caught in the "system," as empowered feminists—however, these assumptions are rarely, if ever, based on sex workers' actual lived experiences.

Because of the illegality of sex work, and the women's desire to maintain a "normal" lifestyle, sex workers often choose to live a double life—known as a sex worker only to clients, and as sister, daughter, mother, or friend to most everyone else in their lives. They seldom get to tell their own stories, and the silence perpetuates the mystery, intrigue, and downright fascination that Western society seems to have with them. The Internet's seeming anonymity makes blog forums a site of potential empowerment for this silenced segment of society.

Sex worker blogs may be read to imply that sex workers choose to blog because they feel pressure to keep their work a secret, and thus, they have nowhere else to express their working identities other than via disembodied and anonymous communication. Their blogs tend to be a mixture of work-related stories, complaints, anecdotes, insights, fears, worries, humor, and musings. Alongside work-related posts are entries about their friends, family, goals, relationships, and day-to-day mundane stories that occupy any other personal blog.

Many of the women admit to starting the blog for the sole purpose of talking about work, but then realize they cannot really separate their working self from their nonworking self, so that the presentation of identities is carefully negotiated even within the "safe" blog space. Because of the desire to maintain anonymity, some sex worker blogs are closed communities inaccessible to the general public. For example, LiveJournal has a sex worker bulletin board that explicitly states clients, johns, and researchers are not allowed. Applicants are reviewed by a moderator to ensure only sex workers become part of the community. As of 2008, the community had more than 450 members.

Although sex workers' blogs offer a "safe" space for individuals to share their stories, voice their opinions, and find support via an uncensored medium, it is also important to draw attention to the ways in which the medium limits participation. Although digital media access is growing, the Internet still requires money, and blogging itself requires a certain degree of cultural capital as well as technical prowess and leisure time. As a result, sex worker blogs tend to privilege middle-class call girls as opposed to street walkers and less advantaged prostitutes.

Jacqueline Vickery

See also Belle de Jour Blog (United Kingdom); Citizens' Media; Feminist Media: An Overview; Women Bloggers (Egypt)

Further Readings

LiveJournal bulletin board: http://community.livejournal .com/sexworkers/profile

SIXTH GENERATION CINEMA (CHINA)

Also called the independent or urban generation, Chinese cinema's "Sixth Generation" (6thG) emerged soon after the Tiananmen Square incident in 1989. Starting in the early 1990s, a collection of maverick filmmakers confronted contemporary social problems by examining the personal lives of protagonists mostly unseen in Chinese cinema before—dissatisfied and dissolute urban youth, rock musicians, immigrant and migrant workers, and gay and lesbian characters—and 6thG cinema was born.

These emphases were driven partly by the young filmmakers' own experiences and partly by their distinctive mode of production. Technology and the political climate, together with access to foreign audiences and transnational financing, made it possible to cultivate a new, smaller scale filmmaking practice, independent of China's state-run studio system and characterized by low budgets and a documentary/art film/realist aesthetic. 6thG filmmakers were naturally drawn to the low glamour, high candor, socially provocative subjects that established their reputation.

Financed often by overseas investment, early 6thG films mostly offered personal accounts of their own adolescent experiences—narrow slices of life that appealed to equally narrow audiences. Sharply diverging from their elders, they took their stylistic cues from European art film and from documentary filmmaking, featuring goal-less protagonists deployed in episodic narratives. Thematically, films such as *Dirt* (Quan Hu, 1994), *The Days* (Wang Xiaoshuan, 1993), *Little Crazy Thing Called Love* (Li Xing, 1993), and *Rainclouds Over Wushan* (Zhang Ming, 1993) articulated many 6thG directors' pervasive pessimism. More cinematic than dramatic, the films also relied heavily on voice-over narration to piece together disjointed narratives.

The early 6thG obsession with individual expression and its realist aesthetic excited critical acclaim at international film festivals, but the domestic market remained largely closed, whether from poor box office or official bans. 6thG filmmakers succeeded partly by cultivating (apparent) political subversiveness and social progressiveness, exploiting the "banned in China" cachet. As self-packaged dissidents, a few 6thG directors became bankable in overseas art circles and on the domestic black market, keeping the foreign finance coming. Zhang Yuan, for instance, made China's first "gay film," *East Palace, West Palace* (1997), with a grant from the Rockefeller Foundation.

Under these conditions, with only a handful of films officially distributed in China, the new cinema was defined as "underground" or "independent." 6thG is different from "independent" cinema in the West, which means independent from state funding and control rather than from Hollywood's entertainment conglomerates. The Chinese state, meanwhile, has mostly turned a blind eye to 6thG filmmaking, regarding it as nonthreatening at home (small audience, politically mild films), and possibly as a boon for its international image as a tolerant regime.

From the mid-1990s, however, the state began to woo 6thG filmmakers with better domestic market access. 6thG filmmakers have always exercised self-censorship by exploring provocative yet politically safe subjects so as to avoid serious confrontations with the state, even as they maintained their "subversive enough" edge overseas. However, increasing official tolerance has threatened to leave these entrepreneurial cultural dissidents with nothing new to say and little state interference to lament.

This shifting political economy resulted in the emergence of some 6thG filmmakers from the underground. Recent films by Wang Xiaoshuai (*Beijing Bicycle*, 2000), Jia Zhangke (*The World*, 2004), and Zhang Yuan (*Green Tea*, 2003) were released in China, although still not to huge box offices. Others have been successful, including Zhang Yang's *Shower* (1999), Jiang Wen's *In the Heat of the Sun* (1994), Jin Chen's *Love in the Time of the Net* (1999), and Shi Runjui's *A Beautiful New World* (1999).

These films run the gamut from contemplative drama to contemporary romance and upbeat comedy. Lately, some directors have moved into "dialect films" to appeal to regional markets within China. In fact, the 6thG is less homogeneous, with more diverse artistic visions than the preceding Fifth Generation. What they have in common, beyond their age, is the new mode of production that they developed out of necessity and at a time of new opportunity. They are less a social movement than founders of a new production mode.

On the social movement "purity scale," Chinese Sixth Generation cinema would probably score somewhere in the middle, not so much akin to a cold war–era "samizdat" movement or "velvet revolution" as to the more routine and less threatening avant-garde artistic movements of relatively free societies.

Ying Zhu

See also Challenge for Change Film Movement (Canada); Documentary Film for Social Change (India); Online Nationalism (China); Youth Rock Music (China)

Further Readings

Barmé, G. (1999). *In the red*. New York: Columbia University Press.

Pickowicz, P. G., & Zhang, Y. (Eds.). (2006). *From underground to independent: Alternative film culture in contemporary China*. Lanham, MD: Rowman & Littlefield.

Zhang Y. (2006). My camera doesn't lie? Truth, subjectivity, and audience in Chinese independent film and video. In P. G. Pickowicz & Y. Zhang (Eds.), *From underground to independent: Alternative film culture in contemporary China*. Lanham, MD: Rowman & Littlefield.

SMALL MEDIA AGAINST BIG OIL (NIGERIA)

International and Nigerian-based protests against oil drilling in the Niger Delta region provide one of the earliest examples of global political mobilization in cyberspace. The petroleum industry in Nigeria is the main source of the nation's gross domestic product (GDP), and it has been enmeshed in political and economic conflict since the discovery of oil in the late 1950s.

In the middle to late 1990s, numerous webpages were created in support of the Ogoni people, who are indigenous to Nigeria's oil-rich Delta region. Sites were used to protest the disastrous environmental and economic effects of Shell Oil drilling, to urge the boycotting of Shell Oil, and to denounce human rights abuses by the Nigerian government and by Shell. The use of the Internet in formulating an international appeal intensified dramatically after the Nigerian government's November 1995 execution of nine Ogoni activists, including Ken Saro-Wiwa, who was one of the founders of the nonviolent Movement for the Survival of the Ogoni People (MOSOP).

The various Ogoni-related websites exemplify two processes often central to intensely political uses of small media: (1) a multi-sited circulation of material from small media across different media technologies and communication venues and (2) the involvement of international organizations and audiences in making small media communications more visible and effective.

Much of what appeared on the middle to late 1990s webpages supporting Ogoni causes was from other small media such as protest rally leaflets, images from demonstration banners, texts of speeches, and interview transcripts from independent videos. For example, Earthlife Africa's site titled "Factsheet on the Ogoni Struggle" began with an image of the Shell Oil Company logo dripping blood. This image first appeared in a banner used during a protest rally. Earthlife's site also included lyrics from Ogoni protest songs.

Besides Earthlife Africa, other green organizations such as the Sierra Club and Greenpeace had pages supporting Ogoni causes, and many involved direct collaboration with MOSOP activists. By 2009, however, most of these pages had been taken down or archived, with the exception of a MOSOP

homepage. International organizations slowly began to reduce their support of MOSOP not long after the death of Nigerian dictator Abacha in 1999, as both Shell and the new civilian regime appeared to shift their stances on human rights and the environment in the Delta region. In addition, MOSOP increasingly became fraught with internal strife.

Other non–web-based types of Ogoni movement media have also been instrumental in generating support among Nigerian nationals living abroad and other interested parties, including pirated videos of the television program *The Drilling Fields* (Channel 4, London), which was later repackaged as *Delta Force* (CBC, Canada). The program documents the Ogoni people's struggles against the environmental and economic exploitation of their land, as well as their conflicts with the Nigerian state and Shell Oil. Significantly, the documentary also employs small media material, including amateur Ogoni video footage made by MOSOP activists.

Debra Spitulnik

See also *Adivasi* Movement Media (India); Environmental Movement Peoples' Media; Human Rights Media; Indigenous Peoples' Media; Online Diaspora (Zambia); Undocumented Workers' Internet Use (France)

Further Readings

Bob, C. (2005). *The marketing of rebellion: Insurgents, media, and international activism.* Cambridge, UK: Cambridge University Press.
Movement for the Survival of the Ogoni People (MOSOP): http://www.mosop.org
Okonta, I. (2008). *When citizens revolt: Nigerian elites, big oil, and the Ogoni struggle for self-determination.* Trenton, NJ: Africa World Press.
Spitulnik, D. (2002). Alternative small media and communicative spaces. In G. Hyden, M. Leslie, & F. F. Ogundimu (Eds.), *Media and democracy in Africa* (pp. 177–205). New Brunswick, NJ: Transaction.

SOCIAL DEMOCRATIC MEDIA TO 1914 (GERMANY)

The so-called social question—i.e., the rights and needs of the laboring classes—had been on the political agenda since industrialization began. Widespread poverty and deprivation encouraged real fear among privileged classes of social upheaval. The famous uprising of the Silesian weavers in 1844 had demonstrated the fragility of the social order. Media challenging the economic and political order, and specifically political party media, only emerged gradually.

Thus, before and during the 1848 Revolution, there was no socialist party and no socialist press as such. A distinction between radical liberalism, socialism, and communism could not readily be drawn. Radical democrats and socialists intermingled, and so did their ideas and their publications. Even Marx and Engels' *Neue Rheinische Zeitung* (New Rhineland Newspaper) pursued a radical democratic rather than socialist ideology. After the revolution, the free press was suppressed in every German state. Radical sheets and newspapers had been banned even earlier, during summer 1848.

The Initial Phase

The history of socialist parties and their press started more than a decade later with two wings, represented by Ferdinand Lassalle and August Bebel. Lassalle was a jurist, a close follower of Hegel, and a moderate socialist. In 1863, he even had some discussions with Prussia's Prime Minister Otto von Bismarck. In the same year, he founded the *Allgemeiner Deutscher Arbeiterverein* (General German Workers' Association, ADAV).

The ADAV strongly opposed the Liberal parties and their trade unions but supported Prussia's foreign politics in the years of Germany's unification. Its central organ the *Sozial-Demokrat* started in earnest in 1865. In 1871, it was renamed *Neuer Sozial-Demokrat*. The circulation was 5,000 in 1869, 2,800 in 1871, and approximately 14,000 in 1876. The newspaper evinced the same division of opinion typical within the ADAV overall concerning socialist and democratic ideas.

Radical ADAV members left one by one. Some founded another socialist party in 1869, the Sozialdemokratische Arbeiter-Partei (Social Democratic Workers' Party, SADP) in Eisenach, in Thuringia. August Bebel was its first chairman. Wilhelm Liebknecht, who was a former ADAV member, became editor in chief of the party's

central organ *Demokratisches Wochenblatt* (Democratic Weekly, DW). The DW actually started in 1868. Its 1869 successor was called *Volksstaat* (Peoples' State). In Germany in the 19th century, it was customary for the foundation of a newspaper to precede the foundation of a political party.

The *Volksstaat*'s circulation by 1973 was approximately 7,700. It and the *Neuer Sozial-Demokrat* merged in 1876, and the two parties merged the year before. The central organ of the newly founded Social Democratic Party (SPD) was named *Vorwärts* (Ahead!), and by 1877, its circulation reached 12,000.

The *Sozialistengesetz*

In 1870/1871, the war between Prussia, its southern allies, and the French Empire had led to Germany's unification. A postwar bubble caused by a huge amount of French reparations money was followed by a deep economic crisis. That renewed the urgency of the social question, aided the two parties' merger, and last but not least, caused fear of a social uprising similar to the 1871 Paris Commune.

When in 1878 two assassins attempted to shoot Emperor Wilhelm, Chancellor Bismarck tried to ban the SPD. The law was initially blocked in parliament but passed the second time. The notorious law, known as the *Sozialistengesetz* (Law on the Socialists), was aimed mainly at the party, and allowed suppression of its press. In general, the 1874 Press Law stated, "The press is free," but no constitutional clauses anchored this.

The police of the German states were authorized to prohibit propaganda, assemblies, demonstrations, and fund-raising, as well as trade unions, the socialist press, the party, its branches, and local clubs. Nearly 800 "agitators" were arrested by the police. However, SPD elected deputies remained members of parliament, even allowed to run for reelection as independents. Editors or publishers of a banned newspaper could appeal to the *Reichsbeschwerdekommission* (Imperial Commission of Appeals), but this body rarely revised police bans. Within a year, the socialist party, its press, and its clubs had been suppressed.

The Social Democrats immediately sought ways to counter the *Sozialistengesetz*. They reopened magazines and newspapers under new names. Most were suppressed immediately, so from 1879/1880 the party changed its strategy. New press organs now were *farblos* (colorless), trying to keep a low profile and keep their propaganda low-key. But a new newspaper, the *Sozialdemocrat,* was socialist to the core. It was edited and printed across the border in Zürich, and a secret organization called *Rote Feldpost* (red field mail) smuggled its copies into Germany, 12,000 of each issue in 1887.

The Wilhelmine Era

The Reichstag renewed the *Sozialistengesetz* annually until 1890. In that year, Emperor Wilhelm II fired Bismarck and tried a new regimen. Canceling the law was part of his design, not at least because it had almost completely failed: The votes for Social Democrats had risen between 1878 and 1890 from 7.6% (9 deputies) to 19.8% (35). Not even the welfare state provisions under Bismarck had slowed the steady growth of voters' support.

But the new policies under Wilhelm II did not have that effect either. The last pre–World War I election in 1912 registered 34.8% of the votes (110 deputies). Therefore, the Kaiser changed his mind again. Some attempts were made to reenact a new, smaller *Sozialistengesetz,* but all of them failed in parliament. The prosecution of the socialist press remained restricted to criminal law from 1890 on, especially through its libel, slander, and seditious libel clauses.

Prosecutions also had no effect on the socialist press overall. In 1878, there were 42 such newspapers, with an estimated circulation of 150,000–170,000. In 1890, when the *Sozialistengesetz* was canceled, 60 newspapers with an overall circulation of 250,000 were published. Immediately before the Great War, 91 newspapers with an overall circulation of 1,500,000 made propaganda for the SPD, the biggest being *Vorwärts* with a 1912 circulation of 165,000.

These figures are somewhat deceptive. They seem to indicate overwhelming success, especially financially. But the business situation was not as good as it seemed. Most SPD newspapers, on the one hand, depended on party subsidies—*Vorwärts,* on the other hand, supported the party itself. The advertisements were pretty poor—partly because the journalists and editors did not

want to "corrupt" themselves by accepting ads, partly because the firms, tradesmen, and merchants did not want to support these "ugly and ruthless socialists." It was not until the last decade before the Great War that the advertisement situation began to improve.

Conclusion: The Functions of the Socialist Press

What functions did the socialist press have? Three can be mentioned.

First, it propagated socialist politics to a broader public and tried to attract voters in elections. But the press was not the most important propaganda tool, given the millions of voters, just one instrument in an orchestra. The SPD successfully operated a wide range. It distributed leaflets in high volumes, sold books in its bookstores, sent out numerous speakers and agitators, operated a network of *Vertrauensleute* (trusties) under the *Sozialistengesetz,* and organized evening schools and other methods of ideological education.

Thus, a second function might be regarded as more important: the press as a platform for internal debate. From then to now, the socialist movement was not homogenous, always having more and less radical wings. A big issue in the Wilhelmine Era debates around 1900 was the question of whether the party should propagate revolution or evolutionary change. The *Revisionismusstreit* (revisionism debate) started in 1896–1898 with articles from Eduard Bernstein in the SPD weekly *Die Neue Zeit* (The New Time). Bernstein argued that the Party should acknowledge society was reforming, and he recommended a more pragmatic socialist politics. His energetic opponents were August Bebel, Wilhelm Liebknecht, Karl Kautsky, and Rosa Luxemburg.

The socialist press's third function typified all newspapers, namely spreading news of public issues. As in other industrialized countries, German journalism also featured scandal and muckraking, at least to some extent. This scandal journalism had practical and ideological sides. On the one hand, journalists tried to get reforms by reporting local scandals, for example in housing conditions. On the other hand, reports on national strengthened public feeling against the constitutional monarchy and the capitalist economy. As August Bebel put it in an 1896 parliamentary debate: "All that is bad comes from above."

We might conclude by reiterating the strong organization of labor movement culture "from below" during this period, which consisted of clubs both serious and recreational, festivals, singing, poetry, political theater, and numerous educational programs of considerable variety. Together with the press, magazines, and journals, this alternative culture was one of the great strengths of the prewar Social Democracy movement in Germany.

Rudolf Stöber

See also Anarchist and Libertarian Media, 1945–2010 (Federal Germany); Anarchist and Libertarian Press, 1945–1990 (Eastern Germany); Anarchist Media; Labor Media (United States); Leninist Underground Media Model; *Mother Earth* (United States); Political Cartooning, 1870s–Present (India)

Further Readings

Danker, U., Oddey, M., Roth, D., & Schwabe, A. (2003). *Am Anfang standen Arbeitergroschen. 140 Jahre Medienunternehmen der SPD* [At the start it was workers' pennies: 140 years of SPD media projects]. Bonn, Germany: Verlag J. H. W. Dietz Nachf.

Hall, A. (1977). *Scandal, sensation and social democracy. The SPD press and Wilhelmine Germany 1890–1914.* Cambridge, UK: Cambridge University Press.

Held, A. (1873). *Die deutsche Arbeiterpresse der Gegenwart* [Today's German workers' press]. Leipzig, Germany: Duncker & Humblot.

Koszyk, K. (1966). *Deutsche presse im 19. jahrhundert* [The German press in the 19th century]. Berlin, Germany: Colloquium.

Lidtke, V. (1985). *The alternative culture: Socialist labor in imperial Germany.* New York: Oxford University Press.

Offermann, T. (Ed.). (2001). *Die erste deutsche Arbeiterpartei. Organisation, verbreitung und sozialstruktur von ADAV und LADAV* [The First German Workers' Party: Organization, expansion and social structure of ADAV and LADAV]. Bonn, Germany: Verlag J. H. W. Dietz Nachf.

Stöber, R. (2005). *Deutsche pressegeschichte. Von den anfängen bis zur gegenwart* [German press history: From the beginnings to the present] (2nd ed.). Konstanz, Germany: UTB/UVK.

Social Movement and Modern Dance (Bengal)

The English word "Bengal" denotes the dominant historical civilization of northeastern India, although administrative boundaries imposed initially by the British culminated in its current partition between Bangladesh and the Indian state of West Bengal. At the turn of the 19th century and the beginning of the 20th, the chief forms of dance performance prevalent in Bengal were the *bai nach, khemta, raibeshe,* and *bratachari* dances, and the *jatras*. These dances either had the stigma of disrepute attached to them or were considered too unsophisticated for the tastes of urban middle-class Bengalis. Only women from dubious backgrounds, courtesans, and those who came from the fringes of urban centers danced in public.

It was in this atmosphere that Nobel Literature Laureate Rabindranath Tagore not only introduced dance into the curriculum of his Shantiniketan *ashram* for both male and female students but also had them performing his poetry and songs on stage. The *ashram* became the Visva Bharati University in 1918. Even though the emergence of the *Naba Nari* (New Woman) literature in Bengal since the mid-19th century had led to women's higher visibility in the public domain, shifting the morally depraved dancing woman from disgrace to respect meant that the Bengali *bhadramahila* (respectable woman) acquired an altogether new identity.

Tagore's literature and art, as well as his contribution to Bengali modern dance and drama (both performance and pedagogy), were inspired by and responded to the social upheavals of the nationalist movement in India. His portrayal of women in his short stories built on the *Naba Nari* tradition. His dance-drama *Chitrangada* (1936) underscored the arrival of the female hero as active agent on the Bengali stage, and *Chandalika* (The Untouchable Girl, 1938) addressed pertinent social issues such as the Hindu caste system and a woman's rebellion against social marginalization.

Indian Independence and After

As India inched its way toward attaining Independence from colonial rule, the social turbulence prompted other significant creative responses from artists and intellectuals. Some of modern dance-maker Uday Shankar's (1900–1977) works in the 1940s became increasingly political, shaped and informed by the contemporary social milieu he and his colleagues worked in. *Kalpana,* Shankar's 1948 dance film, was intended as a strong political statement. The film's opening message just after the initial credits reads:

> I request you all to be very alert. . . . Some of the events depicted here will reel off at great speed and if you miss any piece you will really be missing a vital aspect of our country's life in its Religion, Politics, Education, Society, Art and Culture, Agriculture and Industry.

Among many things, a critique of capitalism and its discrimination against factory workers is offered in this film via an excerpt from a longer choreographic work titled *Labour and Machinery.* This dance reveals how Shankar was able to translate into movement a concept drawn from contemporary social life. Through choreographing the soot-covered and expressionless faces of the factory workers, their heavy overalls, their staccato movements, and the incessant beating of drums in the background soundscape, Shankar gave a stunning depiction of mechanized labor. Of particular note is a sequence in which the workers, as if automatic machines, move their bodies disjointedly while Shankar as machine worker tries to manipulate them.

In the 1980s, Dr. Manjusri Chaki-Sircar (1934–2000) and her genre of dance *Navanritya* (new dance) used Tagore's works, and particularly his dance-dramas, poems, and songs, as inspiration to assert a distinctively feminist Bengali identity through dance. Her voice was a significant one in the dissenting chorus of contemporary feminist choreographers against the women's representation as meek, submissive, and dolled-up figures on the Indian classical dance stage. Some other outspoken dance makers in India were Chandralekha from Chennai, Mallika Sarabhai from Ahmedabad, and Daksha Sheth from Trivandrum.

Chaki-Sircar's major choreographic works were set during a period that witnessed the upsurge of women's rights movements on the one hand and the rise of right wing antifeminist politics on the other hand. Her, and later her daughter Ranjabati Sircar's (1963–1999) dance became a significant

form of representational practice that challenged and critiqued the patriarchal frameworks governing the production of dance for the Indian stage. The mother–daughter duo's choreographic works such as *Tomari Matir Kanya* (Daughter of the Earth, 1985/1987) and *Aranya Amrita* (Evergreen Forest, 1989) are an invaluable source of knowledge regarding the performance of feminism in South Asia as a social and political movement through the dancing body.

Prarthana Purkayastha

See also Bhangra, Resistance, and Rituals (South Asia/Transnational); Dance as Social Activism (South Asia); Performance Art and Social Movement Media: Augusto Boal; Sarabhai Family and the Darpana Academy (India); Street Theater (India)

Further Readings

Bose, M. (2008). Indian modernity and Tagore's dance. *University of Toronto Quarterly, 77*(4), 1085–1094.

Dutta, K., & Robinson, A. (Eds.). (1997). *Rabindranath Tagore: An anthology.* London: Picador.

López y Royo, A. (2003). Classicism, post-classicism and Ranjabati Sircar's work: Re-defining the terms of Indian contemporary dance discourses. *South Asia Research, 23*(1), 153–169.

Rajadhyaksha, A., & P. Willemen, P. (Eds.). (1999). *Encyclopaedia of Indian cinema.* London: BFI.

Rajan, R. S. (1993). *Real and imagined women: Gender, culture and postcolonialism.* London: Routledge.

SOCIAL MOVEMENT MEDIA (MACEDONIA)

In this republic of the former Yugoslav federal state, independent since 1991, social movement media helped to create crucial social changes, movements, and even emancipation from the state. In the case of community radio station Kanal 103 (www.kanal103.com.mk), its story falls into two main periods. Students initially set it up in 1991 to provide a fresh music alternative. When the Balkan wars began, however, it played a tremendous social and political role in the push for Macedonian independence. It was—and still is—a unique radio station with diverse participatory/community-radio programming that can be heard in Skopje, Macedonia's multi-ethnic capital. It is a so-called low-power radio station in the framework of Macedonian public broadcasting (MTV).

Kanal 103's initial role was to broadcast rock and roll from the United States and England, the only such station, while during the period leading up to independence (1991), it was the only media source that reported promptly on independence issues and other political activities. Today's programming gives listeners a wide musical and cultural spectrum.

Regulation Dilemmas Amid a Broadcasting Wasteland

Kanal 103 was, unusually for the region, included legally under Macedonian public broadcasting (MTV). Yet, its frequency was unlisted in MTV's policy documents, only in the broadcasting law—and no one in power wanted to regularize its status. The Macedonian authorities cancelled the frequency several times, one "abolition" in 2004 lasted 14 days. Macedonia (unlike almost all European states) has no encompassing media law, only the 2005 Broadcasting Law. Participatory/community media were not covered.

Macedonia's media in the 2000s, as elsewhere in southeastern Europe, had shifted from the former state-socialist regime to the euphoric creation of free and independent media, with frequent funding from international foundations. New political elites were trying to use media for their own ends, and the neoliberal rhetoric of deregulated media was championed as paralleling political pluralism and democracy. The media market was a rough one, changing from day to day; as one channel shut down, another opened.

The need for participatory and community media was urgent. Multiple channels did not generate content diversity. Commercial TV stations (with rare exceptions) ran poorly produced soap operas, games of chance, entertainment-music talk shows, and soft news. It was hard to distinguish the content from the sponsorship. Research showed Macedonian public broadcasting, too, did not meet at least three of its five basic goals (universality, quality, diversity, nurturing cultural identity, and giving value for cost).

The significance of social movement media was unclear in Macedonia's media debates. All too often, they were characterized as the "alternative," yet the ways they were "alternative" had still to be thought through. This exercise would pose crucial questions: Who has defined them as "alternative"? What makes them "alternative"? How are they different from public and commercial media? Not least, why would these media characterize *themselves* as "alternative"?

To be sure, participatory media sources are often critiqued for being "unlistenable" or for having small audiences. Yet, conventional audience research, geared to large commercial media purposes, is radically out of step with the world of participatory media (definitely so for *Kanal 103*). The language, aesthetics, and usages of participatory media can be a more complex question than superficial comparisons with mainstream media would suggest.

Mojca Planšak

See also Alternative Media; Citizens' Media; Community Media and the Third Sector; Community Radio (Ireland); Free Radio (Austria); Free Radio Movement (Italy); Free Radio Movement, 1974–1981 (France); Low-Power FM Radio (United States); Radio Student and Radio Mars (Slovenia)

Further Readings

Downing, J. (2003). Audiences and readers of alternative media: The absent lure of the virtually unknown, *Media, Culture & Society*, 25(5), 625–645.

Kanal 103: http://www.kanal103.com.mk

Planšak, M. (2009). *Free and community media through the prism of politics.* MA thesis, University of Nova Gorica, Ljubljana, Slovenia.

Rennie, E. (2006). *Community media: A global introduction.* Lanham, MD: Rowman & Littlefield.

Trpevska, S. (2005). In M. Preoteasa (Ed.), *The business of ethics, the ethics of business.* Bucaresti, Romania: Center for Independent Journalism.

SOCIAL MOVEMENT MEDIA (PHILIPPINES)

The long history of the "alternative press" in the Philippines, and its importance during colonization by the Spanish, the Japanese, and the United States, as well as during martial law (1972–1986), led some Filipino journalists to argue that it is the country's genuinely mainstream press. The publications *La Solidaridad* and *Kalayaan,* for example, are often cited as milestones in the development of the alternative press during the period of Spanish occupation. Teodoro distinguishes between the Philippine press in the image of the American press tradition, which was established during U.S. colonization (1898–1946), and the Filipino press, which was characterized by revolutionary critique and unabashed advocacy. It was the "soft power" of the former, he argues, that helped the U.S. colonization succeed, by buttressing elite and foreign interests and helping to sustain unjust political and social structures. His two categorizations are deployed here.

Despite their reputation as the freest media in Southeast Asia, Philippine media are arguably free only within the narrow constraints established by the country's political and economic structures. The interests they represent preclude any significant public service mission, and the profit motive drives them to prioritize sensationalism and improved ratings or sales, closing off their potential to enable debate among diverse voices. Critics argue they cover movements for social change rarely, especially those that openly critique the impact of neoliberal globalization. Few journalists can make a living wage, especially those in the provinces, which makes them notoriously vulnerable to bribery, not to mention fear of assassination.

The Martial Law Years

Critics of the U.S. alliance under President Marcos (1965–1986) were accused of being part of a "communist threat," which in 1972 became his justification for declaring martial law. It was in the 1960s that the Philippine press style had begun to give ground to the critical Filipino tradition, and serious questioning began of the political and economic structures that kept the country impoverished, as well as the U.S. role in that process. Martial law remained in place until Marcos' 1986 ouster, with him maintaining to the end that the news media were abusing their powers, and that many journalists should be arrested for supporting communism.

During the martial law years, while the revolutionary Filipino press went underground, the Philippine press remained subservient to Marcos, cloaking its cowardice in claims of professionalism and "objectivity." During this time, writers, journalists, and artists operated underground revolutionary newspapers and organized what was described as "Xerox journalism" in the struggle against the dictatorship.

Important sources included *Signs of the Times* (later the Philippine News and Features), the Media Mindanao News Service, the Cordillera News and Features, Cobra-Ans, elements of the campus press such as the *Philippine Collegian,* and the anti-Marcos newspapers *Malaya* and the *Philippine Daily Inquirer.* The Radyo Veritas (Truth) station was also a key player. These media became known as the "alternative press," which was celebrated as new despite its long history. They played a vital role in the events that led to the ouster of Marcos, which were brought about in part by the push to extend the limits of media freedom.

Alternative media are not monolithic, however, and some have argued they fell into two major categories, especially just prior to Marcos' fall: One radically critiqued Philippine society and offered alternative political, economic, and social visions, and another of consisted of more liberal and reformist leanings. After the fall of Marcos, the latter became incorporated into the mainstream press, alongside more conservative viewpoints.

The Post-Dictatorship Years

One of the first acts by the post–martial law government of Corazon Aquino was the promulgation in 1987 of a new constitution, which included the right to freedom of expression and the right to information on matters of public concern. This new constitution was dubbed the "People Power Constitution" to resonate with the mass peaceful protest movement, known today as People Power I, which finally toppled the dictatorship. These changes did not affect media ownership, however, and the powerful families that had controlled the Philippine media emerged once again to reclaim their control.

In 2001, millions took to the streets again in the People Power II protests, calling for the ouster of President Joseph Estrada, president since 1998, who had been impeached by the House of Representatives for illegal gambling. Despite support for Estrada in powerful circles, including some media owners, television images of an impeachment court stacked with Estrada supporters, combined with the popularity, immediacy, and ubiquity of texting, helped mobilize the crowds who eventually forced him out.

Philippine alternative media in the early 21st century included many small publications throughout the country sponsored by people's organizations, local progressive groups, and nonprofit institutions. There were also alternative radio programs, online publications such as *Davao Today, Bulatlat, Mindanews,* and *Pinoy Weekly,* more revolutionary publications such as *Ang Bayan* and *Liberation,* and progressive or militant campus newspapers. A loose alliance of progressive production groups existed, such as Kodao Productions, Southern Tagalog Exposure, May Day Productions, the Amado V. Hernandez Resource Center, and CineKatipunan.

These focused on investigative reporting and critical documentaries about poverty, social injustice, political repression, human rights violations, and other issues. The Internet became crucial, especially under the equally corrupt Arroyo administration, which succeeded Estrada's. Blogging provided the public with important uncensored information, often breaking major news stories later picked up by the mainstream commercial press. The Philippine Center for Investigative Journalism (PCIJ) was especially noteworthy in this regard.

There were also some small-scale, development-oriented radio stations generally funded by international development organizations or linked to larger networks such as the church. The Tambuli network and the GenPeace network, devoted to peace and conflict resolution in the conflict-stricken island of Mindanao, are the best known. Yet these stations were rarely critical political voices. This is best explained by the fact that in the Philippines, critical journalists often became targets of violence.

Culture of Impunity

One of the biggest problems facing the media in the Philippines was the murder of journalists that actually began to escalate after martial law ended. The country unfortunately claimed one of the world's highest rates of journalists killed in the line of duty. These deaths occurred predominantly in the provinces, and it is openly acknowledged that local politicians and the army units loyal to them were often guilty. As of April 2010, the Center for Media Freedom and Responsibility had counted a total of 114 journalists killed in the line of duty since 1986, and 76 killed since the Arroyo administration came to power in 2001, 36 of these in 2009 alone, the worst year to date.

Only a few cases resulted in convictions, and as of early 2009, while efforts were proceeding, no mastermind had been prosecuted successfully. Despite the international attention garnered by these killings, the Arroyo administration remained dismissive, arguing that the problem was one of "perception." Because it was easier and cheaper to hire an assassin than a lawyer to prosecute a libel case, and because there was no punishment, the killings continued unabated. Hence, the culture of impunity.

This culture was especially acute in the provinces, where the corruption of local governments was more difficult to challenge than the federal government in image-conscious Manila and where the influence of the metropolitan media was weak. With minuscule salaries and a pervasive culture of corruption, journalists themselves often succumbed to corrupt practices such as "envelopmental journalism," which is the practice of accepting cash in envelopes for positive coverage after local politicians' press conferences. Of the 77 media practitioners killed in the line of duty since 1986, most were from the provinces.

Antiterrorism Measures and Other Obstacles

The "war on terror" after the September 11, 2001, attacks in the United States provided the Arroyo administration with a justification for increasing pressure on activists. Security forces used vague antiterrorism measures to withhold permits for public demonstrations and threaten legal left-wing groups. Even in the period after martial law, the police and the military labeled without proof several nongovernmental and people's organizations, including media organizations, as "fronts" of the Communist Party of the Philippines.

This pressure has continued steadily. According to the government's own Commission on Human Rights, elements of the police and military have perpetrated human rights violations during long-running conflicts between peasants and landowners in the countryside, rarely distinguishing between armed groups and legitimate, unarmed political parties. In 2005, the National Union of Journalists of the Philippines revealed that along with the PCIJ, they had been listed by the Armed Forces of the Philippines as communist sympathizers and "enemies of the state."

Efforts to involve communities in improving or producing local coverage have also been challenging. Although local print media and networks of local commercial broadcasters do exist, there is no regulatory or legislative provision for community broadcasting. The current licensing system requires a congressional franchise, which is available only to those with financial means, making it difficult for local communities to establish their own community radio stations. In addition, many local communities are struggling with day-to-day survival. And because they advocate for social change and are committed to exposing the truth, local alternative media often face political repression.

For all these reasons, locally controlled, nonprofit community media are rare. Even if there were greater opportunities to become involved in community media, people are understandably discouraged because of the violence that often results from such efforts.

Radyo Cagayano

Radyo Cagayano was a small community radio station based in Baggao, Cagayan province, which is approximately 500 km north of Manila. After several years of saving to buy the necessary equipment, *Kagimungan* (the farmers alliance in Cagayan), established its station in a small, simple building they constructed collectively. From the start, the local military command accused the station of seeking to expand the communist interests of the *Kagimungan*, which although a legally registered organization, had also been branded as a communist front.

The station had been on air for only a few months when before dawn on July 2, 2005, eight unidentified but heavily armed men in ski masks, combat boots, and military-type fatigues broke into the building. They bound and gagged six staff members who had been sleeping that night at the station in order to broadcast an early morning mass. They then poured gasoline on the equipment and set the place on fire, destroying everything. Although the station was less than 300 m from the police station, it took the police more than 3 hours to respond to the attack.

Based on the accounts by the station's staff, the National Union of the Journalists of the Philippines (NUJP) accused the army of involvement, as they were the only group known to have a motive. The NUJP, the World Association of Community Radio Broadcasters (AMARC), and the independent group Kodao Productions, which had helped to train the station's staff, held a press conference condemning the attack. The story garnered some coverage in the mainstream Philippine press, and international groups such as the Committee to Protect Journalists and the International Federation of Journalists also released statements of condemnation.

Yet there was no official follow up, and no charges were ever filed. Unfortunately, this was not an isolated case but one in a series of attacks on local radio stations that year, demonstrating the severe constraints faced by community media and other forms of alternative media in the Philippines.

Lisa Brooten

See also Barricada TV (Argentina); Independent Media (Burma/Myanmar); New Media and Alternative Cultural Sphere (Iran); Peace Media (Colombia); Social Movement Media, 1960s–1980s (Chile); Social Movement Media in 1987 Clashes (Korea)

Further Readings

Arguillas, C. O. (2000). Human rights reporting on the Philippines' rural poor: Focus on Mindinao. In *Media & human rights in Asia: An AMIC compilation* (pp. 31–44). Singapore: Asian Media and Information Centre.

Article 19 and Center for Media Freedom and Responsibility. (2005). *Freedom of expression and the media in the Philippines*. London: Article 19 and CMFR.

Center for Media Freedom and Responsibility: http://www.cmfr-phil.org

Center for Media Freedom and Responsibility. (2009). *Philippine press freedom report 2008*. Manila, Philippines: CMFR.

Coronel, S. (2001). The media, the market and democracy: The case of the Philippines. *Javnost/The Public*, 8(2), 109–124.

Gloria, G. M. (2000). Commentary: Media and democracy in the Philippines. In *Media & democracy in Asia: An AMIC compilation* (pp. 165–179). Singapore: Asian Media and Information Centre.

ISIS-International, Manila. (2006). *Attacks on radio station threaten press freedom*. Retrieved July 22, 2008, from http://www.isiswomen.org/index .php?option=com_content&task=view&id=195&Itemi d=204

Rafael, V. L. (2003). The cell-phone and the crowd: Messianic politics in the contemporary Philippines. *Public Culture*, 15(3), 399–425.

Teodoro, L. (2001). The Philippine press: Between two traditions. In L. Teodoro & M. DeJesus (Eds.), *The Filipino press and media, democracy and development* (pp. 31–35). Quezon City: University of the Philippines Press.

Tuazon, B. (2007). Bourgeois journalism vs. alternative journalism in the Philippines. *Bulatlat*. http://www .bulatlat.com/news/7-10/7-10-journ.htm

SOCIAL MOVEMENT MEDIA, 1915–1970 (HAÏTI)

The revolution in Haïti has been broadcasted, sung, spoken, shouted, blasted on a conch shell, and pounded on drums. Ever since the slaves wrested their freedom from the French slave masters in a 13-year bloody revolt beginning in 1791, giving heart to enslaved Africans throughout the Americas, Haïti's people have been struggling against various oppressors. They have included foreign occupiers, homegrown dictatorships, a tiny and politically shortsighted bourgeoisie, and the terrifying paramilitaries of the 1957–1986 Duvalier regimes (the *Tontons Macoute*, named after a mythical bogeyman who kidnapped children at night).

Centuries of constant oppression, however, have bred a culture of resistance. And although force and violence have always been part of that resistance, Haïti's political and social movements of the past 50 years have privileged the spoken word: to cajole, tease, rally to arms, inspire, threaten, denounce, deplore, and demand.

Anti-Occupation Media

Despite popular mythology's glorification of the revolution and its historic accomplishments, once the fighting ended in 1804, the Haitian masses continued to live in poverty and were often no more than bit players in Haïtian history and politics for the next 200 years.

One exception came during the U.S. occupation (1915–1934) when the *Caco* guerrilla movement sprang up. Before the movement was crushed in 1920, thousands of Haïtian farmer soldiers—historians estimate somewhere between 3,000 and 15,000—died in their attempt to regain sovereignty for their nation. The Marines eliminated the *Cacos*, but not anti-occupation sentiment. A mostly petit-bourgeois movement brought together students, nationalist organizations, and political parties. Newspapers such as *La Patrie* (The Fatherland) and *Haïti Intégral* (All of Haïti) were launched and played important roles, although the facts they were in French and had few readers (approximately 5,000 taken together) confirm that the movement's supporters and readership were generally a tiny sector of the population.

In the United States, an anti-imperialist movement opposing the U.S. presence in Haïti grew up around *The Nation* magazine and *The Crisis*, which was the magazine of the National Association for the Advancement of Colored People (NAACP). Despite opposition inside and outside Haïti, however, Washington did not call the Marines home until 1934.

The U.S. occupation also inspired the Haïtian *noiriste* (Black-focused) and *indigéniste* movements, which both sought to valorize Haïti's African cultural roots in literature, music, and culture. The *noiristes* considered themselves part of the international Négritude movement founded by Martinique's Aimé Césaire and Sénégal's Léopold Senghor, and they gave much greater emphasis to "race." The *indigénistes*, many in the emerging communist movement, placed more emphasis on class.

During the occupation, Kreyòl, which is the indigenous language spoken by all Haitians behind closed doors but heretofore disdained by the educated classes—a Creole based on French, with some words and elements from Spanish and African languages—made inroads into the Haïtian music and literature of the middle and upper class, and was even tangentially part of the anti-occupation movement. The popular anti-occupation song *Angelik–O* (later sung by Harry Belafonte) was in Kreyòl. It called for "Angélique," a new bride who was not good at ironing, to "go home to your mother's house." Most historians believe Angélique was Angelique Cole, the wife of a U.S. Marine commander at the time, and that "home" signified the United States.

Media Under the Duvalier Regime

The post-occupation, pre-Duvalier period (1934–1957) was marked by power struggles between various factions of the elite, including *noiristes*, as well as between different progressive parties and organizations. Haïti's first Communist party was founded in 1934, and various other Marxist-influenced parties and unions were also launched in Haïti's larger cities. In addition to books and tracts, these organizations published a myriad of newspapers and journals with titles like *La Nation*, *Vigie* (Watch), *Le Travailleur* (The Worker), *Combat*, and *L'Assaut* (The Assault). Once again, however, most were in French and reached only a tiny percentage of the public.

When François "Papa Doc" Duvalier seized power in 1957, he immediately began a campaign of repression and censorship, dissolving unions, organizations, and even the university; he closed any nonobsequious newspapers and journals, and sent enemies into "voluntary" exile. Any associations and media allowed to continue had to show deference to the regime and exercise extreme self-censorship.

There were some exceptions, like the young Haïtian and foreign priests who founded a Young People's Library group that hosted discussions and seminars and had a monthly cultural journal, *Rond-Point* (Roundabout). Soon there were chapters all over the country. But by the mid-1960s, Duvalier had expelled all foreign clergy and had embarked on the most systematic and brutal state-terrorist campaign in Haïtian history.

Parties and organizations in exile continued to publish journals and newspapers, some in Kreyòl,

but radio was by far the most important communications tool used by opposition organizations and individual activists. Almost all Haitians involved in politics at the time followed the daily Kreyòl broadcasts beamed from Cuba, on Radio Havana or Radio Moscow. Beginning in 1962, René Dépestre, a Communist poet who fled to Cuba in 1959 and eventually helped found the *Casa de las Américas* publishing house, was heard twice a day on Radio Havana. For several years, his news and commentary provided sometimes the only anti-Duvalier voice Haïtians could hear.

In 1965, the shortwave Radio New York Worldwide hit the airwaves. Hosted by Raymond Joseph, who later founded the New York–based *Haïti Observateur* newspaper, it was nicknamed *Radyo Vonvon* (Radio Bee), after the *vonvon*, a male bee with a loud buzz. People could ask one another if they had heard "the bee" without risk of reprisals. The 6 a.m. broadcast was also nicknamed "six o'clock mass."

During the early years of the dictatorship, exiled resistance groups organized a series of clandestine "invasions" and would-be guerrilla movements, usually composed of no more than one or two dozen men. One after another, they failed because of disunity within the groups; failure of supposed supporters to supply material aid; and persecution by Dominican Republic authorities, from where many "invasions" were launched.

Also missing was popular support. The resistance groups had little connection to the country's impoverished masses. They were made up mostly of young men from the petit bourgeoisie: the sons of army officers or doctors, or students who had been studying in Paris, New York, or Moscow. Most had no strategy even for reaching out to the masses.

The last significant attack was carried out by *Jeune Haïti* (Young Haïti) in 1964. Duvalier's public execution of the group's remaining two members showed his clear understanding of the power of imagery and the mass media. The regime had the young men brought to the capital and shot by a firing squad in front of bused-in school children, photographers, and a cameraman. Overnight, the execution photos were plastered all over the capital. *Télé-Nationale*, which was one of the first state television stations in the Caribbean, broadcasted the execution over and over for weeks. Duvalier even had a pamphlet printed and circulated, complete with photos of the rebels' heads. The text warned that he had "crushed and will always crush the attempts of the opposition. Think well, renegades. Here is the fate awaiting you and your kind." Continued overt resistance would be on hold until his death in 1971.

Jane Regan

See also Community Media (Venezuela); Community Radio (Haïti); Mawonaj (Haïti); Music and Social Protest (Malawi); Popular Music and Protest (Ethiopia); Protest Music (Haïti); Social Movement Media, 1971–1990 (Haïti); Social Movement Media, 1991–2010 (Haïti)

Further Readings

Diederich, B., & Burt, A. (2005). *Papa Doc and the Tonton Macoutes*. Princeton, NJ: Markus Wiener.

Nicholls, D. (1974). Ideology and political protest in Haiti, 1930–46. *Journal of Contemporary History, 9*, 3–26.

Social Movement Media, 1920s–1970s (Japan)

1920s–1945

The social movement media picture in Japan for 50 years was lively at the outset, and then again after World War II once the militarists were out of power. Especially in the 1960s and 1970s, numerous media projects flourished. In the 1920s, many social movements were born in Japan as other countries, after the end of the First World War and the shock of the Russian Revolution. Indeed in 1925, in the commercial magazine *Kaizo* (Remodeling), one of the labor movement's then advisors, Hisashi Aso, later an official labor leader, described the diversity of social movements at that time in the following terms:

> We had to choose among socialism, anarchism, democracy, syndicalism, bolshevism, guild-socialism, nihilism, terrorism, labor union movements, national socialism, social democratic and labor parties. . . . Which was the best ideology or

party to choose, which was the best stance to make our own? (*Kaizo*, 1925)

Among all these, the 1922 birth of the Japanese branch of the Komintern (Communist Party) was probably the most shocking to conservative opinion. The party was dissolved as result of government repression in 1924 (and was subsequently reorganized and then disbanded several times over by the state, but it continued to operate until the mid-1930s). The remaining members of the party core published the magazine *Marukusu Shugi* (Marxism) from May 1924 to April 1929, trying to keep the movement alive.

In 1924, two Social Democratic/radical democratic groups were founded: They were the Japan Fabian Society and *Seiji Kenkyukai* (Political Research), sharing many members. Among them was Isoo Abe, who in 1900 became the chairman of the Socialism Association and, in 1901, launched the Japanese Social Democratic Party; he is considered one of the founders of each group.

The Japan Fabian Society, which followed the model especially of the English Labor Party, launched in May of its foundation year the monthly *Shakaishugi Kenkyu* (Socialism Research), but this ceased publication in 1925. The *Seiji Kenkyukai*, more radical, started the monthly *Seiji Undou* (Political Movement) in 1924 and later changed the title to *Seiji Kenkyu* (Political Research), but this also closed in 1925.

The Japanese Communist Party split into two groups in the latter 1920s. One was the main wing, which intended to be the sole workers' vanguard party. They published intermittently *Sekki* (Red Flag) from 1928. Initially, it was manually produced, but mechanically from 1932. But after continuing government repression, the paper saw its demise in 1935 (a total of 185 issues were published).

The other group was the *Rodo Noumin To* (Labor and Peasants Party), which intended to be a broad front, transversal movement, established in 1926. The monthly *Rono* (Labor and Agriculture), beginning November 1927, was closely related to this party. Also, the coterie magazine *Shakai Shisou* (Social Thought), which was published mainly by left-wing intellectuals and beginning February 1927, had a big impact on this party.

There were also artistic media linked with the left-wing political movement. In 1921, anarchist and socialist artists brought out *Tane Maku Hitobito* (Seed Sowers). It closed in 1924, but *Bungei Sensen* (Artistic Front) continued its work. Moreover, centered on this publication's writers, the *Proletarian Literary League* was set up in 1925. However, this leftist artists movement also split, one faction following the Communist Party, which formed the *Proletarian Artistic League*, and the others, a variety of leftist currents. Japan's leftist artistic movement developed in the rivalry between *Bungei Sensen* (1924–1932), representing Social Democrats, and *Senki* (Battle Flag), a bulletin of the pro-Communist *All-Japan Proletarian Artistic League* (NAP [*Nipponia Artista Proleta Federacio*]) that was published 1928–1931.

Similarly, the anti-establishment students' movement was catalyzed by its link with the left-wing parties. Already in 1918, Tokyo University students had formed the *Shinjinkai* (New Members Association), and in 1919 students at Waseda University formed the *Minjin Domei* (People's League) and the *Kensetsusha Domei* (Social Constructors League), all of which were radical democratic movement organizations. In time, all these organizations leaned to Marxism, and in 1922, the *Gakusei Shakaikagaku Rengoukai* (Students' Social Sciences Federation) was founded. This association, soon abbreviated to *Gakuren*, became very big, comprising 1,600 members in 49 universities and professional and vocational schools throughout Japan.

To popularize Marxism-Leninism, the *Gakuren* distributed a series of pamphlets, placards, and fliers. But during 1925–1926, when *Gakuren* students at Kyoto Imperial University were abruptly arrested, the organization was hit hard. Some jailed students went underground and some were absorbed into the Communist Youth League, which was run by the Communist Party.

Another important event in Japan's social movement history was when in 1922, the historically outcast class *Hisabetu-buraku*, which was living under terrible conditions and was heavily discriminated against, founded the *Zenkoku Suiheisha* (National Horizontal Association), the predecessor of today's *Buraku Kaihou Domei* (Buraku Liberation League). In 1922, they issued the Suiheisha Declaration on *buraku-min* rights,

which can be considered Japan's first human rights declaration.

Since the publication of the magazine *Seitou* (Blue Stocking) in 1911, women's liberation movements started to mobilize, and they displayed in their actions the catalyzing influence of the 1920s socialist wave. Within this context, the formation of the *Sekirankai* (Red Wave Society) in 1921 brought about the first socialist women's organization. By making use of left-leaning commercial papers like *Kaizou* and *Taiyou* (The Sun), they tried to reach women workers as well as women intellectuals.

However, in the mid-1930s, all these anti-establishment social movements became almost voiceless after sweeping and drastic repression by the state apparatus. Despite the state's ideological oppression, leftist and antifascist intellectuals still tried to argue about socialism and antifascism via several research activities and publication campaigns. One was the emergence inside the Marxist wing of *Yuibutsuron Kenkyukai* (Association for Materialism Research, 1932–1938). This initiative, which in preparation for an eventual police crackdown had publicized its role as a research organization based not on Marxism but in materialism research, had a big influence on intellectuals and students at that time, via its publication *Yuibutsuron Kenkyu* (Materialism Research). Nonetheless, this organization too, under the intensifying war preparations, was banned and disbanded in 1938.

In contrast with the Materialism Research Association, which developed its activities based on the Marxist current, the more liberal and populist *Anti-fascist Popular Front* movement published the magazine *Sekai Bunka* (World Culture) and the weekly *Doyobi* (Saturday). *Sekai Bunka*, which started in Kyoto in 1935, had a wide readership ranging from Marxists to liberals. The magazine featured European antifascist movements together with theoretical research on art and philosophy, trying to criticize militarism and the totalitarian regime from a cultural perspective.

Doyobi was modeled on France's Popular Front weekly *Vendredi* (Friday). Its prototype was also a weekly called *Kyoto Sutajio Tsushin* (Kyoto Studio Correspondence) published by the Kyoto Film Studio actor Raitaro Saito, who wanted to provide his colleagues with a newspaper where they could exchange their ideas. *Doyobi* was edited in a more accessible style for general readers, given that its predecessor was heavily focused on movie industry workers. It had a popular presentation with subjects ranging from social and cultural criticism, to movies and commentary on current events, manners, and customs.

It was sold in cafés and bookshops all over Kyoto, with a peak circulation of 7,500 subscribers. This was a large number, surpassing the legal antifascist magazine *Roudou Zasshi* (Work Magazine) published in Tokyo, which had a top circulation of 6,500. For that time, we can say that as anti-totalitarianism mass media went, it was strong. But in 1937, many intellectuals and students around *Sekai Bunka* and *Doyobi* were arrested, and this unique antifascist publication disappeared.

1945–1980

The end of World War II meant that the oppressive media rules of the 1930s were over. Under the occupying Allied forces, the militaristic information system was destroyed, and democratization was deepened rapidly and radically together with Japan's media. As a result, left-wing influence and democratic power were restored after being banned, and their strength was expanded.

In 1945, with the restoration of the Japanese Communist Party, its bulletin *Akahata* (Red Flag) reappeared. It was suspended in 1950 on U.S. orders, but it republished from 1952 to now. The next year, the party launched a monthly publication called *Zen'ei* (Vanguard).

Also in 1945, the Japan Socialist Party was founded with members of several proletarian parties and Labor and Peasants' Party members. Within it coexisted many trends. Marxist-Leninist members, whose movement was the most organized of them, published the monthly theoretical journal *Zenshin* (Progress). This group formed the Socialist Association in 1951, whose bulletin *Shakai Shugi* (Socialism) dominated continuing left-wing activism within the Socialist Party.

During the chaos of the postwar years, besides this category of leftist party-related journals and magazines, there were other anti-establishment media. Of these, the most remarkable might be *Shinso* (True Accounts), beginning in 1946. This was a political scandal magazine that not only sharply criticized the Emperor system and conservative politicians but also included open public critiques of the policies of the occupying forces—many of which the U.S. military censored.

Shisou no Kagaku (The Science of Thinking) was edited by postwar liberal intellectuals like Shunsuke Tsurumi, Masao Maruyama, and Shigeto Tsuru, and it was an example of social movement media. Although the title might suggest it was an elitist ideological publication, this was not the case. Rather, it avoided academic theoreticism, while paying attention to the feelings and intuitions of people's everyday lives, so giving birth to a variety of liberal observations and statements. Its pages were not limited to the magazine's staff writers and intellectuals—ordinary readers contributed too. By covering varied social and cultural phenomena, including popular cultural topics such as movies and comics, and by including penetrating analyses based on people's lives, this magazine's contents anticipated today's cultural studies.

In the latter half of the 1950s was born the Japanese New Left. As the critique of Stalinism spread, the Trotskyist group founded the Japan Trotskyism League in 1957. (In 1958, the name changed to Revolutionary Communists League.) Also, based on student members of the Communist Party, the Communists League made its appearance in 1958. In the 1960s, the members of the Socialism Youth League—the Socialist Party's youth organization, influenced by Rosa Luxemburg—created the Socialism Youth League (Liberation Faction).

Later, the Revolutionary Communists League split into three factions: the Fourth International Japanese Branch, the Core Faction, which prioritized mass movements, and the Revolutionary Marxist Faction, focused on the labor movement. In turn, after 1960, the Communists League split into many rival factions, but in the later 1960s it reunited, reflecting the students' and workers' movements of those years. These New Left groups all had different weekly papers like *Zenshin* (Progress), *Kaihou* (Liberation), *Senki* (Battle Flag), and occasional theoretical publications like *Kyousanshugisha* (Communists) and *Riron Sensen* (Theoretical Front).

The Communist Party faction influenced by the Italian Communist Party (but later expelled from

Japan's Communist Party) published *Gendai no Riron* (Contemporary Theory) from 1959 to 1989, drawing heavily on the left-wing movements in Europe and with a major impact on intellectuals and students. Moreover, the pro-Soviet elements expelled from the Communist Party, then the pro-China members also expelled, and the anarchist movement organizations all had their own bulletins and magazines. The so-called Non-Sectarian Radicals, which included students not affiliated to political parties or organizations, spread a movement to create on every campus a *Zengaku Kyoutou Kaigi* (All-School Common Front Councils, or *Zenkyoto*). These groups in turn made placards, pamphlets and posters and also published their own media. However, the *Minshu Seinen Domei* (Democratic Youth League), the Communist Party's youth organization, vied with the *Zenkyoto* and with the New Left groups.

Many publications appeared in the wake of the 1960s student rebellions. The *Asahi Journal* (1959–1992), which was published by one of Japan's main publishing companies, *Asahi Shimbun*, had a strong impact on the student movements. Also, the monthly publications *Gendai no Me* (Present-day Look; 1961–1983), *Ryudou* (Flow; 1969–1982), and Joukyou (*Situation;* 1968–1975) all had a major influence on the new left-wing student and youth movements.

Under the influence of the women's liberation movement in the latter half of the 1960s, women's liberation movement organizations emerged in different parts of Japan. Most had either regular or intermittent publications.

With the beginning of the 1970s, the spread of political terrorism, frustration, and setbacks meant the disappearance of the radical struggle movement, but environmentalism and local citizens' campaigns started to gain impetus. These groups edited their own mini-media, trying to expand their own movements and struggles. Among them, *Gekkan Chiiki Tousou* (Monthly Local Struggle) emerged in 1970, networking all these local movements and making them known nationally.

The New Left movement had lost its impetus, but many publications appeared in the latter half of the 1970s trying to link the fruits of New Left struggles with citizens' campaigns. One of them is *Inpakushon* (Impaction), published from 1979 until now. Another, relating to new social movements like the ecological movement, was *Kuraishisu* (Crisis; 1980–1989).

Kimio Ito

See also Boxer Rebellion Theater (China); Communist Movement Media, 1950s–1960s (Hong Kong); Independence Movement Media (India); Independence Movement Media (Vietnam); New Culture and May 4th Movements Media (China); Social Movement Media, 1980s–2000s (Japan)

Further Readings

Kurata, K. (1969). *Anpo Zengakuren* [Anti-Security-Treaty National Organization of Students' Councils]. Tokyo: San-ichishobo.

Shiota,S. (1982). *Nihon Shakaiundousi* [The history of Japanese social movements] Tokyo: Iwanamishoten.

Suga, H. (2006). *1968 nen* [The year of 1968]. Tokyo: Chikumashobo.

Takagi, M. (1985). *Zengakuren to Zenkyoto* [National Organization of Students' Councils and All-Campus Joint Struggle Councils]. Tokyo: Koudansha.

Yoshida, H., Sakuta, K., & Ikumatsu, K. (Eds.). (1968). *Kindainihon-Shakaishisousi II* [The history of modern Japanese social thought II]. Tokyo: Yuhikaku.

SOCIAL MOVEMENT MEDIA, 1960s–1980s (CHILE)

Chile has a long and significant tradition of social movements going back to the early 20th century. In every case, grassroots arts and media have played pivotal roles as agents of social change and radical action. Some of the most vigorous processes of grassroots mobilization began in the late 1960s. This entry focuses on the Popular Unity period and the 16-year military dictatorship that followed.

Reform and the Popular Unity Years (1968–1973)

The 1960s saw the upsurge of significant popular social movements in Chile, leading up to Salvador Allende's election as President in September 1970. In the late 1960s, these included massive land seizures and housing mobilizations, and in the early

1970s, factory takeovers and student cooperatives. In 1969, several political parties formed the Popular Unity coalition (*Unidad Popular*) to support Allende's presidential bid, representing movements that at that time were shaking the country's inherited structure.

Among the most important propositions in the *Unidad Popular* program was to "build a new culture for a new society," emphasizing the role of culture, communication, and the arts as key agents of the deep social processes underway. During these years, grassroots arts movements begin to take center stage as instruments for political and social critique, activism, and social change.

Folk and popular music were given a new political and ideological dimension to support the wide movements for equality, participation, and social transformation. The *Nueva Canción* (New Song) movement emerged in the mid-1960s through artists like Violeta Parra, Quilapayún, and Victor Jara, among others, who used their music as a new form of social and political engagement and agency. In 1968, the first festival of New Chilean Song took place. The New Chilean Song movement would have a long and intense influence in other parts of Latin America. At its height in the early 1970s, it was a magnetic project of popular resistance.

A year earlier, Chile had already organized the First Festival of Latin American Cinema, launching the New Latin American Cinema movement. Filmmakers started taking to the streets to shoot the social transformations taking place. Dozens of films documented the powerful social movements of workers, peasants, students, and Indigenous peoples.

Douglas Hubner's 1969 film *Herminda de La Victoria,* exploring the complexity of an illegal land seizure by a group of marginal shanty town dwellers, and Pedro Chaskel and Héctor Rios's *Venceremos* (We Will Win; 1970), a visual montage of the violence and contradictions of everyday life in Chile in the early 1970s, are just two of many documentaries that show the power of the genre in conveying the energy of the social movements at that time. The quintessential film of the period is Patricio Guzmán's three-part *The Battle of Chile* (1973–1979), which constitutes one of the most important examples of political cinema *vérité,* documenting the social movement of a

whole nation for the 2 years preceding the military coup.

In 1968, a group of young activists from the Communist Youth Leagues organized the *Brigada Ramona Parra* (BRP), which was an amazing example of a grassroots organization that took to the streets to use the walls as their media. If the upper classes controlled the newspapers and television stations, the BRP controlled the streets, flooding the city with graffiti art, street murals, and political propaganda. The walls and streets of many cities became the media of the people. During the *Unidad Popular* years, the BRP created massive murals in many parts of Chile, often in collaboration with well-known visual artists. One example is the massive mural titled *El Primer Gol del Pueblo Chileno* (The First Goal of the Chilean People), painted collaboratively by surrealist visual artist Roberto Matta and the Ramona Parra Brigade in 1971 on a municipal swimming pool in the southern suburbs of Santiago.

The 1973–1989 Military Dictatorship

On September 11, 1973, a military coup led by General Pinochet and energetically supported by the U.S. government overthrew the elected government. Almost 1 million people were forced into exile; thousands were arrested, kidnapped, and tortured, and several thousands disappeared, only to be found 30 years later in makeshift graves—or never found. The government's film agency was closed; its director was shot dead. Singer and composer Victor Jara was murdered. Most cultural and sporting centers become detention and torture centers. The famous BRP murals were painted out, the voices of Parra and Jara and dozens of others silenced, and the images of most filmmakers burned and buried. Grassroots and alternative media were completely dismantled.

Meanwhile, the military apparatus set in motion a powerful machine of entertainment television and biased press journalism to erase every experience, memory, and ideal of people's emancipation and of their arts and cultural production. The mainstream press and television reported dutifully on the restoration of economic, political, and social order. However, Chile's social movements, now underground or in exile, persisted in producing many forms of media to challenge the dictatorship. The discussion here focuses on film, video, the BRP, and *arpilleras* (wall hangings).

The Chilean filmmakers forced into exile soon picked up their cameras. In the first years after the coup, Chilean films produced in exile became known as the "cinema of resistance," and they became an important resistance strategy by communicating Chilean realities to an international audience. Between 1973 and 1988, exiled Chilean filmmakers produced more than 200 films in 20 countries. It was the first time a nation's cinema was forged outside its frontiers. This cinema became crucial in generating a powerful international solidarity movement.

Inside the country, from 1982, resistance movements and clandestine organizing begin slowly to emerge, in many cases supported by international solidarity movements. The political parties also started to regroup, and a new alliance formed to overthrow the dictatorship. The BRP was reorganized and the walls become once again sites of resistance and mobilization. The renaissance of political activism and the formation of a broad pro-democracy social movement coincided with the introduction of the portable video camera, which led to a big current of alternative video.

Amid the harshest conditions of censorship and repression a group of journalists created *Teleanálisis,* a video news service in operation between 1984 and 1989. *Teleanálisis* produced monthly video reports linked to the core social organizations engaged with the movement against the dictatorship, producing programs of different style and length on specific actions (rallies, protests, and strikes) and social and cultural events. The programs were distributed to more than 350 social organizations, offering images of an invisible country. Tapes were copied to reach every corner of the social tapestry of activist organizations.

Every program would start with the motto "Public Dissemination in Chile Prohibited," which allowed it to remain clandestine and outside of the tentacles of the censorship apparatus. *Teleanálisis* quickly become an underground network of journalist-activists, always narrating stories from firsthand experience. In many regards, the work of *Teleanálisis* and other similar collectives such as *Grupo Proceso*

were early forms of tactical media and citizen journalism. *Teleanálisis* produced more than 200 programs on human rights and became a true alternative video movement that opened up a counterpublic sphere, telling the unofficial story of the darkest years in Chilean history.

This was especially significant because the film industry was reoriented after the coup toward commercial TV and advertising, and the television industry quickly became the dictatorship's favorite state institution (until its mid-1980s privatization). But video technology provided a completely different cultural logic to mainstream cinema and television. Such was the case of *Grupo Proceso,* an underground collective of media activists who in 1982, using a single borrowed video camera and recorder, began documenting the process of pro-democratic mobilizations, directly contesting the military's project, which Augusto Góngora, one of its founders, described as "atomizing, destroying, taking apart and pulverizing Chile's social fabric."

Video technology also implied a completely different concept of circulation: home video systems. This allowed for intricate networks of underground circulation. Video's immediacy allowed for programs to be shot one day and almost instantly screened in neighborhood streets, offering passers-by the possibility to watch real events unfold almost in real time. The movement filmed successful examples of organization and resistance, such as community kitchens pooling scarce food in poor neighborhoods, and illegal strikes.

Another key group was *Llareta,* a grassroots health group operating in *La Bandera,* a poor settlement in southern Santiago, which had emerged in the late 1960s out of a land seizure by homeless communities. Just as the *Unidad Popular* movement had been captured in 16-mm film, songs, street art, and alternative theater, so resistance to the dictatorship was recorded on ¾-inch videotapes—but also in *arpilleras.*

These tapes were small rectangular wall hangings, made by women's organizations, which narrated stories of repression, violence, and political unrest. Using burlap, leather, and copper, the *arpilleras* were colorful portraits of a drained and stark reality. Women narrated their personal stories and those of their communities and organizations under the terror of repression, becoming in many ways the eyes and windows of a whole sector of society. The women were sheltered by the progressive arm of the Chilean Catholic Church, the Vicaría de la Solidaridad, and the first workshop was held as early as 1974 by mothers, sisters, and wives of the disappeared.

Juan Francisco Salazar

See also Alternative Media Heritage in Latin America; Independence Movement Media (Vietnam); Indigenous Media in Latin America; Mothers of the Plaza de Mayo (Argentina); *Samizdat* Underground Media (Soviet Bloc); Zapatista Media (México)

Further Readings

Agosín, M. (1987). *Scraps of life: Chilean arpilleras.* Trenton, NJ: The Red Sea Press.

Bresnahan, R. (2001). Chile's backyard: Social movements create alternative channels. *New Internationalist, 335.*

Guzmán, P. (1973–1979). *La batalla de Chile* [Battle of Chile] [DVD, in Spanish].

Muesca, J. (2005). *El documental Chileno.* Santiago, Chile: LOM Ediciones.

Pinto Vallejos, J. (Ed.). (2005). *Cuando Hicimos Historia: La experiencia de la Unidad Popular.* Santiago, Chile: LOM Ediciones.

SOCIAL MOVEMENT MEDIA, 1971–1990 (HAÏTI)

After François "Papa Doc" Duvalier's son Jean-Claude Duvalier, widely termed "Baby Doc," succeeded him in power in 1971, a 9-year period followed known as "The Opening." Democratic activists, organizers, and some daring journalists seized the opportunity. Farmers—who made up more than two thirds of the population at that time—began quietly to organize with the help of some Protestant and Catholic clergy, nuns, and laypeople. From 1980 until 1986, when Duvalier junior fled, repression was followed by intensified resistance. A turbulent and heady period ensued from 1986 to 1990 as Haitian individuals and organizations struggled for democracy and against "Duvalierism without Duvalier."

"The Opening" and the Rise of Independent Radio

A few newspapers started up during "the opening." Some Catholic priests launched *Bon Nouvèl* (Good News), a monthly bulletin in Kreyòl (Haïtian Creole) with a liberation theology bent. And a new weekly publication the *Petit Samedi Soir* (Little Saturday Evening) engaged in criticism of "Jean-Claudeism" (Duvalier junior's regime) and helped galvanize nationalist democratic sentiment.

The *Tèt Ansanm* (Heads Together) farmers' movement grew to some 600 chapters by 1985. Engaged in both agricultural and consciousness-raising activities, the groups—supported by Catholic nuns, priests, and laypeople—used popular theater and some "tracts" or leaflets, although the brutal repression and almost 100% illiteracy among their members made the latter of limited value.

The real powerhouse of the emergent democratic movement was radio. The most stunning example was *Radio Haïti Inter*, run by Jean Dominique, an agronomist and filmmaker whose brother had been executed in 1959 after heading a failed anti-Duvalier invasion. (In 2000, Dominique himself would be assassinated as he went into the station to host his daily morning news program.)

In the late 1960s and early 1970s, *Radio Haïti Inter* broke new ground when it began tentatively broadcasting in Kreyòl. Dominique started carefully, first with some *mizik angaje* (politically engaged music) and commentary, then foreign news, and finally social commentary, involving plenty of *mawonaj*, Haïti's allusive linguistic practice where puns, homonyms, and coded messages portray piercing criticism of and stubborn resistance to the powerful. Dominique's listeners knew, for example, that the station's dedication to blow-by-blow coverage of Nicaragua's Sandinista struggle against the Somoza dictatorship in the 1970s was a parable—the Somoza regime represented the Duvalier dictatorship and the rebels were meant to inspire Haïtian revolt.

From 1980 to Duvalier's Departure

"The Opening" closed abruptly in 1980, 3 weeks after Ronald Reagan was elected U.S. president. Some 130 journalists and activists were thrown in jail, and *Radio Haïti Inter* was ransacked. Most people were released and went underground or overseas. The following years saw frenetic exile organizing and several more attempted rebel invasions. Invaders, including *Radio Haïti Inter's* popular on-air host Richard Brisson, were usually captured. Brisson was caught in 1982 and was never heard from again.

The democratic fervor could not be tamped down, however, and after Pope John Paul II visited Haïti in 1983 and announced "things must change," organizers and activists cautiously pushed forward once again. This time, a Catholic radio station *Radio Soleil* (Sun Radio) led the charge. Founded in 1977 with a "distance education" mandate, by the early 1980s it had gotten more politicized, using careful and metaphor-heavy broadcasts influenced by liberation theology. Young journalists broadcasted news and commentary in Kreyòl, as well as popular education radio plays that attempted to heighten listeners' awareness of the injustices in Haïtian society.

The regime cracked down on *Radio Soleil* in 1985, but it was too late. Opposition groupings in exile had founded weekly newspapers like *Haïti Progrès* and *Haïti-en-Marche* (Haïti on the March), and throughout the country, students, workers, and journalists were mobilizing. One of the biggest pushes came from within the Catholic and Protestant churches. Clerics and laypeople influenced by liberation theology were organizing *ti legliz* (little church) political discussion groups thinly disguised as prayer meetings. Students formed associations and published anonymous tracts. Protests and organizing picked up all over the country. Demonstrations and strikes roiled the cities. Finally, Jean-Claude Duvalier left on a U.S.-chartered plane on February 8, 1986.

Baboukèt la Tonbe! (The Muzzle Has Fallen!)

When "Baby Doc" and his family fled into exile in 1986, the long-silenced public rejoiced in their freedom of speech. *Baboukèt la tonbe!* was scrawled on walls and yelled out during massive victory demonstrations. Journalists—and the power of the word—were almost fetishized. When *Radio Haïti Inter's* Dominique returned to Haïti from exile, 50,000 people greeted him at the airport.

The next 5 years saw an explosion of social, political, and cultural movements as different factions struggled for power and the U.S.-backed Haïtian Armed Forces tried to keep the movements from coalescing into a revolutionary front. Unions, farmer organizations, neighborhood associations, *ti legliz* and student groups, petit-bourgeois organizations, and new political parties—more than two dozen—emerged and became part of a social movement clamoring for various versions of democracy.

Throughout this tumultuous period, the provisional governments and military councils more or less continued to represent the interests of Haïti's elite through their economic and social policies, using some of the same repression tactics as the Duvaliers. But they could not control people's rage, especially during the first months and years after the dictator's departure. Crowds carried out necklace (burning tire) lynchings against the former paramilitary (the *Tontons Macoute*) and other collaborators.

The tire—held up during a march, painted on a wall, referred to in speeches and songs—became a symbol both of widespread fury over past abuses and the power of popular justice. Paramilitary death squads fought back with nighttime attacks in poor neighborhoods. People responded with *bat tenèb* (literally: Beat *Tenebrae* [shadows], referring to a Catholic Holy Week service), where entire blocks and then entire neighborhoods would respond to gunfire or an attack by beating metal on metal—a lamppost, a pot, or the rusted-out hulk of a junked car: They did anything to make a racket.

Kreyòl and the Freedom to Speak

The new 1987 constitution made Kreyòl one of two official languages, and it was everywhere. Kreyòl—on the air, at press conferences, on walls, in songs and slogans, photocopies, bulletins, declarations, and manifestos—was the principal weapon of the new parties, movements, and unions. The churches and other organizations launched national literacy campaigns, training thousands in rudimentary reading and writing. Along with the French weeklies flown in from the United States, there was a flourishing of radical bulletins in Kreyòl linked to parties or unions with titles like *Rezistans* (Resistance), *Vwa pa nou* (Our voices), and *Kawotchou* (Tire).

But with an adult literacy rate of only just more than 50% and limited access to television (only approximately 10% of the population officially has electricity, although illegal hookups allow for many more to light a bulb or power a radio), Kreyòl radio broadcasts remained the most powerful communication tool.

More than a dozen new radio stations opened during the post-Duvalier era. And although most were privately owned, many fervently embraced Haïti's democratic movement, and thus they could be characterized as "social movement media." They had *tribin lib* (open tribune) programs where representatives of organizations or anyone with anything to say could call in or show up and speak out. Newscasts and journalists were opinionated and even militant, crying out for the need to respect human rights and economic rights, and demanding democratic reforms and even revolution.

Some journalists and radio stations eventually became associated closely with Father Jean-Bertrand Aristide, the most popular of the liberation theology-inspired priests who would soon announce his candidacy for president. The confusion between social movement, political movement, and—once Aristide took power—the state, would come back to haunt not only the "social movement" media and journalists, but the organizations of the democratic and popular movement as a whole.

On the eve of the 1990 elections, a group of the Holy Ghost Order priests helped found the country's first regular Kreyòl newspaper: *Libète* (Liberty). Written in elementary Kreyòl and aimed at the country's new Kreyòl readers, and with a distinctly liberation theology influence, the journal had political and social news, photographs, and information on health and agriculture. Sold at a nominal fee, *Libète* printed up to 17,000 copies per run.

Kreyòl and freedom of speech were celebrated and even imbued with revolutionary potential. There was also a flourishing of political art on walls. These simple paintings or elaborate murals often appeared overnight and depicted the dreams and aspirations of the democratic and popular movement: the necklacing of soldiers; a rooster, the symbol of Aristide and his party, pecking away at a guinea hen (a noisy and aggressive bird, symbolizing the Duvaliers); or beautifully clean, uniformed school children in neat, airy school rooms. Haïti's political murals represented more than popular exultation; they were what might be called the "Dreams of Democracy," to borrow the title of a documentary U.S. Hollywood filmmaker gave to a documentary he made on Haïti's musicians of the time. Tracts, pamphlets, and press releases simply could not convey the intensity of the vision the ordinary public had of their own movement and its events.

Like much of the communication associated with the democratic and popular movement, the murals were usually a spontaneous expression. That spontaneity characterized much of the communication efforts by Haïti's social movement organizations throughout the late 1980s and 1990s but would eventually contribute to the movement's weaknesses.

Jane Regan

See also Mawonaj (Haïti); Miners' Radio Stations (Bolivia); Murals (Northern Ireland); Protest Music (Haïti); Social Movement Media, 1915–1970 (Haïti); Social Movement Media, 1991–2010 (Haïti); Zapatista Media (México)

Further Readings

Jean, J.-C., & Maesschalk, M. (1999). *Transition politique en Haïti—radiographie du pouvoir politique* [Political transition in Haïti—x-ray of the power structure]. Paris: L'Harmattan.

Regan, J. (2008). Baboukèt la tonbe!—The muzzle has fallen! *Media Development, 2,* 12–17.

René, J. A. (2003). *La séduction populiste: Essai sur la crise systémique haïtienne et le phénomène Aristide, 1986–1991* [The populist seduction: Essay on Haïti's systemic crisis and the Aristide phenomenon]. Port-au-Prince, Haïti: Bibliothèque Nationale d'Haïti.

SOCIAL MOVEMENT MEDIA, 1980s–2000s (JAPAN)

By the mid-2000s, Japan was a highly commercialized information society. Social movements operated at the margins and mostly continued to use staid media formats: talks, symposia, books, newspapers, journals, small-scale print media (*mini comi*), and information packets (*shiryoushuu*). However, some Japanese social movements, as outlined below, had made pioneering uses of electronic media.

Micro-Radio and Computer Networks: The Economic Bubble Decade

In the 1980s, the Japanese economy peaked. Tokyo real estate became the most expensive on earth. Global analysts studied Japanese management methods. Yet while the overall culture reveled in hedonistic groupthink, a few alienated Tokyoites, inspired by the Italian Autonomist movement and equipped with cheap consumer electronics, set up unlicensed mini FM (microradio) stations. Groups like Setagaya Mama and Radio Homerun broadcasted an eclectic mix of talk by local people, and underground music.

Peace Boat was set up in 1983 as a floating alternative medium for radical culture and peace education. By the mid-2000s, it had developed into a major, horizontally organized nonprofit organization (NPO), which took 3,500 people annually on educational cruises to promote global justice.

The 1986 Chernobyl disaster and continuing concerns about pollution reinvigorated environmental movements against dams, construction projects, and nuclear reactors. This coincided with the emergence of local/regional computer networks, first established by civic-minded technology enthusiasts. Companies soon began providing electronic bulletin board services.

PC-VAN offered the Third World Networking (DAISAN) forum, whereas NIFTY-Serve offered the Civic Movement Lively Net (FSSHIMIN). Prominent grassroots networks included IGON Ikego Forest Network, which developed around a citizens' group resisting a U.S. Army housing construction project, and Renkon Net, which promoted civic monitoring of radiation levels. In 1988, the environmental movement mobilized 20,000 people for the Hibiya Rally to Stop Nuclear Power.

From the 1990s, onward, policies of privatization, deregulation, pressure on labor unions, the dismantling of social services and Japan's lifetime employment system gave the impetus, and newly inexpensive video equipment the technology, for a "self-taught documentary" movement (*jishuu dokyumentarii undou*). This addressed the plight of workers and other social issues.

Media reform and media literacy movements also matured in the course of that decade, as misreporting and overreporting scandals continued to shake public confidence in mainstream media and concerns rose about the social effects of media commercialization and homogenization. Many cable channels began by promising local services and citizen outlets, but few ever offered a platform for social movements or open channels for local citizenry. By the 1990s, most were fully commercialized. Still, cable offered some openings for ethnic and social minorities, for example JBS, which was a channel for the visually impaired.

The Early Internet Boom and Video Activism in the 1990s

The economic crash in 1991 ushered in a "lost decade" of corporate restructuring and loss of jobs. The 1995 Great Hanshin earthquake sparked an NPO boom: When government and mass media responded poorly, people realized the value of volunteering, NPO activities, and of nonmainstream media and computer networks. In the hardest-hit part of Kobe, FM YY provided multilingual survival information and cultural programming to ethnic minority residents who faced language barriers and feared discrimination. During the next decade, FM YY became a widely noted example of multicultural grassroots media, a key institution in the emerging citizens' media movement.

People with hearing disabilities also faced life-threatening situations in the quake's aftermath. Information about explosion dangers, evacuation, water supplies, and shelters was often transmitted only on radio or TV, or by loudspeaker, with neither subtitles nor sign language interpretation. Nationwide, thousands were left uninformed as public television had cancelled its sign language news program *Shuwa News* to allow intensive coverage of the disaster. This convinced the Japanese Federation of the Deaf to establish their own news program called *Me de kiku terebi* (TV you can hear with your eyes). By the mid-2000s, this was distributed nationwide via satellite, cable, and UHF.

Media for migrant minorities also grew via local radio, cable, and satellite. Although focused on basic survival information for newcomers, they occasionally touched on political issues. In the north and south, Indigenous minorities began to stir. The severely ostracized Ainu in Hokkaido—Ainu Mosir, Land of Human Beings, being the Ainu name—began to reaffirm their identity. Resistance to a dam project in the remote village of Nibutani became linked to a fight for linguistic and cultural rights under the leadership of Ainu artist and author Shigeru Kayano, who founded the first Ainu newspaper, a museum, and a micro-radio station.

In the far south, the long political movement of Okinawans against U.S. military bases—Okinawa Prefecture accounts for more than 70% of military bases but only 1% of the population—was reignited by a 1995 U.S. military rape incident. The movement and its major mobilizations at the time of the G8 summit, which was hosted in the prefectural capital Naha, was supported by the local newspapers but ignored by national news media. Despite lack of political recognition, appreciation of Okinawa's cultural legacy began to grow. By the late 1990s, a revival of Okinawan music, language, and culture had developed around local radio stations within the prefecture and also the urban centers of central Japan.

The women's movement in the 1990s focused on institutional change, especially the passage of gender equality legislation and the establishment of municipal women's centers. An issue that required intensive media work, however, was the "comfort women" issue. Survivors of an institutionalized sexual slavery system during the Asia-Pacific War, especially Philippinas and Koreans, began to demand redress publicly. As they were much maligned in the mainstream media, feminist Japanese video activists and filmmakers rose to document their stories and support their case.

Religious movements also used video for missionary activities and inspiring followers. The Aum Shinrikyo sect made liberal use of special effects to proclaim its leader's superhuman powers, selling the tapes for fund-raising. After the leadership perpetrated sarin gas attacks in the Tokyo subway in 1995, the sect also distributed video news releases with its version, which many rank-and-file followers still believe. Most religious sects continued to rely on text-based print media, but some turned to popular culture formats, such as comic books (manga).

Social movements embraced computer networks and the Internet, broadcasting being mostly closed to them. The 1992 Rio Earth Summit underscored environmentalist groups' needs for computer-mediated communication, and in 1993, JCA (later JCAFE) was set up as a nonprofit Internet service provider for social movements and NPOs. JCA offered server space, site rental, e-mail hosting, and bulletin boards, and they ran workshops and demonstrations. It also supported civic groups' participation in international meetings, especially the Beijing Women's Conference and the Kyoto Protocol summit. The feminist paper *Femin* launched its website when mainstream newspapers still saw the Internet as an enemy. Civic groups were a significant presence among early Japanese websites, and e-mail helped their international networks grow.

Although movement videos circulated in small informal networks, wider distribution remained a problem. The call emerged for a system of public access television, together with a culture of *joeikai*, public screenings for videos and films without commercial distribution because of their social movement content. When the Japanese government supported the First Gulf War, viewed by many as violating the constitution's "Peace Article" (Article 9), a Paper Tiger TV member visited Tokyo in 1992 to speak about the U.S. cable access system and Paper Tiger's Gulf War Project. The spark caught. The People's Media Network (PMN) formed to promote video activism, public access, and movement documentaries. PMN's mailing list had 400 members, and was active until the early 2000s. PMN members published a book outlining the 1990s' video and net-based activism, and in 1998 launched the video distribution service *VIDEO ACT!*, which by the late 2000s was distributing approximately 150 independent videos produced by some 50 groups.

2000s: Citizens' Journalism and Alternative Media Networking

The Koizumi (2001–2006) and Abe (2006–2007) administrations pushed a free market and culturally conservative agenda. The wartime flag and anthem were declared official symbols of state, and efforts were redoubled to amend the constitutional articles on peace and gender equality. The

Fundamental Law on Education was revised to emphasize patriotism. The Ministry of Education ordered sensitive textbook passages revised on Japanese wartime policies. Some school boards followed suit, requiring teachers to stand in honor of the flag and anthem. After the 9/11 massacres, emergency legislation was passed to broaden the military's mandate and support U.S. wars in Afghanistan and Iraq.

The right also targeted mainstream media, resulting in increased media self-censorship regarding feminist issues, Japanese war crimes, the emperor system, and the military. Because of pressure from high-ranking politicians and grassroots right-wing groups, the public service broadcaster NHK distorted a documentary on the 2001 Women's International War Crimes Tribunal on Japan's Military Sexual Slavery. Rightists also tried to intimidate independent media makers with mixed results. Attempts to suppress distribution of the film *Yasukuni,* about the Shinto shrine especially dear to ultra-nationalists, resulted in the film gaining widespread attention. The rightist movement continued to rely on mainstream media, but rightist youth culture also spawned *manga* and pop music. Rightist activism also became prevalent in many online fora.

Social movements on the left organized resistance against these developments and blamed neoliberal policies for a spate of pressing social issues: growing job insecurity, youth unemployment, a rise in homelessness, and the growing income gap. Ironically, spreading this critique was cheap, as neoliberal deregulation had cut broadband rates.

Many alternative media projects took inspiration from abroad. Z-net/Japan (2001–2003) translated articles on Iraq and Colombia, and helped popularize the work of intellectuals such as Noam Chomsky and Edward Said. Indymedia Jp (IMCjp) was started to report on the huge 2002–2004 antiwar protests. The *Democracy Now* Japan site was launched in 2007, translating audio and video of the U.S.-based program. Inspired by Korean activists, a Media Center movement developed (e.g., MediR in Tokyo and the G8 Citizens Media Center in Sapporo).

In the 1990s, the Internet had mostly been used for networking and "talking within and among" different social movement groups. In the 2000s, Net journalism gained attention. Although some projects, notably *OhmyNews Japan* and *PJnews* (launched by Internet giant Livedoor) exploited "alternative" and "citizen participation" rhetoric as part of their business model, others had primarily civic goals. *Nikkan Berita* was launched in 1998 by critical mainstream journalists to report what they could not write elsewhere. Other notable sites included *Labornet Japan, Japan Alternative News for Justice and New Cultures* (JANJAN), and *News for the People in Japan* (NJP, launched by young lawyers critical of the legal system).

Print continued popular with left movements, the many new ones including the *People's Plan Japonesia* (in English) and *Oruta* (Alter). Many older journals went online, including the *Jinmin Shinbun* (People's Newspaper), *People's Plan Kenkyuu* (People's Plan Research), and *Impaction.* These spurred a Japan-based alternative globalization movement, which coalesced around the 2008 G8 in Hokkaido/Ainu Mosir.

Free online services (supported by advertising or data mining) became an important tool for financially precarious groups. *Takae no Genjo* (The situation in Takae), a mobile weblog (moblog), gave casual diary-style updates and soft-focus pictures from a sit-in against helicopter pad construction in an Okinawa environmental protection area. More radical examples included the websites and blogs of young people shut out of steady employment (such as PAFF, a network for non-regular and foreign workers) and homeless support groups (such as Association of Poor Peoples in Nagai Park), which gave blow-by-blow updates of clashes with authorities.

Faster Internet connections helped ease vexed distribution problems. *Ourplanet-TV* was set up in 2001 as an online public access TV station and training center for video activists. *Labornet* staff started *Uniontube,* a kind of noncommercial video sharing site using free and open source software. However, other problems remained. Many projects continued to face severe difficulties, most importantly funding, space and legal recognition, and many failed or curtailed their activities. The *Jumin Media Toshokan* (Citizens' Media Library), which had archived social movement materials since the 1970s, shut down in 2001. Others started with a business perspective to assure sustainability, limiting their scope from the get go. Ecological media, especially, became commercialized.

Although most social movement media remained preoccupied with critiquing the status quo, a new kind of positively oriented "cultural movement" emerged. The revitalized peace and antinuclear movement (especially the *Stop Rokkasho* campaign protesting nuclear reprocessing in rural Aomori), the "slow life" movement spearheaded by the Sloth Club, and the Buy Nothing Day Japan campaign all focused on building an alternative culture around sociopolitical issues.

Despite great efforts, at the end of the 2000s, Japan still lacked alternative media with wide appeal, like the Canadian magazine *Adbusters,* the U.S. *Democracy Now!* radio program, or *Emma, Ms.* magazine's German cousin. There were neither minority-ethnic media distributed to newsstands nor a legislative category for noncommercial, nongovernmental community broadcasting. Cultural factors, combined with state and corporate policies, limited the reach of social movement media. However, a citizens' (*shimin*) media movement was beginning to lobby and network on these issues.

Gabriele Hadl

See also Alternative Media; Citizens' Media; Environmental Movement Media; Indigenous Peoples' Media; Indymedia: East Asia; MediACT (Korea); Social Movement Media, 1920s–1970s (Japan)

Further Readings

Chan, J. (Ed.). (2008). *Another Japan is possible: New social movements and global citizenship education.* Stanford, CA: Stanford University Press.

Hadl, G., & Hamada, T. (2009). Policy convergence and online civil society media (CSM) in Japan. *International Journal of Media and Cultural Politics,* 5(1).

Hamada, T., & Onoda, M. (2003). *Internet to shimin* [Internet and citizens]. Tokyo: Maruzen.

Hasegawa, K. (2004). *Constructing civil society in Japan.* Melbourne, Australia: Trans Pacific Press.

Kogawa, T. (1993). *Free radio in Japan: The mini FM boom.* Retrieved April 29, 2008, from http://anarchy.translocal.jp/non-japanese/1993radiotext.html

Koyama, O., & Matsuura, S. (Eds.). (2008). *Hi-eiri hoso towa nani ka?* [What is nonprofit broadcasting?]. Kyoto, Japan: Minerva Shobo.

Pekkanen, R. (2006). *Japan's dual civil society.* Stanford, CA: Stanford University Press.

PMN (Minshunomedia Renrakukai [People's Media Network]) (Ed.). (1996). *Shimin media nyuumon* [Introduction to citizens' media]. Tokyo: Zoufuusha.

Tsuda, M., & Hiratsuka, C. (Eds.). (2006). *Paburikku akusesu wo manabu hito tame ni Shinpan* [For people studying public access] (2nd ed.). Kyoto, Japan: Sekaishisousha.

Vinken, H. (in press). *Civic engagement in Japan.* New York: Springer.

SOCIAL MOVEMENT MEDIA, 1991–2010 (HAÏTI)

When Jean-Bertrand Aristide was elected Haitian president in a landslide in December 1990, people all over the country went wild with joy, celebrating with music, demonstrations, and murals on the walls in cities and towns across the country. But just 7 months after he was inaugurated, Aristide was overthrown by a U.S.-backed military coup. Army-backed regimes ran Haïti for 3 years, crushing opposition and eliminating critics.

The return of constitutional order in late 1994 did not put an end to resistance and contestation. To the dismay of many of his supporters, Aristide had cut a deal with Washington in exchange for his return to power. In the shadow of heavy U.S. and then U.N. presence, and with "advisors" from the International Monetary Fund and other agencies haunting ministry hallways, the Lavalas governments—headed by Aristide until 1995 and then by his former prime minister René Préval (1995–2000)—were soon pushing a full neoliberal menu of economic austerity and privatization.

In 2004, Aristide, again president, was once more ousted from power, this time by a semi-orchestrated, semipopular uprising egged on by foreign-funded political organizations and a band of disgruntled ex-gang members, former soldiers and cashiered policemen. Backed by the United States and the United Nations, a temporary government ran the country until 2005, when Haïtians once again chose Préval as president. From exile in South Africa, Aristide remained a political force, although his Lavalas political party had split into at least two factions.

1991–1994: Social Movement Media Under Siege

Determined to wipe out Haïti's social movement organizations, the military regime went after grassroots leaders and also made a special point of targeting radio stations and journalists. During just the first 12 months of 3 years of junta rule (1991–1994), four journalists were killed, a fifth disappeared, and more than 30 were arrested. Nine stations were attacked and vandalized, including *Radio Haïti Inter* and *Radio Cacique,* which closed down. More than two dozen journalists fled the country and dozens more went into hiding.

Despite the repressive atmosphere, radio was once again a principal means of mobilization and resistance. When they dared, commercial stations broadcasted news, although sometimes at fatal cost. *Radio Tropic FM* and a few other stations ran abbreviated news programming, but its journalists were constantly threatened, harassed, and even beaten.

Across the border in the western Dominican Republic, Father Pedro Rouquoy and the church-owned Radio Enriquillo, whose signal reached much of eastern Haïti, broke new ground with special anti-junta news programs in Kreyòl (Haitian Creole). Haïtian militants in exile would read the news, sing *mizik angaje* (politically committed) songs, or play tapes smuggled from Haitian grassroots organizations. When the Dominican government outlawed newscasts or any speech in Kreyòl, Rouquoy and the militants *sang* the news. Enriquillo only ended its Kreyòl broadcasts on July 14, 1992, when the country's national telecommunications director and heavily armed soldiers arrived at the station to say that all Kreyòl broadcasts—including the broadcast of music—were now illegal.

Inspired by Enriquillo's reach and impact, in 1993 and 1994 some groups set up clandestine radio stations in the capital with names like *Radio Pèpla* (Radio the People) and *Radyo Solèy Leve* (Radio Rising Sun), a reference to *Radio Soleil,* by then firmly in the Catholic hierarchy's hands and no longer militant. Port-au-Prince would wake up to streets littered with leaflets proclaiming the broadcasts would "take the muzzle out of the people's mouth" and "denounce the enemies of democracy," and listing FM frequencies and program times. The tiny stations played *mizik angaje* and gave news from around the country and from

the growing anti-junta movement in the United States, Canada, and Europe. Some programs and songs also gave instructions on how to make Molotov cocktails or argued the merits of neck lacing (wreaking vengeance on death squad members through setting alight gasoline-soaked tires around their necks).

A few organizations communicated by circulating cassette tapes with recordings of news, *mizik angaje* and calls for resistance. One nongovernmental organization organized a cassette-based program called *Nouvèl Pou N Al Pi Lwen* (News to Take Us Further). Agricultural trainers would collect testimony and news from farmers groups around the country, edit that together with music, and then every 2 weeks quietly distribute a new program to approximately 125 groups across Haiti.

In 1992, the Haïtian Information Bureau (HIB) launched *Haïti Info,* a bi-weekly bulletin for overseas supporters of Haïtian democracy, in Spanish and English versions. A small staff of Haïtian human rights advocates and one foreign journalist wrote articles based on reports from clandestine "grassroots stringers." These were members of unions, rights groups, and farmers and popular organizations, who would collect news and testimony from around the country and deliver it to the capital. Published by a clandestine board of directors drawn from several political and popular organizations, for its first two years *Haiti Info* was not printed in Haïti. Instead, it went via Internet from a clandestine location to volunteers in the United States and Sweden who would print more than 1,000 copies, and then mail or fax them to paying subscribers all over the United States, Europe, and Latin America. When repression eased and the HIB opened an office, its members also briefed numerous "fact-finding" missions from the United States and Europe, put foreign journalists in touch with clandestine groups and activists, and worked with grassroots groups on numerous audio, video, and printed media in Kreyòl.

The Kreyòl newspaper *Libète* had to shut down during part of the coup period because of repression against its vendors, especially in the countryside. They were subject to sometimes brutal attacks by soldiers, police, and paramilitary: beaten, made to eat pages of the paper, and on at least one occasion a vendor's wife was raped. In 1992, the paper reopened, but until the return of constitutional order in 1994, it only printed approximately 2,000 copies for distribution in the capital.

Aristide's government-in-exile also took advantage of creative communication strategies. During the coup period, airplanes dropped fliers with photos of the president and calls for peaceful resistance. Just picking up a flier, however, could result in a beating or arrest. The exiled government also sent in cases of audiotapes and videotapes containing Aristide's speeches. These were played on the pirate radios or listened to by members of grassroots groups at secretly convened meetings. In 1994, with President Bill Clinton in office and when it looked as though Aristide's return to power was inevitable, the Aristide government teamed up with Washington to beam "Radio Democracy" on AM and FM bands into the country, reportedly from a nearby Coast Guard cutter. The content of these broadcasts was not overly revolutionary, however, as Washington officials could censor them.

Several *rasin* (roots) music bands were also part of the democratic resistance. During the 1992 Carnival, the regime shut off the power grid rather than permit RAM from playing its Carnival song *Anbago* (Embargo). This had the line *Kote Moun Yo?* (Where Are the People?), widely reread as "Where is Aristide?" The authorities thought revelers would go on an anti-junta rampage.

The Second, Neoliberal Lavalas Government

Once the coup ended and democratically elected leaders were back in the National Palace, several student groups, social justice nongovernmental organizations (NGOs), musicians, and farmers' organizations saw the neoliberal direction of the government and began mobilizing using the same tools that had worked before the coup: press releases, press conferences, marches, concerts, and strikes.

Musicians who had once risked their lives to sing songs to support Aristide and Lavalas now found themselves on the other side and produced Carnival songs ridiculing politicians' greed or deploring their poor leadership. Unions and farmers organizations continued to publish their small monthly or weekly bulletins. With print runs of between 500 and 2,000, these—with names like

Batay Ouvriye (Workers Struggle) and *Pou Yon Lòt Kalte Jistis* (For Another Kind of Justice) were mostly distributed to members of organizations or their NGOs funders but did not go unnoticed.

Libète did not survive. Founded with foreign funding and never linked to a specific member-based organization, the paper failed to develop a reliable revenue stream. A foreign NGO funded the construction of a printing plant, but between 1995 and 1998, its print run declined from 16,000 to 5,000, and its price tripled.

Beginning in the 2000s, NGOs supporting or associated with social movement organizations began to use the Internet for communicating with one another and the rest of the world. In the capital as well as across Haïti, Internet service was available either via telephone, cellular phone, or satellite connection, although it remained costly. In 2006, the International Telecommunications Union estimated that approximately 6% of the population, some 500,000 people, used the Internet at home, at work, in libraries, or at Internet cafés.

Some social movement-oriented NGOs maintained websites with information about their work and news articles related to social movements. The labor movement support group *Batay Ouvriye* and two NGOs that worked with social movement organizations *Sosyete Animasyon Kominikasyon Sosyal* (Society for Social Communication) and *Institut Culturel Karl Lévêque* had websites with pages in Kreyòl, French, and some English.

In 2001, a group of "alternative" journalists established an Internet-based news service *AlterPresse*, with stories in French, Kreyòl, Spanish, and English. The mission of the site and the journalists—many of whom had "day jobs" at commercial broadcast stations—is to make available vital information about the processes connected with the movements for basic economic, social, and human rights.

Fetishizing the Power of Speech

Nonetheless, toward the end of that decade, social movements were at an ebb, with unions and farmer organizations trying to reinvigorate themselves in a challenging economic, social, and political context. Radio remained the most important communication tool. A 2003 Gallup poll claimed 92% of Haïtians had access to a radio and that some two thirds listened between 2 and 5 hours a day. Although these numbers seemed high for rural citizens, they were believable for the cities, where pervasive unemployment and proximity of living quarters could account for them. But already by 2000, no commercial or state stations and only a few community stations could be called "social movement-oriented."

The heady days of 1986 and *Ayiti libère—Baboukèt la tonbe!* (Haïti is free—The muzzle has fallen!) were past. Organizers were struggling to rebuild organizations and social movements from the ground up, in a context of increasing public poverty and disillusionment, and influential patronage wielding—consciously and overtly by political parties, and less consciously and less conspicuously by foreign-funded NGO development projects.

The greatest factor leading to the disappointments—and, by some standards, failures—of the post-Duvalier movements was undoubtedly foreign intervention in all its forms (political, financial, covert, overt, military, and economic). However, the movement's overwhelming belief in the almost automatic power of the word, of speech, was also to blame. Organizations considered the power to denounce everything and anything and to criticize any maneuver they judged suspect as constituting the essence of democratic activity and struggle, in the process seeming to credit speech with the automatic power to overcome any of the antidemocratic offenses challenging them.

Twenty years after the muzzle was removed, manifestos, position papers, press conferences, and the occasional NGO-backed demonstration remained the privileged forms of mobilizing. Members of social movement organizations were more activists than political actors, and the movement, such as it was, remained a disparate, dispirited, and rather weak collection of unions, women's associations, farmer organizations, student groups, and foreign funded NGOs and their "client" grassroots groups.

In many ways, Haïti's social movement organizations, and their communications efforts, had further to go and more challenges than in 1986, thanks in part to the dependency created or encouraged by foreign funders. And while it remained true that the muzzle was off, and that freedom of speech exists, the overwhelming majority of Haïtians remained oppressed and largely excluded, because of the country's harsh economic and social conditions.

Jane Regan

See also Community Media (Venezuela); Community Radio (Haïti); Community Radio Movement (India); Mawonaj (Haïti); Social Movement Media, 1915–1970 (Haïti); Social Movement Media, 1971–1990 (Haïti); Zapatista Media (México)

Further Readings

Alterpresse: http://www.alterpresse.com
Batay Ouvriye: http://www.batayouvriye.org
Institut Culturel Karl Lévêque: http://www.ickl-Haïti.org
Jean, J.-C., & Maesschalk, M. (1999). *Transition politique en Haïti—radiographie du pouvoir politique* (Political transition in Haïti—x-ray of the power structure]. Paris: L'Harmattan.

SOCIAL MOVEMENT MEDIA, 2001–2002 (ARGENTINA)

Argentina saw tumultuous days in December 2001, when sustained and massive protests at the ruinous economic collapse brought about by the neoliberal regime's policies saw four presidents come and go within a single month, and the president finally in place repudiate the country's colossal International Monetary Fund (IMF) debt. In a country once the most economically advanced in Latin America, unemployment had skyrocketed, middle-class savings had evaporated, and more and more individuals were sorting through garbage dumps. Masses of people were mobilized daily in the streets, chanting "Out with the lot of them!" (¡Que se vayan todos!). Social movement media exploded in volume and impact.

Accumulating Public Frustration

It is impossible to grasp the volatility and variety of alternative communication practices in Argentina in 2001–2002 without reference to the economic, political, and social context, in which regional implementation of the IMF and World Bank monetarist policies led to concentrated wealth and excluded most individuals. As a starting point to consider the role of popular communication within the rebellion of December 19–20, 2001, it is necessary to look back to the desperation and fury generated by the wave of privatizations and unemployment that had plunged the country into extreme poverty.

Concretely, this refers to the 1994 uprising in the quiet northerly province of Santiago del Estero, which opened a phase of struggles characterized by their resistance against the odds to the advance of neoliberalism. Social protest began to grow, from Jujuy and Salta in the far north to Ushuaia in Tierra del Fuego, and from Cruz del Eje in Córdoba province to Patagonia's Cutral Có and Plaza Huincul, putting an emergent social force at the head of the struggle, people who turned their identity into an icon of power and hope for part of the public: the *piquetero* (picketer) movement.

From the second half of the 1990s, unemployed men and women workers took to the streets to make themselves heard. Thrown out of the labor market with no policy solution on the horizon and having to struggle to get something to eat, they confronted their common problems collectively and began to construct a social transformation. Masking their faces to avoid repeated arrests and to make themselves visible, the *piqueteros* saw the fruit of their efforts distorted on TV screens, their struggles demonized, and their reasons obscured or twisted by dominant media.

The power structure's single definition almost seamlessly applied the classic stereotypes of "agitator," "violent," and "infiltrator" to refer to those who were blocking the highways and demanding dignity. Growing media conglomerates applied the same labels without distinction to pensioners' struggles, to the resistance of the first people fired from privatized state firms, to student conflict over public education reform policies, and to the H.I.J.O.S. *escraches*. These demonstrations were by the children of the disappeared outside the residences of the surviving perpetrators of the 1976–1982 genocide, who were living free in their lairs, protected by Argentina's impunity laws.

Development of Social Movement Media

Within this framework, alternative communication began to seem a political necessity, an instrument that would challenge the numbing impact of fast-paced TV dramas and variety shows and expand the terrain of political intervention to the cultural sphere, perceived as a space of class struggle. From this emerged a strategic alliance, especially from the second half of the 1990s, between alternative and counterinformation media, and organizations, movements, community workers, media activists, and students of programs devoted to communication and visual design. The earlier rapid expansion of these programs made their students' prospects seem a mockery in the face of the collapsing economy.

Within these confrontations and alliances, a good part of the alternative media and the richest politico-cultural projects made outstanding contributions to the process of people's struggle, whose highpoint was the rebellion of December 19–20. The rebellion forced President de la Rúa's resignation and challenged the harsh economic policies of the Menem government over the previous decade.

The video and film political intervention groups were a good example of this politics of alliances: *Cine Insurgente* (Rebel Cinema), *Ojo Obrero* (Workers Eye), *Contraimagen* (Counterimage), Boedo Films, *Wayruro Communicación Popular,* or *Alavío* were producing audiovisual materials in concert with or as organic elements within the popular movements, emerging as tools of struggle, organization, and political action. The rebellion's rapid intervention mechanisms were well lubricated. Images of the social explosion multiplied rapidly, widely delegitimating mainstream media discourse. But this response took the form of both a dispute over interpreting the events and the enactment of a politics of confrontation with the media conglomerates. This materialized in different mobilizations and *escraches* at the headquarters of the news companies, denouncing their manipulations and their role in shaping public awareness.

The actions undertaken were not homogeneous but, even with the variations visible in different media (stressing the political or the communication dimension), something similar happened with people's and community radio, which had a long tradition in Argentina (stations such as *Alas* [Wings], *Colectivo La Tribu* [The Tribe Collective], *Aire Libre* [Free Air], and *De La Calle* [Street], among many others). Also, newspapers and news agencies began to make use of the advantages enabled by new information and communication technologies (*Agencia de Noticias Red Acción* [Action Network News Agency], *Red Echo* [Echo Network], and others). They were all clearly committed to a policy of active involvement. All forms of activism encountered and empowered each other on the field of battle.

The dynamic of the political conjuncture in the 2001–2002 biennium, overall, favored the development of three elements: (1) the linkages between different experiences, (2) the birth of new forms of activism and a jump in quality and quantity from earlier forms, and (3) the overflow of small-scale alternative media operations into a mass movement. All this was within the framework of a practice and examination of "the alternative," which in many cases was linked to the necessity of constructing a total mass-based alternative.

Linkages Between Experiences

Linkages and movement growth within larger networks and assemblies were facilitated by a unification of efforts that allowed activist journalists, media, and press leaders of popular organizations to meet in the same spaces. The Documentarists' Association of Argentina (today, DOCA), in terms of documentary and union interventions; *Kino Nuestra Lucha* (Our Struggle Cinema), in terms of videographers, press photographers, workers from factories they had taken over, self-managed workers' committees; or the broader *Argentina Arde* (Argentina Is On Fire), in terms of newspaper, photography, and video: All these were immediate daughters of the December 19–20 rebellion and its assemblies. The activist *piquetero* Darío Santillán, who was killed by police bullets not many days later during a blockage of the big Pueyrredón Bridge in Buenos Aires, had participated in the first assemblies of *Argentina Arde*, representing a sector of the unemployed workers' movement.

Similarly, the Alternative Media Forum *FODEMA* operated as a meeting ground for many media, bringing together groups, individuals, and media in one place with the intention of empowering specific projects through combined activity. FODEMA was a founding member of the *Red de Medios Alternativos* (Alternative Media Network), a national organization that from 2004 proceeded to do battle against the dominant discourse and its individualistic and commercialized practice. That year saw the first conference that brought together counterinformation projects from the entire country in the former Zanón ceramics factory, by then run by its workers as Fasinpat, *Fábrica Sin Patrón* (Factory Without Boss).

New Forms of Activism

There was a surge of fresh media projects and an increase in the size and quality of those that had joined in battle, with extensive production of audiovisual and print materials during the biennium. It was also in this period that the international Indymedia network had its definitive takeoff in Argentina. Many communication activities emerged from the popular assemblies that multiplied especially in the federal capital and in Greater Buenos Aires, although also in other cities such as Rosario. These communication projects were set in motion by employed and unemployed workers, and political art projects, whether performance based or focused on street interventions.

Small-Scale Media in the Mass Movement

The period was marked by a remarkable circulation of alternative media and counter-information, not only inside Argentina's borders but beyond them. But the most interesting aspect here is to lay bare the direct bond between alternative media use and the condition of the class struggle. The mass mobilization meant people could see the sharp difference between the protests they were engaged in and their coverage in mainstream media. This led to a widespread search for other sources of news and perspectives.

Mass action is essential if the objective is to leave the margins, to leave the religion of "small is beautiful," in order to build agreement around a full-scale project for social transformation. However, such mass action cannot be the type of mass behavior imposed by the "culture industry," as described by Adorno and Horkheimer in a famous 1944 essay. They argued that the production of culture in cinema, press, and broadcasting is as much subordinated to market forces as are shoes, cars, and clothes, and that this creation of a "culture industry" crushes the creative spirit, leaving a homogenized mass-produced culture in its place. Rather, intense reflective analysis is needed fundamentally because it is practice in Gramsci's sense: reflective action and reflection on action, which alone can generate a formidable political alternative to the existing order.

From this angle then, the multiplication of counterinformation practices that accompanied and expressed the beginning of the new millennium in Argentina cannot be explained as the result of an "exceptional moment in time" but must be viewed as the result of a dialectical relation between those practices and the popular struggle process, arising out of the first resistance actions against neoliberalism, which peaked in 2001–2002 and then began to ebb. This decline was related clearly to the fact the dominant classes reconstructed their hegemony, as well as to the popular movement's difficulty in putting together an alternative—political and *also* communicative—which would challenge the reactionary forces' handling of events.

The process however is in no way over, though it has a great variety of faces and at times moves slowly. The demands of the moment ceded to both experimentation and the creation of more solid foundations, and many of the seeds flung into the wind during the days of rebellion are germinating. Many argue that the alternative media situation needs analyzing with a view to what was done in previous years, as well as reviving what was learned by older generations in liberation struggles. From that perspective, Latin American history offers much to be mined: In the struggle for independence from Spain, Simón Bolívar, the great anticolonial leader, traveled with a printing press on a mule, asserting that "the press is the artillery of thought."

Natalia Vinelli

See also Alternative Media Heritage in Latin America; Barricada TV (Argentina); Cine Insurgente/Rebel Cinema (Argentina); H.I.J.O.S. and *Escraches* (Argentina); National Alternative Media Network (Argentina); Radio La Tribu (Argentina); Wayruro People's Communication (Argentina); Zapatista Media (México)

Further Readings

Adorno, T., & Horkheimer, M. (1947). *Dialectic of enlightenment*. London: Verso.

Vinelli, N., & Rodríguez Esperón, C. (Eds.). (2004). *Contrainformación: Medios alternativos para la acción política* [Counter-information: Alternative media for political action]. Buenos Aires, Argentina: Ediciones Continente.

SOCIAL MOVEMENT MEDIA, ANTI-APARTHEID (SOUTH AFRICA)

The alternative press in South Africa has a long pedigree. This entry traces its development from the 1860s through the 1990s and its dogged struggle to give voice to the non-White majority.

The Beginnings, 1860–1950

Due to the country's early industrialization and urbanization, and because this process was accompanied by segregation and discrimination against Black South Africans, the Black press developed as a protest press. In the 1860s and 1870s, Africans began publicizing their protests, first in mission journals but after 1880 in independent, African-owned media. Socialist publications targeting the Black urban working classes appeared after 1900, but it was only in the 1950s that a nonracial resistance press emerged. However, targeting a racially and socially heterogeneous readership remained difficult, as evidenced by the experience of the alternative media in the 1980s, a decade of unprecedented popular mobilization.

During the first 50 years of the African protest media, the ideal "progressive African" was a respectable Christian involved in his or her community's welfare. African journalism's pioneer was John Tengo Jabavu. After 4 years editing the mission paper *Isigidimi* (The Xhosa Messenger), his missionary patrons demanded his resignation, objecting to the paper's politicization. In 1884, he founded *Imvo Zabantsundu* (Native Opinion), which continued until 1998. *Imvo* and Jabavu were influential among both Xhosa- and English-speaking Africans, while the newspapers edited by Solomon Tshekisho Plaatje became the voice of African nationalism in Tswana-speaking areas.

Plaatje played a central role in the early years of the South African Native National Congress, later renamed the African National Congress (ANC). Plaatje's first paper, *Koranta ea Becoana* (The Bechuana Gazette) was launched in 1901, and *Ilanga Lase Natal* (The Natal Sun) was started in 1903 by John Langalibalele Dube, a clergyman and educator who became the first president of the South African Native National Congress in 1912. *Ilanga* became the voice of Zulu ethnic nationalism from the 1930s onward.

The news agenda of these and other protest papers was dominated by the 1910 Constitution of the Union of South Africa and the 1913 Natives' Land Act. The British and the Afrikaners—bitter foes in the Anglo-Boer War—worked out a power-sharing deal at the expense of the African majority. The Natives' Land Act confined Africans' land rights to the Native Reserves, later renamed Bantustans, which ultimately covered only 13% of the country.

Other minority groups, notably the Indians and Cape Coloureds, produced their own media. Mahatma Gandhi launched *Indian Opinion* in Durban in 1903, but it was by no means the only Indian voice. The Coloured petite bourgeoisie produced a range of papers, starting in 1909 with the *APO Newspaper,* named after the African Political Organization founded by Abdullah Abdurahman.

Most early nationalist newspapers in Johannesburg were short lived. Their founders participated subsequently in *Abantu-Batho* (The People), launched by Pixley ka Isaka Seme in 1912. Published somewhat irregularly in English, Zulu, Xhosa, and Sotho/Tswana, this was the ANC's first and only official newspaper. It enjoyed its heyday as a militant protest paper when it took up the African workers cause after World War I. However, *Abantu-Batho* lost its militancy in the 1920s and, after its 1931 closure, the ANC never had its own paper again.

Few independent African publications survived the 1930s because of the economic depression and heightened political repression. Between 1930 and 1950, the independent African protest press was gradually replaced by Black commercial publications owned by White business interests. The interests of Black workers were taken up by the *Workers' Herald,* the mouthpiece of the Industrial and Commercial Workers' Union, the largest Black trade union movement prior to World War II.

Opposition voices also found an outlet in socialist journals, notably *Inkululeko* (Freedom), the journal of the Communist Party of South Africa, and the socialist weekly *The Guardian.* The socialist press initially showed little interest in Black community news or in the activities of African nationalist organizations. However, after the Communist Party was banned in 1950, *The Guardian* gave the ANC and its allies extensive coverage. Pioneering work by Ruth First highlighted the plight of Black farmworkers and of African women caught up in the anti–Pass Law campaigns (Africans, under threat of jail, had to carry internal passports at all times).

From Protest to Resistance: The 1950s

The ANC's revival and its transformation into a mass-based movement using confrontational tactics took place amid a rapid process of industrialization and proletarianization in the 1940s and 1950s. The National Party's election victory in 1948 ushered in decades of heightened repression and rigidly applied apartheid policies. Gradually, the ANC moved toward the idea of alliances with other protest movements, but in 1958 part of its leadership broke away and formed the Pan Africanist Congress (PAC) in protest at the joint actions with non-African organizations.

The African nationalist press remained fairly ineffective between 1940 and 1960. The only newspaper with national coverage was *Inkundla ya Bantu* (People's Forum), published in southern Natal. And although White-owned, *Drum* magazine, with its staff of young and talented journalists, writers, and photographers, embodied the aspirations of upwardly mobile Africans more than any other publication. *Drum,* however, shied away from overt political engagement. The unofficial organ of the ANC and its allies in the Congress Alliance was *Fighting Talk,* staffed mainly by members of the banned Communist Party. With the banning of the ANC and the PAC in 1960, the voices of popular protest were effectively silenced.

In the 1970s, African protest media reemerged under the aegis of the Black Consciousness (BC) movement. Although it did not produce much in terms of news media, BC did generate new interest in political and literary protest literature. BC publications included *SASO Newsletter, Essays on Black Theology,* and annual publications like *Black Review* and *Black Viewpoint.*

The *SASO Newsletter* was the voice of the South African Students' Organization that was founded in 1969 when African university students chose to reject White patronage in favor of an affirmative, positive identification with "Black." Steve Biko, BC's most eloquent spokesman, was a prolific writer: His column "I write what I like" under the pseudonym Frank Talk is a valuable source of information about the philosophy and values of BC. With bans coming into place in 1972 and escalating after the 1976 Soweto uprising, media production by the BC movement remained limited. It did, however, exert a formative influence on a new generation of Black journalists, many of whom were working in the White commercial media sector.

Community Papers

The revival of popular protest in the early 1980s was marked by a proliferation of new media. Banners, T-shirts, posters, pamphlets, mass rallies, concerts, funerals, freedom songs, buttons, and newspapers served to popularize the United Democratic Front (UDF), an umbrella movement for hundreds of community organizations, student associations, sports, trade unions, religious groups, and women's groups. Launched in 1983 in protest at a new constitution that introduced separate parliamentary representation for Coloureds and Indians while continuing to exclude Africans, the UDF was easily the most representative mass movement in South African history. Through the UDF and its affiliates, the ANC reemerged as the leading force in the liberation struggle. As a multi-race and multiclass alliance, the UDF made adroit use of the media to mobilize, recruit, organize, and conscientize a broad spectrum of Black and White South Africans.

The UDF produced its own media, notably *UDF News,* a national newsletter with a circulation of 25,000, and the magazine *Isizwe* (The Nation). Edited by Communist Party stalwart Jeremy Cronin, *Isizwe* elaborated on theoretical debates and explained the UDF strategy of building a broad popular alliance and warned against

"errors of populism" and those of "workerism." More importantly, the UDF inspired a new generation of alternative media and had considerable impact on the commercial press.

The pioneer of the new generation of anti-apartheid media was *Grassroots,* a community paper aimed at a Coloured and African readership in the working-class areas around Cape Town. *Grassroots* saw its role as an agent of change: It aspired to interact with its readership and help shape, rather than only report, events. Launched in 1980, it became a model for community papers elsewhere. Most of its funding came from ICCO (Interchurch Organisation for Development Co-operation), an NGO run by Protestant churches in the Netherlands.

A tabloid published every 5 weeks, *Grassroots* had an initial print run of 5,000, which increased initially to 20,000 and then to 40,000 some years later. Its front page usually exposed the apartheid government's scandalous deeds or celebrated a heroic victory by "the people." On its inside pages, *Grassroots* offered advice on pensions, divorce, unemployment benefits, and the prevention of nappie rash; celebrated the ANC heroes of the 1950s; and detailed the everyday struggles of ordinary people. Addressing community issues was not an end in itself but a stepping stone in the process of mobilization against racial and class oppression.

In the second half of the 1980s, its staff became intoxicated by an activist discourse quite remote from ordinary people's daily experiences. *Grassroots* aimed at bridging the divide between Coloureds and Africans by promoting class consciousness, but in doing so, it became increasingly out of touch with ordinary Coloured folks. Attempts to transform the "struggle paper" into a commercial freesheet never took off, and *Grassroots* ceased publication in 1992.

The most important rural offshoot of *Grassroots* was *Saamstaan* (Stand Together), published in Oudtshoorn. Anti-apartheid media in Afrikaans, usually branded "the language of the oppressor," was a novel feature of the 1980s. Both Coloured activists and disenchanted Afrikaners reappropriated Afrikaans as a medium to articulate an alternative worldview, not only in community papers like *Saamstaan* and *Namaqa Nuus* (Namaqa News) but also in publications aimed at a nationwide readership, such as *Vrye Weekblad* (Free Weekly

Paper, 1988–1994) and *Die Suid-Afrikaan* (The South African, 1984–1994). Under its irreverent editor, Max du Preez, *Vrye Weekblad* broke new ground with its investigative journalism that exposed death squads within the police force.

Alternative Newspapers

A similar ambivalence toward the culture of its intended Coloured working-class readership characterized the relatively short but eventful life of the weekly *South,* published in Cape Town from 1987 to 1994. In the political culture of the 1980s, embracing the ideals of nonracialism entailed a denial of Coloured identity, on the grounds that apartheid architects had constructed it to divide and rule the non-White majority. However, with the demise of apartheid, a resurgence of Coloured exclusivity and African–Coloured antagonism could no longer be ignored.

Editor Rashid Seria described the experience of running *South* as "walking a tightrope." The government wanted to bully *South* into compliant reporting, and advertisers shunned the paper. Meanwhile, *South* came under fire from activists who were expecting radical content and were dismissive of the crime, horse racing, fashion, and rock music stories that *South* included to attract a wide readership. A circulation of 70,000 was deemed necessary to be financially independent, but figures hovered between 7,000 and 10,000. With anti-apartheid funding drying up after 1990, not only the community papers but also the alternative weeklies struggled to survive.

Weeklies like *New Nation, Weekly Mail, South,* and *Vrye Weekblad* focused primarily on news. Although broadly sympathetic to the UDF and ANC, they insisted on editorial autonomy and wanted commercial viability. Journalists working for the alternative press routinely suffered personal harassment, searches of their homes and offices, arson, tampering with their cars, and low salaries.

The government came down particularly hard on the weekly *New Nation,* launched in 1986 by the Catholic Bishops' Conference. *New Nation* carried substantial reporting on religious matters, but its focus was on politics and workers' issues, with extensive coverage of the UDF and the COSATU, the trade-union federation. Under its editor Zwelakhe Sisulu, *New Nation*'s editorial line followed a militant socialism. Although it carried little in terms of entertainment and popular fare, it had an estimated circulation of 66,000.

The paper was repeatedly banned, and Zwelakhe Sisulu spent almost 2 years in detention without trial. After the first democratic elections in 1994, the Catholic bishops sold the paper to a Black empowerment consortium. Faced with a declining readership and rising costs, *New Nation* folded in 1997.

The only paper to survive in the post-apartheid era was the *Weekly Mail* (1985–1994), which continued as the *Mail & Guardian* after merging with *The Guardian Weekly* in the United Kingdom. The *Weekly Mail* was launched by journalists from the defunct *Rand Daily Mail,* who used their severance pay to start a new progressive paper. With a broad social-democratic perspective, the *Weekly Mail* focused on opposition politics, trade unions, labor issues, and the security forces' repression and excesses inside and outside South Africa, giving its largely White readership a taste of what was happening in the townships. Its journalistic professionalism and investigative reporting resulted in the *Weekly Mail* having an influence out of all proportion to its 20,000 circulation. After the ANC's 1994 election victory, the newspaper insisted on a more independent editorial policy.

Media played a vital role in the social movements that transformed South African society but, paradoxically, the media of these movements were unable to survive the transition to nonracial democracy.

Ineke van Kessel

See also Anticolonial Press (British Colonial Africa); Independence Movement Media (India); Independence Movement Media (Vietnam); New Culture and May 4th Movements Media (China); Social Movement Media, Post-Apartheid (South Africa)

Further Readings

Limb, P. (1993). *The ANC and Black workers in South Africa, 1912–1992: An annotated bibliography.* London: Hans Zell.

Switzer, L. (Ed.). (1997). *South Africa's alternative press: Voices of protest and resistance, 1880–1960s.* Cambridge, UK: Cambridge University Press.

Switzer, L., & Adhikari, M. (Eds.). (2000). *South Africa's resistance press: Alternative voices in the last generation under apartheid.* Athens: Ohio University Center for International Studies.

Switzer, L., & Switzer, D. (1979). *The Black press in South Africa and Lesotho: A descriptive bibliographical guide to African, Coloured and Indian newspapers, newsletters and magazines 1836–1976.* Boston: Hall.

Tomaselli, K., & Louw, E. P. (Eds.). (1991). *The alternative press in South Africa.* London: James Currey.

Tomaselli, K., Tomaselli, R., & Muller, J. (Eds.). (1987). *The press in South Africa.* London: James Currey.

Van Kessel, I. (2000). *"Beyond our wildest dreams": The United Democratic Front and the transformation of South Africa.* Charlottesville: University Press of Virginia.

SOCIAL MOVEMENT MEDIA, POST-APARTHEID (SOUTH AFRICA)

Social organizations central in the resistance against South Africa's apartheid regime, such as the African National Congress (ANC), the Congress of South African Trade Unions (COSATU), and the United Democratic Front (UDF), effectively mobilized their constituencies through use of alternative media, such as T-shirts, murals, music, pamphlets, and posters. Their tactics, use of alternative media, and strategies of resistance lived on in the new social movements that emerged in South Africa in the early 2000s.

Post-Apartheid Social Movements

These emerged in response to the neoliberal economic policies adopted in the mid-1990s. In 1994, the new ANC government sought to address the huge structural economic inequalities it inherited from its apartheid predecessor through adoption of a social-democratic program named the Reconstruction Development Program (RDP).

But in 1996, policy switched to the neoliberal Growth, Employment, and Redistribution (GEAR) strategy. Although this offered opportunities to a growing urban black middle class as part of the government's Black Economic Empowerment

program, the trade liberalization inherent in GEAR closed a range of uncompetitive industries. The resulting unemployment spikes coincided with a local governments' decision to introduce fees for basic services such as water and electricity.

Several social movements emerged seeking to address government's failure to provide adequate access to basic services for all. These included the Anti-Privatization Forum (APF) in Johannesburg, the Anti-Eviction Campaign (AEC) in Cape Town (both established in 2000), and *Abahlali baseMjondolo* (Shackdwellers in isiZulu, AbM) in Durban (2005) and Cape Town (2008). They challenged local government attempts to evict residents, opposed electricity and water cut-offs, and resisted the enforcement of cost-recovery mechanisms such as the installation of pre-paid water and electricity meters. These movements also highlighted the top-down nature of government housing policy, the lack of consultation in policy formulation, and the state's frequent intimidation of social movements.

Social Movements and Mainstream Media

Although the "new" social movements of the early 2000s opposed the policies introduced after 1994 by the "old" social movements such as the ANC and COSATU (now in government), their media and mobilization strategies bear a strong resemblance to their predecessors'. Like the "old" social movements, the APF, AEC, and AbM had little access to the South Africa Broadcasting Corporation (SABC) and influential national newspapers such as *The Star, The Sunday Times, Mail and Guardian,* and *Business Day.* Mainstream broadcasting and print media often delegitimized the new social movements and framed their actions in terms of "conflict," "troublemakers," or the "ultra-left."

Although some movements managed to build up good relations with individual broadcast and print journalists, locally and even nationally, they perceived the SABC as primarily amplifying the ruling party's voice. They felt the national broadcaster particularly highlighted government achievements in improving the plight of some poor South Africans but failed to expose the negative impact of its policies on the poor at large and rarely accorded airtime to the views of social movements. Although ANC representatives were allocated significant airtime on SABC, representatives from social movements merely featured for a fraction of a second.

As a young AbM activist pointed out in the run-up to the April 2009 national elections:

We have come to understand that the media is not our friend and the media will never be our friend. They will only show the President of Abahlali for one minute and they will show the President of the ANC for two hours, . . . so frustrating. (Focus group discussion with members of Abahlali baseMjondolo, Durban, South Africa, April 4, 2009)

Because of their limited access to formal media at national level, social movements used a range of alternative media to highlight their campaign issues and to draw more activists into their struggles.

Old Media: The March, the T-Shirt, Songs, and Dance

The protest march still constitutes an important medium through which the APF, AEC, and AbM communicate their grievances to government officials and the wider public. Social movements frequently organize demonstrations during which community members deliver memoranda to local and national officials. Marches are announced through posters and pamphlets handed out to the general public and distributed to social movement members, or through door-to-door visits.

T-shirts, songs, and South Africa's distinctive *toyi-toyi* dance—a hallmark of antigovernment demonstrations under apartheid—play a key role during social movement marches. In demonstrations, activists from the APF, AEC, and AbM are easily identifiable by their red T-shirts with slogans about major campaign issues. Under apartheid, political T-shirts were banned as early as 1953. In post-apartheid South Africa, the political T-shirt continued to play an important role.

One AbM activist argued,

It gives you the pride of what is written on it. When it says "No land! No house! No vote!" (the slogan of AbM's election boycott campaign), and you go to a shopping complex or to a hospital or to anywhere else, someone who has not yet gotten the fruits of democracy, can see yes, I have

been doubting who to vote for. But after seeing the T-shirt, someone gets persuaded to vote for the "No land! No house! No vote!" campaign. (Focus group discussion with members of Abahlali baseMjondolo, Durban, South Africa, April 4, 2009)

In South Africa, the red T-shirt has become a symbol of resistance that has enabled social movements to obtain visibility, to gain respect, or to elicit fear from government officials. T-shirts have become the embodied adverts of social movements, continuously communicating the lack of service delivery and the unfulfilled promises of government in the streets of South Africa.

Apart from T-shirts, songs and dances mark most marches organized by the APF, AbM, and the AEC. Activists perform the *toyi-toyi*, and sing powerful songs to highlight the issues. New songs are performed as well as old ones. Social movements have also given liberation songs new meaning to suit the changed political context of the 2000s. In 2007, the APF recorded several songs used during marches on a CD titled "Songs of the Working Class." The liberation song *We Nyamazane Yiyo Ehlala Ehlathini* (A Buck Lives in the Forest, in isiZulu) tells the story of liberation fighters who often spent long stretches of time in the forest. The song has been adapted to call on the post-apartheid government to remain serious about improving the living conditions of the poor.

In another song titled *Amanzi Ngawethu* (Water Is Ours), APF activist-cum-singer Patra Sindane calls on the ANC government, local authorities, and private water companies to accept that access to water is a basic human right and that its provision should not be privatized. APF uses the CD both as a fund-raiser as well as a means to mobilize communities and raise more awareness about the various struggles that the movement is involved in.

Similarly for AbM, songs have been central to mobilize and spread the word. In addition to their own songs, the award-winning Dlamini King Brothers, a 12-member *a capella* choir based in one of AbM's shack settlements in Durban, has advertised AbM's work through their songs. On their album *Hlis'uMoya* (Bringing Salvation), the group laments the conditions faced by poor communities and the failure of government to safeguard their rights. The album also pays tribute to AbM with a song titled *Ablahali*. The song praises the organization for its campaign work on behalf of Durban's poor communities. In the song, the group calls on the government to listen to the needs of impoverished communities, echoing AbM's call to government officials to "talk with us, not for us."

Unlike AbM's own songs that have not yet been recorded, the song *Abahlali* was playlisted in 2009 on Ukhozi FM, the largest radio station in KwaZulu-Natal Province. The increasing popularity of the Dlamini King Brothers contributed to publicize AbM's work to new constituencies. Music then has the power to bring in new activists into local struggles and to fight the stigma attached to squatters and shack dwellers.

New Media: Internet, Video, and Cell Phones

The Internet, video, and cell phones were also crucial in advancing the struggles of social movements in post-apartheid South Africa. APF, AbM, and AEC all had their own websites that collated press statements and articles written about the movements, as well as photos, videos, and statements of solidarity with other movements. Although few social movement members have direct access to the Internet, websites increased the national and international visibility of all three organizations. E-mail distribution lists enabled movements to circulate press statements on marches, arrests of activists, and ongoing court cases to journalists, local and international activists, and friends of the movement. Videos produced by activists about the birth of movements such as AbM were also used to organize new communities and bring their struggles into the movement.

The cell phone was pivotal. Although in 2007, only 8 of 100 South Africans used the Internet, 87% owned a cell phone. Fixed telephone lines in South Africa are only accessible to 10% of the population. Nearly all social movement activists had cell phones, which enabled them to mobilize constituencies effectively. As one AbM activist argued during a focus group discussion, "Without the cellphone, there is no organization. You cannot organize without the cellphone." Another noted, "While I can say the media is not our friend, I can say the cellphone is our friend—not the radio or the TV." Mobile chat technology such as Mixit drastically reduced costs.

Cell phones were used as tools of protest in their own right. For example, after AbM sent a list of grievances to the government, many activists phoned up government offices to request an answer to the communication. The movement managed to block the landline phone connection at the government offices. As a movement representative narrated:

All comrades were phoning, phoning, phoning, comrade after comrade. When they picked up the phone, they hear it's AbM. Everything was blocked in the government office because of AbM. That was another *toyi-toying*, we were protesting using the cellphones. (Focus group discussion with members of Abahlali baseMjondolo, Durban, South Africa, April 4, 2009)

Whereas post-apartheid social movements thus often adopted similar media strategies to their predecessors, the Internet and cell phones publicized their struggles to broader, international audiences and enabled the movements to communicate more frequently with their members and constituencies.

Wendy Willems

See also Eland Ceremony, Abatwa People's (Southern Africa); Online Diaspora (Zambia); Small Media Against Big Oil (Nigeria)

Further Readings

Abahlali baseMjondolo in Durban: http://www.abahlali.org

Abahlali baseMjondolo in Western Cape: http://www.khayelitshastruggles.com

Anti-Eviction Campaign: http://antieviction.org.za

Anti-Privatization Forum: http://apf.org.za

Ballard, R., Habib, A., & Valodia, I. (2006). *Voices of protest: Social movements in post-apartheid South Africa*. Durban, South Africa: University of KwaZulu-Natal Press.

Desai, A. (2002). *We are the poors: Community struggles in post-apartheid South Africa*. New York: Monthly Review Press.

Gibson, N. C. (2006). *Challenging hegemony: Social movements and the quest for a new humanism in post-apartheid South Africa*. Trenton, NJ: Africa World Press.

Olwage, G. (2008). *Composing apartheid: Music for and against apartheid*. Johannesburg, South Africa: Wits University Press.

Robben Island Museum. (2004). *Struggle ink: The poster as a South African cultural weapon, 1982–1994*. Johannesburg, South Africa: Ravan Press.

South African History Archive. (1991). *Images of defiance: South African resistance posters of the 1980s*. Johannesburg, South Africa: Ravan Press.

Wasserman, H. (2005). Connecting African activism with global networks: ICTs and South African social movements. *Africa Development, 30*(1–2), 163–182.

Wasserman, H. (2007). Is a new worldwide web possible? An explorative comparison of the use of ICTs by two South African social movements. *African Studies Review, 50*(1), 109–131.

Williamson, S. (1989). *Resistance art in South Africa*. Cape Town, South Africa: David Philip.

Social Movement Media in 1987 Clashes (Korea)

The year 1987 was a pivotal time of political unrest in South Korea, in which social movement media played a major role. Ever since 1980 when President Chun Doo-Hwan had brutally crushed pro-democracy rebels in the city of Kwangju, opposition had been mounting to his dictatorial rule. Demands to revise the constitution to provide genuine democracy were circulating widely. In February 1987, it came to light that the government had tortured to death a student named Park Jong-Chul, and then had hidden the murder. This sparked a massive national demonstration. In April, when the flames were already high, Chun made the notorious *Hoh-Heon* Declaration (*Hoh-Heon* abbreviates "retaining the constitution as is"), which was like pouring gasoline on a fire.

Chun proceeded to aggravate public hostility even further by engineering his close colleague Roh Tae-woo's election as governing party leader. Under the constitution at that time, this guaranteed that Roh would succeed Chun as the country's president early in 1988, thus extending Chun's influence for another 7 years.

The leader of the popular Kook-Pohn movement (*Kook Min Undong Pohn Pu*, People's Movement Committee for Abolition of *Hoh Heon*

and Winning a Democratic Constitutional Law) chose June 10 for a protest, as it was also the date when the ruling party was scheduled to elect Roh as its candidate. On that day, up to a quarter million people across the country came out to protest the government's election fixing. This resulted in such ongoing violent tumults that on June 29, Roh, at Chun's behest, called for a direct presidential election.

Roh still won, as the progressive wing was divided into two major parties, but the June mobilization was a tremendous popular victory, reflecting the accumulated achievements of past movements and also influencing greatly subsequent progressive ones.

Movement Media

Kook Pohn led the June 1987 movement using forms of alternative media used in Kwangju, but considerably upgraded. Kook Pohn's organizational structure was a mixture of hierarchical and anarchist, loosely assembled from many different sectors and groups. Correspondingly, diverse types of alternative media were in evidence from all progressive sectors, printing their own pamphlets and displaying their own billboards. It was an alternative media explosion.

Pamphlets were used far more widely than in the Kwangju uprising. Countless publishing organizations produced volumes of pamphlets, many of which were subsequently photocopied. As this was a criminal offense, the pamphlets required a systematic and dynamic guerrilla distribution. A team would grab a pile and distribute them quickly to passers-by or bus and subway passengers, while one member of the team made a quick speech. When distribution was complete, the whole team usually shouted out a few slogans in a distinctive rhythm and repetition, punching the air with their right fists. The most popular and important slogan during June 1987 was *Ho Heon Chul Pye Tock Jae Ta Doh* (Abolish *Ho Heon* and Eliminate Dictatorship).

Posters were also important means of distributing news, informing the public, and evaluating the ongoing movement. The main sites were campuses but people also posted them on walls during demonstrations. Most posters would be written on a large white sheet (150 × 80 cm/5 × 3 ft., approximately), with black marker pen, with blue and red for high-lighting. Most posters were one page, but some were as long as dozen.

Alternative media in music had also greatly developed through the Kwangju experience, which provided a rich source of themes for songs and *Noraekeuk* (song-plays, a type of musical). In June 1987, a typical demonstration would begin with singing in an outdoor assembly, led by a team of singers spread out through the crowd. These teams had roots in campus singing clubs that chose music as a form of progressive media. *Undong Kayo* (movement songs) emerged initially during the 1970s but became a force in the 1980s. Some were written in traditional musical style, but most were in the style of 1970s folk songs, whose musical roots were in Western popular songs. Most were short, simple, and lyrical.

From the mid-1980s, songs militant in style and theme were more and more in fashion. These would often be sung without instrumental accompaniment, but when they had some, it was mostly acoustic guitar and traditional drums. Many universities had their own singing teams that collaborated across campus, writing new songs that spread quickly via cassette tapes. Then, the assembly would become a mass of demonstrators and go to the streets singing and shouting slogans.

The lyrics often described the hardship of people's lives, the sorrow and anger of the oppressed, the vow to resist, and hopes for democracy and popular victory. Right after the June 1987 movement, the existing movement singers and campus movement song groups formed a popular movement group called Noh Rae Reul Channeun Sa Ram Deul (those who are trying to find songs, or Noh Chat Sa for short) and released their first LP/cassette in the mainstream music market. They added rock sound (e.g., Western drums and electric guitar), which made the songs more accessible to general audiences but at the same time got them criticized for cheap populism. Their music was indeed distributed widely and successful.

The sites of assemblies were often decorated with giant hanging pictures. One of the most iconic was of Lee Han Yeol, a student killed during a demonstration when shot at close range with a tear gas canister. The press photo showed Lee bleeding from the head, a friend holding him up under his limp arms. The photo was reproduced in countless copies and artifacts, and it became a crucial symbol of June 1987. Tall buildings were the most popular sites to hang these pictures. They were mostly drawn in woodprint fashion, which was believed, after the pioneering works of Oh Yoon (1946–1986), who was a populist print artist, to express the public's powerful and practical aspirations.

Artifacts and methods of demonstration also developed out of Kwangju. A motorcade became a common form of demonstration, and sounding the horn was often done to the same beat as slogan shouting, far more widely even than in Kwangju.

However, a lot of alternative media were invented spontaneously. During a massive street demonstration, countless workers in skyscrapers around the City Hall Plaza threw Kleenex tissues, paper towels, and toilet rolls from on high to help the demonstrators wipe away tears from gas and protect their respiratory organs. The throwing of tons and tons of paper tissues from the air looked like a mass of white petals falling, and certainly it created a memorable scene that communicated ordinary people's support for participants and condemnation of the government. Stacks of bread and drinks were piled on several streets by anonymous passers-by, so the demonstrators could get refreshment. This was a powerful lateral communication of solidarity and hope for victory.

Singing the national anthem and displaying the national flag also became popular. Because the national anthem was not as militant as some other movement songs, many people found it easier to participate. Similarly, people found it easier to celebrate and follow the national flag than other more militant banners.

One of the most impressive alternative media during June 1987 and onward was through dance. *Tal Chum* (the traditional Mask Dance) was studied and practiced as a part of *Madang* street theater during the 1970s and 1980s. Furthermore, Lee Ae Ju, a professional dancer and professor of dance, presented an original dance during Lee Han Yeol's funeral. She was dressed in white traditional dress, a long-sleeved short shirt, and a long skirt. In the tradition of consoling the deceased by various ways (for example, by making the shaman talk to the deceased and dance for him/her), Lee Ae Ju danced for the soul of Lee Han Yeol. She expressed his sorrow, his anger, and his will to fight against the military dictatorship, and ultimately she conveyed the people's inextinguishable will to resist. *Tal Chum* and people's traditional dance had been widely learned and experimented with in the 1970s in the social movement milieu as an alternative medium, and Lee Ae Ju's dance became a catalyst to the dance milieu in establishing progressive dance groups who expressed their political opinions through dance.

As a spectrum of different political groups emerged into the open in 1987, many publications were started. In the 1970s, *Changbi* (abbreviated version of "Creation and Criticism") and *Munji* (abbreviated version of "Literature and Intelligence") had been the two major periodicals for progressive readers. As it was practically forbidden to discuss alternative politics (i.e., politics other than President Park's), they conveyed their political opinions indirectly through writing about modern Korean history or penning progressive literature. Production was not glossy and circulation was small, but they were still precious alternatives for the progressive sector. However, both *Changbi* and *Munji* were banned by President Chun in the early 1980s. Nothing progressive was viable anymore on a regular basis.

Then came *mook*, a word combined from magazine and book, which did what *Changbi* and *Munji* had done but in a guerrilla fashion. June 1987 was an important catalyst for such *mooks*, and they eventually developed into quarterlies. Some *mooks* represented certain political groups, but in general *mooks* became an arena where different groups diagnosed current affairs and circulated action plans and blueprints. Finally, a *mook* appeared for the working class, *Noh Hae Mun* (Literature to Liberate Labor). People began to emerge from their fearful mentality and to express themselves boldly.

Toward the end of the 1980s, *mooks* became the prime arena for debates within the social movement sector: whether Korea was as a neo-colony and to what extent, and what kind of revolutionary strategy was the most viable. Such debates provided a theoretical base for the social movement. June 1987's popular experience on the streets made people confident and politically educated. The site of struggle blended with cultural performance and media art. For example, a typical demonstration would begin by a simple stage performance like singing, dancing, or a simple play (*madang*). Through struggle and movement activism, alternative media also became richer and more expressive.

This tradition continued on well beyond the 1980s; a good example is the 2008 demonstrations against importing American "downer" beef. Many thousands gathered in the City Hall Plaza for weeks with candles and led their demonstration with various cultural performances, such as graffiti, songs, performance, and *madang*, but this time in a relaxed and sometimes humorous way. Even ordinary high-school students put on their own performances, and laughter and jokes, very rare in the tense June 1987 demonstrations, were common.

Eun-ha Oh

See also Madang Street Theater (Korea); Media Activism in the Kwangju Uprising (Korea); MediACT (Korea); Political Song (Northern Ireland); Popular Music and Protest (Ethiopia); Street Theater (Canada); Street Theater (India)

Further Readings

Jung, H., (2004). *Yu-wol Hang-jaeng Kwa Hankook eui Minjujueui* [June 1987 movement and democracy in Korea]. Seoul, South Korea: Minjuhwa Kineom Sa-eop-hoe.

Kang, J. (2003). *Hankook Hyundaesa Sancheck* [A walk through the history of modern Korea] (Vol. 3). Seoul, South Korea: Inmul kwa Sasang.

SOCIAL MOVEMENT MEDIA IN 2009 CRISIS (IRAN)

The June 2009 presidential election triggered unprecedented and impassioned involvement inside Iran. The four approved candidates, vetted from 476 applicants and permitted by the Guardian Council, were announced in mid-May and their colors were distributed. Rapidly, an historic campaign grew in support of Mir-Hussein Mousavi, who put forward a modest, reformist program. This included greater freedom of media and expression, gender equality—prioritized by his wife and public campaigner, Zahra Rahnavard—and a new approach to international affairs.

The "Green" campaign was visible, with bandanas, posters and flags, large rallies, and support mobilized via the Internet. All candidates opened pages on Facebook (which had previously been banned), uploaded photos, and posted statements. Anti-Ahmadinejad sites also proliferated. The women's movement used their various websites to put out statements demanding women's rights. The Iranian diaspora, able to vote, was also addressed, and social networking sites erased the geographical distance between Iran and other countries. *Mowj-e Sabz*, a green wave, was visibly flowing across Iran, in Tehran, in other cities, and beyond.

The overly rapid and unbelievable result of a landslide victory for Ahmadinejad, declared within 2 hours of the polls closing with supposedly 65% of the national and diaspora vote, was immediately rejected by the other three candidates, including the second "conservative" candidate. Quickly, the slogan of a "stolen election" spread and "where is my vote" become a national outcry of many Iranians who believed that their votes were ignored.

In the aftermath, the regime used the *Basij* (Mobilisation Force, a brutal volunteer paramilitary) to crack down violently on demonstrators. It kept foreign journalists sequestered in hotel rooms until their visas ran out, censored the main newspaper of Mousavi's campaign *Kalameh Sabz* (Green Word), and arrested many associated with the Green campaign as well as many who were not.

The Political and Media Buildup

The response of a predominantly (but not solely) young population was astonishing. Politically, such a reaction seemed unlikely. In February 2009, the 30th anniversary of the revolution that brought the Islamic Republic into being, was celebrated in a somewhat low-key fashion. With many journalists and bloggers already in jail and constraints placed on face-to-face politics, young Iranians under 30 (70% of the population) seemed to be more interested in what the regime defined as cultural "deviancy," such as listening to underground music and watching foreign films and satellite TV, than paying much attention to the militant revolutionary rhetoric of President Ahmadinejad.

In media terms, however, Iranians are often early adopters of new technologies, and many were already adept at downloading music and other content from Internet sites, as well as being proficient and prolific bloggers. It was easy and quick for these Internet users to reverse the flow and to become citizen journalists. SMS messages flowed through Twitter and were picked up by external media. Such messages were also picked up by others inside Iran, and Twitter became a useful tool for organizing demonstrations and other activities.

New Media and the Ongoing Challenge to the Regime

Images abounded. Photos of demonstrations were sent out. Short video clips, again often taken from mobile phones, were uploaded to YouTube. Mash-ups of photographs were made into video, accompanied by music. The film of the tragic killing of Neda Agha Soltan, a young woman demonstrator whose death pictures condensed everything enraging world opinion, appeared on YouTube globally available in many different forms and accompanied by different musical scores. One was viewed by more than 500,000 people.

The Green Wave was quick to respond to regime statements and propaganda. Ahmadinejad's comment that those upset at "losing" the election were all *khas o khashak* (dirt and dust), as though they had lost a football match, triggered an anthem that demonstrators sang that turned the jibe back on him. Several versions were made of the original poem by the 13th-century Persian poet Rumi, from which Ahmedinejad had taken the phrase and uploaded to YouTube. Various Iranian singers, including the ever-popular Googoosh, Mohsein Namjoo, Abjeez, and others, recorded solidarity songs and dedicated them to demonstrators.

Global musicians acted in solidarity. Joan Baez sang *We Shall Overcome* in Persian and Andy, a well-known Iranian pop star, recorded *Stand By Me* with Bon Jovi, who also attempted some Persian. U2 played a Green concert. The democratization process belonged not only to Iran but also to the rest of the world.

Global news media, which could not cover the story themselves, relied on these nonprofessional sources, triggering many media debates about the changing nature of journalism. Young Iranians in the diaspora set themselves up as distribution nodes, sending information out to mainstream media sources. *Tehranbureau.com* provided a continuous feed of stories, whereas bloggers at *Huffington Post* and elsewhere kept up regular information and commentary on events. The global commentariat buzzed with alacrity, so it seemed that anyone who had ever eaten *chelo kebab* had something to say (and thought that everyone else wanted to hear it).

Much material was reposted to Facebook, which turned green; Iranians identified with a green square that asked "where is my vote?" whereas others in solidarity asked "where is their vote?" Profile pictures were amended as events unfolded, in themselves a fascinating record of the process.

Comparing 2009 With 1978–1979

Thirty years ago, a different set of small media—audiocassettes, leaflets, graffiti, posters, songs, and word-of-mouth—helped mobilize the overthrow of the Shah that became the revolution of 1979. Then, too, the comic, the violent, the mediated, and the face-to-face all jostled for existence. Nighttime in 2009 found people once again on their rooftops shouting *Allah o akbar* (God is great), as they did 30 years before.

In 2009, acts of solidarity continued around the world. Inside Iran, the Shi'ite ritual lament cycle provided moments of gathering and repetition. Demonstrations were organized in many countries for July 9 to commemorate the protesting Tehran university students whom the regime had killed in 1999, and for July 25, as a last challenge before Ahmadinejad was sworn in for a second term.

All these new communication technologies were no substitute for face-to-face politics. But they were used to remarkable effect. The sense of mutual fear and mistrust inculcated under Ahmadinejad was broken, and a remarkable spontaneous solidarity was fired up among Iranians, as if it had always been under the surface waiting to be rekindled. These new forms of political action showed Iranian creativity in music, in image making, and in widespread competencies in digital mash-ups. New linkages were forged between Iranians inside and outside, whereas new cracks

appeared among the clerical elites who rule Iran. It was a moment of both opportunity and threat.

Annabelle Sreberny

See also BİA Independent Communication Network (Turkey); December 2008 Revolt Media (Greece); Media Activism in the Kwangju Uprising (Korea); New Media and Alternative Cultural Sphere (Iran); Social Movement Media, 1960s–1980s (Chile); Women Bloggers (Egypt)

Further Readings

Khiabany, G., & Sreberny, A. (2007). The politics of/in blogging in Iran. *Comparative Studies of South Asia, Africa and the Middle East, 27*(3), 563–579.

Sreberny, A., & Khiabany, G. (2007). Becoming intellectual: The blogestan and public political space in the Islamic Republic. *British Journal of Middle Eastern Studies, 34*(2), 267–286.

Sreberny-Mohammadi, A., & Mohammadi, A. (1994). *Small media, big revolution: Communication, culture, and the Iranian revolution.* Minneapolis: University of Minnesota Press.

SOCIAL MOVEMENT MEDIA IN THE EMERGENCY (INDIA)

From June 25, 1975, to March 1977, Prime Minister Indira Gandhi declared India in a State of Emergency and suspended the constitution. She blamed the Opposition parties for the country's unrest, which encompassed the 1974 railway workers' strike, Jayaprakash Narayan's nonviolent JP Movement, student demonstrations in Gujarat and Bihar, and the Naxalite movement. The Emergency was declared within a fortnight of Indira Gandhi's conviction for election fraud, which would have required her to resign and banned her from office for 6 years. In January 1977, she scheduled elections but was definitively defeated by a temporary coalition involving every other major party.

This period was marked by fear, limitations on freedom, and a consolidation of power in the person of the prime minister. Gandhi imprisoned more than 100,000 political opponents and detained them without trial under laws such as MISA (Maintenance of Internal Security Act) and DIR (Defense of India Rules) for unspecified crimes, "unpatriotic tendencies," or breaking new laws passed by the much-diminished Parliament. The Emergency is remembered for excess and brutality, particularly associated with City Beautification (slum clearance), Family Planning (forced sterilization), censorship of "objectionable material," and torture of political prisoners.

The oppression experienced during the Emergency is often compared with the colonial period, and Narayan was referred to as the "Father of the Second Indian Freedom Struggle." The government declared several organizations as antinational, such as the extreme rightist RSS, the extremist Jamaat-e-Islami, the Ananda Marga cult, and the Communist Party of India (Marxist-Leninist), and majority of their leaders were arrested. Two major leaders who initially escaped arrest and coordinated underground opposition efforts were George Fernandes (socialist leader) and Nanaji Deshmukh (Jana Sangh), each of whom supported a civil disobedience campaign. They mirrored Mahatma Gandhi's *satyagraha* tactics, such as courting arrest, closing shops, abstaining from work, silent marches, student processions, sit-ins in public places, and hunger strikes (particularly on Gandhi's birthday).

The press was censored heavily and the national broadcast outlets (Doordarshan TV and All India Radio), then monopolies, became government mouthpieces. There was talk of setting up an underground radio station, but it never materialized. The film industry was forced to produce government messages under threat of withholding censor certificates, retribution for "unpatriotic" or "un-nationalistic" tendencies, charges of income tax evasion, and threats of arrest under MISA.

There was some street theater, but members of the major troupe (Janam), fearing arrest and torture, dispersed at this time, reconvening only after the Emergency was lifted. Some people went underground or used camouflage strategies such as allegory, obscure symbolism, secret codes, and anonymity to evade censorship. An example would be Khaliq Abdullah's "A Dirty Poem," written in Urdu in 1976, which is superficially about the Mongols. Some protest poetry, drama, essays,

prison letters, art, songs, and folk sayings circulated underground, but much of this came to light only after March 1977.

Kristen Rudisill

See also Independence Movement Media (India); Madang Street Theater (Korea); Media Activism in the Kwangju Uprising (Korea); Resistance through Ridicule (Africa); Social Movement Media in 2009 Crisis (Iran)

Further Readings

Nayar, K. (1977). *The Judgement: Inside story of the emergency in India*. New Delhi, India: Vikas.
Perry, J. O. (1983). *Voices of emergency: An all-India anthology of protest poetry of the 1975–1977 Emergency*. Bombay, India: Popular Prakashan.
Sahgal, N. (1977). *A voice for freedom*. Delhi, India: Hind Pocket Books.
Tarlo, E. (2003). *Unsettling memories: Narratives of the Emergency in Delhi*. Delhi, India: Permanent Black.
Vasudev, A. (1978). *Liberty and license in the Indian cinema*. New Delhi, India: Vikas.

SOCIAL MOVEMENT MEDIA IN THE SANDINISTA ERA (NICARAGUA)

In 1979, a wide coalition of political forces—high-school and university students, women, farmers, workers, educators, journalists, devout Catholics, Marxists, and business owners—succeeded in overthrowing the long-reigning and tyrannical Somoza dynasty in Nicaragua. President Somoza's dictatorship was marked by tyrannical torture and liquidation of political challengers, including leading journalists and teenage rebels; his orders to bomb rebel neighborhoods from the air; and his personal grip on the nation's finances. Somoza and his father had long enjoyed the friendly tolerance of the U.S. government, but the Carter administration at the end of the 1970s was pressing for human rights globally and suspended military aid to Nicaragua.

The roles of media in this process were fast changing and sharply contested. The new "Sandinista" regime—Augusto Sandino had led a rebellion in the years 1927–1933 against the U.S. Marines' occupation of Nicaragua, but was murdered in cold blood by Somoza senior in 1934—took over a desperately poor and illiterate country, which had been bled dry by Somoza's rapacity. Somoza went into exile, but his feared and despised National Guard soon regrouped with the active support of the new Reagan administration, which in frequent secret defiance of the U.S. Congress armed and supplied a large counter-Sandinista force based across the northern border in Honduras (the "Contras"). Argentinean torture and murder experts, seasoned in their military regime's unspeakable domestic repression of 1976–1982, were shipped in as trainers.

In the decades before the revolution, for both political and underdevelopment reasons, Sandinista forces had had little or no access to major media technologies. However, *pintas* (graffiti, sometimes mural designs) and *consignas* (slogans) frequently appeared on walls, both in the countryside and in the towns. A common slogan in the 1960s was simply *Sandino Lives*, but as the revolutionary front expanded into the towns, this changed to *Long live the people's Sandinista insurrection* and similar messages. In one case, a group of bullet marks in a wall was arrowed: *The Somoza dictatorship's last bullets.* Common were *pintas* serving as memorial plaques: *Freedom for the Fatherland or death—here fell* (name/date).

Radio—there was little television outside Managua and some towns before 1979—was deployed late by the Sandinistas. Although some sympathizers in commercial stations would broadcast coded messages at certain times, Radio Sandino began broadcasting, irregularly, from Costa Rica at the end of 1977, but only really swung into action with daily broadcasts morning and evening in mid-1978. It ran reports, interviews with Sandinista leaders, appeals for a general mobilization, weapon-handling instructions, appeals to National Guard soldiers to desert, and—not least—"new song" numbers, encouraging rebellion. Those inside Nicaragua supplying the station with information ran dire risks, and listeners (if caught) were in severe trouble.

In the months before the revolution, new stations sprouted in towns that had come under Sandinista control: Radio Insurrección in northerly Matagalpa and Radio Venceremos (we will win) in León, although it had to keep changing

location because of Somoza's bombardments. And then in the weeks before, Radio Liberación (Estelí), Radio Revolución (Juigalpa), and Radio Libertad (Jinotepe) were established. Others popped up in the weeks following. Often, the stations' workers would protect the equipment from its owners, who were feverishly trying to dismantle it before the Sandinista forces arrived.

Newspaper journalism had to face strict censorship and worse. The Sandinistas and pre-Sandinista groups had all produced occasional underground publications for decades, but a defining moment was the January 1978 murder of the editor of *La Prensa,* Nicaragua's leading daily, who had steadily critiqued, so far as he could, Somoza's brutal repression. In the protests that followed, four radio stations were closed and a state of emergency was declared. There emerged "catacombs journalism," redolent of persecuted Christians in ancient Rome, where no less than 24 churches in Managua and others around the country began operating as people's information centers.

Poetry has long been a defining mark of Nicaraguan culture, and rebellious poetry played a significant long-term role in the emergence of the revolution beginning in the 1950s. Between 1962 and 1979, no less than four collections of rebel poetry were printed clandestinely in thousands of copies. Many of these rebel poets had been killed by the National Guard while still in their 20s. Their message had especially focused on the necessity to free Nicaragua from U.S. domination, as well as the readiness to sacrifice all for that end. One famous rebel poet, the Marxist priest Ernesto Cardenal, survived to become first minister of culture in the Sandinista regime. The 1970s saw a significant number of women rebel poets surface.

Popular theater also contributed in the early-mid 1970s after the devastating 1972 Managua earthquake. The *Gradas* (steps) group, bringing together poets, sociologists, painters, designers, sculptors, actors, singers, and musicians, began performing in 1973 on the steps of churches. During their short existence, before they were forcibly dispersed, they also performed at factory gates and in schools, and they succeeded in sparking a series of other similar projects in and beyond Managua.

From 1979 through 1990, when the Sandinista government was voted out by a public exhausted from the violence and economic disruption mostly caused by the U.S.-backed forces operating out of Honduras and hoping for a period of peace, the attempts to organize media differently took a great variety of forms. Given that the 1979 revolution had opened up space only temporarily for such experimentation, that war soon became a constant drain on morale and the economy, that a new battery of Cuban advisors viewed themselves as senior brothers in the practice of "how to do it," and that the revolution had been a front composed of many different perspectives, it is not surprising that the record of achievement was mixed on this as other fronts. The Reagan administration and the Vatican loathed the Christian-activist component, viewing it as a dangerous message to many Latin Americans.

Thus, experiments with grassroots correspondents became skewed toward training them to defeat the Contras' propaganda and support the regime. Disproportionate funds were sunk into some expensive 35-mm films, such as *Alsino and the Condor,* rather than short, cheap films addressing the country's critical problems. University education in communication and journalism struggled with pitiful resources, traditionalist approaches, the Cuban advisors' conviction that large chunks of typing and shorthand were essential, and the continuing plague of poor to no literacy, despite the Sandinistas' energetic literacy campaign. Their public commitment to pluralism and the pressures of war were constantly at loggerheads.

As of 1985, more than 70 foreign AM and FM stations were broadcasting into Nicaragua, whereas the national stations, using old equipment, numbered 15, and had correspondingly poor communication with the north and the northwest, plagued by Contra bombings and murders. Some foreign stations, including some clandestine ones, were consistently hostile, as predictably was Voice of America. The ongoing war was also a media war.

John D. H. Downing

See also Alternative Media; COR TV, 2006, Oaxaca (México); Mothers of the Plaza de Mayo (Argentina); Social Movement Media, 1960s–1980s (Chile)

Further Readings

Bar, L. (2004). *Communication et résistance populaire au Nicaragua.* Paris: L'Harmattan.

Brentlinger, J. (1995). *The best of what we are: Reflections on the Nicaraguan revolution.* Amherst: University of Massachusetts Press.
Mattelart, A. (Ed.). (1986). *Communicating in popular Nicaragua.* New York: International General.
O'Donnell, P. (1995). *Dar la palabra al pueblo: La enseñanza-aprendizaje de la comunicación en Nicaragua durante la Revolución Popular Sandinista* [Giving voice to the people: Communication teaching/learning in Nicaragua during the people's Sandinista revolution]. México City: Universidad Iberoamericana.
Rodríguez, C. (2001). *Fissures in the mediascape: An international study of citizens' media* (Ch. 3). Cresskill, NJ: Hampton Press.

SOUTHERN PATRIOT, THE, 1942–1973 (UNITED STATES)

The Southern Patriot was a small but significant monthly newspaper that reported southern civil rights news to several thousand national readers and recruited white support for desegregation both before and after the mass civil rights movement of 1955–1968. After the student sit-ins swept the region in 1960, the newspaper provided the early Student Nonviolent Coordinating Committee (SNCC), the most militant anti-segregation force, its first sympathetic but analytical coverage. Julian Bond, an early SNCC communication director, testified that the *Patriot's* in-depth coverage helped the new generation of 1960s activists to "define who we were . . . as this vanguard challenging not just the segregation system but older organizations too."

The *Patriot* coverage of the new youth-led movement gave student activists a regional and national platform. Indeed, the Southern Conference Educational Fund (SCEF) that published *The Southern Patriot,* and in particular its editor, white southern journalist Anne Braden, provided crucial media training and contacts with a national network of religious, labor, African American, liberal, left, and student news outlets. Anne and her husband Carl Braden—SCEF field organizers and later its directors—were experienced newspaper journalists and longtime civil/labor rights activists. The Bradens and the *Patriot* played key support roles in the growth of SNCC.

The SCEF was a carryover of the New Deal era southern liberal/left cooperation known as the "Popular Front"—part of what historians often call the "Old Left." Established in 1946, SCEF was among the first southern interracial groups to condemn racial segregation openly. It survived its parent organization's fate, the Southern Conference for Human Welfare (SCHW), which First Lady Eleanor Roosevelt had helped to found in 1938 but became an early casualty of the post–World War II Red Scare. The anticommunist hysteria of that period had special force in the South, where conservatives smeared all dissent from the region's rigid racial segregation as "communistic."

The founding executive director of both SCHW and SCEF was James Dombrowski, a white, Florida-born reformer who had been active in southern causes since the 1920s. Dombrowski, a self-proclaimed Christian socialist, also proposed the publication in 1942. The name *Southern Patriot* was adopted to deflect Red-baiting and to reflect love of country. It was nonetheless subjected to years of vitriolic verbal attacks by Senators Joseph McCarthy of Wisconsin and James Eastland of Mississippi, who claimed it was Communist controlled.

The SCHW ended in 1948 under the brunt of those repeated attacks. SCEF, however, would emerge as a leader in the fight against racial segregation. In the late 1940s, SCEF organized the first-ever gathering of professors from 116 southern colleges and universities to oppose segregation in admissions to graduate and professional schools. The *Patriot* also covered campaigns against discrimination in medical care, transportation, public facilities, voting rights, criminal justice, and public education.

The Southern Patriot became such a target in part because it was perhaps the most consistent voice against racial segregation in the South. SCEF had also refused to adopt an anti-Communist stance and so became a more vulnerable target as the cold war wore on. The *Patriot* became one of the few liberal/left news organs to survive the cold war's domestic purges.

SCEF lost its tax-exempt status in 1951 and teetered on the edge of ruin, but it fought back. By spreading the word about grassroots efforts to dismantle Jim Crow segregation, the *Patriot* helped build the southern civil rights movement while informing and garnering support from sympathetic readers outside the South, who formed a large part of its readership.

Dombrowski functioned both as chief SCEF organizer and *Patriot* editor from its founding until the late 1950s. He occasionally broke stories missed by the mainstream press, such as Alabama Governor Thomas Dixon's refusal during World War II to let prison inmates make tents the army badly needed, because he rejected the nondiscrimination clause in federal contracts.

As Dombrowski looked in the mid-1950s for successors to carry on SCEF and the *Patriot*, he found a young couple in Louisville, Kentucky, facing sedition charges for buying a house in an all-white neighborhood and turning it over to a black family, which triggered a campaign of harassment that resulted in the home's dynamiting.

Carl and Anne Braden were white Kentucky natives who had rejected racism and, from that point on, would devote their lives to defeating it. Carl lost his job at the Louisville *Courier Journal* as a result of the sedition trial, in which he was publicly labeled a communist. Anne, already a reporter in Alabama and Kentucky for several years, publicized the civil rights and civil liberties violations in the incident, ultimately writing a 1958 memoir (*The Wall Between*) about their case. Dombrowski was one of the first fellow southerners to offer help, and the *Patriot* covered their case.

Carl served 8 months in prison before the U.S. Supreme Court reversed his conviction. Dombrowski then convinced the Bradens to join the SCEF staff, to find other white southerners like themselves. By then, the energy unleashed by the 1955 Montgomery Bus Boycott, in which the African American public walked to work and back for 11 months to protest segregation on the city's buses, had caught fire in other southern cities. "Jim Crow" segregation laws were under attack from legal and grassroots efforts across the South, and the Bradens supported those efforts through reporting on them in the *Patriot*.

The Bradens' energy reinvigorated SCEF and the *Patriot*. Their journalism backgrounds made the *Patriot* far more than a typical movement newsletter. It was written and designed from journalistic principles but in service of ending racial discrimination and segregation.

The couple used the *Patriot* as an organizing tool, with multiple copies sent to groups and people whose stories it reported. It also became a news service, keeping the mainstream, African American, labor, and alternative media updated on southern racial news. In 1959, the *Patriot* doubled its size to a tabloid.

The stronger the *Patriot* and the movement for change grew, the more intense grew repressive measures by right-wing officials. Carl Braden, along with Frank Wilkinson of the National Committee to Abolish HUAC (i.e., the most actively Red-baiting of the Congress committees), was held in contempt by Congress after Braden told the HUAC hearing in Atlanta that his political beliefs were "none of the committee's business." The U.S. Supreme Court, in a 5–4 decision, upheld the contempt order, and both went to prison for 10 months.

But the *Patriot* was part of a tide that repression could not hold back. Although some established civil rights organizations distanced themselves from SCEF because of the Red-baiting charges, the Bradens—and through them, SCEF, and the *Patriot*—allied themselves with the emerging southern "New Left" grassroots and student movements. Anne Braden worked closely with Dr. Martin Luther King Jr. and the Southern Christian Leadership Conference (SCLC). The dynamic leader of the Birmingham movement, Rev. Fred Shuttlesworth, who was on the SCLC Board, became president of SCEF.

Always emphasizing the power of media, the Bradens became bridges between "Old" and "New" Lefts. They aided and mentored student activists, white and black, in SNCC and, later, the Southern Student Organizing Committee (SSOC), namely those who organized a predominantly white southern counterpart to the black-led SNCC. The SSOC published the *New South Student* from 1964 to 1969.

Repression continued. In 1963, SCEF's New Orleans headquarters was raided and its local leaders (including Dombrowski and the staff attorney) were arrested. The arrests and seizure of SCEF assets led ultimately to an important Supreme Court decision in *Dombrowski v. Pfister,* which overturned the Louisiana anti-subversion laws used to justify the raid and opened the way for

victims of political repression to take their cases straight to federal courts to lessen the "chilling effect" such actions had on First Amendment rights.

When the Bradens moved the SCEF office to Louisville in 1966, federal and state forces also mobilized against them in the coal regions of Kentucky, bringing a second sedition charge in 1967 against the couple and their young staffers. The Bradens became experts at organizing what they called "fightbacks" by turning such efforts at repression into opportunities to defend civil liberties as cornerstones for civil and human rights, using media tools such as the *Patriot* as well as a flurry of news releases and pamphlets. Yet, those battles took their toll.

Amid continued repression, infiltration of the movement by government agents, and the splintering of the early "beloved community" vision of interracial unity that had characterized the early 1960s, internecine divisions among New Leftists who had become enamored of various strains of Marxist-Leninism led to the demise of SCEF. By 1973, the Bradens had left SCEF, now controlled by the Maoist-leaning October League, who moved both it and the *Patriot* to Atlanta. The paper's name was changed to *Southern Struggle*—a smaller, more ideological in-house organ of a short-lived Marxist-Leninist sect. The records of SCEF and *The Southern Patriot* are housed primarily at the Wisconsin Historical Society and secondarily at the Anne Braden Institute for Social Justice Research at the University of Louisville.

Tom Gardner and Catherine A. Fosl

See also Black Press (United States); Citizens' Media; Cultural Front (Canada); Media Justice Movement (United States)

Further Readings

Adams, F. (1992). *James A. Dombrowski, an American heretic, 1897–1983.* Knoxville: University of Tennessee Press.

Barnard, H. F. (Ed.). (1985). *Outside the magic circle: The autobiography of Virginia Foster Durr.* Tuscaloosa: University of Alabama Press.

Brown, C. S. (2002). *Refusing racism: White allies and the struggle for civil rights.* New York: Teachers College Press.

Fosl, C. (2006). *Subversive southerner: Anne Braden and the struggle for racial justice in the cold war South* (reprint). Lexington: University Press of Kentucky.

Klibaner, I. (1990). Southern conference educational fund. In M. J. Buhle, P. Buhle, & D. Georgakas (Eds.), *Encyclopedia of the American left*. Urbana: University of Illinois Press.

Zellner, B., with C. Curry. (2008). *The wrong side of murder creek: A White southerner in the freedom movement*. Montgomery, AL: New South Books.

SPARE RIB MAGAZINE (UNITED KINGDOM)

The British feminist magazine *Spare Rib* started in 1972 as an "alternative" women's magazine. The name, which is a tongue-in-cheek reference to the biblical myth that women were fashioned from one of Adam's ribs, was deliberately light-hearted. The pages were meant to be thought provoking but fun: a good read rather than a political tract. It lasted 24 years, collapsing in 1996 from underfunding and internal disputes.

"Underground" magazines were thriving in Britain in the late 1960s and early 1970s: *Private Eye, Oz, Friends* (then *Frendz*), *IT* (*International Times*), *Black Dwarf, Ink,* and *Seven Days* all set up their stalls, giving a voice to a postwar generation desperate to be heard and impatient with drab politics. But most voices turned out to be male.

Marsha Rowe, a *Spare Rib* founding editor, had worked at *Oz*, first in Australia and then in the United Kingdom. She remembers:

> There were women on the alternative press but always in a service role. Even with the exceptions, like Germaine Greer, author of international best-seller *The Female Eunuch*, their contribution was always sexual—like Germaine's 'Cunt Power' edition of *Oz*. In fact the underground press was even more exploitative than the straight press. If I had wanted to progress I might have done better to stay on working for *Vogue*. (Phillips, 2008, p. 50)

Rozie Boycott, her co-editor, was just out of a girl's boarding school and worked at *Frendz*. Her memories were similar:

> The underground . . . pretended to be alternative but it wasn't providing an alternative for women. It was providing an alternative to men in that there were no problems about screwing around or being who you wanted. . . . Women were the typists, men were the bosses. (Green, 1988, p. 409)

Over at *Black Dwarf*, feminist historian Sheila Rowbotham was the only female editorial member. She resigned in December 1969 with a letter asking her (mostly white) male comrades to "Imagine you are black, not white, imagine you have cunts not cocks." It caused a sensation but no discernable action. In the next February, *Oz* recognized the coming of women's liberation with an edition titled "Pussy Power."

Gradually the anger built up. Women working across the underground press started comparing their experiences, and late in 1971, Rowe and Boycott decided to start an alternative magazine for women. It was the high point of the Women's Liberation Movement, but they were clear that this was not so much a "feminist magazine" as an alternative magazine. They wanted it to be up on the shelves of newsagents, alongside all the other magazines that women bought every week, tackling similar issues but in a different way. It would be a magazine that took women seriously not just as consumers but as thinking, active human beings.

Spare Rib Begins

Starting with donations of only £2000 (from people Rowe had met through *Oz* and *Ink*), the first print run was 15,000, rising at its peak to 30,000 and read by many, many more. Said Rowe, "I have met lots of women who said that their only contact with the women's movement was through *Spare Rib*" (Phillips, 2008, p. 50). She remembers that "established women journalists couldn't write the 'new' way." But most of the underground press women had been making tea and typing—they had never written. She found herself working with complete novices, helping them with their ideas and then helping to shape them.

There needed to be a new kind of imagery. Women's magazines were always sold with a single, glamorous, image on the cover. *Spare Rib* tried to find other formulations: two women, older women, and graphic covers. For the first edition, two women were taken makeup-free to a park, and tried to create something positive and joyful that spoke of female friendship rather than objectification. (This writer took the first few cover photographs.)

Downing writes of a "pre-figurative politics" in which those running alternative publications attempt to live the politics they preach. British feminist politics were militantly egalitarian. Hierarchies of any kind were constantly questioned, even if they were headed by women.

Within a year, the editor's roles had disappeared, and *Spare Rib* became a collective. Shortly afterward, Boycott left, uneasy about the turn the magazine was taking. Rowe stayed on as a member of the collective. Decisions were now discussed at meetings (which were often far from harmonious). The boundary between reader and writer started to dissolve. Readers wrote articles and then rang up to complain trenchantly if a word was tampered with. It was exhausting but exhilarating.

But in attempting to "live" their politics the collective were inevitably confronted with a contradiction. They wanted to write about the lives of mothers and of black and working-class women but the magazine never made enough money to pay anyone properly. The level of self-exploitation excluded many people who could have made a contribution because they simply could not afford to work for so little. The problem was not resolvable. The magazine was selling well but the cover price was kept at a level affordable for women on low (or no) incomes. For most women's magazines, lucrative cosmetic advertising provides a regular subsidy, but advertisers were not going to spend their money on a magazine that published articles attacking the cosmetics industry.

Spare Rib was prepared to be frank about issues that conventional women's magazines would not touch. Advertisements for vibrators appeared regularly after an early feature explaining just how they should be used—but along with adverts for books and records, they were never really going to make up the difference. Benefit concerts were organized to boost finances. For a brief period during the 1980s, the magazine was supported by a grant from the Greater London Council (GLC). The grant died, however, when the GLC was abolished in 1985.

By the end of the 1970s, feminist politics had moved on from the euphoric period in which sisterhood seemed to transcend all barriers. Mainstream publications had started to take on many previously excluded subjects. *Cosmopolitan* magazine happily discussed work and orgasms but emphasized individual rather than collective solutions to women's dilemmas. Neoliberal politics stalked the world stage, and internally the women's movement was starting to factionalize. As the more light-hearted aspects of *Spare Rib* were taken up in the mainstream, the magazine became the space in which internal political divisions found voice.

Sue O'Sullivan was a member of the collective until 1984 and witnessed the effect of these pressures.

A kind of moralism developed with a tendency to harden experience and identity into rigid hierarchies. This, too, took more and more space in the magazine, as we compulsively washed our dirty linen in public. . . . A proliferation of claimed differences between women defined the big questions and clamoured for attention. The anger women had directed so confidently at the perpetrators of sexism was now ricocheting within the movement and *Spare Rib*, the most wide-reaching feminist publication, became the forum or repository for many of these struggles. (Phillips, 2008, p. 50)

The magazine was damaged by these internal wrangles but nevertheless survived into the 1990s when all the other alternatives had long since died.

Angela Phillips

See also Barbie Liberation Organization (United States); Feminist Media, 1960–1990 (Germany); Feminist Media: An Overview; Feminist Movement Media (United States); Women's Movement Media (India); Women's Radio (Austria)

Further Readings

Downing, J. D. H. (1984). *Radical media* (1st ed.). Boston: South End Press.

Downing, J. D. H. (2001). *Radical media* (2nd rev. ed.). Thousand Oaks, CA: Sage.

Fountain, N. (1988). *Underground: The London alternative press, 1966–74*. London: Routledge.

Green, J. (1988). *Days in the life: Voices from the English Underground*. London: Heinemann.

Greer, G. (1970). *The female eunuch*. London: MacGibbon & Kee.

O'Sullivan, S. (2002). *Feminists and flour bombs*. Retrieved April 4, 2009, from http://www.channel4.com/history/microsites/F/flourbombs/essay.html

Phillips, A. (2008). The alternative press. In K. Coyer, T. Dowmunt, & A. Fountain (Eds.), *The alternative media handbook* (pp. 47–95). London: Routledge.

$PREAD MAGAZINE (UNITED STATES)

Founders Rachel Aimee, Rebecca Lynn, and Raven Strega first had the idea for *$pread* Magazine in 2004. They were frustrated by negative misrepresentations of sex workers (including call girls, prostitutes, strippers, porn stars, and phone sex workers, among others) within mainstream media and decided to create a space for sex workers to represent themselves. The founders had no experience in publishing, but with the help of design software classes and benefit fund-raisers they published their first issue of *$pread* on March 15, 2005, and went on to win the *Utne* Independent Press Award for Best New Title. Their mission statement is as follows:

> We believe that all sex workers have a right to self-determination; to choose how we make a living and what we do with our bodies. We aim to build community and destigmatize sex work by providing a forum for the diverse voices of individuals working in the sex industry.

Their submission policy purports to be open minded: They will publish any perspective so long as it is the view of a current or former sex worker. The magazine accepts article submissions, editorials, photographs, and creative artistic expressions. Issues are published quarterly, are available via subscription, and are sold in many independently owned bookstores in the United States, the Netherlands, and shortly in Canada.

The magazine's cover is full color, and the inside is glossy black and white with an artistic and slightly edgy aesthetic. In addition to subscription fees, *$pread* generates revenue from advertising. Not surprisingly, much of the advertising is for sex products, escort services, and pornography, but also it includes advertisements from legal services, therapists, occupational health specialists, and other non–sex-related services. Each issue includes the following sections, many of which contain reader-submitted content: Indecent Proposals (readers send in the funniest or weirdest client request), Scene Report (readers send in stories about their working environments), Media Whore (looks at mainstream media attention towards the sex industry), Cunning Linguist (defines terms of the trade), Double Take (interviews with a sex worker—both his/her non-working and working persona), On the Street (asks random people on the street a question about sex work), Consumer Report (rates various sex products), Positions (asks a debatable question and offers two different perspectives), Hot Topic (reader responses to various "hot topic" questions), Intercourses (interviews with lawyers, advocates, etc.), and Classifieds. Additionally, each issue dedicates space to creative artistic submissions, feature articles, news articles, reviews (books, films, and CDs), and a resource section. Articles are often presented in a humorous, tongue-in-cheek manner, using double entendres to address serious legal and health concerns as well as the more mundane ins and outs of being a sex worker.

Although the magazine certainly provides sex workers with a space for self-representation in uncensored ways that challenge hegemonic notions of sex work, *$pread* also serves as a valuable resource for sex workers. Approximately 1/8 of each issue is dedicated to the Resource section at the back of the magazine. Resources include advice columns, health tips for hookers, legal advice, and online resources such as the International Committee on the Rights of Sex Workers in Europe, Escort Support Resource Portal, and U.S. Database of HIV Testing Sites. Physical resource centers such as Sex Worker Advocates of Tomorrow (Cleveland, Ohio), Working Men Project (United Kingdom), and The Coalition for the Rights of Sex Workers (Montreal, Canada), are listed for the United States, Latin America, Europe, Asia/Pacific Islands, and Africa.

In addition to the physical magazine, *$pread* also has a companion website that lists resources, excerpts from the magazine, information about how to subscribe and contribute, as well as information for the press and potential distributors. The website features a blog that focuses on sex worker–related news stories and events. Although the blog has a comments feature, it seems that few readers leave a comment (most entries range from zero to three comments). However, given that a large proportion of the physical magazine is dedicated to reader-generated content, it would seem that readers are more interested in submitting to the magazine than interacting on the blog. *$pread* achieves its goal of offering sex workers a space to speak for themselves, voice their opinions, ask their questions, and represent themselves in ways not accounted for in mainstream media representations and portrayals of sex workers.

Jacqueline Vickery

See also *Belle de Jour* Blog (United Kingdom); Feminist Media, 1960–1990 (Germany); Gay Press (Canada, United Kingdom, United States); Sex Workers' Blogs; *Spare Rib* Magazine (United Kingdom); Women's Radio (Austria)

Further Readings

$pread Magazine: http://www.spreadmagazine.org

Stay Free! Magazine (United States)

In a culture saturated with magazines reliant on advertising and marketing for survival, *Stay Free!* provides an alternative. A nonprofit independent magazine, it explores consumer culture, the media, and other cultural issues in the United States. Based in Brooklyn, *Stay Free!* began in 1993 as a print zine and later became a magazine with color artwork, published once or twice a year with a circulation of 14,000.

Stay Free! generates enough money from sales to cover the cost of publishing, yet the staff is all volunteer. As of 2008, the print magazine had ceased publication, yet the creators of maintained a website. In addition, in May 2009, publishing company Farrar, Straus, and Giroux released a book by the *Stay Free!* creators called *Ad Nauseam: A survivor's guide to consumer culture.*

Readers can find many back issues of *Stay Free!* online at the website, yet the online versions do not have most of the artwork and photographs found in the print editions. The artwork often provided trenchant cultural critique. Articles were analytical in style. Sample topics included psychology and advertising, pranks, McDonald's commercials, dog breeding, mental illness, the history of advertising, and pop music advertising.

Stay Free! also maintained a blog titled *Stay Free! Daily media criticism, consumer culture & Brooklyn curiosities from Stay Free! magazine.* It was receiving 2000 hits daily as of 2008. People could subscribe to the blog feed.

Moreover, *Stay Free!* sponsored the art exhibit *Illegal Art: Freedom of Expression in the Corporate Age.* The exhibit was in keeping with *Stay Free!*'s vision to expose corporate media and advertising as culturally oppressive. The art explores problems of intellectual property and artwork, asserting that copyright law that once protected artists now is used to silence artists. Some pieces of artwork have appeared in court proceedings.

In keeping with its desire to educate people about the media, *Stay Free!* also created a media literacy curriculum that has been used in high schools and colleges across the United States. Several hundred teachers have used the curriculum, which is distributed without charge through the website. The curriculum aims to teach students about the influence of advertising and media in their lives and draws on real world examples taken from the *Wall Street Journal*, the *Washington Post*, *Harper's Magazine*, and other mainstream news sources. Their book also serves as a resource for educators.

Adrienne Claire Harmon

See also Adbusters Media Foundation (Canada); *Ballyhoo* Magazine (United States); Church of Life After Shopping (United States); Media Education Foundation (United States)

Further Readings

McLaren, C., & J. Torchinsky. (2009). *Ad nauseam: A survivor's guide to consumer culture.* New York: Faber & Faber.

Stay Free! http://www.stayfreemagazine.org

STONEWALL INCIDENT (UNITED STATES)

Although many details surrounding the initial uprising are disputed, the Stonewall incident is commonly viewed as a major turning point in the struggle for lesbian, gay, bisexual, transgendered, and queer (LGBTQ) liberation and rights in the United States. The riots were certainly not the first altercation between the LGBTQ community and New York City's police department, but the events of the weekend remain some of the most written about, as well as some of the most broadly known, even outside of gay and lesbian activist circles.

Just after 1 a.m. on June 28, 1969, the Stonewall Inn, a popular bar and dance club on Christopher Street in Greenwich Village, was raided. Deputy police inspector Seymour Pine and other officers arrived that evening to serve the owners a warrant for unlicensed liquor sales. Pine was the first to enter the establishment to determine that liquor was, indeed, being served. Plainclothes and uniformed officers followed the inspector into the bar where they began arresting employees and forcing patrons out onto the street one by one.

As the police continued, a small crowd began to grow outside. The assembly, which had begun as a celebratory scene, complete with cheers as each patron was ejected from the bar, quickly turned to combat. As one bar-goer resisted arrest, the crowd began throwing coins and stones at the police.

There are competing accounts of precisely what sparked and then sustained the explosion, but considerable agreement that long-sustained anger at anti-gay violence and discrimination was by then very near the surface. The crowd overturned a police wagon. Outnumbered, the officers on the scene barricaded themselves inside of the Stonewall Inn. Someone threw a torch into the bar, igniting a fire. The police called for backup. By the time support arrived, four officers had sustained minor injuries. Men dressed in women's clothing formed a kick line, mocking the officers with chants of "We are the Stonewall girls / We wear our hair in curls / We don't wear underwear / We show our pubic hairs." The rioting continued through the night and through the weekend.

Although it received little mainstream media coverage outside of New York, word of the uprising spread throughout LGBTQ communities across the United States. Underground gay and lesbian publications such as the Gay Liberation Front's *Come Out! Gay Power,* and *Gay* helped disseminate information about the event to gay and lesbian communities in the early 1970s, sparking calls for organizing and revolt.

The Christopher Street Commemoration Day, a march held 1 year after the riots at the site of the uprising, is typically viewed as the beginning of annual Gay Pride events in the United States. Since 1970, these celebrations have spread across the world. In 1999, 51 and 53 Christopher Street, the original site, was declared a National Historic Landmark by the U.S. Department of the Interior. It is the first major government landmark recognizing the struggles of LGBTQ people.

Ricky Hill

See also *Advocate, The* (United States); Alternative Media; Citizens' Media; DIVA TV and ACT UP (United States); Gay Press (Canada, United Kingdom, United States); *Gay USA*

Further Readings

Carter, D. (2004). *Stonewall: The riots that sparked the gay revolution*. New York: St. Martin's.

Chauncey, G. (1995). *Gay New York: Gender, urban culture, and the making of the gay male world, 1890–1940*. New York: Basic Books.

Duberman, M. (1994). *Stonewall*. New York: Plume.

Dunlap, D. (1999, June 26). Stonewall, gay bar that made history, is made a landmark. *New York Times*, p. B6.

Teal, D. (1971). *The gay militants*. New York: St. Martin's.

STREET THEATER (CANADA)

From the raucous parades at protests, to quiet, ritual gatherings, to public performances of unearthed stories that work to heal communities or help stall the privatization of health care, street theater in Canada exists in many forms and brings together a diverse group of people. It spans the country from small rural communities to large urban centers, addressing the many cultures and conflicts of Canada.

In the 1990s and 2000s, street theater became an increasingly popular mode of political expression. Arising in moments of transition, street performances create visions of what society might be and develops challenges to the status quo. The street provides an opportunity to address the relationship between people and authority, for this is where political drama plays out. The "street" is not necessarily literally a street but can be any public, accessible space. In community centers, homeless shelters, union halls, and on farms, people can tell forgotten, local stories and make their voices heard. Street theater addresses injustice and expresses opportunities for different ways of living.

Canada's street theater can be traced to early agitprop pieces such as *Eight Men Speak*, which was performed to protest the imprisonment and attempted murder of Communist Party leader Tim Buck in 1933. And later, as elsewhere, the 1960s and 1970s were a particularly fruitful time in experimental performance. This was partly because of several reasons: (a) a growing national identity, (b) English-speaking Canada was no longer culturally dependent on Britain, (c) Quebec asserted its sovereignty through growing nationalization, and (d) the inspiration of radical performance elsewhere in the world (especially workers' theaters in Germany, Britain, the USSR, and the United States).

Latin American popular theater, and other forms of radical pedagogy and protest, greatly influenced Canadian street theater. The writings of both Paulo Freire and Augusto Boal helped develop political intervention methods that were performative, engaged, and engaging; these writings were a revitalization of the political environment where a seasoned activist or a 5-year-old child could learn, participate, and laugh. These influences from other countries were prominent but were adapted to respond to local contexts and concerns.

Street theater in Canada continues to grow and expand, experimenting with new forms and re-enacting the old. From direct action pieces to longer term community engagement, it works to bring provocation and nuance into politics, with puppets, marching bands, and parades, as well as drama, engaging the tensions and power dynamics of the many different people living in this country. In the following concentrated examination of Canadian street theater, the examples illustrate particular genres, ways of working, and best practices, and they reflect a range of regions and interests.

Agitprop

The most easily recognizable form of street theater is agitprop, which uses theatrical form to grab bypassers' attention to bring focus to a particular issue. Political activists mobilizing around a particular event or cause favor this form of street theater.

As part of the larger global social justice movement, the Toronto Mobilization for Global Justice (or Mob4Glob) formed in 2000, with key members David Anderson (of Clay and Paper Theatre) and Maggie Hutcheson. Their primary sites of action were at Québec City in 2001 for the Free Trade Summit of the Americas, and in 2002 when they organized in Calgary, Toronto, and Ottawa in protest of the G8 Summit held in Kananaskis, Alberta. They created large-scale puppets that sought to convey the political complexity of their opposition with a powerful, accessible image.

Their most recognized and widely used puppet was a 14-foot tall Gaia (a figure symbolizing the Earth). In 2003, the group shifted to become Paperfire, which is an arts collective for social justice, and participated in the peace demonstrations that took place in Toronto against the Iraq war. After the war began, the boisterous colorful puppets no longer seemed appropriate. Instead, the group opted for a simple, somber protest, donning death masks and marching, mechanically, in front of the U.S. Consulate. The tactics of Mob4Glob and later Paperfire sought to engage the public more accessibly and meaningfully than traditional protest culture.

Similarly, ATSA (Action Terroriste Socialement Acceptable or Quand L'art passe à l'action/Socially Acceptable Terrorist Action or When art becomes action) is a street theater group based out of Montréal that devised political interventions in public space. ATSA was founded in 1997 by artists Pierre Allard and Annie Roy, with a mandate to open up urban public space to dialogue through theatrical performance. Their first action consisted of handing out warm soup and socks to the city's homeless.

Since then, they have used a burned-out SUV as a fake "terrorist attack," to stand in for the social and environmental consequences of overdependence on oil and car culture, and "polar squat," which retells the Goldilocks story as a tale of the displacement of polar bears because of global warming. Since 1998, they turned a major square in downtown Montréal into a refugee camp for the homeless—*L'État d'urgence* (State of Emergency). The week-long event was both a performance in itself and hosted numerous other artists and street theater troupes including: *Mise au jeu* (Put in play), a theater- and circus-based performance group in the service of human rights; *Toxique Trottoir* (Toxic Sidewalk), who create public interventions addressing social and environmental issues; and *Les Vidanges en cavale* (Wastepipes on the run), who work collectively with youth to create theater for social change.

Popular Theater

Popular theater extends street theater by working with communities to stage performances in which their political and social concerns are reflected. It aims to demystify the theater process by bringing community members into the scene (literally and figuratively) to tell local stories that speak to the present moment.

The Mummers Troupe from Newfoundland is one of the best-known examples. The company was founded by Chris Brookes and Lynn Lunde, and it performed from 1972 to 1982. Its first production was a short agitprop in a shopping mall in support of a cinema projectionists' strike. The Troupe is best known for its political productions that drew heavily on local histories.

In the 1980s, Ground Zero (founded and directed by Don Bouzek and based out of Toronto and later Edmonton) took up this tradition. Productions involved trade unions in an attempt to mobilize people around health care concerns. In unprecedented coalitions, the group managed to mobilize various unions and professional associations to put on a mobile play *Where's the Care?* The play, which was performed by health care workers, was scripted and adapted loosely to local contexts as it moved throughout Ontario. Its success was felt through the attention given the issues, resulting in a (temporary) victory when Ontario subsequently elected the more left-leaning New Democratic Party.

Many other theater companies worked directly with unions. *Running*, produced in 1995 by Jane Heather, recreated dialogues with unions and workers about working conditions in Alberta. The piece was staged with professional actors for the Edmonton Fringe Festival. This reflects diverse strategies for street theater, even as all styles seek to open up a space for dialogue and political expression.

Everybody's Theatre Company (ETC) has produced plays about local histories and politics since 1990 in Eden Mills, Ontario. It gives a role to everyone in the audience, providing a place for people to tell their own stories in their own voice. It performs plays outdoors, requiring audience members to move from scene to scene, using landscapes and streetscapes as ready-made backdrops. This continues a tradition in Canada of making theater with communities, outdoors. Additional examples include the following: Robert Winslow's 4th Line theater, located on a family farm near Peterborough, Ontario; Murray Schaffer's outdoor operas in Peterborough; Blyth Festival Theatre's outdoor Donnelly series; Caravan Theatre in Armstrong, British Columbia; Fort Qu'Appelle produced by Common Weal Community Arts in Saskatchewan; and Toronto Island's Shadowland theater.

Community-Engaged Theater

Following the ETC example, community-engaged theater often blends into community organizing. Community-engaged theater seeks to expand artistic creation to systemically marginalized communities to produce theater for social justice.

One of the most innovative and successful examples is Jumblies Theatre in Toronto. Ruth Howard, its artistic director, works in collaboration with the Davenport-Perth Neighborhood Community Center. They are committed to participatory, direct engagement with community members to provide a voice for new immigrants and low-income earners. They develop plays where the main content comes from nonprofessional participants, to reflect the realities of the community.

Rural communities in Canada also make community-engaged theater. Runaway Moon Theatre is one example that performs the histories of the remote area. Their community play was remarkable for weaving together the stories of the mainly white residents of Enderby, British Columbia, with the people from the neighboring Spallumcheen Band of the Shuswap First Nation. In most of Canada, the ongoing history of colonialism has left many scars and divides between Aboriginal peoples and the rest of the population. To move beyond this legacy and to comprehend the role of colonial policies in the present day, an understanding of the ways in which the communities are interwoven can help move to a place of healing.

Using street performance as public ritual aids helps with environmental issues as well. Carmen Rosen, a performance artist and founder of Still Moon Arts Society and Mortal Coil Performance Society, created a community performance and parade to address the biosphere damage to a ravine in her Vancouver neighborhood. By integrating Chinese- and white-Canadian traditions, the parade mobilized the entire community.

As one of their tactics, community-engaged theaters often create sacred, secular celebrations. Red Pepper Spectacle Arts work both in Toronto and in Nibinamik in Northern Ontario to create spectacle-based festivals. Their most popular community festival is the Festival of Lights, which is held annually in Kensington Market, Toronto to celebrate the winter solstice. Clay and Paper Theatre, based out of Dufferin Grove Park, also participate in the Festival of Lights as well as hosting an annual Halloween parade, and it produces plays about local histories. Paulina Jardine creates public rituals and performances to acknowledge the dead at Mountainview Cemetery in Vancouver, among other creations of community-engaged theater. Both rituals and festivals help to build community by encouraging and supporting social engagement.

Theater of the Oppressed

Headlines Theatre in Vancouver has been working since 1981 to help communities tell their stories. They use Power Plays and Forum Theatre, drawing on Augusto Boal as a mode of healing. Working with multicultural and First Nations communities on issues ranging from violence and suicide prevention, to bullying, antiracism, youth empowerment, and community development, their method of working called "Theater for Living" is about empowering communities through active dialogue.

Mixed Company in Toronto also develops methods of engaging people, including homeless and street-involved adults and youth, through Augusto Boal's techniques. They became the first company in North America to be certified to teach Forum Theatre.

Heather Davis

See also Angry Buddhist Monk Phenomenon (Southeast Asia); Cultural Front (Canada); First Peoples' Media (Canada); Indian People's Theatre Association; Madang Street Theater (Korea); Moon River Movement Media (Thailand); Performance Art and Social Movement Media: Augusto Boal; Street Theater (India)

Further Readings

Burnham, L. F. (2009). *Social imagination: Documenting engagement in Canada.* Retrieved March 17, 2009, from http://www.communityarts.net/readingroom/archivefiles/2009/02/social_imaginat.php

Cohen-Cruz, J. (1998). *Radical street performance: An international anthology.* London: Routledge.

Filewod, A. (1987). *Collective encounters: Documentary theatre in English Canada.* Toronto, ON, Canada: University of Toronto Press.

Filewod, A. (2001). Coalitions of resistance: Ground zero's community mobilization. In S. C. Haedicke & T. Nellhaus (Eds.), *Performing democracy: International perspectives on urban community-based performance* (pp. 89–103). Ann Arbor: University of Michigan Press.

Hamilton, D. (2006). *Two decades of community-engaged theatre or why I see ghosts.* Retrieved March 17, 2009, from http://www.communityengagedtheatre.ca/articles.html

Heather, J. (2001). Dramatic union: Worker's theatre in the 1990s. In S. C. Haedicke & T. Nellhaus (Eds.), *Performing democracy: International perspectives on urban community-based performance* (pp. 159–165). Ann Arbor: University of Michigan Press.

Hutcheson, M. (2006). Demechanizing our politics: Street performance and making change. In D. Barndt (Ed.), *Wild fire: Art as activism* (pp. 79–88). Toronto, ON, Canada: Sumach.

Paré, A.-L. (2005). Shawinigan street theatre festival. *Espace, 70,* 14–19.

Zwarenstein, C. (2001). All the world's a stage: Theatre as a political tool. *Fuse Magazine, 23*(3), 21–27.

STREET THEATER (INDIA)

Although the names of many folk theaters in India translate directly as "street theater" (*terukkuttu* in Tamilnadu, *veethi natakam* in Andhra Pradesh), they do not conform to common definitions of street theater. Street theater is a combination of theater and activism, performed in an open space such as the street, open lot, slum, in front of a factory or workers' quarters, a temple, church, warehouse, tent, exhibition site, university campus, park, or railway station, where actors can interact directly with the audiences. Street theater should not only entertain but also educate audiences about social issues and hopefully effect social and/or political change. It is about empowerment of the oppressed, although often facilitated by middle-class educated urbanites. In Indian street theater, most activists view themselves as part of a wider social and political movement, supplementing theatrical activities with film societies, library movements, pamphlets on political and cultural issues, revolutionary songs and poetry, workshops, and discussions.

Although there is a lot of formal and linguistic variety, street theater has some typical aesthetic features. It is often experimental and eclectic: The plays were written collaboratively using colloquial language and humor; performed with minimal or absent sets, props, and costumes; and made use of familiar forms of music, dance, and folk performance to connect to the audience and make the message more entertaining. Besides Indian folk and classical forms, major influences on Indian street theater include Bertolt Brecht, Augusto Boal, Badal Sircar, and Utpal Dutt. The form is mobile and the group can perform almost anywhere. Plays might not be announced beforehand; the actors simply show up and attract viewers through drumming or other means (one example is Habib Tanvir's 1948 *Shantidut Kamgar* [One Who Works as a Messenger of Peace], where actors stage a quarrel to attract people's interest, then involve them in a dialogue).

This community-based theater uses familiar stories based on real-life experiences, either of the audience members or of current events. The plays are short to allow for discussion of the controversial social issue presented (dowry, women's education, low wages, AIDS awareness, etc.). Street theater requires participation from the audience and tends to be judged not on financial earnings or aesthetics, but on efficacy. Because of this, governmental and nongovernmental organizations (NGOs) now use street theater. During elections and when an NGO is doing a big campaign, there is a lot of street theater activity in India, but most of these efforts are short lived.

Origins of Street Theater in India

Scholars pinpoint different plays and moments in history as the beginning of street theater in India, depending on how they define the form. The one constant is that there is a deep connection with the Left; many groups are associated explicitly with the Communist Party of India (CPI). Marxist movements in the 1930s politicized aspects of folk theater, using it to raise critical consciousness and mobilize communities. The Indian People's Theatre Association (IPTA) was founded in 1943 in Bombay as a wing of the Communist Party of India, parallel to the Progressive Writers Association (PWA). Most early IPTA productions were for the proscenium theater, but when the CPI and IPTA were banned (1948–1951), the plays went underground and to the streets. Utpal Dutt identifies Panu Pal's 1951 presentation of *Chargesheet*, on Communist leaders imprisoned without trial, as the first street theater play. Many troupes throughout the country still perform under the IPTA banner, particularly after IPTA's golden jubilee celebrations.

There was a lull in street theater productions between 1952 and the 1975 Emergency. Two major groups were founded in 1974 (*Jana Natya Manch* [People's Theater Front] and *Samudaya* [Community]), reflecting the political unrest of the time. Neither turned to the street theater form until 1978, after the Emergency, when the unions that had financially supported them collapsed. They inspired other groups, and there was a spurt of street theater activity in the early 1980s, when groups were formed and journals (such as *Uttarardh* [Second Half]) published street plays.

Leading Street Theater Groups

The name Safdar Hashmi is near-synonymous with street theater in India. He was a founding member of *Jana Natya Manch* (*Janam* [New Birth]) in Delhi and was instrumental in creating their first street play *Machine*. He was attacked, beaten, and dragged through the streets by Congress (I)-supported rowdies during a 1989 performance of *Halla Bol* (Charge!), which is about an industrial strike led by the Center of Indian Trade Unions, which is attached to the Communist Party of India (Marxist). He died the next day, a reminder of the power of street theater.

A surge of street theater activity occurred in India after Hashmi's death; his birthday, April 12, is observed as National Street Theatre Day. Janam is one of the most active street theater groups in India, producing original street and proscenium shows as well as quarterly workshops, and discussions. In addition, Janam managed the Safdar Hashmi Memorial Trust. Sudhanva Deshpande described their 1979 *Aurat* (Woman), on the oppression of women, as "the most popular street theater play to date." The name Jana Natya Manch has also been appropriated by several street theater groups.

Samudaya was founded in 1975 in Bangalore by RP Prasanna. Their first street play *Belchi* was based on the burning of Harijan agricultural laborers in 1977 in the town of Belchi in Bihar. This group is known for their practice of sending out touring groups to perform around the state—a strategy later used by other theater groups and NGOs, particularly effectively by the Kerala Shastra Sahitya Parishad (Kerala People's Science and Art Forum) for the literacy movement.

Jana Sanskriti (People's Culture) was founded in 1985 by Shujoy Bannerji and has many branches. They use Augusto Boal's ideas about the "theater of the oppressed," combined with Indian folk forms, to help villagers to form their own theater groups. *Jana Sanskriti* performs each play twice, and the second time audience members ("spectactors") take the actors' places and play out alternative resolutions.

Chennai Kalai Kuzhu (Chennai Arts Group), associated with the Progressive Writer's Association, was formed in 1984 and was led by Pralayan. The group has done mostly street plays, drawing inspiration from traditional forms and popular media. *Koothu-p-Pattarai* (Theater Workshop) was founded in 1977 under N. Muthusamy, presenting "folk" plays for urban audiences. Their street theater now

consists mostly of awareness plays funded by the city government.

Kristen Rudisill

See also Community Radio Movement (India); Indian People's Theatre Association; Performance Art and Social Movement Media: Augusto Boal; Sarabhai Family and the Darpana Academy (India); Social Movement and Modern Dance (Bengal)

Further Readings

Deshpande, S. (Ed.). (2007). *Theatre of the streets: The Jana Natya Manch experience.* Delhi, India: Janam.

Garlough, C. L. (2008). On the political uses of folklore: Performance and grassroots feminist activism in India. *Journal of American Folklore, 121,* 167–191.

Katyal, A. (Ed.). (1997). *Seagull Theatre Quarterly, Kolkata, 16,* Special issue on street theatre. Retrieved June 2, 2010, from http://www.seagullindia.com/stq/issueframe3.html

Mangai, A. (2006). Street theater in India: With special reference to Tamil Nadu. In P. C. Ramakrishna (Ed.), *Bring down the house lights: 50 years of the Madras players* (pp. 82–92). Chennai, India: The Madras Players.

Mohan, D. (2004). *Jana Sanskriti*'s theatre and political practice in rural Bengal: The making of popular culture. *South Asian Popular Culture, 2*(1), 39–53.

Srampickal, J. (1994). *Voice to the voiceless: The power of people's theatre in India.* London: Hurst & Company.

SUARA INDEPENDEN (INDONESIA)

The Indonesian military under General Soeharto (Suharto) seized power in 1966, with the active involvement and blessing of the U.S. government. A bloodbath ensued, costing perhaps half a million lives, aimed both at leftists and more generally at the community of Chinese descent. Significant organized opposition took almost 20 years to form, of which underground publications were an important component. Extraordinary pressure on Indonesia's press freedom in Indonesia during President Soeharto's regime eventually gave birth to the monthly underground newspaper *Suara Independen* (Independent Voice).

In Soeharto's regime, which was also termed the "New Order," the government was backed up by the military, the civil service, and the powerful official political party *Golkar* (*Golongan Karya*, literally "Functional Groups"). The two other political parties, the Development Unity Party and the Indonesian Democratic Party, had been forcibly constituted by the government from many other parties and completely lacked clout.

During Soeharto's 32 years in office, nearly 300 commercial newspapers and magazines were threatened repeatedly not to publish sensitive news, which forced them to self-censor. All publishing companies had to get a government permit.

This was in a country of 230 million people, with multiple languages and varying religious beliefs. In the 1990s, however, some movements began to challenge the authorities. In 1987–1990, there were not less than 155 demonstrations. University students in Bandung protested land dispossessions in Badega and Cimacan, whereas students in Yogyakarta assisted the people forced off their land in the Kedung Ombo dam project. Several Gadjah Mada University students established their own Student Council (DEMA UGM) in opposition to the government-sponsored one. In some areas, especially in 1995–1996, independent alternative student committees emerged. One was Solidaritas Mahasiswa Indonesia untuk Demokrasi (Indonesian Student Solidarity for Democracy, SMID). SMID and other committee organizations vigorously critiqued the New Order corporatist regime.

In June 1994, in the midst of his proclamations of Indonesia's "openness," Soeharto abruptly canceled permits for three weeklies: *Tempo* (Time), *Editor*, and *DeTik* (Second). They had been reporting the bitter conflict between two government ministers concerning the purchase of decommissioned East German warships. Doing so did not result in political calm as the authorities expected; instead, this action destabilized the country because the public objected to the government locking down its information rights.

Protests and demonstrations broke out in many cities, especially in Java, indicating that not only journalists but also the public objected. In July, approximately 200 journalists came to the office of the Central Indonesian Journalists Association to submit a statement headed "Indonesian Journalists Stance" that was signed by 370 journalists from all parts of Indonesia. Independent journalist groups also organized solidarity actions (e.g., the Independent Journalists Forum in Bandung, the Surabaya Press Club, the Yogyakarta Journalists Discussion Forum, and Jakarta's Independent Journalists Solidarity). In Madura, East Java, approximately 100 Moslem Leaders and 3,000 *santris* (devoutly orthodox Muslims) held a major assembly, signifying that press freedom was not just a big city issue.

On August 7, 1994, many journalists, whether from the banned media or not, politicians of different allegiances, *Muhammadiyah* (reformist) and *Nahdlatul Ulama* (orthodox Sunni) adherents, artists, cultural commentators, and community leaders met in Sirnagalih, West Java. Approximately 100 individuals were present, and half of them were willing to sign the meeting's declaration. This requested the public's right to information, opposed press curbs, rejected a single coordinating journalists' body, and announced the foundation of the Independent Journalists Alliance. The alliance was supported by *Masyarakat Indonesia Peminat Pers Alternatif* (Indonesian Community Interested in Alternative Press-MIPPA) headquartered in Melbourne, Australia, which initially brought out *Independen* that later changed to *Suara Independen* (*SI*).

Under pressure of ongoing mass demonstrations by university students and the economic crisis, on May 21, 1998, Soeharto resigned, and the new government held a democratic general election the next year. Media moved fast toward diversity and pluralism, but the end of authoritarian rule was not translated into democratic pluralism as understood in the West.

Doing Guerrilla Media, Enacting Press Independence

Suara Independen definitely was considered radical, as it reported sensitive issues never covered by mainstream media: the case of East Timor (Timor Leste), violence against farmers in Nipah (East Java), repression of Kedung Ombo basin communities in Central Java, religious humiliation by the Minister of Information, and Indonesian workers abroad. It carried artistic cartoons as well as articles. The publication was noncommercial, because its managers received donations from its supporters. Likewise, its journalists and distributors were unpaid. *SI* used offset printing in a printshop owned by Andi Syahputra, a Muslim Student Association activist in Jakarta.

After *SI* was distributed by its journalists and other activists, readers also made copies. For example, as an *SI* reader from 1996 to 1997, every time this writer got his copy, he would then give it to the campus photocopy officer. After making copies, he would leave the publication there so other interested people, whether lecturers, students or employees, could make their own copies. Only "subscribers" knew to ask the campus photocopy officer: "Is *Independen* in yet?"

A journalist who was also an *SI* activist, Ignatius Haryanto, told the writer:

> I had a quota of 30 to 100 copies, so I offered them to reliable friends in my professional circle. I also left them in offices along Sudirman and Thamrin streets (Jakarta). We also worked with the cell system, where reporting was just reporting and editing was only editing.

In Surabaya, according to Mochammad Faried Cahyono, a former *SI* journalist, there was a senior high-school student, Andi Ardiasto, who distributed copies at traffic lights.

Most *SI* writers were student or media activists. The magazine operated horizontally, making use of activist networks and media professionals in different campuses and cities in Indonesia. Ardiasto reported that from its first appearance soon after the three magazines were shut down until the fall of Soeharto, *SI* published approximately 20 issues. Andreas Harsono, a journalist and Sirnagalih Declaration signatory, mentions a circulation of 15,000, whereas Stanley suggests 8,000, but it was actually read by approximately 250,000 people in different Indonesian cities. In September 1995, *SI* won the Index of Censorship award.

This publication revealed information the authoritarian regime kept secret for decades. Its strength lay in its bravery, because its journalists had to use careful tactics to avoid jail. Their resistance helped delegitimate the New Order regime. Later on, this gave birth to alternative interpretations of mainstream media reports, so that the public would perform oppositional readings, using perspectives they found in alternative media. For the New Order authorities, the presence of *SI* meant a challenge to their hegemony of authority and information. Its influence extended to mainstream media and society at large.

Information Guerrillas

Journalists also carried out a "press guerrilla" strategy, namely tracking down government officials when sensitive issues such as East Timor appeared in international media. *SI* tried to do investigative journalism and was keen to cross-check with often reluctant government sources, including military circles.

Cahyono, another Sirnagalih Declaration signatory, publicized that at a major public occasion, the then Minister of Information, who was well known for prosecuting citizens on charges of insulting Islam, had mispronounced the last line of *al fatikah*—the short prayer that opens the *Qur'an* and which observant Muslims recite many times a day. This remarkable lapse appeared in some media, but they only wrote "slip of the tongue," and so the minister was not accused of having insulted the faith. However, the self-same minister had jailed a then-prominent supporter of Megawati Soekarnoputri—the politically powerful widow of president Soekarno, deposed by Soeharto's 1966 military coup—on the charge of insulting Islam when giving a speech in the federal capital.

On the one hand, the *SI* spirit of rebellion was also expressed by sending every edition to the editorial desk of domestic and foreign news media, and all foreign embassies. On the other hand, journalists also tested out sending articles to mainstream media. When they were rejected, they published them in *SI*. For this reason, several newspapers often referred to *SI* as their source.

For Indonesian media circles, the publication of *SI* fanned the flames of developing an independent, uncurbed press. Cartoons and illustrations in SI were artworks with the nuance of opposition, freedom, and critique. One of its editions in 1995 wrote about Pramoedya Ananta Toer, an iconic author within Indonesia who was long imprisoned and whose works were banned, but who had been translated into more than 20 languages. Responding to *SI* concerning his feelings after receiving the 1995 Magsaysay Award (Asia's Literature Nobel equivalent, awarded for journalism, literature, and creative communication), he said:

> Of course I am happy because there are people who greatly appreciate what I have been doing. Moreover given my current condition—I have been sequestered, defamed, accused of many things and could not defend myself—after 30 years it turns out people really appreciate my works. (Interview with Pramoedya Ananta Toer on Radio Nederland/Antenna Foundation "Weekend Focus," 1995)

Finally, on October 28, 1996, the authority seized Andi Syahputra, the owner of the printing shop, and Nasrul, his employee. The police confiscated 5,000 copies of *SI* 2/III, which included an article titled "Suharto in the Process of Becoming a Naked King" and a news item titled "Mr. Bintang Challenges Soeharto to Direct Election." Syahputra was accused of "offending the President" and "deploying the feeling of hatred to the government," and he was sentenced to 2 years and 6 months for distributing materials endangering Soeharto.

Not too long afterward, in May 1998, the opposition movements against the authoritarian regime got stronger and *Suara Independen* persisted in its challenges to the system. *SI*'s spirit inspired numerous social movements against repression in Indonesia.

Lukas S. Ispandriarno

See also Alternative Media; Community Radio and Natural Disasters (Indonesia); Independent Media (Burma/Myanmar); Internet and the Fall of Dictatorship (Indonesia); Social Movement Media (Macedonia); Social Movement Media in 1987 Clashes (Korea)

Further Readings

Aliansi Jurnalis Independen: http://www.ajiindonesia.org/index.php?fa=org.main

Alternative press challenges information blockade. Retrieved March 17, 2009, from http://insideindonesia.org/index.php?option=com_content&task=view&id=918

Pram: "…Tutup Buku dengan Kekuasaan" [Pram: "…Cover Book with Power"]: http://www.antenna.nl/wvi/bi/puis/pram/suarai.html

Radio Nederland/Antenna Foundation "Weekend Focus" interview with Pramoedya Ananta Toer. (1995). Retrieved June 1, 2010, from http://www.antenna.nl/~fwillems/eng/poet/pram/mag3.html

Rodan, G. (1996). *Political opposition in industrialising Asia.* London: Routledge.

Sanit, A. (1999). *Pergolakan melawan kekuasaan. Gerakan mahasiswa antara aksi moral dan politik* (Rebellion against Power. Student movements among Morale Action and Politics). Yogyakarta, Indonesia: INSIST.

Utami, A., Budiman, A., Mohammad, G., Surukusuma, J. I., Dhakidae, D., Ramli, R., et al. (1994). *Bredel 1994* (The bridle 1994). Jakarta, Indonesia: Aliansi Jurnalis Independen.

Wartawan, T. (1994). *Buku Putih TEMPO: Pembredelan itu* (The White Book of TEMPO: That Bridled). Jakarta, Indonesia: Alumni Majalah TEMPO.

Tamil Nationalist Media (Sri Lanka/Transnational)

Sri Lanka is diverse in language, religion, and culture. British colonial rule began in 1802 but ended in 1948. Sinhalese constitute the majority; Sri Lankan Tamils live predominantly in the northeast and are approximately 13% of the population. Violent confrontations between the Tamil nationalist movement and the Sri Lanka government lasted some two decades, from the late 1980s through 2009. Media were an important dimension of the nationalist movement's activities, not least internationally.

Tamil political nationalism began in the 19th century with a Hindu religious awakening, which was a reaction against Christian missionary activity. Gradually Tamil national consciousness shifted focus and came to include both Hindus and Christians. The nationalist movement in the late 19th century was based among the middle class in the northern town of Jaffna. In the mid-20th century, the movement became political. Ethnically based representation in the Legislative Council, created by the British, prompted the creation of Tamil political parties.

The movement continued to grow in response to Sinhalese nationalism. Independence in 1948 brought a majoritarian democratic system, and the Sri Lankan Tamils lost their relatively privileged position during colonial rule. The 1956 declaration of Sinhala as the sole official language, the changes in university admissions, and the settlement of Sinhalese in traditionally Tamil areas contributed to a feeling among the Tamils of being second-class citizens. The struggle for Tamil rights was initially waged within the political system and through nonviolent protests. However, political negotiations gained little results, and demonstrations were violently repressed.

In 1976, the main Tamil political party declared its intention to form an independent Tamil state. Gradually, several militant groups formed by Tamil youth in the 1970s became increasingly important. After large-scale politically instigated violence against Tamils across Sri Lanka in 1983, India extended its support to the Tamil militants. New recruits joined in large numbers. In the late 1980s, the Liberation Tigers of Tamil Eelam (LTTE) established itself as the supreme advocate of Tamil nationalism, largely by violence. The LTTE took control of substantial areas in northern and eastern Sri Lanka, where it established state-like structures.

When the LTTE was finally defeated by the Sri Lankan government in 2009, the war had claimed at least 70,000 lives and had severely limited the political space for nonviolent social and political movements. Tamil civilians and civil society leaders had been targeted by the Sri Lankan government forces, pro-government Tamil paramilitaries, and the LTTE itself. The latter had claimed to be the Tamils' sole representative and had been criticized for assassinating political opponents, carrying out terror attacks against civilians, and recruiting children. With the killing of the LTTE leadership, the Tamil diaspora gained more importance in pursuing the Tamil nationalist cause.

Communicating Resistance

The early Tamil nationalism had the Tamil language and literary production at its center. Also, Karnatic music and the *bharathanathyam* dance were endorsed as expressions of Tamil national identity, closely connected with Tamil identity in southern India. The first Tamil language newspaper, *Virakesari* (Brave Lion), was founded in the early 1900s by a Tamil Nadu businessman. Since then, several Tamil weeklies and dailies were established, as well as radio stations and television channels.

Although Tamil media in Sri Lanka were not necessarily products of the movement, they came to be used as its important tools and reflected its views and internal contradictions. Early on, they played an important role communicating and promoting a Tamil consciousness. As the conflict escalated, increasingly Tamil newspapers, radio, TV, and later Internet-based media and film became a way to express and encourage Tamil nationalist sentiments. Most Tamil media reflected a nationalist view, although the extent to which different newspapers, for instance, expressed support for the LTTE varied—among the most LTTE-supportive *Suderoli* (Light of Flame), the more moderate *Thinakkural* (Daily Voice) and *Virakesari*, and the anti-LTTE *Thinamurusu* (Daily Drum).

Some media outlets were also produced directly by the LTTE, such as the radio station *Voice of the Tigers* and the *National Tamil Eelam Television*, which were broadcasted from LTTE-controlled areas. Poetry played an important role for the nationalist movement, and several poets (including LTTE cadres) depicted, justified, and encouraged armed struggle. Street drama, art, and traditional dance were also used to commemorate martyrs of the struggle, protest against the government, and recruit new fighters. It is reported that hand signs for "Tiger" and "gunfire" have made their way into the *bharathanathyam* dance.

Preserving Tamil culture, perceived to be under threat, and mobilizing for the continued struggle were important motivations for the movement's use of cultural expressions. Safeguarding the Tamil language from distortion (for instance, by using English words) and promoting women's adherence to traditional dress codes was on the LTTE agenda too. Moreover, the LTTE had a media unit that produced films of real-life battles, which were distributed within the movement, among civilians, and in the diaspora.

Media in the Diaspora

Tamil migrants have played an important role in preserving Tamil culture and in supporting the nationalist struggle, not least economically. Within the diaspora, rumored to be almost one million, media production became vast. In the early days of the war, LTTE channels provided scarce information to the migrants. More recently, the explosion of information sources in the Internet age has made it easier for the diaspora to stay updated and to maintain Tamil nationalist consciousness.

The LTTE dominated the information flow, and most Sri Lankan Tamil media were more or less supportive of the LTTE-led struggle. The LTTE was banned as a terrorist organization in 28 countries, but this did not hamper their use of the Internet to spread information and canvass support. The multimillion-dollar Tamil film industry in India increasingly also came to portray and get involved in the struggle in Sri Lanka. People connected to the LTTE were believed to have invested in the industry, and the Sri Lankan Tamil diaspora became an increasingly important market, leading to the production of movies supportive of the movement.

Most websites did not primarily aim to convey news but to legitimize Tamil claims to national status. One exception was *Tamilnet.com*, which succeeded in speaking not only to the diaspora but also to Western media and other international actors, using professional journalism to communicate Tamil concerns. The media produced in the diaspora played an important role in the struggle as they could circumvent the Sri Lankan government.

The Internet was also an important tool for Tamil groups who wished to criticize the LTTE. Diaspora opposition to the LTTE was also expressed through drama, literature, and poetry. The LTTE's lack of tolerance for dissenting voices was, however, extended to the diaspora, and the organization actively prevented the publication of critical views, at times going as far as physically attacking journalists.

An Information War

The war in Sri Lanka was also a war over information. In 1997, the LTTE was reported to have carried out the first ever cyber-terrorist attack, bombarding the Sri Lankan embassy and consulate networks with junk e-mails and thereby swamping up the computers for 2 weeks.

Both Tamil and Sinhalese media in Sri Lanka were colonized by ethnic and party-political interests, and their reporting reflected the polarization. Sri Lanka's Prevention of Terrorism Act restricted media coverage of the conflict, and the freedom of the press was further compromised as access to conflict zones was tightly controlled. The *Voice of the Tigers* was attacked several times, as were Tamil newspapers and journalists believed to be close to the LTTE. Just between January 2006 and mid-2008, the Free Media Movement in Sri Lanka documented 16 cases of journalists and media workers being killed, 15 cases of abductions, and several cases of detentions and attacks on media workers—a reality that qualified Sri Lanka as one of the four most dangerous countries for journalists.

Camilla Orjuela

See also Community Radio (Sri Lanka); Khalistan Movement Media (India/Transnational); Naxalite Movement Media (India); Peace Media (Colombia); Zapatista Media (México)

Further Readings

Amnesty International. (2008). *Sri Lanka: Silencing dissent*. London: Author.

Balasingham, A. (2001). *A will to freedom: An inside view of Tamil resistance*. Mitcham, UK: Fairmax.

Calvert, B. (2008). Sri Lanka's information war: Part II. *World Politics Review*. Retrieved December 18, 2008, from http://www.worldpoliticsreview.com/article .aspx?id=3059

Kandiah, T. (2001). *The media and the ethnic conflict in Sri Lanka* [Marga Monograph Series on Ethnic Reconciliation]. Colombo, Sri Lanka: Marga Institute.

Ranganathan, M. (2002). Nurturing a nation on the net: The case of Tamil Eelam. *Nationalism and Ethnic Politics, 8*(2), 51–66.

Swamy, M. R. N. (2002). *Tigers of Lanka: From boys to guerrillas* (3rd ed.). Delhi, India: Konark.

Whitaker, M. (2004). Tamilnet.com: Some reflections on popular anthropology, nationalism, and the Internet. *Anthropological Quarterly, 77*(3), 469–498.

Wilson, A. J. (2000). *Sri Lankan Tamil nationalism: Its origins and developments in the 19th and 20th centuries*. London: Hurst.

TEHELKA MAGAZINE (INDIA)

Founded by Tarun Tejpal in 2000, *Tehelka*'s reputation has matched the very definition of the Urdu word from which it takes its name: a tumult, rumpus, or sensational piece of writing. Originating as the investigative news website Tehelka.com, *Tehelka* attracted attention first in 2001 by exposing match-fixing in cricket, India's iconic national game.

The organization's name recognition grew that same year with its involvement in the biggest political scandal in India's history to date: Operation West End. This sting operation revealed corruption in the awarding of Indian defense contracts, reaching the upper echelons of the Indian government. Wired *Tehelka* reporters posed as arms suppliers from a fictional company, West End, and the resulting "*Tehelka* Tapes," as they became known, revealed political figures accepting large-scale bribes for contracts. Defense Minister George Fernandes resigned, although further investigation exonerated him.

As a result, the Indian government launched a nearly 3-year campaign against *Tehelka*, using search warrants for income tax compliance to access Tehelka.com offices. Its ranks were decimated by governmental repression. Its staff of 120 dwindled to 1, and the company faced bankruptcy.

Undeterred, Tejpal relaunched *Tehelka* in 2003 as a weekly newspaper funded by donations. In 2007, *Tehelka* added a revamped web news portal. In late 2007, the organization became involved in another well-known sting: Operation Kalank. This time, *Tehelka* reporters captured on-tape confessions of those who had perpetrated violence during the 2002 anti-Muslim pogroms in Gujarat State. These pogroms followed a devastating fire that killed dozens of Hindu pilgrims, including 20 children, in a train carriage at Godhra railway station, Gujarat, in February 2002. *Tehelka* reporters discovered that what had been officially defined as spontaneous revenge riots were part of a state-sanctioned conspiracy: a pogrom against Muslims supported by the Gujarat State government. Members of the *Sangh Parivar,* a rightist Hindu nationalist organization very active in Gujarat, denied involvement despite being caught on tape bragging about their roles in the riots.

Labeled by the Indian government as muckraking journalism for its use of hidden cameras in undercover investigations, and repeatedly harassed by government authorities, *Tehelka*'s commitment to uncovering truth and promoting justice through its exposés did not waiver. *Tehelka* billed itself "The People's Paper," and the term fits. The organization earned the respect of vocal Indian activists, such as Arundhati Roy. The British newspaper *The Guardian* called *Tehelka* one of India's best news sources, whereas the BBC acknowledged that *Tehelka*'s trenchant journalism had pushed the boundaries of Indian news. *Time* magazine, too, suggested that *Tehelka* lived up to its name. *Tehelka*'s brand stands for independence and fearlessness in public interest journalism and suggests that independent media can fight endemic corruption. As it exposes the challenges to freedom and democracy in India today, *Tehelka*'s very existence indicates that democracy is indeed possible.

Roopika Risam

See also BIA Independent Communication Network (Turkey); Moon River Movement Media (Thailand); Sarabhai Family and the Darpana Academy (India); Social Movement Media, 1980s–2000s (Japan); *Suara Independen* (Indonesia); Women's Movement Media (India)

Further Readings

Thomas, P. (2005). Contested futures: Indian media at the crossroads. In R. Hackett & Y. Zhao (Eds.), *Democratizing global media: One world, many struggles* (pp. 81–100). Lanham, MD: Rowman & Littlefield.

THIRD CINEMA

The term *Third Cinema* was coined in a long and much-read 1969 article by Argentinean political activist filmmakers Fernando Solanas and Octavio Getino that focused mostly on documentary film, albeit in numerous formats. It emerged from the continuing political and economic convulsions in Argentina and more widely through Latin America and across the planet in that decade and the one that followed.

Brazilian filmmaker Glauber Rocha's brief "Esthetic of hunger" manifesto preceded the article. It based its title on a famous 1952 book, *The Geography of Hunger,* by Josué de Castro, the Brazilian director of the Food and Agriculture Organization, who argued that the fundamental causes of global starvation and malnutrition were political, not a lack of resources. Cuban filmmaker Julio García Espinosa's 1969 essay "For an imperfect cinema" also fed that debate, and much of the debate about the term since drew in one way or another on these three Latin American contributions.

The call for a *Third Cinema* was a revolutionary response by filmmakers to global poverty and oppressive structures. It was a call for guerrilla filmmaking, with "the camera as our rifle . . . a gun that can shoot 24 frames a second." There was a real urban guerrilla movement in Argentina at the time, and indeed armed guerrilla politics was then widespread in Latin America, with Cuba and Vietnam as models. Repressive U.S.-backed and -trained military regimes were common. To many, even if not involved directly, guerrilla action seemed the only option remaining to achieve constructive change. The filmmakers' battle, in their words, was against "the enemy's ideas and models to be found inside each one of us" and "for what each one of us has the possibility of becoming."

The term *guerrilla video* as used by the Top Value Television (aka TVTV) collective and similar U.S. movements in the 1970s was somewhat different, referring as much to using cheap portable video and low-to-no budgets as it did to rebellious politics.

Solanas and Getino used the adjective *Third* to distinguish the type of filmmaking that they argued was urgently needed from both Hollywood (First Cinema) and art films, stamped by a particular movie director's personal vision (Second Cinema). The fundamental mission of this Third Cinema was to decolonize culture, strip out U.S. and Western cultural dominance and consumerist ideology in the third world, and replace it with films conveying "a throbbing, living reality which recaptures truth in any of its expressions." As García Espinosa also argued, such films would boldly use the minimal resources available and would feel no need to apologize for not matching up to the affluent West's technical standards.

Beyond content, the production, distribution, and exhibition of Third Cinema films was also defined differently. Solanas and Getino stressed the need to be able to work collectively, to operate underground, to embrace very small screening locations, and to organize screenings to include pauses for audience discussion (along the lines of Brecht's theater). They exemplified this approach in their epic 4.5-hour documentary on Argentina's history and politics, *La Hora de los Hornos* (Hour of the Furnaces, 1969).

John D. H. Downing

See also Activist Cinema in the 1970s (France); Barricada TV (Argentina); Cine Insurgente/Rebel Cinema (Argentina); Documentary Film for Social Change (India); Medvedkine Groups and Workers' Cinema (France); Workers' Film and Photo League (United States)

Further Readings

Boyle, D. (1997). *Subject to change: Guerrilla television revisited*. New York: Oxford University Press.

Gabriel, T. (1982). *Third Cinema in the third world: The aesthetic of liberation*. Ann Arbor, MI: UMI Research Press.

García Espinosa, J. (1983). For an imperfect cinema. In S. Siegelaub & A. Mattelart (Eds.), *Communication and class struggle* (Vol. 2, pp. 295–300). New York: International General. (Original work published 1969)

Gunaratne, A. R., & Dissanayake, W. (Eds.). (2003). *Rethinking Third Cinema*. London: Routledge.

Pines, J. & Willeman, P. (Eds.). (1989). *Questions of Third Cinema*. London: British Film Institute.

Rocha, G. (1995). An esthetic of hunger. In R. Johnson & R. Stam (Eds.), *Brazilian cinema* (2nd ed., pp. 68–71). New York: Columbia University Press. (Original work published 1965)

Solanas, F., & Getino, O. (1983). Towards a Third Cinema. In S. Siegelaub & A. Mattelart (Eds.), *Communication and class struggle* (Vol. 2, pp. 220–230). New York: International General. (Original work published 1969)

Wayne, M. (2001). *Political film: The dialectics of Third Cinema*. London: Pluto Press.

THIRD WORLD NETWORK (MALAYSIA)

Third World Network (TWN) is an independent, nonprofit, international network of individuals and organizations. TWN's mission is to engender a better understanding of the needs and rights of people in the global South, create a more just distribution of world resources, and enable more ecologically sustainable and socially fulfilling modes of development. Founded in 1984 in Penang, Malaysia, TWN is directed by Martin Khor, a journalist, economist, and global civil society activist.

True to its mission, the organization has established bases in different continents that comprise the third world. Unlike similar organizations that are primarily based in the global North, TWN's International Secretariat is in Penang, with regional secretariats in Montevideo, Uruguay (Third World Network Latin America), and Accra, Ghana (Third World Network Africa). Other offices are in Goa and Geneva. TWN is affiliated with organizations in Bangladesh, South Africa, México, and Perú and collaborates with organizations in the global North.

TWN has numerous publications mainly focused on development issues. Although the mostly black-and-white, text-laden pages of their publications are not necessarily alternative in aesthetic, their contents and viewpoints are. They present information about global South issues by individuals and groups of the third world. These perspectives are rare because knowledge about the third world has so far largely emerged from centers of knowledge production in the global North.

Among TWN's publications are *Third World Resurgence*, a monthly on development, ecology, and economics, and *Third World Economics*, a bimonthly on economics, especially on the World Trade Organization, the World Bank, and the International Monetary Fund. Its Geneva office publishes *SUNS Bulletin*, a daily print or e-mail newsletter that monitors key North–South development issues. Averaging 10 pages per issue, this service is distributed on a cost-sharing basis and on a subscriber's ability to pay.

TWN Features Service provides features on development concerns to the media. Offering an average of three features per issue, it strives to be a voice for nongovernmental organizations in the global South, emphasizing collection of stories from grassroots groups. TWN also has several publication series. Its director contributes a weekly essay for the *Global Trends Series.* The organization publishes books by third world authors through TWN's other book series on the global economy, trade and development, intellectual property rights, environment and development, and biotechnology and biosafety.

Some materials for the monthly and fortnightly magazines, features service, and global trends series are available for free on the TWN website. TWN's website is accessible in English, Spanish, and Chinese. Each regional office has its own website.

Lena Khor

See also Alternative Media (Malaysia); Alternative Media in the World Social Forum; Arab Bloggers as Citizen Journalists (Transnational); *Le Monde diplomatique* (France/Transnational))

Further Readings

Third World Network. (1985). *Third world: Development or crisis?* Penang, Malaysia: Author.
Third World Network: http://www.twnside.org.sg

Undocumented Workers' Internet Use (France)

In France, the mobilization of undocumented workers has a long history, with the most recent cycle of mobilization events dating back to 1996. This entry describes the ways in which workers and their supporters have used the Internet in their campaigns for workers' rights. It also examines how the undocumented workers' movement has created a digital tool—their dedicated website—to communicate the workers' stories and to reach and use the mainstream press.

Immigrant workers have staged sit-ins to challenge the arrests, imprisonments, and deportations to which the workers have been subjected. In 1996, some of these protests took the form of sit-ins inside churches (first Saint Ambroise's and then Saint Bernard's in rue Pajol, Paris). The government's response was to eject them forcibly from these sanctuaries, in the face of at least 10 activist organizations seeking to defend their human rights.

In turn, the College of Mediators (CM), a volunteer body of distinguished human rights activists, academics, clergy, journalists, and French Resistance veterans, formed to try to defend the migrant workers. Among its initiatives was a website (http://bok.net/pajol) that quickly became a key element in the struggle waged by the undocumented workers and their supporters. Its listserv, *Z_pajol,* became an indispensable tool of the movement, as well as a showcase of legal expertise.

It equally served as a forum, for instance, to prepare for the Immigration Symposia (*Assises de l'Immigration*) organized by CM. And its webmaster, Marc Chemillier, was very clear that it had a vital role to play in regard to mainstream media and public information on the struggle.

The undocumented workers inside Saint Bernard's consistently showed great skill in using whatever means they could to amplify their struggle as widely as possible. The image of "cyber-illegals" using mobile phones and laptops was part of their media game plan, generating an image of refugees from global poverty adapting sophisticated high-tech tools to their needs. The site also gave them the opportunity to publish their commentaries, most of them taken up voluntarily or at our request on mainstream media sites. These were complemented by documentaries on the struggle, and books on the state's immigration policies, many written in the wake of the struggle.

The website was then a crucial means of allowing the undocumented workers to share fully in how their case was framed and articulated. It permitted them to come across as individuals with thoughts and ideas, not as the undifferentiated group portrayed by mainstream media. Even the undocumented workers' movement leaders, such as Ababacar Diop or Madjiguène Cissé, were little known to the public at large. But with these tools, mainstream media could be bypassed 24/7.

At the same time, this did not shut out working with professional journalists. The strategy was not to oppose mainstream media but to mesh with them. The CM website was hosted on a server in San Francisco in the United States, and its URL was provided in a CM communiqué from August 7. One French national daily took it up on August 10, and a second on August 11. Support postings soon followed. As time went by, international newspapers ran articles on the undocumented workers' struggle, in the United States, Japan, and Germany. This almost certainly fed back into French government circles via diplomatic reports from its embassies.

Some of the material posted online, because of its unusual or dramatic qualities, fit fairly straightforwardly into professional criteria for headline news, over which mainstream journalists routinely compete with each other. The fact that there were messages posted in Wolof (the majority language of Sénégal) was in reality much less relevant for native Wolof speakers among the undocumented workers than for professional journalists, who now had a story that upended conventional notions about Africans and technology. One Internet magazine even titled its story in Wolof.

Indeed the undocumented workers' cause was significantly taken up by the "multimedia" press (a frequent term for digital communication at that time) and by special supplements on digital media in the regular press. When the movement scanned a crop of the official government letters to undocumented Paris workers rejecting their applications for legalization, and put them up on the Web, it was the digital media supplement of *Le Monde* (France's newspaper of record) that reproduced them. The standard commentary pages rarely addressed the issue. Of course, welcome as the attention was, it came on the basis of editorial priorities over which the movement had no ongoing leverage, especially in terms of day-to-day turns of events.

The saga did not completely come to a halt after this upsurge was over. A new collaborative site (http://pajol.eu.org) was opened up to replace the *Pajol* site that had also sparked other social movements' Internet uses during the later 1990s.

Fabien Granjon
(translated by John D. H. Downing)

See also December 2008 Revolt Media (Greece); Migrant Workers' Television (Korea); New Media and Alternative Cultural Sphere (Iran); *OhmyNews* (Korea); Online Diaspora (Zambia)

Further Readings

Chemillier, M. (2001). Cyberéflexion du mouvement social: Un site internet, miroir de la lutte des sans-papiers [Social movement cyber-reflection: A website, mirror of the undocumented workers' struggle]. *Hommes et liberté, 112*. http://www.ldh-france .org/docu_hommeliber3.cfm?idhomme=561&idpere= 541

Dobry, M. (1990). Calcul, concurrence et gestion du sens. Quelques réflexions à propos des manifestations étudiantes de novembre–décembre 1986 [Calculation, competition and the management of meaning. Some reflections considering the student demonstrations of November–December 1986]. In P. Favre (Ed.), *La Manifestation* [The demonstration] (pp. 357–371). Paris: PFNSP.

Siméant, J. (1998). *La cause des sans-papiers* [The undocumented workers' case]. Paris: Presses de Sciences Po.

V

VERNACULAR POETRY AUDIOTAPES IN THE ARAB WORLD

Vernacular poetry in this region refers to a specific form of sung, usually written, verses that often touch on themes of nationalism, activism, morality, and traditional lifestyle. Since the late 1960s, various forms of vernacular poetry have widely circulated on audiotapes. Yemen's *Bid' wa jiwab*, Lebanon's *Zajal,* and Egypt's *Sha'bi* all circulate as well among the Diaspora.

Although these poems' structures and their performance sites may vary across the region, the production and circulation of the audiotapes are similar. A collection of *qassa'ed* (poems, sg. *qassidah*) is recorded, usually during a public performance using conventional recorders, and then circulated through stores, and more recently over the Internet. At times musical instruments are used with an identical composition, although the poets change the lyrics, thus creating multiple variations over a familiar tune. This entry focuses on experiences in Yemen, Lebanon, and Egypt, though audiotaped vernacular poetry is common in different forms and for a variety of purposes in much of the Arab world. Their audiences are mostly within poor rural, tribal, or urban communities.

In Yemen, the most common form is *Bid' wa jiwab* (initiation and response); a poet composes a *qasidah* and addresses it to another poet, who then responds with another *qasidah* that matches the former in style and theme. This became popular in the 1950s during the rise of nationalist discourse,

with poet/singers such as Muhammad Murshed Naji. He was also a writer who compared these "folk songs" to a weapon against colonialism. Since the 1970s, *bid' wa jiwab* became organized with audiotapes distributed to a range of shops that usually make duplicates for sale. The frequency of new releases depends on the themes, whether political, social, or of general community interest. Certain themes are serialized. One of the longest is by Abd al-Naser, which started in 1970 and by 1996 made it to cassette 105. More than 64 poets responded to the original.

In Lebanon, *Zajal* is a form of improvised poetry in which two poets, or teams, challenge each other with verses and are usually followed by a male chorus, the *Reddadeh* (the repeaters). This verbal duel takes the shape of various poetic styles and themes within established conventions. *Zajal* is not just folkloric but challenges the erosion of social values and reasserts cultural authenticity. The verses address the plight of the poor and disenfranchised, the injustices of those in power, and reinforce political or national sentiments. Taxi drivers, construction workers, and farmers are often heard blasting their radios to the sounds of Mousa Zgheyb and Tali' Hamdan, or repeating from memory verses from As'ad al-Khuri al-Feghali (1894–1937), known as *Shahrur al-Wadi* (Merle of the Valley). His verses criticizing merchants' greed still resonate vividly in an older generation.

To understand the central role played by vernacular poetry in Arab social movements, the Egyptian experience is noteworthy. Vernacular poets, known as *Sha'bi* (populist/popular), have captured the political, social, and cultural changes that marked 20th-century Egypt. Under British colonial rule, especially Naguib al-Rihani and Badi' Khayri (songwriters) and Sayyid Darwish (composer) composed popular songs that challenged the British and developed a grassroots musical genre (neither Ottoman/Turkish nor Occidental) with lyrics anchored in the lower classes, not in the elites. With songs like *Salma Ya Salama* (Safe or safety), *Zuruni Kulli Sana Marra* (Visit me once a year), or *al-Hilwa Diy Qamit Ti'gin* (This beautiful woman woke up to bake), they mixed everyday working-class experience with words of defiance, resilience, and pride.

The Arab–Israeli war of 1967 resulted in *al-nakssa* (the setback) for the Arab nationalist movement, led by Egyptian president Abdul Nasser, leading to the pro-Western, free market or *Infitaf* policies of his successor Anwar al-Sadat. Street frustrations with *al-nakssa, Infitaf,* and lack of political freedom were articulated by the duo Ahmad Fouad Negm (poet) and Sheikh Imam (singer). The result was a flow of songs that fueled the imagination of traditional nationalists and disillusioned student activists. Negm spent time in prison, where he continued to write and publish.

During the 1980s, with the rise of Islamic currents, the implementation of the unpopular Israeli–Egyptian peace accord, and the neoliberal policies of President Mubarak, the *sha'bi* singer Ahmad 'Adawiya, singing of traffic jams, class differences, and economic hardships, articulated working-class frustrations. His song *Zahma ya Dunia Zahma* (Traffic, oh world there's traffic) is still taxi drivers' mantra in Cairo even today. Despite a state-owned radio and television ban, 'Adawiya's popularity was strengthened by movie appearances and massive audiotape sales.

In the 2000s, Shaaban Abdel Raheem seemed to continue this tradition with his breakthrough hit *Ana Bakrah Israel* (I hate Israel), yet departed from his predecessors by shifting working-class attention from social, economic, and cultural frustrations to a nationalist pro-regime discourse. The same song that proclaims his hatred for Israel continues with the refrain "But I love Amr Moussa" (Mubarak's hand-picked minister of foreign affairs and later secretary general of the Arab League). Singing about the 9/11 attacks, the war in Iraq, the Muhammad cartoon controversy, and the Hezbollah–Israel war,

Sha'boola (as his fans call him) perhaps regained the nationalist flair of *sha'bi* songs but in the process shunned criticizing the regime.

Additionally, these movements developed from religious traditions. In Yemen, religious scholars used poems to engage in debates about Muslim jurisprudence outside official channels. In Lebanon, *Zajal* was originally promoted by Christian clergy to preserve cultural traditions during the 1975–1990 civil war and to preserve a distinctive nationalist identity. In Egypt, *Sha'bi* departed from its religious origins to diversify in both aesthetics to include different musical genres and purposes to make social and political commentary.

Vernacular poems on audiotapes are also to be found in Palestine, where forms of *Zajal* are used to maintain a collective memory, whereas North African Indigenous Berber populations have used poems, songs, and audiotapes to maintain distinct non-Arab identities.

Joe F. Khalil

See also Alternative Media; Ankara Trash-Sorters' Media (Turkey); Audiocassettes and Political Critique (Kenya); Berber Video-Films (Morocco); Music and Social Protest (Malawi); Women Bloggers (Egypt)

Further Readings

Ghazaleh, P. (1999). The voice of the people. *Al-Ahram Weekly,* p. 422. Retrieved March 10, 2009, from http://weekly.ahram.org.eg/1999/422/cu2.htm

Gordon, J. (2003). Singing the pulse of the Egyptian-Arab street: Shaaban Abd al-Rahim and the geo-pop-politics of fast food. *Popular Music, 22*(1), 73–88.

Haydar, A. (1989). The development of Lebanese *Zajal:* Genre, meter, and verbal duel. *Oral Tradition, 4*(1–2), 159–212.

Miller, F. (2007). *The moral resonance of Arab media: Audiocassette poetry and culture in Yemen.* Cambridge, MA: Harvard University Press.

Sbait, D. H. (1993). Debate in the improvised-sung poetry of the Palestinians. *Asian Folklore Studies, 52*(1), 93–117.

Wahibeh M. E. (1952). *Al-Zajal, its history, literature, and masters in old and modern times.* Harisa, Lebanon: The Pauline Press.

Yaqub, N. G. (2006). *Pens, swords and the springs of art: The oral poetry dueling of Palestinian weddings in the Galilee.* Leiden, the Netherlands: Brill.

VIDEO SEWA (INDIA)

The Self Employed Women's Association (SEWA) is a trade union formed in 1972 in Ahmedabad, Gujarat, India, to fight for the rights of women workers, who are the majority in the self-employed sector. It is both an organization and a movement, each strengthening and carrying forward the other. Gandhian philosophy is the inspiration for SEWA; the poor self-employed SEWA members organize for social change through the path of nonviolence and truth. The struggle is against the many constraints and limitations imposed on them by society and the economy, whereas their development activities strengthen their bargaining power and offer them new alternatives.

Among the most emblematic and pioneering participatory video experiences worldwide, Video SEWA is a cooperative started in 1984 when the late Martha Stuart, an international video communications consultant, held a 3-week video production workshop at SEWA in Gujarat. Twenty women, most of them illiterate, began to make video documentaries on the daily life of their communities. The group included women of all ages, some Muslims and some Hindus, vendors from the market, as well as senior organizers from SEWA.

For more than 15 years, Video SEWA has shown that even an apparently sophisticated technology like video can be tackled and used effectively by workers. The power of the medium and its potential for organizing the poor by raising awareness and bringing issues to the forefront is beyond doubt.

Initially they shot their videos in sequence, editing in camera, until they received additional training and equipment. By 1999, four permanent staff members were dedicated to video production. Many video documentaries on issues of the self-employed women have been shot, edited, and shown by the workers themselves. The producers of these tapes can conceptualize a script, shoot, record sound, and edit, although many of them cannot find the tape on the shelf when they need it because they cannot read or write. Video has become an important instrument for SEWA and has contributed to the strengthening of the organization.

Video SEWA has proved that video can aid by bridging barriers of distance, class, and culture so that people of very different backgrounds can grasp and empathize with each other's concerns. For the 1991 census, Video SEWA produced *My Work, Myself*, a 15-minute program addressed to Gujarati women, which reached an audience of approximately a half-million women through cassette playbacks and was broadcast on state television. Videos produced by SEWA women are used for different purposes. *Manek Chowk*, a video about the poor conditions of vendors and hawkers at Manek Chowk, a vegetable market in Ahmedabad, was an advocacy tool that helped to raise consciousness. Others were training productions, such as videos on oral rehydration therapy and building smokeless stoves.

When organizing in rural villages and urban slums, video can act as a magnet for people to meet and start discussions on the issues portrayed. The instant playback feature is one of its most empowering qualities; it enables continuous participation and immediate feedback. This aspect allows those who are the subject and those who run the technology to collaborate as equals.

Alfonso Gumucio Dagron

See also Adivasi Movement Media (India); Chipko Environmental Movement Media (India); Community Radio in Pau da Lima (Brasil); Community Radio Movement (India); Dalit Movement Media (India); Women's Movement Media (India)

Further Readings

Video SEWA: http://www.videosewa.org

Wartime Underground Resistance Press, 1941–1944 (Greece)

Greece in World War II suffered a triple occupation by the Axis forces. German, Italian, and Bulgarian fascists occupied different parts of the country, with annexation plans. In the face of this triple imperialist onslaught, the Greeks fought back massively and fiercely, never taken in by Nazi propaganda about the Axis being invincible.

The underground free press of the Greek resistance emerged in this spirit to launch the communication battle against torture, crop burning, massacres, and forced labor. By 1936, dictator Ioannis Metaxas had curtailed press freedoms. He prohibited leftist newspapers, such as the Communist Party's *Rizospastis* (The Radical), and he strictly censored the press, theater, plays, and songs. This prewar oppression fostered the spirit of resistance, which gave rise to numerous radical media and strategies soon after the Occupation.

During the Occupation, the underground press, although partisan, remained pluralistic, dedicated to freedom and the restoration of democracy. Thus, it contributed substantially to the great collective effort of the Greek Resistance, focusing on the key objective of freedom. Papers informed and inspired, whereas pamphlets called for action and instigated the passion for freedom, which remained indelible in the minds and hearts of those freedom fighters.

First Steps

Small groups of citizens, spontaneously at first, set up multiple decentralized resistance cells to fend off the Axis forces. These groups began to publish new underground pamphlets, often crudely printed, using amateur presses or even stencil copiers. Gradually, the resistance formed networks that spread across the country, federating into pan-Hellenic organizations, such as the leftist National Liberation Front (EAM) and its associated Hellenic People's Liberation Army (ELAS), together composing the EAM/ELAS. Alongside EAM/ELAS emerged other peripheral organizations, such as the rightist National Republican Greek League (EDES).

For its titanic achievement, the Greek Resistance movement depended on this array of journals, pamphlets, and fliers published and distributed underground. It owed a great debt to graffiti and to the nightly cardboard megaphone appeals against the enemy, shouted out often by girls over the Athens rooftops. Such media and incendiary daily messages played an essential role in the massive mobilization of momentum. The underground press orchestrated liaisons among the civilians' actions and those of partisan fighters, binding people morally together in a secret yet public sphere. This was primarily the responsibility of leading organizations, such as the EAM/ELAS, but it was generated out of spontaneous risky initiatives by ordinary Greeks.

Eleftheria in Thessaloniki and Its Peers

The resistance movement was sustained by people and organizations such as those who launched *Eleftheria* (Freedom), the first underground newspaper to be published in Thessaloniki as early as January 1942. In its third issue on January 22, *Eleftheria* was emphasizing poignantly,

> Our people know that we are still irrigating the tree of freedom with our blood. Every terrorist act, every oppressive measure by the dynastic occupants make our hatred, our resolve and indignation against them grow wilder. They push us further into greater rallying and solidification of national forces.

Indeed, this spirit of intransigent defiance and rallying was duly recorded by enemy accounts. Historian Mark Mazower cites Gestapo reports that Greeks were more outspokenly anti-Nazi, than, say, the Italians, French, or Czechs.

Pamphlets and more regular newspapers were published all over the country, particularly in Athens and Thessaloniki, as well as in smaller towns such as Volos, Ioannina, and Serres, as related by the historian and poet Giorgos Kaftantzis, who dedicated his *Ode to Kerdilia* to the first Nazi reprisal massacre. In the village of *Kerdilia*, the Germans killed all the male population aged between 7 and 77, in one of the most cruel massacres ever. That bitter news spread throughout the country at lightning speed, sounding the alarm among Greeks.

In northern Greece alone, comprising Macedonia and Thrace, as many as 167 newspapers might have been published during the 4 years of the triple occupation. These papers were printed under extremely dangerous conditions and with handmade, utterly primitive technology and materials. The danger was particularly acute during editing and printing, as well as during distribution of forbidden material, which took place under curfew and with enemy informers lurking around every corner. Given the conditions under which such propaganda activity took place, free underground publications could not help but be erratic and irregular in many aspects. However, archival evidence shown in a recent exhibition in the Cultural Foundation of the Macedonia and Thrace Daily Press Journalists' Association demonstrates that many achieved considerable circulation regularity.

The free underground press featured news about the Allies' successes and reverses on the war's various fronts. They gave information about local achievements, such as successful sabotage actions and Partisan Army counteroffensives. They analyzed the moves, strategic abilities, and weaknesses of both sides. They tried consistently to increase awareness of the importance of *resistance*, while stressing practical social and humanitarian self-help measures. Underground papers were also crucial to the intricate sabotage actions and sophisticated resistance operations that were either communicated straightforwardly or signaled in coded messages, so as to prepare the people psychologically and to involve them actively in the operations. Their role in raising the people's morale was paramount, considering the conditions of imprisonment, terror, routine executions, and famine. Overall, the numerous free publications encouraged people continuously, calling them to fight back, not to give up, but to hope and to organize instead.

Every Public Mourning, a Resistance Rally

In short, the free press's impact on battle operations is indisputable. In a similar vein, every ordinary public event, including funerals, was converted into an opportunity for rallying and resistance movement actions. To achieve these objectives, the underground press ceaselessly and secretly prepared the ground. The Greek novelist Giorgos Theotokas testifies how the funeral of Costis Palamas, who was then Greece's most revered poet, was converted into a tremendous public lament and protest. Palamas died in 1942, and his funeral was turned into a mass rally, the most magnificent civic denouncement of the war and of the occupation that heralded the rapid growth of nationalist defiance.

At his requiem, Eleni Sikélianòs, who was another greatly revered Greek poet, read Palamas' encomium and urged people to the fight for freedom with this summons: "Echo your trumpets! Thundering bells, shake the country bodily from end to end!" With the shout of *eleftheria*, he led the procession to the graveside. This became a tumultuous pan-Athens anti-Nazi manifestation that turned into a key moment of the Resistance.

The Greek resurgence was immense, indeed, unprecedented, and also it cut across class and gender. That short-lived unity of the Greeks before the common peril created great civic participation combined with partisan leadership and forged through the free press and underground media.

The Greek Situation Is Continuously Worsening

Such strategic underground activity had severe repercussions on the enemy. Mark Mazower cites Nazi official reports stating that enemy propaganda was becoming more intense and developing with great intensity, becoming extreme, and from ongoing radio broadcasts to graffiti, pamphlets, and fliers, both communist and nationalist, stirring up insurrection. One report observed that subversive messages were constantly being written upon walls, denouncing the arrest of hostages taken by the Nazi authorities, against the Axis powers overall, and not least against the collaborator government for its timidity and its responsibility for the terrible food situation. The greatest achievement of the free press was to raise the public's morale and to even inspire enthusiasm for fighting against overwhelming odds. By creating high morale and inspiring conviction in the final victory of freedom fighters, these underground newspapers simultaneously constructed the public face and the underground public space of the Resistance.

Sophia Kaitatzi-Whitlock

See also Anticolonial Press (British Colonial Africa); Independence Movement Media (India); Peace Media (Colombia); Political Graffiti (Greece); Revolutionary Media, 1956 (Hungary); Social Movement Media, Anti-Apartheid (South Africa)

Further Readings

ESIEMTH (Cultural Foundation of the Macedonia and Thrace Daily Press Journalists' Association). (2009). *Ethniki Antistasi 1941–1944: The underground press in northern Greece* [in Greek]. Thessaloniki, Greece: ESIEMTH.

Forward always, intransigently and courageously! (1942, January 22). *Eleftheria,* headline.

Kaftantzis, G. (2001). The press of Thessaloniki, legal and underground, during the German Occupation (1941–1944); and Appendix, The resistance press of Serres under the occupation. *Meta* (contemporary Serraic magazine [in Greek]).

Kouzinopoulos, S. (1986). *"Freedom": The unknown history of the first underground organization and newspaper of the occupation* (2nd ed.) [in Greek]. Athens, Greece: Kastaniotis.

Mazower, M. (1993). *Inside Hitler's Greece: The experience of occupation 1941–1944.* London: Yale University Press.

Voitsidis, M. (2009). Introduction. In ESIEMTH (Ed.), *Ethniki Antistasi 1941–1944. The underground press in northern Greece* (pp. 1–8). Thessaloniki, Greece: ESIEMTH.

WAYRURO PEOPLE'S COMMUNICATION (ARGENTINA)

The Wayruro People's Communication project began in the early 1990s in the far northwestern Argentinean province of Jujuy, which is located some 1,000 miles from Buenos Aires and borders Bolivia to the north and the Andes and Chile to the west. More than many countries, much of government decision making is concentrated in the capital, which is home to one third of the population. As a result, political realities in distant provinces often fail to receive national news coverage. The need for independent media in these remote areas is, therefore, particularly strong. The project involved a print magazine, video documentaries, and from 1997, an Internet presence.

The activists chose the word *wayruro* because it denotes a red-black seed that has a deep mythical significance among Quechua and Aymara aboriginal peoples, who also traditionally believed that if *wayruro* seeds were placed together in a bowl, then they would grow in size and number. Red and black are also, of course, the anarchist colors.

The initial nucleus of the group was drawn from anthropology students at Jujuy University, who first sharpened their political teeth in campus struggles. At the time, the province was run by a corrupt administration wedded to "structural adjustment" policies, and the group soon linked up with a major wave of union challenges to the provincial governor. They were never tied organizationally, however, to any particular union or political party.

In 1992, they bought their first Super VHS equipment with one of their members' severance pay and set about making documentaries. Completely without funds, they raised additional funds a small amount at a time, through making videos of baptisms, weddings, and publicity materials.

In spring 1994, the group became heavily involved in union battles in the province, which often involved violent confrontations with the police. These events eventually brought about the governor's removal from office. Their first major documentary was titled *Struggle Notes I and II* (*Apuntes de Lucha I y II*). Some months later, they were involved in a huge nationwide march that converged on the Plaza de Mayo in Buenos Aires, challenging the harsh free-market policies of Argentina's government. From that they made *The North on the March* (*Norte en Marcha*). This experience also brought them in contact with many other militant groups nationwide, including the Mothers of the Plaza de Mayo.

They then brought out the first issue, just 16 pages, of the *Wayruro* review, focusing on union issues. However, the gap between issues began quickly to lengthen, in part because the union battles were slowing down. From 1995 through 1997, they spent the time making new connections with activists outside Argentina, such as Brazil's Landless Workers movement, and at Spain's University of Andalucía, making more video documentaries. One of these focused on health issues (*Health and Social Struggles*), a second on the impact on children of "Structural Adjustment" policies (*The Budget Cut Children*), and a third on the protests of the Mothers of the Plaza de Mayo against official silence concerning their children's abduction and disappearance during the 1976–1982 military dictatorship (*Headscarf Revolution*).

More documentaries continued to appear on topics as different as a mountain farm family's life; an annual northern popular song contest, whose lyrics often contested the rich and powerful; and popular religious practices that blended devotion to the Virgin Mary with fealty to Pachamama, the Earth Mother.

In 1998, the collective first began using the Internet, finding it a valuable method of connecting up to activists nationally and globally without incurring impossible travel and telephone expenses. By 2002, there were several sites, one for the magazine, another for the video documentaries, another a mirror site, and one devoted specifically to a documentary, *Unemployed Workers and Highway Blockades in Northwest Argentina*. They also published two primers, *What to Do if You Are Arrested* and *Human Rights and Structural Adjustment*; a notebook commemorating 1969's epic labor confrontations in Córdoba; and two pocket books, *Brazil's Landless Workers Movement* and *Latin America in Struggle*.

In 2002, *wayruro* was again involved in major demonstrations of unemployed workers in the province, in which two individuals were shot dead by the police. But because of the presence of their movement photographers and filmmakers, there were dozens of images that one by one reconstructed how the police infiltrated the demonstrators' ranks, how they used live ammunition, and how they murdered unemployed workers in cold blood. These images flooded the Internet and provided an entirely different account from the impersonal "Crisis claims two victims" headline in the mainstream news.

The Wayruro project never had any funds to speak of, and on this level, it was a testament to what can be done with slender resources. On another level, however, it was a constant source of frustration to the group not to be able to take on much-needed projects. The group's mode of organization was classically libertarian, with individuals pitching in their talents, time, and energy in an emergent division of labor, while having no hierarchical structure in place to set policy from above.

Ariel Ogando
(translated by John D. H. Downing)

Note: Originally published in Wayruro comunicación popular. In N. Vinelli & C. Rodríguez Esperón (Eds.), *Contrainformación: Medios alternativos para la acción política* (pp. 134–142). Buenos Aires, Argentina: Ediciones Continente, 2004.

See also Barricada TV (Argentina); Cine Insurgente/Rebel Cinema (Argentina); December 2008 Revolt Media (Greece); November–December 1995 Social Movement Media (France); *Suara Independen* (Indonesia)

Further Readings

Ogando, A. (2004). Wayruro comunicación popular. In N. Vinelli & C. Rodríguez Esperón (Eds.), *Contrainformación: Medios alternativos para la acción política* (pp. 134–142). Buenos Aires, Argentina: Ediciones Continente.

WEIMAR REPUBLIC DISSIDENT CULTURES (GERMANY)

The "Weimar" Republic era ran from the end of World War I through the Nazis' ascent to power in 1933. Its years were marked by the collapse of the rigidly reactionary Imperial Monarchy and the emergence of republican democracy, social chaos and near revolution in 1918–1919, the vindictive Versailles Treaty powers' dictates over the following decade, an extreme-rightist coup attempt in 1920, the disastrous hyper-inflation of 1923, the crippling impact of the Depression, and the rise of the Nazis—as well as an intensely creative and progressive cultural scene, especially in the capital Berlin, then a city of 4 million. This scene—fueled by the factors mentioned and by the searing memory of the war—served as source for visions and practices of alternative media that retain much of their influence today.

Notable artistic "formations," to use Raymond Williams' term, succeeded each other rapidly in Berlin in that period. During the war, some of the later Expressionists, such as Max Beckmann, Otto Dix, and Georg Grosz, savagely attacked its monumental destructiveness and the obscenity of militaristic propaganda. As the war staggered to its close, however, and as Expressionism began to lose ground, the "dada" movement arose, which was famous for declaring that all art to date had comprehensively failed to inspire the mass public against protracted purposeless slaughter (and for submitting a lavatory pedestal and a mustachioed reproduction of Leonardo da Vinci's iconically "beautiful" Mona Lisa to art exhibitions to make their point).

This movement had circles in several major cities, including New York, but its Berlin circle was especially active and especially connected to revolutionary artistic currents emanating from Moscow in cinema (especially Sergei Eisenstein), photography (especially Aleksandr Rodchenko), and theater (especially Vsevolod Meyerhold). The Russian Constructivist movement also had its impact, defining machine structures and patterns as a central topic for contemporary painting and photography because they evoked the construction of a socialist utopia via industrialization. As "dada" flamed and then died away, Surrealist currents also began to circulate in the mid-1920s from Paris, where the formation was involved increasingly with the political left (its leader André Breton a case in point).

It was also a period in time, however, when, even more intensively than other national publics, Germans flocked to cinemas, embraced home photography and the record player, and listened avidly to the radio. These then-new media, which were largely abhorred by the traditional cultural elite, were being used freely and imaginatively in the USSR at that time. Bertolt Brecht and others projected film in some of their theatrical productions, and he also argued notably for the interactive possibilities of radio that were being eroded by top-down, one-to-many deployment of the technology. His close friend Walter Benjamin later argued these technologies had enormous potential—in dialectical conjunction with the growth of mass political consciousness—to extend public understanding of the meaning and intricacies of human life.

John Heartfield, originally with dada and considerably influenced by Georg Grosz's work attacking war and fascism, was one of a group of artists who took Soviet artists' experiments with photomontage and set up an illustrated monthly of the left, the Workers Illustrated Newspaper (*Arbeiter-Illustrierte-Zeitung*, *AIZ*). He, like his fellow photomontagists, would cut images out of newspapers, magazines, and advertising copy and reassemble them for a political purpose. A classic, borrowed from Grosz, was an image of Hitler standing with his standard salute, right palm upturned, declaring "millions are behind me." Three times his size behind him stands a wealthy industrialist putting a sheaf of bank bills into Hitler's upturned hand.

Hannah Höch, who is less well known today and was less tied to the Communist party, also produced extraordinarily powerful images. Before the ferocious assaults of today's intellectual property laws were ever in place, it was possible for cheap but powerful imagery to be created this way. When the Nazis came to power, Heartfield moved to Prague and continued to publish *AIZ* underground from there (until they took Czechoslovakia as well in 1938). At its height, before 1933, *AIZ* sold more than one third of a million copies.

The workers' photography movement, although producing a considerable volume of undistinguished work, also encouraged members of the public to take visual media technology into their own hands and use it for political purposes to document their lives and collective struggles. Many other examples could be cited, from Brecht's and Kurt Weill's 1928 *Threepenny Opera*, which imported street language and jazz musical idioms, to Käthe Kollwitz's powerful pacifist woodcuts and other work featuring women and their rights, the ravages of mass unemployment.

In the end, however, once the Nazis had won 18% of the popular vote in the 1930 election, much of the freedom and vitality described began to drain away as cinema owners, art patrons, and state radio officials became overwhelmed by their fear of violent assaults on their premises and even their persons—and by the specter of a potential Nazi government.

John D. H. Downing

See also Black Atlantic Liberation Media (Transnational); Cultural Front (Canada); Culture Jamming; Social Democratic Media to 1914 (Germany); Workers' Film and Photo League (United States)

Further Readings

Antonowa, I., & Merkert, J. (Eds.). (1995). *Berlin Moskau 1900–1950*. München, Germany: Prestel-Verlag.

Guttsmann, W. L. (1990). *Workers' culture in Weimar Germany: Between tradition and containment*. New York: Berg.

Jelavich, P. (2006). *Berlin Alexanderplatz: Radio, film, and the death of Weimar culture*. Berkeley: University of California Press.

Ohrn, K. B., & Hardt, H. (1980, August). *Who photographs us? The workers' photography movement in Weimar Germany*. Paper presented at the 63rd Annual Meeting of the Association for Education in Journalism Conference, Boston, MA. http://www.eric.ed.gov/ERICDocs/data/ericdocs2sql/content_storage_01/0000019b/80/3f/2a/77.pdf

Weitz, E. D. (2007). *Weimar Germany: Promise and tragedy*. Princeton, NJ: Princeton University Press.

WHITE SUPREMACIST TATTOOS (UNITED STATES)

White supremacist groups view non-Caucasians as inferior beings, but they vary in certain respects.

Examples of these groups include Public Enemy Number 1 (PENI), Church of the Creator, Ku Klux Klan (KKK), White Peoples' Party, Nazi Low Riders (NLR), The Silent Brotherhood, White Aryan Resistance, American Nazi Party, Aryan Nations, and National Socialists. These groups are not simply driven by their instant emotions but by rational actors, whose practices are embedded within their coherent sociopolitical ideology.

The foundational ideological specifics that drive White supremacists' agenda generally are not shared by mainstream society. Conventional media outlets do not routinely articulate White supremacists' views and activities in detail as they do with some other social movements. In the face of such media marginalization, how do White supremacists disseminate their ideas to the wider public? One way is through their tattoos—body art mediates their ideologies and practices in an alternative semiotic.

Brief History of Tattoos

The word *tattoo* originates from the Tahitian word *ta-tu*, but tattooing exists in most cultures around the world, dating back to ancient times. Evidence of tattooing is available from 4000 BCE in Europe as well as about 2000 BCE in Egypt. Peruvian excavations show evidence of extensively tattooed mummies dating from the 1st century CE. Tattoo art was initially stereotyped negatively as primitive and pathological, but mainstream contemporary U.S. and European culture has largely come to accept the practice. Even social elites now embrace it. A very visible number of U.S. and European college students in the 2000s adorned various parts of their body with tattoos.

White Supremacist Tattoos as Alternative Media

Tattoos have received little attention in alternative media research. We also need to know much more than we do about how alternative media users actually engage with such media. The discussion within this entry initiates a dialogue between these two research areas. White supremacist groups resort to a variety of alternative media outlets, from the Internet to shortwave radio, from rock music to fliers, and from video games to newspapers. One medium is tattoos. Some examples follow from the U.S. Anti-Defamation League online database.

White Supremacist groups tattoo acronyms that reflect aspects of their racist worldview. For instance, some neo-Nazis and racist skinheads are tattooed with the symbol known as *SS Thunderbolts*, which is an acronym for the Nazi police force *Schutzstaffel* (shield squadron, SS). The SS eventually included the secret police and extermination camp guards. Other group members and some members of the World Church of the Creator tattoo *RAHOWA* on themselves which represents Racial Holy War. This phrase expresses belief in the battle between non-Whites and the White race, which will end in Aryan world domination.

Some also tattoo the acronym *SWP*, which signifies "Supreme White Power," which captures the core ideological belief system of White supremacists as superior beings. In addition, group members also might tattoo the acronym *CI*, which represents "Christian Identity." The CI is a religious ideological perspective among extreme right-wing groups. Group members espouse racist, anti-Semitic beliefs and also claim that the real biblical "Chosen People" are Europeans because of their inherent superiority over Blacks and Jews.

Other tattoos that White supremacists use to communicate aspects of their beliefs are graphic symbols. Thus, Neo-Nazis and Skinheads tattoo the *Iron Cross* with a swastika in its middle portion, *the Swastika*, and *the Iron Eagle* that Hitler used for the Third Reich. Familiarity with these symbols cues the observer to these tattoos as signifying anti-Semitism, violence, White supremacy, and fascism. Another tattoo popular with the Aryan Nation and the KKK is a Confederate flag with a noose lying below it. This tattoo alludes to the many lynching murders of African Americans during the century after the Civil War.

Some tattoos signify specific groups. For example, the tattoo of a giant bird-skeleton into whose midsection is inserted a Swastika with NLR written below it demonstrates an affiliation with the Nazi Low Riders. Racist skinheads also signify their affiliation with tattoo of a fist with the letters "s-k-i-n" written on it.

White supremacists tattoos also include "coded" numbers. For example, the tattoo *100%* worn by supremacists expresses the ideology that they are of a pure Aryan "stock." The tattoo *14 Words* is known to signify "We must secure the existence of our people and a future for white children." Also, White supremacists tattoo the numbers *88*, which correspond to the position of H in the English alphabet to signify the Nazi greeting "Heil Hitler."

The KKK also uses the number *311* as an alternative for their acronym *KKK*. The number is derived from the 11th position of the letter K in the alphabet. Thus to insiders, the number signifies affiliation with the KKK. Racist Supremacists also use *4/19* and *4/20* tattoos to commemorate anniversaries they deem historically significant. The former commemorates the 1993 Branch Davidian siege in Waco Texas as well as Timothy McVeigh's bombing of the Oklahoma City Federal Building in 1995. The latter memorializes Adolf Hitler's birthday.

Thus, the tattoos of White supremacist groups forcefully articulate their racist ideologies. Hence, it is not surprising that mainstream media institutions do not participate in promoting their agenda. For White supremacist groups, the embodied tattoos rebalance mainstream media marginalization and offer a visible alternative medium to promote their concerns.

Such tattoos have other functions too. They intimidate people who do not share their worldview, express defiance of current conventions of intergroup relations, and convey a literally enduring commitment to their bigoted belief system. Their transgressive character enables people who subscribe to such beliefs to identify allies and fellow conspirators quickly, to identify signal club membership for safety's sake in violent jails, and to celebrate being a marginalized group whose cause they believe most Whites will eventually accept as visionary and brave.

Thus, these embodied tattoos largely function as an alternative medium to spread White supremacist ideologies and practices. However, one wonders whether White supremacists have given thought to the fact that the tattoo media through which they express their bigotry derive originally from cultures they despise as primitive.

Joseph Oduro-Frimpong

See also Alternative Media; Beheading Videos (Iraq/Transnational); Paramilitary Media (Northern Ireland); Radio Mille Collines and *Kangura* Magazine (Rwanda)

Further Readings

Hilliard, R. L., & Keith, M. C. (1999). *Waves of rancor: Tuning in the radical right*. Armonk, NY: M. E. Sharpe.

Sanders, C. R., & Vail, D. A. (2008). *Customizing the body: The art and culture of tattooing*. Philadelphia, PA: Temple University Press.

WHOLE EARTH CATALOG (UNITED STATES)

The *Whole Earth Catalog* (WEC) was an American counterculture print publication. Against the dominant culture of an industrial America that seemed to flatten individuality, the WEC sought to promote ways of thinking and living as independent individuals. Besides being hugely popular during its relatively short 4-year lifetime, the catalog left a wide and deep legacy.

Founded by Stewart Brand in 1968, its purpose was to provide "access to tools," as its slogan claimed. The Stanford-educated Brand combined his knowledge of biology, artistic interests, and experience with the U.S. military to create a medium for communicating innovative ideas and items that would help individuals create better ways of living. The catalog began as a self-published affair with no advertising. It initially sold 1,000 copies at $5.

The WEC was published regularly from 1968 to 1972 and sporadically after that, based on popular demand. In 1985, it was revived as *Whole Earth Review* after it merged with a sister publication, *CoEvolution Quarterly*. The title was shortened later to *Whole Earth*.

Publication ceased in 2003 when the Point Foundation running the catalog ran out of funds. Later, philanthropist Samuel B. Davis took over the enterprise and published the *Whole Earth Catalog* under its original title through the company New Whole Earth, LLC.

Unlike most of its peer publications that focused on one topic like politics or farming, WEC sought to address all ideas and tools for better living. It housed articles under broad categories such as understanding whole systems, shelter and land use, industry and craft, and communications. The topics were as varied as species preservation, organic farming, and alternative energy, whereas the tools showcased ranged from Buddhist economics and nanotechnology to the double-bubble wheel engine.

Atypical also was WEC's collaborative publication process: One year after its initial printing, the catalog became a forum where readers exchanged ideas and heresies. The catalog even went so far as to keep typos and grammar errors from earlier drafts in the final publication. It also spearheaded financial disclosure, publishing its annual financial reports in the catalog itself.

WEC's goals also differed from mainstream publications that sought longevity and profit. Brand ceased publication once the *Catalog* won the National Book Award in 1972, expecting that similar publications would spring up based on WEC's success. But as no likely offspring emerged and sales continued at 5,000 per week for WEC's last publication—the *Last Whole Earth Catalog*. Brand resumed publication with the paradoxically titled *Updated Last Whole Earth Catalog*.

WEC contributed to the development of social movements in terms of creating communities out of disparate individuals and providing media for communication and tools to transform ideals into reality. The influence of WEC on alternative media and social movements carries on in politics, information and technology, environmentalism, cyberculture, and do-it-yourself culture.

Lena Khor

See also Alternative Media; Chipko Environmental Movement Media (India); Church of Life After Shopping (United States); Citizens' Media; Environmental Movement Media

Further Readings

Kirk, A. (2007). *Counterculture green: The* Whole Earth Catalogue *and American environmentalism*. Lawrence: Kansas University Press.

Turner, F. (2006). *From counterculture to cyberculture: Stewart Brand, the* Whole Earth *network, and the rise of digital utopianism*. Chicago: University of Chicago Press.

Whole Earth Catalog: http://www.wholeearth.com/index.php

WITNESS VIDEO (UNITED STATES)

WITNESS is an independent, nonprofit organization that uses video and online technologies to raise awareness worldwide about human rights violations. Based in Brooklyn, New York, the organization partners with individuals and groups from across the world to defend human rights.

Founded in 1992 by musician-activist Peter Gabriel as a project of the Lawyers Committee for Human Rights (now Human Rights First), WITNESS's form of video advocacy does not simply mean handing a video camera to people. The organization adopts a more instructional and strategic approach. It not only provides its partners with cameras and editing tools but also trains them how to transform plain testimony and stark images into moving narratives. WITNESS also works with its partners to channel these videos to appropriate audiences. They help build advocacy campaigns around these video creations that strategically target particular locales or specific audiences.

There are two main partnering initiatives. The first, Core Partnerships, is longer term, involving 2–3 years of intensive training with a group on a given human rights issue. The second, Seeding Video Advocacy, is shorter term, comprising brief training in production, distribution, and campaign organization.

Under these initiatives, WITNESS has collaborated with groups on a variety of issues, including the mistreatment of internally displaced people and refugees in Burma (Myanmar), child soldiers in the Democratic Republic of Congo, the advocacy of mental disability rights in México and Paraguay, landmines in Sénégal, and inmate abuse in Californian youth prisons.

WITNESS videos have been deployed successfully as evidence in court and quasi-judicial hearings, as sources for news broadcasts, and as resources for grassroots education and social mobilization. For instance, the short film *Operation Fine Girl: Rape Used as a Weapon of War in Sierra Leone*, which was coproduced by WITNESS filmmaker Lilibet Foster and a Sierra Leonean gender specialist, Binta Mansaray, was distributed and screened to nongovernmental organization (NGO) representatives, government officials, and the general public across Sierra Leone. It was also shown to powerful decision makers, including members of the Sierra Leone Truth and Reconciliation Commission (TRC), judicial officials, and traditional local leaders. The film led to the TRC including sexual violence and gender-based crimes in their investigations, and it played a significant role in changing attitudes on gender and sexuality in Sierra Leonean communities.

In 2008, WITNESS launched a global participatory online platform dedicated to human rights media and action, the Hub. Referred to as the YouTube of human rights, the Hub invites individuals and groups from around the globe to upload and share video and information. It provides a global space through which individuals and groups focused on human rights can inform, advocate, campaign, and take action.

Lena Khor

See also Feminist Media: An Overview; Human Rights Media; Independent Media (Burma/Myanmar); Indigenous Media (Burma/Myanmar); Political Song (Liberia and Sierra Leone)

Further Readings

Gregory, S. (2006). Transnational storytelling: Human rights, WITNESS, and video advocacy, *American Anthropologist, 108*(1), 195–204.
Gregory, S., Caldwell, G., Avni, R., & Harding, T. (Eds.). (2005). *Video for change: A guide for advocacy and activism.* London: Pluto Press.
WITNESS 11: http://www.witness.org/index.php

WOMEN BLOGGERS (EGYPT)

On January 22, 2008, Dar Al Shorouk, which is one of the leading publishing houses in Egypt, published the works of three young Egyptian female bloggers. Their books—which are the texts of their personal blogs—were included on lists of currently top-selling titles in Egypt. For approximately 2 months, newspapers, magazines, and prominent television talk shows interviewed those three young women bloggers in an attempt to understand why their books were best sellers.

Some regarded the blogs as a threat to society and literature, condemning bloggers for writing colloquial language or for focusing on their own lives. Others perceived the blogs as a new genre and were excited about them.

Such a division in views is present in the literature on women's blogs. Women are often considered incapable of serious writing because their blogs focus mainly on their own lives, which are so less significant than men's. Thus, diary-style blogs receive little attention, although research shows they are the most popular form of blogging. This entry describes the perceptions of women's blogs in Egypt, discusses the relationship between blogs and cultural citizenship, and summarizes several studies that address the motivations of Egyptian women bloggers and the impact of writing blogs on the women's sense of psychological empowerment impact, self-awareness, and tolerance.

"The Personal Is Political"

A familiar assertion from the "second wave" of feminism (1960s–1970s) was that the personal is political. This slogan encouraged women to make those in power pay attention to their personal lives and acknowledge personal issues such as sexual harassment and domestic abuse as political, for these experiences affect society as a whole.

The lack of a clear understanding of what the "personal" includes has contributed to the negative perception of personal blogs in Egypt. For example, in an entry called "Warmth," the author of the "With Me" blog described a situation she encountered while riding a microbus. The man next to her was leaning heavily into her, so the woman sitting next to her put her arms around her to protect her from the man. Then another girl got on, and the man made himself equally objectionable to her, and so in response, all three women just hugged one another. The story is about the sexual harassment to which women are subjected, but it presents the subject in an indirect and soft way. Given the politics of gender, such writing can hardly be demoted to the "purely personal."

Personal Blogging and Cultural Citizenship

The Egyptian Cabinet Information and Decision Support Center (IDSC) 2008 report showed that nearly 40% of Egyptian blogs focused on personal issues related to the bloggers' daily lives and thoughts, compared with less than 20% that are focused on political matters. These data contradicted frequent claims that political blogs are the most common type in Egypt.

In addition, the IDSC report showed that women mostly created personal blogs. Some of the Egyptian female bloggers used Arabic, others used English or both, and few wrote in French.

Cultural citizenship, a term that extends citizens' rights and agency beyond a purely legal definition of citizenship, is regarded as a vital form of citizenship in contemporary societies. Jean Burgess, Marcus Foth, and Helen Klaebe (2006) argue that information and communication technologies, particularly the Internet, open up opportunities for cultural citizenship practices, which is mainly about "the learning of self and of the relation of self and other," as Gerard Delanty (2002) explains. They conclude that daily Internet practices like chatting, photo sharing, and storytelling could lead to cultural citizenship practices.

Nine Egyptian Women Bloggers

One study by Shokry conducted in-depth structured interviews with nine female bloggers in October and November 2007. They were all from the middle class, had a Bachelor of Arts degree, and were aged 21–30. They all wrote a mix of personal/social/literary blogs except for the author of the *Whada-Masrya* (Egyptian Woman) blog, which includes political topics. The nine women were asked about the reasons for blogging, the impact of blogging on the informants' lives, and the issues addressed in their blogs. Some bloggers asked to be identified in the study by their blog name.

Interacting with others, sharing thoughts with others, and understanding oneself through writing were among their motivations for blogging. Rehab Basam, who is the author of *Hadouta* (Story), liked to share with others new things she has come across. She liked to tell about books she read, a piece of music she heard, or an experience she went through as it might help somebody or make someone happy. *Hadouta* also reported that some people had told her that her postings inspired them.

The nine women interviewed confirmed that blogging had positive effects on their self-development and their social relations. For example, the author of the *Maat* blog, who named her blog after the Pharaonic goddess of law, order, and truth, said that blogging helped her to understand herself more and extended her circle of friends. She hoped her blog would be a way to document the changes in her life and her character development. She commented, "maybe 3 years from now I would be clear about my political views and the things I want to do." She said she gained confidence when people comment on her writings. Their comments gave her insight. Similarly, the author of *Maa-nafsi* (With Me) found blogging helped her to understand herself and to have more friends.

Eman, who is the author of *Eman's blog*, said that being a blogger was sort of a mental boost. Her blog, mainly literary, made her more confident in her writing, as she usually received positive comments. She also mentioned that she was now more tolerant toward other people's convictions. Blogging introduced her to some atheists who were good people, and she respected them regardless of their beliefs.

The author of *Lasto Adri* (I Don't Know) said that, through blogging, she started to be more tolerant, to accept the differences between people, and to view people as humans regardless of the way they dress, their gender, or their religion.

The author of the *Aweza Atgawez* (Wanna be a Bride) blog lived in *Al-Mahala* Governorate, which is a traditional region. She did not have the courage to go Cairo to study because it was not considered appropriate for a girl to travel on her own. However, blogging somehow gave her the strength to do so. She is now taking a screenwriting course in Cairo, as many readers encouraged her to do because her writings were good, amusing, and funny.

For Dina El-Hawary, the author of *Dido's blog*, being a blogger created a form of parallel universe for her where she enjoyed writing and learning about other people's views. She said that readers' positive feedbacks made her consider publishing her work. She was also considering working as a freelance journalist and obtaining a journalism degree.

The author of *Whada-Masrya* was the only political female blogger within the nine participants. She was an active member of the antiregime movement *Kefaya* (Enough). Her motivation for blogging basically was to express her opinions on political issues. Being a political blogger affected her life as well in that she became a more dynamic activist. Now more than ever she wanted to keep up with current trends and attend events to write about in her blog.

The author of the *Ultima Rosa* blog was the only one who took issue with this view. She did not deny that blogging had helped her to understand herself better and had encouraged her to write. However, she said that it had impacted her writing negatively. She tended now to write shorter texts to suit the blog readers, but she felt this was cramping her imagination. She also criticized the blogosphere because there was no code of ethics; this allowed many bloggers to lapse into obscenity, which then became a cheap, trendy way to write.

Sixty-Six Egyptian Women Bloggers

A second study by Shokry was based on 66 responses to a web questionnaire sent to 120 women bloggers in October and November 2008. The study was to try to understand the levels of pluralistic tolerance, self-awareness, and psychological empowerment, which are engendered for women in blogging. All three elements are components of cultural citizenship.

The responses indicated that these women bloggers were more open than many members of the public to people's differences. Learning self-awareness, which is the subjective component of cultural citizenship, was the second indicator. Learning about the other, which includes understanding the shared values that connect people together, the intersubjectivity component, was the last indicator.

These findings do not mean that practicing blogging in itself would actually trigger these changes. The gratifications these women obtained from blogging activity triggered their cultural citizenship practices and, consequently, psychologically empowered them. It also means that they learned more about their personal views and could think critically about their lives in relation to the society they inhabit.

The research showed that personal blogging helped the respondents to feel socially integrated, to register their personal development, and to feel they wielded influence. This opened up opportunities for them to practice cultural citizenship in the sense that they became more tolerant and aware of the values and meanings they share with others, as well as more aware of their attitudes, feelings, and thoughts in relation to the environment they inhabit. This was also a sign for psychological empowerment among the respondents.

Although these findings cannot be generalized to all Egyptian women bloggers, they provide strong insight into some processes—undramatic, but significant—which were helping Egyptian women empower themselves.

Lobna Abd Elmageed Shokry

See also Citizen Journalism; Citizens' Media; Feminist Media: An Overview; Kefaya Movement Media (Egypt); *OhmyNews* (Korea)

Further Readings

Abdulla, R. (2007). *The Internet in the Arab world: Egypt and beyond.* New York: Peter Lang.

Burgess, J., Foth, M., & Klaebe, H. (2006, September). *Everyday creativity as civic engagement: A cultural citizenship view of new media.* Paper presented at the Communication Policy & Research Forum, Sydney, Australia. Retrieved April 19, 2010, from http:// eprints.qut.edu.au/archive/00005056

Delanty, G. (2002). Two conceptions of cultural citizenship: A review of recent literature on culture and citizenship [Electronic version]. *The Global Review of Ethnopolitics*, p. 60.

Hamdy, N. (2006). *Alternate Arab voices: A depiction of the usage of blogs in cyberspace.* Paper presented at the International Association for Mass Communication Research, Cairo, Egypt. Retrieved April 12, 2007, from http://www.docstoc.com/ docs/23024328/Arab-Citizen-Journalism-Shaped-by-Technology-Creates-a-Challenge

Hermes, J. (2006). Citizenship in the age of the Internet. *European Journal of Communication, 21*(3), 295–309.

Herring, S., Scheidt, L., Bonus, S., & Wright, E. L. (2004). *Bridging the gap: A genre analysis of weblogs.* In Proceedings of the 37th Annual Hawaii International Conference on System Sciences, Big Island. Retrieved March 12, 2008, from http://www .ics.uci.edu/~jpd/classes/ics234cw04/herring.pdf

Somolu, O. (2007). Telling our own stories: African women blogging for social change. *Gender & Development, 15*(3), 477–489.

Stavrositu, C., & Sundar, S. (2008, April). *Can blogs empower women? Designing agency-enhancing and community-building interfaces.* Paper presented at the Work in Progress session, Conference on Human Factors in Computing Systems, Florence, Italy. http://doi.acm.org/10.1145/1358628.1358761

Women's Movement Media (India)

The media and cultural productions of the women's movement in India crisscross the subcontinent's ethnic, linguistic, regional, caste, and class divisions, challenging patriarchal norms in India's legal, political, and cultural arenas. They range from speeches, pamphlets, posters, opinion essays and columns, theatrical forms of resistance, songs, and plays to periodicals, books, videos, and online resources.

Historical Background

The women's movement in India can be traced to the early 19th century. Jayawardena's canonic cross-national survey of the emergence of women's movements in global South anticolonial activism combats the misconception that feminism was an alien Western ideology in South Asia. In the early to mid-19th century, public consciousness of women's emancipation spread as Indian male social reformers campaigned to liberate Indian women from practices that the British colonizers had deemed "barbaric"—*sati* or widow burning, isolation of widows, child marriage, and polygamy.

Gradually, the more pressing issue of women's education began to take center stage, and as women gained the benefits of literacy and forms of public participation, the seeds were sown for the rise of the modern women's movement in postcolonial India. Mahatma Gandhi's ascent within the independence movement during the first half of the 20th century and his "indigenous" articulation of Indian women's equality within the patriarchal logic of Hinduism brought a much larger and more diverse group of ordinary urban and rural women into the nationalist movement.

Although male reformers in the urban centers of India initially were the primary agents of change, educated middle- and upper-class/caste Indian women in urban centers across India began to assume leadership roles in the movement by the end of the 19th century. The establishment of women's service associations like the Women's Indian Association, *Sakhi Samiti*, *Arya Mahila Samaj*, *Seva Sadan*, *Prayag Mahila Samithi*, *Mahila Seva Samaj*, and the Hindu Ladies Social and Literary Club extended the movement into wider regional and national networks.

A burgeoning body of women's print culture emerged from this closely knit web of pioneering women leaders and formal women's organizations. Women's periodicals, non-fiction books, novels, memoirs, essays, poetry, and letters and columns in the mainstream press transported the ideas and philosophies of the nascent Indian women's movement into hundreds of homes, clubs, and libraries. Women's literature addressed a range of topics and issues, from more conservative material on domesticity and culinary skills to more radical ideas on women's education and economic independence, religion's oppression of women, widows' rights to remarry, and women's participation in the political and legal realms of public life.

Vernacular language periodicals in Marathi (*Arya Bhagini*, *Swadesh Bhagini*, and *Subodhini*), Hindi (*Stree Darpan*, *Grihalkashmi*, and *Mahila Sarvasv*), Telugu (*Hindu Sundari*, *Savithri*, and *Anasuya*), Bengali (*Bharati*), and Tamil (*Penn Kalvi*, *Kirahalakshmi*, and *Matar Marumanam*) enabled ordinary women to critique patriarchy and debate strategies to improve women's lives.

Matar Marumanam (Widow Remarriage) was unique for its attention to transgressive issues of romantic love, companionate marriage, emotion, and sexual pleasure in women's lives. *Stri Dharma* (Women's Duty, 1918–1930s), an English and vernacular periodical originally founded by Indian, British, and Irish women in Madras (now Chennai), was among the most feminist in tone of these periodicals, with editorial content that described international advances in women's legal rights and in women's campaigns for suffrage. Pandita Ramabai's feminist albeit Orientalist tract *The High Caste Hindu Woman* (1887) offered a searing critique of Indian women's oppression in Hinduism's patriarchal traditions. Tarabai Shinde's *Stree Purush Tulana* (A Comparison Between Women and Men) argued that negative qualities attributed to women, such as superstition, suspicion, and treachery, were in reality more prevalent among men.

Equally important were working-class and poor rural and urban Indian women's oral traditions of protest and contestation. In the urban space of 19th-century Calcutta, lower-class rural migrant women's folk doggerels and poems, songs, and theatrical performances generated narratives that were sensuous and bawdy and mocked patriarchal control over women's bodies, subjectivities, and behaviors.

Postcolonial Women's Movement Activism

A series of overlapping social, political, and economic developments—early socialist and development programs, rural–urban migration, women's participation in the workforce and in state politics, legislative and policy initiatives, the rise of progressive political parties, and the spread of education—have accelerated the steady expansion of the Indian women's movement in postcolonial India. Numerous other social movements and nongovernmental organizations (NGOs) including Dalit anti-caste movements, gay and lesbian activism, radical separatist regional movements, the environmental movement, consumer rights organizations, trade unions, and peasant and workers' rights movements, have also fueled the growing momentum and relevance of feminist agendas for social change.

From the 1970s onward and in the wake of Indira Gandhi's imposition of Emergency (1975–1977), when civil liberties were suspended, the establishment of autonomous organizations and NGOs devoted to women's issues registered the formal institutional trajectories of the women's movement's evolution. These included Video SEWA (Self Employed Women's Alternative), *Aalochana*, *Akshara*, *Majlis*, *Vimochana*, *Pennurimai Iyyakam*, *Saheli*, *Stree Shakti Sanghatana*, Progressive Organization of Women, *Stree Jagruti Samiti*, *Sabla Mahila Sangh*, Forum against the Oppression of Women, *Jagori*, and *Shramik Sanghatana*.

The decades of the 1980s and 1990s witnessed the creation of women's studies academic units (Jadavpur University, Shivaji University, Pondicherry University, University of Delhi,

Shreemati Nathibai Damodar Thackersey [SNDT] Women's University, Tata Institute of Social Sciences, Maharaja Sayajirao [M.S.] University, and the Centre for Women's Development Studies) and research and documentation centers (*Vacha*, Women's Library, *Anveshi*, *Akshara*, and Sound and Picture Archives for Research on Women [SPARROW]).

Mirroring patterns elsewhere, the Indian women's movement has also ebbed and flowed in response to events and crises. These have encompassed the rise of rightist religious fundamentalism; physical abuses of women, including sexual harassment, "eve-teasing" (sexual molestation in public places), and assault; rape by policemen; dowry-dispute murders; wives' economic inequality in divorce; *sati*; displacement by government construction projects; anti-price rise and anti-alcohol protest campaigns; declining sex ratio as a result of sex-selective abortions of female fetuses; and beauty pageant controversies. Formal and informal women's movement media in formats ranging from print and electronic to plays and performative expressions offer evidence of the movement's political agency and its vibrant creativity.

Print Media

Among formal print media, the first feminist periodical was *Feminist Network* started by the Socialist Women's Group in 1977. The journal *Manushi* (English and Hindi), which was founded in 1979, has attained national and international prominence for articulating the concerns of a broad range of Indian women, with a strong mandate to cover the struggles of the urban and rural poor. *Baijia* (Marathi), *Aurat Ki Awaz* (Hindi), *Nari Mukti* (Hindi), *Sachetana* (Bengali), and *Aeideor Jonaki Bat* (Assamese) are examples of vernacular newsletters and magazines from the 1980s that raised awareness of ordinary women's concerns.

The bimonthly *Antarang Sangini* (Close Female Friend) has gained tremendous respect as the only Hindi-language women's studies journal. The feminist publisher Kali for Women, which eventually spilt into Zubaan and Women Unlimited, has published canonical academic and activist books on feminism and women's issues (authors include Maria Mies, Radha Kumar, and Vandana Shiva). Along with producing academic books in English,

Stree Publishers in Calcutta is committed to promoting feminist authorship in Bengali and to translating vernacular Indian feminist work into English.

Khabar Lahariya (News Waves), which is a fortnightly Bundeli newspaper, is among the most notable of rural women's print media productions. Dalit and newly literate women in the Bundelkhand region report and write stories on public health, state apathy, education, and police neglect and atrocities, winning national recognition for investigative style reporting.

Colorful posters produced for a series of women's movement protest campaigns capture the immense creative energy and artistic skills of women artists, designers, and printers, as in the Mathura and Rameeza Bee rape cases, Bhanwari Devi's gang rape, Roop Kanwar's forced widow immolation, the Shah Bano refusal of alimony case, and Sudha Goel's dowry-related death. Creative posters also publicized feminist campaigns on female feticide, political participation, domestic violence, women's health, sex workers' rights, and literacy.

Novels authored by Indian women, including diasporic writers like Anu Subramanian, Anita Desai, Bapsi Sidhwa, Arundhati Roy, Kamala Das, Shobha De, and Manju Kapoor, have translated Indian women's historical and everyday experiences of oppression, negotiation, and liberation into the vivid and inventive language of fiction.

Theater and Performances

In a similar vein, protest campaigns and social injustices have also motivated the women's movement to produce plays, songs, and novel forms of theatrical resistance. Dr. Vibhuti Patel's well-known 1990 play *Naari Itihas Ki Talash Me* (Women in Search of Their History) stages a series of episodes that capture the interpenetration of private and public spheres, home and politics, individual and community. The Jan Natya Manch's (People's Theater Group) 1979 play *Aurat* (Woman), which illuminates women's invisible labor at home and in fields and factories, has had more than 2,500 performances and has been performed in Pakistan, Bangladesh, and Sri Lanka. Stree Sangarsh's play *Om Swaha* (Ritual Sanskrit Chant) and Stree Mukti Sanghatana's play *Mulghi*

Jhali Ho (A Girl Is Born) parody and attack the practice of dowry and the cruelty of women's dowry-related murders.

The Mumbai feminist organization *Majlis* supported the production of plays and other artistic ventures that combat normative conventions of gender and the surveillance of women's sexuality. *Vanangana* (Forest Courtyard), a women's organization in the rural Bundelkhand region, scripted a play *Mujhe Jawab Do* (Answer Me!) and a *Phad*, a picture story painted on cloth, to contest domestic violence and to involve grassroots workers in community theater. The Vacha Documentation Center 's *Kishori Geet* (Songs of Girlhood) is an audio album of folk songs aimed to build girls' self-esteem and nourish their interest in education and economic self-sufficiency.

The feminist activists' campaign against the 1996 Miss World pageant in Bangalore included satirical reenactments of contests in which women were crowned "Miss Landless" or "Miss Poverty." In Maharashtra State, the United Anti-Price Rise Front, a coalition of women's groups that opposed merchants' hoarding and rising food prices, often demonstrated in front of government buildings by beating metal plates with rolling pins.

Radio, Cinema, and Internet

Indian women's radio and film productions have extended the imaginative and community-building impulses of theatrical traditions into new regional, national, and global spaces. Rural women's participation in recent community radio projects in villages in Andhra Pradesh, Gujarat, Karnataka, and Jharkand states has resulted in need-based vernacular language programming on crops, ecology, health, and childcare. The international films of Aparna Sen, Gurindher Chaddha, Meera Nair, and Deepa Mehta have probed tensions in gender, religion, nation, diaspora, and sexuality that ripple through the cultural and ideological space labeled "India."

Documentary filmmakers—Pratibha Parmar, Madhusree Dutta, Vismita Gupta Smith, Deepa Dhanraj, Madhu Kishwar, Aisha Gazdar, Paromita Vohra, Gargi Sen, and Bishakha Datta—have tackled difficult and taboo subjects that include the chilling effects of government population control programs, feminist history, gay and lesbian life, sex work, women's acts of resistance, workers' struggles, and tribal communities' rights.

The Internet has helped to promote women's print and audiovisual productions, collate women's media work to make it more accessible, provide archives of feminist work, and create legal, professional, and feminist networks of support. Mumbai-based SPARROW hosts an exemplary website with a rich sample of free oral history recordings, videos, journal articles, and photographic images and illustrations. The volunteer South Asian Women's Network gathers together links and materials on arts and entertainment, news, domestic violence, and divorce. Network of Women in Media in India acts as a forum for women in media professions to share information and resources and work for gender equality and justice within the media and society.

Finally, outside of these alternative and independent media ventures, the voices of the women's movement have even gained traction within state and commercial media. A spate of women-oriented television serials beginning with *Hum Log* (People Like Us) and *Rajani* (name of female protagonist) to more recent productions like *Hamare Tumhare* (Ours, Yours), *Panaah* (Refuge), and *Kasturi* (Musk) have explored women's education, activism, relationships, economic independence, and struggles to balance domestic life with careers.

Radhika Parameswaran and Sunitha Chitrapu

See also Dance as Social Activism (South Asia); Documentary Film for Social Change (India); Feminist Media, 1960–1990 (Germany); Feminist Movement Media (United States); Sarabhai Family and the Darpana Academy (India); Social Movement and Modern Dance (Bengal); Women Bloggers (Egypt)

Further Readings

Gandhi, N., & Shah, N. (1992). *The issues at stake: Theory and practice in the contemporary women's movement in India*. New Delhi, India: Kali for Women.

Garlough, C. (2008). On the political uses of folklore: Performance and grassroots activism in India. *Journal of American Folklore, 121*(480), 167–191.

Jayawardena, K. (1986). *Feminism and nationalism in the Third World*. London: Zed Books.

Kumar, R. (1993). *The history of doing*. New Delhi, India: Kali for Women.

Nagar, R. (2002). Women's theater and the redefinitions of public, private and politics in North India. *ACME: An International E-Journal for Critical Geographers, 1*(1), 55–72.

Parameswaran, R. (2001). Global media events in India: Contests over beauty, gender, and nation. *Journalism & Communication Monographs, 3*(2), 53–105.

Patel, V. (2002). *Women's challenges of the new millennium*. New Delhi, India: Gyan Publications.

Pavarala, V., & Malik, K. K. (2007). *Other voices: The struggle for community radio in India*. New Delhi, India: Sage Publications.

WOMEN'S RADIO (AUSTRIA)

Until the state's broadcasting monopoly ended in 1993, civic movements from two different camps had critiqued Austria's hegemonic and one-dimensional media landscape. For one, commercial broadcasting licenses were the goal; the other sought social, media-political, and cultural change. Whereas the first camp pivoted its licenses on mainstream commercial music, the second built up a solid, networked, nonprofit structure to promote diversity both in content and participation.

From the beginning, feminist ideas were brought into the project by women activists and artists, who argued that if marginalized groups were to participate fully, then specific, viable, and sustainable structures would be needed. Their aim was to ensure that there women-related content would be broadcasted and women's participation would be ensured, with women having regular shows and serving as management and technical staff members.

In terms of content, one idea was to reserve parts of the schedule for women's shows, for instance, one whole day per week or sections of the daily schedule. Discussions about organizational arrangements also developed from early on and are still relevant today. As Vienna's Radio Orange manager has stressed, ensuring participation by marginalized groups is the responsibility of everyone involved in the station.

To promote open access actively, a strategy tried at the outset was to "take the radio outside." Broadcasting equipment was brought to women's locales such as feminist centers, meetings, and events to arouse interest. Personal networks also brought new participants into the studios. From the beginning, the activists' reputation in certain communities for striving to establish a space for "genuine" women's politics, queer politics, and liberation facilitated the entry of new volunteers. Part of this credibility was because of gender-equal representation at all kinds of executive levels in the stations, as well as a result of the symbolic representation of women and all genders in radio language, press releases, and overall.

A recent international project at Radio Orange promoted antisexist consciousness and strategy development for a more gender-equal radio landscape. Frequently, European funding serves radio stations' networking concerns, joins local and international perspectives, and enables trans-local activities. Via the medium of radio, diverse European women's projects are linked together, and this exchange enriches the stations' experiences. In 2008, a new AMARC-Europe Women's Network was launched to facilitate mutual exchange and cooperation.

Interviews in the 2008 radio study referenced subsequently showed that women's radio initiatives were especially concerned with developing new knowledge, skills, and efficient resource use to improve their shows. Particularly in volunteer training, empowerment and autonomous expression were of central concern. Women's collectives were actively developing appropriate concepts or broadcasting formats and were questioning modes of expression and communicative routines to adapt them to changing needs.

One example in which women in a radio collective attempted to position themselves as mediators of empathetic encounters was the project *Fremd bin ich eingezogen* (I came here as a stranger) in the *Frauenzimmer* (Women's Room) program at Free Radio Freistadt. Through radio portraits, it introduced women who had moved to Austria at a certain point in their life. The idea behind the series was to challenge prejudices through acoustic encounters between the listeners and the women narrating their personal history.

The interviewees met with the producers for conversations and were invited to become involved in editing the hour-long piece. One woman who conducted some of the interviews concluded that whereas she particularly appreciated learning about another person, relating to her, and constructing together a retelling of her life, the interviewees might equally have appreciated the space to reflect, the impact of listening to their own story on the radio, and receiving CDs as a permanent demonstration of the process.

For some women, this was the first occasion to talk about their biography and migration experience in detail. Some reported that they subsequently received encouraging spontaneous reactions and unexpected expressions of empathy from their environment and the listeners. The artistic and aesthetic production of these acoustic encounters would merit additional exploration.

Another remarkable broadcast was "Talk about it—radio against sexual abuse," based at the *Radiofabrik* (Radio Factory) station in Salzburg. The show set out from the idea that media have a responsibility to talk (repeatedly) about taboo topics, thus offering victims orientation and information about help. For the victims, an important step is to overcome their isolation. In cooperation with a support group for sexual abuse victims, "Talk about it" reported on different aspects of abuse and support structures and offered a safe space for the women to talk about their experiences.

Producing a radio broadcast or participating in it can also be used (after a certain point in the process) as a practicable strategy to overcome the silence that often follows traumatic experiences and to attain more control over one's own story. The radio volunteers interviewed for the study and who worked with support groups offered their interviewees security through an environment that to a great extent the latter could control. Interviewees, for example, could decide on whether they wanted to speak live in the studio or pre-produce the interview in a self-paced way, and joint production allowed what was said to be revised.

The range of concepts, feminisms, and imagined audiences among women's radio shows was broad. It included active feminist collectives, such as "SPACEfemFM" in Linz, whose shows are aired on many other Austrian free radio stations. It included young feminist sound art and radio performance, as produced by *Schwestern Brüll* (Brüll

Sisters), and queer feminist shows featuring women artists, politics, and music, such as *Bauch Bein Po* (Belly Leg Bum), both at Radio Orange. And it went from women's collectives, which addressed their topics without an explicitly feminist agenda, to queer radio programs such as *queer durch*—a play on *quer durch*, which means "straight across"—that tried to engage with the lesbian, gay, bisexual, transgender, and queer communities in Klagenfurt.

In several free radio stations, there have been summer holiday radio workshops for girls that attempt to get groups of girls to experience all aspects of radio production. *Fortgeschrittene Verwirrung* (Advanced Babel) is one such show that developed out of a girls' radio project at Radio Helsinki in Graz. Also, youth centers like to use open access to the medium and host regular radio shows produced by girls' groups.

Once again, it is important that radio allows for public expression while offering a certain anonymity and safety for the hosts. The trainers report that researching their own information and transforming it into a broadcast is a particularly rewarding activity for the young women. They enjoy playing with identities and roles in a self-managed environment, and overcoming anxiety about technology seems to work better in girls-only groups.

Through participation in radio production, the girls learned that belonging to a media project might facilitate access to people and information. They learned about communicative routines and discovered the technical manipulation of sound and music—not to forget the experience of power from broadcasting their message via a microphone.

Thus, although there is certainly room for growth, the women's scene in Austrian free radio is diverse, and women activists have initiated important structural, conceptual, and social innovations in the stations.

Petra Pfisterer, Judith Purkarthofer,
and Brigitta Busch

See also Community Media and the Third Sector; Community Radio (Ireland); Community Radio Movement (India); Feminist Media: An Overview; Free Radio (Austria); Free Radio Movement (Italy); Free Radio Movement, 1974–1981 (France); Radio La Tribu (Argentina)

Further Readings

AMARC Women's International Network: http://win
   .amarc.org/index.php?p=home&l=EN
Association of Free Radio in Austria: http://www.freie-
   radios.at
Purkarthofer, J., Pfisterer, P., & Busch, B. (2008). 10
   Jahre freies radio in Österreich. Offener zugang,
   meinungsvielfalt und soziale kohäsion—eine
   explorative studie (Ten years of free radio in Austria:
   Open access, opinion diversity and social cohesion).
   *RTR: Nichtkommerzieller Rundfunk in Österreich
   und Europa, Schriftenreihe Band, 3,* 11–113.
   http://www.rtr.at/de/komp/SchriftenreiheNr32008

Workers' Film and Photo League (United States)

The Workers' Film and Photo League (WFPL) emerged in the early 1930s as an alliance of local groups in the United States, Europe, and Asia. Building on earlier independent media models, their efforts during the early years of the Great Depression helped to define social documentary film and photography as a genre, while advancing independent media practices that survived long after. The Film and Photo League (as it was alternately known) was a multifaceted organization. Members documented social conditions; exhibited films in a network of alternative spaces, published articles, and a newsletter; held photo exhibits; and critiqued mainstream Hollywood films.

The New York Film and Photo League is the best documented of the Film and Photo League chapters, and it was probably the first to form in 1930. Founding members had been active in the late 1920s productions of *Passaic Textile Strike* and *Gastonia*, which are "labor" feature films. The Workers International Relief (WIR) organization helped create the league and develop exhibition activities. WIR's primary role was to provide relief funds to striking workers around the world.

In the later 1930s, the New York Workers' Film and Photo League members split into different activities, some creating other film production units, some going to work for New Deal government agencies, and others transforming the FPL into the Photo League, dedicated to still photography in the same vein.

There were also many local chapters of the Workers Film and Photo League outside New York City. Groups of alternative "media activists" working under the Film and Photo League name could be found in Detroit, Chicago, Ohio, Pennsylvania, and California, as well as in Japan, Germany, Holland, and Britain. Rebelling against mass media institutions that reflected capitalist values, the local Leagues shared a common philosophy, yet maintained their local character. Some writers have associated the Film and Photo League with the Communist Party, but the loose alliances, varied activities, and non-Communist members indicate multiple affiliations.

Working alongside cultural groups such as the Blue Blouse players, the Red Dancers, and the John Reed Clubs of writers, Film and Photo League members saw themselves as cultural workers engaged in political combat. As declared in the opening frames of some of their films, they used the "camera as a weapon" mentality to produce newsreels and longer films on social conditions and workers' struggles. Members published *Filmfront* and *Experimental Film*, and their articles and pictorials appeared in *New Theatre,* the *Daily Worker,* and *Labor Defender.* Not least, the WFPL saw the importance of building distribution networks and worked to create alternative exhibition spaces, as well as organize tours of leftist films.

Like the Workers' Film Societies in England and the Amis de Spartacus in France, the Workers' Film and Photo League sponsored exhibitions of Soviet films such as *Battleship Potemkin, Mother, Storm Over Asia,* and *The End of St. Petersburg.* From Germany, Communist activist and leader Willi Münzenberg's *Internationale Arbeiterhilfe* (Worker's International Relief, in German) often provided the films for these exhibitions. Admission fees benefited groups such as WIR. Short newsreels produced by the WFPL frequently opened the feature film screenings, attracting a wider audience to these events.

None of the WFPL chapters were well funded, although many were self-sustaining, relying on film screenings and local donations to continue their activities. Local branches were often housed in cultural centers run by the Communist Party. For example, in San Francisco, the WFPL had a darkroom in the Ruthenberg House, which also housed a soup kitchen, theater, library, and workers' school.

Many films produced by the Film and Photo League are said to have been destroyed in a storage room fire in New Jersey. During the McCarthy era, others were actually destroyed or hidden to protect the people who had participated in leftist activism from being identified in them. Many WFPL members distanced themselves from the League at that time for the same reason. It was only in the 1970s that research and excavation of the lost films and "lost history" of the Film and Photo League began.

Carla Leshne

See also Activist Cinema in the 1970s (France); Cine Insurgente/Rebel Cinema (Argentina); Citizens' Media; DIVA TV and ACT UP (United States); Documentary Film for Social Change (India); Labor Media (United States); Medvedkine Groups and Workers' Cinema (France); Third Cinema

Further Readings

Alexander, W. (1981). *Film on the left: American documentary film from 1931 to 1942*. Princeton, NJ: Princeton University Press.

Brandon, T. (1992). Survival list: Films of the Great Depression. In D. Platt (Ed.), *Celluloid power: Social film criticism from "The Birth of a Nation" to "Judgment at Nuremberg."* Metuchen, NJ: Scarecrow Press.

Campbell, R. (1982). *Cinema strikes back: Radical filmmaking in the United States 1930–1942*. Ann Arbor, MI: UMI Research Press.

Denning, M. (1997). *The cultural front: The laboring of American culture in the twentieth century*. London: Verso.

Leshne, C. (2006). The Film & Photo League of San Francisco. *Film History, 18*, 361–373.

Slide, A. (1986). *Filmfront 1934–1935*. Reprint edition annotated by Anthony Slide. Metuchen, NJ: Scarecrow Press.

YES MEN, THE (UNITED STATES)

The Yes Men are a group of activists who engage in what they call "identity correction," an activity where they represent an organization or corporation in a particular way in order to spur public critique of them. Since 2000, The Yes Men have "represented" several entities, both public (e.g., the U.S. Department of Housing and Urban Development) and private (e.g., Dow Chemical) in different venues, such as lectures at trade conferences, on television, and on the World Wide Web. In these spaces, The Yes Men craft presentations intended to shock their audience.

Although they do not work alone, the most visible members of The Yes Men are Andy Bichlbaum and Mike Bonanno. In 1999, they created their first action, a website mocking Republican presidential nominee G. W. Bush. The website, gwbush.com, was an exact replica of the official website of the Bush Campaign except that it contained information very critical of the nominee. The Bush campaign filed an injunction to force The Yes Men's ISP to take the website offline. When this failed, Bush famously remarked, "There ought to be limits to freedom."

Websites such as this are how The Yes Men got many of their identity correction opportunities. In 2000, for instance, Bichlbaum and Bonanno created the website gatt.org, a site very similar to the official World Trade Organization (WTO) website, yet containing information critical of globalization policy. The website proved such an effective copy that The Yes Men began receiving invitations for then WTO director-general Mike Moore to speak at various events. The Yes Men would then send a "representative," that person always being Bichlbaum.

Bichlbaum has also appeared on CNBC as a WTO representative and as a Dow Chemical spokesman on BBC World. The latter opportunity came when The Yes Men were contacted through their fake Dow Chemical site (dowethics.com). Dow had bought Union Carbide (international) in 2001 and had refused any financial responsibility for India's 1984 Bhopal factory toxic leak disaster, when thousands died immediately and 200,000 were injured, with many more thousands dying prematurely over the years that followed, and with serious ongoing environmental destruction. Union Carbide had settled claims, but it was too little, too late for The Yes Men. Taking the opportunity in 2004 to speak for Dow on the 20th anniversary, they told the world Dow was selling Union Carbide and donating the resulting $12 billion to victims. The hoax was revealed about an hour later, but not until Dow stock briefly lost $2 billion in value.

The Yes Men rely to a large degree on media coverage to reach a larger audience. Critics argue that this is risky because there is no guarantee mainstream media will cover their activity in a favorable light, or at all. In this regard, The Yes Men's own media become extremely important as they help ensure that their message about the reasons for their actions are plainly expressed. Among The Yes Men's own media are two documentaries,

The Yes Men (released with a companion book in 2003) and *The Yes Men Fix the World* (2009), as well as a website with pages detailing their numerous actions and the reasons for them.

Afsheen Nomai

See also Adbusters Media Foundation (Canada); Alternative Media; *Ballyhoo* Magazine (United States); Church of Life After Shopping (United States); Culture Jamming; Installation Art Media

Further Readings

Bichlbaum, A., Bonanno, M., & Spunkmeyer, B. (2004). *The Yes Men: The true story of the end of the World Trade Organization*. New York: The Disinformation Company.

Harold, C. (2004). Pranking rhetoric: "Culture Jamming" as media activism. *Critical Studies in Media Communication, 21*(3), 198–211.

Harold, C. (2007). *Our space: Resisting the corporate control of culture*. Minneapolis: University of Minnesota Press.

Nethaway, R. (2000, April). Bush's web of limited freedom. *Plain Dealer*, 5F.

Nomai, A. J. (2008). *Culture jamming: Ideological struggle and the possibilities for social change*. PhD dissertation, University of Texas, Austin.

The Yes Men: http://www.theyesmen.org

The Yes Men [DVD]. (2003). Yes Men Films, LLC.

YOUTH MEDIA

Youth media encompass a wide range of media and creative practices, directed at young people for their benefit, or run by young people as autonomous community-based enterprises. Young people do not necessarily have anything in common with each other apart from age, making youth media an infinitely varied field.

"Youth" is a politically fraught concept used to reinforce intergenerational differences and tensions. Some youth media projects buy into the politicized field of "youth," whereas others actively seek to reclaim youth identities. The field of youth media has therefore become a distinct, yet divided, part of alternative media, which has been examined and theorized in its own right.

Public Definitions of "Youth"

The many representations of "youth" are central to understanding this segment of community-based media. The term "youth" is often used to indicate dysfunction. Young people are mostly called "youth" when they do something improper or illegal (smashing bottles, stealing cars, or wearing unusual clothes). In some populist accounts, youth live in an alien and untamed state, hazardous to themselves and to society. It is the opposite of "adulthood"—a time of life associated with maturity and responsibility.

In relation to media policy, young people have been invoked in contradictory and problematic ways—as victims, criminals, or "digital natives." High-stakes enforcement issues such as Internet censorship, piracy, and cyber-bullying are pursued "for the good of young people." Critics have observed that in many instances, young people are merely used as an emotive and symbolic device, disguising other legal, corporate, or government agendas resulting in Internet control.

At the other end of the spectrum, appealing to youth is a marketing and design device. Ideas and trends that emerge in the cultural spheres inhabited by young people get reappropriated for the purposes of fashion, advertising, and branding on a much wider scale. In this way, the inventions of a youth subculture (such as punks, skaters, and hip hop) are made part of the mainstream.

The Many Facets of Youth Media

Youth media are simultaneously a reaction to and disavowal of these various representations of youth. However, it should also be acknowledged that many media organizations run by young people do not use the label "youth media" either because their content is not specifically about "youth" or because they reject the term.

A large segment of the youth media sphere seeks to address youth dysfunction or disadvantage, operating under the "development" umbrella. Media production, in this case, becomes a social welfare tool, prescribed for (re)educational purposes and positive transformation at the individual level. This strand of youth media has its historical roots in pastoral care and evangelical social work projects, designed to equip young people with the personal, social, and cognitive skills required to participate as responsible citizens. The projects are administered by reflective practitioners, usually within social work charities and nongovernmental organizations.

Youth media can therefore be a technique of self-conduct, dedicated to well-being and provided through the bonds and support of the community sphere. There are many successful and interesting examples of youth media projects involving underprivileged or "at-risk" young people (for example, the WAC Performing Arts and Media College in London). By giving young people on the margins a voice, these projects provide a space for various cultures, experiences, and ideas that might not otherwise get produced and circulated.

However, this form of community media has received criticism for reinforcing "youth" as in need of direction and for privileging therapy-like outcomes over media involvement. For instance, some youth development projects are run as short-term programs and do not provide an ongoing means for young people to participate in the media.

Autonomous youth media are something different. Generally run by young people, these organizations provide an avenue for youth culture (in all its forms) and seek to give young people greater control over their media participation and training. Advocates believe mainstream media exclude young people from production and management. Authors such as Mark Davis have argued that the baby boomer cultural elite maintains a hold over defining public issues, to the exclusion of younger generations. Some organizations groom individuals to speak for this underrepresented population, encouraging them to take on ambassador-like roles in the media or in politics.

Digital Media Technologies

These have dramatically changed the youth media landscape. Around the year 2000, a sweep of websites marketed at young people began to appear. Based on a typical, traditional magazine media interface, various for-profit enterprises told kids what to wear and listen to, attracting heavy investment only to disappear again a few months later. The sites had no invitation for people to contribute and very little politics.

In response, groups of young people began to develop their own websites. One was *Vibewire*,

established in Sydney, Australia, in 2002, which rapidly became an active online forum for young people to express ideas, discuss issues, and get involved in creative projects. The core principle of *Vibewire* is user-generated content. However, as the term did not exist when they started up, they called it "democratic media." It worked on the principle that everything is there to be discussed, everything is contestable, and no one is allowed to dictate how things should be.

Although young people can now participate in digital media through commercial social networking sites, blogs, and wikis, youth media organizations generally aim to provide a different kind of engagement. For instance, they might provide access to broadcast audiences, participation in the governance of the organization, training, or a real-life social environment alongside the virtual.

As Sonia Livingstone has written, young people's media participation is often discussed in terms of their civic rights and responsibilities. Web-based communication is promoted as a means to combat political apathy, particularly among younger voters. Such discourses often assume that young people are more naturally adept at online communication than their elders and that online use draws people into political participation. Although there are many youth media projects that focus on political participation, significant questions remain as to whether participants are "converts" or already active in other spheres. Moreover, there are no significant guidelines as to what qualifies as participation or what young people must do before society judges them to be "politically active."

New Dimensions of Youth Media

Youth media organizations have increasingly emphasized training and digital literacy as their main purpose and, in some instances, revenue model. Many participants get involved in youth media for work experience, using it as an avenue to paid media industries work, rather than as a political commitment to counter-hegemonic media activism. Youth media is therefore becoming an important site for research and experimentation in digital literacy education.

Digital literacy denotes fluent communication via the technologies and forms of digital media. Some commentators believe it to be as important to the knowledge economy as print literacy was to the industrial era—an educational imperative with potentially major economic and social consequences, especially if broadly disseminated. Philip W. Graham and Abby A. Goodrum observe that to understand digital literacy fully, we need to think about what it means for people to have a widespread potential to write themselves into global, multimediated conversations, including the necessary technical, cultural, discursive, and aesthetic knowledges, and their political and economic implications. The issue of digital literacy, therefore, spans media power and education. The question for education institutions becomes: How do people become competent in their use of digital media technologies and able to write, not just read, in the "languages" of digital media?

The Educational Video Center

Steve Goodman has observed that media education works best in the context of community organizations where real media outcomes are possible. Schools have traditionally treated media education as a kind of "critical thinking" exercise, where students are taught to analyze texts but not to create their own media. Moreover, modern education puts greater weight on the written word than it does on visual or multimodal communication forms.

Goodman claims that American education ignores the socioeconomic dynamics of the home and neighborhood, expecting kids to see that environment as a deficit, an obstacle to overcome because of "inferior" language use. For him, media production can bring relevance back into education and enable communication beyond dominant ways of writing and speaking—applying visual forms, music, and local speech to the learning process. In this way, youth media organizations are engaging in broader educational debates through the development of courseware, providing access to training and promoting media participation.

The Educational Video Centre (EVC), where Goodman works, is located in New York City and was founded in 1984. EVC serves predominantly low-income communities and young people from diverse ethnic backgrounds. Students learn documentary making from the research stage to

production and post-production. EVC's 20-week school program teaches 60 public high-school students in four afternoon workshops a week. EVC also arranges internships for a small number of its graduates.

Furthermore, EVC works with teachers, delivering professional development programs in media literacy. Goodman argues that the *process* of EVC's workshops has an impact magnified a 1,000-fold on the individual youth participants when the *products*—EVC's library of youth-produced documentaries—are distributed and seen by thousands of other at-risk youth across the country.

The Student Youth Network

Another impressive example of a youth-run media organization is the Student Youth Network (SYN) in Melbourne, Australia. SYN is a full-time, city-wide radio broadcaster, producing two live television programs and various text-based media (online and print). The organization is run by people under the age of 26 (the majority being under 21), although they do use occasional help from older experts. SYN requires that all on-air presenters fall within their age range and stays young by limiting the period that producers can have a show on air, thereby making way for new participants.

Since the station commenced full-time radio broadcasts in 2003, thousands have come through SYN's doors, either as programmers or as station volunteers. The majority of SYN's income is sourced through education and training programs, whereby the young "SYNners" train school groups in media production. The programming is eclectic, confirming that "youth" is not a singular culture. SYN nonetheless manages to attract large radio audiences through its raw sound and surprising programming mix.

Conclusion

As these examples demonstrate, youth media can be both ambitious and progressive, addressing serious concerns such as social welfare and education. In many instances, youth media is a space for young people to be responsible for their own learning, organization, and representation. The difficult issue facing youth media is how to remain participatory and open while providing adequate structures and resources to fulfill such bold agendas.

Ellie Rennie

See also Participatory Media; Political Song (Liberia and Sierra Leone); Popular Music and Political Expression (Côte d'Ivoire); Youth Protest Media (Switzerland); Youth-Generated Media

Further Readings

Buckingham, D. (2007). *Beyond technology: Children's learning in the age of digital culture.* Cambridge, UK: Polity.

Davis, M. (1997). Gangland: *Cultural elites and the new generationalism.* Sydney, Australia: Allen & Unwin.

Giroux, H. A. (1996). *Fugitive cultures: Race, violence, and youth.* New York: Routledge.

Goodman, S. (2003). *Teaching youth media: A critical guide to literacy, video production, & social change.* New York: Teachers College Press.

Graham, P. W., & Goodrum, A. A. (2007). New media literacies: At the intersection of technical, cultural, and discursive knowledges. In R. Mansell, C. Avgerou, D. Quah, & R. Silverstone (Eds.), *The Oxford handbook of information and communication technologies* (pp. 473–493). Oxford, UK: Oxford University Press.

Hebdige, D. (1988). *Hiding in the light: On images and things.* London: Routledge.

Livingstone, S. (2007). Youthful experts? A critical appraisal of children's emerging Internet literacy. In R. Mansell, C. Avgerou, D. Quah, & R. Silverstone (Eds.), *The Oxford handbook of information and communication technologies* (pp. 494–514). Oxford, UK: Oxford University Press.

Montgomery, K. C. (2007). *Generation digital: Politics, commerce, and childhood in the age of the Internet.* Cambridge, MA: MIT Press.

Osgerby, B. (2004). *Youth media.* London: Routledge.

YOUTH PROTEST MEDIA (SWITZERLAND)

The youth riots in Switzerland, beginning on May 30, 1980, hit the international news. They began with a rally in front of the Zürich opera house, where hundreds of young people protested against Zürich City Council's unfair cultural policies. The authorities strongly subsidized opera and classical music, but they were more or less neglecting pop and punk music, as well as experimental and community arts projects. The demonstration escalated into a night of street fighting, which was followed by more riots in the weeks and months to come.

No one understood why such an outburst of violence took place in Zürich, the headquarters of Swiss banking and commerce. But the young protesters were driven by an impulse for cultural revolt and the vision of a life beyond mundane materialism. Their drive for self-realization was a passionate response to what they considered the cold, puritan mentality of the "Gnomes of Zürich" (a popular term for Swiss bankers obsessed with their riches, rather than looking after their young people's well-being).

Out of the riots evolved a youth protest movement active in imaginative uses of alternative media. Pirate radio, action video, street theater, and other forms of media expression like flyers, underground newspapers, and photo documentations were used to highlight the aims of youth protest: the creation of autonomous youth and cultural centers, more space for experimental art forms, free universities, liberal cannabis policies, better housing and living conditions in inner city Zürich, more public transport, no more motorways cutting through the city of Zürich, and other ecological goals, anticipating the green movement of today.

The Eighties Movement

The Eighties Movement, as it called itself, spread to Berne, Basel, St. Gallen, Lausanne, and other places. Young people occupied disused factories and abandoned houses to establish their own autonomous communal living, self-organized music, film and theater events, discussions, and exhibitions. Self-help groups became part of the movement too: young people trying to wean themselves from serious drug addiction, assisted by volunteer community workers; and young women creating their own spaces in the autonomous youth centers, secure from male dominance and violence. The Eighties Movement became a platform for cultural as well as for social experimentation for young people with different upbringings and educational backgrounds: kids from the streets, apprentices, students, and artists.

Older activists from the youth protest movements of the sixties and seventies showed their solidarity. Young second-generation immigrants—the "secondos"—participated in the Eighties Movement as well. For some of them, collective action provided a sense of belonging to Switzerland for the first time in their lives, helping them overcome their alienation in a society that had not really welcomed them.

The impact of the Eighties Movement lasted into the early 1990s and was manifold: More young people in Switzerland became creative in working with drug addicts, in urban struggles, and in the development of independent art cinemas, music labels, and new arts centers, which were now open to pop and politics. People involved in pirate radio stations, video, and photo projects became journalists and filmmakers. The movement was also a wake-up call for young people to get involved in trade unions or in nongovernmental organizations like the anti-apartheid solidarity committee. It was not just about cultural self-expression but a genuine desire to change the world. Activists gained new insights into the political process. Many realized that a society must be capable of change and of finding new approaches to conflict resolution—without falling back on repression.

Communication and Symbolic Resistance

The Eighties Movement did not have a homogeneous logic. It was pragmatic in obtaining its tactical goals, utopian in its claim to change the world, and hostile to the local state, which was perceived by many activists as oppressive. A common language of protest and the shared experience of challenging the authorities unified the disparate groups. Punks, hippies, freaks, dropouts, students, and intellectuals alike felt attracted by the movement. In the buildings they occupied and in the many squats, they exchanged news and experiences.

These places also became centers for independent media production. Important movement events were reported and commented on in underground papers, magazines, and videotapes. This enabled activists to position their practice within a larger debate on living conditions in Swiss society and the necessity for change. Victims of police brutality

and repressive court decisions, as well as teachers fired from universities and high schools, also received coverage in the underground press and in videos shot by movement activists.

Action Video

Video was relatively cheap. Tapes could be recorded over, saving expensive film processing. The rushes could be viewed instantly. After a short training, camera and recording equipment could be handled easily, including by nonprofessionals. Screenings could be in meeting rooms, bars, on the streets, or at home. This made video attractive for political groups and artists who wanted to operate in everyday settings, without inflated art ambitions.

Video played a major role in the Eighties Movement. All important happenings, demos, and surprise interventions were documented by video collectives. The exchange of tapes containing news, solidarity messages, and political statements traveled fast and effectively throughout the country and to Germany, Austria, the Netherlands, Italy, France, and Britain. Like the youth protests in the sixties and seventies, the Eighties Movement became transnational. The movement also highlighted for the first time in Switzerland an independent video sector outside the art world and the established film scene.

Zürich Is Burning was the most widely circulated movement tape. It is a 90-minute documentation of the first year of the riots, filmed by the movement collective Videoladen (Videostore). *Zürich Is Burning* was valued for its subjective montage, which managed to communicate the full power of the protest movement. The tape's ironic commentary, the soundtrack with Zürich punk music, and the elaborate application of special effects (cross-fades, double exposure, overexposure, and use of inter-titles and speech bubbles) made *Zürich Is Burning* a polemical pamphlet far removed from TV documentary aesthetics.

The commentary was crucial in creating an image of Zürich's underground completely different from the tourist perception of Switzerland as the cleanest place in the world:

Deep down where the plaster begins to crumble, and embarrassed trickles from super-clean human bums flow together into a smelly sewer, here live the rats since time immemorial: wild, rambling and cheerful. They speak a new tongue. And when this language bursts into the open, everything that's been said will not be done and gone, black on white not clear as daylight, old and new will be one thing.

TV Interventions

Another way the Eighties Movement shocked the public and appealed to its sympathizers was through nude demonstrations—"We are the naked chaos!"—and witty interventions in established media. A good example of the latter was the so-called "Mueller Show." Swiss television had organized a talk show to discuss the youth riots with two Zürich City Council representatives, a politician, and the city police chief. The youth movement had been asked to send two delegates, who appeared in the talk show under the names of Mr. and Mrs. Mueller, a widespread Swiss surname.

"Mr. and Mrs. Mueller" spoke as two right-wing citizens frustrated by soft police tactics, pleading for the army to crush the youth rebels once and for all, using any means necessary. As "Mr. and Mrs. Mueller," the two activists managed to irritate and disrupt the panel and unmask what in their opinion was a heavy-handed approach the city council was using for the unrest in Zürich's streets.

TV interventions like the "Mueller Show" were effective attacks on the symbolic order in state and society. The "Mueller Show" principle was also introduced in numerous flyers and newspapers of the movement such as *Stilett* (Stiletto), *Eisbrecher* (Icebreaker), and *Brecheisen* (Crowbar). The editors of these papers loved to play on words, to cut up articles and photos from the established journals, and to assemble them in provocative and amusing collages.

Heinz Nigg

See also EuroMayDay; Free Radio Movement (Italy); May 1968 Poetry and Graffiti (France/Transnational); Radio Student and Radio Mars (Slovenia); Yes Men, The (United States); Youth Media

Further Readings

Grand, L. (Ed.). (2006). *Hot love—Swiss punk & wave 1976–1980*. Zürich, Switzerland: Edition Patrick Frey. (Out of print)

Hänny, R. (1981). *Zürich, anfang September* [Zürich, at the beginning of September]. Frankfurt am Main, Germany: Suhrkamp-Verlag.

Koopmans, R., Kriesi, H., Duyvendak, J. W., & Giugni, M. G. (1995). *New social movements in Western Europe. A comparative analysis.* Minneapolis: University of Minnesota Press.

Kriesi, H. (1984). *Die Zürcher bewegung. Bilder, interaktionen, zusammenhänge* [The Zürich movement: Pictures, interactions, contexts]. Frankfurt am Main, Germany: Campus Verlag.

Nigg, H. (2001). *Wir wollen alles, und zwar subito! Die achtziger jugendunruhen in der Schweiz und ihre folgen* [We want everything, and we want it now! The 80s youth unrest in Switzerland and its consequences]. Zürich, Switzerland: Limmat Verlag.

Nigg, H. (2004). Express yourself. Video als widerständische praxis in der jugendbewegung der 1980er jahre [Express yourself: Video as a practice of resistance in the 1980s youth movement]. In A. Broeckmann & R. Frieling (Eds.), *Bandbreite. Medien zwischen kunst und politik* [Bandwidths: Media between art and politics] (pp. 69–73). Berlin, Germany: Kulturverlag Kadmos.

Nigg, H. (2008). Violence and symbolic resistance in the youth unrest of the eighties. In S. Gau & K. Schlieben (Eds.), *Spectacle, pleasure principle or the carnivalesque? A reader on possibilities, experiences of difference and strategies of the carnivalesque in cultural/political practise* (pp. 151–166). Berlin, Germany: b_books.

Archives

Audios: http://www.av-produktionen.ch/80/doku/audio.html

Audiovisual and other materials from the youth protests in Switzerland are located in the Schweizerisches Sozialarchiv in Zürich, covering all events from the 1960s to the present. Schweizerisches Sozialarchiv, Zürich: http://www.sozialarchiv.ch/Bestaende/film_bestand.html

Flyers: http://www.av-produktionen.ch/80/doku/flugis.html

Photos: http://www.av-produktionen.ch/80/doku/foto.html

Stadt in Bewegung [City on the Move]: 110 videos produced during the 1980s in Zürich, Berne, and Basel. A website of the Sozialarchiv and AV-Produktionen Heinz Nigg presents examples of Swiss youth protest media of the 1980s: http://www.av-produktionen.ch/80/doku/video.html

Underground papers: http://www.av-produktionen.ch/80/doku/zeit.html

Videoladen (Ed.). (1981). *Züri brännt* [Zürich is burning]. Switzerland. 2 DVDs, 190 min (including bonus tracks). German, Swiss-German, and subtitles in German, English, French, and Italian.

YOUTH ROCK MUSIC (CHINA)

When rock legend Cui Jian gained national fame in 1986 with his song "Nothing to My Name," a rock culture was born in China. Since then, numerous bands have followed his example, exploring sounds that range from heavy metal to urban folk, and from hip-hop to Britpop, with Beijing as the epicenter of China's rock culture. At times these sounds have had clear political implications: During the spring 1989 student protests, leading to the June 4th Tiananmen massacre, Cui Jian's songs were used by the students as protest songs. The frequent banning of concerts, the difficulty of organizing large stadium concerts, and the continuous censorship of both sound and lyrics attest to the political relevance of rock music in China.

However, over the years, with the gradual opening up of China, the situation has improved significantly. Independent record companies are now allowed to exist, Cui Jian appears on national television talk shows, and there are annual large outdoor rock festivals like the MIDI festival and the Modern Sky Music festival, attracting thousands of fans.

Dakou Culture

After a peak in the early 1990s, the popularity of rock gradually declined. But changes taking place at the end of the 1990s—in particular the intertwined processes of globalization and commercialization—paved the way for a rebirth. This was epitomized by the emergence of *dakou* (nick) culture after the mid-1990s. This culture is named after the illegally imported CDs with a nick clipped from the edge, the *dakou* CDs as they soon became known among Chinese youth and musicians. *Dakou* became the label for a new and vibrant urban youth culture that emerged in China. Yan

Jun, the main Chinese chronicler of the *dakou* generation, claimed it was a generation that would not be silenced, always open, operating under the radar, creating marginal culture and lifestyles, stubbornly pursuing its visions.

But how valid is such a celebration of the marginal, not only as it dismisses the more popular Hong Kong and Taiwan pop, but also ignores the less marginal and rebellious aspects of Chinese rock culture? Chinese youth cultures revolve, in particular since the turn of the century's staggering economic growth, around pleasure and consumption, rather than around politics and rebellion. With the digitization of music, the availability of sounds and images from all over the world has amplified, from which has profited especially the generation born in the 1980s (the *balinghou* generation). This new generation of "little emperors," as they are often cynically referred to, consists of single children, born after the Cultural Revolution. For them, China has always been a country that is opening up, a place of rapid economic progress and modernization, and a place of prosperity and increased abundance, in particular in the urban areas.

Rethinking Politics and Movements

For fans of Chinese rock, the sound is part and parcel of their everyday lifestyles. One cannot speak of Chinese rock culture as if it were a social movement, consisting of a group of young activists who clearly resist dominant culture. Even the live performances of more politically inclined bands like Tongue, PK14, and Carsick Cars are generally saturated by a spirit of pleasure rather than of rebellion, just as Cui Jian's songs are now sung as romantic classics in karaoke bars.

In translating the meanings of this culture solely into political terms, one runs the danger of ignoring the pleasure that comes with the music and its performances. It would generate reductionist readings of a profoundly multivocal culture. Furthermore, a solely political reading reinforces dominant stereotypes about rock, as if it were inherently political or rebellious.

Furthermore, valorizing Chinese rock solely in terms of politics runs the danger of presenting a very simplistic and monolithic picture of China. Different factions exist within the Chinese Communist Party, just as the tremendous regional differences produce specific regional political climates—what is banned in Beijing may be allowed in Kunming and vice versa. Finally, by reducing Chinese rock to solely a matter of politics one may fall in the imperialistic trap of imposing without any reflexivity a rather specific frame of reference, related to notions of "democracy," "freedom," and "human rights," upon another locality.

However, this does not render Chinese rock insignificant for social movements. It may inspire us to rethink politics and to take issues of pleasure and humor—two important characteristics of Chinese rock—more seriously. When young bands often express feelings of anxiety about the future, and the burden they experience from the parents and the school, such expressions do carry a political edge as they challenge the obedience demanded from students. Reading rock in China as a social movement may also inspire a cross-cultural dialogue that can help us to rethink concepts like rebellion, democracy, human rights, and freedom. It should above all push us to think of politics and activism as being highly contingent on the socioeconomic and political context, *both* there and "here."

Jeroen de Kloet

See also Bhangra, Resistance, and Rituals (South Asia/Transnational); Dance as Social Activism (South Asia); Online Nationalism (China); Popular Music and Political Expression (Côte d'Ivoire); Popular Music and Protest (Ethiopia); Sixth Generation Cinema (China)

Further Readings

Baranovitch, N. (2003). *China's new voices—popular music, ethnicity, gender, and politics, 1978–1997.* Berkeley: University of California Press.

de Kloet, J. (2009). *China with a cut—globalisation, urban youth and popular music.* Amsterdam: Amsterdam University Press.

Field, A., & Groenewegen, J. (2008). Explosive acts: Beijing's punk rock scene. *Berliner China Hefte, 34,* 8–26.

Jones, A. F. (1992). *Like a knife—ideology and genre in contemporary Chinese popular music.* Ithaca, NY: Cornell University Press.

Steen, A. (2000). Sounds, protest and business—Modern Sky Co. and the new ideology of Chinese rock. *Berliner China Hefte, 19,* 40–64.

Yan, J. (2004). Yongyuan nianqing, youngyuan relei ningkang—2002 midi yinyuejie jishi [Forever young, forever crying—notes on Midi 2002 music festival]. In G. Chen, W. Liao, & J. Yan (Eds.), *Boximiya Zhongguo* [Bohemian China] (pp. 161–177). Hong Kong: Hong Kong University Press.

YOUTH-GENERATED MEDIA

Broadly defined as self-expressive media and communication artifacts, youth-generated media have long existed and have been associated with specific social movements, such as the 1960s U.S. and French student movements. Since then, media produced by young people for young people have become more ubiquitous as media-making tools became cheaper, smaller, and more accessible. In the process, youth-generated media are redefining the utility and usage of media-making tools from the photocopy machine (zines) to mobile phones (video uploading sites). This entry summarizes some different approaches to youth media and then identifies the characteristics of youth-generated media through case studies from the Arab world.

Youth-generated media are self-expressive, diverse, vibrant, and internally contested. They figure in industrial and developing societies and have also been flourishing in both progressive and extremist circles. Youth-generated media are the outcome of historical processes of reappropriation of multiplatform media—from graffiti to blogs, flyers to online videos.

Today's youth may have rediscovered the power of "DIY" (do-it-yourself). During the 1970s, the term "DIY" gained the status of a subculture with the punk movement's reliance on self-promotion by producing flyers, self-publishing, self-distributing, and the feminist movement (developing ways for "consciousness-raising"). The "DIY" ethos is perhaps resurrected now because cheap access to technology increases opportunities to produce and distribute media. But "DIY" is not just a by-product of new technologies. Whether individually or collectively produced, youth-generated media are often done without any framing adult involvement—not even financial.

However, to see youth-generated media as completely independent is also misleading. They closely interact with political, cultural, economic, and social structures. In some cases, young people may have started with some adult support because access to production means is closely linked to financial independence—rarely available to youth. In other cases, youth-generated media may be part of organized social, religious, or political activities, such as the range of media developed by young people in organizations like Boy/Girl Scouts, Bible study groups, or political party chapters. It can also be argued that youth-generated media are often entangled with mainstream media; their ideas are featured in newspapers and cable shows, their makers are interviewed in newscasts, and their artifacts are often circulated on commercial video web portals.

Youth and Media

Definitions of "youth" often reflect and refract adult society's "moral panics" about the younger generation. Thus, "youth" and "adulthood" can never be completely separated. A trend in policy and census circles positions youth as a demographic category—people between the ages of 14 and 24. Yet this clarity may easily obscure more than it reveals. One of the most often cited examples is the case of African child soldiers who are forced to kill like adults.

Debate about media and youth has raged on since the 1950s, often split between the traditional social-scientific and the critical-cultural. Although the first argues that "youth" is an important period or stage in acquiring specific cognitive and emotional skills, the latter regards young people as active social members with self-developed cultural politics. Echoing the arguments of cognitive and developmental psychology, the empiricist social-science tradition tends to consider children and youth as "in transition" to becoming adults. In contrast, critical-cultural theory considers youth as variously a consumer or resistant group.

Interestingly, both traditions primarily address flaws in policies toward youth or support interventions by parents, educators, or governments. Also their concentration on youth-oriented media, usually mass-produced, has left the area of youth-*generated* media relatively under-researched.

Understandings of "youth" are generationally defined by economic conditions, political structures, and geo-cultural landscapes, and need to be historically informed. Terms such "tweenagers," "middle youth," "kidults," and "adultescents" are a constant reminder of how marketers are blurring distinctions among children, youths, and adults, and in the process are creating images based on lifestyle choices. Researchers of the NetGeners (the current generation) suggest that youth today can be defined as those between the ages of 12 and 30.

The term "youth media" almost always describes media produced *for* youth, primarily by mainstream media. Occasionally, "youth media" refers to media developed for young people under adult supervision with or without the assistance of youth. To center the debate purely on youth-*oriented* media misses the wide array of graffiti, video, music, zines, posters, and other elements often produced autonomously.

Certain important features characterize today's media culture. First, although media texts are produced for press, radio, television, the Internet, and video games, the ubiquity of media products makes reproduction easier; yet this often results in highly contested artifacts—especially in the form of pastiche, collage, homage, and mash-up. Second, young people, particularly but not solely in the West, have significant media choices: multisource, multiplatform interactive possibilities and the ability to produce their own media. Compounding this image is a range of social venues, technological advances, increased global interconnectedness, political awareness, and cultural awakening that provide a context and an impetus for young people's media development.

Creativity, Artifacts, Energy, and Sequence Among Arab Youth

At 60 percent of the population, Arab youth are at the center of divisive and assimilating forces (traditional families, repressive states, terrorism accusations, and rampant unemployment). This youth "bulge" is an overwhelming feature of much of the developing world, but these young people are also growing up in a pervasive media environment, especially satellite television and the Internet. All these factors have created an environment where Arab youth like their peers elsewhere are developing alternative media artifacts to convey their views to each other and the world. Such youth-generated media have four distinctive characteristics to be discussed using case studies from the Arab world.

Creativity

The first is *creativity*, whereby the end result is a unique product of young people's experiences, perspectives, and emotions. Traditional creative attributes (style, feel, and genre) are irrelevant to the extent that young people do not follow market logic or professional dictates (fads, institutional routines, and corporate image), motivated by either "fame or fortune." These young media-makers positively engage in re-examining the world and in the process develop creative images, sounds, language, and tunes.

When youth organizations in Lebanon decided to respond to the massive bomb that assassinated Prime Minister Rafik Hariri in 2005, they planned and organized a series of activities as part of a social movement dubbed the "Cedar Revolution." In articulating their plight, they sought creatively to mobilize the population through participatory media and to attract the attention of local and international mainstream media.

For example, they dedicated Saturday afternoons to media events that called for popular participation in a colorful and auditory activity. On February 28, 2005, they organized a human chain where thousands of participants chanted slogans and held hands linking the city center to the bomb site some 1.5 miles away. On March 12, 2005, more than 10,000 participants stood in carefully arranged positions, holding up pieces of cardboard in the air in the Lebanese flag's colors, including its world-famous cedar emblem. Dubbed the "human flag," these bodies constituted an immense banner, asserting national unity among the components of Lebanon's social mosaic. The event was staged for still and video cameras, whereas young leaders made themselves available for interviews.

Simultaneously, some young Saudis, caught between satellite entertainment images of sexual license and rigid Islamic calls for piety, are increasingly relaxing their social mores and re-articulating religious practices. A former marketing and advertising executive decided to put his talent to the service of a socio-religious call during Ramadan. With the help of his wife and some friends, Ibrahim Abbas developed a character, *Abaleeso* (the tempting devil), to be featured in video vignettes. In one vignette, *Abaleeso* encourages a young man to harass two girls, whereas another vignette showcases how *Abaleeso* convinces a young married woman to distrust her husband's actions. Abbas invested his personal money in a co-production with an Islamic television channel, *al-Risalah* (The Message). When initially judged too risky to broadcast, these vignettes found their way to the Internet but then, based on their popular appeal, were featured as segments in highly commercialized television fare. They reflected an alternative socio-religious approach developed by young people, which resonated with a youthful generation inside and outside Saudi Arabia.

Artifacts

The second characteristic concerns young people's ability to render this creativity into an *artifact*, a self-expressive product of individual or collective experiences such as pictures, blogs, and performances. Distributed primarily through local, regional, and global networks, these media are often de-territorial and multi-territorial. Their aesthetic form, content, and appeal often transcend national borders and develop an almost universal youth discourse.

Recent cases in the Arab world revealed how blogging about Iraq, Lebanon, Palestine, and the Egyptian *Kefaya* movement echoed an antiwar and pro-democracy discourse across the region and the world. By posting pictures, videos, and personal accounts, young Arabs were able to transcend their immediate nation-state boundaries to create a following in the Diaspora and beyond.

The so-called July 06 War between Israel and the radical Lebanese group Hezbollah lasted 34 days and included a blockade of Lebanon in its entirety. Alternative media, particularly blogging, provided a sense of solidarity and maintained connection among the homeland, other Arabs, and the Diaspora. An anonymous group of bloggers developed the "UN" Campaign: screen savers, poster material, and viral images calling attention to the United Nations' slow and inadequate response to the war. Combining mimicry and graffiti, these pictures featured a blue graffiti wall displaying the UN logo and the letters UN followed by sprayed painted letters that read "UNethical," "UNjust," and "UNfair." Others, such as graphic designer Nadine from Arabictype.com, provided free designs that could be used for T-shirts, posters, flyers, or just e-mail.

Energy

The third characteristic is the huge *energy* that motivates young people's personal and collective investment in the development and distribution of youth-generated media. However, this intensity and passion seems often short-lived.

To pursue her stories, Haifa al-Mansour had to relocate from Saudi Arabia, her home country, to Egypt, and then to the United States to learn film-making. As a woman, her social interactions in Saudi Arabia were governed by numerous restrictions enforced on male–female interaction. Thus, to film, al-Mansour had to train her family members in basic acting and technical skills.

Despite her family's support, al-Mansour had problems exhibiting her films outside the international film circuit. The biggest issue was Saudi Arabia's prohibition of movie theaters. To circumvent this, al-Mansour resorted to a virtual online theater where she could share her short films with other Saudis. Between 2003 and 2006, al-Mansour wrote, directed, produced, and promoted four movies before being recruited as a consultant and television host (and finally retiring from media). Her intense energy and passion paid off, with a generation of other young Saudi women trying to break into a virtually uncharted territory.

Sequence

The fourth characteristic reveals that youth-generated media are, in many cases, part of a *sequence* of activities, usually combining with other forms of youth cultural politics.

Against the backdrop of the July 06 War, a New York–based blogging collective, the *Lebanon Chronicle*, launched an "I ♥ Beirut" sticker campaign. However, it was Lebanon-based blogger Fink Ployd of bloggingbeirut.com who promoted and steered the campaign to more than 25 world cities, from Auckland to San Francisco. The sequence in this case had blog followers downloading the rebus, printing it on a sticker, putting it on a particular city's representative landmark, photographing it, and then e-mailing the picture to Fink Ployd. Within hours, a collage of these pictures would appear on the blog coupled with individual pictures and commentary, demonstrating solidarity with the city and its people. From July 26 until August 14, 2006, this solidarity campaign meshed both producer and consumer in participatory activities that formed an orchestrated sequence.

Future Questions

There are two interconnected issues. First, the widespread portrayal of youth as victims of oppressive, hyper-commercialized media is countered with evidence that young people can be agents of free, noncommercial alternative media. However, the cases also give a sense of the sporadic and precarious nature of youth-generated media. Are youth-generated media basically re-interpreting the mainstream media world for a post-mass-audience generation, comprising media creators as well as readers, viewers, and listeners?

Second, whereas youth-oriented media tell us much about adult fears, preoccupations, and anxieties, youth-generated media are the outcome of young people's emotions, experiences, and perspectives. They may serve as catalysts for social, political, economic, and cultural change. Therefore, it becomes imperative to ask which alternatives are provided and which new challenges are being developed. Youth-generated media offer an opportunity to advance our understanding and treatment of youth as social actors and of social movement media. Yet they resist rigid theorizing, fixed methodologies, and permanent conclusions.

Joe F. Khalil

See also Arab Bloggers as Citizen Journalists (Transnational); BİA Independent Communication Network (Turkey); Citizens' Media; December 2008 Revolt Media (Greece); Kefaya Movement Media (Egypt); New Media and Alternative Cultural Sphere (Iran); Women Bloggers (Egypt); Youth Media; Youth Protest Media (Switzerland)

Further Readings

Duncombe, S. (1997). *Notes from underground: Zines and the politics of alternative culture.* London: Verso.

Khalil, J. (2010). *Youth-generated media in Lebanon and Saudi Arabia.* PhD dissertation, Southern Illinois University, Carbondale.

Livingstone, S. (2002). *Young people and new media: Childhood and the changing media environment.* London: Sage.

Tapscott, D. (2009). *Grown up digital: How the net generation is changing your world.* New York: McGraw-Hill.

Z

ZAPATISTA MEDIA (MÉXICO)

The Zapatista National Liberation Army (Ejército Zapatista de Liberación Nacional, or EZLN) is an armed organization that was created in 1984 by Indigenous peoples from the Tzeltal, Tzotzil, Chol, Tojolabal, and Mame ethnic groups in the southeastern state of Chiapas, México. On January 1, 1994, the EZLN initiated armed struggle against the México government and made its cause a public matter. The Zapatistas, led by its spokesperson Subcomandante Marcos, have been able to communicate effectively through the mass media.

1984–1994

Before 1994, the Zapatistas had an official publication named *El Despertador Mexicano* (The México alarm clock). It was published and distributed among the Zapatista communities to keep them informed about the war they would declare against the México government. It did not aim to reach the non-Indigenous population, nor the Indigenous communities that were not Zapatistas.

On January 1, 1994, at the time of the offensive that started the rebellion, the Zapatistas took over two radio stations, the FM indigenist station XEVFS *La Voz de la Frontera Sur* (Southern Frontier Voice), located in the town of Las Margaritas and owned by the México federal government, and XEOCH, an AM radio station located in the town of Ocosingo and owned by the state government. The Zapatistas used these radio stations to inform the inhabitants of the occupied towns in Chiapas about their rebellion and their organization.

The Zapatistas were aware of the importance of making their voice public and relied on outside media to let people in México and the world know about their struggle. The Zapatistas first turned their attention to the media when the government declared a cease-fire on January 12, 1994. The rebels recognized that some media were reporting their struggle and thus gaining the support of the México population who insisted on a peaceful solution for the conflict. The next day the EZLN wrote a letter to four print media requesting them to publish a series of communiqués. These were the México national newspapers *La Jornada* and *El Financiero*, the national newsmagazine *Proceso*, and the local newspaper *El Tiempo* (San Cristóbal de las Casas in Chiapas).

On January 29, 1994, the EZLN established what they called an "open door" policy in another communiqué, which was applicable to media the EZLN considered objective. The policy allowed free access to the press in Zapatista zones, with official ID, and when possible, they would personally accompany the journalists. As part of the media policy, the insurgents selected the media they accredited to cover their events, including special invitations to the four chosen media to which they addressed their communiqués as well as the México newspaper *El Norte* (from the northern industrial city of Monterrey), the *New York Times*, the *Washington Post*, the *Los Angeles Times*, the

Houston Chronicle, and *Le Monde*. They also listed *Siempre!* and *Mira* news magazines.

Furthermore, their list included the independent México video production company Canal 6 de Julio, the television stations Multivisión and Canal 11, and CNN along with AP, UPI, AFP, Reuters, and Prensa Latina. Finally they mentioned the México radio stations Radio Educación, WM (San Cristóbal de las Casas), XEVA (from the neighboring state of Tabasco), Radio Red, and Grupo Acir. The media policy of the Zapatistas also stated that they reserved the right to give interviews or make statements to any media but banned the main private television channels, Televisa and Televisión Azteca, and their subsidiaries.

Over the years Zapatista media policy has held steady, although the General Command has acknowledged the need to expand their media selection, addressing their communiqués, letters, documents, and declarations to the México and international media in general. By 1997, the EZLN also started addressing social movement media around the world.

Internet and Video Uses

Internet use was not direct until 2002, as many Zapatista communities still do not have electricity or phone lines. Yet, the EZLN has been online. The original website (www.ezln.org) was created in 1994 by Justin Paulson at the University of California, Santa Cruz. It was originally published in English but, by 1995, many Méxicanos consulted it and it had to start posting its information in Spanish, too.

The site posted information gathered by Paulson through organizations like the Zapatista National Liberation Front, Enlace Civil (Civil Link), or the Fray Bartolomé Human Rights Commission, as well as *La Jornada* and *Proceso*. In 1999, Paulson obtained authorization from the Zapatistas to use the acronym EZLN as the domain name for the website while he kept on managing the site. By 2006, the site www.ezln.org.mx became devoted to the Sixth Declaration from the Lacandón Jungle, which launched *La Otra Campaña* tour of Subcomandante Marcos throughout México (termed *the Other Campaign* in opposition to the presidential election under way that year, and designating grassroots mobilization).

Most print, electronic, or digital publications about the Indigenous rebellion were produced by people who did not belong to the Indigenous communities in struggle. However, the constant presence of individuals with media technology in rebel Indigenous communities awakened the Zapatistas to the importance and the power of video cameras, tape recorders, digital cameras, and microphones.

In 1998, the Zapatistas started their own independent video-making project called the Chiapas Media Project (Proyecto de Medios de Comunicación Comunitaria)/Promedios. It was a collective initiative that provided Indigenous Zapatista communities with tools and training to produce their own videos instead of depending on outsiders. The Project emerged from the encounter between the peasant and Indigenous communities in southeastern México and civil society activists from the United States, México City, and Oaxaca. It was a bi-national and multicultural initiative.

From its beginning, the Chiapas Media Project/Promedios worked with Indigenous communities on video production according with the needs, culture, and form of community organization of the Zapatistas. Through their traditional assembly system, the Indigenous communities decided they wanted to participate in this communication project and selected those who would be trained in video making.

The Chiapas Media Project/Promedios was coordinated from the United States by Alexandra Halkin, a U.S. videomaker who initially conceptualized the project in 1995. She was in charge of fund-raising, organizing tours, and international exhibitions. The coordinator of the project in San Cristóbal de las Casas was Paco Vázquez, an Indigenous Nahua with vast experience in Indigenous communication projects. Both were in constant communication with the different Indigenous Zapatista communities. However, neither one interfered with decisions on equipment use, video distribution, or the themes or subjects of the videos that the Indigenous communities make. At the time of writing, regional coordinators from the Zapatista communities trained their fellow Zapatistas in camera, editing, and Internet workshops, whereas advanced training was provided still by Indigenous and non-Indigenous instructors from outside Chiapas.

Radio Insurgente

In 2002, the EZLN started Radio Insurgente, *La voz de los sin voz* (Insurgent Radio, voice of the voiceless). The station's purpose is to broadcast the ideas and contents of the Zapatista struggle, including progress in the construction of autonomy in Zapatista zones, Zapatista thinking, and the traditional music of the Zapatista communities via FM, shortwave, the Internet, and CDs.

In December 2005, the EZLN started handing over the FM stations to the Autonomous Rebel Zapatista Municipalities (MAREZ, from their initials in Spanish). In the zone of Los Altos, there were two FM community radio stations already operating: (1) Radio Amanecer de los Pueblos (Radio Peoples' Dawn), broadcasting from the MAREZ of San Andrés Sak'amchén de los Pobres; and (2) Radio Resistencia, Voz Digna de los Pueblos en Lucha (Resistance Radio, worthy voice of the peoples in struggle), broadcasting from the MAREZ Magdalena de la Paz. The goal was to cover the five Zapatista zones with community radios that produce their own shows according to the needs and languages of the Zapatista communities in each zone.

The Radio Insurgente team was still responsible for shortwave emissions, administering the website, and CD production. The weekly 1-hour shortwave program was transmitted on Saturdays. It was targeted nationally and to the rest of the planet. It discussed current events in Chiapas and the history of the EZLN, as well as broadcast local music and stories. On the website, it was possible to listen to and download the weekly shortwave show as well as special programs, plus samples of the shows produced by the community stations. The website also had recordings with traditional Zapatista music and stories, as well as the speeches of Zapatista authorities and Subcomandante Marcos.

Claudia Magallanes-Blanco

See also COR TV, 2006, Oaxaca (México); Indigenous Media (Burma/Myanmar); Indigenous Media in Latin America; Indigenous Radio Stations (México); Peace Media (Colombia)

Further Readings

Bob, C. (2005). *The marketing of rebellion: Insurgents, media and international activism.* Cambridge, UK: Cambridge University Press.

Chiapas Media Project/PROMEDIOS: http://www.chiapasmediaproject.org

Darling, J. (2008). *Latin America, media and revolution: Communication in modern Mesoamerica.* New York: Palgrave Macmillan.

EZLN. (1994). *EZLN: Documentos y Comunicados 1 de enero /8 de agosto 1994* (Vol. 1.). México D.F.: Ediciones Era.

Hackett, R., & Carroll, W. (2006). *Remaking media. The struggle to democratize public communication.* New York: Routledge.

Halkin, A. (2006). Outside the indigenous lens: Zapatistas and autonomous videomaking. *Revista Chilena de Antropología Visual, 7,* 71–92.

Hayden, T. (Ed.). (2002). *The Zapatista reader.* New York: Thunder's Mouth Press/Nation Books.

Magallanes-Blanco, C. (2008). *The use of video for political consciousness-raising in México: An analysis of independent videos about the Zapatistas.* Lewiston, ME: The Edwin Mellen Press.

Radio Insurgente: http://www.radioinsurgente.org

Rovira, G. (2009). *Zapatistas sin fronteras. Las redes de solidaridad con Chiapas y el altermundismo.* México D.F.: Ediciones Era.

ZINES

The term *zine* was established in the 1980s to refer to an extremely wide range of amateur publications, usually written, edited, and published by one person. The word itself is a truncation of *fanzine* (itself abbreviating *fan magazine*). Fanzines are primarily concerned with the object of their attention (works of literature, music, films, or other cultural activities). This is not to say that they are solely about consumption. Cultural studies researchers have argued that fans are cultural producers, forming an alternative social community where their activities build and sustain solidarity within the fan community.

In the case of zines, we find a similar impulse toward community, although there is less focus on primary texts (television programs, films, music, and sport). In many cases, those who produce zines (*zinesters*) turn to themselves, to their own lives and experiences. At the heart of zine culture is not the study of celebrity, cultural product, or activity, but the study of self, of personal expression, and of the building of community.

The result of this means that the zine—with its emphasis on the personal—might explore any subjects that take the writer's fancy. It therefore becomes difficult to categorize zines by subject. In an attempt to do so, Stephen Duncombe presents a range of categories drawn from the American "clearing-house zine" *Factsheet Five*—a "zine taxonomy" that goes beyond fan writing to cover extremely widespread subjects, including politics, the personal (known as "perzines"), "fringe culture," sexuality and sexual practices, and life at work. Even this list Duncombe feels is insufficient, merely an attempt to discipline undisciplined subjects.

Zines and Communication

The small circulation of many zines, the infrequency of their publication, and the short life that most have make it almost redundant to identify key titles and editors. This is perhaps rather appropriate because there is a democracy within zine culture that seems disinterested in success (at least in terms of circulation, readership, and "fame"). During the 1980s and 1990s, the barter system was common. Zines were traded between editors not necessarily by price; a single copy of an extensive, highly professional zine might attract in return several issues of another editor's smaller, more cheaply produced publication. Others were simply happy to swap one zine for another.

The zine as a medium stands in for a social relationship: It is a token to be exchanged. Even when the zine is part of a commodity transaction, it carries with it something of the obligation that a gift exchange carries. Rather than being bought from a vendor, the zine is almost invariably bought from an individual and is a product of that individual's labor, a sign of their individuality. The acquisition of zines was surrounded by its own etiquette that expected readers to be patient—it takes time to make zines, answer mail, and fill out orders. During the 1980s and 1990s, surface mail was at the heart of this amateur enterprise.

Although the term *zine* has become a catchall for any self-published or small-circulation periodical, its origins—and arguably its most powerful form—lie in this emphasis on the personal. This is not to say that the only zines that matter are perzines. In general, the zine seems more interested in the lived relationship of the individual zine writer to the world. There is an emphasis here on the act over the result, to the degree that success is not to be measured by quantity of circulation. The British songwriter Momus reworked Andy Warhol's statement about fame for zines: "In the future everyone will be famous for fifteen people."

The content of many zines is hardly politically or socially transforming in itself, but it is not simply the content of a zine and its distribution that are evidence of their radical nature. There were exceptions, such as *Riot Grrrl* zines, which promoted a punk feminism, and activist gay zines. Whether political, solipsistic, or simply banal, the zine contributed to the construction of personal identity. In an echo of Clemencia Rodríguez's notion of citizens' media, zinesters were more interested in using their publications to understand themselves than in communicating a message to a wide audience.

Nevertheless, networks of zines emerged where horizontal communication between zine editors and readers became perhaps as important as the content of the zine itself. Perzines were often the product of individuals who found themselves isolated and marginalized in large urban—and, occasionally, rural—communities. The zine offered an opportunity to "meet" people in a similar situation (it is no surprise that zine culture developed in the United States with its geographically dispersed communities). The very format of the zine—with design and production values that owed more to the copy shop than to the printing press—encouraged readers to become editors themselves. Through that emulation comes an engagement with the social: Zines promote community as well as individual identity, solidarity, and solipsism.

Zine Culture and E-Zines

The late 1990s saw the move of many zines to the Internet. There is evidence to suggest, however, that the e-zine is not an equal replacement for its printed precursor. When the editor of *For the*

Clerisy moved his zine to the Internet, he found that he not only lost readers who lacked access to the technology, but he also lost readers who preferred the tactile and portable nature of the printed publication. After a few issues of the *Clerisy* e-zine, readership had dropped so low that it returned to print.

Here we see the rehearsal of common arguments about portability and physicality familiar from any champion of the printed page. What is also absent in e-zine culture is the notion of zine etiquette, to be replaced by the generalities of "netiquette." Although this may not seem an irreparable loss, it at least extends one set of defining social relations from zine culture and moves the enterprise that bit closer to the mainstream. Its ways of "doing business" become less distinguishable from the dominant practices in cyberspace.

For some zine commentators, the late 1990s saw the "death of the zine." They argue that the distinctiveness of zine culture—as a print-based culture centered on nonprofessional, single editors within a community of other similar producers—was being eroded by bandwagon-jumpers, corporate co-optation, and zinesters only interested in publishing as a fashion statement. They also acknowledge that zinesters (the majority of whom appeared in their teens or early 20s) grow up, take on careers and families, and find it more difficult to find the time and money for a perhaps futile activity (are 15 people worth it?).

Although zines survive in printed form and show no signs of disappearing, in cyberspace, it is often difficult to separate e-zine's "proper" from other forms of "personal publishing." The rise of social networking sites in the 2000s has arguably refocused the energies of individuals to explore their own identities and to seek out like-minded others. The standardized layout of the Facebook page reduces the possibility of individual creativity. Where radical media so often fail because of poor circulation and small audiences, the printed zine might well survive because of its marginality, its limited reach, and its antiquated physicality.

Chris Atton

See also Alternative Comics (United States); Alternative Media; Culture Jamming; Parodies of Dominant Discourse (Zambia); Political Jokes (Zimbabwe); Youth Media

Further Readings

Atton, C. (2002). *Alternative media*. London: Sage.

Burt, S. (1999). Amateurs. *Transition, 77*, 148–171.

Duncombe, S. (1997). *Notes from underground: Zines and the politics of alternative culture*. London: Verso.

Marr, J. (1999). Zines are dead. *Bad Subjects, 46* (unpaginated).

Rodríguez, C. (2000). *Fissures in the mediascape: An international study of citizens' media*. Cresskill, NJ: Hampton Press.

Yorke, C. (2000). Zines are dead: The six deadly sins that killed zinery. *Broken Pencil, 12*, 18–19.

ZIONIST MOVEMENT MEDIA, PRE-1948

Zionism is the movement that from the late 19th to the mid-20th century led the charge to create a Jewish state in Palestine. Although the movement coalesced around the formation of the World Zionist Organization (WZO) in 1897 under the secular leadership of Theodor Herzl, its origins can be traced to the messianic fervor of certain sects of religious Jews who advocated for a Jewish return to the land promised them by God. Secular Zionists drew on these symbols but replaced the messianic rhetoric with an agenda rooted in both nationalism and socialism.

The Zionist movement used a variety of media to realize both its internal communication and public relations goals, including print, still images, film, and broadcasting. Zionists typically targeted non-Zionist Jews as well as non-Jewish populations to build political alliances, inform about and encourage empathy for the Zionist cause, and raise money for repopulation and infrastructure projects in Palestine. This entry examines the development of Zionism and the roles played by Zionist movement media beginning in the late 19th century until the establishment of Israel in 1948.

Zionism was a by-product of the larger 19th-century push toward establishing the nation-state as the world's primary sociopolitical unit but equally a defense against the European nationalisms, which equated each nation with a single cultural/ethnic group—often through virulently excluding minority-ethnic groups such as the Jews.

Zionists asserted that even as Jews remained marginalized and victimized within newly emergent nation-states, the Jewish people also faced dissolution of their values and cultural heritage through assimilation. Zionists proposed that a Jewish state would offer Jews a sovereign homeland, equal to the other nation-states, but also unique.

Although socialism seeks to transcend nationality and address global class inequalities, Zionism meshed socialism and nationalism, encouraging Jewish populations, regardless of their country of origin, to form a separate national culture that would at last grant Jews equality of opportunity and the prospect of building socialist principles into a new state.

The WZO sought to unite these different strands around the shared conviction that the Jewish people needed a homeland. Even as the movement's political leadership considered several possible territories for establishing a Jewish state, including Argentina and Uganda, Palestine remained its primary focus because of the biblical and historical ties of the Jewish people to that body of land.

Zionism and Non-Zionists

Margalit Toledano argues that Zionism's success was rooted in its ability to sway public opinion and to make the topic of a Jewish homeland a matter of public conversation outside the Jewish community. Although Herzl launched the Zionist newspaper *Die Welt* (The World) in 1897 to promote the movement's causes among Jewish supporters, it was Herzl's continued work for *Die Neue Freie Presse* (The New Free Press) that provided him access to audiences beyond the community.

Not only did Herzl publish pro-Zionist articles, but his journalist credentials gave him entry to political arenas normally barred to Jews. At the same time, *Die Welt* regularly published columns by non-Jews supporting the creation of a separate Jewish state. Although rationales in these columns ranged from empathetic to xenophobic, Alan Levenson asserts that *Die Welt* repurposed any piece in favor of a separate Jewish homeland to cultivate philosemitism among Europe's political elite, who might not have read *Die Welt* but were likely to hear about these aggregated columns by

proxy and lend their support for the Zionist cause. Undoubtedly, many of these same repurposed articles also encouraged Jewish readers to embrace Zionism as a necessary response to anti-Semitism. The WZO expected the Jewish press to be uncritical of the Zionist mission or the conditions in Palestine. Its purpose was to explain the Zionist project, while avoiding publishing any information that might place that mission at risk of failure.

Zionism also believed in the unique and exclusive attributes of Jewish nationalism. The exclusivity sanctified the Zionist cause, and indeed, the movement employed a zealous and polarizing vocabulary in describing its mission. "Ascent" to the land of Israel was not only a divine right of the Jews but a mission on par with the holiest of pilgrimages. Likewise, those Jews who left Palestine were derisively described as "descenders" who had turned their backs on the righteous values of their fellow pioneers. The Diaspora Jew was likewise vilified as unwilling to sacrifice to restore the Jewish nation.

Forging a National Culture

Zionists also used media internally as a means of promoting unity among the movement's various factions (religious, nationalist, and socialist). In its early years, secular Zionists needed religious support to maintain the movement's numbers and momentum. Although the old vanguard, led by Herzl, continued to push for a political solution, others lobbied to create a Zionist cultural and educational infrastructure that would stir the imagination of Europe's Jewry so that the land of Israel would come to be recognized as the only viable national solution. "Cultural" Zionism saw fostering this shared identification as a precursor to any nationalist endeavor.

Cultural Zionists saw particular aspects of Judaism as valuable tools in fostering a collective national imaginary. Zionism, they thought, needed to inspire fanatical devotion. Judaism, selectively reworked as culture, history, and tradition—as opposed to religion—provided the means of achieving this. They stressed the importance of reviving Hebrew as a shared national language among all Jews, both in Palestine and in the Diaspora. They became heavily involved in publishing Hebrew journals, setting up of Hebrew schools, and creating art and other visual aids that would capture the spirit and heroic legacy of life in Israel before Roman emperor Titus's forcible dispersion of the Jewish people in 70 CE.

Cultural Zionists chose Hebrew precisely because they saw in it the ability to break European Jews of their previous national-linguistic imaginings, which were focused on their host nations, and to create a new national imagination directly connected to a "free" and "heroic" Jewish past. The language of the Bible served to remind Jews that they had a national imaginary that preceded and superseded their current national loyalties, one that grounded Jewish nationalism in both history and predestination. But Hebrew was now transmitted, of course, through modern printing and broadcast technologies.

Radio served as an important nationalizing tool within Palestine, partnering with the press and formal educational institutions in fostering a Hebrew vernacular and promoting a Zionist culture. Radio both modernized and standardized the Hebrew language, educating a multilingual immigrant population on how to use the language of the Bible in everyday communication. The first Zionist radio broadcast occurred in 1932, but it was not until 1936, with the establishment of the Palestine Broadcast Service (PBS), that Zionists were granted an official space on Palestine's airwaves.

Although the British mandate saw radio as a tool that might alleviate tensions among Zionist settlers, Palestinians, and the British occupying forces, Zionists continued to use the airwaves to promote a national Jewish culture, often covering Kibbutz (cooperative farm) ceremonies and other cultural events and even injecting Zionist content into its children's programming. The blatant nationalist rhetoric often raised Arab and British ire, although PBS was tame compared with the underground radio channels operated by the militant Jewish resistance movements in Palestine from 1938 to 1947.

Although Zionist radio both directly and indirectly opposed British political control over Palestine, programming often combined Hebrew nationalism with European high culture through classical music and the translation of European literary works into Hebrew radio dramas. In this way, radio served as an intermediary between Zionist and European cultures, stressing their shared heritage while either ignoring or deploring shared cultural roots between Sephardi Jews (Jews of Middle Eastern descent) and the Arab world.

The Zionist movement in Palestine was divided into various political factions, some more militant in their efforts to drive out the British than others, and all used radio to varying degrees to mobilize clandestine support, provide the Palestinian Jewish population with alternative news and information related to the Statist cause, and stir up nationalist sentiments among settlers. The three largest underground broadcasting operations were run by the resistance groups: the *Haganah* (defense), the *Irgun* (acronym for National Military Organization), and the *Lechi* (acronym for Fighters for the Freedom of Israel).

They each employed different strategies and encountered varying levels of resistance. Although it first used radio in 1940 to protest British efforts to curtail land sales to Jewish organizations, the Haganah was generally the most centrist and least militant of the three organizations. Like Irgun and Lechi, Haganah radio was a fairly mobile operation, regularly moving transmitter sites and using elaborate security measures to keep broadcast locations secret, but because of their comparatively milder approach, they were generally permitted to broadcast without reprisals from British authority, particularly after World War II. Haganah radio first included some Arabic programming as early as 1945 in an attempt to win over Arab populations in Palestine to the Zionist cause.

Irgun and Lechi were much more militant than Haganah in their efforts to oust the British and to terrorize Arab populations into submission. Irgun used radio to report on events such as its members' bombing of an Arab market and to recruit new members. Irgun's radio efforts were sporadic compared with those of Lechi. As the smallest but also the most extremist of the three resistance groups, Lechi relied on radio to report on its activities because its members could rarely meet publicly without risking British (and even Haganah) crackdowns. Lechi advocated for the creation of a "Hebrew kingdom from the Euphrates to the Nile" and the use of violence against the British occupiers. Although Haganah and Irgun ceased their broadcasts during World War II in support of the British war efforts, Lechi continued to broadcast anti-British reports and discouraged listeners from enlisting in the British Armed Forces.

Still, even as the various factions of the Jewish underground used radio to sway listeners to their particular points of view, radio would become increasingly important in unifying the Jewish population in Palestine, as well as in informing them of the rise in anti-Semitism in Europe throughout the late 1930s and early 1940s. Correspondingly, the number of radio receivers also dramatically increased throughout the decade from an estimated 5,000 in 1931 to 37,000 by the end of the 1930s and 110,000 by 1943.

Mythmaking and the New Hebrew

More than just providing a lingua franca for a dispersed and diverse Jewish population in Palestine and in Europe, the ideas expressed through the Hebrew language reawakened the imaginations of Europe's Jews to the glory of Israel's past. They also addressed a community grounded in European values, promising that the past could be revived through the natural progression of the Jewish people into modernity. Cultural Zionists regularly dipped into the Bible and other aspects of Judaism to appropriate narratives and symbols that could reawaken a sense of Jewish national continuity, interrupted by the Exile, which would be restored through the re-establishment of a Jewish homeland.

The Zionist mission was imbued with mythical dimensions—in Roland Barthes' sense of the word "myth"—drawn directly from the Bible. Oz Almog identifies five key biblical myths appropriated by Zionism: the myths of deliverance from enemies; the few facing the many; Abraham's readiness to sacrifice his son Isaac at God's command; the redemption of Israel; and the biblical right to the land of Israel. The deliverance myth is rooted in the oft-repeated biblical narrative of God saving the Jews from certain annihilation. Similarly, the myth of the few versus the many is drawn from the miraculous victories of the Hebrews against armies that far outnumbered theirs. In both cases, however, the myths

were carefully recast to exclude divine intervention and to emphasize the courage and power of Hebrew will.

Zionists were quick to point to the recurrence of these biblical narratives in the pioneers' struggles in pre-state Palestine. The story of Joseph Trumpeldor and the battle of Tel Chai evoked the "deliverance" and "the few" elements, as well as the Isaac story. In Zionism, Isaac is willing to sacrifice himself for the sake of his homeland. According to legend, Trumpeldor was a one-armed pioneer who, together with a ragtag group of fellow Jews, defended the settlement of Tel Chai against Arab attackers. Killed during the attack, Trumpeldor's dying words were purportedly "it doesn't matter. It is good to die for your country."

The inaccuracies of this account are not as important as the evocation of national sacrifice and Jewish deliverance from their many enemies through self-defense and strength of will. The redemption of Israel and the belief that the Jews would once again live in their God-given land were initial catalysts for messianic Zionism. Cultural Zionism shifted the emphasis to a secular redemption but did not repudiate the religious elements of Jewish culture. The divine right of return remained, but it was now understood as emanating from political action and human agency rather than from mystical intervention. Similarly, the moral right of the Jews to the State of Israel was never an issue of debate within the WZO.

Negotiating Religious and Secular Identities

Zionist art and other cultural products, such as film, postcards, and magazines, were intended both to sustain solidarity within the movement and to attract potential converts. Cultural production was also perceived as a viable means of soliciting money or political support from both Zionists and non-Zionists, Jewish or otherwise. This often meant treading a slippery representational slope between tradition and modernity, nostalgia and politics.

Many of the biblical elements that Zionism refurbished were evoked through religious visual imagery. Zionists appropriated the menorah (seven-branched candelabrum) as a symbol to connect the new Hebrews with their past glory. The menorah had primarily been associated with the miracle of Chanukah (Festival of Lights). After the Maccabee rebel guerrilla victory over the Syrian Seleucid imperial army in 164 BCE, the priests entered the great temple to relight the menorah but found that there was not enough oil for more than a single day, and the nearest source was 8 days away. Miraculously, the candelabrum burned for those 8 days. Zionists reinterpreted this as a story of Jewish revolt against oppression and for national sovereignty. The menorah was featured prominently on many Zionist cultural artifacts.

The very first postcard from the 1897 WZO congress, drawn by Carl Pollack, is revealing of early Zionist attempts to both appropriate and negotiate tensions between past and present, religious and secular images of the movement. The postcard depicts two separate scenes on opposing edges of the frame. On the left, several orthodox Jews are praying at the Western Wall. On the right, a pioneer is toiling the land. At the top, between these two images, is written in Hebrew, "Who will bring from Zion the redemption of Israel?"

The postcard suggests that both the religious Jew and the pioneer will bring about the redemption, an acknowledgment of religious Zionism rather than its rejection. At the same time, the two images remain separate, coexisting but not necessarily cooperating. Zionist representations repeatedly evidenced such binaries. Religious Zionists were always elderly and depicted as passive, whereas secular Zionist pioneers were young and often shown actively toiling on the land.

In reality, religious Zionists often opposed secular co-optation practices, and overwhelmingly, anti-Zionist Jews were religious. Yet later imagery often depicted religious and secular Zionists occupying the same space, while sidestepping these tensions, instead representing elderly religious Zionists as symbolically passing the torch to a younger, secular generation (or, at least, passively supporting the pioneering cause through prayer). The imagery oscillated between representing the two groups as separate yet equal and suggesting that secular Zionism was taking up the mantle willingly offered to them by its religious forebears.

These postcards must also be understood as produced for particular audiences. The commemorative function of the postcards, coupled with their emphasis on depicting the WZO leadership, suggests that they were intended for internal use, serving as symbolic reminders of the WZO's mission and strengthening the bonds between members by providing cultural artifacts to take home. WZO congresses took place annually and were often the only opportunity for Zionists to come together.

The other potential audience for these postcards would have been non-Zionist Jews. Postcards were easily portable. As non-Zionists were less likely to subscribe to Zionist journals, postcards provided another means of circulating the movement's message. As many non-Zionists were also religious Jews, postcards sought to legitimate the movement by pointing to Zionism's continuity with Jewish tradition.

Showing Off the Land and Its Inhabitants

Whereas artwork, newspapers, and radio were key to Zionist communication strategies, filmmaking played a very small part, with only approximately 20 travelogue films shot in Palestine from 1899 to 1948, accompanied by three fictional shorts. The Jewish National Fund and the Palestinian Foundation Fund funded filmmaking in Palestine. As these two organizations were primarily engaged with land purchases and development, the objectives of these early films were to showcase the land and the New Hebrew pioneer's mastery over it, to alleviate concerns among Jews in Europe that Palestine was unfit to inhabit. They also publicized the work of the two funds and raised money.

Their producers recognized that international audiences, consisting of wealthy Jews and non-Jewish supporters, could be swayed to donate by an appeal to nostalgia and spiritual sentiment as much as the modern project of building Tel Aviv city. These films would usually begin with religious sites, reserving the pioneers' efforts for the films' climaxes. This suggested a progression from antiquity into modernity. Quite often, the travelogues depicted pioneers as inheriting of their forefathers' biblical land, left barren since the Exile. These images usually excluded Arab inhabitants, or depicted Arabs as nomadic, and therefore possessing no legitimate claim to Palestine.

Avi Santo

See also Alternative Information Center (Israel and Palestine); Alternative Media; Berber Video-Films (Morocco); Citizens' Media; Palestinian Interwar Press; Pirate Radio (Israel)

Further Readings

Berkowitz, M. (1993). *Zionist culture and West European Jewry before the First World War*. Chapel Hill: University of North Carolina Press.

Boyd, D. A. (1999). Hebrew-language clandestine radio broadcasting during the British Palestine mandate. *Journal of Radio Studies, 6*(1), 101–115.

Levenson, A. (2002). Gentile reception of Herzlian Zionism, a reconsideration. *Jewish History, 16,* 187–211.

Penslar, D. J. (2003). Transmitting Jewish culture: Radio in Israel. *Jewish Social Studies, 10*(1), 1–29.

Toledano, M. (2005). Challenging accounts: Public relations and a tale of two revolutions. *Public Relations Review, 31,* 463–470.

Tryster, H. (1995). *Israel before Israel: Silent cinema in the Holy Land*. Jerusalem, Israel: Steven Spielberg Jewish Film Archive of the Avraham Harmon Institute of Contemporary Jewry, Hebrew University of Jerusalem, and the Central Zionist Archives.

Index

Entry titles and their page numbers are in **bold**.

Reign of Terror beheadings in, 70
Revue du Monde Noir publication
movement in, 78
Société nouvelle in, 88
undocumented workers' Internet use
in, 525–526
Vietnam independence movement and,
240–242
Frauen gemeinsam sind stark feminist
magazine (Germany), 188
Frauen und Film feminist magazine
(Germany), 188
Frauen-Zeitung feminist newspaper
(Germany), 188
Frazier, Susan, 276
Frederick Douglass' Paper Black
newspaper, 81
Free and Open Source Software
(FLOSS), 268, 270
Free Burma Coalition, 243
Free China monthly magazine
(Taiwan), 158
Free radio (Austria), 201–205. *See also*
Women's radio (Austria)
Free radio movement (Italy), 205–208
**Free radio movement, 1974–1981
(France), 208–211.** *See also* **Radio
Lorraine Coeur d'Acier (France)**
Free Radios Charter (Austria), 202
Free Software Foundation, 142
Free Speech TV (Paper Tiger Television,
U.S.), 215, 384
**Free Tibet movement's publicity,
211–212**
angry Buddhist monk phenomenon
and, 51–52
See also Tibet
Free Trade of the Americas, 268
Freedom Files human rights TV program
(U.S.), 227, 232
Freedom's Journal Black
newspaper, 81
Freire, Paulo, 31, 99, 510
Frick, Henry Clay, 342
Friedan, Betty, 196
From Hecabe dance (Bengal), 157
*From Reverence to Rape: The Treatment
of Women in Movies* (Haskell), 197
Fronta, Monica, 287
Fu Sinian, 361

G8/G20
Indymedia opposition to, 268, 272
protests against, 318, 336
Gabriel, Peter, 539
Gambrell, Dorothy, 11
*Game Over: Gender, Race, and Violence
in Video Games* MEF video, 322
Gandhi, Indira, 92
imposition of Emergency
(1975–1977) by, 499–500, 543
Gandhi, Mahatma, 237, 238, 239, 406,
489, 529, 542
Gandhiji Vijayam independence play
(India), 239

Gandy, Oscar, 324–325
Gangopadhyay, Sunil, 360
Garvey, Marcus, 77, 439
Gay and lesbian media and issues
The Advocate (U.S.), 6–7
DIVA TV and ACT UP (U.S.),
165–166
Focus on the Family radio talk show
opposed by, 94
Gay Liberation Front and, 509
Pride gay and lesbian pride movement
documentary, 166
Stonewall incident (U.S.) and, 509
See also **Gay press (Canada, United
Kingdom, United States);
Gay USA**
Gay Cable Network (GCN), 215
Gay Community News weekly
newspaper (Boston), 213, 214
Gay Flames gay militant press, 213
Gay News (London), 213, 214
**Gay press (Canada, United Kingdom,
United States), 213–215**
The Advocate United States,
6–7, 213
Christopher Street Commemoration
Day march, 509
Come Out! gay militant press,
213, 215, 509
DIVA TV and ACT UP (U.S.),
165–166
Stonewall incident (U.S.) and, 509
See also AIDS activist movement,
advocacy; **Gay USA**
Gay Sunshine gay militant
press, 213
Gay USA, 215
Gender. *See* Feminist media; **Feminist
media, 1960–1990 (Germany);
Feminist media: an overview;
Feminist movement media (United
States); Feminist movement media
(United States); Indymedia and
gender; Women bloggers (Egypt);**
Women's rights, women's issues,
women's media
Gere, Richard, 211
Germany
feminist media, 1960–1990, in, 188–191
National Socialist German Workers'
Party (Nazi Party) to 1933 in,
356–358
social democratic media to 1914 in,
459–462
Weimar Republic dissident cultures in,
535–536
See also Eastern Germany; Federal
Germany
Getino, Octavio, 1, 2, 522, 523
Ghana
music and dissent in, 346–347
Third World Network Africa and, 462
Western Echo Gold Coast anticolonial
newspaper, 56
Ghatak, Manish, 359

Ghose, Gautam, 167
Ghost World comics, 11
Giáp, Võ Nguyên, 241
Gijsels, Hugo, 183
Gillette, Frank, 429
Gilman Street Project community
project, 304
Gincoff, Teo, 216
Ginsburg, Faye, 201, 257, 261, 262, 263
Glasgow News alternative
press (U.K.), 14
Gleyzer, Raymundo, 69
Global South
community media, democracy in,
118–119
feminism in, 542
Indymedia and, 269
political movements, NGOs and,
23–24
Third World Network (TWN) in, 22,
523–524
World Social Forum (WSF) and, 30
See also specific country
GNU Free Documentation
License, 142
GNU General Public License (GPL),
142, 146
Godard, Jean-Luc, 3
The Godfather (film), 80
Godmilow, Jill, 383
Goebbels, Joseph, 358
Goldman, Emma, 341–342
Gone Gitmo virtual Guantánamo
prison, 233
Góngora, Augusto, 475
González, Juan, 163, 164
Goodman, Amy, 162, 163, 164
Goodman, Steve, 554
Goodrum, Abby A., 554
Goodstein, David B., 6
Google Maps, 26
Goolarri Television (Australia), 249
Graham, Philip W., 554
Gramsci, Antonio, 16, 17, 69
Gran Fury artistic group, 277–278
**Grandmothers of the Plaza de Mayo
(Argentina), 216–217.** *See also*
**H.I.J.O.S. and *Escraches*
(Argentina); Mothers of the Plaza
de Mayo (Argentina)**
**Grassroots tech activists and media
policy, 217–221**
community media and the Third
Sector and, 115–121, 218
mobile communication and social
movements and, 335–338
See also **Media activists and
communication policy
processes; Media infrastructure
policy and media activism; Media
justice movement (MJM) (United
States)**
Graswurzelrevolution (Grassroots
revolution), 38–39
Graziano, Margarita, 29